Bass
Family Record

A Genealogy report of the family of Wilson Bass, born about 1785.
Born in North Carolina and migrated to the area of Covington County Alabama about 1820.

Prepared by
Nicholas Bruce Bass

© 2023 by Nicholas Bruce Bass. All rights reserved.
Primary content organized with "Complete Genealogy Reporter".
Fifty-Fifth Anniversary edition, Bass Family Record June 2023.
Printed in the United States of America.
Design by Nicholas Bruce Bass.

All images are from personal collection with the intent of including them in this record, or had already been publicly released through various media. Numerous people have contributed to this collection of data and all involved are greatly appreciated for their contribution and support.

This volume is intended as a historical document to present and preserve as a genealogical record. Without doubt, there are errors. If you find an error, please submit corrections or suggestions though contacts at www.BassFamilyRecord.com.

ISBN-13: 979-8844061080

BISAC: Reference / Genealogy

Forward

Many of you may be aware that in my first attempt at creating a genealogical document I included information going all the way back to the 1400s. It was, and is, fascinating. French Huguenots fleeing to England and then to the Colonies in the 1620s, in prominent fashion. Right there near Jamestown in Virginia, Basse was a well-known name. Basse's Choice was land granted to the family, Indian raids and a few surviving Basse boys seem to have become almost members of the tribe somehow. John Bass married the chief's daughter, and Bass is still a prominent name in the Nansemond Tribe today. Many chiefs and tribe members to this day are Basses.

It's a great history, and I believe that we are part of that history. Though reality is the evidence to support that belief just isn't something that I've found. What evidence that is available on several family trees that include our line, on Ancestry and other sites, does more to disprove the connection they present than to support it. Like, supposedly, listing Wilson as an orphan of Augustin Bass named Bennett in South Carolina dated 1814. Wilson at that time would have been a minimum of 24 years old, had served in the Georgia Militia, and had two children of his own. This just obviously doesn't work.

So, this document follows the line of Wilson Bass who was born in North Carolina between 1780 and 1790 under circumstances that we cannot yet confirm but have genetic evidence through DNA showing that his father was likely a Bridges or Bridgers rather than a Bass. This makes Wilson our brick wall that we can't get past. I have made and continue to make efforts, along with others, to break down this wall. For now, though this is where we start, and I hope that you will find it as fascinating a start as I do.

It's fun to speculate on possibilities. Wilson's mother could have been a Bass or could have married a Bass after he was born. It was a tumultuous time in the history of our nation and the people of that time also faced many of the same challenges and temptations we see around us today. Life then was much different than today, but people were still people. The possibilities are almost endless.

Something that does seem obvious though is that Wilson knew. The primary reason I have that belief is that he named his oldest son Bennett Bridges Bass. This also suggests, to me at least, the likelihood of an unfortunate reason for this break in paternity rather than some of the more traumatic possibilities.

Regardless of the circumstances Wilson's life seems to have started in North Carolina. From there he almost certainly followed the common movements of the time by moving to South Carolina, and definitely later moved to Georgia, where he is recorded as a member of the militia on the rolls of the Georgia militia of Pulaski County entered June 10, 1809.

Entered this 10th day of June 1809
RICHD. H. THOMAS, CLK.
GEORGIA, PULASKI COUNTY

The following list contains the names of persons selected to serve as pettit juriors for said county agreeable to an act of the general assembly passed the seventh day of December 1805

1. John Yon
2. John McCray
3. Nathaniel Harthhorn
4. Isham Jordin
5. Robirt Thompson
6. Moses Kirkland
7. William Wynn
8. John Scarborough
9. Joel Ellis
10. Thomas Coats
11. Leonard Stringer
12. Paskil Hammick
27. John Grinsted
28. Isaac Dyekes
29. John Gilstrap
30. William Grinsted
31. John Smith
32. William Taylor Sr.
33. Edward Lassiter
34. Henry Dewit
35. Arthor Jones
36. Haywood Jones
37. Benjaman Roberson
38. Jacob Taylor
60. Isham McDaniel
61. George Kelley
62. Maliciah Kelley
63. William Kelley
64. Edward Bryant
65. Bartholomuw Lungino
66. William Johnson
67. Joseph Regan
68. Nathan Sowel
69. Luster Crafford
70. Jessee Livily
71. Thomas Adams
72. Thomas Baggot
73. Drewry Mimms
74. John Coleman
75. John Vass
76. Stephen Mitchell
77. Abraham Hollady
97. Isaac Phillips
98. Jonathan Peacock
99. Samuel Peacock
100. Samuel Hart
101. Barney Hart
102. Neile McAlssin
193. Archabal Thompson
104. Nimrod Smith
105. Benjaman Posey
106. William Dreadin
107. John Moses
108. Samuel King
109. Bolin Swearingin
110. Richd Thomas
111. William Pearce
112. Wilson Bass
113. Archabald Jones
114. Thomas Franklin
115. Amos Wheelar

On Aug. 14, 1813, he's listed again in the Pulaski militia muster roll as a Corporal along with Solomon Franklin, son of Thomas Franklin listed above.

Later in October of 1814 Wilson is listed in a document from Pulaski County GA where he is mentioned as "retailing spiritus liquor without a license and keeping a riotous house on the sabbath".

Wilson is again listed on a court document from Pulaski, along with Thomas Franklin. This seems to be some sort of land dispute or sale and is dated Apr 29th, 1817. This suggest to me that this is about the time Wilson and Thomas were leaving Georgia.

Wilson and Thomas are again listed on an undated court document that I can't Identify.

Daniel Rhodes Adm?
vs
Wilson Bass and Wm Garlit — Case — Settled & Cost paid

Daniel Rhodes Adm?
vs
Wilson Bass and
Thomas Franklin — Case — Settled & Cost paid

William Lester
vs
William Canton — debt — Settled & Cost paid

Thomas Mathew
vs
Henry Fulgham — Case — Settled

Jueto H. Mordant
vs
Thomas Butler — Case — Settled at mutual Costs

Compto to
vs
Needham Stephen — debt — Settled & Cost paid

Commster &c
vs
Thomas Mills &
Joseph Mort — debt — Settled at defts Cost

Wilson purchased land in Covington County in December of 1823 and again in January of 1824. He and his son Bennett bought several pieces of land over the years.

Bass, Bennett B.	Cov.	11/29/33	NE¼ofSE¼	28-3-14
		03/16/37	SE¼ofNE¼	14-3-14
Bass, Willson	Cov.	12/22/23	E½ofSE¼	20-3-14
			E½ofNE¼	25-3-13
		01/01/24	W½ofSE¼	29-3-14
		02/16/36	SW¼ofNE¼	28-3-14
		05/03/37	NW¼ofNE¼	28-3-14

Then in January of 1825 Wilson and Thomas Franklin's son Solomon Franklin are found on a militia vote in Covington County. Along with prominent names from the area, Jerimiah Dixon, and our family, Holland Middleton Hogg.

Wilson shows up on census records through 1840, but not after that. His home is listed as a voting location between Jan. 27, 1845, and Feb. 29, 1848, as "Beat No. 2 Voting Precinct titled Wilson Bass'".

Beyond this I'm unaware of any records of Wilson Bass, but since this document includes records of over four thousand of his descendants and relations, his story is not over.

Voting Precincts Established by State Legislature in Covington County 1819-1852

Location	Date Established	Date Abolished
Beat No. 1		
John Fannin	12/13/1819	
Aaron Lockhart's	12/18/1821	
County Seat	12/12/1822	
County Court House (Montezuma)	1824	
Brewer's Old Gin	02/03/1840	01/27/1845
County Court House (Andalusia)	1845	
Beat No. 2		
John E. Sentell's	12/24/1824	12/22/1826
Thomas Franklin's	12/22/1826	01/22/1829
William Padgett's	01/22/1829	01/12/1833
William Summerford's Mill	01/12/1833	02/02/1839
Carria Jernigan's	02/02/1839	01/27/1845
Wilson Bass'	01/27/1845	02/29/1848
Elizabeth Paget's	02/29/1848	
Thomas Lloyd's	02/03/1840	12/29/1841
Reubin Hart's	12/29/1841	01/27/1845
Reubin Hart's	02/29/1848	

This image and the land purchase image are from Wyley Ward's books.

Email: nik@bassfamilyrecord.com   Facebook: https://www.facebook.com/BassFamilyRecord/
Web: bassfamilyrecord.com

CONTENTS

1. INTRODUCTION

2. DESCENDANTS

3. DIRECT RELATIONS

4. INDEX

Acknowledgment

Thank you for your interest in our family. Whether you are a part of the Bass family or not I hope that you will enjoy and be informed by what has been put together here. The Bass Family Record is a compilation of the efforts of many people over the years. I am aware of three previous, significant, records prepared and printed at different times and one book of family stories.

Much of these texts have been included, at least in part. As with so many things in our family, I feel it is a blessing to have more information than you can reasonably include in one publication.

Thank you is not enough to express the appreciation I have for the work done to make my work in preserving and maintaining these records possible and so much more productive than I could have done on my own.

Genola Bass Spence and Glynda Wilkinson Cupp assembled the foundation of this record and published it for the family in 1968. The very document I based the 55th anniversary edition and cover design on. There was an update of that record published in July of 2000 but no part of that record indicated an individual taking credit for the update, only to contact Kim Cupp DiMaria if you would like a copy. The title of those records was "Bass Family Record", and I have titled my record and web site in honor of the work and love they put into creating those original documents that mean so much to me.

Another record was printed for the James Bennet Bass Family (my family), I am not sure of the timing of that one, though I do have a copy. I understand that Faye Hammack Bass updated and published another version in the late 80s, but I do not have a copy.

Hazel Bass Trawick compiled the book of Bass family stories in 1994. With her permission, many of the stories are included on my website, with more to come.

Kris Gresko Crowther, contributed significantly to the line of Wilson Bennett Bass born 1840.

Allen Gindlesperger shared his information on the Shug Bass line, which was a tremendous help.

To those of you that shared updates, corrections, and additions on you imediat line or family, I can't thank you enough. This document could not be what it is without you.

It is my goal and hope to continue working on these records, to update them as the family grows, associate relationships and family history with documentation as well as personal accounts and pictures.

The printed copy many of you have from June of 2016 represents my initial effort. The book represented the compilation and reorganization of previous documents as well as some added discoveries and documentation, some now removed due to inconsistent documentation.

Since that time, I have updated my records with family additions of which I am aware. The additions are from personal correspondents with the family involved and online resources, such as census records and other digital documents. This book, the 2017 edition of my records and BassFamilyRecord.com are, as with all records of its kind, a work in progress. Documenting, expanding, and proving the legitimacy of the data will be ongoing.

These records are both incomplete and imperfect; in my work I have found and corrected errors in dates, spelling, gender, relationship and names. It is inevitable that I have also duplicated and created other mistakes of the same kinds. If you notice any mistakes, missing information or individuals omitted from this record please let me know.

God Bless,

Nicholas Bruce Bass

1. INTRODUCTION

STATISTICS

This document reports the details of 4056 individuals, of which 2085 are male and 1938 are female. Of the 860 individuals with recorded birth and death dates, the average lifespan was 65.4 years. Of these, 479 males averaged 61.7 years, and 381 females averaged 70 years.

The longest living male was Charles Augustus Gregory Sr.[120], who died aged 104. The longest living female was Corinne Gregory[548], who died aged 103.

There are 1440 families reported. 1058 of these families are reported as having children, with an average of 2.6 children per family.

THE NARRATIVE SECTIONS

The "Direct Relations" section reports the details of individuals who have a direct family connection to Wilson Bass[1]. The section is broken into sub-sections for each generation, within which the individuals are listed in order of closeness of relationship. The sequence numbers are used throughout the document to cross-reference back to the detailed entry of an individual.

With a narrative section, each generation is shown as a separate subsection, within which the individuals are listed in order of the closeness of their relationship to Wilson Bass[1].

COUSIN RELATIONSHIPS

Cousin relationships are determined by distance (first, second, third, etc.), and times removed.

Distance is determined as one less than the lower number of the previous generations traversed back from each of the individuals until the first common ancestor is found. Thus, if two people of the same generation have a common great-grandparent (three generations back), they are second cousins.

Removal is determined by the number of generations which separate the two people. For example, consider your first cousin's children. Because your common ancestor with them is your grandfather (two generations back) and their great-grandfather (three generations back), you are first cousins, once removed.

How to find people with reference numbers.

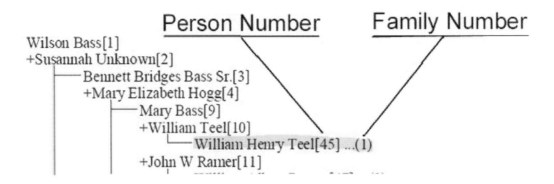

Go to the DESCENDANTS section and find Family Number 1, you'll find more info on Henry's family.

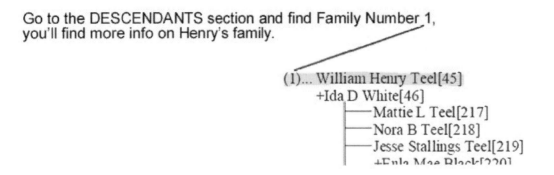

Go to the DIRECT RELATIONS section and find the Person Number 45, and you will find even more details on Henry and his family.

3rd Generation of Descendants

45. WILLIAM HENRY TEEL (see Descendants) was born on January 7, 1863.
Teel[10] and Mary Bass[9]

2. DESCENDANTS

```
Wilson Bass[1]
+Susannah ?[2]
        ├── Bennett Bridges Bass Sr.[3]
        │   +Mary Elizabeth Hogg[4]
        │           ├── Mary Bass[9]
        │           │   +William Teel[10]
        │           │           └── William Henry Teel[45] ...(1)
        │           │   +John W Ramer[11]
        │           │           ├── William Albert Ramer[47] ...(2)
        │           │           ├── John Ramer[49] ...(3)
        │           │           ├── Jacob D Ramer[51] ...(4)
        │           │           ├── James W Ramer[54]
        │           │           ├── Nancy Elizabeth Ramer[55] ...(5)
        │           │           ├── Alfred Calvin Ramer[57]
        │           │           └── Mae Ramer[58] ...(6)
        │           ├── Wilson Bennett Bass[12]
        │           │   +Jane Teel[13]
        │           │           ├── Benjamin Wilson Bass[60] ...(7)
        │           │           └── William Riley Bass[64] ...(8)
        │           ├── Nancy Bass[14]
        │           │   +James Teel[15]
        │           │           ├── Bennett B. Teel[66]
        │           │           ├── Bruner Teel[67]
        │           │           ├── Melvine Lavina Teel[68] ...(9)
        │           │           ├── Annie Teel[70]
        │           │           ├── Elizabeth Teel[71] ...(10)
        │           │           ├── John Teel[73] ...(11)
        │           │           ├── Nancy Viola Teel[75] ...(12)
        │           │           ├── William Riley Teel[77] ...(13)
        │           │           ├── Henry Vauceous Teel[79] ...(14)
        │           │           └── Mattie Teel[81] ...(15)
        │           ├── Levina Bass[16]
        │           ├── Holland Middleton Bass[17] ...(16)
        │           ├── James Hilliard Bass[19]
        │           ├── Bennett Bridges Bass Jr.[20] ...(17)
        │           ├── Elizabeth Bass[24]
        │           │   +Jake Ramer[25]
        │           │           ├── Nancy A. Ramer[137] ...(18)
        │           │           └── John Ramer[139] ...(19)
        │           ├── Martha Jane Bass[26] ...(20)
        │           └── William Riley Bass[28] ...(21)
        ├── Nancy Bass[5]
        │   +William Padgett[6]
        │           ├── Jane Padgett[30]
        │           │   +William Forman Ward[31]
        │           │           └── Margaret Jane Ward[185] ...(22)
        │           ├── Henry Padgett[32]
        │           ├── Levinta Padgett[33] ...(23)
        │           ├── Elizabeth H. Padgett[36] ...(24)
        │           └── Nancy Ann Padgett[38] ...(25)
        └── William Riley Bass[7]
            +Mary Straughn[8]
                    ├── James W. Bass[40]
                    ├── John Bass[41]
                    ├── William M. Bass[42] ...(26)
                    └── Riley Bass[44]
```

Wilson Bass

```
(1)... William Henry Teel[45]
   +Ida D White[46]
         ├── Mattie L Teel[213]
         ├── Nora B Teel[214]
         ├── Jesse Stallings Teel[215]
         │   +Eula Mae Black[216]
         │      └── Myrtice Mae Teel[823]
         ├── James Bennett Teel[217]
         ├── Oliver B Teel[218]
         └── Aaron Teel[219]
             +Bessie Harrelson[220]
                   ├── Mary Ethel Teel[824]
                   │   +J. B. Brooks[825]
                   │         ├── Lester Brooks[2012]
                   │         ├── Sue Brooks[2013]
                   │         ├── Sherry Brooks[2014]
                   │         └── Sandra Brooks[2015]
                   ├── Marie Teel[826]
                   │   +Pete Armstrong[827]
                   │      └── Troyce Armstrong[2016]
                   ├── Vera Merle Teel[828]
                   │   +Cecil Cross[829]
                   │         ├── Jerry Cross[2017]
                   │         ├── Donna Cross[2018]
                   │         └── Billy Cross[2019]
                   ├── Aaron Teel Jr.[830]
                   │   +Jean Childs[831]
                   │         ├── Dexter Teel[2020]
                   │         ├── Debra Kay Teel[2021]
                   │         └── Keneth Ra Teel[2022]
                   └── Frances Ida Teel[832]
                       +Quinton Gene Bass[444]
                             ├── Beverly Lynn Bass[1326]
                             │   +Anthony Scott[1327]
                             │   +William Bryan Rogers Jr.[1328]
                             │      └── William Bryan Rogers III[2618]
                             └── Wesley Alan Bass[1329]
                                 +Donna Chrzastek[1330]
                                    └── Joseph Blaze Chrzastek Bass[2619]
                                        +Alyssa Stark[2620]
                                           └── Emberlynn Crystal Chrzastek-Bass[3601]
                       +Richard Junior Patterson[833]
                       +Bennie Bozeman[834]
```

Left: Ida D. White, wife of William Henry Teel.

Below: Mary Ethel Teel, daughter of Aaron and Bessie Teel.

Left: William and Beverly Rogers with their son William Rogers.

Descendants

```
(2)... William Albert Ramer[47]
     +Florence Missouri Howard[48]
              ├── James William Ramer[221]
              ├── Dewey William Ramer[222]
              │   +Mattie Lucile Johnson[223]
              │            ├── Winford Eugene Ramer Sr.[835]
              │            │   +Nancy Yates[836]
              │            │            ├── Jerry Edward Ramer[2023]
              │            │            ├── Winford Eugene Ramer Jr.[2024]
              │            │            │   +Linda Mead[2025]
              │            │            │            ├── Justin Ramer[3268]
              │            │            │            └── Jennifer Ramer[3269]
              │            │            │                +Mr. Perez[3270]
              │            │            │                         └── Mr. Perez[3938]
              │            │            └── Margaret Ramer[2026]
              │            ├── James Ramer[837]
              │            ├── Ms. Ramer[838]
              │            ├── Buddy Ramer[839]
              │            └── Mildred Ramer[840]
              ├── Lena Zelma Ramer[224]
              ├── Athon Ramer Sr.[225]
              ├── John Bennett Ramer[226]
              │   +Vera Clark[227]
              ├── Mary E Ramer[228]
              ├── William Calvin Ramer[229]
              ├── Albert Farrell Ramer[230]
              │   +Mamie Ada ?[231]
              │            ├── Dorothy Ramer[841]
              │            └── Derward Ramer[842]
              ├── Jesse C Ramer[232]
              │   +H. Closon[233]
              ├── Homer Closon Ramer[234]
              ├── Savannah Irene Ramer[235]
              └── Walter Otis Ramer[236]

(3)... John Ramer[49]
      +Ella Melissa Howard[50]
              ├── James W Ramer[237]
              └── Claude A Ramer[238]
```

Wilson Bass

```
(4)... Jacob D Ramer[51]
    +Illinoy Bulger[52]
            ├── Beulah Ramer[239]
            │   +Amos White[240]
            │       └── James Thomas White Sr.[843]
            │           +Marvette Faye Davis[909]
            │               ├── Steve White[2027]
            │               │   +Casey ?[2028]
            │               │       ├── Mr. White[3271]
            │               │       └── Mr. White[3272]
            │               ├── Mr. White[2029]
            │               │   +Ms. ?[2030]
            │               │       └── Mr. White[3273]
            │               ├── Mr. White[2031]
            │               └── Mr. White[2032]
            │                   +Ms. ?[2033]
            ├── Major Ramer[241]
            ├── Mary Dovie Ramer[242]
            │   +William Travis Wallace[243]
            │       └── Richard Wallace[844]
            └── Millard Ramer[244]
    +Savannah Odom[53]
            └── Maggie Mae Ramer[245]

(5)... Nancy Elizabeth Ramer[55]
    +Wes Lindsey[56]

(6)... Mae Ramer[58]
    +Mr. Forman[59]
```

Descendants

```
(7)... Benjamin Wilson Bass[60]
    +Matilda Hall[61]
            ── Cynthia Lillian Bass[246]
              +John Curtis Barneycastle[247]
                    ── Ester C Barneycastle[845]
                      +Alford L Marcontell[846]
            ── Mr. Bass[248]
            ── Mr. Bass[249]
            ── Martin Luther Bass[250]
              +Marvel May Murphy[251]
            ── Susan Viola Bass[252]
              +Elzie Barneycastle[253]
                    ── Cynthia Lillian Barneycastle[847]
                    ── Benjamin Wilson Barneycastle[848]
                      +Lola Mae Keels[849]
                            ── Hazel Marie Barneycastle[2034]
                            ── Sue Adele Barneycastle[2035]
                              +Edmond Hardcastle[2036]
                                    ── Edmond Hardcastle Jr.[3274]
                                      +Rose ?[3275]
                                    ── Susan Hardcastle[3276]
                                      +Tony ?[3277]
                                    ── Timothy Hardcastle[3278]
                                    ── Pamela Hardcastle[3279]
                                      +Todd ?[3280]
                                    ── Greta Hardcastle[3281]
                            ── Bennie Mae Barneycastle[2037]
                              +Louis George Willis Jr.[2038]
                    ── James William Barneycastle[850]
                    ── Martin Luther Barneycastle[851]
                      +Prudie Lee Fairclothe[852]
                    ── Nobie Barneycastle[853]
                    ── Isabelle Barneycastle[854]
                      +Clarence Johnnie[855]
                            ── Ms. Johnnie[2039]
                    ── L. C. Barneycastle[856]
                      +Inez Hooks[857]
                    ── Todd Barneycastle[858]
                    ── Lula Barneycastle[859]
                    ── Eula Barneycastle[860]
                      +Walter Lee Neel[861]
            ── Wilson Lafayette Bass[254]
              +Nannie Witt[255]
                    ── Alvin Leon Bass[862]
            ── Thomas Watson Bass[256]
            ── Benjamin Eli Bass[257]
              +Bernice Mitchell[258]
    +Frieda Kamilla Schmitt[62]
            ── Douglas U Bass[259]
            ── Thelma B Bass[260]
            ── Louis O Bass[261]
            ── Gustavus Bass[262]
    +E. A. Cameron[63]
```

Sue Adele Barneycastle

Bennie Mae Barneycastle

(8)... William Riley Bass[64]
    +Frances Elizabeth Collins[65]
- Mary Susannah Bass[263]
- Eliza Jane Bass[264]
- Allen Milford Bass[265]
  - +Minnie Horton[266]
    - William Andrew Bass[863]
    - Sarah Francis Bass[864]
- John Riley Bass[267]
  - +Viola Mae Shaw[268]
    - Joyce Imogene Bass[865]
    - Dorothy Bass[866]
    - Margaret Bass[867]
    - Glenn Donald "Johnny" Bass[868]
      - +Olis Geneva Butler[869]
    - Gwendolyn Bass[870]
- Daniel Materson Bass[269]
  - +Ione Shafer[270]
    - Mr. Bass[871]
  - +Katherine Gladys Lee[271]
    - Mr. Bass[872]
    - Katherine Gladys Bass[873] ...(27)
    - Daniel Materson Bass Jr.[875] ...(28)
    - Ray Leonard Bass[877]
    - Kenneth Riley Bass Sr.[878] ...(29)
- Benjamin Edward Bass[272]
  - +Hazel Mae Laughlin[273]
    - Hazel Louise Bass[881]
      - +John Henry Harrel[882]
    - Dorothy Bass[883] ...(30)
    - Ben E Bass[885]
- Etta Mary Bass[274]
  - +Alexander Gilbert Ralston[275]
    - Jean Ralston[886] ...(31)
    - Mark Ralston[888]
  - +Alpha B. Barton[276]
    - A. Bruce Barton[889]
    - Grant B Barton[890]
    - Mary Etta Barton[891]
    - Dixie Barton[892]
- Mary Etta Bass[277]
  - +Joseph Doyle Harris[278]
    - Vincent Harris[893]
    - Leo Patrick Harris[894]
    - Joseph Riley Harris[895]
    - Mary Patricia Harris[896]
    - David Joseph Harris[897]
    - Michael James Harris[898] ...(32)
    - Mary Etta Harris[900]
    - Bernadette Harris[901]
    - John Paul Harris[902]
    - Robert Thomas Harris[903]
- Joseph Carson Bass[279]
  - +Winnetta Cash[280]
- Eva Elizabeth Bass[281] ...(33)
- Martha Bass[283]

(9)... Melvine Lavina Teel[68]
    +James A. Floyd[69]
- Bennett Abner Floyd[284]

William Riley Bass and Frances Elizabeth Collins on their homestead in Utah.

William Riley "Bill" Bass Store in Saratoga Texas.

Left: Melvine Lavina Teel, wife of James A. Floyd.

```
(10)... Elizabeth Teel[71]
    +John Walter Davis[72]
        ├── Lena Mae Davis[285]
        ├── Willie Ophellia Davis[286]
        ├── Nora Davis[287]
        ├── John Sumpter Davis[288]
        ├── Mirtice Davis[289]
        ├── Athen Davis[290]
        │   +Lottie Johnson Hall[291]
        │       ├── Louvenia Davis[908]
        │       ├── Marvette Faye Davis[909]
        │       └── James C Davis[910]
        ├── Elma Davis[292]
        └── Ethel Louise Davis[293]

(11)... John Teel[73]
    +Margaret Josephine Hart[74]
        ├── William Greeley Teel[294]
        │   +Rubie L Kelley[792]
        │       ├── Dorothy Helen Teel[911]
        │       │   +Orange Arnold Herrington[912]
        │       │       ├── Larry Bradley Herrington[2076]
        │       │       │   +Patricia June Wiggins[2077]
        │       │       │       └── Ella Alesia Clauser[3294]
        │       │       ├── Jimmie T Herrington[2078]
        │       │       └── Joseph A Herrington[2079]
        │       └── William Olen Teel[913]
        ├── James Samuel Teel[295]
        ├── George Fred Teel[296]
        ├── Alex Richard Teel[297]
        │   +Annie Bell Padgett[298]
        │       ├── Richard Alex Teel Jr.[914]
        │       │   +Jewel Gertrude Fuqua[915]
        │       ├── Donald Teel[916]
        │       └── Rufus Arnold Teel Teel[917]
        ├── Mayme Lee Teel[299]
        │   +George Henry Godwin[300]
        ├── Corine Virginia Teel[301]
        ├── Dora Margaret Teel[302]
        │   +Rupert Harrelson Blair[303]
        ├── Martha Lena Teel[304]
        │   +Autrey Lewis Johnson[305]
        │       └── Wayne Carroll Johnson[918]
        ├── Ruben Everett Teel[306]
        │   +Eula May Jackson[307]
        │       ├── John Everette Teel[919]
        │       └── James Jery Teel Teel[920]
        └── Bernice Cathleen Teel[308]
            +Orlando Dudley Cary[309]
                ├── Carolyn Cary[921]
                └── Richard Derhyl Cary[922]
                    +Henryetta Nadine Bradley[923]
                        └── Edwin Kieth Cary[2080]

(12)... Nancy Viola Teel[75]
    +Rob Hart[76]
```

John Teel and Margaret Josephine Hart

Rupert Harrelson Blair, husband of Dora Margaret Teel

(13)... William Riley Teel[77]
+Addie Augusta Stokes[78]
├── Willie Samson Teel[310]
│   +Margaret Mae Padgett[311]
├── Atress Teel[312]
├── Jimie L Teel[313]
└── Gladys Teel[314]
    +Fredrick Harling Schmidt[315]
    ├── Carol Jean Hassell[924]
    └── Barbara Burns Schmidt[925]
    +Frank Pete Hassell[316]
    ├── Jimmie Joe Hassell[926]
    ├── Jerry Donald Hassell[927]
    └── Sharon A Hassell[928]
    +Hyram Hayes Straughter[317]

(14)... Henry Vauceous Teel[79]
+Ella Padgett[80]
├── Addie Lee Teel[318]
├── James Vauciuos Teel[319]
└── James Elijah Teel[320]
    +Sara Nancy Teel[321]
    └── Mary Jane Teel[929]

(15)... Mattie Teel[81]
+John Kirklin[82]

Holland Middleton Sr. and Christian (Ward) Bass

(16)... Holland Middleton Bass[17]
    +Christian Ward[18]
- Levina Bass[83]
- William Bennett Bass[84]
  - +Emily Estelle Jordan[85]
    - Genola Bass[322] ...(34)
    - Maxie Milo Bass[324] ...(35)
    - Martha Naomi Bass[327] ...(36)
    - Christian Ottie Lee Bass[329] ...(37)
    - Ossie Mae Bass[331] ...(38)
- Nancy Jane Middleton Bass[86]
  - +James Egie Nardis McGlaun[87]
    - James Hollie McGlaun[333] ...(39)
    - Willie Oscar McGlaun[335] ...(40)
    - Virgil Lee McGlaun[337] ...(41)
    - Ineta McGlaun[340]
    - Orbey Ray McGlaun[341] ...(42)
    - Orion T McGlaun[343] ...(43)
- Catherine Elizabeth Bass[88]
- Isabell Bass[89]
  - +James Henry Rowell[90]
    - Ida Mae Rowell[345] ...(44)
    - Lettie V. Rowell[347] ...(45)
    - Leroy Rowell[348] ...(46)
    - Eva Mae Rowell[350] ...(47)
  - +William Benjamin Huckabaa[91]
    - Eugene Huckaba[353] ...(48)
    - Addie Irene Huckaba[355] ...(49)
- James Dallas Bass[92]
  - +Amie Isabel Bedgood[93]
    - Bessie Luvine Bass[357] ...(50)
    - James Henry Bass[359] ...(51)
    - Hillary J. Bass[362]
    - Magdaline Bass[363]
    - Ray-Monde Bass[364] ...(52)
    - John Clayton Bass[366] ...(53)
    - Marvin Dallas Bass Sr.[368] ...(54)
    - Sarah Christian Bass[370] ...(55)
    - Gerald Howard Bass Sr.[372] ...(56)
- Mary Alice Bass[94]
  - +Martin Edward Posey[95]
    - Mae Belle Posey[374] ...(57)
    - Clifton Posey[376]
    - Preston Dallas Posey[377] ...(58)
    - Chester Posey[379] ...(59)
    - Holland Middleton Posey[381]
    - Stacy Denton Posey[382] ...(60)
    - Bonnie Lee Posey[384] ...(61)
    - Cora Lee Posey[386]
    - Mary Evelyn Posey[387] ...(62)
    - Cleavy Edward Posey Sr.[389] ...(63)
- Holley Middleton Bass[96] ...(64)
- Joseph Alexander Bass[98] ...(65)
- John Riley Bass[100] ...(66)
- Stacy Bibner Bass[102] ...(67)
- Martha Christian Bass[104] ...(68)

Standing left to right: John, Holley, Joe, Stacy Bass
Sitting left to right: Christian, Bill, Nancy, Dallas Bass

Holland M. Bass and Christian Ward, with grandson Maxie Milo Bass.

(17)... Bennett Bridges Bass Jr.[20]
    +Julia Padgett[21]
    +Mary Frances Padgett[22]
        ├── Bennett Bridges Bass III[106]
        │   +Alice Kinlaw[107]
        │   ├── Earnest True Bass Sr.[454] ...(69)
        │   ├── Richard Carl Bass Sr.[458] ...(70)
        │   └── William Bennett Bass[461] ...(71)
        │   +Jonnie Lillian Ballard[108]
        │   ├── Mary Leona Bass[464] ...(72)
        │   └── Henry Obie Bass[466] ...(73)
        │   +Rosa Lee Shuler[109]
        │   └── Morgan Bennett Bass[468]
        ├── Mary Elizabeth Bass[110]
        │   +William Henry Williams[111]
        │   ├── Vinnie Janice Williams[469] ...(74)
        │   ├── Ada Ola Williams[471]
        │   │   +Grover Cleveland Cobb[472]
        │   ├── Francis Folsam Williams[473] ...(75)
        │   ├── Mattie Dora Williams[475] ...(76)
        │   ├── Laura May Williams Williams[477] ...(77)
        │   ├── Henry Gordon Williams[479] ...(78)
        │   ├── William Marcus Williams[481] ...(79)
        │   ├── Naomi Williams[483] ...(80)
        │   ├── Annie Ruth Williams[485] ...(81)
        │   ├── Wilmer Newton Williams[487] ...(82)
        │   ├── Lillian Elizabeth Williams[489] ...(83)
        │   └── Buna Lucille Williams[491] ...(84)
        ├── Elijah L. Bass[112]
        ├── James Wilson Bass[113]
        │   +Emmie Cornelia Hutto[114]
        │   ├── Arrie Bernice Bass[493] ...(85)
        │   ├── Ollie Albert Bass[495]
        │   ├── Eva Allie Bass[496] ...(86)
        │   ├── Jamie Ike Bass[498] ...(87)
        │   ├── Joseph Aaron Bass[500]
        │   ├── Julius Clarence Bass[501] ...(88)
        │   ├── Mary Annie Bass[503] ...(89)
        │   ├── Jessie D Bass[505] ...(90)
        │   ├── Leon Pendry Bass[507] ...(91)
        │   ├── Snyder Clayton Bass[509] ...(92)
        │   ├── Velma Bertha Bass[511] ...(93)
        │   └── Edith Inez Bass[513] ...(94)
        ├── John Bridges Bass[115] ...(95)
        ├── Laura Lee Bass[117] ...(96)
        ├── Sheila Josephine Bass[119] ...(97)
        ├── Henry Harrelson Bass[121] ...(98)
        ├── Riley B Bass[123]
        │   +Gussie Palmer[124]
        ├── Dennis Bridges Bass[125] ...(99)
        ├── Katie Bass[127]
        ├── Bertie B Bass[128] ...(100)
        ├── Florence Bass[130] ...(101)
        └── Lawrence Bass[134]
    +Josiphine Padgett[23]
        └── Thomas Sonny Padgett[135] ...(102)

Bennett Bridges Bass III with his wife Rosa Lee Edwards

(18)... Nancy A. Ramer[137]
　　　+George W. Hart[138]
　　　　　── Grover Cleveland Hart[609]
　　　　　　　+Katie Vera Dobbs[610]
　　　　　　　+Cora Mattie Nichols[611]
　　　　　── Marshall Hart[612]
　　　　　── Ivey W Hart[613]
　　　　　── Ina May Hart[614]
　　　　　── Maggie Hart[615]
　　　　　── Dewey H Hart[616]

(19)... John Ramer[139]
　　　+Nettie Pippins[140]

Emmie Cornelia Hutto, wife of James Wilson Bass, with her family at a reunion. Emmie is the lady seated far right.

(20)... Martha Jane Bass[26]
    +George Washington Parrish[27]
        ├── Mary Ellen Parrish[141]
        +Leonard Destin Jr.[142]
            ├── Mary Ellen Destin[617]
            +Odem Thomas Melvin Sr.[618]
                ├── Odem Thomas Melvin Jr.[1639]
                +Beulah Petit[1640]
                    └── Merwyn T. Melvin I[2960] ...(103)
                ├── Gwen Melvin[1641] ...(104)
                ├── Carolyn Melvin[1643] ...(105)
                └── Bennie Margaret Melvin[1645] ...(106)
            └── Leonard Destin III[619]
            +Viola B Oglesby[620]
                ├── Sylvia Destin[1647]
                └── Linda Destin[1648]
        ├── Emeline Parrish[143]
        +George Sanford Marler[144]
            ├── Aquilla Marler[621]
            +Charlotte Marilla Barnes[622]
                ├── Audrey Marler[1649]
                └── Aquilla Jr Marler[1650]
            ├── Pricilla Marler[623]
            +Andrew Gay Hogeboom[624]
            └── Madeline M Marler[625]
            +Jesse E Brunson[626]
                └── Jean Brunson[1651]
        ├── Charles W. Parrish[145]
        +Lucy L Etheridge[146]
        ├── Martha Jane Parrish[147]
        +Bealaster S. Spence[148]
        ├── John Robert Parrish[149]
        +Patsy Mae Simmons[150]
            └── Bobbie Parrish[627]
        ├── Tolbert Tillis Parrish[151]
        +Laura L. Brown[152]
        ├── Fanny A. Parrish[153]
        ├── Leanna Parrish[154]
        +James Ottis Gunter[155]
            ├── Charles Clyde Gunter[628]
            └── Otto Lee Gunter[629]
        ├── Ella Parrish[156]
        +James E Jerauld[157]
            └── James E Jerauld Jr.[630]
        └── James Albert Parrish[158]
        +Maggie Lou Etheridge[159]
            ├── Genevieve Parrish[631]
            +Rex Ray Kohr[632]
                ├── Patricia Tracie Kohr[1652]
                └── Mr./Ms. Kohr[1653]
            ├── Geraldine Parrish[633]
            +Frank Brown[634]
                ├── Mr./Ms. Brown[1654]
                └── Mr./Ms. Brown[1655]
            └── James Albert Parrish Jr.[635] ...(107)

Mary Parrish   Leonard Destin, Jr.

Capt. James Albert Parrish and Maggie Lou Etheridge

```
(21)... William Riley Bass[28]
     +Nancy Jane Ward[29]
          ├── Mary Elizabeth Bass[160]
          │   +James Hillard Cason[161]
          │        ├── Mary Florence Cason[637] ...(108)
          │        ├── Zonnie Bell Cason[639] ...(109)
          │        ├── William Charles Cason[641] ...(110)
          │        ├── Grady J. Cason[643] ...(111)
          │        ├── John F. Cason[645] ...(112)
          │        └── Coleman R. Cason[647] ...(113)
          ├── William Henry Bass[162]
          │   +Dora Alice Purvis[163]
          │        ├── Veilla Maine Bass[650] ...(114)
          │        ├── Leilla Mae Bass[652] ...(115)
          │        ├── Henry Grady Bass[655] ...(116)
          │        ├── Clyde Kermit Bass Sr.[657] ...(117)
          │        ├── Beatrice Izora Bass[659] ...(118)
          │        ├── Mary Bonnie Bass[661] ...(119)
          │        ├── Floyd Irwin Bass[663] ...(120)
          │        ├── Autray Alto Bass[665] ...(121)
          │        ├── Fannie Esther Bass[667] ...(122)
          │        └── Nannie Ruth Bass[669] ...(123)
          ├── Catherine Emma Bass[164]
          │   +Elzy Henderson Garvin[165]
          │        ├── Nancy Christian Garvin[671] ...(124)
          │        ├── Willier Garvin[673] ...(125)
          │        ├── Sherman Garvin[675] ...(126)
          │        ├── Ollie Garvin[677]
          │        └── Odessa Garvin[678] ...(127)
          ├── Savannah Bass[166]
          │   +James Ocie Posey[167]
          │        ├── Cora Nolia Posey[680] ...(128)
          │        ├── Pearlie Mae Posey[682] ...(129)
          │        ├── Gussie Lee Posey[684] ...(130)
          │        ├── Mary Francis Posey[686] ...(131)
          │        ├── William Albert Posey[688] ...(132)
          │        └── Vianna Catherine Posey[690] ...(133)
          ├── Nancy Jane Bass[168]
          │   +Leslie Riley Edwards Sr.[169]
          │        ├── Josephine E Edwards[692] ...(134)
          │        ├── Janie Edwards[694] ...(135)
          │        ├── Rossa Edwards[696] ...(136)
          │        ├── Harry Edwards[699] ...(137)
          │        ├── Early Edwards[701] ...(138)
          │        ├── Murry Edwards[703]
          │        ├── Correne Edwards[704] ...(139)
          │        └── Ervin Hartley Edwards[706] ...(140)
          ├── Minnie Josephine Bass[170]
          ├── Florence Bass[171]
          ├── Riley John Bass[172] ...(141)
          ├── James Bennett Bass[174] ...(142)
          ├── Charles Bass[176]
          ├── Mattie O. Bass[177] ...(143)
          ├── Flora Bass[179] ...(144)
          ├── Florine Dorothy Bass[181] ...(145)
          └── Lillie May Bass[183] ...(146)
```

William Riley Bass and Nancy Jane Ward

Savannah Bass Posey

(22)... Margaret Jane Ward[185]
+ Oscar H. Reeves[186]
├── William Reeves[764]
├── Priscilla Reeves[765]
├── Johnnie Reeves[766]
└── Oscar B Reeves[767]

(23)... Levinta Padgett[33]
+ Samuel Godwin[34]
├── Nancy G. Godwin[187]
└── Lucy Godwin[188]
+ Robert Francis Jordan[35]
├── Ida Jordan[189]
└── Henry Jordan[190]

(24)... Elizabeth H. Padgett[36]
+ John Elbert Jordan[37]
├── Della Jordan[191]
│   + Thomas Rueben Roberts[192]
│   ├── Thomas H Roberts[768]
│   ├── Mary K Roberts[769]
│   └── Marguerite E Roberts[770]
└── Mary Jordan[193]

Columbus Daniel Hart and Nancy Padgett Hart and family c. 1905-06. Left to Right (back row) Alice Hart Kelley and G. W. Kelley, Ader Hart Campbell and William N. Campbell. Virginia Hart Goodlet and Charles Goodlet and dtr Lucille. Rubin Hart and Leila Cross Hart. John Hart, Nancy Lena (Babe) and Mary Nora (Sweet) Hart. (front row) Allen Kelley (son of Alice &. G. W.) Aline Hart (dtr. of Jim). Ruby Kelley (dtr. of Alice &. G. W.), Columbus Daniel Hart, Lella (dtr. of Jim), Nancy (Nannie) Hart, Jim Hart and son Dan, Flossie and dtr. Birdie and Fred Columbus Kelley (son of Alice & G. W.)

Descendants

```
(25)... Nancy Ann Padgett[38]
    +Columbus Daniel Hart[39]
        ├─James William Hart[194]
        │  +Flossie Bell[195]
        │      ├─Maudie Aline Hart[771]
        │      ├─Lella Mae Hart[772]
        │      ├─Ellen Hart[773]
        │      ├─William Daniel Hart[774]
        │      │  +Eva Irene Durden[775]
        │      │      ├─William Daniel Hart[1982]
        │      │      ├─Eugene Hart[1983]
        │      │      └─Mabel Erline Hart[1984]
        │      ├─Birdie H Hart[776]
        │      │  +Charlie C Davis[777]
        │      ├─James Travis Hart[778]
        │      │  +Delia Adeline Bradley[779]
        │      │      ├─James B Hart[1985]
        │      │      └─Sherley L Hart[1986]
        │      ├─Allen Trammel Hart[780]
        │      │  +Annie P Perry[781]
        │      │      └─Julia A Hart[1987]
        │      ├─Leonard V. Hart[782] ...(147)
        │      ├─W C Hart[784]
        │      └─Jynelle Hart[785] ...(148)
        ├─John C Hart[196]
        ├─Virginia Hart[197]
        │  +Charles Henry Goodlett[198]
        │      └─Lucille Goodlett[787]
        ├─Alice Rebecca Hart[199]
        │  +George Washington Kelley[200]
        │      ├─Fred Columbus Kelley[788] ...(149)
        │      ├─William Allen Kelley[790]
        │      ├─Daniel Kelley[791]
        │      ├─Rubie L Kelley[792]
        │      ├─John Kelley[793]
        │      ├─Columbus Daniel Kelley[794] ...(150)
        │      └─Mildred Hazel Kelley[797]
        ├─Rubin Richard Hart[201]
        │  +Laura Elizabeth Cross[202]
        ├─Ada Alabama Hart[203]
        │  +William Nicholas Campbell[204]
        │      ├─Claude C. Campbell[798]
        │      ├─Mary R Campbell[799]
        │      └─William Nicholas Campbell Jr.[800]
        ├─Nancy Lena Hart[205]
        │  +John Jefferson Cushing[206]
        │      ├─William D "Willie" Cushing[801]
        │      ├─Woodrow Cushing[802]
        │      ├─John Jefferson Cushing[803]
        │      └─Clyde L Cushing[804]
        └─Mary Nora Hart[207]
           +Joseph Josh Davis[208]
               ├─Eleanor D. Hart[805]
               ├─Jack Columbus Davis[806]
               ├─James Rudalph Davis[807]
               └─Nannie Ruth Davis[808]
```

Wilson Bass

(26)... William M. Bass[42]
    +Abigail Welch[43]
        ├── Mary A. Bass[209]
        │   +Liston Thomas Hutcheson[210]
        │   ├── William E Hutchison[809]
        │   ├── Harris G Hutchison[810]
        │   ├── Harold A Hutchison[811]
        │   └── Myrtle E Hutchison[812]
        └── William Riley Bass[211]
            +Augusta Cooper[212]
            ├── Velma Bass[813]
            │   +Horace E Poole[814]
            │   ├── Max Earl Poole[2001]
            │   │   +Mary Ann Smith[2002]
            │   │   ├── Brenda Poole[3264]
            │   │   └── Debbie Poole[3265]
            │   ├── Eddie Poole[2003]
            │   └── Carroll Poole[2004]
            ├── William Barney Bass[815]
            │   +Ruby Lena Padgett[816]
            ├── Maggie M Bass[817]
            ├── Clara M Bass[818]
            ├── Eva Mae Bass[819]
            │   +Dallas Clinton Fowler[820]
            │   └── Mr. Fowler[2005]
            │   +Ms. Gunnis[2006]
            │   └── Mr. Fowler[3266]
            │   +Ms. Owens[2007]
            │   └── Stanley Ray Fowler[3267]
            └── Horace Presley Bass[821]
                +Avie Brooks[822]
                ├── Judith Ellica Bass[2008]
                │   +Richard Ronald Rodgers Sr.[2009]
                └── Tommy Author Bass[2010]
                    +Kathy Ann Medows[2011]

(27)... Katherine Gladys Bass[873]
    +Kenneth Lynell Blume[874]
        └── Donna Lee Blume[2040]

(28)... Daniel Materson Bass Jr.[875]
    +Dorothy Victoria Farris[876]
        ├── Daniel S Bass[2041]
        │   +Barbara ?[2042]
        │   ├── Steve Bass[3282]
        │   ├── Casandra Bass[3283]
        │   └── Seth Bass[3284]
        ├── Brenda Bass[2043]
        │   +Ivar Weierholt[2044]
        ├── John Bass[2045]
        │   +Rachel ?[2046]
        ├── Nita Bass[2047]
        │   +Jim Evans[2048]
        └── Annette Bass[2049]
            +Les Torrey[2050]

Augusta Cooper, wife of William Riley Bass [211]

(29)... Kenneth Riley Bass Sr.[878]
    +Martha L. Batten[879]
        ├─Kenneth Riley Bass Jr.[2051]
        │ +Joy ?[2052]
        │ +Ms. ?[2053]
        │   ├─Gary Bass[3285]
        │   └─Terry Bass[3286]
        ├─Sharon Bass[2054]
        │ +Thomas McKinney[2055]
        └─Timothy Bass[2056]
          +Juanita Labove[2057]
    +Catherine ?[880]

(30)... Dorothy Bass[883]
    +Mr. Lasker[884]
        └─Mr. Lasker[2058]
          +Ms. ?[2059]
            ├─Mr. Lasker[3287]
            ├─Mr./Ms. Lasker[3288]
            ├─Mr./Ms. Lasker[3289]
            └─Mr. Lasker[3290]

(31)... Jean Ralston[886]
    +William Gresko[887]
        ├─Myrna E Gresko[2060]
        ├─William Mark Gresko[2061]
        │ +Ms. ?[2062]
        ├─Ronald Kay Gresko[2063]
        │ +Ms. ?[2064]
        │   ├─Ronald Kay Gresko[3291]
        │   └─Chastity Deannia Inez Gresko[3292]
        │   +Mr. ?[3293]
        ├─Edward Cecil Gresko[2065]
        ├─Etta Celia Gresko[2066]
        └─Mr. Gresko[2067]

(32)... Michael James Harris[898]
    +Betty Jean Flickinger[899]
        ├─Janis Mary Harris[2068]
        └─Nancy Kathryn Harris[2069]
          +Kevin Myers[2070]

(33)... Eva Elizabeth Bass[281]
    +Leonard Merrill Stevens[282]
        ├─Merrillyn Stevens[904]
        │ +Ronald Perkins Guymon[905]
        └─William Reed Stevens[906]
          +Betty Ann Jones[907]
            ├─Mr. Stevens[2071]
            ├─Ms. Stevens[2072]
            ├─Ms. Stevens[2073]
            ├─Mr. Stevens[2074]
            └─Mr. Stevens[2075]

Kenneth Riley Bass Sr.

Michael James Harris and Betty Jean Flickinger

Wilson Bass

```
(34)... Genola Bass[322]
     +Floyd S Spence[323]
          ├── Opal Virginia Spence[930]
          │   +Billie Batson[931]
          │        ├── David Jonathan Batson[2081]
          │        │   +Paula Jean Johnson[2082]
          │        │        └── Zackareah Jonathan Batson[3295]
          │        └── Robin Mario Batson[2083]
          │   +Oscar L. Brock[932]
          │        └── Dawn Denise Brock[2084]
          │            +Chuck Wallace[2085]
          │                 ├── Steven Wallace[3296]
          │                 └── Kevin Wallace[3297]
          └── Clyde Autry Spence[933]
              +Phyllis D. Baughman[934]
                   ├── Carl Leon Spence[2086]
                   ├── Dixie Irene Spence[2087]
                   │   +Timmy Wayne Burlison[2088]
                   │        ├── Timmy Wayne Burlison II[3298]
                   │        │   +Holly Christina Lord[3299]
                   │        │        └── Hannah Danielle Burlison[3939]
                   │        └── Shaun Michael Burlison[3300]
                   ├── Rhonda Sue Spence[2089]
                   │   +Kenneth A. Cain[2090]
                   │        ├── Renee S. Cain[3301]
                   │        │   +Ryan Winters[3302]
                   │        │        ├── Alysa L. Winters[3940]
                   │        │        ├── Tyler R. Winters[3941]
                   │        │        └── Logan Taylor Winters[3942]
                   │        │   +Renee S. Cain[3303]
                   │        ├── Kacey A. Cain[3304]
                   │        │   +Ms. Hendrix[3305]
                   │        │        ├── Damion T. Hendrix[3943]
                   │        │        └── Elijah Hendrix[3944]
                   │        └── Kenneth A. Cain II[3306]
                   ├── Robert Leon Spence[2091]
                   │   +Corinne Sue Smith[2092]
                   │        ├── Shannon Robert Spence[3307]
                   │        └── Cara Leane Spence[3308]
                   ├── James Scott Spence[2093]
                   ├── Floyd Colon Spence[2094]
                   │   +Terri S. Clark[2095]
                   │        └── Tabitha S. Spence[3309]
                   └── Clyde Autry Spence Jr.[2096]

(35)... Maxie Milo Bass[324]
     +Mollie Raley[325]
     +Lucile Byrd[326]
```

Genola Bass wife of Floyd S. Spence Genealogist for the original Bass Family Record.

(36)... Martha Naomi Bass[327]
   +Woodrow A. Wilkinson[328]
         ─── Wade Nathan Wilkinson[935]
            +Nellie Henry[936]
                  ─── Deborah Ann Wilkinson[2097]
                     +Frank James Milstead[2098]
                           ─── Aubrey Gene Milstead[3310] ...(151)
                           ─── Danita Ann Milstead[3312] ...(152)
                  ─── Delmus Nathan Wilkinson[2099]
                     +Mary Belinda Jordan[2100]
                           ─── Jordan Alexander Wilkinson[3314]
                     +Tamara Sue Landis[2101]
                  ─── Joy Denise Wilkinson[2102]
                     +Ecki Alexander Prater[2103]
                           ─── Wade Nathan Prater[3315]
                           ─── Isla Noel Prater[3316]
                           ─── Robert Calvin Prater[3317]
                  ─── Janet Lee Wilkinson[2104]
                     +John Ernest Balius[2105]
                           ─── Justin Eugene Balius[3318]
                           ─── Megan Catherine Balius[3319]
         ─── Floyce Genelle Wilkinson[937]
            +Joseph Shoven Steele[938]
                  ─── Joseph Wayne Steele[2106]
                     +Donna Lee Good[2107]
                           ─── Stephanie Ann Steele[3320]
                     +Kelli Ann Ottley[2108]
                           ─── Rebecca Ann Steele[3321]
                  ─── Larry Dale Steele[2109] ...(153)
                  ─── Donna Marie Steele[2111] ...(154)
                  ─── Terry Michael Steele[2113] ...(155)
         ─── Lorine Annette Wilkinson[939]
            +Roy H. Johnson[940]
                  ─── Lois Anette Johnson[2115] ...(156)
         ─── Judith Elaine Wilkinson[941]
            +Billy Register[942]
                  ─── Marcus Dean Register[2117] ...(157)
                  ─── Matthew Ward Register[2119] ...(158)
                  ─── Martha Grace Register[2121] ...(159)
         ─── Irma Arleen Wilkinson[943]
            +Eugene Fleming[944]
                  ─── Phillip Eugene Fleming[2123] ...(160)
                  ─── Laura Lenelle Fleming[2126] ...(161)
                  ─── Karen Lorine Fleming[2128] ...(162)
         ─── Roland Douglas Wilkinson[945]
            +Judith Harness[946]
                  ─── Rachel Wilkinson[2130]
                  ─── Joshua Wilkinson[2131]
         ─── Linda Aletha Wilkinson[947]
            +William Mooney[948]
         ─── Marcia Glendolyn Wilkinson[949]
            +Jerry Dotson[950]
                  ─── Ted Dotson[2132] ...(163)
                  ─── Tracy Dotson[2134] ...(164)
         ─── Neil Keith Wilkinson[951]

Martha Naomi Bass with her husband Woodrow A. Wilkinson.

(37)... Christian Ottie Lee Bass[329]
 +Glen Curtis Wilkinson[330]
  ├── Wenton Curtis Wilkinson[952]
  │ +Eloise Henry[953]
  │ +Mary Sue Walkup[954]
  │ ├── Ronald Daune Tuley[2136]
  │ ├── Pamela Ann Tuley[2137] ...(165)
  │ ├── Robert Tuley[2140]
  │ ├── Randall Glen Wilkinson[2141] ...(166)
  │ └── Warren Craig Wilkinson[2144]
  │   +April Lee Crabill[2145]
  │   └── Taylor Wilkinson[3356]
  ├── Dorothy Joan Wilkinson[955]
  │ +Eugene Odell Woodard[956]
  │ └── Gail Denise Woodard[2146] ...(167)
  ├── Ina Mae Wilkinson[957]
  │ +Donnie Jay Walters[958]
  │ ├── Don Monwell Walters[2150] ...(168)
  │ ├── Rodrick Jerome Walters[2152] ...(169)
  │ ├── Kenneth Layne Walters[2154] ...(170)
  │ └── Kim Dawn Walters[2156]
  │   +William Mills[2157]
  ├── Mona Idez Wilkinson[959]
  │ +Alfred Cook Jr.[960]
  │ ├── Lisa Marie Cook[2158] ...(171)
  │ ├── Yevette Lee Cook[2160]
  │ └── Jennifer Nell Cook[2161]
  ├── Lary Rodney Wilkinson[961]
  │ +Marie Antonette Cascone[962]
  │ ├── Lary Rodney Wilkinson Jr.[2162]
  │ ├── Brett Alan Wilkinson[2163]
  │ ├── Lisa Marie Wilkinson[2164]
  │ └── Katrina Marie Wilkinson[2165]
  ├── Chadrick Earl Wilkinson[963]
  │ +Judy Gail Kennedy[964]
  │ ├── Dena Gail Wilkinson[2166] ...(172)
  │ └── Christopher Del Wilkinson[2168] ...(173)
  ├── Glynda Carol Wilkinson[965]
  │ +James Charles Cupp[966]
  │ ├── Kimberly Ann Cupp[2170] ...(174)
  │ ├── James Landre Cupp[2172] ...(175)
  │ └── Dorothy Leigh Cupp[2173]
  ├── Norman Curtis Wilkinson[967]
  │ +Wanda Procktor[968]
  │ ├── Candace Delane Wilkinson[2174] ...(176)
  │ └── Shane Curtis Wilkinson[2176] ...(177)
  │ +Roberta Marie Ogle[969]
  │ +Tammy Sue Beasley[970]
  │ ├── Candace Delane Wilkinson[2178] ...(178)
  │ └── Shane Curtis Wilkinson[2180] ...(179)
  ├── Selina Benita Wilkinson[971]
  │ +Duane Allen Dawson Jr.[972]
  │ └── Duane Allen Dawson III[2182]
  └── Rebecca Louise Wilkinson[973]
   +Donnie Leroy Salter[974]
    └── Demetrius LaRoy Salter[2183]

Glynda Carol Wilkinson on the right, with her daughter Kimberly Ann Cupp. Both of these ladies made significant contripution to maintaining Bass family history through there work on various editions and updates of the Bass Family Record.

(38)... Ossie Mae Bass[331]
    +Jesse David Summerlin Jr.[332]
        └──Clarence Devon Summerlin[975]
            +Mary Beth Burnett[976]
                ├──Charles David Summerlin[2184]
                │   +Mary Jo Williamson[2185]
                │   ├──Sarah M. Summerlin[3384]
                │   └──Chad David Summerlin[3385]
                ├──Kathy Ann Summerlin[2186]
                │   └──Jason Sloan Leger[3386]
                └──Kimberly Jan Summerlin[2187]
    +Mary Annice Cotton[977]

(39)... James Hollie McGlaun[333]
    +Anna Reeder[334]
        └──Bobby McGlaun[978]
            +Betty Henley[979]
                ├──Joel Ray McGlaun[2188]
                ├──Mike Dewayne McGlaun[2189]
                ├──Randy Lamar McGlaun[2190]
                │   +Carin ?[2191]
                │   ├──Martial McGlaun[3387]
                │   └──Holly McGlaun[3388]
                └──Erin McGlaun[2193]
                    +Mr. Polzin[2194]
                        └──Mr./Ms. Polzin[3389]

Ossie May Bass

(40)... Willie Oscar McGlaun[335]
  +Clara Mae Schofield[336]
        ├── Ruby Nell McGlaun[980]
        │   +Ray Causie[981]
        │   └── Judy Ann Causie[2195]
        │   +Clyde Henry Mims Jr.[2196]
        │   └── Deborah Jane Causie[3390]
        ├── Mary Etta McGlaun[982]
        │   +Horace Worley[983]
        │   ├── Gary Wayne Worley[2197]
        │   ├── Pamela Jun Worley[2198]
        │   ├── Danny David Worley[2199]
        │   └── Robin Don Worley[2200]
        └── James Kenneth McGlaun[984]
            +Bonnie Brown[985]
                ├── Vickey Yvone McGlaun[2201]
                │   +David Lee Causey[2202]
                │   ├── Tawana Lynn Causey[3391]
                │   │   +Stanley Adam Sherrer[3392]
                │   └── Brandon Lee Causey[3393]
                │   +Michael C. Ferguson[2203]
                │   └── Lena LaRae Ferguson[3394]
                ├── James Tony McGlaun[2204]
                ├── James Kenny McGlaun Jr.[2205]
                │   +Lisa Perl Champion[2206]
                │   ├── James Kenneth McGlaun III[3395]
                │   └── Kimberly Ann McGlaun[3396]
                └── Lisa Rena McGlaun[2207]
                    +Kenneth A. Floyd Jr.[2208]
                        └── Kenneth A. Floyd III[3397]
                    +Ronald Leon O'neil[2209]
                        ├── Ronald Joseph O'neil[3398]
                        ├── Hope Rena O'neil[3399]
                        └── Joshua Aaron O'neil[3400]

James Egie McGlaun with his wife Nancy Jane Middleton Bass, parents of the McGlaun siblings listed on these pages.

(41)... Virgil Lee McGlaun[337]
    +Eula Lee Maughon[338]
        ├── Margie Ree McGlaun[986]
        │   +Bobby Wayne Elmore[987]
        │   ├── John Thomas Wade Elmore[2210]
        │   ├── Clayborn Lee Elmore[2211]
        │   └── Robert L. Elmore[2212]
        ├── Patricia Ann McGlaun[988]
        │   +Ricard Edward Messick[989]
        │   ├── James Edward Messick[2213]
        │   │   +Sheivella Maria Norris[2214]
        │   │   └── Amber Maria Messick[3401]
        │   └── Richard Brian Messick[2215]
        ├── Joyce Marie McGlaun[990]
        │   +Marzette Alford Lawson[991]
        │   ├── Sandra Dianne Lawson[2216]
        │   │   +Michael Todd Inabinett[2217]
        │   │   ├── Kayla Lynn Inabinett[3402]
        │   │   │   +Brett Aubrey Hudson[3403]
        │   │   │   └── Dutton Lee Hudson[3950]
        │   │   ├── Dallas Lawson Inabinett[3404]
        │   │   └── Brayden John Inabinett[3405]
        │   └── Karen Lynn Lawson[2218]
        │   +John Jeffery Sowell ?[2219]
        └── Sheila Dianne McGlaun[992]
            +Thomas Randall Mancil[993]
                ├── Kelley Michelle Mancil[2220]
                └── Mendy Leigh Mancil[2221]
    +Mary L. Holloway[339]

(42)... Orbey Ray McGlaun[341]
    +Helen Henderson[342]
        ├── Doris Irene McGlaun[994]
        │   +Bobby D. Henderson[995]
        │   ├── Laura Rebecca Henderson[2222]
        │   ├── Rhonda Leigh Henderson[2223]
        │   └── Sonia Denise Henderson[2224]
        └── Lamar Ray McGlaun[996]
            +Sara Ann Hair[997]
                └── Carol Ann McGlaun[2225]

(43)... Orion T McGlaun[343]
    +Evelyn Thompson[344]
        ├── Guinda McGlaun[998]
        └── Orion Dewayne McGlaun[999]

(44)... Ida Mae Rowell[345]
 +William Martin Huckabaa[346]
         ─── Martin Van Buren Huckabaa Sr.[1000]
           +Hazel Bass[1451]
                 ─── Mary Evelyn Huckabaa[2226]
                   +Edward Davidson[2227]
                         ─── Elizabeth Ann Davidson[3406] ...(180)
                 ─── Jerry Wayne Huckabaa[2228]
                   +Betty ?[2229]
                         ─── Tina Huckabaa[3408]
                 ─── Charlene Huckabaa[2230]
                   +Wayne Bradley[2231]
                         ─── Tony Wayne Bradley[3409]
                         ─── Crystal Darlene Bradley[3410]
                 ─── Martin Van Buren Huckabaa Jr.[2232] ...(181)
                 ─── Jack Berry Huckabaa[2234]
                 ─── Curtis Huckabaa[2235]
                 ─── James Larry Huckabaa[2236]
         ─── Allie Mae Dukes Ward[1001]
           +James Henry Ward[1002]
           +Hubert Dukes[1003]
                 ─── Alta Dukes[2237] ...(182)
                 ─── Audi Mae Dukes[2239] ...(183)
                 ─── Hubet C. Huckabaa[2241] ...(184)
         ─── Lener Bell Huckabaa[1004]
         ─── L. B. Huckabaa[1005]
           +Betty Jean Bass[1457]
                 ─── Randall Ike Huckabaa[2243] ...(185)
                 ─── Oscar Cleveland Huckabaa[2245] ...(186)
                 ─── Gordon Huckabaa[2247] ...(187)
                 ─── Beverly Jean Huckabaa[2250] ...(188)
                 ─── Rusty Lamar Huckabaa[2253] ...(189)
         ─── Daris Lee Huckabaa[1006]
           +Homer Kimbril[1007]
                 ─── Sandra Elaine Kimbril[2255] ...(190)
                 ─── Timmy Lamar Kimbril[2258] ...(191)
         ─── Baby Huckabaa[1008]
         ─── Henry Clayton Huckabaa[1009]
           +Johnnie Mae Douglas[1010]
                 ─── Carolyn Dianne Huckabaa[2260]
                 ─── Linda Joyce Huckabaa[2261]
                 ─── Dorthy Jean Huckabaa[2262]
                 ─── Henry Clayton Huckabaa Jr.[2263]
         ─── Donald Travis Huckabaa[1011]
           +Viola Byers[1012]
         ─── Earl C. Huckabaa[1013]
           +Mamie Louise Hayes[1014]
                 ─── Teresa Jane Huckabaa[2264] ...(192)
                 ─── Donald Earl Huckabaa[2266] ...(193)
                 ─── Redda Kay Huckabaa[2268] ...(194)
         ─── William Ray Huckabaa[1015]
           +Iver June Jackson[1016]
                 ─── Laura Lynn Huckabaa[2271] ...(195)
                 ─── Eddie Ray Huckabaa[2273] ...(196)
                 ─── Tracy Lamar Huckabaa[2275] ...(197)
         ─── Robert Thomas Huckabaa[1017]

William Martin Huckabaa and Ida Mae Rowell

(45)... Lettie V. Rowell[347]
```
         ├── Trudy Rowell[1018]
         │   +Thomas Jefferson Garrett[1019]
         │         ├── Thomas Jefferson Garrett Jr.[2278]
         │         │   +Helen Adkison[2279]
         │         ├── Nellie June Garrett[2280]
         │         │   +Sherward Gomillion[2281]
         │         └── Peggy Joyce Garrett[2282]
         │             +Clifford Schofield[2283]
         │                   ├── Leslie Ann Schofield[3451]
         │                   │   +Hayward Clarence Norris[3452]
         │                   │         └── Tiffany Ann Norris[3965]
         │                   └── Thomas Jefferson Schofield[3453]
         ├── Willie V. Rowell[1020]
         │   +Mack Smith[1021]
         │         ├── Billie Mack Smith[2284]
         │         │   +Shirley ?[2285]
         │         │         └── Sharlene Suzette Smith[3454]
         │         └── Billie Jo Smith[2286]
         │             +Fenton Broome Cook[2287]
         │                   ├── Rodney Fenton Cook[3455]
         │                   │   +Ms. ?[3456]
         │                   │         └── Christopher M. Cook[3966]
         │                   └── Arnold Randall Cook[3457]
         │   +Harold D. Rowell[1022]
         ├── Eva Mae Rowell[1023]
         └── Bobbie Jean Smith[1024]
             +Russell Lee Gilmen[1025]
                   ├── Barbara Payline Gilmen[2288]
                   │   +Mr. ?[2289]
                   │         └── Nicholas Tyler Gilmen[3458]
                   ├── Russell Lee Gilmen Jr.[2290]
                   └── Deborah Leigh Gilmen[2291]
```

(46)... Leroy Rowell[348]
    +Laura Pittman[349]
```
         ├── Henry Eral Rowell[1026]
         │   +Rhonda Lombard[1027]
         │         ├── April Rowell[2292]
         │         ├── Gary Rowell[2293]
         │         ├── Kimberly Rowell[2294]
         │         ├── Hope Rowell[2295]
         │         ├── Coreen Rowell[2296]
         │         └── Tereasa Rowell[2297]
         ├── Ervunus Rowell[1028]
         │   +Shelby D. Pierson[1029]
         │         ├── Russell Edward Rowell[2298]
         │         │   +Kathy Renee Joyner[2299]
         │         │         ├── Jason Derek Rowell[3459]
         │         │         └── Christopher M. Rowell[3460]
         │         └── James Randall Rowell[2300]
         │             +Jennifer Morris[2301]
         └── Ray Lee Rowell[1030]
```

(47)... Eva Mae Rowell[350]
+Ruben A. Money[351]
  ├── Billie Jean Johnson[1031]
  ├── Ruben Arnold Money Jr.[1032]
  │   +Hitomi Tsurski[1033]
  │   ├── Sherri Money[2302]
  │   └── Scott Money[2303]
  ├── Eva Rosalind Money[1034]
  │   +James B. Roeting[1035]
  │   └── James Phillop Roeting[2304]
  │   +Thomas Lee Rine[1036]
  │   └── Kristopher Lee Rine[2305]
  └── Jimmy Ronald Money[1037]
      +Darlene Eldridge[1038]
        └── Ronald Dewayne Money[2306]
      +Delores J Alford[1039]
        └── Kelli Kaye Money[2307]
+James T. Jinks[352]

(48)... Eugene Huckaba[353]
+Joyce Collinsworth[354]
  ├── Willie Eugene Huckaba[1040]
  ├── John Russell Huckaba[1041]
  └── Robin Rena Huckaba[1042]

(49)... Addie Irene Huckaba[355]
+Troy Davis[356]
  ├── Hazel Alita Davis[1043]
  ├── Georgiann Isabel Davis[1044]
  ├── Troy Davis Jr.[1045]
  ├── Benjamin Franklin Davis[1046]
  └── Terry Allen Davis[1047]

(50)... Bessie Luvine Bass[357]
    +John Henry Crawford[358]
        ├── Lonnie Crawford[1048]
            +Genevieve Langley[1049]
                ├── Nancy Lee Crawford[2308]
                ├── Lonnie Ray Crawford Jr.[2309]
                ├── Eugene Crawford[2310]
                ├── Tina Crawford[2311]
                ├── Sandra Crawford[2312]
                └── Debbie Crawford[2313]
        ├── Edna Mae Crawford[1050]
            +Robert Mason[1051]
                ├── Shirley Mason[2314]
                    +Harry Alverez[2315]
                └── Barbara Payline Mason[2316]
        ├── James Edmund Crawford[1052]
            +Ola Bell Madden[1053]
                ├── Juanita Gale Crawford[2317]
                ├── Patricia Jane Crawford[2318]
                ├── Anita Marie Crawford[2319]
                └── Cheryl Lynn Crawford[2320]
        ├── Herbert L Crawford[1054]
            +Peggy Hatchcock[1055]
                ├── Deborah Ann Crawford[2321]
                └── Herbert Crawford Jr.[2322]
        ├── Betty Jean Crawford[1056]
            +Merlin Barnhill[1057]
                ├── Merlin Barnhill[2323]
                ├── Mikie Barnhill[2324]
                ├── Tammie Barnhill[2325]
                ├── Angelia Barnhill[2326]
                └── Darlene Barnhill[2327]
        ├── John Dallas Crawford[1058]
            +Faye Yawn[1059]
                └── John Kenneth Crawford[2328]
                    +Carol Yvonne Morgan[2329]
                        ├── Ashlyn Morgan Crawford[3461]
                        ├── Apryl Michelle Crawford[3462]
                        ├── Jesse Tanner Crawford[3463]
                        └── Dillon John Crawford[3464]
        ├── Glinda Crawford[1060]
        │   +Johnny Newmann[1061]
        └── Gerald H Crawford[1062]

Wilson Bass

(51)... James Henry Bass[359]
 +Margaret Charity Franklin[360]
  ├── Billy Ray Bass[1063]
  │ +Joyce Merline Russell[1064]
  │ ├── Cynthia Renee Bass[2330]
  │ ├── Michael Zoree Bass[2331]
  │ └── Richard Allen Bass[2332]
  │ +Nancy Lee Carswell Ray[1065]
  ├── Theresa Bass[1066]
  └── Thomas Bass[1067]
 +Minnie Walton McKnight Smith[361]
  ├── Theresa Annette Bass[1068]
  │ +Horace Emmete Jones[1069]
  │ ├── Theresa Darlyne Jones[2333]
  │ └── Connie Denise Jones[2334]
  │ +Eurado Eurigue Urgelles[1070]
  │ +George Jakubcin[1071]
  ├── Thomas Franklin Bass[1072]
  │ +Bobbie Ann Pruitt[1073]
  │ ├── Rickey Thomas Bass[2335]
  │ └── Becky Rene Bass[2336]
  ├── Jasper Daniel Bass[1074]
  │ +Judith Ann Lewis[1075]
  │ ├── Rhonda Elaine Bass[2337]
  │ ├── Susan Elizabeth Bass[2338]
  │ └── Jasper Danniel Bass Jr.[2339]
  │ +Maurine Beth Buckley[1076]
  └── James Dallas Bass[1077]

(52)... Ray-Monde Bass[364]
 +Albert Bartley Curbello[365]
  ├── Joel Maurice Curbello[1078]
  └── Albert Curbello[1079]

(53)... John Clayton Bass[366]
 +Louise Griffith[367]
  ├── William Dallas Bass[1080]
  │ +Patricia Ann Smith[1081]
  │ └── Janet Louise Bass[2340]
  ├── Paul Howard Bass[1082]
  ├── Debbie Sue Bass[1083]
  └── Johnny Ray Bass[1084]

```
(54)... Marvin Dallas Bass Sr.[368]
      +Kathleen L Heath[369]
           ├──Marvin Dallas Bass Jr.[1085]
           │   +Sharon Treasa Barrow[1086]
           │        ├──Robert Dom Bass[2341]
           │        │   +Debbie Lynn Smith[2342]
           │        ├──Hank Dallas Bass Sr.[2343]
           │        │   +Mary Ann Behm[2344]
           │        │        ├──Hank Dallas Bass Jr.[3465]
           │        │        │   +Brittany Leann Vadino[3466]
           │        │        │        ├──Leanne Avery Bass[3967]
           │        │        │        ├──Connor Matthew Bass[3968]
           │        │        │        └──Payton Harper Bass[3969]
           │        │        ├──Michael Anthony Bass[3467]
           │        │        ├──Treasa Ann Bass[3468]
           │        │        └──Zachary Daniel Bass[3469]
           │        └──Joshua Edmund Bass[2345]
           ├──Jimmie Ray Bass[1087]
           └──James Edward Bass[1088]
               +Linda Cook[1089]
                   └──James Edward Bass Jr.[2346]

(55)... Sarah Christian Bass[370]
      +Victor Eugene Nall[371]
           ├──Ronald Duane Nall[1090]
           │   +Dena Glover[1091]
           │        └──Ronnie Duane Nall II[2347]
           ├──Terry Maurice Nall[1092]
           └──Dennis Ray Nall[1093]

(56)... Gerald Howard Bass Sr.[372]
      +Doris Ray[373]
           ├──Gerald Howard Bass Jr.[1094]
           │   +Teresa Griffin[1095]
           │        ├──Melissa Bass[2348]
           │        ├──Chad Howard Bass[2349]
           │        └──Kyle Bass[2350]
           ├──Wanda Bass[1096]
           │   +James Anthony McGill[1097]
           │        ├──Anthony McGill[2351]
           │        └──Aaron McGill[2352]
           ├──Rhonda Bass[1098]
           │   +Mr. Ceurvels[1099]
           │        ├──Heather Lee Ceurvels[2353]
           │        └──Jessica Ceurvels[2354]
           └──Tonya Bass[1100]
               +Steven C. Morrell[1101]
                   ├──Kaitlyn Morrell[2355]
                   └──Brittany Morrell[2356]
```

Gerald Howard Bass Sr.

```
(57)... Mae Belle Posey[374]
     +James Edgar Huckaba[375]
         ├── James Harold Huckaba[1102]
         │   +Cora Lee Wilcox[1103]
         │       ├── Peggy Lee Huckabaa[2357]
         │       │   +William Earl Newmann[2358]
         │       │       ├── William Issac Newmann[3470]
         │       │       └── Lorrie Leigh Newmann[3471]
         │       ├── Donnie Lee Huckabaa[2359]
         │       │   +Shiela Little[2360]
         │       │       ├── David Lee Huckabaa[3472]
         │       │       └── Billy J Huckabaa[3473]
         │       │   +Susan Simon[2361]
         │       ├── Demas Mark Huckabaa[2362]
         │       │   +Deborah Ingram[2363]
         │       │       └── Deborah Sue Huckabaa[3474]
         │       │   +Teresa Hargabus[2364]
         │       │       └── Demas James Huckabaa[3475]
         │       ├── Phyllis Ann Huckabaa[2365]
         │       │   +Mark Macko[2366]
         │       │       └── Cora Marie Macko[3476]
         │       ├── Edgar Hugh Huckabaa[2367]
         │       │   +Beverly Lynn Wittmyer[2368]
         │       │       ├── Jason Hugh Huckabaa[3477]
         │       │       └── Crystal Lynn Huckabaa[3478]
         │       └── James Rudolf Huckabaa[2369]
         │           +Ms. Trisha[2370]
         │               └── Ashli Chere Huckabaa[3479]
         ├── Clara Mae Huckabaa[1104]
         │   +Coley Joseph Snellgrove[1105]
         │       ├── Betty June Snellgrove[2371] ...(198)
         │       ├── Rudy Von Snellgrove[2373] ...(199)
         │       ├── Roger Henry Snellgrove[2375] ...(200)
         │       └── Judy Ann Snellgrove[2377] ...(201)
         ├── Edward Ervin Huckaba[1106]
         │   +Betty Jean Harrison[1107]
         │       ├── Randy Michael Huckaba[2379]
         │       ├── Craig Alan Huckaba[2380]
         │       ├── Karen Elizabeth Huckaba[2381]
         │       ├── Connie Arlene Huckaba[2382]
         │       └── Myra Lorraine Huckaba[2383]
         │   +Gayle Prater[1108]
         ├── Mary Opal Huckabaa[1109]
         │   +James Walter Ansley[1110]
         │       ├── Sherri Leigh Wilson[2384] ...(202)
         │       ├── Dale Edgar Ansley[2385] ...(203)
         │       ├── Joanne Marie Ansley[2387] ...(204)
         │       ├── Lyvon Walter Ansley[2390] ...(205)
         │       └── James William Ansley[2392] ...(206)
         ├── Earl Flyn Huckaba[1111]
         │   +Angela Crusel Nix[1112]
         │       ├── Shonda Denise Huckaba[2394] ...(207)
         │       ├── Tiresa Lynn Huckaba[2398] ...(208)
         │       └── Earl Flyn Huckaba II[2403] ...(209)
         │   +Donna Ann Cummings[1113]
         └── Jimmy David Huckaba[1114]
```

Mae Belle Posey, showing off her hair.

Edward Earl Huckaba as a young man

(58)... Preston Dallas Posey[377]
    +Laura Stiller[378]
        └─ James Edward Posey[1115]
            +Janice Turner[1116]
                ├─ Kimmie Dallas Posey[2407]
                │   +Pamela Hicks[2408]
                │   ├─ Sarah Jane Posey[3514]
                │   └─ James Preston Friday Posey[3515]
                ├─ Mary Katherine Posey[2409]
                │   +Bobby Benoit[2410]
                │   ├─ Matthew Paul Benoit[3516]
                │   └─ Caleb Joseph Benoit[3517]
                └─ Diane Faye Posey[2411]
                    +Joe Booker[2412]
                        └─ Jenny Nicole Booker[3518]
            +Brenda F. Hope[1117]
                ├─ Shawn Michael Posey[2413]
                └─ Hope Mychelle Posey[2414]

(59)... Chester Posey[379]
    +Addie Lee Johnson[380]
        ├─ Mary Jane Posey[1118]
        │   +John Richard McKee[1119]
        └─ Dorothy Faye Posey[1120]
            +William Alexander[1121]

(60)... Stacy Denton Posey[382]
    +Juanita Palmer[383]
        ├─ Linda Louise Posey[1122]
        │   +Patrick Bernard Moylan[1123]
        │   └─ Brett Bernard Moylan[2415]
        ├─ Martin James Posey[1124]
        │   +Linda Mobley[1125]
        │   ├─ Shanna Michelle Posey[2416]
        │   └─ Casey Lauren Posey[2417]
        ├─ Larry Denton Posey[1126]
        │   +Jacqueline Dianne Barron[1127]
        │   ├─ William Denton Posey[2418]
        │   │   +Laurin Botts[2419]
        │   └─ Nathan Edward Posey[2420]
        └─ Debra K. Posey[1128]
            +Walter William Lurton[1129]
            +Mr. Crumpler[1130]

Standing: Clevey, Stacy Denton, Preston Dallas Posey
Seated: Mary Evelyn, Bonnie Lee, and Maebelle Posey

(61)... Bonnie Lee Posey[384]
    +Ernest Stewart[385]
        ├─ Patriciea Ernestine Stewart[1131]
        │ +Hudson Woodfin Sr.[1132]
        │   ├─ Hudson Woodfin Jr.[2421]
        │   │ +Jennifer Denise Cotton[2422]
        │   ├─ Robert Lee Woodfin[2423]
        │   └─ Martin Edward Woodfin[2424]
        │   +Melanie Jean Adams[2425]
        ├─ Barbara Ann Stewart[1133]
        │ +Ronnie Madron[1134]
        │ +Don P. Diegleman[1135]
        │   ├─ Barbara Renee Diegleman[2426]
        │   ├─ Bonnie Marie Diegleman[2427]
        │   ├─ Rhondel London Diegleman[2428]
        │   └─ Brian Scott Diegleman[2429]
        │ +Donald Harris[1136]
        ├─ Betty Sue Stewart[1137]
        │   └─ Clifton Veal Stewart[2430]
        │   +Denise ?[2431]
        │ +Thurman Paul Cook[1138]
        │   ├─ Jason Wayne Cook[2432]
        │   └─ Terry Lynn Cook[2433]
        ├─ Ernest Dewayne Stewart[1139]
        │ +Mary Jo Taylor[1140]
        │   └─ Shelia Diane Stewart[2434]
        │   +Christopher John Deaton[2435]
        │   ├─ Aaron Lee Deaton[3519]
        │   └─ Cory Eugene Deaton[3520]
        │ +Patricia Elaine Tomlins[1141]
        │   └─ Rachel Lee Stewart[2436]
        ├─ Shirley Jane Stewart[1142]
        │ +Mikeal Wayne Danley[1143]
        │   ├─ Michelle Lane Danley[2437]
        │   └─ Sherry Denise Danley[2438]
        ├─ Bonnie Mae Stewart[1144]
        ├─ Mary Elizabeth Stewart[1145]
        │ +Roger Dishman[1146]
        │   └─ Angela Crystal Dishman[2439]
        │ +Kenny Westervelt[1147]
        │   └─ Heather Lynn Westervelt[2440]
        │ +Thomas Short[1148]
        └─ Ernest Stewart Jr.[1149]
           +Ms. Nolana[1150]
               ├─ Derrick Stewart[2441]
               └─ Steven Stewart[2442]
           +Judy Sable[1151]
               └─ LeaAnne Stewart[2443]

Bonnie Lee Posey and Ernest Stewart

Patricia Ernestine Stewart

(62)... Mary Evelyn Posey[387]
+James Edward Taylor Sr.[388]
- Evelyn Elaine Taylor[1152]
- +Jerry N. Murdy[1153]
- Gloria Jean Taylor[1154]
- +Gary Lefebvre[1155]
- Sherry Diane Taylor[1156]
- +Roger Painter[1157]
- James Edward Taylor Jr.[1158]
- Daniel Richard Taylor[1159]
- Thomas Patrick Taylor[1160]
- +Bobbie Stout[1161]
- David Allen Taylor[1162]
- +Julie Mysik[1163]

(63)... Cleavy Edward Posey Sr.[389]
+Ida May Busby[390]
- Joyce Marie Posey[1164]
- +Lynn Jesse Garrett Sr.[1165]
  - Lynn Jesse Garrett Jr.[2444]
  - +Tracy Clark[2445]
  - Lana Joyce Posey Garrett[2446]
  - +Joel Linam[2447]
- Marsha Ann Posey[1166]
- +Jeffery Alan Johns[1167]
  - Jeffery Alan Johns Jr.[2448]
  - Joseph Aaron Johns[2449]
- Ceavie Edward Posey Jr.[1168]
- +Deborah Joann Bradley[1169]
  - Stacie LeAnn Posey[2450]
  - Jason Edward Posey[2451]
- Jennifer Kim Posey[1170]
- +William Jesse Howard[1171]
  - Stefanie Marshann Howard[2452]
- +Mr. Lazzaro[1172]

Cleavy Edward Posey Sr. and Ida May Busby

Image from the Posey Reunion held annually at the Martin Posey and Mary Alace Bass old place in Holt Florida.

(64)... Holley Middleton Bass[96]
    +Jessie Savage[97]
        |—— Dewey Franklin Bass[391]
        |—— Edith Florine Bass[392]
        | +Aurthor Wallace[393]
        | |—— Sandra Ann Wallace[1173]
        | | +William J. Barksdale[1174]
        | | |—— Susan Claire Barksdale[2453]
        | |—— Phillip Aurthur Wallace[1175]
        | | +Pamela Jane Murphree[1176]
        | | |—— Amy Melissa Wallace[2454]
        | | |—— Andrew Middleton Wallace[2455]
        | |—— William Holley Wallace[1177]
        | +Jada Harvey[1178]
        | |—— Charles William Wallace[2456]
        | |—— Christopher Edward Wallace[2457]
        | |—— Chad Alexander Wallace[2458]
        |—— James Verlin Bass[394]
        | +Jane Lee Tart[395]
        | |—— James Michael Bass[1179]
        | | +Linda Ridge[1180]
        | | |—— James Holley Bass[2459]
        | | |—— Brian Bass[2460]
        | |—— Patricia Annelle Bass[1181]
        | | +John Richard Lincoln[1182]
        | | |—— John Stephen Lincoln[2461]
        | | |—— Elizabeth Annelle Lincoln[2462]
        | |—— Roger Douglas Bass[1183]
        | +Pamela Nunn[1184]
        | |—— Eric Douglas Bass[2463]
        |—— Marlin Holley Bass[396]
        | +Charlotte Atkins[397]
        | |—— Jeffrey Marlin Bass[1185]
        | | +Susan Wittman[1186]
        | | |—— Seth Jeffrey Bass[2464]
        | |—— Dottie Lynn Bass[1187]
        | | +Jerry Degraaf[1188]
        | | |—— Jason Kyle Degraaf[2465]
        | | |—— Amanda Michelle Degraaf[2466]
        | |—— Dudley Dean Bass[1189]
        | +Donna Cook[1190]
        | |—— Adam Dean Bass[2467]
        | |—— Erin Leigh Bass[2468]
        | |—— Lorin Holly Bass[2469]
        | |—— Janet Kay Bass[2470]
        | |—— Amy Elizabeth Bass[2471]
        | +Debra Harris[1191]
        |—— Eula Virginia Bass[398]
            +Glenn Dotson[399]
                |—— Gloria Sue Dotson[1192]

Holley Middleton Bass as a young man.

Marlin Holley Bass and Charlotte Atkins with their grandson Seth Bass.

Gloria Sue Dotson and Eula Virginia Bass

```
(65)... Joseph Alexander Bass[98]
    +Carrie Lou Mount[99]
            ├── Carolyn Bass[400]
            │   +Otis C Griffith[401]
            │       ├── Carl Manuel Griffith[1193]
            │       ├── Roger Joseph Griffith[1194]
            │       ├── Ronald Lawrence Griffith[1195]
            │       ├── Stephen Dale Griffith[1196]
            │       │   +Pam Nichols[1197]
            │       │       ├── Joanna Nichole Griffith[2472] ...(210)
            │       │       └── Stacie Renee Griffith[2474]
            │       └── Theresa Ann Griffith[1198]
            │           +Anthony F. Ermy[1199]
            │               ├── Michael A. Ermy[2475]
            │               └── Daniel P. Ermy[2476]
            ├── Calvin Winston Bass[402]
            │   +Marilyn Sanford[403]
            │       ├── Kathy Bass[1200]
            │       │   +Kenny Lowery[1201]
            │       │   +Jerry Carroll[1202]
            │       ├── Brenda Bass[1203]
            │       │   +Roger Hooks[1204]
            │       │       └── Nathinal Hooks[2477]
            │       └── Yvonne Bass[1205]
            │           +John L. Tobias[1206]
            │               └── Ashton Tobias[2478]
            ├── Stephen Durward Bass[404]
            │   +Loretta Griffith[405]
            │       ├── Steve Elvin Bass[1207]
            │       └── Michael Douglas Bass[1208]
            │           +Suzanne Rankin[1209]
            │               ├── Sam Michael Bass[2479]
            │               └── Elizabeth Ann Bass[2480]
            ├── Charity Delores Bass[406]
            │   +Harold Jack Adams[407]
            │       ├── Sharon Adams[1210] ...(211)
            │       ├── Harold DeWayne Adams[1213]
            │       ├── Walter Dean Adams[1214] ...(212)
            │       └── William Aaron Adams[1217]
            │   +William Aaron[408]
            ├── Farrell Dale Bass[409]
            │   +Barbara Kay Sees[410]
            │       └── Roger Dale Bass[1218] ...(213)
            │   +Carol Gries[411]
            │       ├── Robert Bass[1220]
            │       └── Thomas Matthew Bass[1221]
            ├── Joe Farris Bass[412]
            │   +Kay Jorgenson[413]
            │       └── Danne Louise Bass[1222]
            │   +Betty Courtney[414]
            │       └── James Farris Bass[1223]
            │           └── Tammy Spithouler[2489]
            └── Harvey Middleton Bass[415]
                +Aleatha Nixon[416]
                    ├── Brian Joseph Bass[1224]
                    └── Eric Richard Bass[1225]
```

Joseph Alexander Bass and Carrie Lou Mount

Charity Deloris Bass with two of her children Walter Dean and Sharon Adams.

(66)... John Riley Bass[100]
    +Mayme Annie Hassel[101]
        ├──Joel Sidney Bass[417]
          +Mary Elizabeth Henderson[418]
            ├──John William Bass Sr.[1226]
              +Celia Anne Farrar[1227]
                ├──John William Bass Jr.[2490] ...(214)
                └──Joel Farrar Bass[2492] ...(215)
            └──Joel Sidney Bass Jr.[1228]
              +Gina Joy Behr[1229]
              ├──Joel Sidney Bass III[2494]
              └──Julia Elizabeth Bass[2495]
        ├──Margueritte Catherine Bass[419]
          +Mark Anthony Bolding[420]
            └──Margueritte Dawn Bolding[1230]
              +Dennis Paul Olvany[1231]
              ├──Dennis Michael Olvany[2496]
              └──Matthew Stephen Olvany[2497]
        ├──Martha Ann Bass[421]
          +William Mullina Byrd[422]
            ├──Lynda Ann Byrd[1232]
              +Gary Glenn Kinman[1233]
              └──Heather Amanda Kinman[2498]
                +Bo Manry[2499]
            ├──?
            ├──Mychaelle Joy Byrd[1234]
              +Gary Anthony Monarch[1235]
              └──Jennifer Michelle Monarch[2500] ...(216)
            └──Nancy Jane Byrd[1236]
              +Sidney T. McGlamery[1237]
              ├──Amanda Ryan McGlamery[2502]
              └──Mychaelle Ann McGlamery[2503]
          +James Woodrow Kilcrease[423]
            ├──George Stephen Kilcrease[1238]
            ├──Kathleen Ann Kilcrease[1239]
              +Mr. Smith[1240]
            ├──Phillip Wayne Kilcrease[1241]
            └──Angelia Renee Kilcrease[1242]
              +Paul Heal[1243]
              +Herman Edward Chelette III[1244]
              └──Bronwyn Elise Chelette[2504]
          +T. D. Helms[424]
        └──John Thomas Bass[425]
          +Roberta Howell[426]
            ├──Judith Bass[1245]
              +Ray Elliot Anderson[1246]
              ├──Sean Anderson[2505]
              └──Ashley Leigh Anderson[2506]
              +Rick Casey[1247]
            ├──Jacqueline Bass[1248]
              +Charles Manuel Messick[1249]
              ├──Russell Eastman Bass Messick[2507]
              └──Roberta Ruth Messick[2508]
            ├──John Thomas Bass Jr.[1250] ...(217)
            └──Janet Bass[1253] ...(218)

John Riley Bass and Mayme Annie Hassell

John Thomas Bass Sr. as a young man in uniform.

(67)... Stacy Bibner Bass[102]
    +Alline Naomi Rowell[103]
- Mavis Earline Bass[427]
  +Gaston Durell McVay[428]
  - Loyce Elaine McVay[1255]
  - Richard Wayne McVay[1256] ...(219)
  - Joan Marie McVay[1258] ...(220)
  - Michael Ray McVay[1260] ...(221)
  - Samuel Paul McVay[1262] ...(222)
  - David Micah McVay[1264] ...(223)
  - Nathaniel Joel McVay[1267] ...(224)
  - Miriam Lois McVay[1269]
    +Matthew Wayne Cunningham[1270]
  - Jonathan Mark McVay[1271] ...(225)
- James Marcus Bass[429]
  +Mary Louise Johnson[430]
  - Stephen Gene Bass[1274] ...(226)
  - Susan Lynn Bass[1279] ...(227)
- Cecil Edwin Bass[431]
- Sibyl Louise Bass[432]
  +Cecil Larry Day[433]
  - Barbara Elaine Day[1281] ...(228)
  - Cecil Larry Day II[1284]
  - George Anthony Day[1285] ...(229)
  - Tammy Joy Day[1287] ...(230)
- Grover Alcus Bass[434]
  +Dorothy June Rusk[435]
  - Gary Wayne Bass[1288] ...(231)
  - Kathy Jean Bass[1290] ...(232)
  - Gregory Alan Bass[1292] ...(233)
  - Karen Mae Bass[1295] ...(234)
- Margueritte Elizabeth Bass[436]
  +Willard Daniel Martin[437]
  - Deborah Lee Martin[1297] ...(235)
  - Danna Elizabeth Martin[1299] ...(236)
  - Willard Daniel Martin Jr.[1301] ...(237)
- Betty Irene Bass[438]
  +Gerald Wilson Wood[439]
  - JoAnn Wood[1303] ...(238)
  - Connie Gail Wood[1305] ...(239)
  - Rebecca Gaye Wood[1307] ...(240)
  - Pamela Ellen Wood[1309] ...(241)
  - Russel Stacy Wood[1311] ...(242)
  - Joyce Marie Wood[1313] ...(243)
- Audrey Rebecca Bass[440]
  +John Lewis Wilson[441]
  - Sheila Diane Wilson[1315] ...(244)
  - Michail Lewis Wilson[1317] ...(245)
  - Audrey Michelle Wilson[1319] ...(246)
- Hubert Lee Bass[442]
  +Shirley Seiwell[443]
  - Leland Samuel Bass[1321] ...(247)
  - Robin Naomi Bass[1323] ...(248)
  - Maurice Seiwell Bass[1325]
- Quinton Gene Bass[444]
  +Patricia Lucille Bass[1548]

Stacy Bass and Alline Rowell with their sons Hubert Lee and Quinton Bass.

Stacy Bass and Alline Rowell with their daughters Audrey and Betty Bass.

(68)... Martha Christian Bass[104]
```
    +Forman Edward Ward[105]
        ├──Harvey Clinton Ward[445]
        │   +Vivian Jo Fredrick[446]
        ├──William Charles Ward Sr.[447]
        │   +Lelia Murray[448]
        │       ├──Betty Jane Ward[1331]
        │       │   +Johnny McCarsey Adkins[1332]
        │       │       └──Shannon Michele Adkins[2621]
        │       ├──William Charles Ward Jr.[1333]
        │       │   +Kathy Raby[1334]
        │       │       ├──William Charles Ward III[2622]
        │       │       └──David Carter Ward[2623]
        │       │           +Lorena Williamson[2624]
        │       │           +Anita ?[2625]
        │       │               ├──Seth Ward[3602]
        │       │               └──Sydney Taylor Ward[3603]
        │       │           +Vicki ?[2626]
        │       │   +Brenda Henry[1335]
        │       ├──Mary Ann Ward[1336]
        │       │   +Allen R. Stuart[1337]
        │       │       ├──Jeffery Allen Stuart[2627]
        │       │       ├──Bethany Ann Stuart[2628]
        │       │       │   +Nate Moorman[2629]
        │       │       │       ├──Lincoln Nathan Moorman[3604]
        │       │       │       └──Bennett Owen Moorman[3605]
        │       │       └──Suzanne Marie Stuart[2630]
        │       └──Shirley Ward[1338]
        │           +Jeffery Lee Coffman[1339]
        │               └──Gregory Cline Coffman[2631]
        │                   +Angel ?[2632]
        │                       ├──Elijah Coffman[3606]
        │                       └──Cartur Coffman[3607]
        │                   +Amanda ?[2633]
        ├──DeLeon Edward Ward[449]
        │   +Emma June Campbell[450]
        │       ├──Fred Anthony Ward[1340]
        │       ├──Joseph Dale Ward[1341]
        │       │   +Jackie Elaine Crabtree[1342]
        │       │       ├──Joseph Brandon Ward[2634]
        │       │       ├──Maletha Adele Ward[2635]
        │       │       ├──Brooke Michelle Ward[2636]
        │       │       └──Emily June Ward[2637]
        │       ├──Rose Marie Ward[1343]
        │       │   └──Deidre Nicole Ward[2638]
        │       └──Chris Lorraine Ward[1344]
        │           +Daniel Hal Steverson[1345]
        │               └──Shelby Daniel Steverson[2639]
        │   +Elizabeth Virginia Cadenhead[451]
        └──Anna Faye Ward[452]
            +Henry Eugene Fredrick[453]
                ├──Marilyn Fredrick[1346]
                ├──Martin Eugene Fredrick[1347]
                └──Mark Forman Fredrick[1348]
```

William Charles Ward and wife Lelia Murray

Fred Anthoney "Buzz", DeLeon Edward, and Joseph Dale Ward

```
(69)... Earnest True Bass Sr.[454]
     +Lillian Morgan[455]
          ├── Ernest True Bass Jr.[1349]
          └── Mr. Bass[1350]
     +Ruth Valentine Morgan[456]
          ├── Earnest True Bass Jr.[1351]
          │    +Catherine Nadine Ireland[1352]
          │         └── Robert Ernest Bass[2640]
          ├── Donald Willis Bass[1353]
          ├── Ennis Rudolph Bass[1354]
          │    +Linda Barbara Borgioli[1355]
          │         └── Linda Ann Bass[2641]
          │              +Robert Olds[2642]
          │                   └── Morgan E. Olds[3608]
          ├── Mary Ruth Bass[1356]
          ├── Morgan Bennett Bass[1357]
          │    +Minnie M Harrison[1358]
          ├── Alice Nanette Bass[1359]
          ├── William Walter Bass[1360]
          ├── Robert Earl Bass[1361]
          └── Obbie Bass[1362]
     +Ms. Brady[457]
```

William Charles and DeLeon Edward Ward

Chris Lorraine, DeLeon Edward, and Joseph Dale Ward

(70)... Richard Carl Bass Sr.[458]
    +Alice Lucille Beasley[459]
        ├── Alice Lillian Bass[1363]
        │   +Elwynne Phillip Peterson[1364]
        │   └── Elizabeth Sharon Peterson[2643]
        ├── Richard Carle Bass Jr.[1365]
        │   +Mary Elizabeth Hale[1366]
        │   ├── Richard Edward Bass[2644]
        │   │   +Denese McIntire[2645]
        │   │   ├── Erin Lenae Bass[3609]
        │   │   └── Matthew Evan Bass[3610]
        │   │   +Monica ?[3611]
        │   ├── Charles Edward Bass[2646]
        │   │   +Barbara Jones[2647]
        │   │   ├── Patricia Ann Bass[3612]
        │   │   └── Rachel Suzanne Bass[3613]
        │   ├── Linda Elizabeth Bass[2648]
        │   │   +Alvin Donnald Lewis[2649]
        │   │   └── Brook Renee Lewis[3614]
        │   └── Robert Carl Bass[2650]
        ├── Olive Marie Bass[1367]
        ├── Catherine Carlene Bass[1368]
        ├── Charles Edward Bass[1369]
        │   +Mae Burk[1370]
        │   ├── Rhonda Theresa Bass[2651]
        │   └── Richard Charles Bass[2652]
        ├── Nell Bass[1371]
        │   +O. C. Rinehart[1372]
        │   ├── Donna Marie Rinehart[2653]
        │   └── Myra Nell Rinehart[2654]
        └── Betty Bass[1373]
            +Lewis Westbury[1374]
                ├── Gary Westbury[2655]
                └── Donnie Westbury[2656]
    +Hadassah Stautimire[460]
        ├── JoAnne Charlotte Bass[1375]
        │   +Leslie Clayton Cox[1376]
        │   ├── June Lorraine Cox[2657]
        │   │   +Art Richard[2658]
        │   ├── Edward Clayton Cox[2659]
        │   │   +Denise Dels[2660]
        │   └── Carel Jeanette Cox[2661]
        │   +Ricky Allen Langston[2662]
        ├── Kenneth Kirby Bass[1377]
        │   +Barbara Sue Smith[1378]
        │   +Jane Rowe[1379]
        │   +Beth Cockerham[1380]
        ├── Harold Eugene Bass[1381]
        │   +Thelina Gail Kilpratrie[1382]
        │   ├── Karan Lainye Bass[2665]
        │   │   +Scott Bailey[2666]
        │   └── Sabin Craig Bass[2667]
        └── Betty June Bass[1383]
            +John Joseph Koval[1384]
                └── Joseph Kenneth Koval[2668]

Richard Carl Bass Jr. repairing roof damage after Hurricane Kate 1985.

Kenneth Kirby Bass

(71)... William Bennett Bass[461]
    +Ora Della Hare[462]
- William Edward Bass[1385]
  - +Margaret Louise Pearl[1386]
  - +Betty ?[1387]
- Edwin Durwood Bass Sr.[1388]
  - +Margaret Louise Powell[1389]
    - Cynthia Louise Bass[2669]
      - +Raymon Johnson[2670]
        - Melissa Kay Johnson[3617]
          - +Thomas W Babbinton[3618]
        - Raymon Brian Johnson[3619]
      - +Reggie Lawshe Powell[2671]
    - Edwin Durwood Bass Jr.[2672]
    - Susan Dianne Bass[2673]
      - +Gary Allen McCurley[2674]
        - Joshua Adam McCurley[3623]
        - Towanna Joy McCurley[3624]

    +Betty Jean Hawkins[463]
- Donald Gene Bass[1390]
  - +Pamela Jane Hayerberg[1391]
    - William Bennett Bass[2675]
    - Alicia Marie Bass[2676]
    - Shawn Lee Bass[2677]
  - +Bok Suk Choi[1392]
    - Donnie Lee Bass[2678]
- Alice Marie Bass[1393]
  - +Gerald Van Horn[1394]
  - +John A Orback[1395]
  - +Rudy Salaiz[1396]

(72)... Mary Leona Bass[464]
    +Boone Mercer[465]
- Mary Margaret Mercer[1397]
  - +Robert Shores[1398]
- James B. Mercer[1399]
  - +Margie Prolist[1400]

(73)... Henry Obie Bass[466]
    +Ajetta Bodiford[467]
- Trina Elaine Bass[1401]
  - +Bruce R Kain[1402]
- Janiee Marilyn Bass[1403]
  - +Richard Kennel[1404]
- Cheryl Dianne Bass[1405]
  - +Lee Clifton[1406]
- Linda Kay Bass[1407]
  - +Ronnie Leak[1408]

Cpt. Henry Obi Bass

(74)... Vinnie Janice Williams[469]
+William Albert Biggs[470]
├── Minnie Elizabeth Biggs[1409]
├── Beulah Mae Biggs[1410]
│   +Charles D McDonald[1411]
│   ├── Robert McDonald[2679]
│   ├── Lucille McDonald[2680]
│   ├── Voncille McDonald[2681]
│   └── Junior McDonald[2682]
└── Lessie Myrl Biggs[1412]
    +Jay Theron Whatley[1413]
    ├── Myrtice Edna Whatley[2683]
    ├── Myrtle Maxine Whatley[2684]
    └── Gordon Lavaughn Whatley[2685]

(75)... Francis Folsam Williams[473]
+Newton Dudley Bryan[474]
├── Zella Bryan[1414]
├── Judson Bryan[1415]
├── Edwin Bryan[1416]
└── Loraine Bryan[1417]

(76)... Mattie Dora Williams[475]
+Andrew Erastus Anderson[476]
├── Swenson Edwin Anderson[1418]
├── Lucine Dalton Anderson[1419]
├── William F Anderson[1420]
│   +Ms. McCain[1421]
└── Elna F Anderson[1422]

(77)... Laura May Williams Williams[477]
+John W Robinson[478]
└── Jane Robinson[1423]

(78)... Henry Gordon Williams[479]
+Caudie Newman[480]
└── Lester Williams[1424]
    +Ms. Dortch[1425]
    ├── Rebecca Williams[2686]
    │   +Stan Tindal[2687]
    ├── Susan Elizabeth Williams[2688]
    │   +Chuck Epley[2689]
    ├── Johnny Ray Williams[2690]
    │   +Shirley Day[2691]
    │   +Shirley Ann Day[2692]
    ├── Ronald Gordon Williams[2693]
    │   +Marilyn Watts[2694]
    ├── Jo Ann Williams[2695]
    │   +James Jones[2696]
    ├── David Marcus Williams[2697]
    │   +Sue Blackwell[2698]
    └── Angela Maria Williams[2699]

(79)... William Marcus Williams[481]
+Kathleen Hedgekoff[482]

(80)... Naomi Williams[483]
+Frank A. Fuqua[484]
├── Deward Fuqua[1426]
└── Evelyn Fuqua[1427]

(81)... Annie Ruth Williams[485]
	+Benjamin Morris Tatum[486]

(82)... Wilmer Newton Williams[487]
	+Nell Godwin[488]

(83)... Lillian Elizabeth Williams[489]
	+William Frank Timmerman[490]

(84)... Buna Lucille Williams[491]
	+Auburn E. McGraw[492]

(85)... Arrie Bernice Bass[493]
  +Luie Claude Adams[494]
     ┌── Arlis Chapman Adams Sr.[1428]
     │   +Annie Maude Hassell[1429]
     │   ┌── Arlis Chapman Adams Jr.[2700]
     │   │   +Mary Rogers[2701]
     │   ├── Anthony Phillip Adams[2702]
     │   │   +Dianne Logan[2703]
     │   │   ┌── Brook Adams[3625]
     │   │   └── Aric Adams[3626]
     │   └── Angina Valentine Adams[2704]
     ├── Atris C Adams[1430]
     │   +Jessie Beckworth[1431]
     ├── Annette Adams[1432]
     │   +Frank Jackson[1433]
     │   ┌── Deborah Jackson[2705]
     │   ├── Dewayne Jackson[2706]
     │   └── Louis Jackson[2707]
     │   +Ms. ?[2708]
     │   ┌── Mr. Jackson[3627]
     │   ├── Danny Jackson[3628]
     │   ├── David Jackson[3629]
     │   └── Christy Jackson[3630]
     ├── Aaron Lee Adams[1434]
     │   +Betty Jean Brown[1435]
     │   ┌── Danny Lee Adams[2709]
     │   │   +Deborah Babb[2710]
     │   ├── Angela Patrice Adams[2711]
     │   │   +Harvey Valnor Smith[2712]
     │   ├── Pamela Jean Adams[2713]
     │   │   +Donald Raymond Moncrief[2714]
     │   └── Timothy Alan Adams[2715]
     │   +Cynthia Delores Brock[2716]
     └── Audie Mae Adams[1436]
         +Charles Wood Thomasson[1437]
            ┌── Cynthia Mae Thomasson[2717]
            │   +James Marvin Harrison[2718]
            │   ┌── James Brett Harrison[3631]
            │   ├── Charles Brian Harrison[3632]
            │   └── Brittney Lauren Harrison[3633]
            ├── Charles Rocky Thomasson[2719]
            │   +Kimberly Ann Walker[2720]
            │   ┌── Charles Michael Thomasson[3634]
            │   └── Cassandra Nicole Thomasson[3635]
            ├── Celia Lynn Thomasson[2721]
            │   +Mark Nelson Tate[2722]
            │   ┌── Amber Lynell Tate[3636]
            │   ├── Adam Nelson Tate[3637]
            │   ├── Aric Charles Tate[3638]
            │   └── Andrew Nelson Tate[3639]
            └── Carol Sue Thomasson[2723]
                +James Robert Hancock[2724]
                   ┌── Jerrod Randal Hancock[3640]
                   ├── Jordan Robert Hancock[3641]
                   ├── James Ryne Hancock[3642]
                   └── Hailey Hancock[3643]

Arrie Bernice Bass

```
(86)... Eva Allie Bass[496]
    +John Thomas Evans Rodgers[497]
        ─── Thomas Lloyd Rodgers[1438]
        ─── Sibyl Rodgers[1439]
            +John Mandrak Jacobs[1440]
                ─── Sherry Jacobs[2725]
                    +Jim Garner[2726]
                ─── Ronald Jacobs[2727]
                ─── Tim Jacobs[2728]
                ─── Donna Jacobs[2729]
        ─── Evans Rodgers[1441]
            +Fannie Merle Holland[1442]
            +Annice Henderson[1443]
                ─── Thomas Rodgers[2730]
                    +Dorothy ?[2731]
                ─── Alvin Rodgers[2732]
                    +Jana ?[2733]
                        ─── Lori Rogers[3644]
                ─── John Glenn Rodgers[2734]
                    +Bonnie ?[2735]
                ─── Jo Anne Rodgers[2736]
                    +Jimmy Hall[2737]
                ─── Joyce Rodgers[2738]
                    +Jerry Hall[2739]
                        ─── Kim Hall[3645]
                        ─── Greg Hall[3646]
                    +Mr. Little[2740]
                ─── Brenda Rodgers[2741]
            +Opal Hall[1444]
        ─── Ollie Kenneth Rodgers[1445]
        ─── Ross Burton Rodgers[1446]
```

Thomas Lloyd Rodgers PFC 82nd Airborne US Army, KIA. Earned the Distinguished Service Cross, making him the most hightly decorated Pathfinder of the 82nd Airborne in WWII.

Standing: Snyder Clayton Bass, Leon Pendry Bass, Jessie D. "J.D." Bass, Julius Clarence Bass, and Jamie Ike Bass

Seated: Edith Inez, Velma Bertha, Mary Ann, Eva Allie, Arrie Bernice Adams Bass, and Mrs Emmie Hutto

(87)... Jamie Ike Bass[498]
   +Cleo Gunter[499]
      ├── James Ivey Bass[1447]
      │   +Fay Agnes Jones[1448]
      ├── James Ervin Bass[1449]
      │   +Opal Louise King[1450]
      │   └── James Dewayne Bass[2742]
      ├── Hazel Bass[1451]
      ├── Christine Bass[1452]
      │   +W. Edward Blackwell[1453]
      │   ├── Aletha Jean Blackwell[2743]
      │   │   +Josheph Byran Thompson[2744]
      │   │   ├── Joseph Byron Thompson Jr.[3647] ...(249)
      │   │   ├── Sonya Michelle Thompson[3649] ...(250)
      │   │   ├── Kimberly Nicole Thompson[3651] ...(251)
      │   │   └── Capers Thompson[3653]
      │   └── Demisia Blackwell[2745]
      │   +Allen Jack Lee[2746]
      │   ├── Christopher Allen Lee Sr.[3654] ...(252)
      │   └── Casey Lee[3657] ...(253)
      │   +Steve Peacock[2747]
      │   └── Michael Steven Peacock[3659] ...(254)
      │   +Jack Smith[1454]
      ├── Voncile Bass[1455]
      │   +Clifton Curtis Blackwell[1456]
      │   ├── Cornelia Ann Blackwell[2748]
      │   │   +Al Boyett[2749]
      │   │   ├── Tony Boyett[3661] ...(255)
      │   │   └── Al Boyett Jr.[3663]
      │   ├── Deborah Lynn Blackwell[2750]
      │   │   +Doug Findley[2751]
      │   │   └── Delores Findley[3664] ...(256)
      │   │   +George William Evans Jr.[2752]
      │   │   ├── George William Evans III[3666] ...(257)
      │   │   ├── Crystal Gail Evans[3668] ...(258)
      │   │   └── Rebecca Lynn Evans[3670] ...(259)
      │   ├── Teresa Blackwell[2753]
      │   │   +James Randall Cannon[2754]
      │   │   ├── Susan Michelle Cannon[3673] ...(260)
      │   │   ├── Jennifer Nicole Cannon[3677] ...(261)
      │   │   └── Stephanie Dyan Cannon[3679]
      │   ├── Clifton Joseph Blackwell[2755]
      │   └── Shela Dianna Blackwell[2756]
      │   +Ferrell Rabon[2757]
      │   └── Melissa Rabon[3680]
      │   +Charles Greer[2758]
      ├── Betty Jean Bass[1457]
      ├── Emmie Elvira Bass[1458]
      └── Julius Ike Bass[1459]
         +Carolyn Garvin[1460]
            ├── Donna Carol Bass[2759]
            │   +Mr. Maraman[2760]
            └── Waymon Julius Bass[2761]
         +Fay Mitchell[1461]
         +Donna Dorman[1462]

Jamie Ike Bass

Clifton Curtis Blackwell and Voncile Bass

(88)... Julius Clarence Bass[501]
　　+Mildred Nall[502]
　　　├─Beatrice Lucile Bass[1463]
　　　│　　+Ralph Levon Patterson Sr.[1464]
　　　│　　　└─Ralph Levon Patterson Jr.[2762]
　　　│　　　　　+Patricia Smith Lewis[2763]
　　　├─Robert Julius Bass[1465]
　　　│　　+Doris Jean Stokes[1466]
　　　│　　　├─Sharon Jean Bass[2764]
　　　│　　　│　　+Ralph Donald Ekhomm[2765]
　　　│　　　│　　　├─Lindsey Ekhomm[3681]
　　　│　　　│　　　└─Mark Ekhomm[3682]
　　　│　　　└─Julius Randall Bass[2766]
　　　│　　　　　+Shirley Ann Bennett[2767]
　　　│　　　　　　└─Robert Julius Bass II[3683]
　　　│　　　　　+Connie Sue West[2768]
　　　│　　　　　　└─Megan Christina Bass[3684]
　　　│　　　　　　　　+David Dixon[3685]
　　　│　　+Barbara Ann Tisdale[1467]
　　　│　　　└─Edward Michael Bass[2769]
　　　│　　　　　+Donna Denise Rushing[2770]
　　　│　　　　　　└─Phillip Le Brandon Barry[3687]
　　　│　　+Peggy Ducker[1468]
　　　│　　　└─Robin Taiwan Bass[2771]
　　　│　　　　　+Wesley Darryl King[2772]
　　　│　　　　　　├─Wesley Daryl King II[3688]
　　　│　　　　　　├─Justin Lee King[3689]
　　　│　　　　　　└─Zachary Ryan King[3690]
　　　│　　+Sara Moore[1469]
　　　├─Richard Clarence Bass[1470]
　　　│　　+Maxine C ?[1471]
　　　│　　　├─Richard Christopher Bass[2773]
　　　│　　　│　　+Randi Elizabeth Robertson[2774]
　　　│　　　│　　　├─Jason Christopher Bass[3691]
　　　│　　　│　　　└─Joshua Ryan Bass[3692]
　　　│　　　└─Kimberly Ruth Bass[2775]
　　　│　　　　　+George John Nienhouse Jr.[2776]
　　　│　　　　　　├─Amanda Lynn Nienhouse[3693]
　　　│　　　　　　└─Travis George Nienhouse[3694]
　　　└─Gayle Ann Bass[1472]
　　　　　+Terry Lee Cobb[1473]
　　　　　+Thomas Eugene Williams[1474]
　　　　　　├─Leigh Ann Williams[2777]
　　　　　　│　　+James Edward Bachus[2778]
　　　　　　│　　　├─Mclain A Bachus[3695]
　　　　　　│　　　└─Mary Alexandra Bachus[3696]
　　　　　　└─Thomas Eugene Williams II[2779]

(89)... Mary Annie Bass[503]
+George Rufus Harrelson[504]
- Olen Rex Harrelson[1475]
  +Betty Jean Bearden[1476]
  - Rhonda Lynn Harrelson[2780]
    +Sydney Long[2781]
    - Ashley Long[3697]
    - Jennifer Lynn Long[3698]
    +Gary Scroggins[2782]
  - Regina Harrelson[2783]
  - Robert Olen Harrelson[2784]
    +Laurie ?[2785]
    - Erica Harrelson[3699]
    - Leigh Ann Harrelson[3700]
  - Cindy Rene Harrelson[2786]
    +Mochael McLeod[2787]
    - Allison McLeod[3701]
    - Emily Brook McLeod[3702]
    +Tim Mullen[2788]
  - Russel Allen Harrelson[2789]
    +Laura Jeanette Haslip[2790]
    - Peyton Michelle Harrelson[3703]
  - Charles Rhett Harrelson[2791]
    +Stephanie ?[2792]
    - Carolina Harrelson[3704]
    - CJ Harrelson[3705]
    +Vicky Vincent[2793]
    +Barbara Ann Ziverink[2794]
  +Christine Reba Eiland[1477]
  - Michael Rex Harrelson[2795]
    +Shirley Ann Mmith[2796]
- Ralph Marlon Harrelson[1478]
  +Betty June Ganus[1479]
  - Randall Keith Harrelson[2797]
    +Sandra Elaine Douglas[2798]
    - Jeffery Allen Douglas Harrelson[3706]
    - James Travis Harrelson[3707]
    - Randi Nicole Harrelson[3708]
    +Rebecca Ann Lowery[2799]
  - Rae Suzanne Harrelson[2800]
  - James Ricky Harrelson[2801]
    +Mary Beth Walker[2802]
    - Hannah Elizabeth Harrelson[3709]
- Ramond Teuell Harrelson[1480]
  +Shirley Stokes[1481]
  - Jacqueline Carolyn Harrelson[2803]
- Ronnie Ray Harrelson[1482]
  +Barbara Sue Duke[1483]
  - Renda Sue Harrelson[2804]
    - Jessica Sueann Harrelson[3710]
      +Stewart Brandon Carr[3711]
      - Jackson Alexander Carr[4024]
      - Renleigh Elizabeth Carr[4025]
    +James Harris[2805]
  - Rita Ann Harrelson[2806]
    +Carl Marvin Lawson Jr.[2807]

Descendants

(90)... Jessie D Bass[505]
   +Eileen Head[506]
        ├── Charlotte Bass[1484]
        │ +Lloyd Mathew Smith[1674]
        │   ├── Lloyde Mathew Smith Jr.[2808]
        │   │ +Stephanie Sue Powell[2809]
        │   │   ├── Douglas Mathew Smith[3712]
        │   │   └── Katelyn Sue Smith[3713]
        │   ├── Gregory Keith Smith[2810]
        │   │ +Cynthia Denise Tisdale[2811]
        │   │   ├── Jonathan Keith Smith[3714]
        │   │   ├── Zachary Paul Smith[3715]
        │   │   ├── Megan Rebecca Smith[3716]
        │   │   └── Sara Grace Smith[3717]
        │   ├── Jason Darren Smith[2812]
        │   │ +Natasha Lynn[2813]
        │   │   ├── Trever Kyle Williams[3718]
        │   │   ├── Shelby Breanna Smith[3719]
        │   │   └── Jessica Daily Smith[3720]
        │   +Phylis Sorrell[2814]
        │   +Christine Lee[2815]
        └── Elizabeth Louise Bass[1485]
           +Harold Jerome Barrow[1486]
              ├── Melinda Gayle Barrow[2816]
              │ +Robert Lamar Burton[2817]
              │   ├── Garrett Lamar Burton[3721]
              │   └── John Grant Burton[3722]
              ├── Angela Lynn Barrow[2818]
              │ +James William Wismer[2819]
              │   ├── Emily Kay Wismer[3723]
              │   ├── Hannah Elizabeth Wismer[3724]
              │   └── Madalyn Jean Wismer[3725]
              └── Kevin Jerome Barrow[2820]

(91)... Leon Pendry Bass[507]
   +Clipp F Merrill[508]
       ├── Barbara Eleanor Bass[1487]
       └── David Leon Bass[1488]

(92)... Snyder Clayton Bass[509]
   +Viola Ruth Coulter[510]
       └── Roger Clayton Bass[1489]
          +Lily Esther Rice[1490]
              └── Angela Beth Bass[2821]
                  +Mike James[2822]
          +Rhonda Herring[1491]

Jessie D Bass and Eileen Head

Lloyd Mathew Smith and Charlotte Bass

Snyder Clayton Bass

(93)... Velma Bertha Bass[511]
 +William Turner Henderson[512]
   ├── Redessa L Henderson[1492]
   │ +Darrell Wiggins[1493]
   │ ├── Melony Wiggins[2823]
   │ ├── Sylvia Wiggins[2824]
   │ ├── Shannon Wiggins[2825]
   │ └── Connie Wiggins[2826]
   │   +Denny Nall[2827]
   │   ├── Amber Nall[3726]
   │   └── Tanner Nall[3727]
   │   +Tanna ?[3728]
   │   ├── Mr. Nall[4026]
   │   └── Mr. Nall[4027]
   ├── Fredrick Henderson[1494]
   │ +Jeanette Robinson[1495]
   │ ├── Robin Denise Henderson[2828]
   │ │ +Martin Eugene Stacey[2829]
   │ │ ├── Robin Renee Stacey[3729]
   │ │ └── Seth Eugene Stacey[3730]
   │ └── Donna Katrise Henderson[2830]
   │   +Kenneth Charles Murphy[2831]
   │   └── Katherine Marie Murphy[3731]
   ├── Judith Lynn Henderson[1496]
   │ +Ronnie Lewis[1497]
   │ └── Stephanie Lewis[2832]
   └── Phillip Henderson[1498]
    +Rebecca Riley[1499]
     ├── Eric Henderson[2833]
     └── Chad Henderson[2834]
    +Alice ?[1500]

(94)... Edith Inez Bass[513]
 +Homer Huckabaa[514]
 +Allan Butkiss[515]
 +Millard Allison Ott[516]
   ├── Millard Allison Ott Jr.[1501]
   │ +Jerrie Ellen Vandiver[1502]
   │ +Joann Merrel[1503]
   │ ├── Todd Allison Ott[2835]
   │ │ +Stacey Jean Blair[2836]
   │ │ ├── Austin Thomas Ott[3732]
   │ │ └── Carlie Cierra Ott[3733]
   │ ├── Kam Renae Ott[2837]
   │ │ +John Franklin Smith Jr.[2838]
   │ │ ├── Justin Todd Smith[3734]
   │ │ ├── Aaron Hope Inez Smith[3735]
   │ │ ├── Dylan McKay Smith[3736]
   │ │ └── Madison Taylor Smith[3737]
   │ └── William Gilbert Ott[2839]
   ├── James Allen Ott Sr.[1504]
   │ +Karren Regina Henry[1505]
   │ ├── James Allen Ott Jr.[2840]
   │ │ +Vicky Renee Matheny[2841]
   │ │ └── Heather Ott[3738]
   │ ├── Reagan Edward Ott[2842]
   │ └── Karren Michelle Ott[2843]
   └── John Byron Ott[1506]

Velma Bertha Bass

Tanner Nall singing and playing guitar.

Tanner and Tanna Nall with their boys.

Descendants

```
(95)... John Bridges Bass[115]
      +Nancy Amy Carroll[116]
          ├─Frank Stewart Bass[517]
          │ +Ms. Josey[518]
          ├─Claude Bruce Bass[519]
          │ +Marline White[520]
          │     ├─Richard Bass[1507]
          │     │ +Milli Cooper[1508]
          │     ├─Bob Bass[1509]
          │     │ +Ruth ?[1510]
          │     ├─Greg Bass[1511]
          │     │ +Peggy ?[1512]
          │     └─Jeffery W. Bass[1513]
          ├─Sarah Clyde Law[521]
          │ +Cecil Athaniel Law[522]
          │     ├─Mr./Ms. Law[1514]
          │     ├─Mr./Ms. Law[1515]
          │     ├─Mr./Ms. Law[1516]
          │     └─Mr./Ms. Law[1517]
          ├─Bennett Ray Bass[523]
          │ +Mary Rae Parrish[524]
          │     ├─Linda Bass[1518]
          │     │ +James Harold Crews[1519]
          │     │     ├─Michael Allen Crews[2844]
          │     │     │ +Dana Butler[2845]
          │     │     │     ├─Michael Bennett Crews[3739] ...(262)
          │     │     │     └─Summer Crews[3741]
          │     │     └─Angie Crews[2846]
          │     │       +Mr. Barker[2847]
          │     │           ├─Mr./Ms. Barker[3742]
          │     │           ├─Mr./Ms. Barker[3743]
          │     │           └─Mr./Ms. Barker[3744]
          │     └─Gary Dean Bass[1520]
          │       +Dora Mapes[1521]
          │           └─Shawn Bass[2848]
          │             +Ms. ?[2849]
          │                 └─Austin Bass[3745] ...(263)
          │ +Frances Alice Hester Chesser[525]
          ├─Bessie May Bass[526]
          │ +Lucian Hibbard Andrews Jr.[527]
          │     ├─Lucian Hibbard Andrews III[1522]
          │     │ +Elaine ?[1523]
          │     ├─Lucia Dianne Andrews[1524]
          │     │ +Ben Smith III[1525]
          │     ├─Deborah Andrews[1526]
          │     │ +Joe Smith[1527]
          │     └─Rebecca Andrews[1528]
          │       +Andy Rumbaugh[1529]
          ├─John Irvin Bass[528]
          │ +Minnie Jewel McCorquodal[529]
          │     ├─Ronald Bass[1530]
          │     ├─Carol Bass[1531]
          │     ├─Cheryl Bass[1532]
          │     └─Nancy Bass[1533]
          ├─Jesse Ruban Bass[530]
          └─Annie Laura Bass[531]
```

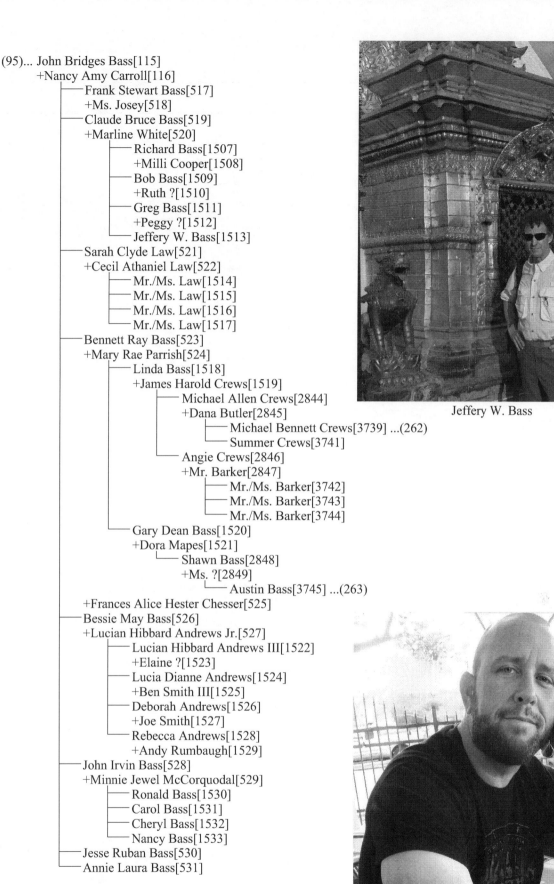

Jeffery W. Bass

Michael Allen Crews

(96)... Laura Lee Bass[117]
```
        ├── Andrew Bennett Bass[532]
        │   +Florence Perdue[533]
        │       ├── Marlon Jerome Bass[1534]
        │       │   +Betty J. ?[1535]
        │       │       └── Marla Kim Bass[2850]
        │       │           +Matthew Mangham[2851]
        │       │               ├── Mathew Mangham[3747]
        │       │               └── Michelle Mangham[3748]
        │       │           +Mr. Barelare[2852]
        │       ├── Doris Jean Bass[1536]
        │       │   +Albert T Tyler[1537]
        │       │       └── Michael Wayne Tyler[2853]
        │       │           +Barbara Ann Fairman[2854]
        │       │               ├── Jessica Ann Tyler[3749]
        │       │               ├── Cathleen Doren Tyler[3750]
        │       │               │   +Rodger Caffey[3751]
        │       │               ├── Justin Fairman Tyler[3752]
        │       │               └── Michael Fairman Tyler[3753]
        │       │   +Henry Albert Tyler[1538]
        │       │       └── Anita Kaye Tyler[2855]
        │       │           +Mark Edward Pruit[2856]
        │       └── Shirley Ann Bass[1539]
        │           +Bruce Veasey Jr.[1540]
        │               ├── Bruce Kelley Veasey[2857]
        │               │   +Melissa Bates[2858]
        │               │       ├── Hanna Elizabeth Veasey[3754]
        │               │       │   +William Allen Bumpers III[3755]
        │               │       │       ├── Caroline Elizabeth Bumpers[4029]
        │               │       │       └── Charlotte Clair Bumpers[4030]
        │               │       └── Andrew Bruce Veasey[3756]
        │               │           +Taylor Lynn Donaldson[3757]
        │               │               └── Katherine Elizabeth Veasey[4031]
        │               └── Brandon Keith Veasey[2859]
        +Morgan Jerome Johnson[118]
            ├── Gussie Josephine Johnson[534]
            │   +William A. Tart[535]
            │       └── Olivia Tart[1541]
            ├── Willie Morgan Johnson[536]
            ├── Addie Lee Johnson Johnson[537]
            ├── Bernice Johnson[538]
            │   +Morris Edwin Watson[539]
            ├── Bert Jerome Johnson[540]
            └── Martha Lou Johnson[541]
                └── Marcus Gene Johnson[1542]
```

Andrew Bennett Bass and Dinnis Bridges Bass

Morgan Jerome Johnson and Laura Lee Bass with one of their daughters.

Descendants

```
(97)... Sheila Josephine Bass[119]
     +Charles Augustus Gregory Sr.[120]
         ├── Garvin Gregory[542]
         ├── Henry Ervin Gregory[543]
         ├── Lloyd Edison Gregory[544]
         │   +Juliatte C Gregory[545]
         ├── Martha Kathleen Gregory[546]
         │   +Stanislaw Edward Davis[547]
         └── Corinne Gregory[548]
             +Robert H Olive[549]
                 ├── Ann Olive[1543]
                 └── Bobby Olive[1544]
                     +Becky ?[1545]
                         ├── Chris Olive[2860]
                         └── Ann Olive[2861]
```

Sheila Josephine Bass

Left: Charles Augustus Gregory Sr as a young man.

Lloyd Edison Gregory

Above and Below: Charles Augustus Gregory Sr.

(98)... Henry Harrelson Bass[121]
    +Katie Mae Gillis[122]
        ├── Donald Bass[550]
        │   +Virginia Bass[551]
        ├── Henry Walton Bass[552]
        ├── William Columbus Bass[553]
        │   +Clara V Stokes[554]
        │   ├── Shelia Pamelia Bass[1546]
        │   │   +Carmon Lee Parrish[1547]
        │   │   ├── Anthony Lee Parrish[2862]
        │   │   │   +Kara Mixson[2863]
        │   │   │   +Belinda Crawford[2864]
        │   │   │   ├── Laura Amanda Parrish[3758]
        │   │   │   │   +Jeremy McDade[3759]
        │   │   │   ├── Celeste Parrish[3760]
        │   │   │   │   +Zachary Morant[3761]
        │   │   │   │   └── Kaden Morant[4032]
        │   │   │   └── Shelby Anne Parrish[3762]
        │   │   ├── Rebecca Lynn Parrish[2865]
        │   │   │   +Danny Ward Holland[2866]
        │   │   │   ├── Hope Danielle Holland[3763]
        │   │   │   ├── Hannah Elizabeth Holland[3764]
        │   │   │   └── Heather Lee Holland[3765] ...(264)
        │   │   └── Jon Kevin Parrish[2867]
        │   ├── Patricia Lucille Bass[1548]
        │   │   +Kenneth Lavon Grissett[1549]
        │   │   ├── Ritchie Dean Grissett[2868]
        │   │   ├── Marquita Lynn Grissett[2869]
        │   │   └── Keith Lavon Grissett[2870]
        │   ├── James William Bass[1550]
        │   │   +Louise Kelley[1551]
        │   │   ├── Donna Lynne Bass[2871]
        │   │   ├── Pamela Renea Bass[2872]
        │   │   └── Paula Kay Bass[2873]
        │   ├── Mathew Gerald Bass[1552]
        │   │   +Mary Lou Bush[1553]
        │   │   ├── Michael Gerald Bass[2874]
        │   │   ├── William Henry Bass[2875]
        │   │   ├── Katie Diane Bass[2876]
        │   │   └── James Lynn Bass[2877]
        │   └── Jerry Bass[1554]
        │   +Ms. ?[1555]
        │   ├── Michael Bass[2878]
        │   └── Mr. Bass[2879]
        ├── Howard Eugine Bass[555]
        │   +Annie M Maud[556]
        │   ├── Donald Bass[1556]
        │   └── Bobby Bass[1557]
        ├── Mary Idell Bass[557]
        ├── Ruby Lee Bass[558]
        │   +O.B. O'Brien[559]
        │   └── Dianna O'Brien[1558]
        ├── Virginia Bass[560]
        │   +Allen Batzinger[561]
        └── Addie Ruth Bass[562]
             +Ellis Lovell[563]

Descendants

```
(99)... Dennis Bridges Bass[125]
    +Lillie Lee Thomas[126]
        ├── Edna Inez Bass[564]
        ├── Kenneth Bridges Bass[565]
        │   +Nancy Ruth Walden[566]
        │       ├── Steve Walden Bass[1559]
        │       │   +Saundra Gail Harris[1560]
        │       │       ├── Brett Zan Bass[2880] ...(265)
        │       │       └── Brandy Lane Bass[2883] ...(266)
        │       │   +Paula Simpson[1561]
        │       │       └── Nanci L. Bass[2885]
        │       ├── Danny Kay Bass[1562]
        │       │   +Vicky Walker[1563]
        │       │       └── Erin Lynn Bass[2886]
        │       ├── Kenneth Lee Bass[1564] ...(267)
        │       └── Randy Lynn Bass[1567] ...(268)
        ├── Mildred E. Griffen Bass[567]
        │   +Glenn M Abney Jr.[568]
        │       ├── Glenn Maurice Abney III[1570] ...(269)
        │       ├── Ann Abney[1572] ...(270)
        │       └── Glenda Abney[1574] ...(271)
        │   +Mr. Griffin[569]
        │   +Fred Randall[570]
        ├── George Washington Bass[571]
        │   +Lorretta Voncile Driggers[572]
        │       ├── John Dennis Bass[1576] ...(272)
        │       ├── William Gary Bass[1578] ...(273)
        │       └── Emily Gwendolyn Bass[1581] ...(274)
        │   +Mary Emma Lawson[573]
        ├── Laura Frances Bass[574]
        │   +George R Barnett[575]
        │       ├── Rickie Donnel Barnett Sr.[1583] ...(275)
        │       ├── Gloria Dianne Barnett[1587] ...(276)
        │       ├── Teresa LaGail Barnett[1589] ...(277)
        │       └── Wanda June Barnett[1592] ...(278)
        ├── Rossie Lee Bass[576]
        │   +Dale Allen Gindlesperger Sr.[577]
        │       └── Dale Allen Gindlesperger Jr.[1595] ...(279)
        │   +Otis RC Mann[578]
        │       ├── Dale Allen Gindlesperger Jr.[1595]
        │       ├── Sue Ann Mann[1597] ...(280)
        │       ├── Barbara Jane Mann[1599] ...(281)
        │       ├── Betty Jean Mann[1601] ...(282)
        │       ├── Dennis Keith Mann[1605] ...(283)
        │       └── Michael Wayne Mann[1608] ...(284)
        ├── Melisa Juanita Bass[579]
        │   +Columbus Franklin Maund[580]
        │       ├── Linda Fay Maund[1610] ...(285)
        │       └── Amelia Delaine Maund[1613] ...(286)
        ├── Winston Byran Bass[581]
        │   +Mary Nell Baker[582]
        │       └── Wendy Brynell Bass[1615] ...(287)
        └── Murry Cecil Bass[583]
            +Elizabeth Ann Jackson[584]
                ├── Alivia LaShelle Bass[1617] ...(288)
                └── Murry Lamar Bass[1619] ...(289)
```

Kenneth Bridges Bass with his wife Nancy Ruth Walden and two of his son's Kenneth Lee and Randy Lynn Bass

Doris Jean Bass, Melisa Juanita Bass, John Dennis Bass, and Dale Allen Gindlesperger Jr.

Wilson Bass

(100)... Bertie B Bass[128]
    +Obie Lucille Walker[129]
- Lewis W Bass[585]
  - +Avis Hutto[586]
    - Linda C Bass[1621]
      - +Vic LaKotos[1622]
- Marjorie Bass[587]
  - +Albert R. Douglas Sr.[588]
    - Albert R. Douglas Jr.[1623]
    - Jo Carrol Douglas[1624]
- Mary Elizabeth Bass[589]
  - +Jerry W Gwin[590]
- Esther Frances Bass[591]
  - +Leonard Raymond Previto Sr.[592]
    - Leonard Raymond Previto Jr.[1625]
      - +Ms. Beverly[1626]
        - Trey Previto[2951]
          - +Ms. ?[2952]
            - Landon Previto[3805]
            - Joey Previto[3806]
        - Leah E Previto[2953]
        - Kristina Previto[2954]

(101)... Florence Bass[130]
    +William Chester Curtis[131]
- James Harold Curtis[593]
- Thelma Olline Curtis[594]
  - +Cary Preston Turner[595]
    - Rex Turner[1627]
    - Jackie Turner[1628]
    - Ruby Jean Turner[1629]
      - +Norman Russell Findley[1630]
        - Troy Lynne Findley[2955]
        - Michael Rena Findley[2956]
        - Robby Lynn Findley[2957]
- Clifford M Curtis[596]

+Dennis William Clary[132]
- William D Clary[597]
- John D Clary[598]
- Mary Frances Clary[599]

+William Thompson[133]

(102)... Thomas Sonny Padgett[135]
    +Loula Jean Welch[136]
            — Marvin Greely Padgett[600]
            — Willie Thermon Padgett[601]
             +Nannie Jewl Hoomes[602]
                    — William Thomas Padgett[1631]
                    — O. B. Padgett[1632]
                    — James Clinton Padgett[1633]
                    — Ivalou Jeanetta Padgett[1634]
                    — William Thomas Padgett[1635]
                     +Mary Louise Poucher[1636]
                            — Mr. Padgett[2958]
                            — Mr. Padgett[2959]
                    — Herbert Wayne Padgett[1637]
                    — Jimmy Cecil Padgett[1638]
             +Myrtle Summerlin[603]
             +Grace Ross Barlow[604]
            — Narvi Lee Padgett[605]
            — Willia Daisy Padgett[606]
            — Claude Ray Padgett[607]
            — Clyde Dean Padgett[608]

(103)... Merwyn T. Melvin I[2960]
    +Louise Adams[2961]
            — Julia Melvin[3807]
             +Timothy Peltier[3808]
            — Merwyn T. Melvin II[3809]
             +Marcie Dupuy[3810]
            — Vincent J. Melvin[3811]
             +Daphne Theriot[3812]
            — Aaron Melvin[3813]
             +Charlene Chiasson[3814]

(104)... Gwen Melvin[1641]
    +Theo Shaw[1642]
            — Ellen Francis Shaw[2962]
             +Roy Simmons[2963]
                    — Treg Simmons[3815]
                     +Kevin Corrigan[3816]

William Thomas Padgett [1635] and Mary Louise Poucher with their boys.

William Thomas Padgett [1635] and Mary Louise Poucher

(105)... Carolyn Melvin[1643]
    +Louis Vagias[1644]
        ┌── Artemis Diane Vagias[2964]
        │   +Richard Sadlier[2965]
        │   ┌── Mr. Sadlier[3817]
        │   ├── Mr./Ms. Sadlier[3818]
        │   ├── Mr./Ms. Sadlier[3819]
        │   └── Mr./Ms. Sadlier[3820]
        │   +Mr. Wayman[2966]
        │   ┌── Carolyn Wayman[3821]
        │   │   +Eric Blaylock[3822]
        │   │   ┌── Mr. Blaylock[4036]
        │   │   └── Mr. Blaylock[4037]
        │   └── Katherine Wayman[3823]
        │   +Randy Main[3824]
        │   ┌── Mr. Main[4038]
        │   ├── Mr. Main[4039]
        │   └── Ms. Main[4040]
        └── Louis Vagias Jr.[2967]
            +Janet Casselberry[2968]
                └── Louis Vagias III[3825]

Carolyn Melvin and Louis Vagias

(106)... Bennie Margaret Melvin[1645]
    +Harry Quinn[1646]
        ┌── Hary Quinn Jr.[2969]
        └── Joan Quinn[2970]
            +Arthur Valdes[2971]
                ┌── Mary Valdes[3826]
                │   +Mr. ?[3827]
                │   └── Mr./Ms. ?[4041]
                └── Arthur Valdes[3828]
                    +Elizabeth ?[3829]
                        ┌── Ms. Valdes[4042]
                        ├── Ms. Valdes[4043]
                        └── Mr. Valdes[4044]

Louis Vagias and Carolyn Melvin

(107)... James Albert Parrish Jr.[635]
    +Zelma Elizabeth Webb[636]
        ┌── Mr. Parrish[1656]
        ├── James Albert Parrish III[1657]
        │   +Ms. ?[1658]
        ├── Mr. Parrish[1659]
        │   +Mr./Ms. ?[1660]
        │   └── Mr./Ms. Parrish[2972]
        └── Mr. Parrish[1661]

(108)... Mary Florence Cason[637]
 +Hollie Matthew Smith[638]
   ├── Dasy May Cason[1662]
   │ +Mr. Smith[1663]
   ├── Rosa Bell Smith[1664]
   │ +Mr. Chaver[1665]
   ├── Gladys Smith[1666]
   │ +Mr. Sanders[1667]
   ├── Bonnie Smith[1668]
   ├── Nellie Ruth Smith[1669]
   │ +Mr. Creech[1670]
   ├── Clenna Smith[1671]
   ├── Annice Smith[1672]
   │ +Mr. Little[1673]
   ├── Lloyd Mathew Smith[1674]
   ├── Bessie Smith[1675]
   │ +Andrew Orsa[1676]
   └── Gary Smith[1677]

Mary Florence Cason

(109)... Zonnie Bell Cason[639]
 +Daniel L Raley[640]
   ├── Clement Raley[1678]
   ├── Douglas Raley[1679]
   ├── Muriel Raley[1680]
   │ +Ms. Bennett[1681]
   ├── Audry Raley[1682]
   │ +Mr. Broadway[1683]
   └── Patricia Ann Raley[1684]

(110)... William Charles Cason[641]
 +Mary Ann Smith[642]
   ├── Kathleen Cason[1685]
   │ +Mr. Suggs[1686]
   ├── Lindsey Cason[1687]
   │ +Rita ?[1688]
   │   └── Mr. Cason[2973]
   └── Carolyn Cason[1689]

(111)... Grady J. Cason[643]
 +Emmie Scoffield[644]
   └── Grady J. Cason Jr.[1690]

(112)... John F. Cason[645]
 +Flora Mavis Little[646]
   ├── Johnny Ray Cason[1691]
   └── Robert Gerald Cason[1692]
     +Sandra J. ?[1693]

(113)... Coleman R. Cason[647]
 +Runell Neese[648]
   ├── Leon Cason[1694]
   ├── Sylvia Jean Cason[1695]
   ├── James David Cason[1696]
   └── Jimmy Ray Cason[1697]
 +Syble G. Cason[649]
   └── Rhett Cason[1698]

(114)... Veilla Maine Bass[650]
    +William Lester Raley[651]
        ├── Addie Vivian Raley[1699]
        │   +James Calvin Little[1700]
        │   ├── Chester Dale Little[2974]
        │   ├── James Curtis Little[2975]
        │   ├── Lanney Ray Little[2976]
        │   └── Karen Regina Little[2977]
        ├── Lois Jewel Raley[1701]
        │   +Roy C. Uptagraft[1702]
        │   ├── Stevan Uptagraft[2978]
        │   └── Lisa Ann Uptagraft[2979]
        ├── Mary Alice Raley[1703]
        │   +Fredrick Harold Powell[1704]
        │   └── Michelle Katherine Powell[2980]
        ├── Julia Yuvone Raley[1705]
        │   +James Dale Andrews[1706]
        │   └── Kelly Lynn Andrews[2981]
        ├── Henry Edgar Raley[1707]
        └── Alvin Lester Raley[1708]

(115)... Leilla Mae Bass[652]
    +Robert Lehmon Foxworth[653]
        ├── Ruby Mildred Foxworth[1709]
        └── Mary Jane Foxworth[1710]
            +Andy Deaton[1711]
    +Edward L. Miller[654]
        ├── Mary Deborah Miller[1712]
        │   +Mr. Manning[1713]
        └── William Michael Miller[1714]

Leilla Mae Bass

(116)... Henry Grady Bass[655]
    +Ruth A Nemet[656]
        ├── Greer Ellen Bass[1715]
        │   +Bill Knipp[1716]
        │   └── Michael Henry Knipp Knipp[2982]
        └── Jennifer Lee Bass[1717]

(117)... Clyde Kermit Bass Sr.[657]
    +Mamie Lelie Hayes[658]
        ├── Judson Levon Bass[1718]
        │   +Alice Floyd[1719]
        │   ├── Judson Levon Bass Jr.[2983]
        │   └── Joseph Michael Bass[2984]
        ├── Marron Grady Bass[1720]
        │   +Carolyn O. Ward[1721]
        │   └── Ronald Joe Bass[2985]
        ├── Vonda Vinor Bass[1722]
        ├── Clyde Kermit Bass Jr.[1723]
        ├── Lewis Arnold Bass[1724]
        ├── Mark Napoleon Bass[1725]
        └── Riley Bennett Bass[1726]

(118)... Beatrice Izora Bass[659]
    +Grover Bozeman[660]
        └── Margaret Ann Bozeman[1727]
            +Hubert Paul[1728]

Clyde Kermit Bass Sr. and Mamie Lelie Hayes

(119)... Mary Bonnie Bass[661]
    +Joe M. Brooks[662]

(120)... Floyd Irwin Bass[663]
 +Avis Carroll[664]

(121)... Autray Alto Bass[665]
 +Joyce Carroll[666]

(122)... Fannie Esther Bass[667]
 +James Donald Wise[668]
 ├── Brenda Gail Wise[1729]
 ├── Myra Lynn Wise[1730]
 └── Tracy Nanette Wise[1731]
 +Mr. Smith[1732]

(123)... Nannie Ruth Bass[669]
 +Joseph Farrel Walice[670]
 └── Jeff Alex Walice[1733]

Henry Grady Bass

Leilla Mae Bass, Veilla Maine Bass, Beatrice Izora Bass, Fannie Esther Bass, Nannie Ruth Bass, Mary Bonnie Bass, Autray Alto Bass, Floyd Irwin Bass

(124)... Nancy Christian Garvin[671]
 +Ernest Terry Beck[672]
    ├── Janice L Beck[1734]
    │   +Stanley Cook[1735]
    │   ├── Karen Cook[2986]
    │   │   +George Brown[2987]
    │   │   +Jerry McLeod[2988]
    │   │   └── Jonathan Eric McLeod[3830]
    │   │   +Donald Wayne Adams[2989]
    │   │   └── Brandon Dewayne Adams[3831]
    │   │   +Billy Simmons[2990]
    │   ├── Keith Cook[2991]
    │   │   +Kathy Douglas[2992]
    │   │   ├── Kenyon Kole Cook[3832]
    │   │   ├── Kayla Michelle Cook[3833]
    │   │   └── Kristopher Lynn Cook[3834]
    │   └── Kenyon Cook[2993]
    ├── Shirley A Beck[1736]
    │   +James Newton[1737]
    │   ├── James Jerry Newton[2994]
    │   ├── Ernest Leroy Newton[2995]
    │   │   +Christine Roderus[2996]
    │   │   ├── Melinda Roderus[3835]
    │   │   └── Christy Lynn Newton[3836]
    │   ├── Bridget Belinda Newton[2997] ...(290)
    │   ├── Missouri Mae Newton[2999] ...(291)
    │   └── Sherry Denise Newton[3001] ...(292)
    ├── Reginald E Beck[1738]
    │   +Geraldine Demoris[1739]
    │   +Shelia Davis[1740]
    │   ├── Alan Beck[3004]
    │   └── Barabara Sue Beck[3005] ...(293)
    │   +Dorothy Howell[1741]
    │   +JoAnn Fuqua[1742]
    ├── Quinton W Beck[1743]
    │   +Judy Golden[1744]
    │   +Linda Lee Jones[1745]
    │   └── Tamara Michelle Beck[3007] ...(294)
    ├── Theron Leon Beck[1746]
    │   +Ola Mae Gainey[1747]
    │   +Ms. Carolyn[1748]
    │   +Brenda Richards[1749]
    │   ├── Shannon Leon Beck[3009]
    │   ├── Christopher Shane Beck[3010]
    │   └── Margaret Beck[3011]
    ├── Ronald Eugene Beck[1750]
    │   +Velma Blocker[1751]
    │   └── Rickey Davon Beck[3012]
    └── Vivian Diane Beck[1752]
        +Jerry Chessher[1753]
            ├── Terry Lee Chessher[3013] ...(295)
            ├── Nolan Dewrell Chessher[3016]
            └── Michael Anthony Chessher[3017]
        +Charles Cook[1754]
            └── Alician Dian Cook[3018]
        +Aubrey Lee[1755]

Left to Right: Nancy Christian Garvin, Elzy Henderson Garvin, Willer Garvin, Catherine Emma Garvin, and Ollie Garvin

(125)... Willier Garvin[673]
+Benjamin Otis Beck[674]
├── Marie Beck[1756]
│   +Lamar Nelson[1757]
│   ├── Carolyn Nelson[3019]
│   ├── Carlton Nelson[3020]
│   ├── Ralph Nelson[3021]
│   ├── Brenda Nelson[3022]
│   ├── Franklin Nelson[3023]
│   └── Wanda Nelson[3024]
├── Collie Beck[1758]
│   +Virginia Elmore[1759]
│   ├── Deborah Elaine Beck[3025]
│   ├── Cindy Lynn Beck[3026]
│   └── Sandra Beck[3027]
├── Edward C Beck[1760]
│   +Ms. ?[1761]
│   └── Marilyn Beck[3028]
└── Marylin Maxine Beck[1762]

(126)... Sherman Garvin[675]
+Unogar Johnson[676]
├── Yvonne Garvin[1763]
│   +Roland Jordan[1764]
│   ├── Gail Jordan[3029]
│   ├── Ronald Sherman Jordan[3030]
│   └── Melissa Glyn Jordan[3031]
├── Laverne Fay Garvin[1765]
├── Therese Garvin[1766]
└── Lonia Garvin[1767]

(127)... Odessa Garvin[678]
+Walun Nick Johnson[679]
├── Joel Johnson[1768]
├── Nick Johnson[1769]
│   +Kathryn Kenney[1770]
│   ├── Carrol Johnson[3032]
│   │   +Jimmy Daw[3033]
│   └── Crista Johnson[3034]
│   +Kathryn Gibson[1771]
├── Sheila Johnson[1772]
│   +Ronnie Henderson[1773]
│   └── Danae Henderson[3035]
│   +Darin Southhard[3036]
│   +Ronnie Morris[1774]
│   ├── Michael Zoree Morris[3037]
│   └── Jeffery Morris[3038]
├── Luvert Johnson[1775]
│   +Dollie Colvin[1776]
│   ├── Danny Johnson[3039]
│   │   +Belinda Speis[3040]
│   └── Dallas Johnson[3041]
│   +Deborah Cahill[3042]
│   └── Aaron Johnson[3848]
└── Gary Lynn Johnson[1777]
    +Faye Golson[1778]
    └── Gary Lynn Johnson Jr.[3043]

Back Row: Nancy Christian Garvin, Willer Garvin, Odessa Garvin
Front Row: Ollie Garvin, Sherman Garvin

(128)... Cora Nolia Posey[680]
        +John Lee Thames[681]
            ├──Ruby Nell Thames[1779]
            │ +Arlee Franklin[1780]
            │   ├── Leigh Ann Franklin[3044]
            │   │   +Dale Chesser[3045]
            │   └── Tracey Lynn Franklin[3046]
            │ +Max McCarty[1781]
            └──Billy Joe Thames[1782]
               +Dale Dixon[1783]
                  └── Christopher Thames[3047]
                      +Karen Schofield[3048]
                          ├── Hillary Page Thames[3849]
                          ├── Clay Daniel Thames[3850]
                          └── Dustin Micheal Thames[3851]

(129)... Pearlie Mae Posey[682]
        +Amos Vincent Turner[683]
            ├──Hyram Walace Turner[1784]
            │ +Dorothy McCurley[1785]
            │   └── Pamela Nell Turner[3049]
            │   +Brandy Keith Owens[3050]
            └──Amos Dalton Turner Sr.[1786]
               +Emma Viola McClintock[1787]
                  ├── Lynda Jeanne Turner[3051]
                  │   +William Todd Martin[3052]
                  │   +James Micheal Carnley[3053]
                  │   ├── Tabitha Dawn Carnley[3852]
                  │   │   +John Raymond Wiggins[3853]
                  │   │   ├── Kenly Madison Wiggins[4045]
                  │   │   ├── Michael Layne Grantham[4046]
                  │   │   ├── Kaden Andrew Wiggins[4047]
                  │   │   ├── Emma-Leigh Katherine Grantham[4048]
                  │   │   ├── Heidi Rae Wiggins[4049]
                  │   │   └── Saydee Mae Wiggins[4050]
                  │   └── Trenton Michael Carnley[3854]
                  │   +Sera Pelham[3855]
                  ├── Amos Dalton Turner Jr.[3054]
                  │   +Brenda Gail Booker[3055]
                  │   ├── Madison Jade Turner[3856]
                  │   │   +Sterling Jo Huggins[3857]
                  │   └── Taylor Grace Turner[3858]
                  └── Beverly Shea Turner[3056]
                      +Mr. Jaynes[3057]
                          └── Tyler Jaynes[3859]

Amos Vincent Turner

Amos Dalton Turner Sr.

Hyram Wallace "Carthell" Turner

(130)... Gussie Lee Posey[684]
    +Charles Oresta Mills[685]
        ┌── William James Mills[1788]
        │   +Martha Ray Carr[1789]
        │   ┌── James Allen Mills[3058]
        │   │   +Jody Lynn Touchton[3059]
        │   │   +Jacqueline Kay Mullinnex[3060]
        │   │   ┌── Joshua Allen Mills[3860]
        │   │   └── Michael Adams Mills[3861]
        │   ├── John Douglas Mills[3061]
        │   └── Joseph Donald Mills[3062]
        │   +Angela Rene Elliot[3063]
        │   ┌── Johnathan David Mills[3862]
        │   └── Jordan Nonovon Mills[3863]
        ├── Evelyn Juanita Mills[1790]
        │   +Dewey Wendell Holmes Sr.[1791]
        │   ┌── Dewey Wendell Holmes Jr.[3064]
        │   │   +Corrie L. Campbell[3065]
        │   │   └── Dewey Wendell Holmes III[3864]
        │   ├── Melinda Dianna Holmes[3066]
        │   │   +Wendell Gene Hunt[3067]
        │   │   ┌── Dillon Gene Hunt[3865]
        │   │   └── Trenton Wayne Hunt[3866]
        │   └── Patricia Gail Holmes[3068]
        │   +Kevin Shawn Bloomfield Sr.[3069]
        │   ┌── Jennifer Nichole Bloomfield[3867]
        │   ├── Kevin Shawn Bloomfield Jr.[3868]
        │   └── Craig Allen Bloomfield[3869]
        ├── Charles Earl Mills[1792]
        │   +Gloria Jean Glover[1793]
        │   ┌── Lena Dianne Mills[3070]
        │   │   +Garry Thomas Walker[3071]
        │   │   ┌── Tera Lynn Walker[3870]
        │   │   ├── Brannon Chase Walker[3871]
        │   │   └── Trista Shealynn Walker[3872]
        │   ├── Richard Earl Mills[3072]
        │   └── Shawnee Lynn Mills[3073]
        │   +Robert Kenner Rathburn[3074]
        │   └── Broc Jordan Rathburn[3873]
        ├── Gene Verlon Mills[1794]
        │   +Patricia Ann Johnson[1795]
        │   ┌── Debbie Diane Mills[3075]
        │   └── Daniel Edward Mills[3076]
        │   +Mary Ellen Smith[1796]
        │   └── Sean Verlon Mills[3077]
        ├── Donell Franklin Mills[1797]
        │   +Brenda Kay Gulett[1798]
        │   ┌── Donna Kay Mills[3078] ...(296)
        │   └── Donell Joseph Mills[3080]
        │   +Stephanie ?[3081]
        │   └── Tracie Renae Mills[3878]
        │   +Judith A. Kucera[1799]
        │   └── Darla Lynn Mills[3082] ...(297)
        │   +Peggy Jean Stallard[1800]
        └── Oresta Mills Jr.[1801]

Gussie Lee Posey and Charles Oresta Mills

Donell Franklin Mills, Gene Verlon Mills, Gussie Lee Posey, Evelyn Juanita Mills, and Charles Earl Mills

(131)... Mary Francis Posey[686]
+Bartlett Lorenzo Cobb[687]
├── Annie Pearl Cobb[1802]
│   +Edward Earl Phillips[1803]
│   ├── Gregory Scott Phillips[3084]
│   └── Kenneth Paul Phillips[3085]
│   +Sonia Darlene Homan[3086]
│   └── Kyle Kenneth Phillips[3882]
└── James Bartlett Cobb Sr.[1804]
    +Janet Bowman[1805]
    ├── James Bartlett Cobb Jr.[3087]
    │   +Jacky Mondora[3088]
    │   ├── Aaron Florence Cobb[3883]
    │   └── Anthony Joseph Cobb[3884]
    ├── Martine Michelle Cobb[3089]
    │   +Gary Hunt[3090]
    │   └── Zackery Tyler Hunt[3885]
    └── Victoria Amanda Cobb[3091]

(132)... William Albert Posey[688]
+Jewel Creech[689]
├── Althea Darlene Posey[1806]
│   +Jerome Aubray Edmondson[1807]
│   ├── Michael Jerome Edmondson[3092]
│   │   +Stephanie Lynn Swaney[3093]
│   │   ├── Logan Swaney Edmondson[3886]
│   │   ├── Zackary Michael Edmondson[3887]
│   │   ├── Ethan Jack Edmondson[3888]
│   │   └── Brock Martin Edmondson[3889]
│   └── Jason Lee Edmondson[3094]
│   +Misty Sue Abrams[3095]
│   ├── Jason Wyatt Edmondson[3890]
│   └── Laken Grace Edmondson[3891]
└── Carolyn Dianne Posey[1808]
    +Fred Charles Weems Jr.[1809]
    ├── Charles Paul Weems[3096]
    │   +Brandy ?[3097]
    ├── Perry Matthew Weems[3098]
    │   +Kenya ?[3099]
    └── Justin Albert Weems[3100]
        +Whitney ?[3101]

Mary Francis Posey

William Albert Posey

Jewel Creech

(133)... Vianna Catherine Posey[690]
....+Dewey Turbeville[691]
........|——Doris Jene Turbeville[1810]
........|....+Robert Dwayne Collier[1811]
........|........|——Robert Dwayne Collier[3102]
........|........|....+Joanna Lee Scoffield[3103]
........|........|........|——Joshua Dwayne Collier[3892]
........|........|........|——Jessie Lee Collier[3893]
........|........|........|——Angelica Lynn Collier[3894]
........|........|........|——Christy Alayne Collier[3895]
........|........|——Rhonda Delaine Collier[3104]
........|........|....+Joesph Porter[3105]
........|........|........|——Timothy Ian Porter[3896]
........|........|........|——Joesph Cameron Porter[3897]
........|——Jimmie Nell Turbeville[1812]
........|....+Earl Harrison[1813]
........|........|——Michael Earl Harrison[3106]
........|——Jerry Lamar Turbeville[1814]
........|——Elaine Turbeville[1815]
........|....+Jimmy Powell[1816]
........|........|——Angie Powell[3107]
........|........|....+Jeffery Pratt[3108]
........|........|........|——Shannon Nicole Pratt[3898]
........|——Dewey Wayne Turbeville[1817]
........|....+Judy Louis Davis[1818]
........|........|——Kim Turbbeville[3109]
........|........|....+Jeffery Fleming[3110]
........|........|——Tracey Turbbeville[3111]
........|........|....+Hank Harrison[3112]
........|........|——Dewey Wayne Turbbeville Jr.[3113]
........|....+Andrea Pate[1819]
........|........|——Hunter Wayne Turbbeville[3114]

Vianna Catherine Posey

(134)... Josephine E Edwards[692]
+William Roy Busbee[693]
```
├── Thelma Lee Busbee[1820]
│   +Porter Everidge[1821]
│       └── Chris Everidge[3115]
├── Elton Busbee[1822]
├── Noma Busbee[1823]
│   +Donnell Gilley[1824]
│       ├── Sheila Gilley[3116]
│       ├── Carol Gilley[3117]
│       ├── Mike Gilley[3118]
│       ├── Gary Gilley[3119]
│       └── Gloria Gilley[3120]
├── James Curtis Busbee[1825]
│   +Betty Helms[1826]
│       ├── Janet Busbee[3121]
│       ├── Sue Busbee[3122]
│       ├── Peggie Busbee[3123]
│       ├── Donald Eugene Busbee[3124]
│       └── Wanda Busbee[3125]
├── Shelby Ray Busbee[1827]
│   +Roslyn Walters[1828]
│       ├── Angie Busbee[3126]
│       ├── Rusty Busbee[3127]
│       └── Rickie Busbee[3128]
├── Eula Vee Busbee[1829]
│   +Roy Frank Gilley[1830]
│       ├── Kathy Gilley[3129]
│       └── Deborah Gilley[3130]
├── Winnie Fay Busbee[1831]
│   +Carl Downs[1832]
│       └── Alan Downs[3131]
├── Polly Busbee[1833]
│   +James T. Williams[1834]
│       ├── Dean Williams[3132]
│       ├── Rita Lynn Williams[3133]
│       └── Douglas Williams[3134]
├── Walan Busbee[1835]
│   +Rochella Hope[1836]
│       ├── Randy Busbee[3135]
│       └── Tonya Busbee[3136]
└── Jean Busbee[1837]
    +Larry L. White[1838]
```

(135)... Janie Edwards[694]
+Fletcher Johnson[695]
- Heyward Ivin Johnson[1839]
  +Essie Orene Bozeman[1840]
  - Hardy Lee Johnson[3137]
  - Patrisha Ann Johnson[3138]
  - Lesley Mitchel Johnson[3139]
- Lewis Edward Johnson[1841]
  +Sylvia ?[1842]
  - Lewis Edward Johnson Jr.[3140]
  - Elaine Johnson[3141]
- Dalton Lee Johnson[1843]
  +Annie Louise Bishop[1844]
- Frances Elaine Johnson[1845]
  +Duval Milford Oglesby[1846]
  - Riley Lee Oglesby[3142]
  - Nancy Elizabeth Oglesby[3143]
  - Sharron Oglesby[3144]
  - Milford Gene Oglesby[3145]
- Cleveland Johnson[1847]
  +Virginia Harris[1848]
  - Patrisha Lee Johnson[3146]
- Roseliner Johnson[1849]
  +Dave Hataway[1850]
- Charles Mitchell Johnson[1851]
- Jean Ray Johnson[1852]
  +Franklin Henry Swanson[1853]

(136)... Rossa Edwards[696]
+M. A. Turner[697]
- Sylvia Turner[1854]
  +George Boshell[1855]
  - Gregory Alan Boshell[3147]
- William Amos Turner[1856]
  +Patricia Winspur[1857]
  - Derrel Turner[3148]
  - Dale Turner[3149]
  - Tracy Turner[3150]
- Jeff Wendell Turner[1858]
  +Janice Frances Davis[1859]
  - Jeffery Wade Turner[3151]
    +Janet Sexton[3152]
    - Jeffery Wade Turner II[3899]
    - Lilli Roseann Turner[3900]
    +Donna L. ?[3153]
  - Jack Milton Turner[3154]
  - Janet Sylvia Turner[3155]
    +Hershel E. Harper[3156]
    - Joshua B. Harper[3901]
    - Jeremy W. Harper[3902]
    - F. Nicole Harper[3903]
+Walter Sahria[698]

(137)... Harry Edwards[699]
    +Pearl Cannon[700]
            ┌── Edna Pearl Edwards[1860]
            │   +Edwin Parker[1861]
            │   ┌── Tim Morroll[3157]
            │   ├── Debbie Morroll[3158]
            │   └── Rickey Morroll[3159]
            ├── Harry Edwards Jr.[1862]
            │   +Edwina Parker[1863]
            │   ┌── Rhett Edwards[3160]
            │   └── Rick Edwards[3161]
            └── Lesley Riley Edwards Jr.[1864]
                +Ms. ?[1865]
                    ┌── Pauline Edwards[3162]
                    │   +Floyd Locke[3163]
                    ├── Ruby Carol Edwards[3164]
                    ├── James Edwards[3165]
                    ├── Kenneth Edwards[3166]
                    ├── Eugene Edwards[3167]
                    ├── Roy Edwards[3168]
                    └── Jerry Edwards[3169]

(138)... Early Edwards[701]
    +Mattilene Covington[702]
            ┌── Margarette Edwards[1866]
            │   +James York[1867]
            │   ┌── Lajaun York[3170]
            │   └── James York Jr.[3171]
            ├── Billie Wayne Edwards[1868]
            ├── Martha Jane Edwards[1869]
            └── Murray Edwards[1870]
                +Annis Creech[1871]
                    ┌── James Murriell Edwards[3172]
                    │   +Phyllis Jane Parks[3173]
                    │   └── James Murray Edwards[3904]
                    ├── Donald Eugene Edwards[3174]
                    │   +Sarah Aldie Qualls[3175]
                    │   └── Steven Murriell Edwards[3905]
                    ├── Sheryl Diane Edwards[3176]
                    └── Judith Ann Edwards[3177]

(139)... Correne Edwards[704]
+Burris Clyde Jernigan[705]
- Phyllis Jernigan[1872]
  +Carl Webster[1873]
  - Tracey Rochelle Webster[3178]
    +Michael McNear[3179]
    +Phillip Farmer[3180]
  - Stive Webster[3181]
  - Denise Webster[3182]
  - Scott Webster[3183]
  - Tim Webster[3184]
  - Carrie Webster[3185]
- Ronnie Jernigan[1874]
  +Janie Gilmore[1875]
  - Lindsey Jernigan[3186]
  - Britton Jernigan[3187]
  - Melissa Jernigan[3188]
- Larry Jernigan[1876]
  +Teresa Hagce[1877]
  - Darren Jernigan[3189]
- Roger Jernigan[1878]
  +Janet Sylvia Hill[1879]

(140)... Ervin Hartley Edwards[706]
+Arlene Crawford[707]
- Linda Edwards[1880]
- Diane Edwards[1881]
- Barbara Ann Edwards[1882]

(141)... Riley John Bass[172]
+Maggie Smith[173]
- Wylene Bass[708]
  +Fred Williams[709]
  - Linda Williams[1883]
    +Jimmy Lassiter[1884]
- Myrtice Bass[710]
  +Jean Padgett[711]
  - Dorothy Jean Padgett[1885]
    +Daniel A. Seckler[1886]
  - D. Jerome Padgett[1887]
  - Gwendolyn J. Padgett[1888]
  - Steven Wayne Padgett[1889]
- Hiram J Bass[712]
  +L. Ruth Howell[713]
  - Randy Joe Bass[1890]
  - Hiram Bass Jr.[1891]
- Clinton Albert Bass[714]
  +Cozette Cushing[715]
  - Clinton Duranne Bass[1892]
    +Ms. ?[1893]
    - Serrie Bass[3190]
  - Nancy Carolyn Bass[1894]
- Gordon L. Bass[716]
  +Joyce Clements[717]
  - Sue Marie Bass[1895]
  - Mike Bass[1896]
- Wayne Bass[718]
  +Dewayne Worrells[719]
  - Marlon Hugh Bass[1897]

Wilson Bass

```
(142)... James Bennett Bass[174]
    +Flara Annie Rowell[175]
        ├── Bruce James Bass[720]
        │   +Catherine Lawson[721]
        │       ├── Wanda Arlene Bass[1898]
        │       │   +Billy Gray Barnes[1899]
        │       │       ├── David Brian Barnes[3191]
        │       │       ├── Phillip Michael Barnes[3192] ...(298)
        │       │       └── Samuel Brad Barnes[3194] ...(299)
        │       ├── Ricky Bruce Bass[1900]
        │       │   +Donna Rena Canant[1901]
        │       │       ├── Nicholas Bruce Bass[3196] ...(300)
        │       │       └── Ashly Rena Bass[3198] ...(301)
        │       ├── Don Jeffery Bass I[1902]
        │       │   +Treva Partain[1903]
        │       │       └── Stacie Partain Bass[3201] ...(302)
        │       │   +Gail Norsworthy[1904]
        │       │       └── Don Jeffery Bass II[3203] ...(303)
        │       └── Janet Marie Bass[1905] ...(304)
        │   +Mildred Carlise Newton[722]
        ├── Eunice Bass[723]
        │   +Thomas Harold Henderson I[724]
        │       └── Thomas Harold Henderson II[1907] ...(305)
        ├── Ralph Caephus Bass[725]
        │   +Annie Joyce Morris[726]
        │       ├── Vivian Ann Bass[1909]
        │       ├── Randall Ralph Bass[1910] ...(306)
        │       ├── Nancy Madonna Bass[1911]
        │       │   +Gerry Russell[1912]
        │       ├── James Benny Bass[1913] ...(307)
        │       ├── Royce Caephus Bass[1915]
        │       └── Winfred Lynn Bass[1916] ...(308)
        ├── Edd Bass[727]
        │   +Learvene Trawick[728]
        │       ├── Anthony Edd Bass[1918] ...(309)
        │       └── Wendy Learvene Bass[1920] ...(310)
        ├── Wavie Lee Bass[729]
        │   +Leon Gade Mims[730]
        │       └── Tony Leon Mims[1923] ...(311)
        ├── Hazel Bass[731]
        │   +Eugene Trawick[732]
        │       ├── Diane Trawick[1926] ...(312)
        │       ├── Charlotte Trawick[1928] ...(313)
        │       ├── Lisa Trawick[1930] ...(314)
        │       └── Gena Trawick[1932] ...(315)
        ├── Herman Bass[733]
        │   +Mary Ann Blair[734]
        │       └── Cynthia Michelle Bass[1935] ...(316)
        ├── Coy Bennett Bass[735]
        │   +Margaret Faye Hammock[736]
        │       ├── Coy Bennett Bass Jr.[1937] ...(317)
        │       └── Columbus Barry Bass[1940] ...(318)
        └── Franklin Jerry Bass[737]
            +Barbara Barton[738]
                ├── Franklin Scott Bass[1943]
                └── Stanley Brian Bass[1944] ...(319)
```

James Bennett Bass and Flara Annie Rowell

Bruce James Bass

Edd Bass

All children of J. Bennett and Flara Rowell in order of age left to right, front row first.

```
(143)... Mattie O. Bass[177]
    +John Henry Johnson[178]
         ├── Dudley Sadie Johnson[739]
         │    +Julia Ann Barrow[740]
         │         ├── John Taft Johnson M.D.[1946]
         │         │    +Karen Ohlmeyer[1947]
         │         │         ├── Christopher Johnson[3254]
         │         │         │    +Kathryn Wilken[3255]
         │         │         │         └── Roy Taft Johnson[3937]
         │         │         └── Julia Adele Johnson[3256]
         │         ├── Dudley Franklin Johnson[1948]
         │         └── Christy Johnson[1949]
         │              +Graham Temple[1950]
         ├── Kenneth Ray Johnson[741]
         │    +Sally Marilyn Simmons[742]
         │         ├── Sally Johnson[1951]
         │         └── Nancy Ann Johnson[1952]
         │              +Todd Pierson[1953]
         │                   ├── Vivian Pierson[3257]
         │                   └── Roland Pierson[3258]
         └── Monia Ruth Johnson[743]
```

Florence and Mattie O. Bass with "Ben"

```
(144)... Flora Bass[179]
    +Quillie Jackson[180]
         ├── Hollis Mitchell Jackson Sr.[744]
         │    +Annie Ruth Gunner[745]
         │         ├── Martha Judson Jackson[1954]
         │         │    +Larry Bolling[1955]
         │         └── Hollis Mitchell Jackson Jr.[1956]
         ├── Horris Carson Jackson[746]
         │    +Jeanette Howard[747]
         │         ├── Loretta Jackson[1957]
         │         ├── Carson Jackson[1958]
         │         └── Tony Ray Jackson[1959]
         ├── Hillary Dalton Jackson[748]
         │    +Margaret Futual[749]
         │         └── James Dalton Jackson[1960]
         │    +Betty Hawkins[750]
         │         ├── Hillary Kim Jackson[1961]
         │         ├── Richard Todd Jackson[1962]
         │         ├── Richard Tad Jackson[1963]
         │         ├── Tracy Allen Jackson[1964]
         │         └── Tammy Gayle Jackson[1965]
         ├── Haward James Jackson[751]
         │    +Nora Fay Roberts[752]
         │         ├── Alex Neal Jackson[1966]
         │         ├── Debra Lynn Jackson[1967]
         │         ├── Dale O'Marr Jackson[1968]
         │         ├── Eric James Jackson[1969]
         │         └── Kimberly K. Jackson[1970]
         └── Florine Jackson Jackson[753]
              +William Adolphus Parker[754]
                   ├── Mitchell Quillie Parker[1971]
                   └── Carrie Elaine Parker[1972]
```

Haward James Jackson

(145)... Florine Dorothy Bass[181]
+Everett Stanley Murphy[182]
├── Dorthy E. Murphy[755]
│   +Arnold Harbuck[756]
│   ├── Frankie Harbuck[1973]
│   │   +Diane Coon[1974]
│   ├── Johnnie Harbuck[1975]
│   └── Allen Harbuck[1976]
├── Charles Alton Murphy[757]
│   +Katheryn Elizabeth Hendrix[758]
│   ├── Charles Alton Murphy II[1977]
│   ├── Daniel Patrick Murphy[1978]
│   └── Bobby Murphy[1979]
├── Lilly May Murphy[759]
├── Bobby Euell Murphy[760]
└── Edna Earl Murphy[761]
    +James Chapple[762]
        ├── Linda James Chapple[1980]
        └── James Douglas Chapple[1981]

(146)... Lillie May Bass[183]
+T. Laban Crosby[184]
└── Baby Crosby[763]

(147)... Leonard V. Hart[782]
+Ferol Janice Stokes[783]

(148)... Jynelle Hart[785]
+Alton Gillis[786]

(149)... Fred Columbus Kelley[788]
+Rachel Davidson[789]
├── Eloise Kelley[1988]
│   +George J. Bicanek Sr.[1989]
│   ├── George J. Bicanek Jr.[3259]
│   ├── Joan Diane Bicanek[3260]
│   └── Carol Jean Bicanek[3261]
├── Ruth Hazel Kelley[1990]
├── Wynelle D Kelley[1991]
├── +Mr. Bailey[1992]
├── Joyce Marie Kelley[1993]
│   +Mr. ?[1994]
│   ├── Betty ?[3262]
│   └── Tommy ?[3263]
├── Fred Ronald Kelley[1995]
├── Barbara Gene Kelley[1996]
├── George D Kelley[1997]
├── Patricia Ann Kelley[1998]
├── James Kelley[1999]
└── Mr. Kelley[2000]

(150)... Columbus Daniel Kelley[794]
+Gladys Herring[795]
+Bertha Lois Bradley[796]

(151)... Aubrey Gene Milstead[3310]
+Heather ?[3311]
└── Blayne Christian Milstead[3945]

Charles Alton Murphy

Fred Columbus Kelley with his

(152)... Danita Ann Milstead[3312]
　　　+Andrew Baylis[3313]
　　　└── Brooke Leighanne Baylis[3946]

(153)... Larry Dale Steele[2109]
　　　+Christina Van Sickler[2110]
　　　├── Kathryn Leanne Steele[3322]
　　　└── David Austin Steele[3323]

(154)... Donna Marie Steele[2111]
　　　+V. W. Kennedy[2112]
　　　├── Kristen Nicole Kennedy[3324]
　　　└── Stephanie Michelle Kennedy[3325]

(155)... Terry Michael Steele[2113]
　　　+Patricia Ann Kilcrease[2114]
　　　├── Jeremy Michael Steele[3326]
　　　├── Bradley Shoven Steele[3327]
　　　├── Kevin Charles Steele[3328]
　　　├── Emily Ann Steele[3329]
　　　└── Erin Elizabeth Steele[3330]

(156)... Lois Anette Johnson[2115]
　　　+Leonard Lee[2116]
　　　├── Jason Lee[3331]
　　　└── Nathan Lee[3332]

(157)... Marcus Dean Register[2117]
　　　+Susan Ward[2118]
　　　├── Alisha Register[3333]
　　　├── Jessica E. Register[3334]
　　　└── Jeremiah D. Register[3335]

(158)... Matthew Ward Register[2119]
　　　+Christy Rene Bennett[2120]
　　　├── Augusta Grace Register[3336]
　　　└── Mattilyn Rose Register[3337]

(159)... Martha Grace Register[2121]
　　　+Mr. ?[2122]
　　　└── Brandie Register[3338]

(160)... Phillip Eugene Fleming[2123]
　　　+Linda Henderson[2124]
　　　└── Phillip Logan Fleming[3339]
　　　+Cindy Borders[2125]
　　　└── Alex Fleming[3340]

(161)... Laura Lenelle Fleming[2126]
　　　+David Eugene Shaud[2127]
　　　└── Matthew Reed Shaud[3341]

(162)... Karen Lorine Fleming[2128]
　　　+Lance Perry[2129]
　　　├── Magnolia Perry[3342]
　　　└── Wyatt Chance Perry[3343]

(163)... Ted Dotson[2132]
+Teresa Allen[2133]
- Dixie Lee Dotson[3344]
- Amber Nicole Dotson[3345]
- Morgan Bailey Dotson[3346]
- Neil Dotson[3347]

(164)... Tracy Dotson[2134]
+Tamara Lynn Simmons[2135]
- Amanda Lynn Dotson[3348]

(165)... Pamela Ann Tuley[2137]
+Mr. ?[2138]
- Melynda Reanee Riggins[3349]
  +Kenneth Demon Lewis[3350]
  - Kenneth Renee Lewis[3947]
+Haywood Riggins[2139]
- Kirstie Lea Riggins[3351]
- Brandon Haywood Riggins[3352]

(166)... Randall Glen Wilkinson[2141]
+Nancy Hale[2142]
- Rhainnon Rose Wilkinson[3353]
+Patti Miller[2143]
- Jeremy Curtis Wilkinson[3354]
- Alicia Raye Wilkinson[3355]

(167)... Gail Denise Woodard[2146]
+Joe Haveard[2147]
- Shaun Michelle Haveard[3357]
  +Chris Sautter[3358]
  - Calli Sautter[3948]
  - Joseph Edwin Haveard[3949]
  +Michael David Reddick[3359]
+Kevin Mcauliffe[2148]
- Kristen Leigh Mcauliffe[3360]
+Will Dunlap[2149]
- Gabrie Coen Dunlap[3361]

(168)... Don Monwell Walters[2150]
+Debra Jean Nolan[2151]
- Lauren Ashley Walters[3362]
- Joshua Walters[3363]
- Tristin Walters[3364]

(169)... Rodrick Jerome Walters[2152]
+Anna Loftus[2153]
- Adam Alexander Walters[3365]
- Roderick Jay Walters[3366]

(170)... Kenneth Layne Walters[2154]
+Sandra Estelle Ellis[2155]
- Kenneth Layne Walters Jr.[3367]

(171)... Lisa Marie Cook[2158]
+Chris Hankins[2159]
- Kaliee Hankins[3368]

(172)... Dena Gail Wilkinson[2166]
+Robert Lee Mathis[2167]

(173)... Christopher Del Wilkinson[2168]
　　　+Lori Caprice Tilley[2169]
　　　　　├─ Erika Jenelle Wilkinson[3369]
　　　　　└─ Jessie Cordel Wilkinson[3370]

(174)... Kimberly Ann Cupp[2170]
　　　+John Paul Victor Dimaria Jr.[2171]
　　　　　├─ Sarah Lindsay Dimaria[3371]
　　　　　└─ Jackson Phillip Dimaria[3372]

(175)... James Landre Cupp[2172]
　　　　　└─ Lindsey Danielle Cupp[3373]

(176)... Candace Delane Wilkinson[2174]
　　　+Mr. Herrin[2175]
　　　　　├─ Mr./Ms. Herrin[3374]
　　　　　├─ Mr./Ms. Herrin[3375]
　　　　　├─ Mr./Ms. Herrin[3376]
　　　　　└─ Mr./Ms. Herrin[3377]

(177)... Shane Curtis Wilkinson[2176]
　　　+Ms. ?[2177]
　　　　　└─ Mr./Ms. Wilkinson[3378]

(178)... Candace Delane Wilkinson[2178]
　　　+Mr. Herrin[2179]
　　　　　├─ Mr./Ms. Herrin[3379]
　　　　　├─ Mr./Ms. Herrin[3380]
　　　　　├─ Mr./Ms. Herrin[3381]
　　　　　└─ Mr./Ms. Herrin[3382]

(179)... Shane Curtis Wilkinson[2180]
　　　+Ms. ?[2181]
　　　　　└─ Mr./Ms. Wilkinson[3383]

(180)... Elizabeth Ann Davidson[3406]
　　　+Guy Kervin[3407]
　　　　　├─ Dana Kervin[3951]
　　　　　├─ Patrick Kervin[3952]
　　　　　└─ Corbrey Kervin[3953]

(181)... Martin Van Buren Huckabaa Jr.[2232]
　　　+Cynthia J. Carpenter[2233]
　　　　　├─ Marsha Huckabaa[3411]
　　　　　├─ William Huckabaa[3412]
　　　　　├─ Brenda Huckabaa[3413]
　　　　　├─ Dennis Huckabaa[3414]
　　　　　└─ Derek Huckabaa[3415]

(182)... Alta Dukes[2237]
　　　+Winfred Davis[2238]
　　　　　├─ Glenda Fay Davis[3416]
　　　　　│　+Bobby Fuller[3417]
　　　　　│　　　├─ Jessica Daniel Fuller[3954]
　　　　　│　　　└─ Andrew Sery Fuller[3955]
　　　　　└─ J. W. Davis[3418]
　　　　　　　+Allie Margent Carrington[3419]
　　　　　　　　　└─ John Aubrey Davis[3956]

(183)... Audi Mae Dukes[2239]
+Jimmy Junior Harris[2240]
├── James Edward Harris[3420]
│   +Rebecca Merritte[3421]
│   ├── James Brandon Harris[3957]
│   └── Krystal Dianna Harris[3958]
└── Cindy Renae Harris[3422]

(184)... Hubet C. Huckabaa[2241]
+Mary Coburn[2242]

(185)... Randall Ike Huckabaa[2243]
+Syble Diane Morgan[2244]
├── Gregory Randall Huckabaa[3423]
│   +Teresa Brady[3424]
│   ├── Joseph Michael Huckabaa[3959]
│   ├── Tessa Leann Huckabaa[3960]
│   ├── Brett Allen Huckabaa[3961]
│   └── Brent Randall Huckabaa[3962]
└── Angelea Huckabaa[3425]

(186)... Oscar Cleveland Huckabaa[2245]
+Lyndell Freeman[2246]
├── Lesia Nicole Huckabaa[3426]
└── Christi Lynn Huckabaa[3427]

(187)... Gordon Huckabaa[2247]
+Emily Henderson[2248]
└── Gordon Heath Huckabaa[3428]
    +Heather ?[3429]
    ├── Shelby Huckabaa[3963]
    └── Jamison Huckabaa[3964]
+Rebecca Dean[2249]
└── Bobby Wayne Huckabaa[3430]

(188)... Beverly Jean Huckabaa[2250]
+Ronnie Creech[2251]
└── Kerry Lynn Creech[3431]
+Lamar Sanders[2252]
└── Amanda Kay Sanders[3432]

(189)... Rusty Lamar Huckabaa[2253]
+Dorthy Ann Kendrix[2254]
├── Kayla Ann Huckabaa[3433]
└── Christopher Allen Huckabaa[3434]

(190)... Sandra Elaine Kimbril[2255]
+Glen Paulk[2256]
+Leon Petty[2257]
└── Christopher Shane Petty[3435]

(191)... Timmy Lamar Kimbril[2258]
+Erldean Carowell[2259]
├── Daniel Lamar Kimbril[3436]
├── Joseph Lokesh Kimbril[3437]
├── Samuel Lakshaw Kimbril[3438]
├── Andrew Lucas Kimbril[3439]
└── Grace Loraine Kimbril[3440]

Shelby, Heather, Gordon Heath, and Jamison Huckabaa

(192)... Teresa Jane Huckabaa[2264]
　　　+Jimmy Ray Boutwell[2265]
　　　└── Jimmy Earl Boutwell[3441]

(193)... Donald Earl Huckabaa[2266]
　　　+Tamela Renee Blair[2267]

(194)... Redda Kay Huckabaa[2268]
　　　+Glen Day Biddle[2269]
　　　├── Glen Day Biddle Jr.[3442]
　　　│　　+Terri ?[3443]
　　　└── Shon Lee Biddle[3444]
　　　　　　+BJ ?[3445]
　　　+Kenneth James White[2270]

(195)... Laura Lynn Huckabaa[2271]
　　　+Dan Howard Lucas[2272]
　　　├── Lori Lucas[3446]
　　　│　　+David Brent Glidewell[2927]
　　　│　　├── Jayden Glidewell[3797]
　　　│　　└── Daughton Glidewell[3798]
　　　└── Amanda Dawn Lucas[3447]

(196)... Eddie Ray Huckabaa[2273]
　　　+Angelia Renee Ramsey[2274]
　　　└── Aaron R Huckabaa[3448]

(197)... Tracy Lamar Huckabaa[2275]
　　　+Kimberly Dawn Wise[2276]
　　　└── Ciji Huckabaa[3449]
　　　+Sandra Fay Butts[2277]
　　　└── Bridget Rochell Huckabaa[3450]

(198)... Betty June Snellgrove[2371]
　　　+Michael C. Walters[2372]
　　　├── David C. Snellgrove[3480]
　　　└── Michael Shane Walters[3481]

(199)... Rudy Von Snellgrove[2373]
　　　+Ms. ?[2374]
　　　├── Travis Snellgrove[3482]
　　　└── Tristan L. Snellgrove[3483]

(200)... Roger Henry Snellgrove[2375]
　　　+Rebecca Lonoel[2376]
　　　├── Amanda Mae Snellgrove[3484]
　　　└── Katie Lucrieta Snellgrove[3485]

(201)... Judy Ann Snellgrove[2377]
　　　+John William Scott[2378]
　　　├── Keisha Lynn Barnes[3486]
　　　├── Crystal Sheree Barnes[3487]
　　　├── Sharley Jo Scott[3488]
　　　└── John Timberlake Scott[3489]

(202)... Sherri Leigh Wilson[2384]
　　　├── Randy Scarbrough[3490]
　　　├── Eric ?[3491]
　　　├── Tiffany ?[3492]
　　　└── Timothy ?[3493]

Wilson Bass

(203)... Dale Edgar Ansley[2385]
　　+Christine Alford[2386]
　　　├── Dale Edgar Ansley[3494]
　　　└── Tiffany Leighann Ansley[3495]

(204)... Joanne Marie Ansley[2387]
　　+Kenneth Allen Guthrie[2388]
　　　├── Mary Elizabeth Guthrie[3496]
　　　└── Jacqueline Marie Guthrie[3497]
　　+Wayne Stokes[2389]

(205)... Lyvon Walter Ansley[2390]
　　+Celetha Dianne Schofield[2391]
　　　├── Carrie Denise Ansley[3498]
　　　└── Summer Lyvon Ansley[3499]

(206)... James William Ansley[2392]
　　+Chandra Jean De Sheppra[2393]

(207)... Shonda Denise Huckaba[2394]
　　+Chris Camp[2395]
　　+Mr. ?[2396]
　　　└── Brittany Nash Huckaba[3500]
　　　　　+Joey Rodrigues[3501]
　　　　　　├── Tenley Martin Rodrigues[3970]
　　　　　　├── Evelee Ember Rodrigues[3971]
　　　　　　└── Huxley Nash Rodrigues[3972]
　　+Mr. ?[2397]
　　　└── Zachariah Tyler Permenter[3502]

(208)... Tiresa Lynn Huckaba[2398]
　　+David Bigger[2399]
　　　├── Amber Lynn Bigger[3503]
　　　│　+Eric Gillis[3504]
　　　│　　├── Elisha Levi Gillis[3973]
　　　│　　└── Ezekiel Isaiah Gillis[3974]
　　　└── Angela Tonya Bigger[3505]
　　　　　+Mr. ?[3506]
　　　　　　├── Molly Madison Sheffield[3975]
　　　　　　└── Mason James Patriquin[3976]
　　+Kurt Allen Stout[2400]
　　　└── Aaron Eli Stout[3507]
　　+David Pool[2401]
　　+Jerry Edwards[2402]

(209)... Earl Flyn Huckaba II[2403]
　　+Tanya Rae Ceynar[2404]
　　　├── Austen James Huckaba[3508]
　　　└── Jayden Earl Huckaba[3509]
　　+Amy Micha Windham[2405]
　　　├── Harlee Fay Huckaba[3510]
　　　└── Samantha Diane Huckaba[3511]
　　　　　+Brandon Mulkey[3512]
　　　　　　├── Braydon Noah Mulkey[3977]
　　　　　　└── Khloe Autumn Mulkey[3978]
　　　　　+Ryan DeVane[3513]
　　　　　　└── Bentley Greyson Huckaba[3979]
　　+Bobbie Fay Roper[2406]

Earl Flyn Huckaba II

(210)... Joanna Nichole Griffith[2472]
　　　+Dusty W. Adams[2473]
　　　└── Dillon Wayne Adams[3521]

(211)... Sharon Adams[1210]
　　　+Thomas White[1211]
　　　+Larry Lahammann[1212]

(212)... Walter Dean Adams[1214]
　　　+Mary Jo[1215]
　　　├── Devin Phillips Adams[2481]
　　　│　　+Ms. ?[2482]
　　　│　　└── Layla Adams[3522]
　　　└── Lindsey Nichole Adams[2483]
　　　　　　+Christopher Willis[2484]
　　　　　　├── Nathan Willis[3523]
　　　　　　└── Candace Willis[3524]
　　　+Tammy Theford Blair[1216]
　　　├── Devin Randal Adams[2485]
　　　│　　+Ashley Johnson Adams[2486]
　　　│　　├── Hudson Adams[3525]
　　　│　　└── Everett Adams[3526]
　　　└── Kayla Danielle Adams[2487]

(213)... Roger Dale Bass[1218]
　　　+Donna ?[1219]
　　　└── Roger Dale Bass Jr.[2488]

(214)... John William Bass Jr.[2490]
　　　+Kelly Pusey[2491]
　　　├── William Cooper Bass[3527]
　　　├── Alexander Riley Bass[3528]
　　　└── Ava Claire Bass[3529]

(215)... Joel Farrar Bass[2492]
　　　+Allison McCorkle[2493]
　　　├── Farrar Courtney Bass[3530]
　　　└── Dray Rolen Bass[3531]

(216)... Jennifer Michelle Monarch[2500]
　　　+Mr. Leonard[2501]
　　　└── Mr./Ms. Leonard[3532]

(217)... John Thomas Bass Jr.[1250]
　　　+Dorothy King[1251]
　　　└── Alanna Nicole Bass[2509]
　　　　　　+Mr. Moore[2510]
　　　　　　├── Amberly Kira Moore[3533]
　　　　　　└── Lakin Moore[3534]
　　　+Freida Rabren[1252]

(218)... Janet Bass[1253]
　　　+Lynn David Reddish[1254]
　　　├── Kristina Lynn Reddish[2511]
　　　└── Shane Stelmon Reddish[2512]
　　　　　　+Lorena Wilkinson[2513]

Sharon Adams

John Thomas Bass Jr.

(219)... Richard Wayne McVay[1256]
    +Alice Drucilla Short[1257]
    └── Stacey Elaine McVay[2514]
        +Nathan Michael Gladson[2515]
        └── Edith Marie Gladson[3535]

(220)... Joan Marie McVay[1258]
    +Charles Herbert Williamson[1259]
    └── Shane Eric Williamson[2523]
        +Traci Locklar[2524]
        ├── Liam Wyatt Williamson[3549]
        └── Finley Scott Williamson[3550]

(221)... Michael Ray McVay[1260]
    +Nancy Runae Nelson[1261]
    ├── Jeffery Michael McVay[2525]
    │   +Traci Beth Thorne[2526]
    │   └── Ethan Michael McVay[3551]
    └── Jeremy Wayne McVay[2527]
        +Chelsi Nicole Garrett[2528]
        ├── Micah Runae McVay[3552]
        │   +Nicholas Price[3553]
        │   └── Nicholas Layne McVay[3992]
        └── Garrett Wayne McVay[3554]
            +Madison Clair Newell[3555]

Richard Wayne McVay

(222)... Samuel Paul McVay[1262]
    +Mary June Picirilli[1263]
    ├── Stephanie Jane McVay[2529]
    └── Suzanne Lea McVay[2530]
        +Jonathan Owens[2531]
        ├── Elijah Adam Owens[3556]
        ├── Josiah Samuel Owens[3557]
        └── Izabela Clair Owens[3558]

(223)... David Micah McVay[1264]
    +Judith Ann Pittman[1265]
    ├── Julie Crystal Qualls[2532]
    │   +Abraham Joshua Moyer[2533]
    │   ├── Hailey June Moyer[3559]
    │   └── Lily Jaicyn Moyer[3560]
    │   +Mr. ?[2534]
    │   └── Cassandra Jai Moyer[3561]
    └── Cody Allen Qualls[2535]
        +Jennifer Christine ?[2536]
        ├── Landon Allen Qualls[3562]
        └── Everhett Stone Qualls[3563]
    +Tracie Renea Dubose[1266]
    ├── Talitha Renea McVay[2537]
    │   +Mr. ?[2538]
    └── Malesha Nicole McVay[2539]
        +Mr. ?[2540]

Michael Ray McVay, dressed as the Laurel Hill Hobo. Well know for this role, proudly used to minister and encourage many that would not likely interact with him dressed as a preacher. Really a beautiful thing.

Descendants

```
(224)... Nathaniel Joel McVay[1267]
        +Linda Gail McLeod[1268]
              ┌── Natalie Melinda McVay[2541]
              │   +Zachary Reese McCarver[2542]
              │        ┌── Mackenzie Grace McCarver[3564]
              │        └── Macon Reese McCarver[3565]
              ├── Nathan Jared McVay[2543]
              │   +Britney Suzanne Gregory[2544]
              │        ┌── Nolan Jared McVay[3566]
              │        └── Braelyn Sadie McVay[3567]
              └── Alexander Jace McVay[2545]

(225)... Jonathan Mark McVay[1271]
        +Tammy E. Daniels[1272]
              ┌── Joshua Mark McVay[2546]
              │   +Taylor Nicole Jackson[2547]
              │        └── Westlynn Grace McVay[3568]
              │   +Ms. ?[2548]
              │        └── Hannah Marie McVay[3569]
              │   +Kayla ?[2549]
              │        ┌── Brenton Mark Lane McVay[3570]
              │        └── Baisley Renee McVay[3571]
              └── Jacob Daniel McVay[2550]
                  +Sara Brisolara[2551]
                  +Deidre Harrison[2552]
        +Debbie Burgdorf[1273]

(226)... Stephen Gene Bass[1274]
        +Josephine Anne Darst[1275]
              ┌── Marcus Stephen Bass[2553]
              │   +Melanie Hoffman[2554]
              │        ┌── Meredith Hope Bass[3572]
              │        ├── Marcus Christian Bass[3573]
              │        └── John Stephen Bass[3574]
              ├── James Scott Bass[2555]
              │   +Elizabeth Mancuso[2556]
              │        ┌── Hunter Scott Bass[3575]
              │        └── Holly Suzanne Bass[3576]
              ├── Jeffery Philip Bass[2557]
              │   +Renee Cancilla[2558]
              └── Kelly Suzanne Bass[2559]
                  +Christopher Aaron Smith[2560]
                       ┌── Eden Kelly Smith[3577]
                       └── Hudson Smith[3578]
        +Susan Malphrus[1276]
        +Terry Carol Nallen[1277]
        +Cathrine Spivey[1278]

(227)... Susan Lynn Bass[1279]
        +Marshall Lee Stockton[1280]
              ┌── Lori Marie Stockton[2561]
              │   +Jerry Kozak[2562]
              │        ┌── Nicholas Kozak[3579]
              │        └── Dylan Kozak[3580]
              └── Marshall Kevin Stockton[2563]
                  +Suzy Fuqua[2564]
                       ┌── Shawn Thomas Stockton[3581]
                       └── Levi Stockton[3582]
```

Nathaniel Joel McVay with Linda Gail McLeod

Debbie Burgdorf and Jonathan Mark McVay

Stephen Gene Bass with Cathrin Spivey

(228)... Barbara Elaine Day[1281]
    +William Dwight Henderson[1282]
    +Larry Van[1283]
        ├── Larry Van Jr.[2565]
        └── Scarlet Van[2566]
            +Cliff Ellis[2567]

(229)... George Anthony Day[1285]
    +Joyce King[1286]
        ├── Timothy Patrick Day[2568]
        └── Christopher Stacy Day[2569]

(230)... Tammy Joy Day[1287]
    +Royce Caephus Bass[1915]
        ├── Brian Royce Bass[2570]
            +Marlee Fuqua[2571]
                ├── Beckham Ceese Bass[3583]
                ├── August Beau Bass[3584]
                └── Eliza Bray Bass[3585]
        └── Holley Alaine Bass[2572]
            +Tyler Joel Wingard[2573]
                ├── Rylee Alaine Wingard[3586]
                ├── Wyatt Carl Wingard[3587]
                └── Coy Bennett Wingard[3588]

(231)... Gary Wayne Bass[1288]
    +Ann Allport[1289]
        ├── Sara Suzanne Bass[2574]
        └── Mark Daron William Bass[2575]

(232)... Kathy Jean Bass[1290]
    +Richard Kenneth Baehr[1291]
        ├── James Richard Baehr[2576]
            +Amy A Democker[2577]
                ├── Sadie E Baehr[3589]
                ├── Annie O. Baehr[3590]
                └── Mya M. Baehr[3591]
        └── Susan Jean Baehr[2578]
            +Mr. Beiswenger[2579]
            +Mr. Nolette[2580]
                └── Benjamin R. Nolette[3592]

(233)... Gregory Alan Bass[1292]
    +Yvonna Christine Hopkins[1293]
        ├── Joshua Alan Bass[2581]
            +Ondrea Leturgey[2582]
                └── Cory Joe Leturgey[3593]
                      +Sierra Resendiz[3594]
                          └── Lilith Ella Leturgey[3993]
            +Nicole ?[2583]
                └── Jaxon Riley Bass[3595]
        └── Teri Lyn Bass[2584]
            +Benjamin Daved Montague[2585]
    +Kimberly Layne Hopkins[1294]

George Anthony Day

Tyler Joel Wingard and Holley Alaine Bass with their children.

Gregory Alan Bass at the entrance of the court room named in his honor after his retirement.

(234)... Karen Mae Bass[1295]
  +David Laverne Maclam[1296]
    ├── Stacie Ann Maclam[2586]
    │   +Joseph F. Volpe[2587]
    │   ├── Tegan Jo Volpe[3596]
    │   └── Anthony Volpe[3597]
    └── Bethany Marie Maclam[2588]

(235)... Deborah Lee Martin[1297]
  +William F. Hooper[1298]
    ├── William Adam Hooper[2589]
    └── Christopher Lindsay Hooper[2590]

(236)... Danna Elizabeth Martin[1299]
  +G. Douglas Williams[1300]
    ├── Danae Elizabeth Williams[2591]
    └── Andrew Douglas Williams[2592]

(237)... Willard Daniel Martin Jr.[1301]
  +Tamara Leigh Clark[1302]
    ├── Elizabeth Leigh Martin[2593]
    └── Whitney Danielle Martin[2594]

(238)... JoAnn Wood[1303]
  +James Mcaleer[1304]

(239)... Connie Gail Wood[1305]
  +Jeffery Ted Knowles[1306]
    ├── Samantha Gail Wood[2595]
    └── Andrea Rebecka Wood[2596]

(240)... Rebecca Gaye Wood[1307]
  +Billy Shannon Wilson[1308]
    ├── Michael Shawn Wilson[2597]
    ├── Courtney Shanna Wilson[2598]
    └── William Daryl Wilson[2599]

(241)... Pamela Ellen Wood[1309]
  +John Gianetto[1310]

(242)... Russel Stacy Wood[1311]
  +Andrea Leedy Self[1312]
    ├── Luke Wood[2600]
    ├── Katherine Mary Wood[2601]
    └── Emily Grace Wood[2602]

(243)... Joyce Marie Wood[1313]
  +John Richard Mandelville[1314]
    └── Matthew Tyler Mandelville[2603]

(244)... Sheila Diane Wilson[1315]
  +Richard Curtis Rhea[1316]
    ├── Jenny Lynn Rhea[2604]
    ├── Amanda Kate Rhea[2605]
    ├── Richard Zachary Rhea[2606]
    └── John Spencer Rhea[2607]
        +Christy ?[2608]
          ├── Ms. Rhea[3598]
          ├── Abelia Jane Rhea[3599]
          └── Mr. Rhea[3600]

Rebecca Gaye, Gerald Wilson, Pamela Ellen, Russel Stacy, Connie Gail, Betty Irene Bass, Joyce Marie, and JoAnn Wood

A young Sheila Diane Wilson

(245)... Michail Lewis Wilson[1317]
 +Zelda Lynn Tweedy[1318]
    ├── Timothy Nicholas Wilson[2609]
    ├── Tiffany Nichole Wilson[2610]
    ├── ReTessa Lyne Wilson[2611]
    └── Michael Travis Wilson[2612]

(246)... Audrey Michelle Wilson[1319]
 +Austin Lamar Dozier[1320]
    ├── John Tyler Dozier[2613]
    └── Kathryn Rebecca Dozier[2614]

(247)... Leland Samuel Bass[1321]
 +Cheri Lynn Ducote[1322]
    ├── Christopher Troy Bass[2615]
    └── Jasmine Leigh Bass[2616]
       +Mr. Greene[2617]

(248)... Robin Naomi Bass[1323]
 +Johnny Jason Missildine[1324]

(249)... Joseph Byron Thompson Jr.[3647]
 +Becky Jean Spivey[3648]
    └── Joseph Byron Thompson III[3994]

(250)... Sonya Michelle Thompson[3649]
 +Donald Kevin Butler[3650]
    └── Kyle Butler[3995]
       +Jessica Faye ?[3996]
          ├── Mr./Ms. Butler[4051]
          └── Mr./Ms. Butler[4052]

(251)... Kimberly Nicole Thompson[3651]
 +Charis Weaver[3652]
    ├── Andrew O'Neal Weaver[3997]
    └── Kayden Weaver[3998]

(252)... Christopher Allen Lee Sr.[3654]
 +Kalise Erwin[3655]
    └── DeAnna Michelle Lee[3999]
       +Jacob Bishop[4000]
          ├── McKinlee Bishop[4053]
          └── Mr./Ms. Bishop[4054]
 +Tasha Nicole Piland[3656]
    ├── Kaitlin Labecca Lee[4001]
    │ +Hunter Demond Johns[4002]
    │   └── Sawyer Allen Johns[4055]
    │ +Evan Kade Mercer[4003]
    │   └── Katalena Eloise Mercer[4056]
    ├── Christopher Allen Lee Jr.[4004]
    ├── Corey Dewayne Lee[4005]
    ├── Shaun Even Lee[4006]
    ├── Chrislyn Skyler Shyann Lee[4007]
    └── Tony Kyler Lee[4008]

(253)... Casey Lee[3657]
 +Joshua Garrett[3658]
    └── Allen Garrett[4009]

Leland Samuel "Lee" Bass

(254)... Michael Steven Peacock[3659]
+Ms. ?[3660]
├── Cody Peacock[4010]
└── Caleb Peacock[4011]

(255)... Tony Boyett[3661]
+Ms. ?[3662]
├── Ms. Boyett[4012]
├── Ms. Boyett[4013]
└── Ms. Boyett[4014]

(256)... Delores Findley[3664]
+Johnny Lamar Douglas[3665]
├── Courtney Douglas[4015]
└── Caylee Douglas[4016]

(257)... George William Evans III[3666]
+Carmen ?[3667]
└── Anna Evans[4017]

(258)... Crystal Gail Evans[3668]
+John Nalley[3669]
├── Mallorie Nalley[4018]
└── Tyler Nalley[4019]

(259)... Rebecca Lynn Evans[3670]
+Troy Stinson[3671]
+Steven Cender[3672]
└── Trenton Stone Cender[4020]

(260)... Susan Michelle Cannon[3673]
+Derek Adams[3674]
└── Hailey Michelle Adams[4021]
+Ronald Whitehurst[3675]
└── Abby Suzann Whitehurst[4022]
+Dustin Fontenot[3676]

(261)... Jennifer Nicole Cannon[3677]
+Robert Eric Trahan[3678]
└── Kyra Trahan[4023]

(262)... Michael Bennett Crews[3739]
+Ms. ?[3740]
└── Brayden Michael Crews[4028]

(263)... Austin Bass[3745]
+Shelby ?[3746]

(264)... Heather Lee Holland[3765]
+Mr. ?[3766]
└── Haylee Elizabeth ?[4033]

(265)... Brett Zan Bass[2880]
+Amy Hawks[2881]
└── Brett Andrew Bass[3767]
    +Francis ?[3768]
    └── Zane Andrew Bass[4034]
+Becky Parker[2882]
└── Camrin Zan Bass[3769]

Kyra Trahan with Jennifer Nicole Cannon

(266)... Brandy Lane Bass[2883]
 +Stephen Michael Scott[2884]
  — Dylan Wayne Scott[3770]

(267)... Kenneth Lee Bass[1564]
 +Tammy C Sorrells[1565]
  — Devin Lee Bass[2887]
   +Ms. Watson[2888]
    — Diesel Wayne Bass[3771]
  — Sheleiah Lynn Bass[2889]
   +Constantinos Argeris[2890]
    — Constantinos Argeris[3772]
    — Hristos Argeris[3773]
 +Jennifer Jernigan[1566]

(268)... Randy Lynn Bass[1567]
 +Kimi Sue Adams[1568]
  — Miranda Bass[2891]
   +Mr. ?[2892]
    — Jameson ?[3774]
  — Randi Lynn Bass[2893]
 +Carry Ann ?[1569]
  — Waylon Bass[2894]

(269)... Glenn Maurice Abney III[1570]
 +Ruth ?[1571]

(270)... Ann Abney[1572]
 +Kenneth Bevers[1573]

(271)... Glenda Abney[1574]
 +Darrell Riegel[1575]

(272)... John Dennis Bass[1576]
 +Janice Darlene Owens[1577]
  — Hannah LeNelle Bass[2895]
   +Jeffery Scott Tutterow[2896]
    — Jackson Tutterow[3775]
  — Kevin Bass[2897]
  — Tina Darlene Bass[2898]
   +Kevin Vance Himes[2899]
    — Cameron Himes[3776]
    — Kendrick Himes[3777]
   +Shawn Patrick O'Connor[2900]
    — Patrick O'Connor[3778]

(273)... William Gary Bass[1578]
 +Louise Watkins[1579]
 +Patricia ?[1580]

(274)... Emily Gwendolyn Bass[1581]
 +Kenneth E Lee[1582]
  — Lori Nicole Lee[2901]
   +William McVay[2902]
    — Loretta Voncile McVay[3779]
    — Ms. McVay[3780]
  +Willis Gene Jackson[2903]
  — Tanner Lee[2904]

Descendants

```
(275)... Rickie Donnel Barnett Sr.[1583]
      +Doris Ann Dubose[1584]
            ├── LaDonice Darnell Barnett[2905]
               +Tony Ingram[2906]
                     ├── Courtney Ingram[3781]
                     └── Joshua Tyler Ingram[3782]
                        +Ms. ?[3783]
                              └── Joshua Brody Ingram[4035]
      +Barbara Gambells[1585]
            ├── Buffie Deanna Barnett[2907]
            └── Rickey Darnell Barnett Jr.[2908]
      +Sandra Adams[1586]
            ├── Gloria Lynn Barnett[2909]
               +Steve Queens[2910]
            └── Melissa Ann Barnett[2911]
               +Daniel ?[2912]

(276)... Gloria Dianne Barnett[1587]
      +Arthur Lynn Presley[1588]
            ├── Brandi Lee Presley[2913]
               +Johnny Robert Boles Sr.[2914]
                     ├── Johnny Robert Boles Jr.[3784]
                     └── Brooklynn Lee Boles[3785]
            ├── Christopher Edwin Presley[2915]
               +Donna Wise[2916]
                     ├── Ciera Elizabeth Presley[3786]
                     └── Cheyenne Erin Presley[3787]
               +Dorenda Richards[2917]
                     └── Brianna Tegan Presley[3788]
            └── Lindsey Presley[2918]
               +John Michael Morris[2919]
               +Mr. Crawford[2920]
                     └── Sydney Nicole Crawford Morris[3789]
```

Gloria Dianne Barnett with her granddaughter and Artur Lynn Presley

```
(277)... Teresa LaGail Barnett[1589]
      +Raymond Randall Russell[1590]
            ├── Starlette Dawn Russell[2921]
               +Casey Levon Ray[2922]
                     └── Emmaleigh Maddison Ray[3790]
            ├── Raymond Randall Russell Jr.[2923]
               +Mary Ann Chance[2924]
                     ├── Kip Riley Russell[3791]
                     ├── Amber Nicole Russell[3792]
                     ├── Payton Breanna Russell[3793]
                     └── Kayla Brook Russell[3794]
            └── Sonya Leann Russell[2925]
               +Michael Dewayne Goodson[2926]
                     ├── Michael Tyler Goodson[3795]
                     └── Cory Ryan Goodson[3796]
      +Richard Dewight Lassiter[1591]
```

Cheyenne Erin, Christopher Edwin, Brianna Tegan, Dorenda Richards, Ciera Elizabeth Presley

```
(278)... Wanda June Barnett[1592]
      +David Glidewell[1593]
            ├── David Brent Glidewell[2927]
            └── Christy Lee Glidewell[2928]
               +Jerry Kilpatrick[2929]
                     └── Caden Kilpatrick[3799]
      +Donald Baker[1594]
```

(279)... Dale Allen Gindlesperger Jr.[1595]
 +Belinda Jo Boney[1596]
  ├── Mitchell Allen Gindlesperger[2930]
  │   +Melissa Ann Boles[2931]
  │   ├── Mason Allen Gindlesperger[3800]
  │   ├── Miles Avery Gindlesperger[3801]
  │   └── Merritt Anderson Gindlesperger[3802]
  ├── Andrew Grant Gindlesperger[2932]
  │   +Amanda Leigh Grider[2933]
  └── Derek Ashley Gindlesperger[2934]
      +Kelly Melissa Raw[2935]

(280)... Sue Ann Mann[1597]
 +James B King[1598]
  └── April Ann King[2936]
      +Michael Maddox[2937]
        ├── Dalto Michael Maddox[3803]
        └── Brodie James Maddox[3804]

(281)... Barbara Jane Mann[1599]
 +Gary Wayne Pelham[1600]

(282)... Betty Jean Mann[1601]
 +Randel Glenn Cornell[1602]
  └── Angela Kay Cornell[2938]
      +Clay Lehmann[2939]
 +Ronald Reed[1603]
 +Patrick McCoy[1604]

(283)... Dennis Keith Mann[1605]
 +Cindy Calhoun[1606]
  └── Ashton Nicole Mann[2940]
 +Brenda Davis[1607]

(284)... Michael Wayne Mann[1608]
 +Sandra Elaine Coleman[1609]
  ├── Seth Allen Mann Mann[2941]
  ├── Cole Michael Mann[2942]
  ├── Dakota Mann[2943]
  ├── Piper Mann[2944]
  └── Taylor Mann[2945]

(285)... Linda Fay Maund[1610]
 +Ansel Hogan[1611]
  └── Tyler Ansel Hogan[2946]
 +Terry Bullard[1612]

(286)... Amelia Delaine Maund[1613]
 +Daniel Lewellyn Beasley[1614]

(287)... Wendy Brynell Bass[1615]
 +David Miles[1616]
  ├── Mary Miles[2947]
  └── Brian Miles[2948]

(288)... Alivia LaShelle Bass[1617]
 +Johnny Mack Danford[1618]
  └── Randy Danford[2949]

(289)... Murry Lamar Bass[1619]
+Donna Theresa Stacks[1620]
└── Derrick Lamar Bass[2950]

(290)... Bridget Belinda Newton[2997]
+Lionel McCombs[2998]
├── Joseph McCombs[3837]
└── Jessica McCombs[3838]

(291)... Missouri Mae Newton[2999]
+Mr. ?[3000]
└── Heather ?[3839]

(292)... Sherry Denise Newton[3001]
+Jay Oliver Spicer[3002]
├── Jay Fletcher Spicer[3840]
└── Phillip Clayton[3841]
+Raymond Chessher[3003]

(293)... Barabara Sue Beck[3005]
+Darrell Gainey[3006]
├── Waylon Gainey[3842]
└── Nicole Gainey[3843]

(294)... Tamara Michelle Beck[3007]
+Alan Landingham[3008]
└── Brittany Landingham[3844]

(295)... Terry Lee Chessher[3013]
+Sandra Hudson[3014]
├── Natasha Chessher[3845]
└── Christina Chessher[3846]
+Ann Edge[3015]
└── Chelsey Leanne Chessher[3847]

(296)... Donna Kay Mills[3078]
+Thomas Patterson[3079]
├── Joshua Alan Silva Patterson[3874]
├── Amber Brook Patterson[3875]
├── Thomas Chester Patterson[3876]
└── Shane Donovan Patterson[3877]

(297)... Darla Lynn Mills[3082]
+Eric Jensen[3083]
├── Edward Clifton Jensen[3879]
├── Matthew Alan Jensen[3880]
└── Paula Marian Lynn Jensen[3881]

(298)... Phillip Michael Barnes[3192]
+Cheryl Anne Kemp[3193]
├── Mary Katherine Barnes[3906]
└── Hannah Marie Barnes[3907]

(299)... Samuel Brad Barnes[3194]
+Bethany Hope Bochette[3195]
├── Benson Gray Barnes[3908]
└── Troy Barnes[3909]

Phillip Michael Barnes, Hannah Marie, May Katherine, and Cheryl Anne Kemp Barnes

Wilson Bass

(300)... Nicholas Bruce Bass[3196]
　　+Elizabeth Corinne Barringer[3197]
　　├── Willson Bruce Bass[3911]
　　└── Joel Ryan Bass[3910]

(301)... Ashly Rena Bass[3198]
　　+Paul Edwin Powell Jr.[3199]
　　├── Aubree Claire Powell[3912]
　　└── Paul Edwin Powell III[3913]
　　+Barney Kieth Ray[3200]
　　└── Riggs Roosivelt Ray[3914]

(302)... Stacie Partain Bass[3201]
　　+John Joe Lamb[3202]
　　└── Brodie Lawson Lamb[3915]

(303)... Don Jeffery Bass II[3203]
　　+Bethany Whitehead[3204]

(304)... Janet Marie Bass[1905]
　　+Benjamin Doyle Kinsaul[1906]
　　├── Kayla Kinsaul[3205]
　　│　　+Jeffrey Douglas Gorum[3206]
　　│　　├── Harper Kate Gorum[3916]
　　│　　└── Stella Ruth Gorum[3917]
　　├── Hunter Doyle Kinsaul[3207]
　　└── Rollin Benjamin Kinsaul[3208]

Left to right back row first.
Nicholas Bruce, Stacie Partain, Ashly Rena Bass, Phillip Michael Barnes, Kala, Hunter Kinsaul, Samuel Brad Barnes, and Don Jeffery Bass II

(305)... Thomas Harold Henderson II[1907]
　　+Carol Jane Jordan[1908]
　　├── Tera Ashleigh Henderson[3209]
　　│　　+Damon Andrew Patrick[3210]
　　│　　└── Clare Elizabeth Patrick[3918]
　　├── Bret Thomas Henderson[3211]
　　│　　+Emily Jean Youngblood[3212]
　　│　　└── Mason Thomas Henderson[3919]
　　├── Kyle Jordan Henderson[3213]
　　│　　+McLean Hickman[3214]
　　└── Erin Lajune Henderson[3215]
　　　　+Mr. Tredwell[3216]
　　　　├── Iris Tredwell[3920]
　　　　└── Elle Tredwell[3921]

(306)... Randall Ralph Bass[1910]
　　+Treva Partain[1903]
　　└── Laura Bass[3217]
　　　　+Anthony Taylor[3218]
　　　　└── Emily Taylor[3922]

(307)... James Benny Bass[1913]
　　+Marie Stokes[1914]
　　├── Johnathan Blake Bass[3220]
　　│　　+Brittany Edwards[3221]
　　│　　├── Blakelee Bass[3925]
　　│　　├── Emerson Bass[3926]
　　│　　├── Bentlee Bass[3927]
　　│　　├── Aniston Bass[3928]
　　│　　└── Leeam Hudson Bass[3929]
　　└── Mandie Marie Bass[3222]
　　　　├── Trey ?[3930]
　　　　└── Charlie ?[3931]

Thomas Harold Henderson II and Carol Jane Jordan

(308)... Winfred Lynn Bass[1916]
    +Rhonda Davis[1917]
        ├─ Zach Bass[3223]
        │   +Janet Lee Taylor[3224]
        │   ├─ Cheston Bass[3932]
        │   └─ Embrie Lynn Bass[3933]
        └─ Allison Bass[3225]
            +Cody Helms[3226]
            +Cole Mock[3227]
                └─ Lynnli Kate Mock[3934]
            +Devin Dye[3228]

(309)... Anthony Edd Bass[1918]
    +Sherry Lynn Scroggins[1919]
        ├─ Anthony Gabriel Bass[3229]
        │   +Whitney Greene[3230]
        │   └─ Declan Ryan Bass[3935]
        └─ Nathaniel Drew Bass[3231]
            +Micgayle Holmes[3232]
                └─ Josiah Samuel Bass[3936]

Rhonda Davis, Winfred Lynn, and Allison Bass

(310)... Wendy Learvene Bass[1920]
    +Sheng Xiang Peng[1921]
    +Jay Jordan[1922]
        └─ Annette Eula Jordan[3233]

(311)... Tony Leon Mims[1923]
    +Jeanie Lorene Douglas[1924]
        ├─ Eric Michael Mims[3234]
        ├─ Tony Justin Mims[3235]
        ├─ William Brandon Mims[3236]
        └─ Megan Hayley Mims[3237]
    +Monette Legg[1925]

(312)... Diane Trawick[1926]
    +Jerral Lynn Taylor[1927]
        └─ Laura Elizabeth Taylor[3238]

(313)... Charlotte Trawick[1928]
    +Larry Dilmore[1929]
        ├─ Nathaniel Hayes Dilmore[3239]
        └─ Timothy Dilmore[3240]

(314)... Lisa Trawick[1930]
    +Gregory Paul Wade[1931]
        └─ Paul Joshua Wade[3241]

(315)... Gena Trawick[1932]
    +David Jernigan[1933]
        ├─ Myranda Nichole Jernigan[3242]
        │   +Sam Soutullo[3243]
        ├─ Natalie Danielle Jernigan[3244]
        ├─ Ethan Tyler Jernigan[3245]
        └─ Kylee Jernigan[3246]
    +Joe Murphy[1934]

Gena Trawick and Joe Murphy

(316)... Cynthia Michelle Bass[1935]
    +Jeffery Lee Switzer[1936]
        — Hannah Leigh Switzer[3247]
          +Ike Collins Dulin III[3248]
        — Timothy Michael Switzer[3249]
        — Jonathan David Switzer[3250]

(317)... Coy Bennett Bass Jr.[1937]
    +Kelly Ann Rusk[1938]
        — James Bennett Bass[3251]
        — Kameron Baylea Bass[3252]
        — Karson Ann Bass[3253]
    +Candy M. Fowler Frantz[1939]

(318)... Columbus Barry Bass[1940]
    +Tamera Renee Wallace[1941]
    +Terri Stone[1942]

(319)... Stanley Brian Bass[1944]
    +Ms. ?[1945]

Stanley Brian Bass, cruzing.

Coy Bennett Jr., Coy Bennett Sr., Margaret Faye Hammock, Columbus Barry Bass

3. DIRECT RELATIONS

Generation of Peers

1. WILSON BASS was born about 1785, in North Carolina, USA.
    - He was recorded in the census in 1830, aged about 45, in Covington, Alabama, USA.
    - He was recorded in the census in 1840, aged about 55, in Covington, Alabama, United States.
    - He died about 1850, aged about 65, in Covington, Alabama, USA.

   The following information is also recorded for Wilson:
    - Military Service in 1813, aged about 28, in Pulaski, Georgia, USA.
    - Crime in October 1814, aged about 29, in Pulaski, Georgia, USA.
    - Property: Purchased the East half of the Southeast quarter 20-3-14 and East half of the Northeast quarter 25-3-14 on December 22, 1823, aged about 38, in Covington, Alabama, USA.
    - Property: West half of Southeast quarter 29-3-14 on January 1, 1824, aged about 38, in Covington, Alabama, USA.
    - Property: Southwest quarter of Northeast quarter 28-3-14 on February 16, 1836, aged about 50, in Covington, Alabama, USA.
    - Property: Northwest quarter of Northeast quarter 28-3-14 on May 3, 1837, aged about 51, in Covington, Alabama, USA.
    - Community Service between January 27, 1845 and February 29, 1848, aged about 61, in Covington, Alabama, United States.

   Notes:
    - *Wilson Bass, father of Bennett Bridges, Nancy, and William Riley Bass, grandfather of Holland M. and William Riley Bass, moved from North to South Carolina, then to Georgia, and later to Covington County, Alabama. Census records show Wilson Bass was born between 1780 and 1790. There were three named children: Bennett, Nancy, and Riley. Census records show Bennett was born in Georgia in 1808, Nancy was born in Georgia around 1813, and William Riley was born in the area of Andalusia, Alabama in 1824. Mr. Bass moved to Montezuma, a small town between Andalusia and River Falls. This town is no longer in existence. He later moved to a farm near the Carolina Community, south of Andalusia, Alabama. The farm is on the right of the Brewton-Andalusia highway. At his death, before 1850, he was buried under a Mulberry tree, as was the custom in those days. There was not a marker, and the grave is now part of a farm. – Original Bass Family Record by Genola Bass Spence and Glynda Wilkinson Cupp.*
    - *Georgia Militia.*
      (Military Service)
    - *...Wilson Bass for retailing spiritous liquers without license and also for keeping a riotus house on the Sabbath day. (Crime)*
    - *Beat No. 2 Voting Precent titled Wilson Bass'.*
      (Community Service)

2. SUSANNAH ? was born about 1790, in North Carolina, USA. She died about 1850, aged about 60, in Covington, Alabama, USA.

   Note: *The name Susannah, as Wilson's wife comes from the family of William Riley Bass b. 1862, son of Wilson Bennett Bass b. 1840. William Riley Bass was a member of the LDS church, known for their commitment to geneology, also named his first daughter Mary Susannah, which gives some credence to the idea of his grandmother also being Susannah. To my knowledge, no documentatin has been found to confirm.*

   Wilson Bass[1] married Susannah ?. They had three children:
   > Bennett Bridges Bass Sr.[3] born on February 17, 1808 in Georgia, USA; died after June 1, 1870 in Andalusa, Alabama, USA
   > Nancy Bass[5] born in 1813 in Georgia, USA; died in 1885 in Falls, Texas, USA
   > William Riley Bass[7] born in 1824 in Andalusia, Covington, Alabama, USA; died on March 18, 1864 in Niceville, Okaloosa, Florida, USA

1st Generation of Descendants

3. BENNETT BRIDGES BASS SR. (see Descendants) was born on February 17, 1808, in Georgia, USA, to Wilson Bass[1] and Susannah ?[2].
    - He was recorded in the census in 1840, aged about 32, in Covington, Alabama, United States.
    - He was recorded in the census in 1850, aged about 42, in Covington county, Covington, Alabama, USA.
    - He was recorded in the census in 1860, aged about 52, in Covington, Alabama, USA.
    - He was recorded in the census on June 1, 1870, aged 62, in Florida, USA.
    - He died after June 1, 1870, when older than 62, in Andalusa, Alabama, USA.
    - He was buried in Walton County, Florida, USA.

    The following information is also recorded for Bennett Bridges:
    - Property: Northeast quarter of Southeast quarter 28-3-14 on November 29, 1833, aged 25, in Covington, Alabama, USA.
    - Property: Southeast quarter of Northeast quarter 14-3-14 on March 16, 1837, aged 29, in Covington, Alabama, USA.
    - Military Service.

    Notes:
    - *Bennett Bridges Bass had a cattle ranch south of Andalusia in the Carolina community. He lost his ranch soon after the Civil War began and moved with his family to Rocky Bayou near Niceville, FL. Two of his sons James and Wilson and his brother William Riley were killed near Niceville, FL at Boggy Bayou during the Civil War by Mississippi cavalrymen. Information found suggest that the Basses were killed helping a "union sympathizer", and local politician named Alfred Holley (state representative), escape to the Union lines. Bennett remained in Walton County, Florida after the war and died there around 1874. Information from the book "Early History of Covington County" by Wyley Donald Ward claims in late 1863 there were growing numbers of deserters and Union sympathizers in Southern Alabama & Western Florida. In order to deal with this, Governor Shorter of Alabama instructed the Confederate Army to attempt to crush deserters and Union sympathy in that region. Col. Holland of the confederate army was a leader of one of the groups assigned to this task. Apparently one of the first moves of Col. Holland was to trap Alfred Holley, state representative of Covington County. Who was thought to be assisting the deserters. An attempt was made on March 15, 1864 which was reported in the Montgomery Weekly Advertiser on April 20, 1864 to trap and arrest Alfred Holley. Although they did not arrest him, they took his son Alfred D. Holley a Lieutenant in the 40 Alabama infantry and held him for a period of time before releasing him after determining his loyalty to the confederacy. Only three days later reported in General Maury's activity report to General Cooper, Col. Holland's expedition had an encounter on the Choctawhatchee Bay and he claimed the entire boat crew of about 25 were killed & drowned with no loss on the Confederate side. Col. Holland was leader of the 37 MS regiment. The event was also mentioned in the April 4, 1864 report of Gen. Asboth, Union Commander at Ft. Barrancas. It stated that "Mr. Alfred Holley came in yesterday, reporting that while leaving Boggy Bayou for East Pass in a skiff with five others (all members of the Bass family residing there), the rebels fired upon them killing 3 and wounding 2, who we now have in our hospital". All the men on the skiff were natives and or longtime residents of Covington County, Alabama. Those killed were William Riley Bass (the youngest son of Wilson Bass) and 2 nephews, Wilson & James H. Bass, sons of Bennett Bridges Bass. Many of the cattle taken by Col. Holland's troops in Florida, were owned by William Ward, also a former resident of Covington County, Alabama. -Copied From Horace P. Bass Family Tree.*
    - *Alabama Malitia 1837.*
      (Military Service)

4. MARY ELIZABETH HOGG was born on October 15, 1818, in Alabama, USA, to Holland Middleton Hogg and Mary Polly Mixon.
    - She was recorded in the census in 1850, aged about 31, in Covington county, Covington, Alabama, USA.
    - She was recorded in the census in 1860, aged about 41, in Covington, Alabama, USA.
    - She was recorded in the census on June 1, 1870, aged 51, in Florida, USA.
    - She died after 1870, when older than 52, in Andalusa, Alabama, USA.
    - She was buried in Conecuh River Baptist Cemetery, Andalusia, Covington, Alabama, USA.

    Bennett Bridges Bass Sr.[3], aged about 29, married Mary Elizabeth Hogg, aged about 18, about March 2, 1837 in Andalusia, Covington, Alabama, USA. They had ten children:

    Mary Bass[9] born on October 3, 1838 in Andalusia, Alabama, USA; died in 1912 in Covington County, Alabama

    Wilson Bennett Bass[12] born on February 17, 1840 in Andalusia, Alabama, USA; died on March 18, 1864 in Niceville, Florida, USA

    Nancy Bass[14] born on March 2, 1842 in Covington, Alabama, USA; died on April 26, 1916 in Covington, Alabama, USA

    Levina Bass[16] born on January 23, 1843 in Covington, Alabama, USA; died on July 18, 1866 in Andalusia, Covington, Alabama, USA

Holland Middleton Bass[17] born on December 21, 1845 in Andalusa, Alabama, USA; died on July 31, 1934 in Okaloosa, Florida, USA

James Hilliard Bass[19] born on April 25, 1847 in Covington County, Alabama, USA; died on March 18, 1864 in Okaloosa County, Florida, USA

Bennett Bridges Bass Jr.[20] born on June 13, 1848 in Covington, Alabama, USA; died on August 10, 1930 in Covington, Alabama, USA

Elizabeth Bass[24] born on October 14, 1850 in Andalusia, Covington, Alabama, USA; died on December 11, 1943 in Niceville, Florida, USA

Martha Jane Bass[26] born on February 13, 1852 in Andalusia, Covington, Alabama, USA; died on December 11, 1943 in Niceville, Okaloosa, Florida, United States

William Riley Bass[28] born on May 28, 1854 in Covington County, Alabama, United States; died on June 19, 1933 in Covington County, Alabama, USA

5. NANCY BASS (see Descendants) was born in 1813, in Georgia, USA, to Wilson Bass[1] and Susannah ?[2].
- She was recorded in the census in 1850, aged about 37, in Covington county, Covington, Alabama, USA.
- She died in 1885, aged about 72, in Falls, Texas, USA.

6. WILLIAM PADGETT was born on May 28, 1811, in Darlington, Darlington, South Carolina, USA, to William Henry Padgett and Elizabeth Dixon. William became known as "Bill".
- He was recorded in the census in 1850, aged about 39, in Covington county, Covington, Alabama, USA.
- He died on August 11, 1855, aged 44 years, in Covington, Alabama, USA.

William Padgett, aged about 26, married Nancy Bass[5], aged about 24, in 1837 in Covington, Alabama, USA. They had five children:

Jane Padgett[30] born on March 18, 1838 in Alabama, USA; died in December 1927

Henry Padgett[32] born on June 18, 1844 in Alabama, United States; died on December 15, 1861 in Mobile, Alabama, USA

Levinta Padgett[33] born about 1847 in Alabama, United States; died in 1900

Elizabeth H. Padgett[36] born on December 3, 1850 in Covington, Alabama, USA; died on July 15, 1931 in Lott, Falls, Texas, USA

Nancy Ann Padgett[38] born on April 16, 1855 in Alabama, USA; died on January 7, 1952 in Andalusia, Covington, Alabama, USA

7. WILLIAM RILEY BASS (see Descendants) was born in 1824, in Andalusia, Covington, Alabama, USA, to Wilson Bass[1] and Susannah ?[2].
- He was recorded in the census in 1860, aged about 36, in Covington, Alabama, USA.
- He died (Killed by Confederate Soldiers) on March 18, 1864, aged about 39, in Niceville, Okaloosa, Florida, USA.

The following information is also recorded for William Riley:
- Military Service in Covington, Alabama, USA.

Notes:
- *There has been some debate, which I am aware of through notes in the margins of documents in libraries, as to the date of William Riley Bass' time of death. These notes in the margins suggest he passed before 1860, because he is not listed on the 1860 census with his wife and children. At first glance this seems to be true, but my research has found that he is listed on the last row of a census page and his wife and children are listed on the next page. My beliefe is that Mr. Riley Bass died on March 18th 1864, along with two of his nephews in an attack by Confederate forces, in their pursuit of State Rep. Alfred Holley. This beliefe is reinforced knowing that just days later his son James W. Bass enlisted in the Union Army in Pensacola Florida, right where Mr. Holley was headed. (Death)*
- *Said to have defected from the Confederat army near the end of the war to go back to Florida with his family. (I've found no record of him ever serving.) Was killed as a Union sympothiser near Niceville. (Military Service)*

8. MARY STRAUGHN was born about 1820, in Alabama, USA.
- She was recorded in the census in 1860, aged about 40, in Covington, Alabama, USA.
- She was recorded in the census in 1880, aged about 60, in Harts And Red Level, Covington, Alabama, USA.
- She died after 1880, when older than 60.

William Riley Bass[7] married Mary Straughn. They had four sons:

James W. Bass[40] born about 1847 in Alabama, United States; died on November 25, 1864 in Barraugas, Santa Rosa, Florida, USA

John Bass[41] born on December 13, 1849 in Alabama, USA

William M. Bass[42] born on August 2, 1852 in Alabama, United States; died on February 20, 1913

Riley Bass[44] born on December 2, 1856 in Alabama, United States; died on February 23, 1915 in Covington, Alabama, USA

The Charleston Mercury

MATRIMONY BY WHOLESALE.—In the Southwestern (Ala.) *Baptist*, we find the following announcement:

"About eight miles southeast from Andalusia, on Thursday, October 16th, were married at the residence of B. B. Bass, by G. A. Snowden, Judge of Probate, James Teel to Nancy Bass, William Teel to Mary Bass, and Wilson Bass to Jane Teel; James, William, and Jane Teel, are all sons and daughter of John and Anna Teel; Wilson, Nancy, and Mary Bass, are all daughters and son of B. B. and Elizabeth Bass, all of Covington County, Alabama. The above connubial attachments were all formed, and but one ceremony delivered—a nuptial phenomenon perhaps unequalled in this State or the South."

VICKSBURG, MISSISSIPPI, JULY 10th A. D. 1863.

TO ALL WHOM IT MAY CONCERN, KNOW YE THAT:

I *Wilson Bass* a *Private* of Co. *E, 42* Reg't *Alabama* Vol., C. S. A., being a Prisoner of War, in the hands of the United States Forces, in virtue of the capitulation of the City of Vicksburg and its Garrison, by Lieut. Gen. John C. Pemberton, C. S. A., Commanding, on the 4th day of July, 1863, do in pursuance of the terms of said capitulation, give this my solemn parole under oath—

That I will not take up arms again against the United States, nor serve in any military, police, or constabulary force in any Fort, Garrison or field work, held by the Confederate States of America, against the United States of America, nor as guard of prisons, depots or stores, nor discharge any duties usually performed by officers or soldiers against the United States of America until duly exchanged by the proper authorities. *Wilson his X Bass mark*

Sworn to and subscribed before me at Vicksburg, Miss., this *10th* day of July, 1863

Geo. W. _____
Lieut. 31st Reg't *Ill.* Vols.,

AND PAROLLING OFFICER.

Wilson Bass' loyalty oath.

VICKSBURG, MISSISSIPPI, JULY 10th A. D. 1863.

TO ALL WHOM IT MAY CONCERN, KNOW YE THAT:

I *Henry Teel* a *Private* of Co. *E, 42* Reg't *Ala* Vol., C. S. A., being a Prisoner of War, in the hands of the United States Forces, in virtue of the capitulation of the City of Vicksburg and its Garrison, by Lieut. Gen. John C. Pemberton, C. S. A., Commanding, on the 4th day of July, 1863, do in pursuance of the terms of said capitulation, give this my solemn parole under oath—

That I will not take up arms again against the United States, nor serve in any military, police, or constabulary force in any Fort, Garrison or field work, held by the Confederate States of America, against the United States of America, nor as guard of prisons, depots or stores, nor discharge any duties usually performed by officers or soldiers against the United States of America until duly exchanged by the proper authorities.

Henry his X Teel mark

Sworn to and subscribed before me at Vicksburg, Miss., this *10th* day of July, 1863

Geo W _____
Capt 31st Reg't *Ill.* Vols.

AND PAROLLING OFFICER.

Henry Teel's loyalty oath. Wilson's brother-in-law.

2nd Generation of Descendants

9. MARY BASS (see Descendants) was born on October 3, 1838, in Andalusa, Alabama, USA, to Bennett Bridges Bass Sr.[3] and Mary Elizabeth Hogg[4].
    - She was recorded in the census in 1850, aged about 11, in Covington county, Covington, Alabama, USA.
    - She was recorded in the census in 1900, aged about 61, in Andalusia town, Covington, Alabama, USA.
    - She was recorded in the census in 1910, aged about 71, in Andalusia, Covington, Alabama, USA.
    - She died in 1912, aged about 73, in Covington County, Alabama.
    - She was buried in Carolina Baptist Church Cemetery, Covington, Alabama, USA.

    Mary married twice. She was married to William Teel[10] and John W Ramer[11].

10. WILLIAM TEEL was born on January 27, 1841, in Covington, Alabama, USA, to John Teel Sr. and Anna Padgett. William became known as "Bill".
    - He was recorded in the census in 1850, aged about 9, in Covington county, Covington, Alabama, USA.
    - He died (At War) on August 11, 1863, aged 22, in Vicksburg, Warren, Missisippi, USA.
    - He was buried in Unknown Grave, Civil War.

    The following information is also recorded for Bill:
    - Military Service.

    Notes:
    - *Due to sickness after reliese from a POW camp.*
    (Death)
    - *Civil War 42nd Alabama.*
    (Military Service)

    William Teel, aged 18, married Mary Bass[9], aged 21, on October 16, 1859. They had one son:

    William Henry Teel[45] born on January 7, 1863 in Florida, United States; died on December 7, 1938 in Andalusia, Covington, Alabama, USA

    Note: *Two Bass sisters and one Bass brother, married two Teel brothers and one Teel sister in the same wedding ceremony.*

    In the Charleston Mercury on December 19, 1859, entitled "Matrimony by Wholesale". It was found in the Southwestern Alabama Baptist with the following statement: "About eight miles southeast from Andalusia, on Thursday, October 16, were married at the residence of B.B. Bass, by G.A. Snowden, Judge of Probate, James Teel to Nancy Bass, William Teel to Mary Bass and Wilson Bass to Jane Teel. James, William and Jane are all sons and daughter of John and Anna Teel. Wilson, Nancy and Mary Bass are all daughters and son of B.B. and Elizabeth Bass, all of Covington County, Ala. The above connubial attachments were all formed one ceremony delivered—a nuptial phenomenon perhaps unequaled in this state or the South.".

11. JOHN W RAMER was born in June 1845, in Covington, Alabama, USA. John W became known as "Bud".
    - He was recorded in the census in 1900, aged about 55, in Andalusia town, Covington, Alabama, USA.
    - He was recorded in the census in 1910, aged about 65, in Andalusia, Covington, Alabama, USA.
    - He died on August 14, 1916, aged 71 years, in Carolina Community, Covington, Alabama, USA.
    - He was buried in Carolina Baptist Church Cemetery, Covington, Alabama, USA.

    The following information is also recorded for Bud:
    - Military Service.

    Note: *Co. I 40 AL Inf CSA, Civil War.*
    (Military Service)

    John W Ramer, aged about 20, married Mary Bass[9], aged about 26, about 1865. They had seven children:

    William Albert Ramer[47] born in August 1870 in Alabama, USA; died on December 25, 1934 in Opp, Covington, Alabama, USA

    John Ramer[49] born on February 22, 1872 in Florida, USA; died on July 17, 1955 in Alabama, USA

    Jacob D Ramer[51] born on February 22, 1872 in Alabama, United States; died on July 17, 1955 in Andalusia, Covington, Alabama, USA

    James W Ramer[54] born in March 1874 in Florida, USA

    Nancy Elizabeth Ramer[55] born in December 1875 in Florida, USA; died in 1963 in Andalusia, Covington, Alabama, USA

    Alfred Calvin Ramer[57] born in August 1882 in Alabama, USA

    Mae Ramer[58]

12. WILSON BENNETT BASS (see Descendants) was born on February 17, 1840, in Andalusa, Alabama, USA, to Bennett Bridges Bass Sr.[3] and Mary Elizabeth Hogg[4].
    - He was recorded in the census in 1850, aged about 10, in Covington county, Covington, Alabama, USA.
    - He was recorded in the census in 1860, aged about 20, in Covington, Alabama, USA.

- He died (Killed by Confederate Soldiers) on March 18, 1864, aged 24 years, in Niceville, Florida, USA.
- He was buried in Niceville, Florida, USA.

The following information is also recorded for Wilson Bennett:
- Military Service in 1862, aged about 22, in Alabama, USA.

Notes:
- *Wilson Bennett Bass, born 1840, enlisted in Captain Brady's Company, Company E., 42nd Alabama Infantry Regiment on April 1, 1862. The 42nd Alabama Infantry Regiment was organized at Columbus, Miss., in May 1862, composed principally of men who reorganized, in two or three instances, as entire companies after serving a year as the 42nd Alabama Infantry Regiment. Members came primarily from Conecuh, Fayette, Marion, Mobile, Monroe, Pickens, Talladega, and Wilcox counties. The regiment joined Generals Price and Van Dorn at Ripley in September and was brigaded under General John C. Moore of Texas. A month later, the 42nd went into the Battle of Corinth with 700 men (losing 98 killed and about 250 wounded or captured) and later wintered in Mississippi. Moore's Brigade was reorganized with the 37th, 40th and 42nd Alabama, and the 2nd Texas regiments. It was part of the garrison of Vicksburg and lost 10 killed and about 50 wounded there, with the remainder captured at the surrender of the fortress. The 42nd was in parole camp at Demopolis and then joined the Army of Tennessee. It fought with severe losses at Lookout Mountain and Mission Ridge, and it wintered at Dalton, Ga. General Baker of Barbour then took command of the brigade, (Clayton's [Stewart's] Division, Polk's Corps). In the spring, the 42nd fought at Resaca with a loss of 59 killed and wounded. It was then continually skirmishing until the battle of New Hope, where its loss was comparatively light as it was at Atlanta on July 22. On July 28, the loss was heavy. A few days later, the regiment was sent to Spanish Fort where it remained on garrison duty during the fall and until January 1865. It then moved into North Carolina, participated in the battle of Bentonville, and surrendered with the army. Field and staff officers were Cols. John W. Portis (Clarke; wounded, Corinth; resigned); Thomas C. Lanier (Pickens; wounded, New Hope); Lt. Col. Thomas C. Lanier (wounded, Corinth; promoted); Major W. C. Fergus (Mobile; captured, Missionary Ridge); and Adjutants Thomas J. Portis (Dallas; resigned); and Thomas Gaillard (Mobile). The 42nd Alabama Infantry was involved in the following battles while the Teel and Bass family members were present: Corinth, Miss., October 3-4, 1862; engagement at Hatchie Bridge "Davis Bridge," Big Hatchie, Metamora, Tenn., Oct. 6, 1862; retreat to the Hatchie River, Miss., Oct. 5-12, 1862; operations on the Mississippi Central R.R. from Bolivar, Tenn., to Coffeeville, Miss.; "Grant's Central Mississippi Campaign," Oct. 31, 1862, through Jan. 10, 1863; skirmishes, 40 Hills and Hankinson's Ferry, Miss., May 3-4, 1863; siege at Vicksburg, Miss., May 18-July 4, 1863; assault, Vicksburg, Miss., May 19 and 22, 1863; and surrender, Vicksburg, July 4, 1863. The Teel brothers and Wilson Bennett Bass survived these campaigns; however, after being required to take the loyalty oath on July 7, 1863, only Henry Teel and Wilson Bennett Bass made it home. William Teel had apparently been ill, and died soon after taking this oath, leaving a young widow, Mary Bass Teel, and son William Henry Teel at home. The actual oath of loyalty signed by William Teel, Henry Teel, and Wilson Bennett Bass is as follows: "I will not take up arms against the United States, nor serve in any military, police, or constabulary force in any fort, garrison, or field work held by the Confederate States of America against the United States of America, nor as guard of prisons, depots, or stores, nor discharged any duties usually performed by officers or soldiers against the United States of America until duly exchanged by the proper authorities." The source is the writings of Linda Kaple, a descendant of this Teel family.*
- *Wilson Bennett Bass was killed in 1864 along with his brother and uncle, March 18, 1864.*
- *Pvt 42nd Alabama Inf CSA.*
(Military Service)

13. JANE TEEL was born on January 27, 1839, in Andalusa, Alabama, USA, to John Teel Sr. and Anna Padgett.
    - She was recorded in the census in 1850, aged about 11, in Covington county, Covington, Alabama, USA.
    - She died (Drowned) in 1864, aged about 25, in Niceville, Florida, USA.
    - She was buried in Niceville, Florida, USA.

    Notes:
    - *Jane Teel, born in 1839. She was residing in her parents' home in 1850, but she was married in 1859 to Wilson Bennett Bass, son of Bennett Bridges and Mary Elizabeth (Hogg) Bass. In 1860, the young couple was living in his father's household in Covington County. In 1862, he enlisted as a private in Company E, 42nd Alabama Infantry Regiment, C.S.A. He was captured and paroled in 1863 during the siege of Vicksburg along with two of his wife's brothers, John and Henry Teel. Upon returning home, he moved with his father and family to Boggy Bayou, Fla. He was killed in 1864 by the Confederate Army. His wife, Jane, drowned maybe a couple of years later along with her sister, Elizabeth, on their way to another sister's wedding.*

    Jane and Wilson B. Bass had only two young children who were left as orphans upon their parents' deaths. Benjamin Wilson Bass was born in 1859 and died in 1935 in Texas where he had married Matilda Hall (1858-1903). William Riley Bass, born in 1862 and died in 1948, was married to Frances Elizabeth Collins, a native of Mississippi (1866-1949). At some point, this couple moved to Utah where they lived out their lives.
    - *Drowned on the way to a sisters wedding due to an accident.*
    (Death)

Wilson Bennett Bass[12], aged 19, married Jane Teel, aged 20, on October 16, 1859. They had two sons:
> Benjamin Wilson ("Ben") Bass[60] born on October 17, 1860 in Mayfield, Alabama, USA; died on May 29, 1935 in Votaw, Hardin, Texas, USA
>
> William Riley ("Bill") Bass[64] born on September 15, 1862 in Pensacola, Escambia, Florida, USA; died on November 19, 1948 in Monticello, San Juan, Utah, USA

Note: *Two Bass sisters and one Bass brother, married two Teel brothers and one Teel sister in the same wedding ceremony.*

In the Charleston Mercury on December 19, 1859, entitled "Matrimony by Wholesale". It was found in the Southwestern Alabama Baptist with the following statement: "About eight miles southeast from Andalusia, on Thursday, October 16, were married at the residence of B.B. Bass, by G.A. Snowden, Judge of Probate, James Teel to Nancy Bass, William Teel to Mary Bass and Wilson Bass to Jane Teel. James, William and Jane are all sons and daughter of John and Anna Teel. Wilson, Nancy and Mary Bass are all daughters and son of B.B. and Elizabeth Bass, all of Covington County, Ala. The above connubial attachments were all formed one ceremony delivered—a nuptial phenomenon perhaps unequaled in this state or the South.".

14. NANCY BASS (see Descendants) was born on March 2, 1842, in Covington, Alabama, USA, to Bennett Bridges Bass Sr.[3] and Mary Elizabeth Hogg[4].
    - She was recorded in the census in 1850, aged about 8, in Covington county, Covington, Alabama, USA.
    - She was recorded in the census in 1860, aged about 18, in Covington, Alabama, USA.
    - She was recorded in the census in 1880, aged about 38, in Harts And Red Level, Covington, Alabama, USA.
    - She was recorded in the census in 1910, aged about 68, in Fairfield, Covington, Alabama, USA.
    - She died on April 26, 1916, aged 74 years, in Covington, Alabama, USA.
    - She was buried in Teel Cemetary, Covington, Alabama, USA.

15. JAMES TEEL was born on November 17, 1830, in Alabama, United States, to John Teel Sr. and Anna Padgett.
    - He was recorded in the census in 1850, aged about 19, in Covington county, Covington, Alabama, USA.
    - He was recorded in the census in 1860, aged about 29, in Covington, Alabama, USA.
    - He was recorded in the census in 1880, aged about 49, in Harts And Red Level, Covington, Alabama, USA.
    - He died on October 19, 1904, aged 73.
    - He was buried in Teel Cemetery, Covington, Alabama, USA.

The following information is also recorded for James:
- Injury on March 18, 1864, aged 33.

Note: *James Teel, was shot through the thigh, by Confederate Soldiers, with a minory ball and remained a cripple all of his life.*
(Injury)

James Teel, aged 28, married Nancy Bass[14], aged 17, on October 16, 1859. They had ten children:
> Bennett B. Teel[66] born on June 28, 1860 in Alabama, USA; died on December 10, 1884 in Alabama, USA
>
> Bruner Teel[67] born in 1861 in Alabama, United States
>
> Melvine Lavina Teel[68] born in 1863 in Alabama, United States; died on November 21, 1949 in Andalusia, Covington, Alabama, USA
>
> Annie Teel[70] born in April 1864 in Alabama, USA; died on March 2, 1941 in Covington, Alabama, USA
>
> Elizabeth Teel[71] born on October 1, 1866 in Alabama, United States; died on February 11, 1949
>
> John Teel[73] born on February 6, 1872 in Alabama, United States; died on May 4, 1958 in Andalusia, Covington, Alabama, USA
>
> Nancy Viola Teel[75] born in 1875 in Alabama, United States
>
> William Riley Teel[77] born on November 2, 1877 in Alabama, USA; died on December 31, 1924 in Andalusia, Covington, Alabama, USA
>
> Henry Vauceous Teel[79] born on June 27, 1881; died on June 6, 1937 in Alabama, USA
>
> Mattie Teel[81] born in 1885 in Alabama, USA; died on March 30, 1974 in Covington, Alabama, USA

Note: *Two Bass sisters and one Bass brother, married two Teel brothers and one Teel sister in the same wedding ceremony.*

In the Charleston Mercury on December 19, 1859, entitled "Matrimony by Wholesale". It was found in the Southwestern Alabama Baptist with the following statement: "About eight miles southeast from Andalusia, on Thursday, October 16, were married at the residence of B.B. Bass, by G.A. Snowden, Judge of Probate, James Teel to Nancy Bass, William Teel to Mary Bass and Wilson Bass to Jane Teel. James, William and Jane are all sons and daughter of John and Anna Teel. Wilson, Nancy and Mary Bass are all daughters and son of B.B. and Elizabeth Bass, all of Covington County, Ala. The above connubial attachments were all formed one ceremony delivered—a nuptial phenomenon perhaps unequaled in this state or the South.".

Notes:

Above: Holland Middleton "Sonk" Bass with his sons. From Left to Right, Back row: John, Stacey, Joseph A. "Joe" Front row: Holly M. "Bud" Jr., William B. "Bill", Holly M. Sr., Dallas

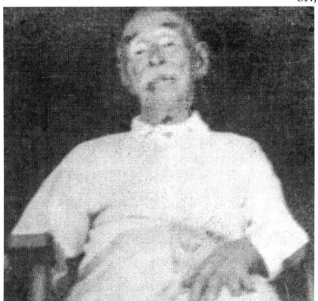

Holland Middleton Bass

Christian Ward Bass with her daughters an others. Not enough confidence to label any of them.

16. LEVINA BASS (see Descendants) was born on January 23, 1843, in Covington, Alabama, USA, to Bennett Bridges Bass Sr.[3] and Mary Elizabeth Hogg[4]. Levina became known as "Winny".
- She was recorded in the census in 1850, aged about 7, in Covington county, Covington, Alabama, USA.
- She was recorded in the census in 1860, aged about 17, in Covington, Alabama, USA.
- She died (At young age) on July 18, 1866, aged 23 years, in Andalusia, Covington, Alabama, USA.

17. HOLLAND MIDDLETON BASS (see Descendants) was born on December 21, 1845, in Andalusa, Alabama, USA, to Bennett Bridges Bass Sr.[3] and Mary Elizabeth Hogg[4]. Holland Middleton became known as "Holley".
- He was recorded in the census in 1850, aged about 4, in Covington county, Covington, Alabama, USA.
- He was recorded in the census in 1860, aged about 14, in Covington, Alabama, USA.
- He was recorded in the census on June 1, 1870, aged 24, in Florida, USA.
- He was recorded in the census in 1900, aged about 54, in Precincts 10, 19 Hart, George, Covington, Alabama, USA.
- He was recorded in the census in 1920, aged about 74, in Precinct 21, Covington, Alabama, USA.
- He died on July 31, 1934, aged 88 years, in Okaloosa, Florida, USA.
- He was buried in Zion Rock Cemetery, Beda, Covington, Alabama, USA.

The following information is also recorded for Holley:
- Description: 5' 5"DarkGrayLight complexion.
- Namesake.
- Military Service in Florida.

Notes:
- *Holly M. Bass Sr. Enlisted in the Union Army on January 19th of 1864, at the age of 19. He was mustered into the First Florida Calvary Co. B as a Privat, on March 23 1864 at Fort Barraicas, Pensicola Florida. Descrived as 5' 5" Tall, Gray Eyes, Dark Hair, Light Complection. He qualified for a $300 bounty at Enlistment and was Paid $25 of that amount. When he mustered out he was still owed $120 of the original $300.*

  He was mustered out on March 17th 1865 at Tallahassee Florida.

  He lost an eye or use of an eye in battle. Per family records, and his pention records do indicate him qualifying as an "Invalid". He farmed the rest of his life and raised a larg family, so the eye injury would fit in his history.
- *Holland M. Bass funeral story as told by different ones of his grandchildren. On July 21 1934 Holland M. Bass passed away at the home of his son William (Bill) in Holt FL. He was 88 and 6 month of age. He was buried at the Zion Rock Cemetery just south of Open Pond in Covington County Ala. Mr. Bass was taken from Holt to Zion Rock Church on the back of a flatbed truck. Preston Posey was driving, and some of the grandsons were on the back with him. When they got to the church there was a man standing in the door and he said you can bring the body inside and the family can come in, but then he pointed at the preacher and said "but he can not come in". So the service was held under an Oak Tree. - Anthony "Buzz" Ward.*
  (Death)
- *His mothers father Holland Middleton Hogg, who was named after his mothers father Holland Middleton.*
  (Namesake)
- *Enlisted at Pensacola, Florida and was discharged at St. Marks, Florida. 1st Cavalry, B.*
  (Military Service)

18. CHRISTIAN WARD was born on October 21, 1847, in Rocky Bayou, Walton, Florida, USA, to William Marion Ward and Catherin Campbell.
- She was recorded in the census in 1850, aged about 2, in Walton county, Walton, Florida, USA.
- She was recorded in the census in 1860, aged about 12, in Walton, Florida, USA.
- She was recorded in the census in 1870, aged about 22, in Florida, USA.
- She was recorded in the census in 1900, aged about 52, in Precincts 10, 19 Hart, George, Covington, Alabama, USA.
- She died on October 3, 1917, aged 69 years, in Walton County, Florida, USA.
- She was buried in Zion Rock Cemetery, Beda, Covington, Alabama, USA.

Note: *Mrs. Christian Bass was born Oct. 21 1847. She was reared in Walton County, Florida, near Laurelhill. She was married to H.M. Bass and lived for sometime near Boggy, Florida, later moving to Covington county and lived here the remainder of her life. She was the Mother of 12 children. Ten of whom are living. Her husband and children and a host of friends mourn her death. .*
(Death)

Holland Middleton Bass[17], aged about 24, married Christian Ward, aged about 22, about 1870. They had twelve children:

Levina Bass[83] born before December 14, 1871

William Bennett Bass[84] born on December 14, 1871 in Uchee Anna, Walton, Florida, USA; died on April 15, 1965 in Holt, Okaloosa, Florida, USA

Nancy Jane Middleton Bass[86] born on March 9, 1873 in Uchee Anna, Walton, Florida, USA; died on November 13, 1947 in Andalusia, Covington, Alabama, USA

Catherine Elizabeth Bass[88] born on February 10, 1877 in Walton County, Florida, USA; died on July 23, 1909 in Andalusia, Covington, Alabama, USA

Isabell Bass[89] born on January 2, 1880 in Florida, United States; died on August 14, 1965 in Dorcus, Okaloosa, Florida, USA

James Dallas Bass[92] born on September 17, 1883 in Andalusia, Covington, Alabama, USA; died on January 27, 1976 in Pensacola, Escambia, Florida, USA

Mary Alice Bass[94] born on September 17, 1883 in Andalusia, Covington, Alabama, USA; died on January 23, 1964 in Holt, Okaloosa, Florida, USA

Holley Middleton ("Bud") Bass[96] born on April 29, 1885 in Covington, Alabama, USA; died on March 4, 1973 in Holt, Okaloosa, Florida, USA

Joseph Alexander ("Joe") Bass[98] born on April 14, 1888 in Andalusia, Covington, Alabama, USA; died on May 25, 1984 in Fort Walton Beach, Okaloosa, Florida, USA

John Riley Bass[100] born on March 8, 1890 in Andalusia, Covington, Alabama, USA; died on September 26, 1987 in Crestview, Okaloosa, Florida, USA

Stacy Bibner ("Uncle Stacie") Bass[102] born on April 21, 1892 in Carolina Community, Covington, Alabama, USA; died on August 21, 1993 in Carolina Community, Covington, Alabama, USA

Martha Christian ("Sister") Bass[104] born on July 18, 1894 in Andalusia, Covington, Alabama, USA; died on February 11, 1989 in Crestview, Okaloosa, Florida, USA

Note: *Holland Middleton Bass married Christian Bass [Ward] and William Riley Bass married Nancy Jane Bass [Ward]The two Bass brothers where married to two ward sisters and they lived and raised their families on ajoining farms. Holly had 12 children and Riley had 14, they lived and worked together for many years. Much of their land is still owed by their decendants.*

19. JAMES HILLIARD BASS (see Descendants) was born on April 25, 1847, in Covington County, Alabama, USA, to Bennett Bridges Bass Sr.[3] and Mary Elizabeth Hogg[4].
- He was recorded in the census in 1850, aged about 3, in Covington county, Covington, Alabama, USA.
- He was recorded in the census in 1860, aged about 13, in Covington, Alabama, USA.
- He died (Killed by Confederate Soldiers) on March 18, 1864, aged 16 years, in Okaloosa County, Florida, USA.
- He was buried in Okaloosa County, Florida, USA.

Note: *Killed by Confederat Soldiers while trying to cross Boggy Bayou with his father.*
(Death)

20. BENNETT BRIDGES BASS JR. (see Descendants) was born on June 13, 1848, in Covington, Alabama, USA, to Bennett Bridges Bass Sr.[3] and Mary Elizabeth Hogg[4]. Bennett Bridges became known as "Shug".
- He was recorded in the census in 1850, aged about 2, in Covington county, Covington, Alabama, USA.
- He was recorded in the census in 1860, aged about 12, in Covington, Alabama, USA.
- He was recorded in the census in 1880, aged about 32, in Harts And Red Level, Covington, Alabama, USA.
- He was a Farmer.
- He was recorded in the census in 1900, aged about 52, in Precincts 2, 6, 18 Fairfield, Loango, River Falls, Covington, Alabama, USA.
- He was recorded in the census in 1910, aged about 62, in Fairfield, Covington, Alabama, USA.
- He was recorded in the census in 1920, aged about 72, in Fairfield Precinct Beat No 2, Covington, Alabama, USA.
- He was recorded in the census in 1930, aged about 82, in Fairfield, Covington, Alabama, USA.
- He died on August 10, 1930, aged 82 years, in Covington, Alabama, USA.
- He was buried in Carolina Baptist Church Cemetery, Covington, Alabama, USA.

The following information is also recorded for Shug:
- Military Service.

Bennett Bridges had three partnerships. He was married to Julia Padgett[21] and Mary Frances Padgett[22]. He was also the partner of Josiphine Padgett[23].

Note: *Civil War - Confederat Navy, possibly enlisted late and young.*
(Military Service)

21. JULIA PADGETT was born about 1852 to Wiley Paget and Caroline Barrow. She died (At young age) about 1868, aged about 16.

Bennett Bridges Bass Jr.[20], when younger than 21, married Julia Padgett, when younger than 17, before 1870.
The following information is also recorded for this family:
- Death of Spouse.

22. MARY FRANCES PADGETT was born on August 15, 1855, in Covington, Alabama, USA, to William Henry Padgett and Roxanne Diamond.

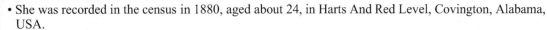

- She was recorded in the census in 1880, aged about 24, in Harts And Red Level, Covington, Alabama, USA.
- She was recorded in the census in 1900, aged about 44, in Precincts 2, 6, 18 Fairfield, Loango, River Falls, Covington, Alabama, USA.
- She was recorded in the census in 1910, aged about 54, in Fairfield, Covington, Alabama, USA.
- She was recorded in the census in 1920, aged about 64, in Fairfield Precinct Beat No 2, Covington, Alabama, USA.
- She was recorded in the census in 1930, aged about 74, in Fairfield, Covington, Alabama, USA.
- She died on November 16, 1937, aged 82 years.
- She was buried in Carolina Baptist Church Cemetery, Covington, Alabama, USA.

Bennett Bridges Bass Jr.[20], aged about 22, married Mary Frances Padgett, aged about 14, about 1870. They had fourteen children:

- Bennett Bridges Bass III[106] born on July 20, 1870 in Andalusia, Covington, Alabama, USA; died on March 12, 1958 in Hosford, Liberty, Florida, USA
- Mary Elizabeth Bass[110] born on January 20, 1871 in Andalusia, Covington, Alabama, USA; died on October 25, 1960 in Andalusia, Covington, Alabama, USA
- Elijah L. Bass[112] born in 1877 in Florida, USA; died in January 1880 in Covington, Alabama, USA
- James Wilson Bass[113] born on March 24, 1878 in Andalusia, Covington, Alabama, USA; died on January 11, 1919 in Covington, Alabama, USA
- John Bridges Bass[115] born on June 11, 1881 in Alabama, USA; died on December 16, 1953
- Laura Lee Bass[117] born on July 24, 1883 in Alabama, USA; died on February 12, 1978 in Andalusia, Covington, Alabama, USA
- Sheila Josephine Bass[119] born on June 11, 1887 in Andalusia, Covington, Alabama, USA; died on November 7, 1922 in USA
- Henry Harrelson Bass[121] born on March 4, 1888 in Andalusia, Covington, Alabama, USA; died on October 29, 1970 in Andalusia, Covington, Alabama, USA
- Riley B Bass[123] born on April 17, 1891 in Covington, Alabama, USA; died on October 4, 1933 in Covington, Alabama, USA
- Dennis Bridges Bass[125] born on April 3, 1893 in Covington, Alabama, USA; died on July 30, 1967 in Andalusia, Covington, Alabama, USA
- Katie Bass[127] born in 1894
- Bertie B Bass[128] born on January 21, 1896 in Alabama, United States; died on February 27, 1982 in Montgomery, Montgomery County, Alabama, USA
- Florence Bass[130] born on March 3, 1899 in Alabama, USA; died on January 23, 1955 in Okaloosa, Florida, USA
- Lawrence Bass[134] born in March 1899

23. JOSIPHINE PADGETT was born in February 1858, in Alabama, United States, to William Henry Padgett and Roxanne Diamond.
- She was recorded in the census in 1900, aged about 42, in Precinct 9 Oldtown, Conecuh, Alabama, USA.
- She died in 1946, aged about 88, in Santa Rosa, Florida, USA.

Josiphine had two partners. She was the partner of Bennett Bridges Bass Jr.[20] and Ephraim Ward.

Bennett Bridges Bass Jr.[20] and Josiphine Padgett had one son:
- Thomas Sonny Padgett[135] born on December 17, 1874 in Covington, Alabama, USA; died on March 3, 1962 in Conecuh, Alabama, USA

The following information is also recorded for this family:
- Unknown Relationship.

Ephraim Ward and Josiphine Padgett had six children:
- James Moses Ward born on March 1, 1881 in Conecuh, Alabma, USA; died on February 7, 1956 in Evergreen, Conecuh, Alabama, USA
- Moses Ward born in March 1884 in Alabama, United States
- Lula B Ward born in 1884; died in 1913
- Arthur Ward born in September 1892 in Alabama, United States
- Clifford Ward born in July 1894 in Old Town, Conecuh, Alabama, USA
- Annie Ward born on January 31, 1898 in Conecuh, Alabma, USA; died on July 7, 1958 in Brewton, Escambia, Alabama, USA

24. ELIZABETH BASS (see Descendants) was born on October 14, 1850, in Andalusia, Covington, Alabama, USA, to Bennett Bridges Bass Sr.[3] and Mary Elizabeth Hogg[4].

- She was recorded in the census in 1850, aged 0, in Covington county, Covington, Alabama, USA.
- She was recorded in the census in 1860, aged about 9, in Covington, Alabama, USA.
- She died on December 11, 1943, aged 93 years, in Niceville, Florida, USA.

25. JAKE RAMER was born in 1848.
> Jake Ramer married Elizabeth Bass[24]. They had two children:
>> Nancy A. Ramer[137] born in January 1870 in Alabama, United States; died on May 28, 1933 in Brantley, Crenshaw, Alabama
>>
>> John Ramer[139]

26. MARTHA JANE BASS (see Descendants) was born on February 13, 1852, in Andalusia, Covington, Alabama, USA, to Bennett Bridges Bass Sr.[3] and Mary Elizabeth Hogg[4].
- She was recorded in the census in 1860, aged about 8, in Covington, Alabama, USA.
- She was recorded in the census in 1860, aged about 8, in Covington, Alabama, USA.
- She was recorded in the census on June 1, 1870, aged 18, in Florida, USA.
- She was recorded in the census in 1940, aged about 88, in Camp Nine, Elec Prec 14 Niceville, Okaloosa, Florida, USA.
- She died on December 11, 1943, aged 91 years, in Niceville, Okaloosa, Florida, United States.
- She was buried in Rocky Memorial Cemetery, Niceville, Okaloosa, Florida, USA.

27. REV. GEORGE WASHINGTON PARRISH was born on September 30, 1844, in Henry, Alabama United States.
- He died on November 27, 1918, aged 74, in Niceville, Okaloosa, Florida, United States.
- He was buried in Rocky Memorial Cemetery, Niceville, Okaloosa, Florida, USA.

> Note: *"A Neighborly Murder" Taken from Troy Messenger 8/28/1873 - Typed by Tonia Porter 2005 Intelligence of a very sociable murder comes from Walton County, Florida. Following, as it does, close upon the heels of another tragedy, and as a woman, whether lovely or not, is at the bottom thereof, the facts in the case are perhaps worth relating. Some months ago, Mr. George Parish, having some misunderstanding with is brother-in-law, a Mr. Leyden, armed himself with a shot-gun and promptly put his recalcitrant relative out of the way. Shortly after this sanguinary affray, which made Mrs. Leyden a widow, she doffed her weeds for the legendary orange-blossom, and became the bride of Mr. Robert Bell. The honeymoon sped by without a ripple on the surface of the placid stream of domestic felicity. In a short time, however, Mrs. Bell made complaint to her husband of the amorous advances of one Mr. William Nathie, a neighbor, and afterwards made the same complaint in the presence of Mr. Nathie. Mr. Bell simply requested her to stop her noise, intimating if this reasonable demand was not complied with, he would be under the painful necessity of severing the marital tie. Whereupon Mr. Nathie remarked that Mrs. Bell could always find a shelter under his hospitable thatch. This remark upon the part of Mr. Nathie roused the sleeping demon of jealousy in the breast of Bell, and an old-fashioned scuffle ensued; in which Nathie was somewhat worsted. His two sons appeared at this juncture, and they made a united effort to suffocate Bell by shutting off his wind, while their respected parent sauntered into the house after a gun for the purpose of putting an end to the pleasantry. Bell managed to break away from his friends and went to his own domain for a shot-gun. He procured his armament and appeared on the scene just in time to receive three buckshot in his head from Nathie s artillery which brought him to the round. Recovering, Bell saluted his opponent with one barrel and mortally wounded him. Nathie died in thirty minutes, while Bell recovered sufficiently to attend the funeral the next day where, according to all accounts, he was the most prominent mourner. The little community has relapse into its former pastoral peacefulness, and all hands are probably satisfied with the situation.   -Savannah News.*
>
> George Washington Parrish, aged 26, married Martha Jane Bass[26], aged 18, on November 1, 1870 in Escambia, Florida, United States. They had ten children:
>> Mary Ellen Parrish[141] born on August 7, 1871 in Florida, United States; died on January 10, 1969 in Ft. Walton Beach, Okaloosa, Florida, USA
>>
>> Emeline Parrish[143] born on May 11, 1873 in Niceville, Okaloosa, Florida, United States; died on November 21, 1965 in Destin, Okaloosa, Florida, USA
>>
>> Charles W. Parrish[145] born on July 4, 1875 in Niceville, Okaloosa, Florida, United States; died on August 26, 1958 in Niceville, Okaloosa, Florida, United States
>>
>> Martha Jane Parrish[147] born on January 3, 1878 in Walton, Florida, USA; died on September 30, 1968 in Niceville, Okaloosa, Florida, United States
>>
>> John Robert Parrish[149] born on June 8, 1881 in Niceville, Okaloosa, Florida, USA; died on April 1, 1951 in Niceville, Okaloosa, Florida, United States
>>
>> Tolbert Tillis Parrish[151] born on September 6, 1883 in Walton, Florida, USA; died on April 2, 1915 in Honduras
>>
>> Fanny A. Parrish[153] born on December 4, 1885 in Walton, Florida, USA; died on April 11, 1887 in Walton, Florida, USA
>>
>> Leanna Parrish[154] born on September 6, 1888 in Boggy Bayou, Walton, Florida, USA; died on July 25, 1988 in Pensacola, Escambia, Florida, USA

Ella Parrish[156] born on March 27, 1892 in Glimer, Georgia, USA; died on
November 26, 1974 in Pensacola, Escambia, Florida, USA
James Albert Parrish[158] born on August 10, 1895 in Niceville, Okaloosa, Florida, USA; died on October
18, 1985 in Niceville, Okaloosa, Florida, United States

28. WILLIAM RILEY BASS (see Descendants) was born on May 28, 1854, in Covington County, Alabama, United States, to Bennett Bridges Bass Sr.[3] and Mary Elizabeth Hogg[4].
- William Riley was a Farmer.
- He was recorded in the census in 1860, aged about 6, in Covington, Alabama, USA.
- He was recorded in the census on June 1, 1870, aged 16, in Florida, USA.
- He was recorded in the census in 1880, aged about 26, in Harts And Red Level, Covington, Alabama, USA.
- He was recorded in the census in 1900, aged about 46, in Precincts 10, 19 Hart, George, Covington, Alabama, USA.
- He was recorded in the census in 1910, aged about 56, in Hart, Covington, Alabama, USA.
- He was recorded in the census in 1920, aged about 66, in Precinct 21, Covington, Alabama, USA.
- He was recorded in the census in 1930, aged about 76, in Carolina, Covington, Alabama, USA.
- He died on June 19, 1933, aged 79 years, in Covington County, Alabama, USA.
- He was buried in Carolina Baptist Church Cemetery, Covington, Alabama, USA.

Note: *William Riley Bass, aged 79, honored and respected citizen, and one of the pioneer citizens of Covington County, died at his home on Rt. 5, Andalusia Monday morning, June 18th. He was... Mr. Bass wielded a potent influence in his section of the county and his service to the community and to his numerous relatives and friends made his passing a matter of sincere regret in the whole section.*
(Death)

29. NANCY JANE WARD was born on March 21, 1860, in Florida, USA, to William Marion Ward and Catherin Campbell.
- She was recorded in the census on June 30, 1860, as an infant, in Walton, Florida, USA.
- She was recorded in the census in 1870, aged about 10, in Florida, USA.
- She was recorded in the census in 1880, aged about 20, in Harts And Red Level, Covington, Alabama, USA.
- She was recorded in the census in 1900, aged about 40, in Precincts 10, 19 Hart, George, Covington, Alabama, USA.
- She was recorded in the census in 1910, aged about 50, in Hart, Covington, Alabama, USA.
- She was recorded in the census in 1920, aged about 60, in Precinct 21, Covington, Alabama, USA.
- She was recorded in the census in 1930, aged about 70, in Carolina, Covington, Alabama, USA.
- She was recorded in the census in 1940, aged about 80, in Beat 21 Carolina, Covington, Alabama, USA.
- She died on September 1, 1945, aged 85 years, in Andalusia, Covington, Alabama, USA.
- She was buried in Carolina Baptist Church Cemetery, Covington, Alabama, USA.

William Riley Bass[28], aged about 23, married Nancy Jane Ward, aged about 17, about 1877. They had fourteen children:
Mary Elizabeth Bass[160] born on October 16, 1878 in Andalusia, Covington, Alabama, USA; died on
July 8, 1974 in Andalusia, Covington, Alabama, USA
William Henry Bass[162] born on January 6, 1880 in Alabama, United States; died on February 15, 1970
Catherine Emma Bass[164] born on October 26, 1881 in Alabama, United States; died on August 18, 1951
Savannah Bass[166] born on September 11, 1884 in Alabama, United States; died on November 20, 1970
in Lockhart, Covington, Alabama, USA
Nancy Jane Bass[168] born on February 6, 1886 in Alabama, USA; died on November 13, 1959 in Walton
County, Florida, USA
Minnie Josephine Bass[170] born on March 31, 1888 in Alabama, United States; died on October 16, 1924
in Covington, Alabama
Florence Bass[171] born on January 1, 1890 in Covington, Alabama, USA; died on January 23, 1982
Riley John Bass[172] born on January 2, 1892 in Alabama, United States; died on December 16, 1979
James Bennett Bass[174] born on March 23, 1893 in Alabama, United States; died on June 4, 1962 in
Carolina Community, Covington, Alabama, USA
Charles Bass[176] born on March 19, 1896; died before 1900
Mattie O. Bass[177] born on August 16, 1897 in Covington, Alabama, USA; died on December 8, 1977 in
Colbert, Alabama, USA
Flora Bass[179] born on April 30, 1899 in Alabama, United States; died in 1981
Florine Dorothy Bass[181] born on April 30, 1899 in Covington, Alabama, USA; died on February 18,
1981 in Covington, Alabama, USA
Lillie May Bass[183] born on January 25, 1902 in Alabama, United States; died on April 3, 1925

Note: *Holland Middleton Bass married Christian Bass [Ward] and William Riley Bass married Nancy Jane Bass [Ward]. The two Bass brothers where married to two ward sisters and they lived and raised their families on ajoining farms and had a very close relationship. -Genoloa Bass Spence Holly had 12 children and Riley had 14, they lived and worked together for many years. Much of their land is still owed by their decendants.*

30. JANE PADGETT (see Descendants) was born on March 18, 1838, in Alabama, USA, to William Padgett[6] and Nancy Bass[5].
   - She was recorded in the census in 1850, aged about 12, in Covington county, Covington, Alabama, USA.
   - She was recorded in the census in 1880, aged about 42, in Falls, Texas, USA.
   - She died in December 1927, aged 89 years.
   - She was buried in Phillips Cemetery, Travis, Texas, USA.
31. WILLIAM FORMAN WARD was born in 1835, in Alabama, USA.
   - William Forman was a Laborer.
   - He was recorded in the census in 1880, aged about 45, in Falls, Texas, USA.
   - He died in 1912, aged about 77, in Falls, Texas, USA.
      William Forman Ward, aged about 30, married Jane Padgett[30], aged about 27, about 1865. They had one daughter:
         Margaret Jane Ward[185] born on July 18, 1875 in Texas, USA; died on June 4, 1955

32. HENRY PADGETT (see Descendants) was born on June 18, 1844, in Alabama, United States, to William Padgett[6] and Nancy Bass[5].
   - He was recorded in the census in 1850, aged about 6, in Covington county, Covington, Alabama, USA.
   - He died (At War) on December 15, 1861, aged 17 years, in Mobile, Alabama, USA.
   The following information is also recorded for Henry:
   - Military Service.
   Note: *Civil War.*
      (Military Service)

33. LEVINTA PADGETT (see Descendants) was born about 1847, in Alabama, United States, to William Padgett[6] and Nancy Bass[5].
   - She was recorded in the census in 1850, aged about 3, in Covington county, Covington, Alabama, USA.
   - She died in 1900, aged about 53.
   Levinta married twice. She was married to Samuel Godwin[34] and Robert Francis Jordan[35].
34. SAMUEL GODWIN was born '1843 or 1845', in Alabama, USA.
      Samuel Godwin married Levinta Padgett[33], aged about 20, on December 26, 1867. They had two daughters:
         Nancy G. Godwin[187] born in 1869
         Lucy Godwin[188] born in 1871
35. ROBERT FRANCIS JORDAN was born in 1843.
      Robert Francis Jordan, when younger than 33, married Levinta Padgett[33], when younger than 29, before 1877. They had two children:
         Ida Jordan[189] born in 1877
         Henry Jordan[190] born in 1879

36. ELIZABETH H. PADGETT (see Descendants) was born on December 3, 1850, in Covington, Alabama, USA, to William Padgett[6] and Nancy Bass[5].
   - She was recorded in the census in 1900, aged about 49, in Lott town, Falls, Texas, USA.
   - She died on July 15, 1931, aged 81 years, in Lott, Falls, Texas, USA.
   - She was buried in Clover Hill Cemetery, Lott, Falls, Texas, USA.
37. JOHN ELBERT JORDAN was born on November 30, 1849, in Covington, Alabama, USA.
   - He was recorded in the census in 1900, aged about 50, in Lott town, Falls, Texas, USA.
   - He died on November 1, 1927, aged 77 years, in Lott, Falls, Texas, USA.
   - He was buried in Clover Hill Cemetery, Lott, Falls, Texas, USA.
      John Elbert Jordan, aged about 25, married Elizabeth H. Padgett[36], aged about 24, about 1875 in Falls County, Texas, USA. They had two daughters:
         Della Jordan[191] born on June 12, 1882 in Texas, USA; died on March 2, 1953
         Mary Jordan[193] born in August 1885 in Texas, United States

I've spoken to several folks in their 90s that clam to have attended "First Sunday in June" for their whole life, and that their parents attended well before them. The picture above was the old Bass School and Church building.

The Sacred Harp singing at Shady Hill Church was always one of the most important days of the year for our family. Mama always started food preparations days ahead of time. The boys would take a bead on the head of a big fat hen with the rifle. One shot would do it. It was a little more difficult to shoot a couple of fryers but the boys very proudly managed that, too. These would be cleaned, cut up, and refrigerated. Turnips were cleaned and made ready for the pot ahead of time too. Mama made the best tarts of anybody I ever knew. She put any kind of preserves inside and then fried or baked them. A cake was baked and iced. Tea cakes were baked. We had enough of these even though Ralph always managed to snitch a few while they were still hot.

Mama would start the cooking of dinner early Sunday morning with the help of Daddy. They cooked breakfast and dinner at the same time. We might even get a piece of fried chicken for breakfast. What a treat! Later Mama would leave Daddy with the cooking long enough to see that the younger children were bathed and dressed for church. As we got older, we girls helped with the cooking instead of Daddy. The boys always had to see about filling the water barrel on the back of the truck for drinking at the singing.

Kinfolks would often stop by before going on to church. We'd be singing together as we worked in the kitchen. When any family member came through, they'd join in too. Sometimes the kinfolks would be inside the house joining in the singing before we knew they were on the place. Oh, what fun times!

We nearly always got a new suit of clothing in the spring. That was Easter. If we were lucky, and we usually were, we got more new clothing for the first Sunday in June. We proudly showed off our new clothes on this day when we saw so many people in one day.

The singing started about 9:30 to 10:00 a.m. Daddy always went ahead of time; the rest of the family would try to get there by 10:00. Many people went and stayed outside the church the whole time, visiting from one group of people to the other. They'd even carry lawn chairs and quilts to sit on beside their parked cars. All of Mama and Daddy's children were expected to go inside the church at least for part of the time. We could all sing sacred harp, some of us better than others. Some of us attended singing school for Sacred Harp at Beda church one summer. Learning to read the notes and then sing the words was easy for us because we already knew most of the tunes. So we were often asked to lead a couple of songs at the singing.

At noon the singers would dismiss for about an hour. That was long enough to unpack dinner and eat. Mama always had her dinner in large boxes. One year she even emptied the old trunk and carried her dinner in that. We children helped Mama spread the dinner.

Some of us would take paper plates and plastic spoons and forks and pass them out to any visitors standing around. Most drinks were moved to a certain area of the long table or to a separate table. Several people would fill cups with ice and pour different kinds of drinks for the people to pick up. After the blessing was offered by the pastor, everyone converged on the long table to fill plates and get a drink. The people would sit or stand to eat. The front of a car, the back of a truck, or a quilt could be used for a table to eat.

After dinner the singers would go back inside to sing until 3:00 to 3:30. Each leader would lead two songs. The last hour or so was used to sing favorite songs in memory of departed loved ones. -Hazel Bass Trawick

Notes:

Direct Relations

38. NANCY ANN PADGETT (see Descendants) was born on April 16, 1855, in Alabama, USA, to William Padgett[6] and Nancy Bass[5]. Nancy Ann became known as "Nannie".
    - She was recorded in the census in 1880, aged about 25, in Harts And Red Level, Covington, Alabama, USA.
    - She was recorded in the census in 1900, aged about 45, in Precincts 10, 19 Hart, George, Covington, Alabama, USA.
    - She died on January 7, 1952, aged 96 years, in Andalusia, Covington, Alabama, USA.
    - She was buried in Pleasant Home Baptist Church Cemetery, Covington, Alabama, USA.

39. COLUMBUS DANIEL HART was born on April 7, 1852, in Alabama, USA, to Isaac Hart and Mary McArthur.
    - He was recorded in the census in 1860, aged about 8, in Covington, Alabama, USA.
    - He was recorded in the census on June 1, 1870, aged 18, in Alabama, USA.
    - He was recorded in the census in 1880, aged about 28, in Harts And Red Level, Covington, Alabama, USA.
    - He was a Farmer.
    - He was recorded in the census in 1900, aged about 48, in Precincts 10, 19 Hart, George, Covington, Alabama, USA.
    - He died on December 21, 1910, aged 58 years, in Covington, Alabama, USA.
    - He was buried in 1910 in Pleasant Home Baptist Church Cemetery, Covington, Alabama, USA.

    Columbus Daniel Hart, aged about 20, married Nancy Ann Padgett[38], aged about 17, in 1872. They had eight children:
    James William Hart[194] born on December 3, 1873 in Covington, Alabama, USA; died on November 14, 1961 in Andalusia, Covington, Alabama, USA
    John C Hart[196] born on August 15, 1876 in Alabama, USA; died on March 9, 1953 in Andalusia, Covington, Alabama, USA
    Virginia Hart[197] born on May 18, 1879 in Alabama, USA; died on April 7, 1958 in Greenville, Butler, Alabama, USA
    Alice Rebecca Hart[199] born on August 8, 1881 in Covington, Alabama, USA; died on May 22, 1962 in Pleasant Home, Covington, Alabama
    Rubin Richard Hart[201] born on November 20, 1883 in Alabama, USA; died on September 25, 1926 in Covington, Alabama, USA
    Ada Alabama Hart[203] born on May 4, 1886 in Alabama, USA; died on July 18, 1975 in Covington, Alabama
    Nancy Lena Hart[205] born on June 24, 1888 in Alabama, United States; died in 1979 in Escambia, Florida, United States
    Mary Nora Hart[207] born on October 10, 1890 in Covington, Alabama, USA; died on October 7, 1973 in Florala, Covington, Alabama, USA

40. JAMES W. BASS (see Descendants) was born about 1847, in Alabama, United States, to William Riley Bass[7] and Mary Straughn[8].
    - He was recorded in the census in 1860, aged about 13, in Covington, Alabama, USA.
    - He died (At War) on November 25, 1864, aged about 17, in Barraugas, Santa Rosa, Florida, USA.

    The following information is also recorded for James W.:
    - Description: 5' 7"LightBlueLight Complexion.
    - Military Service.
    Note: *Co. E 1st Regiment, Florida Cavalry, Union, Civil War.*
    (Military Service)

41. JOHN BASS (see Descendants) was born on December 13, 1849, in Alabama, USA, to William Riley Bass[7] and Mary Straughn[8].
    - He was recorded in the census in 1860, aged about 10, in Covington, Alabama, USA.
    - He was recorded in the census in 1880, aged about 30, in Harts And Red Level, Covington, Alabama, USA.
    - He was recorded in the census in 1910, aged about 60, in Loango, Covington, Alabama, USA.
    Note: *John signed as a witness on a deed for his Franklin "cousins" on 16 Feb 1883, Covington County, Alabama for the sale of land by John & Celia Franklin to their son Jackson Magilbry Franklin. On 01 Sep 1887, he again signed as a witness when Jackson Franklin sold this same land to his brother William J. Franklin.*

42. WILLIAM M. BASS (see Descendants) was born on August 2, 1852, in Alabama, United States, to William Riley Bass[7] and Mary Straughn[8].
    - He was recorded in the census in 1860, aged about 7.
    - He was recorded in the census in 1880, aged about 27, in Harts And Red Level, Covington, Alabama, USA.
    - He died on February 20, 1913, aged 60 years.
    - He was buried in Bass Cemetary.

43. ABIGAIL WELCH was born in October 1854, in Alabama, USA, to Charles Welch and Louis Goff. Abigail became known as "Abbie".
- She died on August 7, 1933, aged 78, in Ft. Lauderdale, Broward, Florida, USA.
- She was buried in Bass Family Cemetery, Andalusia, Covington, Alabama, USA.

Note: *Her father was born in Ireland, her mother in South Carolina.*

William M. Bass[42] married Abigail Welch. They had two children:
Mary A. Bass[209] born in December 1881 in Alabama, United States; died in 1940 in Red Level, Covington, Alabama, USA
William Riley Bass[211] born on August 28, 1882 in Alabama, United States; died on November 17, 1966 in Andalusia, Covington, Alabama, USA

44. RILEY BASS (see Descendants) was born on December 2, 1856, in Alabama, United States, to William Riley Bass[7] and Mary Straughn[8].
- He was recorded in the census in 1860, aged about 3, in Covington, Alabama, USA.
- He was recorded in the census in 1910, aged about 53, in Loango, Covington, Alabama, USA.
- He died (Medical Problem) on February 23, 1915, aged 58 years, in Covington, Alabama, USA.

Notes:
- *Riley Bass died from inflammation of the stomach on Feb. 23, 1915 in Covington County. According to his death certificate he was single. He was buried in Covington County. John appears with Riley showing John as head of household on 1870 census and on thru the 1910. On the 1910 Loango census John is 61 and single and Riley is 54 and also single. Also listed in the household is an aunt Sirena Franklin listed as single and age 82.*
- *Inflamation of Stomach.*
  (Death)

3rd Generation of Descendants

45. WILLIAM HENRY TEEL (see Descendants) was born on January 7, 1863, in Florida, United States, to William Teel[10] and Mary Bass[9].
    - He was recorded in the census in 1910, aged about 47, in Andalusia, Covington, Alabama, USA.
    - He was recorded in the census in 1920, aged about 57, in Precinct 1, Covington, Alabama, USA.
    - He was recorded in the census in 1930, aged about 67, in Andalusia, Covington, Alabama, USA.
    - He died on December 7, 1938, aged 75, in Andalusia, Covington, Alabama, USA.
    - He was buried in Carolina Baptist Church Cemetery, Covington, Alabama, USA.
46. IDA D WHITE was born on March 29, 1872, in Alabama, United States.

    - She was recorded in the census in 1910, aged about 38, in Andalusia, Covington, Alabama, USA.
    - She was recorded in the census in 1920, aged about 48, in Precinct 1, Covington, Alabama, USA.
    - She was recorded in the census in 1930, aged about 58, in Andalusia, Covington, Alabama, USA.
    - She died on March 28, 1954, aged 81, in Prichard, Mobile, Alabama, USA.
    - She was buried in Carolina Baptist Church Cemetery, Covington, Alabama, USA.

    William Henry Teel[45] married Ida D White. They had six children:
    Mattie L Teel[213] born about 1891 in Alabama, United States
    Nora B Teel[214] born about 1895 in Alabama, United States
    Jesse Stallings Teel[215] born on December 8, 1896 in Andalusia, Covington, Alabama, USA; died on December 17, 1962 in Andalusia, Covington, Alabama, USA
    James Bennett Teel[217] born on December 15, 1899 in Alabama, United States; died on December 16, 1962
    Oliver B Teel[218] born about 1902 in Alabama, United States
    Aaron Teel[219] born on July 2, 1907 in Alabama, United States; died on July 19, 1991

47. WILLIAM ALBERT RAMER (see Descendants) was born in August 1870, in Alabama, USA, to John W Ramer[11] and Mary Bass[9].
    - He was recorded in the census in 1900, aged about 29, in Precincts 10, 19 Hart, George, Covington, Alabama, USA.
    - He was a Farmer in Alabama.
    - He was recorded in the census in 1910, aged about 39, in George, Covington, Alabama, USA.
    - He died on December 25, 1934, aged 64, in Opp, Covington, Alabama, USA.
    - He was buried in Carolina Baptist Church Cemetery, Covington, Alabama, USA.
48. FLORENCE MISSOURI HOWARD was born in August 1876, in Alabama, USA.
    - She was recorded in the census in 1900, aged about 23, in Precincts 10, 19 Hart, George, Covington, Alabama, USA.
    - She was recorded in the census in 1910, aged about 33, in George, Covington, Alabama, USA.
    - She died in November 1918, aged 42, in Andalusia, Covington, Alabama, USA.
    - She was buried in Carolina Baptist Church Cemetery, Covington, Alabama, USA.

    William Albert Ramer[47], aged about 25, married Florence Missouri Howard, aged about 19, about 1896. They had twelve children:
    James William Ramer[221] born on January 25, 1897 in Alabama, USA; died about March 1982 in Opp, Covington, Alabama, USA
    Dewey William Ramer[222] born on August 6, 1898 in Alabama, USA; died about July 1981 in Orlando, Orange, Florida, USA
    Lena Zelma Ramer[224] born in April 1900 in Alabama, USA; died on October 7, 1965 in Montgomery, Montgomery, Alabama, USA
    Athon Ramer Sr.[225] born on August 16, 1901 in Alabama, USA; died about February 1979 in Opp, Covington, Alabama, USA
    John Bennett Ramer[226] born on November 19, 1902 in Alabama, United States; died on October 15, 1987 in Opp, Covington, Alabama, USA
    Mary E Ramer[228] born about 1906 in Alabama, United States
    William Calvin Ramer[229] born on May 14, 1907 in Alabama, United States; died on April 10, 2001 in Opp, Covington, Alabama, USA
    Albert Farrell Ramer[230] born on August 8, 1907 in Alabama, United States; died on October 1, 1974 in Opp, Covington, Alabama, USA
    Jesse C Ramer[232] born on May 19, 1909 in Alabama, United States; died in June 1984
    Homer Closon Ramer[234] born on October 4, 1913 in Alabama, United States; died on November 4, 1987 in Opp, Covington, Alabama, USA
    Savannah Irene Ramer[235] born on November 22, 1913 in Andalusia, Covington, Alabama, USA; died on July 25, 2001
    Walter Otis Ramer[236] born on February 14, 1916; died about June 1955 in Opp, Covington, Alabama, USA

49. JOHN RAMER (see Descendants) was born on February 22, 1872, in Florida, USA, to John W Ramer[11] and Mary Bass[9]. John became known as "Bud". He died on July 17, 1955, aged 83 years, in Alabama, USA.
50. ELLA MELISSA HOWARD. Ella Melissa became known as "Lisa".
John Ramer[49] married Ella Melissa Howard. They had two sons:
James W Ramer[237] born on January 10, 1901; died on November 3, 1956 in Andalusia, Covington, Alabama, USA
Claude A Ramer[238] born on January 15, 1902; died on December 22, 1990 in Opp, Covington County, Alabama

51. JACOB D RAMER (see Descendants) was born on February 22, 1872, in Alabama, United States, to John W Ramer[11] and Mary Bass[9]. Jacob D became known as "Jako".
- He was recorded in the census on April 1, 1950, aged 78, in Carolina, Covington, Alabama, United States.
- He died on July 17, 1955, aged 83 years, in Andalusia, Covington, Alabama, USA.
- He was buried in Carolina Baptist Church Cemetery, Covington, Alabama, USA.

Jacob D married twice. He was married to Illinoy Bulger[52] and Savannah Odom[53].
Jacob D Ramer and ? became partners.
52. ILLINOY BULGER was born on March 4, 1876.
- She died on July 14, 1911, aged 35.
- She was buried in Red Oak Baptist Church Cemetery, Red Oak, Covington, Alabama, USA.

Jacob D Ramer[51] married Illinoy Bulger. They had four children:
Beulah Ramer[239] born on July 11, 1902; died on December 19, 1997
Major Ramer[241] born on September 7, 1902; died on May 21, 1963
Mary Dovie Ramer[242] born on September 27, 1904 in Ohio, United States; died on September 14, 1996
Millard Ramer[244] born on March 7, 1909 in Alabama, USA; died on February 26, 1995 in Brooksville, Florida, USA

53. SAVANNAH ODOM was born on November 4, 1874, in Alabama, United States.
- She was recorded in the census on April 1, 1950, aged 75, in Carolina, Covington, Alabama, United States.
- She died on June 21, 1968, aged 93.
- She was buried in Carolina Baptist Church Cemetery, Covington, Alabama, USA.

Jacob D Ramer[51] married Savannah Odom. They had one daughter:
Maggie Mae Ramer[245] born on January 2, 1911; died on February 26, 2003

54. JAMES W RAMER (see Descendants) was born in March 1874, in Florida, USA, to John W Ramer[11] and Mary Bass[9].
- He was recorded in the census in 1900, aged about 26, in Andalusia town, Covington, Alabama, USA.

55. NANCY ELIZABETH RAMER (see Descendants) was born in December 1875, in Florida, USA, to John W Ramer[11] and Mary Bass[9]. Nancy Elizabeth became known as "Sis". She died in 1963, aged about 87, in Andalusia, Covington, Alabama, USA.
56. WES LINDSEY. Wes became known as "Sis".
Wes Lindsey married Nancy Elizabeth Ramer[55].

57. ALFRED CALVIN RAMER (see Descendants) was born in August 1882, in Alabama, USA, to John W Ramer[11] and Mary Bass[9].
- He was recorded in the census in 1900, aged about 17, in Andalusia town, Covington, Alabama, USA.
- He was recorded in the census in 1910, aged about 27, in Andalusia, Covington, Alabama, USA.

58. MAE RAMER (see Descendants) was born to John W Ramer[11] and Mary Bass[9].
59. MR. FORMAN.
Mr. Forman married Mae Ramer[58].

60. BENJAMIN WILSON BASS (see Descendants) was born on October 17, 1860, in Mayfield, Alabama, USA, to Wilson Bennett Bass[12] and Jane Teel[13]. Benjamin Wilson became known as "Ben".
- He was recorded in the census in 1900, aged about 39, in Justice Precinct 4, Hardin, Texas, USA.
- He was recorded in the census in 1910, aged about 49, in Justice Precinct 8, Hardin, Texas, USA.
- He died on May 29, 1935, aged 74 years, in Votaw, Hardin, Texas, USA.
- He was buried on May 30, 1935 in Thicket, Hardin, Texas.

Benjamin Wilson married three times. He was married to Matilda Hall[61], Frieda Kamilla Schmitt[62] and E. A. Cameron[63].
Note: *Moved to Texas to live with relatives after his father was killed in the Civil War and mother drowned on her way to a wedding.*

61. MATILDA HALL was born on June 2, 1858, in Newton, Texas, USA.
- She was recorded in the census in 1900, aged about 42, in Justice Precinct 4, Hardin, Texas, USA.
- She died on May 20, 1903, aged 44 years, in Votaw, Hardin, Texas, USA.

Benjamin Wilson Bass[60], aged about 24, married Matilda Hall, aged about 27, about 1885. They had eight children:
- Cynthia Lillian Bass[246] born on December 28, 1885 in Kountze, Hardin, Texas, USA; died on June 22, 1953
- Mr. Bass[248] born in 1886 in Kountze, Texas, USA; died in 1887
- Mr. Bass[249] born in 1887 in Texas, USA; died in 1887 in Texas, USA
- Martin Luther Bass[250] born on September 8, 1889 in Beaumont, Texas, USA; died on November 7, 1953 in Votaw, Hardin, Texas, USA
- Susan Viola Bass[252] born on January 20, 1891 in Votaw, Hardin, Texas, USA; died on October 21, 1962 in Baytown, Harris, Texas, USA
- Wilson Lafayette Bass[254] born on July 13, 1892 in Votaw, Hardin, Texas, USA; died on December 9, 1943
- Thomas Watson Bass[256] born on December 9, 1894 in Votaw, Hardin, Texas, USA
- Benjamin Eli Bass[257] born on January 30, 1895 in Votaw, Hardin, Texas, USA; died on July 31, 1951 in Hardin, Texas, United States

62. FRIEDA KAMILLA SCHMITT was born in 1864, in Germany.
- In 1889, aged about 25, she immigrated.
- She was recorded in the census in 1910, aged about 46, in Justice Precinct 8, Hardin, Texas, USA.
- She died in 1918, aged about 54, in San Jacinto County, Texas, USA.

Benjamin Wilson Bass[60] married Frieda Kamilla Schmitt. They had four children:
- Douglas U Bass[259] born about 1903 in Texas, United States
- Thelma B Bass[260] born in 1905 in Texas, USA
- Louis O Bass[261] born in 1907 in Texas, United States
- Gustavus Bass[262] born in 1909 in Batson, Hardin, Texas; died on October 22, 1983 in Maize, Sedgwick, Kansas, USA

63. E. A. CAMERON.
Benjamin Wilson Bass[60] married E. A. Cameron.

64. WILLIAM RILEY BASS (see Descendants) was born on September 15, 1862, in Pensacola, Escambia, Florida, USA, to Wilson Bennett Bass[12] and Jane Teel[13]. William Riley became known as "Bill".
- He was recorded in the census in 1910, aged about 47, in Justice Precinct 7, Hardin, Texas, USA.
- He was recorded in the census in 1920, aged about 57, in San Juan, Utah, USA.
- He died (Natural / Old Age) on November 19, 1948, aged 86 years, in Monticello, San Juan, Utah, USA.
- He was buried on November 21, 1948 in La Sal Cemetery, La Sal, Utah, USA.

Note: *Moved to Texas to live with relatives after his father was killed in the Civil War and mother drowned on her way to a wedding.*

65. FRANCES ELIZABETH COLLINS was born on April 22, 1866, in Paulding, Jasper, Mississippi, USA, to James Madison Collins and Caroline Mahuldy Matthews.
- She was recorded in the census in 1880, aged about 14, in Hardin, Texas, USA.
- She was recorded in the census in 1910, aged about 44, in Justice Precinct 7, Hardin, Texas, USA.
- She was recorded in the census in 1920, aged about 54, in San Juan, Utah, USA.
- She died on July 11, 1949, aged 83 years, in Monticello, San Juan, UT.
- She was buried on July 14, 1949 in La Sal Cemetery, La Sal, Utah, USA.

William Riley Bass[64], aged 26, married Frances Elizabeth Collins, aged 22, on January 23, 1889 in Hardin, Texas. They had eleven children:
- Mary Susannah Bass[263] born on October 26, 1889 in White Oak, Hardin, Texas, USA; died on September 7, 1919 in La Sal, San Juan, Utah, USA
- Eliza Jane Bass[264] born on November 20, 1891 in White Oak, Hardin, Texas, USA; died on December 31, 1891
- Allen Milford Bass[265] born on August 11, 1893 in White Oak, Hardin, Texas, USA; died on September 19, 1944 in Mount Pleasant, Titus, Texas, United States
- John Riley Bass[267] born on August 19, 1895 in Votaw, Hardin, Texas, United States; died on July 10, 1978 in Sweeny, Brazoria, Texas, USA
- Daniel Materson Bass[269] born on November 23, 1897 in Votaw, Hardin, Texas, USA; died on January 11, 2000 in Many, Sabine, Louisiana, USA
- Benjamin Edward Bass[272] born on April 10, 1900 in Votaw, Hardin, Texas, USA; died on August 19, 1956

*William Riley Bass was born in Pensacola, Florida, on the 15t.h of September 1862 during the American Civil War. He was the youngest of two boys born to Wilson Bennet Bass and Jane Teel. His brother, Benjamin Wilson Bass was three years older.

Life for Grandpa Bass was difficult right from the very beginning. In 1864, just a few months before the civil war ended, his father, Wilson, and his Uncle James Bass and Uncle James Teel were crossing the Pensacola Bay in a small boat. They were going to hunt wild turkeys on the other side of the bay. Tragedy struck when some men, whom Grandpa refers to as "Seesech" (Secessionists) rode up close to the water and opened fire on three men in the boat. Great-grandfather Wilson Bass, and his brother James Bass, were killed. Grandpa's uncle, James Teel, was shot through the thigh with a minory ball and remained a cripple all of his life.

Grandpa was probably close to three years old when his father was killed. From our records, it appears that he went with his mother, Jane Teel Bass, to live with her mother, Anna Padgett Teel, in Andalusia, Alabama.

About three years later his mother, along with three other people, were crossing the Pensacola Bay on their way to a wedding when a heavy wind came up, capsizing the small boat and drowning all the occupants but one. So at the tender age of six, Grandpa and his brother were orphans. Of his mother's death, grandpa says that he remembers three open graves, but he and his brother were not allowed to see their mother, because the tarpons had eaten her nose and part of her chin.

At the approximate age of 63, his grandmother Teel was left with the care of two little boys. She must have been a truly wonderful woman because she was also caring for the orphaned children of John Teel. Her daughter, Martha, who was about 21 years old at the time, also helped her raise them.

Grandpa's uncle, Richard Teel, was the second settler in a place called Saratoga, Texas. He settled there in 1860, but left for a period of time while he was serving with the Confederate Army. In 1867 he returned to build a new house about 2 miles from the site of his first. Then he sent for Great-Grandma Teel, Martha, Grandpa and his brother, and the cousins who were also living with them. The journeyed from Andalusia, Alabama to Brewton, Alabama where the nearest railroad was. From Brewton they traveled by train to New Orleans. At New Orleans, Grandpa said they ran the train up onto the ship and then they traveled by ship around the Gulf of Mexico to Galveston, Texas. From Galveston the went up the Trinity River to Liberty, Texas, where some of the family of Uncle Richard's met them. They went over land to Saratoga and there Grandpa Lived with Uncle Richard's Family of eleven children, plus all the children Great-Grandmother Teel was caring for.

Grandpa told Uncle Dan some of the pranks he and his Teel cousins pulled as they were growing up in Texas. One such prank was chasing the pigs into the water. Since a pig isn't able to swim very long before it cuts it's own throat with it's hooves, Grandpa and his cousins were responsible for drowning a few of Uncle Richard's pigs. Another example was when they had to hoe the corn, Grandpa said that ever so often he'd dig down and cut the main roots of the stalk of corn to kill it. Killing some of the corn meant that he wouldn't have so much corn to hoe the next time!

-Merrillyn Stevens Guymon daughter of Evyie Elizabeth Bass Stevens (This is only an excerpt)

*The bio of William Riley Bass is presented as provided by his family. It seems crucial to point out that the Turkey Hunt mentioned was more than that. The men when attached, by the official Confederate Army on order, were transporting Alabama State Rep. Alfred Holley. Holley was an anti-secession politician, from Covington County, elected during the war. He was being pursued as a trader to the Confederacy, and the Basses were helping him get to Pensacola. Overall, they were successful in getting him there, though the three men mentioned did die in the process.

Notes:

Etta Mary Bass[274] born on January 14, 1903 in White Oak, Hardin, Texas, USA; died on May 26, 1986 in Gilbert, Maricopa, Arizona, USA

Mary Etta Bass[277] born on January 14, 1903 in White Oak, Hardin, Texas, USA; died on September 14, 1993 in Norwalk, Los Angeles, California, USA

Joseph Carson Bass[279] born on March 2, 1905 in Saratoga, Hardin, Texas, USA; died on September 5, 1925 in Westlake, Calcasieu, Louisiana, USA

Eva Elizabeth ("Evvie") Bass[281] born on March 18, 1907 in Saratoga, Hardin, Texas, USA; died on January 22, 1999 in St. George, Washington, Utah, USA

Martha Bass[283] born on July 27, 1909 in Saratoga, Hardin, Texas, USA; died on July 27, 1909 in Saratoga, Hardin, Texas, USA

66. BENNETT B. TEEL (see Descendants) was born on June 28, 1860, in Alabama, USA, to James Teel[15] and Nancy Bass[14].
- He died on December 10, 1884, aged 24 years, in Alabama, USA.
- He was buried in Teel Cemetery, Covington, Alabama, USA.

67. BRUNER TEEL (see Descendants) was born in 1861, in Alabama, United States, to James Teel[15] and Nancy Bass[14].
- He was recorded in the census in 1880, aged about 19, in Harts And Red Level, Covington, Alabama, USA.

68. MELVINE LAVINA TEEL (see Descendants) was born in 1863, in Alabama, United States, to James Teel[15] and Nancy Bass[14]. Melvine Lavina became known as "Sis".
- She was recorded in the census in 1880, aged about 17, in Harts And Red Level, Covington, Alabama, USA.
- She was recorded in the census in 1940, aged about 77, in 403 Perry Street, Andalusia, Covington, Alabama, USA.
- She died on November 21, 1949, aged about 86, in Andalusia, Covington, Alabama, USA.
- She was buried in Conecuh River Baptist Cemetery, Andalusia, Covington, Alabama, USA.

? and Melvine Lavina Teel became partners.

69. JAMES A. FLOYD was born on February 4, 1861.
- He died on January 27, 1936, aged 74.
- He was buried in Conecuh River Baptist Cemetery, Andalusia, Covington, Alabama, USA.

James A. Floyd married Melvine Lavina Teel[68]. They had one son:
Bennett Abner Floyd[284] born on July 4, 1888 in Alabama, USA; died on October 3, 1949

70. ANNIE TEEL (see Descendants) was born in April 1864, in Alabama, USA, to James Teel[15] and Nancy Bass[14].
- She was recorded in the census in 1880, aged about 16, in Harts And Red Level, Covington, Alabama, USA.
- She was recorded in the census in 1910, aged about 46, in Fairfield, Covington, Alabama, USA.
- She died on March 2, 1941, aged 76, in Covington, Alabama, USA.
- She was buried in Conecuh River Baptist Cemetery, Andalusia, Covingtton, Alabama, USA.

71. ELIZABETH TEEL (see Descendants) was born on October 1, 1866, in Alabama, United States, to James Teel[15] and Nancy Bass[14]. Elizabeth became known as "Lizzie".
- She was recorded in the census in 1880, aged about 13, in Harts And Red Level, Covington, Alabama, USA.
- She died on February 11, 1949, aged 82 years.

72. JOHN WALTER DAVIS was born on October 20, 1870, in Alabama, United States, to James Wadsworth Davis and Rebecca P Ward. He died on October 24, 1939, aged 69.

John Walter Davis married Elizabeth Teel[71]. They had eight children:
Lena Mae Davis[285] born on April 17, 1891 in Anderson, Anderson, South Carolina, USA; died on March 24, 1944 in Anderson, Anderson, South Carolina, USA

Willie Ophellia Davis[286] born in October 1891 in Alabama, USA; died on December 13, 1970 in Anderson, Anderson, South Carolina, USA

Nora Davis[287] born in 1893 in Alabama, USA; died on September 17, 1978 in Anderson, Anderson, South Carolina, USA

John Sumpter Davis[288] born on November 30, 1895 in Fairfield, Covington, Alabama, USA; died on September 8, 1954 in Anderson, Anderson, South Carolina, USA

Mirtice Davis[289] born in 1900; died on July 19, 1982 in Red Level, Covington, Alabama, USA

Athen Davis[290] born on October 19, 1903 in Fairfield, Covington, Alabama, USA; died on August 3, 1964 in Andalusia, Covington, Alabama, USA

Elma Davis[292] born in 1905 in Alabama, USA; died in 1994 in Mobile, Mobile, Alabama, USA

Ethel Louise Davis[293] born on November 30, 1910 in Fairvield, Covington, Alabama, USA; died on January 11, 2001 in Pensacola, Escambia, Florida, USA

Notes:

Small boy with Ruben Teel and John Teel

Mayme Lee Teel

William Greeley Teel

Bernice Cathleen Teel

73. JOHN TEEL (see Descendants) was born on February 6, 1872, in Alabama, United States, to James Teel[15] and Nancy Bass[14].
   - He was recorded in the census in 1880, aged about 8, in Harts And Red Level, Covington, Alabama, USA.
   - He was recorded in the census in 1910, aged about 38, in Fairfield, Covington, Alabama, USA.
   - He was recorded in the census in 1930, aged about 58, in Fairfield, Covington, Alabama, USA.
   - He was recorded in the census in 1940, aged about 68, in Conecuh Church Road, Election Precinct 2 Fairfield, Covington, Alabama, USA.
  - He was recorded in the census on April 1, 1950, aged 78, in 401 Avdon St, Andalusia, Covington, Alabama, United States.
  - He died on May 4, 1958, aged 86 years, in Andalusia, Covington, Alabama, USA.
  - He was buried in Andalusia Memorial Cemetery, Covington, Alabama, USA.
74. MARGARET JOSEPHINE HART was born on October 12, 1875, in Alabama, United States, to William D. Hart and Virginia Foshee.
   - She was recorded in the census in 1910, aged about 34, in Fairfield, Covington, Alabama, USA.
   - She was recorded in the census in 1930, aged about 54, in Fairfield, Covington, Alabama, USA.
   - She was recorded in the census in 1940, aged about 64, in Conecuh Church Road, Election Precinct 2 Fairfield, Covington, Alabama, USA.
   - She was recorded in the census on April 1, 1950, aged 74, in 401 Avdon St, Andalusia, Covington, Alabama, United States.
  - She died on April 5, 1956, aged 80.
  - She was buried in Andalusia Memorial Cemetery, Andalusia, Covington, Alabama, USA.
     John Teel[73] married Margaret Josephine Hart. They had ten children:
       William Greeley Teel[294] born on December 18, 1893 in Covington, Alabama, United States; died on April 10, 1979 in Alabama, United States
       James Samuel Teel[295] born on December 6, 1895 in Covington, Alabama, United States; died on August 6, 1896
       George Fred Teel[296] born about 1897 in Covington, Alabama, United States; died on June 26, 1986
       Alex Richard Teel[297] born about 1900 in Alabama, United States; died on November 27, 1935 in Andalusia, Covington, Alabama, USA
       Mayme Lee Teel[299] born on June 1, 1902 in Alabama, United States; died on June 19, 1993
       Corine Virginia Teel[301] born on April 12, 1904 in Alabama, United States; died on May 2, 1999 in Andalusia, Covington, Alabama, United States
       Dora Margaret Teel[302] born on February 25, 1906 in Alabama, United States; died on April 11, 1992 in Alabama, United States
       Martha Lena Teel[304] born on February 6, 1908 in Alabama, United States; died on November 9, 1994 in Shelby, Richland, Ohio, United States
       Ruben Everett Teel[306] born on November 22, 1912 in Alabama, United States; died on August 24, 1975 in Alabama, United States
       Bernice Cathleen Teel[308] born on August 10, 1916 in Alabama, United States; died on July 25, 1995 in Alabama, United States

75. NANCY VIOLA TEEL (see Descendants) was born in 1875, in Alabama, United States, to James Teel[15] and Nancy Bass[14]. Nancy Viola became known as "Vi".
  - She was recorded in the census in 1880, aged about 5, in Harts And Red Level, Covington, Alabama, USA.
76. ROB HART.
    Rob Hart married Nancy Viola Teel[75].

77. WILLIAM RILEY TEEL (see Descendants) was born on November 2, 1877, in Alabama, USA, to James Teel[15] and Nancy Bass[14]. William Riley became known as "Bill".
   - He was recorded in the census in 1880, aged about 2, in Harts And Red Level, Covington, Alabama, USA.
   - He was recorded in the census in 1910, aged about 32, in Fairfield, Covington, Alabama, USA.
   - He died on December 31, 1924, aged 47 years, in Andalusia, Covington, Alabama, USA.
   - He was buried in Conecuh River Baptist Cemetery, Andalusia, Covington, Alabama, USA.
78. ADDIE AUGUSTA STOKES was born on January 25, 1883.
   - She was recorded in the census in 1910, aged about 27, in Fairfield, Covington, Alabama, USA.
   - She died on October 13, 1962, aged 79.
   - She was buried in Conecuh River Baptist Cemetery, Andalusia, Covington, Alabama, USA.
     William Riley Teel[77] married Addie Augusta Stokes. They had four children:
       Willie Samson Teel[310] born on May 16, 1904 in Alabama, USA; died on December 10, 1982
       Atress Teel[312] born about 1906 in Alabama, United States
       Jimie L Teel[313] born about 1908 in Alabama, United States

Gladys Teel[314] born on April 15, 1915 in Alabama, USA; died on March 2, 1998 in Covington, Alabama, USA

79. HENRY VAUCEOUS TEEL (see Descendants) was born on June 27, 1881 to James Teel[15] and Nancy Bass[14].
- He died on June 6, 1937, aged 55, in Alabama, USA.
- He was buried in Conecuh River Baptist Cemetery, Andalusia, Covington, Alabama, USA.
80. ELLA PADGETT was born on September 7, 1882.
- She died on May 21, 1964, aged 81.
- She was buried in Conecuh River Baptist Cemetery, Andalusia, Covington, Alabama, USA.
Henry Vauceous Teel[79] married Ella Padgett. They had three children:
Addie Lee Teel[318] born on October 23, 1908; died on December 21, 1988
James Vauciuos Teel[319] born in 1915; died in October 1934 in Covington, Alabama, USA
James Elijah Teel[320] born on May 5, 1924 in Covington, Alabama, USA; died on July 2, 1977 in Burtonsville, Montgomery, Maryland, USA

81. MATTIE TEEL (see Descendants) was born in 1885, in Alabama, USA, to James Teel[15] and Nancy Bass[14].
- She was recorded in the census in 1910, aged about 25, in Fairfield, Covington, Alabama, USA.
- She died on March 30, 1974, aged about 88, in Covington, Alabama, USA.
- She was buried in Conecuh River Baptist Cemetery, Andalusia, Covington, Alabama, USA.
82. JOHN KIRKLIN was born in 1887.
- He died in 1979, aged about 92.
- He was buried in Conecuh River Baptist Cemetery, Andalusia, Covington, Alabama, USA.
The following information is also recorded for John:
- Military Service.
Note: *Pvt U.S. Army WWI.*
(Military Service)
John Kirklin married Mattie Teel[81].

83. LEVINA BASS (see Descendants (16)) was born before December 14, 1871 to Holland Middleton Bass[17] and Christian Ward[18]. She died (At young age).
Notes:
- *The story of Holley and Christian's first child comes from the Parish family (relayed to me through Anthony "Buzz" Ward), reporting that Martha Jane Parish [Bass] indicated that an unmarked childs grave was the daughter of her brother Holley, and that she'd been named after thier sister Levina. This story, especially combined with Christian's obituary crediting her with 12 children, seems to ring true.*
- *Before her parents moved back to Alabama.*
(Death)

84. WILLIAM BENNETT BASS (see Descendants (16)) was born on December 14, 1871, in Uchee Anna, Walton, Florida, USA, to Holland Middleton Bass[17] and Christian Ward[18].
- He was recorded in the census in 1900, aged about 28, in Precincts 10, 19 Hart, George, Covington, Alabama, USA.
- He was recorded in the census in 1910, aged about 38, in Hart, Covington, Alabama, USA.
- He was recorded in the census in 1920, aged about 48, in Precinct 21, Covington, Alabama, USA.
- He died on April 15, 1965, aged 93 years, in Holt, Okaloosa, Florida, USA.
- He was buried in New Bethany Cemetery, Holt, Okaloosa, Florida, USA.
85. EMILY ESTELLE JORDAN was born on June 2, 1881, in Andalusa, Alabama, USA, to Lewin Monrow Jordan and Martha Ann Watson.
- She was recorded in the census in 1900, aged about 19, in Andalusia town, Covington, Alabama, USA.
- She was recorded in the census in 1910, aged about 29, in Hart, Covington, Alabama, USA.
- She was recorded in the census in 1920, aged about 39, in Precinct 21, Covington, Alabama, USA.
- She died on March 10, 1936, aged 54 years, in Holt, Okaloosa, Florida, USA.
- She was buried in New Bethany Cemetery, Holt, Okaloosa, Florida, USA.
William Bennett Bass[84], aged 32, married Emily Estelle Jordan, aged 23, on October 27, 1904 in Andalusia, Covington, Alabama, USA. They had five children:
Genola Bass[322] born on December 11, 1905 in Andalusia, Covington, Alabama, USA; died on February 5, 1969
Maxie Milo Bass[324] born on May 7, 1906 in Andalusia, Covington, Alabama, USA; died on January 19, 1984 in Andalusia, Covington, Alabama, USA
Martha Naomi Bass[327] born on April 7, 1910 in Andalusia, Covington, Alabama, USA; died on November 16, 2006

Christian Ottie Lee Bass[329] born on November 18, 1912 in Andalusia, Covington, Alabama, USA; died on September 11, 1993 in Pensacola, Escambia, Florida, USA

Ossie Mae Bass[331] born on September 9, 1917 in Andalusia, Covington, Alabama, USA; died on April 2, 2013 in Pensacola, Escambia, Florida, USA

86. NANCY JANE MIDDLETON BASS (see Descendants (16)) was born on March 9, 1873, in Uchee Anna, Walton, Florida, USA, to Holland Middleton Bass[17] and Christian Ward[18].
    - She was recorded in the census in 1930, aged about 57, in Carolina, Covington, Alabama, USA.
    - She died (Natural / Old Age) on November 13, 1947, aged 74 years, in Andalusia, Covington, Alabama, USA.
    - She was buried in Shiloh Cemetery.

    Note: *Nancy Jane Bass McGlaun was the second child of Holland and Christian Bass. She was born on March 9, 1873 in Walton County Florida. In about 1881, the Bass family moved to Covington County Alabama at the fork of Five Runs and Hogfoot Creek. This is where she lived until she married. On March 18, 1900, she married James Egie McGlaun and they lived across the creek from the Bass family home. All there children were born here. I've been told they lived for some time in Santa Rosa County Florida but the 1930 census show them living in Covington County. Egie and Nancy had 5 sons and 1daughter. Nancy McGlaun died November 13, 1947 and was buried at Shiloh Cemetery. Egie died May 9, 1970 and was buried at Shiloh Cemetery.*

87. JAMES EGIE NARDIS MCGLAUN was born on September 19, 1876, in Barbour, Alabama, USA.
    - He was recorded in the census in 1930, aged about 53, in Carolina, Covington, Alabama, USA.
    - He died (Natural / Old Age) on May 9, 1970, aged 93 years, in Covington, Alabama, USA.
    - He was buried in Shiloh Cemetery.

    James Egie Nardis McGlaun, aged 23, married Nancy Jane Middleton Bass[86], aged 27, on March 18, 1900. They had six children:

    James Hollie McGlaun[333] born on January 22, 1901 in Alabama, USA; died on June 8, 1979 in Andalusia, Covington, Alabama, USA

    Willie Oscar McGlaun[335] born on August 8, 1903 in Covington, Alabama, USA; died on August 30, 1997 in Andalusia, Covington, Alabama, USA

    Virgil Lee McGlaun[337] born on January 18, 1906 in Alabama, USA; died on February 3, 2004 in Andalusia, Covington, Alabama, USA

    Ineta McGlaun[340] born on July 29, 1909 in Alabama, USA; died on December 25, 1997 in Andalusia, Covington, Alabama, USA

    Orbey Ray McGlaun[341] born on July 29, 1911 in Alabama, United States

    Orion T McGlaun[343] born on December 10, 1916 in Alabama, United States

88. CATHERINE ELIZABETH BASS (see Descendants (16)) was born on February 10, 1877, in Walton County, Florida, USA, to Holland Middleton Bass[17] and Christian Ward[18].
    - She was recorded in the census in 1900, aged about 23, in Precincts 10, 19 Hart, George, Covington, Alabama, USA.
    - She died on July 23, 1909, aged 32 years, in Andalusia, Covington, Alabama, USA.
    - She was buried in Zion Rock Cemetery, Beda, Covington, Alabama, USA.

89. ISABELL BASS (see Descendants (16)) was born on January 2, 1880, in Florida, United States, to Holland Middleton Bass[17] and Christian Ward[18].
    - She was recorded in the census in 1900, aged about 20, in Precincts 10, 19 Hart, George, Covington, Alabama, USA.
    - She was recorded in the census in 1910, aged about 30, in Hart, Covington, Alabama, USA.
    - She was recorded in the census in 1920, aged about 40, in Precinct 21, Covington, Alabama, USA.
    - She was recorded in the census in 1930, aged about 50, in Red Rock, Santa Rosa, Florida, USA.
    - She was recorded in the census in 1940, aged about 60, in Second Street, Precinct 20, Walton, Florida, USA.
    - She was recorded in the census on April 1, 1950, aged 70, in 10 7/10 Mi End Pine Grove High Way and Pine Grove Settlement to Highway 83, Liberty, Walton, Florida, United States.
    - She died (Natural / Old Age) on August 14, 1965, aged 85 years, in Dorcus, Okaloosa, Florida, USA.
    - She was buried in Alaqua Methodist Church Cemetery, Steele Church, Walton, Florida, USA.

    Isabell married twice. She was married to James Henry Rowell[90] and William Benjamin Huckabaa[91].

90. JAMES HENRY ROWELL was born on March 6, 1870, in Alabama, USA, to James Edmund Rowell and Mary Ann Frances Jackson.
    - He was recorded in the census in 1880, aged about 10, in Rose Hill, Covington, Alabama, USA.
    - He was recorded in the census in 1910, aged about 40, in Hart, Covington, Alabama, USA.
    - He died on August 5, 1910, aged 40 years, in Covington, Alabama, USA.

Note: *The family story says, James was on his way back home from Andalusia when he was kicked in the chest by a mule and killed.*

James Henry Rowell, aged 31, married Isabell Bass[89], aged 22, on January 12, 1902. They had four children:
 Ida Mae Rowell[345] born on November 4, 1902 in Andalusia, Covington, Alabama, USA; died on December 23, 1986 in Andalusia, Covington, Alabama, United States
 Lettie V. Rowell[347] born on June 15, 1906 in Covington, Alabama, USA; died on July 27, 1994 in Walton County, Florida, USA
 Leroy Rowell[348] born on January 5, 1909 in Alabama, United States; died in October 1977
 Eva Mae Rowell[350] born on October 23, 1927 in Holt, Okaloosa, Florida, USA; died on August 22, 1999

The following information is also recorded for this family:
- Death of Spouse.

91. WILLIAM BENJAMIN HUCKABAA was born on March 31, 1875, in Akin, South Carolina, USA. William Benjamin became known as "Willie".
- He was recorded in the census in 1920, aged about 45, in Precinct 21, Covington, Alabama, USA.
- He was recorded in the census in 1930, aged about 55, in Red Rock, Santa Rosa, Florida, USA.
- He was recorded in the census in 1940, aged about 65, in Second Street, Precinct 20, Walton, Florida, USA.
- He was recorded in the census on April 1, 1950, aged 75, in 10 7/10 Mi End Pine Grove High Way and Pine Grove Settlement to Highway 83, Liberty, Walton, Florida, United States.
- He died (Natural / Old Age) on June 3, 1959, aged 84 years, in Dorcus, Okaloosa, Florida, USA.
- He was buried in Alaqua Methodist Church Cemetery, Steele Church, Walton, Florida, USA.

William Benjamin had three partnerships. He was married to Stella Gunter and Isabell Bass[89]. He was also the partner of Mary Chesre.

William Benjamin Huckabaa, when younger than 40, married Stella Gunter, when younger than 44, before 1916. They had seven children:
 Hattie Eveline Huckaba born on June 20, 1893 in Akin, South Carolina, USA; died on July 11, 1982 in DeFuniak Springs, Walton, Florida, USA
 William Martin Huckabaa[346] born on June 1, 1895 in Wagener, Aiken, South Carolina, United States; died on September 9, 1985 in Andalusia, Covington, Alabama, United States
 Gettice Huckaba born on April 27, 1898 in South Carolina, USA; died on July 15, 1918
 Collie Calhoun Huckabaa born on February 13, 1900 in Aiken, South Carolina, USA; died on March 8, 1964 in Florala, Covington, Alabama, USA
 James Edgar Huckaba[375] born on February 22, 1903 in Covington, Alabama, United States; died on July 12, 1991 in Walton County, Florida, USA
 Acre Huckaba born on October 30, 1904 in Alabama, United States; died on March 23, 1975
 Icelean Huckaba born on December 26, 1906; died on October 27, 1942

The following information is also recorded for this family:
- Death of Spouse.

William Benjamin Huckabaa, aged 42, married Isabell Bass[89], aged 37, on June 10, 1917 in Andalusia, Covington, Alabama, USA. They had two children:
 Eugene Huckaba[353] born on April 7, 1918 in Alabama, United States; died on December 15, 1993 in Siler City, Chatham, North Carolina
 Addie Irene Huckaba[355] born on November 10, 1920 in Andalusia, Covington, Alabama, USA; died on March 16, 1994 in Escambia County, Florida, USA

William Benjamin Huckabaa and Mary Chesre had one daughter:
 Babe Huckaba born on November 15, 1915 in Andalusia, Covington, Alabama, USA; died on August 6, 2016 in Crestview, Okaloosa, Florida, USA

The following information is also recorded for this family:
- Unknown Relationship.

92. JAMES DALLAS BASS (see Descendants (16)) was born on September 17, 1883, in Andalusia, Covington, Alabama, USA, to Holland Middleton Bass[17] and Christian Ward[18].
- He was recorded in the census in 1900, aged about 16, in Precincts 10, 19 Hart, George, Covington, Alabama, USA.
- He was recorded in the census in 1930, aged about 46, in Holt, Okaloosa, Florida, USA.
- He was recorded in the census in 1940, aged about 56, in Okaloosa, Florida, USA.
- He died (Natural / Old Age) on January 27, 1976, aged 92 years, in Pensacola, Escambia, Florida, USA.
- He was buried in New Bethany Cemetery, Holt, Okaloosa, Florida, USA.

The following information is also recorded for James Dallas:
Twin.

Note: *Mary Alice Posey [Bass] - Twin Sister.*
(Twin)

93. AMIE ISABEL BEDGOOD was born on March 27, 1895, in Rose Hill, Covington, Alabama, USA, to Samuel Lawson Bedgood and Sarah Caroline Rowell.
- She was recorded in the census in 1930, aged about 35, in Holt, Okaloosa, Florida, USA.
- She was recorded in the census in 1940, aged about 45, in Okaloosa, Florida, USA.
- She died (Natural / Old Age) on February 11, 1989, aged 93 years, in Pensacola, Escambia, Florida, USA.
- She was buried in New Bethany Cemetery, Holt, Okaloosa, Florida, USA.

James Dallas Bass[92], aged about 41, married Amie Isabel Bedgood, aged about 30, about 1925 in Okaloosa, Florida, USA. They had nine children:

Bessie Luvine Bass[357] born on January 27, 1911 in Florida, United States; died on January 17, 1984
James Henry Bass[359] born on May 1, 1913 in Holt, Okaloosa, Florida, USA; died on September 28, 1988 in Fruitland Park, Lake, Florida, USA
Hillary J. Bass[362] born on January 26, 1916 in Florida, USA; died on October 16, 1916 in Holt, Okaloosa, Florida, USA
Magdaline Bass[363] born on December 14, 1918
Ray-Monde Bass[364] born on February 19, 1920 in Florida, United States
John Clayton Bass[366] born on March 26, 1922 in Florida, United States; died on December 24, 2012
Marvin Dallas Bass Sr.[368] born on March 6, 1924 in Holt, Okaloosa, Florida, USA; died on December 29, 2002 in Crestview, Okaloosa County, Florida, USA
Sarah Christian Bass[370] born on July 17, 1926 in Holt, Okaloosa, Florida, USA; died on August 8, 2015 in Pensacola, Escambia, Florida, USA
Gerald Howard Bass Sr.[372] born on December 10, 1928 in Florida, United States; died on April 30, 2017

94. MARY ALICE BASS (see Descendants (16)) was born on September 17, 1883, in Andalusia, Covington, Alabama, USA, to Holland Middleton Bass[17] and Christian Ward[18].
- She was recorded in the census in 1900, aged about 16, in Precincts 10, 19 Hart, George, Covington, Alabama, USA.
- She was recorded in the census in 1910, aged about 26, in Hart, Covington, Alabama, USA.
- She died on January 23, 1964, aged 80 years, in Holt, Okaloosa, Florida, USA.
- She was buried in New Holt Cemetery, Holt, Okaloosa, Florida, USA.

The following information is also recorded for Mary Alice:

Twin.
Note: *James Dallas Bass - Twin Brother.*
(Twin)

95. MARTIN EDWARD POSEY was born on January 28, 1883, in South Carolina, USA, to Elias H Posey and Vianah Catherine Horsie.
- He was recorded in the census in 1900, aged about 17, in Precincts 2, 6, 18 Fairfield, Loango, River Falls, Covington, Alabama, USA.
- He was recorded in the census in 1910, aged about 27, in Hart, Covington, Alabama, USA.
- He died on November 12, 1958, aged 75 years, in Escambia County, Florida, USA.
- He was buried in New Holt Cemetery, Holt, Okaloosa, Florida, USA.

Martin Edward Posey, aged 24, married Mary Alice Bass[94], aged 24, in January 1908. They had ten children:

Mae Belle Posey[374] born on December 20, 1908 in Covington, Alabama, USA; died on May 29, 2000 in Laurell Hill, Walton, Florida, USA
Clifton Posey[376] born on October 16, 1910; died on February 13, 1913
Preston Dallas Posey[377] born in 1912 in Alabama, USA; died on March 9, 2005
Chester Posey[379] born on February 16, 1914; died on July 28, 1949
Holland Middleton Posey[381] born on May 27, 1916; died on September 20, 1916
Stacy Denton Posey[382] born on August 6, 1917 in Holt, Okaloosa, Florida, USA; died on March 1, 2004
Bonnie Lee Posey[384] born on July 12, 1921 in Holt, Okaloosa, Florida, USA; died in 2008
Cora Lee Posey[386] born on February 2, 1923; died on December 12, 1927
Mary Evelyn Posey[387] born on June 7, 1925 in Holt, Okaloosa, Florida, USA; died on February 10, 2012 in Pensacola, Escambia, Florida, USA
Cleavy Edward Posey Sr.[389] born on September 16, 1927 in Holt, Okaloosa, Florida, USA; died on August 4, 2011 in Pensacola, Escambia, Florida, USA

96. HOLLEY MIDDLETON BASS (see Descendants (16)) was born on April 29, 1885, in Covington, Alabama, USA, to Holland Middleton Bass[17] and Christian Ward[18]. Holley Middleton became known as "Bud".
   - He was recorded in the census in 1900, aged about 15, in Precincts 10, 19 Hart, George, Covington, Alabama, USA.
   - He was recorded in the census in 1940, aged about 55, in E Precinct 6 Red Rock, Santa Rosa, Florida, USA.
   - He was recorded in the census on April 1, 1950, aged 64, in Chestnut St, Crestview, Okaloosa, Florida, United States.
   - He died on March 4, 1973, aged 87 years, in Holt, Okaloosa, Florida, USA.
   - He was buried in New Holt Cemetery, Holt, Okaloosa, Florida, USA.

97. JESSIE SAVAGE was born on October 5, 1893, in Alabama, United States, to James Elija Savage and Nancy Morning Jordan.
   - She was recorded in the census in 1910, aged about 16, in Fairfield, Covington, Alabama, USA.
   - She was recorded in the census in 1940, aged about 46, in E Precinct 6 Red Rock, Santa Rosa, Florida, USA.
   - She was recorded in the census on April 1, 1950, aged 56, in Chestnut St, Crestview, Okaloosa, Florida, United States.
   - She died on September 20, 1950, aged 56 years.
   - She was buried in New Holt Cemetery, Holt, Okaloosa, Florida, USA.

   Holley Middleton Bass[96], aged 29, married Jessie Savage, aged 21, on February 7, 1915. They had five children:
   Dewey Franklin Bass[391] born on December 2, 1915; died on October 20, 1916
   Edith Florine Bass[392] born on April 25, 1918 in Florida, United States; died on March 4, 2003
   James Verlin Bass[394] born on July 29, 1920 in Florida, United States; died on May 20, 2009
   Marlin Holley Bass[396] born on January 16, 1923 in Holt, Okaloosa, Florida, USA; died on January 16, 2016 in Holt, Okaloosa, Florida, USA
   Eula Virginia Bass[398] born on August 24, 1927 in Florida, United States; died on August 28, 2018

98. JOSEPH ALEXANDER BASS (see Descendants (16)) was born on April 14, 1888, in Andalusia, Covington, Alabama, USA, to Holland Middleton Bass[17] and Christian Ward[18]. Joseph Alexander became known as "Joe".
   - He was recorded in the census in 1900, aged about 12, in Precincts 10, 19 Hart, George, Covington, Alabama, USA.
   - He was recorded in the census in 1920, aged about 32, in Precinct 21, Covington, Alabama, USA.
   - He was recorded in the census in 1930, aged about 42, in Holt, Okaloosa, Florida, USA.
   - He was recorded in the census in 1940, aged about 52, in E Precint 9 Holt, Okaloosa, Florida, USA.
   - He was recorded in the census on April 1, 1950, aged 61, in 1/4 Miles Proceeding South on Blockwater Bass Road, Milligan, Okaloosa, Florida, United States.
   - He died on May 25, 1984, aged 96 years, in Fort Walton Beach, Okaloosa, Florida, USA.
   - He was buried in New Bethany Cemetery, Holt, Okaloosa, Florida, USA.

   The following information is also recorded for Joe:
   - Military Service.
   Note: *U.S. Army WWI.*
      (Military Service)

99. CARRIE LOU MOUNT was born on March 18, 1911, in Baker, Okaloosa, Florida, USA.
   - She was recorded in the census in 1930, aged about 19, in Holt, Okaloosa, Florida, USA.
   - She was recorded in the census in 1940, aged about 29, in E Precint 9 Holt, Okaloosa, Florida, USA.
   - She was recorded in the census on April 1, 1950, aged 39, in 1/4 Miles Proceeding South on Blockwater Bass Road, Milligan, Okaloosa, Florida, United States.
   - She died on June 13, 1970, aged 59 years, in Pensacola, Escambia, Florida, USA.
   - She was buried in New Bethany Cemetery, Holt, Okaloosa, Florida, USA.

   Joseph Alexander Bass[98], aged 38, married Carrie Lou Mount, aged 15, on September 19, 1926. They had seven children:
   Carolyn Bass[400] born on March 26, 1928 in Florida, United States
   Calvin Winston Bass[402] born on October 26, 1929 in Florida, United States; died on August 27, 1990
   Stephen Durward Bass[404] born on December 16, 1931 in Holt, Okaloosa, Florida, USA; died on March 5, 2012
   Charity Delores Bass[406] born on October 23, 1933 in Florida, USA
   Farrell Dale Bass[409] born on January 12, 1936 in Florida, USA
   Joe Farris Bass[412] born on February 14, 1938 in Florida, USA
   Harvey Middleton Bass[415] born on August 28, 1940 in Florida, United States; died on December 21, 1985

Direct Relations

100. JOHN RILEY BASS (see Descendants (16)) was born on March 8, 1890, in Andalusia, Covington, Alabama, USA, to Holland Middleton Bass[17] and Christian Ward[18].
- He was recorded in the census in 1900, aged about 10, in Precincts 10, 19 Hart, George, Covington, Alabama, USA.
- He was recorded in the census in 1930, aged about 40, in Carolina, Covington, Alabama, USA.
- He was recorded in the census in 1940, aged about 50, in Election Prect 21 Carolina, Covington, Alabama, USA.
- He was recorded in the census on April 1, 1950, aged 60, in Carolina, Covington, Alabama, United States.
- He died (Natural / Old Age) on September 26, 1987, aged 97 years, in Crestview, Okaloosa, Florida, USA.
- He was buried in Smith Cemetery, Covington, Alabama, USA.

101. MAMIE ANNIE HASSEL was born on August 9, 1893, in Andalusia, Covington, Alabama, USA.
- She was recorded in the census in 1930, aged about 36, in Carolina, Covington, Alabama, USA.
- She was recorded in the census in 1940, aged about 46, in Election Prect 21 Carolina, Covington, Alabama, USA.
- She was a Teacher.
- She was recorded in the census on April 1, 1950, aged 56, in Carolina, Covington, Alabama, United States.
- She died on July 19, 1977, aged 83 years, in Andalusia, Covington, Alabama, USA.
- She was buried in Smith Cemetery, Covington, Alabama, USA.

John Riley Bass[100], aged 26, married Mamie Annie Hassel, aged 23, on February 4, 1917 in Covington County, Alabama. They had four children:
- Joel Sidney Bass[417] born on November 21, 1917 in Alabama, USA; died on February 4, 1996 in Fort Walton Beach, Okaloosa, Florida, USA
- Margueritte Catherine Bass[419] born on January 21, 1919 in Alabama, United States; died on February 13, 2012
- Martha Ann Bass[421] born on December 9, 1921 in Andalusia, Covington, Alabama, USA
- John Thomas Bass[425] born on April 20, 1924 in Alabama, USA

102. STACY BIBNER BASS (see Descendants (16)) was born on April 21, 1892, in Carolina Community, Covington, Alabama, USA, to Holland Middleton Bass[17] and Christian Ward[18]. Stacy Bibner became known as "Uncle Stacie".
- He was recorded in the census in 1900, aged about 8, in Precincts 10, 19 Hart, George, Covington, Alabama, USA.
- He was recorded in the census in 1920, aged about 28, in Precinct 21, Covington, Alabama, USA.
- He was recorded in the census in 1930, aged about 38, in Carolina, Covington, Alabama, USA.
- He was recorded in the census in 1940, aged about 48, in Election Prect 21 Carolina, Covington, Alabama, USA.
- He was recorded in the census on April 1, 1950, aged 57, in Carolina, Covington, Alabama, United States.
- He died (Natural / Old Age) on August 21, 1993, aged 101 years, in Carolina Community, Covington, Alabama, USA.
- He was buried in Shady Hill Church Cemetery.

The following information is also recorded for Uncle Stacie:
- Military Service.

Note: *U.S. Army WWI.*
(Military Service)

103. ALLINE NAOMI ROWELL was born on February 17, 1901, in Alabama, USA, to Alonzo Franklin Rowell and Mattie Virginia Jordan.
- She was recorded in the census in 1910, aged about 9, in Hart, Covington, Alabama, USA.
- She was recorded in the census in 1920, aged about 19, in Precinct 21, Covington, Alabama, USA.
- She was recorded in the census in 1930, aged about 29, in Carolina, Covington, Alabama, USA.
- She was recorded in the census in 1940, aged about 39, in Election Prect 21 Carolina, Covington, Alabama, USA.
- She was recorded in the census on April 1, 1950, aged 49, in Carolina, Covington, Alabama, United States.
- She died on March 11, 1974, aged 73 years, in Andalusia, Covington, Alabama, USA.
- She was buried in Shady Hill Church Cemetery.

Stacy Bibner Bass[102] married Alline Naomi Rowell. They had ten children:
- Mavis Earline Bass[427] born on March 17, 1922 in Alabama, United States; died on December 26, 2016 in Andalusia, Covington, Alabama, USA
- James Marcus Bass[429] born on January 26, 1924 in Alabama, United States; died on October 8, 1999
- Cecil Edwin Bass[431] born on February 11, 1925; died on March 28, 1926
- Sibyl Louise Bass[432] born on February 9, 1927 in Alabama, United States; died on April 7, 2014 in Andalusia, Covington, Alabama, United States

Grover Alcus Bass[434] born on January 7, 1929 in Covington, Alabama, USA; died on April 22, 1987 in Newfane, Niagara, New York, USA
Margueritte Elizabeth Bass[436] born on January 9, 1931
Betty Irene Bass[438] born on January 13, 1933 in Andalusia, Covington, Alabama, USA
Audrey Rebecca Bass[440] born on January 16, 1935 in Alabama, United States
Hubert Lee Bass[442] born on December 19, 1936 in Andalusia, Covington, Alabama, USA; died on September 1, 2007
Quinton Gene Bass[444] born on November 6, 1938 in Covington, Alabama, USA; died on August 7, 2019 in Florala, Covington, Alabama, USA

104. MARTHA CHRISTIAN BASS (see Descendants (16)) was born on July 18, 1894, in Andalusia, Covington, Alabama, USA, to Holland Middleton Bass[17] and Christian Ward[18]. Martha Christian became known as "Sister".
- She was recorded in the census in 1900, aged about 5, in Precincts 10, 19 Hart, George, Covington, Alabama, USA.
- She was recorded in the census in 1940, aged about 45, in E P 15 Crestview, Okaloosa, Florida, USA.
- She died (Natural / Old Age) on February 11, 1989, aged 94 years, in Crestview, Okaloosa, Florida, USA.
- She was buried in Live Oak Baptist Church Cemetery, Crestview, Okaloosa, Florida, USA.

105. FORMAN EDWARD WARD was born on October 25, 1882, in Alabama, USA, to Jesse Ward and Lurena Lofton.
- He was recorded in the census in 1940, aged about 57, in E P 15 Crestview, Okaloosa, Florida, USA.
- He died on January 5, 1967, aged 85 years.
- He was buried in Live Oak Baptist Church Cemetery, Crestview, Okaloosa, Florida, USA.

Forman Edward Ward, aged 33, married Martha Christian Bass[104], aged 21, on April 16, 1916. They had four children:
Harvey Clinton Ward[445] born on July 20, 1918 in Alabama, USA
William Charles Ward Sr.[447] born on November 21, 1921 in Florida, USA; died on November 8, 2022 in Tennessee, USA
DeLeon Edward Ward[449] born on August 10, 1924 in Andalusia, Covington, Alabama, USA; died on January 26, 2022 in Crestview, Okaloosa County, Florida, USA
Anna Faye Ward[452] born on January 27, 1932 in Florida, USA; died in 1984

106. BENNETT BRIDGES BASS III (see Descendants (17)) was born on July 20, 1870, in Andalusia, Covington, Alabama, USA, to Bennett Bridges Bass Jr.[20] and Mary Frances Padgett[22].
- He was recorded in the census in 1880, aged about 9, in Harts And Red Level, Covington, Alabama, USA.
- He was recorded in the census in 1940, aged about 69, in Hosford, E Precinct 4 Hosford, Liberty, Florida, USA.
- He was recorded in the census on April 1, 1950, aged 79, in 4th Direct Road, Bristol, Liberty, Florida, United States.
- He died on March 12, 1958, aged 87 years, in Hosford, Liberty, Florida, USA.
- He was buried in Hosford Cemetery, Hosford, Florida, United States.

Bennett Bridges married three times. He was married to Alice Kinlaw[107], Jonnie Lillian Ballard[108] and Rosa Lee Shuler[109].

107. ALICE KINLAW was born on January 28, 1875, in Alabama, USA.
- She died on November 25, 1948, aged 73, in Tuscolusa, Alabama, USA.
- She was buried in Adellum Cemetery, Andalusia, Covington, Alabama, USA.

Alice married twice. She was married to Bennett Bridges Bass III[106] and R. T. Lolly.
Bennett Bridges Bass III[106], aged about 23, married Alice Kinlaw, aged about 19, about 1894, and they were divorced. They had three sons:
Earnest True Bass Sr.[454] born on October 14, 1894 in Andalusia, Covington, Alabama, USA; died on September 5, 1959 in Lake City, Columbia, Florida, USA
Richard Carl Bass Sr.[458] born on November 14, 1897 in Alabama, USA; died on December 30, 1951 in Tallahassee, Leon, Florida, USA
William Bennett Bass[461] born on August 16, 1899 in Alabama, USA; died on August 14, 1963 in Polk County, Florida, USA
Note: *Bennett Bridges Bass III, left Alice Bass Lolly [Kinlaw] but reportedly did not divorce her. Both were remarried. - as told by Kirby Bass.*
R. T. Lolly married Alice Kinlaw, aged 47, on January 17, 1923.

108. JONNIE LILLIAN BALLARD was born in 1886, in Alabama, USA.
- She died on December 13, 1945, aged about 59, in Escambia County, Florida, USA.
- She was buried in Hosford Cemetery, Hosford, Liberty, Florida, USA.

Bennett Bridges Bass III[106] married Jonnie Lillian Ballard. They had two children:
    Mary Leona Bass[464] born on September 12, 1911 in Telogia, Liberty, Florida, USA; died on November 16, 1986
    Henry Obie Bass[466] born on August 2, 1917 in Telogia, Liberty, Florida, USA; died on February 26, 1992 in Panama City, Bay, Florida, USA

109. ROSA LEE SHULER was born on July 5, 1888, in Florida, USA.

- She was recorded in the census in 1940, aged about 51, in Hosford, E Precinct 4 Hosford, Liberty, Florida, USA.
- She was recorded in the census on April 1, 1950, aged 61, in 4th Direct Road, Bristol, Liberty, Florida, United States.
- She died on November 23, 1974, aged 86 years.
- She was buried in Hosford Cemetery, Hosford, Florida, USA.

Bennett Bridges Bass III[106] married Rosa Lee Shuler. They had one son:
    Morgan Bennett Bass[468] born in 1928; died in 2001

110. MARY ELIZABETH BASS (see Descendants (17)) was born on January 20, 1871, in Andalusia, Covington, Alabama, USA, to Bennett Bridges Bass Jr.[20] and Mary Frances Padgett[22].
- She was recorded in the census in 1880, aged about 9, in Harts And Red Level, Covington, Alabama, USA.
- She died on October 25, 1960, aged 89 years, in Andalusia, Covington, Alabama, USA.
- She was buried in Magnolia Cemetery, Andalusia, Covington, Alabama, USA.

111. WILLIAM HENRY WILLIAMS was born on February 10, 1865, in Andalusia, Covington, Alabama, USA.
- He died on March 21, 1940, aged 75 years, in Andalusia, Covington, Alabama, USA.
- He was buried in Magnolia Cemetery, Andalusia, Covington, Alabama, USA.

William Henry Williams married Mary Elizabeth Bass[110]. They had twelve children:
    Vinnie Janice Williams[469] born in 1884 in Covington, Alabama, USA; died on April 7, 1942 in Andalusia, Covington, Alabama, USA
    Ada Ola Williams[471] born on July 28, 1890 in Covington, Alabama, USA; died on July 28, 1978
    Francis Folsam Williams[473] born on November 6, 1892 in Covington, Alabama, USA; died on April 4, 1969
    Mattie Dora Williams[475] born on December 4, 1894 in Andalusia, Covington, Alabama, USA; died on February 9, 1990 in Atmore, Escambia, Alabama, USA
    Laura May Williams Williams[477] born on July 27, 1897 in Covington, Alabama, USA; died on February 27, 1979
    Henry Gordon Williams[479] born on September 10, 1899 in Andalusia, Covington, Alabama, USA; died on December 19, 1946
    William Marcus Williams[481] born on July 28, 1902 in Andalusia, Covington, Alabama, USA; died on February 6, 1971
    Naomi Williams[483] born on September 14, 1904 in Covington, Alabama, United States
    Annie Ruth Williams[485] born on December 24, 1906 in Andalusia, Covington, Alabama, USA
    Wilmer Newton Williams[487] born on May 10, 1909 in Andalusia, Covington, Alabama, USA; died on January 15, 1993
    Lillian Elizabeth Williams[489] born on September 24, 1911 in Andalusia, Covington, Alabama, USA; died on September 27, 1945
    Buna Lucille Williams[491] born on January 30, 1914 in Andalusia, Covington, Alabama, USA

112. ELIJAH L. BASS (see Descendants (17)) was born in 1877, in Florida, USA, to Bennett Bridges Bass Jr.[20] and Mary Frances Padgett[22].
- He was recorded in the census in 1880, in Harts And Red Level, Covington, Alabama, USA.
- He died (Burnt to Death) in January 1880, aged about 2, in Covington, Alabama, USA.

113. JAMES WILSON BASS (see Descendants (17)) was born on March 24, 1878, in Andalusia, Covington, Alabama, USA, to Bennett Bridges Bass Jr.[20] and Mary Frances Padgett[22]. James Wilson became known as "Jim".
- He was recorded in the census in 1880, aged about 2, in Harts And Red Level, Covington, Alabama, USA.
- He was recorded in the census in 1900, aged about 22, in Precincts 2, 6, 18 Fairfield, Loango, River Falls, Covington, Alabama, USA.
- He was recorded in the census in 1910, aged about 32, in Fairfield, Covington, Alabama, USA.
- He died on January 11, 1919, aged 40 years, in Covington, Alabama, USA.
- He was buried in Carolina Baptist Church Cemetery, Covington, Alabama, USA.

114. EMMIE CORNELIA HUTTO was born on August 17, 1882, in Aiken, South Carolina, USA, to Joseph Aaron Hutto and Nancy I. Gunter.
- She was recorded in the census in 1900, aged about 17, in Precincts 2, 6, 18 Fairfield, Loango, River Falls, Covington, Alabama, USA.
- She was recorded in the census in 1910, aged about 27, in Fairfield, Covington, Alabama, USA.
- She was recorded in the census in 1920, aged about 37, in Precinct 21, Covington, Alabama, USA.
- She was recorded in the census in 1930, aged about 47, in Carolina, Covington, Alabama, USA.
- She was recorded in the census on April 1, 1950, aged 67, in Carolina, Covington, Alabama, United States.
- She died on June 30, 1965, aged 82 years, in Andalusia, Covington, Alabama, USA.
- She was buried in Carolina Baptist Church Cemetery, Covington, Alabama, USA.

The following information is also recorded for Emmie Cornelia:
- Death of Spouse on January 11, 1919, aged 36.

Note: *Emmie never remarried, and finished raising 10 children on her own.*
   (Death of Spouse)

James Wilson ("Jim") Bass[113], aged about 21, married Emmie Cornelia Hutto, aged about 16, about 1899. They had twelve children:

   Arrie Bernice ("Emma") Bass[493] born on May 20, 1900 in Alabama, United States; died on May 15, 1987
   Ollie Albert Bass[495] born on August 16, 1901 in Covington, Alabama, United States; died on July 30, 1904 in Covington, Alabama, United States
   Eva Allie ("Ev 'er") Bass[496] born on November 29, 1902 in Alabama, United States; died on July 31, 2001
   "Jamie" Ike Bass[498] born on December 22, 1904 in Covington, Alabama, United States; died on February 9, 1978 in Andalusia, Covington, Alabama, United States
   Joseph Aaron Bass[500] born on January 24, 1907 in Covington, Alabama, United States; died on September 5, 1919 in Covington, Alabama, USA
   Julius Clarence Bass[501] born on August 26, 1908 in Alabama, United States; died on May 21, 1994
   Mary Annie Bass[503] born on November 13, 1910 in Alabama, United States; died on October 8, 1992
   Jessie D Bass[505] born on August 5, 1912 in Anniston, Calhoun, AL; died on January 13, 1991
   Leon Pendry Bass[507] born on October 27, 1913 in Alabama, USA; died on June 22, 1995 in Andalusa, Covington, Alabama, USA
   Snyder Clayton Bass[509] born on January 29, 1915 in Alabama, United States; died on January 28, 1993
   Velma Bertha Bass[511] born on October 16, 1917 in Alabama, United States; died on October 30, 1995 in Covington, Alabama, United States
   Edith Inez Bass[513] born on September 5, 1919 in Covington, Alabama, United States; died on June 14, 2004 in Covington, Alabama, United States

The following information is also recorded for this family:
- Death of Spouse.

115. JOHN BRIDGES BASS (see Descendants (17)) was born on June 11, 1881, in Alabama, USA, to Bennett Bridges Bass Jr.[20] and Mary Frances Padgett[22].
- He was recorded in the census in 1900, aged about 19, in Precincts 2, 6, 18 Fairfield, Loango, River Falls, Covington, Alabama, USA.
- He was recorded in the census in 1940, aged about 59, in 1 Range 14, Covington, Alabama, USA.
- He died on December 16, 1953, aged 72 years.
- He was buried in Carolina Baptist Church Cemetery, Covington, Alabama, USA.

116. NANCY AMY CARROLL was born on November 3, 1883, in Dothan, Alabama, USA.
- She was recorded in the census in 1930, aged about 46, in Hart, Covington, Alabama, USA.
- She was recorded in the census in 1940, aged about 56, in 1 Range 14, Covington, Alabama, USA.
- She died on June 4, 1960, aged 76 years, in Fairhope, Baldwin, Alabama, USA.
- She was buried in Carolina Baptist Church Cemetery, Covington, Alabama, USA.

John Bridges Bass[115] married Nancy Amy Carroll. They had eight children:

   Frank Stewart Bass[517] born on April 9, 1914 in Andalusia, Covington, Alabama, USA; died on September 6, 1994 in Orlando, Orange, Florida, USA
   Claude Bruce Bass[519] born on June 14, 1916 in Alabama, United States; died on December 1, 1991 in Pensacola, Escambia, Florida, USA
   Sarah Clyde Law[521] born about 1918 in Andalusia, Covington, Alabama, USA; died on May 13, 1980 in Andalusia, Covington, Alabama, USA
   Bennett Ray Bass[523] born on August 19, 1920 in Alabama, USA; died on February 23, 2003
   Bessie May Bass[526] born on August 19, 1920 in Alabama, USA; died on March 23, 2010 in Fairhope, Baldwin, Alabama, USA

Direct Relations

John Irvin Bass[528] born on February 10, 1922 in Andalusia, Covington, Alabama, USA; died on April 22, 2002 in Lancaser, Los Angeles, California, USA

Jesse Ruban Bass[530] born on February 2, 1924 in Alabama, USA; died on January 24, 1952 in Phenix City, Russell, Alabama, USA

Annie Laura Bass[531] born on September 13, 1927 in Andalusia, Covington, Alabama, USA; died on December 5, 1927 in Andalusia, Covington, Alabama, USA

117. LAURA LEE BASS (see Descendants (17)) was born on July 24, 1883, in Alabama, USA, to Bennett Bridges Bass Jr.[20] and Mary Frances Padgett[22].
- She was recorded in the census in 1900, aged about 16, in Precincts 2, 6, 18 Fairfield, Loango, River Falls, Covington, Alabama, USA.
- She died on February 12, 1978, aged 94 years, in Andalusia, Covington, Alabama, USA.
- She was buried in Andalusia Memorial Cemetery, Covington, Alabama, USA.

Laura Lee had two partnerships; including Morgan Jerome Johnson[118].
Laura Lee gave birth to one son:
Andrew Bennett Bass[532] born on November 25, 1900 in Andalusia, Covington, Alabama, USA; died on June 13, 1971 in Montgomery, Montgomery, Alabama, USA

The following information is also recorded for this family:
- Unknown Relationship.

118. MORGAN JEROME JOHNSON was born on September 17, 1884, in Aiken, South Carolina, USA.
- He died on September 17, 1959, aged 75 years, in Andalusia, Covington, Alabama, USA.
- He was buried in Andalusia Memorial Cemetery, Covington, Alabama, USA.

The following information is also recorded for Morgan Jerome:
- Description: ShortStoutBrownBlueFrom WWI Draft Card.

Morgan Jerome Johnson married Laura Lee Bass[117]. They had six children:
Gussie Josephine Johnson[534] born on June 21, 1906 in Andalusia, Covington, Alabama, USA; died on November 29, 2002 in Pensacola, Escambia, Florida, USA

Willie Morgan Johnson[536] born on May 18, 1908 in Andalusia, Covington, Alabama, USA; died on March 2, 1994 in Mobile, Alabama, USA

Addie Lee Johnson Johnson[537] born on December 3, 1910 in Andalusia, Covington, Alabama, USA; died on November 22, 2007 in Pensacola, Escambia, Florida, USA

Bernice Johnson[538] born on November 17, 1913 in Andalusia, Covington, Alabama, USA; died on September 9, 1991 in Orange County, Florida, USA

Bert Jerome Johnson[540] born on November 17, 1913 in Andalusia, Covington, Alabama, USA; died on May 18, 1992 in Volusia, Florida, USA

Martha Lou Johnson[541] born on December 22, 1914 in Andalusia, Covington, Alabama, USA; died on March 19, 2005 in Andalusia, Covington, Alabama, USA

Note: *This marriage is mentioned in the December 15th 1905 Andalusia Star News. No dates.*

119. SHEILA JOSEPHINE BASS (see Descendants (17)) was born on June 11, 1887, in Andalusia, Covington, Alabama, USA, to Bennett Bridges Bass Jr.[20] and Mary Frances Padgett[22]. Sheila Josephine became known as "Josie".
- She was recorded in the census in 1900, aged about 13, in Precincts 2, 6, 18 Fairfield, Loango, River Falls, Covington, Alabama, USA.
- She died on November 7, 1922, aged 35 years, in USA.
- She was buried in Carolina Baptist Church Cemetery, Covington, Alabama, USA.

120. CHARLES AUGUSTUS GREGORY SR. was born on November 29, 1881, in Worth County, Georgia, USA, to William Gregory.
- He died on April 29, 1986, aged 104 years, in Orlando, Orange, Florida, USA.
- He was buried in Carolina Baptist Church Cemetery, Covington, Alabama, USA.

The following information is also recorded for Charles Augustus:
- Military Service.

Charles Augustus Gregory Sr. married Sheila Josephine Bass[119]. They had five children:
Garvin Gregory[542] born in 1908
Henry Ervin Gregory[543] born on July 27, 1908 in Alabama, USA; died on March 7, 1992 in Chase City, Mecklenburg, Virginia, USA

Lloyd Edison Gregory[544] born on October 14, 1910 in Alabama, USA; died on July 31, 1992 in Victoria, Lunenburg, Virginia, USA

Martha Kathleen Gregory[546] born on September 12, 1914 in Florida, USA; died on August 11, 1950 in Dade, Florida, USA

Corinne Gregory[548] born on December 6, 1916 in Florida, United States; died on November 14, 2020

121. HENRY HARRELSON BASS (see Descendants (17)) was born on March 4, 1888, in Andalusia, Covington, Alabama, USA, to Bennett Bridges Bass Jr.[20] and Mary Frances Padgett[22].
- He was recorded in the census in 1900, aged about 12, in Precincts 2, 6, 18 Fairfield, Loango, River Falls, Covington, Alabama, USA.
- He was recorded in the census in 1910, aged about 22, in Fairfield, Covington, Alabama, USA.
- He was recorded in the census in 1930, aged about 42, in Fairfield, Covington, Alabama, USA.
- He was recorded in the census in 1940, aged about 52, in Brewton Highway, Election Precinct 2 Fairfield, Covington, Alabama, USA.
- He died on October 29, 1970, aged 81 years, in Andalusia, Covington, Alabama, USA.
- He was buried in Carolina Baptist Church Cemetery, Covington, Alabama, USA.

122. KATIE MAE GILLIS was born on October 28, 1889, in Alabama, USA.
- She was recorded in the census in 1930, aged about 40, in Fairfield, Covington, Alabama, USA.
- She was recorded in the census in 1940, aged about 50, in Brewton Highway, Election Precinct 2 Fairfield, Covington, Alabama, USA.
- She died on June 14, 1969, aged 79 years, in Andalusia, Covington, Alabama, USA.
- She was buried in Carolina Baptist Church Cemetery, Covington, Alabama, USA.

Henry Harrelson Bass[121], aged 21, married Katie Mae Gillis, aged 20, on December 13, 1909. They had eight children:

Donald Bass[550] died on February 1, 2002 in Douglasville, GA, USA

Henry Walton Bass[552] born on March 24, 1911 in Andalusia, Covington, Alabama, USA; died on May 23, 1988 in Andalusia, Covington, Alabama, USA

William Columbus Bass[553] born on September 21, 1914 in Andalusia, Covington, Alabama, USA; died on May 9, 1981 in Andalusia, Covington, Alabama, USA

Howard Eugine Bass[555] born on September 2, 1918 in Covington, Alabama, USA; died on September 18, 1997 in Pensacola, Escambia, Florida, USA

Mary Idell Bass[557] born on June 1, 1923 in Covington, Alabama, USA; died on November 25, 1923 in Covington, Alabama, USA

Ruby Lee Bass[558] born in 1926 in Alabama, United States

Virginia Bass[560] born about 1933 in Andalusia, Covington, Alabama, USA

Addie Ruth Bass[562]

123. RILEY B BASS (see Descendants (17)) was born on April 17, 1891, in Covington, Alabama, USA, to Bennett Bridges Bass Jr.[20] and Mary Frances Padgett[22].
- He was recorded in the census in 1900, aged about 9, in Precincts 2, 6, 18 Fairfield, Loango, River Falls, Covington, Alabama, USA.
- He was recorded in the census in 1910, aged about 19, in Fairfield, Covington, Alabama, USA.
- He died on October 4, 1933, aged 42 years, in Covington, Alabama, USA.
- He was buried in Carolina Baptist Church Cemetery, Covington, Alabama, USA.

124. GUSSIE PALMER was born on September 3, 1898, in Andalusia, Covington, Alabama, USA.
- She died on January 3, 1996, aged 97 years, in Pensacola, Escambia, Florida, USA.
- She was buried in Eastern Gate Memorial Gardens, Pensacola, Escambia, Florida, USA.

Riley B Bass[123], aged 21, married Gussie Palmer, aged 13, on September 1, 1912 in Covington, Alabama.

125. DENNIS BRIDGES BASS (see Descendants (17)) was born on April 3, 1893, in Covington, Alabama, USA, to Bennett Bridges Bass Jr.[20] and Mary Frances Padgett[22].
- He was recorded in the census in 1900, aged about 7, in Precincts 2, 6, 18 Fairfield, Loango, River Falls, Covington, Alabama, USA.
- He was recorded in the census in 1910, aged about 17, in Fairfield, Covington, Alabama, USA.
- He was recorded in the census in 1920, aged about 27, in Fairfield Precinct Beat No 2, Covington, Alabama, USA.
- He was recorded in the census in 1930, aged about 37, in Fairfield, Covington, Alabama, USA.
- He was recorded in the census on April 1, 1950, aged 56, in On Audalina and Bruckar Hway on West Side Iraveling South, Fairfield, Covington, Alabama, United States.
- He died on July 30, 1967, aged 74 years, in Andalusia, Covington, Alabama, USA.
- He was buried in Carolina Baptist Church Cemetery, Covington, Alabama, USA.

The following information is also recorded for Dennis Bridges:
- Military Service.

Direct Relations

Note: *PVT, 325 Ambulance Co. - WWI.*
(Military Service)

126. LILLIE LEE THOMAS was born on October 8, 1897, in Alabama, USA.
- She was recorded in the census in 1930, aged about 32, in Fairfield, Covington, Alabama, USA.
- She was recorded in the census on April 1, 1950, aged 52, in On Audalina and Bruckar Hway on West Side Iraveling South, Fairfield, Covington, Alabama, United States.
- She died on March 26, 1960, aged 62 years, in Alabama, USA.
- She was buried in Carolina Baptist Church Cemetery, Covington, Alabama, USA.

Dennis Bridges Bass[125], aged 27, married Lillie Lee Thomas, aged 22, on June 29, 1920 in Okaloosa, Florida, USA. They had nine children:

Edna Inez Bass[564] born in 1920 in Andalusia, Covington, Alabama, USA; died in March 1924 in Andalusia, Covington, Alabama, USA

Kenneth Bridges Bass[565] born on February 7, 1923 in Crestview, Okaloosa County, Florida, USA

Mildred E. Griffen Bass[567] born on January 2, 1925 in Andalusia, Covington, Alabama, USA; died on June 22, 2009 in Brenham, Washington, Texas, USA

George Washington Bass[571] born on February 20, 1927 in Covington, Alabama, USA; died on January 12, 2012

Laura Frances Bass[574] born on February 25, 1929 in Andalusia, Covington, Alabama, USA

Rossie Lee Bass[576] born on August 15, 1931 in Andalusia, Covington, Alabama, USA; died on August 9, 2004 in Montgomery, Montgomery, Alabama, USA

Melisa Juanita Bass[579] born on May 27, 1933 in Andalusia, Covington, Alabama, USA

Winston Byran Bass[581] born on December 5, 1935 in Alabama, USA; died on September 13, 2004 in Alabama, USA

Murry Cecil Bass[583] born on November 13, 1937 in Carolina Community, Covington, Alabama, USA; died on June 20, 2016 in Andalusia, Covington, Alabama, USA

127. KATIE BASS (see Descendants (17)) was born in 1894 to Bennett Bridges Bass Jr.[20] and Mary Frances Padgett[22].

128. BERTIE B BASS (see Descendants (17)) was born on January 21, 1896, in Alabama, United States, to Bennett Bridges Bass Jr.[20] and Mary Frances Padgett[22].
- He was recorded in the census in 1900, aged about 4, in Precincts 2, 6, 18 Fairfield, Loango, River Falls, Covington, Alabama, USA.
- He was recorded in the census in 1910, aged about 14, in Fairfield, Covington, Alabama, USA.
- He was recorded in the census in 1920, aged about 24, in Precinct 21, Covington, Alabama, USA.
- He was recorded in the census in 1930, aged about 34, in Carolina, Covington, Alabama, USA.
- He was recorded in the census in 1940, aged about 44, in Election Prect 21 Carolina, Covington, Alabama, USA.
- He died on February 27, 1982, aged 86 years, in Montgomery, Montgomery County, Alabama, USA.
- He was buried in Greenwood Cemetery, Montgomery, Montgomery, Alabama, USA.

129. OBIE LUCILLE WALKER was born on October 4, 1899, in Alabama, USA.
- She was recorded in the census in 1920, aged about 20, in Precinct 21, Covington, Alabama, USA.
- She was recorded in the census in 1930, aged about 30, in Carolina, Covington, Alabama, USA.
- She was recorded in the census in 1940, aged about 40, in Election Prect 21 Carolina, Covington, Alabama, USA.
- She died on May 11, 1988, aged 88 years, in Montgomery, Montgomery, Alabama, USA.
- She was buried in Greenwood Cemetery, Montgomery, Montgomery, Alabam.

Bertie B Bass[128] married Obie Lucille Walker. They had four children:

Lewis W Bass[585] born on November 7, 1916 in Alabama, United States; died on June 28, 1991

Marjorie Bass[587] born about 1922 in Alabama, USA

Mary Elizabeth Bass[589] born on September 9, 1924 in Alabama, USA; died on August 23, 1988

Esther Frances Bass[591] born about 1928 in Alabama, United States; died on September 19, 2007 in Montgomery, Montgomery, Alabama, USA

130. FLORENCE BASS (see Descendants (17)) was born on March 3, 1899, in Alabama, USA, to Bennett Bridges Bass Jr.[20] and Mary Frances Padgett[22].
- She was recorded in the census in 1910, aged about 11, in Fairfield, Covington, Alabama, USA.
- She was recorded in the census in 1920, aged about 21, in Pricint 18 River Falls Town, Covington, Alabama, USA.
- She was recorded in the census in 1930, aged about 31, in Florala, Covington, Alabama, USA.
- She died on January 23, 1955, aged 55 years, in Okaloosa, Florida, USA.
- She was buried in Carolina Baptist Church Cemetery, Carolina, Covington, Alabama, USA.

Florence had three partnerships. She was married to Dennis William Clary[132] and William Thompson[133]. She was also the partner of William Chester Curtis[131].

131. WILLIAM CHESTER CURTIS was born on February 2, 1889, in Medicine Lodge, Barber, Kansas, USA.
    - He was recorded in the census in 1920, aged about 31, in Pricint 18 River Falls Town, Covington, Alabama, USA.
    - He died on April 19, 1953, aged 64 years, in Montgomery, Montgomery, Alabama, USA.
    - He was buried in Liveoak Park Memorial Cemetery, Crestview, Okaloosa, Florida, USA.
    The following information is also recorded for William Chester:
    - Military Service.
    Note: *HQ CO 353 INF 89 DIV - WWI.*
    (Military Service)
    William Chester Curtis and Florence Bass[130] had three children:
    James Harold Curtis[593] born on November 22, 1919 in Covington, Alabama, USA; died on April 7, 1977 in Okaloosa, Florida, USA
    Thelma Olline Curtis[594] born about November 7, 1922 in Alabama, United States
    Clifford M Curtis[596] born on June 13, 1926 in Alabama, United States; died on November 26, 1981
    The following information is also recorded for this family:
    - Unknown Relationship.

132. DENNIS WILLIAM CLARY was born on July 7, 1875, in Alabama, USA.
    - He was recorded in the census in 1930, aged about 54, in Florala, Covington, Alabama, USA.
    - He died on December 28, 1930, aged 55, in Falco, Covington, Alabama, USA.
    - He was buried in Beda Cemetery, Beda, Covington, Alabama, USA.
    Dennis William Clary married Florence Bass[130]. They had three children:
    William D Clary[597] born on January 9, 1925 in Alabama, United States; died on November 12, 1948
    John D Clary[598] born about 1929 in Alabama, United States
    Mary Frances Clary[599]

133. WILLIAM THOMPSON.
    William Thompson married Florence Bass[130].

134. LAWRENCE BASS (see Descendants (17)) was born in March 1899 to Bennett Bridges Bass Jr.[20] and Mary Frances Padgett[22].
    - He was recorded in the census in 1900, aged about 1, in Precincts 2, 6, 18 Fairfield, Loango, River Falls, Covington, Alabama, USA.
    Note: *Records of a Lawrence Bass, born to Bennett "Shug" Bass, where found on the internet through multiple sources but with little information. It is possible he was a twin of Florence since they are usually listed with the same birth month and year. It's also possible that at some point Florence was misinterpreted as Lawrence in a record and the name was added in error.It seems that Florence was listed as Lawrence on the 1900 Census, in error. I have a copy of the Census document. However, that same census says she mothered 14 children with only 11 living, with out Lawrence I only have names for 13.*

135. THOMAS SONNY PADGETT (see Descendants (17)) was born on December 17, 1874, in Covington, Alabama, USA, to Bennett Bridges Bass Jr.[20] and Josiphine Padgett[23]. Thomas Sonny became known as "Sonny".
    - He died on March 3, 1962, aged 87, in Conecuh, Alabama, USA.
    - He was buried in Flat Rock Cemetery, Conecuh, Alabama, USA.
    Note: *Sonny, as he was known, was born to Josephine Paget before she was married to Ephriam Ward. It is believed that his real father was Bennett B. (Shug) Bass (this according to my father, Willie Thermon Padgett). And, as of 2016, the fact that the father of Thomas Sonny was, indeed, Shug Bass has been confirmed by DNA test matches. The DNA results show that I, William. Thomas Padgett is a 2nd or 3rd cousin to several Shug Bass descendants, and the only way that could be is that Shug is my great grandfather! -Tom Padgett.*

136. LOULA JEAN WELCH was born on May 21, 1871, in Covington, Alabama, USA. She died on May 21, 1937, aged 66, in Conecuh, Alabama, USA.
    Thomas Sonny Padgett[135], aged 21, married Loula Jean Welch, aged 25, on June 18, 1896 in Covington, Covington, Alabama, USA. They had six children:
    Marvin Greely Padgett[600] born in 1899 in Alabama, United States; died on March 15, 1943 in Evergreen, Conecuh, Alabama, USA
    Willie Thermon Padgett[601] born on February 9, 1903 in Covington, Alabama, USA; died on October 29, 1984 in Conecuh, Alabama, USA
    Narvi Lee Padgett[605] born in 1905; died in 1971
    Willia Daisy Padgett[606] born on March 21, 1907
    Claude Ray Padgett[607] born on January 2, 1909; died on February 7, 1996 in Conecuh, Alabama, USA
    Clyde Dean Padgett[608] born on August 7, 1916 in Alabama, United States; died on May 10, 1973

137. NANCY A. RAMER (see Descendants) was born in January 1870, in Alabama, United States, to Jake Ramer[25] and Elizabeth Bass[24]. Nancy A. became known as "Nannie".
    - She was recorded in the census in 1900, aged about 30, in Precinct 12 Aiken, Crenshaw, Alabama, USA.

- She was recorded in the census in 1920, aged about 50, in Precinct 12 Aiken And Pleasant Home, Crenshaw, Alabama, USA.
- She died on May 28, 1933, aged 63 years, in Brantley, Crenshaw, Alabama.
- She was buried on May 30, 1933 in Pleasant Home Baptist Church Cemetery, Covington, Alabama, USA.

138. GEORGE W. HART was born in March 1858, in Alabama, United States.
- He was recorded in the census in 1900, aged about 42, in Precinct 12 Aiken, Crenshaw, Alabama, USA.
- He was recorded in the census in 1920, aged about 62, in Precinct 12 Aiken And Pleasant Home, Crenshaw, Alabama, USA.
- He died on April 5, 1933, aged 75 years, in Montgomery, Montgomery, Alabama.
- He was buried in Pleasant Home Baptist Church Cemetery, Covington, Alabama, USA.

George W. Hart, aged about 30, married Nancy A. Ramer[137], aged about 18, about 1888. They had six children:

Grover Cleveland Hart[609] born on June 26, 1888 in Alabama, United States; died on March 17, 1969 in Luverne, Crenshaw, Alabama, USA
Marshall Hart[612] born in February 1892 in Alabama, United States
Ivey W Hart[613] born in May 1893 in Alabama, United States
Ina May Hart[614] born in May 1894 in Alabama, United States
Maggie Hart[615] born in May 1896 in Alabama, United States
Dewey H Hart[616] born in August 1898 in Alabama, United States

139. JOHN RAMER (see Descendants) was born to Jake Ramer[25] and Elizabeth Bass[24].
140. NETTIE PIPPINS.
John Ramer[139] married Nettie Pippins.

141. MARY ELLEN PARRISH (see Descendants (20)) was born on August 7, 1871, in Florida, United States, to George Washington Parrish[27] and Martha Jane Bass[26].
- She was recorded in the census in 1900, aged about 28, in West Bay, Washington, Florida, USA.
- She was recorded in the census in 1910, aged about 38, in Point Washington, Washington, Florida, USA.
- She died on January 10, 1969, aged 97, in Ft. Walton Beach, Okaloosa, Florida, USA.
- She was buried in Marler Memorial Cemetery, Destin, Okaloosa, Florida, USA.

142. LEONARD DESTIN JR. was born on July 6, 1860, in Freeport, Walton, Florida, United States, to Leonard Destin and Martha J McCullom.
- He was recorded in the census in 1900, aged about 39, in West Bay, Washington, Florida, USA.
- He was recorded in the census in 1910, aged about 49, in Point Washington, Washington, Florida, USA.
- He died on November 27, 1916, aged 56, in East Pass, Okaloosa, Florida, USA.
- He was buried in Marler Memorial Cemetery, Destin, Okaloosa, Florida, USA.

Leonard Destin Jr., aged 30, married Mary Ellen Parrish[141], aged 19, on March 18, 1891 in Freeport, Walton, Florida, United States. They had two children:

Mary Ellen Destin[617] born on June 26, 1892 in Florida, United States; died on November 8, 1982
Leonard Destin III[619] born on July 4, 1905 in Walton County, Florida, USA; died on August 5, 1982 in Fort Walton Beach, Okaloosa, Florida, USA

143. EMELINE PARRISH (see Descendants (20)) was born on May 11, 1873, in Niceville, Okaloosa, Florida, United States, to George Washington Parrish[27] and Martha Jane Bass[26]. Emeline became known as "Emma". She died on November 21, 1965, aged 92, in Destin, Okaloosa, Florida, USA.
144. GEORGE SANFORD MARLER was born on April 4, 1873, in Coffee, Alabama, USA. He died on April 21, 1953, aged 80, in Destin, Okaloosa, Florida, USA.

George Sanford Marler, aged about 20, married Emeline Parrish[143], aged about 20, in 1893 in Destin, Okaloosa, Florida, USA. They had three children:

Aquilla Marler[621] born on March 25, 1896 in Destin, Okaloosa, Florida, USA; died on September 19, 1985
Pricilla Marler[623] born on February 5, 1898 in Florida, United States; died on March 15, 1995
Madeline M Marler[625] born on August 16, 1902 in Destin, Okaloosa, Florida, USA; died on September 5, 1986

145. CHARLES W. PARRISH (see Descendants (20)) was born on July 4, 1875, in Niceville, Okaloosa, Florida, United States, to George Washington Parrish[27] and Martha Jane Bass[26].
- He was recorded in the census in 1930, aged about 54, in Niceville, Okaloosa, Florida, USA.

- He was recorded in the census in 1940, aged about 64, in Camp Nine, Elec Prec 14 Niceville, Okaloosa, Florida, USA.
- He died on August 26, 1958, aged 83, in Niceville, Okaloosa, Florida, United States.
- He was buried in Rocky Memorial Cemetery, Niceville, Okaloosa, Florida, USA.

146. LUCY L ETHERIDGE was born on March 29, 1905, in MacClenny, Baker, Florida, USA.
- She was recorded in the census in 1930, aged about 25, in Niceville, Okaloosa, Florida, USA.
- She was recorded in the census in 1940, aged about 35, in Camp Nine, Elec Prec 14 Niceville, Okaloosa, Florida, USA.
- She died on October 16, 2000, aged 95, in Crestview, Okaloosa, Florida, USA.

Charles W. Parrish[145], aged 47, married Lucy L Etheridge, aged 17, on August 16, 1922 in Escambia, Florida, United States.

147. MARTHA JANE PARRISH (see Descendants (20)) was born on January 3, 1878, in Walton, Florida, USA, to George Washington Parrish[27] and Martha Jane Bass[26]. Martha Jane became known as "Mattie".
- She died on September 30, 1968, aged 90, in Niceville, Okaloosa, Florida, United States.
- She was buried in Rocky Memorial Cemetery, Niceville, Okaloosa, Florida, USA.

148. BEALASTER S. SPENCE was born on May 13, 1878, in Glimer County, Georgia, USA. Bealaster S. became known as "Burl".
- He died on December 23, 1938, aged 60, in Niceville, Okaloosa, Florida, United States.
- He was buried in Rocky Memorial Cemetery, Niceville, Okaloosa, Florida, USA.

Bealaster S. Spence, aged 23, married Martha Jane Parrish[147], aged 23, on December 25, 1901 in Walton, Florida, USA.

149. JOHN ROBERT PARRISH (see Descendants (20)) was born on June 8, 1881, in Niceville, Okaloosa, Florida, USA, to George Washington Parrish[27] and Martha Jane Bass[26]. John Robert became known as "Bob".
- He was recorded in the census in 1940, aged about 59, in Camp Nine, Elec Prec 14 Niceville, Okaloosa, Florida, USA.
- He died on April 1, 1951, aged 69, in Niceville, Okaloosa, Florida, United States.
- He was buried in Rocky Memorial Cemetery, Niceville, Okaloosa County, Florida, USA.

150. PATSY MAE SIMMONS was born on December 19, 1902, in Glimer County, Georgia, USA. Patsy Mae became known as "Patsie".
- She was recorded in the census in 1940, aged about 37, in Camp Nine, Elec Prec 14 Niceville, Okaloosa, Florida, USA.
- She died in September 1963, aged 60, in Niceville, Okaloosa, Florida, United States.
- She was buried in Rocky Memorial Cemetery, Niceville, Okaloosa County, Florida, USA.

John Robert Parrish[149], aged 38, married Patsy Mae Simmons, aged 16, on December 2, 1919 in New Orleans, Jefferson, Louisiana, USA. They had one son:
> Bobbie Parrish[627] born about 1924 in Florida, USA

151. CAPT. TOLBERT TILLIS PARRISH (see Descendants (20)) was born on September 6, 1883, in Walton, Florida, USA, to George Washington Parrish[27] and Martha Jane Bass[26]. He died on April 2, 1915, aged 31, in Honduras.
Note: *Lost At Sea Off The Coast of Honduras.*
(Death)

152. LAURA L. BROWN was born in September 1883, in Walton, Florida, USA. She died on April 2, 1915, aged 31, in Honduras.
Note: *Lost At Sea Off The Coast of Honduras.*
(Death)

Tolbert Tillis Parrish[151], aged about 17, married Laura L. Brown, aged about 17, in 1901 in Walton, Florida, USA.

153. FANNY A. PARRISH (see Descendants (20)) was born on December 4, 1885, in Walton, Florida, USA, to George Washington Parrish[27] and Martha Jane Bass[26]. She died on April 11, 1887, aged 1, in Walton, Florida, USA.

154. LEANNA PARRISH (see Descendants (20)) was born on September 6, 1888, in Boggy Bayou, Walton, Florida, USA, to George Washington Parrish[27] and Martha Jane Bass[26]. Leanna became known as "Anna". She died on July 25, 1988, aged 99, in Pensacola, Escambia, Florida, USA.

155. JAMES OTTIS GUNTER was born on September 26, 1885, in Aiken County, South Carolina, USA. He died on March 27, 1970, aged 84, in Pensacola, Escambia, Florida, USA.

James Ottis Gunter, aged 28, married Leanna Parrish[154], aged 25, on October 21, 1913 in Escambia, Florida, United States. They had two children:
> Charles Clyde Gunter[628]
> Otto Lee Gunter[629]

Direct Relations

156. ELLA PARRISH (see Descendants (20)) was born on March 27, 1892, in Glimer, Georgia, USA, to George Washington Parrish[27] and Martha Jane Bass[26].
- She died on November 26, 1974, aged 82, in Pensacola, Escambia, Florida, USA.
- She was buried in Saint John's Cemetery, Pensacola, Escambia, Florida, USA.

157. CAPT. JAMES E JERAULD was born on December 19, 1888, in Peoria, Peoria, Illinois, USA.
- He died on July 22, 1970, aged 81, in Pensacola, Escambia, Florida, USA.
- He was buried in Saint John's Cemetery, Pensacola, Escambia, Florida, USA.

James E Jerauld married Ella Parrish[156]. They had one son:
James E Jerauld Jr.[630] born on July 2, 1915; died on October 21, 1933

158. CAPT. JAMES ALBERT PARRISH (see Descendants (20)) was born on August 10, 1895, in Niceville, Okaloosa, Florida, USA, to George Washington Parrish[27] and Martha Jane Bass[26].
- He was recorded in the census in 1920, aged about 24, in Okaloosa, Florida, USA.
- He was recorded in the census in 1940, aged about 44, in Grey Moss Point, Elec Prec 14 Niceville, Okaloosa, Florida, USA.
- He died on October 18, 1985, aged 90, in Niceville, Okaloosa, Florida, United States.
- He was buried.

159. MAGGIE LOU ETHERIDGE was born on July 23, 1892, in Troy, Pike, Alabama, United States.
- She was recorded in the census in 1920, aged about 27, in Okaloosa, Florida, USA.
- She was recorded in the census in 1940, aged about 47, in Grey Moss Point, Elec Prec 14 Niceville, Okaloosa, Florida, USA.
- She died on February 8, 1962, aged 69, in Niceville, Okaloosa, Florida, USA.
- She was buried in Niceville, Okaloosa, Florida, USA.

James Albert Parrish[158], aged 21, married Maggie Lou Etheridge, aged 24, on March 8, 1917 in Niceville, Okaloosa, Florida, United States. They had three children:
Genevieve Parrish[631] born in February 1918 in Florida, United States
Geraldine Parrish[633] born in November 1919 in Florida, United States; died in 2000
James Albert Parrish Jr.[635] born on October 30, 1923 in Niceville, Okaloosa, Florida, United States; died on February 8, 2008 in Niceville, Okaloosa, Florida, United States

160. MARY ELIZABETH BASS (see Descendants (21)) was born on October 16, 1878, in Andalusia, Covington, Alabama, USA, to William Riley Bass[28] and Nancy Jane Ward[29]. Mary Elizabeth became known as "Lizzy".
- She was recorded in the census in 1880, aged about 1, in Harts And Red Level, Covington, Alabama, USA.
- She was recorded in the census in 1900, aged about 21, in Precincts 10, 19 Hart, George, Covington, Alabama, USA.
- She was recorded in the census in 1930, aged about 51, in Hart, Covington, Alabama, USA.
- She was recorded in the census in 1940, aged about 61, in Precinct 10 Hart, Covington, Alabama, USA.
- She was recorded in the census on April 1, 1950, aged 71, in Boggon Level to Open Pond Rd. on Hyw on 88, Hart, Covington, Alabama, United States.
- She died on July 8, 1974, aged 95 years, in Andalusia, Covington, Alabama, USA.
- She was buried on July 10, 1974 in Zion Rock Cemetery, Beda, Covington, Alabama, USA.

161. JAMES HILLARD CASON was born on November 15, 1879, in Quewhiffle Township, Cumberland, North Carolina, USA. James Hillard became known as "Jim".
- He was recorded in the census in 1930, aged about 50, in Hart, Covington, Alabama, USA.
- He was recorded in the census in 1940, aged about 60, in Precinct 10 Hart, Covington, Alabama, USA.
- He died on June 4, 1946, aged 66 years.
- He was buried in Zion Rock Cemetery, Beda, Covington, Alabama, USA.

Note: *James Hillary Cason, aged 67, whose body was recovered from Yellow River Friday, June 14th, drowned June 4th. He is survived by his wife, Mrs. Mary F. Cason, two daughters, Mrs. Florence Smith, Andalusia Route One, Mrs. Zonie Bell Raley, Therosa, Fla., four sons, Coleman, Charles, and J.P. Cason, all of Andalusia Route 1, Grady J. Cason, U.S. Army. One sister, Mrs. Catherine Cason, Andalusia Route 1, and 16 grandchildren. Funeral Services were held at Zion Rock Church Friday at 10 a.m. with Rev. G.H.-officiating. Pallbearers were-Floyd and Autrey B-, Samuel and Daniel Barrow and L.A. Stokes. Burial was in the church cemetery with Benson Funeral Homes in charge.*
(Death)

James Hillard Cason, aged 29, married Mary Elizabeth Bass[160], aged 30, on January 10, 1909. They had six children:
Mary Florence Cason[637] born on November 29, 1909 in Alabama, United States; died on December 18, 1996
Zonnie Bell Cason[639] born on December 8, 1911 in Alabama, United States

William Charles Cason[641] born on September 29, 1913 in Covington, Alabama, USA; died on May 4, 1990 in Alabama, USA
Grady J. Cason[643] born on September 25, 1915 in Alabama, United States; died in April 1980
John F. Cason[645] born on July 25, 1917 in Andalusia, Covington, Alabama, United States; died on March 4, 2005 in Robertsdale, Baldwin, Alabama, United States
Coleman R. Cason[647] born on November 16, 1919 in Andalusia, Covington, Alabama, United States; died on May 23, 1987 in Covington, Alabama, United States

162. WILLIAM HENRY BASS (see Descendants (21)) was born on January 6, 1880, in Alabama, United States, to William Riley Bass[28] and Nancy Jane Ward[29].
- He was recorded in the census in 1880, aged 0, in Harts And Red Level, Covington, Alabama, USA.
- He was recorded in the census in 1900, aged about 20, in Precincts 10, 19 Hart, George, Covington, Alabama, USA.
- He was recorded in the census in 1920, aged about 40, in Precinct 21, Covington, Alabama, USA.
- He was recorded in the census in 1940, aged about 60, in Precinct 10 Hart, Covington, Alabama, USA.
- He was recorded in the census on April 1, 1950, aged 70, in Beda Church Road to Boggon Level, Hart, Covington, Alabama, United States.
- He died on February 15, 1970, aged 90 years.
- He was buried in Zion Rock Cemetery, Beda, Covington, Alabama, USA.

The following information is also recorded for William Henry:
Injury.
Notes:
- *William Henry Bass is listed on the 1880 Census as "Not Named" with an age of 5/12. The 5/12 indicates 5 out of 12 months, so William seems to have spent the first several months of his life without a name.*
- *I met him once or twice when I was a kid, he used to scare the snot out of me! He was so strong, when he hugged me, I thought he was going to break my ribs! - Lisa Uptagrafft.*
- *Lost an arm.*
  (Injury)
- *My Mom, Henrys daughter Beatrice, told me that he lost his hand when he threw some dynamite in the river to stun some fish then you go and pick the fish up. This one time the dynamite didn't go off, and he went back and picked up the dynamite and it exploded in his hand. - Margaret Bozeman.*
  (Injury)

163. DORA ALICE PURVIS was born on December 15, 1891, in Florida, United States.
- She was recorded in the census in 1920, aged about 28, in Precinct 21, Covington, Alabama, USA.
- She was recorded in the census in 1940, aged about 48, in Precinct 10 Hart, Covington, Alabama, USA.
- She was recorded in the census on April 1, 1950, aged 58, in Beda Church Road to Boggon Level, Hart, Covington, Alabama, United States.
- She died in 1961, aged about 69.
- She was buried in Zion Rock Cemetery, Beda, Covington, Alabama, USA.

William Henry Bass[162], aged 29, married Dora Alice Purvis, aged 17, on April 25, 1909. They had ten children:
Veilla Maine Bass[650] born on March 7, 1912 in Alabama, United States; died on October 2, 1995
Leilla Mae Bass[652] born on February 7, 1914 in Covington, Alabama, USA; died on August 31, 1998
Henry Grady Bass[655] born on November 21, 1915 in Alabama, United States; died in June 1982 in Missouri, USA
Clyde Kermit Bass Sr.[657] born on February 1, 1918 in Alabama, United States; died on June 28, 1961 in Birmingham, Jefferson, Alabama, USA
Beatrice Izora Bass[659] born on August 14, 1921 in Alabama, USA
Mary Bonnie Bass[661] born on June 6, 1924 in Alabama, USA; died on October 5, 1992
Floyd Irwin Bass[663] born on March 26, 1926 in Alabama, USA; died on October 26, 2009
Autray Alto Bass[665] born on April 3, 1928 in Alabama, USA; died on May 20, 2012
Fannie Esther Bass[667] born on November 10, 1931 in Alabama, USA; died on April 3, 2018 in Covington, Alabama, USA
Nannie Ruth Bass[669] born on August 8, 1934 in Alabama, USA

164. CATHERINE EMMA BASS (see Descendants (21)) was born on October 26, 1881, in Alabama, United States, to William Riley Bass[28] and Nancy Jane Ward[29]. Catherine Emma became known as "Emmer".
- She was recorded in the census in 1900, aged about 18, in Precincts 10, 19 Hart, George, Covington, Alabama, USA.
- She was recorded in the census in 1910, aged about 28, in Hart, Covington, Alabama, USA.
- She was recorded in the census in 1920, aged about 38, in Okaloosa, Florida, USA.
- She was recorded in the census in 1930, aged about 48, in Carolina, Covington, Alabama, USA.

- She was recorded in the census in 1940, aged about 58, in Open Pond Road, Election Precinct 7 Watkins, Covington, Alabama, USA.
- She was recorded in the census on April 1, 1950, aged 68, in Mt Olive Church Road, Blackman, Okaloosa, Florida, United States.
- She died on August 18, 1951, aged 69 years.
- She was buried in Carolina Baptist Church Cemetery, Covington, Alabama, USA.

165. ELZY HENDERSON GARVIN was born on May 4, 1880, in South Carolina, United States. Elzy Henderson became known as "Elzy".
- He was recorded in the census in 1910, aged about 30, in Hart, Covington, Alabama, USA.
- He was recorded in the census in 1920, aged about 40, in Okaloosa, Florida, USA.
- He was recorded in the census in 1930, aged about 50, in Carolina, Covington, Alabama, USA.
- He was recorded in the census in 1940, aged about 60, in Open Pond Road, Election Precinct 7 Watkins, Covington, Alabama, USA.
- He was recorded in the census on April 1, 1950, aged 69, in Mt Olive Church Road, Blackman, Okaloosa, Florida, United States.
- He died on November 19, 1956, aged 76 years.
- He was buried in Carolina Baptist Church Cemetery, Covington, Alabama, USA.

Elzy Henderson Garvin, aged 28, married Catherine Emma Bass[164], aged 27, on March 6, 1909 in Covington, Alabama, USA. They had five children:
Nancy Christian Garvin[671] born on February 24, 1911 in Alabama, United States; died on September 11, 1994
Willier Garvin[673] born on December 3, 1914 in Alabama, United States; died on November 25, 2003
Sherman Garvin[675] born on January 18, 1917 in Alabama, United States; died on February 7, 2006
Ollie Garvin[677] born on March 16, 1919 in Alabama, United States; died on September 2, 1987
Odessa Garvin[678] born on February 26, 1923 in Alabama, United States

166. SAVANNAH BASS (see Descendants (21)) was born on September 11, 1884, in Alabama, United States, to William Riley Bass[28] and Nancy Jane Ward[29].
- She was recorded in the census in 1900, aged about 15, in Precincts 10, 19 Hart, George, Covington, Alabama, USA.
- She was recorded in the census in 1920, aged about 35, in Precinct 21, Covington, Alabama, USA.
- She was recorded in the census in 1930, aged about 45, in Hart, Covington, Alabama, USA.
- She was recorded in the census on April 1, 1950, aged 65, in 28 Seminale Ave., Lockhart, Covington, Alabama, United States.
- She died on November 20, 1970, aged 86 years, in Lockhart, Covington, Alabama, USA.
- She was buried on November 24, 1970 in Carolina Baptist Church Cemetery, Andalusia, Covington, Alabama, USA.

167. JAMES OCIE POSEY was born on February 7, 1887, in South Carolina, United States, to Elias H Posey and Vianah Catherine Horsie.
- He was recorded in the census in 1900, aged about 13, in Precincts 2, 6, 18 Fairfield, Loango, River Falls, Covington, Alabama, USA.
- He was recorded in the census in 1920, aged about 33, in Precinct 21, Covington, Alabama, USA.
- He was recorded in the census in 1930, aged about 43, in Hart, Covington, Alabama, USA.
- He died on May 22, 1949, aged 60 years, in Lockhart, Covington, Alabama, USA.
- He was buried on May 24, 1949 in Carolina Baptist Church Cemetery, Andalusia, Alabama, USA.

James Ocie Posey, aged 21, married Savannah Bass[166], aged 23, on March 22, 1908. They had six children:
Cora Nolia Posey[680] born on January 1, 1909 in Covington, Alabama, USA; died on January 17, 1996 in Panama City, Bay, Florida, USA
Pearlie Mae Posey[682] born on September 10, 1911 in Covington, Alabama, USA; died on April 17, 1933 in Okaloosa, Florida, USA
Gussie Lee Posey[684] born on April 3, 1914 in Alabama, United States; died on March 20, 1999 in Fort Walton Beach, Okaloosa, Florida, USA
Mary Francis Posey[686] born on October 8, 1916 in Andalusia, Covington, Alabama, USA; died on September 16, 1999
William Albert Posey[688] born on January 4, 1920 in Alabama, United States; died on May 19, 1951 in Montgomery, Montgomery, Alabama, USA
Vianna Catherine Posey[690] born on April 30, 1922 in Covington, Alabama, USA; died on January 3, 2005 in Lakeland, Polk, Florida, USA

168. NANCY JANE BASS (see Descendants (21)) was born on February 6, 1886, in Alabama, USA, to William Riley Bass[28] and Nancy Jane Ward[29]. Nancy Jane became known as "Jennie".
- She was recorded in the census in 1900, aged about 14, in Precincts 10, 19 Hart, George, Covington, Alabama, USA.

- She was recorded in the census in 1930, aged about 44, in Watkins, Covington, Alabama, USA.
- She died on November 13, 1959, aged 73 years, in Walton County, Florida, USA.
- She was buried in Shiloh Cemetery, Florala, Covington, Alabama, USA.

169. **LESLIE RILEY EDWARDS SR.** was born on February 10, 1883, in Hartsville, Darlington, South Carolina, United States, to Elson Julian Edwards and Martha Jane Jones. Leslie Riley became known as "Les".
- He was recorded in the census in 1930, aged about 47, in Watkins, Covington, Alabama, USA.
- He was recorded in the census in 1935, aged about 52, in Laurel Hill, Okaloosa, Florida.
- He died on April 26, 1944, aged 61 years, in Laurel Hill, Okaloosa, Florida, USA.
- He was buried in Shiloh Cemetery, Andalusia, Covington, Alabama, USA.

Leslie Riley Edwards Sr., aged 24, married Nancy Jane Bass[168], aged 21, on August 4, 1907 in Covington, Alabama, USA. They had eight children:

Josephine E Edwards[692] born on June 4, 1908 in Covington, Alabama, United States; died on March 27, 1993 in Crestview, Okaloosa, Florida, United States
Janie Edwards[694] born on May 13, 1910 in Florala, Covington, Alabama, USA
Rossa Edwards[696] born on January 8, 1912 in Florala, Covington, Alabama, USA; died on June 2, 1988
Harry Edwards[699] born on March 11, 1915 in Florala, Covington, Alabama, USA
Early Edwards[701] born on December 16, 1916 in Florala, Covington, Alabama, USA
Murry Edwards[703] born about 1922 in Alabama, United States
Correne Edwards[704] born about 1927 in Alabama, United States
Ervin Hartley Edwards[706] born on November 9, 1928 in Alabama, United States

170. **MINNIE JOSEPHINE BASS** (see Descendants (21)) was born on March 31, 1888, in Alabama, United States, to William Riley Bass[28] and Nancy Jane Ward[29].
- She was recorded in the census in 1900, aged about 12, in Precincts 10, 19 Hart, George, Covington, Alabama, USA.
- She was recorded in the census in 1910, aged about 22, in Hart, Covington, Alabama, USA.
- She was recorded in the census in 1920, aged about 32, in Precinct 21, Covington, Alabama, USA.
- She died (Accident) on October 16, 1924, aged 36 years, in Covington, Alabama.
- She was buried on October 17, 1924 in Carolina Baptist Church Cemetery, Covington, Alabama, USA.

Note: *Minnie Josephine died at around 36 years of age, possibly in an accident involving a logging train. She reportedly suffered from some type of disability.*

171. **FLORENCE BASS** (see Descendants (21)) was born on January 1, 1890, in Covington, Alabama, USA, to William Riley Bass[28] and Nancy Jane Ward[29].
- She was recorded in the census in 1900, aged about 10, in Precincts 10, 19 Hart, George, Covington, Alabama, USA.
- She was recorded in the census in 1910, aged about 20, in Hart, Covington, Alabama, USA.
- She was recorded in the census in 1920, aged about 30, in Precinct 21, Covington, Alabama, USA.
- She was recorded in the census in 1930, aged about 40, in Carolina, Covington, Alabama, USA.
- She was recorded in the census in 1940, aged about 50, in Beat 21 Carolina, Covington, Alabama, USA.
- She was recorded in the census on April 1, 1950, aged 60, in 40 Osage Ave, Lockhart, Covington, Alabama, United States.
- She died on January 23, 1982, aged 92 years.
- She was buried in Shady Hill Church Cemetery.

Notes:
- *Florence never married, her "sister" said "she did love one man but her father didn't like him and ran him off. She never dated again." - Not sure which sister.*
- *Spent a lot of time caring for her mother after her health began to fail. Later Florence was very close with her sister Mattie O. Bass Johnson, especially after she was widowed.*

172. **RILEY JOHN BASS** (see Descendants (21)) was born on January 2, 1892, in Alabama, United States, to William Riley Bass[28] and Nancy Jane Ward[29].
- He was recorded in the census in 1900, aged about 8, in Precincts 10, 19 Hart, George, Covington, Alabama, USA.
- He was recorded in the census in 1910, aged about 18, in Hart, Covington, Alabama, USA.
- He was recorded in the census in 1920, aged about 28, in Precinct 21, Covington, Alabama, USA.
- He was recorded in the census in 1930, aged about 38, in Hart, Covington, Alabama, USA.
- He died on December 16, 1979, aged 87 years.
- He was buried in Zion Rock Cemetery.

The following information is also recorded for Riley John:
- Military Service.
- Description: TallSlenderBlackBrownFrom WWI Draft Card.

Notes:
- *The way I heard it, while in France, Bennett heard a familiar voice and knew exactly who it was. He jumped up on a nearby stump and started hollering, Riley Bass! Before too long, Riley Bass was hollering back, and come to join Bennett at the stump. Two brothers, so far from home, found each other during a war on another continent.*
- U.S. Army WWI.
  (Military Service)

173. MAGGIE SMITH was born on March 26, 1903, in Alabama, United States.
- She was recorded in the census in 1930, aged about 27, in Hart, Covington, Alabama, USA.
- She died on August 27, 1991, aged 88 years.
- She was buried in Zion Rock Cemetery.

    Riley John Bass[172] married Maggie Smith '5th Sunday in Feb'. They had six children:
    Wylene Bass[708] born about 1921 in Alabama, United States
    Myrtice Bass[710] born about 1923 in Alabama, United States
    Hiram J Bass[712] born on June 7, 1924 in Alabama, United States; died on January 13, 1997
    Clinton Albert Bass[714] born on April 11, 1926 in Alabama, United States; died on December 26, 2020 in Andalusia, Covington, Alabama, USA
    Gordon L. Bass[716] born on September 4, 1931; died on March 14, 1982
    Wayne Bass[718]

174. JAMES BENNETT BASS (see Descendants (21)) was born on March 23, 1893, in Alabama, United States, to William Riley Bass[28] and Nancy Jane Ward[29].
- He was recorded in the census in 1900, aged about 7, in Precincts 10, 19 Hart, George, Covington, Alabama, USA.
- He was recorded in the census in 1910, aged about 17, in Hart, Covington, Alabama, USA.
- He was recorded in the census in 1920, aged about 27, in Precinct 21, Covington, Alabama, USA.
- He was recorded in the census in 1930, aged about 37, in Carolina, Covington, Alabama, USA.
- He was recorded in the census in 1940, aged about 47, in Election Prect 21 Carolina, Covington, Alabama, USA.
- He was a Farmer.
- He was recorded in the census on April 1, 1950, aged 57, in Carolina, Covington, Alabama, United States.
- He died (Cancer) on June 4, 1962, aged 69 years, in Carolina Community, Covington, Alabama, USA.
- He was buried in 1962 in Shady Hill Church Cemetery, Covington, Alabama, USA.

The following information is also recorded for James Bennett:
- Military Service.
- Description: MediumMediumBlackBlueFrom WWI draft card.

Notes:
- *J. Bennett Bass, while in the army during WWI, served in an engineering company working supply lines. His sons usually add that it was the most dangerous job you could have, and there is some merit to that view.*

The way I heard it, while in France, Bennett heard a familiar voice and knew exactly who it was. He jumped up on a nearby stump and started hollering, Riley Bass! Before too long, Riley Bass was hollering back, and come to join Bennett at the stump. Two brothers, so far from home, found each other during a war on another continent.
- U.S. Army WWI.
  (Military Service)

175. FLARA ANNIE ROWELL was born on February 9, 1908, in Alabama, USA, to Alonzo Franklin Rowell and Mattie Virginia Jordan.
- She was recorded in the census in 1910, aged about 2, in Hart, Covington, Alabama, USA.
- She was recorded in the census in 1920, aged about 12, in Precinct 21, Covington, Alabama, USA.
- She was recorded in the census in 1930, aged about 22, in Carolina, Covington, Alabama, USA.
- She was recorded in the census in 1940, aged about 32, in Election Prect 21 Carolina, Covington, Alabama, USA.
- She was recorded in the census on April 1, 1950, aged 42, in Carolina, Covington, Alabama, United States.
- She died (Natural / Old Age) in October 1986, aged 78 years, in Carolina Community, Covington, Alabama, USA.
- She was buried in Shady Hill Church Cemetery, Covington, Alabama, USA.

Notes:
- *When these ladies were younger, Hazel, Wavie, Granny, and Eunice would be cooking or cleaning the kitchen. They would be singing beautiful hymns while they happily worked together. - Wanda Barnes [Bass].*
- *I alway thought being at Grannie was special. After I got drivers license she would ask me to drive her to visit her children (my aunts and uncles) in Auburn and Fort Rucker. I was always thrilled to do so. She taught me so much about life. -Ricky Bass.*
- *Oh, so many memories when we (cousins) stayed with her. One memory: Granny took all us girls to Hogfoot to swim. We were in the white Mustang. Diane, Charlotte and Lisa were having a sibling argument in the back seat.*

Granny kept turning around trying to stop the arguing. We ended up in the ditch. Granny was pretty upset. I can't remember how we got out of the ditch. When we went to town, or anywhere, Granny would kneel by her car a pray, aloud, that we would have a safe trip. She was a saint - Jan Kinsaul [Bass].

- *Aunt Flara. She used to give me a few 22 bullets to shoot rabbits from the garden when I was a boy. It was like I was big game hunting! Always good to me. -Robert Wilcox.*

James Bennett Bass[174], aged 33, married Flara Annie Rowell, aged 19, on March 11, 1927 in Andalusia, Covington, Alabama, USA. They had nine children:

- Bruce James Bass[720] born on May 7, 1927 in Carolina Community, Covington, Alabama, USA; died on July 23, 1988 in Andalusa, Alabama, USA
- Eunice Bass[723] born on February 24, 1929 in Covington, Alabama, USA; died on May 30, 2022 in Brewton, Escambia, Alabama, USA
- Ralph Caephus Bass[725] born on May 20, 1931 in Alabama, USA; died on October 19, 2019 in Carolina Community, Covington, Alabama, USA
- Edd Bass[727] born on April 28, 1933 in Carolina Community, Covington, Alabama, USA; died on December 20, 2016 in Andalusia, Covington, Alabama, USA
- Wavie Lee Bass[729] born on February 14, 1935 in Carolina Community, Covington, Alabama, USA
- Hazel Bass[731] born on November 19, 1936 in Carolina Community, Covington, Alabama, USA; died on April 25, 2023
- Herman Bass[733] born on November 29, 1939 in Carolina Community, Covington, Alabama, USA
- Coy Bennett Bass[735] born on August 4, 1942 in Carolina Community, Covington, Alabama, USA
- Franklin Jerry ("Franky") Bass[737] born on August 1, 1944 in Andalusia, Covington, Alabama, USA

176. CHARLES BASS (see Descendants (21)) was born on March 19, 1896 to William Riley Bass[28] and Nancy Jane Ward[29]. He died (Accident) before 1900, when younger than 3.

Note: *There is a story that Charles Bass, son of William Riley and Nancy Bass [Ward], Who died at a young age. Saying that he was burned in an accident that involved the making cane syrup. This lines up with Charles not being on any of the census records that I have found.*

177. MATTIE O. BASS (see Descendants (21)) was born on August 16, 1897, in Covington, Alabama, USA, to William Riley Bass[28] and Nancy Jane Ward[29].
    - She was recorded in the census in 1900, aged about 2, in Precincts 10, 19 Hart, George, Covington, Alabama, USA.
    - She was recorded in the census in 1910, aged about 12, in Hart, Covington, Alabama, USA.
    - She was recorded in the census in 1920, aged about 22, in Precinct 21, Covington, Alabama, USA.
    - She was recorded in the census on April 1, 1950, aged 52, in 40 Osage Ave, Lockhart, Covington, Alabama, United States.
    - She died on December 8, 1977, aged 80 years, in Colbert, Alabama, USA.
    - She was buried in Beda Cemetery, Andalusia, Alabama, United States.

178. JOHN HENRY JOHNSON was born on March 11, 1884, in Monroe, Alabama, USA.
    - He died on January 29, 1940, aged 55 years, in Falco, Covington, Alabama, USA.
    - He was buried in Beda Cemetery, Andalusia, Alabama, United States.

    John Henry Johnson married Mattie O. Bass[177]. They had three children:
    - Dudley Sadie Johnson[739] born in May 1925 in Andalusia, Covington, Alabama, USA; died on December 8, 1987 in Texas, USA
    - Kenneth Ray Johnson[741] born on December 10, 1927 in Covington, Alabama, USA; died on October 17, 2016
    - Monia Ruth Johnson[743] born on October 4, 1930 in Covington, Alabama, USA; died on December 2, 1931 in Covington, Alabama, USA

179. FLORA BASS (see Descendants (21)) was born on April 30, 1899, in Alabama, United States, to William Riley Bass[28] and Nancy Jane Ward[29].
    - She was recorded in the census in 1910, aged about 11, in Hart, Covington, Alabama, USA.
    - She was recorded in the census in 1930, aged about 31, in Florala, Covington, Alabama, USA.
    - She was recorded in the census in 1940, aged about 41, in Beat 21 Carolina, Covington, Alabama, USA.
    - She died in 1981, aged about 82.

180. QUILLIE JACKSON was born on June 2, 1901, in Alabama, United States, to Jim Jackson and Arlina Jackson.
    - He was recorded in the census in 1910, aged about 9, in Opp, Covington, Alabama, USA.
    - He was recorded in the census in 1920, aged about 19, in Precinct 13, Covington, Alabama, USA.
    - He was recorded in the census in 1930, aged about 29, in Florala, Covington, Alabama, USA.
    - He was recorded in the census in 1940, aged about 39, in Beat 21 Carolina, Covington, Alabama, USA.
    - He died on August 9, 1959, aged 58 years, in Opelika, Lee, Alabama, United States.

Quillie married twice. He was married to Martha Coon and Flora Bass[179].

Quillie Jackson, aged 22, married Martha Coon, aged about 21, on September 16, 1923 in Covington, Alabama.
Quillie Jackson, aged 25, married Flora Bass[179], aged 27, on March 6, 1927 in Covington, Alabama, United States. They had five children:
> Hollis Mitchell Jackson Sr.[744] born on November 1, 1925 in Alabama, USA; died on February 22, 1961 in Opelika, Lee, Alabama, United States
> Horris Carson Jackson[746] born on March 23, 1929 in Opelika, Lee, Alabama, USA; died on February 20, 2019 in Opelika, Lee, Alabama, USA
> Hillary Dalton Jackson[748] born about 1932 in Alabama, USA; died in 2014
> Haward James Jackson[751] born on April 29, 1934 in Alabama, USA; died on April 9, 2018
> Florine Jackson Jackson[753] born on December 14, 1936 in Alabama, USA

181. **FLORINE DOROTHY BASS** (see Descendants (21)) was born on April 30, 1899, in Covington, Alabama, USA, to William Riley Bass[28] and Nancy Jane Ward[29]. Florine Dorothy became known as "Dora".
    - She was recorded in the census in 1900, aged about 1, in Precincts 10, 19 Hart, George, Covington, Alabama, USA.
    - She was recorded in the census in 1910, aged about 11, in Hart, Covington, Alabama, USA.
    - She was recorded in the census in 1920, aged about 21, in Precinct 21, Covington, Alabama, USA.
    - She was recorded in the census in 1930, aged about 31, in Opp, Covington, Alabama, USA.
    - She was recorded in the census in 1940, aged about 41, in Election Precinct No 3 Beaver Creek, Okaloosa, Florida, USA.
    - She died (Natural / Old Age) on February 18, 1981, aged 81 years, in Covington, Alabama, USA.
    - She was buried in Shady Hill Church Cemetery, Covington, Alabama, USA.
182. **EVERETT STANLEY MURPHY** was born on October 26, 1910, in Alabama, United States.
    - He was recorded in the census in 1930, aged about 19, in Opp, Covington, Alabama, USA.
    - He was recorded in the census in 1940, aged about 29, in Election Precinct No 3 Beaver Creek, Okaloosa, Florida, USA.
    - He died on October 7, 1966, aged 55 years.
    - He was buried in Liveoak Park Memorial Cemetery, Crestview, Okaloosa, USA (Garden of Comfort Section).

    The following information is also recorded for Everett Stanley:
    - Military Service.

    Note: *Sgt Btry 603 Coast Arty, WWII.*
    (Military Service)

    Everett Stanley Murphy married Florine Dorothy Bass[181]. They had five children:
    > Dorthy E. Murphy[755] born on March 20, 1929 in Alabama, United States; died on August 26, 2003
    > Charles Alton Murphy[757] born on January 11, 1931 in Covington, Alabama, USA; died on December 13, 2017 in Covington, Alabama, USA
    > Lilly May Murphy[759] born on May 15, 1933 in Covington, Alabama, USA; died on May 1, 1935 in Covington, Alabama, USA
    > Bobby Euell Murphy[760] born on May 14, 1939 in Covington, Alabama, USA; died on June 21, 1956 in Hampton, South Carolina, USA
    > Edna Earl Murphy[761] born on October 20, 1944

183. **LILLIE MAY BASS** (see Descendants (21)) was born on January 25, 1902, in Alabama, United States, to William Riley Bass[28] and Nancy Jane Ward[29].
    - She was recorded in the census in 1910, aged about 8, in Hart, Covington, Alabama, USA.
    - She was recorded in the census in 1920, aged about 18, in Precinct 21, Covington, Alabama, USA.
    - She died (At young age) on April 3, 1925, aged 23 years.
    - She was buried in Carolina Baptist Church Cemetery.

    Note: *Probably during child birth.*
    (Death)
184. **T. LABAN CROSBY**.
    T. Laban Crosby married Lillie May Bass[183]. They had one daughter:
    > Baby Crosby[763] born about 1926; died about 1926

185. **MARGARET JANE WARD** (see Descendants) was born on July 18, 1875, in Texas, USA, to William Forman Ward[31] and Jane Padgett[30].
    - She was recorded in the census in 1880, aged about 4, in Falls, Texas, USA.
    - She was recorded in the census in 1910, aged about 34, in Justice Precinct 7, Falls, Texas, USA.
    - She died on June 4, 1955, aged 79 years.
186. **OSCAR H. REEVES** was born on November 7, 1873, in Georgia, USA.
    - He was recorded in the census in 1910, aged about 36, in Justice Precinct 7, Falls, Texas, USA.
    - He died on June 4, 1955, aged 81 years.

Oscar H. Reeves, aged about 19, married Margaret Jane Ward[185], aged about 17, about 1893 in Falls County, TX, USA. They had four children:
> William Reeves[764] born about 1897 in Texas, United States
> Priscilla Reeves[765] born about 1901 in Texas, United States
> Johnnie Reeves[766] born about 1905 in Texas, United States
> Oscar B Reeves[767] born about 1907 in Texas, United States

187. NANCY G. GODWIN (see Descendants (23)) was born in 1869 to Samuel Godwin[34] and Levinta Padgett[33].

188. LUCY GODWIN (see Descendants (23)) was born in 1871 to Samuel Godwin[34] and Levinta Padgett[33].

189. IDA JORDAN (see Descendants (23)) was born in 1877 to Robert Francis Jordan[35] and Levinta Padgett[33].

190. HENRY JORDAN (see Descendants (23)) was born in 1879 to Robert Francis Jordan[35] and Levinta Padgett[33].

191. DELLA JORDAN (see Descendants (24)) was born on June 12, 1882, in Texas, USA, to John Elbert Jordan[37] and Elizabeth H. Padgett[36].
- She was recorded in the census in 1900, aged about 18, in Lott town, Falls, Texas, USA.
- She was recorded in the census in 1920, aged about 38, in Falls, Texas, USA.
- She was recorded in the census in 1940, aged about 58, in 5th St, Lott, Precinct No 4, Falls, Texas, USA.
- She died on March 2, 1953, aged 70 years.
- She was buried in Clover Hill Cemetery, Lott, Falls, Texas, USA.

192. THOMAS RUEBEN ROBERTS was born on September 21, 1880, in Texas, United States. Thomas Rueben became known as "Tom".
- He was recorded in the census in 1920, aged about 39, in Falls, Texas, USA.
- He was recorded in the census in 1940, aged about 59, in 5th St, Lott, Precinct No 4, Falls, Texas, USA.
- He died on April 11, 1949, aged 68 years.
- He was buried in Clover Hill Cemetery, Lott, Texas, USA.

Thomas Rueben Roberts married Della Jordan[191]. They had three children:
> Thomas H Roberts[768] born about 1904 in Texas, United States
> Mary K Roberts[769] born about 1907 in Texas, United States
> Marguerite E Roberts[770] born about 1911 in Texas, United States

193. MARY JORDAN (see Descendants (24)) was born in August 1885, in Texas, United States, to John Elbert Jordan[37] and Elizabeth H. Padgett[36].
- She was recorded in the census in 1900, aged about 14, in Lott town, Falls, Texas, USA.

194. JAMES WILLIAM HART (see Descendants (25)) was born on December 3, 1873, in Covington, Alabama, USA, to Columbus Daniel Hart[39] and Nancy Ann Padgett[38]. James William became known as "Jim".
- He was recorded in the census in 1880, aged about 6, in Harts And Red Level, Covington, Alabama, USA.
- He was recorded in the census in 1900, aged about 26, in Precincts 10, 19 Hart, George, Covington, Alabama, USA.
- He was recorded in the census in 1920, aged about 46, in Precinct 10, Co, Alabama, USA.
- He was recorded in the census in 1930, aged about 56, in Hart, Covington, Alabama, USA.
- He died on November 14, 1961, aged 87 years, in Andalusia, Covington, Alabama, USA.
- He was buried in Pleasant Home Baptist Church Cemetery, Covington, Alabama, USA.

195. FLOSSIE BELL was born on October 19, 1882, in Covington, Alabama, USA.
- She was recorded in the census in 1900, aged about 17, in Precincts 10, 19 Hart, George, Covington, Alabama, USA.
- She was recorded in the census in 1920, aged about 37, in Precinct 10, Co, Alabama, USA.
- She was recorded in the census in 1930, aged about 47, in Hart, Covington, Alabama, USA.
- She died on February 21, 1957, aged 74 years, in Andalusia, Covington, Alabama, USA.
- She was buried in Pleasant Home Baptist Church Cemetery, Covington, Alabama, USA.

James William Hart[194], aged 24, married Flossie Bell, aged 15, on June 30, 1898 in Covington, Alabama. They had ten children:

Maudie Aline Hart[771] born on April 22, 1899 in Alabama, United States; died on January 23, 1984 in Andalusia, Covington, Alabama, United States

Lella Mae Hart[772] born on December 23, 1900 in Covington, Alabama, United States; died on June 4, 1966 in Alabama, United States

Ellen Hart[773] born about 1901 in Alabama, United States

William Daniel Hart[774] born on December 25, 1902 in Covington, Alabama, United States; died on July 5, 1987 in Andalusia, Covington, Alabama, United States

Birdie H Hart[776] born on November 3, 1904 in Covington, Alabama, United States; died on November 23, 1975 in Lockhart, Covington, Alabama, United States

James Travis Hart[778] born on January 7, 1907 in Alabama, USA; died on August 22, 1985 in Okaloosa, FL, USA

Allen Trammel Hart[780] born on March 8, 1910 in Covington, Alabama, USA; died on July 9, 1994 in Hernando County, Florida, USA

Leonard V. Hart[782] born on September 24, 1918 in Falco, Covington, Alabama, United States; died on February 20, 1998 in De Land, Volusia, Florida, United States

W C Hart[784] born about 1919 in Alabama, United States

Jynelle Hart[785] born on August 28, 1922; died on March 15, 2008

196. JOHN C HART (see Descendants (25)) was born on August 15, 1876, in Alabama, USA, to Columbus Daniel Hart[39] and Nancy Ann Padgett[38].
- He was recorded in the census in 1880, aged about 3, in Harts And Red Level, Covington, Alabama, USA.
- He was recorded in the census in 1900, aged about 23, in Precincts 10, 19 Hart, George, Covington, Alabama, USA.
- He died on March 9, 1953, aged 76 years, in Andalusia, Covington, Alabama, USA.
- He was buried in Covington, Alabama.
- He was buried in Pleasant Home Baptist Cemetery, Covington, Alabama, USA.

197. VIRGINIA HART (see Descendants (25)) was born on May 18, 1879, in Alabama, USA, to Columbus Daniel Hart[39] and Nancy Ann Padgett[38].
- She was recorded in the census in 1880, aged about 1, in Harts And Red Level, Covington, Alabama, USA.
- She was recorded in the census in 1900, aged about 21, in Precincts 10, 19 Hart, George, Covington, Alabama, USA.
- She was recorded in the census in 1940, aged about 61, in 26 Sawmill Street, Chapman Town, Butler, Alabama, USA.
- She was recorded in the census on April 1, 1950, aged 70, in 49 Near Rock Crek Iane, Georgiana, Butler, Alabama, United States.
- She died on April 7, 1958, aged 78 years, in Greenville, Butler, Alabama, USA.
- She was buried in Pleasant Home Baptist Church Cemetery, Covington, Alabama, USA.

198. CHARLES HENRY GOODLETT was born on September 30, 1879, in Alabama, USA.
- He was recorded in the census in 1940, aged about 60, in 26 Sawmill Street, Chapman Town, Butler, Alabama, USA.
- He was recorded in the census on April 1, 1950, aged 70, in 49 Near Rock Crek Iane, Georgiana, Butler, Alabama, United States.
- He died on June 15, 1959, aged 79 years, in Alabama, USA.
- He was buried in Pleasant Home Baptist Cemetery, Covington, Alabama, USA.

Charles Henry Goodlett married Virginia Hart[197]. They had one daughter:
Lucille Goodlett[787]

199. ALICE REBECCA HART (see Descendants (25)) was born on August 8, 1881, in Covington, Alabama, USA, to Columbus Daniel Hart[39] and Nancy Ann Padgett[38].
- She was recorded in the census in 1900, aged about 18, in Precincts 10, 19 Hart, George, Covington, Alabama, USA.
- She was recorded in the census in 1920, aged about 38, in Precinct 10, Covington, Alabama, USA.
- She was recorded in the census in 1930, aged about 48, in Hart, Covington, Alabama, USA.
- She was recorded in the census in 1940, aged about 58, in Precinct 10 Hart, Covington, Alabama, USA.
- She was recorded in the census on April 1, 1950, aged 68, in Pleasant Home to Darble Port Road, Hart, Covington, Alabama, United States.
- She died on May 22, 1962, aged 80 years, in Pleasant Home, Covington, Alabama.
- She was buried in Pleasant Home Baptist Church Cemetery, Covington, Alabama, USA.

Notes:

William Allen Kelley, John Kelley, George Washington Kelley, Rubie L. Kelley, Alice Rebeca Hart, Mildred Hazel Kelley, and Fred Columbus Kelley

200. GEORGE WASHINGTON KELLEY was born on January 12, 1880, in Covington, Alabama, United States, to William Henry Kelley and Effie Gobson.
- He was recorded in the census in 1900, aged about 20, in Precincts 10, 19 Hart, George, Covington, Alabama, USA.
- He was recorded in the census in 1920, aged about 40, in Precinct 10, Covington, Alabama, USA.
- He was recorded in the census in 1930, aged about 50, in Hart, Covington, Alabama, USA.
- He was recorded in the census in 1940, aged about 60, in Precinct 10 Hart, Covington, Alabama, USA.
- He was recorded in the census on April 1, 1950, aged 70, in Pleasant Home to Darble Port Road, Hart, Covington, Alabama, United States.
- He died on January 23, 1955, aged 75 years, in Andalusia, Covington, Alabama, United States.
- He was buried in Pleasant Home Baptist Church Cemetery, Covington, Alabama, USA.

George Washington Kelley, aged about 17, married Alice Rebecca Hart[199], aged about 15, about 1897. They had seven children:

Fred Columbus Kelley[788] born on August 15, 1898 in Covington, Alabama, United States; died on November 28, 1984 in Covington, Alabama, United States

William Allen Kelley[790] born on April 7, 1901 in Covington, Alabama; died on December 22, 1985 in Covington, Alabama

Daniel Kelley[791] born about 1902 in Alabama, United States; died about 1902

Rubie L Kelley[792] born on April 17, 1904 in Covington, Alabama, USA; died on August 30, 2002 in Alabama, United States

John Kelley[793] born on February 18, 1907 in Covington, Alabama, United States; died on March 1, 1996 in Florida, United States

Columbus Daniel Kelley[794] born on June 29, 1912 in Covington, Alabama; died on September 19, 1947 in Covington, Alabama

Mildred Hazel Kelley[797] born on February 3, 1919 in Alabama, United States; died on August 28, 1986

201. RUBIN RICHARD HART (see Descendants (25)) was born on November 20, 1883, in Alabama, USA, to Columbus Daniel Hart[39] and Nancy Ann Padgett[38].
- He was recorded in the census in 1900, aged about 16, in Precincts 10, 19 Hart, George, Covington, Alabama, USA.
- He died on September 25, 1926, aged 42 years, in Covington, Alabama, USA.
- He was buried on September 26, 1926 in Pleasant Home Baptist Church Cemetery, Covington, Alabama, USA.

202. LAURA ELIZABETH CROSS was born on May 19, 1885, in Alabama, USA, to John Wesley Cross and Nancy Caroline Hart. Laura Elizabeth became known as "Leila".
- She died (Complications from childbirth (family stories)) on May 13, 1908, aged 22 years, in Birmingham, Jefferson, Alabama, United States.
- She was buried in Pleasant Home Baptist Church Cemetery, Covington, Alabama, USA.

Rubin Richard Hart[201], aged 22, married Laura Elizabeth Cross, aged 20, on April 25, 1906 in Covington, Alabama, United States.

203. ADA ALABAMA HART (see Descendants (25)) was born on May 4, 1886, in Alabama, USA, to Columbus Daniel Hart[39] and Nancy Ann Padgett[38].
- She was recorded in the census in 1900, aged about 14, in Precincts 10, 19 Hart, George, Covington, Alabama, USA.
- She was recorded in the census in 1910, aged about 24, in Andalusia, Covington, Alabama, USA.
- She was recorded in the census in 1920, aged about 34, in Precinct 1, Covington, Alabama, USA.
- She was recorded in the census in 1930, aged about 44, in Hollywood, Broward, Florida, USA.
- She was recorded in the census in 1940, aged about 54, in East 2238 Hollywood Blvd, Hollywood, Election Precinct 11 Hollywood, Broward, Florida, USA.
- She died on July 18, 1975, aged 89 years, in Covington, Alabama.
- She was buried in Pleasant Home Baptist Church Cemetery, Covington, Alabama, USA.

204. WILLIAM NICHOLAS CAMPBELL was born about 1882, in Alabama, USA. William Nicholas became known as "Nick".
- He was recorded in the census in 1910, aged about 28, in Andalusia, Covington, Alabama, USA.
- He was recorded in the census in 1920, aged about 38, in Precinct 1, Covington, Alabama, USA.
- He was recorded in the census in 1930, aged about 48, in Hollywood, Broward, Florida, USA.
- He died on October 16, 1938, aged about 56, in Tuscaloosa, Tuscaloosa, Alabama, USA.
- He was buried in Pleasant Home Baptist Church Cemetery, Covington, Alabama, USA.

William Nicholas Campbell, aged about 24, married Ada Alabama Hart[203], aged 20, on December 9, 1906 in Covington, Alabama. They had three children:
> Claude C. Campbell[798] born about 1908 in Alabama, USA; died on March 8, 1998 in Alabama, USA
> Mary R Campbell[799] born about 1917 in Alabama, United States
> William Nicholas Campbell Jr.[800] born in November 1919 in Alabama, United States

205. NANCY LENA HART (see Descendants (25)) was born on June 24, 1888, in Alabama, United States, to Columbus Daniel Hart[39] and Nancy Ann Padgett[38]. Nancy Lena became known as "Babe".
   - She was recorded in the census in 1900, aged about 12, in Precincts 10, 19 Hart, George, Covington, Alabama, USA.
   - She was recorded in the census on April 1, 1950, aged 61, in 1006 E De Soto, Pensacola, Escambia, Florida, United States.
   - She died in 1979, aged about 91, in Escambia, Florida, United States.

206. JOHN JEFFERSON CUSHING was born on March 5, 1885, in Blackman, Okaloosa, Florida, United States.
   - He was recorded in the census on April 1, 1950, aged 65, in 1006 E De Soto, Pensacola, Escambia, Florida, United States.
   - He died on November 13, 1963, aged 78, in Pensacola, Escambia, Florida, United States.
   John Jefferson Cushing, aged about 21, married Nancy Lena Hart[205], aged about 18, in 1906 in Covington County, Alabama. They had four sons:
   > William D "Willie" Cushing[801] born in 1911 in Covington County, Alabama; died in 2008 in Pensacola, Escambia County, Florida
   > Woodrow Cushing[802] born in 1917 in Covington County, Alabama; died on July 12, 1994 in Milton, Santa Rosa County, Florida
   > John Jefferson Cushing[803] born on July 18, 1922 in Pensacola, Escambia County, Florida; died on October 14, 1983 in Pensacola, Escambia County, Florida
   > Clyde L Cushing[804] born on October 11, 1925 in Pensacola, Escambia County, Florida; died on June 17, 1980 in Florida

207. MARY NORA HART (see Descendants (25)) was born on October 10, 1890, in Covington, Alabama, USA, to Columbus Daniel Hart[39] and Nancy Ann Padgett[38]. Mary Nora became known as "Sweet".
   - She was recorded in the census in 1900, aged about 9, in Precincts 10, 19 Hart, George, Covington, Alabama, USA.
   - She died on October 7, 1973, aged 82 years, in Florala, Covington, Alabama, USA.
   - She was buried on October 9, 1973 in Covington, Alabama, USA.

208. JOSEPH JOSH DAVIS was born on August 10, 1888, in Covington, Alabama, USA.
   - He died on August 16, 1963, aged 75 years.
   - He was buried on August 17, 1963 in Wing, Covington, Alabama, USA.
   Joseph Josh Davis, aged 20, married Mary Nora Hart[207], aged 18, on February 21, 1909 in Laural Hill, Florida, USA. They had four children:
   > Eleanor D. Hart[805] born on December 21, 1909 in Falco, Covington, Alabama, USA; died on August 12, 1959 in Pensacola, Escambia, Florida, USA
   > Jack Columbus Davis[806] born on May 20, 1914 in Covington, Alabama, USA; died on January 23, 1989 in Crestview, Okaloosa, Florida, USA
   > James Rudalph Davis[807] born on October 24, 1923 in Falco, Covington, Alabama, USA; died on July 19, 1988 in Crestview, Okaloosa, Florida, USA
   > Nannie Ruth Davis[808] born on September 30, 1925 in River Falls, Covington, Alabama, USA; died on July 7, 2010

209. MARY A. BASS (see Descendants (26)) was born in December 1881, in Alabama, United States, to William M. Bass[42] and Abigail Welch[43].
   - She was recorded in the census in 1920, aged about 38, in Beat 6 Loango, Covington, Alabama, USA.
   - She died in 1940, aged about 58, in Red Level, Covington, Alabama, USA.
   - She was buried in Fairmount Baptist Curch Cemetery, Red Level, Covington, Alabama, USA.

210. LISTON THOMAS HUTCHESON was born on January 3, 1880, in Alabama, USA.
   - He was recorded in the census in 1920, aged about 40, in Beat 6 Loango, Covington, Alabama, USA.
   - He died on January 6, 1975, aged 95 years, in Red Level, Covington, Alabama, USA.
   - He was buried in Fairmount Baptist Curch Cemetery, Red Level, Covington, Alabama, USA.
   Liston Thomas married twice. He was married to Mary A. Bass[209] and Maggie Mae Acree.

Notes:
- *From Covington County History, 1821-1976 by Gus Bryan: "Liston T. Hutcheson the oldest citizen in the Red Level – Loango area. Hutcheson was a three mule farmer, operated a sawmill and a cotton gin. In 1925 he moved to Fort Lauderdale, Florida where he worked as a carpenter and later operated a gas station. When he retired he returned to Loango. After his wife's death he remarried Maggie Lindsey Acree and the two resided in Loango."*
- *From his obituary from Audrey Ard Tschirhat: "Liston was not slim but not portly. Somewhere in between. And I imagine about 5 foot 9 inches tall with a ruddy Complexion. He did not wear a hat when he was at church. Of course, he was a Baptist; very polite and friendly. Always had on a white shirt."*

(Death)

Liston Thomas Hutcheson, aged 19, married Mary A. Bass[209], aged 17, on July 2, 1899. They had four children:
  William E Hutchison[809] born about 1901 in Alabama, United States
  Harris G Hutchison[810] born about 1906 in Alabama, United States
  Harold A Hutchison[811] born about 1909 in Alabama, United States
  Myrtle E Hutchison[812] born about 1913 in Alabama, United States

Liston Thomas Hutcheson married Maggie Mae Acree.

211. WILLIAM RILEY BASS (see Descendants (26)) was born on August 28, 1882, in Alabama, United States, to William M. Bass[42] and Abigail Welch[43].
- He was recorded in the census in 1930, aged about 47, in Fairfield, Covington, Alabama, USA.
- He died on November 17, 1966, aged 84 years, in Andalusia, Covington, Alabama, USA.
- He was buried in Andalusia Memorial Cemetery, Covington, Alabama, USA.

212. AUGUSTA COOPER was born on August 28, 1882, in Alabama, United States. Augusta became known as "Gusta".
- She was recorded in the census in 1930, aged about 47, in Fairfield, Covington, Alabama, USA.
- She died on November 17, 1966, aged 84 years, in Andalusia Memorial Cemetery, Covington, Alabama, USA.
- She was buried in Andalusia Memorial Cemetery, Covington, Alabama, USA.

William Riley Bass[211], aged 23, married Augusta Cooper, aged 23, in December 1905. They had six children:
  Velma Bass[813] born on December 23, 1906 in Alabama, United States; died on May 2, 1996 in Bibb County, Georgia, USA
  William Barney Bass[815] born on July 25, 1910 in Alabama, United States; died on November 7, 1995
  Maggie M Bass[817] born about 1913 in Alabama, United States
  Clara M Bass[818] born about 1915 in Alabama, United States
  Eva Mae Bass[819] born on May 9, 1918 in Alabama, United States; died on December 29, 2012 in Andalusia, Covington, Alabama, USA
  Horace Presley Bass[821] born on October 29, 1921 in Alabama, United States; died on March 30, 1993

Note: *"Miss Gusta Cooper and Riley Bass were married one day last week." The Andalusia Star News: January, 8th 1906.* .

Augusta Cooper

James Bennett Teel

Direct Relations

4th Generation of Descendants

213. MATTIE L TEEL (see Descendants (1)) was born about 1891, in Alabama, United States, to William Henry Teel[45] and Ida D White[46].
    • She was recorded in the census in 1910, aged about 19, in Andalusia, Covington, Alabama, USA.

214. NORA B TEEL (see Descendants (1)) was born about 1895, in Alabama, United States, to William Henry Teel[45] and Ida D White[46].
    • She was recorded in the census in 1910, aged about 15, in Andalusia, Covington, Alabama, USA.

215. JESSE STALLINGS TEEL (see Descendants (1)) was born on December 8, 1896, in Andalusia, Covington, Alabama, USA, to William Henry Teel[45] and Ida D White[46].
    • He was recorded in the census in 1910, aged about 13, in Andalusia, Covington, Alabama, USA.
    • He was recorded in the census in 1940, aged about 43, in 338 Dunson, Andalusia, Covington, Alabama, USA.
    • He died on December 17, 1962, aged 66, in Andalusia, Covington, Alabama, USA.
    • He was buried in Carolina Baptist Church Cemetery, Covington, Alabama, USA.
    The following information is also recorded for Jesse Stallings:
    • Military Service.
    Note: *Pvt. 40 Co. 157 Depot Brig, WWI.*
    (Military Service)

216. EULA MAE BLACK was born on March 8, 1901, in Luverne, Crenshaw, Alabama, USA.
    • She was recorded in the census in 1940, aged about 39, in 338 Dunson, Andalusia, Covington, Alabama, USA.
    • She died on April 7, 1989, aged 88, in Greenville, Butler, Alabama, USA.
        Jesse Stallings Teel[215] married Eula Mae Black. They had one daughter:
            Myrtice Mae Teel[823] born about 1932 in Alabama, USA

217. JAMES BENNETT TEEL (see Descendants (1)) was born on December 15, 1899, in Alabama, United States, to William Henry Teel[45] and Ida D White[46].
    • He was recorded in the census in 1910, aged about 10, in Andalusia, Covington, Alabama, USA.
    • He was recorded in the census in 1920, aged about 20, in Precinct 1, Covington, Alabama, USA.
    • He was recorded in the census in 1930, aged about 30, in Andalusia, Covington, Alabama, USA.
    • He died on December 16, 1962, aged 63.
    • He was buried in Carolina Baptist Church Cemetery, Covington, Alabama, USA.

218. OLIVER B TEEL (see Descendants (1)) was born about 1902, in Alabama, United States, to William Henry Teel[45] and Ida D White[46].
    • He was recorded in the census in 1910, aged about 8, in Andalusia, Covington, Alabama, USA.

219. AARON TEEL (see Descendants (1)) was born on July 2, 1907, in Alabama, United States, to William Henry Teel[45] and Ida D White[46].
    • He was recorded in the census in 1910, aged about 2, in Andalusia, Covington, Alabama, USA.
    • He was recorded in the census in 1920, aged about 12, in Precinct 1, Covington, Alabama, USA.
    • He was recorded in the census in 1940, aged about 32, in Election Precinct 1 Andalusia, Covington, Alabama, USA.
    • He was recorded in the census on April 1, 1950, aged 42, in Andalusia, Covington, Alabama, United States.
    • He died on July 19, 1991, aged 84.
    • He was buried in Carolina Baptist Church Cemetery, Covington, Alabama, USA.
220. BESSIE HARRELSON was born on February 7, 1912, in Alabama, United States.
    • She was recorded in the census in 1940, aged about 28, in Election Precinct 1 Andalusia, Covington, Alabama, USA.
    • She was recorded in the census on April 1, 1950, aged 38, in Andalusia, Covington, Alabama, United States.
    • She died on June 17, 1986, aged 74.
    • She was buried in Carolina Baptist Church Cemetery, Covington, Alabama, USA.
        Aaron Teel[219], aged 21, married Bessie Harrelson, aged 16, on November 4, 1928. They had five children:
            Mary Ethel Teel[824] born in 1929 in Alabama, USA
            Marie Teel[826] born in 1932 in Alabama, USA
            Vera Merle Teel[828] born on December 14, 1936 in Andalusia, Covington, Alabama, USA; died on November 16, 2014 in Irving, Dallas, Texas, USA
            Aaron Teel Jr.[830] born in 1939 in Alabama, United States
            Frances Ida Teel[832] born in 1948 in Alabama, United States

221. JAMES WILLIAM RAMER (see Descendants (2)) was born on January 25, 1897, in Alabama, USA, to William Albert Ramer[47] and Florence Missouri Howard[48]. James William became known as "Pete".
    • He was recorded in the census in 1900, aged about 3, in Precincts 10, 19 Hart, George, Covington, Alabama, USA.

- He was recorded in the census in 1910, aged about 13, in George, Covington, Alabama, USA.
- He was recorded in the census on April 22, 1930, aged 33 years, in Watkins, Covington County, Alabama.
- He died about March 1982, aged about 85, in Opp, Covington, Alabama, USA.

222. DEWEY WILLIAM RAMER (see Descendants (2)) was born on August 6, 1898, in Alabama, USA, to William Albert Ramer[47] and Florence Missouri Howard[48].
- He was recorded in the census in 1900, aged about 1, in Precincts 10, 19 Hart, George, Covington, Alabama, USA.
- He was recorded in the census in 1910, aged about 11, in George, Covington, Alabama, USA.
- He was recorded in the census on April 19, 1930, aged 31 years, in Niceville, Okaloosa County, Florida.
- He was recorded in the census in 1940, aged about 41, in Orlando Road, Taft, Precinct 42, Orange, Florida, USA.
- He died about July 1981, aged about 82, in Orlando, Orange, Florida, USA.

223. MATTIE LUCILE JOHNSON was born about 1906, in Alabama, USA. She was recorded in the census in 1940, aged about 34, in Orlando Road, Taft, Precinct 42, Orange, Florida, USA.

Dewey William Ramer[222] married Mattie Lucile Johnson. They had five children:
Winford Eugene Ramer Sr.[835] born on August 24, 1925 in Florida, USA; died on June 11, 1986
James Ramer[837] born about 1928 in Alabama, USA
Ms. Ramer[838] born about 1932 in Alabama, USA
Buddy Ramer[839] born in 1934; died in 1938
Mildred Ramer[840] born about 1938 in Florida, USA

224. LENA ZELMA RAMER (see Descendants (2)) was born in April 1900, in Alabama, USA, to William Albert Ramer[47] and Florence Missouri Howard[48].
- She was recorded in the census in 1900, aged 0, in Precincts 10, 19 Hart, George, Covington, Alabama, USA.
- She was recorded in the census in 1910, aged about 10, in George, Covington, Alabama, USA.
- She died on October 7, 1965, aged 65 years, in Montgomery, Montgomery, Alabama, USA.

225. ATHON RAMER SR. (see Descendants (2)) was born on August 16, 1901, in Alabama, USA, to William Albert Ramer[47] and Florence Missouri Howard[48].
- He was recorded in the census in 1910, aged about 8, in George, Covington, Alabama, USA.
- He was recorded in the census on April 12, 1930, aged 28 years, in George, Covington County, Alabama.
- In 1930, aged about 28, he was a Transportation Laborer in George, Covington County, Alabama.
- He died about February 1979, aged about 77, in Opp, Covington, Alabama, USA.

226. JOHN BENNETT RAMER (see Descendants (2)) was born on November 19, 1902, in Alabama, United States, to William Albert Ramer[47] and Florence Missouri Howard[48].
- He was recorded in the census in 1910, aged about 7, in George, Covington, Alabama, USA.
- He died on October 15, 1987, aged 84 years, in Opp, Covington, Alabama, USA.
- He was buried in Peaceful Acres Memorial Gardens, Opp, Covington, Alabama, USA.

227. VERA CLARK was born on August 4, 1916, in USA.
- She died on November 9, 1997, aged 81, in USA.
- She was buried in Peaceful Acres Opp, AL.

John Bennett Ramer[226] married Vera Clark.

228. MARY E RAMER (see Descendants (2)) was born about 1906, in Alabama, United States, to William Albert Ramer[47] and Florence Missouri Howard[48].
- She was recorded in the census in 1910, aged about 4, in George, Covington, Alabama, USA.

229. WILLIAM CALVIN RAMER (see Descendants (2)) was born on May 14, 1907, in Alabama, United States, to William Albert Ramer[47] and Florence Missouri Howard[48].
- He was recorded in the census in 1910, aged about 3, in George, Covington, Alabama, USA.
- He died on April 10, 2001, aged 93 years, in Opp, Covington, Alabama, USA.

230. ALBERT FARRELL RAMER (see Descendants (2)) was born on August 8, 1907, in Alabama, United States, to William Albert Ramer[47] and Florence Missouri Howard[48].
- He was recorded in the census in 1910, aged about 2, in George, Covington, Alabama, USA.
- He was recorded in the census on April 18, 1930, aged 22 years, in Andalusia, Covington County, Alabama.
- He was recorded in the census in 1940, aged about 32, in Railroad Avenue, Opp, Precinct 3, Covington, Alabama, USA.
- He died on October 1, 1974, aged 67 years, in Opp, Covington, Alabama, USA.

231. MAMIE ADA ? was born on July 28, 1907, in Alabama, USA.
- She was recorded in the census in 1940, aged about 32, in Railroad Avenue, Opp, Precinct 3, Covington, Alabama,

Direct Relations

USA.
- She died on December 31, 1989, aged 82.
- She was buried in Peaceful Acres Memorial Gardens, Opp, Covington County, Alabama, USA.

Albert Farrell Ramer[230] married Mamie Ada ?. They had two children:
- Dorothy Ramer[841] born about 1928 in Alabama, USA
- Derward Ramer[842] born about 1937 in Alabama, USA

232. JESSE C RAMER (see Descendants (2)) was born on May 19, 1909, in Alabama, United States, to William Albert Ramer[47] and Florence Missouri Howard[48].
- He was recorded in the census in 1910, aged about 1, in George, Covington, Alabama, USA.
- He died in June 1984, aged 75.
- He was buried in Peaceful Acres Memorial Gardens, Opp, Covington, Alabama, USA.

233. H. CLOSON was born in 1914. She died in 1987, aged about 73.

Jesse C Ramer[232] married H. Closon.

234. HOMER CLOSON RAMER (see Descendants (2)) was born on October 4, 1913, in Alabama, United States, to William Albert Ramer[47] and Florence Missouri Howard[48].
- He was recorded in the census on April 18, 1930, aged 16 years, in Andalusia, Covington County, Alabama.
- He died on November 4, 1987, aged 74 years, in Opp, Covington, Alabama, USA.
- He was buried in Carolina Baptist Church Cemetery, Covington, Alabama, USA.

235. SAVANNAH IRENE RAMER (see Descendants (2)) was born on November 22, 1913, in Andalusia, Covington, Alabama, USA, to William Albert Ramer[47] and Florence Missouri Howard[48].
- She was recorded in the census on April 18, 1930, aged 16 years, in Andalusia, Covington County, Alabama.
- She died on July 25, 2001, aged 87 years.

236. WALTER OTIS RAMER (see Descendants (2)) was born on February 14, 1916 to William Albert Ramer[47] and Florence Missouri Howard[48].
- He was recorded in the census on April 18, 1930, aged 14 years, in Andalusia, Covington County, Alabama.
- He died about June 1955, aged about 39, in Opp, Covington, Alabama, USA.

237. JAMES W RAMER (see Descendants (3)) was born on January 10, 1901 to John Ramer[49] and Ella Melissa Howard[50]. James W became known as "Bud".
- He died on November 3, 1956, aged 55 years, in Andalusia, Covington, Alabama, USA.
- He was buried about January 1956 in Carolina Baptist Church Cemetery, Carolina, Covington County, Alabama.

238. CLAUDE A RAMER (see Descendants (3)) was born on January 15, 1902 to John Ramer[49] and Ella Melissa Howard[50]. He died on December 22, 1990, aged 88 years, in Opp, Covington County, Alabama.

239. BEULAH RAMER (see Descendants (4)) was born on July 11, 1902 to Jacob D Ramer[51] and Illinoy Bulger[52].
- She died on December 19, 1997, aged 95.
- She was buried in Carolina Baptist Church Cemetery, Covington, Alabama, USA.

240. AMOS WHITE.

Amos White married Beulah Ramer[239]. They had one son:
- James Thomas White Sr.[843] born on July 16, 1927 in Andalusia, Covington, Alabama, USA; died on October 26, 2014 in Pensacola, Escambia, Florida, USA

241. MAJOR RAMER (see Descendants (4)) was born on September 7, 1902 to Jacob D Ramer[51] and Illinoy Bulger[52].
- He died on May 21, 1963, aged 60.
- He was buried in Carolina Baptist Church Cemetery, Covington, Alabama, USA.

The following information is also recorded for Major:
- Military Service.

Note: *Pvt 6 QM Training Regt, WWII.*
(Military Service)

242. MARY DOVIE RAMER (see Descendants (4)) was born on September 27, 1904, in Ohio, United States, to Jacob D Ramer[51] and Illinoy Bulger[52].
- She was recorded in the census on April 1, 1950, aged 45, in 2 1/2 Mile Zenohia Road, Hartland Township, Huron, Ohio, United States.
- She died on September 14, 1996, aged 91.
- She was buried in Adellum Cemetery, Andalusia, Covington, Alabama, USA.

243. WILLIAM TRAVIS WALLACE was born on December 17, 1903, in South Dakota, United States.
- He was recorded in the census on April 1, 1950, aged 46, in 2 1/2 Mile Zenohia Road, Hartland Township, Huron, Ohio, United States.
- He died on September 21, 1986, aged 82.
- He was buried in Adellum Cemetery, Andalusia, Covington, Alabama, USA.
    William Travis Wallace married Mary Dovie Ramer[242]. They had one son:
        Richard Wallace[844] born about 1944 in Ohio, United States

244. MILLARD RAMER (see Descendants (4)) was born on March 7, 1909, in Alabama, USA, to Jacob D Ramer[51] and Illinoy Bulger[52].
- He died on February 26, 1995, aged 85, in Brooksville, Florida, USA.
- He was buried in Greenwood Cemetery, Eustis, Lake, Florida, USA.

245. MAGGIE MAE RAMER (see Descendants (4)) was born on January 2, 1911 to Jacob D Ramer[51] and Savannah Odom[53].
- She died on February 26, 2003, aged 92.
- She was buried in Red Oak Baptist Church Cemetery, Red Oak, Covington, Alabama, USA.

246. CYNTHIA LILLIAN BASS (see Descendants (7)) was born on December 28, 1885, in Kountze, Hardin, Texas, USA, to Benjamin Wilson Bass[60] and Matilda Hall[61].
- She was recorded in the census in 1900, aged about 14, in Justice Precinct 4, Hardin, Texas, USA.
- She was recorded in the census in 1940, aged about 54, in Votaw Qt, Justice Precinct, Hardin, Texas, USA.
- She died on June 22, 1953, aged 67 years.
- She was buried in Hall Cemetery, Thicket, Hardin, Texas, USA.

247. JOHN CURTIS BARNEYCASTLE was born on August 15, 1882, in Alabama, USA.
- He was recorded in the census in 1940, aged about 57, in Votaw Qt, Justice Precinct, Hardin, Texas, USA.
- He was recorded in the census in 1940, aged about 57, in Votaw Qt, Justice Precinct, Hardin, Texas, USA.
- He died on February 12, 1962, aged 79 years.
- He was buried in Hall Cemetery, Thicket, Hardin, Texas, USA.
    John Curtis Barneycastle married Cynthia Lillian Bass[246]. They had one daughter:
        Ester C Barneycastle[845]

248. MR. BASS (see Descendants (7)) was born in 1886, in Kountze, Texas, USA, to Benjamin Wilson Bass[60] and Matilda Hall[61]. He died (At young age) in 1887, aged about 1.

249. MR. BASS (see Descendants (7)) was born in 1887, in Texas, USA, to Benjamin Wilson Bass[60] and Matilda Hall[61]. He died (Stillborn) in 1887, aged 0, in Texas, USA.

250. MARTIN LUTHER BASS (see Descendants (7)) was born on September 8, 1889, in Beaumont, Texas, USA, to Benjamin Wilson Bass[60] and Matilda Hall[61].
- He was recorded in the census in 1900, aged about 10, in Justice Precinct 4, Hardin, Texas, USA.
- He died on November 7, 1953, aged 64 years, in Votaw, Hardin, Texas, USA.
- He was buried in Votaw, Hardin County, Texas, USA.

The following information is also recorded for Martin Luther:
- Military Service.
Note: *F I USNRF WWI.*
    (Military Service)

251. MARVEL MAY MURPHY was born on September 2, 1888, in Kountz, Texas, USA.
- Marvel May graduated.
- She died on March 30, 1969, aged 80 years.
- She was buried.
Notes:
- *Graduate of the North Louisiana State Hospital School of Nursing.*
    (Graduation)
- *Mrs. Bass was born, reared and educated in East Texas and was a graduate of the North Louisiana State Hospital School of Nursing. She married M.L. Bass in Hillsboro in 1921. Mr. Bass was a drilling contractor. He died in 1958. Mrs. Bass was a former resident of LaPorte and had lived in Waco since September of 1968.*
    (Death)
        Martin Luther Bass[250], aged 32, married Marvel May Murphy, aged 33, on October 21, 1921.

252. SUSAN VIOLA BASS (see Descendants (7)) was born on January 20, 1891, in Votaw, Hardin, Texas, USA, to Benjamin Wilson Bass[60] and Matilda Hall[61].
- She was recorded in the census in 1900, aged about 9, in Justice Precinct 4, Hardin, Texas, USA.

- She was recorded in the census in 1940, aged about 49, in Votaw Qt, Justice Precinct, Hardin, Texas, USA.
- She died on October 21, 1962, aged 71 years, in Baytown, Harris, Texas, USA.
- She was buried in Votaw Cemetery, Votaw, Hardin, Texas, USA.

253. ELZIE BARNEYCASTLE was born on June 7, 1879, in Alabama, USA.
- He was recorded in the census in 1940, aged about 61, in Votaw Qt, Justice Precinct, Hardin, Texas, USA.
- He died on June 14, 1945, aged 66 years, in Votaw, Hardin, Texas, USA.
- He was buried in Votaw Cemetery, Votaw, Hardin, Texas, USA.

Elzie Barneycastle married Susan Viola Bass[252]. They had ten children:
Cynthia Lillian Barneycastle[847] born on August 25, 1905 in Votaw, Hardin, Texas, USA; died on September 4, 1907 in Votaw, Hardin, Texas, USA
Benjamin Wilson Barneycastle[848] born on September 4, 1907 in Duncan, Oklahoma, USA; died on December 29, 1962 in Votaw, Hardin, Texas, USA
James William Barneycastle[850] born on May 24, 1910 in Votaw, Hardin, Texas, USA; died on November 21, 1938 in Liberty, Texas, USA
Martin Luther Barneycastle[851] born on April 8, 1912 in Votaw, Hardin, Texas, USA; died on April 1, 1984
Nobie Barneycastle[853] born on October 25, 1913 in Votaw, Hardin, Texas, USA; died on April 14, 1916 in Votaw, Hardin, Texas, USA
Isabelle Barneycastle[854] born on September 28, 1917 in Votaw, Hardin, Texas, USA; died on June 17, 1968 in Houston, Texas, USA
L. C. Barneycastle[856] born on October 1, 1920 in Votaw, Hardin, Texas, USA; died on December 24, 1944 in Saint-Vith, Arrondissement de Verviers, Liège, Belgium
Todd Barneycastle[858] born on June 1, 1922 in Votaw, Hardin, Texas, USA; died on February 1, 1944 in At Sea
Lula Barneycastle[859] born on November 14, 1926 in Votaw, Hardin, Texas, USA; died on September 27, 2000 in West Jordan, Salt Lack, Utah, USA
Eula Barneycastle[860] born on February 24, 1928 in Votaw, Hardin, Texas, USA; died on May 28, 2005 in Taylorsville, Salt Lack, Utah, USA

254. WILSON LAFAYETTE BASS (see Descendants (7)) was born on July 13, 1892, in Votaw, Hardin, Texas, USA, to Benjamin Wilson Bass[60] and Matilda Hall[61].
- He was recorded in the census in 1900, aged about 7, in Justice Precinct 4, Hardin, Texas, USA.
- He was recorded in the census in 1910, aged about 17, in Justice Precinct 8, Hardin, Texas, USA.
- He died on December 9, 1943, aged 51 years.
- He was buried in Hall Cemetery, Thicket, Hardin, Texas, USA.

255. NANNIE WITT.
Wilson Lafayette Bass[254] married Nannie Witt. They had one son:
Alvin Leon Bass[862] born on October 5, 1928; died on July 29, 1952 in La Porte, Texas, USA

256. THOMAS WATSON BASS (see Descendants (7)) was born on December 9, 1894, in Votaw, Hardin, Texas, USA, to Benjamin Wilson Bass[60] and Matilda Hall[61]. He died (At young age) in Votaw, Hardin, Texas, USA.

257. BENJAMIN ELI BASS (see Descendants (7)) was born on January 30, 1895, in Votaw, Hardin, Texas, USA, to Benjamin Wilson Bass[60] and Matilda Hall[61].
- In 1900, aged about 5, he resided at Marital Status: SingleRelation to Head of House: Son, Justice Precinct 4, Hardin, Texas, USA.
- He was recorded in the census in 1900, aged about 5, in Justice Precinct 4, Hardin, Texas, USA.
- In 1910, aged about 15, he resided at Marital Status: SingleRelation to Head of House: Brother-in-law, Justice Precinct 6, Hardin, Texas, USA.
- He was recorded in the census in 1910, aged about 15, in Justice Precinct 6, Hardin, Texas, USA.
- Between 1917 and 1918, from the age of about 22, he resided at Caddo, Louisiana.
- In 1942, aged about 47, he resided at Shreveport, Louisiana, USA.
- He died on July 31, 1951, aged 56 years, in Hardin, Texas, United States.
- He was buried in Thicket, Hardin County, Texas, USA.

258. BERNICE MITCHELL.
Benjamin Eli Bass[257] married Bernice Mitchell.

259. DOUGLAS U BASS (see Descendants (7)) was born about 1903, in Texas, United States, to Benjamin Wilson Bass[60] and Frieda Kamilla Schmitt[62].
- He was recorded in the census in 1910, aged about 7, in Justice Precinct 8, Hardin, Texas, USA.

260. THELMA B BASS (see Descendants (7)) was born in 1905, in Texas, USA, to Benjamin Wilson Bass[60] and Frieda Kamilla Schmitt[62].
- She was recorded in the census in 1910, aged about 5, in Justice Precinct 8, Hardin, Texas, USA.

261. LOUIS O BASS (see Descendants (7)) was born in 1907, in Texas, United States, to Benjamin Wilson Bass[60] and Frieda Kamilla Schmitt[62].
- He was recorded in the census in 1910, aged about 3, in Justice Precinct 8, Hardin, Texas, USA.

262. GUSTAVUS BASS (see Descendants (7)) was born in 1909, in Batson, Hardin, Texas, to Benjamin Wilson Bass[60] and Frieda Kamilla Schmitt[62].
- In 1910, aged about 1, he resided at Marital Status: SingleRelation to Head of House: Son, Justice Precinct 8, Hardin, Texas, USA.
- He was recorded in the census in 1910, aged about 1, in Justice Precinct 8, Hardin, Texas, USA.
- He died on October 22, 1983, aged about 74, in Maize, Sedgwick, Kansas, USA.
- He was buried in Midland, Midland County, Texas, USA.

263. MARY SUSANNAH BASS (see Descendants (8)) was born on October 26, 1889, in White Oak, Hardin, Texas, USA, to William Riley Bass[64] and Frances Elizabeth Collins[65].
- She was recorded in the census in 1910, aged about 20, in Justice Precinct 7, Hardin, Texas, USA.
- She died (Unknown) on September 7, 1919, aged 29 years, in La Sal, San Juan, Utah, USA.
- She was buried on September 8, 1919 in La Sal Cemetery, La Sal, San Juan, Utah, USA.

264. ELIZA JANE BASS (see Descendants (8)) was born on November 20, 1891, in White Oak, Hardin, Texas, USA, to William Riley Bass[64] and Frances Elizabeth Collins[65]. She died on December 31, 1891, aged 0.

265. ALLEN MILFORD BASS (see Descendants (8)) was born on August 11, 1893, in White Oak, Hardin, Texas, USA, to William Riley Bass[64] and Frances Elizabeth Collins[65].
- He was recorded in the census in 1910, aged about 16, in Justice Precinct 7, Hardin, Texas, USA.
- He was recorded in the census in 1930, aged about 36, in Police Jury Ward 2, Caddo, Louisiana, USA.
- He was recorded in the census in 1940, aged about 46, in Oil, Ward 2, Caddo, Louisiana, USA.
- He died on September 19, 1944, aged 51 years, in Mount Pleasant, Titus, Texas, United States.
- He was buried in Forest Park East Cemetery, Shreveport, Caddo Parish, Louisiana, USA.

266. MINNIE HORTON was born on November 14, 1881, in Alabama, United States, to Terah Andrew Horton and Sarah Elizabeth Johnson.
- She was recorded in the census in 1920, aged about 38, in VOL10ES36SH20L16.
- About 1920, aged about 38, she was employed in Boarding House: Oil workers.
- She was recorded in the census in 1940, aged about 58, in Oil, Ward 2, Caddo, Louisiana, USA.
- She died after 1940, when older than 59, in Titus Co., Texas.
- She was buried in Nevills Chapel Cemetery, Mount Pleasant, Titus Co., Texas.

The following information is also recorded for Minnie:
- 1900 US Census on June 22, 1900, aged 18, in Armour, JP #7 Precinct, Limestone Co., Texas T623 #1655 p. 284.
- 1910 US Census on April 26, 1910, aged 28, in South West 1/2, Ward #2, Caddo Parish, Louisiana T624 #510 p. 4.
- 1920 US Census on January 12, 1920, aged 38, in PJ Ward #2, Caddo Co., Oklahoma T625 #609 p. 20.
- 1930 US Census on April 11, 1930, aged 48, in Oil City, Ward #2, Caddo Co., Louisiana T626 #786 p. 138.
- Birth Info in (census 00: TX 10: AL 20: AL 30: AL).

Minnie married twice. She was married to David Allen Nordyke and Allen Milford Bass[265].
    David Allen Nordyke, aged about 18, married Minnie Horton, aged about 16, in 1898 in Limestone Co., Texas. They had two children:
        Childone Nordyke born between 1898 and 1900 in Limestone Co., Texas; died before 1900 in Limestone Co., Texas
        Marshall Nordyke Bass born about 1902 in Texas; died after 1924
    Allen Milford Bass[265], aged about 24, married Minnie Horton, aged about 36, in 1918. They had two children:
        William Andrew Bass[863] born on July 15, 1921 in Arkansas, United States; died on January 25, 1993 in Everett, Washington
        Sarah Francis Bass[864] born on October 23, 1925

267. JOHN RILEY BASS (see Descendants (8)) was born on August 19, 1895, in Votaw, Hardin, Texas, United States, to William Riley Bass[64] and Frances Elizabeth Collins[65]. John Riley became known as "Pop".
- He was christened on March 6, 1904, aged 8, in Hardin, Texas, United States.
- He was recorded in the census in 1910, aged about 14, in Justice Precinct 7, Hardin, Texas, USA.
- He was recorded in the census on April 1, 1950, aged 54, in Wesley Road, Brenham, Washington,

Texas, United States.
- He died on July 10, 1978, aged 82 years, in Sweeny, Brazoria, Texas, USA.
- He was buried on July 11, 1978 in Guedry Cemetery, Batson, Hardin, Texas, United States.

268. VIOLA MAE SHAW was born on January 1, 1896, in Hardin, Texas, USA.

- She was recorded in the census on April 1, 1950, aged 54, in Wesley Road, Brenham, Washington, Texas, United States.
- She died on December 6, 1968, aged 72 years, in Brenham, Washington, Texas, USA.
- She was buried on December 9, 1968 in Guedry Cemetery, Batson, Hardin, Texas, United States.

John Riley Bass[267], aged 20, married Viola Mae Shaw, aged 20, on July 12, 1916 in Kountze, Hardin, Texas, United States. They had five children:

Joyce Imogene Bass[865] born on September 19, 1917 in Saratoga, Hardin Co., TX; died on November 9, 1998 in Brazoria, Texas

Dorothy Bass[866] born on January 3, 1919 in Saratoga, Hardin, Texas; died on December 11, 1919

Margaret Bass[867] born on May 1, 1920 in Saratoga, Hardin, Texas; died on December 18, 1920 in Harris, Texas

Glenn Donald "Johnny" Bass[868] born on March 16, 1922 in Saratoga, Hardin, Texas; died on December 1, 1970

Gwendolyn Bass[870] born on March 16, 1922 in Hardin, Texas, United States; died on September 29, 2014 in Austin, Travis, Texas, United States

269. DANIEL MATERSON BASS (see Descendants (8)) was born on November 23, 1897, in Votaw, Hardin, Texas, USA, to William Riley Bass[64] and Frances Elizabeth Collins[65].
- He was recorded in the census in 1910, aged about 12, in Justice Precinct 7, Hardin, Texas, USA.
- He died on January 11, 2000, aged 102 years, in Many, Sabine, Louisiana, USA.
- He was buried in Magnolia Cemetery, Westlake, Calcasieu Parish, Louisiana, United States of America.

The following information is also recorded for Daniel Materson:
- Injury about 1940, aged about 42.

Daniel Materson married twice. He was married to Ione Shafer[270] and Katherine Gladys Lee[271].
Note: *In the late 1940's he wanted to use an old gas tank for something, and he was trying to cut it in half with a welders torch, and it exploded on him. His injuries resulted in a lost leg.- Warren Ward.*
(Injury)

270. IONE SHAFER was born on November 23, 1893, in Moab, Grand, Utah, United States.
- She died on January 6, 1919, aged 25 years, in Moab, Grand, Utah, United States.
- She was buried in Grand Valley Cemetery, Moab, Utah, United States.

Note: *Ione passed from the Flu while on a visiting with her family for Christmas. She was buried with her premature son in her arms.*
(Death)

Daniel Materson Bass[269], aged 20, married Ione Shafer, aged 24, on February 23, 1918 in Moab, Grand, Utah. They had one son:

Mr. Bass[871] born in 1919; died in 1919

271. KATHERINE GLADYS LEE was born on July 4, 1907, in Hecker, Calcasieu, Louisiana, USA. She died on October 6, 1985, aged 78 years, in Lake Charles, Calcasieu, Louisiana, USA.

Daniel Materson Bass[269], aged 26, married Katherine Gladys Lee, aged 17, on October 9, 1924 in Lake Charles, Louisiana, USA. They had five children:

Mr. Bass[872] born on January 6, 1919 in Moab, Grand, Utah, United States; died on January 6, 1919 in Moab, Grand, Utah, United States

Katherine Gladys Bass[873] born on September 6, 1925 in Westlake, Calcasieu, Louisiana; died on August 15, 2012 in Ragley Beauregard, Louisiana, United States

Daniel Materson Bass Jr.[875] born on October 7, 1926 in West Lake, Calcasieu, LA; died on September 4, 1994

Ray Leonard Bass[877] born on May 28, 1928 in Westlake, Calcasieu, Louisianna; died on July 4, 1928

Kenneth Riley Bass Sr.[878] born on December 19, 1938 in Lake Charles, Calcasieu, Louisiana, United States; died on November 22, 2016 in Houston, Harris, Texas, United States

272. BENJAMIN EDWARD BASS (see Descendants (8)) was born on April 10, 1900, in Votaw, Hardin, Texas, USA, to William Riley Bass[64] and Frances Elizabeth Collins[65].
- He was recorded in the census in 1910, aged about 10, in Justice Precinct 7, Hardin, Texas, USA.
- He was recorded in the census in 1920, aged about 20, in San Juan, Utah, USA.
- He was recorded in the census in 1940, aged about 40, in Westlake, Police Jury Ward 4, Calcasieu, Louisiana, USA.
- He died on August 19, 1956, aged 56.

- He was buried in Magnolia Cemetery, Westlake, Clcs, Lsn.

Note: *Remembered by his children as very sensitive and caring, and very devoted to his familly. -per bio writen by his daugher Louise Bass Harrell.*

273. HAZEL MAE LAUGHLIN was born on September 3, 1912, in Egan, Acadia, Louisiana, USA.
- She was recorded in the census in 1940, aged about 27, in Westlake, Police Jury Ward 4, Calcasieu, Louisiana, USA.
- She died on March 7, 1945, aged 32 years, in Westlake, Calcasieu, Louisiana, USA.

Benjamin Edward Bass[272], aged 26, married Hazel Mae Laughlin, aged 14, on April 5, 1927 in Westlake, Calcasieu, Louisiana, USA. They had three children:

Hazel Louise Bass[881] born on July 28, 1933 in Westlake, Calcausieu, Louisiana, USA; died on January 22, 2012

Dorothy Bass[883] born on March 2, 1935 in Lake Charles, Calcasieu, Louisiana, USA; died on June 18, 2018 in Fernandia Beach, Nassau, Florida, USA

Ben E Bass[885] born about 1938 in Louisiana, USA

274. ETTA MARY BASS (see Descendants (8)) was born on January 14, 1903, in White Oak, Hardin, Texas, USA, to William Riley Bass[64] and Frances Elizabeth Collins[65].
- She was recorded in the census in 1910, aged about 7, in Justice Precinct 7, Hardin, Texas, USA.
- She was recorded in the census in 1940, aged about 37, in Montecello Town, E Precinct 2, San Juan, Utah, USA.
- She was recorded in the census on April 1, 1950, aged 47, in Hard Rd, Monticello, San Juan, Utah, United States.
- She died on May 26, 1986, aged 83 years, in Gilbert, Maricopa, Arizona, USA.
- She was buried on May 28, 1986 in Monticello City Cemetery, Monticello, San Juan, Utah, USA.

The following information is also recorded for Etta Mary:
Twin.

Etta Mary married twice. She was married to Alexander Gilbert Ralston[275] and Alpha B. Barton[276].

275. ALEXANDER GILBERT RALSTON was born on March 18, 1876, in Deer Lodge, Powell, Montana, USA.
- He died on October 19, 1935, aged 59 years, in Denver, Denver, Colorado, USA.
- He was buried on October 22, 1935 in Tobias, Saline, Ne.

Alexander Gilbert Ralston, aged 44, married Etta Mary Bass[274], aged 18, on March 12, 1921 in Salt Lake City, Salt Lake, UT, and they were divorced. They had two children:

Jean Ralston[886] born on February 20, 1922 in Salt Lake City, Salt Lake, Utah, USA; died on September 26, 2005 in Mesa, Maricopa, Arizona, USA

Mark Ralston[888] born on September 15, 1923 in Moab, Grand, Utah, United States; died on December 23, 1936 in Wellington, Carbon, Utah, USA

276. ALPHA B. BARTON was born on March 23, 1885, in Molen, Emery, Utah, USA.
- He was recorded in the census in 1940, aged about 55, in Montecello Town, E Precinct 2, San Juan, Utah, USA.
- He was recorded in the census on April 1, 1950, aged 65, in Hard Rd, Monticello, San Juan, Utah, United States.
- He died on February 10, 1976, aged 90 years, in Hunter, Salt Lake, Utah, USA.
- He was buried in Monticello City Cemetery, Monticello, San Juan, Utah, USA Plot: A-170-07.

Alpha B. married twice. He was married to Etta Mary Bass[274] and Ms. Barton.

Alpha B. Barton, aged 52, married Etta Mary Bass[274], aged 34, on September 10, 1937 in Manti, Sanpete, Utah. They had four children:

A. Bruce Barton[889] born about 1939 in Utah, United States

Grant B Barton[890] born about 1940 in Utah, United States

Mary Etta Barton[891] born about 1942 in Utah, United States

Dixie Barton[892] born about 1944 in Utah, United States

Alpha B. Barton married Ms. Barton. They had two children:

Rex Barton born about 1924 in Utah, USA

Clyda Barton born about 1925 in Utah, United States

277. MARY ETTA BASS (see Descendants (8)) was born on January 14, 1903, in White Oak, Hardin, Texas, USA, to William Riley Bass[64] and Frances Elizabeth Collins[65].
- She was recorded in the census in 1910, aged about 7, in Justice Precinct 7, Hardin, Texas, USA.
- She was recorded in the census on April 1, 1950, aged 47, in Carbonville, Carbon, Utah, United States.
- She died on September 14, 1993, aged 90 years, in Norwalk, Los Angeles, California, USA.

The following information is also recorded for Mary Etta:
Twin.

Note: *First of all I give thanks for the wonderful mother and father that God gave me the privilege of being born to. I was very happy all during my childhood. I just remember my father spanking me one time and that is when we were hoeing weds in the cotton fields in Texas when I missed a few weeds. I don't remember my mother spanking me, however my older sister Susanna gave me a few slaps. I was born January 14, 1903 along with my twin sister Etta (she was born first) to William Riley Bass and Fannie Elizabeth Collins Bass. We were the seventh and eighth born. We were born in a little farm settlement called White Oak near Saratoga, Texas. The doctor was a couple hours away. My father went to get the doctor but by the time he got back we had already been born. My first recollection was crawling around under the house and seeing a snake. Needles to say I didn't venture under the house anymore. My next recollection was my father building a two-story store with the family living upstairs and a general store on the ground floor. Upstairs had a balcony and I remember standing there and watching Haley's Comet go by. The general store failed due to oil workers leaving town without paying their bills. This forced Dad to return to farming in a nearby area. We continued to live over the store. In 1915 my sister Etta and I were baptized in the church by the traveling Mormon Missionaries. I recall attending school in Saratoga, Texas where I enjoyed playing basketball. I was teased and shunned by other students for our religious beliefs. In 1916 at age thirteen, we came by train to Thompson, Utah. We stopped in Denver and mother bought us all a straw hat with a ribbon on top and boy did we think we were elegantly dressed. When we got to Thompson, we went by stagecoach to Moab where dad bought a team and wagon to take the thirty mile trip to LaSal. We were given 160 acres by the Elders of the church. There was no water on the land. We set up a tent Dad had brought with us. I recall Dad and the boys bringing logs down from the mountain and building a log hous with a fireplace for heat. We cleared the land and attempted to grow crops but couldn't because of the arid climate. Dad went to Moab once a month to buy groceries with money that brother Milford set us. We stayed in LaSal until I graduated from eighth grade. Etta and I went to Moab where I worked at the hotel making beds. A short time later Etta and I moved to Thompson, Ugah were we worked for Dr. Ralston at a hotel. After a short time there, Dr. Ralston moved to Logan and Etta went to work for him there and I went to work at a boarding home in Price, Utah where brother Dan had gotten me a job. In December of 1920 or January of 1921, I met J. D. Harris at the boarding home. A few months later I moved to Helper, Utah were I worked at a hotel making beds. J. D. and I were courting at this time. I remember going with him a few trips moving oil field equipment in the San Rafael Valley. We were married on Jun 20, 1921 at Notre Dame Catholic Church in Price, Utah by Msgr. Giovananni. After the wedding we went to dinner, the trucks were already loaded. I changed from my wedding driss and we left for San Rafael Valley with two truckloads of oil equipment. We camped on the San Rafael River.We bought our first home on 3rd Street in Price, Utah about a week later. It was furnished. J. D. had four children by his first wife who died of the flu. They were Lyman, Doyle, Bill, and Alene. A short time after we moved into the house, Lyman and Doyle came to live with us. In April of 1922 our first child Vincent was born. A short time later Bill came from South Dakota to live with us. Children born to J. D. and I were: 1) Vincent Paul 2) Leo P. 3) Joseph Riley 4) Mary Patricia 5) David Joseph 6) Michael James 7) Mary Etta 8) Bernadetta 9) John Paul 10) Robert Thomas Approximately 1939 we moved to Carbonville which is about three miles west of Price. Our three bedroom home was moved in two parts by J. D. and the boys from Soldier Summit to Carbonville. It was placed on a full basement that was previously there. I had a serious operation in 1947 in which the doctor said that I was not to do any work. I could not sit around idly so I thought this was a good time for me to go back to school. I took my GED at Carbon College and then went on to receive a two year Business Administration Certificate. Following this due to the generosity of my boys, I was able to go to the University of Utah where I received my B. S. Degree in Teaching. I tough for many years at Norte Dam and Durant Schools in Price, Utah and also Montezuma Creek School in San Juan County. I retired from teaching at age 65. In April of 1966, we lost J. D. to cancer. In November of 1972 I sold my home in Carbonville and moved to Norwalk, California where I had purchased a two bedroom mobile home. I lived there until November of 1987 when I sold my home and moved to a retirement home in Los Angeles. I lost two infant sons, Joseph in 1926 and Robert in 1946. In April of 1977 I lost my son David to cancer. In January of 1987 I lost my son Leo in a construction accident in Alaska. - Mary Etta Harris [Bass].*

278. **JOSEPH DOYLE HARRIS** was born on September 11, 1886, in Anaconda, Deer Lodge, Montana, USA.
- He was recorded in the census on April 1, 1950, aged 63, in Carbonville, Carbon, Utah, United States.
- He died (Cancer) on April 29, 1966, aged 79 years, in Helper, Carbon, Utah, USA.
- He was buried in Price City Cemetery (Plot: 1-N-046-05), Price City, Carbon, Utah, USA.

Joseph Doyle married twice. He was married to Blanche M. Vercoe and Mary Etta Bass[277].

Joseph Doyle Harris, aged 21, married Blanche M. Vercoe, aged 20, on August 26, 1908 in Galena, Lawrence, South Dakota, USA. They had four children:
- Lyman Harris
- Doyle Harris
- Bill Harris born in 1916
- Alene Harris

The following information is also recorded for this family:
- Death of Spouse.

Joseph Doyle Harris, aged 34, married Mary Etta Bass[277], aged 18, on June 20, 1921 in Price, Carbon, Utah, USA. They had ten children:
>
> Vincent Harris[893] born in April 1922; died in 2016
> Leo Patrick Harris[894] born on January 19, 1925 in Price, Carbon, Utah, USA; died in January 1987
> Joseph Riley Harris[895] born on June 3, 1926 in Price, Carbon, Utah, USA; died on November 27, 1926 in Carbon, Utah, USA
> Mary Patricia Harris[896] born in 1928 in Utah, USA
> David Joseph Harris[897] born on September 19, 1929 in Price, Carbon, Utah, USA; died on April 9, 1977 in Orange, Calafornia, USA
> Michael James ("Jim and MJ") Harris[898] born on December 3, 1933 in Utah, USA; died on June 17, 2017 in Alaska, USA
> Mary Etta Harris[900] born about 1937 in Utah, United States
> Bernadette Harris[901] born about 1939 in Utah, United States; died in 2016
> John Paul Harris[902] born about 1942 in Utah, United States
> Robert Thomas Harris[903] born on July 22, 1946 in Price, Carbon, Utah, USA; died on January 20, 1947

279. JOSEPH CARSON BASS (see Descendants (8)) was born on March 2, 1905, in Saratoga, Hardin, Texas, USA, to William Riley Bass[64] and Frances Elizabeth Collins[65].
    - He was recorded in the census in 1910, aged about 5, in Justice Precinct 7, Hardin, Texas, USA.
    - He was recorded in the census in 1920, aged about 15, in San Juan, Utah, USA.
    - He died (Drowned) on September 5, 1925, aged 20 years, in Westlake, Calcasieu, Louisiana, USA.
    - He was buried in Orange Grove Cemetery, Calcasieu, Louisiana, United States.
    Note: *Drown while swimming with his brothers in the Calcasieu River.*
    (Death)

280. WINNETTA CASH.
    Joseph Carson Bass[279], aged 20, married Winnetta Cash on August 24, 1925.
    The following information is also recorded for this family:
    - Death of Spouse.

281. EVA ELIZABETH BASS (see Descendants (8)) was born on March 18, 1907, in Saratoga, Hardin, Texas, USA, to William Riley Bass[64] and Frances Elizabeth Collins[65]. Eva Elizabeth became known as "Evvie".
    - She was recorded in the census in 1910, aged about 3, in Justice Precinct 7, Hardin, Texas, USA.
    - She was recorded in the census in 1920, aged about 13, in San Juan, Utah, USA.
    - She died on January 22, 1999, aged 91 years, in St. George, Washington, Utah, USA.
    - She was buried in Saint George, Washington, Utah, United States.

282. LEONARD MERRILL STEVENS was born on January 21, 1907, in Fruitland, San Juan, Utah, USA.
    - He died on December 20, 1992, aged 86 years, in Tempe, Maricopa, Arizona, USA.
    - He was buried on December 23, 1992 in Saint George City Cemetery, St. George, Washington, Utah, United States.
    Leonard Merrill Stevens, aged 31, married Eva Elizabeth Bass[281], aged 31, on June 1, 1938 in Manti, Sanpete, Utah, United States. They had two children:
    > Merrillyn Stevens[904] born on May 9, 1939 in Provo, Utah, Utah, United States; died on January 4, 2021 in St. George, Washington, Utah, United States
    > William Reed Stevens[906] born on June 2, 1942 in Moab, Grand, Utah, USA; died on January 23, 1997 in Chandler, Maricopa, Arizona, USA

283. MARTHA BASS (see Descendants (8)) was born on July 27, 1909, in Saratoga, Hardin, Texas, USA, to William Riley Bass[64] and Frances Elizabeth Collins[65]. She died (At young age) on July 27, 1909, aged 0, in Saratoga, Hardin, Texas, USA.

284. BENNETT ABNER FLOYD (see Descendants (9)) was born on July 4, 1888, in Alabama, USA, to James A. Floyd[69] and Melvine Lavina Teel[68].
    - He was recorded in the census in 1940, aged about 51, in 403 Perry Street, Andalusia, Covington, Alabama, USA.
    - He died on October 3, 1949, aged 61.
    - He was buried in Bethesda Cemetery, Loango, Covington, Alabama, USA.

285. LENA MAE DAVIS (see Descendants (10)) was born on April 17, 1891, in Anderson, Anderson, South Carolina, USA, to John Walter Davis[72] and Elizabeth Teel[71]. She died on March 24, 1944, aged 52, in Anderson, Anderson, South Carolina, USA.

286. WILLIE OPHELLIA DAVIS (see Descendants (10)) was born in October 1891, in Alabama, USA, to John Walter

Davis[72] and Elizabeth Teel[71]. She died on December 13, 1970, aged 79, in Anderson, Anderson, South Carolina, USA.

287. NORA DAVIS (see Descendants (10)) was born in 1893, in Alabama, USA, to John Walter Davis[72] and Elizabeth Teel[71]. She died on September 17, 1978, aged about 85, in Anderson, Anderson, South Carolina, USA.

288. JOHN SUMPTER DAVIS (see Descendants (10)) was born on November 30, 1895, in Fairfield, Covington, Alabama, USA, to John Walter Davis[72] and Elizabeth Teel[71]. He died on September 8, 1954, aged 58, in Anderson, Anderson, South Carolina, USA.

289. MIRTICE DAVIS (see Descendants (10)) was born in 1900 to John Walter Davis[72] and Elizabeth Teel[71]. She died on July 19, 1982, aged about 82, in Red Level, Covington, Alabama, USA.

290. ATHEN DAVIS (see Descendants (10)) was born on October 19, 1903, in Fairfield, Covington, Alabama, USA, to John Walter Davis[72] and Elizabeth Teel[71]. He died on August 3, 1964, aged 60, in Andalusia, Covington, Alabama, USA.

291. LOTTIE JOHNSON HALL was born on July 4, 1909, in Alabama, USA. She died on February 20, 1967, aged 57, in Pleasant Home, Covington, Alabama, USA.
> Athen Davis[290], aged 23, married Lottie Johnson Hall, aged 18, on August 13, 1927 in Covington, Alabama, USA. They had three children:
>> Louvenia Davis[908] born on December 10, 1928 in Alabama, USA; died on December 30, 2008 in Andalusia, Covington, Alabama, USA
>> Marvette Faye Davis[909] born on November 3, 1930 in Alabama, USA; died on December 4, 2014 in Pensacola, Escambia, Florida, USA
>> James C Davis[910] born about 1933

292. ELMA DAVIS (see Descendants (10)) was born in 1905, in Alabama, USA, to John Walter Davis[72] and Elizabeth Teel[71]. She died in 1994, aged about 89, in Mobile, Mobile, Alabama, USA.

293. ETHEL LOUISE DAVIS (see Descendants (10)) was born on November 30, 1910, in Fairvield, Covington, Albama, USA, to John Walter Davis[72] and Elizabeth Teel[71]. She died on January 11, 2001, aged 90, in Pensacola, Escambia, Florida, USA.

294. WILLIAM GREELEY TEEL (see Descendants (11)) was born on December 18, 1893, in Covington, Alabama, United States, to John Teel[73] and Margaret Josephine Hart[74].
- He was recorded in the census in 1910, aged about 16, in Fairfield, Covington, Alabama, USA.
- He was recorded in the census in 1940, aged about 46, in 1 Range 14, Covington, Alabama, USA.
- He was recorded in the census on April 1, 1950, aged 56, in Proceeding South West from Pleasant Home School of Fales, Hart, Covington, Alabama, United States.
- He died on April 10, 1979, aged 85, in Alabama, United States.
- He was buried in Pleasant Home Baptist Cemetery, Covington, Alabama, USA.

The following information is also recorded for William Greeley:
- Military Service.

William Greeley had two partnerships; including Rubie L Kelley[792] (his second cousin).
Note: *US Army WWI.*
  (Military Service)
  William Greeley Teel was married.

295. JAMES SAMUEL TEEL (see Descendants (11)) was born on December 6, 1895, in Covington, Alabama, United States, to John Teel[73] and Margaret Josephine Hart[74].
- He died (At young age) on August 6, 1896, as an infant.
- He was buried in Conecuh River Baptist Cemetery, Andalusia, Covington, Alabama, USA.

296. GEORGE FRED TEEL (see Descendants (11)) was born about 1897, in Covington, Alabama, United States, to John Teel[73] and Margaret Josephine Hart[74].
- He was recorded in the census in 1910, aged about 13, in Fairfield, Covington, Alabama, USA.
- He was recorded in the census in 1930, aged about 33, in Fairfield, Covington, Alabama, USA.
- He was recorded in the census in 1940, aged about 43, in Conecuh Church Road, Election Precinct 2 Fairfield, Covington, Alabama, USA.
- He was recorded in the census on April 1, 1950, aged about 52, in 401 Avdon St, Andalusia, Covington, Alabama, United States.

297. ALEX RICHARD TEEL (see Descendants (11)) was born about 1900, in Alabama, United States, to John Teel[73] and Margaret Josephine Hart[74].
- He was recorded in the census in 1910, aged about 10, in Fairfield, Covington, Alabama, USA.
- He was recorded in the census in 1930, aged about 30, in Fairfield, Covington, Alabama, USA.
- He died on November 27, 1935, aged about 35, in Andalusia, Covington, Alabama, USA.
- He was buried in Conecuh River Baptist Cemetery, Andalusia, Covington, Alabama, United States.

298. ANNIE BELL PADGETT was born on February 5, 1906.
- She was recorded in the census in 1930, aged about 24, in Fairfield, Covington, Alabama, USA.
- She died on August 16, 1993, aged 87.
- She was buried in Conecuh River Baptist Cemetery, Andalusia, Covington, Alabama, USA.

Annie Bell married twice. She was married to Elijah Elbert Williams and Alex Richard Teel[297].
Elijah Elbert Williams married Annie Bell Padgett. They had one daughter:
Barbara Ann Williams born on September 27, 1944; died on February 7, 2015
Alex Richard Teel[297] married Annie Bell Padgett. They had three sons:
Richard Alex Teel Jr.[914] born on March 30, 1928; died on May 29, 1983
Donald Teel[916] born on May 14, 1930; died on May 19, 1998
Rufus Arnold Teel Teel[917] born on February 4, 1934; died on May 30, 1936

299. MAYME LEE TEEL (see Descendants (11)) was born on June 1, 1902, in Alabama, United States, to John Teel[73] and Margaret Josephine Hart[74].
- She was recorded in the census in 1910, aged about 8, in Fairfield, Covington, Alabama, USA.
- She died on June 19, 1993, aged 91.
- She was buried.

300. GEORGE HENRY GODWIN was born on May 8, 1901.
- He died on June 28, 1975, aged 74.
- He was buried in Andalusia Memorial Cemetery, Andalusia, Covington, Alabama, USA.
George Henry Godwin, aged 73, married Mayme Lee Teel[299], aged 72, on August 29, 1974.

301. CORINE VIRGINIA TEEL (see Descendants (11)) was born on April 12, 1904, in Alabama, United States, to John Teel[73] and Margaret Josephine Hart[74].
- She was recorded in the census in 1910, aged about 6, in Fairfield, Covington, Alabama, USA.
- She was recorded in the census in 1930, aged about 26, in Fairfield, Covington, Alabama, USA.
- She was recorded in the census on April 1, 1950, aged 45, in 401 Avdon St, Andalusia, Covington, Alabama, United States.
- She died on May 2, 1999, aged 95, in Andalusia, Covington, Alabama, United States.
- She was buried in Andalusia Memorial Cemetery, Andalusia, Covington, Alabama, USA.

302. DORA MARGARET TEEL (see Descendants (11)) was born on February 25, 1906, in Alabama, United States, to John Teel[73] and Margaret Josephine Hart[74].
- She was recorded in the census in 1910, aged about 4, in Fairfield, Covington, Alabama, USA.
- She was recorded in the census in 1930, aged about 24, in Fairfield, Covington, Alabama, USA.
- She was recorded in the census in 1940, aged about 34, in Travis Road, Election Precinct 3 Brewton, Escambia, Alabama, USA.
- She died on April 11, 1992, aged 86, in Alabama, United States.
- She was buried in Brooklyn Baptist Church Cemetery, Evergreen, Conecuh County, Alabama, USA.

303. RUPERT HARRELSON BLAIR was born on September 9, 1910, in Alabama, USA.
- He was recorded in the census in 1940, aged about 29, in Travis Road, Election Precinct 3 Brewton, Escambia, Alabama, USA.
- He died on September 24, 1984, aged 74.
- He was buried in Brooklyn Baptist Church Cemetery, Evergreen, Conecuh County, Alabama, USA.
Rupert Harrelson Blair married Dora Margaret Teel[302].

- He died on June 26, 1986, aged about 88.
- He was buried in 1986 in Andalusia Memorial Cemetery, Andalusia, Covington, Alabama, USA.

Direct Relations

304. MARTHA LENA TEEL (see Descendants (11)) was born on February 6, 1908, in Alabama, United States, to John Teel[73] and Margaret Josephine Hart[74]. Martha Lena became known as "Jack".
- She was recorded in the census in 1910, aged about 2, in Fairfield, Covington, Alabama, USA.
- She was recorded in the census in 1930, aged about 22, in Fairfield, Covington, Alabama, USA.
- She died on November 9, 1994, aged 86, in Shelby, Richland, Ohio, United States.
- She was buried in Pleasant Home Baptist Cemetery, Covington, Alabama, USA.

305. AUTREY LEWIS JOHNSON was born on July 30, 1907, in Alabama, United States, to James H. Johnson and Essie E. Campbell.
- He was recorded in the census in 1930, aged about 22, in Hart, Covington, Alabama, USA.
- He died on July 12, 1967, aged 59.
- He was buried in Pleasant Home Baptist Cemetery, Covington, Alabama, USA.

The following information is also recorded for Autrey Lewis:
- Military Service.
Note: *F1 US Navy WWII.*
(Military Service)

Autrey Lewis Johnson married Martha Lena Teel[304]. They had one son:
    Wayne Carroll Johnson[918] born on April 3, 1936 in Andalusia, Covington, Alabama, USA; died on April 8, 2002 in Fort Walton Beach, Okaloosa, Florida, USA

306. RUBEN EVERETT TEEL (see Descendants (11)) was born on November 22, 1912, in Alabama, United States, to John Teel[73] and Margaret Josephine Hart[74].
- He was recorded in the census in 1930, aged about 17, in Fairfield, Covington, Alabama, USA.
- He died on August 24, 1975, aged 62, in Alabama, United States.
- He was buried in 1975 in Andalusia Memorial Cemetery, Andalusia, Covington, Alabama, USA.

307. EULA MAY JACKSON was born on March 31, 1914.
- She died on December 29, 1991, aged 77, in Alabama, United States.
- She was buried in Andalusia Memorial Cemetery, Andalusia, Covington, Alabama, USA.

Ruben Everett Teel[306] married Eula May Jackson. They had two sons:
    John Everette Teel[919] born on January 9, 1942; died on July 31, 1986
    James Jery Teel Teel[920] born on September 21, 1951; died on November 6, 2013 in Opelika, Lee, Alabama, USA

308. BERNICE CATHLEEN TEEL (see Descendants (11)) was born on August 10, 1916, in Alabama, United States, to John Teel[73] and Margaret Josephine Hart[74].
- She was recorded in the census in 1930, aged about 13, in Fairfield, Covington, Alabama, USA.
- She was recorded in the census in 1940, aged about 23, in Conecuh Church Road, Election Precinct 2 Fairfield, Covington, Alabama, USA.
- She was recorded in the census on April 1, 1950, aged 33, in Castleberry Brooklyn Rd., Brooklyn, Conecuh, Alabama, United States.
- She died on July 25, 1995, aged 78, in Alabama, United States.
- She was buried in Brooklyn Baptist Church Cemetery, Evergreen, Conecuh County, Alabama, USA.

309. ORLANDO DUDLEY CARY was born on April 10, 1909, in Alabama, United States.
- He was recorded in the census on April 1, 1950, aged 40, in Castleberry Brooklyn Rd., Brooklyn, Conecuh, Alabama, United States.
- He died on May 25, 1978, aged 69.
- He was buried in Brooklyn Baptist Church Cemetery, Evergreen, Conecuh County, Alabama, USA.

Orlando Dudley Cary married Bernice Cathleen Teel[308]. They had two children:
    Carolyn Cary[921] born about 1943 in Alabama, United States
    Richard Derhyl Cary[922] born on November 14, 1944 in Alabama, United States; died on November 20, 1996

310. WILLIE SAMSON TEEL (see Descendants (13)) was born on May 16, 1904, in Alabama, USA, to William Riley Teel[77] and Addie Augusta Stokes[78].
- He was recorded in the census in 1910, aged about 6, in Fairfield, Covington, Alabama, USA.
- He was recorded in the census in 1940, aged about 36, in Conecuh Church Road, Election Precinct 2 Fairfield, Covington, Alabama, USA.
- He died on December 10, 1982, aged 78.
- He was buried in Conecuh River Baptist Cemetery, Andalusia, Covington, Alabama, USA.

311. MARGARET MAE PADGETT was born on April 13, 1904, in Alabama, USA. Margaret Mae became known as "Maggie".
- She was recorded in the census in 1940, aged about 36, in Conecuh Church Road, Election Precinct 2 Fairfield, Covington, Alabama, USA.
- She died on December 21, 1968, aged 64.
- She was buried in Conecuh River Baptist Cemetery, Andalusia, Covington, Alabama, USA.
    Willie Samson Teel[310], aged 32, married Margaret Mae Padgett, aged 32, on October 31, 1936.

312. ATRESS TEEL (see Descendants (13)) was born about 1906, in Alabama, United States, to William Riley Teel[77] and Addie Augusta Stokes[78]. She was recorded in the census in 1910, aged about 4, in Fairfield, Covington, Alabama, USA.

313. JIMIE L TEEL (see Descendants (13)) was born about 1908, in Alabama, United States, to William Riley Teel[77] and Addie Augusta Stokes[78]. He was recorded in the census in 1910, aged about 2, in Fairfield, Covington, Alabama, USA.

314. GLADYS TEEL (see Descendants (13)) was born on April 15, 1915, in Alabama, USA, to William Riley Teel[77] and Addie Augusta Stokes[78].
- She was recorded in the census in 1940, aged about 25, in Carlton La???, Andalusia, Covington, Alabama, USA.
- She was recorded in the census on April 1, 1950, aged 34, in Andalusia, Covington, Alabama, United States.
- She died on March 2, 1998, aged 82, in Covington, Alabama, USA.
- She was buried in Bethany Baptist Church Cemetery, Andalusia, Alabama, USA.

Gladys married three times. She was married to Fredrick Harling Schmidt[315], Frank Pete Hassell[316] and Hyram Hayes Straughter[317].

315. LT COL FREDRICK HARLING SCHMIDT was born on March 26, 1922, in Starkvill, Oktibbeha, Missisippi, USA.
- He died on March 2, 2003, aged 80, in Andalusia, Covington, Alabama, USA.
- He was buried in Bethany Baptist Church Cemetery, Andalusia, Alabama, USA.

The following information is also recorded for Fredrick Harling:
- Military Award.
Note: *Lt Col, U.S. Air Force WWII.*
    (Military Award)
        Fredrick Harling Schmidt married Gladys Teel[314]. They had two daughters:
            Carol Jean Hassell[924] born about 1941 in Alabama, United States
            Barbara Burns Schmidt[925] born on November 17, 1947 in Pittsboro, Chatham, North Carolina, USA; died on November 28, 1992

316. FRANK PETE HASSELL was born about 1912, in Alabama, United States.
- He was recorded in the census in 1940, aged about 28, in Carlton La???, Andalusia, Covington, Alabama, USA.
- He was recorded in the census on April 1, 1950, aged about 37, in Andalusia, Covington, Alabama, United States.
    Frank Pete Hassell married Gladys Teel[314]. They had three children:
        Jimmie Joe Hassell[926] born about 1936 in Alabama, United States
        Jerry Donald Hassell[927] born about 1939 in Alabama, United States
        Sharon A Hassell[928]

317. HYRAM HAYES STRAUGHTER.
    Hyram Hayes Straughter married Gladys Teel[314].

318. ADDIE LEE TEEL (see Descendants (14)) was born on October 23, 1908 to Henry Vauceous Teel[79] and Ella Padgett[80].
- She died on December 21, 1988, aged 80.
- She was buried in Conecuh River Baptist Cemetery, Andalusia, Covington, Alabama, USA.

319. JAMES VAUCIUOS TEEL (see Descendants (14)) was born in 1915 to Henry Vauceous Teel[79] and Ella Padgett[80].
- He died in October 1934, aged about 19, in Covington, Alabama, USA.
- He was buried in Conecuh River Baptist Cemetery, Andalusia, Covington, Alabama, USA.

320. JAMES ELIJAH TEEL (see Descendants (14)) was born on May 5, 1924, in Covington, Alabama, USA, to Henry Vauceous Teel[79] and Ella Padgett[80]. James Elijah became known as "Lige".
- He died on July 2, 1977, aged 53, in Burtonsville, Montgomery, Maryland, USA.
- He was buried in Woodfield Cemetery, Galesville, Anne Arudel, Maryland, USA.

The following information is also recorded for Lige:
- Military Service.

Notes:

Left to right back row first: Maxie Milo, Martha Naomi, Christian Ottie Lee, Ossie Mae, Genola, and William Bennett Bass.

2nd Row
6th child Ottie Lee Bass
7th child Naomi Bass
3rd Row
5th boy Maxie Bass
4th Row
Middle child - Genola Bass
Shady Hill School/Church

Direct Relations

Note: *Pfc U.S. Army, WWII.*
(Military Service)

321. SARA NANCY TEEL.
James Elijah Teel[320] married Sara Nancy Teel. They had one daughter:
Mary Jane Teel[929]

322. GENOLA BASS (see Descendants (16)) was born on December 11, 1905, in Andalusia, Covington, Alabama, USA, to William Bennett Bass[84] and Emily Estelle Jordan[85].
- She was recorded in the census in 1910, aged about 4, in Hart, Covington, Alabama, USA.
- She was recorded in the census in 1920, aged about 14, in Precinct 21, Covington, Alabama, USA.
- She was recorded in the census in 1940, aged about 34, in Spring Street, Crestview, 3, Okaloosa, Florida, USA.
- She died on February 5, 1969, aged 61 years.
- She was buried in New Bethany Cemetery, Holt, Okaloosa, Florida, USA.

Note: *Genola is the primary person responsible for the original Bass Family Record distributed in 1968. The work she did in collecting the information for that first book required a great deal more effort than anything I have done so far. The dedication required on her part far exceeds what has been required of me, and she has my unending gratitude for the spark her work was for mine. - Nicholas Bruce Bass.*

323. FLOYD S SPENCE was born on August 6, 1907.
- He was recorded in the census in 1940, aged about 32, in Spring Street, Crestview, 3, Okaloosa, Florida, USA.
- He died on December 8, 1952, aged 45.
- He was buried in New Bethany Cemetery, Holt, Okaloosa, Florida, USA.

Floyd S Spence married Genola Bass[322]. They had two children:
Opal Virginia Spence[930] born on August 24, 1934 in Florida, USA; died on March 5, 1969
Clyde Autry Spence[933] born on October 17, 1937 in Florida, USA; died on September 10, 1987

324. MAXIE MILO BASS (see Descendants (16)) was born on May 7, 1906, in Andalusia, Covington, Alabama, USA, to William Bennett Bass[84] and Emily Estelle Jordan[85].
- He was recorded in the census in 1910, aged about 4, in Hart, Covington, Alabama, USA.
- He was recorded in the census in 1920, aged about 14, in Precinct 21, Covington, Alabama, USA.
- He died on January 19, 1984, aged 77 years, in Andalusia, Covington, Alabama, USA.
- He was buried in New Bethany Cemetery, Holt, Okaloosa County, Florida, USA.

The following information is also recorded for Maxie Milo:
- Military Service.

Maxie Milo had two partnerships. He was married to Lucile Byrd[326]. He was also the partner of Mollie Raley[325].

Note: *Pvt. U.S. Army WWII.*
(Military Service)

325. MOLLIE RALEY was born on March 29, 1911. She died on July 2, 1998, aged 87 years.
Maxie Milo Bass[324] and Mollie Raley became partners.
The following information is also recorded for this family:
- Unknown Relationship.

326. LUCILE BYRD.
Maxie Milo Bass[324], aged about 54, married Lucile Byrd in 1960.

327. MARTHA NAOMI BASS (see Descendants (16)) was born on April 7, 1910, in Andalusia, Covington, Alabama, USA, to William Bennett Bass[84] and Emily Estelle Jordan[85].
- She was recorded in the census in 1910, aged 0, in Hart, Covington, Alabama, USA.
- She was recorded in the census in 1920, aged about 10, in Precinct 21, Covington, Alabama, USA.
- She was recorded in the census in 1940, aged about 30, in Precinct, Santa Rosa, Florida, USA.
- She was recorded in the census on April 1, 1950, aged 39, in Penny Creek Road Between Sections 14 and 15 Proceeding North, Milligan, Okaloosa, Florida, United States.
- She died on November 16, 2006, aged 96 years.
- She was buried in New Bethany Cemetery, Holt, Okaloosa, Florida, USA.

328. WOODROW A. WILKINSON was born on March 29, 1912, in Florida, USA.

- He was recorded in the census in 1940, aged about 28, in Precinct, Santa Rosa, Florida, USA.
- He was recorded in the census on April 1, 1950, aged 38, in Penny Creek Road Between Sections 14 and 15 Proceeding North, Milligan, Okaloosa, Florida, United States.
- He died on March 26, 1996, aged 84 years, in Crestview, Okaloosa, Florida, USA.
- He was buried in New Bethany Cemetery, Holt, Okaloosa, Florida, USA.

Woodrow A. Wilkinson, aged 19, married Martha Naomi Bass[327], aged 21, on October 18, 1931 in Holt, Okaloosa, Florida, USA. They had nine children:
- Wade Nathan Wilkinson[935] born on July 11, 1932 in Holt, Okaloosa, Florida, USA
- Floyce Genelle Wilkinson[937] born on February 12, 1934 in Holt, Okaloosa, Florida, USA
- Lorine Annette Wilkinson[939] born on January 12, 1936 in Holt, Okaloosa, Florida, USA
- Judith Elaine Wilkinson[941] born on January 27, 1938 in Cold Water, Santa Rosa, Florida, USA; died on March 18, 2012
- Irma Arleen Wilkinson[943] born on September 12, 1940 in Cold Water, Santa Rosa, Florida, USA; died on May 24, 2004
- Roland Douglas Wilkinson[945] born on March 17, 1942 in Holt, Okaloosa, Florida, USA
- Linda Aletha Wilkinson[947] born on April 5, 1943 in Holt, Okaloosa, Florida, USA
- Marcia Glendolyn Wilkinson[949] born on April 24, 1947 in Baker, Okaloosa, Florida, USA
- Neil Keith Wilkinson[951] born on September 6, 1951 in Florala, Covington, Alabama, USA; died on April 30, 1971 in United States and Territory

329. **CHRISTIAN OTTIE LEE BASS** (see Descendants (16)) was born on November 18, 1912, in Andalusia, Covington, Alabama, USA, to William Bennett Bass[84] and Emily Estelle Jordan[85].
- She was recorded in the census in 1920, aged about 7, in Precinct 21, Covington, Alabama, USA.
- She was recorded in the census on April 1, 1950, aged 37, in S on Blockwater Boss Road, Milligan, Okaloosa, Florida, United States.
- She died on September 11, 1993, aged 80 years, in Pensacola, Escambia, Florida, USA.
- She was buried in New Bethany Cemetery, Holt, Okaloosa, Florida, USA.

330. **GLEN CURTIS WILKINSON** was born on January 21, 1914, in Florida, United States.
- He was recorded in the census on April 1, 1950, aged 36, in S on Blockwater Boss Road, Milligan, Okaloosa, Florida, United States.
- He died on November 3, 1981, aged 67 years, in Holt, Okaloosa, Florida, USA.
- He was buried in New Bethany Cemetery, Holt, Okaloosa, Florida, USA.

Glen Curtis Wilkinson, aged 18, married Christian Ottie Lee Bass[329], aged 19, on October 10, 1932 in Baker, Okaloosa, Florida, USA. They had ten children:
- Wenton Curtis Wilkinson[952] born on February 15, 1934 in Florida, United States
- Dorothy Joan Wilkinson[955] born on April 8, 1936 in Holt, Okaloosa, Florida, USA
- Ina Mae Wilkinson[957] born on March 19, 1938 in Milton, Santa Rosa, Florida, USA
- Mona Idez Wilkinson[959] born on February 8, 1940 in Florida, United States; died on June 2, 1985 in Niceville, Okaloosa, Florida, USA
- Lary Rodney Wilkinson[961] born on June 16, 1942 in Holt, Okaloosa, Florida, USA
- Chadrick Earl Wilkinson[963] born on November 6, 1944 in Holt, Okaloosa, Florida, USA
- Glynda Carol Wilkinson[965] born on January 2, 1947 in Holt, Okaloosa, Florida, USA
- Norman Curtis Wilkinson[967] born on March 30, 1954 in Florala, Covington, Alabama, USA; died on May 5, 2007 in Holt, Okaloosa, Florida, USA
- Selina Benita Wilkinson[971] born on June 25, 1957 in Florala, Covington, Alabama, USA
- Rebecca Louise Wilkinson[973] born on March 4, 1959 in Milton, Santa Rosa, Florida, USA

331. **OSSIE MAE BASS** (see Descendants (16)) was born on September 9, 1917, in Andalusia, Covington, Alabama, USA, to William Bennett Bass[84] and Emily Estelle Jordan[85].
- She was recorded in the census in 1920, aged about 2, in Precinct 21, Covington, Alabama, USA.
- She was recorded in the census on April 1, 1950, aged 32, in South on Summerlin Road in Section 22, Milligan, Okaloosa, Florida, United States.
- She died on April 2, 2013, aged 95 years, in Pensacola, Escambia, Florida, USA.
- She was buried on April 5, 2013 in Old Holt Cemetery, Hold, Okaloosa, Florida, USA.

Note: *Ossie M. Bass Summerlin, age 95, of Holt, went home to be with the Lord on Tuesday, April 2, 2013, in Pensacola. She was born September 9, 1917, in Andalusia, AL, to the late William and Estelle Jordan Bass, and moved to this area in 1925, living in Holt and Milton. Ossie worked as a ward clerk at Okaloosa Memorial Hospital, and was an active member of the Holt Assembly of God until she became ill. She had also been a member of the Baker (Blossom) Garden Club. She was preceded in death by her husband, J. D. Summerlin, her parents, a brother, Maxie Bass, and sisters, Genola Spence, Naomi Wilkinson and Ottie Lee Wilkinson. Ossie is survived by her son and his wife, Devon and Mary Summerlin; a grandson and his wife, David and Mary Jo; granddaughter, Kathy; and great grandchildren, Jason, Sarah, Chad and Caleb; and several much-loved nieces and nephews. A time of visitation will be held from 6-8 PM on Thursday at the chapel of Whitehurst Powell Funeral Home. Funeral Services will be held at 11 AM Friday at the funeral home, with Rev. Alton Nixon officiating. Burial will follow at Old Holt Cemetery. Arrangements are entrusted*

to Whitehurst Powell Funeral Home in Crestview. Guest book and condolences are available online at www.whitehurstpowellfuneralhome.com.
(Death)

332. JESSE DAVID SUMMERLIN JR. was born on May 30, 1916, in Holt, Okaloosa, Florida, USA. Jesse David became known as "J.D.".
- He was recorded in the census on April 1, 1950, aged 33, in South on Summerlin Road in Section 22, Milligan, Okaloosa, Florida, United States.
- He died on December 10, 1987, aged 71 years, in Holt, Okaloosa, Florida, USA.
- He was buried in Old Holt Cemetery, Holt, Okaloosa, Florida, USA.

   Jesse David Summerlin Jr., aged about 20, married Ossie Mae Bass[331], aged about 18, in 1936. They had one son:

   Clarence Devon Summerlin[975] born on March 7, 1937 in Holt, Okaloosa, Florida, USA

333. JAMES HOLLIE MCGLAUN (see Descendants (16)) was born on January 22, 1901, in Alabama, USA, to James Egie Nardis McGlaun[87] and Nancy Jane Middleton Bass[86]. He died on June 8, 1979, aged 78 years, in Andalusia, Covington, Alabama, USA.

334. ANNA REEDER.
   James Hollie McGlaun[333] married Anna Reeder. They had one son:
   Bobby McGlaun[978] born on September 24, 1933; died on June 5, 1985

335. WILLIE OSCAR MCGLAUN (see Descendants (16)) was born on August 8, 1903, in Covington, Alabama, USA, to James Egie Nardis McGlaun[87] and Nancy Jane Middleton Bass[86].
- He was recorded in the census on April 1, 1950, aged 46, in Sanford, Covington, Alabama, United States.
- He died on August 30, 1997, aged 94 years, in Andalusia, Covington, Alabama, USA.

336. CLARA MAE SCHOFIELD was born about 1906, in Alabama, United States.
- She was recorded in the census on April 1, 1950, aged about 43, in Sanford, Covington, Alabama, United States.
- She died on May 22, 1975, aged about 68.

   Willie Oscar McGlaun[335] married Clara Mae Schofield. They had three children:
   Ruby Nell McGlaun[980] born on November 7, 1925
   Mary Etta McGlaun[982] born on January 5, 1928 in Alabama, United States
   James Kenneth McGlaun[984] born on June 25, 1930 in Andalusia, Covington, Alabama, USA

337. VIRGIL LEE MCGLAUN (see Descendants (16)) was born on January 18, 1906, in Alabama, USA, to James Egie Nardis McGlaun[87] and Nancy Jane Middleton Bass[86].
- He was recorded in the census in 1930, aged about 24, in Carolina, Covington, Alabama, USA.
- He died on February 3, 2004, aged 98 years, in Andalusia, Covington, Alabama, USA.

   Virgil Lee married twice. He was married to Eula Lee Maughon[338] and Mary L. Holloway[339].

338. EULA LEE MAUGHON was born on September 28, 1909.
- She died on February 21, 1981, aged 71 years, in Covington, Alabama, USA.
- She was buried in Covington, Alabama, USA.

   Virgil Lee McGlaun[337], aged 24, married Eula Lee Maughon, aged 21, on January 13, 1931 in Covington, Alabama, USA. They had four daughters:
   Margie Ree McGlaun[986] born on February 3, 1940 in Covington, Alabama, USA
   Patricia Ann McGlaun[988] born on October 24, 1943 in Andalusia, Covington, Alabama, USA
   Joyce Marie McGlaun[990] born on July 21, 1946 in Covington, Alabama, USA
   Sheila Dianne McGlaun[992] born on November 23, 1949 in Covington, Alabama, USA

339. MARY L. HOLLOWAY.
   Virgil Lee McGlaun[337], aged about 86, married Mary L. Holloway in 1992.

340. INETA MCGLAUN (see Descendants (16)) was born on July 29, 1909, in Alabama, USA, to James Egie Nardis McGlaun[87] and Nancy Jane Middleton Bass[86].
- She was recorded in the census in 1930, aged about 20, in Carolina, Covington, Alabama, USA.
- She died on December 25, 1997, aged 88 years, in Andalusia, Covington, Alabama, USA.

341. ORBEY RAY MCGLAUN (see Descendants (16)) was born on July 29, 1911, in Alabama, United States, to James Egie Nardis McGlaun[87] and Nancy Jane Middleton Bass[86].
- He was recorded in the census in 1930, aged about 18, in Carolina, Covington, Alabama, USA.

342. HELEN HENDERSON.
   Orbey Ray McGlaun[341] married Helen Henderson. They had two children:
   Doris Irene McGlaun[994] born on April 16, 1936
   Lamar Ray McGlaun[996] born on January 13, 1941

343. ORION T MCGLAUN (see Descendants (16)) was born on December 10, 1916, in Alabama, United States, to James Egie Nardis McGlaun[87] and Nancy Jane Middleton Bass[86].
- He was recorded in the census in 1930, aged about 13, in Carolina, Covington, Alabama, USA.

344. EVELYN THOMPSON.
Orion T McGlaun[343] married Evelyn Thompson. They had two children:
Guinda McGlaun[998] born on July 27, 1947
Orion Dewayne McGlaun[999] born on September 8, 1954

345. IDA MAE ROWELL (see Descendants (16)) was born on November 4, 1902, in Andalusia, Covington, Alabama, USA, to James Henry Rowell[90] and Isabell Bass[89].
- She was recorded in the census in 1910, aged about 7, in Hart, Covington, Alabama, USA.
- She was recorded in the census in 1920, aged about 17, in Precinct 10, Covington, Alabama, USA.
- She was recorded in the census in 1930, aged about 27, in Red Rock, Santa Rosa, Florida, USA.
- She was recorded in the census in 1940, aged about 37, in Election Prect 21 Carolina, Covington, Alabama, USA.
- She was recorded in the census on April 1, 1950, aged 47, in Carolina, Covington, Alabama, United States.
- She died on December 23, 1986, aged 84 years, in Andalusia, Covington, Alabama, United States.
- She was buried.

346. WILLIAM MARTIN HUCKABAA was born on June 1, 1895, in Wagener, Aiken, South Carolina, United States, to William Benjamin Huckabaa[91] and Stella Gunter.
- He was recorded in the census in 1920, aged about 25, in Precinct 10, Covington, Alabama, USA.
- He was recorded in the census in 1930, aged about 35, in Red Rock, Santa Rosa, Florida, USA.
- In 1935, aged about 40, he resided at R, Covington, Alabama.
- He was recorded in the census in 1940, aged about 45, in Election Prect 21 Carolina, Covington, Alabama, USA.
- He was recorded in the census on April 1, 1950, aged 54, in Carolina, Covington, Alabama, United States.
- He died on September 9, 1985, aged 90 years, in Andalusia, Covington, Alabama, United States.
- He was buried in Shady Hill Church Cemetery, Covington, Alabama, USA.

The following information is also recorded for William Martin:
- Military Service.
Note: *U.S. Army WWI.*
(Military Service)
William Martin Huckabaa, aged 23, married Ida Mae Rowell[345], aged 16, on May 31, 1919 in Covington County, Alabama. They had eleven children:
Martin Van Buren Huckabaa Sr.[1000] born on September 2, 1921 in Holt, Okaloosa, Florida, USA; died on April 19, 1998
Allie Mae Dukes Ward[1001] born on October 29, 1923 in Holt, Okaloosa, Florida, USA; died on August 9, 2017 in Okaloosa, Florida, United States
Lener Bell Huckabaa[1004] born on November 22, 1925 in Holt, Okaloosa, Florida, USA; died on January 31, 1929
L. B. Huckabaa[1005] born on January 14, 1928 in Holt, Okaloosa, Florida, USA; died on March 31, 2015
Daris Lee Huckabaa[1006] born on May 6, 1930 in Milton, Santa Rosa, Florida, USA
Baby Huckabaa[1008] born on January 6, 1933 in Holt, Okaloosa, Florida, USA; died on January 10, 1933 in Holt, Okaloosa, Florida, USA
Henry Clayton Huckabaa[1009] born on February 16, 1934 in Holt, Okaloosa, Florida, USA; died on January 17, 2010
Donald Travis Huckabaa[1011] born on September 10, 1936 in Andalusia, Covington, Alabama, USA; died on July 3, 1997
Earl C. Huckabaa[1013] born on February 28, 1939 in Andalusia, Covington, Alabama, USA; died on October 3, 1979 in Andalusia, Covington, Alabama, USA
William Ray Huckabaa[1015] born on January 15, 1942 in Andalusia, Covington, Alabama, USA
Robert Thomas Huckabaa[1017] born on March 21, 1944 in Andalusia, Covington, Alabama, USA; died on December 9, 1945

347. LETTIE V. ROWELL (see Descendants (16)) was born on June 15, 1906, in Covington, Alabama, USA, to James Henry Rowell[90] and Isabell Bass[89].
- She was recorded in the census in 1910, aged about 4, in Hart, Covington, Alabama, USA.
- She was recorded in the census in 1920, aged about 14, in Precinct 21, Covington, Alabama, USA.
- She was recorded in the census in 1940, aged about 34, in Second Street, E Preinct 20 West De Funiak Springs,

Walton, Florida, USA.
- She died on July 27, 1994, aged 88 years, in Walton County, Florida, USA.
- She was buried in Sunset Cemetery, Valparaiso, Okaloosa, Florida, USA.
    Lettie V. gave birth to four daughters:
        Trudy Rowell[1018] born on November 26, 1921 in Holt, Okaloosa, Florida, USA; died on February 13, 2012
        Willie V. Rowell[1020] born on July 5, 1924 in Holt, Okaloosa, Florida, USA; died on July 18, 1980 in Niceville, Okaloosa, Florida, USA
        Eva Mae Rowell[1023] born about 1928 in Florida, USA
        Bobbie Jean Smith[1024] born on July 21, 1951 in DeFuniak Springs, Walton, Florida, USA
    The following information is also recorded for this family:
    - Unspecified Relationship.

348. LEROY ROWELL (see Descendants (16)) was born on January 5, 1909, in Alabama, United States, to James Henry Rowell[90] and Isabell Bass[89].
- He was recorded in the census in 1910, aged about 1, in Hart, Covington, Alabama, USA.
- He was recorded in the census in 1920, aged about 11, in Precinct 21, Covington, Alabama, USA.
- He was recorded in the census in 1940, aged about 31, in West 5th Avenue, Florala, Covington, Alabama, USA.
- He was recorded in the census on April 1, 1950, aged 41, in 2606 East Ave, Panama City, Bay, Florida, United States.
- He died in October 1977, aged 68 years.
- He was buried in Greenwood Cemetery, Panama City, Bay, Florida, USA.
Note: *Plot: Section 144 Lot 1.*
    (Burial)
349. LAURA PITTMAN was born on May 7, 1908, in Florida, United States.
- She was recorded in the census in 1940, aged about 32, in West 5th Avenue, Florala, Covington, Alabama, USA.
- She was recorded in the census on April 1, 1950, aged 41, in 2606 East Ave, Panama City, Bay, Florida, United States.
- She died on September 19, 1998, aged 90.
- She was buried in Greenwood Cemetery, Panama City, Bay, Florida, USA.
Note: *Plot: Section 144 Lot 1.*
    (Burial)
    Leroy Rowell[348] married Laura Pittman. They had three sons:
        Henry Eral Rowell[1026] born on May 5, 1937 in Florala, Covington, Alabama, USA
        Ervunus Rowell[1028] born on April 9, 1939 in Florala, Covington, Alabama, USA
        Ray Lee Rowell[1030] born on June 22, 1943 in Florala, Covington, Alabama, USA; died on July 22, 1943 in Florala, Covington, Alabama, USA

350. EVA MAE ROWELL (see Descendants (16)) was born on October 23, 1927, in Holt, Okaloosa, Florida, USA, to James Henry Rowell[90] and Isabell Bass[89].
- She was recorded in the census on April 1, 1950, aged 22, in Bruce and Illinois, Defuniak Springs, Walton, Florida, United States.
- She died on August 22, 1999, aged 71 years.
- She was buried in Sunset Cemetery, Valparaiso, Okaloosa, Florida, USA.
Eva Mae married twice. She was married to Ruben A. Money[351] and James T. Jinks[352].
351. RUBEN A. MONEY was born on January 31, 1919, in Alabama, United States.
- He was recorded in the census on April 1, 1950, aged 31, in 3r Bruce and Illinois, Defuniak Springs, Walton, Florida, United States.
- He died on October 7, 1981, aged 62.
- He was buried in Sandy Creek Cemetery, Ponce de Leon, Holmes, Florida, USA.
    Ruben A. Money, aged 27, married Eva Mae Rowell[350], aged 18, on September 2, 1946. They had four children:
        Billie Jean Johnson[1031] born about 1933 in Louisiana, United States
        Ruben Arnold Money Jr.[1032] born on June 23, 1947 in DeFuniak Springs, Walton, Florida, USA
        Eva Rosalind Money[1034] born on July 9, 1948 in DeFuniak Springs, Walton, Florida, USA; died on May 1, 2009
        Jimmy Ronald Money[1037] born on August 27, 1949 in Florala, Covington, Alabama, USA
352. JAMES T. JINKS was born on April 17, 1930, in Knoxville, Knox, Tennessee, USA.
- He died on January 31, 2003, aged 72.
- He was buried in Sunset Cemetery, Valparaiso, Okaloosa, Florida, USA.

James T. Jinks, aged 30, married Eva Mae Rowell[350], aged 32, on August 19, 1960.

353. EUGENE HUCKABA (see Descendants (16)) was born on April 7, 1918, in Alabama, United States, to William Benjamin Huckabaa[91] and Isabell Bass[89].
- He was recorded in the census in 1920, aged about 2, in Precinct 21, Covington, Alabama, USA.
- He was recorded in the census in 1930, aged about 12, in Red Rock, Santa Rosa, Florida, USA.
- He was recorded in the census in 1940, aged about 22, in Second Street, Precinct 20, Walton, Florida, USA.
- He was a Painter.
- He was recorded in the census on April 1, 1950, aged 31, in 10 7/10 Mi End Pine Grove High Way and Pine Grove Settlement to Highway 83, Liberty, Walton, Florida, United States.
- He died on December 15, 1993, aged 75 years, in Siler City, Chatham, North Carolina.
- He was buried in Guilford Cremation Service Cemetery, Greensboro, Nc.

354. JOYCE COLLINSWORTH was born about 1934, in Florida, United States. She was recorded in the census on April 1, 1950, aged about 15, in 10 7/10 Mi End Pine Grove High Way and Pine Grove Settlement to Highway 83, Liberty, Walton, Florida, United States.

Eugene Huckaba[353] married Joyce Collinsworth. They had three children:
Willie Eugene Huckaba[1040] born on May 20, 1953
John Russell Huckaba[1041] born on October 1, 1953
Robin Rena Huckaba[1042] born on September 10, 1961

355. ADDIE IRENE HUCKABA (see Descendants (16)) was born on November 10, 1920, in Andalusia, Covington, Alabama, USA, to William Benjamin Huckabaa[91] and Isabell Bass[89].
- She was recorded in the census in 1930, aged about 9, in Red Rock, Santa Rosa, Florida, USA.
- She was recorded in the census in 1940, aged about 19, in Second Street, Precinct 20, Walton, Florida, USA.
- She died on March 16, 1994, aged 73 years, in Escambia County, Florida, USA.

356. TROY DAVIS.
Troy Davis married Addie Irene Huckaba[355]. They had five children:
Hazel Alita Davis[1043] born on May 18, 1950
Georgiann Isabel Davis[1044] born on February 19, 1952
Troy Davis Jr.[1045] born on June 2, 1953
Benjamin Franklin Davis[1046] born on June 28, 1955
Terry Allen Davis[1047] born on June 23, 1957

357. BESSIE LUVINE BASS (see Descendants (16)) was born on January 27, 1911, in Florida, United States, to James Dallas Bass[92] and Amie Isabel Bedgood[93].
- She was recorded in the census in 1940, aged about 29, in Crestview, 3, Okaloosa, Florida, USA.
- She was recorded in the census on April 1, 1950, aged 39, in 692 700 Block E. Chestnut Ave., Crestview, Okaloosa, Florida, United States.
- She died on January 17, 1984, aged 72 years.
- She was buried on January 20, 1984 in New Bethany Cemetery, Holt, Okaloosa, Florida, United States.

358. JOHN HENRY CRAWFORD was born on January 27, 1911, in Florida, United States.
- He was recorded in the census in 1940, aged about 29, in Crestview, 3, Okaloosa, Florida, USA.
- He was recorded in the census on April 1, 1950, aged 39, in 692 700 Block E. Chestnut Ave., Crestview, Okaloosa, Florida, United States.
- He died on March 28, 1982, aged 71.
- He was buried in New Bethany Cemetery, Holt, Okaloosa, Florida, United States.

John Henry Crawford married Bessie Luvine Bass[357]. They had eight children:
Lonnie Crawford[1048] born on May 23, 1929 in Florida, USA; died on June 8, 2002
Edna Mae Crawford[1050] born on June 3, 1930 in Florida, United States
James Edmund Crawford[1052] born on June 12, 1932 in Florida, United States; died in August 1978
Herbert L Crawford[1054] born on February 20, 1934 in Florida, United States
Betty Jean Crawford[1056] born on April 17, 1936 in Florida, United States
John Dallas Crawford[1058] born on May 20, 1939 in Crestview, Okaloosa, Florida, USA
Glinda Crawford[1060] born on July 24, 1945 in Florida, United States
Gerald H Crawford[1062] born on March 31, 1947 in Florida, United States

359. JAMES HENRY BASS (see Descendants (16)) was born on May 1, 1913, in Holt, Okaloosa, Florida, USA, to James Dallas Bass[92] and Amie Isabel Bedgood[93].
- He was recorded in the census in 1930, aged about 17, in Holt, Okaloosa, Florida, USA.
- He was recorded in the census in 1940, aged about 27, in State Highway, Merritt Island, Precinct 11, Brevard, Florida, USA.

Direct Relations

- He died on September 28, 1988, aged 75 years, in Fruitland Park, Lake, Florida, USA.
- He was buried in Shiloh Cemetery, Fruitland Park, Lake, Florida, USA.

James Henry married twice. He was married to Margaret Charity Franklin[360] and Minnie Walton McKnight Smith[361].

360. MARGARET CHARITY FRANKLIN was born about 1920, in Florida, USA.
- She was recorded in the census in 1940, aged about 20, in State Highway, Merritt Island, Precinct 11, Brevard, Florida, USA.

The following information is also recorded for Margaret Charity:
Twin.

Margaret Charity married twice. She was married to James Henry Bass[359] and James T McKnight Sr.
Note: *Mary Alice Bass - Twin Sister.*
(Twin)

James Henry Bass[359], when younger than 21, married Margaret Charity Franklin, when younger than 14, before 1935. They had three children:
Billy Ray Bass[1063] born on October 12, 1935 in Florida, USA; died on June 14, 2004
Theresa Bass[1066] born about 1938 in Florida, USA
Thomas Bass[1067] born about 1939 in Florida, USA

James T McKnight Sr. married Margaret Charity Franklin.

361. MINNIE WALTON MCKNIGHT SMITH was born on March 16, 1916, in Fruitland Park, Lake, Florida, USA.
- She died on January 26, 2009, aged 92 years, in Fruitland Park, Lake, Florida, USA.
- She was buried in Shiloh Cemetery, Fruitland Park, Lake, Florida, USA.

James Henry Bass[359], when older than 24, married Minnie Walton McKnight Smith, when older than 21, after 1937. They had four children:
Theresa Annette Bass[1068] born on July 9, 1937 in Florida, USA
Thomas Franklin Bass[1072] born on November 21, 1939 in Florida, USA
Jasper Daniel Bass[1074] born on March 29, 1943
James Dallas Bass[1077] born on January 20, 1951

362. HILLARY J. BASS (see Descendants (16)) was born on January 26, 1916, in Florida, USA, to James Dallas Bass[92] and Amie Isabel Bedgood[93]. She died on October 16, 1916, aged 0, in Holt, Okaloosa, Florida, USA.

363. MAGDALINE BASS (see Descendants (16)) was born on December 14, 1918 to James Dallas Bass[92] and Amie Isabel Bedgood[93].

364. RAY-MONDE BASS (see Descendants (16)) was born on February 19, 1920, in Florida, United States, to James Dallas Bass[92] and Amie Isabel Bedgood[93]. She was recorded in the census in 1930, aged about 10, in Holt, Okaloosa, Florida, USA.

365. ALBERT BARTLEY CURBELLO.
Albert Bartley Curbello married Ray-Monde Bass[364]. They had two sons:
Joel Maurice Curbello[1078] born on September 17, 1948 in Houston, Harris, Texas 77251, USA
Albert Curbello[1079]

366. JOHN CLAYTON BASS (see Descendants (16)) was born on March 26, 1922, in Florida, United States, to James Dallas Bass[92] and Amie Isabel Bedgood[93].
- He was recorded in the census in 1930, aged about 8, in Holt, Okaloosa, Florida, USA.
- He was recorded in the census in 1940, aged about 18, in Okaloosa, Florida, USA.
- He was recorded in the census on April 1, 1950, aged 28, in Mirror Lake, Fruitland Park, Lake, Florida, United States.
- He died on December 24, 2012, aged 90 years.

367. LOUISE GRIFFITH was born about 1927, in Florida, United States. She was recorded in the census on April 1, 1950, aged about 22, in Mirror Lake, Fruitland Park, Lake, Florida, United States.
John Clayton Bass[366] married Louise Griffith. They had four children:
William Dallas Bass[1080] born on March 3, 1947 in Florida, United States; died on July 30, 1999
Paul Howard Bass[1082] born on May 12, 1948 in Florida, United States
Debbie Sue Bass[1083] born on September 18, 1952
Johnny Ray Bass[1084] born on December 6, 1962

368. MARVIN DALLAS BASS SR. (see Descendants (16)) was born on March 6, 1924, in Holt, Okaloosa, Florida, USA, to James Dallas Bass[92] and Amie Isabel Bedgood[93].
- He was recorded in the census in 1930, aged about 6, in Holt, Okaloosa, Florida, USA.
- He was recorded in the census in 1940, aged about 16, in Okaloosa, Florida, USA.
- He was recorded in the census on April 1, 1950, aged 26, in Dixie Highway, Fruitland Park, Lake, Florida, United

States.
- He died on December 29, 2002, aged 78 years, in Crestview, Okaloosa County, Florida, USA.
- He was buried in Live Oak Park Cemetery, Crestview, Florida, USA.

The following information is also recorded for Marvin Dallas:
- Military Service.

Note: *WWII Vet.*
(Military Service)

369. KATHLEEN L HEATH was born about 1929, in Florida, United States. She was recorded in the census on April 1, 1950, aged about 20, in Dixie Highway, Fruitland Park, Lake, Florida, United States.

Marvin Dallas Bass Sr.[368] married Kathleen L Heath. They had three sons:
Marvin Dallas Bass Jr.[1085] born on June 9, 1947 in Florida, United States
Jimmie Ray Bass[1087] born on August 14, 1948 in Florida, United States
James Edward Bass[1088] born on January 25, 1950 in Florida, United States

370. SARAH CHRISTIAN BASS (see Descendants (16)) was born on July 17, 1926, in Holt, Okaloosa, Florida, USA, to James Dallas Bass[92] and Amie Isabel Bedgood[93].
- She was recorded in the census in 1930, aged about 3, in Holt, Okaloosa, Florida, USA.
- She was recorded in the census in 1940, aged about 13, in Okaloosa, Florida, USA.
- She died on August 8, 2015, aged 89 years, in Pensacola, Escambia, Florida, USA.

371. VICTOR EUGENE NALL was born on May 13, 1924.
- He died on December 1, 1990, aged 66 years.
- He was buried in Barrancas National Cemetery, Naval Air Station, 1 Cemetery Road, Pensacola, Florida 32508, USA.

The following information is also recorded for Victor Eugene:
- Military Service.

Note: *U.S. Army WWII.*
(Military Service)

Victor Eugene Nall married Sarah Christian Bass[370]. They had three sons:
Ronald Duane Nall[1090] born on November 15, 1947
Terry Maurice Nall[1092] born on November 9, 1949
Dennis Ray Nall[1093] born on May 12, 1954

372. GERALD HOWARD BASS SR. (see Descendants (16)) was born on December 10, 1928, in Florida, United States, to James Dallas Bass[92] and Amie Isabel Bedgood[93].
- He was recorded in the census in 1930, aged about 1, in Holt, Okaloosa, Florida, USA.
- He was recorded in the census in 1940, aged about 11, in Okaloosa, Florida, USA.
- He died on April 30, 2017, aged 88.

373. DORIS RAY was born on October 8, 1932, in Panama City, Florida, USA. She died on January 9, 2019, aged 86.

Note: *Doris Bass, 86, of Lynn Haven, Florida passed away Saturday January 19, 2019 at home surrounded by family. Doris was born in Panama City, Florida. She graduated from Bay High School in 1950. Doris owned and managed Bass Grocery in West Bay, Florida until 1971. She was a life-member of West Bay Advent Christian Church, where she served as a Deaconess, Treasurer, and was actively involved in the Women's Home and Foreign Mission Society. Doris had an extraordinary love for her family, friends and church. She was deeply loved and respected for her Christian faith and kindness to all. Doris was preceded in death by her husband of 66 years, Gerald H. Bass, Sr, son Gerald H. (Howie) Bass, Jr., sons-in-law Larry Striplin and Anthony (Tony) McGill and sister Inez Kirtsinger. She is survived by her daughters, Wanda McGill, Rhonda Striplin and Tonya Wagner; grandchildren Melissa Dudley, Chad Bass (Carrie), Kyle Bass, Delilah Bass, Josh Jackson (Tiffany), Anthony McGill, Aharon McGill (Amber), Heather Gentry (Wayne), Jessica Ceurvels, Kaitlyn Rodriguez (A.J.) and Brittney Latta (Austin); siblings Roy Ray (Myrtle), Delma Ruth Jordan, John Ray (Donna); and 19 great grandchildren.Funeral services held 1:30 P.M. Tuesday, January 22, 2019 at West Bay Advent Christian Church. Serving as pallbearers are Donald Wayne Miller, Brigham Bass, Kenny Ray, Greg Ray, A.J. Rodriguez, and Aharon McGill.*
(Death)

Gerald Howard Bass Sr.[372] married Doris Ray. They had four children:
Gerald Howard Bass Jr.[1094] born on April 29, 1953; died on May 19, 2008
Wanda Bass[1096] born on September 3, 1956
Rhonda Bass[1098] born on April 5, 1958
Tonya Bass[1100] born on October 6, 1968

374. MAE BELLE POSEY (see Descendants (16)) was born on December 20, 1908, in Covington, Alabama, USA, to Martin Edward Posey[95] and Mary Alice Bass[94].
- She was recorded in the census in 1910, aged about 1, in Hart, Covington, Alabama, USA.
- She was recorded in the census in 1930, aged about 21, in Mary Esther, Okaloosa, Florida, USA.
- She was recorded in the census in 1940, aged about 31, in Election Prect 21 Carolina, Covington, Alabama, USA.
- She died on May 29, 2000, aged 91 years, in Laurell Hill, Walton, Florida, USA.
- She was buried in J.E. Huckaba Cemetery, Defuniak Springs, Walton, Florida, USA.

375. JAMES EDGAR HUCKABA was born on February 22, 1903, in Covington, Alabama, United States, to William Benjamin Huckabaa[91] and Stella Gunter.
- He was recorded in the census in 1920, aged about 17, in Precinct 21, Covington, Alabama, USA.
- He was recorded in the census in 1930, aged about 27, in Mary Esther, Okaloosa, Florida, USA.
- He was recorded in the census in 1940, aged about 37, in Election Prect 21 Carolina, Covington, Alabama, USA.
- He died on July 12, 1991, aged 88 years, in Walton County, Florida, USA.
- He was buried in J.E. Huckaba Cemetery, Defuniak Springs, Walton, Florida, USA.

The following information is also recorded for James Edgar:
- Military Service.

James Edgar Huckaba, aged 22, married Mae Belle Posey[374], aged 16, on July 8, 1925. They had six children:
James Harold Huckaba[1102] born on April 3, 1926 in Mossy Head, Walton, Florida, USA; died on July 17, 2011
Clara Mae Huckabaa[1104] born on June 10, 1928 in Alabama, United States
Edward Ervin Huckaba[1106] born on March 18, 1932 in Alabama, USA
Mary Opal Huckabaa[1109] born on April 18, 1940
Earl Flyn Huckaba[1111] born on February 14, 1944
Jimmy David Huckaba[1114] born on June 18, 1948

376. CLIFTON POSEY (see Descendants (16)) was born on October 16, 1910 to Martin Edward Posey[95] and Mary Alice Bass[94]. He died on February 13, 1913, aged 2.

377. PRESTON DALLAS POSEY (see Descendants (16)) was born in 1912, in Alabama, USA, to Martin Edward Posey[95] and Mary Alice Bass[94]. He died on March 9, 2005, aged about 92.

378. LAURA STILLER was born on May 31, 1909, in Geneva, Geneva, Alabama, USA.
- She died on April 17, 1990, aged 80 years, in Baker, Okaloosa, Florida, USA.
- She was buried in Holt Cemetery.

Preston Dallas Posey[377], aged about 28, married Laura Stiller, aged 31, on September 22, 1940. They had one son:
James Edward Posey[1115] born on June 14, 1942 in Holt, Okaloosa, Florida, USA; died on August 21, 2007

379. CHESTER POSEY (see Descendants (16)) was born on February 16, 1914 to Martin Edward Posey[95] and Mary Alice Bass[94]. He died on July 28, 1949, aged 35.

380. ADDIE LEE JOHNSON was born on April 24, 1915.
- She died on December 12, 2000, aged 85.
- She was buried in Bethel Cemetery, Escambia County, Alabama, USA.

Chester Posey[379] married Addie Lee Johnson. They had two daughters:
Mary Jane Posey[1118] born on July 8, 1938; died on December 6, 2006 in Pensacola, Escambia, Florida, USA
Dorothy Faye Posey[1120] born on April 26, 1942

381. HOLLAND MIDDLETON POSEY (see Descendants (16)) was born on May 27, 1916 to Martin Edward Posey[95] and Mary Alice Bass[94]. He died on September 20, 1916, as an infant.

382. STACY DENTON POSEY (see Descendants (16)) was born on August 6, 1917, in Holt, Okaloosa, Florida, USA, to Martin Edward Posey[95] and Mary Alice Bass[94].
- He died on March 1, 2004, aged 86.

The following information is also recorded for Stacy Denton:
- Military Service.

383. JUANITA PALMER was born on December 2, 1931, in Laurel Hill, Okaloosa, Florida, USA.
Stacy Denton Posey[382] married Juanita Palmer. They had four children:
Linda Louise Posey[1122] born on August 10, 1949
Martin James Posey[1124] born on September 8, 1952
Larry Denton Posey[1126] born on October 13, 1956
Debra K. Posey[1128] born on March 12, 1958

384. BONNIE LEE POSEY (see Descendants (16)) was born on July 12, 1921, in Holt, Okaloosa, Florida, USA, to Martin Edward Posey[95] and Mary Alice Bass[94].
- She died in 2008, aged about 86.
- She was buried in Bayview Memoial Park, Pensacola, Escambia, Florida, USA.

385. ERNEST STEWART was born on March 2, 1913, in Laurel Hill, Okaloosa, Florida, USA. He died on October 12, 1983, aged 70 years, in Escambia, Florida, USA.
Ernest Stewart married Bonnie Lee Posey[384]. They had eight children:
Patriciea Ernestine Stewart[1131] born on January 27, 1942 in Montgomery County, Alabama, USA; died on September 18, 2020 in Pensacola, Escambia, Florida, USA
Barbara Ann Stewart[1133] born on July 28, 1944
Betty Sue Stewart[1137] born on November 15, 1945; died on April 10, 2008
Ernest Dewayne Stewart[1139] born on November 2, 1947 in Florala, Covington, Alabama, USA
Shirley Jane Stewart[1142] born on July 30, 1949
Bonnie Mae Stewart[1144] born on April 20, 1953 in Florala, Covington, Alabama, USA
Mary Elizabeth Stewart[1145] born on December 23, 1955 in Escambia, Florida, USA
Ernest Stewart Jr.[1149] born on March 19, 1961

386. CORA LEE POSEY (see Descendants (16)) was born on February 2, 1923 to Martin Edward Posey[95] and Mary Alice Bass[94]. She died on December 12, 1927, aged 4.

387. MARY EVELYN POSEY (see Descendants (16)) was born on June 7, 1925, in Holt, Okaloosa, Florida, USA, to Martin Edward Posey[95] and Mary Alice Bass[94].
- She died on February 10, 2012, aged 86, in Pensacola, Escambia, Florida, USA.
- She was buried in New Holt Cemetery, Holt, Okaloosa, Florida, USA.

388. JAMES EDWARD TAYLOR SR. was born on September 16, 1923, in Poarch, Indian Reservation, Alabama, USA.
- He died in 1997, aged about 73.
- He was buried in New Holt Cemetery, Holt, Okaloosa, Florida, USA.

The following information is also recorded for James Edward:
- Military Service.
- Military Service.

Note: *U.S. Navy WWII.*
(Military Service)
James Edward Taylor Sr., aged 22, married Mary Evelyn Posey[387], aged 20, on March 30, 1946 in Brewton, Escambia, Alabama, USA. They had seven children:
Evelyn Elaine Taylor[1152] born on May 5, 1947 in Pensacola, Escambia, Florida, USA; died on July 31, 2021
Gloria Jean Taylor[1154] born on June 11, 1948 in Florala, Covington, Alabama, USA
Sherry Diane Taylor[1156] born on May 20, 1949 in Florala, Covington, Alabama, USA

James Edward Taylor Jr.[1158] born on July 20, 1952 in Pensacola, Escambia, Florida, USA
Daniel Richard Taylor[1159] born on June 8, 1953 in Pensacola, Escambia, Florida, USA
Thomas Patrick Taylor[1160] born on June 13, 1954
David Allen Taylor[1162] born on March 4, 1957 in Pensacola, Escambia, Florida, USA

389. CLEAVY EDWARD POSEY SR. (see Descendants (16)) was born on September 16, 1927, in Holt, Okaloosa, Florida, USA, to Martin Edward Posey[95] and Mary Alice Bass[94].
- He was recorded in the census on April 1, 1950, aged 22, in 12 Applegate Courts, Brownsville-Brent-Goulding, Escambia, Florida, United States.
- He died on August 4, 2011, aged 83, in Pensacola, Escambia, Florida, USA.
- He was buried in New Holt Cemetery, Holt, Okaloosa, Florida, USA.

The following information is also recorded for Cleavy Edward:
- Military Service.

Notes:
- *He retired as an insurance salesman with Gulf Life Insurance Company and was a member of Milligan Assembly of God. He was a veteran of the U. S. Army.*
- *U.S. Army.*
  (Military Service)

390. IDA MAY BUSBY was born on March 7, 1928, in Florida, United States, to Vernon Edward Busby.
- She was recorded in the census on April 1, 1950, aged 22, in 12 Applegate Courts, Brownsville-Brent-Goulding, Escambia, Florida, United States.
- She died on July 21, 2004, aged 76.
- She was buried in New Holt Cemetery, Holt, Okaloosa, Florida, USA.

Cleavy Edward Posey Sr.[389] married Ida May Busby. They had four children:
Joyce Marie Posey[1164] born on July 13, 1947 in Florida, United States
Marsha Ann Posey[1166] born on August 6, 1953
Ceavie Edward Posey Jr.[1168] born on April 26, 1956
Jennifer Kim Posey[1170] born on September 13, 1961

391. DEWEY FRANKLIN BASS (see Descendants (64)) was born on December 2, 1915 to Holley Middleton Bass[96] and Jessie Savage[97]. He died on October 20, 1916, aged 0.

392. EDITH FLORINE BASS (see Descendants (64)) was born on April 25, 1918, in Florida, United States, to Holley Middleton Bass[96] and Jessie Savage[97].
- She was recorded in the census on April 1, 1950, aged 31, in 407 Church Street, Andalusia, Covington, Alabama, United States.
- She died on March 4, 2003, aged 84.

393. AURTHOR WALLACE was born on October 20, 1917, in Alabama, United States, to Mr. Wallace and Ms. Wallace.
- He was recorded in the census on April 1, 1950, aged 32, in 407 Church Street, Andalusia, Covington, Alabama, United States.

Aurthor Wallace, aged 25, married Edith Florine Bass[392], aged 24, on November 29, 1942. They had three children:
Sandra Ann Wallace[1173] born on November 8, 1943 in Alabama, United States; died on September 17, 2000
Phillip Aurthur Wallace[1175] born on April 26, 1947 in Alabama, United States
William Holley Wallace[1177] born on July 4, 1950

394. JAMES VERLIN BASS (see Descendants (64)) was born on July 29, 1920, in Florida, United States, to Holley Middleton Bass[96] and Jessie Savage[97].
- He was recorded in the census on April 1, 1950, aged 29, in 601 W Jordan, Brownsville-Brent-Goulding, Escambia, Florida, United States.
- He died on May 20, 2009, aged 88 years.
- He was buried in Andalusia Memorial Cemetery, Covington, Alabama, USA.

395. JANE LEE TART was born on May 1, 1920, in Florida, United States.
- She was recorded in the census on April 1, 1950, aged 29, in 601 W Jordan, Brownsville-Brent-Goulding, Escambia, Florida, United States.
- She died on May 3, 2010, aged 90 years.
- She was buried in Andalusia Memorial Cemetery, Covington, Alabama, USA.

James Verlin Bass[394], aged 48, married Jane Lee Tart, aged 49, on May 31, 1969. They had three children:
James Michael Bass[1179] born on August 10, 1945
Patricia Annelle Bass[1181] born on March 3, 1950 in Florida, United States
Roger Douglas Bass[1183] born on April 8, 1952

396. MARLIN HOLLEY BASS (see Descendants (64)) was born on January 16, 1923, in Holt, Okaloosa, Florida, USA, to Holley Middleton Bass[96] and Jessie Savage[97].
- He was recorded in the census in 1940, aged about 17, in E Precinct 6 Red Rock, Santa Rosa, Florida, USA.
- He was recorded in the census on April 1, 1950, aged 27, in 5 3/10 from Okaloss Line on The Right Leaving Okaloosa County Line Proceeding West on No. 4highway No 4, Jay, Santa Rosa, Florida, United States.
- He died on January 16, 2016, aged 93, in Holt, Okaloosa, Florida, USA.
- He was buried in Liveoak Park Memorial Cemetery, Crestview, Okaloosa, Florida, USA.

Notes:
- "I'm Marlin Bass, I have two fish names." A frequent introduction used.
- *Marlin Bass, age 93 of Crestview went to his heavenly home on Tuesday, April 26, 2016. He was born in Holt, FL on January 16, 1923, and has been a lifelong resident of the area. He graduated from Munson High School class of 1941. Marlin served his country in the United States Army and fought in World War II. He was a member of First Baptist Church of Crestview. Marlin loved to go to bluegrass festivals and loved to camp. He was a gifted story teller and talker who never met a stranger, always introducing himself saying, "I'm Marlin Bass, I have two fish names". Most of all he loved his family and loved his grandchildren.
(Death)*

397. CHARLOTTE ATKINS was born on October 26, 1925, in Florida, United States.
- She was recorded in the census on April 1, 1950, aged 24, in 5 3/10 from Okaloss Line on The Right Leaving Okaloosa County Line Proceeding West on No. 4highway No 4, Jay, Santa Rosa, Florida, United States.
- She died on October 27, 2022, aged 97.

Marlin Holley Bass[396], aged 49, married Charlotte Atkins, aged 46, on March 18, 1972. They had three children:
Jeffrey Marlin Bass[1185] born on March 10, 1949 in Florida, United States
Dottie Lynn Bass[1187] born on November 4, 1951
Dudley Dean Bass[1189] born on October 28, 1956

398. EULA VIRGINIA BASS (see Descendants (64)) was born on August 24, 1927, in Florida, United States, to Holley Middleton Bass[96] and Jessie Savage[97].
- She was recorded in the census in 1940, aged about 12, in E Precinct 6 Red Rock, Santa Rosa, Florida, USA.
- She was recorded in the census on April 1, 1950, aged 22, in Chestnut St, Crestview, Okaloosa, Florida, United States.
- She died on August 28, 2018, aged 91.

399. GLENN DOTSON was born on April 4, 1928. He died on September 1, 2017, aged 89.

Glenn Dotson, aged 20, married Eula Virginia Bass[398], aged 21, on December 24, 1948. They had one daughter:
Gloria Sue Dotson[1192] born on February 11, 1951
Note: *Daddy (Glenn) came in from overseas. He didn't even sit down. My aunt and uncle took them to Mississippi to get married. That was the only way they could get married before January 1st so he could get the $200 refund in income tax. -Gloria Dotson.*

400. CAROLYN BASS (see Descendants (65)) was born on March 26, 1928, in Florida, United States, to Joseph Alexander Bass[98] and Carrie Lou Mount[99].
- She was recorded in the census in 1930, aged about 2, in Holt, Okaloosa, Florida, USA.
- She was recorded in the census in 1940, aged about 12, in E Precint 9 Holt, Okaloosa, Florida, USA.
- She was recorded in the census on April 1, 1950, aged 22, in Florida Highway 4 South of Baker, Milligan, Okaloosa, Florida, United States.

401. OTIS C GRIFFITH was born on March 26, 1928, in Holt, Okaloosa, Florida, USA.
- He was recorded in the census on April 1, 1950, aged 22, in Florida Highway 4 South of Baker, Milligan, Okaloosa, Florida, United States.

Otis C Griffith married Carolyn Bass[400]. They had five children:
Carl Manuel Griffith[1193] born on July 6, 1948 in Florida, United States
Roger Joseph Griffith[1194] born on September 5, 1949; died on September 28, 1949
Ronald Lawrence Griffith[1195] born on September 5, 1949; died on September 29, 1949
Stephen Dale Griffith[1196] born on January 22, 1952
Theresa Ann Griffith[1198] born on December 5, 1956

Direct Relations

402. CALVIN WINSTON BASS (see Descendants (65)) was born on October 26, 1929, in Florida, United States, to Joseph Alexander Bass[98] and Carrie Lou Mount[99].
- He was recorded in the census in 1930, as an infant, in Holt, Okaloosa, Florida, USA.
- He was recorded in the census in 1940, aged about 10, in E Precint 9 Holt, Okaloosa, Florida, USA.
- He was recorded in the census on April 1, 1950, aged 20, in 1/4 Miles Proceeding South on Blockwater Bass Road, Milligan, Okaloosa, Florida, United States.
- He died on August 27, 1990, aged 60 years.
- He was buried in Shady Grove Cemetery, Baker, Okaloosa, Florida, USA.

403. MARILYN SANFORD was born on June 10, 1935, in Okaloosa, Florida, USA.
- She died on September 19, 1989, aged 54 years, in Escambia, Florida, USA.
- She was buried in Shady Grove Cemetery, Baker, Okaloosa, Florida, USA.

Calvin Winston Bass[402] married Marilyn Sanford. They had three daughters:
Kathy Bass[1200] born on December 11, 1956
Brenda Bass[1203] born on March 27, 1959
Yvonne Bass[1205] born on May 30, 1965

404. STEPHEN DURWARD BASS (see Descendants (65)) was born on December 16, 1931, in Holt, Okaloosa, Florida, USA, to Joseph Alexander Bass[98] and Carrie Lou Mount[99].
- He was recorded in the census in 1940, aged about 8, in E Precint 9 Holt, Okaloosa, Florida, USA.
- He was recorded in the census on April 1, 1950, aged 18, in 1/4 Miles Proceeding South on Blockwater Bass Road, Milligan, Okaloosa, Florida, United States.
- He died on March 5, 2012, aged 80 years.

405. LORETTA GRIFFITH was born on March 6, 1936.

Stephen Durward Bass[404] married Loretta Griffith. They had two sons:
Steve Elvin Bass[1207] born on February 3, 1965
Michael Douglas Bass[1208] born on December 4, 1966

406. CHARITY DELORES BASS (see Descendants (65)) was born on October 23, 1933, in Florida, USA, to Joseph Alexander Bass[98] and Carrie Lou Mount[99].
- She was recorded in the census in 1940, aged about 6, in E Precint 9 Holt, Okaloosa, Florida, USA.
- She was recorded in the census on April 1, 1950, aged 16, in 1/4 Miles Proceeding South on Blockwater Bass Road, Milligan, Okaloosa, Florida, United States.

Charity Delores married twice. She was married to Harold Jack Adams[407] and William Aaron[408].

407. HAROLD JACK ADAMS was born on October 23, 1933. Harold Jack became known as "Dude". He died on November 3, 2019, aged 86.

Harold Jack Adams married Charity Delores Bass[406]. They had four children:
Sharon Adams[1210] born on December 31, 1953
Harold DeWayne Adams[1213] born on March 15, 1956; died on August 8, 2008
Walter Dean Adams[1214] born on October 20, 1961
William Aaron Adams[1217] died on October 25, 2010

408. WILLIAM AARON.
William Aaron married Charity Delores Bass[406], aged 48, on May 22, 1982.

409. FARRELL DALE BASS (see Descendants (65)) was born on January 12, 1936, in Florida, USA, to Joseph Alexander Bass[98] and Carrie Lou Mount[99].
- He was recorded in the census in 1940, aged about 4, in E Precint 9 Holt, Okaloosa, Florida, USA.
- He was recorded in the census on April 1, 1950, aged 14, in 1/4 Miles Proceeding South on Blockwater Bass Road, Milligan, Okaloosa, Florida, United States.

Farrell Dale married twice. He was married to Barbara Kay Sees[410] and Carol Gries[411].

410. BARBARA KAY SEES.
Farrell Dale Bass[409] married Barbara Kay Sees. They had one son:
Roger Dale Bass[1218] born on February 21, 1962

411. CAROL GRIES.
Farrell Dale Bass[409], aged 40, married Carol Gries on February 14, 1976. They had two sons:
Robert Bass[1220] born on October 7, 1979
Thomas Matthew Bass[1221] born on January 8, 1983

412. JOE FARRIS BASS (see Descendants (65)) was born on February 14, 1938, in Florida, USA, to Joseph Alexander Bass[98] and Carrie Lou Mount[99].

- He was recorded in the census in 1940, aged about 2, in E Precinct 9 Holt, Okaloosa, Florida, USA.
- He was recorded in the census on April 1, 1950, aged 12, in 1/4 Miles Proceeding South on Blockwater Bass Road, Milligan, Okaloosa, Florida, United States.

Joe Farris married twice. He was married to Kay Jorgenson[413] and Betty Courtney[414].

413. KAY JORGENSON.

Joe Farris Bass[412] married Kay Jorgenson. They had one daughter:
Danne Louise Bass[1222] born on February 21, 1967

414. BETTY COURTNEY.

Joe Farris Bass[412] married Betty Courtney. They had one son:
James Farris Bass[1223]

415. HARVEY MIDDLETON BASS (see Descendants (65)) was born on August 28, 1940, in Florida, United States, to Joseph Alexander Bass[98] and Carrie Lou Mount[99].
- He was recorded in the census on April 1, 1950, aged 9, in 1/4 Miles Proceeding South on Blockwater Bass Road, Milligan, Okaloosa, Florida, United States.
- He died on December 21, 1985, aged 45 years.

416. ALEATHA NIXON.

Harvey Middleton Bass[415] married Aleatha Nixon. They had two sons:
Brian Joseph Bass[1224] born on March 14, 1970
Eric Richard Bass[1225] born on January 15, 1972

417. JOEL SIDNEY BASS (see Descendants (66)) was born on November 21, 1917, in Alabama, USA, to John Riley Bass[100] and Mamie Annie Hassel[101].
- He was recorded in the census in 1930, aged about 12, in Carolina, Covington, Alabama, USA.
- He was recorded in the census in 1940, aged about 22, in Election Prect 21 Carolina, Covington, Alabama, USA.
- He was recorded in the census on April 1, 1950, aged 32, in 1c Granes Apartments, Auburn, Lee, Alabama, United States.
- He died on February 4, 1996, aged 78 years, in Fort Walton Beach, Okaloosa, Florida, USA.
- He was buried in Carolina Baptist Church Cemetery.

The following information is also recorded for Joel Sidney:
- Military Service.
- Description: 5' 11.5"165BrownGrayThree inch scar running back on the right side of his face, about the hair line. From WWII Draft Card.

Note: *CPL. US Army World War II.*
(Military Service)

418. MARY ELIZABETH HENDERSON was born on June 24, 1930, in Andalusia, Covington, Alabama, USA.
- She was recorded in the census on April 1, 1950, aged 19, in 1c Granes Apartments, Auburn, Lee, Alabama, United States.
- She died on January 21, 2017, aged 86 years, in Magnolia Place, Cairo, Georgia, USA.
- She was buried in Carolina Baptist Church Cemetery, Covington, Alabama, USA.

Joel Sidney Bass[417], aged 29, married Mary Elizabeth Henderson, aged 16, on March 6, 1947 in Andalusia, Covington, Alabama, USA. They had two sons:
John William Bass Sr.[1226] born on March 6, 1949 in Andalusia, Covington, Alabama, USA
Joel Sidney Bass Jr.[1228] born on March 6, 1954

419. MARGUERITTE CATHERINE BASS (see Descendants (66)) was born on January 21, 1919, in Alabama, United States, to John Riley Bass[100] and Mamie Annie Hassel[101].
- She was recorded in the census in 1930, aged about 11, in Carolina, Covington, Alabama, USA.
- She was recorded in the census in 1940, aged about 21, in Election Prect 21 Carolina, Covington, Alabama, USA.
- She died on February 13, 2012, aged 93 years.

420. MARK ANTHONY BOLDING was born on April 28, 1922, in Fort Valley, Peach, Georgia, USA.
- He died on September 7, 1990, aged 68 years, in Metairie, Jefferson Parish, Louisianna, USA.
- He was buried in Pine Log Cemetery, Bartow, Gorgia, USA.

Mark Anthony Bolding, aged 23, married Margueritte Catherine Bass[419], aged 26, on November 5, 1945. They had one daughter:
Margueritte Dawn Bolding[1230] born on September 20, 1950 in New Orleans, Louisiana, USA

421. MARTHA ANN BASS (see Descendants (66)) was born on December 9, 1921, in Andalusia, Covington, Alabama, USA, to John Riley Bass[100] and Mamie Annie Hassel[101].

- She was recorded in the census in 1930, aged about 8, in Carolina, Covington, Alabama, USA.
- She was recorded in the census in 1940, aged about 18, in Election Prect 21 Carolina, Covington, Alabama, USA.
- She was recorded in the census on April 1, 1950, aged 28, in Chattahoochee, Gadsden, Florida, United States.

Martha Ann married three times. She was married to William Mullina Byrd[422], James Woodrow Kilcrease[423] and T. D. Helms[424].

422. **WILLIAM MULLINA BYRD** was born about 1926, in Florida, United States.
- He was recorded in the census on April 1, 1950, aged about 23, in Chattahoochee, Gadsden, Florida, United States.

William Mullina Byrd, aged about 20, married Martha Ann Bass[421], aged 24, in September 1946. They had four children:

Lynda Ann Byrd[1232] born on June 19, 1947 in Chattahoochee, Gadsden, Florida, USA
?
Mychaelle Joy Byrd[1234] born on December 7, 1955
Nancy Jane Byrd[1236] born on June 17, 1957

423. **JAMES WOODROW KILCREASE**.

James Woodrow Kilcrease married Martha Ann Bass[421], aged about 44, in 1966. They had four children:
George Stephen Kilcrease[1238] born on October 12, 1950
Kathleen Ann Kilcrease[1239] born on September 26, 1952
Phillip Wayne Kilcrease[1241] born on December 24, 1955
Angelia Renee Kilcrease[1242] born on June 17, 1967 in Fort Walton Beach, Okaloosa, Florida, USA

424. **T. D. HELMS**.

T. D. Helms married Martha Ann Bass[421], aged 68, on July 5, 1990.

425. **JOHN THOMAS BASS** (see Descendants (66)) was born on April 20, 1924, in Alabama, USA, to John Riley Bass[100] and Mamie Annie Hassel[101]. John Thomas became known as "T".
- He was recorded in the census in 1930, aged about 6, in Carolina, Covington, Alabama, USA.
- He was recorded in the census in 1940, aged about 16, in Election Prect 21 Carolina, Covington, Alabama, USA.
- He was recorded in the census on April 1, 1950, aged 25, in 30 Panama City, Bay, Florida, United States.

The following information is also recorded for T:
- Military Service.

Notes:
- *Easter Sunday.*
(Birth)
- *WWII.*
(Military Service)

426. **ROBERTA HOWELL** was born on January 15, 1927, in Andalusia, Covington, Alabama, USA.
- She was recorded in the census on April 1, 1950, aged 23, in 30 Panama City, Bay, Florida, United States.
- She died on August 10, 2005, aged 78 years.

John Thomas Bass[425] married Roberta Howell. They had four children:
Judith Bass[1245] born on November 24, 1947 in Troy, Pike, Alabama, USA
Jacqueline Bass[1248] born on August 29, 1950 in Panama City, Bay, Florida, USA; died on August 21, 2018 in Pensacola, Santa Rosa, Florida, USA
John Thomas Bass Jr.[1250] born on September 5, 1952 in Panama City, Bay, Florida, USA; died on October 30, 2014
Janet Bass[1253] born on March 13, 1957 in Panama City, Bay, Florida, USA

427. **MAVIS EARLINE BASS** (see Descendants (67)) was born on March 17, 1922, in Alabama, United States, to Stacy Bibner Bass[102] and Alline Naomi Rowell[103].
- She was recorded in the census in 1930, aged about 8, in Carolina, Covington, Alabama, USA.
- She was recorded in the census in 1940, aged about 18, in Election Prect 21 Carolina, Covington, Alabama, USA.
- She died (Natural / Old Age) on December 26, 2016, aged 94, in Andalusia, Covington, Alabama, USA.
- She was buried on December 31, 2016 in Shady Hill Church Cemetery, Covington, Alabama, USA.

Notes:
- *It is not every day that you are allowed the privilege to witness the absolute favor of God on any one person. Not to say that God doesn't grant his favor, peace, or tender mercy to many on a daily basis. However, more often than not we find ourselves rationalizing terrible situations saying (he/she isn't suffering anymore) or having to make difficult decisions on hospice care or whether or not to place a loved one in a home where they could struggle and languish for years with no quality of life. Well tonight I had the privilege to witness Gods favor poured out on my Granny Mac. She has traveled to many different places, visiting various different ones of her children for a few months here and there. At 94 yrs old it would have been no surprise to anyone if she'd answered the call of the master to come*

home at any given time or place from Florida, to North Carolina, to Pleasant View, Tn. After all no one lives forever and 94 these days seems way above average. Especially to be 94 and sharp as a tac. A living family tree that you only need ask and she could give you more genealogy than most online server's could about who belonged to who or married who, etc.. Tonight as she sat in her house in the Shady Hill, Al community surrounded by her 8 Children and several of her grandchildren and great grandchildren after a weekend of celebrating the birth of Jesus Christ, the call that she'd longed for so many years began to ring through. Mere moments after discussing how good she felt with her children and grand/greatgrand children. Some 45min to an hour later (give or take) after being accompanied by a grandson on the transport to the hospital, Granny lay in the trauma unit, eyes looking toward heaven as Micah and myself visited with her. I gently leaned over and kissed her forhead, told her we loved her and she slowly closed her eyes and recieve the greatest Christmas Gift of all. God allowed Granny an express ticket to the one place she's longed for all her life. After a week of what she would consider heaven on earth, which merely consisted of being home with her children and grandchildren. With no suffering she experienced the perfect peace that is to be absent from this body and to be present with the Lord. Thank you Lord for the Favor you've shared with Granny. If God were to allow us to write the script for our last day's, I don't believe there would be much that she would have changed. She will be sorely missed. Thank you Lord for allowing me the privilege fo being her grandson. Till we meet again, we love you Granny Mac..

- Jeremy McVay.
- *"The most amazing, wonderful, caring, loving, saint there ever was......so blessed to call her my Momma!" -Joan Williamson [McVay].*
- *She loved to read her Bible and do her daily devotions. She attended church every time the doors were open and encouraged everyone else to do the same. She loved sewing, crocheting, cooking, gardening, reading, word search, and watching Wheel of Fortune and Hallmark movies. She loved traveling and had been to many places in the USA, as well as Spain and Portugal. She loved singing gospel music with the family at family gatherings. She was a long standing faithful member of Shady Hill Free Will Baptist Church, a long-time supporter of Welch College (and was an honorary alumnus), and Free Will Baptist International Missions.*

She taught us how to live the Christian life by example, and showed us the meaning of "actions speak louder than words." She was a fervent prayer warrior.
(Death)

428. **GASTON DURELL MCVAY** was born on January 7, 1924. He died on December 15, 2014, aged 90.
    Gaston Durell McVay, aged 18, married Mavis Earline Bass[427], aged 20, on December 6, 1942, and they were divorced. They had nine children:
    Loyce Elaine McVay[1255] born on December 25, 1944
    Richard Wayne McVay[1256] born on October 26, 1946 in Andalusia, Covington, Alabama, USA
    Joan Marie McVay[1258] born on February 22, 1949 in Andalusia, Covington, Alabama, USA
    Michael Ray McVay[1260] born on February 28, 1951 in Andalusia, Covington, Alabama, USA
    Samuel Paul McVay[1262] born on September 7, 1955 in Andalusia, Covington, Alabama, USA
    David Micah McVay[1264] born on October 24, 1956 in Andalusia, Covington, Alabama, USA
    Nathaniel Joel McVay[1267] born on July 26, 1958 in Andalusia, Covington, Alabama, USA
    Miriam Lois McVay[1269] born on May 31, 1962 in Andalusia, Covington, Alabama, USA
    Jonathan Mark McVay[1271] born on November 11, 1964 in Andalusia, Covington, Alabama, USA

429. **JAMES MARCUS BASS** (see Descendants (67)) was born on January 26, 1924, in Alabama, United States, to Stacy Bibner Bass[102] and Alline Naomi Rowell[103].
    - He was recorded in the census in 1930, aged about 6, in Carolina, Covington, Alabama, USA.
    - He was recorded in the census in 1940, aged about 16, in Election Prect 21 Carolina, Covington, Alabama, USA.
    - He was recorded in the census on April 1, 1950, aged 26, in 1718 Ashland Ave., Niagara Falls, Niagara, New York, United States.
    - He died on October 8, 1999, aged 75 years.
    The following information is also recorded for James Marcus:
    • Military Service.
    Note: *WWII.*
    (Military Service)

430. **MARY LOUISE JOHNSON** was born on June 5, 1928, in Andalusia, Covington, Alabama, USA. She was recorded in the census on April 1, 1950, aged 21, in 1718 Ashland Ave., Niagara Falls, Niagara, New York, United States.
    James Marcus Bass[429], aged 21, married Mary Louise Johnson, aged 16, on May 3, 1945 in Andalusia, Covington, Alabama, USA. They had two children:
    Stephen Gene Bass[1274] born on March 12, 1947 in Montgomery, Montgomery, Alabama, USA; died on November 6, 2022 in Abbeville, Henry, Alabama, USA
    Susan Lynn Bass[1279] born on August 29, 1950

Stacy Bibner Bass and Alline Naomi Rowell, with their children standing in age order.

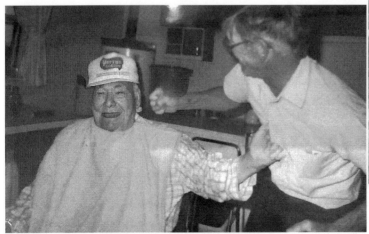

Stacy Bibner and Quinton Gene Bass

Cecil Larry Day and Sibyl Louise Bass

Margueritte Elizabeth, Betty Irene, Mavis Earline, Sibyl Louise, and Audrey Rebecca Bass

Natalie Melinda McVay and Mavis Earline Bass

Betty Irene Bass and Gerald Wilson Wood

431. CECIL EDWIN BASS (see Descendants (67)) was born on February 11, 1925 to Stacy Bibner Bass[102] and Alline Naomi Rowell[103].
- He died (At young age) on March 28, 1926, aged 1 years.
- He was buried in Carolina Baptist Church Cemetery.

432. SIBYL LOUISE BASS (see Descendants (67)) was born on February 9, 1927, in Alabama, United States, to Stacy Bibner Bass[102] and Alline Naomi Rowell[103].
- She was recorded in the census in 1930, aged about 3, in Carolina, Covington, Alabama, USA.
- She was recorded in the census in 1940, aged about 13, in Election Prect 21 Carolina, Covington, Alabama, USA.
- She was recorded in the census on April 1, 1950, aged 23, in 6437 Division Ave., Birmingham, Jefferson, Alabama, United States.
- She died on April 7, 2014, aged 87, in Andalusia, Covington, Alabama, United States.
- She was buried in Andalusia Memorial Cemetery, Andalusia, Covington, Alabama, USA.

433. CECIL LARRY DAY was born on December 15, 1923, in Barbour, Alabama, USA.
- He was recorded in the census on April 1, 1950, aged 26, in 6437 Division Ave., Birmingham, Jefferson, Alabama, United States.

The following information is also recorded for Cecil Larry:
   Membership.
   Note: *Alabama Board of Pharmacy.*
      (Membership)

Cecil Larry Day, aged 22, married Sibyl Louise Bass[432], aged 19, on August 10, 1946. They had four children:
   Barbara Elaine Day[1281] born about 1945 in Alabama, United States
   Cecil Larry Day II[1284] born on November 17, 1951 in Topeka, Shawnee, Kansas, USA; died on April 26, 2015 in Andalusia, Covington, Alabama, United States
   George Anthony Day[1285] born on December 26, 1953 in Montgomery, Montgomery, Alabama, USA
   Tammy Joy Day[1287] born on July 8, 1962

434. GROVER ALCUS BASS (see Descendants (67)) was born on January 7, 1929, in Covington, Alabama, USA, to Stacy Bibner Bass[102] and Alline Naomi Rowell[103].
- He was recorded in the census in 1930, aged about 1, in Carolina, Covington, Alabama, USA.
- He was recorded in the census in 1940, aged about 11, in Election Prect 21 Carolina, Covington, Alabama, USA.
- He was recorded in the census on April 1, 1950, aged 21, in Santa Anna, San Antonio, Bexar, Texas, United States.
- He died on April 22, 1987, aged 58 years, in Newfane, Niagara, New York, USA.
- He was buried in Shady Hill Church Cemetery.

435. DOROTHY JUNE RUSK was born on April 22, 1931, in New York, United States. She was recorded in the census on April 1, 1950, aged 18, in Santa Anna, San Antonio, Bexar, Texas, United States.

Grover Alcus Bass[434], aged 19, married Dorothy June Rusk, aged 17, on August 5, 1948 in Mississippi, USA. They had four children:
   Gary Wayne Bass[1288] born on June 15, 1949 in Niagara Falls, Niagara, New York, USA
   Kathy Jean Bass[1290] born on August 6, 1950
   Gregory Alan Bass[1292] born on August 2, 1952
   Karen Mae Bass[1295] born on September 10, 1954 in Lockport, Niagara, New York, USA

436. MARGUERITTE ELIZABETH BASS (see Descendants (67)) was born on January 9, 1931 to Stacy Bibner Bass[102] and Alline Naomi Rowell[103]. She was recorded in the census in 1940, aged about 9, in Election Prect 21 Carolina, Covington, Alabama, USA.

437. WILLARD DANIEL MARTIN was born on July 8, 1928.

Willard Daniel Martin, aged 21, married Margueritte Elizabeth Bass[436], aged 18, on December 17, 1949 in Birmingham, Jefferson, Alabama, USA. They had three children:
   Deborah Lee Martin[1297] born on December 19, 1951
   Danna Elizabeth Martin[1299] born on November 17, 1955
   Willard Daniel Martin Jr.[1301] born on March 9, 1959 in Montgomery, Montgomery, Alabama, USA

438. BETTY IRENE BASS (see Descendants (67)) was born on January 13, 1933, in Andalusia, Covington, Alabama, USA, to Stacy Bibner Bass[102] and Alline Naomi Rowell[103].
- She was recorded in the census in 1940, aged about 7, in Election Prect 21 Carolina, Covington, Alabama, USA.
- She was recorded in the census on April 1, 1950, aged 17, in Carolina, Covington, Alabama, United States.

439. GERALD WILSON WOOD was born on August 19, 1929, in Clifton Forge, Virginia, USA. Gerald Wilson became known as "Son".
- He died on July 28, 2017, aged 87, in Millboro, Bath, Virginia, USA.
- He was buried in Horeb Baptist Church Cemetery, Millboro, Bath, Virginia, USA.

Note: *He was a retired Tech Sargent serving in the United States Air Force for over 20 years and spent 17 years working for the United States Government in Civil Service. He was a past Commander of the Veterans of Foreign Wars Post 10773 of Millboro and Goshen, Past President of the Millboro Ruritan Club and was active in Bath County meals on wheels. He was a deacon of the Horeb Baptist Church and served as cemetery sexton of the cemetery. He was an active member of the Bent Rod Hunt Club at Nimrod.*
(Death)

Gerald Wilson Wood, aged 23, married Betty Irene Bass[438], aged 20, on May 8, 1953. They had six children:
- JoAnn Wood[1303] born on January 5, 1954
- Connie Gail Wood[1305] born on December 12, 1954
- Rebecca Gaye Wood[1307] born on March 19, 1957 in Columbus Air Force Base, Columbus, Ohio, USA
- Pamela Ellen Wood[1309] born on March 21, 1959
- Russel Stacy Wood[1311] born on April 7, 1960 in Newfoundland Air Force Base
- Joyce Marie Wood[1313] born on March 11, 1967 in Newfoundland Air Force Base

440. AUDREY REBECCA BASS (see Descendants (67)) was born on January 16, 1935, in Alabama, United States, to Stacy Bibner Bass[102] and Alline Naomi Rowell[103].
- She was recorded in the census in 1940, aged about 5, in Election Prect 21 Carolina, Covington, Alabama, USA.
- She was recorded in the census on April 1, 1950, aged 15, in Carolina, Covington, Alabama, United States.

441. JOHN LEWIS WILSON was born on August 18, 1935.
- He died on May 14, 1997, aged 61 years.
- He was buried in Andalusia Memorial Cemetery, Covington, Alabama, USA.

The following information is also recorded for John Lewis:
- Military Service.

Note: *Pvt U.S. Army, Korea.*
(Military Service)

John Lewis Wilson married Audrey Rebecca Bass[440]. They had three children:
- Sheila Diane Wilson[1315] born on August 13, 1955
- Michail Lewis Wilson[1317] born on July 17, 1959
- Audrey Michelle Wilson[1319] born on August 12, 1966 in Andalusia, Covington, Alabama, USA

442. HUBERT LEE BASS (see Descendants (67)) was born on December 19, 1936, in Andalusia, Covington, Alabama, USA, to Stacy Bibner Bass[102] and Alline Naomi Rowell[103].
- He was recorded in the census in 1940, aged about 3, in Election Prect 21 Carolina, Covington, Alabama, USA.
- He was recorded in the census on April 1, 1950, aged 13, in Carolina, Covington, Alabama, United States.
- He died on September 1, 2007, aged 70 years.
- He was buried in Shady Hill Church Cemetery, Covington, Alabama, USA.

443. SHIRLEY SEIWELL was born on July 17, 1941, in Niagara Falls, Niagara, New York, USA.

Hubert Lee Bass[442], aged 21, married Shirley Seiwell, aged 16, on May 1, 1958 in Niagara Falls, Niagara, New York, USA. They had three children:
- Leland Samuel Bass[1321] born on November 9, 1958 in Niagara Falls, Niagara, New York, USA
- Robin Naomi Bass[1323] born on August 23, 1960
- Maurice Seiwell Bass[1325] born on May 12, 1962

Note: *Hubert and Shirley met while Hubert was visiting his brother Grover who had moved up around Niagara Falls, New York. –Maurice Seiwell Bass.*

444. QUINTON GENE BASS (see Descendants (67)) was born on November 6, 1938, in Covington, Alabama, USA, to Stacy Bibner Bass[102] and Alline Naomi Rowell[103].
- He was recorded in the census in 1940, aged about 1, in Election Prect 21 Carolina, Covington, Alabama, USA.
- He was recorded in the census on April 1, 1950, aged 11, in Carolina, Covington, Alabama, United States.
- He died on August 7, 2019, aged 80, in Florala, Covington, Alabama, USA.

The following information is also recorded for Quinton Gene:
- Military Service.

Quinton Gene married twice. He was married to Frances Ida Teel[832] (his second cousin, once removed) and Patricia Lucille Bass[1548] (his second cousin, once removed).

Note: *U.S. Army.*
(Military Service)

445. HARVEY CLINTON WARD (see Descendants (68)) was born on July 20, 1918, in Alabama, USA, to Forman Edward Ward[105] and Martha Christian Bass[104].
- He was recorded in the census in 1940, aged about 21, in E P 15 Crestview, Okaloosa, Florida, USA.
- He was recorded in the census on April 1, 1950, aged 31, in 4w Esthere, Orlando, Orange, Florida, United States.

The following information is also recorded for Harvey Clinton:
- Military Service.

446. VIVIAN JO FREDRICK was born about 1926, in Indiana, United States. She was recorded in the census on April 1, 1950, aged about 23, in 4w Esthere, Orlando, Orange, Florida, United States.

Harvey Clinton Ward[445] married Vivian Jo Fredrick.

447. REV. WILLIAM CHARLES WARD SR. (see Descendants (68)) was born on November 21, 1921, in Florida, USA, to Forman Edward Ward[105] and Martha Christian Bass[104]. William Charles became known as "Bill".
- He was recorded in the census in 1940, aged about 18, in E P 15 Crestview, Okaloosa, Florida, USA.
- He died on November 8, 2022, aged 100, in Tennessee, USA.
- He was buried in Oak Ridge Memorial Park, Oak Ridge, Anderson, Tennessee, USA.

The following information is also recorded for Bill:
- Military Service.

Notes:
- *Bill Ward might have trouble drifting off to sleep Wednesday night. It's been that way every Dec. 6 for more than three-quarters of a century.Waking to a savage attack will do that — which is how Ward was welcomed to the U.S. naval base at Pearl Harbor on the Hawaiian island of Oahu."I'll never forget that day," he said, slowly and sadly shaking his head. "I was scared from that moment on. I didn't quit being scared 'til I saw the Golden Gate Bridge" (near the end of his service in the U.S. Navy.).Ward, 96, is among the sparse group of survivors from the "date which will live in infamy," as President Franklin Roosevelt labeled Dec. 7, 1941.He was aboard the destroyer O'Brien during the assault, which killed 2,403 servicemen and civilians and marked America's entry into World War II.The O'Brien had sailed into Pearl Harbor less than 24 hours earlier. What began as a peaceful night, turned into hell on earth.As the old sailor recalled: "We were anchored only about a quarter-mile away from the Arizona" (the battleship which suffered the greatest casualties.) "The (Japanese) planes flew right over us."The O'Brien wasn't struck during the surprise raid. It pursued a Japanese submarine, overtaking it near Waikiki Beach.After Pearl Harbor, the O'Brien was involved in heavy fighting during battles of the Coral Sea, Midway and Solomon Sea.It was during one of those encounters that Ward, manning a 20-millimeter gun, took a near-direct hit."The man next to me was blown to bits," he said. "I wound up with 111 pieces of shrapnel in my body."On another occasion, Ward and other crewmen thwarted an attack from five Japanese soldiers. He was struck in the leg."We were shooting at each other from about 75 yards apart," he said. "We killed them all."Ward was awarded a Purple Heart, but the medal was quickly rescinded."They said we were hit by 'friendly fire,'" he said, eyes ablaze at the memory. "Friendly fire, nothin'! It took 64 years for the Navy to finally give it to me!"After the war, Ward learned pipefitting in his native Florida and came to Oak Ridge to work at the Y-12 facility. He also pastored two Baptist churches.Lela, his wife of 68 years, died in 2012. He has four children, nine grandchildren and "too many great-grandkids to count."Ward resides at Meadowview Senior Living Center in Clinton, where the walls of his room are decorated with numerous family photos and citations from governmental and civilian organizations. "When I was in the seventh grade, the class voted me 'Most Likely To Not Succeed,'" he says with a chuckle.Wow. Talk about an election gone wrong.Published 7:00 a.m. ET Dec. 5, 2017 in Knox News.*

- *William Charles Ward Sr. age 100, went to be with his lord and savior on November 8, 2022. He was thirteen days shy of his 101st birthday.William was born on November 21, 1921, in Andalusia, Alabama to his mother and father; Foman Ward and Martha Bass Ward. William fought in World War II, The Battel of The Coral Sea, Battle of Midway, and is a Pearl Harbor Veteran.William was ordained as a Baptist minister at Blowing Springs Baptist church in Clinton, TN. on January 29, 1961. He pastored and preached at numerous churches and was a loyal member of the Evangelist team. William never failed to show others his love for the lord and to share the word of God with them.*
  (Death)
- *U.S. Navy - USS O'Brien - Pearl Harbor Survivor.*
  (Military Service)

448. **LELIA MURRAY** was born on January 28, 1919, in Faceville, Decatur, Georgia, USA.

William Charles Ward Sr.[447], aged 22, married Lelia Murray, aged 25, on May 7, 1944 in Pensacola, Escambia, Florida, USA. They had four children:
- Betty Jane Ward[1331] born on August 15, 1945 in Bainbridge, Decatur, Georgia, USA; died on February 11, 2022
- William Charles Ward Jr.[1333] born on October 25, 1948
- Mary Ann Ward[1336] born in April 1952 in Crestview, Okaloosa, Florida, USA
- Shirley Ward[1338] born in January 1960

449. **DELEON EDWARD WARD** (see Descendants (68)) was born on August 10, 1924, in Andalusia, Covington, Alabama, USA, to Forman Edward Ward[105] and Martha Christian Bass[104].
- He was recorded in the census in 1935, aged about 10, in Holt, Santa Rosa, Florida.
- He was recorded in the census in 1940, aged about 15, in E P 15 Crestview, Okaloosa, Florida, USA.
- He died (Natural / Old Age) on January 26, 2022, aged 97, in Crestview, Okaloosa County, Florida, USA.

The following information is also recorded for DeLeon Edward:
- Military Service.

DeLeon Edward married twice. He was married to Emma June Campbell[450] and Elizabeth Virginia Cadenhead[451].

Notes:
- *I met Mr. DeLeon Ward at the First Sunday in June Sacred Harp singing and reunion, Jun 5th 2016. He was just shy of 92 years old at the time and we had a very plesant conversation. His wit was sharp and his since of humor was refreshing. He said he'd been coming to the First Sunday singings for his whole life and always enjoyed them. He invited me to the annual Bass reuninon in Baker Florida on the 4th Saturday in July. Mr. Ward also commented that he hoped to "live to be 100 years old, unless Jesus returned first". That year was the first year I went to the reunion he invited me to, and so far I've not missed one since. Lucky enough Mr. Ward was with us for several more years and I built many fond memories with him. He was a genuine treasure that blessed my life. While he didn't make his 100 year goal, he seemed blessed to maintain his wit and enjoyed life, especially when family was around. - Nicholas Bruce Bass.*
- *DeLeon Ward age 97 of Crestview stepped into the arms of his Savior on Wednesday January 26, 2022. He was born in Andalusia, AL on August 10, 1924, to Foman & Martha Ward. He was a lifelong resident of Crestview. DeLeon served his country in the United States Navy during World War II. He was assigned to the USS Yorktown and participated in the Battle of the Coral Sea and the Battle of Midway. After leaving the service, Mr. Ward returned to Okaloosa County where he spent the remainder of his life. He whittled wooden chains & was lovingly called "the chain man".*
  (Death)
- *U.S. Navy - Yorttown - WWII.*
  (Military Service)

450. **EMMA JUNE CAMPBELL** was born on June 12, 1933, in Tennessee, USA.
- She died on October 2, 1982, aged 49 years, in Crestview, Okaloosa, Florida, USA.
- She was buried in Shoal River Cemetery.

DeLeon Edward Ward[449] married Emma June Campbell. They had four children:
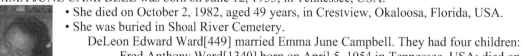
- Fred Anthony Ward[1340] born on April 5, 1954 in Tennessee, USA; died on June 30, 2021 in Crestview, Okaloosa County, Florida, USA
- Joseph Dale Ward[1341] born on May 14, 1955 in Tennessee, USA; died on June 12, 2021 in Florida, United States
- Rose Marie Ward[1343] born on October 2, 1956 in Crestview, Okaloosa, Florida, USA
- Chris Lorraine Ward[1344] born on November 16, 1958 in Pensacola, Escambia, Florida, USA

451. **ELIZABETH VIRGINIA CADENHEAD**.

DeLeon Edward Ward[449], aged 59, married Elizabeth Virginia Cadenhead on December 17, 1983 in Okaloosa, Florida, USA.

William Charles Ward Sr.

William Charles Ward Sr. with his children.

Lelia Murry

DeLeon Edward Ward

Emma June Campbell

Notes:

452. ANNA FAYE WARD (see Descendants (68)) was born on January 27, 1932, in Florida, USA, to Forman Edward Ward[105] and Martha Christian Bass[104].
- She was recorded in the census in 1940, aged about 8, in E P 15 Crestview, Okaloosa, Florida, USA.
- She was recorded in the census on April 1, 1950, aged 18, in 432 Barron, Crestview, Okaloosa, Florida, United States.
- She died in 1984, aged about 52.

453. HENRY EUGENE FREDRICK was born about 1929, in Washington, United States.
- He was recorded in the census on April 1, 1950, aged about 20, in 432 Barron, Crestview, Okaloosa, Florida, United States.

The following information is also recorded for Henry Eugene:
- Military Service.

Henry Eugene Fredrick married Anna Faye Ward[452]. They had three children:
Marilyn Fredrick[1346] born on September 15, 1951
Martin Eugene Fredrick[1347] born on June 6, 1956 in Ohio, USA
Mark Forman Fredrick[1348] born on October 2, 1958

454. EARNEST TRUE BASS SR. (see Descendants (17)) was born on October 14, 1894, in Andalusia, Covington, Alabama, USA, to Bennett Bridges Bass III[106] and Alice Kinlaw[107].
- He was recorded in the census in 1920, aged about 25, in Liberty, Florida, USA.
- He was recorded in the census in 1930, aged about 35, in Telogia, Liberty, Florida, USA.
- He was recorded in the census in 1940, aged about 45, in Telogia, Precinct 6, Liberty, Florida, USA.
- He died on September 5, 1959, aged 64 years, in Lake City, Columbia, Florida, USA.

Earnest True married three times. He was married to Lillian Morgan[455], Ruth Valentine Morgan[456] and Ms. Brady[457].

455. LILLIAN MORGAN was born on August 22, 1902, in Liberty, Florida, USA. Lillian became known as "Lila".
- She was recorded in the census in 1920, aged about 17, in Liberty, Florida, USA.
- She died (In Childbirth) on February 12, 1921, aged 18, in Hosford, Liberty, Florida, USA.
- She was buried in Lake Mystic Cemetery, Bristol, Liberty, Florida, USA.

Earnest True Bass Sr.[454] married Lillian Morgan. They had two sons:
Ernest True Bass Jr.[1349] born on January 17, 1919 in Liberty, Florida, USA; died on March 15, 1920 in Liberty, Florida, USA
Mr. Bass[1350] born on February 12, 1921 in Liberty, Florida, USA; died on February 12, 1921 in Liberty, Florida, USA

456. RUTH VALENTINE MORGAN was born on February 14, 1904, in Florida, USA.
- She was recorded in the census in 1930, aged about 26, in Telogia, Liberty, Florida, USA.
- She was recorded in the census in 1940, aged about 36, in Telogia, Precinct 6, Liberty, Florida, USA.
- She died on March 23, 1946, aged 42 years, in Leon, Florida, USA.
- She was buried in Lake Mystic Cemetery, Bristol, Liberty, Florida, USA.

Earnest True Bass Sr.[454], when older than 27, married Ruth Valentine Morgan, when older than 17, after 1921. They had nine children:
Earnest True Bass Jr.[1351] born on July 2, 1922 in Telogia, Liberty, Florida, USA; died on June 7, 2009 in Tallahassee, Leon, Florida, USA
Donald Willis Bass[1353] born on November 11, 1923 in Florida, USA; died on August 18, 1989
Ennis Rudolph Bass[1354] born on May 28, 1925 in Crawfordville, Florida, USA; died on October 19, 2004 in Tallahassee, Leon, Florida, USA
Mary Ruth Bass[1356] born on December 13, 1926 in Florida, USA
Morgan Bennett Bass[1357] born on May 28, 1928 in Telogia, Liberty, Florida, USA; died on December 3, 2001 in Orange Heights, Alachua, Florida, USA
Alice Nanette Bass[1359] born on March 9, 1931 in Florida, USA
William Walter Bass[1360] born on February 6, 1934 in Florida, USA
Robert Earl Bass[1361] born on February 6, 1934; died on February 6, 1934
Obbie Bass[1362] born on February 6, 1934 in Liberty, Florida, USA; died on February 6, 1934 in Liberty, Florida, USA

457. MS. BRADY was born in Havana, Florida, USA.

Earnest True Bass Sr.[454], when younger than 53, married Ms. Brady before 1948, and they were divorced.

458. RICHARD CARL BASS SR. (see Descendants (17)) was born on November 14, 1897, in Alabama, USA, to Bennett Bridges Bass III[106] and Alice Kinlaw[107].
- He was recorded in the census in 1940, aged about 42, in Crawfordville, E Precinct 2, Wakulla, Florida, USA.

- He was recorded in the census on April 1, 1950, aged 52, in Wakula Road, Tallahassee, Leon, Florida, United States.
- He died on December 30, 1951, aged 54 years, in Tallahassee, Leon, Florida, USA.
- He was buried in Oakland Cemetery, Tallahassee, Leon, Florida, USA.

Richard Carl married twice. He was married to Alice Lucille ("Olive") Beasley[459] and Hadassah Stautimire[460].

459. ALICE LUCILLE BEASLEY was born on September 26, 1902, in Thomasville, Georgia, USA. Alice Lucille became known as "Olive".

Richard Carl Bass Sr.[458] married Alice Lucille Beasley, and they were divorced. They had seven children:
- Alice Lillian Bass[1363] born on April 20, 1919 in Hosford, Liberty, Florida, USA; died on April 29, 2003 in Northport, Tuscaloosa, Alabama, USA
- Richard Carle Bass Jr.[1365] born on October 24, 1920 in Leon, Florida, USA; died on December 29, 1999 in Tallahassee, Leon, Florida, USA
- Olive Marie Bass[1367] born in 1921
- Catherine Carlene Bass[1368] born in 1923
- Charles Edward Bass[1369] born on January 19, 1925 in Telogia, Liberty, Florida, USA
- Nell Bass[1371] born in 1927
- Betty Bass[1373] born in 1929

460. HADASSAH STAUTIMIRE was born on June 25, 1915, in Florida, United States.
- She was recorded in the census in 1940, aged about 25, in Crawfordville, E Precinct 2, Wakulla, Florida, USA.
- She was recorded in the census on April 1, 1950, aged 34, in Wakula Road, Tallahassee, Leon, Florida, United States.

Richard Carl Bass Sr.[458], aged 36, married Hadassah Stautimire, aged 18, on March 10, 1934. They had four children:
- JoAnne Charlotte Bass[1375] born on April 19, 1935 in Arran, Florida, USA
- Kenneth Kirby Bass[1377] born on September 11, 1936 in Arran, Wakulla, Florida, USA; died on May 26, 2018 in Tallahassee, Florida, USA
- Harold Eugene Bass[1381] born on November 12, 1937 in Crawfordville, Florida, USA
- Betty June Bass[1383] born on May 12, 1942 in Florida, United States

461. WILLIAM BENNETT BASS (see Descendants (17)) was born on August 16, 1899, in Alabama, USA, to Bennett Bridges Bass III[106] and Alice Kinlaw[107].
- He was recorded in the census in 1930, aged about 30, in Fairfield, Covington, Alabama, USA.
- He was recorded in the census on April 1, 1950, aged 50, in 1144 W Olive St, Lakeland, Polk, Florida, United States.
- He died on August 14, 1963, aged 63 years, in Polk County, Florida, USA.
- He was buried in New Home Baptist Church Cemetery, Lakeland, Polk County, Florida, USA.

William Bennett married twice. He was married to Ora Della Hare[462] and Betty Jean Hawkins[463].

462. ORA DELLA HARE was born on July 20, 1905, in Covington, Alabama, United States.
- She was recorded in the census in 1930, aged about 24, in Fairfield, Covington, Alabama, USA.
- She died on February 17, 1986, aged 80, in Covington, Alabama, United States.

William Bennett Bass[461], aged 23, married Ora Della Hare, aged 17, on December 24, 1922 in Covington, Alabama. They had two sons:
- William Edward Bass[1385] born on September 18, 1923 in Andalusia, Covington, Alabama, USA; died on May 28, 1987
- Edwin Durwood Bass Sr.[1388] born on March 9, 1926 in Andalusia, Covington, Alabama, USA

463. BETTY JEAN HAWKINS. She was recorded in the census on April 1, 1950, in 1144 W Olive St, Lakeland, Polk, Florida, United States.

William Bennett Bass[461] married Betty Jean Hawkins. They had two children:
- Donald Gene Bass[1390] born on October 16, 1947 in Dade City, Pasco, Florida, USA
- Alice Marie Bass[1393] born on June 19, 1949 in Lakeland, Polk, Florida, USA

464. MARY LEONA BASS (see Descendants (17)) was born on September 12, 1911, in Telogia, Liberty, Florida, USA, to Bennett Bridges Bass III[106] and Jonnie Lillian Ballard[108].
- She was recorded in the census in 1940, aged about 28, in Hosford, E Precinct Hosford, Liberty, Florida, USA.
- She was recorded in the census on April 1, 1950, aged 38, in State Road No 65, Bristol, Liberty, Florida, United States.
- She died on November 16, 1986, aged 75.

465. BOONE MERCER was born about 1910, in Florida, United States.
- He was recorded in the census in 1940, aged about 30, in Hosford, E Precinct Hosford, Liberty, Florida, USA.
- He was recorded in the census on April 1, 1950, aged about 39, in State Road No 65, Bristol, Liberty, Florida, United States.
- He died in Hasford, Liberty, Florida, USA.

Direct Relations

Boone Mercer, aged about 20, married Mary Leona Bass[464], aged about 18, in 1930. They had two children:
Mary Margaret Mercer[1397] born in 1931 in Hasford, Liberty, Florida, USA
James B. Mercer[1399] born on January 9, 1933 in Hasford, Liberty, Florida, USA

466. CAPTAIN HENRY OBIE BASS (see Descendants (17)) was born on August 2, 1917, in Telogia, Liberty, Florida, USA, to Bennett Bridges Bass III[106] and Jonnie Lillian Ballard[108].

- He was recorded in the census on April 1, 1950, aged 32, in 610 2nd Court, Panama City, Bay, Florida, United States.
- He died on February 26, 1992, aged 74 years, in Panama City, Bay, Florida, USA.
- He was buried in Evergreen Memorial Gardens, Panama City, Bay, Florida, USA.

The following information is also recorded for Henry Obie:
- Military Service in 1979, aged about 61, in Panama City, Florida, USA.

Note: *610 E 2nd CT.*
(Military Service)

467. AJETTA BODIFORD was born on August 23, 1921, in Hosford, Liberty, Florida, USA.
- She was recorded in the census on April 1, 1950, aged 28, in 610 2nd Court, Panama City, Bay, Florida, United States.
- She died on November 25, 2015, aged 94 years.
- She was buried in Evergreen Memorial Gardens, Panama City, Bay, Florida, USA.

Henry Obie Bass[466], aged 22, married Ajetta Bodiford, aged 18, on March 31, 1940 in Donaldsonville, Georgia, USA. They had four daughters:
Trina Elaine Bass[1401] born on August 19, 1941 in Fort Benning, Georgia, USA
Janiee Marilyn Bass[1403] born on August 9, 1943 in Temple, Texas, USA
Cheryl Dianne Bass[1405] born on July 20, 1950 in Panama City, Bay, Florida, USA
Linda Kay Bass[1407] born on September 21, 1956 in Panama City, Bay, Florida, USA

468. MORGAN BENNETT BASS (see Descendants (17)) was born in 1928 to Bennett Bridges Bass III[106] and Rosa Lee Shuler[109]. He died in 2001, aged about 73.

469. VINNIE JANICE WILLIAMS (see Descendants (17)) was born in 1884, in Covington, Alabama, USA, to William Henry Williams[111] and Mary Elizabeth Bass[110]. She died on April 7, 1942, aged about 57, in Andalusia, Covington, Alabama, USA.

470. WILLIAM ALBERT BIGGS was born on June 25, 1884, in Andalusia, Covington, Alabama, USA, to Christania B Biggs.
- He was recorded in the census in 1920, aged about 36, in Precinct 16 Stangler School House, Covington, Alabama, USA.
- He died on September 24, 1939, aged 55 years, in Andalusia, Covington, Alabama, USA.

William Albert Biggs married Vinnie Janice Williams[469]. They had three daughters:
Minnie Elizabeth Biggs[1409] born on February 26, 1907 in Alabama, USA; died on April 23, 1991 in Luverne, Crenshaw, Alabama, USA
Beulah Mae Biggs[1410] born on August 10, 1909 in Andalusia, Covington, Alabama, USA; died on March 29, 1971 in Elba, Coffee, Alabama, USA
Lessie Myrl Biggs[1412] born on December 19, 1914 in Tuscolusa, Alabama, USA; died on June 26, 1991 in Alabama, USA

471. ADA OLA WILLIAMS (see Descendants (17)) was born on July 28, 1890, in Covington, Alabama, USA, to William Henry Williams[111] and Mary Elizabeth Bass[110]. She died on July 28, 1978, aged 88.

472. GROVER CLEVELAND COBB.
Grover Cleveland Cobb married Ada Ola Williams[471], aged 18, on November 6, 1908 in Andalusia, Covington, Alabama, USA.

473. FRANCIS FOLSAM WILLIAMS (see Descendants (17)) was born on November 6, 1892, in Covington, Alabama, USA, to William Henry Williams[111] and Mary Elizabeth Bass[110].
- She was recorded in the census in 1940, aged about 47, in 3024 Bishop, Little Rock, Big Rock Twp, Pulaski, Arkansas, USA.
- She died on April 4, 1969, aged 76.

474. NEWTON DUDLEY BRYAN was born about 1886, in Florida, USA.
- He was recorded in the census in 1940, aged about 54, in 3024 Bishop, Little Rock, Big Rock Twp, Pulaski, Arkansas, USA.

Newton Dudley Bryan, aged about 26, married Francis Folsam Williams[473], aged 20, on February 10, 1913. They had four children:

Zella Bryan[1414] born about 1915 in Alabama, USA
Judson Bryan[1415] born about 1919 in Alabama, USA
Edwin Bryan[1416] born about 1921 in Alabama, USA
Loraine Bryan[1417] born about 1930 in Arkansas, USA

475. MATTIE DORA WILLIAMS (see Descendants (17)) was born on December 4, 1894, in Andalusia, Covington, Alabama, USA, to William Henry Williams[111] and Mary Elizabeth Bass[110].
- She was recorded in the census in 1930, aged about 35, in Andalusia, Covington, Alabama, USA.
- She was recorded in the census in 1940, aged about 45, in 940 River Falls Street, Andalusia, Covington, Alabama, USA.
- She died on February 9, 1990, aged 95 years, in Atmore, Escambia, Alabama, USA.

476. ANDREW ERASTUS ANDERSON was born on April 5, 1886, in Andalusia, Covington, Alabama, USA.
- He was recorded in the census in 1930, aged about 44, in Andalusia, Covington, Alabama, USA.
- He was recorded in the census in 1940, aged about 54, in 940 River Falls Street, Andalusia, Covington, Alabama, USA.
- He died on September 19, 1963, aged 77 years, in New Orleans, Louisiana, USA.

Andrew Erastus Anderson, aged 26, married Mattie Dora Williams[475], aged 17, on October 27, 1912 in Andalusia, Covington, Alabama, USA. They had four children:
Swenson Edwin Anderson[1418] born on December 29, 1914 in Covington, Alabama, USA; died on December 24, 1977 in Covington, Alabama, USA
Lucine Dalton Anderson[1419] born on November 9, 1916 in Alabama, United States; died on December 25, 1998 in Mobile, Alabama, USA
William F Anderson[1420] born on July 6, 1921 in Andalusia, Covington, Alabama, USA; died on October 6, 1974 in Foley, Baldwin, Alabama, USA
Elna F Anderson[1422] born about 1924 in Alabama, United States

477. LAURA MAY WILLIAMS WILLIAMS (see Descendants (17)) was born on July 27, 1897, in Covington, Alabama, USA, to William Henry Williams[111] and Mary Elizabeth Bass[110].
- She was recorded in the census in 1940, aged about 42, in West Jackson Street, Pensacola, E P 38, Escambia, Florida, USA.
- She was recorded in the census on April 1, 1950, aged 52, in Pensacola, Escambia, Florida, United States.
- She died on February 27, 1979, aged 81 years.
- She was buried in Magnolia Cemetery, Andalusia, Covington, Alabama, USA.

478. JOHN W ROBINSON was born about 1897, in Alabama, United States.
- He was recorded in the census in 1940, aged about 43, in West Jackson Street, Pensacola, E P 38, Escambia, Florida, USA.
- He was recorded in the census on April 1, 1950, aged about 52, in Pensacola, Escambia, Florida, United States.

John W Robinson married Laura May Williams Williams[477]. They had one daughter:
Jane Robinson[1423] born about 1926 in Alabama, United States

479. HENRY GORDON WILLIAMS (see Descendants (17)) was born on September 10, 1899, in Andalusia, Covington, Alabama, USA, to William Henry Williams[111] and Mary Elizabeth Bass[110]. He died on December 19, 1946, aged 47.

480. CAUDIE NEWMAN.
Henry Gordon Williams[479] married Caudie Newman. They had one son:
Lester Williams[1424] born on January 8, 1935 in Andalusia, Covington, Alabama, USA

481. WILLIAM MARCUS WILLIAMS (see Descendants (17)) was born on July 28, 1902, in Andalusia, Covington, Alabama, USA, to William Henry Williams[111] and Mary Elizabeth Bass[110]. He died on February 6, 1971, aged 68.

482. KATHLEEN HEDGEKOFF.
William Marcus Williams[481] married Kathleen Hedgekoff.

483. NAOMI WILLIAMS (see Descendants (17)) was born on September 14, 1904, in Covington, Alabama, United States, to William Henry Williams[111] and Mary Elizabeth Bass[110].
- She was recorded in the census in 1940, aged about 35, in South Three Notch Street, Andalusia, Covington, Alabama, USA.

484. FRANK A. FUQUA was born about 1898, in Alabama, USA.
- He was recorded in the census in 1940, aged about 42, in South Three Notch Street, Andalusia, Covington, Alabama, USA.

Frank A. Fuqua married Naomi Williams[483]. They had two children:
Deward Fuqua[1426] born about 1923 in Alabama, USA
Evelyn Fuqua[1427] born about 1925 in Alabama, USA

485. ANNIE RUTH WILLIAMS (see Descendants (17)) was born on December 24, 1906, in Andalusia, Covington, Alabama, USA, to William Henry Williams[111] and Mary Elizabeth Bass[110].
• She was recorded in the census on April 1, 1950, aged 43, in Prestwood Bridge Road, Andalusia, Covington, Alabama, United States.

486. BENJAMIN MORRIS TATUM was born about 1903, in Alabama, United States.
• He was recorded in the census on April 1, 1950, aged about 46, in Prestwood Bridge Road, Andalusia, Covington, Alabama, United States.
Benjamin Morris Tatum, aged about 24, married Annie Ruth Williams[485], aged 20, on August 5, 1927.

487. WILMER NEWTON WILLIAMS (see Descendants (17)) was born on May 10, 1909, in Andalusia, Covington, Alabama, USA, to William Henry Williams[111] and Mary Elizabeth Bass[110]. He died on January 15, 1993, aged 83.

488. NELL GODWIN.
Wilmer Newton Williams[487] married Nell Godwin.

489. LILLIAN ELIZABETH WILLIAMS (see Descendants (17)) was born on September 24, 1911, in Andalusia, Covington, Alabama, USA, to William Henry Williams[111] and Mary Elizabeth Bass[110]. She died on September 27, 1945, aged 34.

490. WILLIAM FRANK TIMMERMAN.
William Frank Timmerman married Lillian Elizabeth Williams[489].

491. BUNA LUCILLE WILLIAMS (see Descendants (17)) was born on January 30, 1914, in Andalusia, Covington, Alabama, USA, to William Henry Williams[111] and Mary Elizabeth Bass[110].

492. AUBURN E. MCGRAW.
Auburn E. McGraw married Buna Lucille Williams[491], aged 26, on April 21, 1940.

493. ARRIE BERNICE BASS (see Descendants (17)) was born on May 20, 1900, in Alabama, United States, to James Wilson Bass[113] and Emmie Cornelia Hutto[114]. Arrie Bernice became known as "Emma".
• She was recorded in the census in 1900, aged 0, in Precincts 2, 6, 18 Fairfield, Loango, River Falls, Covington, Alabama, USA.
• She was recorded in the census in 1910, aged about 10, in Fairfield, Covington, Alabama, USA.
• She was recorded in the census in 1920, aged about 20, in Precinct 21, Covington, Alabama, USA.
• She was recorded in the census in 1930, aged about 30, in Carolina, Covington, Alabama, USA.
• She was recorded in the census in 1940, aged about 40, in Beat 21 Carolina, Covington, Alabama, USA.
• She was recorded in the census on April 1, 1950, aged 49, in Carolina, Covington, Alabama, United States.
• She died on May 15, 1987, aged 86 years.
• She was buried in Carolina Baptist Church Cemetery, Covington, Alabama, USA.

494. LUIE CLAUDE ADAMS was born on December 15, 1893, in Alabama, USA.
• He was recorded in the census in 1930, aged about 36, in Carolina, Covington, Alabama, USA.
• He was recorded in the census in 1940, aged about 46, in Beat 21 Carolina, Covington, Alabama, USA.
• He was recorded in the census on April 1, 1950, aged 56, in Carolina, Covington, Alabama, United States.
• He died on January 20, 1956, aged 62 years, in Covington, Alabama, United States.
• He was buried in Carolina Baptist Church Cemetery, Covington, Alabama, USA.
Luie Claude Adams, aged 27, married Arrie Bernice Bass[493], aged 21, on November 5, 1921. They had five children:
Arlis Chapman Adams Sr.[1428] born about 1925 in Alabama, USA
Atris C Adams[1430] born about 1927 in Alabama, USA
Annette Adams[1432] born about 1928 in Alabama, USA
Aaron Lee Adams[1434] born on March 6, 1930 in Andalusia, Covington, Alabama, USA; died on December 1, 2011 in Macon, Bibb, Georgia, USA
Audie Mae Adams[1436] born on June 12, 1934 in Alabama, USA

495. OLLIE ALBERT BASS (see Descendants (17)) was born on August 16, 1901, in Covington, Alabama, United States, to James Wilson Bass[113] and Emmie Cornelia Hutto[114].
• He died on July 30, 1904, aged 2 years, in Covington, Alabama, United States.
• He was buried in Carolina Baptist Church Cemetery, Covington, Alabama, USA.

496. EVA ALLIE BASS (see Descendants (17)) was born on November 29, 1902, in Alabama, United States, to James Wilson Bass[113] and Emmie Cornelia Hutto[114]. Eva Allie became known as "Ev 'er".
- She was recorded in the census in 1910, aged about 7, in Fairfield, Covington, Alabama, USA.
- She was recorded in the census in 1920, aged about 17, in Precinct 21, Covington, Alabama, USA.
- She was recorded in the census in 1930, aged about 27, in Andalusia, Covington, Alabama, USA.
- She died on July 31, 2001, aged 98 years.
- She was buried in Carolina Baptist Church Cemetery, Covington, Alabama, USA.

497. JOHN THOMAS EVANS RODGERS was born on January 4, 1897, in Alabama, United States.
- He was recorded in the census in 1930, aged about 33, in Andalusia, Covington, Alabama, USA.
- He died on November 21, 1970, aged 73 years.
- He was buried in Carolina Baptist Church Cemetery, Covington, Alabama, USA.

The following information is also recorded for John Thomas Evans:
- Military Service.

Note: *HQ Co. 106 Ammo Train - WWI.*
(Military Service)

John Thomas Evans Rodgers married Eva Allie Bass[496]. They had five children:
- Thomas Lloyd Rodgers[1438] born on April 5, 1921 in Alabama, United States; died on June 15, 1944 in Normandy, France
- Sibyl Rodgers[1439] born on November 6, 1922 in Alabama, United States; died on May 23, 2011 in Carolina Community, Covington, Alabama, USA
- Evans Rodgers[1441] born on April 21, 1924 in Alabama, United States; died on March 8, 2008 in Walton County, Florida, USA
- Ollie Kenneth Rodgers[1445] born about 1926 in Alabama, United States; died in 1997
- Ross Burton Rodgers[1446] born on October 14, 1927 in Alabama, United States; died on January 25, 1997

498. JAMIE IKE BASS (see Descendants (17)) was born on December 22, 1904, in Covington, Alabama, United States, to James Wilson Bass[113] and Emmie Cornelia Hutto[114]. Jamie Ike became known as "Jamie".
- He was recorded in the census in 1910, aged about 5, in Fairfield, Covington, Alabama, USA.
- He was recorded in the census in 1920, aged about 15, in Precinct 21, Covington, Alabama, USA.
- He was recorded in the census in 1930, aged about 25, in Carolina, Covington, Alabama, USA.
- He was recorded in the census in 1940, aged about 35, in Election Prect 21 Carolina, Covington, Alabama, USA.
- He was recorded in the census on April 1, 1950, aged 45, in Carolina, Covington, Alabama, United States.
- He died on February 9, 1978, aged 73 years, in Andalusia, Covington, Alabama, United States.
- He was buried in Carolina Baptist Church Cemetery, Covington, Alabama, USA.

499. CLEO GUNTER was born on December 23, 1908, in Covington, Alabama, United States.
- She was recorded in the census in 1930, aged about 21, in Carolina, Covington, Alabama, USA.
- She was recorded in the census in 1940, aged about 31, in Election Prect 21 Carolina, Covington, Alabama, USA.
- She was recorded in the census on April 1, 1950, aged 41, in Carolina, Covington, Alabama, United States.
- She died on April 10, 1991, aged 82 years, in Covington, Alabama, United States.
- She was buried in Carolina Baptist Church Cemetery, Covington, Alabama, USA.

Jamie Ike Bass[498], aged 18, married Cleo Gunter, aged 14, on April 6, 1923 in Covington, Alabama, United States. They had eight children:
- James Ivey Bass[1447] born on April 5, 1924 in Carolina, Covington, Alabama, United States; died on July 29, 2001 in Florala, Covington, Alabama, United States
- James Ervin Bass[1449] born on October 25, 1925 in Covington, Alabama, USA; died on March 15, 1971
- Hazel Bass[1451] born on August 14, 1927 in Andalusia, Covington, Alabama, USA; died on August 15, 2013
- Christine Bass[1452] born on July 29, 1929 in Carolina Community, Covington, Alabama, USA; died about 2005
- Voncile Bass[1455] born on September 21, 1931 in Carolina, Covington, Alabama, United States; died on September 23, 2008 in Covington, Alabama, United States
- Betty Jean Bass[1457] born on May 23, 1933 in Covington, Alabama, USA; died on December 9, 2007 in Covington, Alabama, United States
- Emmie Elvira Bass[1458] born about 1944 in Alabama, United States
- Julius Ike Bass[1459] born on October 23, 1946 in Alabama, United States

500. JOSEPH AARON BASS (see Descendants (17)) was born on January 24, 1907, in Covington, Alabama, United States, to James Wilson Bass[113] and Emmie Cornelia Hutto[114].

- He was recorded in the census in 1910, aged about 3, in Fairfield, Covington, Alabama, USA.
- He died on September 5, 1919, aged 12 years, in Covington, Alabama, USA.
- He was buried in Carolina Baptist Church Cemetery, Covington, Alabama, USA.

501. JULIUS CLARENCE BASS (see Descendants (17)) was born on August 26, 1908, in Alabama, United States, to James Wilson Bass[113] and Emmie Cornelia Hutto[114].
   - He was recorded in the census in 1910, aged about 1, in Fairfield, Covington, Alabama, USA.
   - He was recorded in the census in 1920, aged about 11, in Precinct 21, Covington, Alabama, USA.
   - He was recorded in the census in 1930, aged about 21, in Niagara Falls, Niagara, New York, USA.
   - He was recorded in the census in 1940, aged about 31, in Creekside Parkway, Niagara Town, Niagara, New York, USA.
   - He was recorded in the census on April 1, 1950, aged 41, in 2 Mil on Pleas and Nome and Coneuch Church Iraveling Sousth East, Fairfield, Covington, Alabama, United States.
   - He died on May 21, 1994, aged 85 years.
   - He was buried in Carolina Baptist Church Cemetery, Covington, Alabama, USA.

502. MILDRED NALL was born on July 21, 1910, in Alabama, United States.
   - She was recorded in the census in 1930, aged about 19, in Niagara Falls, Niagara, New York, USA.
   - She was recorded in the census in 1940, aged about 29, in Creekside Parkway, Niagara Town, Niagara, New York, USA.
   - She was recorded in the census on April 1, 1950, aged 39, in On Pleas and Nome and Coneuch Church Iraveling Sousth East, Fairfield, Covington, Alabama, United States.
   - She died on December 21, 1997, aged 87 years.
   - She was buried in Carolina Baptist Church Cemetery, Covington, Alabama, USA.

   Julius Clarence Bass[501] married Mildred Nall. They had four children:
   Beatrice Lucile Bass[1463] born on July 1, 1930 in Niagra Falls, New York, USA
   Robert Julius Bass[1465] born on March 21, 1938 in Niagra Falls, New York, USA; died on April 23, 1981
   Richard Clarence Bass[1470] born on October 2, 1940 in Niagra Falls, New York, USA; died on March 14, 2008 in Lorida, Highlands, Florida, USA
   Gayle Ann Bass[1472] born on November 13, 1947 in Andalusa, Covington, Alabama, USA

503. MARY ANNIE BASS (see Descendants (17)) was born on November 13, 1910, in Alabama, United States, to James Wilson Bass[113] and Emmie Cornelia Hutto[114].
   - She was recorded in the census in 1920, aged about 9, in Precinct 21, Covington, Alabama, USA.
   - She was recorded in the census on April 1, 1950, aged 39, in Carolina, Covington, Alabama, United States.
   - She died on October 8, 1992, aged 81.
   - She was buried in Carolina Baptist Church Cemetery, Covington, Alabama, USA.

504. GEORGE RUFUS HARRELSON was born on December 16, 1904, in Alabama, United States.
   - He was recorded in the census on April 1, 1950, aged 45, in Carolina, Covington, Alabama, United States.
   - He died on January 8, 1991, aged 86.
   - He was buried in Carolina Baptist Church Cemetery, Covington, Alabama, USA.

   George Rufus Harrelson, aged 21, married Mary Annie Bass[503], aged 15, on June 30, 1926 in Andalusia, Ala. They had four sons:
   Olen Rex Harrelson[1475] born on April 29, 1927 in Andalusa, Covington, Alabama, USA; died on December 20, 1983 in Andalusa, Covington, Alabama, USA
   Ralph Marlon Harrelson[1478] born on January 11, 1929 in Carolina, Covington, Alabama, USA; died on December 25, 1994 in Carolina, Covington, Alabama, USA
   Ramond Teuell Harrelson[1480] born on January 10, 1934 in Andalusa, Covington, Alabama, USA
   Ronnie Ray Harrelson[1482] born on October 3, 1943 in Andalusa, Covington, Alabama, USA

505. JESSIE D BASS (see Descendants (17)) was born on August 5, 1912, in Anniston, Calhoun, AL, to James Wilson Bass[113] and Emmie Cornelia Hutto[114].
   - He was recorded in the census in 1920, aged about 7, in Precinct 21, Covington, Alabama, USA.
   - He was recorded in the census in 1930, aged about 17, in Carolina, Covington, Alabama, USA.
   - He was recorded in the census on April 1, 1950, aged 37, in Carolina, Covington, Alabama, United States.
   - He died on January 13, 1991, aged 78 years.
   - He was buried in Carolina Baptist Church Cemetery, Covington, Alabama, USA.

506. EILEEN HEAD was born on January 23, 1916, in Black Rock, Crenshaw, Alabama, USA, to Byron Head and Mamie Head.
- She was recorded in the census in 1930, aged about 14, in Staughns Schoolhouse, Covington, Alabama, USA.
- She was recorded in the census on April 1, 1950, aged 34, in Carolina, Covington, Alabama, United States.
- She died on October 30, 1982, aged 66 years, in Birmingham, Jefferson, AL.
- She was buried in Carolina Baptist Church Cemetery, Andalusia, Covington, Alabama, USA.

Jessie D Bass[505], aged 24, married Eileen Head, aged 21, on March 27, 1937 in Covington, Alabama, USA. They had two daughters:
Charlotte Bass[1484] born on February 28, 1945 in Andalusia, Covington, Alabama, USA
Elizabeth Louise Bass[1485] born on May 20, 1947 in Niagra Falls, New York, USA

507. LEON PENDRY BASS (see Descendants (17)) was born on October 27, 1913, in Alabama, USA, to James Wilson Bass[113] and Emmie Cornelia Hutto[114].
- He was recorded in the census in 1920, aged about 6, in Precinct 21, Covington, Alabama, USA.
- He was recorded in the census in 1930, aged about 16, in Carolina, Covington, Alabama, USA.
- He was recorded in the census in 1940, aged about 26, in Election Prect 21 Carolina, Covington, Alabama, USA.
- He was recorded in the census on April 1, 1950, aged 36, in Carolina, Covington, Alabama, United States.
- He died on June 22, 1995, aged 81 years, in Andalusa, Covington, Alabama, USA.
- He was buried in Carolina Baptist Church Cemetery, Covington, Alabama, USA.

508. CLIPP F MERRILL was born on April 11, 1916, in Alabama, USA.
- She was recorded in the census in 1940, aged about 24, in Election Prect 21 Carolina, Covington, Alabama, USA.
- She was recorded in the census on April 1, 1950, aged 33, in Carolina, Covington, Alabama, United States.
- She died on August 17, 1988, aged 72 years.
- She was buried in Carolina Baptist Church Cemetery, Covington, Alabama, USA.

Leon Pendry Bass[507] married Clipp F Merrill. They had two children:
Barbara Eleanor Bass[1487] born on September 10, 1938 in Alabama, USA; died in 1945
David Leon Bass[1488] born on November 26, 1948 in Alabama, United States

509. SNYDER CLAYTON BASS (see Descendants (17)) was born on January 29, 1915, in Alabama, United States, to James Wilson Bass[113] and Emmie Cornelia Hutto[114].
- He was recorded in the census in 1920, aged about 5, in Precinct 21, Covington, Alabama, USA.
- He was recorded in the census in 1930, aged about 15, in Carolina, Covington, Alabama, USA.
- He was recorded in the census in 1940, aged about 25, in Creekside Parkway, Niagara Town, Niagara, New York, USA.
- He died on January 28, 1993, aged 77.
- He was buried in Carolina Baptist Church Cemetery, Covington, Alabama, USA.

The following information is also recorded for Snyder Clayton:
- Military Service.

Note: *U.S. Army WWII - New Guinea.*
(Military Service)

510. VIOLA RUTH COULTER was born on September 3, 1921.
- She died on August 13, 1986, aged 64.
- She was buried.

Snyder Clayton Bass[509] married Viola Ruth Coulter. They had one son:
Roger Clayton Bass[1489] died on June 3, 1991 in Andalusa, Covington, Alabama, USA

511. VELMA BERTHA BASS (see Descendants (17)) was born on October 16, 1917, in Alabama, United States, to James Wilson Bass[113] and Emmie Cornelia Hutto[114].
- She was recorded in the census in 1920, aged about 2, in Precinct 21, Covington, Alabama, USA.
- She was recorded in the census in 1930, aged about 12, in Carolina, Covington, Alabama, USA.
- She was recorded in the census on April 1, 1950, aged 32, in Carolina, Covington, Alabama, United States.
- She died on October 30, 1995, aged 78, in Covington, Alabama, United States.

512. WILLIAM TURNER HENDERSON was born about 1906, in Alabama, United States.
- He was recorded in the census on April 1, 1950, aged about 43, in Carolina, Covington, Alabama, United States.

William Turner Henderson, aged about 28, married Velma Bertha Bass[511], aged 16, on July 16, 1934. They had four children:
Redessa L Henderson[1492] born about 1936 in Alabama, United States
Fredrick Henderson[1494] born on February 28, 1943 in Andalusia, Covington, Alabama, USA
Judith Lynn Henderson[1496] born about 1949 in Alabama, United States

Direct Relations

Phillip Henderson[1498]

513. EDITH INEZ BASS (see Descendants (17)) was born on September 5, 1919, in Covington, Alabama, United States, to James Wilson Bass[113] and Emmie Cornelia Hutto[114].
- She was recorded in the census in 1920, as an infant, in Precinct 21, Covington, Alabama, USA.
- She was recorded in the census in 1930, aged about 10, in Carolina, Covington, Alabama, USA.
- She died on June 14, 2004, aged 84, in Covington, Alabama, United States.

Edith Inez had three partnerships. She was married to Millard Allison Ott[516]. She was also the partner of Homer Huckabaa[514] and Allan Butkiss[515].

514. HOMER HUCKABAA.
Homer Huckabaa and Edith Inez Bass[513] became partners.
The following information is also recorded for this family:
- Unknown Relationship.

515. ALLAN BUTKISS.
Allan Butkiss and Edith Inez Bass[513] became partners.
The following information is also recorded for this family:
- Unknown Relationship.

516. MILLARD ALLISON OTT.
Millard Allison Ott married Edith Inez Bass[513], aged about 22, in 1942. They had three sons:
Millard Allison Ott Jr.[1501] born on January 7, 1946 in Cleveland, Liberty, Texas, USA
James Allen Ott Sr.[1504] born on January 3, 1948 in Cleveland, Liberty, Texas, USA
John Byron Ott[1506] born on July 3, 1949 in Conroe, Montgomery, Texas, USA

517. FRANK STEWART BASS (see Descendants (95)) was born on April 9, 1914, in Andalusia, Covington, Alabama, USA, to John Bridges Bass[115] and Nancy Amy Carroll[116].
- He was recorded in the census in 1930, aged about 16, in Hart, Covington, Alabama, USA.
- He died on September 6, 1994, aged 80, in Orlando, Orange, Florida, USA.

518. MS. JOSEY.
Frank Stewart Bass[517], aged 25, married Ms. Josey in October 1939 in Covington, Alabama, USA.

519. CLAUDE BRUCE BASS (see Descendants (95)) was born on June 14, 1916, in Alabama, United States, to John Bridges Bass[115] and Nancy Amy Carroll[116].
- He was recorded in the census in 1930, aged about 14, in Hart, Covington, Alabama, USA.
- He was educated (3 Years of High School).
- He died on December 1, 1991, aged 75, in Pensacola, Escambia, Florida, USA.
- He was buried in Pensacola Memorial Gardens, Pensacola, Escambia County, Florida, USA.

The following information is also recorded for Claude Bruce:
- Military Enlistment on September 1, 1945, aged 29, in Atlanta, Georgia, USA.
- Military Service.

Note: *1st Sgt US Army WWII.*
(Military Service)

520. MARLINE WHITE was born on November 23, 1920, in Andalusia, Covington, Alabama, USA. She died on November 1, 2013, aged 92, in Pensacola, Escambia, Florida, USA.
Claude Bruce Bass[519], aged 25, married Marline White, aged 21, on December 25, 1941 in Covington, Alabama, USA. They had four sons:
Richard Bass[1507]
Bob Bass[1509] born in October 23 A.D.
Greg Bass[1511]
Jeffery W. Bass[1513] born in March 31 A.D.

521. SARAH CLYDE LAW (see Descendants (95)) was born about 1918, in Andalusia, Covington, Alabama, USA, to John Bridges Bass[115] and Nancy Amy Carroll[116].
- She was recorded in the census in 1930, aged about 12, in Hart, Covington, Alabama, USA.
- She was recorded in the census in 1940, aged about 22, in East Ends State High # 12, Elec Prec 1 Andalusia, Covington, Alabama, USA.
- She died on May 13, 1980, aged about 61, in Andalusia, Covington, Alabama, USA.
- She was buried in Adellum Cemetery, Andalusia, Covington County, Alabama, USA.

522. CECIL ATHANIEL LAW was born on August 28, 1908, in Troy, Pike, Alabama, USA.
- He died on January 6, 1969, aged 60, in Andalusia, Covington, Alabama, USA.
- He was buried in Adellum Cemetery, Andalusia, Covington County, Alabama, USA.

Cecil Athaniel Law, aged 31, married Sarah Clyde Law[521], aged about 21, on January 1, 1940 in Covington, Alabama, USA. They had four children:
>Mr./Ms. Law[1514]
>Mr./Ms. Law[1515]
>Mr./Ms. Law[1516]
>Mr./Ms. Law[1517]

523. BENNETT RAY BASS (see Descendants (95)) was born on August 19, 1920, in Alabama, USA, to John Bridges Bass[115] and Nancy Amy Carroll[116].
- He was recorded in the census in 1930, aged about 9, in Hart, Covington, Alabama, USA.
- He was recorded in the census in 1940, aged about 19, in 1 Range 14, Covington, Alabama, USA.
- He was recorded in the census on April 1, 1950, aged 29, in 127 A Ingram, Norfolk, Norfolk City, Virginia, United States.
- He died on February 23, 2003, aged 82 years.
- He was buried in Pigeon Creek Baptist Church Memorial Cemetery, Red Level, Covington, Alabama, USA.

Bennett Ray married twice. He was married to Mary Rae Parrish[524] and Frances Alice Hester Chesser[525].

524. MARY RAE PARRISH was born on September 21, 1924, in Andalusia, Covington, Alabama, USA.
- She was recorded in the census on April 1, 1950, aged 25, in 127 A Ingram, Norfolk, Norfolk City, Virginia, United States.
- She died on February 22, 2009, aged 84, in Palm Bay, Brevard, Florida, USA.

Bennett Ray Bass[523], aged 22, married Mary Rae Parrish, aged 18, on April 26, 1943, and they were divorced. They had two children:
>Linda Bass[1518] born in August 27 A.D. in Alabama, United States
>Gary Dean Bass[1520] born on July 1, 1950 in Norfolk, Virginia, USA; died on July 27, 2019 in Mims, Brevard, Florida, USA

525. FRANCES ALICE HESTER CHESSER was born on December 9, 1921, in Alabama, USA.
- She was recorded in the census on April 1, 1950, aged 28, in 321 C Academy, Geneva, Geneva, Alabama, United States.
- She died on April 29, 2006, aged 84 years, in Red Level, Covington, Alabama, USA.
- She was buried in Pigeon Creek Baptist Church Memorial Cemetery, Red Level, Covington, Alabama, USA.

Frances Alice Hester married twice. She was married to Bennett Ray Bass[523] and Noble Clark Hester Sr.
Bennett Ray Bass[523], aged 49, married Frances Alice Hester Chesser, aged 47, on November 22, 1969 in Andalusia, Covington, Alabama, USA.
Noble Clark Hester Sr. married Frances Alice Hester Chesser. They had two sons:
>C Frankie Hester born about 1946 in Alabama, United States
>Noble Clark Hester Jr.

526. BESSIE MAY BASS (see Descendants (95)) was born on August 19, 1920, in Alabama, USA, to John Bridges Bass[115] and Nancy Amy Carroll[116].
- She was recorded in the census in 1930, aged about 9, in Hart, Covington, Alabama, USA.
- She was recorded in the census in 1940, aged about 19, in 1 Range 14, Covington, Alabama, USA.
- She was recorded in the census on April 1, 1950, aged 29, in 903 New Jersey., Mobile, Mobile, Alabama, United States.
- She died on March 23, 2010, aged 89, in Fairhope, Baldwin, Alabama, USA.
- She was buried in Belforest Community Cemetery, Belforest, Baldwin, Alabama, USA.

Note:

She was a former member of the Business & Professional Women's Club. One of her passions was working at Brookley Air Force Base in Mobile. She also worked at Pensacola Naval Air Station helping military families relocate. She was a master gardener and loved being outdoors.

(Death)

527. LUCIAN HIBBARD ANDREWS JR. was born on August 30, 1921, in Daphne, Baldwin, Alabama, USA, to Lucian Hibbard Andrews Sr. and Birdie Idett Wright.
- He was recorded in the census in 1930, aged about 8, in Daphne, Baldwin, Alabama, USA.
- He was recorded in the census on April 1, 1950, aged 28, in 903 New Jersey., Mobile, Mobile, Alabama, United States.
- He died on February 3, 1969, aged 47, in Daphne, Baldwin, Alabama, USA.
- He was buried in Belforest Community Cemetery, Belforest, Baldwin, Alabama, USA.

Direct Relations

    Lucian Hibbard Andrews Jr. married Bessie May Bass[526]. They had four children:
        Lucian Hibbard Andrews III[1522]
        Lucia Dianne Andrews[1524] born about 1948 in California, United States
        Deborah Andrews[1526]
        Rebecca Andrews[1528]

528. JOHN IRVIN BASS (see Descendants (95)) was born on February 10, 1922, in Andalusia, Covington, Alabama, USA, to John Bridges Bass[115] and Nancy Amy Carroll[116].
- He was recorded in the census in 1930, aged about 8, in Hart, Covington, Alabama, USA.
- He was recorded in the census in 1940, aged about 18, in 1 Range 14, Covington, Alabama, USA.
- He was recorded in the census on April 1, 1950, aged 28, in 1938 So Huron, Denver, Denver, Colorado, United States.
- He died on April 22, 2002, aged 80, in Lancaser, Los Angeles, California, USA.

529. MINNIE JEWEL MCCORQUODAL was born on December 16, 1926, in Salitpa, Clark, Alabama, USA.
- She was recorded in the census on April 1, 1950, aged 23, in 1938 So Huron, Denver, Denver, Colorado, United States.
- She died on March 13, 1999, aged 72, in Lancaser, Los Angeles, California, USA.

    John Irvin Bass[528], aged 22, married Minnie Jewel McCorquodal, aged 17, on February 24, 1944. They had four children:
        Ronald Bass[1530] born about 1945 in Alabama, United States
        Carol Bass[1531] born about 1947 in Alabama, United States
        Cheryl Bass[1532] born about 1947 in Alabama, United States
        Nancy Bass[1533] born about 1949 in Colorado, United States

530. JESSE RUBAN BASS (see Descendants (95)) was born on February 2, 1924, in Alabama, USA, to John Bridges Bass[115] and Nancy Amy Carroll[116].
- He was recorded in the census in 1930, aged about 6, in Hart, Covington, Alabama, USA.
- He was recorded in the census in 1940, aged about 16, in 1 Range 14, Covington, Alabama, USA.
- He was educated (1 Year of High School).
- He died on January 24, 1952, aged 27 years, in Phenix City, Russell, Alabama, USA.
- He was buried in Carolina Baptist Church Cemetery, Covington, Alabama, USA.

The following information is also recorded for Jesse Ruban:
- Military Service.
- Military Enlistment on July 25, 1944, aged 20, in Ft McClellan, Alabama, USA.

Note: *S. SGT 695 QM TRUCK Co. WWII.*
    (Military Service)

531. ANNIE LAURA BASS (see Descendants (95)) was born on September 13, 1927, in Andalusia, Covington, Alabama, USA, to John Bridges Bass[115] and Nancy Amy Carroll[116].
- She died on December 5, 1927, aged 0, in Andalusia, Covington, Alabama, USA.
- She was buried in Carolina Baptist Church Cemetery, Covington, Alabama, USA.

532. ANDREW BENNETT BASS (see Descendants (96)) was born on November 25, 1900, in Andalusia, Covington, Alabama, USA, to Laura Lee Bass[117]. Andrew Bennett became known as "Ander".
- He was recorded in the census on April 1, 1950, aged 49, in 1ar River Falls Street, Andalusia, Covington, Alabama, United States.
- He died on June 13, 1971, aged 70, in Montgomery, Montgomery, Alabama, USA.
- He was buried in Andalusia Memorial Cemetery, Andalusia, Covington, Alabama, USA.

533. FLORENCE PERDUE was born on July 28, 1906, in Alabama, United States.
- She was recorded in the census on April 1, 1950, aged 43, in 1ar River Falls Street, Andalusia, Covington, Alabama, United States.
- She died on March 21, 1980, aged 73.
- She was buried in Andalusia Memorial Cemetery, Andalusia, Covington, Alabama, USA.

    Andrew Bennett Bass[532], aged 26, married Florence Perdue, aged 21, on October 26, 1927. They had three children:
        Marlon Jerome Bass[1534] born on November 1, 1928 in Andalusia, Covington, Alabama, USA; died on January 5, 2006 in Andalusia, Covington, Alabama, USA
        Doris Jean Bass[1536] born on February 18, 1932 in Charlottsville, VA, USA
        Shirley Ann Bass[1539] born on March 24, 1940 in Andalusia, Covington, Alabama, USA

534. GUSSIE JOSEPHINE JOHNSON (see Descendants (96)) was born on June 21, 1906, in Andalusia, Covington, Alabama, USA, to Morgan Jerome Johnson[118] and Laura Lee Bass[117]. She died on November 29, 2002, aged 96 years, in Pensacola, Escambia, Florida, USA.
535. WILLIAM A. TART was born in 1908. William A. became known as "Alf". He died in 1987, aged about 79.
William A. Tart married Gussie Josephine Johnson[534]. They had one daughter:
Olivia Tart[1541]

536. WILLIE MORGAN JOHNSON (see Descendants (96)) was born on May 18, 1908, in Andalusia, Covington, Alabama, USA, to Morgan Jerome Johnson[118] and Laura Lee Bass[117]. He died on March 2, 1994, aged 85 years, in Mobile, Alabama, USA.

537. ADDIE LEE JOHNSON JOHNSON (see Descendants (96)) was born on December 3, 1910, in Andalusia, Covington, Alabama, USA, to Morgan Jerome Johnson[118] and Laura Lee Bass[117]. She died on November 22, 2007, aged 96 years, in Pensacola, Escambia, Florida, USA.

538. BERNICE JOHNSON (see Descendants (96)) was born on November 17, 1913, in Andalusia, Covington, Alabama, USA, to Morgan Jerome Johnson[118] and Laura Lee Bass[117].
- She was recorded in the census on April 1, 1950, aged 36, in 407 North Deland, Volusia, Florida, United States.
- She died on September 9, 1991, aged 77 years, in Orange County, Florida, USA.
- She was buried in Andalusia Memorial Garden, Andalusia, Alabama, USA.
539. MORRIS EDWIN WATSON was born on July 4, 1910, in Dozier, Crenshaw, Alabama, USA.
- He was recorded in the census on April 1, 1950, aged 39, in 407 North Deland, Volusia, Florida, United States.
- He died on June 24, 1974, aged 63 years, in Andalusia, Covington, Alabama, USA.
- He was buried in Andalusia Memorial Cemetery, Andalusia, Covington, Alabama, USA.
Morris Edwin Watson married Bernice Johnson[538].

540. BERT JEROME JOHNSON (see Descendants (96)) was born on November 17, 1913, in Andalusia, Covington, Alabama, USA, to Morgan Jerome Johnson[118] and Laura Lee Bass[117]. He died on May 18, 1992, aged 78 years, in Volusia, Florida, USA.

541. MARTHA LOU JOHNSON (see Descendants (96)) was born on December 22, 1914, in Andalusia, Covington, Alabama, USA, to Morgan Jerome Johnson[118] and Laura Lee Bass[117]. She died on March 19, 2005, aged 90 years, in Andalusia, Covington, Alabama, USA.
Martha Lou gave birth to one son:
Marcus Gene Johnson[1542]

542. GARVIN GREGORY (see Descendants (97)) was born in 1908 to Charles Augustus Gregory Sr.[120] and Sheila Josephine Bass[119].

543. HENRY ERVIN GREGORY (see Descendants (97)) was born on July 27, 1908, in Alabama, USA, to Charles Augustus Gregory Sr.[120] and Sheila Josephine Bass[119]. He died on March 7, 1992, aged 83 years, in Chase City, Mecklenburg, Virginia, USA.

544. LLOYD EDISON GREGORY (see Descendants (97)) was born on October 14, 1910, in Alabama, USA, to Charles Augustus Gregory Sr.[120] and Sheila Josephine Bass[119].
- He died on July 31, 1992, aged 81 years, in Victoria, Lunenburg, Virginia, USA.
- He was buried in Trinity Memorial Gardens, Rice, Prince Edward County, Virginia, USA.

545. JULIATTE C GREGORY was born in 1908.
- She died in 1985, aged about 77.
- She was buried in Trinity Memorial Gardens, Rice, Prince Edward County, Virginia, USA.
Lloyd Edison Gregory[544] married Juliatte C Gregory.

546. MARTHA KATHLEEN GREGORY (see Descendants (97)) was born on September 12, 1914, in Florida, USA, to Charles Augustus Gregory Sr.[120] and Sheila Josephine Bass[119]. She died on August 11, 1950, aged 35 years, in Dade, Florida, USA.
547. STANISLAW EDWARD DAVIS.
Stanislaw Edward Davis married Martha Kathleen Gregory[546], aged about 33, in 1948.

548. CORINNE GREGORY (see Descendants (97)) was born on December 6, 1916, in Florida, United States, to Charles Augustus Gregory Sr.[120] and Sheila Josephine Bass[119].
- She was recorded in the census on April 1, 1950, aged 33, in 189- S Collinswath, El Paso, El Paso, Texas, United States.
- She died on November 14, 2020, aged 103.

549. CAPT. ROBERT H OLIVE was born on August 11, 1912, in Stafford, Virginia, United States, to Henry C. Olive and Emma Limerick.
- He was recorded in the census on April 1, 1950, aged 37, in 189- S Collinswath, El Paso, El Paso, Texas, United States.
- He died on January 21, 1994, aged 81, in Orlando, Orange, Florida, United States.
- He was buried in Palm Cemetery, Winter Park, Orange, Florida, USA.

The following information is also recorded for Robert H:
- Military Service.

Note: *Capt. U.S. Air Force WWII.*
(Military Service)

Robert H Olive married Corinne Gregory[548]. They had two children:
  Ann Olive[1543] born about 1945 in Virginia, United States
  Bobby Olive[1544] born on April 2, 1952 in USA; died on October 27, 2002 in Richmond, Virginia, USA

550. DONALD BASS (see Descendants (98)) was born 'Ju 14 1929', in Andalusia, Covington, Alabama, USA, to Henry Harrelson Bass[121] and Katie Mae Gillis[122].
- He was recorded in the census in 1930, in Fairfield, Covington, Alabama, USA.
- He was recorded in the census in 1940, in Brewton Highway, Election Precinct 2 Fairfield, Covington, Alabama, USA.
- He died on February 1, 2002 in Douglasville, GA, USA.
- He was buried in Griffin Memorial Gardens, Griffin, Spalding County, Georgia, USA.

551. VIRGINIA BASS.
Donald Bass[550] married Virginia Bass.

552. HENRY WALTON BASS (see Descendants (98)) was born on March 24, 1911, in Andalusia, Covington, Alabama, USA, to Henry Harrelson Bass[121] and Katie Mae Gillis[122]. Henry Walton became known as "Walt".
- He was recorded in the census in 1930, aged about 19, in Fairfield, Covington, Alabama, USA.
- He died on May 23, 1988, aged 77 years, in Andalusia, Covington, Alabama, USA.

553. WILLIAM COLUMBUS BASS (see Descendants (98)) was born on September 21, 1914, in Andalusia, Covington, Alabama, USA, to Henry Harrelson Bass[121] and Katie Mae Gillis[122]. William Columbus became known as "Bill".
- He was recorded in the census in 1930, aged about 15, in Fairfield, Covington, Alabama, USA.
- He was recorded in the census on April 1, 1950, aged 35, in 304 Woodrow Ave, Andalusia, Covington, Alabama, United States.
- He died on May 9, 1981, aged 66 years, in Andalusia, Covington, Alabama, USA.
- He was buried in Cedar Grove Cemetery, Andalusia, Alabama, United States.

554. CLARA V STOKES was born on August 3, 1917, in Alabama, United States.
- She was recorded in the census on April 1, 1950, aged 32, in 304 Woodrow Ave, Andalusia, Covington, Alabama, United States.
- She died on November 12, 2014, aged 97 years, in Alabama, USA.
- She was buried in Cedar Grove Church of Christ Cemetery, Andalusia, Covington, Alabama, USA.

William Columbus Bass[553] married Clara V Stokes. They had five children:
  Shelia Pamelia Bass[1546] born on June 15, 1937 in Andalusia, Covington, Alabama, USA
  Patricia Lucille Bass[1548] born on October 22, 1939 in Alabama, United States
  James William Bass[1550] born on November 11, 1942 in Andalusia, Covington, Alabama, USA
  Mathew Gerald Bass[1552] born on April 6, 1948 in Andalusia, Covington, Alabama, USA
  Jerry Bass[1554]

555. HOWARD EUGINE BASS (see Descendants (98)) was born on September 2, 1918, in Covington, Alabama, USA, to Henry Harrelson Bass[121] and Katie Mae Gillis[122]. Howard Eugine became known as "Runt".
- He was recorded in the census in 1930, aged about 11, in Fairfield, Covington, Alabama, USA.
- He was recorded in the census in 1940, aged about 21, in Brewton Highway, Election Precinct 2 Fairfield, Covington, Alabama, USA.
- He died on September 18, 1997, aged 79 years, in Pensacola, Escambia, Florida, USA.

556. ANNIE M MAUD was born on October 16, 1923. She died on November 1, 2003, aged 80, in Pensacola, Escambia, Florida, USA.
>Howard Eugine Bass[555] married Annie M Maud. They had two sons:
>>Donald Bass[1556]
>>Bobby Bass[1557]

557. MARY IDELL BASS (see Descendants (98)) was born on June 1, 1923, in Covington, Alabama, USA, to Henry Harrelson Bass[121] and Katie Mae Gillis[122].
- She died on November 25, 1923, aged 0, in Covington, Alabama, USA.
- She was buried in Carolina Baptist Church Cemetery, Covington, Alabama, USA.

558. RUBY LEE BASS (see Descendants (98)) was born in 1926, in Alabama, United States, to Henry Harrelson Bass[121] and Katie Mae Gillis[122].
- She was recorded in the census in 1930, aged about 4, in Fairfield, Covington, Alabama, USA.
- She was recorded in the census in 1940, aged about 14, in Brewton Highway, Election Precinct 2 Fairfield, Covington, Alabama, USA.

559. O.B. O'BRIEN.
>O.B. O'Brien married Ruby Lee Bass[558]. They had one daughter:
>>Dianna O'Brien[1558]

560. VIRGINIA BASS (see Descendants (98)) was born about 1933, in Andalusia, Covington, Alabama, USA, to Henry Harrelson Bass[121] and Katie Mae Gillis[122]. Virginia became known as "Ginny".
- She was recorded in the census in 1940, aged about 7, in Brewton Highway, Election Precinct 2 Fairfield, Covington, Alabama, USA.
- She was recorded in the census in 1940, aged about 7, in Brewton Highway, Election Precinct 2 Fairfield, Covington, Alabama, USA.

561. ALLEN BATZINGER.
>Allen Batzinger married Virginia Bass[560].

562. ADDIE RUTH BASS (see Descendants (98)) was born in Andalusia, Covington, Alabama, USA to Henry Harrelson Bass[121] and Katie Mae Gillis[122].

563. ELLIS LOVELL.
>Ellis Lovell married Addie Ruth Bass[562].

564. EDNA INEZ BASS (see Descendants (99)) was born in 1920, in Andalusia, Covington, Alabama, USA, to Dennis Bridges Bass[125] and Lillie Lee Thomas[126]. She died in March 1924, aged about 3, in Andalusia, Covington, Alabama, USA.

565. KENNETH BRIDGES BASS (see Descendants (99)) was born on February 7, 1923, in Crestview, Okaloosa County, Florida, USA, to Dennis Bridges Bass[125] and Lillie Lee Thomas[126].
- He was recorded in the census in 1930, aged about 7, in Fairfield, Covington, Alabama, USA.
- He was recorded in the census on April 1, 1950, aged 27, in Quida, Enterprise, Coffee, Alabama, United States.

566. NANCY RUTH WALDEN was born on December 30, 1924, in Daleville, Coffee, Alabama, USA. She was recorded in the census on April 1, 1950, aged 25, in Quida, Enterprise, Coffee, Alabama, United States.
>Kenneth Bridges Bass[565], aged 18, married Nancy Ruth Walden, aged 16, on December 25, 1941. They had four sons:
>>Steve Walden Bass[1559] born on May 26, 1946 in Hartford, Geneva County, Alabama, United States; died on May 24, 1999 in Milton, Florida USA
>>Danny Kay Bass[1562] born in 1954
>>Kenneth Lee Bass[1564] born in 1960
>>Randy Lynn Bass[1567] born in 1963

567. MILDRED E. GRIFFEN BASS (see Descendants (99)) was born on January 2, 1925, in Andalusia, Covington, Alabama, USA, to Dennis Bridges Bass[125] and Lillie Lee Thomas[126].
- She was recorded in the census in 1930, aged about 5, in Fairfield, Covington, Alabama, USA.
- She died on June 22, 2009, aged 84 years, in Brenham, Washington, Texas, USA.
- She was buried in Chappell Hill Masonic Cemetery, Chapell Hill, Washington, Texas, USA.

Mildred E. Griffen married three times. She was married to Glenn M Abney Jr.[568], Mr. Griffin[569] and Fred Randall[570].

568. GLENN M ABNEY JR. was born on August 16, 1920, in Donna, Hidalgo, Texas, USA.
- He was recorded in the census in 1940, aged about 19, in Conway Blvd, Justice Precinct 4, Hidalgo, Texas, USA.
- He died on August 12, 2004, aged 83 years, in Brenham, Washington, Texas, USA.

Glenn M Abney Jr., aged 78, married Mildred E. Griffen Bass[567], aged 74, on February 12, 1999 in Washington, Texas, USA. They had three children:
> Glenn Maurice Abney III[1570]
> Ann Abney[1572]
> Glenda Abney[1574]

569. MR. GRIFFIN.
> Mr. Griffin married Mildred E. Griffen Bass[567].

570. FRED RANDALL.
> Fred Randall married Mildred E. Griffen Bass[567].

571. GEORGE WASHINGTON BASS (see Descendants (99)) was born on February 20, 1927, in Covington, Alabama, USA, to Dennis Bridges Bass[125] and Lillie Lee Thomas[126].
- He was recorded in the census in 1930, aged about 3, in Fairfield, Covington, Alabama, USA.
- He died on January 12, 2012, aged 84 years.
- He was buried in Carolina Baptist Church Cemetery, Covington, Alabama, USA.

George Washington married twice. He was married to Lorretta Voncile Driggers[572] and Mary Emma Lawson[573].

572. LORRETTA VONCILE DRIGGERS was born on May 22, 1926, in Andalusia, Covington, Alabama, USA, to James R. Lawson Sr. and Malissa Frances Spears. She died on April 22, 1984, aged 57, in Andalusia, Covington, Alabama, USA.
> George Washington Bass[571] married Lorretta Voncile Driggers. They had three children:
> > John Dennis Bass[1576] born in December 1951 in Covington, Alabama, USA
> > William Gary Bass[1578] born on June 27, 1955 in Covington, Alabama, USA
> > Emily Gwendolyn Bass[1581] born on August 1, 1956 in Covington, Alabama, USA

573. MARY EMMA LAWSON was born on June 24, 1932, in Alabama, USA, to James R. Lawson Sr. and Malissa Frances Spears. She was recorded in the census in 1940, aged about 8, in 1 Range 14, Covington, Alabama, USA.
> George Washington Bass[571], aged 73, married Mary Emma Lawson, aged 67, on June 16, 2000 in Cert: 063859, Santa Rosa, Florida, USA.

574. LAURA FRANCES BASS (see Descendants (99)) was born on February 25, 1929, in Andalusia, Covington, Alabama, USA, to Dennis Bridges Bass[125] and Lillie Lee Thomas[126].
- She was recorded in the census in 1930, aged about 1, in Fairfield, Covington, Alabama, USA.
- She was recorded in the census on April 1, 1950, aged 21, in Albritton Rd., Andalusia, Covington, Alabama, United States.

575. GEORGE R BARNETT was born on June 24, 1923, in Wildfork, Covington, Alabama, USA. He was recorded in the census on April 1, 1950, aged 26, in Albritton Rd., Andalusia, Covington, Alabama, United States.
> George R Barnett married Laura Frances Bass[574]. They had four children:
> > Rickie Donnel Barnett Sr.[1583] born on July 24, 1946 in Andalusia, Covington, Alabama, USA
> > Gloria Dianne Barnett[1587] born on October 17, 1949 in Andalusia, Covington, Alabama, USA
> > Teresa LaGail Barnett[1589] born on April 23, 1952 in Andalusia, Covington, Alabama, USA
> > Wanda June Barnett[1592] born on June 12, 1955

576. ROSSIE LEE BASS (see Descendants (99)) was born on August 15, 1931, in Andalusia, Covington, Alabama, USA, to Dennis Bridges Bass[125] and Lillie Lee Thomas[126].
- She died on August 9, 2004, aged 72 years, in Montgomery, Montgomery, Alabama, USA.
- She was buried in Carolina Baptist Church Cemetery, Covington, Alabama, USA.

Rossie Lee married twice. She was married to Dale Allen Gindlesperger Sr.[577] and Otis RC Mann[578].

577. DALE ALLEN GINDLESPERGER SR. was born on December 12, 1928. He died on April 28, 1980, aged 51, in Miami, Dade, Florida, USA.
> Dale Allen Gindlesperger Sr., aged 21, married Rossie Lee Bass[576], aged 18, on February 4, 1950. They had one son:
> > Dale Allen Gindlesperger Jr.[1595] born on January 6, 1951 in Andalusia, Covington, Alabama, USA

578. OTIS RC MANN was born on May 15, 1926, in Andalusia, Covington, Alabama, USA.
- He died on September 7, 2004, aged 78 years, in Montgomery, Montgomery, Alabama, USA.
- He was buried in Carolina Baptist Church Cemetery, Covington, Alabama, USA.

> Otis RC Mann, aged 27, married Rossie Lee Bass[576], aged 22, on December 5, 1953. They had six children:
> > Dale Allen Gindlesperger Jr.[1595] born on January 6, 1951 in Andalusia, Covington, Alabama, USA
> > Sue Ann Mann[1597] born on April 11, 1954 in Andalusia, Covington, Alabama, USA
> > Barbara Jane Mann[1599] born on August 15, 1956 in Andalusia, Covington, Alabama, USA
> > Betty Jean Mann[1601] born on August 15, 1956 in Andalusia, Covington, Alabama, USA
> > Dennis Keith Mann[1605] born on August 28, 1961 in Milton, Florida USA
> > Michael Wayne Mann[1608] born on November 6, 1964 in Milton, Florida USA

579. MELISA JUANITA BASS (see Descendants (99)) was born on May 27, 1933, in Andalusia, Covington, Alabama, USA, to Dennis Bridges Bass[125] and Lillie Lee Thomas[126].
580. COLUMBUS FRANKLIN MAUND was born on December 17, 1929, in Dale County, Alabama, USA. He died on February 15, 1992, aged 62, in Slocomb, Geneva, Alabama, USA.
> Columbus Franklin Maund, aged 20, married Melisa Juanita Bass[579], aged 17, on July 22, 1950 in Dale County, Alabama, USA. They had two daughters:
>> Linda Fay Maund[1610] born on August 25, 1951 in Genvea, Geneva, Alabama, USA
>> Amelia Delaine Maund[1613] born on June 14, 1957 in Enterprise, Coffee, Alabama, USA

581. WINSTON BYRAN BASS (see Descendants (99)) was born on December 5, 1935, in Alabama, USA, to Dennis Bridges Bass[125] and Lillie Lee Thomas[126].
- He was recorded in the census on April 1, 1950, aged 14, in On Audalina and Bruckar Hway on West Side Iraveling South, Fairfield, Covington, Alabama, United States.
- He died on September 13, 2004, aged 68 years, in Alabama, USA.
- He was buried in Carolina Baptist Church Cemetery, Covington, Alabama, USA.
582. MARY NELL BAKER was born on January 8, 1940.
- She died on January 4, 1998, aged 57 years.
- She was buried in Carolina Baptist Church Cemetery, Covington, Alabama, USA.
> Winston Byran Bass[581] married Mary Nell Baker, and they were divorced. They had one daughter:
>> Wendy Brynell Bass[1615]

583. MURRY CECIL BASS (see Descendants (99)) was born on November 13, 1937, in Carolina Community, Covington, Alabama, USA, to Dennis Bridges Bass[125] and Lillie Lee Thomas[126].
- He was recorded in the census on April 1, 1950, aged 12, in On Audalina and Bruckar Hway on West Side Iraveling South, Fairfield, Covington, Alabama, United States.
- He died on June 20, 2016, aged 78, in Andalusia, Covington, Alabama, USA.
- He was buried in Carolina Baptist Church Cemetery, Covington, Alabama, USA.

Note: *Mr. Murry Cecil Bass, 78, of the Carolina community, passed away Monday June 20, 2016 at the Andalusia Hospital.*

Funeral services will be at 10 AM Wednesday June 22, 2016 from Foreman Funeral Home Chapel with interment in Carolina Cemetery. Visitation will be from 5:30 – 8 PM Tuesday at Foreman Funeral Home.

He is survived by his son and daughter-in-law, Lamar and Donna Bass of Andalusia; his daughter, Sherry Danford of Red Level; two grandchildren J-Mack (Lakelyn) Danford and Derrick Bass; a brother and sister-in-law, Kenneth and Nancy Bass of Milton; and two sisters, Laura Barnett of Andalusia and Juanita Maund of Lake Park, GA

He is preceded in death by his wife, Elizabeth Ann Jackson Bass; two brothers, Winston Bass and George Bass; and two sisters, Mildred Abner and Rossie Mann.
(Death)

584. ELIZABETH ANN JACKSON was born on October 3, 1942, in Covington, Alabama, USA. She died on November 10, 2006, aged 64, in Montgomery, Montgomery, Alabama, USA.

Note: *Eulogy for Elizabeth Ann Bass November 14,2006 Allen Gindlesperger (Nephew) We arrive here today in honor, respect, and remembrance of the life of the life of Elizabeth Ann Bass. We arrive from many different places and backgrounds....but all having at least this one common bond……the love of this wonderful lady of great substance in our lives. Good Morning. I am Allen Gindlesperger. Ann Bass is my Aunt. I am honored to have been asked to share a few thoughts and remembrances of my beloved Aunt. I will try to do so without crying. Aunt Ann always said I was tenderhearted.....but deep down, I think we both knew I was just a crybaby. Never the less, I shall try....but if I do cry, I ask your forgiveness in advance. While I know she resides in a far better, pain free place on this day....we are none the less saddened by her absence from us......saddened, but not diminished by her passing-------for you see each of us has been made the more complete...and better because of her presence in our lives. We have gained and been made richer because of our association with her. She was that kind of person. We know she is absent from the body....yet her presence remains.....In the lives she touched and the lives she brought into the world. As long as we who were touched by her, hold onto the same kind of love and the same kind of kindness that was Ann Bass,.... she will remain. I know her legacy will live on. She will live on thru us....Her husband, her children, her grandchildren and their children for generations yet to come. Ann Bass made a difference that will be felt for years to come. Nieces, Nephews, other family and friends are much richer in generosity because of her example. A few months a go, Aunt Ann helped me fill in a few of the blanks in her family tree. She was born Elizabeth Ann Jackson on October 3, 1942 right here in Covington County. She was the youngest daughter of Homer Clarence Jackson and Linnie Bell Strickland Jackson Ann is preceded in her death by both parents and three siblings. Two brothers, Lamar and Edward Jackson and a sister Mary Frances Jackson Kirkland. Ann is survived by her husband of 46 years, my Uncle Murry Cecil Bass and two adult children and two grand children... Daughter Shelly Carroll and her son J-Mack Danford and son Lamar Bass and his wife Donna and their son Derrick. In addition to numerous other family members and friends that Ann considered part of her family. Aunt Ann Loved her family. All of you know you were loved. But the neat thing was, You didn't have to have to be born with Jackson or Bass after your name to be included...to be part of her family. If you were around her anytime at all,...she made sure you were part of her extended family......family or not......you were always treated with a kindness and familiarity that made you feel warm and welcomed and important to her. I still remember when Uncle Murry brought Aunt home to Ma and Pa Bass's house for the first time. She took to us kids in a heartbeat. She picked at us and we picked at us and we picked right back. She was fun and she loved to laugh and we kept something going on most of the time. I think we had picked her as our aunt Ann even before Uncle Murry had picked her for a wife. She made us feel important even back then. It was a trait that would follow her all her life. She had a way of making people feel good about themselves and I am forever grateful for her confidence. A hallmark of her life......and the home of Murry and Ann Bass was kindness and benevolence to others. If you had need for something and they had it to give, they gave it. If they didn't have it,....An Bass still found a way to share..."Murry, get some of those peas, peanuts, okra or deer meat out of the freezer and five it to"...whoever had happened by. You couldn't refuse it...You couldn't say no...they wouldn't let you! You can imagine...a lot of people came by to visit with Aunt Ann and Uncle Murry. However, it wasn't the stuff out of the freezer or Aunt Ann's good cooking that made folks want to stop by. Aunt Ann's house was a friendly meeting place for the community and extended family. A place for a cup of coffee – or even a whole pot- and a glass of tea....Just to sit and talk. The door was always open. "Y'all come on in and make yourself at home" The people closest to them, benefited the most from their generosity. And as I look across the room, that was just about all of us. "Come on in" - She always had a listening ear, a sympathetic ear and a caring ear ready to just listen. However, she was not bashful or timid about sharing her opinion, (especially if she thought you were wrong), or giving a little sage, but, loving advice. Some might say she was highly opinionated or at times even stubborn. She had her standard and she usually stuck to it. The great thing is........she was generally right in her pronouncements. Whatever it was.....you could be sure it was with love. She loved a lot and she enjoyed a lot of things in her life. Things she enjoyed and enjoyed doing, she would say she loved. She would tell you she loved Christmas.......... and just about any other holiday where family got together. She loved to cook and feed the whole bunch, she loved her crafts and she loved to read. She loved to have fun and figure things out. She really loved people and...She loved her family....She loved those grand boys...they hung the moon and stars for her. She loved to play her piano especially if she could get one of her grandsons to join her. That just made her love it the more. She loved Hugs. "Come here, gimme a hug"....Coming and going....and sometimes in between, "'Gimme a hug" Not like the air kisses of today....but a genuine, heartfelt, up close and personal HUU..UG. Aunt Ann gave great hugs and for her, the more the better. While in the hospital, Aunt Ann recounted again and again, the number of hugs Lamar had given her before going back out on the oil rig. She said she had gotten more hugs on his last visit home than ever before. She was elated. She remembered those hugs and it gave her such joy...and peace... and happiness. For her, these hugs were timely...and under the circumstance....it was as if that had been the plan all along. Just part of getting ready... Lamar, your Mama loved you and she took pride in you...and your family ..and their accomplishments. In that Montgomery hospital ...full of pain....and medications to keep her more comfortable, Aunt Ann listened with her eyes closed to Donna as she recounted the phone conversation she had had with you. "Lamar said to tell you he loved you and he would be home tomorrow" Even through the din of pain and drugs, Lamar, your Mama struggled to open one eye.....and she smiled. In that moment, her joy at hearing your name ...brought a peaceful smile to her face. You brought her happiness and Joy. Likewise, Shelly, her first born...You hold a place - no other can. She loved you and admired you and her pride was evidenced by everything she said about you. She took personal pride in your accomplishments and the strength and determination you've shown in your life even in the face of your own adversity. You gave her strength. She saw in you many of her own traits and your daddy's strengths. In these last days she knew you would be OK....and it gave her comfort. Like you Shelly, your Mom had an inner strength and tenacity - it was not in her nature to give up or say I can't. It was also not in her nature to let YOU give up or say I can't. it was part of her strength that rubbed of on those she cared about. Ann Bass found a way....if there was a way to be found. After years of working in progressively more responsible positions at Alatax, Andala Shaw, Columbia and Amoco fibers, Ann Bass ....on the over the hill side of 50....went to college. She earned a degree in accounting and put that knowledge to work. Tenacity....Stick-to-itiveness. She was proud of her accomplishments as well. Fact is, ..her family and friends were proud of her too. .... Not surprised .....but clearly proud of her drive and indominatable spirit. She passed that kind of determination on to her family and that too gave her comfort and a peace about what was happening to her. She wasn't happy about it, but she knew her family would be ok. Uncle Murry, I wouldn't presume to tell you what Aunt Ann held in her heart for you. You know that already....and you know she loves you still....even beyond her last breath. I do know what she shared with other family members in quiet conversation. Her thoughts were of you. She knew you would hurt...and feel her absence...but she also knew the strength of your character. Even in this occasion, ...she knew your nature as a fighter and survivor and that you would be ok. Shelly and Lamar still need their Dad and the boy's will still need the strength of example and relationship of their Grand Dad. I think she would tell you to take care of yourself - for their sake – and hers. Hold onto each other……You'll be holding onto her. No one will ever fill the special place in our lives that Ann Bass did. A wife - The perfect wife for Murry Bass. The perfect complement*

and counter balance. A Mother - There is no other for Shelly and Lamar. Lamar said it best……when asked what was most special about Aunt Ann, he simply and quietly ….with reverence said,…"She is my Mom" No one will be a grand mother like she was. With great pride and joy in her grandchildren she had great positive impact in their lives and marveled at the fine young men J-Mack and Derrick have become. Boys, your Grand Mother Bass loved you and held each of you in esteemed positions in her heart. She always had high praise for you but above all she wanted you to be good and kind people….and to be happy……. Do that for her. Ann was a mother-in law like no other. When Lamar brought Donna home….his Mom made it clear….If Lamar didn't Marry her,….She was! Instant bond. Relationship forged. Donna was a daughter long before she was a daughter – in law. Aunt Ann was a sister in law to many. But all will tell you.. with honesty…..Ann was their sister. As a friend, there was none better…..there will never be another like her,..but I think she would want us all to try. Make friendships count. In the end…..Aunt Ann was very pragmatic and practical. Her pain, her suffering and her worsening condition was more than her body could bear……..Even then she did not give up. She made peace with with it, She accepted it and moved beyond this life into the next. Into a place with no more suffering. No more pain. Finally, rest. Finally……. at peace. She exchanged her body racked with pain for a new one…….A perfect one made to last forever. Whatever that new body looks like,….I believe she's got on a pair of pink Pajamas. In her last days, She let Donna and Shelly know, "I want to be buried in my pajamas. I like my pajamas. My pajamas are comfortable." Ann Bass is wearing pink pajamas. She was unique here…She will remain unique in our hearts forever. She will always be my Aunt Ann. I'll not say good bye. For I will see her again. Sleep well my dear Aunt - I love you. We will see you in the morning.
(Death)

Murry Cecil Bass[583], aged 22, married Elizabeth Ann Jackson, aged 17, on April 22, 1960 in Andalusia, Covington, Alabama, USA. They had two children:
    Alivia LaShelle Bass[1617] born on December 7, 1961 in Andalusia, Covington, Alabama, USA
    Murry Lamar Bass[1619] born on March 10, 1965 in Andalusia, Covington, Alabama, USA

585. **LEWIS W BASS** (see Descendants (100)) was born on November 7, 1916, in Alabama, United States, to Bertie B Bass[128] and Obie Lucille Walker[129].
- He was recorded in the census in 1920, aged about 3, in Precinct 21, Covington, Alabama, USA.
- He was recorded in the census in 1930, aged about 13, in Carolina, Covington, Alabama, USA.
- He was recorded in the census in 1940, aged about 23, in Allen, Andalusia, Covington, Alabama, USA.
- He was recorded in the census on April 1, 1950, aged 33, in 101b Meaher Ave, Prichard, Mobile, Alabama, United States.
- He died on June 28, 1991, aged 74.
- He was buried in Greenwood Cemetery, Montgomery, Montgomery, Alabama, USA.

586. **AVIS HUTTO** was born on August 28, 1916, in Alabama, USA.
- She was recorded in the census in 1940, aged about 23, in Allen, Andalusia, Covington, Alabama, USA.
- She was recorded in the census on April 1, 1950, aged 33, in 101b Meaher Ave, Prichard, Mobile, Alabama, United States.
- She died on December 18, 2019, aged 103, in Pensacola, Escambia, Florida, USA.
- She was buried in Cremated.

Note: *Avis H. Bass was born Aug 28, 1916 in Andalusia, AL. After High School she married Lewis Bass and moved to Mobile, AL. She had one child, Linda Bass Lakatos. Avis worked at Brookley AFB. until they closed. In 1964 she moved to San Antoinio, TX to work at Kelly AFB. She lived there until Jan 2000. At that time she moved to Pensacola, FL to be near her Daughter, Linda. She had three Grand Children,11 Great Grand Children, and 3 Great Great Grand Children. Avis had a long and very interesting life. After her retirement in 1978, she was able to travel for 10 years to many foreign countries and all areas of the US.*
(Death)

Lewis W Bass[585] married Avis Hutto. They had one daughter:
    Linda C Bass[1621] born about 1943 in Alabama, United States

587. **MARJORIE BASS** (see Descendants (100)) was born about 1922, in Alabama, USA, to Bertie B Bass[128] and Obie Lucille Walker[129].
- She was recorded in the census in 1930, aged about 8, in Carolina, Covington, Alabama, USA.
- She was recorded in the census in 1940, aged about 18, in Election Prect 21 Carolina, Covington, Alabama, USA.

588. **ALBERT R. DOUGLAS SR.**
Albert R. Douglas Sr. married Marjorie Bass[587]. They had two children:
    Albert R. Douglas Jr.[1623]
    Jo Carrol Douglas[1624]

589. MARY ELIZABETH BASS (see Descendants (100)) was born on September 9, 1924, in Alabama, USA, to Bertie B Bass[128] and Obie Lucille Walker[129].
- She was recorded in the census in 1930, aged about 5, in Carolina, Covington, Alabama, USA.
- She was recorded in the census in 1940, aged about 15, in Election Prect 21 Carolina, Covington, Alabama, USA.
- She died on August 23, 1988, aged 63.
- She was buried in Greenwood Cemetery, Montgomery, Montgomery County, Alabama, USA.

590. JERRY W GWIN.
Jerry W Gwin married Mary Elizabeth Bass[589].

591. ESTHER FRANCES BASS (see Descendants (100)) was born about 1928, in Alabama, United States, to Bertie B Bass[128] and Obie Lucille Walker[129].
- She was recorded in the census in 1930, aged about 2, in Carolina, Covington, Alabama, USA.
- She was recorded in the census in 1940, aged about 12, in Election Prect 21 Carolina, Covington, Alabama, USA.
- She was recorded in the census on April 1, 1950, aged about 21, in High Power Radio Station No Severn, Anne Arundel, Maryland, United States.
- She died on September 19, 2007, aged about 79, in Montgomery, Montgomery, Alabama, USA.

592. LEONARD RAYMOND PREVITO SR. was born about 1923, in Alabama, United States. He was recorded in the census on April 1, 1950, aged about 26, in High Power Radio Station No Severn, Anne Arundel, Maryland, United States.
Leonard Raymond Previto Sr., aged about 21, married Esther Frances Bass[591], aged about 16, on February 25, 1945 in Montgomery, Montgomery, Alabama, USA. They had one son:
Leonard Raymond Previto Jr.[1625] born in December 1945 in Alabama, United States

593. JAMES HAROLD CURTIS (see Descendants (101)) was born on November 22, 1919, in Covington, Alabama, USA, to William Chester Curtis[131] and Florence Bass[130].
- He was recorded in the census in 1920, as an infant, in Pricint 18 River Falls Town, Covington, Alabama, USA.
- He was recorded in the census in 1930, aged about 10, in Florala, Covington, Alabama, USA.
- He died on April 7, 1977, aged 57 years, in Okaloosa, Florida, USA.
- He was buried in Liveoak Park Memorial Cemetery, Crestview, Okaloosa, USA.

The following information is also recorded for James Harold:
- Military Service.
Note: *U.S. Navy WWII.*
(Military Service)

594. THELMA OLLINE CURTIS (see Descendants (101)) was born about November 7, 1922, in Alabama, United States, to William Chester Curtis[131] and Florence Bass[130].
- She was recorded in the census in 1930, aged about 7, in Florala, Covington, Alabama, USA.

595. CARY PRESTON TURNER.
Cary Preston Turner married Thelma Olline Curtis[594]. They had three children:
Rex Turner[1627]
Jackie Turner[1628]
Ruby Jean Turner[1629] born on November 14, 1942; died in 2005

596. CLIFFORD M CURTIS (see Descendants (101)) was born on June 13, 1926, in Alabama, United States, to William Chester Curtis[131] and Florence Bass[130].
- He was recorded in the census in 1930, aged about 4, in Florala, Covington, Alabama, USA.
- He died on November 26, 1981, aged 55 years.
- He was buried in Liveoak Park Memorial Cemetery, Crestview, Okaloosa, Florida, USA.

The following information is also recorded for Clifford M:
- Military Service.
Note: *U.S. Army.*
(Military Service)

597. WILLIAM D CLARY (see Descendants (101)) was born on January 9, 1925, in Alabama, United States, to Dennis William Clary[132] and Florence Bass[130].
- He was recorded in the census in 1930, aged about 5, in Florala, Covington, Alabama, USA.
- He was recorded in the census in 1930, aged about 5, in Florala, Covington, Alabama, USA.
- He died on November 12, 1948, aged 23 years.
- He was buried in Carolina Baptist Church Cemetery, Covington, Alabama, USA.

The following information is also recorded for William D:
- Military Service.

Note: *DET FIELD ARTILLERY - WWII.*
(Military Service)

598. JOHN D CLARY (see Descendants (101)) was born about 1929, in Alabama, United States, to Dennis William Clary[132] and Florence Bass[130]. He was recorded in the census in 1930, aged about 1, in Florala, Covington, Alabama, USA.

599. MARY FRANCES CLARY (see Descendants (101)) was born in Alabama, United States to Dennis William Clary[132] and Florence Bass[130]. She was recorded in the census in 1930, in Florala, Covington, Alabama, USA.

600. MARVIN GREELY PADGETT (see Descendants (102)) was born in 1899, in Alabama, United States, to Thomas Sonny Padgett[135] and Loula Jean Welch[136]. He died on March 15, 1943, aged about 43, in Evergreen, Conecuh, Alabama, USA.

601. WILLIE THERMON PADGETT (see Descendants (102)) was born on February 9, 1903, in Covington, Alabama, USA, to Thomas Sonny Padgett[135] and Loula Jean Welch[136].
- He was recorded in the census in 1940, aged about 37, in Conecuh, Alabama, USA.
- He died on October 29, 1984, aged 81, in Conecuh, Alabama, USA.

Willie Thermon had three partnerships. He was married to Myrtle Summerlin[603] and Grace Ross Barlow[604]. He was also the partner of Nannie Jewl Hoomes[602].

602. NANNIE JEWL HOOMES was born on July 15, 1906, in Escambia, Alabama, USA.
- She was recorded in the census in 1940, aged about 33, in Conecuh, Alabama, USA.
- She died on January 18, 1970, aged 63, in Montgomery, Alabama, United States.

Willie Thermon Padgett[601] and Nannie Jewl Hoomes had seven children:

William Thomas Padgett[1631] born on August 15, 1926 in Conecuh, Alabama, USA; died on August 26, 1936 in Conecuh, Alabama, USA

O. B. Padgett[1632] born on March 18, 1930 in Jefferson, Alabama, USA; died on July 22, 1985 in Seminole County, Georgia, USA

James Clinton Padgett[1633] born on May 10, 1932 in Conecuh, Alabama, USA

Ivalou Jeanetta Padgett[1634] born on July 2, 1936 in Conecuh, Alabama, USA; died on June 30, 2016 in Marietta, Georgia, USA

William Thomas Padgett[1635] born on December 5, 1939 in Conecuh, Alabama, USA

Herbert Wayne Padgett[1637] born on May 31, 1943 in Jefferson, Alabama, USA; died on December 15, 2006 in Conecuh, Alabama, USA

Jimmy Cecil Padgett[1638] born on October 9, 1945 in Conecuh, Alabama, USA; died on January 9, 1949 in Conecuh, Alabama, USA

603. MYRTLE SUMMERLIN. She died in 1975.

Willie Thermon Padgett[601], aged about 69, married Myrtle Summerlin in 1972 in Montgomery, Alabama, United States.

604. GRACE ROSS BARLOW.

Willie Thermon Padgett[601], aged about 73, married Grace Ross Barlow in 1976 in Evergreen, Conecuh, Alabama, USA.

605. NARVI LEE PADGETT (see Descendants (102)) was born in 1905 to Thomas Sonny Padgett[135] and Loula Jean Welch[136]. He died in 1971, aged about 66.

606. WILLIA DAISY PADGETT (see Descendants (102)) was born on March 21, 1907 to Thomas Sonny Padgett[135] and Loula Jean Welch[136].

607. CLAUDE RAY PADGETT (see Descendants (102)) was born on January 2, 1909 to Thomas Sonny Padgett[135] and Loula Jean Welch[136]. He died on February 7, 1996, aged 87, in Conecuh, Alabama, USA.

608. CLYDE DEAN PADGETT (see Descendants (102)) was born on August 7, 1916, in Alabama, United States, to Thomas Sonny Padgett[135] and Loula Jean Welch[136]. He died on May 10, 1973, aged 56.

609. GROVER CLEVELAND HART (see Descendants (18)) was born on June 26, 1888, in Alabama, United States, to George W. Hart[138] and Nancy A. Ramer[137].
- He was recorded in the census in 1900, aged about 12, in Precinct 12 Aiken, Crenshaw, Alabama, USA.
- He was recorded in the census on April 1, 1950, aged 61, in Aiken, Crenshaw, Alabama, United States.
- He died on March 17, 1969, aged 80 years, in Luverne, Crenshaw, Alabama, USA.
- He was buried in Pleasant Home Baptist Church Cemetery, Covington, Alabama, USA.

Grover Cleveland married twice. He was married to Katie Vera Dobbs[610] and Cora Mattie Nichols[611].

610. KATIE VERA DOBBS was born on February 25, 1899.
- She died on March 26, 1934, aged 35 years.
- She was buried in Pleasant Home Baptist Church Cemetery, Covington, Alabama, USA.
  Grover Cleveland Hart[609], when younger than 45, married Katie Vera Dobbs, when younger than 34, before 1934.

611. CORA MATTIE NICHOLS was born on September 9, 1897.
- She was recorded in the census on April 1, 1950, aged 52, in Aiken, Crenshaw, Alabama, United States.
- She died on December 31, 1988, aged 91 years.

Cora Mattie married twice. She was married to Grover Cleveland Hart[609] and Mr. Shows.
  Grover Cleveland Hart[609], when older than 46, married Cora Mattie Nichols, when older than 37, after 1934.
  Mr. Shows married Cora Mattie Nichols. They had one son:
    R. J. Shows born on August 18, 1925 in Florala, Covington, Alabama, USA; died on May 4, 1934 in Pensacola, Escambia, Florida, USA

612. MARSHALL HART (see Descendants (18)) was born in February 1892, in Alabama, United States, to George W. Hart[138] and Nancy A. Ramer[137].
- He was recorded in the census in 1900, aged about 8, in Precinct 12 Aiken, Crenshaw, Alabama, USA.

613. IVEY W HART (see Descendants (18)) was born in May 1893, in Alabama, United States, to George W. Hart[138] and Nancy A. Ramer[137].
- He was recorded in the census in 1900, aged about 7, in Precinct 12 Aiken, Crenshaw, Alabama, USA.

614. INA MAY HART (see Descendants (18)) was born in May 1894, in Alabama, United States, to George W. Hart[138] and Nancy A. Ramer[137].
- She was recorded in the census in 1900, aged about 6, in Precinct 12 Aiken, Crenshaw, Alabama, USA.
- She was recorded in the census in 1920, aged about 26, in Precinct 12 Aiken And Pleasant Home, Crenshaw, Alabama, USA.

615. MAGGIE HART (see Descendants (18)) was born in May 1896, in Alabama, United States, to George W. Hart[138] and Nancy A. Ramer[137].
- She was recorded in the census in 1900, aged about 4, in Precinct 12 Aiken, Crenshaw, Alabama, USA.

616. DEWEY H HART (see Descendants (18)) was born in August 1898, in Alabama, United States, to George W. Hart[138] and Nancy A. Ramer[137].
- He was recorded in the census in 1900, aged about 1, in Precinct 12 Aiken, Crenshaw, Alabama, USA.

617. MARY ELLEN DESTIN (see Descendants (20)) was born on June 26, 1892, in Florida, United States, to Leonard Destin Jr.[142] and Mary Ellen Parrish[141].
- She was recorded in the census in 1900, aged about 8, in West Bay, Washington, Florida, USA.
- She was recorded in the census in 1910, aged about 18, in Point Washington, Washington, Florida, USA.
- She died on November 8, 1982, aged 90.
- She was buried in Marler Memorial Cemetery, Destin, Okaloosa, Florida, USA.

618. CAPT. ODEM THOMAS MELVIN SR. was born on March 10, 1893.
- He died on February 9, 1975, aged 81.
- He was buried in Marler Memorial Cemetery, Destin, Okaloosa, Florida, USA.
- Note: *Capt. O.T. was a tough and tenacious Man who worked hard, took care of his family and looked after his neighbors. When asked, if you could relive your life what would you do? His reply was "I would do the same thing. I have never wanted to do anything but fish, it was a good life, and the harvest of the sea was bountiful!" - Destin History and Fishing Museum.*

Odem Thomas Melvin Sr. married Mary Ellen Destin[617]. They had four children:
  Odem Thomas Melvin Jr.[1639] born on March 15, 1915 in Florida, United States; died on August 9, 2004 in Larose, Lafourche Parish, Louisiana, USA
  Gwen Melvin[1641] born on September 7, 1925; died on June 27, 1998
  Carolyn Melvin[1643] born on April 22, 1927; died on December 18, 2013
  Bennie Margaret Melvin[1645]

619. LEONARD DESTIN III (see Descendants (20)) was born on July 4, 1905, in Walton County, Florida, USA, to Leonard Destin Jr.[142] and Mary Ellen Parrish[141].
- He was recorded in the census in 1910, aged about 4, in Point Washington, Washington, Florida, USA.
- He was recorded in the census on April 1, 1950, aged 44, in Brook Street, Fort Walton Beach, Okaloosa, Florida,

United States.
- He died on August 5, 1982, aged 77, in Fort Walton Beach, Okaloosa, Florida, USA.
- He was buried in Beal Memorial Cemetery, Fort Walton Beach, Okaloosa, Florida, USA.

620. VIOLA B OGLESBY was born on April 15, 1914, in Florida, United States.
- She was recorded in the census on April 1, 1950, aged 35, in Brook Street, Fort Walton Beach, Okaloosa, Florida, United States.
- She died on March 6, 1989, aged 74, in Leon, Florida, USA.
- She was buried in Beal Memorial Cemetery, Fort Walton Beach, Okaloosa, Florida, USA.

  Leonard Destin III[619], aged 24, married Viola B Oglesby, aged 15, on July 31, 1929. They had two daughters:
  Sylvia Destin[1647] born about 1942 in Florida, United States
  Linda Destin[1648] born about 1945 in Florida, United States

621. AQUILLA MARLER (see Descendants (20)) was born on March 25, 1896, in Destin, Okaloosa, Florida, USA, to George Sanford Marler[144] and Emeline Parrish[143].
- He was recorded in the census in 1940, aged about 44, in Fraser Township, Colleton, South Carolina, USA.
- He died on September 19, 1985, aged 89.
- He was buried in Marler Memorial Cemetery, Destin, Okaloosa, Florida, USA.

The following information is also recorded for Aquilla:
- Military Service.

Note: *Sgt. U.S. Army.*
(Military Service)

622. CHARLOTTE MARILLA BARNES was born on October 28, 1893, in Vancleave, Jackson, Mississippi, USA.
- She was recorded in the census in 1940, aged about 46, in Fraser Township, Colleton, South Carolina, USA.
- She died on August 26, 1968, aged 74.
- She was buried in Marler Memorial Cemetery, Destin, Okaloosa, Florida, USA.

  Aquilla Marler[621] married Charlotte Marilla Barnes. They had two children:
  Audrey Marler[1649] born about 1921 in South Carolina, USA
  Aquilla Jr Marler[1650] born about 1928 in South Carolina, USA

623. PRICILLA MARLER (see Descendants (20)) was born on February 5, 1898, in Florida, United States, to George Sanford Marler[144] and Emeline Parrish[143].
- She was recorded in the census on April 1, 1950, aged 52, in Going West on Highway 30, Niceville, Okaloosa, Florida, United States.
- She died on March 15, 1995, aged 97.
- She was buried in Marler Memorial Cemetery, Destin, Okaloosa, Florida, USA.

624. ANDREW GAY HOGEBOOM was born on June 16, 1895, in Florida, United States.
- He was recorded in the census on April 1, 1950, aged 54, in Going West on Highway 30, Niceville, Okaloosa, Florida, United States.
- He died on July 24, 1963, aged 68.
- He was buried in Marler Memorial Cemetery, Destin, Okaloosa, Florida, USA.

  Andrew Gay Hogeboom married Pricilla Marler[623].

625. MADELINE M MARLER (see Descendants (20)) was born on August 16, 1902, in Destin, Okaloosa, Florida, USA, to George Sanford Marler[144] and Emeline Parrish[143].
- She was recorded in the census on April 1, 1950, aged 47, in 1/2 a Mile North Coast on Destin Road, Niceville, Okaloosa, Florida, United States.
- She died on September 5, 1986, aged 84.
- She was buried in Marler Memorial Cemetery, Destin, Okaloosa, Florida, USA.

626. JESSE E BRUNSON was born on August 16, 1902, in Florida, United States.
- He was recorded in the census on April 1, 1950, aged 47, in 1/2 a Mile North Coast on Destin Road, Niceville, Okaloosa, Florida, United States.
- He died on September 5, 1986, aged 84.
- He was buried in Marler Memorial Cemetery, Destin, Okaloosa, Florida, USA.

  Jesse E Brunson married Madeline M Marler[625]. They had one daughter:
  Jean Brunson[1651] born about 1937 in Florida, United States

627. BOBBIE PARRISH (see Descendants (20)) was born about 1924, in Florida, USA, to John Robert Parrish[149] and Patsy Mae Simmons[150]. He was recorded in the census in 1940, aged about 16, in Camp Nine, Elec Prec 14 Niceville, Okaloosa, Florida, USA.

628. CHARLES CLYDE GUNTER (see Descendants (20)) was born to James Ottis Gunter[155] and Leanna Parrish[154].

Direct Relations

629. OTTO LEE GUNTER (see Descendants (20)) was born to James Ottis Gunter[155] and Leanna Parrish[154].

630. JAMES E JERAULD JR. (see Descendants (20)) was born on July 2, 1915 to James E Jerauld[157] and Ella Parrish[156].
- He died on October 21, 1933, aged 18.
- He was buried in Saint John's Cemetery, Pensacola, Escambia, Florida, USA.

631. GENEVIEVE PARRISH (see Descendants (20)) was born in February 1918, in Florida, United States, to James Albert Parrish[158] and Maggie Lou Etheridge[159].
- She was recorded in the census in 1920, aged about 2, in Okaloosa, Florida, USA.
- She was recorded in the census on April 1, 1950, aged 32, in Bay Side Taun* Ct, Pensacola, Escambia, Florida, United States.

632. REX RAY KOHR was born in 1916, in Indiana, United States.
- He was recorded in the census on April 1, 1950, aged about 33, in Bay Side Taun* Ct, Pensacola, Escambia, Florida, United States.
- He died in 2010, aged about 94.
    Rex Ray Kohr married Genevieve Parrish[631]. They had two children:
        Patricia Tracie Kohr[1652] born in 1940 in Florida, United States; died in 2010
        Mr./Ms. Kohr[1653]

633. GERALDINE PARRISH (see Descendants (20)) was born in November 1919, in Florida, United States, to James Albert Parrish[158] and Maggie Lou Etheridge[159].
- She was recorded in the census in 1920, as an infant, in Okaloosa, Florida, USA.
- She was recorded in the census in 1940, aged about 20, in Grey Moss Point, Elec Prec 14 Niceville, Okaloosa, Florida, USA.
- She died in 2000, aged about 80.

634. FRANK BROWN was born in 1920. He died in 2006, aged about 86.
    Frank Brown married Geraldine Parrish[633]. They had two children:
        Mr./Ms. Brown[1654]
        Mr./Ms. Brown[1655]

635. JAMES ALBERT PARRISH JR. (see Descendants (20)) was born on October 30, 1923, in Niceville, Okaloosa, Florida, United States, to James Albert Parrish[158] and Maggie Lou Etheridge[159].
- He was recorded in the census in 1940, aged about 16, in Grey Moss Point, Elec Prec 14 Niceville, Okaloosa, Florida, USA.
- He died on February 8, 2008, aged 84, in Niceville, Okaloosa, Florida, United States.

636. ZELMA ELIZABETH WEBB was born on September 26, 1923, in Pennsylvania, USA. She died (Cancer) on February 28, 2016, aged 92, in Niceville, Okaloosa, Florida, United States.
Note: *Bladder Cancer.*
    (Death)
    James Albert Parrish Jr.[635], aged 20, married Zelma Elizabeth Webb, aged 21, on October 7, 1944 in Gulfport, Mississippi, USA. They had four sons:
        Mr. Parrish[1656]
        James Albert Parrish III[1657] born on October 9, 1946
        Mr. Parrish[1659]
        Mr. Parrish[1661]

637. MARY FLORENCE CASON (see Descendants (21)) was born on November 29, 1909, in Alabama, United States, to James Hillard Cason[161] and Mary Elizabeth Bass[160].
- She died on December 18, 1996, aged 87 years.
- She was buried in Beda Cemetery, Wing, Covington, Alabama, USA.

638. HOLLIE MATTHEW SMITH was born on January 1, 1909.
- He died on May 1, 1982, aged 73 years.
- He was buried in Beda Cemetery, Wing, Covington, Alabama, USA.
    Hollie Matthew Smith married Mary Florence Cason[637]. They had ten children:
        Dasy May Cason[1662] born on January 21, 1928
        Rosa Bell Smith[1664] born on June 29, 1930
        Gladys Smith[1666] born on November 27, 1932

Bonnie Smith[1668] born on September 10, 1933
Nellie Ruth Smith[1669] born on February 26, 1936
Clenna Smith[1671] born on March 12, 1938
Annice Smith[1672] born on December 17, 1940
Lloyd Mathew Smith[1674] born on November 7, 1942
Bessie Smith[1675] born on March 10, 1944
Gary Smith[1677] born on February 28, 1946

639. ZONNIE BELL CASON (see Descendants (21)) was born on December 8, 1911, in Alabama, United States, to James Hillard Cason[161] and Mary Elizabeth Bass[160].
- She was recorded in the census in 1940, aged about 28, in Putnam Hall, Lives in Grandin, E P 19 Grandin, Putnam, Florida, USA.

640. DANIEL L RALEY was born about 1902, in Alabama, USA.
- He was recorded in the census in 1940, aged about 38, in Putnam Hall, Lives in Grandin, E P 19 Grandin, Putnam, Florida, USA.

Daniel L Raley married Zonnie Bell Cason[639]. They had five children:
Clement Raley[1678] born about 1931 in Alabama, USA
Douglas Raley[1679] born on July 25, 1932
Muriel Raley[1680] born about 1933 in Alabama, USA
Audry Raley[1682]
Patricia Ann Raley[1684]

641. WILLIAM CHARLES CASON (see Descendants (21)) was born on September 29, 1913, in Covington, Alabama, USA, to James Hillard Cason[161] and Mary Elizabeth Bass[160]. William Charles became known as "Charlie".
- He was recorded in the census in 1930, aged about 16, in Hart, Covington, Alabama, USA.
- He died on May 4, 1990, aged 76 years, in Alabama, USA.
- He was buried in Zion Rock Cemetery, Beda, Covington, Alabama, USA.

642. MARY ANN SMITH was born on May 15, 1915.
- She died on May 27, 1996, aged 81 years.
- She was buried in Zion Rock Cemetery, Beda, Covington, Alabama, USA.

William Charles Cason[641] married Mary Ann Smith. They had three children:
Kathleen Cason[1685] born on November 19, 1947
Lindsey Cason[1687] born on March 14, 1949
Carolyn Cason[1689] born on February 7, 1954

643. GRADY J. CASON (see Descendants (21)) was born on September 25, 1915, in Alabama, United States, to James Hillard Cason[161] and Mary Elizabeth Bass[160].
- He was recorded in the census in 1930, aged about 14, in Hart, Covington, Alabama, USA.
- He died in April 1980, aged 64 years.

644. EMMIE SCOFFIELD.
Grady J. Cason[643] married Emmie Scoffield. They had one son:
Grady J. Cason Jr.[1690] born in August 1953

645. JOHN F. CASON (see Descendants (21)) was born on July 25, 1917, in Andalusia, Covington, Alabama, United States, to James Hillard Cason[161] and Mary Elizabeth Bass[160].
- He was recorded in the census in 1930, aged about 12, in Hart, Covington, Alabama, USA.
- He was recorded in the census in 1940, aged about 22, in Precinct 10 Hart, Covington, Alabama, USA.
- He was recorded in the census on April 1, 1950, aged 32, in Proceeding North on Hyway 88 from Beda Church, Hart, Covington, Alabama, United States.
- He died on March 4, 2005, aged 87 years, in Robertsdale, Baldwin, Alabama, United States.
- He was buried in Zion Rock Cemetery, Beda, Covington, Alabama, USA.

646. FLORA MAVIS LITTLE was born on January 12, 1926, in Covington, Alabama, USA.

- She was recorded in the census on April 1, 1950, aged 24, in Proceeding North on Hyway 88 from Beda Church, Hart, Covington, Alabama, United States.
- She died on July 31, 2015, aged 89, in Andalusia, Covington, Alabama, United States.
- She was buried in Zion Rock Cemetery, Beda, Covington, Alabama, USA.

John F. Cason[645] married Flora Mavis Little. They had two sons:
Johnny Ray Cason[1691] born on October 12, 1943 in Alabama, United States; died on August 2, 1989
Robert Gerald Cason[1692] born on February 24, 1945 in Covington, Alabama, USA; died on July 11, 1985

647. COLEMAN R. CASON (see Descendants (21)) was born on November 16, 1919, in Andalusia, Covington, Alabama, United States, to James Hillard Cason[161] and Mary Elizabeth Bass[160].
- He was recorded in the census in 1930, aged about 10, in Hart, Covington, Alabama, USA.
- He was recorded in the census on April 1, 1950, aged 30, in Boggon Level to Open Pond Rd. on Hyw on 88, Hart, Covington, Alabama, United States.
- He died on May 23, 1987, aged 67 years, in Covington, Alabama, United States.
- He was buried in Zion Rock Cemetery, Beda, Covington, Alabama, USA.

The following information is also recorded for Coleman R.:
- Military Service.

Coleman R. married twice. He was married to Runell Neese[648] and Syble G. Cason[649].

Note: *U.S. Army - WWII.*
(Military Service)

648. RUNELL NEESE. Runell became known as "Nelle".

Coleman R. Cason[647] married Runell Neese. They had four children:
Leon Cason[1694] born on October 10, 1950
Sylvia Jean Cason[1695] born in March 1951
James David Cason[1696] born on January 10, 1952
Jimmy Ray Cason[1697] born in November 1953

649. SYBLE G. CASON was born on October 24, 1919.
- She died on April 23, 2003, aged 83 years.
- She was buried in Shady Hill Cemetery, Covington, Alabama, USA.

Syble G. married twice. She was married to Coleman R. Cason[647] and Mr. Morris.

Coleman R. Cason[647] married Syble G. Cason. They had one son:
Rhett Cason[1698] born in November 1963

Mr. Morris married Syble G. Cason. They had four children:
Annie Joyce Morris[726] born on April 4, 1939; died on June 22, 2015 in Andalusia, Covington, Alabama, United States
Darrell Morris born on July 19, 1948; died on June 28, 1975
Emmett Morris
David Morris

650. VEILLA MAINE BASS (see Descendants (21)) was born on March 7, 1912, in Alabama, United States, to William Henry Bass[162] and Dora Alice Purvis[163].
- She was recorded in the census in 1920, aged about 8, in Precinct 21, Covington, Alabama, USA.
- She was recorded in the census on April 1, 1950, aged 38, in Beda Church Road to Boggon Level, Hart, Covington, Alabama, United States.
- She died on October 2, 1995, aged 83 years.

651. WILLIAM LESTER RALEY was born about 1906, in Alabama, United States.
- He was recorded in the census on April 1, 1950, aged about 43, in Beda Church Road to Boggon Level, Hart, Covington, Alabama, United States.

William Lester Raley married Veilla Maine Bass[650]. They had six children:
Addie Vivian Raley[1699] born on February 19, 1933 in Alabama, United States
Lois Jewel Raley[1701] born on April 21, 1935 in Alabama, United States
Mary Alice Raley[1703] born on May 12, 1938 in Florida, United States
Julia Yuvone Raley[1705] born on October 7, 1941 in Florida, United States
Henry Edgar Raley[1707] born on September 5, 1944 in Florida, United States
Alvin Lester Raley[1708] born on March 11, 1953

652. LEILLA MAE BASS (see Descendants (21)) was born on February 7, 1914, in Covington, Alabama, USA, to William Henry Bass[162] and Dora Alice Purvis[163].
- She was recorded in the census in 1920, aged about 6, in Precinct 21, Covington, Alabama, USA.
- She was recorded in the census in 1930, aged about 16, in Hart, Covington, Alabama, USA.
- She was recorded in the census in 1940, aged about 26, in Open Pond Road, Beat 7, Covington, Alabama, USA.
- She died on August 31, 1998, aged 84 years.
- She was buried in Zion Rock Cemetery, Beda, Covington, Alabama, USA.

Leilla Mae married twice. She was married to Robert Lehmon Foxworth[653] and Edward L. Miller[654].

Note: *Clipping, I assume, from the Andalusia paper of the time. Aug. 3 or 8 1938....The writer was especially deeply impressed with the next family that was visited on the tour, for more than one reason. This particular man was Mr. Robert Foxworth, of Andalusia, route 1, (near Open Pond). Mr. Foxworth age 25, has a wife and one small child that are dependent upon him.Before the writer ventures any further in praising Mr. and Mrs. Foxworth, he would like to tell of some of their accomplishments.In 1937 Mr. Foxworth estimated his worth above his liabilities at only $15.00, having had two previous years' bad crops. He had only a steer as a work stock these* *two years, but at the end of 1937 Mr. Foxworth's net worth dropped down to a mere $8.07. Yet Mr. and Mrs. Foxworth weren't ready to call it quits—nay, by a long shot.He determined to try again this year and the FSA again stepped in... (obscured in image) ...money to buy a mare, wagon, seeds, feed and enough cash to pay living expenses.On reason that this particulare case impressed the writer so was the fact that Mr. Foxworth rented about 30 acres of land and a pasture—and note, you, this Mr. Foxworth rented land that didn't have a sign of a building on it, but he said that the set right in and build a neat two... (obscured) ...ing, a smokehouse, chicken house, and a barn entirely of logs and rough boards, furnished by the landowner.Another thing that left a very impressing mark was the fin display of canned food that was canned and neatly arranged in the smokehouse by Mr. Foxworth. Being that Mrs. Foxworth had been very sick most of the year didn't stop Mr. Foxworth from having a good supply of canned food for winter use on hand. He rolled up his sleeves and set into canning the vegetables and the fruits like nobody's business and at the present time has about 210 quarts canned up, and hear ye... I'll wager that many a female would turn green with envy upon looking at the outcome of Mr. Foxworths culinary ability.Mrs. Foxworth not being physically able to be on her feet any of the time, didn't let that fact bother her for she set right in and... gents...his lady really has the... (obscured)... the lau...good sized...to quilting a...was really a...some of the...that she had...quilts that sh...while she wa...work. -Clipping shared by Bill Miller, son of Mae Foxworth Miller [Bass].*

653. ROBERT LEHMON FOXWORTH was born on March 15, 1910, in Alabama, United States, to R.L. Foxworth and Mattie Snellgrove.
- He was recorded in the census in 1920, aged about 10, in Santa Rosa, Florida, USA.
- He was recorded in the census in 1930, aged about 20, in Hart, Covington, Alabama, USA.
- He was recorded in the census in 1940, aged about 30, in Open Pond Road, Beat 7, Covington, Alabama, USA.
- He died on September 4, 1948, aged 38 years, in Florala, Covington, Alabama, USA.
- He was buried in Zion Rock Cemetery, Beda, Covington, Alabama, USA.

Robert Lehmon Foxworth married Leilla Mae Bass[652]. They had two daughters:
Ruby Mildred Foxworth[1709] born about 1933 in Alabama, USA
Mary Jane Foxworth[1710] born about 1940 in Alabama, USA

654. EDWARD L. MILLER was born on February 19, 1904.
- He died on November 25, 1989, aged 85.
- He was buried in Chapel Hill Baptist Church Cemetery, Chapel Hill, Covington County, Alabama, USA.

Edward L. married twice. He was married to Ilene Sawyer and Leilla Mae Bass[652].
Edward L. Miller, aged about 20, married Ilene Sawyer, aged about 19, in 1924. They had one son:
Clyde F. Miller born on March 18, 1927; died on February 28, 1932
Edward L. Miller, aged 50, married Leilla Mae Bass[652], aged 40, on December 26, 1954. They had two children:
Mary Deborah Miller[1712]
William Michael Miller[1714]

655. HENRY GRADY BASS (see Descendants (21)) was born on November 21, 1915, in Alabama, United States, to William Henry Bass[162] and Dora Alice Purvis[163]. Henry Grady became known as "Tough".
- He was recorded in the census in 1920, aged about 4, in Precinct 21, Covington, Alabama, USA.
- He was recorded in the census in 1930, aged about 14, in Hart, Covington, Alabama, USA.
- He was recorded in the census on April 1, 1950, aged 34, in 1111 Ware Ave, Sedalia, Pettis, Missouri, United States.
- He died in June 1982, aged 66 years, in Missouri, USA.
- He was buried in Masonic Cemetery Tipton, Moniteau, Missouri, USA.

The following information is also recorded for Tough:
- Military Service.

Notes:
- *Henry Grady Bass was born Nov. 21 1915 to William Henry and Dora Bass [Purvis]. Acording to his WWII draft Registration Card, by age 24 he was working for Frank Horton Engineering Co. in Lamar, Barton County, Missouri. On his draft card, he is listed as 5' 5" tall, 155lb, Blue eyes, and Brown hair, with a ruddy complexion. He married twice, first to a lady named Edith and finally to Ruth Bass [Nemet] in Kansas City on Aug. 26 1946.Mr. Bass was a veteran of WWII, a Sgt. In the 145th Armored Infantry, and brought back many pictures of his time in Europe and Germany. After the war he returned to Missouri and was active in his community, a member of the United Methodist Church, a trustee and board member of the Masonic Lodge AF&AM No. 56, VFW, served on the City Council, and even Mayor of Tipton Missouri. Mr. Bass died in a Boone County, MO hospital on Monday Jun. 21 1982 and was buried in the Masonic Cemetery Tipton, Moniteau, Missouri, USA.*
- *Sgt. 145th ARMd. Sig. Co. - WWII.*
(Military Service)

Direct Relations

656. RUTH A NEMET was born on October 4, 1912, in Cleveland, Case, Missouri, USA.
• She was recorded in the census on April 1, 1950, aged 37, in 1111 Ware Ave, Sedalia, Pettis, Missouri, United States.
• She died on July 7, 2000, aged 87, in Versailles, Morgan, Missouri, USA.
• She was buried in Masonic Cemetery Tipton, Moniteau, Missouri, USA.
Note: *She served on the advisory board for the Tipton Library and Moniteau County Extension. She was a past Girl Scout leader and had been involved with the PTA. She was a member of the United Methodist Church, Tipton, and the Eastern Star. She was a past president of the American Legion Auxiliary.*
(Death)

Henry Grady Bass[655], aged 30, married Ruth A Nemet, aged 33, on August 26, 1946. They had two daughters:
Greer Ellen Bass[1715] born about 1948 in Missouri, United States
Jennifer Lee Bass[1717]

657. CLYDE KERMIT BASS SR. (see Descendants (21)) was born on February 1, 1918, in Alabama, United States, to William Henry Bass[162] and Dora Alice Purvis[163].
• He was recorded in the census in 1920, aged about 2, in Precinct 21, Covington, Alabama, USA.
• He was recorded in the census in 1930, aged about 12, in Hart, Covington, Alabama, USA.
• He was recorded in the census in 1940, aged about 22, in Precinct 10 Hart, Covington, Alabama, USA.
• He died (Illness) on June 28, 1961, aged 43 years, in Birmingham, Jefferson, Alabama, USA.
• He was buried in Zion Rock Cemetery, Beda, Covington, Alabama, USA.
The following information is also recorded for Clyde Kermit:
• Military Service.
Notes:
• *Died of Tuberculosis he contracted during the war.*
(Death)
• *1322 Service Unit - WWII.*
(Military Service)

658. MAMIE LELIE HAYES.

Clyde Kermit Bass Sr.[657] married Mamie Lelie Hayes. They had seven children:
Judson Levon Bass[1718] born on April 21, 1942; died on March 8, 2013
Marron Grady Bass[1720] born on December 2, 1944
Vonda Vinor Bass[1722] born on April 6, 1947
Clyde Kermit Bass Jr.[1723] born on August 31, 1949
Lewis Arnold Bass[1724] born on June 1, 1957
Mark Napoleon Bass[1725] born on November 28, 1959
Riley Bennett Bass[1726]

659. BEATRICE IZORA BASS (see Descendants (21)) was born on August 14, 1921, in Alabama, USA, to William Henry Bass[162] and Dora Alice Purvis[163].
• She was recorded in the census in 1930, aged about 8, in Hart, Covington, Alabama, USA.
• She was recorded in the census in 1940, aged about 18, in Precinct 10 Hart, Covington, Alabama, USA.

660. GROVER BOZEMAN was born on October 31, 1913. He died on October 22, 1993, aged 79.
Grover Bozeman, aged about 26, married Beatrice Izora Bass[659], aged about 18, in 1940. They had one daughter:
Margaret Ann Bozeman[1727] born on September 28, 1959

661. MARY BONNIE BASS (see Descendants (21)) was born on June 6, 1924, in Alabama, USA, to William Henry Bass[162] and Dora Alice Purvis[163].
• She was recorded in the census in 1930, aged about 6, in Hart, Covington, Alabama, USA.
• She was recorded in the census in 1940, aged about 16, in Precinct 10 Hart, Covington, Alabama, USA.
• She died on October 5, 1992, aged 68 years.
• She was buried in Stone Lake Gardens Cemetery, Andalusia, Covington, Alabama, USA.

662. JOE M. BROOKS was born on August 22, 1922.
Joe M. Brooks married Mary Bonnie Bass[661].

663. FLOYD IRWIN BASS (see Descendants (21)) was born on March 26, 1926, in Alabama, USA, to William Henry Bass[162] and Dora Alice Purvis[163].
• He was recorded in the census in 1940, aged about 14, in Precinct 10 Hart, Covington, Alabama, USA.

- He was recorded in the census on April 1, 1950, aged 24, in Beda Church Road to Boggon Level, Hart, Covington, Alabama, United States.
- He died on October 26, 2009, aged 83 years.
- He was buried in Zion Rock Cemetery, Beda, Covington, Alabama, USA.

The following information is also recorded for Floyd Irwin:
Injury.
Notes:
- *Lost his left arm.*
  (Injury)
- *He was crossing a fence and his gun discharged, striking him in the arm. After his arm had to be removed, a funeral service was held for the arm, and it was buried in Zion Rock Cemetery, Beda, Covington, Alabaman, USA.*
  (Injury)

664. AVIS CARROLL.
Floyd Irwin Bass[663] married Avis Carroll.

665. AUTRAY ALTO BASS (see Descendants (21)) was born on April 3, 1928, in Alabama, USA, to William Henry Bass[162] and Dora Alice Purvis[163].
- He was recorded in the census in 1930, aged about 2, in Hart, Covington, Alabama, USA.
- He was recorded in the census in 1940, aged about 12, in Precinct 10 Hart, Covington, Alabama, USA.
- He was recorded in the census on April 1, 1950, aged 21, in Boggon Level to Open Pond Rd. on Hyw on 88, Hart, Covington, Alabama, United States.
- He died on May 20, 2012, aged 84.
- He was buried in Shady Hill Church Cemetery, Covington, Alabama, USA.

666. JOYCE CARROLL.
Autray Alto Bass[665] married Joyce Carroll.

667. FANNIE ESTHER BASS (see Descendants (21)) was born on November 10, 1931, in Alabama, USA, to William Henry Bass[162] and Dora Alice Purvis[163].
- She was recorded in the census in 1940, aged about 8, in Precinct 10 Hart, Covington, Alabama, USA.
- She was recorded in the census on April 1, 1950, aged 18, in Boggon Level to Open Pond Rd. on Hyw on 88, Hart, Covington, Alabama, United States.
- She died on April 3, 2018, aged 86, in Covington, Alabama, USA.
- She was buried in Chapel Hill Baptist Church Cemetery, Chapel Hill, Covington, Alabama, United States.

Notes:
- *No one could have asked for a better mother-in-law. She raised two beautiful daughters that she was very proud of. She'll be missed, but I'm confident that she's comfortable, able to move around without any pain, and probably tending to her garden in heaven. I'm glad I could be one of the ones to make her laugh. Her laugh was infectious and was always a highlight of our visits. - Jim Smith.*
- *Mrs. Esther was a sweet lady. She loved the Lord and shared that love with everyone that she met. Knowing Mrs. Esther was a true blessing from Heaven. Prayers are going up for her family. - Terry Spader.*
- *She worked at Franklin Ferguson Company in Florala and was a member of the First Baptist Church of Florala.*

  She was the ultimate description of a Christian woman. In the 70s, she taught 2 and 3-year-olds in nursery school at the First Baptist Church and was ever patient and loving. She was a kind-hearted woman who always put others first. For those that knew her, you know that she loved to laugh, she loved to watch comedies and she loved to hear funny stories and jokes. At times you would think she had stopped breathing she was laughing so hard and you would find yourself laughing at her laughing.

  She had been suffering the last few years of her life after having two hip replacement surgeries and surgery to repair fractures in her back. She is suffering no more and is basking in the glory of Heaven with her family and friends.
  (Death)

668. JAMES DONALD WISE was born on October 17, 1928, in Hacoda, Geneva, Alabama, United States, to Donly R.Q. Wise and Sallie May Holman.
- He was recorded in the census in 1940, aged about 11, in Hacoda Road, Beat 22, Covington, Alabama, USA.
- He was recorded in the census on April 1, 1950, aged 21, in No Nour for Road, Hacoda, Geneva, Alabama, United States.
- He died on December 14, 1997, aged 69.
- He was buried in Chapel Hill Baptist Church Cemetery, Chapel Hill, Covington, Alabama, USA.

James Donald Wise married Fannie Esther Bass[667]. They had three daughters:
Brenda Gail Wise[1729] born on June 19, 1957; died on June 19, 1957
Myra Lynn Wise[1730] born on November 16, 1960
Tracy Nanette Wise[1731] born on March 26, 1963

669. NANNIE RUTH BASS (see Descendants (21)) was born on August 8, 1934, in Alabama, USA, to William Henry Bass[162] and Dora Alice Purvis[163].
- She was recorded in the census in 1940, aged about 5, in Precinct 10 Hart, Covington, Alabama, USA.
- She was recorded in the census on April 1, 1950, aged 15, in Boggon Level to Open Pond Rd. on Hyw on 88, Hart, Covington, Alabama, United States.

670. JOSEPH FARREL WALICE.
Joseph Farrel Walice married Nannie Ruth Bass[669]. They had one son:
Jeff Alex Walice[1733] born on December 18, 1963

671. NANCY CHRISTIAN GARVIN (see Descendants (21)) was born on February 24, 1911, in Alabama, United States, to Elzy Henderson Garvin[165] and Catherine Emma Bass[164].
- She was recorded in the census in 1920, aged about 9, in Okaloosa, Florida, USA.
- She was recorded in the census in 1930, aged about 19, in Carolina, Covington, Alabama, USA.
- She was recorded in the census on April 1, 1950, aged 39, in Mt Olive Church Road, Blackman, Okaloosa, Florida, United States.
- She died on September 11, 1994, aged 83 years.

672. ERNEST TERRY BECK was born on June 7, 1917, in Florida, United States, to John I Beck and Agnus Amanda Turner.
- He was recorded in the census on April 1, 1950, aged 32, in Mt Olive Church Road, Blackman, Okaloosa, Florida, United States.
- He died on February 10, 1981, aged 63 years, in Okaloosa, Florida, United States.
- He was buried in Okaloosa, Florida, United States.

Ernest Terry Beck married Nancy Christian Garvin[671]. They had seven children:
Janice L Beck[1734] born on July 16, 1934 in Alabama, United States
Shirley A Beck[1736] born on September 5, 1936 in Alabama, United States
Reginald E Beck[1738] born on December 23, 1938 in Alabama, United States
Quinton W Beck[1743] born on May 25, 1942 in Alabama, United States
Theron Leon Beck[1746] born on March 26, 1945 in Alabama, United States
Ronald Eugene Beck[1750] born on February 16, 1947 in Alabama, United States
Vivian Diane Beck[1752] born on August 17, 1949 in Alabama, United States

673. WILLIER GARVIN (see Descendants (21)) was born on December 3, 1914, in Alabama, United States, to Elzy Henderson Garvin[165] and Catherine Emma Bass[164].
- She was recorded in the census in 1920, aged about 5, in Okaloosa, Florida, USA.
- She was recorded in the census in 1930, aged about 15, in Carolina, Covington, Alabama, USA.
- She was recorded in the census on April 1, 1950, aged 35, in 1/2 Mile Left from Red Oak to Mountain City Road Traveling Toward Red Oak from Blackman, Blackman, Okaloosa, Florida, United States.
- She died on November 25, 2003, aged 88.
- She was buried in Red Oak Cemetery, Christview, Okaloosa, Florida, USA.

674. BENJAMIN OTIS BECK was born on July 18, 1914, in Alabama, United States.
- He was recorded in the census on April 1, 1950, aged 35, in 1/2 Mile Left from Red Oak to Mountain City Road Traveling Toward Red Oak from Blackman, Blackman, Okaloosa, Florida, United States.
- He died on January 26, 2005, aged 90.
- He was buried in Red Oak Cemetery, Christview, Okaloosa, Florida, USA.

Benjamin Otis Beck married Willier Garvin[673]. They had four children:
Marie Beck[1756] born on September 21, 1936 in Alabama, United States
Collie Beck[1758] born on August 2, 1938
Edward C Beck[1760] born on December 25, 1943 in Alabama, United States
Marylin Maxine Beck[1762]

675. SHERMAN GARVIN (see Descendants (21)) was born on January 18, 1917, in Alabama, United States, to Elzy Henderson Garvin[165] and Catherine Emma Bass[164].
- He was recorded in the census in 1920, aged about 3, in Okaloosa, Florida, USA.
- He was recorded in the census in 1930, aged about 13, in Carolina, Covington, Alabama, USA.
- He was recorded in the census in 1940, aged about 23, in Open Pond Road, Election Precinct 7 Watkins, Covington, Alabama, USA.

- He died on February 7, 2006, aged 89 years.
- He was buried in Greenwood Cemetery, Florala, Covington, Alabama, USA.

676. UNOGAR JOHNSON was born on April 21, 1920, in Alabama, USA, to Nicholas Reese Johnson and Matilda Jane Barnes.
- She was recorded in the census in 1940, aged about 20, in Open Pond Road, Election Precinct 7 Watkins, Covington, Alabama, USA.
- She died on June 5, 2003, aged 83.
- She was buried in Eastern Gate Memorial Gardens, Pensacola, Escambia, Florida, USA.

Sherman Garvin[675], aged 20, married Unogar Johnson, aged 17, on May 1, 1937. They had four daughters:
- Yvonne Garvin[1763]
- Laverne Fay Garvin[1765]
- Therese Garvin[1766]
- Lonia Garvin[1767]

677. OLLIE GARVIN (see Descendants (21)) was born on March 16, 1919, in Alabama, United States, to Elzy Henderson Garvin[165] and Catherine Emma Bass[164].
- He was recorded in the census in 1920, aged about 1, in Okaloosa, Florida, USA.
- He was recorded in the census in 1930, aged about 11, in Carolina, Covington, Alabama, USA.
- He was recorded in the census in 1940, aged about 21, in Open Pond Road, Election Precinct 7 Watkins, Covington, Alabama, USA.
- He died on September 2, 1987, aged 68.
- He was buried in Greenwood Memorial Cemetery, Florala, Covington, Alabama, USA.

678. ODESSA GARVIN (see Descendants (21)) was born on February 26, 1923, in Alabama, United States, to Elzy Henderson Garvin[165] and Catherine Emma Bass[164].
- She was recorded in the census in 1930, aged about 7, in Carolina, Covington, Alabama, USA.
- She was recorded in the census in 1940, aged about 17, in Open Pond Road, Election Precinct 7 Watkins, Covington, Alabama, USA.

679. WALUN NICK JOHNSON was born on October 10, 1923, in Covington, Alabama, United States, to Nicholas Reese Johnson and Matilda Jane Barnes.
- He died on August 13, 2000, aged 76.
- He was buried in Eastern Gate Memorial Gardens, Pensacola, Escambia, Florida, USA.
- He was buried in Eastern Gate Memorial Gardens, Pensacola, Escambia, Florida, United States.

The following information is also recorded for Walun Nick:
- Death(?) on August 13, 2000, aged 76, in Pensacola, Escambia, Florida, United States.

Walun Nick married twice. He was married to Odessa Garvin[678] and Lucille Waldroup.
Walun Nick Johnson married Odessa Garvin[678]. They had five children:
- Joel Johnson[1768] born on April 14, 1944
- Nick Johnson[1769] born on February 11, 1946
- Sheila Johnson[1772] born on October 6, 1947
- Luvert Johnson[1775]
- Gary Lynn Johnson[1777]

Walun Nick Johnson, aged 61, married Lucille Waldroup on March 21, 1985 in Jackson, Florida, USA.

680. CORA NOLIA POSEY (see Descendants (21)) was born on January 1, 1909, in Covington, Alabama, USA, to James Ocie Posey[167] and Savannah Bass[166].
- She was recorded in the census in 1920, aged about 11, in Precinct 21, Covington, Alabama, USA.
- She was recorded in the census in 1930, aged about 21, in Hart, Covington, Alabama, USA.
- She died on January 17, 1996, aged 87 years, in Panama City, Bay, Florida, USA.
- She was buried in Greenwood Memorial Cemetery, Florala, Covington, Alabama, USA.

Note: *Nolie was the wife of John Lee Thames and the daughter of James Ocey & Savannah Bass Posey. She worked at Franklin-Ferguson Sawing factor in Florala, Alabama for 40 years.*

681. JOHN LEE THAMES was born on December 15, 1907, in Coffee, Alabama, USA.
- He died on June 11, 1986, aged 78 years.
- He was buried in Greenwood Memorial Cemetery, Florala, Covington, Alabama, USA.

John Lee Thames married Cora Nolia Posey[680]. They had two children:
- Ruby Nell Thames[1779] born in 1943
- Billy Joe Thames[1782] born on January 27, 1949; died on December 12, 2014

682. PEARLIE MAE POSEY (see Descendants (21)) was born on September 10, 1911, in Covington, Alabama, USA, to James Ocie Posey[167] and Savannah Bass[166].
- She was recorded in the census in 1920, aged about 8, in Precinct 21, Covington, Alabama, USA.
- She was recorded in the census in 1930, aged about 18, in Hart, Covington, Alabama, USA.
- She died on April 17, 1933, aged 21 years, in Okaloosa, Florida, USA.
- She was buried in Beda Cemetery, Beda, Covington, Alabama, USA.

683. AMOS VINCEN TURNER was born on December 12, 1910, in Wing, Covington, Alabama, USA. Amos Vincen became known as "Buddy".
- He died on June 27, 1967, aged 56 years, in Hillsborough, Florida, USA.
- He was buried in Myrtle Hill Memorial Park, Tampa, Hillsborough, Florida, USA.

Amos Vincen married twice. He was married to Pearlie Mae Posey[682] and Doris Inez Davis.
Amos Vincen Turner married Pearlie Mae Posey[682]. They had two sons:
> Hyram Walace Turner[1784] born on October 3, 1931 in Wing, Covington, Alabama, USA; died on October 15, 2001 in Opp, Covington, Alabama, USA
> Amos Dalton Turner Sr.[1786] born on January 19, 1933 in Baker, Okaloosa, Florida, USA; died on September 24, 2006

Amos Vincen Turner married Doris Inez Davis.

684. GUSSIE LEE POSEY (see Descendants (21)) was born on April 3, 1914, in Alabama, United States, to James Ocie Posey[167] and Savannah Bass[166].
- She was recorded in the census in 1920, aged about 6, in Precinct 21, Covington, Alabama, USA.
- She was recorded in the census in 1930, aged about 16, in Hart, Covington, Alabama, USA.
- She died on March 20, 1999, aged 84 years, in Fort Walton Beach, Okaloosa, Florida, USA.
- She was buried in Beal Memorial Cemetery, Fort Walton Beach, Okaloosa, Florida, USA.

Note: *She moved to Fort Walton Beach in the early 1970s from Lakeland, Fla. She was Baptist by faith and enjoyed spending her time working in the yard and cooking for her family, who she loved very much.*
(Death)

685. CHARLES ORESTA MILLS was born on September 17, 1912.
- He died on April 8, 1986, aged 73 years.
- He was buried in Beal Memorial Cemetery, Fort Walton Beach, Okaloosa, Florida, USA.

Note: *Dad married my mother Gussie Lee Posey on April 17, 1937. They were married by Judge J. R. Roberts, witness's were Frances & Nolie Posey.*

Dad joined the Civilian Conservation Corps on July 7, 1934 in Dothan Alabama .From July 7, 1934 to Jan. 1, 1935 he was under the War Dept. at Old Town, Florida. Type of Work was Conservation. Jan. 1, 1935 to June 30, 1935 he was at Green Cove, Florida. Same type of work. His performance was rated as excellent. Remarks on his discharge was- very good truck driver -- dependable fellow.After Dad and Mom married he did Share Croping for severly years along with other work. Dad had a severe Back injury in the early 1950s, while working in the Ship Yard in Green Cove Springs, Florida (the ship yard is no longer there). He had several surgery's over the years, if it helped him it was very little. He was in a great deal of pain for the rest of his life, but most of the time you would not know it. After his death his Doctor said no one knew how much he had suffered over the years. -Donell Mills.
(Death)

Charles Oresta Mills, aged 44, married Gussie Lee Posey[684], aged 42, on September 22, 1956. They had six children:
> William James Mills[1788] born on January 19, 1938 in Alabama, USA; died on January 19, 2015 in Auburndale, Polk, Florida, USA
> Evelyn Juanita Mills[1790] born on August 9, 1939 in Laurel Hill, Okaloosa, Florida, USA; died on September 8, 2013 in Lakeland, Polk, Florida, USA
> Charles Earl Mills[1792] born on February 26, 1943 in Florala, Covington, Alabama, USA
> Gene Verlon Mills[1794] born on January 11, 1945 in Lockhart, Covington, Alabama, USA; died in November 1995 in Fort Walton Beach, Okaloosa, Florida, USA
> Donell Franklin Mills[1797] born on July 3, 1947 in Lockhart, Covington, Alabama, USA
> Oresta Mills Jr.[1801]

686. **MARY FRANCIS POSEY** (see Descendants (21)) was born on October 8, 1916, in Andalusia, Covington, Alabama, USA, to James Ocie Posey[167] and Savannah Bass[166].
- She was recorded in the census in 1920, aged about 3, in Precinct 21, Covington, Alabama, USA.
- She was recorded in the census in 1930, aged about 13, in Hart, Covington, Alabama, USA.
- She was recorded in the census in 1940, aged about 23, in South 5th Street, Florala, Covington, Alabama, USA.
- She was recorded in the census on April 1, 1950, aged 33, in 28 Seminale Ave., Lockhart, Covington, Alabama, United States.
- She died on September 16, 1999, aged 82 years.
- She was buried in Greenwood Cemetery, Florala, Alabama, United States.

Note: *Frances was the wife of Bartlett "Bart" Cobb. She was retired from Franklin-Ferguson sewing factory in Florala, Alabama, where she worked for about 40 years.*
(Death)

687. **BARTLETT LORENZO COBB** was born on December 25, 1902, in Santa Rosa, Florida, USA. Bartlett Lorenzo became known as "Bart".
- He was recorded in the census in 1940, aged about 37, in South 5th Street, Florala, Covington, Alabama, USA.
- He was recorded in the census on April 1, 1950, aged 47, in 28 Seminale Ave., Lockhart, Covington, Alabama, United States.
- He died on September 4, 1986, aged 83 years, in Pensacola, Escambia, Florida, USA.
- He was buried in Greenwood Memorial Cemetery, Florala, Covington, Alabama, USA.

Note: *He was known as Bart Cobb. he was the husband of Mary Frances Posey. He was a barber in Florala, Al. for many years. He had a way with childern and they always wanted Bart to cut their hair. His wife Frances was my mothers sister. - Donell Mills.*

Bartlett Lorenzo Cobb married Mary Francis Posey[686] in Crestview, Okaloosa, Florida, USA. They had two children:
  Annie Pearl Cobb[1802] born on July 4, 1939 in Florala, Covington, Alabama, USA; died on June 22, 1968
  James Bartlett Cobb Sr.[1804] born on March 9, 1942 in Florala, Covington, Alabama, USA

688. **WILLIAM ALBERT POSEY** (see Descendants (21)) was born on January 4, 1920, in Alabama, United States, to James Ocie Posey[167] and Savannah Bass[166].
- He was recorded in the census in 1920, aged 0, in Precinct 21, Covington, Alabama, USA.
- He was recorded in the census in 1930, aged about 10, in Hart, Covington, Alabama, USA.
- He died (Cancer) on May 19, 1951, aged 31 years, in Montgomery, Montgomery, Alabama, USA.
- He was buried in Carolina Baptist Church Cemetery, Covington, Alabama, USA.

The following information is also recorded for William Albert:
- Military Service.

Notes:
- *Albert Posey was an even-tempered, easy-going, caring, loving handsome family man. He served in World War II, [in the Pacific theater] as A Military Policeman in the U.S. Army. He could have returned home during the four years he served, but he said that he didn't think he would ever be able to go back again once he went home. He once told his mother that he felt like he would not be killed in service, but that he would die of natural causes. He was correct. He died at the very young age of 31 years of colon cancer, leaving behind his young wife Jewel, and two daughters, Darlene age 2 years & 11 months old, and Dianne age 50 days old. At the time he was taken ill, he was working for Booth Drug Store in Florala, Alabama. He has been greatly missed. This was told to me by his sister (my Mother) Gussie Mills Posey - Donell Mills.*
- *PFC 801 MIL POLICE BN - WWII.*
(Military Service)

689. **JEWEL CREECH**, also recorded as and , was born on June 26, 1928. Jewel became known as "Granny Jewel".
- She died on November 1, 2015, aged 87.
- She was buried in Chapel Hill Baptist Church Cemetery, Chapel Hill, Covington, Alabama, USA.

Jewel married twice. She was married to William Albert Posey[688] and Clarence Paul Baker.

Note: *Jewel was a loving wife, mother, grandmother and great grandmother. She love to so sew and make clothes for her children. Jewel enjoyed cooking, (everyone looked forward to her famous pancakes) planting flowers around her home, working outside and decorating for Christmas. Her biggest legacy, however is the unconditional love she had for her family. Known to them as Jewel, Mama, Granny Jewel, "Jew Jew" and "Bubbie", she will forever hold a dear and precious place in each of their hearts.*
(Death)

William Albert Posey[688] married Jewel Creech. They had two daughters:
  Althea Darlene Posey[1806] born on June 22, 1948 in Mcintosh, Marion, Florida, USA

Direct Relations

Carolyn Dianne Posey[1808] born on April 30, 1951 in Florala, Covington, Alabama, USA; died on April 16, 2018
Clarence Paul Baker married Jewel Creech.

690. **VIANNA CATHERINE POSEY** (see Descendants (21)) was born on April 30, 1922, in Covington, Alabama, USA, to James Ocie Posey[167] and Savannah Bass[166].
- She was recorded in the census in 1930, aged about 8, in Hart, Covington, Alabama, USA.
- She was recorded in the census on April 1, 1950, aged 27, in Winston, Polk, Florida, United States.
- She died on January 3, 2005, aged 82 years, in Lakeland, Polk, Florida, USA.
- She was buried in Auburndale Memorial Park, Auburndale, Polk, Florida, USA.

Note: *My aunt Vianna (Anna) was the daughter of James Ocey & Savannah Bass Posey. She was a devoted Christian woman & it was a blessing to be around her. - Donell Mills.*

691. **REV. DEWEY TURBEVILLE** was born on February 6, 1914, in Alabama, United States.
- He was recorded in the census on April 1, 1950, aged 36, in Winston, Polk, Florida, United States.
- He died on July 21, 1979, aged 65 years.
- He was buried in Auburndale Memorial Park, Auburndale, Polk, Florida, USA.

Dewey Turbeville, aged 23, married Vianna Catherine Posey[690], aged 15, on June 12, 1937 in DeFuniak Springs, Walton, Florida, USA. They had five children:
Doris Jene Turbeville[1810] born about 1939 in Alabama, United States
Jimmie Nell Turbeville[1812] born on March 12, 1941 in Ocala, Marion, Florida, USA
Jerry Lamar Turbeville[1814] born on January 19, 1944 in Ocala, Marion, Florida, USA; died on October 24, 1945 in Ocala, Marion, Florida, USA
Elaine Turbeville[1815] born on September 23, 1945; died on April 21, 2006
Dewey Wayne Turbeville[1817] born on October 23, 1948 in Marion County, Florida, USA

692. **JOSEPHINE E EDWARDS** (see Descendants (21)) was born on June 4, 1908, in Covington, Alabama, United States, to Leslie Riley Edwards Sr.[169] and Nancy Jane Bass[168].
- She was recorded in the census in 1940, aged about 32, in Dorcas Svea RD, Dorcas Election Prect # 13, Okaloosa, Florida, USA.
- She died on March 27, 1993, aged 84, in Crestview, Okaloosa, Florida, United States.
- She was buried in March 1993 in Live oak Park Memorial Cemetery, Crestview, Okaloosa, Florida, United States.

693. **WILLIAM ROY BUSBEE** was born on September 5, 1899, in Covington, Alabama, United States, to William Perry Busbee and Fronie Lowery.
- He was recorded in the census in 1940, aged about 40, in Dorcas Svea RD, Dorcas Election Prect # 13, Okaloosa, Florida, USA.
- He died on June 18, 1982, aged 82, in Laurel Hill, Okaloosa, Florida, United States.
- He was buried in June 1982 in Live oak Park Memorial Cemetery, Crestview, Okaloosa, Florida, United States.

William Roy Busbee, aged 23, married Josephine E Edwards[692], aged 14, on April 21, 1923 in Covington, Alabama. They had ten children:
Thelma Lee Busbee[1820] born on September 16, 1924 in Covington, Alabama, United States; died on August 22, 2007 in Freeport, Walton, Florida, United States
Elton Busbee[1822] born in 1925 in Covington, Alabama United States; died in 1926 in Covington, Alabama United States
Noma Busbee[1823] born on September 2, 1926 in Covington, Alabama, United States; died on April 8, 2001 in Crestview, Okaloosa, Florida, United States
James Curtis Busbee[1825] born on July 22, 1930 in Covington, Alabama, United States; died on October 24, 1982 in Crestview, Okaloosa, Florida, United States
Shelby Ray Busbee[1827] born on April 26, 1933 in Okaloosa, Florida, United States; died on November 3, 2009 in Pensacola, Escambia, Florida, United States
Eula Vee Busbee[1829] born on August 8, 1935 in Laural Hill, Okaloosa, Florida, United States; died on September 7, 2016 in Okaloosa, Florida, United States
Winnie Fay Busbee[1831] born about 1938 in Florida, USA
Polly Busbee[1833]
Walan Busbee[1835]
Jean Busbee[1837] died in 2017

694. **JANIE EDWARDS** (see Descendants (21)) was born on May 13, 1910, in Florala, Covington, Alabama, USA, to Leslie Riley Edwards Sr.[169] and Nancy Jane Bass[168].

695. **FLETCHER JOHNSON**.
Fletcher Johnson married Janie Edwards[694]. They had eight children:
Heyward Ivin Johnson[1839]
Lewis Edward Johnson[1841]

Dalton Lee Johnson[1843]
Frances Elaine Johnson[1845] born on August 23, 1934 in Fort Walton Beach, FL; died in 2000 in Defuniak Springs FL
Cleveland Johnson[1847]
Roseliner Johnson[1849]
Charles Mitchell Johnson[1851]
Jean Ray Johnson[1852]

696. ROSSA EDWARDS (see Descendants (21)) was born on January 8, 1912, in Florala, Covington, Alabama, USA, to Leslie Riley Edwards Sr.[169] and Nancy Jane Bass[168].
- She was recorded in the census in 1940, aged about 28, in Open Pond Road, Election Precinct 7 Watkins, Covington, Alabama, USA.
- She was recorded in the census on April 1, 1950, aged 38, in Turner Road, Watkins, Covington, Alabama, United States.
- She died on June 2, 1988, aged 76 years.
- She was buried in Shiloh Cemetery, Florala, Covington, Alabama, USA.

Rossa married twice. She was married to M. A. Turner[697] and Walter Sahria[698].

697. M. A. TURNER was born about 1908, in Alabama, United States.
- He was recorded in the census in 1940, aged about 32, in Open Pond Road, Election Precinct 7 Watkins, Covington, Alabama, USA.
- He was recorded in the census on April 1, 1950, aged about 41, in Turner Road, Watkins, Covington, Alabama, United States.

M. A. Turner married Rossa Edwards[696]. They had three children:
Sylvia Turner[1854] born about 1930 in Alabama, United States
William Amos Turner[1856] born about 1933 in Alabama, United States
Jeff Wendell Turner[1858] born on April 30, 1935 in Covington, Alabama, USA

698. WALTER SAHRIA.
Walter Sahria married Rossa Edwards[696].

699. HARRY EDWARDS (see Descendants (21)) was born on March 11, 1915, in Florala, Covington, Alabama, USA, to Leslie Riley Edwards Sr.[169] and Nancy Jane Bass[168].
- He was recorded in the census in 1930, aged about 15, in Watkins, Covington, Alabama, USA.

700. PEARL CANNON.
Harry Edwards[699] married Pearl Cannon. They had three children:
Edna Pearl Edwards[1860]
Harry Edwards Jr.[1862]
Lesley Riley Edwards Jr.[1864]

701. EARLY EDWARDS (see Descendants (21)) was born on December 16, 1916, in Florala, Covington, Alabama, USA, to Leslie Riley Edwards Sr.[169] and Nancy Jane Bass[168].
- He was recorded in the census in 1930, aged about 13, in Watkins, Covington, Alabama, USA.

702. MATTILENE COVINGTON.
Early Edwards[701] married Mattilene Covington. They had four children:
Margarette Edwards[1866]
Billie Wayne Edwards[1868]
Martha Jane Edwards[1869]
Murray Edwards[1870]

703. MURRY EDWARDS (see Descendants (21)) was born about 1922, in Alabama, United States, to Leslie Riley Edwards Sr.[169] and Nancy Jane Bass[168]. He was recorded in the census in 1930, aged about 8, in Watkins, Covington, Alabama, USA.

704. CORRENE EDWARDS (see Descendants (21)) was born about 1927, in Alabama, United States, to Leslie Riley Edwards Sr.[169] and Nancy Jane Bass[168]. She was recorded in the census in 1930, aged about 3, in Watkins, Covington, Alabama, USA.

705. BURRIS CLYDE JERNIGAN was born on November 9, 1915, in Florala, Covington, Alabama, USA. He died on July 6, 2004, aged 88 years.

Burris Clyde Jernigan, aged 32, married Correne Edwards[704], aged about 20, on December 20, 1947. They had four children:
Phyllis Jernigan[1872] born on December 11, 1949 in Shanely, Oklahoma, USA
Ronnie Jernigan[1874] born on November 20, 1950 in Shanely, Oklahoma, USA
Larry Jernigan[1876] born on December 6, 1954 in Crestview, Okaloosa, Florida, USA

Direct Relations

Roger Jernigan[1878]

706. ERVIN HARTLEY EDWARDS (see Descendants (21)) was born on November 9, 1928, in Alabama, United States, to Leslie Riley Edwards Sr.[169] and Nancy Jane Bass[168]. He was recorded in the census in 1930, aged about 1, in Watkins, Covington, Alabama, USA.

707. ARLENE CRAWFORD.
> Ervin Hartley Edwards[706] married Arlene Crawford. They had three daughters:
>> Linda Edwards[1880]
>> Diane Edwards[1881]
>> Barbara Ann Edwards[1882]

708. WYLENE BASS (see Descendants (141)) was born about 1921, in Alabama, United States, to Riley John Bass[172] and Maggie Smith[173]. She was recorded in the census in 1930, aged about 9, in Hart, Covington, Alabama, USA.

709. FRED WILLIAMS.
> Fred Williams married Wylene Bass[708]. They had one daughter:
>> Linda Williams[1883]

710. MYRTICE BASS (see Descendants (141)) was born about 1923, in Alabama, United States, to Riley John Bass[172] and Maggie Smith[173]. She was recorded in the census in 1930, aged about 7, in Hart, Covington, Alabama, USA.

711. JEAN PADGETT.
> Jean Padgett married Myrtice Bass[710]. They had four children:
>> Dorothy Jean Padgett[1885]
>> D. Jerome Padgett[1887]
>> Gwendolyn J. Padgett[1888]
>> Steven Wayne Padgett[1889]

712. HIRAM J BASS (see Descendants (141)) was born on June 7, 1924, in Alabama, United States, to Riley John Bass[172] and Maggie Smith[173].
- He was recorded in the census in 1930, aged about 6, in Hart, Covington, Alabama, USA.
- He died (Green Valley Cemetery, Big Cove, Madison, Alabama, USA) on January 13, 1997, aged 72.
- He was buried.

The following information is also recorded for Hiram J:
- Military Service.
- Death(?) on January 13, 1997, aged 72.

Note: *S1 US Navy WWII.*
(Military Service)

713. L. RUTH HOWELL was born on May 6, 1922.
- She died on March 23, 1994, aged 71.
- She was buried in Green Valley Cemetery, Big Cove, Madison, Alabama, USA.
> Hiram J Bass[712] married L. Ruth Howell. They had two sons:
>> Randy Joe Bass[1890]
>> Hiram Bass Jr.[1891]

714. CLINTON ALBERT BASS (see Descendants (141)) was born on April 11, 1926, in Alabama, United States, to Riley John Bass[172] and Maggie Smith[173]. Clinton Albert became known as "Clint".
- He was recorded in the census in 1930, aged about 4, in Hart, Covington, Alabama, USA.
- He was recorded in the census on April 1, 1950, aged 23, in 2nd House Carolina, Covington, Alabama, United States.
- He died on December 26, 2020, aged 94, in Andalusia, Covington, Alabama, USA.
- He was buried in Carolina Baptist Church Cemetery, Covington, Alabama, USA.

715. COZETTE CUSHING was born on April 24, 1928.
- She was recorded in the census on April 1, 1950, aged 21, in 2nd House Carolina, Covington, Alabama, United States.
- She died on March 4, 2006, aged 77.
- She was buried.
> Clinton Albert Bass[714] married Cozette Cushing. They had two children:
>> Clinton Duranne Bass[1892] born on March 23, 1949 in Covington county, Covington, Alabama, USA; died on January 2, 2009 in Carolina, Covington, Alabama, USA
>> Nancy Carolyn Bass[1894] born in 1954 in Andalusia, Covington, Alabama, USA; died on March 9, 1954 in Andalusia, Covington, Alabama, USA

716. **GORDON L. BASS** (see Descendants (141)) was born on September 4, 1931 to Riley John Bass[172] and Maggie Smith[173].
- He died on March 14, 1982, aged 50 years.
- He was buried in Zion Rock Cemetery.

717. **JOYCE CLEMENTS.**
>Gordon L. Bass[716] married Joyce Clements. They had two children:
>>Sue Marie Bass[1895]
>>Mike Bass[1896]

718. **WAYNE BASS** (see Descendants (141)) was born to Riley John Bass[172] and Maggie Smith[173].

719. **DEWAYNE WORRELLS.**
>Wayne Bass[718] married Dewayne Worrells. They had one son:
>>Marlon Hugh Bass[1897]

720. **BRUCE JAMES BASS** (see Descendants (142)) was born on May 7, 1927, in Carolina Community, Covington, Alabama, USA, to James Bennett Bass[174] and Flara Annie Rowell[175].
- He was recorded in the census in 1930, aged about 3, in Carolina, Covington, Alabama, USA.
- He was recorded in the census in 1940, aged about 13, in Election Prect 21 Carolina, Covington, Alabama, USA.
- He was an Education Administrator.
- He resided at Clemrus State Ladies College.
- He was recorded in the census on April 1, 1950, aged 22, in Clemrus State Ladies College, Troy, Pike, Alabama, United States.
- He died (Medical Problem) on July 23, 1988, aged 61 years, in Andalusa, Alabama, USA.
- He was buried in Andalusia Memorial Cemetery, Andalusia, Covington, Alabama, USA.

The following information is also recorded for Bruce James:
- Injury.
- Description: 5' 5"115BrownGrayScar under chin. From WWII Draft Card.
- Military Service, aged 18 years.

Bruce James married twice. He was married to Catherine Lawson[721] and Mildred Carlise Newton[722].

Notes:
- *Bruce was the oldest and very often the last to get to the table at meal time. He would invariably go all the way around the table to his chair bumping each of his brothers and sisters head with his hand as he went by. "Blip, blip, blip', he would say as he hit each head. Some would try to dodge his hand but were usually unsuccessful.*

Then the yelling would begin. "Ouch, quit! Mama, Mama, make Bruce quit, we'd yell. We'd be shushed quiet. Bruce would be reprimanded. The blessing would be said and eating would begin. The reprimand did little good though. At the next meal Bruce would take the same route to his seat at the table, hitting heads as he passed.

When Bruce was in senior high school he was drafted into the army. We hated to see him leave home before graduating from high school. We shouldn't have worried. He worked and took an equivalence test. He got his high school diploma. I remember his saying that when he was being examined so that he could get into the army, it was found that he lacked a pound or two weighing enough. The examining officer flipped him a quarter and told him to go buy and eat some bananas so that he could weigh enough.

When Bruce was discharged from the army he wanted to get a job, but Daddy was very persuasive in talking Bruce into going on to college. (He bought extra mules so they could plow more often.) The G.I. Bill would pay his way to go to school. Troy State Teacher's College was nearest so Bruce said he'd just go one quarter to satisfy Daddy. He did go to college one quarter and liked going so well that he continued to the of 4 years and got his degree in education.

Bruce became principal of Babbie School after getting his degree. He also taught a class as well as having the job of being principal. I remember how proud Daddy was of Bruce for graduating from college and for becoming principal of Babbie Elementary School, too. Daddy found time to go to Babbie one time and walk over the school grounds and through the school to see how things were getting along. He was told by the superintendent that Bruce was doing fine. The superintendent said that they liked getting a young man as principal. Then they could train him on the job. This satisfied Daddy enough so that he could stop worrying about Bruce and just be proud of him. - Hazel Bass Trawick

Photos of Bruce James Bass

Flara Annie Rowell holding Hunter Doyle Kensaul, Bruce James Bass holding Samuel Brad Barnes, and Wanda Arlene Bass. Always looked like Granny Bass wanted to be holding both of them.

Catherine Lawson and Bruce James Bass

Catherine Lawson and Bruce James Bass with thier kids.

Catherine Lawson

Bruce James Bass and Mildred Newton

Direct Relations

- *After graduating college his first job in education was as Principle of Babbie School in Covington, Alabama, USA.He was later Principle of Sanford School and then Vice Principle of Straughn School (K-12 at the time) and retired from that position in the late 80s.He recieved a Gold Toothpick as a gift at his retirement ceremony. (Occupation)*
- *Complications from heart surgery in Birmingham Alabama.
(Death)*
- *Bruce lost the end of his middle finger.
(Injury)*
- *As my dad tells the story of my grandfather, he was working on a squeaky water pump. There was a belt attached to a large and small pulley, with the large wheel attached to a hinged arm that drove the pump cylinder. The joint in the arm off the big wheel almost touched the base; everything connected to, on the down stroke. He'd oiled all the rotating and moving connections, and the joint in the arm I mentioned was dripping oil onto the base, and for whatever reason he was wiping the oil of after a drip. He messed up his timing on a wipe and his finger was squished between the arm joint and the base.Granny couldn't drive at the time, so he was going to drive himself to the hospital, but before he got far he felt faint so he stopped at a neighbor's house, and knocked on their door. When the neighbor lady came out, she found him passed out on her porch. They got him to the doctor and he was fine in the end, other than missing the tip of his finger.
(Injury)*
- *U.S. Army Drafted for WWII but the war ended soon after.
(Military Service)*
- *Per verbal record. He returned from his first day of his Sr. year of high school with his draft letter or to find it at home. The war ended before or shortly after he completed boot camp and he seems to have been on his way to the Pacific and ended up in the midwest for a period of time. He lingered a bit visiting family on his way home.
(Military Service)*

721. CATHERINE LAWSON was born on October 31, 1925, in Covington, Alabama, USA, to Dewey Lawson and Ether B Henley.
- She was recorded in the census in 1930, aged about 4, in George, Covington, Alabama, USA.
- She was recorded in the census on April 1, 1950, aged 24, in Clemrus State Ladies College, Troy, Pike, Alabama, United States.
- She died (Cancer) on January 7, 1972, aged 46 years, in Covington, Alabama, USA.
- She was buried in Andalusia Memorial Cemetery, Andalusia, Covington, Alabama, USA.

Note: *Mrs. Bass, a native of Covington county, had lived all of her life in the Andalusia area. She graduated from Straughn High School and served as secretary at the Sanford School for several years prior to her illness. She was a faithful member of the Sanford Baptist Church and taught Sunday school until her health failed. .*
(Death)

Bruce James Bass[720] married Catherine Lawson. They had four children:
Wanda Arlene Bass[1898] born on July 29, 1949 in Andalusia, Covington, Alabama, USA
Ricky Bruce Bass[1900] born on October 14, 1952 in Andalusia, Covington, Alabama, USA
Don Jeffery Bass I[1902] born on February 5, 1958
Janet Marie Bass[1905] born on June 6, 1960 in Andalusa, Alabama, USA

The following information is also recorded for this family:
- Death of Spouse.

Note: *They met at one of the singings that both of their families attended regularly.*

722. MILDRED CARLISE NEWTON was born on July 7, 1931, in Alabama, USA.
- She was recorded in the census on April 1, 1950, aged 18, in Opp, Covington, Alabama, United States.
- She died (Natural / Old Age) on August 14, 2020, aged 89, in Andalusia, Covington, Alabama, USA.
- She was buried on August 15, 2020 in Oakey Ridge Cemetery, Andalusia, Covington, Alabama, USA.

Mildred Carlise married twice. She was married to Thomas Carlise and Bruce James Bass[720].

Note: *Grave side service only, due to COVID-19. Her sister was buried on the 14th, just the day before.*
(Burial)

Thomas Carlise, when younger than 41, married Mildred Carlise Newton, when younger than 38, before 1970. They had one son:
Jimmy Carlise died in 2015

Bruce James Bass[720], when older than 45, married Mildred Carlise Newton, when older than 41, after 1972.

723. **EUNICE BASS** (see Descendants (142)) was born on February 24, 1929, in Covington, Alabama, USA, to James Bennett Bass[174] and Flara Annie Rowell[175].
- She was recorded in the census in 1930, aged about 1, in Carolina, Covington, Alabama, USA.
- She was recorded in the census in 1940, aged about 11, in Election Prect 21 Carolina, Covington, Alabama, USA.
- She was recorded in the census on April 1, 1950, aged 21, in Auburn, Lee, Alabama, United States.
- She died (Natural / Old Age) on May 30, 2022, aged 93, in Brewton, Escambia, Alabama, USA.
- She was buried in Shady Hill Church Cemetery, Covington, Alabama, USA.

The following information is also recorded for Eunice:
  Comment.
Notes:
- *When these ladies were younger, Hazel, Wavie, Granny, and Eunice would be cooking or cleaning the kitchen. They would be singing beautiful hymns while they happily worked together. - Wanda Barnes [Bass].*
- *Some years after Aunt Eunice's husband had passed, and she was living with Tom and Jane. She was driving and somehow managed to get hit by a train and sustain no significant injuries to herself. She was upset with Tom for not fixing the car, which was totaled, because Harold had bought it for her. -Nicholas Bass.*
  (Comment)

724. **THOMAS HAROLD HENDERSON I** was born on July 30, 1924, in Andalusia, Covington County, Alabama, United States, to William Henderson and Daisy Belle Hutto.
- He was recorded in the census in 1940, aged about 15, in Beat 21 Carolina, Covington, Alabama, USA.
- He was recorded in the census on April 1, 1950, aged 25, in Auburn, Lee, Alabama, United States.
- He died on December 5, 2006, aged 82.
- He was buried in Shady Hill Cemetery, Covington, Alabama, USA.

Thomas Harold Henderson I, aged 23, married Eunice Bass[723], aged 19, on March 8, 1948. They had one son:
  Thomas Harold Henderson II[1907] born on January 2, 1949 in Auburn, Lee, Alabama, USA

725. **RALPH CAEPHUS BASS** (see Descendants (142)) was born on May 20, 1931, in Alabama, USA, to James Bennett Bass[174] and Flara Annie Rowell[175].
- He was recorded in the census in 1940, aged about 9, in Election Prect 21 Carolina, Covington, Alabama, USA.
- He was recorded in the census on April 1, 1950, aged 18, in Carolina, Covington, Alabama, United States.
- He died on October 19, 2019, aged 88, in Carolina Community, Covington, Alabama, USA.

The following information is also recorded for Ralph Caephus:
- Military Service.
Notes:
- *Uncle Ralph was always fun to be around. He had a lot of stories and told them well, he had a lot of opinions and shared them freely, and he had a lot of time and love for friends and family whenever they were around. A big thing I remember about visiting Uncle Ralph was that someone else was almost always there too. His house was often a full and busy place. Much of the visiting had to do with him having a bunch of kids and grandkids, and folks that may as well have been his kids and grandkids. Him and Aunt Joyce where lively, welcoming and you'd never leave hungry when both were around. Life has it's challenges for all of us, and I know Uncle Ralph had more than his share, but it's my impression that he enjoyed life right up to the day of his stroke. It's hard to imagine asking for more than that, may we all be so lucky. -Nicholas Bass.*
- *Had a Stroke on Oct. 12 2019, he was back in his home after a few days in the hospital but never recovered.*
  (Death)
- *U.S. Army Korea.*
  (Military Service)

726. **ANNIE JOYCE MORRIS** was born on April 4, 1939 to Mr. Morris and Syble G. Cason[649].
- She died on June 22, 2015, aged 76 years, in Andalusia, Covington, Alabama, United States.
- She was buried in Shady Hill Cemetery, Covington, Alabama, USA.

Ralph Caephus Bass[725] married Annie Joyce Morris. They had six children:
  Vivian Ann Bass[1909] born on March 16, 1957; died on March 29, 1986
  Randall Ralph Bass[1910] born on January 11, 1959
  Nancy Madonna Bass[1911] born on December 24, 1960
  James Benny Bass[1913] born on April 23, 1962
  Royce Caephus Bass[1915] born on July 12, 1963
  Winfred Lynn Bass[1916] born on November 30, 1964

Direct Relations

727. EDD BASS (see Descendants (142)) was born on April 28, 1933, in Carolina Community, Covington, Alabama, USA, to James Bennett Bass[174] and Flara Annie Rowell[175].
- He was recorded in the census in 1940, aged about 7, in Election Prect 21 Carolina, Covington, Alabama, USA.
- He was recorded in the census on April 1, 1950, aged 16, in Carolina, Covington, Alabama, United States.
- He died (Medical Problem) on December 20, 2016, aged 83, in Andalusia, Covington, Alabama, USA.
- He was buried on December 23, 2016 in Shady Hill Church Cemetery, Covington, Alabama, USA.

The following information is also recorded for Edd:
- Military Service.

Notes:
- *Mr. Bass began his career in electrical repairs with Ward Bell Company and then with Covington Electronics where he worked for almost 38 years. He and his wife had been married for 57 years. They had been active members of Shady Hill Baptist Church for many years and for the last couple of years had attended Beda Baptist Church. He loved to whittle woods and make it into all shapes of animals. He took pride in his vegetable garden and enjoyed raising cows.*
- *Edd Bass died after a short illness. He spent a few days in Florala Alabama for treatment at the nursing home there. He was transferred to Andalusia for dialysis and then to Crestview, after a few hours, due to issues with the dialysis machine in Andalusia. Edd passed in the Crestview hospital. Until his illness Edd was generally healthy and he lived his whole life in his own home and did about like he wanted to. During his illness he was visited by many relatives and friends. - Nicholas Bruce Bass.*
(Death)
- *U.S. Army.*
(Military Service)

728. LEARVENE TRAWICK was born to Leonard Bunion Trawick and Eula Free.

Edd Bass[727], aged 52, married Learvene Trawick on June 23, 1985. They had two children:
Anthony Edd Bass[1918] born on September 26, 1962 in Covington, Alabama, USA
Wendy Learvene Bass[1920] born on June 17, 1967 in Covington, Alabama, USA

729. WAVIE LEE BASS (see Descendants (142)) was born on February 14, 1935, in Carolina Community, Covington, Alabama, USA, to James Bennett Bass[174] and Flara Annie Rowell[175].
- She was recorded in the census in 1940, aged about 5, in Election Prect 21 Carolina, Covington, Alabama, USA.
- She was recorded in the census on April 1, 1950, aged 15, in Carolina, Covington, Alabama, United States.

Note: *When these ladies were younger, Hazel, Wavie, Granny, and Eunice would be cooking or cleaning the kitchen. They would be singing beautiful hymns while they happily worked together. - Wanda Barnes [Bass].*

730. LEON GADE MIMS was born on December 25, 1932, in Holmes County, Florida. USA, to James Frances Dan Mims and Lecie Loreney Myers.
- He died on June 7, 2005, aged 72 years, in Andalusia, Covington, Alabama, USA.
- He was buried in Shady Hill Cemetery, Covington County, Alabama, USA.

Leon Gade Mims, aged 32, married Wavie Lee Bass[729], aged 30, on June 10, 1965. They had one son:
Tony Leon Mims[1923] born on December 25, 1971

731. HAZEL BASS (see Descendants (142)) was born on November 19, 1936, in Carolina Community, Covington, Alabama, USA, to James Bennett Bass[174] and Flara Annie Rowell[175].
- She was recorded in the census in 1940, aged about 3, in Election Prect 21 Carolina, Covington, Alabama, USA.
- She was recorded in the census on April 1, 1950, aged 13, in Carolina, Covington, Alabama, United States.
- She died on April 25, 2023, aged 86.
- She was buried in Calvary Baptist Cemetery, Allentown, Santa Rosa County, Florida, USA.

Note: *When these ladies were younger, Hazel, Wavie, Granny, and Eunice would be cooking or cleaning the kitchen. They would be singing beautiful hymns while they happily worked together. - Wanda Barnes [Bass].*

732. EUGENE TRAWICK was born on August 20, 1930 to Leonard Bunion Trawick and Eula Free. Eugene became known as "Gene".
- He died on January 31, 2001, aged 70.
- He was buried in Calvary Baptist Cemetery, Allentown, Santa Rosa County, Florida, USA.

Eugene Trawick married Hazel Bass[731]. They had four daughters:
 Diane Trawick[1926] born on November 6, 1958
 Charlotte Trawick[1928] born on November 5, 1961
 Lisa Trawick[1930] born on April 4, 1963
 Gena Trawick[1932]

733. HERMAN BASS (see Descendants (142)) was born on November 29, 1939, in Carolina Community, Covington, Alabama, USA, to James Bennett Bass[174] and Flara Annie Rowell[175].
- He was recorded in the census in 1940, as an infant, in Election Prect 21 Carolina, Covington, Alabama, USA.
- He was recorded in the census on April 1, 1950, aged 10, in Carolina, Covington, Alabama, United States.

The following information is also recorded for Herman:
- Military Service.

734. MARY ANN BLAIR was born on February 16, 1945.

Herman Bass[733] married Mary Ann Blair. They had one daughter:
 Cynthia Michelle Bass[1935] born on September 25, 1967

735. COY BENNETT BASS (see Descendants (142)) was born on August 4, 1942, in Carolina Community, Covington, Alabama, USA, to James Bennett Bass[174] and Flara Annie Rowell[175].
- He was recorded in the census on April 1, 1950, aged 7, in Carolina, Covington, Alabama, United States.

The following information is also recorded for Coy Bennett:
- Military Service.

736. MARGARET FAYE HAMMOCK was born on November 30, 1942. She died on February 10, 2023, aged 80, in Auburn, Lee, Alabama, USA.

Note: *Faye Bass was a longtime resident of Lee County. Faye was married to Coy Bass for 56 years. Faye is a member of Central Baptist Church. She loved being a homemaker and managing Bass Mobile Estates. She was a loving wife and mother of two children that she raised in a loving home. (Death)*

Coy Bennett Bass[735] married Margaret Faye Hammock. They had two sons:
 Coy Bennett Bass Jr.[1937] born on May 13, 1968
 Columbus Barry Bass[1940] born on May 4, 1972

737. FRANKLIN JERRY BASS (see Descendants (142)) was born on August 1, 1944, in Andalusia, Covington, Alabama, USA, to James Bennett Bass[174] and Flara Annie Rowell[175]. Franklin Jerry became known as "Franky". He was recorded in the census on April 1, 1950, aged 5, in Carolina, Covington, Alabama, United States.

Note: *Only one of his siblings born in a hospital, the rest were born at home with a midwife.*

738. BARBARA BARTON.

Franklin Jerry Bass[737] married Barbara Barton. They had two sons:
 Franklin Scott Bass[1943] born on August 13, 1970; died on August 31, 1990
 Stanley Brian Bass[1944]

739. DR. DUDLEY SADIE JOHNSON (see Descendants (143)) was born in May 1925, in Andalusia, Covington, Alabama, USA, to John Henry Johnson[178] and Mattie O. Bass[177]. Dudley Sadie became known as "Sadie".
- He died on December 8, 1987, aged 62 years, in Texas, USA.
- He was buried in Grace Hill Cemetery, Blanchard, Polk, Texas, USA.

The following information is also recorded for Sadie:
- Military Service.
- Degree.

Notes:
- *U.S. Navy WWII.*
  (Military Service)
- *As a PhD of history he taught at Southeastern Louisiana University.*
  (Degree)

740. JULIA ANN BARROW was born on April 1, 1943.

Dudley Sadie Johnson[739], aged 34, married Julia Ann Barrow, aged 16, on August 5, 1959. They had three children:

John Taft Johnson M.D.[1946] born on May 15, 1960 in Crestview, Okaloosa County, Florida, USA
Dudley Franklin Johnson[1948] born on October 11, 1963 in Tallahassee, Florida, USA; died on January 28, 2017 in Ponchatoula, Louisiana, USA
Christy Johnson[1949]

741. DR. KENNETH RAY JOHNSON (see Descendants (143)) was born on December 10, 1927, in Covington, Alabama, USA, to John Henry Johnson[178] and Mattie O. Bass[177].
- He died on October 17, 2016, aged 88 years.
- He was buried in Beda Cemetery, Beda, Covington, Alabama, USA.

The following information is also recorded for Kenneth Ray:
- Title: Professor Emeritus in 1996, aged about 68, in Univeristy of North Alabama.
- Military Service.

Notes:
- *Dr. Kenneth R. Johnson was born December 10, 1927 to Mattie Bass Johnson and John Henry Johnson, in the logging community of Falco, in Covington County, Alabama.*

  An Army veteran, Dr. Johnson served nearly three years in Korea. He earned degrees from Troy State Teachers College (BS-Social Studies Education), the University of Alabama (MA-School Administration), and Florida State University (MS and PhD-History). Later, he engaged in post-doctoral research in the field of Black Studies with Dr. John Hope Franklin at the University of Chicago.

  He taught in public schools, Young Harris College, and Florida State University. In 1966, Dr. Johnson joined the faculty at the University of North Alabama, teaching several different history courses, specializing in Southern History and Alabama History and later becoming Head of the History Department. He retired in 1996 and holds the title of Professor Emeritus.

  Dr. Johnson researched, wrote and published several articles about southern history with an emphasis on the Muscle Shoals area. In the 1970s he joined with other local historians and began the Journal of Muscle Shoals History.

  In 1994 Dr. Johnson and others interested in Methodist History organized the North Alabama Methodist Conference Historical Society. He served as president of this Society for several years.

  An active member of the community, Dr. Johnson participated and lead in many organizations including the Florence chapter of Civitan International, the Tennessee Valley Historical Society (president), Florence Historical Board, Alabama Humanities Foundation (president), Alabama Historical Association (president), Southern Historical Association (Lifetime Member), Florence Federal Credit Union Board of Directors, Friends of the Public Library and Edgemont United Methodist Church.

  Dr. Johnson was the recipient of the Lifetime Achievement Award from the UNA Alumni Association and the Wheeler Archives and History Award by the North Alabama Conference of the United Methodist Church as well as a member of Phi Kappa Phi.
  (Death)
- *US Army.*
  (Military Service)

742. SALLY MARILYN SIMMONS was born on August 5, 1939, in Rose Hill, Mississippi, USA.
   Kenneth Ray Johnson[741], aged 36, married Sally Marilyn Simmons, aged 24, on June 21, 1964. They had two daughters:
      Sally Johnson[1951] born on June 12, 1966
      Nancy Ann Johnson[1952] born on September 19, 1967

743. MONIA RUTH JOHNSON (see Descendants (143)) was born on October 4, 1930, in Covington, Alabama, USA, to John Henry Johnson[178] and Mattie O. Bass[177].
   • She died (At young age) on December 2, 1931, aged 1 years, in Covington, Alabama, USA.
   • She was buried in Beda Cemetery.

744. HOLLIS MITCHELL JACKSON SR. (see Descendants (144)) was born on November 1, 1925, in Alabama, USA, to Quillie Jackson[180] and Flora Bass[179].
   • He was recorded in the census in 1930, aged about 4, in Florala, Covington, Alabama, USA.
   • He was recorded in the census in 1940, aged about 14, in Beat 21 Carolina, Covington, Alabama, USA.
   • He died on February 22, 1961, aged 35 years, in Opelika, Lee, Alabama, United States.
   • He was buried in Garden Hills Cemetery, Opelika, Lee, Alabama, USA.
The following information is also recorded for Hollis Mitchell:
   • Military Service on October 12, 1944, aged 18.
   • Military Award.
   • Military Award.
Notes:
   • *Seaman, U.S. Navy WWII and an aditional enlistment.*
   (Military Service)
   • *Victory Ribbon.*
   (Military Award)
   • *Asiatic-Pacific Campaign Medal.*
   (Military Award)

745. ANNIE RUTH GUNNER.
   Hollis Mitchell Jackson Sr.[744] married Annie Ruth Gunner. They had two children:
      Martha Judson Jackson[1954] born on May 23, 1948
      Hollis Mitchell Jackson Jr.[1956] born on July 27, 1952

746. HORRIS CARSON JACKSON (see Descendants (144)) was born on March 23, 1929, in Opelika, Lee, Alabama, USA, to Quillie Jackson[180] and Flora Bass[179].
   • He was recorded in the census in 1930, aged about 1, in Florala, Covington, Alabama, USA.
   • He was recorded in the census in 1940, aged about 11, in Beat 21 Carolina, Covington, Alabama, USA.
   • He died on February 20, 2019, aged 89, in Opelika, Lee, Alabama, USA.
   • He was buried in Garden Hills Cemetery. Opelika, Lee County, Alabama, USA.

747. JEANETTE HOWARD was born on August 12, 1933.
   • She died on July 24, 2014, aged 80.
   • She was buried in Garden Hills Cemetery. Opelika, Lee County, Alabama, USA.
      Horris Carson Jackson[746] married Jeanette Howard. They had three children:
         Loretta Jackson[1957] born on July 8, 1951; died on March 14, 2012
         Carson Jackson[1958] born on November 5, 1952
         Tony Ray Jackson[1959] born on April 7, 1960

748. HILLARY DALTON JACKSON (see Descendants (144)) was born about 1932, in Alabama, USA, to Quillie Jackson[180] and Flora Bass[179].
   • He was recorded in the census in 1940, aged about 8, in Beat 21 Carolina, Covington, Alabama, USA.
   • He died in 2014, aged about 82.
Hillary Dalton married twice. He was married to Margaret Futual[749] and Betty Hawkins[750].

749. MARGARET FUTUAL.
   Hillary Dalton Jackson[748] married Margaret Futual. They had one son:
      James Dalton Jackson[1960] born on February 26, 1952

750. BETTY HAWKINS.
   Hillary Dalton Jackson[748] married Betty Hawkins. They had five children:
      Hillary Kim Jackson[1961] born on May 27, 1960
      Richard Todd Jackson[1962] born on July 31, 1961
      Richard Tad Jackson[1963] born on July 28, 1963
      Tracy Allen Jackson[1964] born on April 17, 1964

Tammy Gayle Jackson[1965] born on July 9, 1966

751. MSGT HAWARD JAMES JACKSON (see Descendants (144)) was born on April 29, 1934, in Alabama, USA, to Quillie Jackson[180] and Flora Bass[179].
- He was recorded in the census in 1940, aged about 6, in Beat 21 Carolina, Covington, Alabama, USA.
- He died on April 9, 2018, aged 83.
- He was buried in Garden Hills Cemetery, Opelika, Lee, Alabama, USA.

The following information is also recorded for Haward James:
- Military Service.

Notes:
- *USAF Retired Master Sergeant, Haward James Jackson, 83, was called to his final deployment on Monday, April 9, 2018. Haward served our country for twenty years in the United States Air Force. Haward was a loving husband, father, and grandfather.*
(Death)
- *Master Sergent, USAF Retired with 20 years of service.*
(Military Service)

752. NORA FAY ROBERTS.
Haward James Jackson[751] married Nora Fay Roberts. They had five children:
Alex Neal Jackson[1966] born on January 11, 1954
Debra Lynn Jackson[1967] born on December 27, 1955
Dale O'Marr Jackson[1968] born on December 27, 1955
Eric James Jackson[1969] born on July 8, 1963
Kimberly K. Jackson[1970] born on January 3, 1967

753. FLORINE JACKSON JACKSON (see Descendants (144)) was born on December 14, 1936, in Alabama, USA, to Quillie Jackson[180] and Flora Bass[179]. She was recorded in the census in 1940, aged about 3, in Beat 21 Carolina, Covington, Alabama, USA.

754. WILLIAM ADOLPHUS PARKER.
William Adolphus Parker married Florine Jackson Jackson[753]. They had two children:
Mitchell Quillie Parker[1971] born on January 19, 1958
Carrie Elaine Parker[1972] born on August 14, 1959

755. DORTHY E. MURPHY (see Descendants (145)) was born on March 20, 1929, in Alabama, United States, to Everett Stanley Murphy[182] and Florine Dorothy Bass[181].
- She was recorded in the census in 1930, aged about 1, in Opp, Covington, Alabama, USA.
- She was recorded in the census in 1940, aged about 11, in Election Precinct No 3 Beaver Creek, Okaloosa, Florida, USA.
- She died on August 26, 2003, aged 74 years.
- She was buried in Shady Hill Church Cemetery, Covington, Alabama, USA.

The following information is also recorded for Dorthy E.:
- Military Service.

Note: *U.S. Army - WWII.*
(Military Service)

756. ARNOLD HARBUCK.
Arnold Harbuck married Dorthy E. Murphy[755]. They had three sons:
Frankie Harbuck[1973] born on September 6, 1945
Johnnie Harbuck[1975] born on August 24, 1950
Allen Harbuck[1976] born on April 23, 1952

757. CHARLES ALTON MURPHY (see Descendants (145)) was born on January 11, 1931, in Covington, Alabama, USA, to Everett Stanley Murphy[182] and Florine Dorothy Bass[181]. Charles Alton became known as "Al".
- He was recorded in the census in 1940, aged about 9, in Election Precinct No 3 Beaver Creek, Okaloosa, Florida, USA.
- He died on December 13, 2017, aged 86, in Covington, Alabama, USA.
- He was buried in Shady Hill Church Cemetery, Covington, Alabama, USA.

The following information is also recorded for Al:
- Military Service.

Notes:
- *Al lived a full life, surrounded by those he loved. He began his career at the young age of 16 when he left home to join the military. He served three years before joining the US Merchant Marines. He spent several years travelling the world and providing for his mother and siblings. When he returned home, he settled down and met the love of his life, Beth. He started a new career, working in construction at Eglin Air Force Base, in Niceville, Florida. He*

found much success in commercial construction, and quickly rose up the ranks to General Superintendent. He spent his career building the skyline of Okaloosa Island and Fort-Walton Beach. Al was a devoted family man and strong Christian. He was an active member of Choctaw Beach First Baptist Church and a pillar in his community. -Bio from Obituary.
- Served 3 Years.
(Military Service)

758. KATHERYN ELIZABETH HENDRIX.
Charles Alton Murphy[757], aged 25, married Katheryn Elizabeth Hendrix on December 31, 1956. They had three children:
Charles Alton Murphy II[1977] born on April 24, 1958 in Crestview, Okaloosa, Florida, USA; died on March 21, 2018 in Florida, United States
Daniel Patrick Murphy[1978] born on June 17, 1961
Bobby Murphy[1979]

759. LILLY MAY MURPHY (see Descendants (145)) was born on May 15, 1933, in Covington, Alabama, USA, to Everett Stanley Murphy[182] and Florine Dorothy Bass[181].
- She died (At young age) on May 1, 1935, aged 1 years, in Covington, Alabama, USA.
- She was buried in Shady Hill Church Cemetery, Covington, Alabama, USA.

760. BOBBY EUELL MURPHY (see Descendants (145)) was born on May 14, 1939, in Covington, Alabama, USA, to Everett Stanley Murphy[182] and Florine Dorothy Bass[181].
- He died on June 21, 1956, aged 17 years, in Hampton, South Carolina, USA.
- He was buried in Shady Hill Church Cemetery, Covington, Alabama, USA.

The following information is also recorded for Bobby Euell:
- Military Service.
Note: *U.S. Air Force - A3C 1608 INSTL SQ.*
(Military Service)

761. EDNA EARL MURPHY (see Descendants (145)) was born on October 20, 1944 to Everett Stanley Murphy[182] and Florine Dorothy Bass[181].

762. JAMES CHAPPLE.
James Chapple married Edna Earl Murphy[761]. They had two children:
Linda James Chapple[1980] born on December 26, 1963
James Douglas Chapple[1981] born on April 24, 1966

763. BABY CROSBY (see Descendants (146)) was born about 1926 to T. Laban Crosby[184] and Lillie May Bass[183].
- She died (At young age) about 1926, as an infant.
- She was buried in Carolina Baptist Church Cemetery, Covington, Alabama, USA.

764. WILLIAM REEVES (see Descendants (22)) was born about 1897, in Texas, United States, to Oscar H. Reeves[186] and Margaret Jane Ward[185].
- He was recorded in the census in 1910, aged about 13, in Justice Precinct 7, Falls, Texas, USA.

765. PRISCILLA REEVES (see Descendants (22)) was born about 1901, in Texas, United States, to Oscar H. Reeves[186] and Margaret Jane Ward[185].
- She was recorded in the census in 1910, aged about 9, in Justice Precinct 7, Falls, Texas, USA.

766. JOHNNIE REEVES (see Descendants (22)) was born about 1905, in Texas, United States, to Oscar H. Reeves[186] and Margaret Jane Ward[185].
- He was recorded in the census in 1910, aged about 5, in Justice Precinct 7, Falls, Texas, USA.

767. OSCAR B REEVES (see Descendants (22)) was born about 1907, in Texas, United States, to Oscar H. Reeves[186] and Margaret Jane Ward[185].
- He was recorded in the census in 1910, aged about 3, in Justice Precinct 7, Falls, Texas, USA.

768. THOMAS H ROBERTS (see Descendants (24)) was born about 1904, in Texas, United States, to Thomas Rueben Roberts[192] and Della Jordan[191].
- He was recorded in the census in 1920, aged about 16, in Falls, Texas, USA.

769. MARY K ROBERTS (see Descendants (24)) was born about 1907, in Texas, United States, to Thomas Rueben Roberts[192] and Della Jordan[191].
- She was recorded in the census in 1920, aged about 13, in Falls, Texas, USA.

770. MARGUERITE E ROBERTS (see Descendants (24)) was born about 1911, in Texas, United States, to Thomas Rueben Roberts[192] and Della Jordan[191].
- She was recorded in the census in 1920, aged about 9, in Falls, Texas, USA.

771. MAUDIE ALINE HART (see Descendants (25)) was born on April 22, 1899, in Alabama, United States, to James William Hart[194] and Flossie Bell[195].
- She was recorded in the census in 1900, aged about 1, in Precincts 10, 19 Hart, George, Covington, Alabama, USA.
- She died on January 23, 1984, aged 84 years, in Andalusia, Covington, Alabama, United States.

772. LELLA MAE HART (see Descendants (25)) was born on December 23, 1900, in Covington, Alabama, United States, to James William Hart[194] and Flossie Bell[195]. She died on June 4, 1966, aged 65 years, in Alabama, United States.

773. ELLEN HART (see Descendants (25)) was born about 1901, in Alabama, United States, to James William Hart[194] and Flossie Bell[195].
- She was recorded in the census in 1920, aged about 19, in Precinct 10, Co, Alabama, USA.

774. WILLIAM DANIEL HART (see Descendants (25)) was born on December 25, 1902, in Covington, Alabama, United States, to James William Hart[194] and Flossie Bell[195]. William Daniel became known as "Dan".
- He was recorded in the census in 1930, aged about 27, in Hart, Covington, Alabama, USA.
- He was recorded in the census in 1940, aged about 37, in 1 Range 14, Covington, Alabama, USA.
- He was recorded in the census on April 1, 1950, aged 47, in Proceeding West on Wing to Bradly Road, Hart, Covington, Alabama, United States.
- He died on July 5, 1987, aged 84 years, in Andalusia, Covington, Alabama, United States.
- He was buried in Pleasant Home Baptist Cemetery, Covington, Alabama, USA.

775. EVA IRENE DURDEN was born on October 21, 1906, in Escambia, Alabama, United States. Eva Irene became known as "Eva".
- She was recorded in the census in 1930, aged about 23, in Hart, Covington, Alabama, USA.
- She was recorded in the census in 1940, aged 34 years, in 1 Range 14, Covington, Alabama, USA.
- She was recorded in the census on April 1, 1950, aged 43, in Proceeding West on Wing to Bradly Road, Hart, Covington, Alabama, United States.
- She died on March 4, 1992, aged 85 years, in Andalusia, Covington, Alabama, United States.
- She was buried in Pleasant Home Baptist Cemetery, Covington, Alabama, USA.
William Daniel Hart[774] married Eva Irene Durden. They had three children:
William Daniel Hart[1982] born on June 14, 1925 in Alabama, United States; died on January 6, 2002 in Daytona Beach, Volusia, Florida, United States
Eugene Hart[1983] born in 1928 in Alabama, United States
Mabel Erline Hart[1984] born on July 4, 1929 in Pleasant Home, Covington, Alabama, United States; died on August 9, 2007 in Andalusia, Covington, Alabama, United States

776. BIRDIE H HART (see Descendants (25)) was born on November 3, 1904, in Covington, Alabama, United States, to James William Hart[194] and Flossie Bell[195].
- She was recorded in the census in 1920, aged about 15, in Precinct 10, Co, Alabama, USA.
- She was recorded in the census in 1930, aged about 25, in Hart, Covington, Alabama, USA.
- She died on November 23, 1975, aged 71 years, in Lockhart, Covington, Alabama, United States.
- She was buried in Pleasant Home Baptist Church Cemetery, Covington, Alabama, USA.

777. CHARLIE C DAVIS was born on September 25, 1895, in Alabama, USA.
- He died on April 11, 1974, aged 78 years, in Covington, Alabama, USA.
- He was buried in Pleasant Home Baptist Church Cemetery, Covington, Alabama, USA.
Charlie C Davis married Birdie H Hart[776].

778. JAMES TRAVIS HART (see Descendants (25)) was born on January 7, 1907, in Alabama, USA, to James William Hart[194] and Flossie Bell[195].
- He was recorded in the census in 1920, aged about 13, in Precinct 10, Co, Alabama, USA.
- He was recorded in the census in 1930, aged about 23, in Hart, Covington, Alabama, USA.
- He was recorded in the census on April 1, 1950, aged 43, in Proceeding West on Wing to Bradly Road, Hart, Covington, Alabama, United States.
- He died on August 22, 1985, aged 78 years, in Okaloosa, FL, USA.
- He was buried in Pleasant Home Baptist Church Cemetery, Covington, Alabama, USA.

779. DELIA ADELINE BRADLEY was born on September 5, 1909, in Alabama, USA.
- She was recorded in the census on April 1, 1950, aged 40, in Proceeding West on Wing to Bradly Road, Hart,

Covington, Alabama, United States.
- She died on June 25, 1981, aged 71 years, in Covington, Alabama, USA.
- She was buried in Pleasant Home Baptist Church Cemetery, Covington, Alabama, USA.

James Travis Hart[778] married Delia Adeline Bradley. They had two children:
James B Hart[1985] born about 1939 in Alabama, United States
Sherley L Hart[1986] born about 1949 in Alabama, United States

780. ALLEN TRAMMEL HART (see Descendants (25)) was born on March 8, 1910, in Covington, Alabama, USA, to James William Hart[194] and Flossie Bell[195].
- He was recorded in the census in 1920, aged about 10, in Precinct 10, Co, Alabama, USA.
- He was recorded in the census in 1940, aged about 30, in West Central, Orlando, Elc Prec 18, Orange, Florida, USA.
- He was recorded in the census on April 1, 1950, aged 40, in Oakwood, Crescent City, Putnam, Florida, United States.
- He died on July 9, 1994, aged 84 years, in Hernando County, Florida, USA.
- He was buried in Brooksville Cemetery, Brooksville, Hernando, Florida, USA.

781. ANNIE P PERRY was born on October 18, 1918, in Georgia, USA.
- She was recorded in the census in 1940, aged about 21, in West Central, Orlando, Elc Prec 18, Orange, Florida, USA.
- She was recorded in the census on April 1, 1950, aged 31, in Oakwood, Crescent City, Putnam, Florida, United States.
- She died on July 2, 1992, aged 73 years.
- She was buried in Brooksville Cemetery, Brooksville, Hernando, Flori.

Allen Trammel Hart[780] married Annie P Perry. They had one daughter:
Julia A Hart[1987] born about 1938 in Florida, USA

782. LEONARD V. HART (see Descendants (25)) was born on September 24, 1918, in Falco, Covington, Alabama, United States, to James William Hart[194] and Flossie Bell[195].
- He was recorded in the census on April 1, 1950, aged 31, in 3 Mantaeis Ave, North Deland, Volusia, Florida, United States.
- He died on February 20, 1998, aged 79 years, in De Land, Volusia, Florida, United States.
- He was buried in Pleasant Home Baptist Church Cemetery, Covington, Alabama, USA.

Note: *L. V. Hart is noted as Nephew of James W. and Flossie B. Hart on the 1930 US Census.*

783. FEROL JANICE STOKES was born on February 3, 1919.
- She was recorded in the census on April 1, 1950, aged 31, in 3 Mantaeis Ave, North Deland, Volusia, Florida, United States.
- She died on October 15, 2018, aged 99, in Florida, United States.
- She was buried in Pleasant Home Baptist Church Cemetery, Covington, Alabama, USA.

Leonard V. Hart[782] married Ferol Janice Stokes.

784. W C HART (see Descendants (25)) was born about 1919, in Alabama, United States, to James William Hart[194] and Flossie Bell[195]. He was recorded in the census in 1920, aged about 1, in Precinct 10, Co, Alabama, USA.

785. JYNELLE HART (see Descendants (25)) was born on August 28, 1922 to James William Hart[194] and Flossie Bell[195].
- She was recorded in the census in 1930, aged about 7, in Hart, Covington, Alabama, USA.
- She died on March 15, 2008, aged 85 years.
- She was buried in Weavers Cemetery, Brewton, Escambia, Alabama, USA.

786. ALTON GILLIS was born on November 1, 1911.
- He died on September 9, 1994, aged 82 years.
- He was buried in Weavers Cemetery, Brewton, Escambia, Alabama, USA.

The following information is also recorded for Alton:
- Military Service.

Note: *U.S. Navy WWII.*
(Military Service)

Alton Gillis, aged 49, married Jynelle Hart[785], aged 38, on March 25, 1961.

787. LUCILLE GOODLETT (see Descendants (25)) was born to Charles Henry Goodlett[198] and Virginia Hart[197].

788. FRED COLUMBUS KELLEY (see Descendants (25)) was born on August 15, 1898, in Covington, Alabama, United States, to George Washington Kelley[200] and Alice Rebecca Hart[199].
- He was recorded in the census in 1900, aged about 1, in Precincts 10, 19 Hart, George, Covington, Alabama, USA.
- He was recorded in the census in 1920, aged about 21, in Precinct 10, Covington, Alabama, USA.
- He was recorded in the census in 1930, aged about 31, in Hart, Covington, Alabama, USA.
- He was recorded in the census in 1940, aged about 41, in Precinct 10 Hart, Covington, Alabama, USA.
- He died on November 28, 1984, aged 86, in Covington, Alabama, United States.
- He was buried in 1984 in Pleasant Home Baptist Church Cemetery, Covington, Alabama, USA.

789. RACHEL DAVIDSON was born on November 11, 1900, in Florida, USA.
- She was recorded in the census in 1930, aged about 29, in Hart, Covington, Alabama, USA.
- She was recorded in the census in 1940, aged about 39, in Precinct 10 Hart, Covington, Alabama, USA.
- She died in 1987, aged about 86, in Florida, USA.
- She was buried in Pleasant Home Baptist Church Cemetery, Covington, Alabama, USA.

Fred Columbus Kelley[788], aged 22, married Rachel Davidson, aged 20, on December 2, 1920 in Alabama, United States. They had ten children:

Eloise Kelley[1988] born on October 15, 1921 in Alabama, United States; died on August 17, 2012 in California, USA

Ruth Hazel Kelley[1990] born on February 2, 1924 in Alabama, United States; died in 2000

Wynelle D Kelley[1991] born on February 18, 1926 in Andalusia, Covington, Alabama, United States; died on June 4, 2017 in Warner Robins, Houston, Georgia, USA

Joyce Marie Kelley[1993] born on April 10, 1928 in Alabama, United States; died in 1976

Fred Ronald Kelley[1995] born on June 20, 1930 in Alabama, United States

Barbara Gene Kelley[1996] born on August 24, 1932 in Alabama, USA; died on August 8, 1997 in Covington, Alabama, USA

George D Kelley[1997] born on June 19, 1935 in Alabama, USA

Patricia Ann Kelley[1998] born on October 6, 1937 in Alabama, USA; died in 2020

James Kelley[1999] born in 1943

Mr. Kelley[2000]

790. WILLIAM ALLEN KELLEY (see Descendants (25)) was born on April 7, 1901, in Covington, Alabama, to George Washington Kelley[200] and Alice Rebecca Hart[199]. William Allen became known as "Allen". He died on December 22, 1985, aged 84, in Covington, Alabama.

791. DANIEL KELLEY (see Descendants (25)) was born about 1902, in Alabama, United States, to George Washington Kelley[200] and Alice Rebecca Hart[199]. He died (At young age) about 1902, as an infant.

792. RUBIE L KELLEY (see Descendants (25)) was born on April 17, 1904, in Covington, Alabama, USA, to George Washington Kelley[200] and Alice Rebecca Hart[199].
- She was recorded in the census in 1920, aged about 16, in Precinct 10, Covington, Alabama, USA.
- She was recorded in the census in 1940, aged about 36, in 1 Range 14, Covington, Alabama, USA.
- She was recorded in the census on April 1, 1950, aged 45, in Proceeding South West from Pleasant Home School of Fales, Hart, Covington, Alabama, United States.
- She died on August 30, 2002, aged 98, in Alabama, United States.
- She was buried in 2002 in Covington, Alabama, United States.

Rubie L was the partner of her second cousin, William Greeley Teel[294].

William Greeley Teel[294] and Rubie L Kelley had two children:

Dorothy Helen Teel[911] born on December 20, 1922 in Alabama, United States; died on September 23, 1983 in Alabama, United States

William Olen Teel[913] born on October 25, 1925 in Alabama, United States; died on December 26, 1974 in Wing, Covington, Alabama, United States

793. JOHN KELLEY (see Descendants (25)) was born on February 18, 1907, in Covington, Alabama, United States, to George Washington Kelley[200] and Alice Rebecca Hart[199].
- He was recorded in the census in 1920, aged about 13, in Precinct 10, Covington, Alabama, USA.
- He was recorded in the census in 1930, aged about 23, in Hart, Covington, Alabama, USA.
- He died on March 1, 1996, aged 89, in Florida, United States.

794. COLUMBUS DANIEL KELLEY (see Descendants (25)) was born on June 29, 1912, in Covington, Alabama, to George Washington Kelley[200] and Alice Rebecca Hart[199]. Columbus Daniel became known as "Dan".
- He was recorded in the census in 1920, aged about 8, in Precinct 10, Covington, Alabama, USA.
- He was recorded in the census in 1930, aged about 18, in Hart, Covington, Alabama, USA.
- He died (Illness) on September 19, 1947, aged 35, in Covington, Alabama.

Columbus Daniel had two partnerships. He was married to Gladys Herring[795]. He was also the partner of Bertha Lois Bradley[796].

Note: *Contracted TB or Milaria in Africa or Italy during his time in WWII.*
   (Death)

795. GLADYS HERRING was born in 1913.
   Columbus Daniel Kelley[794] married Gladys Herring.

796. BERTHA LOIS BRADLEY was born on July 12, 1910, in Friendship, Hot Springs, Arkansas, USA, to Charles Franklin Bradley and Arra Loretta Henley.
- She died on July 6, 1997, aged 86, in Palatka, Putnam, Florida, USA.
- She was buried in July 1997 in Red Oak Baptist Church Cemetery, Covington, Alabama.
   Columbus Daniel Kelley[794] and Bertha Lois Bradley became partners.

797. MILDRED HAZEL KELLEY (see Descendants (25)) was born on February 3, 1919, in Alabama, United States, to George Washington Kelley[200] and Alice Rebecca Hart[199].
- She was recorded in the census in 1920, aged about 1, in Precinct 10, Covington, Alabama, USA.
- She was recorded in the census in 1930, aged about 11, in Hart, Covington, Alabama, USA.
- She was recorded in the census in 1940, aged about 21, in Precinct 10 Hart, Covington, Alabama, USA.
- She died on August 28, 1986, aged 67.

798. CLAUDE C. CAMPBELL (see Descendants (25)) was born about 1908, in Alabama, USA, to William Nicholas Campbell[204] and Ada Alabama Hart[203].
- He was recorded in the census in 1910, aged about 2, in Andalusia, Covington, Alabama, USA.
- He was recorded in the census in 1920, aged about 12, in Precinct 1, Covington, Alabama, USA.
- He was recorded in the census in 1930, aged about 22, in Hollywood, Broward, Florida, USA.
- He was recorded in the census in 1940, aged about 32, in East 2238 Hollywood Blvd, Hollywood, Election Precinct 11 Hollywood, Broward, Florida, USA.
- He died on March 8, 1998, aged about 89, in Alabama, USA.
- He was buried in Pleasant Home Baptist Church Cemetery, Covington, Alabama, USA.

The following information is also recorded for Claude C.:
- Military Service.

Note: *U.S. Army - WWII.*
   (Military Service)

799. MARY R CAMPBELL (see Descendants (25)) was born about 1917, in Alabama, United States, to William Nicholas Campbell[204] and Ada Alabama Hart[203].
- She was recorded in the census in 1920, aged about 3, in Precinct 1, Covington, Alabama, USA.
- She was recorded in the census in 1930, aged about 13, in Hollywood, Broward, Florida, USA.

800. WILLIAM NICHOLAS CAMPBELL JR. (see Descendants (25)) was born in November 1919, in Alabama, United States, to William Nicholas Campbell[204] and Ada Alabama Hart[203].
- He was recorded in the census in 1920, as an infant, in Precinct 1, Covington, Alabama, USA.
- He was recorded in the census in 1930, aged about 10, in Hollywood, Broward, Florida, USA.
- He was recorded in the census in 1940, aged about 20, in East 2238 Hollywood Blvd, Hollywood, Election Precinct 11 Hollywood, Broward, Florida, USA.

801. WILLIAM D "WILLIE" CUSHING (see Descendants (25)) was born in 1911, in Covington County, Alabama, to

John Jefferson Cushing[206] and Nancy Lena Hart[205]. William D "Willie" became known as "Willie". He died in 2008, aged about 97, in Pensacola, Escambia County, Florida.

802. WOODROW CUSHING (see Descendants (25)) was born in 1917, in Covington County, Alabama, to John Jefferson Cushing[206] and Nancy Lena Hart[205]. He died on July 12, 1994, aged about 77, in Milton, Santa Rosa County, Florida.

803. JOHN JEFFERSON CUSHING (see Descendants (25)) was born on July 18, 1922, in Pensacola, Escambia County, Florida, to John Jefferson Cushing[206] and Nancy Lena Hart[205]. He died on October 14, 1983, aged 61, in Pensacola, Escambia County, Florida.

804. CLYDE L CUSHING (see Descendants (25)) was born on October 11, 1925, in Pensacola, Escambia County, Florida, to John Jefferson Cushing[206] and Nancy Lena Hart[205].
- He was recorded in the census on April 1, 1950, aged 24, in 1006 E De Soto, Pensacola, Escambia, Florida, United States.
- He died on June 17, 1980, aged 54, in Florida.

805. ELEANOR D. HART (see Descendants (25)) was born on December 21, 1909, in Falco, Covington, Alabama, USA, to Joseph Josh Davis[208] and Mary Nora Hart[207].
- She died on August 12, 1959, aged 49 years, in Pensacola, Escambia, Florida, USA.
- She was buried on August 14, 1959 in Covington, Alabama, USA.

806. JACK COLUMBUS DAVIS (see Descendants (25)) was born on May 20, 1914, in Covington, Alabama, USA, to Joseph Josh Davis[208] and Mary Nora Hart[207].
- He died on January 23, 1989, aged 74 years, in Crestview, Okaloosa, Florida, USA.
- He was buried on January 25, 1989 in Covington, Alabama, USA.

807. JAMES RUDOLPH DAVIS (see Descendants (25)) was born on October 24, 1923, in Falco, Covington, Alabama, USA, to Joseph Josh Davis[208] and Mary Nora Hart[207].
- He died on July 19, 1988, aged 64 years, in Crestview, Okaloosa, Florida, USA.
- He was buried on July 21, 1988 in Covington, Alabama, USA.

808. NANNIE RUTH DAVIS (see Descendants (25)) was born on September 30, 1925, in River Falls, Covington, Alabama, USA, to Joseph Josh Davis[208] and Mary Nora Hart[207]. She died on July 7, 2010, aged 84 years.

809. WILLIAM E HUTCHISON (see Descendants (26)) was born about 1901, in Alabama, United States, to Liston Thomas Hutcheson[210] and Mary A. Bass[209]. He was recorded in the census in 1920, aged about 19, in Beat 6 Loango, Covington, Alabama, USA.

810. HARRIS G HUTCHISON (see Descendants (26)) was born about 1906, in Alabama, United States, to Liston Thomas Hutcheson[210] and Mary A. Bass[209]. He was recorded in the census in 1920, aged about 14, in Beat 6 Loango, Covington, Alabama, USA.

811. HAROLD A HUTCHISON (see Descendants (26)) was born about 1909, in Alabama, United States, to Liston Thomas Hutcheson[210] and Mary A. Bass[209]. He was recorded in the census in 1920, aged about 11, in Beat 6 Loango, Covington, Alabama, USA.

812. MYRTLE E HUTCHISON (see Descendants (26)) was born about 1913, in Alabama, United States, to Liston Thomas Hutcheson[210] and Mary A. Bass[209]. She was recorded in the census in 1920, aged about 7, in Beat 6 Loango, Covington, Alabama, USA.

813. VELMA BASS (see Descendants (26)) was born on December 23, 1906, in Alabama, United States, to William Riley Bass[211] and Augusta Cooper[212].
- She was recorded in the census in 1930, aged about 23, in Andalusia, Covington, Alabama, USA.
- She died on May 2, 1996, aged 89 years, in Bibb County, Georgia, USA.
- She was buried in Glen Haven Memorial Garden, Macon, Bibb, Georgia, USA.

814. HORACE E POOLE was born on February 7, 1909, in Alabama, United States.
- He was recorded in the census in 1930, aged about 21, in Andalusia, Covington, Alabama, USA.
- He died on November 3, 1974, aged 65 years, in Bibb County, Georgia, USA.
- He was buried in Glen Haven Memorial Garden, Macon, Bibb, Georgia, USA.

Horace E Poole, aged about 21, married Velma Bass[813], aged about 23, in 1930. They had three children:
- Max Earl Poole[2001] born on September 22, 1930 in Alabama; died in March 1983 in Houston County, Alabama
- Eddie Poole[2003]
- Carroll Poole[2004]

815. WILLIAM BARNEY BASS (see Descendants (26)) was born on July 25, 1910, in Alabama, United States, to William Riley Bass[211] and Augusta Cooper[212].
- He was recorded in the census in 1930, aged about 19, in Fairfield, Covington, Alabama, USA.
- He was recorded in the census in 1940, aged about 29, in Conecuh Church Road, Election Precinct 2 Fairfield, Covington, Alabama, USA.
- He died on November 7, 1995, aged 85.
- He was buried in Andalus Memorial Cemetery, Andalusia, Covington County, Alabama, USA.

816. RUBY LENA PADGETT was born on July 25, 1910, in Covington, Alabama, USA.
- She was recorded in the census in 1940, aged about 29, in Conecuh Church Road, Election Precinct 2 Fairfield, Covington, Alabama, USA.
- She died on November 11, 1980, aged 70, in Andalusia, Covington, Alabama, USA.
- She was buried in Salem Baptist Church Cemetery, Covington County, Alabama, USA.

William Barney Bass[815] married Ruby Lena Padgett.

817. MAGGIE M BASS (see Descendants (26)) was born about 1913, in Alabama, United States, to William Riley Bass[211] and Augusta Cooper[212].
- She was recorded in the census in 1930, aged about 17, in Fairfield, Covington, Alabama, USA.

818. CLARA M BASS (see Descendants (26)) was born about 1915, in Alabama, United States, to William Riley Bass[211] and Augusta Cooper[212].
- She was recorded in the census in 1930, aged about 15, in Fairfield, Covington, Alabama, USA.

819. EVA MAE BASS (see Descendants (26)) was born on May 9, 1918, in Alabama, United States, to William Riley Bass[211] and Augusta Cooper[212].
- She was recorded in the census in 1930, aged about 12, in Fairfield, Covington, Alabama, USA.
- She was recorded in the census in 1940, aged about 22, in Conecuh Church Road, Election Precinct 2 Fairfield, Covington, Alabama, USA.
- She died (Natural / Old Age) on December 29, 2012, aged 94 years, in Andalusia, Covington, Alabama, USA.
- She was buried in Andalusia Memorial Cemetery, Andalusia, Covington, Alabama, USA.

Note: *She was born May 9, 1918, to the late William Riley Bass and Gusta Cooper Bass. She began work at Andala and Alatex at a very young age. She also worked at Funsten in Andalusia and retired after 20 years of service. She loved to garden and quilt, but especially loved to cook for her family. She loved the Lord and instilled that love in her children, grandchildren, and great grandchildren.*
(Death)

820. DALLAS CLINTON FOWLER. He died on March 21, 1972.

Dallas Clinton Fowler married Eva Mae Bass[819]. They had one son:
- Mr. Fowler[2005]

821. HORACE PRESLEY BASS (see Descendants (26)) was born on October 29, 1921, in Alabama, United States, to William Riley Bass[211] and Augusta Cooper[212].
- He was recorded in the census in 1930, aged about 8, in Fairfield, Covington, Alabama, USA.
- He died on March 30, 1993, aged 71.
- He was buried in Sunrise Memorial Gardens, Lithia Springs, Douglas County, Georgia, USA.

822. AVIE BROOKS was born on February 22, 1924.
- She died on April 24, 1992, aged 68.
- She was buried in Sunrise Memorial Gardens, Lithia Springs, Douglas County, Georgia, USA.

Horace Presley Bass[821] married Avie Brooks. They had two children:
- Judith Ellica Bass[2008] born on November 19, 1944 in Andalusia, Covington, Alabama, United States; died on October 16, 2016
- Tommy Author Bass[2010] born on January 18, 1956 in Columbus, Muscogee, Georgia, United States; died on April 2, 2007

5th Generation of Descendants

823. MYRTICE MAE TEEL (see Descendants (1)) was born about 1932, in Alabama, USA, to Jesse Stallings Teel[215] and Eula Mae Black[216]. She was recorded in the census in 1940, aged about 8, in 338 Dunson, Andalusia, Covington, Alabama, USA.

824. MARY ETHEL TEEL (see Descendants (1)) was born in 1929, in Alabama, USA, to Aaron Teel[219] and Bessie Harrelson[220]. She was recorded in the census in 1940, aged about 11, in Election Precinct 1 Andalusia, Covington, Alabama, USA.

825. J. B. BROOKS was born in 1922.
   J. B. Brooks married Mary Ethel Teel[824]. They had four children:
      Lester Brooks[2012] born in 1947
      Sue Brooks[2013] born in 1950
      Sherry Brooks[2014] born in 1954
      Sandra Brooks[2015] born in 1958

826. MARIE TEEL (see Descendants (1)) was born in 1932, in Alabama, USA, to Aaron Teel[219] and Bessie Harrelson[220]. She was recorded in the census in 1940, aged about 8, in Election Precinct 1 Andalusia, Covington, Alabama, USA.

827. PETE ARMSTRONG was born in 1930. He died in 1995, aged about 65.
   Pete Armstrong married Marie Teel[826]. They had one daughter:
      Troyce Armstrong[2016] born in 1949

828. VERA MERLE TEEL (see Descendants (1)) was born on December 14, 1936, in Andalusia, Covington, Alabama, USA, to Aaron Teel[219] and Bessie Harrelson[220].
   • She was recorded in the census in 1940, aged about 3, in Election Precinct 1 Andalusia, Covington, Alabama, USA.
   • She was recorded in the census on April 1, 1950, aged 13, in Andalusia, Covington, Alabama, United States.
   • She died on November 16, 2014, aged 77, in Irving, Dallas, Texas, USA.
   • She was buried in Carolina Baptist Church Cemetery, Covington, Alabama, USA.

829. CECIL CROSS was born in 1935.
   Cecil Cross married Vera Merle Teel[828]. They had three children:
      Jerry Cross[2017] born in 1955
      Donna Cross[2018] born in 1957
      Billy Cross[2019] born in 1959

830. AARON TEEL JR. (see Descendants (1)) was born in 1939, in Alabama, United States, to Aaron Teel[219] and Bessie Harrelson[220]. Aaron became known as "Junior".
   • He was recorded in the census in 1940, aged about 1, in Election Precinct 1 Andalusia, Covington, Alabama, USA.
   • He was recorded in the census on April 1, 1950, aged about 10, in Andalusia, Covington, Alabama, United States.

831. JEAN CHILDS. She died in 1964.
   Aaron Teel Jr.[830] married Jean Childs. They had three children:
      Dexter Teel[2020] born in 1958; died in 1964
      Debra Kay Teel[2021] born in 1960
      Keneth Ra Teel[2022] born in 1964

832. FRANCES IDA TEEL (see Descendants (1)) was born in 1948, in Alabama, United States, to Aaron Teel[219] and Bessie Harrelson[220]. She was recorded in the census on April 1, 1950, aged about 1, in Andalusia, Covington, Alabama, United States.
   Frances Ida married three times. She was married to Quinton Gene Bass[444] (her second cousin, once removed), Richard Junior Patterson[833] and Bennie Bozeman[834].
      Quinton Gene Bass[444], aged 24, married Frances Ida Teel, aged about 15, on September 1, 1963, and they were divorced. They had two children:
         Beverly Lynn Bass[1326] born on August 20, 1964
         Wesley Alan Bass[1329] born on December 1, 1967

833. RICHARD JUNIOR PATTERSON was born on October 14, 1933. Richard Junior became known as "RJ".
- He died on February 25, 2010, aged 76, in Andalusia, Covington, Alabama, USA.
- He was buried in Buck Creek Baptist Church Cemetery, Covington, Alabama, USA.

Richard Junior married twice. He was married to Frances Ida Teel[832] and Ms. ?.
Richard Junior ("RJ") Patterson married Frances Ida Teel[832].
The following information is also recorded for this family:
- Death of Spouse.

Richard Junior ("RJ") Patterson married Ms. ?. They had two daughters:
  Barbara Patterson
  Angie Patterson

834. BENNIE BOZEMAN.
Bennie Bozeman married Frances Ida Teel[832], aged about 73, on February 12, 2022.

835. WINFORD EUGENE RAMER SR. (see Descendants (2)) was born on August 24, 1925, in Florida, USA, to Dewey William Ramer[222] and Mattie Lucile Johnson[223].
- He was recorded in the census in 1940, aged about 14, in Orlando Road, Taft, Precinct 42, Orange, Florida, USA.
- He died on June 11, 1986, aged 60.
- He was buried in Oak Ridge Cemetery, Orange County, Florida, USA.

836. NANCY YATES.
Winford Eugene Ramer Sr.[835] married Nancy Yates. They had three children:
  Jerry Edward Ramer[2023]
  Winford Eugene Ramer Jr.[2024] died on March 22, 2014 in Marietta, Georgia, USA
  Margaret Ramer[2026]

837. JAMES RAMER (see Descendants (2)) was born about 1928, in Alabama, USA, to Dewey William Ramer[222] and Mattie Lucile Johnson[223]. He was recorded in the census in 1940, aged about 12, in Orlando Road, Taft, Precinct 42, Orange, Florida, USA.

838. MS. RAMER (see Descendants (2)) was born about 1932, in Alabama, USA, to Dewey William Ramer[222] and Mattie Lucile Johnson[223]. She was recorded in the census in 1940, aged about 8, in Orlando Road, Taft, Precinct 42, Orange, Florida, USA.

839. BUDDY RAMER (see Descendants (2)) was born in 1934 to Dewey William Ramer[222] and Mattie Lucile Johnson[223]. He died in 1938, aged about 4.

840. MILDRED RAMER (see Descendants (2)) was born about 1938, in Florida, USA, to Dewey William Ramer[222] and Mattie Lucile Johnson[223]. She was recorded in the census in 1940, aged about 2, in Orlando Road, Taft, Precinct 42, Orange, Florida, USA.

841. DOROTHY RAMER (see Descendants (2)) was born about 1928, in Alabama, USA, to Albert Farrell Ramer[230] and Mamie Ada ?[231]. She was recorded in the census in 1940, aged about 12, in Railroad Avenue, Opp, Precinct 3, Covington, Alabama, USA.

842. DERWARD RAMER (see Descendants (2)) was born about 1937, in Alabama, USA, to Albert Farrell Ramer[230] and Mamie Ada ?[231]. He was recorded in the census in 1940, aged about 3, in Railroad Avenue, Opp, Precinct 3, Covington, Alabama, USA.

843. JAMES THOMAS WHITE SR. (see Descendants (4)) was born on July 16, 1927, in Andalusia, Covington, Alabama, USA, to Amos White[240] and Beulah Ramer[239].
- He died on October 26, 2014, aged 87, in Pensacola, Escambia, Florida, USA.

The following information is also recorded for James Thomas:
- Military Service.
Note: *HA2 US Navy.*
 (Military Service)
James Thomas married his third cousin, Marvette Faye Davis[909].

844. RICHARD WALLACE (see Descendants (4)) was born about 1944, in Ohio, United States, to William Travis Wallace[243] and Mary Dovie Ramer[242]. He was recorded in the census on April 1, 1950, aged about 5, in 2 1/2 Mile Zenohia Road, Hartland Township, Huron, Ohio, United States.

845. ESTER C BARNEYCASTLE (see Descendants (7)) was born to John Curtis Barneycastle[247] and Cynthia Lillian Bass[246].

846. ALFORD L MARCONTELL.
Alford L Marcontell married Ester C Barneycastle[845].

847. CYNTHIA LILLIAN BARNEYCASTLE (see Descendants (7)) was born on August 25, 1905, in Votaw, Hardin, Texas, USA, to Elzie Barneycastle[253] and Susan Viola Bass[252]. She died (At young age) on September 4, 1907, aged 2 years, in Votaw, Hardin, Texas, USA.

848. BENJAMIN WILSON BARNEYCASTLE (see Descendants (7)) was born on September 4, 1907, in Duncan, Oklahoma, USA, to Elzie Barneycastle[253] and Susan Viola Bass[252].
- He was recorded in the census in 1940, aged about 32, in Votaw Qt, Justice Precinct, Hardin, Texas, USA.
- He was recorded in the census on April 1, 1950, aged 42, in 113 2nd Ave No, Texas City, Galveston, Texas, United States.
- He died on December 29, 1962, aged 55 years, in Votaw, Hardin, Texas, USA.
- He was buried in Votaw Cemetery, Votaw, Hardin, Texas, USA.

849. LOLA MAE KEELS was born on March 27, 1909, in Texas, United States.
- She was recorded in the census on April 1, 1950, aged 41, in 113 2nd Ave No, Texas City, Galveston, Texas, United States.
- She died (Cancer) on October 26, 1967, aged 58.
- She was buried in Hayes Grace Memorial Park, Hitchcock, Galveston, Texas, USA.

Benjamin Wilson Barneycastle[848] married Lola Mae Keels. They had three daughters:
Hazel Marie Barneycastle[2034] born on November 12, 1933 in Groveton, Trinity, Texas 75845, USA
Sue Adele Barneycastle[2035] born on April 4, 1942 in Houston, Harris County, Texas, USA; died on December 1, 2015 in Salt Lake City, Salt Lake, Utah, USA
Bennie Mae Barneycastle[2037] born on September 14, 1944 in Texas City, Galveston County, Texas, USA; died on September 22, 2018 in Houston, Harris, Texas, USA

850. JAMES WILLIAM BARNEYCASTLE (see Descendants (7)) was born on May 24, 1910, in Votaw, Hardin, Texas, USA, to Elzie Barneycastle[253] and Susan Viola Bass[252].
- He died on November 21, 1938, aged 28 years, in Liberty, Texas, USA.
- He was buried in Votaw Cemetery, Votaw, Hardin, Texas, USA.

851. MARTIN LUTHER BARNEYCASTLE (see Descendants (7)) was born on April 8, 1912, in Votaw, Hardin, Texas, USA, to Elzie Barneycastle[253] and Susan Viola Bass[252].
- He was recorded in the census in 1940, aged about 28, in Oil Field Settlement Road, Justice Precinct 4, Tyler, Texas, USA.
- He died on April 1, 1984, aged 71 years.

852. PRUDIE LEE FAIRCLOTHE was born about 1917, in Texas, USA. She was recorded in the census in 1940, aged about 23, in Oil Field Settlement Road, Justice Precinct 4, Tyler, Texas, USA.

Martin Luther Barneycastle[851], aged 26, married Prudie Lee Fairclothe, aged about 21, on July 3, 1938.

853. NOBIE BARNEYCASTLE (see Descendants (7)) was born on October 25, 1913, in Votaw, Hardin, Texas, USA, to Elzie Barneycastle[253] and Susan Viola Bass[252].
- She died (At young age) on April 14, 1916, aged 2 years, in Votaw, Hardin, Texas, USA.
- She was buried in Votaw Cemetery, Votaw, Hardin, Texas, USA.

854. ISABELLE BARNEYCASTLE (see Descendants (7)) was born on September 28, 1917, in Votaw, Hardin, Texas, USA, to Elzie Barneycastle[253] and Susan Viola Bass[252].
- She died on June 17, 1968, aged 50 years, in Houston, Texas, USA.
- She was buried in Votaw Cemetery, Votaw, Hardin, Texas, USA.

855. CLARENCE JOHNNIE was born on May 6, 1913, in Orangefield, Orange, Texas, USA.
- He died on September 7, 1959, aged 46 years, in Houston, Texas, USA.
- He was buried in Votaw Cemetery, Votaw, Hardin, Texas, USA.

Clarence Johnnie, aged 28, married Isabelle Barneycastle[854], aged 24, on December 7, 1941. They had one daughter:
Ms. Johnnie[2039]

856. 1ST LT L. C. BARNEYCASTLE (see Descendants (7)) was born on October 1, 1920, in Votaw, Hardin, Texas, USA, to Elzie Barneycastle[253] and Susan Viola Bass[252].
- He was recorded in the census in 1940, aged about 19, in Votaw Qt, Justice Precinct, Hardin, Texas, USA.
- He died (At War) on December 24, 1944, aged 24 years, in Saint-Vith, Arrondissement de Verviers, Liège, Belgium.

- He was buried in Plot G Row 13 Grave 10 Henri-Chapelle American Cemetery and Memorial, Henri-Chapelle, Arrondissement de Verviers, Liège, Belgium.

The following information is also recorded for L. C.:
- Military Service on July 15, 1942, aged 21, in Houston, Texas, USA.
- Military Award.
- Military Award.

Notes:
- *L.C. Barneycastle served as a First Lieutenant & Pilot on B-24J "Lady Lora" #43-50799, 714th Bomber Squadron, 448th Bomber Group, Heavy, U.S. Army Air Force during World War II. He resided in Hardin County, Texas prior to the war. He enlisted in the Army on July 15, 1942 in Houston, Texas. He was noted, at the time of his enlistment, as being employed as a lumbermen and also as Single, without dependents. B-24J #43-50799 took off from Seething, England on a bombing mission over Euskirchen, Germany. They were hit by German ground anti-aircraft fire and crashed near St. Vith, Belgium during the war. L.C. Barneycastle was "Killed In Action" in this crash. He was awarded the Air Medal & the Purple Heart. Service # O-685258 His brother, SSgt Todd Barneycastle, was also Killed In Action during World War II.*
- *WWII.*
  (Death)
- *First Lieutenant & Pilot on B-24J "Lady Lora" #43-50799, 714th Bomber Squadron, 448th Bomber Group, Heavy, U.S. Army Air Force during World War II.*
  (Military Service)
- *Air Medal.*
  (Military Award)
- *Purple Heart.*
  (Military Award)

857. **INEZ HOOKS.**

L. C. Barneycastle[856], aged 22, married Inez Hooks on August 14, 1943.

858. **S SGT TODD BARNEYCASTLE** (see Descendants (7)) was born on June 1, 1922, in Votaw, Hardin, Texas, USA, to Elzie Barneycastle[253] and Susan Viola Bass[252].
- He was recorded in the census in 1940, aged about 18, in Votaw Qt, Justice Precinct, Hardin, Texas, USA.
- He died (At War) on February 1, 1944, aged 21 years, in At Sea.
- He was buried in Florence American Cemetery and Memorial, Florence, Città Metropolitana di Firenze, Toscana, Italy.

The following information is also recorded for Todd:
- Military Service on August 17, 1942, aged 20, in Houston, Texas, USA.
- Military Award.
- Military Award.

Notes:
- *Todd served as a Staff Sergeant & Engineer / Gunner on B-25G #42-64770, 379th Bomber Squadron, 310th Bomber Group, Medium, U.S. Army Air Force during World War II.He resided in Hardin County, Texas prior to the war. He enlisted in the Army on August 17, 1942 in Houston, Texas. He was noted, at the time of his enlistment, as being Single, without dependents. B-25G #42-64770 took off from Gambut, Libya on a shipping bombing mission over Portelargo Bay, near Leros Island, Greece. They were hit by anti-aircraft fire and crash in the sea about two miles of shore during the war. Todd was declared "Missing In Action" in this crash. He was awarded the Air Medal and the Purple Heart. Service # 18117439.*
- *WWII.*
  (Death)
- *Staff Sergeant & Engineer / Gunner on B-25G #42-64770, 379th Bomber Squadron, 310th Bomber Group, Medium, U.S. Army Air Force during World War II.*
  (Military Service)
- *Air Medal.*
  (Military Award)
- *Purple Heart.*
  (Military Award)

859. **LULA BARNEYCASTLE** (see Descendants (7)) was born on November 14, 1926, in Votaw, Hardin, Texas, USA, to Elzie Barneycastle[253] and Susan Viola Bass[252].
- She was recorded in the census in 1940, aged about 13, in Votaw Qt, Justice Precinct, Hardin, Texas, USA.
- She was recorded in the census on April 1, 1950, aged 23, in 3120 Caroline, Houston, Harris, Texas, United States.
- She died on September 27, 2000, aged 73 years, in West Jordan, Salt Lack, Utah, USA.

Note: *Lula is listed as Head and a Eunice Shelton is listed as Partner.*
   (Census)

860. EULA BARNEYCASTLE (see Descendants (7)) was born on February 24, 1928, in Votaw, Hardin, Texas, USA, to Elzie Barneycastle[253] and Susan Viola Bass[252].
    • She was recorded in the census in 1940, aged about 12, in Votaw Qt, Justice Precinct, Hardin, Texas, USA.
    • She died on May 28, 2005, aged 72 years, in Taylorsville, Salt Lack, Utah, USA.
    • She was buried in Votaw Cemetery, Votaw, Hardin County, Texas, USA.
    Note: *She was an active member of the LDS Church and held many positions including those of Stake Young Wo-men's president for 20 years in the Houston, Texas area. Talented Gospel Doctrine teacher, temple worker, and served with Walter as missionaries in the Charleston, West Virginia, Mission.*
    (Death)

861. WALTER LEE NEEL was born on April 17, 1907.
    • He died on December 9, 1982, aged 75.
    • He was buried in Votaw Cemetery, Votaw, Hardin County, Texas, USA.
        Walter Lee Neel, aged 46, married Eula Barneycastle[860], aged 25, on December 18, 1953 in Baytown, Harris, Texas, USA.

862. ALVIN LEON BASS (see Descendants (7)) was born on October 5, 1928 to Wilson Lafayette Bass[254] and Nannie Witt[255]. He died on July 29, 1952, aged 23 years, in La Porte, Texas, USA.

863. WILLIAM ANDREW BASS (see Descendants (8)) was born on July 15, 1921, in Arkansas, United States, to Allen Milford Bass[265] and Minnie Horton[266]. William Andrew became known as "Billy".
    • He was recorded in the census in 1930, aged about 8, in Police Jury Ward 2, Caddo, Louisiana, USA.
    • He was recorded in the census in 1940, aged about 18, in Oil, Ward 2, Caddo, Louisiana, USA.
    • He died on January 25, 1993, aged 71, in Everett, Washington.
    • He was buried in Evergreen Cemetery Everett, Snohomish County, Washington, USA.
    The following information is also recorded for Billy:
    • Military Service.
    Note: *WWII POW.*
        (Military Service)

864. SARAH FRANCIS BASS (see Descendants (8)) was born on October 23, 1925 to Allen Milford Bass[265] and Minnie Horton[266]. She died (At young age).

865. JOYCE IMOGENE BASS (see Descendants (8)) was born on September 19, 1917, in Saratoga, Hardin Co., TX, to John Riley Bass[267] and Viola Mae Shaw[268].
    • She died on November 9, 1998, aged 81, in Brazoria, Texas.
    • She was buried in 1998 in Sweeny, Brazoria, Texas, United States of America.

866. DOROTHY BASS (see Descendants (8)) was born on January 3, 1919, in Saratoga, Hardin, Texas, to John Riley Bass[267] and Viola Mae Shaw[268].
    • She died on December 11, 1919, as an infant.
    • She was buried in Guedry Cemetery, Batson, Hardin, Texas, United States of America.

867. MARGARET BASS (see Descendants (8)) was born on May 1, 1920, in Saratoga, Hardin, Texas, to John Riley Bass[267] and Viola Mae Shaw[268].
    • She died on December 18, 1920, as an infant, in Harris, Texas.
    • She was buried in Guedry Cemetery, Batson, Hardin, Texas, United States.

868. GLENN DONALD "JOHNNY" BASS (see Descendants (8)) was born on March 16, 1922, in Saratoga, Hardin, Texas, to John Riley Bass[267] and Viola Mae Shaw[268]. Glenn Donald "Johnny" became known as "Johnny".
    • He died on December 1, 1970, aged 48.
    • He was buried in Sweeny Cemetery, Sweeny, Brazoria, Texas, United States.

869. OLIS GENEVA BUTLER was born on February 12, 1922, in Eureka, Navarro, Texas, United States.
    • She died on January 25, 2011, aged 88, in Clute, Texas, United States.
    • She was buried in Sweeny Cemetery, Sweeny, Brazoria, Texas, United States.
        Glenn Donald "Johnny" Bass[868], aged 22, married Olis Geneva Butler, aged 22, on June 29, 1944 in Bay City, Matagorda, Texas, United States.

870. GWENDOLYN BASS (see Descendants (8)) was born on March 16, 1922, in Hardin, Texas, United States, to John Riley Bass[267] and Viola Mae Shaw[268].
- She died on September 29, 2014, aged 92, in Austin, Travis, Texas, United States.
- She was buried in 2014 in Lakeland Hills Memorial Park, Burnet, Burnet, Texas, United States.

871. MR. BASS (see Descendants (8)) was born in 1919 to Daniel Materson Bass[269] and Ione Shafer[270]. He died (At young age) in 1919, as an infant.

872. MR. BASS (see Descendants (8)) was born on January 6, 1919, in Moab, Grand, Utah, United States, to Daniel Materson Bass[269] and Katherine Gladys Lee[271].
- He died on January 6, 1919, as an infant, in Moab, Grand, Utah, United States.
- He was buried on January 7, 1919 in Grand Valley Cemetery, Moab, Grand, Utah, United States.

873. KATHERINE GLADYS BASS (see Descendants (8)) was born on September 6, 1925, in Westlake, Calcasieu, Louisiana, to Daniel Materson Bass[269] and Katherine Gladys Lee[271].
- She died on August 15, 2012, aged 86, in Ragley Beauregard, Louisiana, United States.
- She was buried in Westlake, Calcasieu Parish, Louisiana, United States of America.

874. KENNETH LYNELL BLUME was born on March 9, 1922, in Beaumont, Jefferson, Texas, to John Pickney Blume and Ida Merl Newell.
- He died on June 6, 2004, aged 82, in Lake Charles, Louisiana, United States.

The following information is also recorded for Kenneth Lynell:
- Military Service.

Note: *Served in WWII.*
  (Military Service)

Kenneth Lynell Blume, aged 20, married Katherine Gladys Bass[873], aged 16, on May 9, 1942 in St. Charles Missouri, United States. They had one daughter:
> Donna Lee Blume[2040] born on August 6, 1943 in Westlake, Calcasieu, Louisiana, United States; died on April 1, 2020

875. DANIEL MATERSON BASS JR. (see Descendants (8)) was born on October 7, 1926, in West Lake, Calcasieu, LA, to Daniel Materson Bass[269] and Katherine Gladys Lee[271].
- He died on September 4, 1994, aged 67.
- He was buried in Florien Cemetery, Florien, Sabine Parish, Louisiana, USA.

The following information is also recorded for Daniel Materson:
- Military Service.

Note: *U.S. Navy WWII.*
  (Military Service)

876. DOROTHY VICTORIA FARRIS was born on May 5, 1927, in Alco, Vernon Parish, Louisiana, USA. She died on November 14, 2015, aged 88, in Odessa, Ector, Texas, USA.

Daniel Materson Bass Jr.[875] married Dorothy Victoria Farris. They had five children:
> Daniel S Bass[2041] born on June 6, 1950 in Lake Charles, Calcasieu Parish, Louisiana, USA; died on March 1, 2010 in Pennsylvania, USA
> Brenda Bass[2043]
> John Bass[2045]
> Nita Bass[2047]
> Annette Bass[2049]

877. RAY LEONARD BASS (see Descendants (8)) was born on May 28, 1928, in Westlake, Calcasieu, Louisianna, to Daniel Materson Bass[269] and Katherine Gladys Lee[271].
- He died (At young age) on July 4, 1928, as an infant.
- He was buried in Westlake, Calcasieu Parish, Louisiana, United States of America.

878. KENNETH RILEY BASS SR. (see Descendants (8)) was born on December 19, 1938, in Lake Charles, Calcasieu, Louisiana, United States, to Daniel Materson Bass[269] and Katherine Gladys Lee[271]. He died on November 22, 2016, aged 77, in Houston, Harris, Texas, United States.

Kenneth Riley married twice. He was married to Martha L. Batten[879] and Catherine ?[880].

Direct Relations

879. MARTHA L. BATTEN was born in 1941.
> Kenneth Riley Bass Sr.[878] married Martha L. Batten. They had three children:
>> Kenneth Riley Bass Jr.[2051] born on August 5, 1960 in Lake Charles, Calcasieu Parish, Louisiana, USA; died on February 3, 2013 in Mooringsport, Caddo Parish, Louisiana, USA
>> Sharon Bass[2054]
>> Timothy Bass[2056]

880. CATHERINE ?.
> Kenneth Riley Bass Sr.[878] married Catherine ?.

881. HAZEL LOUISE BASS (see Descendants (8)) was born on July 28, 1933, in Westlake, Calcausieu, Louisiana, USA, to Benjamin Edward Bass[272] and Hazel Mae Laughlin[273].
- She was recorded in the census in 1940, aged about 6, in Westlake, Police Jury Ward 4, Calcasieu, Louisiana, USA.
- She died on January 22, 2012, aged 78.

882. JOHN HENRY HARREL.
> John Henry Harrel married Hazel Louise Bass[881], aged 17, on July 7, 1951.

883. DOROTHY BASS (see Descendants (8)) was born on March 2, 1935, in Lake Charles, Calcasieu, Louisiana, USA, to Benjamin Edward Bass[272] and Hazel Mae Laughlin[273].
- She was recorded in the census in 1940, aged about 5, in Westlake, Police Jury Ward 4, Calcasieu, Louisiana, USA.
- She died on June 18, 2018, aged 83, in Fernandia Beach, Nassau, Florida, USA.

884. MR. LASKER.
> Mr. Lasker married Dorothy Bass[883]. They had one son:
>> Mr. Lasker[2058]

885. BEN E BASS (see Descendants (8)) was born about 1938, in Louisiana, USA, to Benjamin Edward Bass[272] and Hazel Mae Laughlin[273]. He was recorded in the census in 1940, aged about 2, in Westlake, Police Jury Ward 4, Calcasieu, Louisiana, USA.

886. JEAN RALSTON (see Descendants (8)) was born on February 20, 1922, in Salt Lake City, Salt Lake, Utah, USA, to Alexander Gilbert Ralston[275] and Etta Mary Bass[274].
- She was recorded in the census on April 1, 1950, aged 28, in Red and Summers Sub Div, Monticello, San Juan, Utah, United States.
- She died on September 26, 2005, aged 83 years, in Mesa, Maricopa, Arizona, USA.

887. WILLIAM GRESKO was born on January 13, 1917, in Forest City, Susquehanna, Pennsylania, USA.
- He was recorded in the census on April 1, 1950, aged 33, in Red and Summers Sub Div, Monticello, San Juan, Utah, United States.
- He died on April 13, 2007, aged 90 years, in Gilbert, Maricopa, Arizona, USA.
> William Gresko, aged about 22, married Jean Ralston[886], aged about 17, in 1939. They had six children:
>> Myrna E Gresko[2060] born about 1942 in New Jersey, United States
>> William Mark Gresko[2061] born on February 9, 1943 in Moab, Grand, Utah, USA; died on September 22, 2013 in Cottonwood, Yavapai, Arizona, USA
>> Ronald Kay Gresko[2063] born on June 23, 1947 in Moab, Grand, Utah, USA; died on February 17, 2017 in Arizona, USA
>> Edward Cecil Gresko[2065] born about 1949 in Utah, United States
>> Etta Celia Gresko[2066] born about 1949 in Utah, United States
>> Mr. Gresko[2067]

888. MARK RALSTON (see Descendants (8)) was born on September 15, 1923, in Moab, Grand, Utah, United States, to Alexander Gilbert Ralston[275] and Etta Mary Bass[274]. He died on December 23, 1936, aged 13 years, in Wellington, Carbon, Utah, USA.

889. A. BRUCE BARTON (see Descendants (8)) was born about 1939, in Utah, United States, to Alpha B. Barton[276] and

Etta Mary Bass[274].
- He was recorded in the census in 1940, aged about 1, in Montecello Town, E Precinct 2, San Juan, Utah, USA.
- He was recorded in the census on April 1, 1950, aged about 10, in Hard Rd, Monticello, San Juan, Utah, United States.

890. GRANT B BARTON (see Descendants (8)) was born about 1940, in Utah, United States, to Alpha B. Barton[276] and Etta Mary Bass[274].
- He was recorded in the census in 1940, as an infant, in Montecello Town, E Precinct 2, San Juan, Utah, USA.
- He was recorded in the census on April 1, 1950, aged about 9, in Hard Rd, Monticello, San Juan, Utah, United States.

891. MARY ETTA BARTON (see Descendants (8)) was born about 1942, in Utah, United States, to Alpha B. Barton[276] and Etta Mary Bass[274]. She was recorded in the census on April 1, 1950, aged about 7, in Hard Rd, Monticello, San Juan, Utah, United States.

892. DIXIE BARTON (see Descendants (8)) was born about 1944, in Utah, United States, to Alpha B. Barton[276] and Etta Mary Bass[274]. She was recorded in the census on April 1, 1950, aged about 5, in Hard Rd, Monticello, San Juan, Utah, United States.

893. VINCENT HARRIS (see Descendants (8)) was born in April 1922 to Joseph Doyle Harris[278] and Mary Etta Bass[277]. He died in 2016, aged about 94.

894. LEO PATRICK HARRIS (see Descendants (8)) was born on January 19, 1925, in Price, Carbon, Utah, USA, to Joseph Doyle Harris[278] and Mary Etta Bass[277]. He died in January 1987, aged 61.

895. JOSEPH RILEY HARRIS (see Descendants (8)) was born on June 3, 1926, in Price, Carbon, Utah, USA, to Joseph Doyle Harris[278] and Mary Etta Bass[277]. He died on November 27, 1926, as an infant, in Carbon, Utah, USA.

896. MARY PATRICIA HARRIS (see Descendants (8)) was born in 1928, in Utah, USA, to Joseph Doyle Harris[278] and Mary Etta Bass[277].

897. DAVID JOSEPH HARRIS (see Descendants (8)) was born on September 19, 1929, in Price, Carbon, Utah, USA, to Joseph Doyle Harris[278] and Mary Etta Bass[277]. He died (Cancer) on April 9, 1977, aged 47, in Orange, Calafornia, USA.

898. MICHAEL JAMES HARRIS (see Descendants (8)) was born on December 3, 1933, in Utah, USA, to Joseph Doyle Harris[278] and Mary Etta Bass[277]. Michael James became known as "Jim and MJ".

- He was recorded in the census on April 1, 1950, aged 16, in Carbonville, Carbon, Utah, United States.
- He died on June 17, 2017, aged 83, in Alaska, USA.

Note: *An original Ice Road Trucker, not from the TV show, the real deal. When oil was first discovered in the Northern Slope area in the 1960s, the family was living in Soldotna, Alaska. Before that he'd worked for the Road Commision in Valdez, Alaska as a heavy equipment operator. This was about 1950 when Alaska was still a territory, not yet a state.*

899. BETTY JEAN FLICKINGER.
Michael James Harris[898], aged 22, married Betty Jean Flickinger on December 29, 1955. They had two daughters:
Janis Mary Harris[2068] born on October 21, 1957 in Glennallen, Alaska, USA
Nancy Kathryn Harris[2069] born on May 18, 1959 in Glennallen, Alaska, USA

900. MARY ETTA HARRIS (see Descendants (8)) was born about 1937, in Utah, United States, to Joseph Doyle Harris[278] and Mary Etta Bass[277]. She was recorded in the census on April 1, 1950, aged about 12, in Carbonville, Carbon, Utah, United States.

901. BERNADETTE HARRIS (see Descendants (8)) was born about 1939, in Utah, United States, to Joseph Doyle Harris[278] and Mary Etta Bass[277].
- She was recorded in the census on April 1, 1950, aged about 10, in Carbonville, Carbon, Utah, United States.
- She died in 2016, aged about 77.

902. JOHN PAUL HARRIS (see Descendants (8)) was born about 1942, in Utah, United States, to Joseph Doyle Harris[278] and Mary Etta Bass[277]. He was recorded in the census on April 1, 1950, aged about 7, in Carbonville, Carbon, Utah, United States.

903. ROBERT THOMAS HARRIS (see Descendants (8)) was born on July 22, 1946, in Price, Carbon, Utah, USA, to Joseph Doyle Harris[278] and Mary Etta Bass[277]. He died on January 20, 1947, as an infant.

904. MERRILLYN STEVENS (see Descendants (33)) was born on May 9, 1939, in Provo, Utah, Utah, United States, to Leonard Merrill Stevens[282] and Eva Elizabeth Bass[281].
- She died on January 4, 2021, aged 81, in St. George, Washington, Utah, United States.
- She was buried on January 11, 2021 in Tonaquint Cemetery, St. George, Washington, Utah, United States.

905. RONALD PERKINS GUYMON was born on August 25, 1938, in Blanding, San Juan, Utah, United States.
- He died on February 3, 2022, aged 83, in St. George, Washington, Utah, United States.
- He was buried on February 11, 2022 in Tonaquint Cemetery, Saint George, Washington, Utah, United States.
  Ronald Perkins Guymon, aged 22, married Merrillyn Stevens[904], aged 21, on February 11, 1961 in Manti, Sanpete, Utah, United States.

906. WILLIAM REED STEVENS (see Descendants (33)) was born on June 2, 1942, in Moab, Grand, Utah, USA, to Leonard Merrill Stevens[282] and Eva Elizabeth Bass[281].
- He died on January 23, 1997, aged 54, in Chandler, Maricopa, Arizona, USA.
- He was buried in Mesa Cemetery, Mesa, Maricopa, Arizona, United States.

907. BETTY ANN JONES.
William Reed Stevens[906] married Betty Ann Jones. They had five children:
Mr. Stevens[2071]
Ms. Stevens[2072]
Ms. Stevens[2073]
Mr. Stevens[2074]
Mr. Stevens[2075]

908. LOUVENIA DAVIS (see Descendants (10)) was born on December 10, 1928, in Alabama, USA, to Athen Davis[290] and Lottie Johnson Hall[291]. She died on December 30, 2008, aged 80, in Andalusia, Covington, Alabama, USA.

909. MARVETTE FAYE DAVIS (see Descendants (10)) was born on November 3, 1930, in Alabama, USA, to Athen Davis[290] and Lottie Johnson Hall[291]. She died on December 4, 2014, aged 84, in Pensacola, Escambia, Florida, USA.
Marvette Faye married her third cousin, James Thomas White Sr.[843].
James Thomas White Sr.[843], aged 23, married Marvette Faye Davis, aged 20, on December 23, 1950 in Andalusia, Covington, Alabama, USA. They had four sons:
Steve White[2027]
Mr. White[2029]
Mr. White[2031]
Mr. White[2032]

910. JAMES C DAVIS (see Descendants (10)) was born about 1933 to Athen Davis[290] and Lottie Johnson Hall[291].

911. DOROTHY HELEN TEEL (see Descendants (11)) was born on December 20, 1922, in Alabama, United States, to William Greeley Teel[294] and Rubie L Kelley[792].
- She was recorded in the census in 1940, aged about 17, in 1 Range 14, Covington, Alabama, USA.
- She was recorded in the census on April 1, 1950, aged 27, in 316 Central Ave, Laurel, Jones, Mississippi, United States.
- She died on September 23, 1983, aged 60, in Alabama, United States.
- She was buried in Pleasant Home Baptist Cemetery, Covington, Alabama, USA.

912. ORANGE ARNOLD HERRINGTON was born on December 12, 1912, in Jones County, Mississippi, USA.
- He was recorded in the census on April 1, 1950, aged 37, in 316 Central Ave, Laurel, Jones, Mississippi, United States.
- He died on November 18, 1985, aged 72, in Alabama, United States.
- He was buried in Pleasant Home Baptist Cemetery, Covington, Alabama, USA.
  Orange Arnold Herrington married Dorothy Helen Teel[911]. They had three sons:
  Larry Bradley Herrington[2076] born on March 10, 1945 in Florida, United States; died on November 29, 2014
  Jimmie T Herrington[2078] born about 1947 in Mississippi, United States

Joseph A Herrington[2079]

913. WILLIAM OLEN TEEL (see Descendants (11)) was born on October 25, 1925, in Alabama, United States, to William Greeley Teel[294] and Rubie L Kelley[792].
- He was recorded in the census in 1940, aged about 14, in 1 Range 14, Covington, Alabama, USA.
- He was recorded in the census on April 1, 1950, aged 24, in Proceeding South West from Pleasant Home School of Fales, Hart, Covington, Alabama, United States.
- He died on December 26, 1974, aged 49, in Wing, Covington, Alabama, United States.
- He was buried in Pleasant Home Baptist Cemetery, Covington, Alabama, USA.

The following information is also recorded for William Olen:
- Military Service.

Note: *Pvt. US Marine Corps.*
(Military Service)

914. RICHARD ALEX TEEL JR. (see Descendants (11)) was born on March 30, 1928 to Alex Richard Teel[297] and Annie Bell Padgett[298].
- He was recorded in the census in 1930, aged about 2, in Fairfield, Covington, Alabama, USA.
- He died on May 29, 1983, aged 55.
- He was buried in Conecuh River Baptist Cemetery, Andalusia, Covington, Alabama, USA.

915. JEWEL GERTRUDE FUQUA was born on February 16, 1936.
- She died on January 14, 1974, aged 37, in Andalusia, Covington, Alabama, USA.
- She was buried in Conecuh River Baptist Cemetery, Andalusia, Covington, Alabama, USA.

Richard Alex Teel Jr.[914], aged 27, married Jewel Gertrude Fuqua, aged 19, on July 1, 1955.

916. DONALD TEEL (see Descendants (11)) was born on May 14, 1930 to Alex Richard Teel[297] and Annie Bell Padgett[298].
- He died on May 19, 1998, aged 68.
- He was buried in Andalusia Memorial Cemetery, Andalusia, Covington, Alabama, USA.

917. RUFUS ARNOLD TEEL TEEL (see Descendants (11)) was born on February 4, 1934 to Alex Richard Teel[297] and Annie Bell Padgett[298].
- He died on May 30, 1936, aged 2.
- He was buried in Conecuh River Baptist Cemetery, Andalusia, Covington, Alabama, USA.

918. WAYNE CARROLL JOHNSON (see Descendants (11)) was born on April 3, 1936, in Andalusia, Covington, Alabama, USA, to Autrey Lewis Johnson[305] and Martha Lena Teel[304]. He died on April 8, 2002, aged 66, in Fort Walton Beach, Okaloosa, Florida, USA.

919. JOHN EVERETTE TEEL (see Descendants (11)) was born on January 9, 1942 to Ruben Everett Teel[306] and Eula May Jackson[307].
- He died on July 31, 1986, aged 44.
- He was buried in Andalusia Memorial Cemetery, Andalusia, Covington, Alabama, USA.

920. JAMES JERY TEEL TEEL (see Descendants (11)) was born on September 21, 1951 to Ruben Everett Teel[306] and Eula May Jackson[307]. He died on November 6, 2013, aged 62, in Opelika, Lee, Alabama, USA.

921. CAROLYN CARY (see Descendants (11)) was born about 1943, in Alabama, United States, to Orlando Dudley Cary[309] and Bernice Cathleen Teel[308]. She was recorded in the census on April 1, 1950, aged about 6, in Castleberry Brooklyn Rd., Brooklyn, Conecuh, Alabama, United States.

922. RICHARD DERHYL CARY (see Descendants (11)) was born on November 14, 1944, in Alabama, United States, to Orlando Dudley Cary[309] and Bernice Cathleen Teel[308].
- He was recorded in the census on April 1, 1950, aged 5, in Castleberry Brooklyn Rd., Brooklyn, Conecuh, Alabama, United States.
- He died on November 20, 1996, aged 52.
- He was buried in Brooklyn Baptist Church Cemetery, Evergreen, Conecuh County, Alabama, USA.

923. HENRYETTA NADINE BRADLEY was born on January 13, 1948.
- She died on July 8, 1998, aged 50.
- She was buried in Brooklyn Baptist Church Cemetery, Evergreen, Conecuh County, Alabama, USA.

Direct Relations

Richard Derhyl Cary[922], aged 21, married Henryetta Nadine Bradley, aged 17, on November 16, 1965. They had one son:
    Edwin Kieth Cary[2080] born on August 4, 1971; died on August 4, 1971

924. CAROL JEAN HASSELL (see Descendants (13)) was born about 1941, in Alabama, United States, to Fredrick Harling Schmidt[315] and Gladys Teel[314]. She was recorded in the census on April 1, 1950, aged about 8, in Andalusia, Covington, Alabama, United States.

925. BARBARA BURNS SCHMIDT (see Descendants (13)) was born on November 17, 1947, in Pittsboro, Chatham, North Carolina, USA, to Fredrick Harling Schmidt[315] and Gladys Teel[314].
- She died on November 28, 1992, aged 45.
- She was buried in Alabama Heritage Cemetery, Montgomery, Alabama, USA.

926. JIMMIE JOE HASSELL (see Descendants (13)) was born about 1936, in Alabama, United States, to Frank Pete Hassell[316] and Gladys Teel[314].
- He was recorded in the census in 1940, aged about 4, in Carlton La???, Andalusia, Covington, Alabama, USA.
- He was recorded in the census on April 1, 1950, aged about 13, in Andalusia, Covington, Alabama, United States.

927. JERRY DONALD HASSELL (see Descendants (13)) was born about 1939, in Alabama, United States, to Frank Pete Hassell[316] and Gladys Teel[314].
- He was recorded in the census in 1940, aged about 1, in Carlton La???, Andalusia, Covington, Alabama, USA.
- He was recorded in the census on April 1, 1950, aged about 10, in Andalusia, Covington, Alabama, United States.

928. SHARON A HASSELL (see Descendants (13)) was born in Alabama, United States to Frank Pete Hassell[316] and Gladys Teel[314]. She was recorded in the census on April 1, 1950, in Andalusia, Covington, Alabama, United States.

929. MARY JANE TEEL (see Descendants (14)) was born to James Elijah Teel[320] and Sara Nancy Teel[321].

930. OPAL VIRGINIA SPENCE (see Descendants (34)) was born on August 24, 1934, in Florida, USA, to Floyd S Spence[323] and Genola Bass[322].
- She was recorded in the census in 1940, aged about 5, in Spring Street, Crestview, 3, Okaloosa, Florida, USA.
- She died on March 5, 1969, aged 34 years.

Opal Virginia married twice. She was married to Billie Batson[931] and Oscar L. Brock[932].

931. BILLIE BATSON.
    Billie Batson married Opal Virginia Spence[930]. They had two sons:
        David Jonathan Batson[2081] born on January 5, 1961
        Robin Mario Batson[2083] born on January 26, 1964

932. OSCAR L. BROCK.
    Oscar L. Brock married Opal Virginia Spence[930]. They had one daughter:
        Dawn Denise Brock[2084] born on August 25, 1966

933. CLYDE AUTRY SPENCE (see Descendants (34)) was born on October 17, 1937, in Florida, USA, to Floyd S Spence[323] and Genola Bass[322].
- He was recorded in the census in 1940, aged about 2, in Spring Street, Crestview, 3, Okaloosa, Florida, USA.
- He died on September 10, 1987, aged 49 years.
- He was buried in New Bethany Cemetery, Holt, Okaloosa, Florida, USA.

934. PHYLLIS D. BAUGHMAN was born on March 1, 1941, in Oklahoma, USA.
    Clyde Autry Spence[933], aged 17, married Phyllis D. Baughman, aged 14, on April 30, 1955. They had seven children:
        Carl Leon Spence[2086] born on May 31, 1956 in Arizona, USA; died on June 11, 1956 in Pima, Arizona, USA
        Dixie Irene Spence[2087] born on September 15, 1957
        Rhonda Sue Spence[2089] born on November 21, 1958
        Robert Leon Spence[2091] born on July 31, 1961
        James Scott Spence[2093] born on September 14, 1962
        Floyd Colon Spence[2094] born on January 28, 1965
        Clyde Autry Spence Jr.[2096] born on August 7, 1966

935. WADE NATHAN WILKINSON (see Descendants (36)) was born on July 11, 1932, in Holt, Okaloosa, Florida, USA, to Woodrow A. Wilkinson[328] and Martha Naomi Bass[327].
- He was recorded in the census in 1940, aged about 7, in Precinct, Santa Rosa, Florida, USA.

- He was recorded in the census on April 1, 1950, aged 17, in Penny Creek Road Between Sections 14 and 15 Proceeding North, Milligan, Okaloosa, Florida, United States.
936. NELLIE HENRY was born on July 11, 1932, in Baker, Okaloosa, Florida, USA.
Wade Nathan Wilkinson[935], aged 17, married Nellie Henry, aged 17, on July 8, 1950 in Baker, Okaloosa, Florida, USA. They had four children:
Deborah Ann Wilkinson[2097] born on August 27, 1951 in Florala, Covington, Alabama, USA
Delmus Nathan Wilkinson[2099] born on March 3, 1953 in Florala, Covington, Alabama, USA
Joy Denise Wilkinson[2102] born on September 10, 1955 in Florala, Covington, Alabama, USA
Janet Lee Wilkinson[2104] born on February 12, 1959 in Florala, Covington, Alabama, USA

937. FLOYCE GENELLE WILKINSON (see Descendants (36)) was born on February 12, 1934, in Holt, Okaloosa, Florida, USA, to Woodrow A. Wilkinson[328] and Martha Naomi Bass[327].
- She was recorded in the census in 1940, aged about 6, in Precinct, Santa Rosa, Florida, USA.
- She was recorded in the census on April 1, 1950, aged 16, in Penny Creek Road Between Sections 14 and 15 Proceeding North, Milligan, Okaloosa, Florida, United States.
938. JOSEPH SHOVEN STEELE was born on July 5, 1926, in Rockingham, Bacon, Georgia, USA. He was recorded in the census on April 1, 1950, aged 23, in Penny Creek Road Between Sections 14 and 15 Proceeding North, Milligan, Okaloosa, Florida, United States.
Joseph Shoven Steele, aged 22, married Floyce Genelle Wilkinson[937], aged 15, on February 25, 1949. They had four children:
Joseph Wayne Steele[2106] born on August 26, 1951 in Florala, Covington, Alabama, USA
Larry Dale Steele[2109] born on November 19, 1953 in Murray, Salt Lake, Utah, USA
Donna Marie Steele[2111] born on January 21, 1957
Terry Michael Steele[2113] born on May 19, 1958; died on May 23, 2000

939. LORINE ANNETTE WILKINSON (see Descendants (36)) was born on January 12, 1936, in Holt, Okaloosa, Florida, USA, to Woodrow A. Wilkinson[328] and Martha Naomi Bass[327].
- She was recorded in the census in 1940, aged about 4, in Precinct, Santa Rosa, Florida, USA.
- She was recorded in the census on April 1, 1950, aged 14, in Penny Creek Road Between Sections 14 and 15 Proceeding North, Milligan, Okaloosa, Florida, United States.
940. ROY H. JOHNSON was born on February 3, 1934.
Roy H. Johnson, aged 23, married Lorine Annette Wilkinson[939], aged 21, on August 24, 1957. They had one daughter:
Lois Anette Johnson[2115] born on August 23, 1958

941. JUDITH ELAINE WILKINSON (see Descendants (36)) was born on January 27, 1938, in Cold Water, Santa Rosa, Florida, USA, to Woodrow A. Wilkinson[328] and Martha Naomi Bass[327].
- She was recorded in the census in 1940, aged about 2, in Precinct, Santa Rosa, Florida, USA.
- She was recorded in the census on April 1, 1950, aged 12, in Penny Creek Road Between Sections 14 and 15 Proceeding North, Milligan, Okaloosa, Florida, United States.
- She died on March 18, 2012, aged 74 years.
942. BILLY REGISTER was born on July 6, 1934.
Billy Register, aged 23, married Judith Elaine Wilkinson[941], aged 19, on November 1, 1957. They had three children:
Marcus Dean Register[2117] born on August 7, 1960
Matthew Ward Register[2119] born on August 24, 1964
Martha Grace Register[2121] born on October 6, 1970

943. IRMA ARLEEN WILKINSON (see Descendants (36)) was born on September 12, 1940, in Cold Water, Santa Rosa, Florida, USA, to Woodrow A. Wilkinson[328] and Martha Naomi Bass[327].
- She was recorded in the census on April 1, 1950, aged 9, in Penny Creek Road Between Sections 14 and 15 Proceeding North, Milligan, Okaloosa, Florida, United States.
- She died on May 24, 2004, aged 63 years.
944. EUGENE FLEMING.
Eugene Fleming married Irma Arleen Wilkinson[943]. They had three children:
Phillip Eugene Fleming[2123] born on December 30, 1958
Laura Lenelle Fleming[2126] born on December 31, 1960
Karen Lorine Fleming[2128] born on January 3, 1964

945. ROLAND DOUGLAS WILKINSON (see Descendants (36)) was born on March 17, 1942, in Holt, Okaloosa, Florida, USA, to Woodrow A. Wilkinson[328] and Martha Naomi Bass[327]. He was recorded in the census on April 1, 1950, aged 8, in Penny Creek Road Between Sections 14 and 15 Proceeding North, Milligan, Okaloosa, Florida, United States.

Direct Relations

946. JUDITH HARNESS.
> Roland Douglas Wilkinson[945] married Judith Harness. They had two children:
>> Rachel Wilkinson[2130]
>> Joshua Wilkinson[2131]

947. LINDA ALETHA WILKINSON (see Descendants (36)) was born on April 5, 1943, in Holt, Okaloosa, Florida, USA, to Woodrow A. Wilkinson[328] and Martha Naomi Bass[327]. She was recorded in the census on April 1, 1950, aged 6, in Penny Creek Road Between Sections 14 and 15 Proceeding North, Milligan, Okaloosa, Florida, United States.

948. WILLIAM MOONEY was born on July 25, 1927.
> William Mooney, aged 37, married Linda Aletha Wilkinson[947], aged 21, on March 3, 1965, and they were divorced.

949. MARCIA GLENDOLYN WILKINSON (see Descendants (36)) was born on April 24, 1947, in Baker, Okaloosa, Florida, USA, to Woodrow A. Wilkinson[328] and Martha Naomi Bass[327]. She was recorded in the census on April 1, 1950, aged 2, in Penny Creek Road Between Sections 14 and 15 Proceeding North, Milligan, Okaloosa, Florida, United States.

950. JERRY DOTSON was born on May 10, 1946.
> Jerry Dotson, aged 17, married Marcia Glendolyn Wilkinson[949], aged 16, on November 1, 1963, and they were divorced. They had two sons:
>> Ted Dotson[2132] born on July 18, 1964
>> Tracy Dotson[2134] born on November 25, 1965

951. NEIL KEITH WILKINSON (see Descendants (36)) was born on September 6, 1951, in Florala, Covington, Alabama, USA, to Woodrow A. Wilkinson[328] and Martha Naomi Bass[327].
• He died on April 30, 1971, aged 19 years, in United States and Territory.
The following information is also recorded for Neil Keith:
• Military Service in 1971.
• Religion: Baptist.

952. WENTON CURTIS WILKINSON (see Descendants (37)) was born on February 15, 1934, in Florida, United States, to Glen Curtis Wilkinson[330] and Christian Ottie Lee Bass[329]. He was recorded in the census on April 1, 1950, aged 16, in S on Blockwater Boss Road, Milligan, Okaloosa, Florida, United States.
Wenton Curtis married twice. He was married to Eloise Henry[953] and Mary Sue Walkup[954].

953. ELOISE HENRY.
> Wenton Curtis Wilkinson[952], aged about 25, married Eloise Henry in 1959.

954. MARY SUE WALKUP was born on January 22, 1934.
> Wenton Curtis Wilkinson[952], aged 25, married Mary Sue Walkup, aged 25, on December 18, 1959. They had five children:
>> Ronald Daune Tuley[2136] born on October 16, 1953 in Dallas, Dallas, Texas, USA; died on September 5, 1990
>> Pamela Ann Tuley[2137] born on March 5, 1955 in Dallas, Dallas, Texas, USA
>> Robert Tuley[2140] born on May 11, 1956 in Dallas, Dallas, Texas, USA; died on May 24, 1974 in Baker, Okaloosa, Florida, USA
>> Randall Glen Wilkinson[2141] born on November 16, 1960 in Dallas, Dallas, Texas, USA
>> Warren Craig Wilkinson[2144] born on December 26, 1962 in Dallas, Dallas, Texas, USA

955. DOROTHY JOAN WILKINSON (see Descendants (37)) was born on April 8, 1936, in Holt, Okaloosa, Florida, USA, to Glen Curtis Wilkinson[330] and Christian Ottie Lee Bass[329]. She was recorded in the census on April 1, 1950, aged 13, in S on Blockwater Boss Road, Milligan, Okaloosa, Florida, United States.

956. EUGENE ODELL WOODARD was born on March 28, 1937, in Jackson City, Madison, Tennessee, USA. He died on April 9, 1991, aged 54 years, in Columbus, Muscogee, Georgia, USA.
> Eugene Odell Woodard, aged 18, married Dorothy Joan Wilkinson[955], aged 19, on December 16, 1955 in Tazwell, Tazewell, Virginia, USA, and they were divorced. They had one daughter:
>> Gail Denise Woodard[2146] born on August 30, 1957 in Pensacola, Escambia, Florida, USA

957. INA MAE WILKINSON (see Descendants (37)) was born on March 19, 1938, in Milton, Santa Rosa, Florida, USA, to Glen Curtis Wilkinson[330] and Christian Ottie Lee Bass[329]. She was recorded in the census on April 1, 1950, aged 12, in S on Blockwater Boss Road, Milligan, Okaloosa, Florida, United States.

958. DONNIE JAY WALTERS was born on January 31, 1939, in Laurel, Jones, Mississippi, USA.
> Donnie Jay Walters, aged 36, married Ina Mae Wilkinson[957], aged 37, on July 30, 1975 in Holt, Okaloosa, Florida, USA. They had four children:

Don Monwell Walters[2150] born on October 20, 1958 in Hattiesburg, Forest, Mississippi, USA
Rodrick Jerome Walters[2152] born on May 17, 1961 in Pensacola, Escambia, Florida, USA
Kenneth Layne Walters[2154] born on October 29, 1963 in Pensacola, Escambia, Florida, USA; died on September 27, 1985 in Philadelphia, Philadelphia, Pennsylvania, USA
Kim Dawn Walters[2156] born in 1966

959. MONA IDEZ WILKINSON (see Descendants (37)) was born on February 8, 1940, in Florida, United States, to Glen Curtis Wilkinson[330] and Christian Ottie Lee Bass[329].
- She was recorded in the census on April 1, 1950, aged 10, in S on Blockwater Boss Road, Milligan, Okaloosa, Florida, United States.
- She died on June 2, 1985, aged 45 years, in Niceville, Okaloosa, Florida, USA.

960. ALFRED COOK JR. was born in November 14 A.D.
Alfred Cook Jr. married Mona Idez Wilkinson[959], and they were divorced. They had three daughters:
Lisa Marie Cook[2158] born on July 31, 1968
Yevette Lee Cook[2160] born on October 1, 1971
Jennifer Nell Cook[2161] born on May 17, 1976

961. LARY RODNEY WILKINSON (see Descendants (37)) was born on June 16, 1942, in Holt, Okaloosa, Florida, USA, to Glen Curtis Wilkinson[330] and Christian Ottie Lee Bass[329]. He was recorded in the census on April 1, 1950, aged 7, in S on Blockwater Boss Road, Milligan, Okaloosa, Florida, United States.

962. MARIE ANTONETTE CASCONE was born on November 23, 1942, in Jacksonville, Duval, Florida, USA.
Lary Rodney Wilkinson[961] married Marie Antonette Cascone. They had four children:
Lary Rodney Wilkinson Jr.[2162] born on November 28, 1968 in Jacksonville, Duval, Florida, USA
Brett Alan Wilkinson[2163] born on November 28, 1972 in Jacksonville, Duval, Florida, USA
Lisa Marie Wilkinson[2164] born on September 27, 1974 in Jacksonville, Duval, Florida, USA
Katrina Marie Wilkinson[2165] born on October 14, 1975 in Jacksonville, Duval, Florida, USA

963. CHADRICK EARL WILKINSON (see Descendants (37)) was born on November 6, 1944, in Holt, Okaloosa, Florida, USA, to Glen Curtis Wilkinson[330] and Christian Ottie Lee Bass[329]. Chadrick Earl became known as "Chad". He was recorded in the census on April 1, 1950, aged 5, in S on Blockwater Boss Road, Milligan, Okaloosa, Florida, United States.

964. JUDY GAIL KENNEDY was born on June 23, 1946.
Chadrick Earl Wilkinson[963], aged 19, married Judy Gail Kennedy, aged 18, on October 22, 1964 in Crestview, Okaloosa, Florida, USA. They had two children:
Dena Gail Wilkinson[2166] born on September 20, 1965
Christopher Del Wilkinson[2168] born on August 1, 1969 in Milton, Santa Rosa, Florida, USA

965. GLYNDA CAROL WILKINSON (see Descendants (37)) was born on January 2, 1947, in Holt, Okaloosa, USA, to Glen Curtis Wilkinson[330] and Christian Ottie Lee Bass[329]. She was recorded in the census on April 1, 1950, aged 3, in S on Blockwater Boss Road, Milligan, Okaloosa, Florida, United States.
Note: *Glynda helped Genola Spence [Bass] with the original Bass Family Record and her and her daughter Kim continued the work and produced updates at least through 2000. We met for the first time at the Baker reunion on July 22, 2017. We had a pleasant chat about family and the work we had each done on the family documents. I was very excited to meet her and wish we had taken the time to talk longer and hope to in the future. -Nicholas Bruce Bass.*

966. JAMES CHARLES CUPP was born on December 14, 1945, in Pensacola, Escambia, Florida, USA.
James Charles Cupp, aged 29, married Glynda Carol Wilkinson[965], aged 28, on December 5, 1975 in Holt, Okaloosa, Florida, USA. They had three children:
Kimberly Ann Cupp[2170] born on June 12, 1968 in Milton, Santa Rosa, Florida, USA
James Landre Cupp[2172] born on August 8, 1972 in Pensacola, Escambia, Florida, USA
Dorothy Leigh Cupp[2173] born on May 2, 1981 in Milton, Santa Rosa, Florida, USA

967. NORMAN CURTIS WILKINSON (see Descendants (37)) was born on March 30, 1954, in Florala, Covington, Alabama, USA, to Glen Curtis Wilkinson[330] and Christian Ottie Lee Bass[329]. He died (Heart Attack) on May 5, 2007, aged 53 years, in Holt, Okaloosa, Florida, USA.
Norman Curtis married three times. He was married to Wanda Procktor[968], Roberta Marie Ogle[969] and Tammy Sue Beasley[970].

968. WANDA PROCKTOR.
Norman Curtis Wilkinson[967], aged about 20, married Wanda Procktor in 1974. They had two children:
Candace Delane Wilkinson[2174] born on May 8, 1981
Shane Curtis Wilkinson[2176] born on July 28, 1983

969. ROBERTA MARIE OGLE. Roberta Marie became known as "Robbie".
> Norman Curtis Wilkinson[967], aged 24, married Roberta Marie Ogle on October 6, 1978 in Okaloosa, Florida, USA, and they were divorced.

970. TAMMY SUE BEASLEY was born in February 3 A.D., in Sulphur, Oklahoma, USA.
> Tammy Sue married twice. She was married to Norman Curtis Wilkinson[967] and Michael Joe Peckham.
>> Norman Curtis Wilkinson[967], aged 26, married Tammy Sue Beasley, aged 1977, on October 31, 1980, and they were divorced. They had two children:
>>> Candace Delane Wilkinson[2178] born on May 8, 1981 in Oklahoma City, Oklahoma, Oklahoma, USA
>>> Shane Curtis Wilkinson[2180] born on July 28, 1983 in Percell, McClain, Oklahoma, USA
>> Michael Joe Peckham married Tammy Sue Beasley.

971. SELINA BENITA WILKINSON (see Descendants (37)) was born on June 25, 1957, in Florala, Covington, Alabama, USA, to Glen Curtis Wilkinson[330] and Christian Ottie Lee Bass[329].
972. DUANE ALLEN DAWSON JR. was born on December 27, 1957, in Cottage Grove, Lane, Oregon, USA.
> Duane Allen Dawson Jr., aged 17, married Selina Benita Wilkinson[971], aged 18, on November 7, 1975 in Milton, Santa Rosa, Florida, USA. They had one son:
>> Duane Allen Dawson III[2182] born on July 12, 1988 in Wahiawa, Honolulu, Hawaii, USA

973. REBECCA LOUISE WILKINSON (see Descendants (37)) was born on March 4, 1959, in Milton, Santa Rosa, Florida, USA, to Glen Curtis Wilkinson[330] and Christian Ottie Lee Bass[329].
974. DONNIE LEROY SALTER was born on February 22, 1958, in Milton, Santa Rosa, Florida, USA.
> Donnie Leroy Salter, aged 21, married Rebecca Louise Wilkinson[973], aged 20, on July 27, 1979 in Milton, Santa Rosa, Florida, USA. They had one son:
>> Demetrius LaRoy Salter[2183] born on April 12, 1979 in Milton, Santa Rosa, Florida, USA

975. CLARENCE DEVON SUMMERLIN (see Descendants (38)) was born on March 7, 1937, in Holt, Okaloosa, Florida, USA, to Jesse David Summerlin Jr.[332] and Ossie Mae Bass[331]. He was recorded in the census on April 1, 1950, aged 13, in South on Summerlin Road in Section 22, Milligan, Okaloosa, Florida, United States.
> Clarence Devon married twice. He was married to Mary Beth Burnett[976] and Mary Annice Cotton[977].
976. MARY BETH BURNETT.
> Clarence Devon Summerlin[975], aged 19, married Mary Beth Burnett in August 1956 in Holt, Okaloosa, Florida, USA, and they were divorced. They had three children:
>> Charles David Summerlin[2184] born on February 1, 1958
>> Kathy Ann Summerlin[2186] born on March 28, 1960
>> Kimberly Jan Summerlin[2187] born on March 11, 1963 in Pensacola, Escambia, Florida, USA; died on March 13, 1963 in Pensacola, Escambia, Florida, USA
977. MARY ANNICE COTTON was born on February 4, 1946, in Baker, Okaloosa, Florida, USA.
> Clarence Devon Summerlin[975], aged 31, married Mary Annice Cotton, aged 22, on November 9, 1968 in Milton, Santa Rosa, Florida, USA.

978. BOBBY MCGLAUN (see Descendants (39)) was born on September 24, 1933 to James Hollie McGlaun[333] and Anna Reeder[334].
> • He died on June 5, 1985, aged 51.
> • He was buried in Andalusia Memorial Cemetery, Andalusia, Covington, Alabama, USA.
979. BETTY HENLEY was born about 1936, in Alabama, United States, to Woodrow Henley and Tessie Jewell Lawson. She was recorded in the census on April 1, 1950, aged about 13, in Breston Road, Andalusia, Covington, Alabama, United States.
> Bobby McGlaun[978] married Betty Henley. They had four children, and assumed parenthood of another one:
>> Joel Ray McGlaun[2188] born on October 25, 1954
>> Mike Dewayne McGlaun[2189] born on October 9, 1957
>> Randy Lamar McGlaun[2190] born on September 11, 1964
>> Lee McGlaun[2192] by adoption
>> Erin McGlaun[2193]

980. RUBY NELL MCGLAUN (see Descendants (40)) was born on November 7, 1925 to Willie Oscar McGlaun[335] and Clara Mae Schofield[336].
981. RAY CAUSIE.
> Ray Causie married Ruby Nell McGlaun[980]. They had one daughter:
>> Judy Ann Causie[2195] born on September 24, 1944

982. MARY ETTA MCGLAUN (see Descendants (40)) was born on January 5, 1928, in Alabama, United States, to Willie Oscar McGlaun[335] and Clara Mae Schofield[336]. She was recorded in the census on April 1, 1950, aged 22, in Sanford, Covington, Alabama, United States.

983. HORACE WORLEY.
> Horace Worley married Mary Etta McGlaun[982]. They had four children:
>> Gary Wayne Worley[2197] born on August 14, 1952
>> Pamela Jun Worley[2198] born on June 15, 1954
>> Danny David Worley[2199] born on May 16, 1957
>> Robin Don Worley[2200] born on January 1, 1959

984. JAMES KENNETH MCGLAUN (see Descendants (40)) was born on June 25, 1930, in Andalusia, Covington, Alabama, USA, to Willie Oscar McGlaun[335] and Clara Mae Schofield[336].
- He was recorded in the census on April 1, 1950, aged 19, in Sanford, Covington, Alabama, United States.

985. BONNIE BROWN was born on October 30, 1937, in Andalusia, Covington, Alabama, USA.
- She died on January 17, 2021, aged 83.
- She was buried in Pine Level Baptist Church Cemetery.

Note: *Bonnie loved her family with all her heart. She was tough as nails on the outside but had a heart of gold and was always willing to help in any way she could. She loved to cook, collecting teddy bears and dolls, and gardening. She is famous for her biscuits, buttermilk pies, cornbread, and most especially her chocolate cakes.She came to faith a little later in life, but she loved the Lord and studied her Bible daily. She was a long time member of Pine Level Baptist Church, where she served in different outreach ministries. She will be missed dearly by her family and friends. But we know that she is with family that have gone on before her and most especially her daughter and husband of 63 years and is now resting in the arms of Jesus.*
(Death)

James Kenneth McGlaun[984] married Bonnie Brown. They had four children:
> Vickey Yvone McGlaun[2201] born on March 27, 1954 in Opp, Covington, Alabama, USA; died on November 18, 1978 in Montgomery, AL
> James Tony McGlaun[2204] born on January 10, 1956
> James Kenny McGlaun Jr.[2205] born on May 21, 1957 in Montgomery, Montgomery, Alabama, USA
> Lisa Rena McGlaun[2207] born on January 16, 1962

986. MARGIE REE MCGLAUN (see Descendants (41)) was born on February 3, 1940, in Covington, Alabama, USA, to Virgil Lee McGlaun[337] and Eula Lee Maughon[338].

987. BOBBY WAYNE ELMORE was born on December 25, 1932, in Covington, Alabama, USA.
> Bobby Wayne Elmore, aged 28, married Margie Ree McGlaun[986], aged 21, on April 13, 1961 in Covington, Alabama, USA. They had three sons:
>> John Thomas Wade Elmore[2210] born on June 14, 1966 in Opp, Covington, Alabama, USA
>> Clayborn Lee Elmore[2211] born on August 28, 1970 in Andalusia, Covington, Alabama, USA
>> Robert L. Elmore[2212] born on August 1, 1971

988. PATRICIA ANN MCGLAUN (see Descendants (41)) was born on October 24, 1943, in Andalusia, Covington, Alabama, USA, to Virgil Lee McGlaun[337] and Eula Lee Maughon[338].

989. RICARD EDWARD MESSICK was born on July 20, 1946, in Opp, Covington, Alabama, USA.
> Ricard Edward Messick married Patricia Ann McGlaun[988]. They had two sons:
>> James Edward Messick[2213] born on August 6, 1969 in Andalusia, Covington, Alabama, USA
>> Richard Brian Messick[2215] born on June 24, 1975 in Andalusia, Covington, Alabama, USA

990. JOYCE MARIE MCGLAUN (see Descendants (41)) was born on July 21, 1946, in Covington, Alabama, USA, to Virgil Lee McGlaun[337] and Eula Lee Maughon[338].

991. MARZETTE ALFORD LAWSON was born on October 4, 1938, in Covington, Alabama, USA, to Connie B Lawson and Nobie Walters.
- He died on January 29, 2014, aged 75.
- He was buried in Andalusia Memorial Cemetery, Andalusia, Covington, Alabama, USA.
> Marzette Alford Lawson, aged about 43, married Joyce Marie McGlaun[990], aged about 35, from June 30, 1967 to October 9, 1998 in Covington, Alabama, USA, and they were divorced. They had two daughters:

Sandra Dianne Lawson[2216] born on March 13, 1971 in Andalusia, Covington, Alabama, USA
Karen Lynn Lawson[2218] born on October 17, 1975

992. SHEILA DIANNE MCGLAUN (see Descendants (41)) was born on November 23, 1949, in Covington, Alabama, USA, to Virgil Lee McGlaun[337] and Eula Lee Maughon[338].

993. THOMAS RANDALL MANCIL was born on November 23, 1950, in Covington, Alabama, USA.
Thomas Randall Mancil, aged 19, married Sheila Dianne McGlaun[992], aged 20, on June 18, 1970 in Covington, Alabama, USA. They had two daughters:
Kelley Michelle Mancil[2220] born on March 10, 1973 in Andalusia, Covington, Alabama, USA
Mendy Leigh Mancil[2221] born on May 16, 1977 in Andalusia, Covington, Alabama, USA

994. DORIS IRENE MCGLAUN (see Descendants (42)) was born on April 16, 1936 to Orbey Ray McGlaun[341] and Helen Henderson[342].

995. BOBBY D. HENDERSON.
Bobby D. Henderson married Doris Irene McGlaun[994]. They had three daughters:
Laura Rebecca Henderson[2222] born on February 9, 1961
Rhonda Leigh Henderson[2223] born on January 19, 1968
Sonia Denise Henderson[2224] born on January 19, 1968

996. LAMAR RAY MCGLAUN (see Descendants (42)) was born on January 13, 1941 to Orbey Ray McGlaun[341] and Helen Henderson[342].

997. SARA ANN HAIR.
Lamar Ray McGlaun[996] married Sara Ann Hair. They had one daughter:
Carol Ann McGlaun[2225] born on March 14, 1967

998. GUINDA MCGLAUN (see Descendants (43)) was born on July 27, 1947 to Orion T McGlaun[343] and Evelyn Thompson[344].

999. ORION DEWAYNE MCGLAUN (see Descendants (43)) was born on September 8, 1954 to Orion T McGlaun[343] and Evelyn Thompson[344].

1000. MARTIN VAN BUREN HUCKABAA SR. (see Descendants (44)) was born on September 2, 1921, in Holt, Okaloosa, Florida, USA, to William Martin Huckabaa[346] and Ida Mae Rowell[345].
- He was recorded in the census in 1930, aged about 8, in Red Rock, Santa Rosa, Florida, USA.
- He was recorded in the census in 1940, aged about 18, in Election Prect 21 Carolina, Covington, Alabama, USA.
- He died on April 19, 1998, aged 76 years.
- He was buried in Shady Hill Church Cemetery, Covington, Alabama, USA.

The following information is also recorded for Martin Van Buren:
- Military Service.
- Military Enlistment on December 18, 1942, aged 21 years, in Ft McClellan, Alabama, USA.

Note: *U.S. Army WWII.*
(Military Service)

Martin Van Buren married his third cousin, Hazel Bass[1451].

1001. ALLIE MAE DUKES WARD (see Descendants (44)) was born on October 29, 1923, in Holt, Okaloosa, Florida, USA, to William Martin Huckabaa[346] and Ida Mae Rowell[345].
- She was recorded in the census in 1930, aged about 6, in Red Rock, Santa Rosa, Florida, USA.
- She was recorded in the census in 1940, aged about 16, in Election Prect 21 Carolina, Covington, Alabama, USA.
- She was recorded in the census on April 1, 1950, aged 26, in Carolina, Covington, Alabama, United States.
- She died on August 9, 2017, aged 93, in Okaloosa, Florida, United States.
- She was buried in 2017 in Alberton Cemetery, Alberton, Coffee, Alabama, United States.

Allie Mae married twice. She was married to James Henry Ward[1002] and Hubert Dukes[1003].

1002. JAMES HENRY WARD.
James Henry Ward married Allie Mae Dukes Ward[1001].

1003. HUBERT DUKES was born on January 28, 1921, in DeFuniak Springs, Walton, Florida, USA. He died about 1989, aged 68 years.
Hubert Dukes, aged 21, married Allie Mae Dukes Ward[1001], aged 18, on April 14, 1942 in Andalusia, Covington, Alabama, USA. They had three children:
Alta Dukes[2237] born on May 26, 1943 in Florala, Covington, Alabama, USA
Audi Mae Dukes[2239] born on September 2, 1946 in Florala, Covington, Alabama, USA; died on January 16, 2020

Hubet C. Huckabaa[2241] born on February 2, 1950 in Andalusia, Covington, Alabama, USA

1004. LENER BELL HUCKABAA (see Descendants (44)) was born on November 22, 1925, in Holt, Okaloosa, Florida, USA, to William Martin Huckabaa[346] and Ida Mae Rowell[345]. He died on January 31, 1929, aged 3 years.

1005. L. B. HUCKABAA (see Descendants (44)) was born on January 14, 1928, in Holt, Okaloosa, Florida, USA, to William Martin Huckabaa[346] and Ida Mae Rowell[345].
- He was recorded in the census in 1930, aged about 2, in Red Rock, Santa Rosa, Florida, USA.
- He was recorded in the census in 1940, aged about 12, in Election Prect 21 Carolina, Covington, Alabama, USA.
- He was recorded in the census on April 1, 1950, aged 22, in Carolina, Covington, Alabama, United States.
- He died on March 31, 2015, aged 87.
- He was buried in Carolina Baptist Church Cemetery, Covington, Alabama, USA.

L. B. married his third cousin, Betty Jean Bass[1457].

1006. DARIS LEE HUCKABAA (see Descendants (44)) was born on May 6, 1930, in Milton, Santa Rosa, Florida, USA, to William Martin Huckabaa[346] and Ida Mae Rowell[345].
- She was recorded in the census in 1940, aged about 10, in Election Prect 21 Carolina, Covington, Alabama, USA.
- She was recorded in the census on April 1, 1950, aged 19, in 8th St, Fort Meade, Polk, Florida, United States.

1007. HOMER KIMBRIL was born on December 6, 1929, in North, Alabama, USA, to Buster E Kimbril and Iola Kimbril.
- He was recorded in the census in 1940, aged about 10, in Andalusia Road, Precinct 7 Watkins, Covington, Alabama, USA.
- He was recorded in the census on April 1, 1950, aged 20, in 8th St, Fort Meade, Polk, Florida, United States.

Homer Kimbril, aged 19, married Daris Lee Huckabaa[1006], aged 19, on October 29, 1949 in Andalusia, Covington, Alabama, USA. They had two children:
Sandra Elaine Kimbril[2255] born on February 10, 1951 in Florala, Covington, Alabama, USA
Timmy Lamar Kimbril[2258] born on September 2, 1955 in DeFuniak Springs, Walton, Florida, USA

1008. BABY HUCKABAA (see Descendants (44)) was born on January 6, 1933, in Holt, Okaloosa, Florida, USA, to William Martin Huckabaa[346] and Ida Mae Rowell[345]. She died (At young age) on January 10, 1933, aged 0, in Holt, Okaloosa, Florida, USA.

1009. HENRY CLAYTON HUCKABAA (see Descendants (44)) was born on February 16, 1934, in Holt, Okaloosa, Florida, USA, to William Martin Huckabaa[346] and Ida Mae Rowell[345].
- He was recorded in the census in 1940, aged about 6, in Election Prect 21 Carolina, Covington, Alabama, USA.
- He was recorded in the census on April 1, 1950, aged 16, in Carolina, Covington, Alabama, United States.
- He died on January 17, 2010, aged 75.

1010. JOHNNIE MAE DOUGLAS.
Henry Clayton Huckabaa[1009] married Johnnie Mae Douglas. They had four children:
Carolyn Dianne Huckabaa[2260] born on August 23, 1956
Linda Joyce Huckabaa[2261] born on June 18, 1959
Dorthy Jean Huckabaa[2262] born on July 2, 1961
Henry Clayton Huckabaa Jr.[2263] born on November 23, 1965

1011. DONALD TRAVIS HUCKABAA (see Descendants (44)) was born on September 10, 1936, in Andalusia, Covington, Alabama, USA, to William Martin Huckabaa[346] and Ida Mae Rowell[345].
- He was recorded in the census in 1940, aged about 3, in Election Prect 21 Carolina, Covington, Alabama, USA.
- He was recorded in the census on April 1, 1950, aged 13, in Carolina, Covington, Alabama, United States.
- He died on July 3, 1997, aged 60 years.
- He was buried in Shady Hill Church Cemetery, Covington, Alabama, USA.

1012. VIOLA BYERS was born in Ohio, USA.
Donald Travis Huckabaa[1011] married Viola Byers.

1013. EARL C. HUCKABAA (see Descendants (44)) was born on February 28, 1939, in Andalusia, Covington, Alabama, USA, to William Martin Huckabaa[346] and Ida Mae Rowell[345].
- He was recorded in the census in 1940, aged about 1, in Election Prect 21 Carolina, Covington, Alabama, USA.
- He was recorded in the census on April 1, 1950, aged 11, in Carolina, Covington, Alabama, United States.
- He died on October 3, 1979, aged 40 years, in Andalusia, Covington, Alabama, USA.
- He was buried in Shady Hill Church Cemetery, Covington, Alabama, USA.

1014. MAMIE LOUISE HAYES was born on August 5, 1925, in Robertsdale, Baldwin, Alabama, USA.
Earl C. Huckabaa[1013], aged 22, married Mamie Louise Hayes, aged 36, on September 12, 1961 in Andalusia, Covington, Alabama, USA. They had three children:

Teresa Jane Huckabaa[2264] born on July 22, 1962 in Andalusia, Covington, Alabama, USA
Donald Earl Huckabaa[2266] born on June 13, 1963 in Robertsdale, Baldwin, Alabama, USA
Redda Kay Huckabaa[2268] born on August 27, 1965 in Andalusia, Covington, Alabama, USA

1015. WILLIAM RAY HUCKABAA (see Descendants (44)) was born on January 15, 1942, in Andalusia, Covington, Alabama, USA, to William Martin Huckabaa[346] and Ida Mae Rowell[345]. He was recorded in the census on April 1, 1950, aged 8, in Carolina, Covington, Alabama, United States.
1016. IVER JUNE JACKSON.
William Ray Huckabaa[1015] married Iver June Jackson. They had three children:
Laura Lynn Huckabaa[2271] born in February 4 A.D.
Eddie Ray Huckabaa[2273] born on August 18, 1963 in Wachula, Hardee, Florida, USA
Tracy Lamar Huckabaa[2275] born on June 23, 1966 in Andalusia, Covington, Alabama, USA

1017. ROBERT THOMAS HUCKABAA (see Descendants (44)) was born on March 21, 1944, in Andalusia, Covington, Alabama, USA, to William Martin Huckabaa[346] and Ida Mae Rowell[345]. He died on December 9, 1945, aged 1 years.

1018. TRUDY ROWELL (see Descendants (45)) was born on November 26, 1921, in Holt, Okaloosa, Florida, USA, to Lettie V. Rowell[347].
- She was recorded in the census in 1940, aged about 18, in Second Street, E Preinct 20 West De Funiak Springs, Walton, Florida, USA.
- She was recorded in the census on April 1, 1950, aged 28, in 1/2 Mi Left Indian Creek Road Off Euchleanna De Funuh Road, Bruce Creek, Walton, Florida, United States.
- She died on February 13, 2012, aged 90 years.
1019. THOMAS JEFFERSON GARRETT was born on July 4, 1920, in DeFuniak Springs, Walton, Florida, USA.
- He was recorded in the census on April 1, 1950, aged 29, in 1/2 Mi Left Indian Creek Road Off Euchleanna De Funuh Road, Bruce Creek, Walton, Florida, United States.
Thomas Jefferson Garrett, aged 21, married Trudy Rowell[1018], aged 20, on December 20, 1941 in DeFuniak Springs, Walton, Florida, USA. They had three children:
Thomas Jefferson Garrett Jr.[2278] born on September 23, 1942 in DeFuniak Springs, Walton, Florida, USA
Nellie June Garrett[2280] born on October 20, 1947 in DeFuniak Springs, Walton, Florida, USA
Peggy Joyce Garrett[2282] born on October 8, 1948 in DeFuniak Springs, Walton, Florida, USA

1020. WILLIE V. ROWELL (see Descendants (45)) was born on July 5, 1924, in Holt, Okaloosa, Florida, USA, to Lettie V. Rowell[347].
- She was recorded in the census in 1940, aged about 15, in Second Street, E Preinct 20 West De Funiak Springs, Walton, Florida, USA.
- She died on July 18, 1980, aged 56 years, in Niceville, Okaloosa, Florida, USA.
Willie V. married twice. She was married to Mack Smith[1021] and Harold D. Rowell[1022].
1021. MACK SMITH was born on December 23, 1917, in Picayune, Pearl River, Mississippi, USA.
Mack Smith, aged 22, married Willie V. Rowell[1020], aged 15, on June 19, 1940 in DeFuniak Springs, Walton, Florida, USA. They had two children:
Billie Mack Smith[2284] born on September 5, 1942 in DeFuniak Springs, Walton, Florida, USA; died on September 3, 1992 in Bruce, Walton, Florida, USA
Billie Jo Smith[2286] born on October 29, 1947 in Eglin Air Force Base, Okaloosa, Florida, USA
1022. HAROLD D. ROWELL.
Harold D. Rowell married Willie V. Rowell[1020], aged 39, on June 18, 1964.

1023. EVA MAE ROWELL (see Descendants (45)) was born about 1928, in Florida, USA, to Lettie V. Rowell[347]. She was recorded in the census in 1940, aged about 12, in Second Street, E Preinct 20 West De Funiak Springs, Walton, Florida, USA.

1024. BOBBIE JEAN SMITH (see Descendants (45)) was born on July 21, 1951, in DeFuniak Springs, Walton, Florida, USA, to Lettie V. Rowell[347].
1025. RUSSELL LEE GILMEN was born on September 26, 1946, in Whitman, Logan, West Virginia, USA. He died on December 5, 1981, aged 35 years, in Chipley, Washington, Florida, USA.
Russell Lee Gilmen, aged 21, married Bobbie Jean Smith[1024], aged 16, on October 16, 1967 in Niceville, Okaloosa, Florida, USA. They had three children:
Barbara Payline Gilmen[2288] born on December 5, 1969 in Homestead Air Force Base, Dade, Florida, USA

Russell Lee Gilmen Jr.[2290] born on December 30, 1980 in Eglin Air Force Base, Okaloosa, Florida, USA

Deborah Leigh Gilmen[2291] born on February 22, 1992 in Homestead Air Force Base, Dade, Florida, USA

1026. HENRY ERAL ROWELL (see Descendants (46)) was born on May 5, 1937, in Florala, Covington, Alabama, USA, to Leroy Rowell[348] and Laura Pittman[349].
- He was recorded in the census in 1940, aged about 3, in West 5th Avenue, Florala, Covington, Alabama, USA.
- He was recorded in the census on April 1, 1950, aged 12, in 2606 East Ave, Panama City, Bay, Florida, United States.

1027. RHONDA LOMBARD. She died in California, USA.

Henry Eral Rowell[1026] married Rhonda Lombard in Las Vegas, Clark, Nevada, USA. They had six children:
April Rowell[2292]
Gary Rowell[2293] born on June 22, 1962
Kimberly Rowell[2294]
Hope Rowell[2295]
Coreen Rowell[2296]
Tereasa Rowell[2297]

1028. ERVUNUS ROWELL (see Descendants (46)) was born on April 9, 1939, in Florala, Covington, Alabama, USA, to Leroy Rowell[348] and Laura Pittman[349].
- He was recorded in the census in 1940, aged about 1, in West 5th Avenue, Florala, Covington, Alabama, USA.
- He was recorded in the census on April 1, 1950, aged 10, in 2606 East Ave, Panama City, Bay, Florida, United States.

1029. SHELBY D. PIERSON was born on October 28, 1939.

Ervunus Rowell[1028], aged 18, married Shelby D. Pierson, aged 17, on August 31, 1957 in Panama City, Bay, Florida, USA. They had two sons:
Russell Edward Rowell[2298] born on August 18, 1959 in Panama City, Bay, Florida, USA
James Randall Rowell[2300] born on September 10, 1961 in Panama City, Bay, Florida, USA

1030. RAY LEE ROWELL (see Descendants (46)) was born on June 22, 1943, in Florala, Covington, Alabama, USA, to Leroy Rowell[348] and Laura Pittman[349]. He died (At young age) on July 22, 1943, aged 0, in Florala, Covington, Alabama, USA.

1031. BILLIE JEAN JOHNSON (see Descendants (47)) was born about 1933, in Louisiana, United States, to Ruben A. Money[351] and Eva Mae Rowell[350]. She was recorded in the census on April 1, 1950, aged about 16, in Bruce and Illinois, Defuniak Springs, Walton, Florida, United States.

1032. RUBEN ARNOLD MONEY JR. (see Descendants (47)) was born on June 23, 1947, in DeFuniak Springs, Walton, Florida, USA, to Ruben A. Money[351] and Eva Mae Rowell[350]. He was recorded in the census on April 1, 1950, aged 2, in Bruce and Illinois, Defuniak Springs, Walton, Florida, United States.

1033. HITOMI TSURSKI was born on January 19, 1952, in Fukoka, Japan.

Ruben Arnold Money Jr.[1032], aged 22, married Hitomi Tsurski, aged 18, on January 22, 1970. They had two children:
Sherri Money[2302] born on January 6, 1971 in Eglin Air Force Base, Okaloosa, Florida, USA
Scott Money[2303] born on October 10, 1975 in Okaloosa, Florida, USA

1034. EVA ROSALIND MONEY (see Descendants (47)) was born on July 9, 1948, in DeFuniak Springs, Walton, Florida, USA, to Ruben A. Money[351] and Eva Mae Rowell[350].
- She was recorded in the census on April 1, 1950, aged 1, in Bruce and Illinois, Defuniak Springs, Walton, Florida, United States.
- She died on May 1, 2009, aged 60.
- She was buried in Heritage Gardens, Niceville, Okaloosa, Florida, USA.

Eva Rosalind married twice. She was married to James B. Roeting[1035] and Thomas Lee Rine[1036].

1035. JAMES B. ROETING.

James B. Roeting married Eva Rosalind Money[1034], aged 18, on May 26, 1967. They had one son:
James Phillop Roeting[2304] born on October 6, 1969 in Columbus, Lowndes, Mississippi, USA; died on March 22, 2006 in Niceville, Okaloosa, Florida, USA

1036. THOMAS LEE RINE was born on November 19, 1945, in Morgantown, Monongalia, West Virginia, USA.

Thomas Lee Rine, aged 31, married Eva Rosalind Money[1034], aged 28, on April 15, 1977 in Niceville, Okaloosa, Florida, USA. They had one son:
Kristopher Lee Rine[2305] born on August 25, 1978 in Fort Walton Beach, Okaloosa, Florida, USA

Direct Relations

1037. JIMMY RONALD MONEY (see Descendants (47)) was born on August 27, 1949, in Florala, Covington, Alabama, USA, to Ruben A. Money[351] and Eva Mae Rowell[350]. He was recorded in the census on April 1, 1950, as an infant, in Bruce and Illinois, Defuniak Springs, Walton, Florida, United States.
Jimmy Ronald married twice. He was married to Darlene Eldridge[1038] and Delores J Alford[1039].

1038. DARLENE ELDRIDGE.
Jimmy Ronald Money[1037], aged 21, married Darlene Eldridge on January 6, 1971. They had one son:
Ronald Dewayne Money[2306] born on October 8, 1972 in Fort Walton Beach, Okaloosa, Florida, USA

1039. DELORES J ALFORD was born on May 1, 1954, in Crestview, Okaloosa, Florida, USA.
Jimmy Ronald Money[1037], aged 23, married Delores J Alford, aged 18, on March 10, 1973. They had one daughter:
Kelli Kaye Money[2307] born on November 2, 1974 in Fort Walton Beach, Okaloosa, Florida, USA

1040. WILLIE EUGENE HUCKABA (see Descendants (48)) was born on May 20, 1953 to Eugene Huckaba[353] and Joyce Collinsworth[354].

1041. JOHN RUSSELL HUCKABA (see Descendants (48)) was born on October 1, 1953 to Eugene Huckaba[353] and Joyce Collinsworth[354].

1042. ROBIN RENA HUCKABA (see Descendants (48)) was born on September 10, 1961 to Eugene Huckaba[353] and Joyce Collinsworth[354].

1043. HAZEL ALITA DAVIS (see Descendants (49)) was born on May 18, 1950 to Troy Davis[356] and Addie Irene Huckaba[355].

1044. GEORGIANN ISABEL DAVIS (see Descendants (49)) was born on February 19, 1952 to Troy Davis[356] and Addie Irene Huckaba[355].

1045. TROY DAVIS JR. (see Descendants (49)) was born on June 2, 1953 to Troy Davis[356] and Addie Irene Huckaba[355].

1046. BENJAMIN FRANKLIN DAVIS (see Descendants (49)) was born on June 28, 1955 to Troy Davis[356] and Addie Irene Huckaba[355].

1047. TERRY ALLEN DAVIS (see Descendants (49)) was born on June 23, 1957 to Troy Davis[356] and Addie Irene Huckaba[355].

1048. LONNIE CRAWFORD (see Descendants (50)) was born on May 23, 1929, in Florida, USA, to John Henry Crawford[358] and Bessie Luvine Bass[357].
- He was recorded in the census in 1940, aged about 11, in Crestview, 3, Okaloosa, Florida, USA.
- He died on June 8, 2002, aged 73.
- He was buried in New Bethany Cemetery, Holt, Okaloosa, Florida, United States.

1049. GENEVIEVE LANGLEY.
Lonnie Crawford[1048] married Genevieve Langley. They had six children:
Nancy Lee Crawford[2308] born on July 9, 1950
Lonnie Ray Crawford Jr.[2309] born on June 18, 1952
Eugene Crawford[2310] born on August 3, 1953
Tina Crawford[2311]
Sandra Crawford[2312]
Debbie Crawford[2313]

1050. EDNA MAE CRAWFORD (see Descendants (50)) was born on June 3, 1930, in Florida, United States, to John Henry Crawford[358] and Bessie Luvine Bass[357].
- She was recorded in the census in 1940, aged about 10, in Crestview, 3, Okaloosa, Florida, USA.
- She was recorded in the census on April 1, 1950, aged 19, in 7th Barnes Lane, Brownsville-Brent-Goulding, Escambia, Florida, United States.

1051. ROBERT MASON was born about 1929, in Florida, United States. He was recorded in the census on April 1, 1950, aged about 20, in 7th Barnes Lane, Brownsville-Brent-Goulding, Escambia, Florida, United States.
Robert Mason married Edna Mae Crawford[1050]. They had two daughters:
Shirley Mason[2314] born on October 22, 1949 in Florida, United States
Barbara Payline Mason[2316] born on October 7, 1951

1052. JAMES EDMUND CRAWFORD (see Descendants (50)) was born on June 12, 1932, in Florida, United States, to John Henry Crawford[358] and Bessie Luvine Bass[357].
- He was recorded in the census in 1940, aged about 8, in Crestview, 3, Okaloosa, Florida, USA.
- He was recorded in the census on April 1, 1950, aged 17, in 692 700 Block E. Chestnut Ave., Crestview, Okaloosa, Florida, United States.
- He died in August 1978, aged 46.

1053. OLA BELL MADDEN.
James Edmund Crawford[1052] married Ola Bell Madden. They had four daughters:
Juanita Gale Crawford[2317] born in March 31 A.D.
Patricia Jane Crawford[2318] born on September 20, 1950
Anita Marie Crawford[2319] born on August 28, 1959
Cheryl Lynn Crawford[2320] born on April 26, 1961

1054. HERBERT L CRAWFORD (see Descendants (50)) was born on February 20, 1934, in Florida, United States, to John Henry Crawford[358] and Bessie Luvine Bass[357].
- He was recorded in the census in 1940, aged about 6, in Crestview, 3, Okaloosa, Florida, USA.
- He was recorded in the census on April 1, 1950, aged 16, in 692 700 Block E. Chestnut Ave., Crestview, Okaloosa, Florida, United States.

1055. PEGGY HATCHCOCK.
Herbert L Crawford[1054] married Peggy Hatchcock. They had two children:
Deborah Ann Crawford[2321]
Herbert Crawford Jr.[2322] born on September 2, 1959

1056. BETTY JEAN CRAWFORD (see Descendants (50)) was born on April 17, 1936, in Florida, United States, to John Henry Crawford[358] and Bessie Luvine Bass[357].
- She was recorded in the census in 1940, aged about 4, in Crestview, 3, Okaloosa, Florida, USA.
- She was recorded in the census on April 1, 1950, aged 13, in 692 700 Block E. Chestnut Ave., Crestview, Okaloosa, Florida, United States.

1057. MERLIN BARNHILL.
Merlin Barnhill married Betty Jean Crawford[1056]. They had five children:
Merlin Barnhill[2323] born on February 7, 1954
Mikie Barnhill[2324]
Tammie Barnhill[2325]
Angelia Barnhill[2326]
Darlene Barnhill[2327]

1058. JOHN DALLAS CRAWFORD (see Descendants (50)) was born on May 20, 1939, in Crestview, Okaloosa, Florida, USA, to John Henry Crawford[358] and Bessie Luvine Bass[357].
- He was recorded in the census in 1940, aged about 1, in Crestview, 3, Okaloosa, Florida, USA.
- He was recorded in the census on April 1, 1950, aged 10, in 692 700 Block E. Chestnut Ave., Crestview, Okaloosa, Florida, United States.

1059. FAYE YAWN was born in Bowling Green, Hardee, Florida, USA.
John Dallas Crawford[1058] married Faye Yawn. They had one son:
John Kenneth Crawford[2328] born on October 15, 1968

1060. GLINDA CRAWFORD (see Descendants (50)) was born on July 24, 1945, in Florida, United States, to John Henry Crawford[358] and Bessie Luvine Bass[357]. She was recorded in the census on April 1, 1950, aged 4, in 692 700 Block E. Chestnut Ave., Crestview, Okaloosa, Florida, United States.

1061. JOHNNY NEWMANN.
Johnny Newmann married Glinda Crawford[1060].

1062. GERALD H CRAWFORD (see Descendants (50)) was born on March 31, 1947, in Florida, United States, to John Henry Crawford[358] and Bessie Luvine Bass[357]. He was recorded in the census on April 1, 1950, aged 3, in 692 700 Block E. Chestnut Ave., Crestview, Okaloosa, Florida, United States.

1063. BILLY RAY BASS (see Descendants (51)) was born on October 12, 1935, in Florida, USA, to James Henry Bass[359] and Margaret Charity Franklin[360].
- He was recorded in the census in 1940, aged about 4, in State Highway, Merritt Island, Precinct 11, Brevard, Florida, USA.
- He died on June 14, 2004, aged 68 years.

Billy Ray married twice. He was married to Joyce Merline Russell[1064] and Nancy Lee Carswell Ray[1065].

Direct Relations

1064. JOYCE MERLINE RUSSELL.
    Billy Ray Bass[1063] married Joyce Merline Russell. They had three children:
        Cynthia Renee Bass[2330] born on July 18, 1955
        Michael Zoree Bass[2331] born on December 4, 1959
        Richard Allen Bass[2332] born on May 18, 1962

1065. NANCY LEE CARSWELL RAY.
    Billy Ray Bass[1063] married Nancy Lee Carswell Ray.

1066. THERESA BASS (see Descendants (51)) was born about 1938, in Florida, USA, to James Henry Bass[359] and Margaret Charity Franklin[360]. She was recorded in the census in 1940, aged about 2, in State Highway, Merritt Island, Precinct 11, Brevard, Florida, USA.

1067. THOMAS BASS (see Descendants (51)) was born about 1939, in Florida, USA, to James Henry Bass[359] and Margaret Charity Franklin[360]. He was recorded in the census in 1940, aged about 1, in State Highway, Merritt Island, Precinct 11, Brevard, Florida, USA.

1068. THERESA ANNETTE BASS (see Descendants (51)) was born on July 9, 1937, in Florida, USA, to James Henry Bass[359] and Minnie Walton McKnight Smith[361]. She was recorded in the census in 1940, aged about 2, in State Highway, Merritt Island, Precinct 11, Brevard, Florida, USA.
    Theresa Annette married three times. She was married to Horace Emmete Jones[1069], Eurado Eurigue Urgelles[1070] and George Jakubcin[1071].

1069. HORACE EMMETE JONES. He died in Florida.
    Horace Emmete Jones married Theresa Annette Bass[1068]. They had two daughters:
        Theresa Darlyne Jones[2333] born on July 29, 1954 in Orlando Regional Hospital, Orlando, Orange Co., Florida
        Connie Denise Jones[2334] born on April 29, 1957

1070. EURADO EURIGUE URGELLES.
    Eurado Eurigue Urgelles married Theresa Annette Bass[1068], aged about 32, in 1970, and they were divorced.

1071. GEORGE JAKUBCIN.
    George Jakubcin married Theresa Annette Bass[1068], aged 42, on August 28, 1979.

1072. THOMAS FRANKLIN BASS (see Descendants (51)) was born on November 21, 1939, in Florida, USA, to James Henry Bass[359] and Minnie Walton McKnight Smith[361]. He was recorded in the census in 1940, as an infant, in State Highway, Merritt Island, Precinct 11, Brevard, Florida, USA.

1073. BOBBIE ANN PRUITT.
    Thomas Franklin Bass[1072] married Bobbie Ann Pruitt. They had two children:
        Rickey Thomas Bass[2335] born on January 3, 1958
        Becky Rene Bass[2336] born on June 22, 1967

1074. JASPER DANIEL BASS (see Descendants (51)) was born on March 29, 1943 to James Henry Bass[359] and Minnie Walton McKnight Smith[361].
    Jasper Daniel married twice. He was married to Judith Ann Lewis[1075] and Maurine Beth Buckley[1076].

1075. JUDITH ANN LEWIS.
    Jasper Daniel Bass[1074] married Judith Ann Lewis. They had three daughters:
        Rhonda Elaine Bass[2337] born on June 1, 1959
        Susan Elizabeth Bass[2338] born on September 2, 1961
        Jasper Danniel Bass Jr.[2339] born on February 12, 1963

1076. MAURINE BETH BUCKLEY.
    Jasper Daniel Bass[1074] married Maurine Beth Buckley.

1077. JAMES DALLAS BASS (see Descendants (51)) was born on January 20, 1951 to James Henry Bass[359] and Minnie Walton McKnight Smith[361].

1078. JOEL MAURICE CURBELLO (see Descendants (52)) was born on September 17, 1948, in Houston, Harris, Texas 77251, USA, to Albert Bartley Curbello[365] and Ray-Monde Bass[364].

1079. ALBERT CURBELLO (see Descendants (52)) was born to Albert Bartley Curbello[365] and Ray-Monde Bass[364].

1080. WILLIAM DALLAS BASS (see Descendants (53)) was born on March 3, 1947, in Florida, United States, to John Clayton Bass[366] and Louise Griffith[367].
- He was recorded in the census on April 1, 1950, aged 3, in Mirror Lake, Fruitland Park, Lake, Florida, United

States.
- He died on July 30, 1999, aged 52 years.
- He was buried in Florida National Cemetery, 6502 Sw. 102nd Ave., Bushnell, Florida 33513, USA.

1081. PATRICIA ANN SMITH.
William Dallas Bass[1080] married Patricia Ann Smith. They had one daughter:
Janet Louise Bass[2340] born on January 6, 1966

1082. PAUL HOWARD BASS (see Descendants (53)) was born on May 12, 1948, in Florida, United States, to John Clayton Bass[366] and Louise Griffith[367]. He was recorded in the census on April 1, 1950, aged 1, in Mirror Lake, Fruitland Park, Lake, Florida, United States.

1083. DEBBIE SUE BASS (see Descendants (53)) was born on September 18, 1952 to John Clayton Bass[366] and Louise Griffith[367].

1084. JOHNNY RAY BASS (see Descendants (53)) was born on December 6, 1962 to John Clayton Bass[366] and Louise Griffith[367].

1085. MARVIN DALLAS BASS JR. (see Descendants (54)) was born on June 9, 1947, in Florida, United States, to Marvin Dallas Bass Sr.[368] and Kathleen L Heath[369]. He was recorded in the census on April 1, 1950, aged 2, in Dixie Highway, Fruitland Park, Lake, Florida, United States.

1086. SHARON TREASA BARROW.
Marvin Dallas Bass Jr.[1085] married Sharon Treasa Barrow. They had three sons:
Robert Dom Bass[2341] born on November 5, 1966
Hank Dallas Bass Sr.[2343] born on September 11, 1969
Joshua Edmund Bass[2345] born on July 23, 1980

1087. JIMMIE RAY BASS (see Descendants (54)) was born on August 14, 1948, in Florida, United States, to Marvin Dallas Bass Sr.[368] and Kathleen L Heath[369]. He was recorded in the census on April 1, 1950, aged 1, in Dixie Highway, Fruitland Park, Lake, Florida, United States.

1088. JAMES EDWARD BASS (see Descendants (54)) was born on January 25, 1950, in Florida, United States, to Marvin Dallas Bass Sr.[368] and Kathleen L Heath[369]. He was recorded in the census on April 1, 1950, as an infant, in Dixie Highway, Fruitland Park, Lake, Florida, United States.

1089. LINDA COOK.
James Edward Bass[1088] married Linda Cook. They had one son:
James Edward Bass Jr.[2346] born on April 2, 1968

1090. RONALD DUANE NALL (see Descendants (55)) was born on November 15, 1947 to Victor Eugene Nall[371] and Sarah Christian Bass[370].

1091. DENA GLOVER.
Ronald Duane Nall[1090] married Dena Glover. They had one son:
Ronnie Duane Nall II[2347]

1092. TERRY MAURICE NALL (see Descendants (55)) was born on November 9, 1949 to Victor Eugene Nall[371] and Sarah Christian Bass[370].

1093. DENNIS RAY NALL (see Descendants (55)) was born on May 12, 1954 to Victor Eugene Nall[371] and Sarah Christian Bass[370].

1094. GERALD HOWARD BASS JR. (see Descendants (56)) was born on April 29, 1953 to Gerald Howard Bass Sr.[372] and Doris Ray[373]. Gerald Howard became known as "Howie".
- He died on May 19, 2008, aged 55 years.
- He was buried in Hurricane Creek Cemetery, Holmes, Florida, USA.
Note: *Howie was a resident of Westville. He was Baptist by faith and a member of Northside Baptist Church in Ponce de Leon, Fla. He owned and operated Advance Copy in DeFuniak Springs, Fla., for 10 years. He was currently working at Reliable Products in Geneva, Ala., as a press operator. He enjoyed hunting and fishing and also enjoyed spending time with his family. He was an avid outdoorsman.*
(Death)

1095. TERESA GRIFFIN was born on November 2, 1961. Teresa became known as "Terry".

Gerald Howard Bass Jr.[1094] married Teresa Griffin. They had three children:
    Melissa Bass[2348] born on December 12, 1972
    Chad Howard Bass[2349] born on June 25, 1975
    Kyle Bass[2350] born on September 13, 1988

1096. WANDA BASS (see Descendants (56)) was born on September 3, 1956 to Gerald Howard Bass Sr.[372] and Doris Ray[373].

1097. JAMES ANTHONY MCGILL.
    James Anthony McGill married Wanda Bass[1096]. They had two sons:
        Anthony McGill[2351]
        Aaron McGill[2352] born on September 12, 1981

1098. RHONDA BASS (see Descendants (56)) was born on April 5, 1958 to Gerald Howard Bass Sr.[372] and Doris Ray[373].

1099. MR. CEURVELS.
    Mr. Ceurvels married Rhonda Bass[1098]. They had two daughters:
        Heather Lee Ceurvels[2353] born on November 18, 1976
        Jessica Ceurvels[2354] born on March 6, 1981

1100. TONYA BASS (see Descendants (56)) was born on October 6, 1968 to Gerald Howard Bass Sr.[372] and Doris Ray[373].

1101. STEVEN C. MORRELL.
    Steven C. Morrell married Tonya Bass[1100]. They had two daughters:
        Kaitlyn Morrell[2355] born on March 28, 1992
        Brittany Morrell[2356] born on May 8, 1995

1102. JAMES HAROLD HUCKABA (see Descendants (57)) was born on April 3, 1926, in Mossy Head, Walton, Florida, USA, to James Edgar Huckaba[375] and Mae Belle Posey[374].
- He was recorded in the census in 1930, aged about 4, in Mary Esther, Okaloosa, Florida, USA.
- He was recorded in the census in 1940, aged about 14, in Election Prect 21 Carolina, Covington, Alabama, USA.
- He died on July 17, 2011, aged 85.
- He was buried in J.E. Huckaba Cemetery, Defuniak Springs, Walton, Florida, USA.

1103. CORA LEE WILCOX was born on August 2, 1936, in Shady Grove, Taylor, Florida, USA.
    James Harold Huckaba[1102], aged 25, married Cora Lee Wilcox, aged 14, on July 18, 1951 in Lucedale, George, Mississippi, USA. They had six children:
        Peggy Lee Huckabaa[2357] born on July 4, 1954 in Florala, Covington, Alabama, USA
        Donnie Lee Huckabaa[2359] born on December 24, 1955 in Tampa, Hillsborough, Florida, USA
        Demas Mark Huckabaa[2362] born on March 7, 1959 in Saint Cloud, Osceola, Florida, USA
        Phyllis Ann Huckabaa[2365] born on December 10, 1960 in Tampa, Hillsborough, Florida, USA
        Edgar Hugh Huckabaa[2367] born on September 1, 1963 in Plant City, Hillsboro, Florida, USA
        James Rudolf Huckabaa[2369] born on October 22, 1964 in Tampa, Hillsborough, Florida, USA

1104. CLARA MAE HUCKABAA (see Descendants (57)) was born on June 10, 1928, in Alabama, United States, to James Edgar Huckaba[375] and Mae Belle Posey[374].
- She was recorded in the census in 1930, aged about 2, in Mary Esther, Okaloosa, Florida, USA.
- She was recorded in the census in 1940, aged about 12, in Election Prect 21 Carolina, Covington, Alabama, USA.

1105. COLEY JOSEPH SNELLGROVE was born on June 6, 1912.
    Coley Joseph Snellgrove married Clara Mae Huckabaa[1104]. They had four children:
        Betty June Snellgrove[2371] born on August 10, 1951
        Rudy Von Snellgrove[2373] born on February 18, 1953
        Roger Henry Snellgrove[2375] born on September 16, 1955
        Judy Ann Snellgrove[2377] born on February 3, 1957

1106. EDWARD ERVIN HUCKABA (see Descendants (57)) was born on March 18, 1932, in Alabama, USA, to James Edgar Huckaba[375] and Mae Belle Posey[374].
- He was recorded in the census in 1940, aged about 8, in Election Prect 21 Carolina, Covington, Alabama, USA.

The following information is also recorded for Edward Ervin:
- Military Service.

Edward Ervin married twice. He was married to Betty Jean Harrison[1107] and Gayle Prater[1108].
Note: *U.S. Army Korea.*
    (Military Service)

1107. BETTY JEAN HARRISON.
> Edward Ervin Huckaba[1106] married Betty Jean Harrison. They had five children:
>> Randy Michael Huckaba[2379] born on November 3, 1956
>> Craig Alan Huckaba[2380] born on May 10, 1958
>> Karen Elizabeth Huckaba[2381] born on November 26, 1959
>> Connie Arlene Huckaba[2382] born on July 31, 1961
>> Myra Lorraine Huckaba[2383] born on June 25, 1963

1108. GAYLE PRATER.
> Edward Ervin Huckaba[1106] married Gayle Prater.

1109. MARY OPAL HUCKABAA (see Descendants (57)) was born on April 18, 1940 to James Edgar Huckaba[375] and Mae Belle Posey[374].

1110. JAMES WALTER ANSLEY was born on December 15, 1927.
> James Walter Ansley married Mary Opal Huckabaa[1109]. They had five children:
>> Sherri Leigh Wilson[2384] born in April 4 A.D.
>> Dale Edgar Ansley[2385] born on January 13, 1960
>> Joanne Marie Ansley[2387] born on November 14, 1960
>> Lyvon Walter Ansley[2390] born on February 23, 1961
>> James William Ansley[2392] born on March 24, 1967

1111. EARL FLYN HUCKABA (see Descendants (57)) was born on February 14, 1944 to James Edgar Huckaba[375] and Mae Belle Posey[374].
> Earl Flyn married twice. He was married to Angela Crusel Nix[1112] and Donna Ann Cummings[1113].

1112. ANGELA CRUSEL NIX.
> Earl Flyn Huckaba[1111], aged about 29, married Angela Crusel Nix from August 7, 1964 to August 4, 1982, and they were divorced. They had three children:
>> Shonda Denise Huckaba[2394] born on October 11, 1965
>> Tiresa Lynn Huckaba[2398] born on December 17, 1967
>> Earl Flyn Huckaba II[2403] born on March 11, 1972

1113. DONNA ANN CUMMINGS.
> Earl Flyn Huckaba[1111], aged 47, married Donna Ann Cummings on August 13, 1991.
> Note: *First married Jun. 18, 1987 and divorced Jun. 1, 1988. They were remarried in 1991 as shown.*

1114. JIMMY DAVID HUCKABA (see Descendants (57)) was born on June 18, 1948 to James Edgar Huckaba[375] and Mae Belle Posey[374].

1115. JAMES EDWARD POSEY (see Descendants (58)) was born on June 14, 1942, in Holt, Okaloosa, Florida, USA, to Preston Dallas Posey[377] and Laura Stiller[378]. He died on August 21, 2007, aged 65.
> James Edward married twice. He was married to Janice Turner[1116] and Brenda F. Hope[1117].

1116. JANICE TURNER. She died on August 19, 1995 in Crestview, Okaloosa, Florida, USA.
> James Edward Posey[1115], aged 19, married Janice Turner on December 12, 1961. They had three children:
>> Kimmie Dallas Posey[2407] born on March 28, 1963 in Crestview, Okaloosa, Florida, USA
>> Mary Katherine Posey[2409] born on September 17, 1966 in Crestview, Okaloosa, Florida, USA
>> Diane Faye Posey[2411] born on September 16, 1967 in Crestview, Okaloosa, Florida, USA

1117. BRENDA F. HOPE.
> James Edward Posey[1115] married Brenda F. Hope. They had two children:
>> Shawn Michael Posey[2413] born on June 5, 1974 in Massachuttes, USA
>> Hope Mychelle Posey[2414] born on May 27, 1980 in Morgan City, St. Mary Parish, Lousiana, USA

1118. MARY JANE POSEY (see Descendants (59)) was born on July 8, 1938 to Chester Posey[379] and Addie Lee Johnson[380].
- She died on December 6, 2006, aged 68, in Pensacola, Escambia, Florida, USA.
- She was buried in Bethel Cemetery, Escambia County, Alabama, USA.

1119. JOHN RICHARD MCKEE was born 'Ma 20 1931', in Covington county, Covington, Alabama, USA.
- He died on June 24, 2022 in Pensacola, Escambia, Florida, USA.
- He was buried in Bayview Memorial Park, Pensacola, Escambia County, Florida, USA.
> Note: *Dick was born May 20, 1931 in Covington County, Alabama, to his parents; John Richard and Bessie McKee. He was the youngest of five brothers and five sisters. He graduated from Crestview High School and later attended college in Orlando. He was a member of the National Guard for eight years, and in 1960, became an agent for Allstate Insurance Company, retiring after 40 years. He had been a Mason for over fifty years in Myrtle Grove Lodge 352; 32° Scottish Rite of Freemasonry and remained a current member of Pensacola Hadji*

Shrine. Number one hobby and pastime was quail hunting, with his buddy, Angus Comerford. Followed closely by his passion for the Florida Gators, golf and freshwater fishing. He loved being outdoors. .
(Birth)
John Richard McKee married Mary Jane Posey[1118].

1120. DOROTHY FAYE POSEY (see Descendants (59)) was born on April 26, 1942 to Chester Posey[379] and Addie Lee Johnson[380].
1121. WILLIAM ALEXANDER.
William Alexander married Dorothy Faye Posey[1120].

1122. LINDA LOUISE POSEY (see Descendants (60)) was born on August 10, 1949 to Stacy Denton Posey[382] and Juanita Palmer[383].

1123. PATRICK BERNARD MOYLAN was born on February 20, 1948.
Patrick Bernard Moylan, aged 38, married Linda Louise Posey[1122], aged 37, in August 1986. They divorced on August 18, 1986, when aged 38 and 37 respectively, in Escambia, Florida, USA. They had one son:
Brett Bernard Moylan[2415] born on July 31, 1972 in Pensacola, Escambia, Florida, USA

1124. MARTIN JAMES POSEY (see Descendants (60)) was born on September 8, 1952 to Stacy Denton Posey[382] and Juanita Palmer[383].
1125. LINDA MOBLEY was born on November 14, 1956, in Atmore, Escambia, Alabama, USA.
Martin James Posey[1124], aged 24, married Linda Mobley, aged 20, on March 5, 1977. They had two daughters:
Shanna Michelle Posey[2416] born on April 10, 1981 in Pensacola, Escambia, Florida, USA
Casey Lauren Posey[2417] born on October 13, 1984 in Pensacola, Escambia, Florida, USA

1126. LARRY DENTON POSEY (see Descendants (60)) was born on October 13, 1956 to Stacy Denton Posey[382] and Juanita Palmer[383].
1127. JACQUELINE DIANNE BARRON was born on September 17, 1959, in Pensacola, Escambia, Florida, USA.
Larry Denton Posey[1126], aged 23, married Jacqueline Dianne Barron, aged 20, on May 24, 1980 in Pensacola, Escambia, Florida, USA. They had two sons:
William Denton Posey[2418] born on July 28, 1982 in Pensacola, Escambia, Florida, USA
Nathan Edward Posey[2420] born on June 25, 1987 in Pensacola, Escambia, Florida, USA

1128. DEBRA K. POSEY (see Descendants (60)) was born on March 12, 1958 to Stacy Denton Posey[382] and Juanita Palmer[383].
Debra K. married twice. She was married to Walter William Lurton[1129] and Mr. Crumpler[1130].
1129. WALTER WILLIAM LURTON was born on November 28, 1948, in Pensacola, Escambia, Florida, USA.
Walter William Lurton, aged 30, married Debra K. Posey[1128], aged 20, on February 3, 1979 in Escambia, Florida, USA, and they were divorced.
1130. MR. CRUMPLER.
Mr. Crumpler married Debra K. Posey[1128].

1131. PATRICIEA ERNESTINE STEWART (see Descendants (61)) was born on January 27, 1942, in Montgomery County, Alabama, USA, to Ernest Stewart[385] and Bonnie Lee Posey[384].
- She died on September 18, 2020, aged 78, in Pensacola, Escambia, Florida, USA.
- She was buried in Pensacola Memorial Gardens, Pensacola, Escambia County, Florida, USA.
Note: *Pat graduated from Tate High School in 1961 and worked in many capacities for the Escambia County School District for over 20 years where she made many friends that she considered family. After retiring, she devoted her time to traveling, sewing and teaching her grand-children to cook and sew. She also taught all of her daughter-in-laws how to cook the special things that her sons loved that only Mom could make.*
(Death)

Wilson Bass

1132. HUDSON WOODFIN SR. was born on February 18, 1939, in Elmore City, Coose, Alabama, USA.

Hudson Woodfin Sr., aged 22, married Patriciea Ernestine Stewart[1131], aged 19, on November 16, 1961 in Pensacola, Escambia, Florida, USA. They had three sons:
- Hudson Woodfin Jr.[2421] born on May 17, 1966 in Escambia, Florida, USA
- Robert Lee Woodfin[2423] born on June 21, 1968 in Escambia, Florida, USA
- Martin Edward Woodfin[2424] born on January 4, 1970 in Escambia, Florida, USA

1133. BARBARA ANN STEWART (see Descendants (61)) was born on July 28, 1944 to Ernest Stewart[385] and Bonnie Lee Posey[384].
Barbara Ann married three times. She was married to Ronnie Madron[1134], Don P. Diegleman[1135] and Donald Harris[1136].

1134. RONNIE MADRON.
Ronnie Madron married Barbara Ann Stewart[1133].

1135. DON P. DIEGLEMAN was born on July 22, 1942.
Don P. Diegleman married Barbara Ann Stewart[1133]. They had four children:
- Barbara Renee Diegleman[2426] born on March 8, 1962
- Bonnie Marie Diegleman[2427] born on August 24, 1964
- Rhondel London Diegleman[2428] born on January 16, 1966
- Brian Scott Diegleman[2429] born in October 1968

1136. DONALD HARRIS.
Donald Harris married Barbara Ann Stewart[1133].

1137. BETTY SUE STEWART (see Descendants (61)) was born on November 15, 1945 to Ernest Stewart[385] and Bonnie Lee Posey[384]. She died (Accident) on April 10, 2008, aged 62.
Betty Sue married twice, including Thurman Paul Cook[1138].
Notes:
- Betty was a very special lady and touched the hearts of many. (Death)
- April 10, 2008 was an unbelievable day. This was the day Betty was taken unexpectedly from this world. We must all go on. Betty was really one of God's special people. She was blind from birth. But, she was as normal as any of us. Yes, she could peel a potato and only peel the skin away. She made the best potato salad, baked beans, and banana pudding. She could sweep the floor as good as I could. She would do this bare footed. She could fill a glass or cup full without running it over. Just, put her finger in the top and feel the liquid when it reached the top. There will be no more pot holders from her. She kept us in good pot holders. I will always Keep her in my memories, also. I Love you. Betty -Pat Woodfin [Stewart]. (Death)

Betty Sue gave birth to one son:
- Clifton Veal Stewart[2430] born on June 14, 1963

1138. THURMAN PAUL COOK was born on August 25, 1946.
Thurman Paul Cook, aged 26, married Betty Sue Stewart[1137], aged 27, on April 3, 1973. They had two sons:
- Jason Wayne Cook[2432] born on April 29, 1975
- Terry Lynn Cook[2433] born on September 29, 1977

The following information is also recorded for this family:
- Death of Spouse.

1139. ERNEST DEWAYNE STEWART (see Descendants (61)) was born on November 2, 1947, in Florala, Covington, Alabama, USA, to Ernest Stewart[385] and Bonnie Lee Posey[384].
Ernest Dewayne married twice. He was married to Mary Jo Taylor[1140] and Patricia Elaine Tomlins[1141].

1140. MARY JO TAYLOR was born on August 5, 1951.
Ernest Dewayne Stewart[1139], aged 19, married Mary Jo Taylor, aged 16, on August 28, 1967 in Pensacola, Escambia, Florida, USA. They had one daughter:
- Shelia Diane Stewart[2434] born on October 14, 1968 in Pensacola, Escambia, Florida, USA

1141. PATRICIA ELAINE TOMLINS was born on May 3, 1952.
Ernest Dewayne Stewart[1139], aged 32, married Patricia Elaine Tomlins, aged 27, in March 1980 in Escambia, Florida, USA. They had one daughter:
- Rachel Lee Stewart[2436] born on January 3, 1982 in Pensacola, Escambia, Florida, USA

1142. SHIRLEY JANE STEWART (see Descendants (61)) was born on July 30, 1949 to Ernest Stewart[385] and Bonnie Lee Posey[384].

Direct Relations

1143. MIKEAL WAYNE DANLEY was born on November 19, 1945.
    Mikeal Wayne Danley, aged 19, married Shirley Jane Stewart[1142], aged 16, on August 20, 1965. They had two daughters:
        Michelle Lane Danley[2437] born on February 7, 1968 in Escambia, Florida, USA
        Sherry Denise Danley[2438] born on August 10, 1972 in Escambia, Florida, USA

1144. BONNIE MAE STEWART (see Descendants (61)) was born on April 20, 1953, in Florala, Covington, Alabama, USA, to Ernest Stewart[385] and Bonnie Lee Posey[384]. Bonnie Mae became known as "Princess".

1145. MARY ELIZABETH STEWART (see Descendants (61)) was born on December 23, 1955, in Escambia, Florida, USA, to Ernest Stewart[385] and Bonnie Lee Posey[384].
    Mary Elizabeth married three times. She was married to Roger Dishman[1146], Kenny Westervelt[1147] and Thomas Short[1148].

1146. ROGER DISHMAN.
    Roger Dishman married Mary Elizabeth Stewart[1145]. They had one daughter:
        Angela Crystal Dishman[2439] born on September 22, 1974

1147. KENNY WESTERVELT.
    Kenny Westervelt married Mary Elizabeth Stewart[1145]. They had one daughter:
        Heather Lynn Westervelt[2440] born on October 22, 1975

1148. THOMAS SHORT was born to Thomas Davis Short and Louise Stanton.
    Thomas Short married Mary Elizabeth Stewart[1145].

1149. ERNEST STEWART JR. (see Descendants (61)) was born on March 19, 1961 to Ernest Stewart[385] and Bonnie Lee Posey[384].
    Ernest married twice. He was married to Ms. Nolana[1150] and Judy Sable[1151].

1150. MS. NOLANA.
    Ernest Stewart Jr.[1149] married Ms. Nolana. They had two sons:
        Derrick Stewart[2441] born in March 2 A.D. in Escambia, Florida, USA
        Steven Stewart[2442]

1151. JUDY SABLE.
    Ernest Stewart Jr.[1149] married Judy Sable. They had one daughter:
        LeaAnne Stewart[2443]

1152. EVELYN ELAINE TAYLOR (see Descendants (62)) was born on May 5, 1947, in Pensacola, Escambia, Florida, USA, to James Edward Taylor Sr.[388] and Mary Evelyn Posey[387].
- She died on July 31, 2021, aged 74.
- She was buried in Barrancas National Cemeery.

1153. JERRY N. MURDY.
    Jerry N. Murdy married Evelyn Elaine Taylor[1152], aged 19, on January 14, 1967.

1154. GLORIA JEAN TAYLOR (see Descendants (62)) was born on June 11, 1948, in Florala, Covington, Alabama, USA, to James Edward Taylor Sr.[388] and Mary Evelyn Posey[387].

1155. GARY LEFEBVRE.
    Gary Lefebvre married Gloria Jean Taylor[1154], aged 45, on June 27, 1993.

1156. SHERRY DIANE TAYLOR (see Descendants (62)) was born on May 20, 1949, in Florala, Covington, Alabama, USA, to James Edward Taylor Sr.[388] and Mary Evelyn Posey[387].

1157. ROGER PAINTER.
    Roger Painter married Sherry Diane Taylor[1156], aged 23, on June 10, 1972.

1158. JAMES EDWARD TAYLOR JR. (see Descendants (62)) was born on July 20, 1952, in Pensacola, Escambia, Florida, USA, to James Edward Taylor Sr.[388] and Mary Evelyn Posey[387].

1159. DANIEL RICHARD TAYLOR (see Descendants (62)) was born on June 8, 1953, in Pensacola, Escambia, Florida, USA, to James Edward Taylor Sr.[388] and Mary Evelyn Posey[387].

1160. THOMAS PATRICK TAYLOR (see Descendants (62)) was born on June 13, 1954 to James Edward Taylor Sr.[388] and Mary Evelyn Posey[387].
1161. BOBBIE STOUT.
> Thomas Patrick Taylor[1160] married Bobbie Stout.

1162. DAVID ALLEN TAYLOR (see Descendants (62)) was born on March 4, 1957, in Pensacola, Escambia, Florida, USA, to James Edward Taylor Sr.[388] and Mary Evelyn Posey[387].
1163. JULIE MYSIK.
> David Allen Taylor[1162] married Julie Mysik.

1164. JOYCE MARIE POSEY (see Descendants (63)) was born on July 13, 1947, in Florida, United States, to Cleavy Edward Posey Sr.[389] and Ida May Busby[390]. She was recorded in the census on April 1, 1950, aged 2, in 12 Applegate Courts, Brownsville-Brent-Goulding, Escambia, Florida, United States.

1165. LYNN JESSE GARRETT SR.
> Lynn Jesse Garrett Sr. married Joyce Marie Posey[1164], aged 16, on October 10, 1963. They had two children:
>> Lynn Jesse Garrett Jr.[2444] born on July 12, 1964
>> Lana Joyce Posey Garrett[2446] born on December 18, 1969

1166. MARSHA ANN POSEY (see Descendants (63)) was born on August 6, 1953 to Cleavy Edward Posey Sr.[389] and Ida May Busby[390].

1167. JEFFERY ALAN JOHNS was born on October 9, 1959.
> Jeffery Alan Johns, aged 20, married Marsha Ann Posey[1166], aged 26, on May 30, 1980. They had two sons:
>> Jeffery Alan Johns Jr.[2448] born on May 23, 1981
>> Joseph Aaron Johns[2449] born on July 3, 1991; died on September 23, 2020

1168. CEAVIE EDWARD POSEY JR. (see Descendants (63)) was born on April 26, 1956 to Cleavy Edward Posey Sr.[389] and Ida May Busby[390].

1169. DEBORAH JOANN BRADLEY was born on October 23, 1953.
> Ceavie Edward Posey Jr.[1168], aged 24, married Deborah Joann Bradley, aged 26, on May 29, 1980. They had two children:
>> Stacie LeAnn Posey[2450] born on January 9, 1981
>> Jason Edward Posey[2451] born on May 18, 1982

1170. JENNIFER KIM POSEY (see Descendants (63)) was born on September 13, 1961 to Cleavy Edward Posey Sr.[389] and Ida May Busby[390].
> Jennifer Kim married twice. She was married to William Jesse Howard[1171] and Mr. Lazzaro[1172].

1171. WILLIAM JESSE HOWARD was born on July 30, 1958. He died on May 7, 1993, aged 34 years.
    William Jesse Howard, aged 21, married Jennifer Kim Posey[1170], aged 18, on November 10, 1979 in Escambia, Florida, USA. They had one daughter:
        Stefanie Marshann Howard[2452] born on August 11, 1980
    The following information is also recorded for this family:
- Death of Spouse.

1172. MR. LAZZARO.
    Mr. Lazzaro married Jennifer Kim Posey[1170].

1173. SANDRA ANN WALLACE (see Descendants (64)) was born on November 8, 1943, in Alabama, United States, to Aurthor Wallace[393] and Edith Florine Bass[392].
- She was recorded in the census on April 1, 1950, aged 6, in 407 Church Street, Andalusia, Covington, Alabama, United States.
- She died on September 17, 2000, aged 56.

1174. WILLIAM J. BARKSDALE was born on June 16, 1942.
    William J. Barksdale, aged 32, married Sandra Ann Wallace[1173], aged 30, on June 29, 1974. They had one daughter:
        Susan Claire Barksdale[2453] born on October 2, 1977

1175. PHILLIP AURTHUR WALLACE (see Descendants (64)) was born on April 26, 1947, in Alabama, United States, to Aurthor Wallace[393] and Edith Florine Bass[392]. He was recorded in the census on April 1, 1950, aged 2, in 407 Church Street, Andalusia, Covington, Alabama, United States.

1176. PAMELA JANE MURPHREE was born on September 12, 1948.
    Phillip Aurthur Wallace[1175], aged 23, married Pamela Jane Murphree, aged 21, on June 13, 1970. They had two children:
        Amy Melissa Wallace[2454] born on October 24, 1976
        Andrew Middleton Wallace[2455] born on April 28, 1981

1177. WILLIAM HOLLEY WALLACE (see Descendants (64)) was born on July 4, 1950 to Aurthor Wallace[393] and Edith Florine Bass[392].

1178. JADA HARVEY was born on September 6, 1949. She died on February 26, 1995, aged 45 years.
    William Holley Wallace[1177], aged 27, married Jada Harvey, aged 28, on February 28, 1978. They had three sons:
        Charles William Wallace[2456] born on October 16, 1978
        Christopher Edward Wallace[2457] born on September 17, 1983
        Chad Alexander Wallace[2458] born on October 7, 1987

1179. JAMES MICHAEL BASS (see Descendants (64)) was born on August 10, 1945 to James Verlin Bass[394] and Jane Lee Tart[395].
- He was recorded in the census on April 1, 1950, aged 4, in 601 W Jordan, Brownsville-Brent-Goulding, Escambia, Florida, United States.

The following information is also recorded for James Michael:
- Military Service from 1966 to June 1969, aged about 22.

Note: *U.S. Army Viet Nam 36th Signal Battalion 1 tour - 2nd Battalion, 36th Inf. Reg. half tour, 101sh Airborn - Special Forces at Command Control North (CNN) half tour.*
(Military Service)

1180. LINDA RIDGE was born on July 8, 1948.
    James Michael Bass[1179], aged 23, married Linda Ridge, aged 20, on May 31, 1969. They had two sons:
        James Holley Bass[2459] born on January 23, 1970
        Brian Bass[2460] born on February 17, 1977

1181. PATRICIA ANNELLE BASS (see Descendants (64)) was born on March 3, 1950, in Florida, United States, to James Verlin Bass[394] and Jane Lee Tart[395]. She was recorded in the census on April 1, 1950, as an infant, in 601 W Jordan, Brownsville-Brent-Goulding, Escambia, Florida, United States.

1182. JOHN RICHARD LINCOLN was born on February 25, 1948.
> John Richard Lincoln, aged 23, married Patricia Annelle Bass[1181], aged 21, on December 18, 1971. They had two children:
>> John Stephen Lincoln[2461] born on June 10, 1975
>> Elizabeth Annelle Lincoln[2462] born on July 6, 1978

1183. ROGER DOUGLAS BASS (see Descendants (64)) was born on April 8, 1952 to James Verlin Bass[394] and Jane Lee Tart[395].

1184. PAMELA NUNN was born on July 30, 1951.
> Roger Douglas Bass[1183], aged 19, married Pamela Nunn, aged 20, on March 18, 1972. They had one son:
>> Eric Douglas Bass[2463] born on April 8, 1974

1185. JEFFREY MARLIN BASS (see Descendants (64)) was born on March 10, 1949, in Florida, United States, to Marlin Holley Bass[396] and Charlotte Atkins[397]. He was recorded in the census on April 1, 1950, aged 1, in 5 3/10 from Okaloss Line on The Right Leaving Okaloosa County Line Proceeding West on No. 4highway No 4, Jay, Santa Rosa, Florida, United States.

1186. SUSAN WITTMAN was born on April 27, 1950.
> Jeffrey Marlin Bass[1185], aged 23, married Susan Wittman, aged 22, on January 27, 1973. They had one son:
>> Seth Jeffrey Bass[2464] born on June 15, 1982

1187. DOTTIE LYNN BASS (see Descendants (64)) was born on November 4, 1951 to Marlin Holley Bass[396] and Charlotte Atkins[397].

1188. JERRY DEGRAAF was born on August 15, 1949.
> Jerry Degraaf, aged -1923, married Dottie Lynn Bass[1187], aged -1925, in January 27 A.D. They had two children:
>> Jason Kyle Degraaf[2465] born on December 25, 1972
>> Amanda Michelle Degraaf[2466] born on March 8, 1975

1189. DUDLEY DEAN BASS (see Descendants (64)) was born on October 28, 1956 to Marlin Holley Bass[396] and Charlotte Atkins[397].
> Dudley Dean married twice. He was married to Donna Cook[1190] and Debra Harris[1191].

1190. DONNA COOK was born on April 12, 1956.
> Dudley Dean Bass[1189], aged 17, married Donna Cook, aged 18, on July 20, 1974. They had five children:
>> Adam Dean Bass[2467] born on February 4, 1975
>> Erin Leigh Bass[2468] born on April 21, 1977
>> Lorin Holly Bass[2469] born on August 19, 1981
>> Janet Kay Bass[2470] born on December 12, 1986
>> Amy Elizabeth Bass[2471] born on November 7, 1988

1191. DEBRA HARRIS.
> Dudley Dean Bass[1189], aged 48, married Debra Harris on June 4, 2005.

1192. GLORIA SUE DOTSON (see Descendants (64)) was born on February 11, 1951 to Glenn Dotson[399] and Eula Virginia Bass[398].

1193. CARL MANUEL GRIFFITH (see Descendants (65)) was born on July 6, 1948, in Florida, United States, to Otis C Griffith[401] and Carolyn Bass[400]. He was recorded in the census on April 1, 1950, aged 1, in Florida Highway 4 South of Baker, Milligan, Okaloosa, Florida, United States.

1194. ROGER JOSEPH GRIFFITH (see Descendants (65)) was born on September 5, 1949 to Otis C Griffith[401] and Carolyn Bass[400]. He died on September 28, 1949, aged 0.

1195. RONALD LAWRENCE GRIFFITH (see Descendants (65)) was born on September 5, 1949 to Otis C Griffith[401] and Carolyn Bass[400]. He died on September 29, 1949, aged 0.

1196. STEPHEN DALE GRIFFITH (see Descendants (65)) was born on January 22, 1952 to Otis C Griffith[401] and Carolyn Bass[400].
1197. PAM NICHOLS.
> Stephen Dale Griffith[1196] married Pam Nichols. They had two daughters:
> Joanna Nichole Griffith[2472] born on December 14, 1971
> Stacie Renee Griffith[2474] born on October 4, 1979

1198. THERESA ANN GRIFFITH (see Descendants (65)) was born on December 5, 1956 to Otis C Griffith[401] and Carolyn Bass[400].
1199. ANTHONY F. ERMY.
> Anthony F. Ermy married Theresa Ann Griffith[1198]. They had two sons:
> Michael A. Ermy[2475] born on June 11, 1979
> Daniel P. Ermy[2476] born on March 10, 1983

1200. KATHY BASS (see Descendants (65)) was born on December 11, 1956 to Calvin Winston Bass[402] and Marilyn Sanford[403].
> Kathy married twice. She was married to Kenny Lowery[1201] and Jerry Carroll[1202].
1201. KENNY LOWERY. He died on November 7, 1988.
> Kenny Lowery married Kathy Bass[1200].
1202. JERRY CARROLL.
> Jerry Carroll married Kathy Bass[1200].

1203. BRENDA BASS (see Descendants (65)) was born on March 27, 1959 to Calvin Winston Bass[402] and Marilyn Sanford[403].
1204. ROGER HOOKS.
> Roger Hooks married Brenda Bass[1203]. They had one son:
> Nathinal Hooks[2477] born on January 10, 1985

1205. YVONNE BASS (see Descendants (65)) was born on May 30, 1965 to Calvin Winston Bass[402] and Marilyn Sanford[403].
1206. JOHN L. TOBIAS.
> John L. Tobias married Yvonne Bass[1205]. They had one son:
> Ashton Tobias[2478] born on December 11, 1989

1207. STEVE ELVIN BASS (see Descendants (65)) was born on February 3, 1965 to Stephen Durward Bass[404] and Loretta Griffith[405].

1208. MICHAEL DOUGLAS BASS (see Descendants (65)) was born on December 4, 1966 to Stephen Durward Bass[404] and Loretta Griffith[405].
1209. SUZANNE RANKIN.
> Michael Douglas Bass[1208] married Suzanne Rankin. They had two children:
> Sam Michael Bass[2479] born on September 2, 1992
> Elizabeth Ann Bass[2480] born on December 2, 1993

1210. SHARON ADAMS (see Descendants (65)) was born on December 31, 1953 to Harold Jack Adams[407] and Charity Delores Bass[406].
> Sharon married twice. She was married to Thomas White[1211] and Larry Lahammann[1212].

1211. THOMAS WHITE. He died in March 1982.
> Thomas White married Sharon Adams[1210], aged 17, on September 1, 1971.
1212. LARRY LAHAMMANN. He died in May 1990.

Larry Lahammann married Sharon Adams[1210], aged 29, in November 1983.

1213. HAROLD DEWAYNE ADAMS (see Descendants (65)) was born on March 15, 1956 to Harold Jack Adams[407] and Charity Delores Bass[406]. He died on August 8, 2008, aged 52.

1214. WALTER DEAN ADAMS (see Descendants (65)) was born on October 20, 1961 to Harold Jack Adams[407] and Charity Delores Bass[406].
Walter Dean married twice. He was married to Mary Jo[1215] and Tammy Theford Blair[1216].

1215. MARY JO. She died in 1991.
Walter Dean Adams[1214], aged about 25, married Mary Jo in 1987. They had two children:
Devin Phillips Adams[2481] born on March 15, 1988
Lindsey Nichole Adams[2483] born on June 16, 1989

1216. TAMMY THEFORD BLAIR was born on March 16, 1967.
Walter Dean Adams[1214], aged 31, married Tammy Theford Blair, aged 25, on November 21, 1992. They had two children:
Devin Randal Adams[2485] born on May 27, 1987
Kayla Danielle Adams[2487] born on February 15, 1989

1217. WILLIAM AARON ADAMS (see Descendants (65)) was born to Harold Jack Adams[407] and Charity Delores Bass[406]. He died on October 25, 2010.

1218. ROGER DALE BASS (see Descendants (65)) was born on February 21, 1962 to Farrell Dale Bass[409] and Barbara Kay Sees[410].

1219. DONNA ?.
Roger Dale Bass[1218] married Donna ?. They had one son:
Roger Dale Bass Jr.[2488] born on June 11, 1985

1220. ROBERT BASS (see Descendants (65)) was born on October 7, 1979 to Farrell Dale Bass[409] and Carol Gries[411].

1221. THOMAS MATTHEW BASS (see Descendants (65)) was born on January 8, 1983 to Farrell Dale Bass[409] and Carol Gries[411].

1222. DANNE LOUISE BASS (see Descendants (65)) was born on February 21, 1967 to Joe Farris Bass[412] and Kay Jorgenson[413].

1223. JAMES FARRIS BASS (see Descendants (65)) was born to Joe Farris Bass[412] and Betty Courtney[414].
James Farris fathered one daughter:
Tammy Spithouler[2489]

1224. BRIAN JOSEPH BASS (see Descendants (65)) was born on March 14, 1970 to Harvey Middleton Bass[415] and Aleatha Nixon[416].

1225. ERIC RICHARD BASS (see Descendants (65)) was born on January 15, 1972 to Harvey Middleton Bass[415] and Aleatha Nixon[416].

1226. JOHN WILLIAM BASS SR. (see Descendants (66)) was born on March 6, 1949, in Andalusia, Covington, Alabama, USA, to Joel Sidney Bass[417] and Mary Elizabeth Henderson[418]. John William became known as "Bill".
  • He was recorded in the census on April 1, 1950, aged 1, in 1c Granes Apartments, Auburn, Lee, Alabama, United States.
The following information is also recorded for Bill:
  • Military Service.

1227. CELIA ANNE FARRAR was born on November 14, 1946, in Atmore, Escambia, Alabama, USA.

John William Bass Sr.[1226], aged 20, married Celia Anne Farrar, aged 22, on August 30, 1969 in Canoe, Escambia, Alabama, USA. They had two sons:
> John William Bass Jr.[2490] born on May 4, 1970 in Auburn, Lee, Alabama, USA
> Joel Farrar Bass[2492] born on January 13, 1975 in Winter Park, Orange, Florida, USA

1228. JOEL SIDNEY BASS JR. (see Descendants (66)) was born on March 6, 1954 to Joel Sidney Bass[417] and Mary Elizabeth Henderson[418]. Joel Sidney became known as "Joe".

1229. GINA JOY BEHR.
Joel Sidney Bass Jr.[1228] and Gina Joy Behr had two children:
> Joel Sidney Bass III[2494]
> Julia Elizabeth Bass[2495]

The following information is also recorded for this family:
- Unknown Relationship.

1230. MARGUERITTE DAWN BOLDING (see Descendants (66)) was born on September 20, 1950, in New Orleans, Louisiana, USA, to Mark Anthony Bolding[420] and Margueritte Catherine Bass[419].

1231. DENNIS PAUL OLVANY was born on June 7, 1948, in Kew Garden, New York, USA.
Dennis Paul Olvany, aged 25, married Margueritte Dawn Bolding[1230], aged 23, on May 11, 1974 in Metairie, Jefferson Parish, Louisianna, USA. They had two sons:
> Dennis Michael Olvany[2496] born on December 17, 1976 in Saint Joe, Gulf, Florida, USA
> Matthew Stephen Olvany[2497] born on December 12, 1979 in Metairie, Jefferson Parish, Louisianna, USA

1232. LYNDA ANN BYRD (see Descendants (66)) was born on June 19, 1947, in Chattahoochee, Gadsden, Florida, USA, to William Mullina Byrd[422] and Martha Ann Bass[421]. She was recorded in the census on April 1, 1950, aged 2, in Chattahoochee, Gadsden, Florida, United States.

1233. GARY GLENN KINMAN was born on September 27, 1948, in Walla Walla, Walla Walla, Washington, USA.
Gary Glenn Kinman, aged 24, married Lynda Ann Byrd[1232], aged 25, on December 20, 1972 in Crestview, Okaloosa, Florida, USA. They had one daughter:
> Heather Amanda Kinman[2498] born on May 15, 1978 in Geneva, Geneva, Alabama, USA

1234. MYCHAELLE JOY BYRD (see Descendants (66)) was born on December 7, 1955 to William Mullina Byrd[422] and Martha Ann Bass[421].

1235. GARY ANTHONY MONARCH was born on September 23, 1945, in Troy, New York, USA.
Gary Anthony Monarch, aged 36, married Mychaelle Joy Byrd[1234], aged 26, on February 14, 1982 in Wakulla Springs, Florida, USA. They had one daughter:
> Jennifer Michelle Monarch[2500] born on February 24, 1985 in Mesa, Maricopa, Arizona, USA

1236. NANCY JANE BYRD (see Descendants (66)) was born on June 17, 1957 to William Mullina Byrd[422] and Martha Ann Bass[421].

1237. SIDNEY T. MCGLAMERY was born on March 12, 1948, in Blakley, Early, Georgia, USA.
Sidney T. McGlamery, aged 31, married Nancy Jane Byrd[1236], aged 22, on December 15, 1979 in Tallahassee, Leon, Florida, USA. They had two daughters:
> Amanda Ryan McGlamery[2502] born on November 23, 1980 in Tallahassee, Leon, Florida, USA
> Mychaelle Ann McGlamery[2503] born on April 19, 1983 in Tallahassee, Leon, Florida, USA

1238. GEORGE STEPHEN KILCREASE (see Descendants (66)) was born on October 12, 1950 to James Woodrow Kilcrease[423] and Martha Ann Bass[421].

1239. KATHLEEN ANN KILCREASE (see Descendants (66)) was born on September 26, 1952 to James Woodrow Kilcrease[423] and Martha Ann Bass[421].

1240. MR. SMITH.
Mr. Smith married Kathleen Ann Kilcrease[1239].

1241. PHILLIP WAYNE KILCREASE (see Descendants (66)) was born on December 24, 1955 to James Woodrow Kilcrease[423] and Martha Ann Bass[421].

1242. ANGELIA RENEE KILCREASE (see Descendants (66)) was born on June 17, 1967, in Fort Walton Beach, Okaloosa, Florida, USA, to James Woodrow Kilcrease[423] and Martha Ann Bass[421].
Angelia Renee married twice. She was married to Paul Heal[1243] and Herman Edward Chelette III[1244].

1243. PAUL HEAL.
    Paul Heal married Angelia Renee Kilcrease[1242].
1244. HERMAN EDWARD CHELETTE III was born on March 23, 1966, in Marquette, Marquette, Michigan, USA.
    Herman Edward Chelette III, aged 23, married Angelia Renee Kilcrease[1242], aged 22, on February 27, 1990 in Tallahassee, Leon, Florida, USA. They had one daughter:
        Bronwyn Elise Chelette[2504] born on September 14, 1994 in Tallahassee, Leon, Florida, USA

1245. JUDITH BASS (see Descendants (66)) was born on November 24, 1947, in Troy, Pike, Alabama, USA, to John Thomas Bass[425] and Roberta Howell[426]. Judith became known as "Judy". She was recorded in the census on April 1, 1950, aged 2, in 30 Panama City, Bay, Florida, United States.
    Judith married twice. She was married to Ray Elliot Anderson[1246] and Rick Casey[1247].
1246. RAY ELLIOT ANDERSON.
    Ray Elliot Anderson married Judith Bass[1245]. They had two children:
        Sean Anderson[2505] born on June 15, 1970 in Shreveport, Caddo Parish, Louisiana, USA
        Ashley Leigh Anderson[2506] born on April 10, 1980 in Enterprise, Coffee, Alabama, USA
1247. RICK CASEY.
    Rick Casey married Judith Bass[1245].

1248. JACQUELINE BASS (see Descendants (66)) was born on August 29, 1950, in Panama City, Bay, Florida, USA, to John Thomas Bass[425] and Roberta Howell[426]. Jacqueline became known as "Jackie".
- She died (Chronic Obstructive Pulmonary Disease) on August 21, 2018, aged 67, in Pensacola, Santa Rosa, Florida, USA.

The following information is also recorded for Jackie:
- Military Service.

1249. CHARLES MANUEL MESSICK was born on March 13, 1948, in Andalusia, Covington, Alabama, USA.
    Charles Manuel Messick, aged 24, married Jacqueline Bass[1248], aged 22, on March 9, 1973. They had two children:
        Russell Eastman Bass Messick[2507] born on September 3, 1971 in Savannah, Chatham, Georgia, USA
        Roberta Ruth Messick[2508] born on July 4, 1975 in Andalusia, Covington, Alabama, USA

1250. JOHN THOMAS BASS JR. (see Descendants (66)) was born on September 5, 1952, in Panama City, Bay, Florida, USA, to John Thomas Bass[425] and Roberta Howell[426]. John Thomas became known as "Johnny". He died on October 30, 2014, aged 62 years.
    John Thomas married twice. He was married to Dorothy King[1251] and Freida Rabren[1252].

1251. DOROTHY KING.
    John Thomas Bass Jr.[1250] married Dorothy King, and they were divorced. They had one daughter:
        Alanna Nicole Bass[2509] born on January 9, 1983
1252. FREIDA RABREN was born on February 11, 1953, in Andalusia, Covington, Alabama, USA.
    Freida married twice. She was married to John Thomas Bass Jr.[1250] and Mr. Morgan.
    John Thomas Bass Jr.[1250], aged 36, married Freida Rabren, aged 36, on March 17, 1989 in Andalusia, Covington, Alabama, USA.
    Mr. Morgan married Freida Rabren. They had two sons:
        John David Morgan born before 1979; died before 1989
        Shaun T. Morgan Bass born on September 17, 1979

1253. JANET BASS (see Descendants (66)) was born on March 13, 1957, in Panama City, Bay, Florida, USA, to John Thomas Bass[425] and Roberta Howell[426]. Janet became known as "Jan".
The following information is also recorded for Jan:
- Military Service.
1254. LYNN DAVID REDDISH was born on September 1, 1955, in Sturart, Martin, Florida, USA.
    Lynn David Reddish, aged 32, married Janet Bass[1253], aged 31, on April 22, 1988 in Andalusia, Covington, Alabama, USA. They had two children:
        Kristina Lynn Reddish[2511] born on January 3, 1989 in Andalusia, Covington, Alabama, USA
        Shane Stelmon Reddish[2512] born on September 13, 1991 in Andalusia, Covington, Alabama, USA

Direct Relations

1255. LOYCE ELAINE MCVAY (see Descendants (67)) was born on December 25, 1944 to Gaston Durell McVay[428] and Mavis Earline Bass[427].

1256. RICHARD WAYNE MCVAY (see Descendants (67)) was born on October 26, 1946, in Andalusia, Covington, Alabama, USA, to Gaston Durell McVay[428] and Mavis Earline Bass[427].
The following information is also recorded for Richard Wayne:
• Military Service.
Note: *USMC Viet Nam.*
(Military Service)

1257. ALICE DRUCILLA SHORT was born on July 8, 1946. Alice Drucilla became known as "Dru".
Richard Wayne McVay[1256], aged 31, married Alice Drucilla Short, aged 31, on July 1, 1978. They had one daughter:
Stacey Elaine McVay[2514] born on February 5, 1980

1258. JOAN MARIE MCVAY (see Descendants (67)) was born on February 22, 1949, in Andalusia, Covington, Alabama, USA, to Gaston Durell McVay[428] and Mavis Earline Bass[427].

1259. CHARLES HERBERT WILLIAMSON was born on March 3, 1943.
• He died on November 27, 2007, aged 64.
• He was buried in Pensacola Memorial Gardens, Pensacola, Escambia County, Florida, USA.
Charles Herbert had two partnerships. He was married to Joan Marie McVay[1258]. He was also the partner of Ms. ?.
Note: *Charles H. Williamson, age 64, of Pensacola, passed away Tuesday, November 27, 2007 at Sacred Heart Hospital. Charles was a lifelong member of Brentwood Assembly of God Church where he was a Trustee. He was a member of the finance committee, Assistant Men's Ministry Leader and a member of the adult choir. He was the owner and operator of Continental Hair Design for over 30 years.*
(Death)
Charles Herbert Williamson, aged 30, married Joan Marie McVay[1258], aged 24, on August 31, 1973. They had one son, and assumed parenthood of another three children:
Charles Anthony Williamson[2516] by adoption
Sandra Michelle Williamson[2519] by adoption
Gordon Michael Williamson[2521] by adoption
Shane Eric Williamson[2523] born on July 18, 1976
Charles Herbert Williamson and Ms. ? had three children:
Charles Anthony Williamson[2516] born on August 3, 1961
Sandra Michelle Williamson[2519] born on July 11, 1963
Gordon Michael Williamson[2521] born on February 24, 1966
The following information is also recorded for this family:
• Unknown Relationship.

1260. MICHAEL RAY MCVAY (see Descendants (67)) was born on February 28, 1951, in Andalusia, Covington, Alabama, USA, to Gaston Durell McVay[428] and Mavis Earline Bass[427].

1261. NANCY RUNAE NELSON was born on December 16, 1954.

Michael Ray McVay[1260], aged 20, married Nancy Runae Nelson, aged 17, on February 26, 1972. They had two sons:
- Jeffery Michael McVay[2525] born on July 19, 1973
- Jeremy Wayne McVay[2527] born on August 20, 1977

1262. SAMUEL PAUL MCVAY (see Descendants (67)) was born on September 7, 1955, in Andalusia, Covington, Alabama, USA, to Gaston Durell McVay[428] and Mavis Earline Bass[427].

1263. MARY JUNE PICIRILLI was born on May 10, 1955.

Samuel Paul McVay[1262], aged 19, married Mary June Picirilli, aged 20, on August 23, 1975. They had two daughters:
- Stephanie Jane McVay[2529] born on December 16, 1978 in Tennessee, USA
- Suzanne Lea McVay[2530] born on July 9, 1982 in Tennessee, USA

1264. DAVID MICAH MCVAY (see Descendants (67)) was born on October 24, 1956, in Andalusia, Covington, Alabama, USA, to Gaston Durell McVay[428] and Mavis Earline Bass[427].
David Micah married twice. He was married to Judith Ann Pittman[1265] and Tracie Renea Dubose[1266].

1265. JUDITH ANN PITTMAN was born on February 9, 1961.
David Micah McVay[1264], aged 22, married Judith Ann Pittman, aged 18, on August 3, 1979 in Santa Rosa, Florida, USA, and they were divorced. They had two children:
- Julie Crystal Qualls[2532] born on July 14, 1982
- Cody Allen Qualls[2535] born on June 22, 1986

1266. TRACIE RENEA DUBOSE was born on January 10, 1967.
David Micah McVay[1264], aged 31, married Tracie Renea Dubose, aged 21, on August 6, 1988. They had two daughters:
- Talitha Renea McVay[2537] born on November 20, 1990
- Malesha Nicole McVay[2539] born on August 9, 1994

1267. NATHANIEL JOEL MCVAY (see Descendants (67)) was born on July 26, 1958, in Andalusia, Covington, Alabama, USA, to Gaston Durell McVay[428] and Mavis Earline Bass[427]. Nathaniel Joel became known as "Nat".

1268. LINDA GAIL MCLEOD was born on December 29, 1960.

Nathaniel Joel McVay[1267], aged 22, married Linda Gail McLeod, aged 20, on April 4, 1981. They had three children:
- Natalie Melinda McVay[2541] born on November 17, 1983
- Nathan Jared McVay[2543] born on November 8, 1985
- Alexander Jace McVay[2545] born on August 7, 2006

1269. MIRIAM LOIS MCVAY (see Descendants (67)) was born on May 31, 1962, in Andalusia, Covington, Alabama, USA, to Gaston Durell McVay[428] and Mavis Earline Bass[427].

1270. MATTHEW WAYNE CUNNINGHAM was born on October 14, 1961.
Matthew Wayne Cunningham, aged 25, married Miriam Lois McVay[1269], aged 24, on November 21, 1986.

1271. **JONATHAN MARK MCVAY** (see Descendants (67)) was born on November 11, 1964, in Andalusia, Covington, Alabama, USA, to Gaston Durell McVay[428] and Mavis Earline Bass[427].
Jonathan Mark married twice. He was married to Tammy E. Daniels[1272] and Debbie Burgdorf[1273].

1272. **TAMMY E. DANIELS** was born on August 4, 1968.
    Jonathan Mark McVay[1271], aged 21, married Tammy E. Daniels, aged 18, on November 5, 1986, and they were divorced. They had two sons:
        Joshua Mark McVay[2546] born on December 17, 1987
        Jacob Daniel McVay[2550] born on May 9, 1989

1273. **DEBBIE BURGDORF** was born on June 28, 1966.
Debbie married twice. She was married to Jonathan Mark McVay[1271] and Mr. ?.
    Jonathan Mark McVay[1271], aged 41, married Debbie Burgdorf, aged 40, on July 5, 2006.
    Mr. ? married Debbie Burgdorf. They had three sons:
        Chris Burgdorf born on March 3, 1984
        David Peek born on April 5, 1985
        T.J. Peek born on May 8, 1990

1274. **STEPHEN GENE BASS** (see Descendants (67)) was born on March 12, 1947, in Montgomery, Montgomery, Alabama, USA, to James Marcus Bass[429] and Mary Louise Johnson[430]. Stephen Gene became known as "Steve".
- He was recorded in the census on April 1, 1950, aged 3, in 1718 Ashland Ave., Niagara Falls, Niagara, New York, United States.
- He died on November 6, 2022, aged 75, in Abbeville, Henry, Alabama, USA.

The following information is also recorded for Steve:
- Military Service.

Stephen Gene married four times. He was married to Josephine Anne Darst[1275], Susan Malphrus[1276], Terry Carol Nallen[1277] and Cathrine Spivey[1278].
Notes:
- *Steve Bass was born in Montgomery and lived in Andalusia before moving to Lake Eufaula in Henry County in 2010. He served his country in the U. S. Air Force during the Vietnam War era. Steve was a member of the Judson Baptist Church. He was retired from Power South in Andalusia as a Heavy Equipment Technician. He was an avid outdoorsman, who loved God, his country, his family and his church.*
(Death)
- *U.S. Airforce, Vietnam Era, Germany.*
(Military Service)

1275. **JOSEPHINE ANNE DARST** was born on November 25, 1950.
    Stephen Gene Bass[1274], aged 24, married Josephine Anne Darst, aged 21, on November 27, 1971 in Palm Beach, Palm Beach, Florida, USA, and they were divorced. They had four children:
        Marcus Stephen Bass[2553] born on April 9, 1973 in Andalusia, Covington, Alabama, USA
        James Scott Bass[2555] born on October 22, 1974 in Andalusia, Covington, Alabama, USA
        Jeffery Philip Bass[2557] born on August 21, 1976 in Andalusia, Covington, Alabama, USA
        Kelly Suzanne Bass[2559] born on January 29, 1981 in Andalusia, Covington, Alabama, USA

1276. **SUSAN MALPHRUS**.
    Stephen Gene Bass[1274], aged 38, married Susan Malphrus in September 1985, and they were divorced.

1277. **TERRY CAROL NALLEN**.
    Stephen Gene Bass[1274], aged 46, married Terry Carol Nallen on December 31, 1993.

1278. **CATHRINE SPIVEY**. Cathrine became known as "Cathy".
    Stephen Gene Bass[1274] married Cathrine Spivey.

1279. **SUSAN LYNN BASS** (see Descendants (67)) was born on August 29, 1950 to James Marcus Bass[429] and Mary Louise Johnson[430].

1280. MARSHALL LEE STOCKTON was born on January 14, 1948, in Conyers, Rockdale, Georgia, USA.
>   Marshall Lee Stockton, aged 23, married Susan Lynn Bass[1279], aged 20, on June 20, 1971 in Conyers, Rockdale, Georgia, USA. They had two children:
>> Lori Marie Stockton[2561] born on October 5, 1973 in Dekalb, Georgia, USA
>> Marshall Kevin Stockton[2563] born on August 27, 1976 in Dekalb, Georgia, USA

1281. BARBARA ELAINE DAY (see Descendants (67)) was born about 1945, in Alabama, United States, to Cecil Larry Day[433] and Sibyl Louise Bass[432]. She was recorded in the census on April 1, 1950, aged about 4, in 6437 Division Ave., Birmingham, Jefferson, Alabama, United States.
Barbara Elaine had two partnerships. She was married to Larry Van[1283]. She was also the partner of William Dwight Henderson[1282].

1282. WILLIAM DWIGHT HENDERSON was born on February 19, 1947, in Pike, Alabama, USA.
>   William Dwight Henderson and Barbara Elaine Day[1281] became partners.
>   The following information is also recorded for this family:
>> • Unknown Relationship.

1283. LARRY VAN.
>   Larry Van married Barbara Elaine Day[1281], aged about 14, on December 23, 1959. They had two children:
>> Larry Van Jr.[2565] born on October 2, 1960
>> Scarlet Van[2566] born on October 24, 1962

1284. CECIL LARRY DAY II (see Descendants (67)) was born on November 17, 1951, in Topeka, Shawnee, Kansas, USA, to Cecil Larry Day[433] and Sibyl Louise Bass[432].
>   • He died on April 26, 2015, aged 63, in Andalusia, Covington, Alabama, United States.
>   • He was buried in Andalusia Memorial Cemetery, Andalusia, Covington, Alabama, USA.

1285. GEORGE ANTHONY DAY (see Descendants (67)) was born on December 26, 1953, in Montgomery, Montgomery, Alabama, USA, to Cecil Larry Day[433] and Sibyl Louise Bass[432]. George Anthony became known as "Tony".
>   The following information is also recorded for Tony:
>   • Military Service.

1286. JOYCE KING was born on January 13, 1956. She died on February 5, 2022, aged 66.
>   George Anthony Day[1285], aged 21, married Joyce King, aged 19, on May 9, 1975. They had two sons:
>> Timothy Patrick Day[2568] born on July 20, 1982
>> Christopher Stacy Day[2569] born on February 1, 1990

1287. TAMMY JOY DAY (see Descendants (67)) was born on July 8, 1962 to Cecil Larry Day[433] and Sibyl Louise Bass[432].
>   Tammy Joy married her second cousin, Royce Caephus Bass[1915].

1288. GARY WAYNE BASS (see Descendants (67)) was born on June 15, 1949, in Niagara Falls, Niagara, New York, USA, to Grover Alcus Bass[434] and Dorothy June Rusk[435]. He was recorded in the census on April 1, 1950, as an infant, in Santa Anna, San Antonio, Bexar, Texas, United States.

1289. ANN ALLPORT was born on June 18, 1949.
>   Gary Wayne Bass[1288], aged 22, married Ann Allport, aged 22, on July 2, 1971. They had two children:
>> Sara Suzanne Bass[2574] born on July 4, 1980
>> Mark Daron William Bass[2575] born on July 23, 1983

1290. KATHY JEAN BASS (see Descendants (67)) was born on August 6, 1950 to Grover Alcus Bass[434] and Dorothy June Rusk[435].

1291. RICHARD KENNETH BAEHR was born on April 9, 1950.

Direct Relations

Richard Kenneth Baehr, aged 21, married Kathy Jean Bass[1290], aged 20, on June 26, 1971. They had two children:
> James Richard Baehr[2576] born on May 26, 1972
> Susan Jean Baehr[2578] born on January 19, 1974

1292. GREGORY ALAN BASS (see Descendants (67)) was born on August 2, 1952 to Grover Alcus Bass[434] and Dorothy June Rusk[435]. Gregory Alan became known as "Greg".
- Greg became a Justic of the Peace.
- In 1974, aged about 21, he was educated in Kentucky, USA (Transylvania University).

Gregory Alan married twice. He was married to Yvonna Christine Hopkins[1293] and Kimberly Layne Hopkins[1294].

Note: *It's the end of an era in Royalton Town Court. Town justice Greg Bass, 65, heard his last cases onTuesday. He's retiring on Dec. 31, after 28 years on the bench, which makes him the longestcontinuously serving justice in the town's history. In recognition of Bass's public service record, theRoyalton Town Board approved naming the town courtroom after him. The nameplate over theentrance, which reads "Gregory A. Bass Courtroom," was unveiled earlier this month, during thetown court's holiday party at the town hall. The unveiling was a surprise for Bass. Traditionally, thecourt's holiday party is held at the Village Eatery in Lockport; but this year, Bass was informed, therestaurant was overbooked, so the party would have to be at the town hall. Bass's relatives from outof state were in on the surprise and were present for the unveiling. Bass said he was "completelyoverwhelmed" by the honor. "Totally unexpected. "James Budde, town board member and townjustice-elect, said the naming celebrates Bass's "unblemished record of service". -"Lockport Journal" Dec 20, 2017.*

1293. YVONNA CHRISTINE HOPKINS was born on September 11, 1951. Yvonna Christine became known as "Chris".
- Chris was educated (Christine received her Bachelor of Arts Degree in Education from Transylvania University in Lexington, KY).
- She died on October 30, 2008, aged 57.

Gregory Alan Bass[1292], aged 21, married Yvonna Christine Hopkins, aged 22, on April 20, 1974. They had two children:
> Joshua Alan Bass[2581] born on November 14, 1976
> Teri Lyn Bass[2584] born on April 14, 1981

The following information is also recorded for this family:
- Death of Spouse.

1294. KIMBERLY LAYNE HOPKINS was born on December 23, 1955. Kimberly Layne became known as "Kim". Kimberly Layne had two partnerships. She was married to Gregory Alan Bass[1292]. She was also the partner of Mr. Lown.

Gregory Alan Bass[1292], aged 60, married Kimberly Layne Hopkins, aged 56, on October 13, 2012.

Mr. Lown and Kimberly Layne Hopkins had two children:
> Justin Reese Lown born on November 8, 1978
> Erin Fatima Lown born on June 6, 1984

The following information is also recorded for this family:
- Unknown Relationship.

1295. KAREN MAE BASS (see Descendants (67)) was born on September 10, 1954, in Lockport, Niagara, New York, USA, to Grover Alcus Bass[434] and Dorothy June Rusk[435].

1296. DAVID LAVERNE MACLAM was born on July 31, 1953.
David Laverne Maclam, aged 20, married Karen Mae Bass[1295], aged 18, on August 5, 1973. They had two daughters:
> Stacie Ann Maclam[2586] born on October 13, 1974
> Bethany Marie Maclam[2588] born on January 8, 1977

1297. DEBORAH LEE MARTIN (see Descendants (67)) was born on December 19, 1951 to Willard Daniel Martin[437] and Margueritte Elizabeth Bass[436].

1298. WILLIAM F. HOOPER.
William F. Hooper married Deborah Lee Martin[1297], aged 20, on November 25, 1972. They had two children:
> William Adam Hooper[2589] born on May 17, 1979 in Troy, Pike, Alabama, USA
> Christopher Lindsay Hooper[2590] born on May 7, 1982 in Troy, Pike, Alabama, USA

1299. DANNA ELIZABETH MARTIN (see Descendants (67)) was born on November 17, 1955 to Willard Daniel Martin[437] and Margueritte Elizabeth Bass[436].

1300. G. DOUGLAS WILLIAMS was born on October 2, 1956, in Shelby, Alabama, USA.
> G. Douglas Williams, aged 28, married Danna Elizabeth Martin[1299], aged 29, on May 4, 1985. They had two children:
>> Danae Elizabeth Williams[2591] born on September 29, 1988 in Huntsville, Madison, Alabama, USA
>> Andrew Douglas Williams[2592] born on April 16, 1991 in Huntsville, Madison, Alabama, USA

1301. WILLARD DANIEL MARTIN JR. (see Descendants (67)) was born on March 9, 1959, in Montgomery, Montgomery, Alabama, USA, to Willard Daniel Martin[437] and Margueritte Elizabeth Bass[436]. Willard Daniel became known as "Danny".

1302. TAMARA LEIGH CLARK was born on February 10, 1962, in Montgomery, Montgomery, Alabama, USA.
> Willard Daniel Martin Jr.[1301], aged 25, married Tamara Leigh Clark, aged 22, on August 4, 1984. They had two daughters:
>> Elizabeth Leigh Martin[2593] born on March 20, 1989 in Montgomery, Montgomery, Alabama, USA
>> Whitney Danielle Martin[2594] born on August 3, 1992 in Montgomery, Montgomery, Alabama, USA

1303. JOANN WOOD (see Descendants (67)) was born on January 5, 1954 to Gerald Wilson Wood[439] and Betty Irene Bass[438].

1304. JAMES MCALEER.
> James Mcaleer married JoAnn Wood[1303], aged 24, on April 20, 1978, and they were divorced.

1305. CONNIE GAIL WOOD (see Descendants (67)) was born on December 12, 1954 to Gerald Wilson Wood[439] and Betty Irene Bass[438].

1306. JEFFERY TED KNOWLES was born on February 10, 1955.
> Jeffery Ted Knowles, aged 19, married Connie Gail Wood[1305], aged 19, on June 6, 1974. They had two daughters:
>> Samantha Gail Wood[2595] born on October 23, 1980
>> Andrea Rebecka Wood[2596] born on February 3, 1984

1307. REBECCA GAYE WOOD (see Descendants (67)) was born on March 19, 1957, in Columbus Air Force Base, Columbus, Ohio, USA, to Gerald Wilson Wood[439] and Betty Irene Bass[438]. Rebecca Gaye became known as "Becky".

1308. BILLY SHANNON WILSON was born on April 19, 1957.
> Billy Shannon Wilson married Rebecca Gaye Wood[1307]. They had three children:
>> Michael Shawn Wilson[2597] born on April 18, 1979
>> Courtney Shanna Wilson[2598] born on May 26, 1981 in Andalusia, Covington, Alabama, USA
>> William Daryl Wilson[2599] born on January 15, 1985 in Andalusia, Covington, Alabama, USA

1309. PAMELA ELLEN WOOD (see Descendants (67)) was born on March 21, 1959 to Gerald Wilson Wood[439] and Betty Irene Bass[438].

1310. JOHN GIANETTO was born in September 1966.

John Gianetto, aged 25, married Pamela Ellen Wood[1309], aged 32, on March 15, 1992.

1311. RUSSEL STACY WOOD (see Descendants (67)) was born on April 7, 1960, in Newfoundland Air Force Base, to Gerald Wilson Wood[439] and Betty Irene Bass[438].

1312. ANDREA LEEDY SELF was born on April 27, 1963.
    Russel Stacy Wood[1311] married Andrea Leedy Self. They had three children:
        Luke Wood[2600] born on January 7, 1993; died on January 7, 1993
        Katherine Mary Wood[2601] born on January 7, 1993
        Emily Grace Wood[2602] born on January 7, 1993

1313. JOYCE MARIE WOOD (see Descendants (67)) was born on March 11, 1967, in Newfoundland Air Force Base, to Gerald Wilson Wood[439] and Betty Irene Bass[438].

1314. JOHN RICHARD MANDELVILLE.
    John Richard Mandelville married Joyce Marie Wood[1313], aged 22, on April 15, 1989. They had one son:
        Matthew Tyler Mandelville[2603] born on March 31, 1993

1315. SHEILA DIANE WILSON (see Descendants (67)) was born on August 13, 1955 to John Lewis Wilson[441] and Audrey Rebecca Bass[440].

1316. RICHARD CURTIS RHEA was born on February 13, 1944, in Knoxville, Knox, Tennessee, USA, to Jack L Rhea and Anne N Rhea.
- He was recorded in the census on April 1, 1950, aged 6, in 2601 Central, Knoxville, Knox, Tennessee, United States.
- He died on December 14, 2021, aged 77, in Dothan, Houston, Alabama, USA.

Note: *Richard was born February 13, 1944, in Knoxville, TN, the son of Jack Lynn and Anna Mae Spencer Rhea. His affinity and natural talent for music began early in life. At age eleven, he played a violin solo when his class orchestra performed at Carnegie Hall in New York City. He attended Fulton County High School, Class of 1962, where he played on the football team and refined his musical talents by performing at sock-hops and other high school events. After graduation and serving his country as a Sergeant in the US Army, Richard worked as a music instructor at Lynn's Guitars in Knoxville, TN and continued to perform locally. He later attended college at the University of Tennessee and graduated in 1972 with a degree in Music Education. Following a brief tenure as a high school band director in Knoxville, Richard began to pursue his music career in earnest. As a full-time professional musician, he performed with such notable artists as Clifford Curry, Ray Charles, Dolly Parton, and more. In 1976, Richard moved to Nashville, TN and co-founded the original Corner Music. He continued to work professionally on stage and in the recording studio. In the early 1980s, Richard began a career as a financial planner and insurance broker, which eventually relocated him to Louisiana in 1995. Throughout this time, he never abandoned his love of music and continued to teach and perform. After retiring from his business career in the early 2000's, Richard returned to his musical roots and founded Creative Soundshop in Alexandria, Louisiana, a retail music store offering music instruction and a professional recording studio.*

Throughout his life, Richard was drawn to music ministry. From St. Bartholomew's Episcopal Church in Nashville to St. Timothy's Episcopal Church in Alexandria, Richard was active in helping to foster the love of Christ through music. His work with Kairos Prison Ministry and his experiences at Cursillo were central to his faith.

For the last decade, Richard made his home in Andalusia, AL, the childhood hometown of his wife, Sheila. Richard and Sheila met in the mid 1970s when she was booked as the new singer for a musical revue that he played every year. Together, they had four children.
(Death)

Richard Curtis Rhea, aged 33, married Sheila Diane Wilson[1315], aged 21, on August 8, 1977. They had four children:
> Jenny Lynn Rhea[2604] born on January 2, 1979 in Nashville, Davidson, Tennessee, USA
> Amanda Kate Rhea[2605] born on June 6, 1983 in Nashville, Davidson, Tennessee, USA
> Richard Zachary Rhea[2606] born on August 22, 1986 in Nashville, Davidson, Tennessee, USA
> John Spencer Rhea[2607] born on November 13, 1991 in Nashville, Davidson, Tennessee, USA

1317. MICHAIL LEWIS WILSON (see Descendants (67)) was born on July 17, 1959 to John Lewis Wilson[441] and Audrey Rebecca Bass[440].
1318. ZELDA LYNN TWEEDY was born on July 29, 1965, in Maryville, Blount, Tennessee, USA.
> Michail Lewis Wilson[1317] married Zelda Lynn Tweedy. They had four children:
> Timothy Nicholas Wilson[2609] born on February 19, 1985
> Tiffany Nichole Wilson[2610] born on February 19, 1985
> ReTessa Lyne Wilson[2611] born on January 19, 1988
> Michael Travis Wilson[2612] born on July 17, 1991

1319. AUDREY MICHELLE WILSON (see Descendants (67)) was born on August 12, 1966, in Andalusia, Covington, Alabama, USA, to John Lewis Wilson[441] and Audrey Rebecca Bass[440].
> The following information is also recorded for Audrey Michelle:
> • Military Service.
1320. AUSTIN LAMAR DOZIER was born on November 28, 1965, in Andalusia, Covington, Alabama, USA.
> Austin Lamar Dozier, aged 20, married Audrey Michelle Wilson[1319], aged 19, on January 31, 1986. They had two children:
> John Tyler Dozier[2613] born on October 10, 1989 in Eglin Air Force Base, Walton, Florida, USA
> Kathryn Rebecca Dozier[2614] born on May 21, 1993 in Andalusia, Covington, Alabama, USA

1321. LELAND SAMUEL BASS (see Descendants (67)) was born on November 9, 1958, in Niagara Falls, Niagara, New York, USA, to Hubert Lee Bass[442] and Shirley Seiwell[443]. Leland Samuel became known as "Lee".
1322. CHERI LYNN DUCOTE was born on November 21, 1963.
> Leland Samuel Bass[1321], aged 24, married Cheri Lynn Ducote, aged 19, on March 4, 1983 in Greer, Greenville/Spartanburg, South Carolina, USA. They had two children:
> Christopher Troy Bass[2615] born on July 6, 1983 in Greer, Greenville/Spartanburg, South Carolina, USA
> Jasmine Leigh Bass[2616] born on May 8, 1991 in Greer, Greenville/Spartanburg, South Carolina, USA

1323. ROBIN NAOMI BASS (see Descendants (67)) was born on August 23, 1960 to Hubert Lee Bass[442] and Shirley Seiwell[443].
1324. JOHNNY JASON MISSILDINE was born on August 28, 1979, in Montgomery, Montgomery, Alabama, USA.
> Johnny Jason Missildine married Robin Naomi Bass[1323] in Montgomery, Montgomery, Alabama, USA.

1325. MAURICE SEIWELL BASS (see Descendants (67)) was born on May 12, 1962 to Hubert Lee Bass[442] and Shirley Seiwell[443].
> The following information is also recorded for Maurice Seiwell:
> • Military Service.
> Notes:
> • *US Army - Iraq two tours. 2003 and 2006 (0859096320450).*
> *(Military Service)*
> • *Served two tours of duty in Iraq, active Military, and a Civilian tour in Iraq as well as Afghanistan. So four times in Combat zones.*
> *(Military Service)*

1326. BEVERLY LYNN BASS (see Descendants (1)) was born on August 20, 1964 to Quinton Gene Bass[444] and Frances Ida Teel[832].
> Beverly Lynn married twice. She was married to Anthony Scott[1327] and William Bryan Rogers Jr.[1328].

1327. ANTHONY SCOTT. He died on October 13, 1987.
>Anthony Scott married Beverly Lynn Bass[1326], aged 17, on June 5, 1982.
>The following information is also recorded for this family:
>- Death of Spouse.

1328. WILLIAM BRYAN ROGERS JR. was born on December 28, 1964, in Crestview, Okaloosa, Florida, USA.
>William Bryan Rogers Jr., aged 26, married Beverly Lynn Bass[1326], aged 26, on January 26, 1991. They had one son:
>>William Bryan Rogers III[2618] born on February 3, 1995 in Crestview, Okaloosa, Florida, USA

1329. WESLEY ALAN BASS (see Descendants (1)) was born on December 1, 1967 to Quinton Gene Bass[444] and Frances Ida Teel[832].
>The following information is also recorded for Wesley Alan:
>- Email: wesley.bass@clearwatersol.com.

1330. DONNA CHRZASTEK.
>Wesley Alan Bass[1329] married Donna Chrzastek, and they were divorced. They had one son:
>>Joseph Blaze Chrzastek Bass[2619] born on April 28, 2000

1331. BETTY JANE WARD (see Descendants (68)) was born on August 15, 1945, in Bainbridge, Decatur, Georgia, USA, to William Charles Ward Sr.[447] and Lelia Murray[448]. She died (Illness) on February 11, 2022, aged 76.

1332. JOHNNY MCCARSEY ADKINS was born on May 3, 1945, in Harrimon, Roane, Tennessee, USA.
>The following information is also recorded for Johnny McCarsey:
>- Military Service.
>Johnny McCarsey Adkins married Betty Jane Ward[1331]. They had one daughter:
>>Shannon Michele Adkins[2621] born on July 6, 1972 in Knoxville, Knox, Tennessee, USA

1333. WILLIAM CHARLES WARD JR. (see Descendants (68)) was born on October 25, 1948 to William Charles Ward Sr.[447] and Lelia Murray[448]. William Charles became known as "Billy".
>The following information is also recorded for Billy:
>- Military Service.
>William Charles had two partnerships. He was married to Brenda Henry[1335]. He was also the partner of Kathy Raby[1334].

1334. KATHY RABY.
>William Charles Ward Jr.[1333] and Kathy Raby had two sons:
>>William Charles Ward III[2622] born on July 5, 1972 in Eglin Air Force Base, Walton, Florida, USA
>>David Carter Ward[2623] born on August 24, 1974 in Wahiawa, Honolulu, Hawaii, USA
>The following information is also recorded for this family:
>- Unknown Relationship.

1335. BRENDA HENRY was born on July 6, 1949, in Cullman, Cullman, Alabama, USA.
>Brenda had two partnerships. She was married to William Charles Ward Jr.[1333]. She was also the partner of Glenn R. Pallicer.
>William Charles Ward Jr.[1333] married Brenda Henry.
>Glenn R. Pallicer and Brenda Henry had three children:
>>Glenn Robert Pallicer born on November 8, 1968 in Haileah, Dade, Florida, USA
>>Sharon Y. Pallicer born on April 27, 1970 in Fort Belvoir, Fairfax, Virginia, USA
>>Tanya J. Pallicer born on November 13, 1972 in Frankfort, Germany
>The following information is also recorded for this family:
>- Unknown Relationship.

1336. MARY ANN WARD (see Descendants (68)) was born in April 1952, in Crestview, Okaloosa, Florida, USA, to William Charles Ward Sr.[447] and Lelia Murray[448].

1337. ALLEN R. STUART was born on July 6, 1946, in Morrestown, Hamblen, Tennessee, USA.
>The following information is also recorded for Allen R.:
>- Military Service.

Allen R. Stuart, aged 29, married Mary Ann Ward[1336], aged 24, on May 31, 1976 in White Pine, Jefferson, Tennessee, USA. They had three children:
> Jeffery Allen Stuart[2627] born on September 8, 1981 in Shenandoah, Page, Iowa, USA
> Bethany Ann Stuart[2628] born on February 21, 1983 in Bristol, Sullivan, Tennessee, USA
> Suzanne Marie Stuart[2630] born on July 2, 1984 in Shenandoah, Page, Iowa, USA

1338. **SHIRLEY WARD** (see Descendants (68)) was born in January 1960 to William Charles Ward Sr.[447] and Lelia Murray[448].

1339. **JEFFERY LEE COFFMAN** was born on January 15, 1965, in Lack City, Anderson, Tennessee, USA.
> Jeffery Lee Coffman, aged 30, married Shirley Ward[1338], aged 35, on February 15, 1995. They had one son:
>> Gregory Cline Coffman[2631] born on December 15, 1994

1340. **FRED ANTHONY WARD** (see Descendants (68)) was born on April 5, 1954, in Tennessee, USA, to DeLeon Edward Ward[449] and Emma June Campbell[450]. Fred Anthony became known as "Buzz".
- He died (Cancer) on June 30, 2021, aged 67, in Crestview, Okaloosa County, Florida, USA.
- He was buried in Shady Hill Cemetery, Covington, Alabama, USA.

The following information is also recorded for Buzz:
- Accomplishment on May 4, 1972, aged 18.
- Title: Bass Family Historian.

Notes:
- *Buz spent a great deal of time researching and seeking out information on the history of his family. Given the opertunity he'd often present the history of various ancestors in character as the person, complete with costume at times. He was a good story teller and a passionate pursuer of history. I hope to oneday know almost as much about our family history as Buzz Ward. - Nicholas Bruce Bass.*
- *Buzz loved Family history and became known as the Bass Family Historian. He worked at Dogwood Acres Veterinary Clinic. He was loved by his co-workers.*
(Death)
- *Eagle Scout Award of the Boy Scouts of America, Troop 30 "Dirty 30".*
(Accomplishment)

1341. **JOSEPH DALE WARD** (see Descendants (68)) was born on May 14, 1955, in Tennessee, USA, to DeLeon Edward Ward[449] and Emma June Campbell[450]. Joseph Dale became known as "Dale".
- He died (Cancer) on June 12, 2021, aged 66, in Florida, United States.
- He was buried in Mossy Head Comunity Cemetery, DeFuniak Springs, Florida, USA.

Note: *Dale loved travelling, hunting, and especially the Mullet Festival. He was an active member of the Boggy Boys social club. He loved hosting gatherings with friends and family and was known for his spicy crawfish.*
(Death)

1342. **JACKIE ELAINE CRABTREE**.
> Joseph Dale Ward[1341], aged 18, married Jackie Elaine Crabtree on March 2, 1974 in Crestview, Okaloosa, Florida, USA. They had four children:
>> Joseph Brandon Ward[2634] born on August 20, 1974 in Fort Walton Beach, Okaloosa, Florida, USA
>> Maletha Adele Ward[2635] born on August 15, 1977
>> Brooke Michelle Ward[2636] born on January 7, 1980
>> Emily June Ward[2637] born on August 30, 1982 in Louisiana, USA

1343. **ROSE MARIE WARD** (see Descendants (68)) was born on October 2, 1956, in Crestview, Okaloosa, Florida, USA, to DeLeon Edward Ward[449] and Emma June Campbell[450].
> Rose Marie gave birth to one daughter:
>> Deidre Nicole Ward[2638] born on November 7, 1984
> The following information is also recorded for this family:
> - Unknown Relationship.

1344. CHRIS LORRAINE WARD (see Descendants (68)) was born on November 16, 1958, in Pensacola, Escambia, Florida, USA, to DeLeon Edward Ward[449] and Emma June Campbell[450].

1345. DANIEL HAL STEVERSON was born on November 1, 1961, in Bonifay, Holmes, Florida, USA.
> Daniel Hal Steverson, aged 26, married Chris Lorraine Ward[1344], aged 29, on December 5, 1987 in Crestview, Okaloosa, Florida, USA. They had one son:
>> Shelby Daniel Steverson[2639] born on March 23, 1993 in Pensacola, Escambia, Florida, USA

1346. MARILYN FREDRICK (see Descendants (68)) was born on September 15, 1951 to Henry Eugene Fredrick[453] and Anna Faye Ward[452].

1347. MARTIN EUGENE FREDRICK (see Descendants (68)) was born on June 6, 1956, in Ohio, USA, to Henry Eugene Fredrick[453] and Anna Faye Ward[452].

1348. MARK FORMAN FREDRICK (see Descendants (68)) was born on October 2, 1958 to Henry Eugene Fredrick[453] and Anna Faye Ward[452].

1349. ERNEST TRUE BASS JR. (see Descendants (69)) was born on January 17, 1919, in Liberty, Florida, USA, to Earnest True Bass Sr.[454] and Lillian Morgan[455].
- He was recorded in the census in 1920, in Liberty, Florida, USA.
- He died on March 15, 1920, aged 1, in Liberty, Florida, USA.
- He was buried in Lake Mystic Cemetery, Bristol, Liberty, Florida, USA.

1350. MR. BASS (see Descendants (69)) was born on February 12, 1921, in Liberty, Florida, USA, to Earnest True Bass Sr.[454] and Lillian Morgan[455].
- He died (Stillborn) on February 12, 1921, aged 0, in Liberty, Florida, USA.
- He was buried in Lake Mystic Cemetery, Bristol, Liberty, Florida, USA.

1351. EARNEST TRUE BASS JR. (see Descendants (69)) was born on July 2, 1922, in Telogia, Liberty, Florida, USA, to Earnest True Bass Sr.[454] and Ruth Valentine Morgan[456].
- He was recorded in the census in 1940, aged about 17, in Telogia, Precinct 6, Liberty, Florida, USA.
- He was recorded in the census on April 1, 1950, aged 27, in Styles Subdivision, Tallahassee, Leon, Florida, United States.
- He died on June 7, 2009, aged 86, in Tallahassee, Leon, Florida, USA.
- He was buried in Culley's MeadowWood Memorial Park, Tallahassee, Leon County, Florida, USA.

The following information is also recorded for Earnest True:
- Military Service.

Notes:
- *He moved to Tallahassee in 1941 and was the former owner of Bass Lighting and Electrical Supply. Mr. Bass was a veteran of World War II and served with the U.S. Marine Corps (CB) in the Pacific Theater. He was a member of a local VFW Post, Civitian Club and the Sertoma Club of Tarpon Springs.*
  (Death)
- *Garden of Peace 9.*
  (Burial)
- *U.S. Navy, 53rd Seabees - 1st Marine, WWII.*
  (Military Service)

1352. CATHERINE NADINE IRELAND was born on August 27, 1923, in Thomasville, Georgia, USA, to Leo Ireland and Ruth Ireland.
- She was recorded in the census in 1930, aged about 6, in Precinct 4, Liberty, Florida, USA.
- She was recorded in the census in 1940, aged about 16, in Hosford, Liberty, Florida, USA.
- She was recorded in the census on April 1, 1950, aged 26, in Styles Subdivision, Tallahassee, Leon, Florida, United States.
- She died on April 20, 2015, aged 91 years, in Tallahassee, Leon, Florida, USA.
- She was buried in Culley's MeadowWood Memorial Park, Tallahassee, Leon County, Florida, USA.

Notes:
- *Nadine Ireland Bass, 91, of Tallahassee died Monday at Big Bend Hospice. Nadine was a native of Thomasville, GA and was raised in Hosford, FL. She was a real estate broker and worked at agencies Jacksonville, Tarpon Springs, as well as Tallahassee. She has been back here in Tallahassee since 1986. She had been a member of the VFW, volunteered at the Tallahassee Memorial Hospital as a Pink Lady, during WW II she worked in the shipyard at Panama City to support the war effort, and was a Welcome Wagon Hostess. She was especially dedicated to her family and had also served as a Cub Scout Leader.*
(Death)
- *Garden of Peace 9.*
(Burial)

Earnest True Bass Jr.[1351] married Catherine Nadine Ireland. They had one son:
Robert Ernest Bass[2640] born about 1946 in Florida, United States

1353. DONALD WILLIS BASS (see Descendants (69)) was born on November 11, 1923, in Florida, USA, to Earnest True Bass Sr.[454] and Ruth Valentine Morgan[456].
- He was recorded in the census in 1930, aged about 6, in Telogia, Liberty, Florida, USA.
- He was recorded in the census in 1940, aged about 16, in Telogia, Precinct 6, Liberty, Florida, USA.
- He died on August 18, 1989, aged 65.

1354. ENNIS RUDOLPH BASS (see Descendants (69)) was born on May 28, 1925, in Crawfordville, Florida, USA, to Earnest True Bass Sr.[454] and Ruth Valentine Morgan[456].
- He was recorded in the census in 1930, aged about 5, in Telogia, Liberty, Florida, USA.
- He was recorded in the census in 1940, aged about 15, in Telogia, Precinct 6, Liberty, Florida, USA.
- He was recorded in the census on April 1, 1950, aged 24, in Chattahoochee, Gadsden, Florida, United States.
- He died on October 19, 2004, aged 79 years, in Tallahassee, Leon, Florida, USA.
- He was buried in Memory Gardens Cemetery, Tallahassee, Leon, Florida, USA.

The following information is also recorded for Ennis Rudolph:
- Military Service.

Notes:
- *Ennis served during, WWII, S Sgt. US Army Co. E 423 Inf., in Germany and his military marker is noted with, "Battle of the Bulge POW".*
- *Co. E 423 INF U.S. Army - WWII Germany Battle of the Bulge POW.*
(Military Service)

1355. LINDA BARBARA BORGIOLI was born on August 24, 1924, in Revere, Suffolk, Massachusetts, USA.
- She was recorded in the census on April 1, 1950, aged 25, in Chattahoochee, Gadsden, Florida, United States.
- She died on December 10, 2010, aged 86 years, in Tallahassee, Leon, Florida, USA.
- She was buried in Memory Gardens Cemetery, Tallahassee, Leon, Florida, USA.

Note: *She was born August 20, 1924, in Revere, Massachusetts, to the late Carlo and Annina Albano Borgioli. She was a registered nurse, having worked with Dr. Frank All and later, as a nurse with the Florida State Legislature. She was active in and an officer with VFW Ladies' Auxiliary Posts 3308 and 4538, an avid Bingo player and active with both the Alzheimer's Association Support Group and the Tallahassee Retired Nurses Association.*
(Death)

Ennis Rudolph Bass[1354] married Linda Barbara Borgioli. They had one daughter:
Linda Ann Bass[2641]

1356. MARY RUTH BASS (see Descendants (69)) was born on December 13, 1926, in Florida, USA, to Earnest True Bass Sr.[454] and Ruth Valentine Morgan[456].
- She was recorded in the census in 1930, aged about 3, in Telogia, Liberty, Florida, USA.
- She was recorded in the census in 1940, aged about 13, in Telogia, Precinct 6, Liberty, Florida, USA.

1357. MORGAN BENNETT BASS (see Descendants (69)) was born on May 28, 1928, in Telogia, Liberty, Florida, USA, to Earnest True Bass Sr.[454] and Ruth Valentine Morgan[456]. Morgan Bennett became known as "Bennie".
- He was recorded in the census in 1940, aged about 12, in Telogia, Precinct 6, Liberty, Florida, USA.
- He died on December 3, 2001, aged 73 years, in Orange Heights, Alachua, Florida, USA.

1358. MINNIE M HARRISON was born on January 31, 1924.
- She died on September 11, 2003, aged 79 years.
- She was buried in Saluda Cemetery, Orange Hights, Alachua, Florida, USA.

Morgan Bennett Bass[1357] married Minnie M Harrison.

1359. ALICE NANETTE BASS (see Descendants (69)) was born on March 9, 1931, in Florida, USA, to Earnest True Bass Sr.[454] and Ruth Valentine Morgan[456]. She was recorded in the census in 1940, aged about 9, in Telogia, Precinct 6, Liberty, Florida, USA.

1360. WILLIAM WALTER BASS (see Descendants (69)) was born on February 6, 1934, in Florida, USA, to Earnest True Bass Sr.[454] and Ruth Valentine Morgan[456]. William Walter became known as "Billy".
- He was recorded in the census in 1940, aged about 6, in Telogia, Precinct 6, Liberty, Florida, USA.

1361. ROBERT EARL BASS (see Descendants (69)) was born on February 6, 1934 to Earnest True Bass Sr.[454] and Ruth Valentine Morgan[456]. He died on February 6, 1934, as an infant.

1362. OBBIE BASS (see Descendants (69)) was born on February 6, 1934, in Liberty, Florida, USA, to Earnest True Bass Sr.[454] and Ruth Valentine Morgan[456].
- He died (Stillborn) on February 6, 1934, as an infant, in Liberty, Florida, USA.
- He was buried in Lake Mystic Cemetery, Bristol, Liberty, Florida, USA.

1363. ALICE LILLIAN BASS (see Descendants (70)) was born on April 20, 1919, in Hosford, Liberty, Florida, USA, to Richard Carl Bass Sr.[458] and Alice Lucille Beasley[459].
- She was recorded in the census in 1940, aged about 21, in 1827 East Prospect Road, East Ashtabula, Ashtabula, Ashtabula, Ohio, USA.
- She was recorded in the census on April 1, 1950, aged 30, in 32 Telegraph Road, Prichard, Mobile, Alabama, United States.
- She died on April 29, 2003, aged 84, in Northport, Tuscaloosa, Alabama, USA.
- She was buried in Catholic Cemetery, Mobile, Mobile, Alabama, USA.

1364. ELWYNNE PHILLIP PETERSON was born on December 12, 1913, in Sturgeon Bay, Door, Wisconsin, USA, to GUST Peterson and Eliza Writt.
- In 1935, aged about 21, he resided at Sandusky, Dorr, Wisconsin.
- He was recorded in the census in 1940, aged about 26, in 1827 East Prospect Road, East Ashtabula, Ashtabula, Ashtabula, Ohio, USA.
- He was recorded in the census on April 1, 1950, aged 36, in 32 Telegraph Road, Prichard, Mobile, Alabama, United States.
- He died on March 3, 1986, aged 72, in Mobile, Mobile, Alabama, USA.
- He was buried in Catholic Cemetery, Mobile, Mobile, Alabama, USA.

Elwynne Phillip Peterson married Alice Lillian Bass[1363]. They had one daughter:
Elizabeth Sharon Peterson[2643] born on July 6, 1947 in Pascagoula, Jackson, Mississippi, USA

1365. RICHARD CARLE BASS JR. (see Descendants (70)) was born on October 24, 1920, in Leon, Florida, USA, to Richard Carl Bass Sr.[458] and Alice Lucille Beasley[459].
- Richard Carle resided at Tallahassee, Florida 32304, USA.
- He was recorded in the census on April 1, 1950, aged 29, in District 4, Tallahassee, Leon, Florida, United States.
- He died on December 29, 1999, aged 79, in Tallahassee, Leon, Florida, USA.
- He was buried in Roselawn Cemetery, Tallahassee, Leon, Florida, USA.

1366. MARY ELIZABETH HALE was born on November 1, 1923, in Tallahassee, Leon, Florida, USA.
- She was recorded in the census on April 1, 1950, aged 26, in District 4, Tallahassee, Leon, Florida, United States.
- She died on March 30, 2007, aged 83, in Tallahassee, Leon, Florida, USA.
- She was buried in Roselawn Cemetery, Tallahassee, Leon, Florida, USA.

Note: *A life long resident of Tallahassee, she will always be remembered as a loving mother, grand mother and good friend to all who knew her. She retired from the State of Florida as a calculations specialist for the Division of Retirement.*

Richard Carle Bass Jr.[1365], aged 24, married Mary Elizabeth Hale, aged 21, on August 8, 1945. They had four children:
Richard Edward Bass[2644] born on February 8, 1950 in Tallahassee, Leon, Florida, USA
Charles Edward Bass[2646] born on July 18, 1954
Linda Elizabeth Bass[2648] born on June 25, 1955 in Tallahassee, Leon, Florida, USA
Robert Carl Bass[2650] born in 1961

1367. OLIVE MARIE BASS (see Descendants (70)) was born in 1921 to Richard Carl Bass Sr.[458] and Alice Lucille Beasley[459].

1368. CATHERINE CARLENE BASS (see Descendants (70)) was born in 1923 to Richard Carl Bass Sr.[458] and Alice Lucille Beasley[459].

1369. CHARLES EDWARD BASS (see Descendants (70)) was born on January 19, 1925, in Telogia, Liberty, Florida, USA, to Richard Carl Bass Sr.[458] and Alice Lucille Beasley[459]. He was recorded in the census on April 1, 1950, aged 25, in Bass Road, Tallahassee, Leon, Florida, United States.

1370. MAE BURK was born about 1927, in Florida, United States. She was recorded in the census on April 1, 1950, aged about 22, in Bass Road, Tallahassee, Leon, Florida, United States.
> Charles Edward Bass[1369], aged about 20, married Mae Burk, aged about 18, in 1945. They had two children:
> Rhonda Theresa Bass[2651] born on October 12, 1965 in Sweinfort, Germany
> Richard Charles Bass[2652] born on October 14, 1966 in Sweinfort, Germany

1371. NELL BASS (see Descendants (70)) was born in 1927 to Richard Carl Bass Sr.[458] and Alice Lucille Beasley[459].

1372. O. C. RINEHART.
> O. C. Rinehart married Nell Bass[1371], aged about 20, in 1947. They had two daughters:
> Donna Marie Rinehart[2653] born in 1955 in Thomasville, Thomas, Georgia, USA
> Myra Nell Rinehart[2654] born in 1961 in Thomasville, Thomas, Georgia, USA

1373. BETTY BASS (see Descendants (70)) was born in 1929 to Richard Carl Bass Sr.[458] and Alice Lucille Beasley[459].

1374. LEWIS WESTBURY.
> Lewis Westbury married Betty Bass[1373], aged about 23, in 1952 in Thomasville. They had two sons:
> Gary Westbury[2655] born in 1957
> Donnie Westbury[2656] born in 1960

1375. JOANNE CHARLOTTE BASS (see Descendants (70)) was born on April 19, 1935, in Arran, Florida, USA, to Richard Carl Bass Sr.[458] and Hadassah Stautimire[460].
- She was recorded in the census in 1940, aged about 5, in Crawfordville, E Precinct 2, Wakulla, Florida, USA.
- She was recorded in the census on April 1, 1950, aged 14, in Wakula Road, Tallahassee, Leon, Florida, United States.

1376. LESLIE CLAYTON COX was born on February 10, 1936, in Smith Creek, Wakulla.
> Leslie Clayton Cox married JoAnne Charlotte Bass[1375]. They had three children:
> June Lorraine Cox[2657] born on May 10, 1951
> Edward Clayton Cox[2659] born on February 18, 1954
> Carel Jeanette Cox[2661] born on April 5, 1956

1377. KENNETH KIRBY BASS (see Descendants (70)) was born on September 11, 1936, in Arran, Wakulla, Florida, USA, to Richard Carl Bass Sr.[458] and Hadassah Stautimire[460].
- He was recorded in the census in 1940, aged about 3, in Crawfordville, E Precinct 2, Wakulla, Florida, USA.
- He was recorded in the census on April 1, 1950, aged 13, in Wakula Road, Tallahassee, Leon, Florida, United States.
- He died on May 26, 2018, aged 81, in Tallahassee, Florida, USA.
- He was buried in Tallahassee National Cemetery, Tallahassee, Leon, Florida, USA.

The following information is also recorded for Kenneth Kirby:
- Military Service.
- Military Award.

Kenneth Kirby married three times. He was married to Barbara Sue Smith[1378], Jane Rowe[1379] and Beth Cockerham[1380].

Notes:
- *Peacefully.*
  (Death)
- *When Kirby was still a young child, he moved with his parents and siblings to Tallahassee, Florida. Kirby was an active member, usher of the Woodville First Baptist Church and was a Christian. He graduated from Leon High School in 1956. He was a U.S. Army veteran, having served actively for six years in numerous locations including Korea, Saudi Arabia, and Kuwait. Afterwards, he had a career in state government in Tallahassee, Florida, retiring on March 1, 1993. He was active in the Florida National Guard in Tallahassee, Florida. He retired from the military as a Sergeant First Class, serving for a total of 27 years. His highest award was the bronze star; this was awarded to Kirby, after being deployed to and serving in Operation Desert Storm.*
  (Death)
- *Sergeant First Class a total of 27 years. U.S. Army.*
  (Military Service)
- *Bronze Star - Operation Desert Storm.*
  (Military Award)

1378. BARBARA SUE SMITH.

Kenneth Kirby Bass[1377] married Barbara Sue Smith.

1379. JANE ROWE was born on June 26, 1952, in Maclenny, Florida, USA, to Benjamine Hopkins Rowe and Sadie Mae Dugger.

Kenneth Kirby Bass[1377], aged 47, married Jane Rowe, aged 31, on May 11, 1984. They assumed parenthood of one daughter:

Cheryl Kaye Bass[2663] by adoption

The following information is also recorded for this family:
• Death of Spouse.

1380. BETH COCKERHAM.

Kenneth Kirby Bass[1377] married Beth Cockerham.

1381. HAROLD EUGENE BASS (see Descendants (70)) was born on November 12, 1937, in Crawfordville, Florida, USA, to Richard Carl Bass Sr.[458] and Hadassah Stautimire[460].
• He was recorded in the census in 1940, aged about 2, in Crawfordville, E Precinct 2, Wakulla, Florida, USA.
• He was recorded in the census on April 1, 1950, aged 12, in Wakula Road, Tallahassee, Leon, Florida, United States.

1382. THELINA GAIL KILPRATRIE.

Harold Eugene Bass[1381], aged 22, married Thelina Gail Kilpratrie on April 23, 1960. They had two children:
Karan Lainye Bass[2665] born on November 2, 1962
Sabin Craig Bass[2667] born on December 21, 1964 in Tallahassee, Leon, Florida, USA

1383. BETTY JUNE BASS (see Descendants (70)) was born on May 12, 1942, in Florida, United States, to Richard Carl Bass Sr.[458] and Hadassah Stautimire[460]. She was recorded in the census on April 1, 1950, aged 7, in Wakula Road, Tallahassee, Leon, Florida, United States.

1384. JOHN JOSEPH KOVAL was born on March 3, 1934.

John Joseph Koval, aged about 29, married Betty June Bass[1383], aged about 21, in 1963. They had one son:
Joseph Kenneth Koval[2668] born on September 30, 1978

1385. WILLIAM EDWARD BASS (see Descendants (71)) was born on September 18, 1923, in Andalusia, Covington, Alabama, USA, to William Bennett Bass[461] and Ora Della Hare[462].
• He was recorded in the census in 1930, aged about 6, in Fairfield, Covington, Alabama, USA.
• He died on May 28, 1987, aged 63.

William Edward married twice. He was married to Margaret Louise Pearl[1386] and Betty ?[1387].

1386. MARGARET LOUISE PEARL.

William Edward Bass[1385], aged 24, married Margaret Louise Pearl on January 9, 1948.

1387. BETTY ?.

William Edward Bass[1385] married Betty ?.

1388. EDWIN DURWOOD BASS SR. (see Descendants (71)) was born on March 9, 1926, in Andalusia, Covington, Alabama, USA, to William Bennett Bass[461] and Ora Della Hare[462]. He was recorded in the census in 1930, aged about 4, in Fairfield, Covington, Alabama, USA.

1389. MARGARET LOUISE POWELL was born on June 6, 1928, in Andalusia, Covington, Alabama, USA.

Edwin Durwood Bass Sr.[1388], aged 21, married Margaret Louise Powell, aged 19, on January 9, 1948 in Andalusia, Covington, Alabama, USA. They had three children:
Cynthia Louise Bass[2669] born on October 15, 1950 in Montgomery, Montgomery, Alabama, USA
Edwin Durwood Bass Jr.[2672] born on May 9, 1953 in Andalusia, Covington, Alabama, USA
Susan Dianne Bass[2673] born on June 11, 1956 in Andalusia, Covington, Alabama, USA

1390. DONALD GENE BASS (see Descendants (71)) was born on October 16, 1947, in Dade City, Pasco, Florida, USA, to William Bennett Bass[461] and Betty Jean Hawkins[463]. He was recorded in the census on April 1, 1950, aged 2, in 1144 W Olive St, Lakeland, Polk, Florida, United States.

Donald Gene married twice. He was married to Pamela Jane Hayerberg[1391] and Bok Suk Choi[1392].

1391. PAMELA JANE HAYERBERG.

Donald Gene Bass[1390], aged 19, married Pamela Jane Hayerberg on November 7, 1966. They had three children:
William Bennett Bass[2675] born on March 20, 1967 in Fort Ord, Monterey, California, USA
Alicia Marie Bass[2676] born on March 12, 1968 in Sarasota, Florida, USA
Shawn Lee Bass[2677] born on May 1, 1983 in Fort Ord, Monterey, California, USA

1392. BOK SUK CHOI was born on May 20, 1955, in Masan, Korea.

Donald Gene Bass[1390], aged 34, married Bok Suk Choi, aged 26, on April 8, 1982. They had one son:
Donnie Lee Bass[2678] born on February 27, 1986 in Seoul, Korea

1393. ALICE MARIE BASS (see Descendants (71)) was born on June 19, 1949, in Lakeland, Polk, Florida, USA, to William Bennett Bass[461] and Betty Jean Hawkins[463]. She was recorded in the census on April 1, 1950, as an infant, in 1144 W Olive St, Lakeland, Polk, Florida, United States.
Alice Marie married three times. She was married to Gerald Van Horn[1394], John A Orback[1395] and Rudy Salaiz[1396].
1394. GERALD VAN HORN.
Gerald Van Horn married Alice Marie Bass[1393].
1395. JOHN A ORBACK.
John A Orback married Alice Marie Bass[1393].
1396. RUDY SALAIZ.
Rudy Salaiz married Alice Marie Bass[1393].

1397. MARY MARGARET MERCER (see Descendants (72)) was born in 1931, in Hasford, Liberty, Florida, USA, to Boone Mercer[465] and Mary Leona Bass[464].
- She was recorded in the census in 1940, aged about 9, in Hosford, E Precinct Hosford, Liberty, Florida, USA.
- She was recorded in the census on April 1, 1950, aged about 18, in State Road No 65, Bristol, Liberty, Florida, United States.

1398. ROBERT SHORES.
Robert Shores married Mary Margaret Mercer[1397].

1399. JAMES B. MERCER (see Descendants (72)) was born on January 9, 1933, in Hasford, Liberty, Florida, USA, to Boone Mercer[465] and Mary Leona Bass[464].
- He was recorded in the census in 1940, aged about 7, in Hosford, E Precinct Hosford, Liberty, Florida, USA.
- He was recorded in the census on April 1, 1950, aged 17, in State Road No 65, Bristol, Liberty, Florida, United States.

1400. MARGIE PROLIST.
James B. Mercer[1399] married Margie Prolist.

1401. TRINA ELAINE BASS (see Descendants (73)) was born on August 19, 1941, in Fort Benning, Georgia, USA, to Henry Obie Bass[466] and Ajetta Bodiford[467]. She was recorded in the census on April 1, 1950, aged 8, in 610 2nd Court, Panama City, Bay, Florida, United States.
1402. BRUCE R KAIN.
Bruce R Kain married Trina Elaine Bass[1401], aged 36, on January 4, 1978.

1403. JANIEE MARILYN BASS (see Descendants (73)) was born on August 9, 1943, in Temple, Texas, USA, to Henry Obie Bass[466] and Ajetta Bodiford[467]. She was recorded in the census on April 1, 1950, aged 6, in 610 2nd Court, Panama City, Bay, Florida, United States.
1404. RICHARD KENNEL.
Richard Kennel married Janiee Marilyn Bass[1403], aged 37, on August 10, 1980.

1405. CHERYL DIANNE BASS (see Descendants (73)) was born on July 20, 1950, in Panama City, Bay, Florida, USA, to Henry Obie Bass[466] and Ajetta Bodiford[467].
1406. LEE CLIFTON.
Lee Clifton married Cheryl Dianne Bass[1405], aged 20, on December 19, 1970.

1407. LINDA KAY BASS (see Descendants (73)) was born on September 21, 1956, in Panama City, Bay, Florida, USA, to Henry Obie Bass[466] and Ajetta Bodiford[467].
1408. RONNIE LEAK was born on March 19, 1977.
Ronnie Leak married Linda Kay Bass[1407].

1409. MINNIE ELIZABETH BIGGS (see Descendants (74)) was born on February 26, 1907, in Alabama, USA, to William Albert Biggs[470] and Vinnie Janice Williams[469].
- She was recorded in the census in 1920, aged about 13, in Precinct 16 Stangler School House, Covington, Alabama, USA.
- She was recorded in the census in 1920, aged about 13, in Precinct 16 Stangler School House, Covington, Alabama, USA.
- She died on April 23, 1991, aged 84 years, in Luverne, Crenshaw, Alabama, USA.

1410. BEULAH MAE BIGGS (see Descendants (74)) was born on August 10, 1909, in Andalusia, Covington, Alabama, USA, to William Albert Biggs[470] and Vinnie Janice Williams[469].
- She was recorded in the census in 1920, aged about 10, in Precinct 16 Stangler School House, Covington, Alabama,

Direct Relations

USA.
- She was recorded in the census in 1940, aged about 30, in E Precinct 3 Brannen, Coffee, Alabama, USA.
- She died on March 29, 1971, aged 61 years, in Elba, Coffee, Alabama, USA.

1411. CHARLES D MCDONALD was born on November 15, 1906, in Alabama, USA.
- He was recorded in the census in 1940, aged about 33, in E Precinct 3 Brannen, Coffee, Alabama, USA.
- He died on May 11, 1968, aged 61.

   Charles D McDonald married Beulah Mae Biggs[1410]. They had four children:
   Robert McDonald[2679] born about 1930 in Alabama, USA
   Lucille McDonald[2680] born about 1933 in Alabama, USA
   Voncille McDonald[2681] born about 1933 in Alabama, USA
   Junior McDonald[2682] born about 1935 in Alabama, USA

1412. LESSIE MYRL BIGGS (see Descendants (74)) was born on December 19, 1914, in Tuscolusa, Alabama, USA, to William Albert Biggs[470] and Vinnie Janice Williams[469].
- She was recorded in the census on April 1, 1950, aged 35, in 11 Dexn Mile Tanetera, Andalusia, Covington, Alabama, United States.
- She died on June 26, 1991, aged 76 years, in Alabama, USA.

1413. JAY THERON WHATLEY was born on June 17, 1915, in Tallapoosa, Alabama, USA.
- He was recorded in the census on April 1, 1950, aged 34, in 11 Dexn Mile Tanetera, Andalusia, Covington, Alabama, United States.
- He died on August 9, 1979, aged 64 years, in Florala, Covington, Alabama, USA.

   Jay Theron Whatley married Lessie Myrl Biggs[1412]. They had three children:
   Myrtice Edna Whatley[2683] born on June 29, 1937 in Covington, Alabama, USA; died on June 13, 1992 in Milledgeville, Baldwin, Georgia, USA
   Myrtle Maxine Whatley[2684] born on October 24, 1941 in Andalusia, Covington, Alabama, USA; died on February 8, 1944 in Andalusia, Covington, Alabama, USA
   Gordon Lavaughn Whatley[2685] born on August 17, 1945 in Mobile, Alabama, USA; died in 1993 in Florala, Covington, Alabama, USA

1414. ZELLA BRYAN (see Descendants (75)) was born about 1915, in Alabama, USA, to Newton Dudley Bryan[474] and Francis Folsam Williams[473]. She was recorded in the census in 1940, aged about 25, in 3024 Bishop, Little Rock, Big Rock Twp, Pulaski, Arkansas, USA.

1415. JUDSON BRYAN (see Descendants (75)) was born about 1919, in Alabama, USA, to Newton Dudley Bryan[474] and Francis Folsam Williams[473]. He was recorded in the census in 1940, aged about 21, in 3024 Bishop, Little Rock, Big Rock Twp, Pulaski, Arkansas, USA.

1416. EDWIN BRYAN (see Descendants (75)) was born about 1921, in Alabama, USA, to Newton Dudley Bryan[474] and Francis Folsam Williams[473]. He was recorded in the census in 1940, aged about 19, in 3024 Bishop, Little Rock, Big Rock Twp, Pulaski, Arkansas, USA.

1417. LORAINE BRYAN (see Descendants (75)) was born about 1930, in Arkansas, USA, to Newton Dudley Bryan[474] and Francis Folsam Williams[473]. She was recorded in the census in 1940, aged about 10, in 3024 Bishop, Little Rock, Big Rock Twp, Pulaski, Arkansas, USA.

1418. SWENSON EDWIN ANDERSON (see Descendants (76)) was born on December 29, 1914, in Covington, Alabama, USA, to Andrew Erastus Anderson[476] and Mattie Dora Williams[475].
- He was recorded in the census in 1930, aged about 15, in Andalusia, Covington, Alabama, USA.
- He died on December 24, 1977, aged 62 years, in Covington, Alabama, USA.

1419. LUCINE DALTON ANDERSON (see Descendants (76)) was born on November 9, 1916, in Alabama, United States, to Andrew Erastus Anderson[476] and Mattie Dora Williams[475].
- He was recorded in the census in 1930, aged about 13, in Andalusia, Covington, Alabama, USA.
- He died on December 25, 1998, aged 82 years, in Mobile, Alabama, USA.

1420. WILLIAM F ANDERSON (see Descendants (76)) was born on July 6, 1921, in Andalusia, Covington, Alabama, USA, to Andrew Erastus Anderson[476] and Mattie Dora Williams[475].
- He was recorded in the census in 1930, aged about 8, in Andalusia, Covington, Alabama, USA.
- He was recorded in the census in 1940, aged about 18, in 940 River Falls Street, Andalusia, Covington, Alabama, USA.
- He died on October 6, 1974, aged 53 years, in Foley, Baldwin, Alabama, USA.

1421. MS. MCCAIN.
> William F Anderson[1420], aged 26, married Ms. McCain on September 13, 1947 in Montgomery, Montgomery County, Alabama, USA.

1422. ELNA F ANDERSON (see Descendants (76)) was born about 1924, in Alabama, United States, to Andrew Erastus Anderson[476] and Mattie Dora Williams[475].
- She was recorded in the census in 1930, aged about 6, in Andalusia, Covington, Alabama, USA.
- She was recorded in the census in 1940, aged about 16, in 940 River Falls Street, Andalusia, Covington, Alabama, USA.

1423. JANE ROBINSON (see Descendants (77)) was born about 1926, in Alabama, United States, to John W Robinson[478] and Laura May Williams Williams[477].
- She was recorded in the census in 1940, aged about 14, in West Jackson Street, Pensacola, E P 38, Escambia, Florida, USA.
- She was recorded in the census on April 1, 1950, aged about 23, in Pensacola, Escambia, Florida, United States.

1424. LESTER WILLIAMS (see Descendants (78)) was born on January 8, 1935, in Andalusia, Covington, Alabama, USA, to Henry Gordon Williams[479] and Caudie Newman[480].

1425. MS. DORTCH was born in Blount County, Alabama, USA.
> Lester Williams[1424] married Ms. Dortch. They had seven children:
>> Rebecca Williams[2686] born on February 25, 1953 in Andalusia, Covington, Alabama, USA
>> Susan Elizabeth Williams[2688] born on May 23, 1954 in Andalusia, Covington, Alabama, USA
>> Johnny Ray Williams[2690] born on March 21, 1956 in Andalusia, Covington, Alabama, USA
>> Ronald Gordon Williams[2693] born on October 26, 1957 in Andalusia, Covington, Alabama, USA
>> Jo Ann Williams[2695] born on July 1, 1959 in Andalusia, Covington, Alabama, USA
>> David Marcus Williams[2697] born on March 26, 1962 in Andalusia, Covington, Alabama, USA
>> Angela Maria Williams[2699] born on October 19, 1964

1426. DEWARD FUQUA (see Descendants (80)) was born about 1923, in Alabama, USA, to Frank A. Fuqua[484] and Naomi Williams[483]. He was recorded in the census in 1940, aged about 17, in South Three Notch Street, Andalusia, Covington, Alabama, USA.

1427. EVELYN FUQUA (see Descendants (80)) was born about 1925, in Alabama, USA, to Frank A. Fuqua[484] and Naomi Williams[483]. She was recorded in the census in 1940, aged about 15, in South Three Notch Street, Andalusia, Covington, Alabama, USA.

1428. ARLIS CHAPMAN ADAMS SR. (see Descendants (85)) was born about 1925, in Alabama, USA, to Luie Claude Adams[494] and Arrie Bernice Bass[493].
- He was recorded in the census in 1930, aged about 5, in Carolina, Covington, Alabama, USA.
- He was recorded in the census in 1940, aged about 15, in Beat 21 Carolina, Covington, Alabama, USA.
- He was recorded in the census on April 1, 1950, aged about 24, in 930d Calber@Calbert@Madison Madison, Chickasaw, Mobile, Alabama, United States.

The following information is also recorded for Arlis Chapman:
- Military Service.

Note: *WWII.*
> *(Military Service)*

1429. ANNIE MAUDE HASSELL was born about 1928, in Alabama, United States. She was recorded in the census on April 1, 1950, aged about 21, in 930d Calber@Calbert@Madison Madison, Chickasaw, Mobile, Alabama, United States.
> Arlis Chapman Adams Sr.[1428] married Annie Maude Hassell. They had three children:
>> Arlis Chapman Adams Jr.[2700] born on February 21, 1947 in Texas, United States
>> Anthony Phillip Adams[2702] born about November 1955
>> Angina Valentine Adams[2704]

1430. ATRIS C ADAMS (see Descendants (85)) was born about 1927, in Alabama, USA, to Luie Claude Adams[494] and Arrie Bernice Bass[493].
- She was recorded in the census in 1930, aged about 3, in Carolina, Covington, Alabama, USA.
- She was recorded in the census in 1940, aged about 13, in Beat 21 Carolina, Covington, Alabama, USA.
- She was recorded in the census on April 1, 1950, aged about 22, in Carolina, Covington, Alabama, United States.

1431. JESSIE BECKWORTH.
> Jessie Beckworth married Atris C Adams[1430].

Notes:

PFC T. L. Rodgers was a decedent of B.B. "Shug" Bass, Jr. The 82nd had long served and endured combat over months of action in Italy leading up to D-Day, when they found themselves in England for rest. Rose Carter describes various indulgences enjoyed by himself and fellow soldiers in the 82nd during this "rest", but his only reference to "Big Rodgers" is to say that he was there to keep an eye on friends, being a teetotaler. Which I'm sure would make his mother proud.

T. L. Rodgers was one of a very few to volunteer to drop with the invasion on D-Day.

Rose Carter documented one of his final exchanges with "Big Rodgers", having told him to be careful Rodgers responded after a pause, that "he'd be as careful as he could, but he may not be careful enough this time". Thomas L. Rodgers who Sgt. McCarthy believed had been killed on June 6th when they both were misdropped on a German Garrison, actually landed in the walled courtyard of the garrison. He managed to deploy his Browning automatic rifle and shoot his way out of the area and get to safety. He served with the 507th in combat until 6/15/1944, when he engaged the Germans heroically and was killed in action. Rodgers' friends received the news in England that T.L. had been killed in action. According to reports received from his 1st Bn C Company Comrades, he had given a good account of himself.

They were told that in action near St. Mere Eglise he slew 40 Germans and received the Distinguished Service Cross for his actions.

Company C 82nd Airborne Fort Brag NC Oct 10 1942.
Thomas Lloyd Rodgers is in the second row directly under the B in Brag.

Jessie Beckworth married Atris C Adams[1430].

1432. ANNETTE ADAMS (see Descendants (85)) was born about 1928, in Alabama, USA, to Luie Claude Adams[494] and Arrie Bernice Bass[493].
- She was recorded in the census in 1930, aged about 2, in Carolina, Covington, Alabama, USA.
- She was recorded in the census in 1940, aged about 12, in Beat 21 Carolina, Covington, Alabama, USA.

1433. FRANK JACKSON.
Frank Jackson married Annette Adams[1432]. They had three children:
Deborah Jackson[2705]
Dewayne Jackson[2706]
Louis Jackson[2707]

1434. AARON LEE ADAMS (see Descendants (85)) was born on March 6, 1930, in Andalusia, Covington, Alabama, USA, to Luie Claude Adams[494] and Arrie Bernice Bass[493].
- Aaron Lee was an Air Force Logistics Specialist.
- He was recorded in the census in 1930, as an infant, in Carolina, Covington, Alabama, USA.
- He was recorded in the census in 1940, aged about 10, in Beat 21 Carolina, Covington, Alabama, USA.
- He died (Illness) on December 1, 2011, aged 81 years, in Macon, Bibb, Georgia, USA.
- He was buried in Glen Haven Memorial Garden, Macon, Bibb County, Georgia, USA.

The following information is also recorded for Aaron Lee:
- Military Service.

Notes:
- *He retired from Robins Air Force Base as a Logistics Specialist. Mr Adams was a member at Northside Baptist Church.*
(Death)
- *WWII.*
(Military Service)

1435. BETTY JEAN BROWN was born on May 29, 1934, in Ashburn, Turner, Georgia, USA.
Aaron Lee Adams[1434], aged 20, married Betty Jean Brown, aged 16, on August 4, 1950. They had four children:
Danny Lee Adams[2709] born on November 26, 1951 in Andalusia, Covington, Alabama, USA
Angela Patrice Adams[2711] born on November 14, 1955 in Mobile, Mobile, Alabama, USA
Pamela Jean Adams[2713] born on July 31, 1962 in Mobile, Mobile, Alabama, USA
Timothy Alan Adams[2715] born on July 31, 1962 in Mobile, Mobile, Alabama, USA

1436. AUDIE MAE ADAMS (see Descendants (85)) was born on June 12, 1934, in Alabama, USA, to Luie Claude Adams[494] and Arrie Bernice Bass[493].
- She was recorded in the census in 1940, aged about 6, in Beat 21 Carolina, Covington, Alabama, USA.
- She was recorded in the census on April 1, 1950, aged 15, in Carolina, Covington, Alabama, United States.

1437. CHARLES WOOD THOMASSON was born on July 31, 1932.
Charles Wood Thomasson, aged -281, married Audie Mae Adams[1436], aged -282, on July 17, 1652. They had four children:
Cynthia Mae Thomasson[2717] born on October 20, 1953 in Andalusia, Covington, Alabama, USA
Charles Rocky Thomasson[2719] born on January 2, 1956 in Andalusia, Covington, Alabama, USA
Celia Lynn Thomasson[2721] born on February 13, 1957 in Andalusia, Covington, Alabama, USA
Carol Sue Thomasson[2723] born on October 29, 1959 in Andalusia, Covington, Alabama, USA

1438. PFC THOMAS LLOYD RODGERS (see Descendants (86)) was born on April 5, 1921, in Alabama, United States, to John Thomas Evans Rodgers[497] and Eva Allie Bass[496]. Thomas Lloyd became known as "Big Rogers".
- He was recorded in the census in 1930, aged about 9, in Andalusia, Covington, Alabama, USA.
- He died (At War) on June 15, 1944, aged 23 years, in Normandy, France.
- He was buried on October 24, 1944 in Carolina Baptist Church Cemetery, Covington, Alabama, USA.

The following information is also recorded for Big Rogers:
- Military Service on November 25, 1940, aged 19.
- Military Award.
- Military Award in Normandy, France.
- Military Award in Normandy, France.

Notes:
- *"Big Rodgers was more than just a member of the platoon. He was a staunch pillar in our ranks both morally and physically. He radiated a quiet encouragement that sustained our confidence. In battle, he manifested a courage*

that translated itself into deeds and a bulwark of security for us all".

Ross Carter in his book, "Those Devils in Baggy Pants."
- *PFC 504th PIR Co. C 82nd Airborn - WWII.*
  (Military Service)
- *Thomas L. Rodgers who Sgt. McCarthy believed had been killed on June 6th when they both were misdropped on a German Garrison, actually landed in the walled courtyard of the garrison. He managed to deploy his Browning automatic rifle and shoot his way out of the area and get to safety. He served with the 507th in combat until 6/15/1944, when he engaged the Germans heroically and was killed in action. Rodgers' friends received the news in England that T.L. had been killed in action. According to reports received from his 1st Bn C Company Comrades, he had given a good account of himself. They were told that in action near St. Mere Eglise he slew 40 Germans and received the Distinguished Service Cross for his actions.*
  (Military Service)
- *Purple Heart.*
  (Military Award)
- *Bronze Star.*
  (Military Award)
- *Distinguished Service Cross.*
  (Military Award)
- *Private First Class Thomas L. Rodgers, 20421704, Infantry, United States Army for extraordinary heroism in connection with military operations against an enemy of the United States. Having jumped into Normandy in the vicinity of Amfresville, France on 6 June 1944, Private First Class Ridgers, observing many of his comrades pinned down by enemy machine gun and small arms fire, moved without hesitation to destroy the enemy. Mounting a stone wall, in full view of the enemy, he neutralized the machine gun position and proceeded forward, driving back the enemy with effective fire from his Browning Automatic Rifle. During this action Private First Class Rodgers killed or wounded 25 of the enemy and made possible the organization and advance of our troops in the area. His personal courage, aggressive leadership and courageous inspiration contributed materially to the success of his comrades and typified the highest traditions of the service. Private First Class Rodgers was later killed in action against the enemy. Entered military service from Alabama. Awarded posthumously.*
  (Military Award)

1439. SIBYL RODGERS (see Descendants (86)) was born on November 6, 1922, in Alabama, United States, to John Thomas Evans Rodgers[497] and Eva Allie Bass[496].
- She was recorded in the census in 1930, aged about 7, in Andalusia, Covington, Alabama, USA.
- She died on May 23, 2011, aged 88 years, in Carolina Community, Covington, Alabama, USA.
- She was buried in Carolina Baptist Church Cemetery, Covington, Alabama, USA.

1440. JOHN MANDRAK JACOBS was born on October 19, 1918.
- He died on October 2, 1999, aged 80 years.
- He was buried in Carolina Baptist Church Cemetery, Covington, Alabama, USA.
  John Mandrak Jacobs married Sibyl Rodgers[1439]. They had four children:
  Sherry Jacobs[2725]
  Ronald Jacobs[2727]
  Tim Jacobs[2728]
  Donna Jacobs[2729]

1441. EVANS RODGERS (see Descendants (86)) was born on April 21, 1924, in Alabama, United States, to John Thomas Evans Rodgers[497] and Eva Allie Bass[496].
- He was recorded in the census in 1930, aged about 6, in Andalusia, Covington, Alabama, USA.
- He died on March 8, 2008, aged 83 years, in Walton County, Florida, USA.
- He was buried in Carolina Baptist Church Cemetery, Covington, Alabama, USA.

The following information is also recorded for Evans:
- Military Service.

Evans married three times. He was married to Fannie Merle Holland[1442], Annice Henderson[1443] and Opal Hall[1444].
Note: *U.S. Navy WWII.*
(Military Service)

1442. FANNIE MERLE HOLLAND was born on September 17, 1925.
- She died on September 26, 1989, aged 64 years.
- She was buried in Beda Cemetery, Beda, Covington, Alabama, USA.

Fannie Merle married twice. She was married to Evans Rodgers[1441] and Virgil Morgan Henley.

Direct Relations

Evans Rodgers[1441] married Fannie Merle Holland.
Virgil Morgan Henley married Fannie Merle Holland.

1443. ANNICE HENDERSON was born on February 20, 1925.
- She died on January 23, 1995, aged 69.
- She was buried in Carolina Baptist Church Cemetery, Covington, Alabama, USA.

Evans Rodgers[1441] married Annice Henderson. They had six children:
Thomas Rodgers[2730]
Alvin Rodgers[2732] born on March 23, 1955
John Glenn Rodgers[2734]
Jo Anne Rodgers[2736]
Joyce Rodgers[2738]
Brenda Rodgers[2741]

1444. OPAL HALL.
Evans Rodgers[1441] married Opal Hall.

1445. OLLIE KENNETH RODGERS (see Descendants (86)) was born about 1926, in Alabama, United States, to John Thomas Evans Rodgers[497] and Eva Allie Bass[496].
- He was recorded in the census in 1930, aged about 4, in Andalusia, Covington, Alabama, USA.
- He died in 1997, aged about 71.

1446. ROSS BURTON RODGERS (see Descendants (86)) was born on October 14, 1927, in Alabama, United States, to John Thomas Evans Rodgers[497] and Eva Allie Bass[496].
- He was recorded in the census in 1930, aged about 2, in Andalusia, Covington, Alabama, USA.
- He died on January 25, 1997, aged 69 years.
- He was buried in Carolina Baptist Church Cemetery, Covington, Alabama, USA.

The following information is also recorded for Ross Burton:
- Military Service.

Note: *U.S. Navy WWII.*
(Military Service)

1447. JAMES IVEY BASS (see Descendants (87)) was born on April 5, 1924, in Carolina, Covington, Alabama, United States, to Jamie Ike Bass[498] and Cleo Gunter[499].
- He was recorded in the census in 1930, aged about 6, in Carolina, Covington, Alabama, USA.
- He was recorded in the census in 1940, aged about 16, in Election Prect 21 Carolina, Covington, Alabama, USA.
- He was recorded in the census on April 1, 1950, aged 25, in Carolina, Covington, Alabama, United States.
- He died on July 29, 2001, aged 77 years, in Florala, Covington, Alabama, United States.
- He was buried in Greenwood Cemetery, Florala, Alabama, United States.

The following information is also recorded for James Ivey:
- Military Service.

Note: *U.S. Army WWII.*
(Military Service)

1448. FAY AGNES JONES was born on January 1, 1936.
- She died on October 30, 2008, aged 72 years.
- She was buried in Greenwood Memorial Cemetery, Florala, Covington, Alabama, USA.

James Ivey Bass[1447] married Fay Agnes Jones.

1449. JAMES ERVIN BASS (see Descendants (87)) was born on October 25, 1925, in Covington, Alabama, USA, to Jamie Ike Bass[498] and Cleo Gunter[499].
- He was recorded in the census in 1940, aged about 14, in Election Prect 21 Carolina, Covington, Alabama, USA.
- He was recorded in the census on April 1, 1950, aged 24, in Baykin and Road Leral Road, Westover, Covington, Alabama, United States.
- He died on March 15, 1971, aged 45.
- He was buried in Carolina Baptist Church Cemetery, Covington, Alabama, USA.

1450. OPAL LOUISE KING was born about 1930, in Alabama, United States. She was recorded in the census on April 1, 1950, aged about 19, in Baykin and Road Leral Road, Westover, Covington, Alabama, United States.

James Ervin Bass[1449] married Opal Louise King. They had one son:
James Dewayne Bass[2742] born on December 16, 1947 in Alabama, United States; died on April 29, 1966

1451. HAZEL BASS (see Descendants (87)) was born on August 14, 1927, in Andalusia, Covington, Alabama, USA, to Jamie Ike Bass[498] and Cleo Gunter[499].
- She was recorded in the census in 1940, aged about 12, in Election Prect 21 Carolina, Covington, Alabama, USA.
- She was recorded in the census on April 1, 1950, aged 22, in Carolina, Covington, Alabama, United States.
- She died on August 15, 2013, aged 86 years.
- She was buried in Shady Hill Church Cemetery, Covington, Alabama, USA.

Hazel married her third cousin, Martin Van Buren Huckabaa Sr.[1000].

Martin Van Buren Huckabaa Sr.[1000], aged 24, married Hazel Bass, aged 18, in February 1946 in Covington, Alabama, United States. They had seven children:

Mary Evelyn Huckabaa[2226] born on December 8, 1946 in Andalusia, Covington, Alabama, USA

Jerry Wayne Huckabaa[2228] born on August 17, 1948 in Andalusia, Covington, Alabama, USA

Charlene Huckabaa[2230] born on February 10, 1950 in Andalusia, Covington, Alabama, USA

Martin Van Buren Huckabaa Jr.[2232] born on October 13, 1951 in Andalusia, Covington, Alabama, USA; died on January 26, 2011

Jack Berry Huckabaa[2234] born on January 29, 1953 in Andalusia, Covington, Alabama, USA; died on December 4, 2013

Curtis Huckabaa[2235] born on August 21, 1955 in Andalusia, Covington, Alabama, USA

James Larry Huckabaa[2236] born on February 27, 1964 in Andalusia, Covington, Alabama, USA

1452. CHRISTINE BASS (see Descendants (87)) was born on July 29, 1929, in Carolina Community, Covington, Alabama, USA, to Jamie Ike Bass[498] and Cleo Gunter[499].
- She was recorded in the census in 1930, as an infant, in Carolina, Covington, Alabama, USA.
- She was recorded in the census in 1940, aged about 10, in Election Prect 21 Carolina, Covington, Alabama, USA.
- She was a Sewing Factory, Blue Lake Methodist Camp, Covington, Alabama, USA.
- She was recorded in the census on April 1, 1950, aged 20, in Carolina, Covington, Alabama, United States.
- She died about 2005, aged about 75.

Christine married twice. She was married to W. Edward Blackwell[1453] and Jack Smith[1454].

1453. W. EDWARD BLACKWELL was born on June 19, 1924, in Covington, Alabama, USA, to James Milton Blackwell and Nancy Viola Jane Lawson. W. Edward became known as "Eddie".
- He was recorded in the census in 1940, aged about 16, in Election Prect 21 Carolina, Covington, Alabama, USA.
- He was recorded in the census on April 1, 1950, aged 25, in Carolina, Covington, Alabama, United States.
- He died on August 15, 1974, aged 50, in Covington, Alabama, USA.

W. Edward Blackwell married Christine Bass[1452]. They had two daughters:

Aletha Jean Blackwell[2743] born on December 31, 1953 in Andalusia, Covington, Alabama, USA; died on November 1, 2006 in Andalusia, Covington, Alabama, USA

Demisia Blackwell[2745]

1454. JACK SMITH.

Jack Smith married Christine Bass[1452].

1455. VONCILE BASS (see Descendants (87)) was born on September 21, 1931, in Carolina, Covington, Alabama, United States, to Jamie Ike Bass[498] and Cleo Gunter[499].
- She was recorded in the census in 1940, aged about 8, in Election Prect 21 Carolina, Covington, Alabama, USA.
- She was recorded in the census on April 1, 1950, aged 18, in Carolina, Covington, Alabama, United States.
- She died on September 23, 2008, aged 77 years, in Covington, Alabama, United States.
- She was buried on September 26, 2008 in Carolina Baptist Church Cemetery, Covington, Alabama, USA.

1456. CLIFTON CURTIS BLACKWELL was born on November 29, 1921, in Carolina Community, Covington, Alabama, USA, to James Milton Blackwell and Nancy Viola Jane Lawson.
- He was recorded in the census in 1940, aged about 18, in Election Prect 21 Carolina, Covington, Alabama, USA.
- He died on September 12, 1988, aged 66, in Carolina Community, Covington, Alabama, USA.
- He was buried in Carolina Baptist Church Cemetery, Covington, Alabama, USA.

Clifton Curtis Blackwell married Voncile Bass[1455]. They had five children:

Cornelia Ann Blackwell[2748] born in May 1953 in Charlottsville, Vaginia, USA; died in May 1983

Deborah Lynn Blackwell[2750] born on February 25, 1955 in Andalusia, Covington, Alabama, USA

Teresa Blackwell[2753] born on September 1, 1959 in Andalusia, Covington, Alabama, USA
Clifton Joseph Blackwell[2755] born on September 2, 1970; died on September 3, 1970
Shela Dianna Blackwell[2756]

1457. BETTY JEAN BASS (see Descendants (87)) was born on May 23, 1933, in Covington, Alabama, USA, to Jamie Ike Bass[498] and Cleo Gunter[499].
- She was recorded in the census in 1940, aged about 7, in Election Prect 21 Carolina, Covington, Alabama, USA.
- She was recorded in the census on April 1, 1950, aged 16, in Carolina, Covington, Alabama, United States.
- She was recorded in the census on April 1, 1950, aged 16, in Carolina, Covington, Alabama, United States.
- She died on December 9, 2007, aged 74 years, in Covington, Alabama, United States.
- She was buried in Carolina Baptist Church Cemetery, Covington, Alabama, USA.

Betty Jean married her third cousin, L. B. Huckabaa[1005].
L. B. Huckabaa[1005], aged 27, married Betty Jean Bass, aged 21, on April 9, 1955 in Lucedale, George, Mississippi, USA. They had five children:
Randall Ike Huckabaa[2243] born on December 31, 1950 in Andalusia, Covington, Alabama, USA
Oscar Cleveland Huckabaa[2245] born on May 18, 1952 in Andalusia, Covington, Alabama, USA
Gordon Huckabaa[2247] born on April 17, 1956 in Andalusia, Covington, Alabama, USA
Beverly Jean Huckabaa[2250] born on October 11, 1957 in Andalusia, Covington, Alabama, USA
Rusty Lamar Huckabaa[2253] born on June 15, 1962 in Andalusia, Covington, Alabama, USA

1458. EMMIE ELVIRA BASS (see Descendants (87)) was born about 1944, in Alabama, United States, to Jamie Ike Bass[498] and Cleo Gunter[499]. She was recorded in the census on April 1, 1950, aged about 5, in Carolina, Covington, Alabama, United States.

1459. JULIUS IKE BASS (see Descendants (87)) was born on October 23, 1946, in Alabama, United States, to Jamie Ike Bass[498] and Cleo Gunter[499]. He was recorded in the census on April 1, 1950, aged 3, in Carolina, Covington, Alabama, United States.
Julius Ike married three times. He was married to Carolyn Garvin[1460], Fay Mitchell[1461] and Donna Dorman[1462].

1460. CAROLYN GARVIN.
Julius Ike Bass[1459] married Carolyn Garvin. They had two children:
Donna Carol Bass[2759]
Waymon Julius Bass[2761]

1461. FAY MITCHELL.
Julius Ike Bass[1459] married Fay Mitchell.

1462. DONNA DORMAN.
Julius Ike Bass[1459] married Donna Dorman.

1463. BEATRICE LUCILE BASS (see Descendants (88)) was born on July 1, 1930, in Niagra Falls, New York, USA, to Julius Clarence Bass[501] and Mildred Nall[502].
- She was recorded in the census in 1940, aged about 9, in Creekside Parkway, Niagara Town, Niagara, New York, USA.
- She was recorded in the census on April 1, 1950, aged 19, in 102 Carolin, Andalusia, Covington, Alabama, United States.

1464. RALPH LEVON PATTERSON SR. was born on November 17, 1930, in Andalusia, Covington, Alabama, USA.
- He was recorded in the census on April 1, 1950, aged 19, in 102 Carolin, Andalusia, Covington, Alabama, United States.
- He died on February 21, 1996, aged 65, in Andalusia, Covington, Alabama, USA.

Ralph Levon Patterson Sr., aged 18, married Beatrice Lucile Bass[1463], aged 18, on June 5, 1949. They had one son:
Ralph Levon Patterson Jr.[2762] born on February 3, 1954 in Andalusia, Covington, Alabama, USA

1465. ROBERT JULIUS BASS (see Descendants (88)) was born on March 21, 1938, in Niagra Falls, New York, USA, to Julius Clarence Bass[501] and Mildred Nall[502].
- He was recorded in the census in 1940, aged about 2, in Creekside Parkway, Niagara Town, Niagara, New York, USA.
- He was recorded in the census on April 1, 1950, aged 12, in On Pleas and Nome and Coneuch Church Iraveling Sousth East, Fairfield, Covington, Alabama, United States.
- He died on April 23, 1981, aged 43 years.

- He was buried in Carolina Baptist Church Cemetery, Covington, Alabama, USA.

The following information is also recorded for Robert Julius:
- Military Service.

Robert Julius married four times. He was married to Doris Jean Stokes[1466], Barbara Ann Tisdale[1467], Peggy Ducker[1468] and Sara Moore[1469].

Note: *U.S. Army.*
(Military Service)

1466. DORIS JEAN STOKES was born on November 20, 1938, in Covington, Alabama, USA.
Robert Julius Bass[1465], aged 18, married Doris Jean Stokes, aged 17, on October 17, 1956 in Pleasant Home Church. They had two children:
Sharon Jean Bass[2764] born on October 10, 1957 in Andalusia, Covington, Alabama, USA
Julius Randall Bass[2766] born on May 9, 1959 in Fort Bragg, Cumberland County, North Carolina, United States; died on July 10, 1998 in Andalusia, Covington, Alabama, USA

1467. BARBARA ANN TISDALE was born on August 20, 1951, in Troy, Pike, Alabama, United States.
Robert Julius Bass[1465], aged 34, married Barbara Ann Tisdale, aged 21, on February 20, 1973 in Enterprise, Coffee, Alabama, USA. They had one son:
Edward Michael Bass[2769] born on June 20, 1970 in Troy, Pike, Alabama, United States

1468. PEGGY DUCKER was born on January 5, 1940, in Enterprise, Coffee, Alabama, USA.
Robert Julius Bass[1465] married Peggy Ducker. They had one daughter:
Robin Taiwan Bass[2771] born on September 29, 1962 in Andalusia, Covington, Alabama, USA

1469. SARA MOORE.
Robert Julius Bass[1465] married Sara Moore.

1470. RICHARD CLARENCE BASS (see Descendants (88)) was born on October 2, 1940, in Niagra Falls, New York, USA, to Julius Clarence Bass[501] and Mildred Nall[502].
- He was recorded in the census on April 1, 1950, aged 9, in On Pleas and Nome and Coneuch Church Iraveling Sousth East, Fairfield, Covington, Alabama, United States.
- He died on March 14, 2008, aged 67 years, in Lorida, Highlands, Florida, USA.
- He was buried in Carolina Baptist Church Cemetery, Covington, Alabama, USA.

1471. MAXINE C ? was born on September 18, 1940.
Richard Clarence Bass[1470], aged 17, married Maxine C ?, aged 17, on May 31, 1958. They had two children:
Richard Christopher Bass[2773] born on October 31, 1961 in Andalusia, Covington, Alabama, USA
Kimberly Ruth Bass[2775] born on July 21, 1963 in Andalusia, Covington, Alabama, USA

1472. GAYLE ANN BASS (see Descendants (88)) was born on November 13, 1947, in Andalusa, Covington, Alabama, USA, to Julius Clarence Bass[501] and Mildred Nall[502]. She was recorded in the census on April 1, 1950, aged 2, in On Pleas and Nome and Coneuch Church Iraveling Sousth East, Fairfield, Covington, Alabama, United States.
Gayle Ann married twice. She was married to Terry Lee Cobb[1473] and Thomas Eugene Williams[1474].

1473. TERRY LEE COBB was born on May 6, 1949.
Terry Lee Cobb, aged 4, married Gayle Ann Bass[1472], aged 5, on September 30, 1953.

1474. THOMAS EUGENE WILLIAMS was born on February 20, 1943, in Sylacauga, Alabama, USA.
Thomas Eugene Williams, aged 23, married Gayle Ann Bass[1472], aged 19, on December 17, 1966. They had two children:
Leigh Ann Williams[2777] born on September 6, 1968 in Birminghame, Jefferson, Alabama, USA
Thomas Eugene Williams II[2779] born on July 8, 1972 in Montgomery, Montgomery, Alabama, USA

1475. OLEN REX HARRELSON (see Descendants (89)) was born on April 29, 1927, in Andalusa, Covington, Alabama, USA, to George Rufus Harrelson[504] and Mary Annie Bass[503].
- He was recorded in the census on April 1, 1950, aged 22, in Carolina, Covington, Alabama, United States.
- He died on December 20, 1983, aged 56, in Andalusa, Covington, Alabama, USA.
- He was buried in Carolina Baptist Church Cemetery, Covington, Alabama, USA.

Olen Rex married twice. He was married to Betty Jean Bearden[1476] and Christine Reba Eiland[1477].

1476. BETTY JEAN BEARDEN was born on January 17, 1935.
Olen Rex Harrelson[1475], aged 27, married Betty Jean Bearden, aged 19, on December 15, 1954. They had six children:
Rhonda Lynn Harrelson[2780] born on October 8, 1955 in Andalusa, Covington, Alabama, USA
Regina Harrelson[2783] born on June 28, 1958 in Andalusa, Covington, Alabama, USA
Robert Olen Harrelson[2784] born on March 17, 1960 in Andalusa, Covington, Alabama, USA
Cindy Rene Harrelson[2786] born on May 16, 1960 in Andalusa, Covington, Alabama, USA
Russel Allen Harrelson[2789] born on June 26, 1964 in Andalusa, Covington, Alabama, USA
Charles Rhett Harrelson[2791] born on October 26, 1966 in Andalusa, Covington, Alabama, USA

1477. CHRISTINE REBA EILAND was born about 1928, in Alabama, United States. She was recorded in the census on April 1, 1950, aged about 21, in Carolina, Covington, Alabama, United States.
> Olen Rex Harrelson[1475] married Christine Reba Eiland. They had one son:
>> Michael Rex Harrelson[2795] born on December 26, 1947 in Alabama, United States; died on February 21, 1969 in Andalusa, Covington, Alabama, USA

1478. RALPH MARLON HARRELSON (see Descendants (89)) was born on January 11, 1929, in Carolina, Covington, Alabama, USA, to George Rufus Harrelson[504] and Mary Annie Bass[503].
- He was recorded in the census on April 1, 1950, aged 21, in Carolina, Covington, Alabama, United States.
- He died on December 25, 1994, aged 65, in Carolina, Covington, Alabama, USA.
- He was buried in Carolina Baptist Church Cemetery, Covington, Alabama, USA.

The following information is also recorded for Ralph Marlon:
- Military Service.

Note: *Cpl. U.S. Army, Korea.*
(Military Service)

1479. BETTY JUNE GANUS was born on February 15, 1936, in Andalusia, Covington, Alabama, USA.
> Ralph Marlon Harrelson[1478], aged 30, married Betty June Ganus, aged 23, on April 11, 1959. They had three children:
>> Randall Keith Harrelson[2797] born on December 30, 1959 in Andalusia, Covington, Alabama, USA
>> Rae Suzanne Harrelson[2800] born on December 18, 1964 in Andalusia, Covington, Alabama, USA
>> James Ricky Harrelson[2801] born on December 18, 1964 in Andalusia, Covington, Alabama, USA

1480. RAMOND TEUELL HARRELSON (see Descendants (89)) was born on January 10, 1934, in Andalusa, Covington, Alabama, USA, to George Rufus Harrelson[504] and Mary Annie Bass[503]. He was recorded in the census on April 1, 1950, aged 16, in Carolina, Covington, Alabama, United States.

1481. SHIRLEY STOKES was born on August 29, 1934.
> Ramond Teuell Harrelson[1480], aged 22, married Shirley Stokes, aged 21, on March 31, 1956. They had one daughter:
>> Jacqueline Carolyn Harrelson[2803] born on September 6, 1957

1482. RONNIE RAY HARRELSON (see Descendants (89)) was born on October 3, 1943, in Andalusa, Covington, Alabama, USA, to George Rufus Harrelson[504] and Mary Annie Bass[503]. He was recorded in the census on April 1, 1950, aged 6, in Carolina, Covington, Alabama, United States.

1483. BARBARA SUE DUKE.
> Ronnie Ray Harrelson[1482] married Barbara Sue Duke. They had two daughters:
>> Renda Sue Harrelson[2804] born on June 24, 1964
>> Rita Ann Harrelson[2806] born on July 22, 1969

1484. CHARLOTTE BASS (see Descendants (90)) was born on February 28, 1945, in Andalusia, Covington, Alabama, USA, to Jessie D Bass[505] and Eileen Head[506]. She was recorded in the census on April 1, 1950, aged 5, in Carolina, Covington, Alabama, United States.
Charlotte married her third cousin, Lloyd Mathew Smith[1674].

1485. ELIZABETH LOUISE BASS (see Descendants (90)) was born on May 20, 1947, in Niagra Falls, New York, USA, to Jessie D Bass[505] and Eileen Head[506]. She was recorded in the census on April 1, 1950, aged 2, in Carolina, Covington, Alabama, United States.

1486. HAROLD JEROME BARROW was born on July 5, 1945.
> Harold Jerome Barrow, aged 22, married Elizabeth Louise Bass[1485], aged 20, on July 14, 1967 in Andalusia, Covington, Alabama, USA. They had three children:
>> Melinda Gayle Barrow[2816] born on January 21, 1972 in Andalusia, Covington, Alabama, USA
>> Angela Lynn Barrow[2818] born on December 15, 1974 in Andalusia, Covington, Alabama, USA
>> Kevin Jerome Barrow[2820] born on July 21, 1978 in Andalusia, Covington, Alabama, USA

1487. BARBARA ELEANOR BASS (see Descendants (91)) was born on September 10, 1938, in Alabama, USA, to Leon Pendry Bass[507] and Clipp F Merrill[508].
- She was recorded in the census in 1940, aged about 1, in Election Prect 21 Carolina, Covington, Alabama, USA.
- She died (At young age) in 1945, aged about 6.

1488. DAVID LEON BASS (see Descendants (91)) was born on November 26, 1948, in Alabama, United States, to Leon Pendry Bass[507] and Clipp F Merrill[508]. He was recorded in the census on April 1, 1950, aged 1, in Carolina, Covington, Alabama, United States.

1489. ROGER CLAYTON BASS (see Descendants (92)) was born to Snyder Clayton Bass[509] and Viola Ruth Coulter[510]. He died on June 3, 1991 in Andalusa, Covington, Alabama, USA.
Roger Clayton married twice. He was married to Lily Esther Rice[1490] and Rhonda Herring[1491].
1490. LILY ESTHER RICE.
    Roger Clayton Bass[1489] married Lily Esther Rice. They had one daughter:
        Angela Beth Bass[2821] born on June 3, 1968
1491. RHONDA HERRING.
    Roger Clayton Bass[1489] married Rhonda Herring.

1492. REDESSA L HENDERSON (see Descendants (93)) was born about 1936, in Alabama, United States, to William Turner Henderson[512] and Velma Bertha Bass[511]. She was recorded in the census on April 1, 1950, aged about 13, in Carolina, Covington, Alabama, United States.
1493. DARRELL WIGGINS.
    Darrell Wiggins married Redessa L Henderson[1492]. They had four children:
        Melony Wiggins[2823]
        Sylvia Wiggins[2824]
        Shannon Wiggins[2825]
        Connie Wiggins[2826]

1494. FREDRICK HENDERSON (see Descendants (93)) was born on February 28, 1943, in Andalusa, Covington, Alabama, USA, to William Turner Henderson[512] and Velma Bertha Bass[511]. He was recorded in the census on April 1, 1950, aged 7, in Carolina, Covington, Alabama, United States.
1495. JEANETTE ROBINSON was born on October 19, 1943, in Opp, Covington, Alabama, USA.
    Fredrick Henderson[1494] married Jeanette Robinson. They had two daughters:
        Robin Denise Henderson[2828] born on January 30, 1964 in Andalusia, Covington, Alabama, USA
        Donna Katrise Henderson[2830] born on June 14, 1966 in Andalusia, Covington, Alabama, USA

1496. JUDITH LYNN HENDERSON (see Descendants (93)) was born about 1949, in Alabama, United States, to William Turner Henderson[512] and Velma Bertha Bass[511]. She was recorded in the census on April 1, 1950, as an infant, in Carolina, Covington, Alabama, United States.
1497. RONNIE LEWIS.
    Ronnie Lewis married Judith Lynn Henderson[1496]. They had one daughter:
        Stephanie Lewis[2832]

1498. PHILLIP HENDERSON (see Descendants (93)) was born to William Turner Henderson[512] and Velma Bertha Bass[511].
Phillip married twice. He was married to Rebecca Riley[1499] and Alice ?[1500].
1499. REBECCA RILEY.
    Phillip Henderson[1498] married Rebecca Riley. They had two sons:
        Eric Henderson[2833]
        Chad Henderson[2834]
1500. ALICE ?.
    Phillip Henderson[1498] married Alice ?.

1501. MILLARD ALLISON OTT JR. (see Descendants (94)) was born on January 7, 1946, in Cleveland, Liberty, Texas, USA, to Millard Allison Ott[516] and Edith Inez Bass[513].
Millard Allison had two partnerships. He was married to Jerrie Ellen Vandiver[1502]. He was also the partner of Joann Merrel[1503].
1502. JERRIE ELLEN VANDIVER was born on April 21, 1951, in Alliance, Nebraska, USA.
    Millard Allison Ott Jr.[1501], aged 34, married Jerrie Ellen Vandiver, aged 29, on November 2, 1980.
1503. JOANN MERREL.
    Millard Allison Ott Jr.[1501] and Joann Merrel had three children:
        Todd Allison Ott[2835] born on April 5, 1965 in Channelview, Harris, Texas, USA
        Kam Renae Ott[2837] born on December 15, 1973 in Conroe, Montgomery, Texas, USA
        William Gilbert Ott[2839] born on January 8, 1975 in Cleveland, Liberty, Texas, USA
    The following information is also recorded for this family:
        • Unknown Relationship.

An image of Jeffery W. Bass' Virginia Hall painting licensed to the International Spy Museum in Washington DC. The original painting resides at CIA headquarters.

Above: Portrait of Barron Hilton by Jeffery W. Bass, the second son and successor to hotelier Conrad Hilton. Barron Hilton was chairman and CEO of Hilton Hotels Corporation.

Left: Portrait of George H. W. Bush, 41st President of the United States. The original portrait by Jeffery W. Bass hangs in the National Museum of Naval Aviation.

Greg Bass (standing) and Courtney Haden of the "Greg and Courtney" morning-show team, a popular radio show in the Birmingham are for many years.

Direct Relations

1504. JAMES ALLEN OTT SR. (see Descendants (94)) was born on January 3, 1948, in Cleveland, Liberty, Texas, USA, to Millard Allison Ott[516] and Edith Inez Bass[513].
The following information is also recorded for James Allen:
• Military Service.

1505. KARREN REGINA HENRY was born on November 28, 1950, in Cleveland, Liberty, Texas, USA.
James Allen Ott Sr.[1504], aged 21, married Karren Regina Henry, aged 18, on May 24, 1969. They had three children:
James Allen Ott Jr.[2840] born on April 12, 1972 in Conroe, Montgomery, Texas, USA
Reagan Edward Ott[2842] born on June 20, 1974 in Cochice, Arazona, USA
Karren Michelle Ott[2843] born on May 23, 1979 in Conroe, Montgomery, Texas, USA

1506. JOHN BYRON OTT (see Descendants (94)) was born on July 3, 1949, in Conroe, Montgomery, Texas, USA, to Millard Allison Ott[516] and Edith Inez Bass[513].

1507. RICHARD BASS (see Descendants (95)) was born to Claude Bruce Bass[519] and Marline White[520].

1508. MILLI COOPER.

Richard Bass[1507] married Milli Cooper.

1509. BOB BASS (see Descendants (95)) was born in October 23 A.D. to Claude Bruce Bass[519] and Marline White[520].
1510. RUTH ?.
Bob Bass[1509] married Ruth ?.

1511. GREG BASS (see Descendants (95)) was born to Claude Bruce Bass[519] and Marline White[520]. Greg was employed.
Note: *"Greg and Courtney" morning-show team on WKXX-FM (Kicks 106) from 1981 to 1984. They moved the show to Rock 99 in 1991-1993. Along with Courtney Haden, Greg produced a documentary about the 16th Street Baptist Church for WBHM-FM which won a regional Edward R. Murrow Award.*
(Occupation)
1512. PEGGY ?.
Greg Bass[1511] and Peggy ? became partners.
The following information is also recorded for this family:
• Unknown Relationship.

1513. JEFFERY W. BASS (see Descendants (95)) was born in March 31 A.D. to Claude Bruce Bass[519] and Marline White[520]. Jeffery W. became known as "Jeff". Jeff was an Artist.
Note: *Jeffrey W. Bass has been painting since age nine, and credits his late mother--an artist herself--as his most significant influence. At age thirteen, he began receiving instruction in drawing and painting from a Scottish portrait painter and teacher. He sold his first painting--a view of Chesapeake Bay as seen from a family residence--at age fourteen. Before he graduated from high school, he was selling prints of his artwork and working as a professional illustrator. Today, Jeff Bass completes fine art portraits as well as historical works for private collections and museums. His work is represented in the United States House of Representatives, the Smithsonian, the Central Intelligence Agency, the National World War II Museum, the National Naval Aviation Museum, the Reagan Presidential Library and Museum and the Hoover Institute, to name a few. He has painted luminaries including President George H. W. Bush, Florida Governor Jeb Bush and former Secretary of State George Shultz. Bass's work has been featured on CNN, Fox News and France 2 Television. His work has also been frequently distributed around the world through major news services such as Reuters and the Associated Press with appearances in the London Sunday Times*

and the UK Daily Mail. Images of his work have also been licensed to publishers and museums worldwide. Although Bass works primarily in oil, he's also adept at aqueous media and holds a signature membership in the National Watercolor Society. -jeffbass.com/about.
(Occupation)

1514. MR./MS. LAW (see Descendants (95)) was born to Cecil Athaniel Law[522] and Sarah Clyde Law[521].

1515. MR./MS. LAW (see Descendants (95)) was born to Cecil Athaniel Law[522] and Sarah Clyde Law[521].

1516. MR./MS. LAW (see Descendants (95)) was born to Cecil Athaniel Law[522] and Sarah Clyde Law[521].

1517. MR./MS. LAW (see Descendants (95)) was born to Cecil Athaniel Law[522] and Sarah Clyde Law[521].

1518. LINDA BASS (see Descendants (95)) was born in August 27 A.D., in Alabama, United States, to Bennett Ray Bass[523] and Mary Rae Parrish[524]. She was recorded in the census on April 1, 1950, aged 1922, in 127 A Ingram, Norfolk, Norfolk City, Virginia, United States.

1519. JAMES HAROLD CREWS. James Harold became known as "Harry".
James Harold Crews married Linda Bass[1518]. They had two children:
Michael Allen Crews[2844] died on June 16, 2016
Angie Crews[2846]

1520. COL. GARY DEAN BASS (see Descendants (95)) was born on July 1, 1950, in Norfolk, Virginia, USA, to Bennett Ray Bass[523] and Mary Rae Parrish[524].
• He died on July 27, 2019, aged 69, in Mims, Brevard, Florida, USA.
• He was buried in Cape Canaveral National Cemetery, Mims, Brevard, Florida, USA.
The following information is also recorded for Gary Dean:
• Military Service.
Note: *LTC US Army.*
(Military Service)

1521. DORA MAPES.
Gary Dean Bass[1520] married Dora Mapes. They had one son:
Shawn Bass[2848]

1522. LUCIAN HIBBARD ANDREWS III (see Descendants (95)) was born to Lucian Hibbard Andrews Jr.[527] and Bessie May Bass[526].
1523. ELAINE ?.
Lucian Hibbard Andrews III[1522] married Elaine ?.

1524. LUCIA DIANNE ANDREWS (see Descendants (95)) was born about 1948, in California, United States, to Lucian Hibbard Andrews Jr.[527] and Bessie May Bass[526]. She was recorded in the census on April 1, 1950, aged about 1, in 903 New Jersey., Mobile, Mobile, Alabama, United States.
1525. BEN SMITH III.
Ben Smith III married Lucia Dianne Andrews[1524].

1526. DEBORAH ANDREWS (see Descendants (95)) was born to Lucian Hibbard Andrews Jr.[527] and Bessie May Bass[526].
1527. JOE SMITH.
Joe Smith married Deborah Andrews[1526].

1528. REBECCA ANDREWS (see Descendants (95)) was born to Lucian Hibbard Andrews Jr.[527] and Bessie May Bass[526].
1529. ANDY RUMBAUGH.
Andy Rumbaugh married Rebecca Andrews[1528].

1530. RONALD BASS (see Descendants (95)) was born about 1945, in Alabama, United States, to John Irvin Bass[528] and Minnie Jewel McCorquodal[529]. He was recorded in the census on April 1, 1950, aged about 4, in 1938 So Huron, Denver, Denver, Colorado, United States.

1531. CAROL BASS (see Descendants (95)) was born about 1947, in Alabama, United States, to John Irvin Bass[528] and Minnie Jewel McCorquodal[529]. She was recorded in the census on April 1, 1950, aged about 2, in 1938 So Huron, Denver, Denver, Colorado, United States.

1532. CHERYL BASS (see Descendants (95)) was born about 1947, in Alabama, United States, to John Irvin Bass[528] and Minnie Jewel McCorquodal[529]. She was recorded in the census on April 1, 1950, aged about 2, in 1938 So Huron, Denver, Denver, Colorado, United States.

1533. NANCY BASS (see Descendants (95)) was born about 1949, in Colorado, United States, to John Irvin Bass[528] and Minnie Jewel McCorquodal[529]. She was recorded in the census on April 1, 1950, as an infant, in 1938 So Huron, Denver, Denver, Colorado, United States.

1534. MARLON JEROME BASS (see Descendants (96)) was born on November 1, 1928, in Andalusia, Covington, Alabama, USA, to Andrew Bennett Bass[532] and Florence Perdue[533].
- He was recorded in the census on April 1, 1950, aged 21, in 1ar River Falls Street, Andalusia, Covington, Alabama, United States.
- He died on January 5, 2006, aged 77, in Andalusia, Covington, Alabama, USA.
- He was buried in Andalusia Memorial Cemetery, Andalusia, Covington, Alabama, USA.

The following information is also recorded for Marlon Jerome:
- Military Service.

Note: *US Airforce and MSG US Army.*
(Military Service)

1535. BETTY J. ? was born on March 13, 1934.
Marlon Jerome Bass[1534], aged about 25, married Betty J. ?, aged about 20, about 1954 in Covington, Alabama, USA. They had one daughter:
Marla Kim Bass[2850]

1536. DORIS JEAN BASS (see Descendants (96)) was born on February 18, 1932, in Charlottsville, VA, USA, to Andrew Bennett Bass[532] and Florence Perdue[533]. She was recorded in the census on April 1, 1950, aged 18, in 1ar River Falls Street, Andalusia, Covington, Alabama, United States.
Doris Jean married twice. She was married to Albert T Tyler[1537] and Henry Albert Tyler[1538].

1537. ALBERT T TYLER was born about 1930, in Charlottsville, VA, USA.
Albert T Tyler married Doris Jean Bass[1536]. They had one son:
Michael Wayne Tyler[2853] born on June 28, 1953 in Charlottsville, VA, USA

1538. HENRY ALBERT TYLER was born on October 26, 1926, in Charlottsville, VA, USA.
Henry Albert Tyler, aged 24, married Doris Jean Bass[1536], aged 19, on March 11, 1951 in Pascagoula, Mississippi, USA. They had one daughter, and assumed parenthood of another one:
Michael Wayne Tyler[2853] by adoption
Anita Kaye Tyler[2855] born on October 17, 1966 in Andalusia, Covington, Alabama, USA

1539. SHIRLEY ANN BASS (see Descendants (96)) was born on March 24, 1940, in Andalusia, Covington, Alabama, USA, to Andrew Bennett Bass[532] and Florence Perdue[533]. She was recorded in the census on April 1, 1950, aged 10, in 1ar River Falls Street, Andalusia, Covington, Alabama, United States.

1540. BRUCE VEASEY JR. was born 'FROM AFT 1930 TO BEF 1940', in Charlottsville, VA, USA. Bruce became known as "Pete".
Bruce Veasey Jr. married Shirley Ann Bass[1539], aged 18, on December 11, 1958 in Andalusia, Covington, Alabama, USA. They had two sons:
Bruce Kelley Veasey[2857] born on September 22, 1961
Brandon Keith Veasey[2859]

1541. OLIVIA TART (see Descendants (96)) was born to William A. Tart[535] and Gussie Josephine Johnson[534].

1542. MARCUS GENE JOHNSON (see Descendants (96)) was born in Andalusia, Covington, Alabama, USA to Martha Lou Johnson[541].

1543. ANN OLIVE (see Descendants (97)) was born about 1945, in Virginia, United States, to Robert H Olive[549] and Corinne Gregory[548]. She was recorded in the census on April 1, 1950, aged about 4, in S Collinswath, El Paso, El Paso, Texas, United States.

1544. BOBBY OLIVE (see Descendants (97)) was born on April 2, 1952, in USA, to Robert H Olive[549] and Corinne Gregory[548]. He died on October 27, 2002, aged 50, in Richmond, Virginia, USA.

1545. BECKY ?.
    Bobby Olive[1544] married Becky ?. They had two children:
        Chris Olive[2860]
        Ann Olive[2861]

1546. SHELIA PAMELIA BASS (see Descendants (98)) was born on June 15, 1937, in Andalusia, Covington, Alabama, USA, to William Columbus Bass[553] and Clara V Stokes[554]. She was recorded in the census on April 1, 1950, aged 12, in 304 Woodrow Ave, Andalusia, Covington, Alabama, United States.

1547. CARMON LEE PARRISH was born on January 8, 1927, in Andalusia, Covington, Alabama, USA.
    Carmon Lee Parrish married Shelia Pamelia Bass[1546]. They had three children:
        Anthony Lee Parrish[2862] born on February 4, 1957 in Andalusia, Covington, Alabama, USA
        Rebecca Lynn Parrish[2865] born on November 15, 1958
        Jon Kevin Parrish[2867] born on November 18, 1963

1548. PATRICIA LUCILLE BASS (see Descendants (98)) was born on October 22, 1939, in Alabama, United States, to William Columbus Bass[553] and Clara V Stokes[554]. She was recorded in the census on April 1, 1950, aged 10, in 304 Woodrow Ave, Andalusia, Covington, Alabama, United States.
Patricia Lucille married twice. She was married to Kenneth Lavon Grissett[1549] and Quinton Gene Bass[444] (her second cousin, once removed).
    Quinton Gene Bass[444], aged about 66, married Patricia Lucille Bass, aged about 65, in 2005.

1549. KENNETH LAVON GRISSETT was born on September 10, 1941.
    Kenneth Lavon Grissett married Patricia Lucille Bass[1548]. They had three children:
        Ritchie Dean Grissett[2868] born on November 14, 1965 in Andalusia, Covington, Alabama, USA
        Marquita Lynn Grissett[2869] born on July 20, 1969 in Andalusia, Covington, Alabama, USA
        Keith Lavon Grissett[2870] born on May 9, 1973 in Andalusia, Covington, Alabama, USA

1550. JAMES WILLIAM BASS (see Descendants (98)) was born on November 11, 1942, in Andalusia, Covington, Alabama, USA, to William Columbus Bass[553] and Clara V Stokes[554]. He was recorded in the census on April 1, 1950, aged 7, in 304 Woodrow Ave, Andalusia, Covington, Alabama, United States.

1551. LOUISE KELLEY.
    James William Bass[1550] married Louise Kelley. They had three daughters:
        Donna Lynne Bass[2871] born on September 4, 1965 in Andalusia, Covington, Alabama, USA
        Pamela Renea Bass[2872] born on January 18, 1967 in Andalusia, Covington, Alabama, USA
        Paula Kay Bass[2873] born on August 25, 1972 in Andalusia, Covington, Alabama, USA

1552. MATHEW GERALD BASS (see Descendants (98)) was born on April 6, 1948, in Andalusia, Covington, Alabama, USA, to William Columbus Bass[553] and Clara V Stokes[554]. He was recorded in the census on April 1, 1950, aged 1, in 304 Woodrow Ave, Andalusia, Covington, Alabama, United States.

1553. MARY LOU BUSH.
    Mathew Gerald Bass[1552] married Mary Lou Bush. They had four children:
        Michael Gerald Bass[2874] born on June 22, 1971 in Andalusia, Covington, Alabama, USA
        William Henry Bass[2875] born on September 23, 1972 in Andalusia, Covington, Alabama, USA
        Katie Diane Bass[2876] born on April 22, 1975 in Andalusia, Covington, Alabama, USA
        James Lynn Bass[2877] born on April 30, 1976 in Andalusia, Covington, Alabama, USA

1554. JERRY BASS (see Descendants (98)) was born to William Columbus Bass[553] and Clara V Stokes[554].

1555. MS. ?.
    Jerry Bass[1554] married Ms. ?. They had two sons:
        Michael Bass[2878]
        Mr. Bass[2879]

1556. DONALD BASS (see Descendants (98)) was born to Howard Eugine Bass[555] and Annie M Maud[556].

Direct Relations

1557. BOBBY BASS (see Descendants (98)) was born to Howard Eugine Bass[555] and Annie M Maud[556].

1558. DIANNA O'BRIEN (see Descendants (98)) was born to O.B. O'Brien[559] and Ruby Lee Bass[558].

1559. STEVE WALDEN BASS (see Descendants (99)) was born on May 26, 1946, in Hartford, Geneva County, Alabama, United States, to Kenneth Bridges Bass[565] and Nancy Ruth Walden[566].
- He was recorded in the census on April 1, 1950, aged 3, in Quida, Enterprise, Coffee, Alabama, United States.
- He died on May 24, 1999, aged 52, in Milton, Florida USA.

Steve Walden married twice. He was married to Saundra Gail Harris[1560] and Paula Simpson[1561].

1560. SAUNDRA GAIL HARRIS was born in 1946.
>Steve Walden Bass[1559] married Saundra Gail Harris. They had two children:
>>Brett Zan Bass[2880] born in 1965 in Hattisburg, Mississippi, USA
>>Brandy Lane Bass[2883] born in 1968

1561. PAULA SIMPSON.
>Steve Walden Bass[1559] married Paula Simpson. They had one daughter:
>>Nanci L. Bass[2885]

1562. DANNY KAY BASS (see Descendants (99)) was born in 1954 to Kenneth Bridges Bass[565] and Nancy Ruth Walden[566].

1563. VICKY WALKER. She died in 1990 in Milton, Florida USA.
>Danny Kay Bass[1562] married Vicky Walker. They had one daughter:
>>Erin Lynn Bass[2886] born on October 18, 1986 in Milton, Florida USA

1564. KENNETH LEE BASS (see Descendants (99)) was born in 1960 to Kenneth Bridges Bass[565] and Nancy Ruth Walden[566].

Kenneth Lee married twice. He was married to Tammy C Sorrells[1565] and Jennifer Jernigan[1566].

1565. TAMMY C SORRELLS.
>Kenneth Lee Bass[1564] married Tammy C Sorrells. They had two children:
>>Devin Lee Bass[2887] born on March 31, 1986
>>Sheleiah Lynn Bass[2889] born on March 11, 1988

1566. JENNIFER JERNIGAN was born on July 16, 1970.
>Jennifer married twice. She was married to Kenneth Lee Bass[1564] and Mr. Rigby.
>Kenneth Lee Bass[1564], aged about 59, married Jennifer Jernigan, aged 49, on December 2, 2019.
>Mr. Rigby married Jennifer Jernigan. They had one daughter:
>>Ellen Grace Rigby born on February 21, 2007

1567. RANDY LYNN BASS (see Descendants (99)) was born in 1963 to Kenneth Bridges Bass[565] and Nancy Ruth Walden[566].

Randy Lynn married twice. He was married to Kimi Sue Adams[1568] and Carry Ann ?[1569].

1568. KIMI SUE ADAMS was born in 1963.
>Randy Lynn Bass[1567], aged about 25, married Kimi Sue Adams, aged about 25, on August 14, 1988 in Santa Rosa, Florida, USA. They had two children:
>>Miranda Bass[2891] born in 1990
>>Randi Lynn Bass[2893] born in 1995

1569. CARRY ANN ?.
>Randy Lynn Bass[1567] married Carry Ann ?. They had one son:
>>Waylon Bass[2894]

1570. GLENN MAURICE ABNEY III (see Descendants (99)) was born in Texas, United States to Glenn M Abney Jr.[568] and Mildred E. Griffen Bass[567]. He was recorded in the census on April 1, 1950, in 8 Mi North West of S B + R G V Rwy, Mission, Hidalgo, Texas, United States.

1571. RUTH ?.
>Glenn Maurice Abney III[1570] married Ruth ?.

1572. ANN ABNEY (see Descendants (99)) was born in Texas, United States to Glenn M Abney Jr.[568] and Mildred E. Griffen Bass[567]. She was recorded in the census on April 1, 1950, in 8 Mi North West of S B + R G V Rwy, Mission, Hidalgo, Texas, United States.

1573. KENNETH BEVERS.
>Kenneth Bevers married Ann Abney[1572].

1574. GLENDA ABNEY (see Descendants (99)) was born to Glenn M Abney Jr.[568] and Mildred E. Griffen Bass[567].

She was recorded in the census on April 1, 1950, in 8 Mi North West of S B + R G V Rwy, Mission, Hidalgo, Texas, United States.

1575. DARRELL RIEGEL.
Darrell Riegel married Glenda Abney[1574].

1576. JOHN DENNIS BASS (see Descendants (99)) was born in December 1951, in Covington, Alabama, USA, to George Washington Bass[571] and Lorretta Voncile Driggers[572].

1577. JANICE DARLENE OWENS.
John Dennis Bass[1576] married Janice Darlene Owens. They had three children:
Hannah LeNelle Bass[2895] born on December 13, 1980 in Atlanta, Georgia, USA
Kevin Bass[2897] born on March 22, 1982 in Atlanta, Georgia, USA
Tina Darlene Bass[2898]

1578. WILLIAM GARY BASS (see Descendants (99)) was born on June 27, 1955, in Covington, Alabama, USA, to George Washington Bass[571] and Lorretta Voncile Driggers[572].
William Gary married twice. He was married to Louise Watkins[1579] and Patricia ?[1580].

1579. LOUISE WATKINS was born on March 22, 1952, in Toccoa, Georgia, USA.
William Gary Bass[1578], aged 41, married Louise Watkins, aged 44, on February 7, 1997.

1580. PATRICIA ?.
William Gary Bass[1578] married Patricia ?.

1581. EMILY GWENDOLYN BASS (see Descendants (99)) was born on August 1, 1956, in Covington, Alabama, USA, to George Washington Bass[571] and Lorretta Voncile Driggers[572].

1582. KENNETH E LEE was born on March 24, 1957.
Kenneth E Lee, aged 23, married Emily Gwendolyn Bass[1581], aged 24, on August 23, 1980. They had two children:
Lori Nicole Lee[2901] born on June 26, 1984 in Montgomery, Montgomery, Alabama, USA
Tanner Lee[2904] born on June 27, 1991 in Andalusia, Covington, Alabama, USA

1583. RICKIE DONNEL BARNETT SR. (see Descendants (99)) was born on July 24, 1946, in Andalusia, Covington, Alabama, USA, to George R Barnett[575] and Laura Frances Bass[574]. He was recorded in the census on April 1, 1950, aged 3, in Albritton Rd., Andalusia, Covington, Alabama, United States.
Rickie Donnel married three times. He was married to Doris Ann Dubose[1584], Barbara Gambells[1585] and Sandra Adams[1586].

1584. DORIS ANN DUBOSE.
Rickie Donnel Barnett Sr.[1583] married Doris Ann Dubose. They had one daughter:
LaDonice Darnell Barnett[2905]

1585. BARBARA GAMBELLS.
Rickie Donnel Barnett Sr.[1583] married Barbara Gambells. They had two children:
Buffie Deanna Barnett[2907]
Rickey Darnell Barnett Jr.[2908]

1586. SANDRA ADAMS.
Rickie Donnel Barnett Sr.[1583] married Sandra Adams. They had two daughters:
Gloria Lynn Barnett[2909]
Melissa Ann Barnett[2911]

1587. GLORIA DIANNE BARNETT (see Descendants (99)) was born on October 17, 1949, in Andalusia, Covington, Alabama, USA, to George R Barnett[575] and Laura Frances Bass[574]. She was recorded in the census on April 1, 1950, as an infant, in Albritton Rd., Andalusia, Covington, Alabama, United States.

1588. ARTHUR LYNN PRESLEY was born on December 4, 1948. He died on January 26, 2021, aged 72.
Arthur Lynn Presley, aged 22, married Gloria Dianne Barnett[1587], aged 22, on December 3, 1971. They had three children:
Brandi Lee Presley[2913] born on February 17, 1977
Christopher Edwin Presley[2915] born on February 17, 1977
Lindsey Presley[2918] born on April 19, 1984

1589. TERESA LAGAIL BARNETT (see Descendants (99)) was born on April 23, 1952, in Andalusia, Covington, Alabama, USA, to George R Barnett[575] and Laura Frances Bass[574].
Teresa LaGail married twice. She was married to Raymond Randall Russell[1590] and Richard Dewight Lassiter[1591].

1590. RAYMOND RANDALL RUSSELL.
Raymond Randall Russell married Teresa LaGail Barnett[1589]. They had three children:
Starlette Dawn Russell[2921]
Raymond Randall Russell Jr.[2923]
Sonya Leann Russell[2925]

1591. RICHARD DEWIGHT LASSITER.
Richard Dewight Lassiter married Teresa LaGail Barnett[1589].

1592. WANDA JUNE BARNETT (see Descendants (99)) was born on June 12, 1955 to George R Barnett[575] and Laura Frances Bass[574].
Wanda June married twice. She was married to David Glidewell[1593] and Donald Baker[1594].

1593. DAVID GLIDEWELL.
David Glidewell married Wanda June Barnett[1592]. They had two children:
David Brent Glidewell[2927]
Christy Lee Glidewell[2928]

1594. DONALD BAKER.
Donald Baker married Wanda June Barnett[1592].

1595. DALE ALLEN GINDLESPERGER JR. (see Descendants (99) and Descendants (99)) was born on January 6, 1951, in Andalusia, Covington, Alabama, USA, to Otis RC Mann[578] and Rossie Lee Bass[576].

1596. BELINDA JO BONEY was born on January 23, 1951, in Jacksonville, Florida, USA.
Dale Allen Gindlesperger Jr.[1595], aged 21, married Belinda Jo Boney, aged 21, on March 18, 1972 in Jacksonville, Florida, USA. They had three sons:
Mitchell Allen Gindlesperger[2930] born on February 27, 1974 in Jacksonville, Florida, USA
Andrew Grant Gindlesperger[2932] born on December 7, 1978 in Jacksonville, Florida, USA
Derek Ashley Gindlesperger[2934] born on November 7, 1983 in Duluth, Georgia, USA

1597. SUE ANN MANN (see Descendants (99)) was born on April 11, 1954, in Andalusia, Covington, Alabama, USA, to Otis RC Mann[578] and Rossie Lee Bass[576].

1598. JAMES B KING was born on April 4, 1951.
James B King, aged 20, married Sue Ann Mann[1597], aged 17, on May 14, 1971 in Montgomery, Montgomery, Alabama, USA. They had one daughter:
April Ann King[2936] born on October 20, 1971 in Montgomery, Montgomery, Alabama, USA

1599. BARBARA JANE MANN (see Descendants (99)) was born on August 15, 1956, in Andalusia, Covington, Alabama, USA, to Otis RC Mann[578] and Rossie Lee Bass[576].

1600. GARY WAYNE PELHAM was born on December 31, 1944, in Montgomery, Montgomery, Alabama, USA.
Gary Wayne Pelham married Barbara Jane Mann[1599].

1601. BETTY JEAN MANN (see Descendants (99)) was born on August 15, 1956, in Andalusia, Covington, Alabama, USA, to Otis RC Mann[578] and Rossie Lee Bass[576].
Betty Jean married three times. She was married to Randel Glenn Cornell[1602], Ronald Reed[1603] and Patrick McCoy[1604].

1602. RANDEL GLENN CORNELL was born on March 17, 1951, in Montgomery, Montgomery, Alabama, USA.
Randel Glenn Cornell, aged 32, married Betty Jean Mann[1601], aged 27, on December 22, 1983. They had one daughter:
Angela Kay Cornell[2938] born on August 28, 1971 in Hopkinsville, Kentucky, USA

1603. RONALD REED.
Ronald Reed married Betty Jean Mann[1601]. They assumed parenthood of one daughter:
Angela Kay Cornell[2938] by adoption

1604. PATRICK MCCOY.
Patrick McCoy married Betty Jean Mann[1601].

1605. DENNIS KEITH MANN (see Descendants (99)) was born on August 28, 1961, in Milton, Florida USA, to Otis RC Mann[578] and Rossie Lee Bass[576].
Dennis Keith married twice. He was married to Cindy Calhoun[1606] and Brenda Davis[1607].

1606. CINDY CALHOUN.
> Dennis Keith Mann[1605] married Cindy Calhoun. They had one daughter:
>> Ashton Nicole Mann[2940] born on October 10, 1986 in Montgomery, Montgomery, Alabama, USA

1607. BRENDA DAVIS.
> Dennis Keith Mann[1605] married Brenda Davis.

1608. MICHAEL WAYNE MANN (see Descendants (99)) was born on November 6, 1964, in Milton, Florida USA, to Otis RC Mann[578] and Rossie Lee Bass[576].

1609. SANDRA ELAINE COLEMAN was born on January 25, 1972, in Greenville, South Carolina, USA.
> Michael Wayne Mann[1608], aged 35, married Sandra Elaine Coleman, aged 28, on October 7, 2000 in Kowliga, Alabama, USA. They had five children:
>> Seth Allen Mann Mann[2941] born on November 2, 2002 in Montgomery, Montgomery, Alabama, USA
>> Cole Michael Mann[2942] born on November 18, 2004 in Montgomery, Montgomery, Alabama, USA; died on December 22, 2004 in Fitzgerald, Georgia, USA
>> Dakota Mann[2943] born on January 6, 2008 in Montgomery, Montgomery, Alabama, USA
>> Piper Mann[2944] born on January 6, 2008 in Montgomery, Montgomery, Alabama, USA
>> Taylor Mann[2945] born on January 6, 2008 in Montgomery, Montgomery, Alabama, USA

1610. LINDA FAY MAUND (see Descendants (99)) was born on August 25, 1951, in Genvea, Geneva, Alabama, USA, to Columbus Franklin Maund[580] and Melisa Juanita Bass[579].
> Linda Fay married twice. She was married to Ansel Hogan[1611] and Terry Bullard[1612].

1611. ANSEL HOGAN.
> Ansel Hogan married Linda Fay Maund[1610]. They had one son:
>> Tyler Ansel Hogan[2946] born on October 2, 1990 in Valdosta, Lowndes, Alabama, USA

1612. TERRY BULLARD.
> Terry Bullard married Linda Fay Maund[1610].

1613. AMELIA DELAINE MAUND (see Descendants (99)) was born on June 14, 1957, in Enterprise, Coffee, Alabama, USA, to Columbus Franklin Maund[580] and Melisa Juanita Bass[579].

1614. DANIEL LEWELLYN BEASLEY.
> Daniel Lewellyn Beasley married Amelia Delaine Maund[1613], aged 45, on April 19, 2003 in Monroe County, Florida, USA.

1615. WENDY BRYNELL BASS (see Descendants (99)) was born in Andalusia, Covington, Alabama, USA to Winston Byran Bass[581] and Mary Nell Baker[582].

1616. DAVID MILES was born in Ramer, Alabama, USA.
> David Miles married Wendy Brynell Bass[1615]. They had two children:
>> Mary Miles[2947]
>> Brian Miles[2948]

1617. ALIVIA LASHELLE BASS (see Descendants (99)) was born on December 7, 1961, in Andalusia, Covington, Alabama, USA, to Murry Cecil Bass[583] and Elizabeth Ann Jackson[584].

1618. JOHNNY MACK DANFORD.
> Johnny Mack Danford married Alivia LaShelle Bass[1617]. They had one son:
>> Randy Danford[2949]

1619. MURRY LAMAR BASS (see Descendants (99)) was born on March 10, 1965, in Andalusia, Covington, Alabama, USA, to Murry Cecil Bass[583] and Elizabeth Ann Jackson[584].

1620. DONNA THERESA STACKS.
> Murry Lamar Bass[1619], aged 23, married Donna Theresa Stacks on June 4, 1988 in Andalusia, Covington, Alabama, USA. They had one son:
>> Derrick Lamar Bass[2950] born on July 7, 1993 in Montgomery, Montgomery, Alabama, USA

1621. LINDA C BASS (see Descendants (100)) was born about 1943, in Alabama, United States, to Lewis W Bass[585] and Avis Hutto[586]. She was recorded in the census on April 1, 1950, aged about 6, in 101b Meaher Ave, Prichard, Mobile, Alabama, United States.

1622. VIC LAKOTOS.
> Vic LaKotos married Linda C Bass[1621].

1623. ALBERT R. DOUGLAS JR. (see Descendants (100)) was born to Albert R. Douglas Sr.[588] and Marjorie Bass[587].

1624. JO CARROL DOUGLAS (see Descendants (100)) was born to Albert R. Douglas Sr.[588] and Marjorie Bass[587].

1625. LEONARD RAYMOND PREVITO JR. (see Descendants (100)) was born in December 1945, in Alabama, United States, to Leonard Raymond Previto Sr.[592] and Esther Frances Bass[591]. He was recorded in the census on April 1, 1950, aged 4, in High Power Radio Station No Severn, Anne Arundel, Maryland, United States.

1626. MS. BEVERLY.
> Leonard Raymond Previto Jr.[1625] married Ms. Beverly. They had three children:
>> Trey Previto[2951]
>> Leah E Previto[2953] born about 1978
>> Kristina Previto[2954]

1627. REX TURNER (see Descendants (101)) was born to Cary Preston Turner[595] and Thelma Olline Curtis[594].

1628. JACKIE TURNER (see Descendants (101)) was born to Cary Preston Turner[595] and Thelma Olline Curtis[594].

1629. RUBY JEAN TURNER (see Descendants (101)) was born on November 14, 1942 to Cary Preston Turner[595] and Thelma Olline Curtis[594]. She died in 2005, aged about 62.

1630. NORMAN RUSSELL FINDLEY was born on June 17, 1938, in Alabama, United States.
> Norman Russell Findley married Ruby Jean Turner[1629]. They had three children:
>> Troy Lynne Findley[2955] born in March 1962; died in January 1968
>> Michael Rena Findley[2956] born on December 3, 1963
>> Robby Lynn Findley[2957] born on May 2, 1969

1631. WILLIAM THOMAS PADGETT (see Descendants (102)) was born on August 15, 1926, in Conecuh, Alabama, USA, to Willie Thermon Padgett[601] and Nannie Jewl Hoomes[602].
- He died (At young age) on August 26, 1936, aged 10, in Conecuh, Alabama, USA.
- He was buried in Carolina Baptist Church Cemetery, Covington, Alabama, USA.

1632. O. B. PADGETT (see Descendants (102)) was born on March 18, 1930, in Jefferson, Alabama, USA, to Willie Thermon Padgett[601] and Nannie Jewl Hoomes[602].
- He was recorded in the census in 1940, aged about 10, in Conecuh, Alabama, USA.
- He died on July 22, 1985, aged 55, in Seminole County, Georgia, USA.

1633. JAMES CLINTON PADGETT (see Descendants (102)) was born on May 10, 1932, in Conecuh, Alabama, USA, to Willie Thermon Padgett[601] and Nannie Jewl Hoomes[602]. He was recorded in the census in 1940, aged about 8, in Conecuh, Alabama, USA.

1634. IVALOU JEANETTA PADGETT (see Descendants (102)) was born on July 2, 1936, in Conecuh, Alabama, USA, to Willie Thermon Padgett[601] and Nannie Jewl Hoomes[602].
- She was recorded in the census in 1940, aged about 3, in Conecuh, Alabama, USA.
- She died on June 30, 2016, aged 79, in Marietta, Georgia, USA.

1635. WILLIAM THOMAS PADGETT (see Descendants (102)) was born on December 5, 1939, in Conecuh, Alabama, USA, to Willie Thermon Padgett[601] and Nannie Jewl Hoomes[602]. He was recorded in the census in 1940, as an infant, in Conecuh, Alabama, USA.

1636. MARY LOUISE POUCHER. Mary Louise became known as "Mary Lou".
> William Thomas Padgett[1635], aged 21, married Mary Louise Poucher on August 26, 1961. They had two sons:
>> Mr. Padgett[2958]
>> Mr. Padgett[2959]

1637. HERBERT WAYNE PADGETT (see Descendants (102)) was born on May 31, 1943, in Jefferson, Alabama, USA, to Willie Thermon Padgett[601] and Nannie Jewl Hoomes[602]. He died on December 15, 2006, aged 63, in Conecuh, Alabama, USA.

1638. JIMMY CECIL PADGETT (see Descendants (102)) was born on October 9, 1945, in Conecuh, Alabama, USA, to Willie Thermon Padgett[601] and Nannie Jewl Hoomes[602]. He died on January 9, 1949, aged 3, in Conecuh, Alabama, USA.

1639. CAPT. ODEM THOMAS MELVIN JR. (see Descendants (20)) was born on March 15, 1915, in Florida, United States, to Odem Thomas Melvin Sr.[618] and Mary Ellen Destin[617]. Odem Thomas became known as "O.T.".
- He died on August 9, 2004, aged 89, in Larose, Lafourche Parish, Louisiana, USA.
- He was buried in Sacred Heart Cemetery, Cut Off, Lafourche, Louisiana, USA.

Note: *No one can fill the shoes of the late Capt. O.T. Melvin Jr., yet visitors at the Destin History and Fishing Museum can stand in the spot where the captain spent nearly three decades of his life at the new Brass Wheelhouse Exhibit. "The fact that it all still works is amazing," said museum director Jean Melvin. The O.T. Melvin tugboat spent most of its days working the waters of Louisiana before the captain sold it in 1974 — not before taking the brass steering wheel, telegraph and magnetic compass with circular azimuth with him. Named after his father who helped dig out the new East Pass, O.T. started his life in Destin born on March 15, 1915, as the first child and only son of Ellen Destin Melvin and O.T. Melvin, Sr. He grew up here and began his career on the water with his father working on all types of boats. At the age of 19, O.T. went to work for American Bridge Company to construct the Destin bridge. The company had O.T. driving tugboats and recruited him to help construct a new bridge over Bayou Bienvenue in Chalmette, La., once the Destin project was completed. Jean said O.T. planned to come home to Destin when the bridge was completed, until he met and married Chalmette local Beulah Petit. The couple had one child, Merwyn Melvin, five grandchildren and nine great-grandchildren. O.T. operated tugboats for the oil rigs off Louisiana during the '30s. He eventually built a shipyard and a fleet of eight tugs that operated until he sold the business in 1974. When the O.T. Melvin tug was sold, the brass instruments were stripped from the wheelhouse and preserved in O.T.'s home. O.T. passed away in 2004, leaving the brass relics to his son Merwyn. O.T. never moved back home to Destin, and Merwyn decided that the fishing village his father was from would be the best place to retire the wheel and instruments. The new permanent view from behind the wheel is a dated panoramic image of East Pass. The steer station, obviously no longer attached to the boat's rudder, is the centerpiece of the exhibit. Looking to the right, just as it appeared in the tug's wheelhouse, is the telegraph the captain used to communicate with the engine room. The captain also used the magnetic compass with azimuth circle for celestial navigation. The exhibit is also sponsored by Jerremy Whitehead of Southern Paradise Homes, which constructed the replica platform that holds the wheelhouse's old setup. It's the museum's first exhibit of its kind. "It adds another facet of life at sea," Jean said. Want to see? Visit the Capt. O.T. Melvin Jr. Brass Wheelhouse Exhibit at the Destin History and Fishing Museum Monday through Saturday from 10 a.m. to 4 p.m. at 108 Stahlman Ave. in Destin. Source: The Destin Log Museum Exhibit.*

1640. BEULAH PETIT was born on January 22, 1913, in Larose, Lafourche Parish, Louisiana, USA.
- She died on August 21, 2007, aged 94, in Cut Off, Lafourche, Louisiana, USA.
- She was buried in Sacred Heart Cemetery, Cut Off, Lafourche, Louisiana, USA.

Odem Thomas Melvin Jr.[1639] married Beulah Petit. They had one son:
Merwyn T. Melvin I[2960]

1641. GWEN MELVIN (see Descendants (20)) was born on September 7, 1925 to Odem Thomas Melvin Sr.[618] and Mary Ellen Destin[617].
- She died on June 27, 1998, aged 72.
- She was buried in Marler Memorial Cemetery, Destin, Okaloosa, Florida, USA.

1642. THEO SHAW was born on November 10, 1920.
- He died on April 4, 2004, aged 83.
- He was buried in Marler Memorial Cemetery, Destin, Okaloosa, Florida, USA.

Theo Shaw married Gwen Melvin[1641]. They had one daughter:
Ellen Francis Shaw[2962]

1643. CAROLYN MELVIN (see Descendants (20)) was born on April 22, 1927 to Odem Thomas Melvin Sr.[618] and Mary Ellen Destin[617].
- She died on December 18, 2013, aged 86.
- She was buried in Barrancas National Cemetery, Pensacola, Escambia, USA.

Note: *Section 54 Site 31.*
(Burial)

1644. LT. COL. LOUIS VAGIAS was born on August 3, 1920.
- He died (Natural / Old Age) on August 15, 2020, aged 100.
- He was buried in Barrancas National Cemetery, Pensacola, Escambia, Florida, USA.

The following information is also recorded for Louis:
- Military Service.

Notes:
- *Section 54 Site 31.*
  (Burial)
- *LTC US AIR FORCE - WORLD WAR II, KOREA, VIETNAM.*
  (Military Service)
- *Honoring Uncle Lou Vegas - A Bomber Pilot on D-DayTo Uncle Lou looking down from above.... "Uncle Lou, do you remember on June 6th, 1996-97 when Marci, Brittany, & I visited with you & Aunt Carolyn, at your home in Destin? I recall, it was on this date June 6th, b/c I asked a few questions about exactly what it was like to fly into Normandy on D-Day. Your response was informative. My questions was stated as this, "it had to be the most dangerous, and challenging flight of your WW II Pilot experience"? To my great surprise, you said, "it was not. """Although it was one of the worst, we had lots of support from the air, from our fellow pilots, in the allied forces, and, I never saw so many ships and boats in my life. In-fact I didn't realize that there were that many ships & boats in existence"". ""No, Mel the absolute very-worst, and most dangerous flight was the bombing of Berlin. The German high command was tipped off by someone, somewhere, and they were "all" waiting for us... Somehow my co-pilot and I completed our mission, and got that plane back to base, but when we got out of the plane, and on the tarmac, we were shocked to see how badly we had been hit by the Germans.... That plane did not have one panel on the body, wings, or tail, that was not missing, or riddled with bullet holes. How we made it back, well, that was miraculous. We lost quite a few friends, and planes, that day. But your point is well taken, D-Day, was "NO" Picnic"""".... Lou Vegas Lt. Col. USAF RET.Uncle Lou lived 100 Years and 1-week... He was a tremendous, family-man, golfer, soldier, sports car enthusiast, and a man who woke up, and went to bed with a CONSTANT "GLUED ON SMILE" I will always admire, and never forget him. -Mel Melvin.*
  (Military Service)

   Louis Vagias married Carolyn Melvin[1643]. They had two children:
   Artemis Diane Vagias[2964]
   Louis Vagias Jr.[2967]

1645. BENNIE MARGARET MELVIN (see Descendants (20)) was born to Odem Thomas Melvin Sr.[618] and Mary Ellen Destin[617].

1646. HARRY QUINN.
   Harry Quinn married Bennie Margaret Melvin[1645]. They had two children:
   Hary Quinn Jr.[2969]
   Joan Quinn[2970]

1647. SYLVIA DESTIN (see Descendants (20)) was born about 1942, in Florida, United States, to Leonard Destin III[619] and Viola B Oglesby[620]. She was recorded in the census on April 1, 1950, aged about 7, in Brook Street, Fort Walton Beach, Okaloosa, Florida, United States.

1648. LINDA DESTIN (see Descendants (20)) was born about 1945, in Florida, United States, to Leonard Destin III[619] and Viola B Oglesby[620]. She was recorded in the census on April 1, 1950, aged about 4, in Brook Street, Fort Walton Beach, Okaloosa, Florida, United States.

1649. AUDREY MARLER (see Descendants (20)) was born about 1921, in South Carolina, USA, to Aquilla Marler[621] and Charlotte Marilla Barnes[622]. She was recorded in the census in 1940, aged about 19, in Fraser Township, Colleton, South Carolina, USA.

1650. AQUILLA JR MARLER (see Descendants (20)) was born about 1928, in South Carolina, USA, to Aquilla Marler[621] and Charlotte Marilla Barnes[622]. He was recorded in the census in 1940, aged about 12, in Fraser Township, Colleton, South Carolina, USA.

1651. JEAN BRUNSON (see Descendants (20)) was born about 1937, in Florida, United States, to Jesse E Brunson[626] and Madeline M Marler[625]. She was recorded in the census on April 1, 1950, aged about 12, in 1/2 a Mile North Coast on Destin Road, Niceville, Okaloosa, Florida, United States.

1652. PATRICIA TRACIE KOHR (see Descendants (20)) was born in 1940, in Florida, United States, to Rex Ray Kohr[632] and Genevieve Parrish[631].
- She was recorded in the census on April 1, 1950, aged about 9, in Bay Side Taun* Ct, Pensacola, Escambia, Florida, United States.
- She died in 2010, aged about 70.

1653. MR./MS. KOHR (see Descendants (20)) was born to Rex Ray Kohr[632] and Genevieve Parrish[631].

1654. MR./MS. BROWN (see Descendants (20)) was born to Frank Brown[634] and Geraldine Parrish[633].

1655. MR./MS. BROWN (see Descendants (20)) was born to Frank Brown[634] and Geraldine Parrish[633].

1656. MR. PARRISH (see Descendants (107)) was born to James Albert Parrish Jr.[635] and Zelma Elizabeth Webb[636].

1657. JAMES ALBERT PARRISH III (see Descendants (107)) was born on October 9, 1946 to James Albert Parrish Jr.[635] and Zelma Elizabeth Webb[636].
1658. MS. ?.
    James Albert Parrish III[1657] married Ms. ?.

1659. MR. PARRISH (see Descendants (107)) was born to James Albert Parrish Jr.[635] and Zelma Elizabeth Webb[636].
1660. MR./MS. ?.
    Mr. Parrish[1659] married Mr./Ms. ?. They had one child:
        Mr./Ms. Parrish[2972]

1661. MR. PARRISH (see Descendants (107)) was born to James Albert Parrish Jr.[635] and Zelma Elizabeth Webb[636].

1662. DASY MAY CASON (see Descendants (108)) was born on January 21, 1928 to Hollie Matthew Smith[638] and Mary Florence Cason[637].
1663. MR. SMITH.
    Mr. Smith married Dasy May Cason[1662].

1664. ROSA BELL SMITH (see Descendants (108)) was born on June 29, 1930 to Hollie Matthew Smith[638] and Mary Florence Cason[637].
1665. MR. CHAVER.
    Mr. Chaver married Rosa Bell Smith[1664].

1666. GLADYS SMITH (see Descendants (108)) was born on November 27, 1932 to Hollie Matthew Smith[638] and Mary Florence Cason[637].
1667. MR. SANDERS.
    Mr. Sanders married Gladys Smith[1666].

1668. BONNIE SMITH (see Descendants (108)) was born on September 10, 1933 to Hollie Matthew Smith[638] and Mary Florence Cason[637].

1669. NELLIE RUTH SMITH (see Descendants (108)) was born on February 26, 1936 to Hollie Matthew Smith[638] and Mary Florence Cason[637].
1670. MR. CREECH.
    Mr. Creech married Nellie Ruth Smith[1669].

1671. CLENNA SMITH (see Descendants (108)) was born on March 12, 1938 to Hollie Matthew Smith[638] and Mary Florence Cason[637].

1672. ANNICE SMITH (see Descendants (108)) was born on December 17, 1940 to Hollie Matthew Smith[638] and Mary Florence Cason[637].
1673. MR. LITTLE.
    Mr. Little married Annice Smith[1672].

1674. LLOYD MATHEW SMITH (see Descendants (108)) was born on November 7, 1942 to Hollie Matthew Smith[638] and Mary Florence Cason[637].
    Lloyd Mathew married his third cousin, Charlotte Bass[1484].
        Lloyd Mathew Smith, aged 20, married Charlotte Bass[1484], aged 18, on June 29, 1963 in Covington county, Covington, Alabama, USA. They had three sons:
            Lloyde Mathew Smith Jr.[2808] born on February 28, 1965
            Gregory Keith Smith[2810] born on November 13, 1967
            Jason Darren Smith[2812] born on March 21, 1973

1675. BESSIE SMITH (see Descendants (108)) was born on March 10, 1944 to Hollie Matthew Smith[638] and Mary Florence Cason[637].

1676. ANDREW ORSA.
>   Andrew Orsa married Bessie Smith[1675].

1677. GARY SMITH (see Descendants (108)) was born on February 28, 1946 to Hollie Matthew Smith[638] and Mary Florence Cason[637].

1678. CLEMENT RALEY (see Descendants (109)) was born about 1931, in Alabama, USA, to Daniel L Raley[640] and Zonnie Bell Cason[639]. He was recorded in the census in 1940, aged about 9, in Putnam Hall, Lives in Grandin, E P 19 Grandin, Putnam, Florida, USA.

1679. DOUGLAS RALEY (see Descendants (109)) was born on July 25, 1932 to Daniel L Raley[640] and Zonnie Bell Cason[639]. He was recorded in the census in 1940, aged about 7, in Putnam Hall, Lives in Grandin, E P 19 Grandin, Putnam, Florida, USA.

1680. MURIEL RALEY (see Descendants (109)) was born about 1933, in Alabama, USA, to Daniel L Raley[640] and Zonnie Bell Cason[639]. He was recorded in the census in 1940, aged about 7, in Putnam Hall, Lives in Grandin, E P 19 Grandin, Putnam, Florida, USA.

1681. MS. BENNETT.
>   Muriel Raley[1680] married Ms. Bennett.

1682. AUDRY RALEY (see Descendants (109)) was born to Daniel L Raley[640] and Zonnie Bell Cason[639].

1683. MR. BROADWAY.
>   Mr. Broadway married Audry Raley[1682].

1684. PATRICIA ANN RALEY (see Descendants (109)) was born to Daniel L Raley[640] and Zonnie Bell Cason[639].

1685. KATHLEEN CASON (see Descendants (110)) was born on November 19, 1947 to William Charles Cason[641] and Mary Ann Smith[642].

1686. MR. SUGGS.
>   Mr. Suggs married Kathleen Cason[1685].

1687. LINDSEY CASON (see Descendants (110)) was born on March 14, 1949 to William Charles Cason[641] and Mary Ann Smith[642].

1688. RITA ?.
>   Lindsey Cason[1687] married Rita ?. They had one son:
>   Mr. Cason[2973]

1689. CAROLYN CASON (see Descendants (110)) was born on February 7, 1954 to William Charles Cason[641] and Mary Ann Smith[642].

1690. GRADY J. CASON JR. (see Descendants (111)) was born in August 1953 to Grady J. Cason[643] and Emmie Scoffield[644].

1691. JOHNNY RAY CASON (see Descendants (112)) was born on October 12, 1943, in Alabama, United States, to John F. Cason[645] and Flora Mavis Little[646].
- He was recorded in the census on April 1, 1950, aged 6, in Proceeding North on Hyway 88 from Beda Church, Hart, Covington, Alabama, United States.
- He died on August 2, 1989, aged 45 years.
- He was buried in Zion Rock Cemetery, Beda, Covington, Alabama, USA.

The following information is also recorded for Johnny Ray:
- Military Service.

Note: *U.S. Army Vietnam.*
(Military Service)

1692. ROBERT GERALD CASON (see Descendants (112)) was born on February 24, 1945, in Covington, Alabama, USA, to John F. Cason[645] and Flora Mavis Little[646].
- He was recorded in the census on April 1, 1950, aged 5, in Proceeding North on Hyway 88 from Beda Church, Hart, Covington, Alabama, United States.
- He died on July 11, 1985, aged 40 years.
- He was buried in Zion Rock Cemetery, Beda, Covington, Alabama, USA.

Wilson Bass

1693. SANDRA J. ? was born on September 19, 1945.
    Robert Gerald Cason[1692] married Sandra J. ?.

1694. LEON CASON (see Descendants (113)) was born on October 10, 1950 to Coleman R. Cason[647] and Runell Neese[648].

1695. SYLVIA JEAN CASON (see Descendants (113)) was born in March 1951 to Coleman R. Cason[647] and Runell Neese[648].

1696. JAMES DAVID CASON (see Descendants (113)) was born on January 10, 1952 to Coleman R. Cason[647] and Runell Neese[648].

1697. JIMMY RAY CASON (see Descendants (113)) was born in November 1953 to Coleman R. Cason[647] and Runell Neese[648].

1698. RHETT CASON (see Descendants (113)) was born in November 1963 to Coleman R. Cason[647] and Syble G. Cason[649].

1699. ADDIE VIVIAN RALEY (see Descendants (114)) was born on February 19, 1933, in Alabama, United States, to William Lester Raley[651] and Veilla Maine Bass[650]. She was recorded in the census on April 1, 1950, aged 17, in Beda Church Road to Boggon Level, Hart, Covington, Alabama, United States.
1700. JAMES CALVIN LITTLE.
    James Calvin Little married Addie Vivian Raley[1699]. They had four children:
        Chester Dale Little[2974] born on April 16, 1952; died on September 3, 1975 in United States and Territory
        James Curtis Little[2975] born on February 5, 1954
        Lanney Ray Little[2976] born on June 4, 1955
        Karen Regina Little[2977] born on March 7, 1960

1701. LOIS JEWEL RALEY (see Descendants (114)) was born on April 21, 1935, in Alabama, United States, to William Lester Raley[651] and Veilla Maine Bass[650]. She was recorded in the census on April 1, 1950, aged 14, in Beda Church Road to Boggon Level, Hart, Covington, Alabama, United States.
1702. ROY C. UPTAGRAFT.
    Roy C. Uptagraft married Lois Jewel Raley[1701]. They had two children:
        Stevan Uptagraft[2978] born on July 28, 1956
        Lisa Ann Uptagraft[2979] born on August 19, 1958

1703. MARY ALICE RALEY (see Descendants (114)) was born on May 12, 1938, in Florida, United States, to William Lester Raley[651] and Veilla Maine Bass[650]. She was recorded in the census on April 1, 1950, aged 11, in Beda Church Road to Boggon Level, Hart, Covington, Alabama, United States.
1704. FREDRICK HAROLD POWELL.
    Fredrick Harold Powell married Mary Alice Raley[1703]. They had one daughter:
        Michelle Katherine Powell[2980] born on December 12, 1965

1705. JULIA YUVONE RALEY (see Descendants (114)) was born on October 7, 1941, in Florida, United States, to William Lester Raley[651] and Veilla Maine Bass[650]. She was recorded in the census on April 1, 1950, aged 8, in Beda Church Road to Boggon Level, Hart, Covington, Alabama, United States.
1706. JAMES DALE ANDREWS.
    James Dale Andrews married Julia Yuvone Raley[1705]. They had one daughter:
        Kelly Lynn Andrews[2981]

1707. HENRY EDGAR RALEY (see Descendants (114)) was born on September 5, 1944, in Florida, United States, to William Lester Raley[651] and Veilla Maine Bass[650]. He was recorded in the census on April 1, 1950, aged 5, in Beda Church Road to Boggon Level, Hart, Covington, Alabama, United States.

1708. ALVIN LESTER RALEY (see Descendants (114)) was born on March 11, 1953 to William Lester Raley[651] and Veilla Maine Bass[650].

1709. RUBY MILDRED FOXWORTH (see Descendants (115)) was born about 1933, in Alabama, USA, to Robert Lehmon Foxworth[653] and Leilla Mae Bass[652]. She was recorded in the census in 1940, aged about 7, in Open Pond Road, Beat 7, Covington, Alabama, USA.

1710. MARY JANE FOXWORTH (see Descendants (115)) was born about 1940, in Alabama, USA, to Robert Lehmon Foxworth[653] and Leilla Mae Bass[652]. She was recorded in the census in 1940, as an infant, in Open Pond Road, Beat 7, Covington, Alabama, USA.

1711. ANDY DEATON.
    Andy Deaton married Mary Jane Foxworth[1710].

1712. MARY DEBORAH MILLER (see Descendants (115)) was born to Edward L. Miller[654] and Leilla Mae Bass[652].

1713. MR. MANNING.
    Mr. Manning married Mary Deborah Miller[1712].

1714. WILLIAM MICHAEL MILLER (see Descendants (115)) was born to Edward L. Miller[654] and Leilla Mae Bass[652].

1715. GREER ELLEN BASS (see Descendants (116)) was born about 1948, in Missouri, United States, to Henry Grady Bass[655] and Ruth A Nemet[656]. She was recorded in the census on April 1, 1950, aged about 1, in 1111 Ware Ave, Sedalia, Pettis, Missouri, United States.

1716. BILL KNIPP.
    Bill Knipp married Greer Ellen Bass[1715]. They had one son:
        Michael Henry Knipp Knipp[2982]

1717. JENNIFER LEE BASS (see Descendants (116)) was born to Henry Grady Bass[655] and Ruth A Nemet[656].

1718. JUDSON LEVON BASS (see Descendants (117)) was born on April 21, 1942 to Clyde Kermit Bass Sr.[657] and Mamie Lelie Hayes[658]. He died on March 8, 2013, aged 70 years.

1719. ALICE FLOYD.
    Judson Levon Bass[1718] married Alice Floyd. They had two sons:
        Judson Levon Bass Jr.[2983] born on November 23, 1962
        Joseph Michael Bass[2984] born on November 23, 1963

1720. MARRON GRADY BASS (see Descendants (117)) was born on December 2, 1944 to Clyde Kermit Bass Sr.[657] and Mamie Lelie Hayes[658].

1721. CAROLYN O. WARD.
    Marron Grady Bass[1720] married Carolyn O. Ward. They had one son:
        Ronald Joe Bass[2985] born on February 13, 1965

1722. VONDA VINOR BASS (see Descendants (117)) was born on April 6, 1947 to Clyde Kermit Bass Sr.[657] and Mamie Lelie Hayes[658].

1723. CLYDE KERMIT BASS JR. (see Descendants (117)) was born on August 31, 1949 to Clyde Kermit Bass Sr.[657] and Mamie Lelie Hayes[658].

1724. LEWIS ARNOLD BASS (see Descendants (117)) was born on June 1, 1957 to Clyde Kermit Bass Sr.[657] and Mamie Lelie Hayes[658].

1725. MARK NAPOLEON BASS (see Descendants (117)) was born on November 28, 1959 to Clyde Kermit Bass Sr.[657] and Mamie Lelie Hayes[658].

1726. RILEY BENNETT BASS (see Descendants (117)) was born to Clyde Kermit Bass Sr.[657] and Mamie Lelie Hayes[658].

1727. MARGARET ANN BOZEMAN (see Descendants (118)) was born on September 28, 1959 to Grover Bozeman[660] and Beatrice Izora Bass[659].

1728. HUBERT PAUL.
    Hubert Paul married Margaret Ann Bozeman[1727].

1729. BRENDA GAIL WISE (see Descendants (122)) was born on June 19, 1957 to James Donald Wise[668] and Fannie Esther Bass[667].
- She died on June 19, 1957, aged 0.
- She was buried.

1730. MYRA LYNN WISE (see Descendants (122)) was born on November 16, 1960 to James Donald Wise[668] and Fannie Esther Bass[667].

1731. TRACY NANETTE WISE (see Descendants (122)) was born on March 26, 1963 to James Donald Wise[668] and Fannie Esther Bass[667].

1732. MR. SMITH.
    Mr. Smith married Tracy Nanette Wise[1731].

1733. JEFF ALEX WALICE (see Descendants (123)) was born on December 18, 1963 to Joseph Farrel Walice[670] and Nannie Ruth Bass[669].

1734. JANICE L BECK (see Descendants (124)) was born on July 16, 1934, in Alabama, United States, to Ernest Terry Beck[672] and Nancy Christian Garvin[671]. She was recorded in the census on April 1, 1950, aged 15, in Mt Olive Church Road, Blackman, Okaloosa, Florida, United States.

1735. STANLEY COOK.
    Stanley Cook married Janice L Beck[1734]. They had three children:
        Karen Cook[2986] born on October 30, 1954
        Keith Cook[2991] born on May 13, 1960
        Kenyon Cook[2993] born on November 21, 1961; died in 1982

1736. SHIRLEY A BECK (see Descendants (124)) was born on September 5, 1936, in Alabama, United States, to Ernest Terry Beck[672] and Nancy Christian Garvin[671]. She was recorded in the census on April 1, 1950, aged 13, in Mt Olive Church Road, Blackman, Okaloosa, Florida, United States.

1737. JAMES NEWTON.
    James Newton married Shirley A Beck[1736]. They had five children:
        James Jerry Newton[2994] born on May 6, 1953
        Ernest Leroy Newton[2995] born on June 2, 1955
        Bridget Belinda Newton[2997] born on February 16, 1957
        Missouri Mae Newton[2999] born on November 11, 1958
        Sherry Denise Newton[3001] born on August 4, 1960

1738. REGINALD E BECK (see Descendants (124)) was born on December 23, 1938, in Alabama, United States, to Ernest Terry Beck[672] and Nancy Christian Garvin[671]. He was recorded in the census on April 1, 1950, aged 11, in Mt Olive Church Road, Blackman, Okaloosa, Florida, United States.
Reginald E married four times. He was married to Geraldine Demoris[1739], Shelia Davis[1740], Dorothy Howell[1741] and JoAnn Fuqua[1742].

1739. GERALDINE DEMORIS.
    Reginald E Beck[1738] married Geraldine Demoris.

1740. SHELIA DAVIS.
    Reginald E Beck[1738] married Shelia Davis. They had two children:
        Alan Beck[3004] born on January 16, 1971
        Barabara Sue Beck[3005] born on January 1, 1973

1741. DOROTHY HOWELL.
    Reginald E Beck[1738] married Dorothy Howell.

1742. JOANN FUQUA.
    Reginald E Beck[1738] married JoAnn Fuqua.

1743. QUINTON W BECK (see Descendants (124)) was born on May 25, 1942, in Alabama, United States, to Ernest Terry Beck[672] and Nancy Christian Garvin[671]. He was recorded in the census on April 1, 1950, aged 7, in Mt Olive Church Road, Blackman, Okaloosa, Florida, United States.
Quinton W married twice. He was married to Judy Golden[1744] and Linda Lee Jones[1745].

1744. JUDY GOLDEN.

Quinton W Beck[1743] married Judy Golden.

1745. LINDA LEE JONES.
Quinton W Beck[1743] married Linda Lee Jones. They had one daughter:
Tamara Michelle Beck[3007] born on September 12, 1968

1746. THERON LEON BECK (see Descendants (124)) was born on March 26, 1945, in Alabama, United States, to Ernest Terry Beck[672] and Nancy Christian Garvin[671]. He was recorded in the census on April 1, 1950, aged 5, in Mt Olive Church Road, Blackman, Okaloosa, Florida, United States.
Theron Leon married three times. He was married to Ola Mae Gainey[1747], Ms. Carolyn[1748] and Brenda Richards[1749].

1747. OLA MAE GAINEY was born in May 1953.
Theron Leon Beck[1746] married Ola Mae Gainey.

1748. MS. CAROLYN.
Theron Leon Beck[1746] married Ms. Carolyn.

1749. BRENDA RICHARDS.
Theron Leon Beck[1746] married Brenda Richards. They had three children:
Shannon Leon Beck[3009] born on July 18, 1969
Christopher Shane Beck[3010]
Margaret Beck[3011]

1750. RONALD EUGENE BECK (see Descendants (124)) was born on February 16, 1947, in Alabama, United States, to Ernest Terry Beck[672] and Nancy Christian Garvin[671]. He was recorded in the census on April 1, 1950, aged 3, in Mt Olive Church Road, Blackman, Okaloosa, Florida, United States.

1751. VELMA BLOCKER.
Ronald Eugene Beck[1750] married Velma Blocker. They had one son:
Rickey Davon Beck[3012] born on February 7, 1974

1752. VIVIAN DIANE BECK (see Descendants (124)) was born on August 17, 1949, in Alabama, United States, to Ernest Terry Beck[672] and Nancy Christian Garvin[671]. She was recorded in the census on April 1, 1950, as an infant, in Mt Olive Church Road, Blackman, Okaloosa, Florida, United States.
Vivian Diane married three times. She was married to Jerry Chessher[1753], Charles Cook[1754] and Aubrey Lee[1755].

1753. JERRY CHESSHER.
Jerry Chessher married Vivian Diane Beck[1752]. They had three sons:
Terry Lee Chessher[3013] born on July 3, 1968
Nolan Dewrell Chessher[3016]
Michael Anthony Chessher[3017]

1754. CHARLES COOK.
Charles Cook married Vivian Diane Beck[1752]. They had one daughter:
Alician Dian Cook[3018]

1755. AUBREY LEE.
Aubrey Lee married Vivian Diane Beck[1752].

1756. MARIE BECK (see Descendants (125)) was born on September 21, 1936, in Alabama, United States, to Benjamin Otis Beck[674] and Willier Garvin[673]. She was recorded in the census on April 1, 1950, aged 13, in 1/2 Mile Left from Red Oak to Mountain City Road Traveling Toward Red Oak from Blackman, Blackman, Okaloosa, Florida, United States.

1757. LAMAR NELSON.
Lamar Nelson married Marie Beck[1756]. They had six children:
Carolyn Nelson[3019] born on September 30, 1953
Carlton Nelson[3020] born on August 16, 1954
Ralph Nelson[3021] born on November 16, 1955
Brenda Nelson[3022] born on February 24, 1957
Franklin Nelson[3023] born on October 11, 1958
Wanda Nelson[3024] born on July 29, 1961

1758. COLLIE BECK (see Descendants (125)) was born on August 2, 1938 to Benjamin Otis Beck[674] and Willier Garvin[673]. He was recorded in the census on April 1, 1950, aged 11, in 1/2 Mile Left from Red Oak to Mountain City Road Traveling Toward Red Oak from Blackman, Blackman, Okaloosa, Florida, United States.

1759. VIRGINIA ELMORE.

Collie Beck[1758] married Virginia Elmore. They had three daughters:
- Deborah Elaine Beck[3025] born on April 9, 1962
- Cindy Lynn Beck[3026] born on October 21, 1963
- Sandra Beck[3027] born on November 25, 1965

1760. EDWARD C BECK (see Descendants (125)) was born on December 25, 1943, in Alabama, United States, to Benjamin Otis Beck[674] and Willier Garvin[673]. He was recorded in the census on April 1, 1950, aged 6, in 1/2 Mile Left from Red Oak to Mountain City Road Traveling Toward Red Oak from Blackman, Blackman, Okaloosa, Florida, United States.

1761. MS. ?.
Edward C Beck[1760] married Ms. ?. They had one daughter:
- Marilyn Beck[3028] born on January 27, 1950

1762. MARYLIN MAXINE BECK (see Descendants (125)) was born in Florida, United States to Benjamin Otis Beck[674] and Willier Garvin[673]. She was recorded in the census on April 1, 1950, in 1/2 Mile Left from Red Oak to Mountain City Road Traveling Toward Red Oak from Blackman, Blackman, Okaloosa, Florida, United States.

1763. YVONNE GARVIN (see Descendants (126)) was born to Sherman Garvin[675] and Unogar Johnson[676].

1764. ROLAND JORDAN.
Roland Jordan married Yvonne Garvin[1763]. They had three children:
- Gail Jordan[3029] born on April 12, 1961
- Ronald Sherman Jordan[3030] born on November 19, 1964
- Melissa Glyn Jordan[3031] born on March 5, 1966

1765. LAVERNE FAY GARVIN (see Descendants (126)) was born to Sherman Garvin[675] and Unogar Johnson[676].

1766. THERESE GARVIN (see Descendants (126)) was born to Sherman Garvin[675] and Unogar Johnson[676].

1767. LONIA GARVIN (see Descendants (126)) was born to Sherman Garvin[675] and Unogar Johnson[676].

1768. JOEL JOHNSON (see Descendants (127)) was born on April 14, 1944 to Walun Nick Johnson[679] and Odessa Garvin[678].

1769. NICK JOHNSON (see Descendants (127)) was born on February 11, 1946 to Walun Nick Johnson[679] and Odessa Garvin[678].
Nick married twice. He was married to Kathryn Kenney[1770] and Kathryn Gibson[1771].

1770. KATHRYN KENNEY.
Nick Johnson[1769] married Kathryn Kenney. They had two daughters:
- Carrol Johnson[3032]
- Crista Johnson[3034]

1771. KATHRYN GIBSON.
Nick Johnson[1769] married Kathryn Gibson.

1772. SHEILA JOHNSON (see Descendants (127)) was born on October 6, 1947 to Walun Nick Johnson[679] and Odessa Garvin[678].
Sheila married twice. She was married to Ronnie Henderson[1773] and Ronnie Morris[1774].

1773. RONNIE HENDERSON.
Ronnie Henderson married Sheila Johnson[1772]. They had one daughter:
- Danae Henderson[3035] born in June 1968

1774. RONNIE MORRIS.
Ronnie Morris married Sheila Johnson[1772]. They had two sons:
- Michael Zoree Morris[3037]
- Jeffery Morris[3038]

1775. LUVERT JOHNSON (see Descendants (127)) was born to Walun Nick Johnson[679] and Odessa Garvin[678]. Luvert became known as "Lou".

1776. DOLLIE COLVIN.
Luvert Johnson[1775] married Dollie Colvin. They had two sons:
- Danny Johnson[3039]
- Dallas Johnson[3041]

1777. GARY LYNN JOHNSON (see Descendants (127)) was born to Walun Nick Johnson[679] and Odessa Garvin[678].
1778. FAYE GOLSON.
Gary Lynn Johnson[1777] married Faye Golson. They had one son:
Gary Lynn Johnson Jr.[3043]

1779. RUBY NELL THAMES (see Descendants (128)) was born in 1943 to John Lee Thames[681] and Cora Nolia Posey[680].
Ruby Nell married twice. She was married to Arlee Franklin[1780] and Max McCarty[1781].
1780. ARLEE FRANKLIN.
Arlee Franklin married Ruby Nell Thames[1779]. They had two daughters:
Leigh Ann Franklin[3044] born on July 8, 1964
Tracey Lynn Franklin[3046] born on July 19, 1968
1781. MAX MCCARTY.
Max McCarty married Ruby Nell Thames[1779].

1782. BILLY JOE THAMES (see Descendants (128)) was born on January 27, 1949 to John Lee Thames[681] and Cora Nolia Posey[680].
• He died on December 12, 2014, aged 65 years.
• He was buried in Greenwood Memorial Cemetery, Florala, Covington, Alabama, USA.
Note: *Billy Joe was employed by Lord and Sons Construction located in Fort Walton Beach until ill health forced his retirement. In his spare time he loved to fish. He loved spending time with his family especially taking his grandchildren camping. He loved being their "PaPa". Nothing was more important to Billy Joe as his faith in Jesus Christ. It sustained him as he bravely fought many health issues. He fought the good fight. He finished the race. He kept the faith.*
(Death)
1783. DALE DIXON.
Billy Joe Thames[1782] married Dale Dixon. They had one son:
Christopher Thames[3047] born on August 15, 1973

1784. HYRAM WALACE TURNER (see Descendants (129)) was born on October 3, 1931, in Wing, Covington, Alabama, USA, to Amos Vincen Turner[683] and Pearlie Mae Posey[682]. Hyram Walace became known as "Carthell".
• Carthell was a Police Officer.
• He died on October 15, 2001, aged 70 years, in Opp, Covington, Alabama, USA.
• He was buried in Blue Springs Church Cemetery, Opp, Covingtion, Alabama, USA.
The following information is also recorded for Carthell:
• Military Service.
Note: *U.S. Army Korea.*
(Military Service)
1785. DOROTHY MCCURLEY was born on November 14, 1933, in Opp, Covington, Alabama, USA.
• She died on June 30, 2016, aged 82, in Andalusia, Covington, Alabama, United States.
• She was buried in Blue Springs Church Cemetery, Opp, Covingtion, Alabama, USA.
Hyram Walace Turner[1784] married Dorothy McCurley. They had one daughter:
Pamela Nell Turner[3049] born on August 26, 1964 in Covington, Alabama, USA; died on September 22, 2011 in Opp, Covington, Alabama, USA

1786. AMOS DALTON TURNER SR. (see Descendants (129)) was born on January 19, 1933, in Baker, Okaloosa, Florida, USA, to Amos Vincen Turner[683] and Pearlie Mae Posey[682].
• He died on September 24, 2006, aged 73 years.
• He was buried in Beda Cemetery, Beda, Covington, Alabama, USA.
The following information is also recorded for Amos Dalton:
• Military Service.
Note: *U.S. Navy Korea.*
(Military Service)
1787. EMMA VIOLA MCCLINTOCK was born on July 27, 1935, in Pennsylvania, USA.

• She died on August 28, 2020, aged 85, in Andalusia, Covington, Alabama, USA.
• She was buried in Beda Cemetery, Beda, Covington, Alabama, USA.
Amos Dalton Turner Sr.[1786], aged 31, married Emma Viola McClintock, aged 29, on October 16, 1964 in Covington, Alabama, USA. They had three children:

Lynda Jeanne Turner[3051] born on July 23, 1965 in Fort Walton Beach, Okaloosa, Florida, USA
Amos Dalton Turner Jr.[3054] born on September 23, 1967 in Fort Walton Beach, Okaloosa, Florida, USA
Beverly Shea Turner[3056] born on April 30, 1974 in Andalusia, Covington, Alabama, USA

1788. WILLIAM JAMES MILLS (see Descendants (130)) was born on January 19, 1938, in Alabama, USA, to Charles Oresta Mills[685] and Gussie Lee Posey[684].
- He died on January 19, 2015, aged 77 years, in Auburndale, Polk, Florida, USA.
- He was buried in Glen Abbey Memorial Gardens, Auburndale, Polk County, Florida, USA.

Note: *William James Mills, 77, of Auburndale, FL passed away on January 19, 2015 at his residence.Born January 19, 1938 in Alabama, he moved here in 1952 from Alabama. He was retired as a Boilermaker and also was a union representative. He was a member of the First Baptist Church at the Mall.Mr. Mills is survived by his wife of 59 years, Martha; 3 sons, Douglas Mills of Auburndale, FL, Don Mills of Mulberry, FL and Allen Mills of Auburndale, FL; 2 brothers, Charles Mills of Missouri and Donnell Mills of Atlanta, GA; and 4 grandchildren.The family will receive friends from 5:00pm till 7:00pm, Thursday, January 22, 2015 at Oak Ridge Funeral Care in Winter Haven. Funeral Services will be held at 10:00am, Friday, January 23, 2015 at the First Baptist Church at the Mall in Lakeland. Interment will follow at Glen Abbey Memorial Gardens.*
(Death)

1789. MARTHA RAY CARR.
William James Mills[1788] married Martha Ray Carr. They had three sons:
James Allen Mills[3058] born on July 16, 1958 in Lakeland, Polk, Florida, USA
John Douglas Mills[3061] born on June 6, 1966 in Lakeland, Polk, Florida, USA
Joseph Donald Mills[3062] born on June 6, 1966 in Lakeland, Polk, Florida, USA

1790. EVELYN JUANITA MILLS (see Descendants (130)) was born on August 9, 1939, in Laurel Hill, Okaloosa, Florida, USA, to Charles Oresta Mills[685] and Gussie Lee Posey[684].
- She died on September 8, 2013, aged 74 years, in Lakeland, Polk, Florida, USA.
- She was buried in Lakeland Memorial Gardens, Lakeland, Polk, Florida, USA.

1791. DEWEY WENDELL HOLMES SR. was born on April 13, 1931, in Elberton, Elbert, Georgia, USA.
- He died on September 3, 2012, aged 81 years, in Murphy, Cherokee, North Carolina, USA.
- He was buried in Lakeland Memorial Gardens, Lakeland, Polk, Florida, USA.

The following information is also recorded for Dewey Wendell:
- Military Service.

Notes:
- *Dewey, a Korean War Air Force Veteran, retired from Butter Crust Bread Co. with 28 years of employment.*
- *Korean War Air Force Veteran.*
(Military Service)

Dewey Wendell Holmes Sr., aged 28, married Evelyn Juanita Mills[1790], aged 20, on March 3, 1960. They had three children:
Dewey Wendell Holmes Jr.[3064] born on December 23, 1960 in Lakeland, Polk, Florida, USA
Melinda Dianna Holmes[3066] born on January 27, 1962 in Lakeland, Polk, Florida, USA
Patricia Gail Holmes[3068] born on October 26, 1963 in Lakeland, Polk, Florida, USA

1792. CHARLES EARL MILLS (see Descendants (130)) was born on February 26, 1943, in Florala, Covington, Alabama, USA, to Charles Oresta Mills[685] and Gussie Lee Posey[684].

1793. GLORIA JEAN GLOVER.
Charles Earl Mills[1792], aged 21, married Gloria Jean Glover on August 3, 1964 in Lakeland, Polk, Florida, USA. They had three children:
Lena Dianne Mills[3070] born on February 25, 1964 in Vandenberg Air Force Base, California, USA
Richard Earl Mills[3072] born on November 12, 1964 in Fort Walton Beach, Okaloosa, Florida, USA; died on November 12, 1964 in Fort Walton Beach, Okaloosa, Florida, USA

Shawnee Lynn Mills[3073] born on September 12, 1966 in Lakeland, Polk, Florida, USA

1794. **GENE VERLON MILLS** (see Descendants (130)) was born on January 11, 1945, in Lockhart, Covington, Alabama, USA, to Charles Oresta Mills[685] and Gussie Lee Posey[684].
- He died in November 1995, aged 50 years, in Fort Walton Beach, Okaloosa, Florida, USA.
- He was buried in Beal Memorial Cemetery, Fort Walton Beach, Okaloosa, Florida, USA.

Gene Verlon married twice. He was married to Patricia Ann Johnson[1795] and Mary Ellen Smith[1796].

1795. **PATRICIA ANN JOHNSON.**
Gene Verlon Mills[1794], aged about 19, married Patricia Ann Johnson in 1964. They had two children:
Debbie Diane Mills[3075] born on October 21, 1965 in Lakeland, Polk, Florida, USA
Daniel Edward Mills[3076] born on November 8, 1967 in Saint Petersburg, Florida, USA

1796. **MARY ELLEN SMITH.**
Gene Verlon Mills[1794], aged 27, married Mary Ellen Smith on July 31, 1972. They had one son:
Sean Verlon Mills[3077] born on February 3, 1973 in Mobile, Mobile, Alabama, USA

1797. **DONELL FRANKLIN MILLS** (see Descendants (130)) was born on July 3, 1947, in Lockhart, Covington, Alabama, USA, to Charles Oresta Mills[685] and Gussie Lee Posey[684].
Donell Franklin married three times. He was married to Brenda Kay Gulett[1798], Judith A. Kucera[1799] and Peggy Jean Stallard[1800].

1798. **BRENDA KAY GULETT.**
Donell Franklin Mills[1797], aged 19, married Brenda Kay Gulett on August 1, 1966. They had two children:
Donna Kay Mills[3078] born on January 10, 1967 in Bartow, Polk, Florida, USA
Donell Joseph Mills[3080] born on August 19, 1973 in Toledo, Lucas, Ohio, USA

1799. **JUDITH A. KUCERA.**
Donell Franklin Mills[1797], aged 21, married Judith A. Kucera on March 22, 1969. They had one daughter:
Darla Lynn Mills[3082] born on August 12, 1970 in Sarasota, Florida, USA

1800. **PEGGY JEAN STALLARD.**
Donell Franklin Mills[1797], aged 44, married Peggy Jean Stallard on April 11, 1992 in Fort Walton Beach, Okaloosa, Florida, USA.

1801. **ORESTA MILLS JR.** (see Descendants (130)) was born to Charles Oresta Mills[685] and Gussie Lee Posey[684].

1802. **ANNIE PEARL COBB** (see Descendants (131)) was born on July 4, 1939, in Florala, Covington, Alabama, USA, to Bartlett Lorenzo Cobb[687] and Mary Francis Posey[686].
- She was recorded in the census in 1940, as an infant, in South 5th Street, Florala, Covington, Alabama, USA.
- She was recorded in the census on April 1, 1950, aged 10, in 28 Seminale Ave., Lockhart, Covington, Alabama, United States.
- She died on June 22, 1968, aged 28 years.

1803. **EDWARD EARL PHILLIPS.**
Edward Earl Phillips married Annie Pearl Cobb[1802], aged 23, on January 20, 1963 in Lockhart, Covington, Alabama, USA. They had two sons:
Gregory Scott Phillips[3084] born on September 7, 1964 in Florala, Covington, Alabama, USA
Kenneth Paul Phillips[3085] born on October 4, 1965 in Florala, Covington, Alabama, USA

1804. **JAMES BARTLETT COBB SR.** (see Descendants (131)) was born on March 9, 1942, in Florala, Covington, Alabama, USA, to Bartlett Lorenzo Cobb[687] and Mary Francis Posey[686]. He was recorded in the census on April 1, 1950, aged 8, in 28 Seminale Ave., Lockhart, Covington, Alabama, United States.

1805. **JANET BOWMAN** was born on August 23, 1946.
James Bartlett Cobb Sr.[1804], aged 21, married Janet Bowman, aged 17, on November 2, 1963 in Andalusia, Covington, Alabama, USA. They had three children:
James Bartlett Cobb Jr.[3087] born on May 22, 1964 in Florala, Covington, Alabama, USA
Martine Michelle Cobb[3089] born on October 21, 1965 in Fort Walton Beach, Okaloosa, Florida, USA
Victoria Amanda Cobb[3091] born on May 28, 1970 in Opp, Covington, Alabama, USA

1806. ALTHEA DARLENE POSEY (see Descendants (132)) was born on June 22, 1948, in Mcintosh, Marion, Florida, USA, to William Albert Posey[688] and Jewel Creech[689].
1807. JEROME AUBRAY EDMONDSON.
> Jerome Aubray Edmondson married Althea Darlene Posey[1806], aged 21, on March 7, 1970 in Florala, Covington, Alabama, USA. They had two sons:
>> Michael Jerome Edmondson[3092] born on October 1, 1970 in Opp, Covington, Alabama, USA
>> Jason Lee Edmondson[3094] born on November 14, 1975 in Geneva, Geneva, Alabama, USA

1808. CAROLYN DIANNE POSEY (see Descendants (132)) was born on April 30, 1951, in Florala, Covington, Alabama, USA, to William Albert Posey[688] and Jewel Creech[689]. She died on April 16, 2018, aged 66.

1809. FRED CHARLES WEEMS JR.
> Fred Charles Weems Jr. married Carolyn Dianne Posey[1808], aged 20, on May 1, 1971 in Florala, Covington, Alabama, USA. They had three sons:
>> Charles Paul Weems[3096] born on December 28, 1973 in Greeneville, Greene, Tennessee, USA
>> Perry Matthew Weems[3098] born on May 23, 1978 in Greeneville, Greene, Tennessee, USA
>> Justin Albert Weems[3100] born on December 11, 1980 in Greeneville, Greene, Tennessee, USA

1810. DORIS JENE TURBEVILLE (see Descendants (133)) was born about 1939, in Alabama, United States, to Dewey Turbeville[691] and Vianna Catherine Posey[690]. She was recorded in the census on April 1, 1950, aged about 10, in Winston, Polk, Florida, United States.
1811. ROBERT DWAYNE COLLIER.
> Robert Dwayne Collier married Doris Jene Turbeville[1810], aged about 17, on June 28, 1957 in Opelika, Lee, Alabama, USA. They had two children:
>> Robert Dwayne Collier[3102] born on September 17, 1959 in Lakeland, Polk, Florida, USA
>> Rhonda Delaine Collier[3104] born on August 10, 1962 in Lakeland, Polk, Florida, USA

1812. JIMMIE NELL TURBEVILLE (see Descendants (133)) was born on March 12, 1941, in Ocala, Marion, Florida, USA, to Dewey Turbeville[691] and Vianna Catherine Posey[690]. She was recorded in the census on April 1, 1950, aged 9, in Winston, Polk, Florida, United States.
1813. EARL HARRISON. He died on May 16, 2012.

> Earl Harrison married Jimmie Nell Turbeville[1812], aged 15, on January 12, 1957 in Opp, Covington, Alabama, USA. They had one son:
>> Michael Earl Harrison[3106] born on May 18, 1959 in Lakeland, Polk, Florida, USA

1814. JERRY LAMAR TURBEVILLE (see Descendants (133)) was born on January 19, 1944, in Ocala, Marion, Florida, USA, to Dewey Turbeville[691] and Vianna Catherine Posey[690].
- He died (At young age) on October 24, 1945, aged 1 years, in Ocala, Marion, Florida, USA.
- He was buried in Anthony Cemetery, Anthony, Marion, Florida, USA.

1815. ELAINE TURBEVILLE (see Descendants (133)) was born on September 23, 1945 to Dewey Turbeville[691] and Vianna Catherine Posey[690].
- She was recorded in the census on April 1, 1950, aged 4, in Winston, Polk, Florida, United States.
- She died on April 21, 2006, aged 60 years.
1816. JIMMY POWELL.
> Jimmy Powell married Elaine Turbeville[1815], aged 18, on December 1, 1963. They had one daughter:
>> Angie Powell[3107] born on June 8, 1964 in Lakeland, Polk, Florida, USA

1817. DEWEY WAYNE TURBEVILLE (see Descendants (133)) was born on October 23, 1948, in Marion County, Florida, USA, to Dewey Turbeville[691] and Vianna Catherine Posey[690]. He was recorded in the census on April 1, 1950, aged 1, in Winston, Polk, Florida, United States.
Dewey Wayne married twice. He was married to Judy Louis Davis[1818] and Andrea Pate[1819].

Direct Relations

1818. JUDY LOUIS DAVIS.
> Dewey Wayne Turbeville[1817], aged 18, married Judy Louis Davis on March 26, 1967 in Auburndale, Polk, Florida, USA. They had three children:
>> Kim Turbbeville[3109] born on January 16, 1968 in Lakeland, Polk, Florida, USA
>> Tracey Turbbeville[3111] born on April 3, 1970 in Lakeland, Polk, Florida, USA
>> Dewey Wayne Turbbeville Jr.[3113] born on November 30, 1976 in Lakeland, Polk, Florida, USA

1819. ANDREA PATE.
> Dewey Wayne Turbeville[1817], aged 44, married Andrea Pate on November 20, 1992 in Tampa, Hillsborough, Florida, USA. They had one son:
>> Hunter Wayne Turbbeville[3114] born on August 14, 1994

1820. THELMA LEE BUSBEE (see Descendants (134)) was born on September 16, 1924, in Covington, Alabama, United States, to William Roy Busbee[693] and Josephine E Edwards[692].
- She was recorded in the census in 1940, aged about 15, in Dorcas Svea RD, Dorcas Election Prect # 13, Okaloosa, Florida, USA.
- She was recorded in the census on April 1, 1950, aged 25, in Laurel Hill, Okaloosa, Florida, United States.
- She died on August 22, 2007, aged 82, in Freeport, Walton, Florida, United States.

1821. PORTER EVERIDGE was born about 1921, in Florida, United States. He was recorded in the census on April 1, 1950, aged about 28, in Laurel Hill, Okaloosa, Florida, United States.
> Porter Everidge married Thelma Lee Busbee[1820]. They had one son:
>> Chris Everidge[3115]

1822. ELTON BUSBEE (see Descendants (134)) was born in 1925, in Covington, Alabama United States, to William Roy Busbee[693] and Josephine E Edwards[692]. He died in 1926, aged about 1, in Covington, Alabama United States.

1823. NOMA BUSBEE (see Descendants (134)) was born on September 2, 1926, in Covington, Alabama, United States, to William Roy Busbee[693] and Josephine E Edwards[692].
- She died on April 8, 2001, aged 74, in Crestview, Okaloosa, Florida, United States.
- She was buried in April 2001 in Liveoak Park Memorial Cemetery, Okaloosa, Florida United States.

1824. DONNELL GILLEY.
> Donnell Gilley married Noma Busbee[1823]. They had five children:
>> Sheila Gilley[3116]
>> Carol Gilley[3117]
>> Mike Gilley[3118]
>> Gary Gilley[3119]
>> Gloria Gilley[3120]

1825. JAMES CURTIS BUSBEE (see Descendants (134)) was born on July 22, 1930, in Covington, Alabama, United States, to William Roy Busbee[693] and Josephine E Edwards[692].
- He was recorded in the census in 1940, aged about 9, in Dorcas Svea RD, Dorcas Election Prect # 13, Okaloosa, Florida, USA.
- He died on October 24, 1982, aged 52, in Crestview, Okaloosa, Florida, United States.
- He was buried in October 1982 in Liveoak Park Memorial Cemetery, Crestview, Okaloosa, Florida United States.

1826. BETTY HELMS.
> James Curtis Busbee[1825] married Betty Helms. They had five children:
>> Janet Busbee[3121]
>> Sue Busbee[3122]
>> Peggie Busbee[3123]
>> Donald Eugene Busbee[3124] born on March 13, 1957
>> Wanda Busbee[3125]

1827. SHELBY RAY BUSBEE (see Descendants (134)) was born on April 26, 1933, in Okaloosa, Florida, United States, to William Roy Busbee[693] and Josephine E Edwards[692].
- She was recorded in the census in 1940, aged about 7, in Dorcas Svea RD, Dorcas Election Prect # 13, Okaloosa, Florida, USA.
- She died on November 3, 2009, aged 76, in Pensacola, Escambia, Florida, United States.
- She was buried in November 2009 in Liveoak Park Memorial Cemetery, Crestview, Okaloosa, Florida United States.

1828. ROSLYN WALTERS.
> Shelby Ray Busbee[1827] married Roslyn Walters. They had three children:
>> Angie Busbee[3126]
>> Rusty Busbee[3127]

Rickie Busbee[3128]

1829. EULA VEE BUSBEE (see Descendants (134)) was born on August 8, 1935, in Laural Hill, Okaloosa, Florida, United States, to William Roy Busbee[693] and Josephine E Edwards[692].
- She was recorded in the census in 1940, aged about 4, in Dorcas Svea RD, Dorcas Election Prect # 13, Okaloosa, Florida, USA.
- She died on September 7, 2016, aged 81, in Okaloosa, Florida, United States.
- She was buried in August 2016 in Liveoak Park Memorial Cemetery, Crestview, Okaloosa, Florida, United States.

1830. ROY FRANK GILLEY.
Roy Frank Gilley married Eula Vee Busbee[1829]. They had two daughters:
Kathy Gilley[3129]
Deborah Gilley[3130]

1831. WINNIE FAY BUSBEE (see Descendants (134)) was born about 1938, in Florida, USA, to William Roy Busbee[693] and Josephine E Edwards[692]. She was recorded in the census in 1940, aged about 2, in Dorcas Svea RD, Dorcas Election Prect # 13, Okaloosa, Florida, USA.

1832. CARL DOWNS.
Carl Downs married Winnie Fay Busbee[1831]. They had one son:
Alan Downs[3131]

1833. POLLY BUSBEE (see Descendants (134)) was born to William Roy Busbee[693] and Josephine E Edwards[692].

1834. JAMES T. WILLIAMS.
James T. Williams married Polly Busbee[1833]. They had three children:
Dean Williams[3132]
Rita Lynn Williams[3133]
Douglas Williams[3134]

1835. WALAN BUSBEE (see Descendants (134)) was born to William Roy Busbee[693] and Josephine E Edwards[692].

1836. ROCHELLA HOPE.
Walan Busbee[1835] married Rochella Hope. They had two children:
Randy Busbee[3135]
Tonya Busbee[3136]

1837. JEAN BUSBEE (see Descendants (134)) was born to William Roy Busbee[693] and Josephine E Edwards[692]. She died in 2017.

1838. LARRY L. WHITE.
Larry L. White married Jean Busbee[1837].

1839. HEYWARD IVIN JOHNSON (see Descendants (135)) was born to Fletcher Johnson[695] and Janie Edwards[694].

1840. ESSIE ORENE BOZEMAN.
Heyward Ivin Johnson[1839] married Essie Orene Bozeman. They had three children:
Hardy Lee Johnson[3137]
Patrisha Ann Johnson[3138]
Lesley Mitchel Johnson[3139]

1841. LEWIS EDWARD JOHNSON (see Descendants (135)) was born to Fletcher Johnson[695] and Janie Edwards[694].

1842. SYLVIA ?.
Lewis Edward Johnson[1841] married Sylvia ?. They had two children:
Lewis Edward Johnson Jr.[3140]
Elaine Johnson[3141]

1843. DALTON LEE JOHNSON (see Descendants (135)) was born to Fletcher Johnson[695] and Janie Edwards[694].

1844. ANNIE LOUISE BISHOP.
Dalton Lee Johnson[1843] married Annie Louise Bishop.

1845. FRANCES ELAINE JOHNSON (see Descendants (135)) was born on August 23, 1934, in Fort Walton Beach, FL, to Fletcher Johnson[695] and Janie Edwards[694]. She died in 2000, aged about 65, in Defuniak Springs FL.

1846. DUVAL MILFORD OGLESBY was born in 1934, in Florida, United States, to Robert R Oglesby and Maxie E ?.
- He was recorded in the census in 1940, aged about 6, in Wright, Okaloosa, Florida, USA.
- He was recorded in the census on April 1, 1950, aged about 15, in Shalimar, Okaloosa, Florida, United States.
- He died on July 5, 1984, aged about 50, in Defuniak Springs FL.

Duval Milford Oglesby, aged about 21, married Frances Elaine Johnson[1845], aged about 20, in 1955. They had four children:
> Riley Lee Oglesby[3142]
> Nancy Elizabeth Oglesby[3143]
> Sharron Oglesby[3144]
> Milford Gene Oglesby[3145]

1847. CLEVELAND JOHNSON (see Descendants (135)) was born to Fletcher Johnson[695] and Janie Edwards[694].
1848. VIRGINIA HARRIS.
> Cleveland Johnson[1847] married Virginia Harris. They had one daughter:
> Patrisha Lee Johnson[3146]

1849. ROSELINER JOHNSON (see Descendants (135)) was born to Fletcher Johnson[695] and Janie Edwards[694].
1850. DAVE HATAWAY.
> Dave Hataway married Roseliner Johnson[1849].

1851. CHARLES MITCHELL JOHNSON (see Descendants (135)) was born to Fletcher Johnson[695] and Janie Edwards[694].

1852. JEAN RAY JOHNSON (see Descendants (135)) was born to Fletcher Johnson[695] and Janie Edwards[694].
1853. FRANKLIN HENRY SWANSON.
> Franklin Henry Swanson married Jean Ray Johnson[1852].

1854. SYLVIA TURNER (see Descendants (136)) was born about 1930, in Alabama, United States, to M. A. Turner[697] and Rossa Edwards[696].
- She was recorded in the census in 1940, aged about 10, in Open Pond Road, Election Precinct 7 Watkins, Covington, Alabama, USA.
- She was recorded in the census on April 1, 1950, aged about 19, in Turner Road, Watkins, Covington, Alabama, United States.

1855. GEORGE BOSHELL.
> George Boshell married Sylvia Turner[1854]. They had one son:
> Gregory Alan Boshell[3147]

1856. WILLIAM AMOS TURNER (see Descendants (136)) was born about 1933, in Alabama, United States, to M. A. Turner[697] and Rossa Edwards[696].
- He was recorded in the census in 1940, aged about 7, in Open Pond Road, Election Precinct 7 Watkins, Covington, Alabama, USA.
- He was recorded in the census on April 1, 1950, aged about 16, in Turner Road, Watkins, Covington, Alabama, United States.

1857. PATRICIA WINSPUR.
> William Amos Turner[1856] married Patricia Winspur. They had three sons:
> Derrel Turner[3148]
> Dale Turner[3149]
> Tracy Turner[3150]

1858. JEFF WENDELL TURNER (see Descendants (136)) was born on April 30, 1935, in Covington, Alabama, USA, to M. A. Turner[697] and Rossa Edwards[696].
- He was recorded in the census in 1940, aged about 5, in Open Pond Road, Election Precinct 7 Watkins, Covington, Alabama, USA.
- He was recorded in the census on April 1, 1950, aged 14, in Turner Road, Watkins, Covington, Alabama, United States.

1859. JANICE FRANCES DAVIS was born on October 20, 1940, in Covington, Alabama, USA.
> Jeff Wendell Turner[1858], aged 23, married Janice Frances Davis, aged 18, on April 11, 1959 in Covington, Alabama, USA. They had three children:
> Jeffery Wade Turner[3151] born on February 1, 1960 in Florala, Covington, Alabama, USA
> Jack Milton Turner[3154] born on July 2, 1961 in Florala, Covington, Alabama, USA; died on November 3, 1979 in Shiloh, Covington, Alabama, USA
> Janet Sylvia Turner[3155] born on June 12, 1964 in Florala, Covington, Alabama, USA; died on June 19, 1982

1860. EDNA PEARL EDWARDS (see Descendants (137)) was born to Harry Edwards[699] and Pearl Cannon[700].

1861. EDWIN PARKER.
>Edwin Parker married Edna Pearl Edwards[1860]. They had three children:
>>Tim Morroll[3157]
>>Debbie Morroll[3158]
>>Rickey Morroll[3159]

1862. HARRY EDWARDS JR. (see Descendants (137)) was born to Harry Edwards[699] and Pearl Cannon[700].
1863. EDWINA PARKER.
>Harry Edwards Jr.[1862] married Edwina Parker. They had two sons:
>>Rhett Edwards[3160]
>>Rick Edwards[3161]

1864. LESLEY RILEY EDWARDS JR. (see Descendants (137)) was born to Harry Edwards[699] and Pearl Cannon[700].
1865. MS. ?.
>Lesley Riley Edwards Jr.[1864] married Ms. ?. They had seven children:
>>Pauline Edwards[3162]
>>Ruby Carol Edwards[3164]
>>James Edwards[3165]
>>Kenneth Edwards[3166]
>>Eugene Edwards[3167]
>>Roy Edwards[3168]
>>Jerry Edwards[3169]

1866. MARGARETTE EDWARDS (see Descendants (138)) was born to Early Edwards[701] and Mattilene Covington[702].
1867. JAMES YORK.
>James York married Margarette Edwards[1866]. They had two sons:
>>Lajaun York[3170]
>>James York Jr.[3171]

1868. BILLIE WAYNE EDWARDS (see Descendants (138)) was born to Early Edwards[701] and Mattilene Covington[702].

1869. MARTHA JANE EDWARDS (see Descendants (138)) was born to Early Edwards[701] and Mattilene Covington[702].

1870. MURRAY EDWARDS (see Descendants (138)) was born to Early Edwards[701] and Mattilene Covington[702].
1871. ANNIS CREECH.
>Murray Edwards[1870] married Annis Creech. They had four children:
>>James Murriell Edwards[3172]
>>Donald Eugene Edwards[3174]
>>Sheryl Diane Edwards[3176]
>>Judith Ann Edwards[3177]

1872. PHYLLIS JERNIGAN (see Descendants (139)) was born on December 11, 1949, in Shanely, Oklahoma, USA, to Burris Clyde Jernigan[705] and Correne Edwards[704].
1873. CARL WEBSTER.
>Carl Webster married Phyllis Jernigan[1872]. They had six children:
>>Tracey Rochelle Webster[3178] born on February 7, 1968
>>Stive Webster[3181] born on April 22, 1969
>>Denise Webster[3182] born on April 6, 1971
>>Scott Webster[3183] born on February 27, 1973
>>Tim Webster[3184] born on July 17, 1980
>>Carrie Webster[3185] born on January 12, 1982

1874. RONNIE JERNIGAN (see Descendants (139)) was born on November 20, 1950, in Shanely, Oklahoma, USA, to Burris Clyde Jernigan[705] and Correne Edwards[704].
1875. JANIE GILMORE.
>Ronnie Jernigan[1874] married Janie Gilmore. They had three daughters:
>>Lindsey Jernigan[3186] born on May 12, 1982
>>Britton Jernigan[3187] born on October 14, 1983
>>Melissa Jernigan[3188] born on July 2, 1985

1876. LARRY JERNIGAN (see Descendants (139)) was born on December 6, 1954, in Crestview, Okaloosa, Florida, USA, to Burris Clyde Jernigan[705] and Correne Edwards[704].
1877. TERESA HAGCE.
> Larry Jernigan[1876] married Teresa Hagce. They had one son:
> Darren Jernigan[3189] born on January 17, 1988

1878. ROGER JERNIGAN (see Descendants (139)) was born to Burris Clyde Jernigan[705] and Correne Edwards[704].
1879. JANET SYLVIA HILL.
> Roger Jernigan[1878] married Janet Sylvia Hill.

1880. LINDA EDWARDS (see Descendants (140)) was born to Ervin Hartley Edwards[706] and Arlene Crawford[707].

1881. DIANE EDWARDS (see Descendants (140)) was born to Ervin Hartley Edwards[706] and Arlene Crawford[707].

1882. BARBARA ANN EDWARDS (see Descendants (140)) was born to Ervin Hartley Edwards[706] and Arlene Crawford[707].

1883. LINDA WILLIAMS (see Descendants (141)) was born to Fred Williams[709] and Wylene Bass[708].
1884. JIMMY LASSITER.
> Jimmy Lassiter married Linda Williams[1883].

1885. DOROTHY JEAN PADGETT (see Descendants (141)) was born to Jean Padgett[711] and Myrtice Bass[710].
1886. DANIEL A. SECKLER.
> Daniel A. Seckler married Dorothy Jean Padgett[1885].

1887. D. JEROME PADGETT (see Descendants (141)) was born to Jean Padgett[711] and Myrtice Bass[710].

1888. GWENDOLYN J. PADGETT (see Descendants (141)) was born to Jean Padgett[711] and Myrtice Bass[710].

1889. STEVEN WAYNE PADGETT (see Descendants (141)) was born to Jean Padgett[711] and Myrtice Bass[710].

1890. RANDY JOE BASS (see Descendants (141)) was born to Hiram J Bass[712] and L. Ruth Howell[713].

1891. HIRAM BASS JR. (see Descendants (141)) was born to Hiram J Bass[712] and L. Ruth Howell[713].

1892. CLINTON DURANNE BASS (see Descendants (141)) was born on March 23, 1949, in Covington county, Covington, Alabama, USA, to Clinton Albert Bass[714] and Cozette Cushing[715]. Clinton Duranne became known as "Dewey".
- He was recorded in the census on April 1, 1950, aged 1, in 2nd House Carolina, Covington, Alabama, United States.
- He died on January 2, 2009, aged 59, in Carolina, Covington, Alabama, USA.
- He was buried in Carolina Baptist Church Cemetery, Covington, Alabama, USA.

The following information is also recorded for Dewey:
- Death(?) on January 2, 2009, aged 59.

1893. MS. ?.
> Clinton Duranne Bass[1892] and Ms. ? had one daughter:
> Serrie Bass[3190]
> The following information is also recorded for this family:
> • Unknown Relationship.

1894. NANCY CAROLYN BASS (see Descendants (141)) was born in 1954, in Andalusia, Covington, Alabama, USA, to Clinton Albert Bass[714] and Cozette Cushing[715]. She died (At young age) on March 9, 1954, as an infant, in Andalusia, Covington, Alabama, USA.

1895. SUE MARIE BASS (see Descendants (141)) was born to Gordon L. Bass[716] and Joyce Clements[717].

1896. MIKE BASS (see Descendants (141)) was born to Gordon L. Bass[716] and Joyce Clements[717].

1897. MARLON HUGH BASS (see Descendants (141)) was born to Wayne Bass[718] and Dewayne Worrells[719].

1898. WANDA ARLENE BASS (see Descendants (142)) was born on July 29, 1949, in Andalusia, Covington, Alabama, USA, to Bruce James Bass[720] and Catherine Lawson[721].
- Wanda Arlene became a Teacher.
- She was recorded in the census on April 1, 1950, as an infant, in Clemrus State Ladies College, Troy, Pike, Alabama, United States.

1899. BILLY GRAY BARNES was born on August 11, 1948.
The following information is also recorded for Billy Gray:
- Military Service.

Billy Gray Barnes married Wanda Arlene Bass[1898]. They had three sons:
David Brian Barnes[3191] born on October 10, 1971 in Andalusia, Covington, Alabama, USA; died on October 10, 1971 in Andalusia, Covington, Alabama, USA
Phillip Michael Barnes[3192] born on January 13, 1974 in Enterprise, Coffee, Alabama, USA
Samuel Brad Barnes[3194] born on August 8, 1986 in Enterprise, Coffee, Alabama, USA

1900. RICKY BRUCE BASS (see Descendants (142)) was born on October 14, 1952, in Andalusia, Covington, Alabama, USA, to Bruce James Bass[720] and Catherine Lawson[721]. Ricky Bruce became a Teacher.

1901. DONNA RENA CANANT was born on May 8, 1957 to George Thomas Canant and Betty Jean Bush.
Ricky Bruce Bass[1900], aged 23, married Donna Rena Canant, aged 18, on November 8, 1975 in Andalusa, Alabama, USA. They had two children:
Nicholas Bruce Bass[3196] born on August 12, 1979 in Selma, Dallas, Alabama, USA
Ashly Rena Bass[3198] born on March 17, 1981 in Thomasville, Clark, Alabama, USA

1902. DON JEFFERY BASS I (see Descendants (142)) was born on February 5, 1958 to Bruce James Bass[720] and Catherine Lawson[721].
Don Jeffery married twice. He was married to Treva Partain[1903] and Gail Norsworthy[1904].

1903. TREVA PARTAIN was born on January 14, 1961.
Treva married twice. She was married to Don Jeffery Bass I[1902] and Randall Ralph Bass[1910].
Don Jeffery Bass I[1902], aged about 20, married Treva Partain, aged about 17, about 1978, and they were divorced. They had one daughter:
Stacie Partain Bass[3201] born on August 29, 1978

1904. GAIL NORSWORTHY was born on June 7, 1956.
Gail married twice. She was married to Don Jeffery Bass I[1902] and Mr. ?.
Don Jeffery Bass I[1902] married Gail Norsworthy. They had one son:
Don Jeffery Bass II[3203] born on December 19, 1986
Mr. ? married Gail Norsworthy.
The following information is also recorded for this family:
- Death of Spouse.

1905. JANET MARIE BASS (see Descendants (142)) was born on June 6, 1960, in Andalusa, Alabama, USA, to Bruce James Bass[720] and Catherine Lawson[721].

Direct Relations

1906. BENJAMIN DOYLE KINSAUL was born on June 1, 1959. Benjamin Doyle became a Coach.

Having become engaged on August 24, 1979 in Florida, Benjamin Doyle Kinsaul married Janet Marie Bass[1905]. They had three children:
Kayla Kinsaul[3205] born on April 20, 1983
Hunter Doyle Kinsaul[3207] born on May 3, 1986 in Andalusia, Covington, Alabama, USA
Rollin Benjamin Kinsaul[3208] born on December 26, 1996 in Andalusia, Covington, Alabama, USA
Note: *Aug 24 1979 From a postcard's note, by Mildred Newton Carlies Bass. (Engagement)*

1907. THOMAS HAROLD HENDERSON II (see Descendants (142)) was born on January 2, 1949, in Auburn, Lee, Alabama, USA, to Thomas Harold Henderson I[724] and Eunice Bass[723].
- Thomas Harold became a Pharmacists.
- He was recorded in the census on April 1, 1950, aged 1, in Auburn, Lee, Alabama, United States.

1908. CAROL JANE JORDAN was born on November 26, 1951. Carol Jane became a Teacher.

Thomas Harold Henderson II[1907], aged 24, married Carol Jane Jordan, aged 21, on September 1, 1973 in First Church of the Nazarene E. Brewton, Escambia, Alabama, USA. They had four children:
Tera Ashleigh Henderson[3209] born on June 13, 1979
Bret Thomas Henderson[3211] born on November 2, 1980
Kyle Jordan Henderson[3213] born on August 27, 1982
Erin Lajune Henderson[3215] born on August 28, 1987

1909. VIVIAN ANN BASS (see Descendants (142)) was born on March 16, 1957 to Ralph Caephus Bass[725] and Annie Joyce Morris[726]. Vivian Ann became known as "Sister". She died (Medical Problem) on March 29, 1986, aged 29 years.

1910. RANDALL RALPH BASS (see Descendants (142)) was born on January 11, 1959 to Ralph Caephus Bass[725] and Annie Joyce Morris[726]. Randall Ralph became known as "Randy".
Randall Ralph Bass, aged 21, married Treva Partain[1903], aged 19, on December 17, 1980. They had one daughter:
Laura Bass[3217] born on February 16, 1983

1911. NANCY MADONNA BASS (see Descendants (142)) was born on December 24, 1960 to Ralph Caephus Bass[725] and Annie Joyce Morris[726]. Nancy Madonna became known as "Donna".

1912. GERRY RUSSELL was born on November 5, 1959.

- He died (Illness) on February 21, 2022, aged 62.
- He was buried in Shady Hill Church Cemetery, Covington, Alabama, USA.
Gerry Russell married Nancy Madonna Bass[1911]. They assumed parenthood of one daughter:
Whittly Vivian Russell[3219] by adoption

1913. JAMES BENNY BASS (see Descendants (142)) was born on April 23, 1962 to Ralph Caephus Bass[725] and Annie Joyce Morris[726].

1914. MARIE STOKES was born to Bill Stokes and Mary ?. She died on July 14, 2022 in Pensacola, Florida, USA.
James Benny Bass[1913], aged 20, married Marie Stokes on September 17, 1982. They had two children:
Johnathan Blake Bass[3220] born on September 27, 1984
Mandie Marie Bass[3222] born on December 2, 1986

1915. ROYCE CAEPHUS BASS (see Descendants (142)) was born on July 12, 1963 to Ralph Caephus Bass[725] and Annie Joyce Morris[726].
Royce Caephus married his second cousin, Tammy Joy Day[1287].
Royce Caephus Bass, aged 21, married Tammy Joy Day[1287], aged 22, on April 26, 1985. They had two children:
Brian Royce Bass[2570] born on October 26, 1987
Holley Alaine Bass[2572] born on October 18, 1989

1916. WINFRED LYNN BASS (see Descendants (142)) was born on November 30, 1964 to Ralph Caephus Bass[725] and Annie Joyce Morris[726].

1917. RHONDA DAVIS.
Winfred Lynn Bass[1916] married Rhonda Davis. They had two children:
Zach Bass[3223]
Allison Bass[3225] born on March 24, 1994

1918. ANTHONY EDD BASS (see Descendants (142)) was born on September 26, 1962, in Covington, Alabama, USA, to Edd Bass[727] and Learvene Trawick[728].

1919. SHERRY LYNN SCROGGINS was born on September 29, 1962.
Anthony Edd Bass[1918], aged 21, married Sherry Lynn Scroggins, aged 21, on July 30, 1984. They had two sons:
Anthony Gabriel Bass[3229] born on May 2, 1986
Nathaniel Drew Bass[3231] born on February 5, 1988

1920. WENDY LEARVENE BASS (see Descendants (142)) was born on June 17, 1967, in Covington, Alabama, USA, to Edd Bass[727] and Learvene Trawick[728].
Wendy Learvene married twice. She was married to Sheng Xiang Peng[1921] and Jay Jordan[1922].

1921. SHENG XIANG PENG.

Sheng Xiang Peng married Wendy Learvene Bass[1920], aged 19, on August 22, 1986, and they were divorced.

1922. JAY JORDAN was born on April 23, 1961.

The following information is also recorded for Jay:
- Military Service between 1984 and 1990, aged about 26, in San Diego, Orange, California, USA and Philadelphia.

Notes:
- *U.S. Navy Hospital Corpsman.*
  (Military Service)
- *"I served from 1984-1990 and left the Navy with a rank of Hospital Corpsman 3rd class (E-4). I was stationed almost 1 year in San Diego and almost 5 years in Philadelphia. I also spent a short time in training in San Antonio and Portsmouth VA. My best time was in Philadelphia because I was there the longest and I had the most friends there. We had to work long hours on swing shifts but Philadelphia was a 24 hour city and no matter when we had to work there was always somewhere to go with friends afterwards to wind down." -Jay Jordan.*
  (Military Service)

Jay Jordan married Wendy Learvene Bass[1920]. They had one daughter:
Annette Eula Jordan[3233] born on July 13, 1996

1923. TONY LEON MIMS (see Descendants (142)) was born on December 25, 1971 to Leon Gade Mims[730] and Wavie Lee Bass[729].

Tony Leon married twice. He was married to Jeanie Lorene Douglas[1924] and Monette Legg[1925].

1924. JEANIE LORENE DOUGLAS.

Tony Leon Mims[1923] married Jeanie Lorene Douglas, and they were divorced. They had four children:
Eric Michael Mims[3234] born on January 30, 1988; died on August 17, 1998 in Andalusia, Covington, Alabama, USA
Tony Justin Mims[3235] born on May 12, 1990; died on August 17, 1998 in Andalusia, Covington, Alabama, USA
William Brandon Mims[3236] born on January 1, 1993
Megan Hayley Mims[3237] born on September 2, 1995

1925. MONETTE LEGG.

Tony Leon Mims[1923] married Monette Legg.

1926. DIANE TRAWICK (see Descendants (142)) was born on November 6, 1958 to Eugene Trawick[732] and Hazel Bass[731].

1927. JERRAL LYNN TAYLOR.

Jerral Lynn Taylor married Diane Trawick[1926]. They had one daughter:
Laura Elizabeth Taylor[3238] born on August 21, 1998

1928. CHARLOTTE TRAWICK (see Descendants (142)) was born on November 5, 1961 to Eugene Trawick[732] and Hazel Bass[731].

1929. LARRY DILMORE was born on May 12, 1962.
> Larry Dilmore married Charlotte Trawick[1928]. They had two sons:
> Nathaniel Hayes Dilmore[3239] born on January 26, 1988
> Timothy Dilmore[3240] born on October 23, 1990

1930. LISA TRAWICK (see Descendants (142)) was born on April 4, 1963 to Eugene Trawick[732] and Hazel Bass[731].

1931. GREGORY PAUL WADE was born on September 3, 1962.
> Gregory Paul Wade married Lisa Trawick[1930]. They had one son:
> Paul Joshua Wade[3241] born on October 10, 1991

1932. GENA TRAWICK (see Descendants (142)) was born to Eugene Trawick[732] and Hazel Bass[731].
> Gena married twice. She was married to David Jernigan[1933] and Joe Murphy[1934].

1933. DAVID JERNIGAN.
> David Jernigan married Gena Trawick[1932], and they were divorced. They had four children:
> Myranda Nichole Jernigan[3242] born in 1994
> Natalie Danielle Jernigan[3244] born in 1995
> Ethan Tyler Jernigan[3245] born in 2003
> Kylee Jernigan[3246] born in 2004

1934. JOE MURPHY.
> Joe Murphy married Gena Trawick[1932] in October 2018.

1935. CYNTHIA MICHELLE BASS (see Descendants (142)) was born on September 25, 1967 to Herman Bass[733] and Mary Ann Blair[734].

1936. JEFFERY LEE SWITZER was born on September 27, 1968.

Jeffery Lee Switzer married Cynthia Michelle Bass[1935]. They had three children:
Hannah Leigh Switzer[3247] born on December 2, 1993 in Fayette, Kentucky 40501, USA
Timothy Michael Switzer[3249] born on May 9, 1995 in Fayette, Kentucky 40501, USA
Jonathan David Switzer[3250] born on July 9, 1999

1937. COY BENNETT BASS JR. (see Descendants (142)) was born on May 13, 1968 to Coy Bennett Bass[735] and Margaret Faye Hammock[736]. Coy Bennett became known as "Ben".
Coy Bennett married twice. He was married to Kelly Ann Rusk[1938] and Candy M. Fowler Frantz[1939].

1938. KELLY ANN RUSK was born on December 22, 1972.
Coy Bennett Bass Jr.[1937], aged 22, married Kelly Ann Rusk, aged 17, on December 7, 1990, and they were divorced. They had three children:
James Bennett Bass[3251] born on June 10, 1994; died on September 30, 1994
Kameron Baylea Bass[3252] born on August 2, 1995
Karson Ann Bass[3253] born on September 6, 1998

1939. CANDY M. FOWLER FRANTZ.
Candy M. married twice. She was married to Coy Bennett Bass Jr.[1937] and Mr. Frantz.
Coy Bennett Bass Jr.[1937], aged 43, married Candy M. Fowler Frantz on November 8, 2011.
Mr. Frantz married Candy M. Fowler Frantz. They had two children:
Brenana N. Frantz born on December 14, 1994
Michael Lee Frantz born on November 12, 2002
The following information is also recorded for this family:
• Unknown Relationship.

1940. COLUMBUS BARRY BASS (see Descendants (142)) was born on May 4, 1972 to Coy Bennett Bass[735] and Margaret Faye Hammock[736]. Columbus Barry became known as "Berry".
Columbus Barry married twice. He was married to Tamera Renee Wallace[1941] and Terri Stone[1942].

1941. TAMERA RENEE WALLACE was born on September 30, 1972.
Columbus Barry Bass[1940] married Tamera Renee Wallace, and they were divorced.

1942. TERRI STONE.

Columbus Barry Bass[1940] married Terri Stone.

1943. FRANKLIN SCOTT BASS (see Descendants (142)) was born on August 13, 1970 to Franklin Jerry Bass[737] and Barbara Barton[738].
• He died (Traffic accident) on August 31, 1990, aged 20.
• He was buried in Shady Hill Church Cemetery, Covington, Alabama, USA.

1944. STANLEY BRIAN BASS (see Descendants (142)) was born to Franklin Jerry Bass[737] and Barbara Barton[738].

Wilson Bass

1945. MS. ?.
> Stanley Brian Bass[1944] married Ms. ?, and they were divorced.

1946. DR. JOHN TAFT JOHNSON M.D. (see Descendants (143)) was born on May 15, 1960, in Crestview, Okaloosa County, Florida, USA, to Dudley Sadie Johnson[739] and Julia Ann Barrow[740]. John Taft became a Medical Doctor.

1947. KAREN OHLMEYER was born on September 14, 1956, in New Orleans, Louisiana, USA.
> John Taft Johnson M.D.[1946], aged 25, married Karen Ohlmeyer, aged 28, on June 22, 1985. They had two children:
>> Christopher Johnson[3254] born on September 4, 1988
>> Julia Adele Johnson[3256] born on December 1, 1994

1948. DUDLEY FRANKLIN JOHNSON (see Descendants (143)) was born on October 11, 1963, in Tallahassee, Florida, USA, to Dudley Sadie Johnson[739] and Julia Ann Barrow[740].
- He died on January 28, 2017, aged 53, in Ponchatoula, Louisiana, USA.
- He was buried in Beta Cemetery.

Note: *Dudley suffered with congenital developmental delay and severe epilepsy due to hypsarrhythmia with profound mental retardation. Dudley became a resident of Hammond State School in 1968 and was a lifelong resident at that facility until it closed in December 2016. Evergreen Life Services began providing care at Hammond State School (now North Lakes Support Services Center) in 2014 and moved resident out to group homes in the community. Dudley's group moved in December 2016 to Wadesboro Group home near Ponchatoula, Louisiana where he received great care. Dudley suffered an apparent stroke and cardiac arrest on the evening of January 28, 2017 and did not survive.*
(Death)

1949. CHRISTY JOHNSON (see Descendants (143)) was born to Dudley Sadie Johnson[739] and Julia Ann Barrow[740].

1950. GRAHAM TEMPLE.
> Graham Temple married Christy Johnson[1949].

1951. SALLY JOHNSON (see Descendants (143)) was born on June 12, 1966 to Kenneth Ray Johnson[741] and Sally Marilyn Simmons[742].

1952. NANCY ANN JOHNSON (see Descendants (143)) was born on September 19, 1967 to Kenneth Ray Johnson[741] and Sally Marilyn Simmons[742].

1953. TODD PIERSON was born on September 7, 1967.
> Todd Pierson married Nancy Ann Johnson[1952]. They had two children:
>> Vivian Pierson[3257]
>> Roland Pierson[3258]

1954. MARTHA JUDSON JACKSON (see Descendants (144)) was born on May 23, 1948 to Hollis Mitchell Jackson Sr.[744] and Annie Ruth Gunner[745].

1955. LARRY BOLLING.
> Larry Bolling married Martha Judson Jackson[1954].

1956. HOLLIS MITCHELL JACKSON JR. (see Descendants (144)) was born on July 27, 1952 to Hollis Mitchell Jackson Sr.[744] and Annie Ruth Gunner[745].

1957. LORETTA JACKSON (see Descendants (144)) was born on July 8, 1951 to Horris Carson Jackson[746] and Jeanette Howard[747].
- She died on March 14, 2012, aged 60.
- She was buried in Garden Hills Cemetery. Opelika, Lee County, Alabam.

1958. CARSON JACKSON (see Descendants (144)) was born on November 5, 1952 to Horris Carson Jackson[746] and Jeanette Howard[747].

1959. TONY RAY JACKSON (see Descendants (144)) was born on April 7, 1960 to Horris Carson Jackson[746] and Jeanette Howard[747].

1960. JAMES DALTON JACKSON (see Descendants (144)) was born on February 26, 1952 to Hillary Dalton Jackson[748] and Margaret Futual[749].

1961. HILLARY KIM JACKSON (see Descendants (144)) was born on May 27, 1960 to Hillary Dalton Jackson[748] and Betty Hawkins[750].

1962. RICHARD TODD JACKSON (see Descendants (144)) was born on July 31, 1961 to Hillary Dalton Jackson[748] and Betty Hawkins[750].

1963. RICHARD TAD JACKSON (see Descendants (144)) was born on July 28, 1963 to Hillary Dalton Jackson[748] and Betty Hawkins[750].

1964. TRACY ALLEN JACKSON (see Descendants (144)) was born on April 17, 1964 to Hillary Dalton Jackson[748] and Betty Hawkins[750].

1965. TAMMY GAYLE JACKSON (see Descendants (144)) was born on July 9, 1966 to Hillary Dalton Jackson[748] and Betty Hawkins[750].

1966. ALEX NEAL JACKSON (see Descendants (144)) was born on January 11, 1954 to Haward James Jackson[751] and Nora Fay Roberts[752].

1967. DEBRA LYNN JACKSON (see Descendants (144)) was born on December 27, 1955 to Haward James Jackson[751] and Nora Fay Roberts[752].
The following information is also recorded for Debra Lynn:
Twin.

1968. DALE O'MARR JACKSON (see Descendants (144)) was born on December 27, 1955 to Haward James Jackson[751] and Nora Fay Roberts[752].
The following information is also recorded for Dale O'Marr:
Twin.

1969. ERIC JAMES JACKSON (see Descendants (144)) was born on July 8, 1963 to Haward James Jackson[751] and Nora Fay Roberts[752].

1970. KIMBERLY K. JACKSON (see Descendants (144)) was born on January 3, 1967 to Haward James Jackson[751] and Nora Fay Roberts[752].

1971. MITCHELL QUILLIE PARKER (see Descendants (144)) was born on January 19, 1958 to William Adolphus Parker[754] and Florine Jackson Jackson[753].

1972. CARRIE ELAINE PARKER (see Descendants (144)) was born on August 14, 1959 to William Adolphus Parker[754] and Florine Jackson Jackson[753].

1973. FRANKIE HARBUCK (see Descendants (145)) was born on September 6, 1945 to Arnold Harbuck[756] and Dorthy E. Murphy[755].
1974. DIANE COON.
Frankie Harbuck[1973] married Diane Coon.

1975. JOHNNIE HARBUCK (see Descendants (145)) was born on August 24, 1950 to Arnold Harbuck[756] and Dorthy E. Murphy[755].

1976. ALLEN HARBUCK (see Descendants (145)) was born on April 23, 1952 to Arnold Harbuck[756] and Dorthy E. Murphy[755].

1977. CHARLES ALTON MURPHY II (see Descendants (145)) was born on April 24, 1958, in Crestview, Okaloosa, Florida, USA, to Charles Alton Murphy[757] and Katheryn Elizabeth Hendrix[758].
• He died on March 21, 2018, aged 59, in Florida, United States.
• He was buried in Shady Hill Church Cemetery, Covington, Alabama, USA.

1978. DANIEL PATRICK MURPHY (see Descendants (145)) was born on June 17, 1961 to Charles Alton Murphy[757] and Katheryn Elizabeth Hendrix[758].

1979. BOBBY MURPHY (see Descendants (145)) was born to Charles Alton Murphy[757] and Katheryn Elizabeth Hendrix[758].

1980. LINDA JAMES CHAPPLE (see Descendants (145)) was born on December 26, 1963 to James Chapple[762] and Edna Earl Murphy[761].

1981. JAMES DOUGLAS CHAPPLE (see Descendants (145)) was born on April 24, 1966 to James Chapple[762] and Edna Earl Murphy[761].

1982. WILLIAM DANIEL HART (see Descendants (25)) was born on June 14, 1925, in Alabama, United States, to William Daniel Hart[774] and Eva Irene Durden[775].
- He was recorded in the census in 1930, aged about 5, in Hart, Covington, Alabama, USA.
- He was recorded in the census in 1940, aged about 15, in 1 Range 14, Covington, Alabama, USA.
- He died on January 6, 2002, aged 76 years, in Daytona Beach, Volusia, Florida, United States.

1983. EUGENE HART (see Descendants (25)) was born in 1928, in Alabama, United States, to William Daniel Hart[774] and Eva Irene Durden[775].
- He was recorded in the census in 1930, aged about 2, in Hart, Covington, Alabama, USA.
- He was recorded in the census in 1940, aged about 12, in 1 Range 14, Covington, Alabama, USA.
- He died in Andalusia, Covington, Alabama, United States.

1984. MABEL ERLINE HART (see Descendants (25)) was born on July 4, 1929, in Pleasant Home, Covington, Alabama, United States, to William Daniel Hart[774] and Eva Irene Durden[775].
- She was recorded in the census in 1930, as an infant, in Hart, Covington, Alabama, USA.
- She was recorded in the census in 1940, aged about 10, in 1 Range 14, Covington, Alabama, USA.
- She died on August 9, 2007, aged 78 years, in Andalusia, Covington, Alabama, United States.

1985. JAMES B HART (see Descendants (25)) was born about 1939, in Alabama, United States, to James Travis Hart[778] and Delia Adeline Bradley[779]. He was recorded in the census on April 1, 1950, aged about 10, in Proceeding West on Wing to Bradly Road, Hart, Covington, Alabama, United States.

1986. SHERLEY L HART (see Descendants (25)) was born about 1949, in Alabama, United States, to James Travis Hart[778] and Delia Adeline Bradley[779]. She was recorded in the census on April 1, 1950, as an infant, in Proceeding West on Wing to Bradly Road, Hart, Covington, Alabama, United States.

1987. JULIA A HART (see Descendants (25)) was born about 1938, in Florida, USA, to Allen Trammel Hart[780] and Annie P Perry[781].
- She was recorded in the census in 1940, aged about 2, in West Central, Orlando, Elc Prec 18, Orange, Florida, USA.
- She was recorded in the census on April 1, 1950, aged about 11, in Oakwood, Crescent City, Putnam, Florida, United States.

1988. ELOISE KELLEY (see Descendants (149)) was born on October 15, 1921, in Alabama, United States, to Fred Columbus Kelley[788] and Rachel Davidson[789].
- She was recorded in the census in 1930, aged about 8, in Hart, Covington, Alabama, USA.
- She was recorded in the census in 1940, aged about 18, in Precinct 10 Hart, Covington, Alabama, USA.
- She was recorded in the census on April 1, 1950, aged 28, in 2508 S. Christiana, Chicago, Cook, Illinois, United States.
- She died on August 17, 2012, aged 90, in California, USA.
- She was buried in Pleasant Home Baptist Church Cemetery, Covington, Alabama, USA.

1989. GEORGE J. BICANEK SR. was born on March 30, 1918, in Illinois, USA, to John Bicanek and Stefie Bicanek.
- He was recorded in the census in 1940, aged about 22, in 7731 Ogden Avenue, Cook, Illinois, USA.
- He was recorded in the census on April 1, 1950, aged 32, in 2508 S. Christiana, Chicago, Cook, Illinois, United States.
- He died on January 1, 2009, aged 90.
- He was buried in Pleasant Home Baptist Church Cemetery, Covington, Alabama, USA.

George J. Bicanek Sr., aged 26, married Eloise Kelley[1988], aged 22, on July 15, 1944. They had three children:
> George J. Bicanek Jr.[3259] born in March 1945 in Florida, United States
> Joan Diane Bicanek[3260] born about 1946 in Chicago, Illinois, USA; died on July 15, 2022
> Carol Jean Bicanek[3261] born about 1948 in Illinois, United States

1990. RUTH HAZEL KELLEY (see Descendants (149)) was born on February 2, 1924, in Alabama, United States, to Fred Columbus Kelley[788] and Rachel Davidson[789].
- She was recorded in the census in 1930, aged about 6, in Hart, Covington, Alabama, USA.
- She was recorded in the census in 1940, aged about 16, in Precinct 10 Hart, Covington, Alabama, USA.
- She died in 2000, aged about 76.

1991. WYNELLE D KELLEY (see Descendants (149)) was born on February 18, 1926, in Andalusia, Covington, Alabama, United States, to Fred Columbus Kelley[788] and Rachel Davidson[789].
- She was recorded in the census in 1940, aged about 14, in Precinct 10 Hart, Covington, Alabama, USA.
- She died on June 4, 2017, aged 91, in Warner Robins, Houston, Georgia, USA.
- She was buried in Magnolia Park Cemetery and Mausoleum, Warner Robins, Houston, Georgia, USA.

Note: *She worked for 35 years at Robins Air Force Base in the morale, welfare and recreation division and at retirement was the food operations manager. She attended Green Acres Baptist Church for many years.*
(Death)

1992. MR. BAILEY.
Mr. Bailey married Wynelle D Kelley[1991].

1993. JOYCE MARIE KELLEY (see Descendants (149)) was born on April 10, 1928, in Alabama, United States, to Fred Columbus Kelley[788] and Rachel Davidson[789].
- She was recorded in the census in 1930, aged about 2, in Hart, Covington, Alabama, USA.
- She was recorded in the census in 1940, aged about 12, in Precinct 10 Hart, Covington, Alabama, USA.
- She died in 1976, aged about 48.

1994. MR. ?.
Mr. ? married Joyce Marie Kelley[1993]. They had two children:
> Betty ?[3262]
> Tommy ?[3263]

1995. FRED RONALD KELLEY (see Descendants (149)) was born on June 20, 1930, in Alabama, United States, to Fred Columbus Kelley[788] and Rachel Davidson[789]. He was recorded in the census in 1940, aged about 10, in Precinct 10 Hart, Covington, Alabama, USA.

1996. BARBARA GENE KELLEY (see Descendants (149)) was born on August 24, 1932, in Alabama, USA, to Fred Columbus Kelley[788] and Rachel Davidson[789].
- She was recorded in the census in 1940, aged about 7, in Precinct 10 Hart, Covington, Alabama, USA.
- She died on August 8, 1997, aged 64, in Covington, Alabama, USA.
- She was buried in Pleasant Home Baptist Church Cemetery, Covington, Alabama, USA.

1997. GEORGE D KELLEY (see Descendants (149)) was born on June 19, 1935, in Alabama, USA, to Fred Columbus Kelley[788] and Rachel Davidson[789]. George D became known as "Pete". He was recorded in the census in 1940, aged about 5, in Precinct 10 Hart, Covington, Alabama, USA.

1998. PATRICIA ANN KELLEY (see Descendants (149)) was born on October 6, 1937, in Alabama, USA, to Fred Columbus Kelley[788] and Rachel Davidson[789].
- She was recorded in the census in 1940, aged about 2, in Precinct 10 Hart, Covington, Alabama, USA.
- She died in 2020, aged about 82.

1999. JAMES KELLEY (see Descendants (149)) was born in 1943 to Fred Columbus Kelley[788] and Rachel Davidson[789].

2000. MR. KELLEY (see Descendants (149)) was born to Fred Columbus Kelley[788] and Rachel Davidson[789]. He died (At young age).

2001. MAX EARL POOLE (see Descendants (26)) was born on September 22, 1930, in Alabama, to Horace E Poole[814] and Velma Bass[813]. He died in March 1983, aged 52, in Houston County, Alabama.

2002. MARY ANN SMITH.
>Max Earl Poole[2001] married Mary Ann Smith. They had two daughters:
>>Brenda Poole[3264]
>>Debbie Poole[3265]

2003. EDDIE POOLE (see Descendants (26)) was born to Horace E Poole[814] and Velma Bass[813].

2004. CARROLL POOLE (see Descendants (26)) was born to Horace E Poole[814] and Velma Bass[813].

2005. MR. FOWLER (see Descendants (26)) was born to Dallas Clinton Fowler[820] and Eva Mae Bass[819].
Mr. Fowler married twice. He was married to Ms. Gunnis[2006] and Ms. Owens[2007].

2006. MS. GUNNIS.
>Mr. Fowler[2005] married Ms. Gunnis. They had one son:
>>Mr. Fowler[3266]

2007. MS. OWENS.
>Mr. Fowler[2005] married Ms. Owens. They had one son:
>>Stanley Ray Fowler[3267]

2008. JUDITH ELLICA BASS (see Descendants (26)) was born on November 19, 1944, in Andalusia, Covington, Alabama, United States, to Horace Presley Bass[821] and Avie Brooks[822].
- She died on October 16, 2016, aged 71.
- She was buried in West Georgia Memorial Park, Carrollton, Carroll County, Georgia, USA.

2009. RICHARD RONALD RODGERS SR.
>Richard Ronald Rodgers Sr. married Judith Ellica Bass[2008].

2010. TOMMY AUTHOR BASS (see Descendants (26)) was born on January 18, 1956, in Columbus, Muscogee, Georgia, United States, to Horace Presley Bass[821] and Avie Brooks[822].
- Tommy Author was a Owner of T. A. Hauling in Douglasville Georgia.
- He died on April 2, 2007, aged 51.

2011. KATHY ANN MEDOWS.
>Tommy Author Bass[2010] married Kathy Ann Medows.

6th Generation of Descendants

2012. LESTER BROOKS (see Descendants (1)) was born in 1947 to J. B. Brooks[825] and Mary Ethel Teel[824].

2013. SUE BROOKS (see Descendants (1)) was born in 1950 to J. B. Brooks[825] and Mary Ethel Teel[824].

2014. SHERRY BROOKS (see Descendants (1)) was born in 1954 to J. B. Brooks[825] and Mary Ethel Teel[824].

2015. SANDRA BROOKS (see Descendants (1)) was born in 1958 to J. B. Brooks[825] and Mary Ethel Teel[824].

2016. TROYCE ARMSTRONG (see Descendants (1)) was born in 1949 to Pete Armstrong[827] and Marie Teel[826].

2017. JERRY CROSS (see Descendants (1)) was born in 1955 to Cecil Cross[829] and Vera Merle Teel[828].

2018. DONNA CROSS (see Descendants (1)) was born in 1957 to Cecil Cross[829] and Vera Merle Teel[828].

2019. BILLY CROSS (see Descendants (1)) was born in 1959 to Cecil Cross[829] and Vera Merle Teel[828].

2020. DEXTER TEEL (see Descendants (1)) was born in 1958 to Aaron Teel Jr.[830] and Jean Childs[831]. He died in 1964, aged about 6.

2021. DEBRA KAY TEEL (see Descendants (1)) was born in 1960 to Aaron Teel Jr.[830] and Jean Childs[831].

2022. KENETH RA TEEL (see Descendants (1)) was born in 1964 to Aaron Teel Jr.[830] and Jean Childs[831].

2023. JERRY EDWARD RAMER (see Descendants (2)) was born to Winford Eugene Ramer Sr.[835] and Nancy Yates[836].

2024. WINFORD EUGENE RAMER JR. (see Descendants (2)) was born to Winford Eugene Ramer Sr.[835] and Nancy Yates[836]. He died on March 22, 2014 in Marietta, Georgia, USA.
2025. LINDA MEAD.
       Winford Eugene Ramer Jr.[2024] married Linda Mead. They had two children:
           Justin Ramer[3268] born about 1980
           Jennifer Ramer[3269]

2026. MARGARET RAMER (see Descendants (2)) was born to Winford Eugene Ramer Sr.[835] and Nancy Yates[836].

2027. STEVE WHITE (see Descendants (4)) was born to James Thomas White Sr.[843] and Marvette Faye Davis[909].
2028. CASEY ?.
       Steve White[2027] married Casey ?. They had two sons:
           Mr. White[3271]
           Mr. White[3272]

2029. MR. WHITE (see Descendants (4)) was born to James Thomas White Sr.[843] and Marvette Faye Davis[909].
2030. MS. ?.
       Ms. ? married twice. She was married to Mr. White[2029] and Mr. ?.
           Mr. White[2029] married Ms. ?. They had one son:
               Mr. White[3273]
           Mr. ? married Ms. ?. They had two children:
               Mr. ?
               Ms. ?

2031. MR. WHITE (see Descendants (4)) was born to James Thomas White Sr.[843] and Marvette Faye Davis[909].

2032. MR. WHITE (see Descendants (4)) was born to James Thomas White Sr.[843] and Marvette Faye Davis[909].
2033. MS. ?.
       Mr. White[2032] married Ms. ?.

2034. HAZEL MARIE BARNEYCASTLE (see Descendants (7)) was born on November 12, 1933, in Groveton, Trinity, Texas 75845, USA, to Benjamin Wilson Barneycastle[848] and Lola Mae Keels[849]. She was recorded in the census on April 1, 1950, aged 16, in 113 2nd Ave No, Texas City, Galveston, Texas, United States.

2035. SUE ADELE BARNEYCASTLE (see Descendants (7)) was born on April 4, 1942, in Houston, Harris County, Texas, USA, to Benjamin Wilson Barneycastle[848] and Lola Mae Keels[849].
- She was recorded in the census on April 1, 1950, aged 7, in 113 2nd Ave No, Texas City, Galveston, Texas, United States.
- She died on December 1, 2015, aged 73, in Salt Lake City, Salt Lake, Utah, USA.
- She was buried in Hayes Grace Memorial Park, Hitchcock, Galveston County, Texas, USA.

Note: *Sue was raised in Texas City, Texas and graduated from Texas City High School. Later she earned her bachelor's degree at the University of Utah. She learned to play piano at an early age and by age 12 she was the church pianist. She danced ballet from her youth through her young adult years. She was an artist with emphasis on landscape oil and southwest water-color paintings. She owned her own art studio where she taught many aspiring artists her trade. She traveled the US selling her paintings at art shows.Sue loved gardening with a rare passion that was evident in the way she could turn any bare spot green. She passed on her love of gardening to her children and grandchildren. If you went to visit Sue and she didn't answer the door, you knew to go around to the back where you would find her out in the garden.Sue enjoyed any good political debate and would tirelessly debate her side. She could cook and loved to cook southern food for her family. She loved baking and even won a blue ribbon at the Utah State Fair for her delicious Mexican wedding cookies. Of all the many things Sue did in her life, the most important thing to her was her family. She loved unconditionally. She made spoiling her grandchildren into an art form. She was self-sacrificing, independent and creative. She would help a stranger as quickly as she would family. Her fighting spirit will forever be cherished by all those lucky enough to have known her.*

2036. EDMOND HARDCASTLE.
Edmond Hardcastle married Sue Adele Barneycastle[2035], aged about 24, from September 21, 1957 to May 22, 1974, and they were divorced. They had five children:
Edmond Hardcastle Jr.[3274]
Susan Hardcastle[3276]
Timothy Hardcastle[3278]
Pamela Hardcastle[3279]
Greta Hardcastle[3281]

2037. BENNIE MAE BARNEYCASTLE (see Descendants (7)) was born on September 14, 1944, in Texas City, Galveston County, Texas, USA, to Benjamin Wilson Barneycastle[848] and Lola Mae Keels[849].
- She was recorded in the census on April 1, 1950, aged 5, in 113 2nd Ave No, Texas City, Galveston, Texas, United States.
- She died (Cancer) on September 22, 2018, aged 74, in Houston, Harris, Texas, USA.
- She was buried in Houston National Cemetery, Houston, Harris County, Texas, USA.

Note: *Bennie loved being a grandmother and always saw the best in everyone she met, an eternal optimist.*
(Death)

2038. LOUIS GEORGE WILLIS JR.
The following information is also recorded for Louis George:
- Military Service.
Note: *EM3, US Navy.*
(Military Service)
Louis George Willis Jr. married Bennie Mae Barneycastle[2037].

2039. MS. JOHNNIE (see Descendants (7)) was born to Clarence Johnnie[855] and Isabelle Barneycastle[854].

2040. DONNA LEE BLUME (see Descendants (27)) was born on August 6, 1943, in Westlake, Calcasieu, Louisiana, United States, to Kenneth Lynell Blume[874] and Katherine Gladys Bass[873].
- She died on April 1, 2020, aged 76.
- She was buried in Westlake, Calcasieu Parish, Louisiana, United States of America.

2041. DANIEL S BASS (see Descendants (28)) was born on June 6, 1950, in Lake Charles, Calcasieu Parish, Louisiana, USA, to Daniel Materson Bass Jr.[875] and Dorothy Victoria Farris[876]. Daniel S became known as "Steve". He died on March 1, 2010, aged 59, in Pennsylvania, USA.

2042. BARBARA ?.
> Daniel S Bass[2041] married Barbara ?. They had three children:
>> Steve Bass[3282]
>> Casandra Bass[3283]
>> Seth Bass[3284]

2043. BRENDA BASS (see Descendants (28)) was born to Daniel Materson Bass Jr.[875] and Dorothy Victoria Farris[876].
2044. IVAR WEIERHOLT.
> Ivar Weierholt married Brenda Bass[2043].

2045. JOHN BASS (see Descendants (28)) was born to Daniel Materson Bass Jr.[875] and Dorothy Victoria Farris[876].
2046. RACHEL ?.
> John Bass[2045] married Rachel ?.

2047. NITA BASS (see Descendants (28)) was born to Daniel Materson Bass Jr.[875] and Dorothy Victoria Farris[876].
2048. JIM EVANS.
> Jim Evans married Nita Bass[2047].

2049. ANNETTE BASS (see Descendants (28)) was born to Daniel Materson Bass Jr.[875] and Dorothy Victoria Farris[876].
2050. LES TORREY.
> Les Torrey married Annette Bass[2049].

2051. KENNETH RILEY BASS JR. (see Descendants (29)) was born on August 5, 1960, in Lake Charles, Calcasieu Parish, Louisiana, USA, to Kenneth Riley Bass Sr.[878] and Martha L. Batten[879]. Kenneth Riley became known as "Kenny".
- He died on February 3, 2013, aged 52, in Mooringsport, Caddo Parish, Louisiana, USA.
- He was buried in Lakeview Memorial Gardens, Oil City, Caddo Parish, Louisiana, USA.

Kenneth Riley had two partnerships. He was married to Joy ?[2052]. He was also the partner of Ms. ?[2053].

2052. JOY ?.
> Kenneth Riley Bass Jr.[2051] married Joy ?.
2053. MS. ?.
> Kenneth Riley Bass Jr.[2051] and Ms. ? had two sons:
>> Gary Bass[3285]
>> Terry Bass[3286]
> The following information is also recorded for this family:
> - Unknown Relationship.

2054. SHARON BASS (see Descendants (29)) was born to Kenneth Riley Bass Sr.[878] and Martha L. Batten[879].

2055. THOMAS MCKINNEY.
> Thomas McKinney married Sharon Bass[2054] on September 9, 2017.

2056. TIMOTHY BASS (see Descendants (29)) was born to Kenneth Riley Bass Sr.[878] and Martha L. Batten[879].

2057. JUANITA LABOVE.

Timothy Bass[2056] married Juanita Labove in 2016.

2058. MR. LASKER (see Descendants (30)) was born to Mr. Lasker[884] and Dorothy Bass[883].
2059. MS. ?.
Mr. Lasker[2058] married Ms. ?. They had four children:
Mr. Lasker[3287]
Mr./Ms. Lasker[3288]
Mr./Ms. Lasker[3289]
Mr. Lasker[3290]

2060. MYRNA E GRESKO (see Descendants (31)) was born about 1942, in New Jersey, United States, to William Gresko[887] and Jean Ralston[886]. She was recorded in the census on April 1, 1950, aged about 7, in Red and Summers Sub Div, Monticello, San Juan, Utah, United States.

2061. WILLIAM MARK GRESKO (see Descendants (31)) was born on February 9, 1943, in Moab, Grand, Utah, USA, to William Gresko[887] and Jean Ralston[886].
• He was recorded in the census on April 1, 1950, aged 7, in Red and Summers Sub Div, Monticello, San Juan, Utah, United States.
• He died on September 22, 2013, aged 70, in Cottonwood, Yavapai, Arizona, USA.

2062. MS. ?.
William Mark Gresko[2061] married Ms. ?.

2063. RONALD KAY GRESKO (see Descendants (31)) was born on June 23, 1947, in Moab, Grand, Utah, USA, to William Gresko[887] and Jean Ralston[886].
• He was recorded in the census on April 1, 1950, aged 2, in Red and Summers Sub Div, Monticello, San Juan, Utah, United States.
• He died on February 17, 2017, aged 69, in Arizona, USA.

2064. MS. ?.
Ronald Kay Gresko[2063], aged 24, married Ms. ? on April 14, 1972. They had two children:
Ronald Kay Gresko[3291] born in 1972; died in 1973
Chastity Deannia Inez Gresko[3292] born on May 30, 1974 in Phoenix, Maricopa, Arizona, USA; died on May 21, 2016 in Arizona, USA

2065. EDWARD CECIL GRESKO (see Descendants (31)) was born about 1949, in Utah, United States, to William Gresko[887] and Jean Ralston[886].
• He was recorded in the census on April 1, 1950, as an infant, in Red and Summers Sub Div, Monticello, San Juan, Utah, United States.
• He was recorded in the census on April 1, 1950, as an infant, in Red and Summers Sub Div, Monticello, San Juan, Utah, United States.

2066. ETTA CELIA GRESKO (see Descendants (31)) was born about 1949, in Utah, United States, to William Gresko[887] and Jean Ralston[886]. She was recorded in the census on April 1, 1950, as an infant, in Red and Summers Sub Div, Monticello, San Juan, Utah, United States.

2067. MR. GRESKO (see Descendants (31)) was born to William Gresko[887] and Jean Ralston[886].

2068. JANIS MARY HARRIS (see Descendants (32)) was born on October 21, 1957, in Glennallen, Alaska, USA, to Michael James Harris[898] and Betty Jean Flickinger[899].

2069. NANCY KATHRYN HARRIS (see Descendants (32)) was born on May 18, 1959, in Glennallen, Alaska, USA, to Michael James Harris[898] and Betty Jean Flickinger[899].

Direct Relations

2070. KEVIN MYERS.
Kevin Myers and Nancy Kathryn Harris[2069] became partners.

2071. MR. STEVENS (see Descendants (33)) was born to William Reed Stevens[906] and Betty Ann Jones[907].

2072. MS. STEVENS (see Descendants (33)) was born to William Reed Stevens[906] and Betty Ann Jones[907].

2073. MS. STEVENS (see Descendants (33)) was born to William Reed Stevens[906] and Betty Ann Jones[907].

2074. MR. STEVENS (see Descendants (33)) was born to William Reed Stevens[906] and Betty Ann Jones[907].

2075. MR. STEVENS (see Descendants (33)) was born to William Reed Stevens[906] and Betty Ann Jones[907].

2076. LARRY BRADLEY HERRINGTON (see Descendants (11)) was born on March 10, 1945, in Florida, United States, to Orange Arnold Herrington[912] and Dorothy Helen Teel[911].
- He was recorded in the census on April 1, 1950, aged 5, in 316 Central Ave, Laurel, Jones, Mississippi, United States.
- He died on November 29, 2014, aged 69.
- He was buried in Carolina Baptist Church Cemetery, Covington, Alabama, USA.

The following information is also recorded for Larry Bradley:
- Military Service.

Note: *SP4 US Army Vietnam.*
(Military Service)

2077. PATRICIA JUNE WIGGINS was born on April 15, 1943.
- She died on February 11, 2016, aged 72.
- She was buried in Carolina Baptist Church Cemetery, Covington, Alabama, USA.

Larry Bradley Herrington[2076], aged about 24, married Patricia June Wiggins, aged about 26, in 1969. They had one daughter:
Ella Alesia Clauser[3294] born on December 21, 1963; died on August 15, 1998

2078. JIMMIE T HERRINGTON (see Descendants (11)) was born about 1947, in Mississippi, United States, to Orange Arnold Herrington[912] and Dorothy Helen Teel[911]. He was recorded in the census on April 1, 1950, aged about 2, in 316 Central Ave, Laurel, Jones, Mississippi, United States.

2079. JOSEPH A HERRINGTON (see Descendants (11)) was born in Mississippi, United States to Orange Arnold Herrington[912] and Dorothy Helen Teel[911]. He was recorded in the census on April 1, 1950, in 316 Central Ave, Laurel, Jones, Mississippi, United States.

2080. EDWIN KIETH CARY (see Descendants (11)) was born on August 4, 1971 to Richard Derhyl Cary[922] and Henryetta Nadine Bradley[923].
- He died on August 4, 1971, as an infant.
- He was buried in Brooklyn Baptist Church Cemetery, Evergreen, Conecuh County, Alabama, USA.

2081. DAVID JONATHAN BATSON (see Descendants (34)) was born on January 5, 1961 to Billie Batson[931] and Opal Virginia Spence[930].

2082. PAULA JEAN JOHNSON.
David Jonathan Batson[2081] married Paula Jean Johnson. They had one son:
Zackareah Jonathan Batson[3295] born on March 15, 1985

2083. ROBIN MARIO BATSON (see Descendants (34)) was born on January 26, 1964 to Billie Batson[931] and Opal Virginia Spence[930].

2084. DAWN DENISE BROCK (see Descendants (34)) was born on August 25, 1966 to Oscar L. Brock[932] and Opal Virginia Spence[930].

2085. CHUCK WALLACE.
Chuck Wallace married Dawn Denise Brock[2084], aged 27, in March 1994. They had two sons:
Steven Wallace[3296] born on September 10, 1977
Kevin Wallace[3297] born on May 1, 1984

2086. CARL LEON SPENCE (see Descendants (34)) was born on May 31, 1956, in Arizona, USA, to Clyde Autry Spence[933] and Phyllis D. Baughman[934]. He died (At young age) on June 11, 1956, aged 0, in Pima, Arizona, USA.

2087. DIXIE IRENE SPENCE (see Descendants (34)) was born on September 15, 1957 to Clyde Autry Spence[933] and Phyllis D. Baughman[934].
2088. TIMMY WAYNE BURLISON.
> Timmy Wayne Burlison married Dixie Irene Spence[2087], aged 16, on August 2, 1974. They had two sons:
>> Timmy Wayne Burlison II[3298] born on April 10, 1976
>> Shaun Michael Burlison[3300] born on February 5, 1979

2089. RHONDA SUE SPENCE (see Descendants (34)) was born on November 21, 1958 to Clyde Autry Spence[933] and Phyllis D. Baughman[934].
2090. KENNETH A. CAIN.
> Kenneth A. Cain married Rhonda Sue Spence[2089], aged 15, on May 1, 1974. They had three children:
>> Renee S. Cain[3301] born on January 29, 1974
>> Kacey A. Cain[3304] born on September 12, 1977
>> Kenneth A. Cain II[3306] born on April 4, 1981

2091. ROBERT LEON SPENCE (see Descendants (34)) was born on July 31, 1961 to Clyde Autry Spence[933] and Phyllis D. Baughman[934].
2092. CORINNE SUE SMITH.
> Robert Leon Spence[2091], aged 19, married Corinne Sue Smith on August 22, 1980 in Okaloosa, Florida, USA. They had two children:
>> Shannon Robert Spence[3307] born on July 29, 1982
>> Cara Leane Spence[3308] born on January 24, 1986

2093. JAMES SCOTT SPENCE (see Descendants (34)) was born on September 14, 1962 to Clyde Autry Spence[933] and Phyllis D. Baughman[934].

2094. FLOYD COLON SPENCE (see Descendants (34)) was born on January 28, 1965 to Clyde Autry Spence[933] and Phyllis D. Baughman[934].
2095. TERRI S. CLARK.
> Floyd Colon Spence[2094], aged 19, married Terri S. Clark on June 15, 1984, and they were divorced. They had one daughter:
>> Tabitha S. Spence[3309] born on October 21, 1984

2096. CLYDE AUTRY SPENCE JR. (see Descendants (34)) was born on August 7, 1966 to Clyde Autry Spence[933] and Phyllis D. Baughman[934].

2097. DEBORAH ANN WILKINSON (see Descendants (36)) was born on August 27, 1951, in Florala, Covington, Alabama, USA, to Wade Nathan Wilkinson[935] and Nellie Henry[936].
2098. FRANK JAMES MILSTEAD was born on November 21, 1950, in Pensacola, Escambia, Florida, USA.
> Frank James Milstead, aged 19, married Deborah Ann Wilkinson[2097], aged 18, on June 5, 1970 in Pensacola, Escambia, Florida, USA. They had two children:
>> Aubrey Gene Milstead[3310] born on August 8, 1974 in Pensacola, Escambia, Florida, USA
>> Danita Ann Milstead[3312] born on December 4, 1977 in Fort Walton Beach, Okaloosa, Florida, USA

2099. DELMUS NATHAN WILKINSON (see Descendants (36)) was born on March 3, 1953, in Florala, Covington, Alabama, USA, to Wade Nathan Wilkinson[935] and Nellie Henry[936].
Delmus Nathan had two partnerships. He was married to Tamara Sue Landis[2101]. He was also the partner of Mary Belinda Jordan[2100].
2100. MARY BELINDA JORDAN was born on July 25, 1955, in Crestview, Okaloosa, Florida, USA.
> Delmus Nathan Wilkinson[2099] and Mary Belinda Jordan had one son:
>> Jordan Alexander Wilkinson[3314] born on August 14, 1996
> The following information is also recorded for this family:
> • Unknown Relationship.
2101. TAMARA SUE LANDIS was born in August 1 A.D.
> Delmus Nathan Wilkinson[2099], aged 40, married Tamara Sue Landis, aged 1992, on September 3, 1993 in Escambia, Florida, USA, and they were divorced.

2102. JOY DENISE WILKINSON (see Descendants (36)) was born on September 10, 1955, in Florala, Covington, Alabama, USA, to Wade Nathan Wilkinson[935] and Nellie Henry[936].
2103. ECKI ALEXANDER PRATER was born on April 22, 1946, in Oklahoma City, Oklahoma, Oklahoma, USA.

Ecki Alexander Prater, aged 27, married Joy Denise Wilkinson[2102], aged 18, on November 17, 1973 in Baker, Okaloosa, Florida, USA. They had three children:
> Wade Nathan Prater[3315] born on May 23, 1978 in Edmond, Oklahoma, Oklahoma, USA
> Isla Noel Prater[3316] born on April 19, 1985 in Edmond, Oklahoma, Oklahoma, USA
> Robert Calvin Prater[3317] born on March 25, 1988 in Edmond, Oklahoma, Oklahoma, USA

2104. JANET LEE WILKINSON (see Descendants (36)) was born on February 12, 1959, in Florala, Covington, Alabama, USA, to Wade Nathan Wilkinson[935] and Nellie Henry[936].

2105. JOHN ERNEST BALIUS was born on February 15, 1947, in Creston, Union, Iowa, USA, to Eugene Balius and Lois Balius. He was recorded in the census on April 1, 1950, aged 3, in 508 Wyoming Ave, Creston, Union, Iowa, United States.
> John Ernest Balius, aged 31, married Janet Lee Wilkinson[2104], aged 19, on October 28, 1978 in Baker, Okaloosa, Florida, USA. They had two children:
>> Justin Eugene Balius[3318] born on February 2, 1989 in Creston, Union, Iowa, USA
>> Megan Catherine Balius[3319] born on November 20, 1990 in Norfolk, Virginia, USA

2106. JOSEPH WAYNE STEELE (see Descendants (36)) was born on August 26, 1951, in Florala, Covington, Alabama, USA, to Joseph Shoven Steele[938] and Floyce Genelle Wilkinson[937].
Joseph Wayne had two partnerships. He was married to Kelli Ann Ottley[2108]. He was also the partner of Donna Lee Good[2107].

2107. DONNA LEE GOOD was born on December 9, 1948, in Guernsey, Platte, Wyoming, USA.
> Joseph Wayne Steele[2106] and Donna Lee Good had one daughter:
>> Stephanie Ann Steele[3320] born on February 12, 1980 in Bountiful, Davis, Utah, USA
> The following information is also recorded for this family:
> • Unknown Relationship.

2108. KELLI ANN OTTLEY was born on September 27, 1960, in Salt Lake City, Salt Lake, Utah, USA.
> Joseph Wayne Steele[2106], aged 28, married Kelli Ann Ottley, aged 19, on August 25, 1980 in Salt Lake City, Salt Lake, Utah, USA. They had one daughter:
>> Rebecca Ann Steele[3321] born on November 21, 1981

2109. LARRY DALE STEELE (see Descendants (36)) was born on November 19, 1953, in Murray, Salt Lake, Utah, USA, to Joseph Shoven Steele[938] and Floyce Genelle Wilkinson[937].

2110. CHRISTINA VAN SICKLER was born on March 10, 1958, in Bangor, Penobscot, Maine, USA, to Robert Van Sickler.
> Larry Dale Steele[2109], aged 30, married Christina Van Sickler, aged 25, on November 25, 1983. They had two children:
>> Kathryn Leanne Steele[3322] born on July 29, 1991 in Montgomery, Montgomery, Alabama, USA
>> David Austin Steele[3323] born on January 11, 1994 in Montgomery, Montgomery, Alabama, USA

2111. DONNA MARIE STEELE (see Descendants (36)) was born on January 21, 1957 to Joseph Shoven Steele[938] and Floyce Genelle Wilkinson[937].

2112. V. W. KENNEDY was born on February 10, 1950.
V. W. married twice. He was married to Donna Marie Steele[2111] and Ms. ?.
> V. W. Kennedy, aged 25, married Donna Marie Steele[2111], aged 18, on August 22, 1975. They had two daughters:
>> Kristen Nicole Kennedy[3324] born on May 27, 1987
>> Stephanie Michelle Kennedy[3325] born on December 28, 1993
> V. W. Kennedy married Ms. ?. They had two sons:
>> Shon Kevin Kennedy born on December 18, 1970
>> Scottie Maurice Kennedy born on February 3, 1972

2113. TERRY MICHAEL STEELE (see Descendants (36)) was born on May 19, 1958 to Joseph Shoven Steele[938] and Floyce Genelle Wilkinson[937]. He died on May 23, 2000, aged 42 years.

2114. PATRICIA ANN KILCREASE.
> Terry Michael Steele[2113], aged 21, married Patricia Ann Kilcrease on May 2, 1980. They had five children:
>> Jeremy Michael Steele[3326] born on May 24, 1981
>> Bradley Shoven Steele[3327] born on September 1, 1983
>> Kevin Charles Steele[3328] born on May 20, 1986
>> Emily Ann Steele[3329] born on September 21, 1987
>> Erin Elizabeth Steele[3330] born on September 21, 1987

2115. LOIS ANETTE JOHNSON (see Descendants (36)) was born on August 23, 1958 to Roy H. Johnson[940] and Lorine Annette Wilkinson[939].
2116. LEONARD LEE was born on December 17, 1953.
> Leonard Lee, aged 22, married Lois Anette Johnson[2115], aged 17, on January 2, 1976. They had two sons:
>> Jason Lee[3331] born on August 1, 1976 in Milton, Santa Rosa, Florida, USA
>> Nathan Lee[3332] born on December 28, 1980 in Milton, Santa Rosa, Florida, USA

2117. MARCUS DEAN REGISTER (see Descendants (36)) was born on August 7, 1960 to Billy Register[942] and Judith Elaine Wilkinson[941].
2118. SUSAN WARD was born on August 23, 1965.
> Marcus Dean Register[2117] married Susan Ward. They had three children:
>> Alisha Register[3333] born on October 23, 1984
>> Jessica E. Register[3334] born on June 13, 1994
>> Jeremiah D. Register[3335] born on October 7, 1996

2119. MATTHEW WARD REGISTER (see Descendants (36)) was born on August 24, 1964 to Billy Register[942] and Judith Elaine Wilkinson[941].
2120. CHRISTY RENE BENNETT.
> Matthew Ward Register[2119], aged 33, married Christy Rene Bennett on April 11, 1998 in Gadsden, Florida, USA. They had two daughters:
>> Augusta Grace Register[3336] born on September 16, 1998
>> Mattilyn Rose Register[3337] born on March 9, 2000

2121. MARTHA GRACE REGISTER (see Descendants (36)) was born on October 6, 1970 to Billy Register[942] and Judith Elaine Wilkinson[941].
2122. MR. ?.
> Mr. ? married Martha Grace Register[2121]. They had one daughter:
>> Brandie Register[3338] born on March 29, 1996

2123. PHILLIP EUGENE FLEMING (see Descendants (36)) was born on December 30, 1958 to Eugene Fleming[944] and Irma Arleen Wilkinson[943].
> Phillip Eugene married twice. He was married to Linda Henderson[2124] and Cindy Borders[2125].
2124. LINDA HENDERSON.
> Phillip Eugene Fleming[2123] married Linda Henderson. They had one son:
>> Phillip Logan Fleming[3339] born on March 15, 1983
2125. CINDY BORDERS.
> Phillip Eugene Fleming[2123] married Cindy Borders. They had one son:
>> Alex Fleming[3340]

2126. LAURA LENELLE FLEMING (see Descendants (36)) was born on December 31, 1960 to Eugene Fleming[944] and Irma Arleen Wilkinson[943].

2127. DAVID EUGENE SHAUD.
> David Eugene Shaud married Laura Lenelle Fleming[2126], aged 19, on August 16, 1980 in Okaloosa, Florida, USA. They had one son:
>> Matthew Reed Shaud[3341] born on September 27, 1989

2128. KAREN LORINE FLEMING (see Descendants (36)) was born on January 3, 1964 to Eugene Fleming[944] and Irma Arleen Wilkinson[943].
2129. LANCE PERRY.
> Lance Perry married Karen Lorine Fleming[2128]. They had two children:
>> Magnolia Perry[3342]
>> Wyatt Chance Perry[3343]

2130. RACHEL WILKINSON (see Descendants (36)) was born to Roland Douglas Wilkinson[945] and Judith Harness[946].

Direct Relations

2131. JOSHUA WILKINSON (see Descendants (36)) was born to Roland Douglas Wilkinson[945] and Judith Harness[946].

2132. TED DOTSON (see Descendants (36)) was born on July 18, 1964 to Jerry Dotson[950] and Marcia Glendolyn Wilkinson[949].
2133. TERESA ALLEN was born on December 2, 1966.
> Ted Dotson[2132], aged 17, married Teresa Allen, aged 15, on March 12, 1982. They had four children:
>> Dixie Lee Dotson[3344] born on April 16, 1984
>> Amber Nicole Dotson[3345] born on April 8, 1986
>> Morgan Bailey Dotson[3346] born on August 12, 1989
>> Neil Dotson[3347] born on September 30, 1991

2134. TRACY DOTSON (see Descendants (36)) was born on November 25, 1965 to Jerry Dotson[950] and Marcia Glendolyn Wilkinson[949].
2135. TAMARA LYNN SIMMONS was born on June 19, 1968.
> Tracy Dotson[2134], aged 30, married Tamara Lynn Simmons, aged 27, on December 27, 1995 in Okaloosa, Florida, USA. They had one daughter:
>> Amanda Lynn Dotson[3348] born on December 3, 1996

2136. RONALD DAUNE TULEY (see Descendants (37)) was born on October 16, 1953, in Dallas, Dallas, Texas, USA, to Wenton Curtis Wilkinson[952] and Mary Sue Walkup[954]. He died on September 5, 1990, aged 36 years.

2137. PAMELA ANN TULEY (see Descendants (37)) was born on March 5, 1955, in Dallas, Dallas, Texas, USA, to Wenton Curtis Wilkinson[952] and Mary Sue Walkup[954].
Pamela Ann married twice. She was married to Mr. ?[2138] and Haywood Riggins[2139].
2138. MR. ?.
> Mr. ? married Pamela Ann Tuley[2137]. They had one daughter:
>> Melynda Reanee Riggins[3349] born on December 12, 1974 in McKinney, Collin, Texas, USA
2139. HAYWOOD RIGGINS was born on October 14, 1957, in Glenwood, Crenshaw, Alabama, USA.
> Haywood Riggins, aged 20, married Pamela Ann Tuley[2137], aged 23, on September 15, 1978. They had two children:
>> Kirstie Lea Riggins[3351] born on November 21, 1979 in Milton, Santa Rosa, Florida, USA
>> Brandon Haywood Riggins[3352] born on February 11, 1988 in Wylie, Colin, Texas, USA

2140. ROBERT TULEY (see Descendants (37)) was born on May 11, 1956, in Dallas, Dallas, Texas, USA, to Wenton Curtis Wilkinson[952] and Mary Sue Walkup[954]. He died on May 24, 1974, aged 18 years, in Baker, Okaloosa, Florida, USA.

2141. RANDALL GLEN WILKINSON (see Descendants (37)) was born on November 16, 1960, in Dallas, Dallas, Texas, USA, to Wenton Curtis Wilkinson[952] and Mary Sue Walkup[954].
Randall Glen married twice. He was married to Nancy Hale[2142] and Patti Miller[2143].
2142. NANCY HALE.
> Randall Glen Wilkinson[2141] married Nancy Hale. They had one daughter:
>> Rhainnon Rose Wilkinson[3353] born on February 12, 1981
2143. PATTI MILLER was born in January 15 A.D.
> Randall Glen Wilkinson[2141], aged 21, married Patti Miller, aged 1966, on December 30, 1981. They had two children:
>> Jeremy Curtis Wilkinson[3354] born on January 25, 1991
>> Alicia Raye Wilkinson[3355] born on March 25, 1993

2144. WARREN CRAIG WILKINSON (see Descendants (37)) was born on December 26, 1962, in Dallas, Dallas, Texas, USA, to Wenton Curtis Wilkinson[952] and Mary Sue Walkup[954].
2145. APRIL LEE CRABILL was born on May 17, 1962.
> Warren Craig Wilkinson[2144], aged 26, married April Lee Crabill, aged 27, on June 24, 1989. They had one son:
>> Taylor Wilkinson[3356] born on August 15, 1993 in Wylie, Colin, Texas, USA

2146. GAIL DENISE WOODARD (see Descendants (37)) was born on August 30, 1957, in Pensacola, Escambia, Florida, USA, to Eugene Odell Woodard[956] and Dorothy Joan Wilkinson[955].
Gail Denise had three partnerships. She was married to Joe Haveard[2147] and Will Dunlap[2149]. She was also the partner of Kevin Mcauliffe[2148].

Wilson Bass

2147. JOE HAVEARD.
    Joe Haveard married Gail Denise Woodard[2146], aged 19, on July 25, 1977, and they were divorced. They had one daughter:
        Shaun Michelle Haveard[3357] born on July 25, 1977

2148. KEVIN MCAULIFFE.
    Kevin Mcauliffe and Gail Denise Woodard[2146] had one daughter:
        Kristen Leigh Mcauliffe[3360] born on April 30, 1983
    The following information is also recorded for this family:
      • Unspecified Relationship.

2149. WILL DUNLAP.
    Will Dunlap married Gail Denise Woodard[2146], aged about 35, in 1993, and they were divorced. They had one son:
        Gabrie Coen Dunlap[3361] born on September 26, 1986

2150. DON MONWELL WALTERS (see Descendants (37)) was born on October 20, 1958, in Hattiesburg, Forest, Mississippi, USA, to Donnie Jay Walters[958] and Ina Mae Wilkinson[957].

2151. DEBRA JEAN NOLAN was born on July 1, 1959, in Morocco, Africa.
    Don Monwell Walters[2150], aged 21, married Debra Jean Nolan, aged 21, on August 31, 1980. They had three children:
        Lauren Ashley Walters[3362] born on July 17, 1984 in Jefferson City, Cole, Missouri, USA
        Joshua Walters[3363] born on September 4, 1985 in Raleigh, Wake, North Carolina, USA
        Tristin Walters[3364] born on December 4, 1986 in Pensacola, Escambia, Florida, USA

2152. RODRICK JEROME WALTERS (see Descendants (37)) was born on May 17, 1961, in Pensacola, Escambia, Florida, USA, to Donnie Jay Walters[958] and Ina Mae Wilkinson[957].

2153. ANNA LOFTUS.
    Rodrick Jerome Walters[2152] married Anna Loftus. They had two sons:
        Adam Alexander Walters[3365] born on May 29, 1985 in Dallas, Dallas, Texas, USA
        Roderick Jay Walters[3366] born on July 20, 1986 in Dallas, Dallas, Texas, USA

2154. KENNETH LAYNE WALTERS (see Descendants (37)) was born on October 29, 1963, in Pensacola, Escambia, Florida, USA, to Donnie Jay Walters[958] and Ina Mae Wilkinson[957].
    • He died on September 27, 1985, aged 21 years, in Philadelphia, Philadelphia, Pennsylvania, USA.
    • He was buried in New Bethany Cemetery, Holt, Okaloosa, Florida, USA.

2155. SANDRA ESTELLE ELLIS.
    Kenneth Layne Walters[2154], aged 20, married Sandra Estelle Ellis on June 29, 1984 in Escambia, Florida, USA. They had one son:
        Kenneth Layne Walters Jr.[3367] born on November 3, 1984 in Pensacola, Escambia, Florida, USA

2156. KIM DAWN WALTERS (see Descendants (37)) was born in 1966 to Donnie Jay Walters[958] and Ina Mae Wilkinson[957].

2157. WILLIAM MILLS.
    William Mills married Kim Dawn Walters[2156].

2158. LISA MARIE COOK (see Descendants (37)) was born on July 31, 1968 to Alfred Cook Jr.[960] and Mona Idez Wilkinson[959].

2159. CHRIS HANKINS.
    Chris Hankins married Lisa Marie Cook[2158], aged about 17, in 1986 in Holt, Okaloosa, Florida, USA. They had one daughter:
        Kaliee Hankins[3368] born on December 4, 1989

2160. YEVETTE LEE COOK (see Descendants (37)) was born on October 1, 1971 to Alfred Cook Jr.[960] and Mona Idez Wilkinson[959].

2161. JENNIFER NELL COOK (see Descendants (37)) was born on May 17, 1976 to Alfred Cook Jr.[960] and Mona Idez Wilkinson[959].

2162. LARY RODNEY WILKINSON JR. (see Descendants (37)) was born on November 28, 1968, in Jacksonville, Duval, Florida, USA, to Lary Rodney Wilkinson[961] and Marie Antonette Cascone[962].

2163. BRETT ALAN WILKINSON (see Descendants (37)) was born on November 28, 1972, in Jacksonville, Duval, Florida, USA, to Lary Rodney Wilkinson[961] and Marie Antonette Cascone[962].

Direct Relations

2164. LISA MARIE WILKINSON (see Descendants (37)) was born on September 27, 1974, in Jacksonville, Duval, Florida, USA, to Lary Rodney Wilkinson[961] and Marie Antonette Cascone[962].

2165. KATRINA MARIE WILKINSON (see Descendants (37)) was born on October 14, 1975, in Jacksonville, Duval, Florida, USA, to Lary Rodney Wilkinson[961] and Marie Antonette Cascone[962].

2166. DENA GAIL WILKINSON (see Descendants (37)) was born on September 20, 1965 to Chadrick Earl Wilkinson[963] and Judy Gail Kennedy[964].
2167. ROBERT LEE MATHIS was born in November 9 A.D.
> Robert Lee Mathis, aged 1979, married Dena Gail Wilkinson[2166], aged 23, on May 20, 1989 in Okaloosa, Florida, USA.

2168. CHRISTOPHER DEL WILKINSON (see Descendants (37)) was born on August 1, 1969, in Milton, Santa Rosa, Florida, USA, to Chadrick Earl Wilkinson[963] and Judy Gail Kennedy[964].
2169. LORI CAPRICE TILLEY was born on March 7, 1968, in Marquette, Michigan, USA.
> Christopher Del Wilkinson[2168], aged 22, married Lori Caprice Tilley, aged 24, on May 16, 1992 in Baker, Okaloosa, Florida, USA. They had two children:
>> Erika Jenelle Wilkinson[3369] born on October 11, 1988 in Milton, Santa Rosa, Florida, USA
>> Jessie Cordel Wilkinson[3370] born on February 11, 1994

2170. KIMBERLY ANN CUPP (see Descendants (37)) was born on June 12, 1968, in Milton, Santa Rosa, Florida, USA, to James Charles Cupp[966] and Glynda Carol Wilkinson[965].
> Note: *Kim and her mom did much to keep the family history up to date and available to the family. -Nicholas Bruce Bass.*

2171. JOHN PAUL VICTOR DIMARIA JR. was born on May 11, 1966, in Hollywood, Broward, Florida, USA.
> John Paul Victor Dimaria Jr., aged 22, married Kimberly Ann Cupp[2170], aged 20, on December 30, 1988 in Holt, Okaloosa, Florida, USA. They had two children:
>> Sarah Lindsay Dimaria[3371] born on November 19, 1992 in Orlando, Orange, Florida, USA
>> Jackson Phillip Dimaria[3372] born on September 28, 1995 in Orlando, Orange, Florida, USA

2172. JAMES LANDRE CUPP (see Descendants (37)) was born on August 8, 1972, in Pensacola, Escambia, Florida, USA, to James Charles Cupp[966] and Glynda Carol Wilkinson[965].
> James Landre fathered one daughter:
>> Lindsey Danielle Cupp[3373] born on February 11, 1993

2173. DOROTHY LEIGH CUPP (see Descendants (37)) was born on May 2, 1981, in Milton, Santa Rosa, Florida, USA, to James Charles Cupp[966] and Glynda Carol Wilkinson[965].

2174. CANDACE DELANE WILKINSON (see Descendants (37)) was born on May 8, 1981 to Norman Curtis Wilkinson[967] and Wanda Procktor[968].
2175. MR. HERRIN.
> Mr. Herrin married Candace Delane Wilkinson[2174]. They had four children:
>> Mr./Ms. Herrin[3374]
>> Mr./Ms. Herrin[3375]
>> Mr./Ms. Herrin[3376]
>> Mr./Ms. Herrin[3377]

2176. SHANE CURTIS WILKINSON (see Descendants (37)) was born on July 28, 1983 to Norman Curtis Wilkinson[967] and Wanda Procktor[968].
2177. MS. ?.
> Shane Curtis Wilkinson[2176] married Ms. ?. They had one child:
>> Mr./Ms. Wilkinson[3378]

2178. CANDACE DELANE WILKINSON (see Descendants (37)) was born on May 8, 1981, in Oklahoma City, Oklahoma, Oklahoma, USA, to Norman Curtis Wilkinson[967] and Tammy Sue Beasley[970].
2179. MR. HERRIN.
> Mr. Herrin married Candace Delane Wilkinson[2178]. They had four children:
>> Mr./Ms. Herrin[3379]
>> Mr./Ms. Herrin[3380]

Wilson Bass

> Mr./Ms. Herrin[3381]
> Mr./Ms. Herrin[3382]

2180. SHANE CURTIS WILKINSON (see Descendants (37)) was born on July 28, 1983, in Percell, McClain, Oklahoma, USA, to Norman Curtis Wilkinson[967] and Tammy Sue Beasley[970].

2181. MS. ?.
> Shane Curtis Wilkinson[2180] married Ms. ?. They had one child:
>> Mr./Ms. Wilkinson[3383]

2182. DUANE ALLEN DAWSON III (see Descendants (37)) was born on July 12, 1988, in Wahiawa, Honolulu, Hawaii, USA, to Duane Allen Dawson Jr.[972] and Selina Benita Wilkinson[971].

2183. DEMETRIUS LAROY SALTER (see Descendants (37)) was born on April 12, 1979, in Milton, Santa Rosa, Florida, USA, to Donnie Leroy Salter[974] and Rebecca Louise Wilkinson[973].

2184. CHARLES DAVID SUMMERLIN (see Descendants (38)) was born on February 1, 1958 to Clarence Devon Summerlin[975] and Mary Beth Burnett[976].

2185. MARY JO WILLIAMSON was born on February 5, 1959, in Pensacola, Escambia, Florida, USA.
> Charles David Summerlin[2184], aged 22, married Mary Jo Williamson, aged 21, on April 12, 1980. They had two children:
>> Sarah M. Summerlin[3384] born on August 19, 1988 in Opelika, Lee, Alabama, USA
>> Chad David Summerlin[3385] born on April 14, 1990 in Pensacola, Escambia, Florida, USA

2186. KATHY ANN SUMMERLIN (see Descendants (38)) was born on March 28, 1960 to Clarence Devon Summerlin[975] and Mary Beth Burnett[976].
> Kathy Ann gave birth to one son:
>> Jason Sloan Leger[3386] born on February 1, 1983 in Pensacola, Escambia, Florida, USA

2187. KIMBERLY JAN SUMMERLIN (see Descendants (38)) was born on March 11, 1963, in Pensacola, Escambia, Florida, USA, to Clarence Devon Summerlin[975] and Mary Beth Burnett[976].
- She died (At young age) on March 13, 1963, aged 0, in Pensacola, Escambia, Florida, USA.
- She was buried in Bayview Pensacola.

2188. JOEL RAY MCGLAUN (see Descendants (39)) was born on October 25, 1954 to Bobby McGlaun[978] and Betty Henley[979].

2189. MIKE DEWAYNE MCGLAUN (see Descendants (39)) was born on October 9, 1957 to Bobby McGlaun[978] and Betty Henley[979].

2190. RANDY LAMAR MCGLAUN (see Descendants (39)) was born on September 11, 1964 to Bobby McGlaun[978] and Betty Henley[979].

2191. CARIN ?.
> Randy Lamar McGlaun[2190] married Carin ?. They had two children:
>> Martial McGlaun[3387]
>> Holly McGlaun[3388]

2192. LEE MCGLAUN.
- Lee was adopted by Bobby McGlaun[978] and Betty Henley[979].

2193. ERIN MCGLAUN (see Descendants (39)) was born to Bobby McGlaun[978] and Betty Henley[979].

2194. MR. POLZIN.
> Mr. Polzin married Erin McGlaun[2193]. They had one child:
>> Mr./Ms. Polzin[3389]

2195. JUDY ANN CAUSIE (see Descendants (40)) was born on September 24, 1944 to Ray Causie[981] and Ruby Nell McGlaun[980].

2196. CLYDE HENRY MIMS JR.
> Clyde Henry Mims Jr. married Judy Ann Causie[2195]. They had one daughter:
>> Deborah Jane Causie[3390] born in June 4 A.D.

2197. GARY WAYNE WORLEY (see Descendants (40)) was born on August 14, 1952 to Horace Worley[983] and Mary Etta McGlaun[982].

2198. PAMELA JUN WORLEY (see Descendants (40)) was born on June 15, 1954 to Horace Worley[983] and Mary Etta McGlaun[982].

2199. DANNY DAVID WORLEY (see Descendants (40)) was born on May 16, 1957 to Horace Worley[983] and Mary Etta McGlaun[982].

2200. ROBIN DON WORLEY (see Descendants (40)) was born on January 1, 1959 to Horace Worley[983] and Mary Etta McGlaun[982].

2201. VICKEY YVONE MCGLAUN (see Descendants (40)) was born on March 27, 1954, in Opp, Covington, Alabama, USA, to James Kenneth McGlaun[984] and Bonnie Brown[985].
- She died on November 18, 1978, aged 24 years, in Montgomery, AL.
- She was buried on November 21, 1978 in Pine Level Baptist Cemetary, Pine Level, Clark, Alabama, USA.

Vickey Yvone married twice. She was married to David Lee Causey[2202] and Michael C. Ferguson[2203].

2202. DAVID LEE CAUSEY.
    David Lee Causey married Vickey Yvone McGlaun[2201], aged about 19, in 1973. They had two children:
        Tawana Lynn Causey[3391] born on November 22, 1970 in Montgomery, AL
        Brandon Lee Causey[3393] born on August 7, 1972

2203. MICHAEL C. FERGUSON was born on June 8, 1952.
    Michael C. Ferguson, aged about 23, married Vickey Yvone McGlaun[2201], aged about 21, in 1975. They had one daughter:
        Lena LaRae Ferguson[3394] born on January 16, 1976

2204. JAMES TONY MCGLAUN (see Descendants (40)) was born on January 10, 1956 to James Kenneth McGlaun[984] and Bonnie Brown[985].

2205. JAMES KENNY MCGLAUN JR. (see Descendants (40)) was born on May 21, 1957, in Montgomery, Montgomery, Alabama, USA, to James Kenneth McGlaun[984] and Bonnie Brown[985].

2206. LISA PERL CHAMPION was born on February 17, 1960.
    James Kenny McGlaun Jr.[2205], aged 21, married Lisa Perl Champion, aged 19, on March 9, 1979. They had two children:
        James Kenneth McGlaun III[3395] born on November 29, 1983
        Kimberly Ann McGlaun[3396] born on November 5, 1991

2207. LISA RENA MCGLAUN (see Descendants (40)) was born on January 16, 1962 to James Kenneth McGlaun[984] and Bonnie Brown[985].

Lisa Rena married twice. She was married to Kenneth A. Floyd Jr.[2208] and Ronald Leon O'neil[2209].

2208. KENNETH A. FLOYD JR.
    Kenneth A. Floyd Jr. married Lisa Rena McGlaun[2207], and they were divorced. They had one son:
        Kenneth A. Floyd III[3397] born on July 11, 1983

2209. RONALD LEON O'NEIL was born on February 15, 1962.
    Ronald Leon O'neil married Lisa Rena McGlaun[2207]. They had three children:
        Ronald Joseph O'neil[3398] born on May 24, 1986
        Hope Rena O'neil[3399] born on October 18, 1987
        Joshua Aaron O'neil[3400] born on May 11, 1992

2210. JOHN THOMAS WADE ELMORE (see Descendants (41)) was born on June 14, 1966, in Opp, Covington, Alabama, USA, to Bobby Wayne Elmore[987] and Margie Ree McGlaun[986].

2211. CLAYBORN LEE ELMORE (see Descendants (41)) was born on August 28, 1970, in Andalusia, Covington, Alabama, USA, to Bobby Wayne Elmore[987] and Margie Ree McGlaun[986].

2212. ROBERT L. ELMORE (see Descendants (41)) was born on August 1, 1971 to Bobby Wayne Elmore[987] and Margie Ree McGlaun[986].

2213. JAMES EDWARD MESSICK (see Descendants (41)) was born on August 6, 1969, in Andalusia, Covington, Alabama, USA, to Ricard Edward Messick[989] and Patricia Ann McGlaun[988].

2214. SHEIVELLA MARIA NORRIS.
    James Edward Messick[2213], aged 23, married Sheivella Maria Norris on September 12, 1992 in Birmingham, Jefferson, Alabama, USA. They had one daughter:
        Amber Maria Messick[3401] born on June 22, 1992

2215. RICHARD BRIAN MESSICK (see Descendants (41)) was born on June 24, 1975, in Andalusia, Covington, Alabama, USA, to Ricard Edward Messick[989] and Patricia Ann McGlaun[988].

2216. SANDRA DIANNE LAWSON (see Descendants (41)) was born on March 13, 1971, in Andalusia, Covington, Alabama, USA, to Marzette Alford Lawson[991] and Joyce Marie McGlaun[990].

2217. MICHAEL TODD INABINETT was born on March 1, 1972.
> Michael Todd Inabinett, aged 22, married Sandra Dianne Lawson[2216], aged 23, on December 3, 1994 in Covington, Alabama, USA. They had three children:
>> Kayla Lynn Inabinett[3402] born on September 8, 1997
>> Dallas Lawson Inabinett[3404] born on January 24, 2001
>> Brayden John Inabinett[3405] born on November 24, 2014

2218. KAREN LYNN LAWSON (see Descendants (41)) was born on October 17, 1975 to Marzette Alford Lawson[991] and Joyce Marie McGlaun[990].

2219. JOHN JEFFERY SOWELL ? was born on February 27, 1972.
> John Jeffery Sowell ?, aged 39, married Karen Lynn Lawson[2218], aged 35, on July 27, 2011.

2220. KELLEY MICHELLE MANCIL (see Descendants (41)) was born on March 10, 1973, in Andalusia, Covington, Alabama, USA, to Thomas Randall Mancil[993] and Sheila Dianne McGlaun[992].

2221. MENDY LEIGH MANCIL (see Descendants (41)) was born on May 16, 1977, in Andalusia, Covington, Alabama, USA, to Thomas Randall Mancil[993] and Sheila Dianne McGlaun[992].

2222. LAURA REBECCA HENDERSON (see Descendants (42)) was born on February 9, 1961 to Bobby D. Henderson[995] and Doris Irene McGlaun[994].

2223. RHONDA LEIGH HENDERSON (see Descendants (42)) was born on January 19, 1968 to Bobby D. Henderson[995] and Doris Irene McGlaun[994].

2224. SONIA DENISE HENDERSON (see Descendants (42)) was born on January 19, 1968 to Bobby D. Henderson[995] and Doris Irene McGlaun[994].

2225. CAROL ANN MCGLAUN (see Descendants (42)) was born on March 14, 1967 to Lamar Ray McGlaun[996] and Sara Ann Hair[997].

2226. MARY EVELYN HUCKABAA (see Descendants (44)) was born on December 8, 1946, in Andalusia, Covington, Alabama, USA, to Martin Van Buren Huckabaa Sr.[1000] and Hazel Bass[1451].

2227. EDWARD DAVIDSON.
> Edward Davidson married Mary Evelyn Huckabaa[2226]. They had one daughter:
>> Elizabeth Ann Davidson[3406] born on June 17, 1968 in Andalusia, Covington, Alabama, USA

2228. JERRY WAYNE HUCKABAA (see Descendants (44)) was born on August 17, 1948, in Andalusia, Covington, Alabama, USA, to Martin Van Buren Huckabaa Sr.[1000] and Hazel Bass[1451].

2229. BETTY ?.
> Jerry Wayne Huckabaa[2228] married Betty ?. They had one daughter:
>> Tina Huckabaa[3408] born in 1977 in Andalusia, Covington, Alabama, USA

2230. CHARLENE HUCKABAA (see Descendants (44)) was born on February 10, 1950, in Andalusia, Covington, Alabama, USA, to Martin Van Buren Huckabaa Sr.[1000] and Hazel Bass[1451].

2231. WAYNE BRADLEY.
> Wayne Bradley married Charlene Huckabaa[2230]. They had two children:
>> Tony Wayne Bradley[3409] born on December 29, 1969 in Andalusia, Covington, Alabama, USA
>> Crystal Darlene Bradley[3410]

2232. MARTIN VAN BUREN HUCKABAA JR. (see Descendants (44)) was born on October 13, 1951, in Andalusia,

Covington, Alabama, USA, to Martin Van Buren Huckabaa Sr.[1000] and Hazel Bass[1451].
- He died on January 26, 2011, aged 59 years.
- He was buried in Shady Hill Church Cemetery, Covington, Alabama, USA.

The following information is also recorded for Martin Van Buren:
- Military Service.

Note: *U.S. Army Vietnam War.*
(Military Service)

2233. CYNTHIA J. CARPENTER was born on August 6, 1957, in Liebing, Ohio, USA.
Martin Van Buren Huckabaa Jr.[2232], aged 22, married Cynthia J. Carpenter, aged 16, on February 17, 1974 in Nework, Licking, Ohio, USA. They had five children:
Marsha Huckabaa[3411] born on October 17, 1975 in Andalusia, Covington, Alabama, USA
William Huckabaa[3412] born on January 7, 1979 in Andalusia, Covington, Alabama, USA
Brenda Huckabaa[3413] born on February 29, 1980 in Andalusia, Covington, Alabama, USA
Dennis Huckabaa[3414] born on December 8, 1981 in Andalusia, Covington, Alabama, USA
Derek Huckabaa[3415] born on May 26, 1989 in Andalusia, Covington, Alabama, USA

2234. JACK BERRY HUCKABAA (see Descendants (44)) was born on January 29, 1953, in Andalusia, Covington, Alabama, USA, to Martin Van Buren Huckabaa Sr.[1000] and Hazel Bass[1451]. Jack Berry became known as "Jackie".
- He died on December 4, 2013, aged 60.
- He was buried in Shady Hill Church Cemetery, Covington, Alabama, USA.

2235. CURTIS HUCKABAA (see Descendants (44)) was born on August 21, 1955, in Andalusia, Covington, Alabama, USA, to Martin Van Buren Huckabaa Sr.[1000] and Hazel Bass[1451].

2236. JAMES LARRY HUCKABAA (see Descendants (44)) was born on February 27, 1964, in Andalusia, Covington, Alabama, USA, to Martin Van Buren Huckabaa Sr.[1000] and Hazel Bass[1451].

2237. ALTA DUKES (see Descendants (44)) was born on May 26, 1943, in Florala, Covington, Alabama, USA, to Hubert Dukes[1003] and Allie Mae Dukes Ward[1001].

2238. WINFRED DAVIS was born on August 24, 1940.
Winfred Davis, aged 19, married Alta Dukes[2237], aged 16, on September 9, 1959. They had two children:
Glenda Fay Davis[3416] born on October 12, 1960
J. W. Davis[3418] born on August 5, 1963 in Opp, Covington, Alabama, USA

2239. AUDI MAE DUKES (see Descendants (44)) was born on September 2, 1946, in Florala, Covington, Alabama, USA, to Hubert Dukes[1003] and Allie Mae Dukes Ward[1001]. She died on January 16, 2020, aged 73.

2240. JIMMY JUNIOR HARRIS was born on June 19, 1944, in Okaloosa, Florida, USA.
Jimmy Junior Harris, aged 19, married Audi Mae Dukes[2239], aged 17, on January 30, 1964 in Andalusia, Covington, Alabama, USA. They had two children:
James Edward Harris[3420] born on August 14, 1965
Cindy Renae Harris[3422] born on July 9, 1976

2241. HUBET C. HUCKABAA (see Descendants (44)) was born on February 2, 1950, in Andalusia, Covington, Alabama, USA, to Hubert Dukes[1003] and Allie Mae Dukes Ward[1001].

2242. MARY COBURN was born on May 7, 1952, in Orlando, Orange, Florida, USA.
Hubet C. Huckabaa[2241] married Mary Coburn.

2243. RANDALL IKE HUCKABAA (see Descendants (44)) was born on December 31, 1950, in Andalusia, Covington, Alabama, USA, to L. B. Huckabaa[1005] and Betty Jean Bass[1457].

2244. SYBLE DIANE MORGAN was born on February 12, 1951.
Randall Ike Huckabaa[2243], aged 18, married Syble Diane Morgan, aged 18, on August 16, 1969 in Andalusia, Covington, Alabama, USA. They had two children:
Gregory Randall Huckabaa[3423] born on April 6, 1971 in Andalusia, Covington, Alabama, USA
Angelea Huckabaa[3425] born on December 27, 1974

2245. OSCAR CLEVELAND HUCKABAA (see Descendants (44)) was born on May 18, 1952, in Andalusia, Covington, Alabama, USA, to L. B. Huckabaa[1005] and Betty Jean Bass[1457].

2246. LYNDELL FREEMAN was born on June 30, 1954, in Andalusia, Covington, Alabama, USA.
Oscar Cleveland Huckabaa[2245], aged 19, married Lyndell Freeman, aged 17, on November 20, 1971. They had two daughters:

Lesia Nicole Huckabaa[3426] born on October 3, 1975
Christi Lynn Huckabaa[3427] born on December 11, 1978

2247. GORDON HUCKABAA (see Descendants (44)) was born on April 17, 1956, in Andalusia, Covington, Alabama, USA, to L. B. Huckabaa[1005] and Betty Jean Bass[1457].
Gordon married twice. He was married to Emily Henderson[2248] and Rebecca Dean[2249].
2248. EMILY HENDERSON was born about October 21, 1959.
Gordon Huckabaa[2247], when younger than 27, married Emily Henderson, when younger than 23, before June 14, 1983. They had one son:
Gordon Heath Huckabaa[3428] born on July 3, 1975 in Andalusia, Covington, Alabama, USA
2249. REBECCA DEAN was born on September 3, 1965, in Andalusia, Covington, Alabama, USA. Rebecca became known as "Becky".
Gordon Huckabaa[2247], aged 27, married Rebecca Dean, aged 17, on June 14, 1983. They had one son:
Bobby Wayne Huckabaa[3430] born on August 15, 1987 in Andalusia, Covington, Alabama, USA

2250. BEVERLY JEAN HUCKABAA (see Descendants (44)) was born on October 11, 1957, in Andalusia, Covington, Alabama, USA, to L. B. Huckabaa[1005] and Betty Jean Bass[1457].
Beverly Jean married twice. She was married to Ronnie Creech[2251] and Lamar Sanders[2252].
2251. RONNIE CREECH.
Ronnie Creech married Beverly Jean Huckabaa[2250]. They had one daughter:
Kerry Lynn Creech[3431] born on May 17, 1975
2252. LAMAR SANDERS was born on March 24, 1946.
Lamar Sanders, aged 37, married Beverly Jean Huckabaa[2250], aged 26, on December 27, 1983. They had one daughter:
Amanda Kay Sanders[3432] born on October 16, 1984 in Montgomery, Montgomery, Alabama, USA

2253. RUSTY LAMAR HUCKABAA (see Descendants (44)) was born on June 15, 1962, in Andalusia, Covington, Alabama, USA, to L. B. Huckabaa[1005] and Betty Jean Bass[1457].
2254. DORTHY ANN KENDRIX was born on April 13, 1966.
Rusty Lamar Huckabaa[2253], aged 20, married Dorthy Ann Kendrix, aged 17, on May 26, 1983 in Andalusia, Covington, Alabama, USA. They had two children:
Kayla Ann Huckabaa[3433] born on December 14, 1983 in Andalusia, Covington, Alabama, USA
Christopher Allen Huckabaa[3434] born on May 14, 1985 in Andalusia, Covington, Alabama, USA

2255. SANDRA ELAINE KIMBRIL (see Descendants (44)) was born on February 10, 1951, in Florala, Covington, Alabama, USA, to Homer Kimbril[1007] and Daris Lee Huckabaa[1006].
Sandra Elaine married twice. She was married to Glen Paulk[2256] and Leon Petty[2257].
2256. GLEN PAULK.
Glen Paulk married Sandra Elaine Kimbril[2255].
2257. LEON PETTY was born in July 5 A.D., in Montgomery, Montgomery, Alabama, USA.
Leon Petty, aged 1976, married Sandra Elaine Kimbril[2255], aged 31, on May 7, 1982 in Montgomery, Montgomery, Alabama, USA. They had one son:
Christopher Shane Petty[3435] born on September 14, 1978 in Montgomery, Montgomery, Alabama, USA

2258. TIMMY LAMAR KIMBRIL (see Descendants (44)) was born on September 2, 1955, in DeFuniak Springs, Walton, Florida, USA, to Homer Kimbril[1007] and Daris Lee Huckabaa[1006].
2259. ERLDEAN CAROWELL was born in April 25 A.D.
Timmy Lamar Kimbril[2258], aged 19, married Erldean Carowell, aged 1950, on July 25, 1975 in Montgomery, Montgomery, Alabama, USA. They had five children:
Daniel Lamar Kimbril[3436] born on July 27, 1978 in Andalusia, Covington, Alabama, USA
Joseph Lokesh Kimbril[3437] born on February 14, 1980 in India
Samuel Lakshaw Kimbril[3438] born on August 15, 1980 in India
Andrew Lucas Kimbril[3439] born on May 9, 1984 in India
Grace Loraine Kimbril[3440] born on June 11, 1987 in Hong Kong

2260. CAROLYN DIANNE HUCKABAA (see Descendants (44)) was born on August 23, 1956 to Henry Clayton Huckabaa[1009] and Johnnie Mae Douglas[1010].

2261. LINDA JOYCE HUCKABAA (see Descendants (44)) was born on June 18, 1959 to Henry Clayton Huckabaa[1009] and Johnnie Mae Douglas[1010].

Direct Relations

2262. DORTHY JEAN HUCKABAA (see Descendants (44)) was born on July 2, 1961 to Henry Clayton Huckabaa[1009] and Johnnie Mae Douglas[1010].

2263. HENRY CLAYTON HUCKABAA JR. (see Descendants (44)) was born on November 23, 1965 to Henry Clayton Huckabaa[1009] and Johnnie Mae Douglas[1010].

2264. TERESA JANE HUCKABAA (see Descendants (44)) was born on July 22, 1962, in Andalusia, Covington, Alabama, USA, to Earl C. Huckabaa[1013] and Mamie Louise Hayes[1014].
2265. JIMMY RAY BOUTWELL was born on April 13, 1956, in Jay, Santa Rosa, Florida, USA.
    Jimmy Ray Boutwell, aged 24, married Teresa Jane Huckabaa[2264], aged 18, on January 8, 1981 in Kirksville, Adair, Missouri, USA. They had one son:
        Jimmy Earl Boutwell[3441] born on May 3, 1982 in Brewton, Escambia, Alabama, USA

2266. DONALD EARL HUCKABAA (see Descendants (44)) was born on June 13, 1963, in Robertsdale, Baldwin, Alabama, USA, to Earl C. Huckabaa[1013] and Mamie Louise Hayes[1014].
2267. TAMELA RENEE BLAIR was born on June 15, 1962, in Brewton, Escambia, Alabama, USA.
    Donald Earl Huckabaa[2266], aged 28, married Tamela Renee Blair, aged 28, on June 14, 1991 in Century, Escambia, Florida, USA.

2268. REDDA KAY HUCKABAA (see Descendants (44)) was born on August 27, 1965, in Andalusia, Covington, Alabama, USA, to Earl C. Huckabaa[1013] and Mamie Louise Hayes[1014].
    Redda Kay married twice. She was married to Glen Day Biddle[2269] and Kenneth James White[2270].
2269. GLEN DAY BIDDLE.
    Glen Day Biddle married Redda Kay Huckabaa[2268]. They had two sons:
        Glen Day Biddle Jr.[3442] born on October 18, 1983 in Geneva, Geneva, Alabama, USA
        Shon Lee Biddle[3444] born on November 20, 1985 in Pensacola, Escambia, Florida, USA
2270. KENNETH JAMES WHITE was born on October 14, 1966, in Century, Escambia, Florida, USA, to James Thomas White and Bertha Marie Park.
    Kenneth James married twice. He was married to Redda Kay Huckabaa[2268] and Cheryl ?.
    Kenneth James White, aged 25, married Redda Kay Huckabaa[2268], aged 26, on March 20, 1992 in Century, Escambia, Florida, USA.
    Kenneth James White married Cheryl ?. They had one son:
        Kenneth Dustin White born on August 9, 1988 in Mobile, Mobile, Alabama, USA

2271. LAURA LYNN HUCKABAA (see Descendants (44)) was born in February 4 A.D. to William Ray Huckabaa[1015] and Iver June Jackson[1016].
2272. DAN HOWARD LUCAS was born on June 10, 1963.
    Dan Howard Lucas, aged 20, married Laura Lynn Huckabaa[2271], aged 1979, on August 12, 1983 in Andalusia, Covington, Alabama, USA. They had two daughters:
        Lori Lucas[3446] born on February 18, 1984
        Amanda Dawn Lucas[3447] born on January 27, 1985

2273. EDDIE RAY HUCKABAA (see Descendants (44)) was born on August 18, 1963, in Wachula, Hardee, Florida, USA, to William Ray Huckabaa[1015] and Iver June Jackson[1016].
2274. ANGELIA RENEE RAMSEY was born on November 7, 1966, in Butler, Alabama, USA.
    Eddie Ray Huckabaa[2273], aged 28, married Angelia Renee Ramsey, aged 25, on July 24, 1992 in Andalusia, Covington, Alabama, USA. They had one son:
        Aaron R Huckabaa[3448] born on December 25, 1990 in Andalusia, Covington, Alabama, USA

2275. TRACY LAMAR HUCKABAA (see Descendants (44)) was born on June 23, 1966, in Andalusia, Covington, Alabama, USA, to William Ray Huckabaa[1015] and Iver June Jackson[1016].
    Tracy Lamar married twice. He was married to Kimberly Dawn Wise[2276] and Sandra Fay Butts[2277].
2276. KIMBERLY DAWN WISE.
    Tracy Lamar Huckabaa[2275] married Kimberly Dawn Wise. They had one daughter:
        Ciji Huckabaa[3449] born on September 14, 1984 in Andalusia, Covington, Alabama, USA
2277. SANDRA FAY BUTTS was born on February 2, 1967.
    Tracy Lamar Huckabaa[2275], aged 16, married Sandra Fay Butts, aged 16, on February 27, 1983 in Andalusia, Covington, Alabama, USA. They had one daughter:
        Bridget Rochell Huckabaa[3450] born on February 2, 1985; died on November 12, 1985

2278. THOMAS JEFFERSON GARRETT JR. (see Descendants (45)) was born on September 23, 1942, in DeFuniak

Springs, Walton, Florida, USA, to Thomas Jefferson Garrett[1019] and Trudy Rowell[1018]. He was recorded in the census on April 1, 1950, aged 7, in 1/2 Mi Left Indian Creek Road Off Euchleanna De Funuh Road, Bruce Creek, Walton, Florida, United States.

2279. HELEN ADKISON was born on December 29, 1946, in DeFuniak Springs, Walton, Florida, USA.
> Thomas Jefferson Garrett Jr.[2278], aged 25, married Helen Adkison, aged 21, on June 3, 1968 in Free Port, Walton, Florida, USA.

2280. NELLIE JUNE GARRETT (see Descendants (45)) was born on October 20, 1947, in DeFuniak Springs, Walton, Florida, USA, to Thomas Jefferson Garrett[1019] and Trudy Rowell[1018]. She was recorded in the census on April 1, 1950, aged 2, in 1/2 Mi Left Indian Creek Road Off Euchleanna De Funuh Road, Bruce Creek, Walton, Florida, United States.

2281. SHERWARD GOMILLION.
> Sherward Gomillion married Nellie June Garrett[2280], aged 18, on July 25, 1966.

2282. PEGGY JOYCE GARRETT (see Descendants (45)) was born on October 8, 1948, in DeFuniak Springs, Walton, Florida, USA, to Thomas Jefferson Garrett[1019] and Trudy Rowell[1018]. She was recorded in the census on April 1, 1950, aged 1, in 1/2 Mi Left Indian Creek Road Off Euchleanna De Funuh Road, Bruce Creek, Walton, Florida, United States.

2283. CLIFFORD SCHOFIELD was born on June 13, 1941, in DeFuniak Springs, Walton, Florida, USA.
> Clifford Schofield, aged 26, married Peggy Joyce Garrett[2282], aged 19, on December 28, 1967 in Geneva, Geneva, Alabama, USA. They had two children:
>> Leslie Ann Schofield[3451] born on September 26, 1975 in Fort Walton Beach, Okaloosa, Florida, USA
>> Thomas Jefferson Schofield[3453] born on January 17, 1979 in Fort Walton Beach, Okaloosa, Florida, USA

2284. BILLIE MACK SMITH (see Descendants (45)) was born on September 5, 1942, in DeFuniak Springs, Walton, Florida, USA, to Mack Smith[1021] and Willie V. Rowell[1020]. He died on September 3, 1992, aged 49 years, in Bruce, Walton, Florida, USA.

2285. SHIRLEY ? was born on September 25, 1947, in Niceville, Okaloosa, Florida, USA.
> Billie Mack Smith[2284] married Shirley ?. They had one daughter:
>> Sharlene Suzette Smith[3454] born on February 9, 1966 in Niceville, Okaloosa, Florida, USA

2286. BILLIE JO SMITH (see Descendants (45)) was born on October 29, 1947, in Eglin Air Force Base, Okaloosa, Florida, USA, to Mack Smith[1021] and Willie V. Rowell[1020].

2287. FENTON BROOME COOK was born on August 25, 1938, in Culpepper, Culpeper, Virginia, USA.
> Fenton Broome Cook, aged 25, married Billie Jo Smith[2286], aged 16, on July 11, 1964 in Andalusia, Covington, Alabama, USA. They had two sons:
>> Rodney Fenton Cook[3455] born on May 11, 1965 in Niceville, Okaloosa, Florida, USA
>> Arnold Randall Cook[3457] born on August 7, 1969 in Fort Walton Beach, Okaloosa, Florida, USA

2288. BARBARA PAYLINE GILMEN (see Descendants (45)) was born on December 5, 1969, in Homestead Air Force Base, Dade, Florida, USA, to Russell Lee Gilmen[1025] and Bobbie Jean Smith[1024].

2289. MR. ?.
> Mr. ? married Barbara Payline Gilmen[2288]. They had one son:
>> Nicholas Tyler Gilmen[3458] born on August 22, 1992 in Eglin Air Force Base, Okaloosa, Florida, USA

2290. RUSSELL LEE GILMEN JR. (see Descendants (45)) was born on December 30, 1980, in Eglin Air Force Base, Okaloosa, Florida, USA, to Russell Lee Gilmen[1025] and Bobbie Jean Smith[1024].

2291. DEBORAH LEIGH GILMEN (see Descendants (45)) was born on February 22, 1992, in Homestead Air Force Base, Dade, Florida, USA, to Russell Lee Gilmen[1025] and Bobbie Jean Smith[1024].

2292. APRIL ROWELL (see Descendants (46)) was born to Henry Eral Rowell[1026] and Rhonda Lombard[1027].

2293. GARY ROWELL (see Descendants (46)) was born on June 22, 1962 to Henry Eral Rowell[1026] and Rhonda Lombard[1027].

2294. KIMBERLY ROWELL (see Descendants (46)) was born to Henry Eral Rowell[1026] and Rhonda Lombard[1027].

2295. HOPE ROWELL (see Descendants (46)) was born to Henry Eral Rowell[1026] and Rhonda Lombard[1027].

2296. COREEN ROWELL (see Descendants (46)) was born to Henry Eral Rowell[1026] and Rhonda Lombard[1027].

2297. TEREASA ROWELL (see Descendants (46)) was born to Henry Eral Rowell[1026] and Rhonda Lombard[1027].

2298. RUSSELL EDWARD ROWELL (see Descendants (46)) was born on August 18, 1959, in Panama City, Bay, Florida, USA, to Ervunus Rowell[1028] and Shelby D. Pierson[1029].
2299. KATHY RENEE JOYNER was born on May 4, 1962, in Panama City, Bay, Florida, USA.
> Russell Edward Rowell[2298], aged 19, married Kathy Renee Joyner, aged 16, on September 16, 1978 in Bay, Florida, USA. They had two sons:
>> Jason Derek Rowell[3459] born on November 18, 1980 in Tallahassee, Leon, Florida, USA
>> Christopher M. Rowell[3460] born on May 4, 1982 in Tallahassee, Leon, Florida, USA

2300. JAMES RANDALL ROWELL (see Descendants (46)) was born on September 10, 1961, in Panama City, Bay, Florida, USA, to Ervunus Rowell[1028] and Shelby D. Pierson[1029].
2301. JENNIFER MORRIS was born on February 7, 1969, in Panama City, Bay, Florida, USA.
> James Randall Rowell[2300], aged 24, married Jennifer Morris, aged 16, on September 13, 1985 in Panama City, Bay, Florida, USA.

2302. SHERRI MONEY (see Descendants (47)) was born on January 6, 1971, in Eglin Air Force Base, Okaloosa, Florida, USA, to Ruben Arnold Money Jr.[1032] and Hitomi Tsurski[1033].

2303. SCOTT MONEY (see Descendants (47)) was born on October 10, 1975, in Okaloosa, Florida, USA, to Ruben Arnold Money Jr.[1032] and Hitomi Tsurski[1033].

2304. JAMES PHILLOP ROETING (see Descendants (47)) was born on October 6, 1969, in Columbus, Lowndes, Mississippi, USA, to James B. Roeting[1035] and Eva Rosalind Money[1034].
- He died on March 22, 2006, aged 36, in Niceville, Okaloosa, Florida, USA.
- He was buried in Garden of Peace, Lot 359, Space B-A.

2305. KRISTOPHER LEE RINE (see Descendants (47)) was born on August 25, 1978, in Fort Walton Beach, Okaloosa, Florida, USA, to Thomas Lee Rine[1036] and Eva Rosalind Money[1034].

2306. RONALD DEWAYNE MONEY (see Descendants (47)) was born on October 8, 1972, in Fort Walton Beach, Okaloosa, Florida, USA, to Jimmy Ronald Money[1037] and Darlene Eldridge[1038].

2307. KELLI KAYE MONEY (see Descendants (47)) was born on November 2, 1974, in Fort Walton Beach, Okaloosa, Florida, USA, to Jimmy Ronald Money[1037] and Delores J Alford[1039].

2308. NANCY LEE CRAWFORD (see Descendants (50)) was born on July 9, 1950 to Lonnie Crawford[1048] and Genevieve Langley[1049].

2309. LONNIE RAY CRAWFORD JR. (see Descendants (50)) was born on June 18, 1952 to Lonnie Crawford[1048] and Genevieve Langley[1049].

2310. EUGENE CRAWFORD (see Descendants (50)) was born on August 3, 1953 to Lonnie Crawford[1048] and Genevieve Langley[1049].

2311. TINA CRAWFORD (see Descendants (50)) was born to Lonnie Crawford[1048] and Genevieve Langley[1049].

2312. SANDRA CRAWFORD (see Descendants (50)) was born to Lonnie Crawford[1048] and Genevieve Langley[1049].

2313. DEBBIE CRAWFORD (see Descendants (50)) was born to Lonnie Crawford[1048] and Genevieve Langley[1049].

2314. SHIRLEY MASON (see Descendants (50)) was born on October 22, 1949, in Florida, United States, to Robert Mason[1051] and Edna Mae Crawford[1050]. She was recorded in the census on April 1, 1950, as an infant, in 7th Barnes Lane, Brownsville-Brent-Goulding, Escambia, Florida, United States.
2315. HARRY ALVEREZ.
> Harry Alverez married Shirley Mason[2314].

2316. BARBARA PAYLINE MASON (see Descendants (50)) was born on October 7, 1951 to Robert Mason[1051] and Edna Mae Crawford[1050].

2317. JUANITA GALE CRAWFORD (see Descendants (50)) was born in March 31 A.D. to James Edmund Crawford[1052] and Ola Bell Madden[1053].

2318. PATRICIA JANE CRAWFORD (see Descendants (50)) was born on September 20, 1950 to James Edmund Crawford[1052] and Ola Bell Madden[1053].

2319. ANITA MARIE CRAWFORD (see Descendants (50)) was born on August 28, 1959 to James Edmund Crawford[1052] and Ola Bell Madden[1053].

2320. CHERYL LYNN CRAWFORD (see Descendants (50)) was born on April 26, 1961 to James Edmund Crawford[1052] and Ola Bell Madden[1053].

2321. DEBORAH ANN CRAWFORD (see Descendants (50)) was born to Herbert L Crawford[1054] and Peggy Hatchcock[1055].

2322. HERBERT CRAWFORD JR. (see Descendants (50)) was born on September 2, 1959 to Herbert L Crawford[1054] and Peggy Hatchcock[1055].

2323. MERLIN BARNHILL (see Descendants (50)) was born on February 7, 1954 to Merlin Barnhill[1057] and Betty Jean Crawford[1056].

2324. MIKIE BARNHILL (see Descendants (50)) was born to Merlin Barnhill[1057] and Betty Jean Crawford[1056].

2325. TAMMIE BARNHILL (see Descendants (50)) was born to Merlin Barnhill[1057] and Betty Jean Crawford[1056].

2326. ANGELIA BARNHILL (see Descendants (50)) was born to Merlin Barnhill[1057] and Betty Jean Crawford[1056].

2327. DARLENE BARNHILL (see Descendants (50)) was born to Merlin Barnhill[1057] and Betty Jean Crawford[1056].

2328. JOHN KENNETH CRAWFORD (see Descendants (50)) was born on October 15, 1968 to John Dallas Crawford[1058] and Faye Yawn[1059].
2329. CAROL YVONNE MORGAN was born on November 28, 1967, in Sweetwater, Monroe/McMinn, Tennesse, USA. John Kenneth Crawford[2328] married Carol Yvonne Morgan. They had four children:
    Ashlyn Morgan Crawford[3461] born on December 4, 1988
    Apryl Michelle Crawford[3462] born on April 26, 1990
    Jesse Tanner Crawford[3463] born on April 17, 1992
    Dillon John Crawford[3464] born on December 15, 1993

2330. CYNTHIA RENEE BASS (see Descendants (51)) was born on July 18, 1955 to Billy Ray Bass[1063] and Joyce Merline Russell[1064].

2331. MICHAEL ZOREE BASS (see Descendants (51)) was born on December 4, 1959 to Billy Ray Bass[1063] and Joyce Merline Russell[1064].

2332. RICHARD ALLEN BASS (see Descendants (51)) was born on May 18, 1962 to Billy Ray Bass[1063] and Joyce Merline Russell[1064].

2333. THERESA DARLYNE JONES (see Descendants (51)) was born on July 29, 1954, in Orlando Regional Hospital, Orlando, Orange Co., Florida, to Horace Emmete Jones[1069] and Theresa Annette Bass[1068]. She was baptized on July 9, 1978, aged 23, in Methodist Church of Pine Castle, Florida.

2334. CONNIE DENISE JONES (see Descendants (51)) was born on April 29, 1957 to Horace Emmete Jones[1069] and Theresa Annette Bass[1068].

2335. RICKEY THOMAS BASS (see Descendants (51)) was born on January 3, 1958 to Thomas Franklin Bass[1072] and Bobbie Ann Pruitt[1073].

2336. BECKY RENE BASS (see Descendants (51)) was born on June 22, 1967 to Thomas Franklin Bass[1072] and Bobbie Ann Pruitt[1073].

2337. RHONDA ELAINE BASS (see Descendants (51)) was born on June 1, 1959 to Jasper Daniel Bass[1074] and Judith Ann Lewis[1075].

Direct Relations

2338. SUSAN ELIZABETH BASS (see Descendants (51)) was born on September 2, 1961 to Jasper Daniel Bass[1074] and Judith Ann Lewis[1075].

2339. JASPER DANNIEL BASS JR. (see Descendants (51)) was born on February 12, 1963 to Jasper Daniel Bass[1074] and Judith Ann Lewis[1075].

2340. JANET LOUISE BASS (see Descendants (53)) was born on January 6, 1966 to William Dallas Bass[1080] and Patricia Ann Smith[1081].

2341. ROBERT DOM BASS (see Descendants (54)) was born on November 5, 1966 to Marvin Dallas Bass Jr.[1085] and Sharon Treasa Barrow[1086].

2342. DEBBIE LYNN SMITH.
> Robert Dom Bass[2341], aged 24, married Debbie Lynn Smith on December 1, 1990.

2343. HANK DALLAS BASS SR. (see Descendants (54)) was born on September 11, 1969 to Marvin Dallas Bass Jr.[1085] and Sharon Treasa Barrow[1086].

2344. MARY ANN BEHM was born on March 8, 1970.
> Hank Dallas Bass Sr.[2343], aged 21, married Mary Ann Behm, aged 21, on September 10, 1991. They had four children:
>> Hank Dallas Bass Jr.[3465] born on March 27, 1992
>> Michael Anthony Bass[3467] born on December 28, 1993
>> Treasa Ann Bass[3468] born on December 14, 1995
>> Zachary Daniel Bass[3469] born on August 28, 1997

2345. JOSHUA EDMUND BASS (see Descendants (54)) was born on July 23, 1980 to Marvin Dallas Bass Jr.[1085] and Sharon Treasa Barrow[1086].

2346. JAMES EDWARD BASS JR. (see Descendants (54)) was born on April 2, 1968 to James Edward Bass[1088] and Linda Cook[1089].

2347. RONNIE DUANE NALL II (see Descendants (55)) was born to Ronald Duane Nall[1090] and Dena Glover[1091].

2348. MELISSA BASS (see Descendants (56)) was born on December 12, 1972 to Gerald Howard Bass Jr.[1094] and Teresa Griffin[1095].

2349. CHAD HOWARD BASS (see Descendants (56)) was born on June 25, 1975 to Gerald Howard Bass Jr.[1094] and Teresa Griffin[1095].

2350. KYLE BASS (see Descendants (56)) was born on September 13, 1988 to Gerald Howard Bass Jr.[1094] and Teresa Griffin[1095].

2351. ANTHONY MCGILL (see Descendants (56)) was born to James Anthony McGill[1097] and Wanda Bass[1096].

2352. AARON MCGILL (see Descendants (56)) was born on September 12, 1981 to James Anthony McGill[1097] and Wanda Bass[1096].

2353. HEATHER LEE CEURVELS (see Descendants (56)) was born on November 18, 1976 to Mr. Ceurvels[1099] and Rhonda Bass[1098].

2354. JESSICA CEURVELS (see Descendants (56)) was born on March 6, 1981 to Mr. Ceurvels[1099] and Rhonda Bass[1098].

2355. KAITLYN MORRELL (see Descendants (56)) was born on March 28, 1992 to Steven C. Morrell[1101] and Tonya Bass[1100].

2356. BRITTANY MORRELL (see Descendants (56)) was born on May 8, 1995 to Steven C. Morrell[1101] and Tonya Bass[1100].

2357. PEGGY LEE HUCKABAA (see Descendants (57)) was born on July 4, 1954, in Florala, Covington, Alabama, USA, to James Harold Huckaba[1102] and Cora Lee Wilcox[1103].

2358. **WILLIAM EARL NEWMANN.**
>William Earl Newmann married Peggy Lee Huckabaa[2357], aged 17, on May 20, 1972 in Madison, Madison, Florida, USA. They had two children:
>>William Issac Newmann[3470] born on October 23, 1973
>>Lorrie Leigh Newmann[3471] born on June 26, 1982 in Clearwater, Pinellas, Florida, USA

2359. **DONNIE LEE HUCKABAA** (see Descendants (57)) was born on December 24, 1955, in Tampa, Hillsborough, Florida, USA, to James Harold Huckaba[1102] and Cora Lee Wilcox[1103]. Donnie Lee became known as "Don". Donnie Lee married twice. He was married to Shiela Little[2360] and Susan Simon[2361].

2360. **SHIELA LITTLE.**
>Donnie Lee Huckabaa[2359], aged -1936, married Shiela Little in April 20 A.D. in Georgia, USA, and they were divorced. They had two sons:
>>David Lee Huckabaa[3472] born on July 12, 1984 in Georgia, USA
>>Billy J Huckabaa[3473] born on December 4, 1986 in Belgium

2361. **SUSAN SIMON.**
>Donnie Lee Huckabaa[2359], aged 38, married Susan Simon on June 10, 1994 in Augusta, Richmond, Georgia, USA.

2362. **DEMAS MARK HUCKABAA** (see Descendants (57)) was born on March 7, 1959, in Saint Cloud, Osceola, Florida, USA, to James Harold Huckaba[1102] and Cora Lee Wilcox[1103].
Demas Mark married twice. He was married to Deborah Ingram[2363] and Teresa Hargabus[2364].

2363. **DEBORAH INGRAM.**
>Demas Mark Huckabaa[2362] married Deborah Ingram. They had one daughter:
>>Deborah Sue Huckabaa[3474] born on October 11, 1981 in Sarasota, Sarasota, Florida, USA

2364. **TERESA HARGABUS** was born on July 28, 1959.
>Demas Mark Huckabaa[2362], aged 33, married Teresa Hargabus, aged 33, on August 10, 1992 in Walton, Florida, USA. They had one son:
>>Demas James Huckabaa[3475] born on September 22, 1993 in Pensacola, Escambia, Florida, USA

2365. **PHYLLIS ANN HUCKABAA** (see Descendants (57)) was born on December 10, 1960, in Tampa, Hillsborough, Florida, USA, to James Harold Huckaba[1102] and Cora Lee Wilcox[1103].

2366. **MARK MACKO.**
>Mark Macko married Phyllis Ann Huckabaa[2365], aged 20, on April 17, 1981. They had one daughter:
>>Cora Marie Macko[3476] born on April 4, 1990 in Ozark, Dale, Alabama, USA

2367. **EDGAR HUGH HUCKABAA** (see Descendants (57)) was born on September 1, 1963, in Plant City, Hillsboro, Florida, USA, to James Harold Huckaba[1102] and Cora Lee Wilcox[1103].

2368. **BEVERLY LYNN WITTMYER.**
>Edgar Hugh Huckabaa[2367], aged 20, married Beverly Lynn Wittmyer on December 3, 1983 in Okaloosa, Florida, USA. They had two children:
>>Jason Hugh Huckabaa[3477] born on March 5, 1984 in Walton, Florida, USA
>>Crystal Lynn Huckabaa[3478] born on July 8, 1988 in Walton, Florida, USA

2369. **JAMES RUDOLF HUCKABAA** (see Descendants (57)) was born on October 22, 1964, in Tampa, Hillsborough, Florida, USA, to James Harold Huckaba[1102] and Cora Lee Wilcox[1103]. James Rudolf became known as "Rudy".

2370. **MS. TRISHA.**
>James Rudolf Huckabaa[2369] married Ms. Trisha. They had one daughter:
>>Ashli Chere Huckabaa[3479] born on January 24, 1986 in Ozark, Dale, Alabama, USA

2371. **BETTY JUNE SNELLGROVE** (see Descendants (57)) was born on August 10, 1951 to Coley Joseph Snellgrove[1105] and Clara Mae Huckabaa[1104].

2372. **MICHAEL C. WALTERS** was born on May 17, 1950.
>Michael C. Walters married Betty June Snellgrove[2371]. They had two sons:
>>David C. Snellgrove[3480] born on October 16, 1970
>>Michael Shane Walters[3481] born on July 26, 1975

2373. **RUDY VON SNELLGROVE** (see Descendants (57)) was born on February 18, 1953 to Coley Joseph Snellgrove[1105] and Clara Mae Huckabaa[1104].

2374. **MS. ?.**
>Rudy Von Snellgrove[2373] married Ms. ?. They had two children:
>>Travis Snellgrove[3482] born on January 11, 1979
>>Tristan L. Snellgrove[3483] born on September 12, 1984

Direct Relations

2375. ROGER HENRY SNELLGROVE (see Descendants (57)) was born on September 16, 1955 to Coley Joseph Snellgrove[1105] and Clara Mae Huckabaa[1104].
2376. REBECCA LONOEL was born on September 20, 1956.
> Roger Henry Snellgrove[2375] married Rebecca Lonoel. They had two daughters:
>> Amanda Mae Snellgrove[3484] born on April 7, 1980
>> Katie Lucrieta Snellgrove[3485] born on December 5, 1983

2377. JUDY ANN SNELLGROVE (see Descendants (57)) was born on February 3, 1957 to Coley Joseph Snellgrove[1105] and Clara Mae Huckabaa[1104].
2378. JOHN WILLIAM SCOTT was born on February 3, 1960.
> John William Scott married Judy Ann Snellgrove[2377]. They had four children:
>> Keisha Lynn Barnes[3486] born on September 23, 1977
>> Crystal Sheree Barnes[3487] born on September 24, 1980
>> Sharley Jo Scott[3488] born on December 10, 1990
>> John Timberlake Scott[3489] born on May 16, 1994

2379. RANDY MICHAEL HUCKABA (see Descendants (57)) was born on November 3, 1956 to Edward Ervin Huckaba[1106] and Betty Jean Harrison[1107].

2380. CRAIG ALAN HUCKABA (see Descendants (57)) was born on May 10, 1958 to Edward Ervin Huckaba[1106] and Betty Jean Harrison[1107].

2381. KAREN ELIZABETH HUCKABA (see Descendants (57)) was born on November 26, 1959 to Edward Ervin Huckaba[1106] and Betty Jean Harrison[1107].

2382. CONNIE ARLENE HUCKABA (see Descendants (57)) was born on July 31, 1961 to Edward Ervin Huckaba[1106] and Betty Jean Harrison[1107].

2383. MYRA LORRAINE HUCKABA (see Descendants (57)) was born on June 25, 1963 to Edward Ervin Huckaba[1106] and Betty Jean Harrison[1107].

2384. SHERRI LEIGH WILSON (see Descendants (57)) was born in April 4 A.D. to James Walter Ansley[1110] and Mary Opal Huckabaa[1109].
> Sherri Leigh gave birth to four children:
>> Randy Scarbrough[3490]
>> Eric ?[3491]
>> Tiffany ?[3492]
>> Timothy ?[3493]

2385. DALE EDGAR ANSLEY (see Descendants (57)) was born on January 13, 1960 to James Walter Ansley[1110] and Mary Opal Huckabaa[1109].
2386. CHRISTINE ALFORD was born on September 28, 1972.
> Dale Edgar Ansley[2385] married Christine Alford. They had two children:
>> Dale Edgar Ansley[3494] born on April 16, 1990
>> Tiffany Leighann Ansley[3495] born on December 12, 1990

2387. JOANNE MARIE ANSLEY (see Descendants (57)) was born on November 14, 1960 to James Walter Ansley[1110] and Mary Opal Huckabaa[1109].
Joanne Marie married twice. She was married to Kenneth Allen Guthrie[2388] and Wayne Stokes[2389].
2388. KENNETH ALLEN GUTHRIE was born on November 14, 1962.
> Kenneth Allen Guthrie married Joanne Marie Ansley[2387]. They had two daughters:
>> Mary Elizabeth Guthrie[3496] born on March 15, 1980
>> Jacqueline Marie Guthrie[3497] born on October 18, 1981

2389. WAYNE STOKES.
> Wayne Stokes married Joanne Marie Ansley[2387].

2390. LYVON WALTER ANSLEY (see Descendants (57)) was born on February 23, 1961 to James Walter Ansley[1110] and Mary Opal Huckabaa[1109].
2391. CELETHA DIANNE SCHOFIELD was born in September 24 A.D.
> Lyvon Walter Ansley[2390] married Celetha Dianne Schofield. They had two daughters:
>> Carrie Denise Ansley[3498] born on January 6, 1983
>> Summer Lyvon Ansley[3499] born on June 12, 1985

2392. JAMES WILLIAM ANSLEY (see Descendants (57)) was born on March 24, 1967 to James Walter Ansley[1110] and Mary Opal Huckabaa[1109].
2393. CHANDRA JEAN DE SHEPPRA was born on April 18, 1970.
   James William Ansley[2392] married Chandra Jean De Sheppra.

2394. SHONDA DENISE HUCKABA (see Descendants (57)) was born on October 11, 1965 to Earl Flyn Huckaba[1111] and Angela Crusel Nix[1112].
   Shonda Denise had three partnerships. She was married to Chris Camp[2395]. She was also the partner of Mr. ?[2396] and Mr. ?[2397].

2395. CHRIS CAMP.
   Chris Camp married Shonda Denise Huckaba[2394], aged about 33, from February 2, 1998 to 2000, and they were divorced.
2396. MR. ?.
   Mr. ? and Shonda Denise Huckaba[2394] had one daughter:
      Brittany Nash Huckaba[3500] born on October 26, 1988
   The following information is also recorded for this family:
      • Unknown Relationship.
2397. MR. ?.
   Mr. ? and Shonda Denise Huckaba[2394] had one son:
      Zachariah Tyler Permenter[3502] born on August 30, 1990
   The following information is also recorded for this family:
      • Unknown Relationship.

2398. TIRESA LYNN HUCKABA (see Descendants (57)) was born on December 17, 1967 to Earl Flyn Huckaba[1111] and Angela Crusel Nix[1112].
   Tiresa Lynn married four times. She was married to David Bigger[2399], Kurt Allen Stout[2400], David Pool[2401] and Jerry Edwards[2402].
2399. DAVID BIGGER. He died in August 1987.
   David Bigger married Tiresa Lynn Huckaba[2398], aged 18, on August 1, 1986. They had two daughters:
      Amber Lynn Bigger[3503] born on June 3, 1986
      Angela Tonya Bigger[3505] born on August 3, 1986
   The following information is also recorded for this family:
      • Death of Spouse.
2400. KURT ALLEN STOUT.
   Kurt Allen Stout married Tiresa Lynn Huckaba[2398], aged about 31, from July 11, 1992 to 2006, and they were divorced. They had one son:
      Aaron Eli Stout[3507] born on January 4, 1993
2401. DAVID POOL.
   David Pool married Tiresa Lynn Huckaba[2398], aged about 46, from February 21, 2013 to 2016, and they were divorced.
2402. JERRY EDWARDS was born on December 11, 1968.
   Jerry married twice. He was married to Tiresa Lynn Huckaba[2398] and Ms. ?.
      Jerry Edwards, aged 48, married Tiresa Lynn Huckaba[2398], aged 49, on July 19, 2017.
      Jerry Edwards married Ms. ?. They had one daughter:
         Emilie Edwards born on July 31, 1996

2403. EARL FLYN HUCKABA II (see Descendants (57)) was born on March 11, 1972 to Earl Flyn Huckaba[1111] and Angela Crusel Nix[1112].
   Earl Flyn married three times. He was married to Tanya Rae Ceynar[2404], Amy Micha Windham[2405] and Bobbie Fay Roper[2406].

2404. TANYA RAE CEYNAR.
   Earl Flyn Huckaba II[2403], aged about 24, married Tanya Rae Ceynar from August 18, 1992 to 1999, and they were divorced. They had two sons:
      Austen James Huckaba[3508] born on March 5, 1993
      Jayden Earl Huckaba[3509] born on March 3, 1994

Direct Relations

2405. AMY MICHA WINDHAM.
> Earl Flyn Huckaba II[2403], aged about 35, married Amy Micha Windham from June 1, 2001 to 2013, and they were divorced. They had two daughters:
>> Harlee Fay Huckaba[3510] born on October 8, 2002
>> Samantha Diane Huckaba[3511]

2406. BOBBIE FAY ROPER was born on December 22, 1978.
> Bobbie Fay had two partnerships. She was married to Earl Flyn Huckaba II[2403]. She was also the partner of Mr. Harris.
> Earl Flyn Huckaba II[2403], aged 43, married Bobbie Fay Roper, aged 36, on June 11, 2015.
> Mr. Harris and Bobbie Fay Roper had one daughter:
>> Kandace Lane Harris born on May 21, 1997
> The following information is also recorded for this family:
> • Unknown Relationship.

2407. KIMMIE DALLAS POSEY (see Descendants (58)) was born on March 28, 1963, in Crestview, Okaloosa, Florida, USA, to James Edward Posey[1115] and Janice Turner[1116].

2408. PAMELA HICKS.
> Kimmie Dallas Posey[2407], aged 18, married Pamela Hicks on October 26, 1981. They had two children:
>> Sarah Jane Posey[3514] born on August 22, 1985 in North Carolina, USA
>> James Preston Friday Posey[3515] born on May 20, 1987 in Raleigh, Wake, North Carolina, USA

2409. MARY KATHERINE POSEY (see Descendants (58)) was born on September 17, 1966, in Crestview, Okaloosa, Florida, USA, to James Edward Posey[1115] and Janice Turner[1116].

2410. BOBBY BENOIT.
> Bobby Benoit married Mary Katherine Posey[2409], aged 20, on January 8, 1987. They had two sons:
>> Matthew Paul Benoit[3516] born on July 21, 1988 in North Carolina, USA
>> Caleb Joseph Benoit[3517] born on March 11, 1992 in North Carolina, USA

2411. DIANE FAYE POSEY (see Descendants (58)) was born on September 16, 1967, in Crestview, Okaloosa, Florida, USA, to James Edward Posey[1115] and Janice Turner[1116].

2412. JOE BOOKER.
> Joe Booker married Diane Faye Posey[2411]. They had one daughter:
>> Jenny Nicole Booker[3518] born on April 29, 1983 in Crestview, Okaloosa, Florida, USA

2413. SHAWN MICHAEL POSEY (see Descendants (58)) was born on June 5, 1974, in Massachuttes, USA, to James Edward Posey[1115] and Brenda F. Hope[1117].

2414. HOPE MYCHELLE POSEY (see Descendants (58)) was born on May 27, 1980, in Morgan City, St. Mary Parish, Lousiana, USA, to James Edward Posey[1115] and Brenda F. Hope[1117].

2415. BRETT BERNARD MOYLAN (see Descendants (60)) was born on July 31, 1972, in Pensacola, Escambia, Florida, USA, to Patrick Bernard Moylan[1123] and Linda Louise Posey[1122].

2416. SHANNA MICHELLE POSEY (see Descendants (60)) was born on April 10, 1981, in Pensacola, Escambia, Florida, USA, to Martin James Posey[1124] and Linda Mobley[1125].

2417. CASEY LAUREN POSEY (see Descendants (60)) was born on October 13, 1984, in Pensacola, Escambia, Florida, USA, to Martin James Posey[1124] and Linda Mobley[1125].

2418. WILLIAM DENTON POSEY (see Descendants (60)) was born on July 28, 1982, in Pensacola, Escambia, Florida, USA, to Larry Denton Posey[1126] and Jacqueline Dianne Barron[1127].

2419. LAURIN BOTTS.
> William Denton Posey[2418] married Laurin Botts.

2420. NATHAN EDWARD POSEY (see Descendants (60)) was born on June 25, 1987, in Pensacola, Escambia, Florida, USA, to Larry Denton Posey[1126] and Jacqueline Dianne Barron[1127].

2421. HUDSON WOODFIN JR. (see Descendants (61)) was born on May 17, 1966, in Escambia, Florida, USA, to Hudson Woodfin Sr.[1132] and Patriciea Ernestine Stewart[1131].

2422. JENNIFER DENISE COTTON was born on November 26, 1968, in Atmore, Escambia, Alabama, USA.
Hudson Woodfin Jr.[2421], aged 27, married Jennifer Denise Cotton, aged 24, on July 17, 1993 in Walnut Hill, Escambia, Florida, USA.

2423. ROBERT LEE WOODFIN (see Descendants (61)) was born on June 21, 1968, in Escambia, Florida, USA, to Hudson Woodfin Sr.[1132] and Patriciea Ernestine Stewart[1131].

2424. MARTIN EDWARD WOODFIN (see Descendants (61)) was born on January 4, 1970, in Escambia, Florida, USA, to Hudson Woodfin Sr.[1132] and Patriciea Ernestine Stewart[1131].

2425. MELANIE JEAN ADAMS was born on March 24, 1966, in Jacksonville, Onslow, North Carolina, USA.
Martin Edward Woodfin[2424] married Melanie Jean Adams.

2426. BARBARA RENEE DIEGLEMAN (see Descendants (61)) was born on March 8, 1962 to Don P. Diegleman[1135] and Barbara Ann Stewart[1133].

2427. BONNIE MARIE DIEGLEMAN (see Descendants (61)) was born on August 24, 1964 to Don P. Diegleman[1135] and Barbara Ann Stewart[1133].

2428. RHONDEL LONDON DIEGLEMAN (see Descendants (61)) was born on January 16, 1966 to Don P. Diegleman[1135] and Barbara Ann Stewart[1133].

2429. BRIAN SCOTT DIEGLEMAN (see Descendants (61)) was born in October 1968 to Don P. Diegleman[1135] and Barbara Ann Stewart[1133].

2430. CLIFTON VEAL STEWART (see Descendants (61)) was born on June 14, 1963 to Betty Sue Stewart[1137].
2431. DENISE ?.
Clifton Veal Stewart[2430] married Denise ?.

2432. JASON WAYNE COOK (see Descendants (61)) was born on April 29, 1975 to Thurman Paul Cook[1138] and Betty Sue Stewart[1137].

2433. TERRY LYNN COOK (see Descendants (61)) was born on September 29, 1977 to Thurman Paul Cook[1138] and Betty Sue Stewart[1137].

2434. SHELIA DIANE STEWART (see Descendants (61)) was born on October 14, 1968, in Pensacola, Escambia, Florida, USA, to Ernest Dewayne Stewart[1139] and Mary Jo Taylor[1140].
2435. CHRISTOPHER JOHN DEATON was born on October 10, 1966, in Shelby, Cleveland, North Carolina, USA.
Christopher John Deaton, aged 21, married Shelia Diane Stewart[2434], aged 19, on September 25, 1988 in Escambia, Florida, USA. They had two sons:
Aaron Lee Deaton[3519] born on June 18, 1989 in Pensacola, Escambia, Florida, USA
Cory Eugene Deaton[3520] born on May 3, 1990 in Pensacola, Escambia, Florida, USA

2436. RACHEL LEE STEWART (see Descendants (61)) was born on January 3, 1982, in Pensacola, Escambia, Florida, USA, to Ernest Dewayne Stewart[1139] and Patricia Elaine Tomlins[1141].

2437. MICHELLE LANE DANLEY (see Descendants (61)) was born on February 7, 1968, in Escambia, Florida, USA, to Mikeal Wayne Danley[1143] and Shirley Jane Stewart[1142].

2438. SHERRY DENISE DANLEY (see Descendants (61)) was born on August 10, 1972, in Escambia, Florida, USA, to Mikeal Wayne Danley[1143] and Shirley Jane Stewart[1142].

2439. ANGELA CRYSTAL DISHMAN (see Descendants (61)) was born on September 22, 1974 to Roger Dishman[1146] and Mary Elizabeth Stewart[1145].

2440. HEATHER LYNN WESTERVELT (see Descendants (61)) was born on October 22, 1975 to Kenny Westervelt[1147] and Mary Elizabeth Stewart[1145].

2441. DERRICK STEWART (see Descendants (61)) was born in March 2 A.D., in Escambia, Florida, USA, to Ernest Stewart Jr.[1149] and Ms. Nolana[1150].

2442. STEVEN STEWART (see Descendants (61)) was born in Escambia, Florida, USA to Ernest Stewart Jr.[1149] and Ms. Nolana[1150].

Direct Relations

2443. LEAANNE STEWART (see Descendants (61)) was born to Ernest Stewart Jr.[1149] and Judy Sable[1151].

2444. LYNN JESSE GARRETT JR. (see Descendants (63)) was born on July 12, 1964 to Lynn Jesse Garrett Sr.[1165] and Joyce Marie Posey[1164].

2445. TRACY CLARK was born on July 25, 1974.
   Lynn Jesse Garrett Jr.[2444], aged 30, married Tracy Clark, aged 20, on October 22, 1994.

2446. LANA JOYCE POSEY GARRETT (see Descendants (63)) was born on December 18, 1969 to Lynn Jesse Garrett Sr.[1165] and Joyce Marie Posey[1164].

2447. JOEL LINAM was born on October 9, 1966.
   Joel Linam, aged 27, married Lana Joyce Posey Garrett[2446], aged 24, on July 23, 1994.

2448. JEFFERY ALAN JOHNS JR. (see Descendants (63)) was born on May 23, 1981 to Jeffery Alan Johns[1167] and Marsha Ann Posey[1166].

2449. JOSEPH AARON JOHNS (see Descendants (63)) was born on July 3, 1991 to Jeffery Alan Johns[1167] and Marsha Ann Posey[1166]. Joseph Aaron became known as "Joey". He died on September 23, 2020, aged 29.

2450. STACIE LEANN POSEY (see Descendants (63)) was born on January 9, 1981 to Ceavie Edward Posey Jr.[1168] and Deborah Joann Bradley[1169].

2451. JASON EDWARD POSEY (see Descendants (63)) was born on May 18, 1982 to Ceavie Edward Posey Jr.[1168] and Deborah Joann Bradley[1169].

2452. STEFANIE MARSHANN HOWARD (see Descendants (63)) was born on August 11, 1980 to William Jesse Howard[1171] and Jennifer Kim Posey[1170].

2453. SUSAN CLAIRE BARKSDALE (see Descendants (64)) was born on October 2, 1977 to William J. Barksdale[1174] and Sandra Ann Wallace[1173].

2454. AMY MELISSA WALLACE (see Descendants (64)) was born on October 24, 1976 to Phillip Aurthur Wallace[1175] and Pamela Jane Murphree[1176].

2455. ANDREW MIDDLETON WALLACE (see Descendants (64)) was born on April 28, 1981 to Phillip Aurthur Wallace[1175] and Pamela Jane Murphree[1176].

2456. CHARLES WILLIAM WALLACE (see Descendants (64)) was born on October 16, 1978 to William Holley Wallace[1177] and Jada Harvey[1178].

2457. CHRISTOPHER EDWARD WALLACE (see Descendants (64)) was born on September 17, 1983 to William Holley Wallace[1177] and Jada Harvey[1178].

2458. CHAD ALEXANDER WALLACE (see Descendants (64)) was born on October 7, 1987 to William Holley Wallace[1177] and Jada Harvey[1178].

2459. JAMES HOLLEY BASS (see Descendants (64)) was born on January 23, 1970 to James Michael Bass[1179] and Linda Ridge[1180].

2460. BRIAN BASS (see Descendants (64)) was born on February 17, 1977 to James Michael Bass[1179] and Linda Ridge[1180].

2461. JOHN STEPHEN LINCOLN (see Descendants (64)) was born on June 10, 1975 to John Richard Lincoln[1182] and Patricia Annelle Bass[1181].

2462. ELIZABETH ANNELLE LINCOLN (see Descendants (64)) was born on July 6, 1978 to John Richard Lincoln[1182] and Patricia Annelle Bass[1181].

2463. ERIC DOUGLAS BASS (see Descendants (64)) was born on April 8, 1974 to Roger Douglas Bass[1183] and Pamela Nunn[1184].

2464. SETH JEFFREY BASS (see Descendants (64)) was born on June 15, 1982 to Jeffrey Marlin Bass[1185] and Susan Wittman[1186].

2465. JASON KYLE DEGRAAF (see Descendants (64)) was born on December 25, 1972 to Jerry Degraaf[1188] and Dottie Lynn Bass[1187].

2466. AMANDA MICHELLE DEGRAAF (see Descendants (64)) was born on March 8, 1975 to Jerry Degraaf[1188] and Dottie Lynn Bass[1187].

2467. ADAM DEAN BASS (see Descendants (64)) was born on February 4, 1975 to Dudley Dean Bass[1189] and Donna Cook[1190].

2468. ERIN LEIGH BASS (see Descendants (64)) was born on April 21, 1977 to Dudley Dean Bass[1189] and Donna Cook[1190].

2469. LORIN HOLLY BASS (see Descendants (64)) was born on August 19, 1981 to Dudley Dean Bass[1189] and Donna Cook[1190].

2470. JANET KAY BASS (see Descendants (64)) was born on December 12, 1986 to Dudley Dean Bass[1189] and Donna Cook[1190].

2471. AMY ELIZABETH BASS (see Descendants (64)) was born on November 7, 1988 to Dudley Dean Bass[1189] and Donna Cook[1190].

2472. JOANNA NICHOLE GRIFFITH (see Descendants (65)) was born on December 14, 1971 to Stephen Dale Griffith[1196] and Pam Nichols[1197].

2473. DUSTY W. ADAMS.
    Dusty W. Adams married Joanna Nichole Griffith[2472]. They had one son:
        Dillon Wayne Adams[3521] born on January 16, 1992

2474. STACIE RENEE GRIFFITH (see Descendants (65)) was born on October 4, 1979 to Stephen Dale Griffith[1196] and Pam Nichols[1197].

2475. MICHAEL A. ERMY (see Descendants (65)) was born on June 11, 1979 to Anthony F. Ermy[1199] and Theresa Ann Griffith[1198].

2476. DANIEL P. ERMY (see Descendants (65)) was born on March 10, 1983 to Anthony F. Ermy[1199] and Theresa Ann Griffith[1198].

2477. NATHINAL HOOKS (see Descendants (65)) was born on January 10, 1985 to Roger Hooks[1204] and Brenda Bass[1203].

2478. ASHTON TOBIAS (see Descendants (65)) was born on December 11, 1989 to John L. Tobias[1206] and Yvonne Bass[1205].

2479. SAM MICHAEL BASS (see Descendants (65)) was born on September 2, 1992 to Michael Douglas Bass[1208] and Suzanne Rankin[1209].

Direct Relations

2480. ELIZABETH ANN BASS (see Descendants (65)) was born on December 2, 1993 to Michael Douglas Bass[1208] and Suzanne Rankin[1209].

2481. DEVIN PHILLIPS ADAMS (see Descendants (212)) was born on March 15, 1988 to Walter Dean Adams[1214] and Mary Jo[1215].
2482. MS. ?.
>   Devin Phillips Adams[2481] and Ms. ? had one daughter:
>   >   Layla Adams[3522]
>   The following information is also recorded for this family:
>   - Unknown Relationship.

2483. LINDSEY NICHOLE ADAMS (see Descendants (212)) was born on June 16, 1989 to Walter Dean Adams[1214] and Mary Jo[1215].
2484. CHRISTOPHER WILLIS. He died in 2015.
>   Christopher Willis married Lindsey Nichole Adams[2483]. They had two children:
>   >   Nathan Willis[3523] born in 2009
>   >   Candace Willis[3524] born in 2012

2485. DEVIN RANDAL ADAMS (see Descendants (212)) was born on May 27, 1987 to Walter Dean Adams[1214] and Tammy Theford Blair[1216].
2486. ASHLEY JOHNSON ADAMS was born on July 26, 1987.
>   Devin Randal Adams[2485], aged 24, married Ashley Johnson Adams, aged 24, on March 24, 2012. They had two sons:
>   >   Hudson Adams[3525] born on May 24, 2013
>   >   Everett Adams[3526] born on March 8, 2020

2487. KAYLA DANIELLE ADAMS (see Descendants (212)) was born on February 15, 1989 to Walter Dean Adams[1214] and Tammy Theford Blair[1216].

2488. ROGER DALE BASS JR. (see Descendants (213)) was born on June 11, 1985 to Roger Dale Bass[1218] and Donna ?[1219].

2489. TAMMY SPITHOULER (see Descendants (65)) was born to James Farris Bass[1223].

2490. JOHN WILLIAM BASS JR. (see Descendants (66)) was born on May 4, 1970, in Auburn, Lee, Alabama, USA, to John William Bass Sr.[1226] and Celia Anne Farrar[1227].
2491. KELLY PUSEY. Kelly became known as "Tiny".
>   John William Bass Jr.[2490], aged 27, married Kelly Pusey on August 16, 1997. They had three children:
>   >   William Cooper Bass[3527] born on May 23, 2000
>   >   Alexander Riley Bass[3528] born on December 5, 2003
>   >   Ava Claire Bass[3529] born on February 14, 2006

2492. JOEL FARRAR BASS (see Descendants (66)) was born on January 13, 1975, in Winter Park, Orange, Florida, USA, to John William Bass Sr.[1226] and Celia Anne Farrar[1227].
2493. ALLISON MCCORKLE.
>   Joel Farrar Bass[2492], aged 24, married Allison McCorkle on June 19, 1999. They had two children:
>   >   Farrar Courtney Bass[3530] born on September 16, 2004
>   >   Dray Rolen Bass[3531] born on October 19, 2007

2494. JOEL SIDNEY BASS III (see Descendants (66)) was born to Joel Sidney Bass Jr.[1228] and Gina Joy Behr[1229].

2495. JULIA ELIZABETH BASS (see Descendants (66)) was born to Joel Sidney Bass Jr.[1228] and Gina Joy Behr[1229].

2496. DENNIS MICHAEL OLVANY (see Descendants (66)) was born on December 17, 1976, in Saint Joe, Gulf, Florida, USA, to Dennis Paul Olvany[1231] and Margueritte Dawn Bolding[1230].

2497. MATTHEW STEPHEN OLVANY (see Descendants (66)) was born on December 12, 1979, in Metairie, Jefferson Parish, Louisianna, USA, to Dennis Paul Olvany[1231] and Margueritte Dawn Bolding[1230].

2498. HEATHER AMANDA KINMAN (see Descendants (66)) was born on May 15, 1978, in Geneva, Geneva, Alabama, USA, to Gary Glenn Kinman[1233] and Lynda Ann Byrd[1232].

2499. BO MANRY.
> Bo Manry married Heather Amanda Kinman[2498].

2500. JENNIFER MICHELLE MONARCH (see Descendants (66)) was born on February 24, 1985, in Mesa, Maricopa, Arizona, USA, to Gary Anthony Monarch[1235] and Mychaelle Joy Byrd[1234].

2501. MR. LEONARD.
> Mr. Leonard married Jennifer Michelle Monarch[2500]. They had one child:
> Mr./Ms. Leonard[3532]

2502. AMANDA RYAN MCGLAMERY (see Descendants (66)) was born on November 23, 1980, in Tallahassee, Leon, Florida, USA, to Sidney T. McGlamery[1237] and Nancy Jane Byrd[1236].

2503. MYCHAELLE ANN MCGLAMERY (see Descendants (66)) was born on April 19, 1983, in Tallahassee, Leon, Florida, USA, to Sidney T. McGlamery[1237] and Nancy Jane Byrd[1236].

2504. BRONWYN ELISE CHELETTE (see Descendants (66)) was born on September 14, 1994, in Tallahassee, Leon, Florida, USA, to Herman Edward Chelette III[1244] and Angelia Renee Kilcrease[1242].

2505. SEAN ANDERSON (see Descendants (66)) was born on June 15, 1970, in Shreveport, Caddo Parish, Louisiana, USA, to Ray Elliot Anderson[1246] and Judith Bass[1245].
The following information is also recorded for Sean:
• Military Service.
Note: *Desert Storm.*
(Military Service)

2506. ASHLEY LEIGH ANDERSON (see Descendants (66)) was born on April 10, 1980, in Enterprise, Coffee, Alabama, USA, to Ray Elliot Anderson[1246] and Judith Bass[1245].
The following information is also recorded for Ashley Leigh:
• Military Service.
Note: *Bosnia and 9/11.*
(Military Service)

2507. RUSSELL EASTMAN BASS MESSICK (see Descendants (66)) was born on September 3, 1971, in Savannah, Chatham, Georgia, USA, to Charles Manuel Messick[1249] and Jacqueline Bass[1248].

2508. ROBERTA RUTH MESSICK (see Descendants (66)) was born on July 4, 1975, in Andalusia, Covington, Alabama, USA, to Charles Manuel Messick[1249] and Jacqueline Bass[1248].

2509. ALANNA NICOLE BASS (see Descendants (217)) was born on January 9, 1983 to John Thomas Bass Jr.[1250] and Dorothy King[1251].

2510. MR. MOORE.
> Mr. Moore married Alanna Nicole Bass[2509]. They had two daughters:
> Amberly Kira Moore[3533] born on August 4, 2002
> Lakin Moore[3534] born on December 23, 2002

2511. KRISTINA LYNN REDDISH (see Descendants (218)) was born on January 3, 1989, in Andalusia, Covington, Alabama, USA, to Lynn David Reddish[1254] and Janet Bass[1253].

2512. SHANE STELMON REDDISH (see Descendants (218)) was born on September 13, 1991, in Andalusia, Covington, Alabama, USA, to Lynn David Reddish[1254] and Janet Bass[1253].

2513. LORENA WILKINSON.
> Shane Stelmon Reddish[2512], aged 26, married Lorena Wilkinson on September 1, 2018.

2514. STACEY ELAINE MCVAY (see Descendants (219)) was born on February 5, 1980 to Richard Wayne McVay[1256] and Alice Drucilla Short[1257].

2515. NATHAN MICHAEL GLADSON was born on October 7, 1982.
>   Nathan Michael Gladson, aged 26, married Stacey Elaine McVay[2514], aged 28, on December 13, 2008. They had one daughter:
>> Edith Marie Gladson[3535] born on February 3, 2016

2516. CHARLES ANTHONY WILLIAMSON was born on August 3, 1961 to Charles Herbert Williamson[1259] and Ms. ?. Charles Anthony became known as "Tony". Tony was adopted by Charles Herbert Williamson[1259] and Joan Marie McVay[1258].
> Charles Anthony married twice. He was married to Beverly ?[2517] and Conny Lynn Joiner[2518].

2517. BEVERLY ?.
> Charles Anthony Williamson[2516], when younger than 43, married Beverly ? before 2005, and they were divorced. They had one daughter:
>> Amanda Lynn Williamson[3536] born on February 5, 1984

2518. CONNY LYNN JOINER was born on March 6, 1974.
> Conny Lynn married twice. She was married to Charles Anthony Williamson[2516] and Mr. Joiner.
> Charles Anthony Williamson[2516], aged 44, married Conny Lynn Joiner, aged 31, on September 24, 2005.
> Mr. Joiner married Conny Lynn Joiner. They had one son:
>> William Bert Joiner born on January 28, 1994

2519. SANDRA MICHELLE WILLIAMSON was born on July 11, 1963 to Charles Herbert Williamson[1259] and Ms. ?. Sandra Michelle was adopted by Charles Herbert Williamson[1259] and Joan Marie McVay[1258].

2520. SHANE BARNHILL.
> Shane Barnhill married Sandra Michelle Williamson[2519], and they were divorced. They had three children:
>> Kristen Michelle Barnhill[3538] born on June 25, 1991
>> Taylor Nicole Barnhill[3540] born on December 12, 1993
>> Chase Allen Barnhill[3542] born on October 22, 1996

2521. GORDON MICHAEL WILLIAMSON was born on February 24, 1966 to Charles Herbert Williamson[1259] and Ms. ?. Gordon Michael was adopted by Charles Herbert Williamson[1259] and Joan Marie McVay[1258].

2522. MARY MICHELLE LUCAS was born on December 22, 1966.
> Gordon Michael Williamson[2521], aged 20, married Mary Michelle Lucas, aged 20, on December 29, 1986. They had two children:
>> Meagan Michelle Williamson[3545] born on February 8, 1989
>> Garrett Michael Williamson[3547] born on December 7, 1991

2523. SHANE ERIC WILLIAMSON (see Descendants (220)) was born on July 18, 1976 to Charles Herbert Williamson[1259] and Joan Marie McVay[1258].

2524. TRACI LOCKLAR was born on April 21, 1978.
> Shane Eric Williamson[2523], aged 29, married Traci Locklar, aged 28, on May 13, 2006. They had two sons:
>> Liam Wyatt Williamson[3549] born on August 27, 2008
>> Finley Scott Williamson[3550] born on January 27, 2012

2525. JEFFERY MICHAEL MCVAY (see Descendants (221)) was born on July 19, 1973 to Michael Ray McVay[1260] and Nancy Runae Nelson[1261].

2526. TRACI BETH THORNE was born on July 20, 1976.
> Jeffery Michael McVay[2525], aged 21, married Traci Beth Thorne, aged 18, on December 30, 1994. They had one son:
>> Ethan Michael McVay[3551] born on July 26, 2001

2527. JEREMY WAYNE MCVAY (see Descendants (221)) was born on August 20, 1977 to Michael Ray McVay[1260] and Nancy Runae Nelson[1261].

2528. CHELSI NICOLE GARRETT was born on January 4, 1974. Chelsi Nicole became known as "Nikki".
> Jeremy Wayne McVay[2527] married Chelsi Nicole Garrett, and they were divorced. They had two children:
>> Micah Runae McVay[3552] born on September 28, 2000
>> Garrett Wayne McVay[3554] born on January 26, 2002

2529. STEPHANIE JANE MCVAY (see Descendants (222)) was born on December 16, 1978, in Tennessee, USA, to Samuel Paul McVay[1262] and Mary June Picirilli[1263].

2530. SUZANNE LEA MCVAY (see Descendants (222)) was born on July 9, 1982, in Tennessee, USA, to Samuel Paul McVay[1262] and Mary June Picirilli[1263].

2531. JONATHAN OWENS was born on February 26, 1979.
> Jonathan Owens, aged 28, married Suzanne Lea McVay[2530], aged 25, on July 21, 2007. They had three children:
>> Elijah Adam Owens[3556] born on March 4, 2009
>> Josiah Samuel Owens[3557] born on May 20, 2011
>> Izabela Clair Owens[3558] born on November 20, 2013

2532. JULIE CRYSTAL QUALLS (see Descendants (223)) was born on July 14, 1982 to David Micah McVay[1264] and Judith Ann Pittman[1265].
Julie Crystal had two partnerships. She was married to Abraham Joshua Moyer[2533]. She was also the partner of Mr. ?[2534].

2533. ABRAHAM JOSHUA MOYER was born on November 22, 1979.
> Abraham Joshua Moyer, aged 29, married Julie Crystal Qualls[2532], aged 26, on March 14, 2009. They had two daughters:
>> Hailey June Moyer[3559] born on September 17, 2009
>> Lily Jaicyn Moyer[3560] born on September 15, 2015

2534. MR. ?.
> Mr. ? and Julie Crystal Qualls[2532] had one daughter:
>> Cassandra Jai Moyer[3561] born on February 3, 2004
> The following information is also recorded for this family:
>> • Unknown Relationship.

2535. CODY ALLEN QUALLS (see Descendants (223)) was born on June 22, 1986 to David Micah McVay[1264] and Judith Ann Pittman[1265].

2536. JENNIFER CHRISTINE ? was born on October 30, 1985. Jennifer Christine became known as "Jenn".
> Cody Allen Qualls[2535], aged 18, married Jennifer Christine ?, aged 18, on October 17, 2004. They had two sons:
>> Landon Allen Qualls[3562] born on March 27, 2015
>> Everhett Stone Qualls[3563] born on February 13, 2019

2537. TALITHA RENEA MCVAY (see Descendants (223)) was born on November 20, 1990 to David Micah McVay[1264] and Tracie Renea Dubose[1266].

2538. MR. ?.
> Mr. ? and Talitha Renea McVay[2537] became partners.
> The following information is also recorded for this family:
>> • Unknown Relationship.

2539. MALESHA NICOLE MCVAY (see Descendants (223)) was born on August 9, 1994 to David Micah McVay[1264] and Tracie Renea Dubose[1266].

2540. MR. ?.
> Mr. ? and Malesha Nicole McVay[2539] became partners.
> The following information is also recorded for this family:
>> • Unknown Relationship.

2541. NATALIE MELINDA MCVAY (see Descendants (224)) was born on November 17, 1983 to Nathaniel Joel McVay[1267] and Linda Gail McLeod[1268].

2542. ZACHARY REESE MCCARVER was born on November 28, 1985.
> Zachary Reese McCarver, aged 19, married Natalie Melinda McVay[2541], aged 21, on November 12, 2005. They had two children:
>> Mackenzie Grace McCarver[3564] born on October 6, 2005
>> Macon Reese McCarver[3565] born on July 1, 2020

2543. NATHAN JARED MCVAY (see Descendants (224)) was born on November 8, 1985 to Nathaniel Joel McVay[1267] and Linda Gail McLeod[1268].

2544. BRITNEY SUZANNE GREGORY.
Nathan Jared McVay[2543], aged 26, married Britney Suzanne Gregory on April 28, 2012. They had two children:
  Nolan Jared McVay[3566] born on January 28, 2009
  Braelyn Sadie McVay[3567] born on September 6, 2012

2545. ALEXANDER JACE MCVAY (see Descendants (224)) was born on August 7, 2006
  Aexander Jace became known as "Alex".

2546. JOSHUA MARK MCVAY (see Descendants (225)) was born on December 17, 1987 to Jonathan Mark McVay[1271] and Tammy E. Daniels[1272].
Joshua Mark had three partnerships. He was married to Taylor Nicole Jackson[2547] and Kayla ?[2549]. He was also the partner of Ms. ?[2548].

2547. TAYLOR NICOLE JACKSON was born on July 12, 1993.
Taylor Nicole had two partnerships. She was married to Joshua Mark McVay[2546]. She was also the partner of Mr. ?.
  Joshua Mark McVay[2546], aged 28, married Taylor Nicole Jackson, aged 22, on December 19, 2015, and they were divorced. They had one daughter:
    Westlynn Grace McVay[3568] born on March 28, 2017
  Mr. ? and Taylor Nicole Jackson had one son:
    Rhyflen Lane McVay born on November 1, 2012
  The following information is also recorded for this family:
    • Unknown Relationship.

2548. MS. ?.
  Joshua Mark McVay[2546] and Ms. ? had one daughter:
    Hannah Marie McVay[3569] born on April 22, 2009
  The following information is also recorded for this family:
    • Unknown Relationship.

2549. KAYLA ?.
  Joshua Mark McVay[2546], aged 22, married Kayla ? on July 24, 2010, and they were divorced. They had two children:
    Brenton Mark Lane McVay[3570] born on December 7, 2011
    Baisley Renee McVay[3571] born on April 28, 2015

2550. JACOB DANIEL MCVAY (see Descendants (225)) was born on May 9, 1989 to Jonathan Mark McVay[1271] and Tammy E. Daniels[1272].
The following information is also recorded for Jacob Daniel:
  • Military Service.
Jacob Daniel married twice. He was married to Sara Brisolara[2551] and Deidre Harrison[2552].

2551. SARA BRISOLARA was born on June 8, 1993.
  Jacob Daniel McVay[2550], aged 31, married Sara Brisolara, aged 27, on November 15, 2020.

2552. DEIDRE HARRISON.
  Jacob Daniel McVay[2550] married Deidre Harrison.

2553. MARCUS STEPHEN BASS (see Descendants (226)) was born on April 9, 1973, in Andalusia, Covington, Alabama, USA, to Stephen Gene Bass[1274] and Josephine Anne Darst[1275]. Marcus Stephen became known as "Marc".
The following information is also recorded for Marc:
  Hobbies.
  Note: *Distance Runner.*
    (Hobbies)

2554. MELANIE HOFFMAN. Melanie became known as "Mel".
    Marcus Stephen Bass[2553] married Melanie Hoffman. They had three children:
        Meredith Hope Bass[3572]
        Marcus Christian Bass[3573]
        John Stephen Bass[3574]

2555. JAMES SCOTT BASS (see Descendants (226)) was born on October 22, 1974, in Andalusia, Covington, Alabama, USA, to Stephen Gene Bass[1274] and Josephine Anne Darst[1275].

2556. ELIZABETH MANCUSO.
    James Scott Bass[2555] married Elizabeth Mancuso. They had two children:
        Hunter Scott Bass[3575]
        Holly Suzanne Bass[3576]

2557. JEFFERY PHILIP BASS (see Descendants (226)) was born on August 21, 1976, in Andalusia, Covington, Alabama, USA, to Stephen Gene Bass[1274] and Josephine Anne Darst[1275].

2558. RENEE CANCILLA.
    Jeffery Philip Bass[2557] married Renee Cancilla.

2559. KELLY SUZANNE BASS (see Descendants (226)) was born on January 29, 1981, in Andalusia, Covington, Alabama, USA, to Stephen Gene Bass[1274] and Josephine Anne Darst[1275].

2560. CHRISTOPHER AARON SMITH.
    Christopher Aaron Smith married Kelly Suzanne Bass[2559]. They had two children:
        Eden Kelly Smith[3577]
        Hudson Smith[3578]

2561. LORI MARIE STOCKTON (see Descendants (227)) was born on October 5, 1973, in Dekalb, Georgia, USA, to Marshall Lee Stockton[1280] and Susan Lynn Bass[1279].

2562. JERRY KOZAK.
> Jerry Kozak married Lori Marie Stockton[2561]. They had two sons:
>> Nicholas Kozak[3579]
>> Dylan Kozak[3580]

2563. MARSHALL KEVIN STOCKTON (see Descendants (227)) was born on August 27, 1976, in Dekalb, Georgia, USA, to Marshall Lee Stockton[1280] and Susan Lynn Bass[1279].
2564. SUZY FUQUA.
> Marshall Kevin Stockton[2563] married Suzy Fuqua. They had two sons:
>> Shawn Thomas Stockton[3581]
>> Levi Stockton[3582]

2565. LARRY VAN JR. (see Descendants (228)) was born on October 2, 1960 to Larry Van[1283] and Barbara Elaine Day[1281].

2566. SCARLET VAN (see Descendants (228)) was born on October 24, 1962 to Larry Van[1283] and Barbara Elaine Day[1281].
2567. CLIFF ELLIS.
> Cliff Ellis married Scarlet Van[2566].

2568. TIMOTHY PATRICK DAY (see Descendants (229)) was born on July 20, 1982 to George Anthony Day[1285] and Joyce King[1286]. Timothy Patrick became known as "Tim".

2569. CHRISTOPHER STACY DAY (see Descendants (229)) was born on February 1, 1990 to George Anthony Day[1285] and Joyce King[1286].

2570. BRIAN ROYCE BASS (see Descendants (230)) was born on October 26, 1987 to Royce Caephus Bass[1915] and Tammy Joy Day[1287].
2571. MARLEE FUQUA was born on October 5, 1990.
> Brian Royce Bass[2570] married Marlee Fuqua. They had three children:
>> Beckham Ceese Bass[3583] born on June 22, 2016
>> August Beau Bass[3584] born on December 9, 2020
>> Eliza Bray Bass[3585]

2572. HOLLEY ALAINE BASS (see Descendants (230)) was born on October 18, 1989 to Royce Caephus Bass[1915] and Tammy Joy Day[1287].

2573. TYLER JOEL WINGARD was born on October 23, 1986.
> Tyler Joel Wingard married Holley Alaine Bass[2572]. They had three children:
>> Rylee Alaine Wingard[3586] born on August 25, 2011
>> Wyatt Carl Wingard[3587] born on March 26, 2013
>> Coy Bennett Wingard[3588] born on April 9, 2016

2574. SARA SUZANNE BASS (see Descendants (231)) was born on July 4, 1980 to Gary Wayne Bass[1288] and Ann Allport[1289].

2575. MARK DARON WILLIAM BASS (see Descendants (231)) was born on July 23, 1983 to Gary Wayne Bass[1288] and Ann Allport[1289].

2576. JAMES RICHARD BAEHR (see Descendants (232)) was born on May 26, 1972 to Richard Kenneth Baehr[1291] and Kathy Jean Bass[1290]. James Richard became known as "Jim".
2577. AMY A DEMOCKER was born on November 16, 1973.
> James Richard Baehr[2576], aged 31, married Amy A Democker, aged 29, on July 1, 2003. They had three daughters:

Sadie E Baehr[3589] born on March 9, 2006
Annie O. Baehr[3590] born on April 26, 2007
Mya M. Baehr[3591] born on August 12, 2009

2578. SUSAN JEAN BAEHR (see Descendants (232)) was born on January 19, 1974 to Richard Kenneth Baehr[1291] and Kathy Jean Bass[1290].
Susan Jean had two partnerships. She was married to Mr. Beiswenger[2579]. She was also the partner of Mr. Nolette[2580].

2579. MR. BEISWENGER.
Mr. Beiswenger married Susan Jean Baehr[2578], and they were divorced.

2580. MR. NOLETTE.
Mr. Nolette and Susan Jean Baehr[2578] had one son:
Benjamin R. Nolette[3592] born on May 7, 2004
The following information is also recorded for this family:
• Unknown Relationship.

2581. JOSHUA ALAN BASS (see Descendants (233)) was born on November 14, 1976 to Gregory Alan Bass[1292] and Yvonna Christine Hopkins[1293]. Joshua Alan became known as "Josh".
Joshua Alan had two partnerships. He was married to Nicole ?[2583]. He was also the partner of Ondrea Leturgey[2582].

2582. ONDREA LETURGEY.
Joshua Alan Bass[2581] and Ondrea Leturgey had one son:
Cory Joe Leturgey[3593] born on August 10, 1994
The following information is also recorded for this family:
• Unspecified Relationship.

2583. NICOLE ?.
Joshua Alan Bass[2581] married Nicole ?, and they were divorced. They had one son:
Jaxon Riley Bass[3595] born on August 5, 2011

2584. TERI LYN BASS (see Descendants (233)) was born on April 14, 1981 to Gregory Alan Bass[1292] and Yvonna Christine Hopkins[1293].

2585. BENJAMIN DAVED MONTAGUE was born about December 1980.
Benjamin Daved Montague, aged about 41, married Teri Lyn Bass[2584], aged 41, on September 10, 2022.

2586. STACIE ANN MACLAM (see Descendants (234)) was born on October 13, 1974 to David Laverne Maclam[1296] and Karen Mae Bass[1295].

2587. JOSEPH F. VOLPE was born on September 5, 1975.
Joseph F. Volpe, aged 24, married Stacie Ann Maclam[2586], aged 24, on September 9, 1999. They had two children:
Tegan Jo Volpe[3596] born on August 30, 1999
Anthony Volpe[3597] born on June 4, 2004

2588. BETHANY MARIE MACLAM (see Descendants (234)) was born on January 8, 1977 to David Laverne Maclam[1296] and Karen Mae Bass[1295].

2589. WILLIAM ADAM HOOPER (see Descendants (235)) was born on May 17, 1979, in Troy, Pike, Alabama, USA, to William F. Hooper[1298] and Deborah Lee Martin[1297].

2590. CHRISTOPHER LINDSAY HOOPER (see Descendants (235)) was born on May 7, 1982, in Troy, Pike, Alabama, USA, to William F. Hooper[1298] and Deborah Lee Martin[1297].

2591. DANAE ELIZABETH WILLIAMS (see Descendants (236)) was born on September 29, 1988, in Huntsville, Madison, Alabama, USA, to G. Douglas Williams[1300] and Danna Elizabeth Martin[1299].

2592. ANDREW DOUGLAS WILLIAMS (see Descendants (236)) was born on April 16, 1991, in Huntsville, Madison, Alabama, USA, to G. Douglas Williams[1300] and Danna Elizabeth Martin[1299].

2593. ELIZABETH LEIGH MARTIN (see Descendants (237)) was born on March 20, 1989, in Montgomery, Montgomery, Alabama, USA, to Willard Daniel Martin Jr.[1301] and Tamara Leigh Clark[1302].

2594. WHITNEY DANIELLE MARTIN (see Descendants (237)) was born on August 3, 1992, in Montgomery, Montgomery, Alabama, USA, to Willard Daniel Martin Jr.[1301] and Tamara Leigh Clark[1302].

Direct Relations

2595. SAMANTHA GAIL WOOD (see Descendants (239)) was born on October 23, 1980 to Jeffery Ted Knowles[1306] and Connie Gail Wood[1305].

2596. ANDREA REBECKA WOOD (see Descendants (239)) was born on February 3, 1984 to Jeffery Ted Knowles[1306] and Connie Gail Wood[1305].

2597. MICHAEL SHAWN WILSON (see Descendants (240)) was born on April 18, 1979 to Billy Shannon Wilson[1308] and Rebecca Gaye Wood[1307].

2598. COURTNEY SHANNA WILSON (see Descendants (240)) was born on May 26, 1981, in Andalusia, Covington, Alabama, USA, to Billy Shannon Wilson[1308] and Rebecca Gaye Wood[1307].

2599. WILLIAM DARYL WILSON (see Descendants (240)) was born on January 15, 1985, in Andalusia, Covington, Alabama, USA, to Billy Shannon Wilson[1308] and Rebecca Gaye Wood[1307].

2600. LUKE WOOD (see Descendants (242)) was born on January 7, 1993 to Russel Stacy Wood[1311] and Andrea Leedy Self[1312].
  • He died (At young age) on January 7, 1993, aged 0.
  • He was buried in Horeb Baptist, Millboro, Virginia, USA.

2601. KATHERINE MARY WOOD (see Descendants (242)) was born on January 7, 1993 to Russel Stacy Wood[1311] and Andrea Leedy Self[1312].

2602. EMILY GRACE WOOD (see Descendants (242)) was born on January 7, 1993 to Russel Stacy Wood[1311] and Andrea Leedy Self[1312].

2603. MATTHEW TYLER MANDELVILLE (see Descendants (243)) was born on March 31, 1993 to John Richard Mandelville[1314] and Joyce Marie Wood[1313].

2604. JENNY LYNN RHEA (see Descendants (244)) was born on January 2, 1979, in Nashville, Davidson, Tennessee, USA, to Richard Curtis Rhea[1316] and Sheila Diane Wilson[1315].

2605. AMANDA KATE RHEA (see Descendants (244)) was born on June 6, 1983, in Nashville, Davidson, Tennessee, USA, to Richard Curtis Rhea[1316] and Sheila Diane Wilson[1315].

2606. RICHARD ZACHARY RHEA (see Descendants (244)) was born on August 22, 1986, in Nashville, Davidson, Tennessee, USA, to Richard Curtis Rhea[1316] and Sheila Diane Wilson[1315].

2607. JOHN SPENCER RHEA (see Descendants (244)) was born on November 13, 1991, in Nashville, Davidson, Tennessee, USA, to Richard Curtis Rhea[1316] and Sheila Diane Wilson[1315].

2608. CHRISTY ?.

John Spencer Rhea[2607] married Christy ?. They had three children:
Ms. Rhea[3598]
Abelia Jane Rhea[3599] born on January 17, 2023
Mr. Rhea[3600]

2609. TIMOTHY NICHOLAS WILSON (see Descendants (245)) was born on February 19, 1985 to Michail Lewis Wilson[1317] and Zelda Lynn Tweedy[1318].

2610. TIFFANY NICHOLE WILSON (see Descendants (245)) was born on February 19, 1985 to Michail Lewis Wilson[1317] and Zelda Lynn Tweedy[1318].

2611. RETESSA LYNE WILSON (see Descendants (245)) was born on January 19, 1988 to Michail Lewis Wilson[1317] and Zelda Lynn Tweedy[1318].

2612. MICHAEL TRAVIS WILSON (see Descendants (245)) was born on July 17, 1991 to Michail Lewis Wilson[1317] and Zelda Lynn Tweedy[1318].

2613. JOHN TYLER DOZIER (see Descendants (246)) was born on October 10, 1989, in Eglin Air Force Base, Walton, Florida, USA, to Austin Lamar Dozier[1320] and Audrey Michelle Wilson[1319].

2614. KATHRYN REBECCA DOZIER (see Descendants (246)) was born on May 21, 1993, in Andalusia, Covington, Alabama, USA, to Austin Lamar Dozier[1320] and Audrey Michelle Wilson[1319].

2615. CHRISTOPHER TROY BASS (see Descendants (247)) was born on July 6, 1983, in Greer, Greenville/Spartanburg, South Carolina, USA, to Leland Samuel Bass[1321] and Cheri Lynn Ducote[1322].

2616. JASMINE LEIGH BASS (see Descendants (247)) was born on May 8, 1991, in Greer, Greenville/Spartanburg, South Carolina, USA, to Leland Samuel Bass[1321] and Cheri Lynn Ducote[1322].

2617. MR. GREENE.
   Mr. Greene married Jasmine Leigh Bass[2616].

2618. WILLIAM BRYAN ROGERS III (see Descendants (1)) was born on February 3, 1995, in Crestview, Okaloosa, Florida, USA, to William Bryan Rogers Jr.[1328] and Beverly Lynn Bass[1326].

2619. JOSEPH BLAZE CHRZASTEK BASS (see Descendants (1)) was born on April 28, 2000 to Wesley Alan Bass[1329] and Donna Chrzastek[1330].
   The following information is also recorded for Joseph Blaze:
   • Military Service.

2620. ALYSSA STARK was born on April 11, 2001.
   Joseph Blaze Chrzastek Bass[2619], aged 22, married Alyssa Stark, aged 21, on July 11, 2022. They had one daughter:
      Emberlynn Crystal Chrzastek-Bass[3601] born on October 20, 2022

2621. SHANNON MICHELE ADKINS (see Descendants (68)) was born on July 6, 1972, in Knoxville, Knox, Tennessee, USA, to Johnny McCarsey Adkins[1332] and Betty Jane Ward[1331].

2622. WILLIAM CHARLES WARD III (see Descendants (68)) was born on July 5, 1972, in Eglin Air Force Base, Walton, Florida, USA, to William Charles Ward Jr.[1333] and Kathy Raby[1334].

2623. DAVID CARTER WARD (see Descendants (68)) was born on August 24, 1974, in Wahiawa, Honolulu, Hawaii, USA, to William Charles Ward Jr.[1333] and Kathy Raby[1334].
   The following information is also recorded for David Carter:
   • Military Service.
   David Carter married three times. He was married to Lorena Williamson[2624], Anita ?[2625] and Vicki ?[2626].

2624. LORENA WILLIAMSON was born on January 3, 1973, in Phoenix, Mesa, Arizona, USA.
   David Carter Ward[2623] married Lorena Williamson, aged 22, about August 16, 1995 (estimated).

2625. ANITA ?.
   David Carter Ward[2623] married Anita ?. They had two children:
      Seth Ward[3602] born on August 6, 1996
      Sydney Taylor Ward[3603] born on September 8, 2000

2626. VICKI ?.
   David Carter Ward[2623] married Vicki ?.

Direct Relations

2627. JEFFERY ALLEN STUART (see Descendants (68)) was born on September 8, 1981, in Shenandoah, Page, Iowa, USA, to Allen R. Stuart[1337] and Mary Ann Ward[1336].

2628. BETHANY ANN STUART (see Descendants (68)) was born on February 21, 1983, in Bristol, Sullivan, Tennessee, USA, to Allen R. Stuart[1337] and Mary Ann Ward[1336].
2629. NATE MOORMAN.
> Nate Moorman married Bethany Ann Stuart[2628], aged 25, on August 3, 2008. They had two sons:
>> Lincoln Nathan Moorman[3604] born on November 23, 2012
>> Bennett Owen Moorman[3605] born on August 13, 2014

2630. SUZANNE MARIE STUART (see Descendants (68)) was born on July 2, 1984, in Shenandoah, Page, Iowa, USA, to Allen R. Stuart[1337] and Mary Ann Ward[1336].

2631. GREGORY CLINE COFFMAN (see Descendants (68)) was born on December 15, 1994 to Jeffery Lee Coffman[1339] and Shirley Ward[1338].
> Gregory Cline married twice. He was married to Angel ?[2632] and Amanda ?[2633].

2632. ANGEL ?.
> Gregory Cline Coffman[2631] married Angel ?, and they were divorced. They had two sons:
>> Elijah Coffman[3606] born in 2013
>> Cartur Coffman[3607] born in 2017
2633. AMANDA ?.
> Gregory Cline Coffman[2631] married Amanda ?.

2634. JOSEPH BRANDON WARD (see Descendants (68)) was born on August 20, 1974, in Fort Walton Beach, Okaloosa, Florida, USA, to Joseph Dale Ward[1341] and Jackie Elaine Crabtree[1342].

2635. MALETHA ADELE WARD (see Descendants (68)) was born on August 15, 1977 to Joseph Dale Ward[1341] and Jackie Elaine Crabtree[1342].

2636. BROOKE MICHELLE WARD (see Descendants (68)) was born on January 7, 1980 to Joseph Dale Ward[1341] and Jackie Elaine Crabtree[1342].

2637. EMILY JUNE WARD (see Descendants (68)) was born on August 30, 1982, in Louisiana, USA, to Joseph Dale Ward[1341] and Jackie Elaine Crabtree[1342].

2638. DEIDRE NICOLE WARD (see Descendants (68)) was born on November 7, 1984 to Rose Marie Ward[1343].

2639. SHELBY DANIEL STEVERSON (see Descendants (68)) was born on March 23, 1993, in Pensacola, Escambia, Florida, USA, to Daniel Hal Steverson[1345] and Chris Lorraine Ward[1344].

2640. ROBERT ERNEST BASS (see Descendants (69)) was born about 1946, in Florida, United States, to Earnest True Bass Jr.[1351] and Catherine Nadine Ireland[1352]. He was recorded in the census on April 1, 1950, aged about 3, in Styles Subdivision, Tallahassee, Leon, Florida, United States.

2641. LINDA ANN BASS (see Descendants (69)) was born in Florida, United States to Ennis Rudolph Bass[1354] and Linda Barbara Borgioli[1355]. She was recorded in the census on April 1, 1950, in Chattahoochee, Gadsden, Florida, United States.
2642. DR. ROBERT OLDS.
> Robert Olds married Linda Ann Bass[2641]. They had one daughter:
>> Morgan E. Olds[3608]

2643. ELIZABETH SHARON PETERSON (see Descendants (70)) was born on July 6, 1947, in Pascagoula, Jackson, Mississippi, USA, to Elwynne Phillip Peterson[1364] and Alice Lillian Bass[1363]. She was recorded in the census on April 1, 1950, aged 2, in 32 Telegraph Road, Prichard, Mobile, Alabama, United States.

2644. RICHARD EDWARD BASS (see Descendants (70)) was born on February 8, 1950, in Tallahassee, Leon, Florida, USA, to Richard Carle Bass Jr.[1365] and Mary Elizabeth Hale[1366]. He was recorded in the census on April 1, 1950, as an infant, in District 4, Tallahassee, Leon, Florida, United States.

2645. DENESE MCINTIRE was born on July 6, 1950, in Tallahassee, Leon, Florida, USA. She died on August 16, 2021, aged 71.
> Richard Edward Bass[2644] married Denese McIntire. They had two children:
>> Erin Lenae Bass[3609] born on May 12, 1973 in Tallahassee, Leon, Florida, USA
>> Matthew Evan Bass[3610] born on November 29, 1979 in Tallahassee, Leon, Florida, USA

2646. CHARLES EDWARD BASS (see Descendants (70)) was born on July 18, 1954 to Richard Carle Bass Jr.[1365] and Mary Elizabeth Hale[1366]. Charles Edward became known as "Chuck".

2647. BARBARA JONES was born on February 6, 1956.
> Charles Edward Bass[2646] married Barbara Jones. They had two daughters:
>> Patricia Ann Bass[3612] born on April 20, 1973 in tallahassee, Leon, Florida, USA
>> Rachel Suzanne Bass[3613] born on June 13, 1984 in Tallahassee, Leon, Florida, USA

2648. LINDA ELIZABETH BASS (see Descendants (70)) was born on June 25, 1955, in Tallahassee, Leon, Florida, USA, to Richard Carle Bass Jr.[1365] and Mary Elizabeth Hale[1366].

2649. ALVIN DONNALD LEWIS was born on May 23, 1951, in Woodville, Florida, USA.
> Alvin Donnald Lewis married Linda Elizabeth Bass[2648]. They had one daughter:
>> Brook Renee Lewis[3614] born on October 22, 1982 in Tallahassee, Leon, Florida, USA

2650. ROBERT CARL BASS (see Descendants (70)) was born in 1961 to Richard Carle Bass Jr.[1365] and Mary Elizabeth Hale[1366].

2651. RHONDA THERESA BASS (see Descendants (70)) was born on October 12, 1965, in Sweinfort, Germany, to Charles Edward Bass[1369] and Mae Burk[1370].

2652. RICHARD CHARLES BASS (see Descendants (70)) was born on October 14, 1966, in Sweinfort, Germany, to Charles Edward Bass[1369] and Mae Burk[1370].

2653. DONNA MARIE RINEHART (see Descendants (70)) was born in 1955, in Thomasville, Thomas, Georgia, USA, to O. C. Rinehart[1372] and Nell Bass[1371].

2654. MYRA NELL RINEHART (see Descendants (70)) was born in 1961, in Thomasville, Thomas, Georgia, USA, to O. C. Rinehart[1372] and Nell Bass[1371].

2655. GARY WESTBURY (see Descendants (70)) was born in 1957 to Lewis Westbury[1374] and Betty Bass[1373].

2656. DONNIE WESTBURY (see Descendants (70)) was born in 1960 to Lewis Westbury[1374] and Betty Bass[1373].

2657. JUNE LORRAINE COX (see Descendants (70)) was born on May 10, 1951 to Leslie Clayton Cox[1376] and JoAnne Charlotte Bass[1375].

2658. ART RICHARD.
> Art Richard married June Lorraine Cox[2657], aged 24, on June 26, 1975.

2659. EDWARD CLAYTON COX (see Descendants (70)) was born on February 18, 1954 to Leslie Clayton Cox[1376] and JoAnne Charlotte Bass[1375].

2660. DENISE DELS.
> Edward Clayton Cox[2659], aged 18, married Denise Dels on September 18, 1972.

2661. CAREL JEANETTE COX (see Descendants (70)) was born on April 5, 1956 to Leslie Clayton Cox[1376] and JoAnne Charlotte Bass[1375].

2662. RICKY ALLEN LANGSTON.
> Ricky Allen Langston married Carel Jeanette Cox[2661], aged 21, on January 7, 1978.

2663. CHERYL KAYE BASS was born on September 7, 1965. Cheryl Kaye was adopted by Kenneth Kirby Bass[1377] and Jane Rowe[1379].

2664. JIMMY HAMILTON.
> Jimmy Hamilton married Cheryl Kaye Bass[2663]. They had two children:
> Josh Strickland[3615]
> Natalie Westerling[3616]

2665. KARAN LAINYE BASS (see Descendants (70)) was born on November 2, 1962 to Harold Eugene Bass[1381] and Thelina Gail Kilpratrie[1382].

2666. SCOTT BAILEY.
> Scott Bailey married Karan Lainye Bass[2665].

2667. SABIN CRAIG BASS (see Descendants (70)) was born on December 21, 1964, in Tallahassee, Leon, Florida, USA, to Harold Eugene Bass[1381] and Thelina Gail Kilpratrie[1382].

2668. JOSEPH KENNETH KOVAL (see Descendants (70)) was born on September 30, 1978 to John Joseph Koval[1384] and Betty June Bass[1383].

2669. CYNTHIA LOUISE BASS (see Descendants (71)) was born on October 15, 1950, in Montgomery, Montgomery, Alabama, USA, to Edwin Durwood Bass Sr.[1388] and Margaret Louise Powell[1389].
> Cynthia Louise married twice. She was married to Raymon Johnson[2670] and Reggie Lawshe Powell[2671].

2670. RAYMON JOHNSON.
> Raymon Johnson married Cynthia Louise Bass[2669], aged 19, on April 4, 1970. They had two children:
> Melissa Kay Johnson[3617] born on June 28, 1971 in Andalusia, Covington, Alabama, USA
> Raymon Brian Johnson[3619] born on May 24, 1973 in Selma, Dallas, Alabama, USA

2671. REGGIE LAWSHE POWELL was born on November 5, 1956, in Andalusia, Covington, Alabama, USA.
> Reggie Lawshe married twice. He was married to Cynthia Louise Bass[2669] and Ms. ?.
> Reggie Lawshe Powell married Cynthia Louise Bass[2669]. They assumed parenthood of two daughters:
> Andrea Nicole Powell[3620] by adoption
> Haley Elyse Powell[3621] by adoption
> Reggie Lawshe Powell married Ms. ?. They had two daughters:
> Andrea Nicole Powell[3620] born on June 23, 1980 in Andalusia, Covington, Alabama, USA
> Haley Elyse Powell[3621] born on July 14, 1987 in Opp, Covington, Alabama, USA

2672. EDWIN DURWOOD BASS JR. (see Descendants (71)) was born on May 9, 1953, in Andalusia, Covington, Alabama, USA, to Edwin Durwood Bass Sr.[1388] and Margaret Louise Powell[1389].

2673. SUSAN DIANNE BASS (see Descendants (71)) was born on June 11, 1956, in Andalusia, Covington, Alabama, USA, to Edwin Durwood Bass Sr.[1388] and Margaret Louise Powell[1389].

2674. GARY ALLEN MCCURLEY was born on August 8, 1957, in California, USA.
> Gary Allen McCurley married Susan Dianne Bass[2673]. They had two children:
> Joshua Adam McCurley[3623] born on January 26, 1978 in Andalusia, Covington, Alabama, USA
> Towanna Joy McCurley[3624] born on July 9, 1979 in Andalusia, Covington, Alabama, USA

2675. WILLIAM BENNETT BASS (see Descendants (71)) was born on March 20, 1967, in Fort Ord, Monterey, California, USA, to Donald Gene Bass[1390] and Pamela Jane Hayerberg[1391].

2676. ALICIA MARIE BASS (see Descendants (71)) was born on March 12, 1968, in Sarasota, Florida, USA, to Donald Gene Bass[1390] and Pamela Jane Hayerberg[1391].

2677. SHAWN LEE BASS (see Descendants (71)) was born on May 1, 1983, in Fort Ord, Monterey, California, USA, to Donald Gene Bass[1390] and Pamela Jane Hayerberg[1391].

2678. DONNIE LEE BASS (see Descendants (71)) was born on February 27, 1986, in Seoul, Korea, to Donald Gene Bass[1390] and Bok Suk Choi[1392].

2679. ROBERT MCDONALD (see Descendants (74)) was born about 1930, in Alabama, USA, to Charles D McDonald[1411] and Beulah Mae Biggs[1410]. He was recorded in the census in 1940, aged about 10, in E Precinct 3 Brannen, Coffee, Alabama, USA.

2680. LUCILLE MCDONALD (see Descendants (74)) was born about 1933, in Alabama, USA, to Charles D McDonald[1411] and Beulah Mae Biggs[1410]. She was recorded in the census in 1940, aged about 7, in E Precinct 3 Brannen, Coffee, Alabama, USA.

2681. VONCILLE MCDONALD (see Descendants (74)) was born about 1933, in Alabama, USA, to Charles D McDonald[1411] and Beulah Mae Biggs[1410]. She was recorded in the census in 1940, aged about 7, in E Precinct 3 Brannen, Coffee, Alabama, USA.

2682. JUNIOR MCDONALD (see Descendants (74)) was born about 1935, in Alabama, USA, to Charles D McDonald[1411] and Beulah Mae Biggs[1410]. He was recorded in the census in 1940, aged about 5, in E Precinct 3 Brannen, Coffee, Alabama, USA.

2683. MYRTICE EDNA WHATLEY (see Descendants (74)) was born on June 29, 1937, in Covington, Alabama, USA, to Jay Theron Whatley[1413] and Lessie Myrl Biggs[1412].
- She was recorded in the census on April 1, 1950, aged 12, in 11 Dexn Mile Tanetera, Andalusia, Covington, Alabama, United States.
- She died on June 13, 1992, aged 54 years, in Milledgeville, Baldwin, Georgia, USA.

2684. MYRTLE MAXINE WHATLEY (see Descendants (74)) was born on October 24, 1941, in Andalusia, Covington, Alabama, USA, to Jay Theron Whatley[1413] and Lessie Myrl Biggs[1412].
- She died (At young age) on February 8, 1944, aged 2 years, in Andalusia, Covington, Alabama, USA.
- She was buried in Bethel Primitive Baptist Church Cemetery, Babbie, Covington, Alabama, USA.

2685. GORDON LAVAUGHN WHATLEY (see Descendants (74)) was born on August 17, 1945, in Mobile, Alabama, USA, to Jay Theron Whatley[1413] and Lessie Myrl Biggs[1412].
- He was recorded in the census on April 1, 1950, aged 4, in 11 Dexn Mile Tanetera, Andalusia, Covington, Alabama, United States.
- He died in 1993, aged about 47, in Florala, Covington, Alabama, USA.

2686. REBECCA WILLIAMS (see Descendants (78)) was born on February 25, 1953, in Andalusia, Covington, Alabama, USA, to Lester Williams[1424] and Ms. Dortch[1425].
2687. STAN TINDAL.
Stan Tindal married Rebecca Williams[2686].

2688. SUSAN ELIZABETH WILLIAMS (see Descendants (78)) was born on May 23, 1954, in Andalusia, Covington, Alabama, USA, to Lester Williams[1424] and Ms. Dortch[1425].
2689. CHUCK EPLEY.
Chuck Epley married Susan Elizabeth Williams[2688].

2690. JOHNNY RAY WILLIAMS (see Descendants (78)) was born on March 21, 1956, in Andalusia, Covington, Alabama, USA, to Lester Williams[1424] and Ms. Dortch[1425].
Johnny Ray had two partnerships. He was married to Shirley Day[2691]. He was also the partner of Shirley Ann Day[2692].
2691. SHIRLEY DAY.
Johnny Ray Williams[2690] married Shirley Day.
2692. SHIRLEY ANN DAY was born on February 27, 1959 to George Andrew Day and Clara Evelyn Jordan.
Johnny Ray Williams[2690] and Shirley Ann Day became partners.

2693. RONALD GORDON WILLIAMS (see Descendants (78)) was born on October 26, 1957, in Andalusia, Covington, Alabama, USA, to Lester Williams[1424] and Ms. Dortch[1425].
2694. MARILYN WATTS.
Ronald Gordon Williams[2693] married Marilyn Watts.

2695. JO ANN WILLIAMS (see Descendants (78)) was born on July 1, 1959, in Andalusia, Covington, Alabama, USA, to Lester Williams[1424] and Ms. Dortch[1425].
2696. JAMES JONES.
James Jones married Jo Ann Williams[2695].

2697. DAVID MARCUS WILLIAMS (see Descendants (78)) was born on March 26, 1962, in Andalusia, Covington, Alabama, USA, to Lester Williams[1424] and Ms. Dortch[1425].
2698. SUE BLACKWELL.
David Marcus Williams[2697] married Sue Blackwell.

2699. ANGELA MARIA WILLIAMS (see Descendants (78)) was born on October 19, 1964 to Lester Williams[1424] and Ms. Dortch[1425].

Direct Relations

2700. ARLIS CHAPMAN ADAMS JR. (see Descendants (85)) was born on February 21, 1947, in Texas, United States, to Arlis Chapman Adams Sr.[1428] and Annie Maude Hassell[1429]. He was recorded in the census on April 1, 1950, aged 3, in Calber@Calbert@Madison Madison, Chickasaw, Mobile, Alabama, United States.
2701. MARY ROGERS.
>Arlis Chapman Adams Jr.[2700] married Mary Rogers.

2702. ANTHONY PHILLIP ADAMS (see Descendants (85)) was born about November 1955 to Arlis Chapman Adams Sr.[1428] and Annie Maude Hassell[1429].
2703. DIANNE LOGAN.
>Anthony Phillip Adams[2702] married Dianne Logan. They had two children:
>>Brook Adams[3625]
>>Aric Adams[3626]

2704. ANGINA VALENTINE ADAMS (see Descendants (85)) was born to Arlis Chapman Adams Sr.[1428] and Annie Maude Hassell[1429].

2705. DEBORAH JACKSON (see Descendants (85)) was born to Frank Jackson[1433] and Annette Adams[1432].

2706. DEWAYNE JACKSON (see Descendants (85)) was born to Frank Jackson[1433] and Annette Adams[1432].

2707. LOUIS JACKSON (see Descendants (85)) was born to Frank Jackson[1433] and Annette Adams[1432].
2708. MS. ?.
>Louis Jackson[2707] married Ms. ?. They had four children:
>>Mr. Jackson[3627]
>>Danny Jackson[3628]
>>David Jackson[3629]
>>Christy Jackson[3630]

2709. DANNY LEE ADAMS (see Descendants (85)) was born on November 26, 1951, in Andalusia, Covington, Alabama, USA, to Aaron Lee Adams[1434] and Betty Jean Brown[1435].
2710. DEBORAH BABB.
>Danny Lee Adams[2709], aged 25, married Deborah Babb on June 15, 1977.

2711. ANGELA PATRICE ADAMS (see Descendants (85)) was born on November 14, 1955, in Mobile, Mobile, Alabama, USA, to Aaron Lee Adams[1434] and Betty Jean Brown[1435].
2712. HARVEY VALNOR SMITH.
>Harvey Valnor Smith married Angela Patrice Adams[2711], aged 44, on April 2, 2000.

2713. PAMELA JEAN ADAMS (see Descendants (85)) was born on July 31, 1962, in Mobile, Mobile, Alabama, USA, to Aaron Lee Adams[1434] and Betty Jean Brown[1435].
2714. DONALD RAYMOND MONCRIEF. Donald Raymond became known as "Don".
>Donald Raymond Moncrief married Pamela Jean Adams[2713], aged 15, on July 7, 1978.

2715. TIMOTHY ALAN ADAMS (see Descendants (85)) was born on July 31, 1962, in Mobile, Mobile, Alabama, USA, to Aaron Lee Adams[1434] and Betty Jean Brown[1435].
2716. CYNTHIA DELORES BROCK.
>Timothy Alan Adams[2715] married Cynthia Delores Brock.

2717. CYNTHIA MAE THOMASSON (see Descendants (85)) was born on October 20, 1953, in Andalusia, Covington, Alabama, USA, to Charles Wood Thomasson[1437] and Audie Mae Adams[1436].
2718. JAMES MARVIN HARRISON.
>James Marvin Harrison married Cynthia Mae Thomasson[2717], aged 20, on August 16, 1974. They had three children:
>>James Brett Harrison[3631] born on March 14, 1977 in Enterprise, Coffee, Alabama, USA
>>Charles Brian Harrison[3632] born on August 9, 1979 in Enterprise, Coffee, Alabama, USA
>>Brittney Lauren Harrison[3633] born on March 6, 1986 in Dothan, Dale, Alabama, USA

2719. CHARLES ROCKY THOMASSON (see Descendants (85)) was born on January 2, 1956, in Andalusia, Covington, Alabama, USA, to Charles Wood Thomasson[1437] and Audie Mae Adams[1436].
2720. KIMBERLY ANN WALKER.

Charles Rocky Thomasson[2719], aged 24, married Kimberly Ann Walker on June 20, 1980. They had two children:
- Charles Michael Thomasson[3634] born on July 25, 1984
- Cassandra Nicole Thomasson[3635] born on January 8, 1990

2721. CELIA LYNN THOMASSON (see Descendants (85)) was born on February 13, 1957, in Andalusia, Covington, Alabama, USA, to Charles Wood Thomasson[1437] and Audie Mae Adams[1436].

2722. MARK NELSON TATE was born on July 3, 1956.
Mark Nelson Tate, aged 22, married Celia Lynn Thomasson[2721], aged 21, on August 4, 1978. They had four children:
- Amber Lynell Tate[3636] born on February 13, 1986
- Adam Nelson Tate[3637] born on April 15, 1989
- Aric Charles Tate[3638] born on March 25, 1992
- Andrew Nelson Tate[3639] born on March 25, 1992

2723. CAROL SUE THOMASSON (see Descendants (85)) was born on October 29, 1959, in Andalusia, Covington, Alabama, USA, to Charles Wood Thomasson[1437] and Audie Mae Adams[1436].

2724. JAMES ROBERT HANCOCK.
James Robert Hancock married Carol Sue Thomasson[2723], aged 22, on July 17, 1982. They had four children:
- Jerrod Randal Hancock[3640] born on February 15, 1985
- Jordan Robert Hancock[3641] born on July 25, 1987
- James Ryne Hancock[3642] born on May 1, 1990
- Hailey Hancock[3643] born on January 12, 1993

2725. SHERRY JACOBS (see Descendants (86)) was born to John Mandrak Jacobs[1440] and Sibyl Rodgers[1439].

2726. JIM GARNER.
Jim Garner married Sherry Jacobs[2725].

2727. RONALD JACOBS (see Descendants (86)) was born to John Mandrak Jacobs[1440] and Sibyl Rodgers[1439].

2728. TIM JACOBS (see Descendants (86)) was born to John Mandrak Jacobs[1440] and Sibyl Rodgers[1439].

2729. DONNA JACOBS (see Descendants (86)) was born to John Mandrak Jacobs[1440] and Sibyl Rodgers[1439].

2730. THOMAS RODGERS (see Descendants (86)) was born to Evans Rodgers[1441] and Annice Henderson[1443].

2731. DOROTHY ?.
Thomas Rodgers[2730] married Dorothy ?.

2732. ALVIN RODGERS (see Descendants (86)) was born on March 23, 1955 to Evans Rodgers[1441] and Annice Henderson[1443].

2733. JANA ? was born on March 29, 1956.
Alvin Rodgers[2732] married Jana ?. They had one daughter:
- Lori Rogers[3644] born on August 24, 1991

2734. JOHN GLENN RODGERS (see Descendants (86)) was born to Evans Rodgers[1441] and Annice Henderson[1443].

2735. BONNIE ?.
John Glenn Rodgers[2734] married Bonnie ?.

2736. JO ANNE RODGERS (see Descendants (86)) was born to Evans Rodgers[1441] and Annice Henderson[1443].

2737. JIMMY HALL.
Jimmy Hall married Jo Anne Rodgers[2736].

2738. JOYCE RODGERS (see Descendants (86)) was born to Evans Rodgers[1441] and Annice Henderson[1443].
Joyce married twice. She was married to Jerry Hall[2739] and Mr. Little[2740].

2739. JERRY HALL.
Jerry Hall married Joyce Rodgers[2738]. They had two children:
- Kim Hall[3645]
- Greg Hall[3646]

2740. MR. LITTLE.
Mr. Little married Joyce Rodgers[2738].

Direct Relations

2741. BRENDA RODGERS (see Descendants (86)) was born to Evans Rodgers[1441] and Annice Henderson[1443].

2742. JAMES DEWAYNE BASS (see Descendants (87)) was born on December 16, 1947, in Alabama, United States, to James Ervin Bass[1449] and Opal Louise King[1450].
- He was recorded in the census on April 1, 1950, aged 2, in Baykin and Road Leral Road, Westover, Covington, Alabama, United States.
- He died on April 29, 1966, aged 18.

2743. ALETHA JEAN BLACKWELL (see Descendants (87)) was born on December 31, 1953, in Andalusia, Covington, Alabama, USA, to W. Edward Blackwell[1453] and Christine Bass[1452]. She died on November 1, 2006, aged 52, in Andalusia, Covington, Alabama, USA.

2744. JOSHEPH BYRAN THOMPSON.
> Josheph Byran Thompson married Aletha Jean Blackwell[2743], aged 18, on January 6, 1972. They had four children:
>> Joseph Byron Thompson Jr.[3647] born on March 21, 1973 in Andalusia, Covington, Alabama, USA
>> Sonya Michelle Thompson[3649] born on September 1, 1974
>> Kimberly Nicole Thompson[3651] born on November 14, 1979
>> Capers Thompson[3653]

2745. DEMISIA BLACKWELL (see Descendants (87)) was born to W. Edward Blackwell[1453] and Christine Bass[1452].
Demisia married twice. She was married to Allen Jack Lee[2746] and Steve Peacock[2747].

2746. ALLEN JACK LEE. Allen Jack became known as "Al".
> Allen Jack Lee married Demisia Blackwell[2745]. They had two children:
>> Christopher Allen Lee Sr.[3654] born on February 19, 1980
>> Casey Lee[3657] born on February 6, 1990

2747. STEVE PEACOCK.
> Steve Peacock married Demisia Blackwell[2745]. They had one son:
>> Michael Steven Peacock[3659] born on August 11, 1974

2748. CORNELIA ANN BLACKWELL (see Descendants (87)) was born in May 1953, in Charlottsville, Vaginia, USA, to Clifton Curtis Blackwell[1456] and Voncile Bass[1455]. She died in May 1983, aged 30.

2749. AL BOYETT.
> Al Boyett married Cornelia Ann Blackwell[2748]. They had two sons:
>> Tony Boyett[3661]
>> Al Boyett Jr.[3663]

2750. DEBORAH LYNN BLACKWELL (see Descendants (87)) was born on February 25, 1955, in Andalusia, Covington, Alabama, USA, to Clifton Curtis Blackwell[1456] and Voncile Bass[1455].
Deborah Lynn married twice. She was married to Doug Findley[2751] and George William Evans Jr.[2752].

2751. DOUG FINDLEY.
> Doug Findley married Deborah Lynn Blackwell[2750]. They had one daughter:
>> Delores Findley[3664]

2752. GEORGE WILLIAM EVANS JR.
> George William Evans Jr. married Deborah Lynn Blackwell[2750]. They had three children:
>> George William Evans III[3666]
>> Crystal Gail Evans[3668]
>> Rebecca Lynn Evans[3670]

2753. TERESA BLACKWELL (see Descendants (87)) was born on September 1, 1959, in Andalusia, Covington, Alabama, USA, to Clifton Curtis Blackwell[1456] and Voncile Bass[1455].

2754. JAMES RANDALL CANNON was born on April 29, 1960, in Pensacola, Escambia, Florida, USA, to James Everett Cannon and Audrey May Penton. James Randall became known as "Randy".
> James Randall Cannon, aged 19, married Teresa Blackwell[2753], aged 19, on May 18, 1979. They had three daughters:
>> Susan Michelle Cannon[3673] born on May 7, 1981
>> Jennifer Nicole Cannon[3677] born on February 10, 1984
>> Stephanie Dyan Cannon[3679] born on January 14, 1990

2755. CLIFTON JOSEPH BLACKWELL (see Descendants (87)) was born on September 2, 1970 to Clifton Curtis Blackwell[1456] and Voncile Bass[1455].

• He died (At young age) on September 3, 1970, as an infant.
• He was buried in Carolina Baptist Church Cemetery, Covington, Alabama, USA.

2756. SHELA DIANNA BLACKWELL (see Descendants (87)) was born in Charlottsville, Vaginia, USA to Clifton Curtis Blackwell[1456] and Voncile Bass[1455].
Shela Dianna married twice. She was married to Ferrell Rabon[2757] and Charles Greer[2758].

2757. FERRELL RABON.
Ferrell Rabon married Shela Dianna Blackwell[2756]. They had one daughter:
Melissa Rabon[3680]

2758. CHARLES GREER. He died in 2006.
Charles Greer married Shela Dianna Blackwell[2756].

2759. DONNA CAROL BASS (see Descendants (87)) was born to Julius Ike Bass[1459] and Carolyn Garvin[1460].

2760. MR. MARAMAN.
Mr. Maraman married Donna Carol Bass[2759].

2761. WAYMON JULIUS BASS (see Descendants (87)) was born to Julius Ike Bass[1459] and Carolyn Garvin[1460].

2762. RALPH LEVON PATTERSON JR. (see Descendants (88)) was born on February 3, 1954, in Andalusia, Covington, Alabama, USA, to Ralph Levon Patterson Sr.[1464] and Beatrice Lucile Bass[1463].

2763. PATRICIA SMITH LEWIS was born on December 23, 1956, in Mobile, Mobile, Alabama, USA.
Ralph Levon Patterson Jr.[2762], aged 34, married Patricia Smith Lewis, aged 31, on July 18, 1988.

2764. SHARON JEAN BASS (see Descendants (88)) was born on October 10, 1957, in Andalusia, Covington, Alabama, USA, to Robert Julius Bass[1465] and Doris Jean Stokes[1466].

2765. RALPH DONALD EKHOMM.
Ralph Donald Ekhomm married Sharon Jean Bass[2764]. They had two children:
Lindsey Ekhomm[3681]
Mark Ekhomm[3682]

2766. JULIUS RANDALL BASS (see Descendants (88)) was born on May 9, 1959, in Fort Bragg, Cumberland County, North Carolina, United States, to Robert Julius Bass[1465] and Doris Jean Stokes[1466]. Julius Randall became known as "Randy".
• He died on July 10, 1998, aged 39, in Andalusia, Covington, Alabama, USA.
• He was buried in Carolina Baptist Church Cemetery, Covington, Alabama, USA.
Julius Randall married twice. He was married to Shirley Ann Bennett[2767] and Connie Sue West[2768].

2767. SHIRLEY ANN BENNETT was born on September 24, 1961.
Julius Randall Bass[2766], aged 18, married Shirley Ann Bennett, aged 16, on December 17, 1977. They had one son:
Robert Julius Bass II[3683]

2768. CONNIE SUE WEST was born on August 30, 1964.
Connie Sue had three partnerships. She was married to Julius Randall Bass[2766] and Mr. Poore. She was also the partner of Mr. Dickhut.
Julius Randall Bass[2766] married Connie Sue West. They had one daughter, and assumed parenthood of another one:
Megan Christina Bass[3684]
Christopher Randall Dickhut[3686] by adoption

Mr. Dickhut and Connie Sue West had one son:
>Christopher Randall Dickhut[3686] born on August 11, 1982 in Rochester, Olmstead, Minnesota, USA

The following information is also recorded for this family:
- Unknown Relationship.

Mr. Poore married Connie Sue West.

2769. EDWARD MICHAEL BASS (see Descendants (88)) was born on June 20, 1970, in Troy, Pike, Alabama, United States, to Robert Julius Bass[1465] and Barbara Ann Tisdale[1467].

2770. DONNA DENISE RUSHING.
Edward Michael Bass[2769], aged 24, married Donna Denise Rushing on December 31, 1994 in Crensaw County, Alabama, USA. They had one son:
>Phillip Le Brandon Barry[3687]

2771. ROBIN TAIWAN BASS (see Descendants (88)) was born on September 29, 1962, in Andalusia, Covington, Alabama, USA, to Robert Julius Bass[1465] and Peggy Ducker[1468].

2772. WESLEY DARRYL KING was born on September 26, 1961.
Wesley Darryl King, aged 21, married Robin Taiwan Bass[2771], aged 20, on April 22, 1983 in Crestview, Okaloosa County, Florida, USA. They had three sons:
>Wesley Daryl King II[3688] born on January 30, 1987
>Justin Lee King[3689] born on January 18, 1989
>Zachary Ryan King[3690] born on June 22, 1996

2773. RICHARD CHRISTOPHER BASS (see Descendants (88)) was born on October 31, 1961, in Andalusia, Covington, Alabama, USA, to Richard Clarence Bass[1470] and Maxine C ?[1471].

2774. RANDI ELIZABETH ROBERTSON was born on November 27, 1961, in West Palm Beach, Florida, USA.
Richard Christopher Bass[2773], aged 20, married Randi Elizabeth Robertson, aged 20, on September 18, 1982 in West Palm Beach, Florida, USA. They had two sons:
>Jason Christopher Bass[3691] born on March 13, 1985 in West Palm Beach, Florida, USA
>Joshua Ryan Bass[3692] born on November 14, 1987 in West Palm Beach, Florida, USA

2775. KIMBERLY RUTH BASS (see Descendants (88)) was born on July 21, 1963, in Andalusia, Covington, Alabama, USA, to Richard Clarence Bass[1470] and Maxine C ?[1471].

2776. GEORGE JOHN NIENHOUSE JR. was born on March 14, 1956, in New Jersey, USA.
George John Nienhouse Jr., aged 24, married Kimberly Ruth Bass[2775], aged 17, on November 18, 1980. They had two children:
>Amanda Lynn Nienhouse[3693] born on September 18, 1981 in West Palm Beach, Florida, USA
>Travis George Nienhouse[3694] born on January 27, 1985 in West Palm Beach, Florida, USA

2777. LEIGH ANN WILLIAMS (see Descendants (88)) was born on September 6, 1968, in Birminghame, Jefferson, Alabama, USA, to Thomas Eugene Williams[1474] and Gayle Ann Bass[1472].

2778. JAMES EDWARD BACHUS was born on September 3, 1947, in Opp, Covington, Alabama, USA.
James Edward Bachus married Leigh Ann Williams[2777]. They had two children:
>Mclain A Bachus[3695] born on June 2, 1995 in Chattanooga, Hamilton, Tennessee, USA
>Mary Alexandra Bachus[3696] born on May 6, 2004 in Chattanooga, Hamilton, Tennessee, USA

2779. THOMAS EUGENE WILLIAMS II (see Descendants (88)) was born on July 8, 1972, in Montgomery, Montgomery, Alabama, USA, to Thomas Eugene Williams[1474] and Gayle Ann Bass[1472].

2780. RHONDA LYNN HARRELSON (see Descendants (89)) was born on October 8, 1955, in Andalusa, Covington, Alabama, USA, to Olen Rex Harrelson[1475] and Betty Jean Bearden[1476].
Rhonda Lynn married twice. She was married to Sydney Long[2781] and Gary Scroggins[2782].

2781. SYDNEY LONG.
Sydney Long married Rhonda Lynn Harrelson[2780]. They had two daughters:
>Ashley Long[3697]
>Jennifer Lynn Long[3698] born on September 28, 1981

2782. GARY SCROGGINS.
Gary Scroggins married Rhonda Lynn Harrelson[2780].

2783. REGINA HARRELSON (see Descendants (89)) was born on June 28, 1958, in Andalusa, Covington, Alabama, USA, to Olen Rex Harrelson[1475] and Betty Jean Bearden[1476].

2784. ROBERT OLEN HARRELSON (see Descendants (89)) was born on March 17, 1960, in Andalusa, Covington, Alabama, USA, to Olen Rex Harrelson[1475] and Betty Jean Bearden[1476].
2785. LAURIE ?.
    Robert Olen Harrelson[2784] married Laurie ?. They had two daughters:
        Erica Harrelson[3699] born on December 12, 1990
        Leigh Ann Harrelson[3700]

2786. CINDY RENE HARRELSON (see Descendants (89)) was born on May 16, 1960, in Andalusa, Covington, Alabama, USA, to Olen Rex Harrelson[1475] and Betty Jean Bearden[1476].
    Cindy Rene married twice. She was married to Mochael McLeod[2787] and Tim Mullen[2788].
2787. MOCHAEL MCLEOD.
    Mochael McLeod married Cindy Rene Harrelson[2786]. They had two daughters:
        Allison McLeod[3701] born on July 1, 1989
        Emily Brook McLeod[3702] born on December 14, 1994
2788. TIM MULLEN.
    Tim Mullen married Cindy Rene Harrelson[2786].

2789. RUSSEL ALLEN HARRELSON (see Descendants (89)) was born on June 26, 1964, in Andalusa, Covington, Alabama, USA, to Olen Rex Harrelson[1475] and Betty Jean Bearden[1476].
2790. LAURA JEANETTE HASLIP.
    Russel Allen Harrelson[2789] married Laura Jeanette Haslip. They had one daughter:
        Peyton Michelle Harrelson[3703] born on April 16, 1994

2791. CHARLES RHETT HARRELSON (see Descendants (89)) was born on October 26, 1966, in Andalusa, Covington, Alabama, USA, to Olen Rex Harrelson[1475] and Betty Jean Bearden[1476].
    Charles Rhett married three times. He was married to Stephanie ?[2792], Vicky Vincent[2793] and Barbara Ann Ziverink[2794].
2792. STEPHANIE ?.
    Charles Rhett Harrelson[2791] married Stephanie ?. They had two children:
        Carolina Harrelson[3704]
        CJ Harrelson[3705]
2793. VICKY VINCENT.
    Charles Rhett Harrelson[2791] married Vicky Vincent.
2794. BARBARA ANN ZIVERINK.
    Charles Rhett Harrelson[2791] married Barbara Ann Ziverink.

2795. MICHAEL REX HARRELSON (see Descendants (89)) was born on December 26, 1947, in Alabama, United States, to Olen Rex Harrelson[1475] and Christine Reba Eiland[1477].
- He was recorded in the census on April 1, 1950, aged 2, in Carolina, Covington, Alabama, United States.
- He died on February 21, 1969, aged 21, in Andalusa, Covington, Alabama, USA.
- He was buried.

2796. SHIRLEY ANN MMITH.
    Michael Rex Harrelson[2795] married Shirley Ann Mmith.

2797. RANDALL KEITH HARRELSON (see Descendants (89)) was born on December 30, 1959, in Andalusia, Covington, Alabama, USA, to Ralph Marlon Harrelson[1478] and Betty June Ganus[1479].
    Randall Keith married twice. He was married to Sandra Elaine Douglas[2798] and Rebecca Ann Lowery[2799].
2798. SANDRA ELAINE DOUGLAS.
    Randall Keith Harrelson[2797] married Sandra Elaine Douglas. They had three children:
        Jeffery Allen Douglas Harrelson[3706] born on September 1, 1978
        James Travis Harrelson[3707] born on October 28, 1983
        Randi Nicole Harrelson[3708] born on March 27, 1990
2799. REBECCA ANN LOWERY.
    Randall Keith Harrelson[2797] married Rebecca Ann Lowery.

2800. RAE SUZANNE HARRELSON (see Descendants (89)) was born on December 18, 1964, in Andalusia, Covington, Alabama, USA, to Ralph Marlon Harrelson[1478] and Betty June Ganus[1479].
    The following information is also recorded for Rae Suzanne:
- Twin on December 18, 1964, as an infant.

2801. JAMES RICKY HARRELSON (see Descendants (89)) was born on December 18, 1964, in Andalusia, Covington,

Direct Relations

Alabama, USA, to Ralph Marlon Harrelson[1478] and Betty June Ganus[1479].
The following information is also recorded for James Ricky:
- Twin on December 18, 1964, as an infant.

2802. MARY BETH WALKER.
James Ricky Harrelson[2801] married Mary Beth Walker. They had one daughter:
Hannah Elizabeth Harrelson[3709] born on October 3, 1989

2803. JACQUELINE CAROLYN HARRELSON (see Descendants (89)) was born on September 6, 1957 to Ramond Teuell Harrelson[1480] and Shirley Stokes[1481].

2804. RENDA SUE HARRELSON (see Descendants (89)) was born on June 24, 1964 to Ronnie Ray Harrelson[1482] and Barbara Sue Duke[1483].
Renda Sue gave birth to one daughter:
Jessica Sueann Harrelson[3710] born on December 11, 1983 in Andalusia, Covington, Alabama, USA

2805. JAMES HARRIS.
James Harris married Renda Sue Harrelson[2804].

2806. RITA ANN HARRELSON (see Descendants (89)) was born on July 22, 1969 to Ronnie Ray Harrelson[1482] and Barbara Sue Duke[1483].

2807. CARL MARVIN LAWSON JR. was born on December 19, 1968, in Covington, Alabama, USA, to Carl Marvin Lawson and Barbara Ann Nelson.
Carl Marvin Lawson Jr., aged 24, married Rita Ann Harrelson[2806], aged 24, on November 20, 1993.

2808. LLOYDE MATHEW SMITH JR. (see Descendants (90)) was born on February 28, 1965 to Lloyd Mathew Smith[1674] and Charlotte Bass[1484].

2809. STEPHANIE SUE POWELL was born on November 21, 1971.
Lloyde Mathew Smith Jr.[2808], aged 29, married Stephanie Sue Powell, aged 23, on December 1, 1994 in Babbie, Covington, Alabama, USA. They had two children:
Douglas Mathew Smith[3712] born on December 6, 1995 in Andalusia, Covington, Alabama, USA
Katelyn Sue Smith[3713] born on April 8, 1997 in Andalusia, Covington, Alabama, USA

2810. GREGORY KEITH SMITH (see Descendants (90)) was born on November 13, 1967 to Lloyd Mathew Smith[1674] and Charlotte Bass[1484].

2811. CYNTHIA DENISE TISDALE was born on October 9, 1969.
Gregory Keith Smith[2810], aged 21, married Cynthia Denise Tisdale, aged 19, on June 24, 1989 in Carolina Baptist Church, Covington, Alabama, USA. They had four children:
Jonathan Keith Smith[3714] born on November 16, 1993 in Dothan, Houston, Alabama, USA
Zachary Paul Smith[3715] born on November 21, 1997 in Dothan, Houston, Alabama, USA
Megan Rebecca Smith[3716] born on October 5, 1999 in Dothan, Houston, Alabama, USA
Sara Grace Smith[3717] born on March 21, 2001 in Dothan, Houston, Alabama, USA

2812. JASON DARREN SMITH (see Descendants (90)) was born on March 21, 1973 to Lloyd Mathew Smith[1674] and Charlotte Bass[1484].
Jason Darren married three times. He was married to Natasha Lynn[2813], Phylis Sorrell[2814] and Christine Lee[2815].

2813. NATASHA LYNN.
Jason Darren Smith[2812] married Natasha Lynn. They had three children:
Trever Kyle Williams[3718] born on December 6, 1997 in Green County, Mississippi, USA
Shelby Breanna Smith[3719] born on April 13, 2004 in Andalusia, Covington, Alabama, USA
Jessica Daily Smith[3720] born on May 22, 2008

2814. PHYLIS SORRELL.
Jason Darren Smith[2812] married Phylis Sorrell.

2815. CHRISTINE LEE.
Jason Darren Smith[2812] married Christine Lee.

2816. MELINDA GAYLE BARROW (see Descendants (90)) was born on January 21, 1972, in Andalusia, Covington, Alabama, USA, to Harold Jerome Barrow[1486] and Elizabeth Louise Bass[1485].

2817. ROBERT LAMAR BURTON.
Robert Lamar Burton married Melinda Gayle Barrow[2816], aged 23, on June 24, 1995. They had two sons:
Garrett Lamar Burton[3721] born on September 21, 1998 in Montgomery, Montgomery, Alabama, USA
John Grant Burton[3722] born on October 30, 2001 in Montgomery, Montgomery, Alabama, USA

2818. ANGELA LYNN BARROW (see Descendants (90)) was born on December 15, 1974, in Andalusia, Covington, Alabama, USA, to Harold Jerome Barrow[1486] and Elizabeth Louise Bass[1485].
2819. JAMES WILLIAM WISMER.
> James William Wismer married Angela Lynn Barrow[2818]. They had three daughters:
>> Emily Kay Wismer[3723] born on August 20, 1999 in Montgomery, Montgomery, Alabama, USA
>> Hannah Elizabeth Wismer[3724] born on August 20, 1999 in Montgomery, Montgomery, Alabama, USA
>> Madalyn Jean Wismer[3725] born on May 29, 2001 in Montgomery, Montgomery, Alabama, USA

2820. KEVIN JEROME BARROW (see Descendants (90)) was born on July 21, 1978, in Andalusia, Covington, Alabama, USA, to Harold Jerome Barrow[1486] and Elizabeth Louise Bass[1485].

2821. ANGELA BETH BASS (see Descendants (92)) was born on June 3, 1968 to Roger Clayton Bass[1489] and Lily Esther Rice[1490].
2822. MIKE JAMES.
> Mike James married Angela Beth Bass[2821], aged 20, in December 1988, and they were divorced.

2823. MELONY WIGGINS (see Descendants (93)) was born to Darrell Wiggins[1493] and Redessa L Henderson[1492].

2824. SYLVIA WIGGINS (see Descendants (93)) was born to Darrell Wiggins[1493] and Redessa L Henderson[1492].

2825. SHANNON WIGGINS (see Descendants (93)) was born to Darrell Wiggins[1493] and Redessa L Henderson[1492].

2826. CONNIE WIGGINS (see Descendants (93)) was born to Darrell Wiggins[1493] and Redessa L Henderson[1492].
2827. DENNY NALL.

> Denny Nall married Connie Wiggins[2826]. They had two children:
>> Amber Nall[3726] born on November 8, 1977
>> Tanner Nall[3727] born about 1981

2828. ROBIN DENISE HENDERSON (see Descendants (93)) was born on January 30, 1964, in Andalusia, Covington, Alabama, USA, to Fredrick Henderson[1494] and Jeanette Robinson[1495].
2829. MARTIN EUGENE STACEY was born on March 25, 1959.
> Martin Eugene Stacey married Robin Denise Henderson[2828]. They had two children:
>> Robin Renee Stacey[3729] born on August 15, 1987 in Warner Robins, Houston, Alabama, USA
>> Seth Eugene Stacey[3730] born on May 9, 1989 in Warner Robins, Houston, Alabama, USA

2830. DONNA KATRISE HENDERSON (see Descendants (93)) was born on June 14, 1966, in Andalusia, Covington, Alabama, USA, to Fredrick Henderson[1494] and Jeanette Robinson[1495].
2831. KENNETH CHARLES MURPHY.
> Kenneth Charles Murphy married Donna Katrise Henderson[2830]. They had one daughter:
>> Katherine Marie Murphy[3731] born on April 7, 1991 in Brunswick, Glenn, Georgia, USA

2832. STEPHANIE LEWIS (see Descendants (93)) was born to Ronnie Lewis[1497] and Judith Lynn Henderson[1496].

2833. ERIC HENDERSON (see Descendants (93)) was born to Phillip Henderson[1498] and Rebecca Riley[1499].

2834. CHAD HENDERSON (see Descendants (93)) was born to Phillip Henderson[1498] and Rebecca Riley[1499].

2835. TODD ALLISON OTT (see Descendants (94)) was born on April 5, 1965, in Channelview, Harris, Texas, USA, to Millard Allison Ott Jr.[1501] and Joann Merrel[1503].
2836. STACEY JEAN BLAIR was born on November 15, 1969.
> Todd Allison Ott[2835], aged 29, married Stacey Jean Blair, aged 25, on March 18, 1995 in Georgetown, Delaware, USA. They had two children:
>> Austin Thomas Ott[3732] born on September 16, 1995 in Christianna, Delaware, USA
>> Carlie Cierra Ott[3733] born on February 12, 1998 in The woods, Montgomery, Texas, USA

2837. KAM RENAE OTT (see Descendants (94)) was born on December 15, 1973, in Conroe, Montgomery, Texas, USA, to Millard Allison Ott Jr.[1501] and Joann Merrel[1503].

2838. JOHN FRANKLIN SMITH JR. was born on November 18, 1971, in Conroe, Montgomery, Texas, USA.
  John Franklin Smith Jr., aged 20, married Kam Renae Ott[2837], aged 18, on January 18, 1992 in Bear Creek, San Jacinto, Texas, USA. They had four children:
    Justin Todd Smith[3734] born on December 9, 1992 in Conroe, Montgomery, Texas, USA
    Aaron Hope Inez Smith[3735] born on November 9, 1996 in Conroe, Montgomery, Texas, USA
    Dylan McKay Smith[3736] born on March 10, 1998 in Woodlands, Montgomery, Texas, USA
    Madison Taylor Smith[3737] born on November 6, 1999 in Conroe, Montgomery, Texas, USA

2839. WILLIAM GILBERT OTT (see Descendants (94)) was born on January 8, 1975, in Cleveland, Liberty, Texas, USA, to Millard Allison Ott Jr.[1501] and Joann Merrel[1503].

2840. JAMES ALLEN OTT JR. (see Descendants (94)) was born on April 12, 1972, in Conroe, Montgomery, Texas, USA, to James Allen Ott Sr.[1504] and Karren Regina Henry[1505].
2841. VICKY RENEE MATHENY was born in Pasadena, Harris, Texas, USA.
  James Allen Ott Jr.[2840], aged 23, married Vicky Renee Matheny on April 15, 1995 in Cleveland, Liberty, Texas, USA. They had one daughter:
    Heather Ott[3738]

2842. REAGAN EDWARD OTT (see Descendants (94)) was born on June 20, 1974, in Cochice, Arazona, USA, to James Allen Ott Sr.[1504] and Karren Regina Henry[1505].

2843. KARREN MICHELLE OTT (see Descendants (94)) was born on May 23, 1979, in Conroe, Montgomery, Texas, USA, to James Allen Ott Sr.[1504] and Karren Regina Henry[1505].

2844. MICHAEL ALLEN CREWS (see Descendants (95)) was born to James Harold Crews[1519] and Linda Bass[1518].

  Michael Allen became known as "Mike". He died on June 16, 2016.
  Note: *Michael Allen Crews, age 47, died suddenly but peacefully from a massive heart attack before sunrise on Thursday, June 16, 2016 in Elliott County, Kentucky. Mike was an avid hunter, fisherman, survivalist, gardener, lover of nature. He was a surveyor for over 20 years and loved his outdoor "office." Mike walked to the beat of his own drummer. He enjoyed every minute of that walk and touched so many people along the way. He will be missed so much by so many.* (Death)

2845. DANA BUTLER.

  Michael Allen Crews[2844] and Dana Butler had two children:
    Michael Bennett Crews[3739]
    Summer Crews[3741]
  The following information is also recorded for this family:
    • Unknown Relationship.

2846. ANGIE CREWS (see Descendants (95)) was born to James Harold Crews[1519] and Linda Bass[1518].

2847. MR. BARKER.
  Mr. Barker married Angie Crews[2846]. They had three children:
    Mr./Ms. Barker[3742]
    Mr./Ms. Barker[3743]
    Mr./Ms. Barker[3744]

2848. SHAWN BASS (see Descendants (95)) was born to Gary Dean Bass[1520] and Dora Mapes[1521].
2849. MS. ?.
  Shawn Bass[2848] married Ms. ?. They had one son:
    Austin Bass[3745]

2850. MARLA KIM BASS (see Descendants (96)) was born to Marlon Jerome Bass[1534] and Betty J. ?[1535].
  Marla Kim married twice. She was married to Matthew Mangham[2851] and Mr. Barelare[2852].

2851. MATTHEW MANGHAM.
> Matthew Mangham married Marla Kim Bass[2850]. They had two children:
>> Mathew Mangham[3747]
>> Michelle Mangham[3748]

2852. MR. BARELARE.
> Mr. Barelare married Marla Kim Bass[2850] on March 29, 2000.

2853. MICHAEL WAYNE TYLER (see Descendants (96)) was born on June 28, 1953, in Charlottsville, VA, USA, to Albert T Tyler[1537] and Doris Jean Bass[1536]. Michael Wayne was adopted by Henry Albert Tyler[1538] and Doris Jean Bass[1536].

2854. BARBARA ANN FAIRMAN was born on July 22, 1953, in Pensylvania, USA.
> Michael Wayne Tyler[2853] married Barbara Ann Fairman. They had four children:
>> Jessica Ann Tyler[3749] born on March 10, 1985 in Dothan, Dale, Alabama, USA
>> Cathleen Doren Tyler[3750] born on March 5, 1987 in Dothan, Dale, Alabama, USA
>> Justin Fairman Tyler[3752] born on November 12, 1989; died on November 12, 1989
>> Michael Fairman Tyler[3753] born on May 8, 1991 in Andalusia, Covington, Alabama, USA

2855. ANITA KAYE TYLER (see Descendants (96)) was born on October 17, 1966, in Andalusia, Covington, Alabama, USA, to Henry Albert Tyler[1538] and Doris Jean Bass[1536].

2856. MARK EDWARD PRUIT.
> Mark Edward Pruit married Anita Kaye Tyler[2855], aged 25, on November 30, 1991 in Andalusia, Covington, Alabama, USA.

2857. BRUCE KELLEY VEASEY (see Descendants (96)) was born on September 22, 1961 to Bruce Veasey Jr.[1540] and Shirley Ann Bass[1539].

2858. MELISSA BATES was born on October 22, 1962.
> Bruce Kelley Veasey[2857], aged 22, married Melissa Bates, aged 21, on June 23, 1984. They had two children:
>> Hanna Elizabeth Veasey[3754] born on October 19, 1987
>> Andrew Bruce Veasey[3756] born on November 2, 1990

2859. BRANDON KEITH VEASEY (see Descendants (96)) was born to Bruce Veasey Jr.[1540] and Shirley Ann Bass[1539].

2860. CHRIS OLIVE (see Descendants (97)) was born to Bobby Olive[1544] and Becky ?[1545].

2861. ANN OLIVE (see Descendants (97)) was born to Bobby Olive[1544] and Becky ?[1545].

2862. ANTHONY LEE PARRISH (see Descendants (98)) was born on February 4, 1957, in Andalusia, Covington, Alabama, USA, to Carmon Lee Parrish[1547] and Shelia Pamelia Bass[1546].
> Anthony Lee married twice. He was married to Kara Mixson[2863] and Belinda Crawford[2864].

2863. KARA MIXSON was born in Moultie, Georgia, USA.
> Anthony Lee Parrish[2862] married Kara Mixson.

2864. BELINDA CRAWFORD.
> Anthony Lee Parrish[2862] married Belinda Crawford. They had three daughters:
>> Laura Amanda Parrish[3758] born on April 17, 1981
>> Celeste Parrish[3760] born on December 19, 1981
>> Shelby Anne Parrish[3762] born on March 29, 1999

2865. REBECCA LYNN PARRISH (see Descendants (98)) was born on November 15, 1958 to Carmon Lee Parrish[1547] and Shelia Pamelia Bass[1546].

2866. DANNY WARD HOLLAND was born on October 16, 1953.
> Danny Ward Holland married Rebecca Lynn Parrish[2865]. They had three daughters:
>> Hope Danielle Holland[3763] born on March 14, 1981
>> Hannah Elizabeth Holland[3764] born on September 10, 1985
>> Heather Lee Holland[3765] born on September 10, 1985

2867. JON KEVIN PARRISH (see Descendants (98)) was born on November 18, 1963 to Carmon Lee Parrish[1547] and Shelia Pamelia Bass[1546].

2868. RITCHIE DEAN GRISSETT (see Descendants (98)) was born on November 14, 1965, in Andalusia, Covington, Alabama, USA, to Kenneth Lavon Grissett[1549] and Patricia Lucille Bass[1548].

2869. MARQUITA LYNN GRISSETT (see Descendants (98)) was born on July 20, 1969, in Andalusia, Covington, Alabama, USA, to Kenneth Lavon Grissett[1549] and Patricia Lucille Bass[1548].

2870. KEITH LAVON GRISSETT (see Descendants (98)) was born on May 9, 1973, in Andalusia, Covington, Alabama, USA, to Kenneth Lavon Grissett[1549] and Patricia Lucille Bass[1548].

2871. DONNA LYNNE BASS (see Descendants (98)) was born on September 4, 1965, in Andalusia, Covington, Alabama, USA, to James William Bass[1550] and Louise Kelley[1551].

2872. PAMELA RENEA BASS (see Descendants (98)) was born on January 18, 1967, in Andalusia, Covington, Alabama, USA, to James William Bass[1550] and Louise Kelley[1551].

2873. PAULA KAY BASS (see Descendants (98)) was born on August 25, 1972, in Andalusia, Covington, Alabama, USA, to James William Bass[1550] and Louise Kelley[1551].

2874. MICHAEL GERALD BASS (see Descendants (98)) was born on June 22, 1971, in Andalusia, Covington, Alabama, USA, to Mathew Gerald Bass[1552] and Mary Lou Bush[1553].

2875. WILLIAM HENRY BASS (see Descendants (98)) was born on September 23, 1972, in Andalusia, Covington, Alabama, USA, to Mathew Gerald Bass[1552] and Mary Lou Bush[1553].

2876. KATIE DIANE BASS (see Descendants (98)) was born on April 22, 1975, in Andalusia, Covington, Alabama, USA, to Mathew Gerald Bass[1552] and Mary Lou Bush[1553].

2877. JAMES LYNN BASS (see Descendants (98)) was born on April 30, 1976, in Andalusia, Covington, Alabama, USA, to Mathew Gerald Bass[1552] and Mary Lou Bush[1553].

2878. MICHAEL BASS (see Descendants (98)) was born to Jerry Bass[1554] and Ms. ?[1555].

2879. MR. BASS (see Descendants (98)) was born to Jerry Bass[1554] and Ms. ?[1555].

2880. BRETT ZAN BASS (see Descendants (99)) was born in 1965, in Hattisburg, Mississippi, USA, to Steve Walden Bass[1559] and Saundra Gail Harris[1560].
Brett Zan married twice. He was married to Amy Hawks[2881] and Becky Parker[2882].
2881. AMY HAWKS.
    Brett Zan Bass[2880] married Amy Hawks. They had one son:
        Brett Andrew Bass[3767] born in 1987
2882. BECKY PARKER.
    Brett Zan Bass[2880] married Becky Parker. They had one daughter:
        Camrin Zan Bass[3769] born in 1993

2883. BRANDY LANE BASS (see Descendants (99)) was born in 1968 to Steve Walden Bass[1559] and Saundra Gail Harris[1560].
2884. STEPHEN MICHAEL SCOTT.
    Stephen Michael Scott married Brandy Lane Bass[2883], aged about 28, from 1993 to 1999, and they were divorced. They had one son:
        Dylan Wayne Scott[3770] born on May 26, 1993 in Milton, Santa Rosa, Florida, USA

2885. NANCI L. BASS (see Descendants (99)) was born to Steve Walden Bass[1559] and Paula Simpson[1561].

2886. ERIN LYNN BASS (see Descendants (99)) was born on October 18, 1986, in Milton, Florida USA, to Danny Kay Bass[1562] and Vicky Walker[1563].

2887. DEVIN LEE BASS (see Descendants (267)) was born on March 31, 1986 to Kenneth Lee Bass[1564] and Tammy C Sorrells[1565].
2888. MS. WATSON.
    Devin Lee Bass[2887] and Ms. Watson had one son:
        Diesel Wayne Bass[3771] born on March 15, 2011
    The following information is also recorded for this family:
      • Unspecified Relationship.

2889. SHELEIAH LYNN BASS (see Descendants (267)) was born on March 11, 1988 to Kenneth Lee Bass[1564] and Tammy C Sorrells[1565].
2890. CONSTANTINOS ARGERIS was born on June 23, 1985. Constantinos became known as "Tino".
Constantinos Argeris married Sheleiah Lynn Bass[2889]. They had two sons:
Constantinos Argeris[3772] born on June 1, 2017
Hristos Argeris[3773] born on November 12, 2019

2891. MIRANDA BASS (see Descendants (268)) was born in 1990 to Randy Lynn Bass[1567] and Kimi Sue Adams[1568].
2892. MR. ?.
Mr. ? married Miranda Bass[2891]. They had one son:
Jameson ?[3774] born in 2010

2893. RANDI LYNN BASS (see Descendants (268)) was born in 1995 to Randy Lynn Bass[1567] and Kimi Sue Adams[1568].

2894. WAYLON BASS (see Descendants (268)) was born to Randy Lynn Bass[1567] and Carry Ann ?[1569].

2895. HANNAH LENELLE BASS (see Descendants (272)) was born on December 13, 1980, in Atlanta, Georgia, USA, to John Dennis Bass[1576] and Janice Darlene Owens[1577].
2896. JEFFERY SCOTT TUTTEROW.
Jeffery Scott Tutterow married Hannah LeNelle Bass[2895], aged 24, on September 10, 2005 in Cannon United Methodist, Snellville, Georgia, USA. They had one son:
Jackson Tutterow[3775]

2897. KEVIN BASS (see Descendants (272)) was born on March 22, 1982, in Atlanta, Georgia, USA, to John Dennis Bass[1576] and Janice Darlene Owens[1577].

2898. TINA DARLENE BASS (see Descendants (272)) was born in Atlanta, Georgia, USA to John Dennis Bass[1576] and Janice Darlene Owens[1577].
Tina Darlene married twice. She was married to Kevin Vance Himes[2899] and Shawn Patrick O'Connor[2900].
2899. KEVIN VANCE HIMES.
Kevin Vance Himes married Tina Darlene Bass[2898] on June 4, 1994 in Level Creek United Methodist, Suwanee, Georgia, USA. They had two sons:
Cameron Himes[3776]
Kendrick Himes[3777]
2900. SHAWN PATRICK O'CONNOR.
Shawn Patrick O'Connor married Tina Darlene Bass[2898]. They had one son:
Patrick O'Connor[3778]

2901. LORI NICOLE LEE (see Descendants (274)) was born on June 26, 1984, in Montgomery, Montgomery, Alabama, USA, to Kenneth E Lee[1582] and Emily Gwendolyn Bass[1581].
Lori Nicole married twice. She was married to William McVay[2902] and Willis Gene Jackson[2903].
2902. WILLIAM MCVAY. William became known as "Will".
William McVay married Lori Nicole Lee[2901]. They had two daughters:
Loretta Voncile McVay[3779]
Ms. McVay[3780]
2903. WILLIS GENE JACKSON.
Willis Gene married twice. He was married to Lori Nicole Lee[2901] and Ms. ?.
Willis Gene Jackson married Lori Nicole Lee[2901].
Willis Gene Jackson married Ms. ?. They had one son:
Chrisitan Jackson

2904. TANNER LEE (see Descendants (274)) was born on June 27, 1991, in Andalusia, Covington, Alabama, USA, to Kenneth E Lee[1582] and Emily Gwendolyn Bass[1581].

2905. LADONICE DARNELL BARNETT (see Descendants (275)) was born to Rickie Donnel Barnett Sr.[1583] and Doris Ann Dubose[1584].
2906. TONY INGRAM.
Tony Ingram married LaDonice Darnell Barnett[2905]. They had two children:
Courtney Ingram[3781]
Joshua Tyler Ingram[3782]

2907. BUFFIE DEANNA BARNETT (see Descendants (275)) was born to Rickie Donnel Barnett Sr.[1583] and Barbara Gambells[1585].

2908. RICKEY DARNELL BARNETT JR. (see Descendants (275)) was born to Rickie Donnel Barnett Sr.[1583] and Barbara Gambells[1585].

2909. GLORIA LYNN BARNETT (see Descendants (275)) was born to Rickie Donnel Barnett Sr.[1583] and Sandra Adams[1586].
2910. STEVE QUEENS.
    Steve Queens married Gloria Lynn Barnett[2909].

2911. MELISSA ANN BARNETT (see Descendants (275)) was born to Rickie Donnel Barnett Sr.[1583] and Sandra Adams[1586].
2912. DANIEL ?.
    Daniel ? married Melissa Ann Barnett[2911].

2913. BRANDI LEE PRESLEY (see Descendants (276)) was born on February 17, 1977 to Arthur Lynn Presley[1588] and Gloria Dianne Barnett[1587].
The following information is also recorded for Brandi Lee:
  Twin.
2914. JOHNNY ROBERT BOLES SR. was born on April 8, 1977. Johnny Robert became known as "Robbie".
    Johnny Robert Boles Sr. married Brandi Lee Presley[2913]. They had two children:
        Johnny Robert Boles Jr.[3784] born on January 6, 2005
        Brooklynn Lee Boles[3785] born on November 1, 2012

2915. CHRISTOPHER EDWIN PRESLEY (see Descendants (276)) was born on February 17, 1977 to Arthur Lynn Presley[1588] and Gloria Dianne Barnett[1587].
The following information is also recorded for Christopher Edwin:
  Twin.
Christopher Edwin married twice. He was married to Donna Wise[2916] and Dorenda Richards[2917].

2916. DONNA WISE.
    Christopher Edwin Presley[2915], aged about 22, married Donna Wise about 1999. They had two daughters:
        Ciera Elizabeth Presley[3786] born on April 12, 1999
        Cheyenne Erin Presley[3787] born on February 12, 2001
2917. DORENDA RICHARDS was born on September 2, 1976.
    Christopher Edwin Presley[2915], aged 33, married Dorenda Richards, aged 33, on May 29, 2010. They had one daughter:
        Brianna Tegan Presley[3788] born on September 4, 2008

2918. LINDSEY PRESLEY (see Descendants (276)) was born on April 19, 1984 to Arthur Lynn Presley[1588] and Gloria Dianne Barnett[1587].
Lindsey had two partnerships. She was married to John Michael Morris[2919]. She was also the partner of Mr. Crawford[2920].
2919. JOHN MICHAEL MORRIS was born on October 21, 1982.
    John Michael Morris, aged 30, married Lindsey Presley[2918], aged 28, on April 12, 2013.
2920. MR. CRAWFORD.
    Mr. Crawford and Lindsey Presley[2918] had one daughter:
        Sydney Nicole Crawford Morris[3789] born on March 2, 2011
    The following information is also recorded for this family:
      • Unknown Relationship.

2921. STARLETTE DAWN RUSSELL (see Descendants (277)) was born to Raymond Randall Russell[1590] and Teresa LaGail Barnett[1589].
2922. CASEY LEVON RAY.
    Casey Levon Ray married Starlette Dawn Russell[2921]. They had one daughter:
        Emmaleigh Maddison Ray[3790]

2923. RAYMOND RANDALL RUSSELL JR. (see Descendants (277)) was born to Raymond Randall Russell[1590] and Teresa LaGail Barnett[1589]. Raymond Randall became known as "Ray".
2924. MARY ANN CHANCE.
> Raymond Randall Russell Jr.[2923] married Mary Ann Chance. They had four children:
>> Kip Riley Russell[3791]
>> Amber Nicole Russell[3792]
>> Payton Breanna Russell[3793]
>> Kayla Brook Russell[3794]

2925. SONYA LEANN RUSSELL (see Descendants (277)) was born to Raymond Randall Russell[1590] and Teresa LaGail Barnett[1589].
2926. MICHAEL DEWAYNE GOODSON.
> Michael Dewayne Goodson married Sonya Leann Russell[2925]. They had two sons:
>> Michael Tyler Goodson[3795]
>> Cory Ryan Goodson[3796]

2927. DAVID BRENT GLIDEWELL (see Descendants (278)) was born to David Glidewell[1593] and Wanda June Barnett[1592].
David Brent was the partner of his fourth cousin, once removed, Lori Lucas[3446].

2928. CHRISTY LEE GLIDEWELL (see Descendants (278)) was born to David Glidewell[1593] and Wanda June Barnett[1592].
2929. JERRY KILPATRICK.
> Jerry Kilpatrick married Christy Lee Glidewell[2928]. They had one daughter:
>> Caden Kilpatrick[3799]

2930. MITCHELL ALLEN GINDLESPERGER (see Descendants (279)) was born on February 27, 1974, in Jacksonville, Florida, USA, to Dale Allen Gindlesperger Jr.[1595] and Belinda Jo Boney[1596].
2931. MELISSA ANN BOLES was born on October 19, 1973, in Georgia, USA.
> Mitchell Allen Gindlesperger[2930], aged 23, married Melissa Ann Boles, aged 23, on August 16, 1997 in L'Ville Chruch of God, Lawranceville, Georgia, USA. They had three sons:
>> Mason Allen Gindlesperger[3800] born on February 23, 2004 in Snellville, Georgia, USA
>> Miles Avery Gindlesperger[3801] born on May 19, 2006 in Snellville, Georgia, USA
>> Merritt Anderson Gindlesperger[3802] born on August 24, 2008 in Snellville, Georgia, USA

2932. ANDREW GRANT GINDLESPERGER (see Descendants (279)) was born on December 7, 1978, in Jacksonville, Florida, USA, to Dale Allen Gindlesperger Jr.[1595] and Belinda Jo Boney[1596].
2933. AMANDA LEIGH GRIDER was born on April 4, 1980, in Loganville, Georga, USA.
> Andrew Grant Gindlesperger[2932], aged 27, married Amanda Leigh Grider, aged 26, on October 21, 2006 in Peachtree Christian Church, Atlanta, Georgia, USA.

2934. DEREK ASHLEY GINDLESPERGER (see Descendants (279)) was born on November 7, 1983, in Duluth, Georgia, USA, to Dale Allen Gindlesperger Jr.[1595] and Belinda Jo Boney[1596].
2935. KELLY MELISSA RAW was born on June 2, 1985, in Florida, USA.
> Derek Ashley Gindlesperger[2934], aged 27, married Kelly Melissa Raw, aged 25, on February 24, 2011 in Tuscawilla Country Club, Oveido, Florida, USA.

2936. APRIL ANN KING (see Descendants (280)) was born on October 20, 1971, in Montgomery, Montgomery, Alabama, USA, to James B King[1598] and Sue Ann Mann[1597].
2937. MICHAEL MADDOX was born on October 14, 1971, in Montgomery, Montgomery, Alabama, USA.
> Michael Maddox married April Ann King[2936] in Pratville, Alabama, USA. They had two sons:
>> Dalto Michael Maddox[3803] born on October 2, 2000 in Montgomery, Montgomery, Alabama, USA
>> Brodie James Maddox[3804] born on April 24, 2004 in Montgomery, Montgomery, Alabama, USA

2938. ANGELA KAY CORNELL (see Descendants (282)) was born on August 28, 1971, in Hopkinsville, Kentucky, USA, to Randel Glenn Cornell[1602] and Betty Jean Mann[1601]. Angela Kay was adopted by Ronald Reed[1603] and Betty Jean Mann[1601].
2939. CLAY LEHMANN.
> Clay Lehmann married Angela Kay Cornell[2938].

2940. ASHTON NICOLE MANN (see Descendants (283)) was born on October 10, 1986, in Montgomery, Montgomery, Alabama, USA, to Dennis Keith Mann[1605] and Cindy Calhoun[1606].

2941. SETH ALLEN MANN MANN (see Descendants (284)) was born on November 2, 2002, in Montgomery, Montgomery, Alabama, USA, to Michael Wayne Mann[1608] and Sandra Elaine Coleman[1609].

2942. COLE MICHAEL MANN (see Descendants (284)) was born on November 18, 2004, in Montgomery, Montgomery, Alabama, USA, to Michael Wayne Mann[1608] and Sandra Elaine Coleman[1609]. He died (At young age) on December 22, 2004, as an infant, in Fitzgerald, Georgia, USA.

2943. DAKOTA MANN (see Descendants (284)) was born on January 6, 2008, in Montgomery, Montgomery, Alabama, USA, to Michael Wayne Mann[1608] and Sandra Elaine Coleman[1609].

2944. PIPER MANN (see Descendants (284)) was born on January 6, 2008, in Montgomery, Montgomery, Alabama, USA, to Michael Wayne Mann[1608] and Sandra Elaine Coleman[1609].

2945. TAYLOR MANN (see Descendants (284)) was born on January 6, 2008, in Montgomery, Montgomery, Alabama, USA, to Michael Wayne Mann[1608] and Sandra Elaine Coleman[1609].

2946. TYLER ANSEL HOGAN (see Descendants (285)) was born on October 2, 1990, in Valdosta, Lowndes, Alabama, USA, to Ansel Hogan[1611] and Linda Fay Maund[1610].

2947. MARY MILES (see Descendants (287)) was born to David Miles[1616] and Wendy Brynell Bass[1615].

2948. BRIAN MILES (see Descendants (287)) was born to David Miles[1616] and Wendy Brynell Bass[1615].

2949. RANDY DANFORD (see Descendants (288)) was born to Johnny Mack Danford[1618] and Alivia LaShelle Bass[1617]. Randy became known as "J-Mack".

2950. DERRICK LAMAR BASS (see Descendants (289)) was born on July 7, 1993, in Montgomery, Montgomery, Alabama, USA, to Murry Lamar Bass[1619] and Donna Theresa Stacks[1620].

2951. TREY PREVITO (see Descendants (100)) was born to Leonard Raymond Previto Jr.[1625] and Ms. Beverly[1626].
2952. MS. ?.
    Trey Previto[2951] married Ms. ?. They had two sons:
        Landon Previto[3805]
        Joey Previto[3806]

2953. LEAH E PREVITO (see Descendants (100)) was born about 1978 to Leonard Raymond Previto Jr.[1625] and Ms. Beverly[1626].

2954. KRISTINA PREVITO (see Descendants (100)) was born to Leonard Raymond Previto Jr.[1625] and Ms. Beverly[1626].

2955. TROY LYNNE FINDLEY (see Descendants (101)) was born in March 1962 to Norman Russell Findley[1630] and Ruby Jean Turner[1629]. She died in January 1968, aged 5.

2956. MICHAEL RENA FINDLEY (see Descendants (101)) was born on December 3, 1963 to Norman Russell Findley[1630] and Ruby Jean Turner[1629].

2957. ROBBY LYNN FINDLEY (see Descendants (101)) was born on May 2, 1969 to Norman Russell Findley[1630] and Ruby Jean Turner[1629].

2958. MR. PADGETT (see Descendants (102)) was born to William Thomas Padgett[1635] and Mary Louise Poucher[1636].

2959. MR. PADGETT (see Descendants (102)) was born to William Thomas Padgett[1635] and Mary Louise Poucher[1636].

2960. MERWYN T. MELVIN I (see Descendants (20)) was born to Odem Thomas Melvin Jr.[1639] and Beulah Petit[1640].
2961. LOUISE ADAMS.
    Merwyn T. Melvin I[2960] married Louise Adams. They had four children:
        Julia Melvin[3807]
        Merwyn T. Melvin II[3809]

Vincent J. Melvin[3811]
Aaron ("Bogie") Melvin[3813]

2962. ELLEN FRANCIS SHAW (see Descendants (104)) was born to Theo Shaw[1642] and Gwen Melvin[1641].
2963. ROY SIMMONS.
Roy Simmons married Ellen Francis Shaw[2962]. They had one daughter:
Treg Simmons[3815]

2964. ARTEMIS DIANE VAGIAS (see Descendants (105)) was born to Louis Vagias[1644] and Carolyn Melvin[1643]. Artemis Diane married twice. She was married to Richard Sadlier[2965] and Mr. Wayman[2966].

2965. RICHARD SADLIER. Richard became known as "Rick".
The following information is also recorded for Rick:
• Military Service.
Notes:
• *Commander U.S. Navy.*
(Military Service)
• *"On Armed Forces Day (2019) Rick was inducted into the Avenue of Heroes in Coronado for his service to country. I suppose the most impressive part of his career is that he flew 483 combat missions in a Huey gun ship, sometimes flying up to 4 combat missions in one day and survived! Not only was he a great pilot but he has been the very best husband and Dad any woman could ever hope for! -Diane Sadlier [Vagias].*
(Military Service)
Richard Sadlier married Artemis Diane Vagias[2964]. They had four children:
Mr. Sadlier[3817]
Mr./Ms. Sadlier[3818]
Mr./Ms. Sadlier[3819]
Mr./Ms. Sadlier[3820]

2966. MR. WAYMAN.
Mr. Wayman married Artemis Diane Vagias[2964]. They had two daughters:
Carolyn Wayman[3821]
Katherine Wayman[3823]

2967. LOUIS VAGIAS JR. (see Descendants (105)) was born to Louis Vagias[1644] and Carolyn Melvin[1643]. Louis became known as "Buz".

2968. JANET CASSELBERRY.
Louis Vagias Jr.[2967] married Janet Casselberry. They had one son:
Louis Vagias III[3825]

2969. HARY QUINN JR. (see Descendants (106)) was born to Harry Quinn[1646] and Bennie Margaret Melvin[1645].

2970. JOAN QUINN (see Descendants (106)) was born to Harry Quinn[1646] and Bennie Margaret Melvin[1645].
2971. ARTHUR VALDES.
Arthur Valdes married Joan Quinn[2970]. They had two children:
Mary Valdes[3826]
Arthur Valdes[3828]

2972. MR./MS. PARRISH (see Descendants (107)) was born to Mr. Parrish[1659] and Mr./Ms. ?[1660].

2973. MR. CASON (see Descendants (110)) was born to Lindsey Cason[1687] and Rita ?[1688].

2974. CHESTER DALE LITTLE (see Descendants (114)) was born on April 16, 1952 to James Calvin Little[1700] and

Direct Relations

Addie Vivian Raley[1699].
- He died on September 3, 1975, aged 23, in United States and Territory.

The following information is also recorded for Chester Dale:
- Military Service in 1975, aged about 23.
- Religion: Baptist-Other Groups.

2975. JAMES CURTIS LITTLE (see Descendants (114)) was born on February 5, 1954 to James Calvin Little[1700] and Addie Vivian Raley[1699].

2976. LANNEY RAY LITTLE (see Descendants (114)) was born on June 4, 1955 to James Calvin Little[1700] and Addie Vivian Raley[1699].

2977. KAREN REGINA LITTLE (see Descendants (114)) was born on March 7, 1960 to James Calvin Little[1700] and Addie Vivian Raley[1699].

2978. STEVAN UPTAGRAFT (see Descendants (114)) was born on July 28, 1956 to Roy C. Uptagraft[1702] and Lois Jewel Raley[1701].

2979. LISA ANN UPTAGRAFT (see Descendants (114)) was born on August 19, 1958 to Roy C. Uptagraft[1702] and Lois Jewel Raley[1701].

2980. MICHELLE KATHERINE POWELL (see Descendants (114)) was born on December 12, 1965 to Fredrick Harold Powell[1704] and Mary Alice Raley[1703].

2981. KELLY LYNN ANDREWS (see Descendants (114)) was born to James Dale Andrews[1706] and Julia Yuvone Raley[1705].

2982. MICHAEL HENRY KNIPP KNIPP (see Descendants (116)) was born to Bill Knipp[1716] and Greer Ellen Bass[1715].

2983. JUDSON LEVON BASS JR. (see Descendants (117)) was born on November 23, 1962 to Judson Levon Bass[1718] and Alice Floyd[1719].

2984. JOSEPH MICHAEL BASS (see Descendants (117)) was born on November 23, 1963 to Judson Levon Bass[1718] and Alice Floyd[1719].

2985. RONALD JOE BASS (see Descendants (117)) was born on February 13, 1965 to Marron Grady Bass[1720] and Carolyn O. Ward[1721].

2986. KAREN COOK (see Descendants (124)) was born on October 30, 1954 to Stanley Cook[1735] and Janice L Beck[1734].
Karen married four times. She was married to George Brown[2987], Jerry McLeod[2988], Donald Wayne Adams[2989] and Billy Simmons[2990].
2987. GEORGE BROWN.
George Brown married Karen Cook[2986].
2988. JERRY MCLEOD.
Jerry McLeod married Karen Cook[2986]. They had one son:
Jonathan Eric McLeod[3830]
2989. DONALD WAYNE ADAMS.
Donald Wayne Adams married Karen Cook[2986]. They had one son:
Brandon Dewayne Adams[3831]
2990. BILLY SIMMONS.
Billy Simmons married Karen Cook[2986].

2991. KEITH COOK (see Descendants (124)) was born on May 13, 1960 to Stanley Cook[1735] and Janice L Beck[1734].
2992. KATHY DOUGLAS.
Keith Cook[2991] married Kathy Douglas. They had three children:
Kenyon Kole Cook[3832]
Kayla Michelle Cook[3833]
Kristopher Lynn Cook[3834]

Page 385

2993. KENYON COOK (see Descendants (124)) was born on November 21, 1961 to Stanley Cook[1735] and Janice L Beck[1734]. He died in 1982, aged about 20.

2994. JAMES JERRY NEWTON (see Descendants (124)) was born on May 6, 1953 to James Newton[1737] and Shirley A Beck[1736].

2995. ERNEST LEROY NEWTON (see Descendants (124)) was born on June 2, 1955 to James Newton[1737] and Shirley A Beck[1736].
2996. CHRISTINE RODERUS.
> Ernest Leroy Newton[2995] married Christine Roderus. They had two daughters:
>> Melinda Roderus[3835]
>> Christy Lynn Newton[3836]

2997. BRIDGET BELINDA NEWTON (see Descendants (124)) was born on February 16, 1957 to James Newton[1737] and Shirley A Beck[1736].
2998. LIONEL MCCOMBS.
> Lionel McCombs married Bridget Belinda Newton[2997]. They had two children:
>> Joseph McCombs[3837] born on January 31, 1977
>> Jessica McCombs[3838] born on June 3, 1981

2999. MISSOURI MAE NEWTON (see Descendants (124)) was born on November 11, 1958 to James Newton[1737] and Shirley A Beck[1736].
3000. MR. ?.
> Mr. ? and Missouri Mae Newton[2999] had one daughter:
>> Heather ?[3839]
>
> The following information is also recorded for this family:
> • Unknown Relationship.

3001. SHERRY DENISE NEWTON (see Descendants (124)) was born on August 4, 1960 to James Newton[1737] and Shirley A Beck[1736].
Sherry Denise married twice. She was married to Jay Oliver Spicer[3002] and Raymond Chessher[3003].
3002. JAY OLIVER SPICER.
> Jay Oliver Spicer married Sherry Denise Newton[3001]. They had two sons:
>> Jay Fletcher Spicer[3840] born on November 8, 1976
>> Phillip Clayton[3841] born on February 10, 1993
3003. RAYMOND CHESSHER.
> Raymond Chessher married Sherry Denise Newton[3001].

3004. ALAN BECK (see Descendants (124)) was born on January 16, 1971 to Reginald E Beck[1738] and Shelia Davis[1740].

3005. BARABARA SUE BECK (see Descendants (124)) was born on January 1, 1973 to Reginald E Beck[1738] and Shelia Davis[1740].
3006. DARRELL GAINEY.
> Darrell Gainey married Barabara Sue Beck[3005]. They had two children:
>> Waylon Gainey[3842]
>> Nicole Gainey[3843]

3007. TAMARA MICHELLE BECK (see Descendants (124)) was born on September 12, 1968 to Quinton W Beck[1743] and Linda Lee Jones[1745].
3008. ALAN LANDINGHAM.
> Alan Landingham married Tamara Michelle Beck[3007]. They had one daughter:
>> Brittany Landingham[3844]

3009. SHANNON LEON BECK (see Descendants (124)) was born on July 18, 1969 to Theron Leon Beck[1746] and Brenda Richards[1749].

3010. CHRISTOPHER SHANE BECK (see Descendants (124)) was born to Theron Leon Beck[1746] and Brenda Richards[1749].

3011. MARGARET BECK (see Descendants (124)) was born to Theron Leon Beck[1746] and Brenda Richards[1749].

Direct Relations

3012. RICKEY DAVON BECK (see Descendants (124)) was born on February 7, 1974 to Ronald Eugene Beck[1750] and Velma Blocker[1751].

3013. TERRY LEE CHESSHER (see Descendants (124)) was born on July 3, 1968 to Jerry Chessher[1753] and Vivian Diane Beck[1752].
Terry Lee married twice. He was married to Sandra Hudson[3014] and Ann Edge[3015].
3014. SANDRA HUDSON.
> Terry Lee Chessher[3013] married Sandra Hudson. They had two daughters:
> > Natasha Chessher[3845]
> > Christina Chessher[3846]
3015. ANN EDGE.
> Terry Lee Chessher[3013] married Ann Edge. They had one daughter:
> > Chelsey Leanne Chessher[3847] born on September 16, 1994

3016. NOLAN DEWRELL CHESSHER (see Descendants (124)) was born to Jerry Chessher[1753] and Vivian Diane Beck[1752].

3017. MICHAEL ANTHONY CHESSHER (see Descendants (124)) was born to Jerry Chessher[1753] and Vivian Diane Beck[1752].

3018. ALICIAN DIAN COOK (see Descendants (124)) was born to Charles Cook[1754] and Vivian Diane Beck[1752].

3019. CAROLYN NELSON (see Descendants (125)) was born on September 30, 1953 to Lamar Nelson[1757] and Marie Beck[1756].

3020. CARLTON NELSON (see Descendants (125)) was born on August 16, 1954 to Lamar Nelson[1757] and Marie Beck[1756].

3021. RALPH NELSON (see Descendants (125)) was born on November 16, 1955 to Lamar Nelson[1757] and Marie Beck[1756].

3022. BRENDA NELSON (see Descendants (125)) was born on February 24, 1957 to Lamar Nelson[1757] and Marie Beck[1756].

3023. FRANKLIN NELSON (see Descendants (125)) was born on October 11, 1958 to Lamar Nelson[1757] and Marie Beck[1756].

3024. WANDA NELSON (see Descendants (125)) was born on July 29, 1961 to Lamar Nelson[1757] and Marie Beck[1756].

3025. DEBORAH ELAINE BECK (see Descendants (125)) was born on April 9, 1962 to Collie Beck[1758] and Virginia Elmore[1759].

3026. CINDY LYNN BECK (see Descendants (125)) was born on October 21, 1963 to Collie Beck[1758] and Virginia Elmore[1759].

3027. SANDRA BECK (see Descendants (125)) was born on November 25, 1965 to Collie Beck[1758] and Virginia Elmore[1759].

3028. MARILYN BECK (see Descendants (125)) was born on January 27, 1950 to Edward C Beck[1760] and Ms. ?[1761].

3029. GAIL JORDAN (see Descendants (126)) was born on April 12, 1961 to Roland Jordan[1764] and Yvonne Garvin[1763].

3030. RONALD SHERMAN JORDAN (see Descendants (126)) was born on November 19, 1964 to Roland Jordan[1764] and Yvonne Garvin[1763].

3031. MELISSA GLYN JORDAN (see Descendants (126)) was born on March 5, 1966 to Roland Jordan[1764] and Yvonne Garvin[1763].

3032. CARROL JOHNSON (see Descendants (127)) was born to Nick Johnson[1769] and Kathryn Kenney[1770].
3033. JIMMY DAW.
> Jimmy Daw married Carrol Johnson[3032].

3034. CRISTA JOHNSON (see Descendants (127)) was born to Nick Johnson[1769] and Kathryn Kenney[1770].

3035. DANAE HENDERSON (see Descendants (127)) was born in June 1968 to Ronnie Henderson[1773] and Sheila Johnson[1772].
3036. DARIN SOUTHHARD.
> Darin Southhard married Danae Henderson[3035].

3037. MICHAEL ZOREE MORRIS (see Descendants (127)) was born to Ronnie Morris[1774] and Sheila Johnson[1772].

3038. JEFFERY MORRIS (see Descendants (127)) was born to Ronnie Morris[1774] and Sheila Johnson[1772].

3039. DANNY JOHNSON (see Descendants (127)) was born to Luvert Johnson[1775] and Dollie Colvin[1776].
3040. BELINDA SPEIS.
> Danny Johnson[3039] married Belinda Speis.

3041. DALLAS JOHNSON (see Descendants (127)) was born to Luvert Johnson[1775] and Dollie Colvin[1776].
3042. DEBORAH CAHILL.
> Dallas Johnson[3041] married Deborah Cahill. They had one son:
> > Aaron Johnson[3848]

3043. GARY LYNN JOHNSON JR. (see Descendants (127)) was born to Gary Lynn Johnson[1777] and Faye Golson[1778].

3044. LEIGH ANN FRANKLIN (see Descendants (128)) was born on July 8, 1964 to Arlee Franklin[1780] and Ruby Nell Thames[1779].
3045. DALE CHESSER.
> Dale Chesser married Leigh Ann Franklin[3044].

3046. TRACEY LYNN FRANKLIN (see Descendants (128)) was born on July 19, 1968 to Arlee Franklin[1780] and Ruby Nell Thames[1779].

3047. CHRISTOPHER THAMES (see Descendants (128)) was born on August 15, 1973 to Billy Joe Thames[1782] and Dale Dixon[1783].
3048. KAREN SCHOFIELD.
> Christopher Thames[3047], aged 19, married Karen Schofield on December 18, 1992. They had three children:
> > Hillary Page Thames[3849] born on November 26, 1992
> > Clay Daniel Thames[3850] born on September 20, 1993
> > Dustin Micheal Thames[3851] born on November 29, 1995

3049. PAMELA NELL TURNER (see Descendants (129)) was born on August 26, 1964, in Covington, Alabama, USA, to Hyram Walace Turner[1784] and Dorothy McCurley[1785].
- She died on September 22, 2011, aged 47 years, in Opp, Covington, Alabama, USA.
- She was buried in Blue Springs Church Cemetery, Opp, Covingtion, Alabama, USA.

3050. BRANDY KEITH OWENS was born on January 7, 1968, in Covington, Alabama, USA.
- He died on April 16, 2003, aged 35 years, in Andalusia, Covington, Alabama, USA.
- He was buried in Bethel Primitive Baptist Church Cemetery, Babbie, Covington, Alabama, USA.
> Brandy Keith Owens married Pamela Nell Turner[3049].

3051. LYNDA JEANNE TURNER (see Descendants (129)) was born on July 23, 1965, in Fort Walton Beach, Okaloosa, Florida, USA, to Amos Dalton Turner Sr.[1786] and Emma Viola McClintock[1787].
> Lynda Jeanne married twice. She was married to William Todd Martin[3052] and James Micheal Carnley[3053].
3052. WILLIAM TODD MARTIN.
> William Todd Martin married Lynda Jeanne Turner[3051].

Direct Relations

3053. JAMES MICHEAL CARNLEY.
>James Micheal Carnley married Lynda Jeanne Turner[3051], aged 21, on May 12, 1987 in Opp, Covington, Alabama, USA. They had two children:
>>Tabitha Dawn Carnley[3852] born on September 16, 1985
>>Trenton Michael Carnley[3854] born on October 2, 1989 in Enterprise, Coffee, Alabama, USA

3054. AMOS DALTON TURNER JR. (see Descendants (129)) was born on September 23, 1967, in Fort Walton Beach, Okaloosa, Florida, USA, to Amos Dalton Turner Sr.[1786] and Emma Viola McClintock[1787].

3055. BRENDA GAIL BOOKER.
>Amos Dalton Turner Jr.[3054], aged 21, married Brenda Gail Booker on July 7, 1989 in Andalusia, Covington, Alabama, USA. They had two daughters:
>>Madison Jade Turner[3856]
>>Taylor Grace Turner[3858] born on January 19, 2000

3056. BEVERLY SHEA TURNER (see Descendants (129)) was born on April 30, 1974, in Andalusia, Covington, Alabama, USA, to Amos Dalton Turner Sr.[1786] and Emma Viola McClintock[1787].

3057. MR. JAYNES.
>Mr. Jaynes married Beverly Shea Turner[3056], and they were divorced. They had one daughter:
>>Tyler Jaynes[3859] born on May 15, 2000

3058. JAMES ALLEN MILLS (see Descendants (130)) was born on July 16, 1958, in Lakeland, Polk, Florida, USA, to William James Mills[1788] and Martha Ray Carr[1789].
>James Allen married twice. He was married to Jody Lynn Touchton[3059] and Jacqueline Kay Mullinnex[3060].

3059. JODY LYNN TOUCHTON.
>James Allen Mills[3058], aged 29, married Jody Lynn Touchton on January 26, 1988 in Zanesville, Muskingum, Ohio, USA.

3060. JACQUELINE KAY MULLINNEX.
>James Allen Mills[3058] married Jacqueline Kay Mullinnex. They had two sons:
>>Joshua Allen Mills[3860] born on August 17, 1988 in Winter Haven, Polk, Florida, USA
>>Michael Adams Mills[3861] born on September 7, 1991 in Canton, Stark, Ohio, USA

3061. JOHN DOUGLAS MILLS (see Descendants (130)) was born on June 6, 1966, in Lakeland, Polk, Florida, USA, to William James Mills[1788] and Martha Ray Carr[1789].

3062. JOSEPH DONALD MILLS (see Descendants (130)) was born on June 6, 1966, in Lakeland, Polk, Florida, USA, to William James Mills[1788] and Martha Ray Carr[1789].

3063. ANGELA RENE ELLIOT.
>Joseph Donald Mills[3062], aged 22, married Angela Rene Elliot on March 31, 1989 in Polk, Florida, USA. They had two sons:
>>Johnathan David Mills[3862] born on January 1, 1992
>>Jordan Nonovon Mills[3863] born on January 31, 1994

3064. DEWEY WENDELL HOLMES JR. (see Descendants (130)) was born on December 23, 1960, in Lakeland, Polk, Florida, USA, to Dewey Wendell Holmes Sr.[1791] and Evelyn Juanita Mills[1790].

3065. CORRIE L. CAMPBELL.
>Dewey Wendell Holmes Jr.[3064], aged 23, married Corrie L. Campbell on May 12, 1984. They had one son:
>>Dewey Wendell Holmes III[3864] born on December 21, 1991 in Lakeland, Polk, Florida, USA

3066. MELINDA DIANNA HOLMES (see Descendants (130)) was born on January 27, 1962, in Lakeland, Polk, Florida, USA, to Dewey Wendell Holmes Sr.[1791] and Evelyn Juanita Mills[1790].

3067. WENDELL GENE HUNT.
>Wendell Gene Hunt married Melinda Dianna Holmes[3066], aged 24, on April 27, 1986. They had two sons:
>>Dillon Gene Hunt[3865] born on January 10, 1990
>>Trenton Wayne Hunt[3866] born on July 20, 1991

3068. PATRICIA GAIL HOLMES (see Descendants (130)) was born on October 26, 1963, in Lakeland, Polk, Florida, USA, to Dewey Wendell Holmes Sr.[1791] and Evelyn Juanita Mills[1790].

3069. KEVIN SHAWN BLOOMFIELD SR.
>   Kevin Shawn Bloomfield Sr. married Patricia Gail Holmes[3068], aged 18, on March 5, 1982. They had three children:
>> Jennifer Nichole Bloomfield[3867] born on August 31, 1982 in Winter Haven, Polk, Florida, USA
>> Kevin Shawn Bloomfield Jr.[3868] born on September 2, 1983 in Lakeland, Polk, Florida, USA
>> Craig Allen Bloomfield[3869] born on October 8, 1984 in Winter Haven, Polk, Florida, USA

3070. LENA DIANNE MILLS (see Descendants (130)) was born on February 25, 1964, in Vandenberg Air Force Base, California, USA, to Charles Earl Mills[1792] and Gloria Jean Glover[1793].

3071. GARRY THOMAS WALKER.
>   Garry Thomas Walker married Lena Dianne Mills[3070], aged 24, on August 3, 1988 in Aurora, Colorado, USA. They had three children:
>> Tera Lynn Walker[3870] born on August 26, 1988 in Las Vegas, Clark, Nevada, USA; died on August 26, 1988 in Las Vegas, Clark, Nevada, USA
>> Brannon Chase Walker[3871] born on October 25, 1990 in Las Vegas, Clark, Nevada, USA
>> Trista Shealynn Walker[3872] born on July 31, 1992 in Las Vegas, Clark, Nevada, USA

3072. RICHARD EARL MILLS (see Descendants (130)) was born on November 12, 1964, in Fort Walton Beach, Okaloosa, Florida, USA, to Charles Earl Mills[1792] and Gloria Jean Glover[1793]. He died (At young age) on November 12, 1964, aged 0, in Fort Walton Beach, Okaloosa, Florida, USA.

3073. SHAWNEE LYNN MILLS (see Descendants (130)) was born on September 12, 1966, in Lakeland, Polk, Florida, USA, to Charles Earl Mills[1792] and Gloria Jean Glover[1793].

3074. ROBERT KENNER RATHBURN.
>   Robert Kenner Rathburn married Shawnee Lynn Mills[3073], aged 22, on June 24, 1989 in Aurora, Colorado, USA. They had one son:
>> Broc Jordan Rathburn[3873] born on April 10, 1991 in Denver, Colorado, USA

3075. DEBBIE DIANE MILLS (see Descendants (130)) was born on October 21, 1965, in Lakeland, Polk, Florida, USA, to Gene Verlon Mills[1794] and Patricia Ann Johnson[1795].

3076. DANIEL EDWARD MILLS (see Descendants (130)) was born on November 8, 1967, in Saint Petersburg, Florida, USA, to Gene Verlon Mills[1794] and Patricia Ann Johnson[1795].

3077. SEAN VERLON MILLS (see Descendants (130)) was born on February 3, 1973, in Mobile, Mobile, Alabama, USA, to Gene Verlon Mills[1794] and Mary Ellen Smith[1796].

3078. DONNA KAY MILLS (see Descendants (130)) was born on January 10, 1967, in Bartow, Polk, Florida, USA, to Donell Franklin Mills[1797] and Brenda Kay Gulett[1798].

3079. THOMAS PATTERSON.
>   Thomas Patterson married Donna Kay Mills[3078], aged 19, on April 12, 1986. They had four children:
>> Joshua Alan Silva Patterson[3874] born on September 27, 1984 in Boca Raton, Palm Beach, Florida, USA
>> Amber Brook Patterson[3875] born on April 20, 1986 in Boca Raton, Palm Beach, Florida, USA
>> Thomas Chester Patterson[3876] born on April 23, 1987 in Jacksonville, Duval, Florida, USA
>> Shane Donovan Patterson[3877] born on May 2, 1988 in Boca Raton, Palm Beach, Florida, USA

3080. DONELL JOSEPH MILLS (see Descendants (130)) was born on August 19, 1973, in Toledo, Lucas, Ohio, USA, to Donell Franklin Mills[1797] and Brenda Kay Gulett[1798].

3081. STEPHANIE ?.
>   Donell Joseph Mills[3080] married Stephanie ?. They had one daughter:
>> Tracie Renae Mills[3878] born on January 11, 1994

3082. DARLA LYNN MILLS (see Descendants (130)) was born on August 12, 1970, in Sarasota, Florida, USA, to Donell Franklin Mills[1797] and Judith A. Kucera[1799].

3083. ERIC JENSEN.
>   Eric Jensen married Darla Lynn Mills[3082], aged 19, on July 7, 1990. They had three children:
>> Edward Clifton Jensen[3879] born on August 2, 1986 in Sarasota, Florida, USA
>> Matthew Alan Jensen[3880] born on November 24, 1989 in Orange Park, Clay, Florida, USA
>> Paula Marian Lynn Jensen[3881] born on October 6, 1991 in Orange Park, Clay, Florida, USA

3084. GREGORY SCOTT PHILLIPS (see Descendants (131)) was born on September 7, 1964, in Florala, Covington, Alabama, USA, to Edward Earl Phillips[1803] and Annie Pearl Cobb[1802].

Direct Relations

3085. KENNETH PAUL PHILLIPS (see Descendants (131)) was born on October 4, 1965, in Florala, Covington, Alabama, USA, to Edward Earl Phillips[1803] and Annie Pearl Cobb[1802].
3086. SONIA DARLENE HOMAN.
> Kenneth Paul Phillips[3085] married Sonia Darlene Homan. They had one son:
>> Kyle Kenneth Phillips[3882] born on March 27, 1996

3087. JAMES BARTLETT COBB JR. (see Descendants (131)) was born on May 22, 1964, in Florala, Covington, Alabama, USA, to James Bartlett Cobb Sr.[1804] and Janet Bowman[1805].
3088. JACKY MONDORA.
> James Bartlett Cobb Jr.[3087] married Jacky Mondora. They had two children:
>> Aaron Florence Cobb[3883] born on September 25, 1990
>> Anthony Joseph Cobb[3884] born on June 3, 1993

3089. MARTINE MICHELLE COBB (see Descendants (131)) was born on October 21, 1965, in Fort Walton Beach, Okaloosa, Florida, USA, to James Bartlett Cobb Sr.[1804] and Janet Bowman[1805].
3090. GARY HUNT.
> Gary Hunt married Martine Michelle Cobb[3089]. They had one son:
>> Zackery Tyler Hunt[3885] born on August 18, 1993

3091. VICTORIA AMANDA COBB (see Descendants (131)) was born on May 28, 1970, in Opp, Covington, Alabama, USA, to James Bartlett Cobb Sr.[1804] and Janet Bowman[1805].

3092. MICHAEL JEROME EDMONDSON (see Descendants (132)) was born on October 1, 1970, in Opp, Covington, Alabama, USA, to Jerome Aubray Edmondson[1807] and Althea Darlene Posey[1806].
3093. STEPHANIE LYNN SWANEY.
> Michael Jerome Edmondson[3092], aged 27, married Stephanie Lynn Swaney on November 1, 1997. They had four sons:
>> Logan Swaney Edmondson[3886] born on May 21, 1999
>> Zackary Michael Edmondson[3887] born on October 12, 2001
>> Ethan Jack Edmondson[3888] born on January 4, 2004
>> Brock Martin Edmondson[3889] born on June 10, 2005

3094. JASON LEE EDMONDSON (see Descendants (132)) was born on November 14, 1975, in Geneva, Geneva, Alabama, USA, to Jerome Aubray Edmondson[1807] and Althea Darlene Posey[1806].
3095. MISTY SUE ABRAMS.
> Jason Lee Edmondson[3094], aged 30, married Misty Sue Abrams on June 17, 2006. They had two children:
>> Jason Wyatt Edmondson[3890] born on February 15, 2008
>> Laken Grace Edmondson[3891] born on November 11, 2015

3096. CHARLES PAUL WEEMS (see Descendants (132)) was born on December 28, 1973, in Greeneville, Greene, Tennessee, USA, to Fred Charles Weems Jr.[1809] and Carolyn Dianne Posey[1808].
3097. BRANDY ?.
> Charles Paul Weems[3096] married Brandy ?.

3098. PERRY MATTHEW WEEMS (see Descendants (132)) was born on May 23, 1978, in Greeneville, Greene, Tennessee, USA, to Fred Charles Weems Jr.[1809] and Carolyn Dianne Posey[1808].
3099. KENYA ?.
> Perry Matthew Weems[3098] married Kenya ?.

3100. JUSTIN ALBERT WEEMS (see Descendants (132)) was born on December 11, 1980, in Greeneville, Greene, Tennessee, USA, to Fred Charles Weems Jr.[1809] and Carolyn Dianne Posey[1808].
3101. WHITNEY ?.
> Justin Albert Weems[3100] married Whitney ?.

3102. ROBERT DWAYNE COLLIER (see Descendants (133)) was born on September 17, 1959, in Lakeland, Polk, Florida, USA, to Robert Dwayne Collier[1811] and Doris Jene Turbeville[1810].
3103. JOANNA LEE SCOFFIELD.
> Robert Dwayne Collier[3102], aged 22, married Joanna Lee Scoffield on June 5, 1982 in Palm Harbor, Pinellas, Florida, USA. They had four children:
>> Joshua Dwayne Collier[3892] born on May 11, 1983
>> Jessie Lee Collier[3893] born on October 22, 1987
>> Angelica Lynn Collier[3894] born on August 26, 1990

Christy Alayne Collier[3895] born on February 2, 1993

3104. RHONDA DELAINE COLLIER (see Descendants (133)) was born on August 10, 1962, in Lakeland, Polk, Florida, USA, to Robert Dwayne Collier[1811] and Doris Jene Turbeville[1810].
3105. JOESPH PORTER.
Joesph Porter married Rhonda Delaine Collier[3104], aged 17, on July 27, 1980 in Lakeland, Polk, Florida, USA. They had two sons:
Timothy Ian Porter[3896] born on March 4, 1981
Joesph Cameron Porter[3897] born on September 7, 1989

3106. MICHAEL EARL HARRISON (see Descendants (133)) was born on May 18, 1959, in Lakeland, Polk, Florida, USA, to Earl Harrison[1813] and Jimmie Nell Turbeville[1812].

3107. ANGIE POWELL (see Descendants (133)) was born on June 8, 1964, in Lakeland, Polk, Florida, USA, to Jimmy Powell[1816] and Elaine Turbeville[1815].
3108. JEFFERY PRATT.
Jeffery Pratt married Angie Powell[3107], aged 19, on December 21, 1983. They had one daughter:
Shannon Nicole Pratt[3898] born on June 23, 1984

3109. KIM TURBBEVILLE (see Descendants (133)) was born on January 16, 1968, in Lakeland, Polk, Florida, USA, to Dewey Wayne Turbeville[1817] and Judy Louis Davis[1818].
3110. JEFFERY FLEMING.
Jeffery Fleming married Kim Turbbeville[3109] in Auburndale, Polk, Florida, USA.

3111. TRACEY TURBBEVILLE (see Descendants (133)) was born on April 3, 1970, in Lakeland, Polk, Florida, USA, to Dewey Wayne Turbeville[1817] and Judy Louis Davis[1818].
3112. HANK HARRISON.
Hank Harrison married Tracey Turbbeville[3111] in Haines City, Polk, Florida, USA.

3113. DEWEY WAYNE TURBBEVILLE JR. (see Descendants (133)) was born on November 30, 1976, in Lakeland, Polk, Florida, USA, to Dewey Wayne Turbeville[1817] and Judy Louis Davis[1818].

3114. HUNTER WAYNE TURBBEVILLE (see Descendants (133)) was born on August 14, 1994 to Dewey Wayne Turbeville[1817] and Andrea Pate[1819].

3115. CHRIS EVERIDGE (see Descendants (134)) was born to Porter Everidge[1821] and Thelma Lee Busbee[1820].

3116. SHEILA GILLEY (see Descendants (134)) was born to Donnell Gilley[1824] and Noma Busbee[1823].

3117. CAROL GILLEY (see Descendants (134)) was born to Donnell Gilley[1824] and Noma Busbee[1823].

3118. MIKE GILLEY (see Descendants (134)) was born to Donnell Gilley[1824] and Noma Busbee[1823].

3119. GARY GILLEY (see Descendants (134)) was born to Donnell Gilley[1824] and Noma Busbee[1823].

3120. GLORIA GILLEY (see Descendants (134)) was born to Donnell Gilley[1824] and Noma Busbee[1823].

3121. JANET BUSBEE (see Descendants (134)) was born to James Curtis Busbee[1825] and Betty Helms[1826].

3122. SUE BUSBEE (see Descendants (134)) was born to James Curtis Busbee[1825] and Betty Helms[1826].

3123. PEGGIE BUSBEE (see Descendants (134)) was born to James Curtis Busbee[1825] and Betty Helms[1826].

3124. DONALD EUGENE BUSBEE (see Descendants (134)) was born on March 13, 1957 to James Curtis Busbee[1825] and Betty Helms[1826].

3125. WANDA BUSBEE (see Descendants (134)) was born to James Curtis Busbee[1825] and Betty Helms[1826].

3126. ANGIE BUSBEE (see Descendants (134)) was born to Shelby Ray Busbee[1827] and Roslyn Walters[1828].

3127. RUSTY BUSBEE (see Descendants (134)) was born to Shelby Ray Busbee[1827] and Roslyn Walters[1828].

Direct Relations

3128. RICKIE BUSBEE (see Descendants (134)) was born to Shelby Ray Busbee[1827] and Roslyn Walters[1828].

3129. KATHY GILLEY (see Descendants (134)) was born to Roy Frank Gilley[1830] and Eula Vee Busbee[1829].

3130. DEBORAH GILLEY (see Descendants (134)) was born to Roy Frank Gilley[1830] and Eula Vee Busbee[1829].

3131. ALAN DOWNS (see Descendants (134)) was born to Carl Downs[1832] and Winnie Fay Busbee[1831].

3132. DEAN WILLIAMS (see Descendants (134)) was born to James T. Williams[1834] and Polly Busbee[1833].

3133. RITA LYNN WILLIAMS (see Descendants (134)) was born to James T. Williams[1834] and Polly Busbee[1833].

3134. DOUGLAS WILLIAMS (see Descendants (134)) was born to James T. Williams[1834] and Polly Busbee[1833].

3135. RANDY BUSBEE (see Descendants (134)) was born to Walan Busbee[1835] and Rochella Hope[1836].

3136. TONYA BUSBEE (see Descendants (134)) was born to Walan Busbee[1835] and Rochella Hope[1836].

3137. HARDY LEE JOHNSON (see Descendants (135)) was born to Heyward Ivin Johnson[1839] and Essie Orene Bozeman[1840].

3138. PATRISHA ANN JOHNSON (see Descendants (135)) was born to Heyward Ivin Johnson[1839] and Essie Orene Bozeman[1840].

3139. LESLEY MITCHEL JOHNSON (see Descendants (135)) was born to Heyward Ivin Johnson[1839] and Essie Orene Bozeman[1840].

3140. LEWIS EDWARD JOHNSON JR. (see Descendants (135)) was born to Lewis Edward Johnson[1841] and Sylvia ?[1842].

3141. ELAINE JOHNSON (see Descendants (135)) was born to Lewis Edward Johnson[1841] and Sylvia ?[1842].

3142. RILEY LEE OGLESBY (see Descendants (135)) was born to Duval Milford Oglesby[1846] and Frances Elaine Johnson[1845].

3143. NANCY ELIZABETH OGLESBY (see Descendants (135)) was born to Duval Milford Oglesby[1846] and Frances Elaine Johnson[1845].

3144. SHARRON OGLESBY (see Descendants (135)) was born to Duval Milford Oglesby[1846] and Frances Elaine Johnson[1845].

3145. MILFORD GENE OGLESBY (see Descendants (135)) was born to Duval Milford Oglesby[1846] and Frances Elaine Johnson[1845].

3146. PATRISHA LEE JOHNSON (see Descendants (135)) was born to Cleveland Johnson[1847] and Virginia Harris[1848].

3147. GREGORY ALAN BOSHELL (see Descendants (136)) was born to George Boshell[1855] and Sylvia Turner[1854].

3148. DERREL TURNER (see Descendants (136)) was born to William Amos Turner[1856] and Patricia Winspur[1857].

3149. DALE TURNER (see Descendants (136)) was born to William Amos Turner[1856] and Patricia Winspur[1857].

3150. TRACY TURNER (see Descendants (136)) was born to William Amos Turner[1856] and Patricia Winspur[1857].

3151. JEFFERY WADE TURNER (see Descendants (136)) was born on February 1, 1960, in Florala, Covington, Alabama, USA, to Jeff Wendell Turner[1858] and Janice Frances Davis[1859].
Jeffery Wade married twice. He was married to Janet Sexton[3152] and Donna L. ?[3153].

3152. JANET SEXTON.
    Jeffery Wade Turner[3151] married Janet Sexton. They had two children:
        Jeffery Wade Turner II[3899] born on June 10, 1982 in Opp, Covington, Alabama, USA
        Lilli Roseann Turner[3900] born on July 26, 1984 in Opp, Covington, Alabama, USA

3153. DONNA L. ?.
   Jeffery Wade Turner[3151], aged 34, married Donna L. ? on June 12, 1994.

3154. JACK MILTON TURNER (see Descendants (136)) was born on July 2, 1961, in Florala, Covington, Alabama, USA, to Jeff Wendell Turner[1858] and Janice Frances Davis[1859]. He died on November 3, 1979, aged 18 years, in Shiloh, Covington, Alabama, USA.

3155. JANET SYLVIA TURNER (see Descendants (136)) was born on June 12, 1964, in Florala, Covington, Alabama, USA, to Jeff Wendell Turner[1858] and Janice Frances Davis[1859]. She died on June 19, 1982, aged 18 years.

3156. HERSHEL E. HARPER.
   Hershel E. Harper married Janet Sylvia Turner[3155]. They had three children:
   Joshua B. Harper[3901] born on May 23, 1984 in Dothan, Houston, Alabama, USA
   Jeremy W. Harper[3902] born on April 23, 1986 in Dothan, Houston, Alabama, USA
   F. Nicole Harper[3903] born on August 6, 1990 in Dothan, Houston, Alabama, USA

3157. TIM MORROLL (see Descendants (137)) was born to Edwin Parker[1861] and Edna Pearl Edwards[1860].

3158. DEBBIE MORROLL (see Descendants (137)) was born to Edwin Parker[1861] and Edna Pearl Edwards[1860].

3159. RICKEY MORROLL (see Descendants (137)) was born to Edwin Parker[1861] and Edna Pearl Edwards[1860].

3160. RHETT EDWARDS (see Descendants (137)) was born to Harry Edwards Jr.[1862] and Edwina Parker[1863].

3161. RICK EDWARDS (see Descendants (137)) was born to Harry Edwards Jr.[1862] and Edwina Parker[1863].

3162. PAULINE EDWARDS (see Descendants (137)) was born to Lesley Riley Edwards Jr.[1864] and Ms. ?[1865].

3163. FLOYD LOCKE.
   Floyd Locke married Pauline Edwards[3162].

3164. RUBY CAROL EDWARDS (see Descendants (137)) was born to Lesley Riley Edwards Jr.[1864] and Ms. ?[1865].

3165. JAMES EDWARDS (see Descendants (137)) was born to Lesley Riley Edwards Jr.[1864] and Ms. ?[1865].

3166. KENNETH EDWARDS (see Descendants (137)) was born to Lesley Riley Edwards Jr.[1864] and Ms. ?[1865].

3167. EUGENE EDWARDS (see Descendants (137)) was born to Lesley Riley Edwards Jr.[1864] and Ms. ?[1865].

3168. ROY EDWARDS (see Descendants (137)) was born to Lesley Riley Edwards Jr.[1864] and Ms. ?[1865].

3169. JERRY EDWARDS (see Descendants (137)) was born to Lesley Riley Edwards Jr.[1864] and Ms. ?[1865].

3170. LAJAUN YORK (see Descendants (138)) was born to James York[1867] and Margarette Edwards[1866].

3171. JAMES YORK JR. (see Descendants (138)) was born to James York[1867] and Margarette Edwards[1866].

3172. JAMES MURRIELL EDWARDS (see Descendants (138)) was born to Murray Edwards[1870] and Annis Creech[1871].

3173. PHYLLIS JANE PARKS.
   James Murriell Edwards[3172] married Phyllis Jane Parks. They had one son:
   James Murray Edwards[3904]

3174. DONALD EUGENE EDWARDS (see Descendants (138)) was born to Murray Edwards[1870] and Annis Creech[1871].

3175. SARAH ALDIE QUALLS.
   Donald Eugene Edwards[3174] married Sarah Aldie Qualls. They had one son:
   Steven Murriell Edwards[3905]

3176. SHERYL DIANE EDWARDS (see Descendants (138)) was born to Murray Edwards[1870] and Annis Creech[1871].

3177. JUDITH ANN EDWARDS (see Descendants (138)) was born to Murray Edwards[1870] and Annis Creech[1871].

Direct Relations

3178. TRACEY ROCHELLE WEBSTER (see Descendants (139)) was born on February 7, 1968 to Carl Webster[1873] and Phyllis Jernigan[1872].
    Tracey Rochelle married twice. She was married to Michael McNear[3179] and Phillip Farmer[3180].

3179. MICHAEL MCNEAR.
    Michael McNear married Tracey Rochelle Webster[3178].

3180. PHILLIP FARMER.
    Phillip Farmer married Tracey Rochelle Webster[3178].

3181. STIVE WEBSTER (see Descendants (139)) was born on April 22, 1969 to Carl Webster[1873] and Phyllis Jernigan[1872].

3182. DENISE WEBSTER (see Descendants (139)) was born on April 6, 1971 to Carl Webster[1873] and Phyllis Jernigan[1872].

3183. SCOTT WEBSTER (see Descendants (139)) was born on February 27, 1973 to Carl Webster[1873] and Phyllis Jernigan[1872].

3184. TIM WEBSTER (see Descendants (139)) was born on July 17, 1980 to Carl Webster[1873] and Phyllis Jernigan[1872].

3185. CARRIE WEBSTER (see Descendants (139)) was born on January 12, 1982 to Carl Webster[1873] and Phyllis Jernigan[1872].

3186. LINDSEY JERNIGAN (see Descendants (139)) was born on May 12, 1982 to Ronnie Jernigan[1874] and Janie Gilmore[1875].

3187. BRITTON JERNIGAN (see Descendants (139)) was born on October 14, 1983 to Ronnie Jernigan[1874] and Janie Gilmore[1875].

3188. MELISSA JERNIGAN (see Descendants (139)) was born on July 2, 1985 to Ronnie Jernigan[1874] and Janie Gilmore[1875].

3189. DARREN JERNIGAN (see Descendants (139)) was born on January 17, 1988 to Larry Jernigan[1876] and Teresa Hagce[1877].

3190. SERRIE BASS (see Descendants (141)) was born to Clinton Duranne Bass[1892] and Ms. ?[1893].

3191. DAVID BRIAN BARNES (see Descendants (142)) was born on October 10, 1971, in Andalusia, Covington, Alabama, USA, to Billy Gray Barnes[1899] and Wanda Arlene Bass[1898].
 • He died (Stillborn) on October 10, 1971, as an infant, in Andalusia, Covington, Alabama, USA.
 • He was buried in Sanford Baptist Church Cemetery, Andalusia, Covington, Alabama, USA.

3192. PHILLIP MICHAEL BARNES (see Descendants (142)) was born on January 13, 1974, in Enterprise, Coffee, Alabama, USA, to Billy Gray Barnes[1899] and Wanda Arlene Bass[1898]. Phillip Michael became known as "Chipper".

3193. CHERYL ANNE KEMP was born on March 2, 1976. Cheryl Anne became a Teacher.
    Phillip Michael Barnes[3192], aged 22, married Cheryl Anne Kemp, aged 20, on July 27, 1996 in Andalusia, Covington, Alabama, USA. They had two daughters:
        Mary Katherine Barnes[3906] born on June 17, 2003 in Homewood, Alabama, USA
        Hannah Marie Barnes[3907] born on December 15, 2008 in Homewood, Alabama, USA

3194. SAMUEL BRAD BARNES (see Descendants (142)) was born on August 8, 1986, in Enterprise, Coffee, Alabama, USA, to Billy Gray Barnes[1899] and Wanda Arlene Bass[1898].

3195. BETHANY HOPE BOCHETTE was born on December 8, 1991. Bethany Hope became a Teacher.
    Samuel Brad Barnes[3194] married Bethany Hope Bochette. They had two sons:
        Benson Gray Barnes[3908] born in 2016
        Troy Barnes[3909]

3196. NICHOLAS BRUCE BASS (see Descendants (142)) was born on August 12, 1979, in Selma, Dallas, Alabama, USA, to Ricky Bruce Bass[1900] and Donna Rena Canant[1901]. Nicholas Bruce became known as "Nik". The following information is also recorded for Nik:
  • Email: nikbass@gmail.com.
Note: *Born in Selma, Alabama due to complications. Thomasville, Alabama is the location of the initial hospital and family residence at the time of birth.*
(Birth)

3197. ELIZABETH CORINNE BARRINGER was born on January 8, 1981, in Phoenixville, Chester, Pennsylvania, USA, to Mark William Barringer and Bonita Mae Schott. Elizabeth Corinne became known as "Liz".
Elizabeth Corinne had two partnerships; including Nicholas Bruce Bass[3196].
    Elizabeth Corinne gave birth to one son:
        Joel Ryan Bass[3910] born on December 25, 1998 in Andalusia, Covington, Alabama, USA
    The following information is also recorded for this family:
    • Unspecified Relationship.
Nicholas Bruce Bass[3196], aged 20, married Elizabeth Corinne Barringer, aged 19, on March 11, 2000 in Andalusa, Alabama, USA. They had one son, and assumed parenthood of another one:
    Joel Ryan Bass[3910] by adoption
    Willson Bruce Bass[3911] born on June 8, 2006 in Opp, Alabama, USA
Note: *This is me and my wife, no citations but I was there. -Nik Bass.*

3198. ASHLY RENA BASS (see Descendants (142)) was born on March 17, 1981, in Thomasville, Clark, Alabama, USA, to Ricky Bruce Bass[1900] and Donna Rena Canant[1901].
Ashly Rena had two partnerships. She was married to Paul Edwin Powell Jr.[3199]. She was also the partner of Barney Kieth Ray[3200].

3199. PAUL EDWIN POWELL JR. was born on October 12, 1980, in Opp, Covington, Alabama, USA. Paul Edwin became a Teacher.
    Paul Edwin Powell Jr., aged about 30, married Ashly Rena Bass[3198], aged about 30, between January 22, 2005 and 2017 in Andalusia, Covington, Alabama, USA, and they were divorced. They had two children:
        Aubree Claire Powell[3912] born on August 3, 2007 in Crestview, Okaloosa, Florida, USA
        Paul Edwin Powell III[3913] born on October 24, 2010 in Crestview, Okaloosa, Florida, USA

3200. BARNEY KIETH RAY was born on March 20, 1979.
    Barney Kieth Ray and Ashly Rena Bass[3198] had one son:
        Riggs Roosivelt Ray[3914] born on January 5, 2023 in Crestview, Okaloosa County, Florida, USA
    The following information is also recorded for this family:
    • Unspecified Relationship.

3201. STACIE PARTAIN BASS (see Descendants (142)) was born on August 29, 1978 to Don Jeffery Bass I[1902] and Treva Partain[1903]. Stacie Partain became a Teacher.

Direct Relations

3202. JOHN JOE LAMB was born on March 13, 1974.

John Joe Lamb, aged -1956, married Stacie Partain Bass[3201], aged -1960, in February 19 A.D. They had one son:
Brodie Lawson Lamb[3915] born on March 19, 2007 in Georgia, USA

3203. DON JEFFERY BASS II (see Descendants (142)) was born on December 19, 1986 to Don Jeffery Bass I[1902] and Gail Norsworthy[1904]. Don Jeffery became known as "Jeff".

3204. BETHANY WHITHEAD was born on July 11, 1991.
Don Jeffery Bass II[3203] married Bethany Whithead.

3205. KAYLA KINSAUL (see Descendants (304)) was born on April 20, 1983 to Benjamin Doyle Kinsaul[1906] and Janet Marie Bass[1905]. Kayla became a Teacher.

3206. JEFFREY DOUGLAS GORUM was born on February 10, 1983.
Jeffrey Douglas Gorum married Kayla Kinsaul[3205]. They had two daughters:
Harper Kate Gorum[3916]
Stella Ruth Gorum[3917] born on December 17, 2016

3207. HUNTER DOYLE KINSAUL (see Descendants (304)) was born on May 3, 1986, in Andalusia, Covington, Alabama, USA, to Benjamin Doyle Kinsaul[1906] and Janet Marie Bass[1905].

3208. ROLLIN BENJAMIN KINSAUL (see Descendants (304)) was born on December 26, 1996, in Andalusia, Covington, Alabama, USA, to Benjamin Doyle Kinsaul[1906] and Janet Marie Bass[1905].

3209. TERA ASHLEIGH HENDERSON (see Descendants (305)) was born on June 13, 1979 to Thomas Harold Henderson II[1907] and Carol Jane Jordan[1908].

3210. DAMON ANDREW PATRICK was born on May 26, 1976 to Bill Andrew Patrick and Debbie ?.
Damon Andrew Patrick, aged 24, married Tera Ashleigh Henderson[3209], aged 21, on June 30, 2000 in First Church of the Nazarene E. Brewton, Escambia, Alabama, USA. They had one daughter:
Clare Elizabeth Patrick[3918]

3211. BRET THOMAS HENDERSON (see Descendants (305)) was born on November 2, 1980 to Thomas Harold Henderson II[1907] and Carol Jane Jordan[1908].

3212. EMILY JEAN YOUNGBLOOD was born on December 17, 1979 to Eddie Youngblood and Louise ?.
Bret Thomas Henderson[3211], aged 22, married Emily Jean Youngblood, aged 23, on July 12, 2003 in St. Maurice's Catholic Church Robertsdale, Baldwin, Alabama, USA. They had one son:
Mason Thomas Henderson[3919] born on April 5, 2007

3213. KYLE JORDAN HENDERSON (see Descendants (305)) was born on August 27, 1982 to Thomas Harold Henderson II[1907] and Carol Jane Jordan[1908].

3214. MCLEAN HICKMAN was born to Frank Hickman and Rebecca McLean.
Kyle Jordan Henderson[3213] married McLean Hickman.

3215. ERIN LAJUNE HENDERSON (see Descendants (305)) was born on August 28, 1987 to Thomas Harold Henderson II[1907] and Carol Jane Jordan[1908].

3216. MR. TREDWELL.
Mr. Tredwell married Erin Lajune Henderson[3215]. They had two daughters:
Iris Tredwell[3920]
Elle Tredwell[3921]

3217. LAURA BASS (see Descendants (306)) was born on February 16, 1983 to Randall Ralph Bass[1910] and Treva Partain[1903].

3218. ANTHONY TAYLOR was born on February 20, 1980.
Anthony Taylor, aged 22, married Laura Bass[3217], aged 19, on November 16, 2002. They had one daughter:
Emily Taylor[3922] born on July 21, 2004

3219. WHITTLY VIVIAN RUSSELL was born on January 31, 1995. Whittly Vivian was adopted by Gerry Russell[1912] and Nancy Madonna Bass[1911].
Whittly Vivian gave birth to two sons:
Jonathan Russell Chrzastek[3923]
Gerry Ethan Russell[3924]

3220. JOHNATHAN BLAKE BASS (see Descendants (307)) was born on September 27, 1984 to James Benny Bass[1913] and Marie Stokes[1914].

3221. BRITTANY EDWARDS.
Johnathan Blake Bass[3220] married Brittany Edwards. They had five children:
Blakelee Bass[3925]
Emerson Bass[3926]
Bentlee Bass[3927]
Aniston Bass[3928]
Leeam Hudson Bass[3929] born on April 24, 2017

3222. MANDIE MARIE BASS (see Descendants (307)) was born on December 2, 1986 to James Benny Bass[1913] and Marie Stokes[1914].
Mandie Marie gave birth to two sons:
Trey ?[3930]
Charlie ?[3931]

3223. ZACH BASS (see Descendants (308)) was born to Winfred Lynn Bass[1916] and Rhonda Davis[1917].
3224. JANET LEE TAYLOR.
Zach Bass[3223] married Janet Lee Taylor. They had two children:
Cheston Bass[3932]
Embrie Lynn Bass[3933] born on September 20, 2016

3225. ALLISON BASS (see Descendants (308)) was born on March 24, 1994 to Winfred Lynn Bass[1916] and Rhonda Davis[1917].
Allison married three times. She was married to Cody Helms[3226], Cole Mock[3227] and Devin Dye[3228].

3226. CODY HELMS was born on June 1, 1992.
Cody Helms, when younger than 25, married Allison Bass[3225], when younger than 23, before 2018, and they were divorced.
3227. COLE MOCK was born on August 3, 1988.
Cole married twice. He was married to Allison Bass[3225] and Ms. ?.
Cole Mock, aged 29, married Allison Bass[3225], aged 23, on February 17, 2018 in Ralph Bass' old place Falco, Covington, Alabama, USA, and they were divorced. They had one daughter:
Lynnli Kate Mock[3934] born in 2018
Cole Mock married Ms. ?, and they were divorced. They had one daughter:
Lily Rae Mock
3228. DEVIN DYE.
Devin Dye married Allison Bass[3225], aged about 29, in 2023.

3229. ANTHONY GABRIEL BASS (see Descendants (309)) was born on May 2, 1986 to Anthony Edd Bass[1918] and Sherry Lynn Scroggins[1919].

3230. WHITNEY GREENE.
Anthony Gabriel Bass[3229], aged 26, married Whitney Greene on October 13, 2012. They had one son:
Declan Ryan Bass[3935] born on October 26, 2015

3231. NATHANIEL DREW BASS (see Descendants (309)) was born on February 5, 1988 to Anthony Edd Bass[1918] and Sherry Lynn Scroggins[1919].

3232. MICGAYLE HOLMES.
Nathaniel Drew Bass[3231], aged 23, married Micgayle Holmes on February 19, 2011. They had one son:
Josiah Samuel Bass[3936] born on February 23, 2014

3233. ANNETTE EULA JORDAN (see Descendants (310)) was born on July 13, 1996 to Jay Jordan[1922] and Wendy Learvene Bass[1920]. Annette Eula became known as "Nettie".

3234. ERIC MICHAEL MIMS (see Descendants (311)) was born on January 30, 1988 to Tony Leon Mims[1923] and Jeanie Lorene Douglas[1924].
• He died (Accident) on August 17, 1998, aged 10 years, in Andalusia, Covington, Alabama, USA.
• He was buried in Shady Hill Cemetery, Covington County, Alabama, USA.

3235. TONY JUSTIN MIMS (see Descendants (311)) was born on May 12, 1990 to Tony Leon Mims[1923] and Jeanie Lorene Douglas[1924].
• He died (Accident) on August 17, 1998, aged 8 years, in Andalusia, Covington, Alabama, USA.
• He was buried in Shady Hill Cemetery, Covington County, Alabama, USA.

3236. WILLIAM BRANDON MIMS (see Descendants (311)) was born on January 1, 1993 to Tony Leon Mims[1923] and Jeanie Lorene Douglas[1924].

3237. MEGAN HAYLEY MIMS (see Descendants (311)) was born on September 2, 1995 to Tony Leon Mims[1923] and Jeanie Lorene Douglas[1924].

3238. LAURA ELIZABETH TAYLOR (see Descendants (312)) was born on August 21, 1998 to Jerral Lynn Taylor[1927] and Diane Trawick[1926].

3239. NATHANIEL HAYES DILMORE (see Descendants (313)) was born on January 26, 1988 to Larry Dilmore[1929] and Charlotte Trawick[1928]. Nathaniel Hayes became known as "Nate".

3240. TIMOTHY DILMORE (see Descendants (313)) was born on October 23, 1990 to Larry Dilmore[1929] and Charlotte Trawick[1928].

3241. PAUL JOSHUA WADE (see Descendants (314)) was born on October 10, 1991 to Gregory Paul Wade[1931] and Lisa Trawick[1930].

3242. MYRANDA NICHOLE JERNIGAN (see Descendants (315)) was born in 1994 to David Jernigan[1933] and Gena Trawick[1932].

3243. SAM SOUTULLO.
Sam Soutullo married Myranda Nichole Jernigan[3242].

3244. NATALIE DANIELLE JERNIGAN (see Descendants (315)) was born in 1995 to David Jernigan[1933] and Gena Trawick[1932].

3245. ETHAN TYLER JERNIGAN (see Descendants (315)) was born in 2003 to David Jernigan[1933] and Gena Trawick[1932].

3246. KYLEE JERNIGAN (see Descendants (315)) was born in 2004 to David Jernigan[1933] and Gena Trawick[1932].

3247. HANNAH LEIGH SWITZER (see Descendants (316)) was born on December 2, 1993, in Fayette, Kentucky 40501, USA, to Jeffery Lee Switzer[1936] and Cynthia Michelle Bass[1935].

3248. IKE COLLINS DULIN III.
Ike Collins Dulin III married Hannah Leigh Switzer[3247], aged 22, on July 2, 2016.

3249. TIMOTHY MICHAEL SWITZER (see Descendants (316)) was born on May 9, 1995, in Fayette, Kentucky 40501, USA, to Jeffery Lee Switzer[1936] and Cynthia Michelle Bass[1935].

3250. JONATHAN DAVID SWITZER (see Descendants (316)) was born on July 9, 1999 to Jeffery Lee Switzer[1936] and Cynthia Michelle Bass[1935].

3251. JAMES BENNETT BASS (see Descendants (317)) was born on June 10, 1994 to Coy Bennett Bass Jr.[1937] and Kelly Ann Rusk[1938].
- He died (Unknown) on September 30, 1994, aged 0.
- He was buried in Garden Hill Cemetary, Opelika, Lee, USA.

3252. KAMERON BAYLEA BASS (see Descendants (317)) was born on August 2, 1995 to Coy Bennett Bass Jr.[1937] and Kelly Ann Rusk[1938].

3253. KARSON ANN BASS (see Descendants (317)) was born on September 6, 1998 to Coy Bennett Bass Jr.[1937] and Kelly Ann Rusk[1938].

3254. DR. CHRISTOPHER JOHNSON (see Descendants (143)) was born on September 4, 1988 to John Taft Johnson M.D.[1946] and Karen Ohlmeyer[1947].

3255. KATHRYN WILKEN.
    Christopher Johnson[3254] married Kathryn Wilken. They had one son:
        Roy Taft Johnson[3937] born in October 2019

3256. JULIA ADELE JOHNSON (see Descendants (143)) was born on December 1, 1994 to John Taft Johnson M.D.[1946] and Karen Ohlmeyer[1947].

3257. VIVIAN PIERSON (see Descendants (143)) was born to Todd Pierson[1953] and Nancy Ann Johnson[1952].

3258. ROLAND PIERSON (see Descendants (143)) was born to Todd Pierson[1953] and Nancy Ann Johnson[1952].

3259. GEORGE J. BICANEK JR. (see Descendants (149)) was born in March 1945, in Florida, United States, to George J. Bicanek Sr.[1989] and Eloise Kelley[1988]. He was recorded in the census on April 1, 1950, aged 5, in 2508 S. Christiana, Chicago, Cook, Illinois, United States.

3260. JOAN DIANE BICANEK (see Descendants (149)) was born about 1946, in Chicago, Illinois, USA, to George J. Bicanek Sr.[1989] and Eloise Kelley[1988].
- She was recorded in the census on April 1, 1950, aged about 3, in 2508 S. Christiana, Chicago, Cook, Illinois, United States.
- She died on July 15, 2022, aged about 76.

3261. CAROL JEAN BICANEK (see Descendants (149)) was born about 1948, in Illinois, United States, to George J. Bicanek Sr.[1989] and Eloise Kelley[1988]. She was recorded in the census on April 1, 1950, aged about 1, in 2508 S. Christiana, Chicago, Cook, Illinois, United States.

3262. BETTY ? (see Descendants (149)) was born to Mr. ?[1994] and Joyce Marie Kelley[1993]. She died (Heart Attack).

3263. TOMMY ? (see Descendants (149)) was born to Mr. ?[1994] and Joyce Marie Kelley[1993].

3264. BRENDA POOLE (see Descendants (26)) was born to Max Earl Poole[2001] and Mary Ann Smith[2002].

3265. DEBBIE POOLE (see Descendants (26)) was born to Max Earl Poole[2001] and Mary Ann Smith[2002].

3266. MR. FOWLER (see Descendants (26)) was born to Mr. Fowler[2005] and Ms. Gunnis[2006].

3267. STANLEY RAY FOWLER (see Descendants (26)) was born to Mr. Fowler[2005] and Ms. Owens[2007].

7th Generation of Descendants

3268. JUSTIN RAMER (see Descendants (2)) was born about 1980 to Winford Eugene Ramer Jr.[2024] and Linda Mead[2025].

3269. JENNIFER RAMER (see Descendants (2)) was born to Winford Eugene Ramer Jr.[2024] and Linda Mead[2025].
3270. MR. PEREZ.
    Mr. Perez married Jennifer Ramer[3269]. They had one son:
        Mr. Perez[3938]

3271. MR. WHITE (see Descendants (4)) was born to Steve White[2027] and Casey ?[2028].

3272. MR. WHITE (see Descendants (4)) was born to Steve White[2027] and Casey ?[2028].

3273. MR. WHITE (see Descendants (4)) was born to Mr. White[2029] and Ms. ?[2030].

3274. EDMOND HARDCASTLE JR. (see Descendants (7)) was born to Edmond Hardcastle[2036] and Sue Adele Barneycastle[2035].
3275. ROSE ?.
    Edmond Hardcastle Jr.[3274] married Rose ?.

3276. SUSAN HARDCASTLE (see Descendants (7)) was born to Edmond Hardcastle[2036] and Sue Adele Barneycastle[2035].
3277. TONY ?.
    Tony ? married Susan Hardcastle[3276].

3278. TIMOTHY HARDCASTLE (see Descendants (7)) was born to Edmond Hardcastle[2036] and Sue Adele Barneycastle[2035].

3279. PAMELA HARDCASTLE (see Descendants (7)) was born to Edmond Hardcastle[2036] and Sue Adele Barneycastle[2035].
3280. TODD ?.
    Todd ? married Pamela Hardcastle[3279].

3281. GRETA HARDCASTLE (see Descendants (7)) was born to Edmond Hardcastle[2036] and Sue Adele Barneycastle[2035].

3282. STEVE BASS (see Descendants (28)) was born to Daniel S Bass[2041] and Barbara ?[2042].

3283. CASANDRA BASS (see Descendants (28)) was born to Daniel S Bass[2041] and Barbara ?[2042].

3284. SETH BASS (see Descendants (28)) was born to Daniel S Bass[2041] and Barbara ?[2042].

3285. GARY BASS (see Descendants (29)) was born to Kenneth Riley Bass Jr.[2051] and Ms. ?[2053].

3286. TERRY BASS (see Descendants (29)) was born to Kenneth Riley Bass Jr.[2051] and Ms. ?[2053].

3287. MR. LASKER (see Descendants (30)) was born to Mr. Lasker[2058] and Ms. ?[2059].

3288. MR./MS. LASKER (see Descendants (30)) was born to Mr. Lasker[2058] and Ms. ?[2059].

3289. MR./MS. LASKER (see Descendants (30)) was born to Mr. Lasker[2058] and Ms. ?[2059].

3290. MR. LASKER (see Descendants (30)) was born to Mr. Lasker[2058] and Ms. ?[2059].

3291. RONALD KAY GRESKO (see Descendants (31)) was born in 1972 to Ronald Kay Gresko[2063] and Ms. ?[2064]. He died in 1973, aged about 1.

Direct Relations

3292. CHASTITY DEANNIA INEZ GRESKO (see Descendants (31)) was born on May 30, 1974, in Phoenix, Maricopa, Arizona, USA, to Ronald Kay Gresko[2063] and Ms. ?[2064]. She died on May 21, 2016, aged 41, in Arizona, USA.

3293. MR. ?.
   Mr. ? married Chastity Deannia Inez Gresko[3292].

3294. ELLA ALESIA CLAUSER (see Descendants (11)) was born on December 21, 1963 to Larry Bradley Herrington[2076] and Patricia June Wiggins[2077].
   • She died on August 15, 1998, aged 34.
   • She was buried in Carolina Baptist Church Cemetery, Covington, Alabama, USA.

3295. ZACKAREAH JONATHAN BATSON (see Descendants (34)) was born on March 15, 1985 to David Jonathan Batson[2081] and Paula Jean Johnson[2082].

3296. STEVEN WALLACE (see Descendants (34)) was born on September 10, 1977 to Chuck Wallace[2085] and Dawn Denise Brock[2084].

3297. KEVIN WALLACE (see Descendants (34)) was born on May 1, 1984 to Chuck Wallace[2085] and Dawn Denise Brock[2084].

3298. TIMMY WAYNE BURLISON II (see Descendants (34)) was born on April 10, 1976 to Timmy Wayne Burlison[2088] and Dixie Irene Spence[2087].
3299. HOLLY CHRISTINA LORD was born on July 22, 1995.
   Timmy Wayne Burlison II[3298] married Holly Christina Lord. They had one daughter:
      Hannah Danielle Burlison[3939]

3300. SHAUN MICHAEL BURLISON (see Descendants (34)) was born on February 5, 1979 to Timmy Wayne Burlison[2088] and Dixie Irene Spence[2087].

3301. RENEE S. CAIN (see Descendants (34)) was born on January 29, 1974 to Kenneth A. Cain[2090] and Rhonda Sue Spence[2089].
   Renee S. married twice. She was married to Ryan Winters[3302] and Renee S. Cain[3303].
3302. RYAN WINTERS.
   Ryan Winters married Renee S. Cain[3301], aged 19, in July 1993. They had three children:
      Alysa L. Winters[3940] born on January 20, 1992
      Tyler R. Winters[3941] born on August 4, 1994
      Logan Taylor Winters[3942] born on September 4, 1996
3303. RENEE S. CAIN.
   Renee S. Cain married Renee S. Cain[3301], aged 22, in June 1996.

3304. KACEY A. CAIN (see Descendants (34)) was born on September 12, 1977 to Kenneth A. Cain[2090] and Rhonda Sue Spence[2089].
3305. MS. HENDRIX.
   Kacey A. Cain[3304] married Ms. Hendrix. They had two sons:
      Damion T. Hendrix[3943] born on May 31, 1996
      Elijah Hendrix[3944] born on May 31, 1998

3306. KENNETH A. CAIN II (see Descendants (34)) was born on April 4, 1981 to Kenneth A. Cain[2090] and Rhonda Sue Spence[2089].

3307. SHANNON ROBERT SPENCE (see Descendants (34)) was born on July 29, 1982 to Robert Leon Spence[2091] and Corinne Sue Smith[2092].

3308. CARA LEANE SPENCE (see Descendants (34)) was born on January 24, 1986 to Robert Leon Spence[2091] and Corinne Sue Smith[2092].

3309. TABITHA S. SPENCE (see Descendants (34)) was born on October 21, 1984 to Floyd Colon Spence[2094] and Terri S. Clark[2095].

3310. AUBREY GENE MILSTEAD (see Descendants (36)) was born on August 8, 1974, in Pensacola, Escambia, Florida, USA, to Frank James Milstead[2098] and Deborah Ann Wilkinson[2097].

3311. HEATHER ?.
> Aubrey Gene Milstead[3310], aged 25, married Heather ? on September 25, 1999. They had one son:
> Blayne Christian Milstead[3945] born on March 13, 2000

3312. DANITA ANN MILSTEAD (see Descendants (36)) was born on December 4, 1977, in Fort Walton Beach, Okaloosa, Florida, USA, to Frank James Milstead[2098] and Deborah Ann Wilkinson[2097].

3313. ANDREW BAYLIS.
> Andrew Baylis married Danita Ann Milstead[3312], aged 21, on December 31, 1998. They had one daughter:
> Brooke Leighanne Baylis[3946] born on May 14, 1999

3314. JORDAN ALEXANDER WILKINSON (see Descendants (36)) was born on August 14, 1996 to Delmus Nathan Wilkinson[2099] and Mary Belinda Jordan[2100].

3315. WADE NATHAN PRATER (see Descendants (36)) was born on May 23, 1978, in Edmond, Oklahoma, Oklahoma, USA, to Ecki Alexander Prater[2103] and Joy Denise Wilkinson[2102].

3316. ISLA NOEL PRATER (see Descendants (36)) was born on April 19, 1985, in Edmond, Oklahoma, Oklahoma, USA, to Ecki Alexander Prater[2103] and Joy Denise Wilkinson[2102].

3317. ROBERT CALVIN PRATER (see Descendants (36)) was born on March 25, 1988, in Edmond, Oklahoma, Oklahoma, USA, to Ecki Alexander Prater[2103] and Joy Denise Wilkinson[2102].

3318. JUSTIN EUGENE BALIUS (see Descendants (36)) was born on February 2, 1989, in Creston, Union, Iowa, USA, to John Ernest Balius[2105] and Janet Lee Wilkinson[2104].

3319. MEGAN CATHERINE BALIUS (see Descendants (36)) was born on November 20, 1990, in Norfolk, Virginia, USA, to John Ernest Balius[2105] and Janet Lee Wilkinson[2104].

3320. STEPHANIE ANN STEELE (see Descendants (36)) was born on February 12, 1980, in Bountiful, Davis, Utah, USA, to Joseph Wayne Steele[2106] and Donna Lee Good[2107].

3321. REBECCA ANN STEELE (see Descendants (36)) was born on November 21, 1981 to Joseph Wayne Steele[2106] and Kelli Ann Ottley[2108].

3322. KATHRYN LEANNE STEELE (see Descendants (153)) was born on July 29, 1991, in Montgomery, Montgomery, Alabama, USA, to Larry Dale Steele[2109] and Christina Van Sickler[2110].

3323. DAVID AUSTIN STEELE (see Descendants (153)) was born on January 11, 1994, in Montgomery, Montgomery, Alabama, USA, to Larry Dale Steele[2109] and Christina Van Sickler[2110].

3324. KRISTEN NICOLE KENNEDY (see Descendants (154)) was born on May 27, 1987 to V. W. Kennedy[2112] and Donna Marie Steele[2111].

3325. STEPHANIE MICHELLE KENNEDY (see Descendants (154)) was born on December 28, 1993 to V. W. Kennedy[2112] and Donna Marie Steele[2111].

3326. JEREMY MICHAEL STEELE (see Descendants (155)) was born on May 24, 1981 to Terry Michael Steele[2113] and Patricia Ann Kilcrease[2114].

3327. BRADLEY SHOVEN STEELE (see Descendants (155)) was born on September 1, 1983 to Terry Michael Steele[2113] and Patricia Ann Kilcrease[2114].

3328. KEVIN CHARLES STEELE (see Descendants (155)) was born on May 20, 1986 to Terry Michael Steele[2113] and Patricia Ann Kilcrease[2114].

3329. EMILY ANN STEELE (see Descendants (155)) was born on September 21, 1987 to Terry Michael Steele[2113] and Patricia Ann Kilcrease[2114].

3330. ERIN ELIZABETH STEELE (see Descendants (155)) was born on September 21, 1987 to Terry Michael Steele[2113] and Patricia Ann Kilcrease[2114].

3331. JASON LEE (see Descendants (156)) was born on August 1, 1976, in Milton, Santa Rosa, Florida, USA, to Leonard Lee[2116] and Lois Anette Johnson[2115].

3332. NATHAN LEE (see Descendants (156)) was born on December 28, 1980, in Milton, Santa Rosa, Florida, USA, to Leonard Lee[2116] and Lois Anette Johnson[2115].

3333. ALISHA REGISTER (see Descendants (157)) was born on October 23, 1984 to Marcus Dean Register[2117] and Susan Ward[2118].

3334. JESSICA E. REGISTER (see Descendants (157)) was born on June 13, 1994 to Marcus Dean Register[2117] and Susan Ward[2118].

3335. JEREMIAH D. REGISTER (see Descendants (157)) was born on October 7, 1996 to Marcus Dean Register[2117] and Susan Ward[2118].

3336. AUGUSTA GRACE REGISTER (see Descendants (158)) was born on September 16, 1998 to Matthew Ward Register[2119] and Christy Rene Bennett[2120].

3337. MATTILYN ROSE REGISTER (see Descendants (158)) was born on March 9, 2000 to Matthew Ward Register[2119] and Christy Rene Bennett[2120].

3338. BRANDIE REGISTER (see Descendants (159)) was born on March 29, 1996 to Mr. ?[2122] and Martha Grace Register[2121].

3339. PHILLIP LOGAN FLEMING (see Descendants (160)) was born on March 15, 1983 to Phillip Eugene Fleming[2123] and Linda Henderson[2124].

3340. ALEX FLEMING (see Descendants (160)) was born to Phillip Eugene Fleming[2123] and Cindy Borders[2125].

3341. MATTHEW REED SHAUD (see Descendants (161)) was born on September 27, 1989 to David Eugene Shaud[2127] and Laura Lenelle Fleming[2126].

3342. MAGNOLIA PERRY (see Descendants (162)) was born to Lance Perry[2129] and Karen Lorine Fleming[2128].

3343. WYATT CHANCE PERRY (see Descendants (162)) was born to Lance Perry[2129] and Karen Lorine Fleming[2128].

3344. DIXIE LEE DOTSON (see Descendants (163)) was born on April 16, 1984 to Ted Dotson[2132] and Teresa Allen[2133].

3345. AMBER NICOLE DOTSON (see Descendants (163)) was born on April 8, 1986 to Ted Dotson[2132] and Teresa Allen[2133].

3346. MORGAN BAILEY DOTSON (see Descendants (163)) was born on August 12, 1989 to Ted Dotson[2132] and Teresa Allen[2133].

3347. NEIL DOTSON (see Descendants (163)) was born on September 30, 1991 to Ted Dotson[2132] and Teresa Allen[2133].

3348. AMANDA LYNN DOTSON (see Descendants (164)) was born on December 3, 1996 to Tracy Dotson[2134] and Tamara Lynn Simmons[2135].

3349. MELYNDA REANEE RIGGINS (see Descendants (165)) was born on December 12, 1974, in McKinney, Collin, Texas, USA, to Mr. ?[2138] and Pamela Ann Tuley[2137].

3350. KENNETH DEMON LEWIS was born on February 18, 1971.
    Kenneth Demon Lewis, aged 25, married Melynda Reanee Riggins[3349], aged 21, on March 15, 1996. They had one son:
        Kenneth Renee Lewis[3947] born on August 3, 1995

3351. KIRSTIE LEA RIGGINS (see Descendants (165)) was born on November 21, 1979, in Milton, Santa Rosa, Florida, USA, to Haywood Riggins[2139] and Pamela Ann Tuley[2137].

3352. BRANDON HAYWOOD RIGGINS (see Descendants (165)) was born on February 11, 1988, in Wylie, Colin, Texas, USA, to Haywood Riggins[2139] and Pamela Ann Tuley[2137].

3353. RHAINNON ROSE WILKINSON (see Descendants (166)) was born on February 12, 1981 to Randall Glen Wilkinson[2141] and Nancy Hale[2142].

3354. JEREMY CURTIS WILKINSON (see Descendants (166)) was born on January 25, 1991 to Randall Glen Wilkinson[2141] and Patti Miller[2143].

3355. ALICIA RAYE WILKINSON (see Descendants (166)) was born on March 25, 1993 to Randall Glen Wilkinson[2141] and Patti Miller[2143].

3356. TAYLOR WILKINSON (see Descendants (37)) was born on August 15, 1993, in Wylie, Colin, Texas, USA, to Warren Craig Wilkinson[2144] and April Lee Crabill[2145].

3357. SHAUN MICHELLE HAVEARD (see Descendants (167)) was born on July 25, 1977 to Joe Haveard[2147] and Gail Denise Woodard[2146].
Shaun Michelle married twice. She was married to Chris Sautter[3358] and Michael David Reddick[3359].

3358. CHRIS SAUTTER.
    Chris Sautter married Shaun Michelle Haveard[3357]. They had two children:
        Calli Sautter[3948]
        Joseph Edwin Haveard[3949] born on April 13, 2000

3359. MICHAEL DAVID REDDICK was born on May 14, 1975.
    Michael David Reddick, aged 22, married Shaun Michelle Haveard[3357], aged 19, on May 31, 1997, and they were divorced.

3360. KRISTEN LEIGH MCAULIFFE (see Descendants (167)) was born on April 30, 1983 to Kevin Mcauliffe[2148] and Gail Denise Woodard[2146].

3361. GABRIE COEN DUNLAP (see Descendants (167)) was born on September 26, 1986 to Will Dunlap[2149] and Gail Denise Woodard[2146].

3362. LAUREN ASHLEY WALTERS (see Descendants (168)) was born on July 17, 1984, in Jefferson City, Cole, Missouri, USA, to Don Monwell Walters[2150] and Debra Jean Nolan[2151].

3363. JOSHUA WALTERS (see Descendants (168)) was born on September 4, 1985, in Raleigh, Wake, North Carolina, USA, to Don Monwell Walters[2150] and Debra Jean Nolan[2151].

3364. TRISTIN WALTERS (see Descendants (168)) was born on December 4, 1986, in Pensacola, Escambia, Florida, USA, to Don Monwell Walters[2150] and Debra Jean Nolan[2151].

3365. ADAM ALEXANDER WALTERS (see Descendants (169)) was born on May 29, 1985, in Dallas, Dallas, Texas, USA, to Rodrick Jerome Walters[2152] and Anna Loftus[2153].

3366. RODERICK JAY WALTERS (see Descendants (169)) was born on July 20, 1986, in Dallas, Dallas, Texas, USA, to Rodrick Jerome Walters[2152] and Anna Loftus[2153].

3367. KENNETH LAYNE WALTERS JR. (see Descendants (170)) was born on November 3, 1984, in Pensacola, Escambia, Florida, USA, to Kenneth Layne Walters[2154] and Sandra Estelle Ellis[2155].

3368. KALIEE HANKINS (see Descendants (171)) was born on December 4, 1989 to Chris Hankins[2159] and Lisa Marie Cook[2158].

3369. ERIKA JENELLE WILKINSON (see Descendants (173)) was born on October 11, 1988, in Milton, Santa Rosa, Florida, USA, to Christopher Del Wilkinson[2168] and Lori Caprice Tilley[2169].

3370. JESSIE CORDEL WILKINSON (see Descendants (173)) was born on February 11, 1994 to Christopher Del Wilkinson[2168] and Lori Caprice Tilley[2169].

3371. SARAH LINDSAY DIMARIA (see Descendants (174)) was born on November 19, 1992, in Orlando, Orange, Florida, USA, to John Paul Victor Dimaria Jr.[2171] and Kimberly Ann Cupp[2170].

Direct Relations

3372. JACKSON PHILLIP DIMARIA (see Descendants (174)) was born on September 28, 1995, in Orlando, Orange, Florida, USA, to John Paul Victor Dimaria Jr.[2171] and Kimberly Ann Cupp[2170].

3373. LINDSEY DANIELLE CUPP (see Descendants (175)) was born on February 11, 1993 to James Landre Cupp[2172].

3374. MR./MS. HERRIN (see Descendants (176)) was born to Mr. Herrin[2175] and Candace Delane Wilkinson[2174].

3375. MR./MS. HERRIN (see Descendants (176)) was born to Mr. Herrin[2175] and Candace Delane Wilkinson[2174].

3376. MR./MS. HERRIN (see Descendants (176)) was born to Mr. Herrin[2175] and Candace Delane Wilkinson[2174].

3377. MR./MS. HERRIN (see Descendants (176)) was born to Mr. Herrin[2175] and Candace Delane Wilkinson[2174].

3378. MR./MS. WILKINSON (see Descendants (177)) was born to Shane Curtis Wilkinson[2176] and Ms. ?[2177].

3379. MR./MS. HERRIN (see Descendants (178)) was born to Mr. Herrin[2179] and Candace Delane Wilkinson[2178].

3380. MR./MS. HERRIN (see Descendants (178)) was born to Mr. Herrin[2179] and Candace Delane Wilkinson[2178].

3381. MR./MS. HERRIN (see Descendants (178)) was born to Mr. Herrin[2179] and Candace Delane Wilkinson[2178].

3382. MR./MS. HERRIN (see Descendants (178)) was born to Mr. Herrin[2179] and Candace Delane Wilkinson[2178].

3383. MR./MS. WILKINSON (see Descendants (179)) was born to Shane Curtis Wilkinson[2180] and Ms. ?[2181].

3384. SARAH M. SUMMERLIN (see Descendants (38)) was born on August 19, 1988, in Opelika, Lee, Alabama, USA, to Charles David Summerlin[2184] and Mary Jo Williamson[2185].

3385. CHAD DAVID SUMMERLIN (see Descendants (38)) was born on April 14, 1990, in Pensacola, Escambia, Florida, USA, to Charles David Summerlin[2184] and Mary Jo Williamson[2185].

3386. JASON SLOAN LEGER (see Descendants (38)) was born on February 1, 1983, in Pensacola, Escambia, Florida, USA, to Kathy Ann Summerlin[2186].

3387. MARTIAL MCGLAUN (see Descendants (39)) was born to Randy Lamar McGlaun[2190] and Carin ?[2191].

3388. HOLLY MCGLAUN (see Descendants (39)) was born to Randy Lamar McGlaun[2190] and Carin ?[2191].

3389. MR./MS. POLZIN (see Descendants (39)) was born to Mr. Polzin[2194] and Erin McGlaun[2193].

3390. DEBORAH JANE CAUSIE (see Descendants (40)) was born in June 4 A.D. to Clyde Henry Mims Jr.[2196] and Judy Ann Causie[2195].

3391. TAWANA LYNN CAUSEY (see Descendants (40)) was born on November 22, 1970, in Montgomery, AL, to David Lee Causey[2202] and Vickey Yvone McGlaun[2201].
- She was christened on March 5, 2015, aged 44, in Ashville Road Church of Christ.
- On May 19, 2014, aged 43, she was a Family Service Counselor in Elmwood Cemetery.

The following information is also recorded for Tawana Lynn:
- Marriages: James Calvin Sargent, III on April 24, 1993, aged 22, in Alexander City, AL.
- Marriages: Stanley Adam Sherrer, he died April 27, 2013 on February 9, 1996, aged 25, in Montgomery, AL.
- Miscarriage on September 12, 1996, aged 25, in Dadeville, AL.
- Children: Hayden Alexander Sherrer made his appearance, 19 days late. He was born with group b strep, transient tykipnea, and jaundice. We were told he'd not make it 48 hours. But he's still with us. on November 19, 1997, aged 26, in Opelika, AL.
- Degree on July 31, 2011, aged 40, in Kaplan University.
- Marriages: James Gregory Cleghorn on January 16, 2015, aged 44, in Ashville, AL.

Notes:
- *Angel Lynn Sherrer.*
  (Miscarriage)
- *Bachelor of Science, Criminal Justice.*
  (Degree)

3392. STANLEY ADAM SHERRER was born on July 31, 1965. He died on April 27, 2013, aged 47.
Stanley Adam Sherrer married Tawana Lynn Causey[3391].

3393. BRANDON LEE CAUSEY (see Descendants (40)) was born on August 7, 1972 to David Lee Causey[2202] and Vickey Yvone McGlaun[2201].

3394. LENA LARAE FERGUSON (see Descendants (40)) was born on January 16, 1976 to Michael C. Ferguson[2203] and Vickey Yvone McGlaun[2201].

3395. JAMES KENNETH MCGLAUN III (see Descendants (40)) was born on November 29, 1983 to James Kenny McGlaun Jr.[2205] and Lisa Perl Champion[2206].

3396. KIMBERLY ANN MCGLAUN (see Descendants (40)) was born on November 5, 1991 to James Kenny McGlaun Jr.[2205] and Lisa Perl Champion[2206].

3397. KENNETH A. FLOYD III (see Descendants (40)) was born on July 11, 1983 to Kenneth A. Floyd Jr.[2208] and Lisa Rena McGlaun[2207].

3398. RONALD JOSEPH O'NEIL (see Descendants (40)) was born on May 24, 1986 to Ronald Leon O'neil[2209] and Lisa Rena McGlaun[2207].

3399. HOPE RENA O'NEIL (see Descendants (40)) was born on October 18, 1987 to Ronald Leon O'neil[2209] and Lisa Rena McGlaun[2207].

3400. JOSHUA AARON O'NEIL (see Descendants (40)) was born on May 11, 1992 to Ronald Leon O'neil[2209] and Lisa Rena McGlaun[2207].

3401. AMBER MARIA MESSICK (see Descendants (41)) was born on June 22, 1992 to James Edward Messick[2213] and Sheivella Maria Norris[2214].

3402. KAYLA LYNN INABINETT (see Descendants (41)) was born on September 8, 1997 to Michael Todd Inabinett[2217] and Sandra Dianne Lawson[2216].

3403. BRETT AUBREY HUDSON was born on June 28, 1995.
Brett Aubrey Hudson, aged 25, married Kayla Lynn Inabinett[3402], aged 22, on July 24, 2020. They had one son:
Dutton Lee Hudson[3950] born on March 28, 2023

3404. DALLAS LAWSON INABINETT (see Descendants (41)) was born on January 24, 2001 to Michael Todd Inabinett[2217] and Sandra Dianne Lawson[2216].

3405. BRAYDEN JOHN INABINETT (see Descendants (41)) was born on November 24, 2014 to Michael Todd Inabinett[2217] and Sandra Dianne Lawson[2216].

3406. ELIZABETH ANN DAVIDSON (see Descendants (44)) was born on June 17, 1968, in Andalusia, Covington, Alabama, USA, to Edward Davidson[2227] and Mary Evelyn Huckabaa[2226].

3407. GUY KERVIN was born on July 21, 1955.
Guy Kervin married Elizabeth Ann Davidson[3406]. They had three children:
Dana Kervin[3951] born on August 20, 1987 in Andalusia, Covington, Alabama, USA
Patrick Kervin[3952] born on September 9, 1988 in Andalusia, Covington, Alabama, USA
Corbrey Kervin[3953] born on November 2, 1989 in Andalusia, Covington, Alabama, USA

3408. TINA HUCKABAA (see Descendants (44)) was born in 1977, in Andalusia, Covington, Alabama, USA, to Jerry Wayne Huckabaa[2228] and Betty ?[2229].

3409. TONY WAYNE BRADLEY (see Descendants (44)) was born on December 29, 1969, in Andalusia, Covington, Alabama, USA, to Wayne Bradley[2231] and Charlene Huckabaa[2230].

3410. CRYSTAL DARLENE BRADLEY (see Descendants (44)) was born in Andalusia, Covington, Alabama, USA to Wayne Bradley[2231] and Charlene Huckabaa[2230].

3411. MARSHA HUCKABAA (see Descendants (181)) was born on October 17, 1975, in Andalusia, Covington, Alabama, USA, to Martin Van Buren Huckabaa Jr.[2232] and Cynthia J. Carpenter[2233].

3412. WILLIAM HUCKABAA (see Descendants (181)) was born on January 7, 1979, in Andalusia, Covington, Alabama, USA, to Martin Van Buren Huckabaa Jr.[2232] and Cynthia J. Carpenter[2233].

3413. BRENDA HUCKABAA (see Descendants (181)) was born on February 29, 1980, in Andalusia, Covington, Alabama, USA, to Martin Van Buren Huckabaa Jr.[2232] and Cynthia J. Carpenter[2233].

3414. DENNIS HUCKABAA (see Descendants (181)) was born on December 8, 1981, in Andalusia, Covington, Alabama, USA, to Martin Van Buren Huckabaa Jr.[2232] and Cynthia J. Carpenter[2233].

3415. DEREK HUCKABAA (see Descendants (181)) was born on May 26, 1989, in Andalusia, Covington, Alabama, USA, to Martin Van Buren Huckabaa Jr.[2232] and Cynthia J. Carpenter[2233].

3416. GLENDA FAY DAVIS (see Descendants (182)) was born on October 12, 1960 to Winfred Davis[2238] and Alta Dukes[2237].
3417. BOBBY FULLER.
> Bobby Fuller married Glenda Fay Davis[3416], aged 25, on January 18, 1986 in Opp, Covington, Alabama, USA. They had two children:
>> Jessica Daniel Fuller[3954] born on August 4, 1988 in Dothan, Houston, Alabama, USA
>> Andrew Sery Fuller[3955] born on April 13, 1990 in Dothan, Houston, Alabama, USA

3418. J. W. DAVIS (see Descendants (182)) was born on August 5, 1963, in Opp, Covington, Alabama, USA, to Winfred Davis[2238] and Alta Dukes[2237].
3419. ALLIE MARGENT CARRINGTON was born on August 15, 1965.
> J. W. Davis[3418], aged 22, married Allie Margent Carrington, aged 20, on October 26, 1985. They had one son:
>> John Aubrey Davis[3956] born on September 28, 1990

3420. JAMES EDWARD HARRIS (see Descendants (183)) was born on August 14, 1965 to Jimmy Junior Harris[2240] and Audi Mae Dukes[2239].
3421. REBECCA MERRITTE was born on March 22, 1967.
> James Edward Harris[3420] married Rebecca Merritte. They had two children:
>> James Brandon Harris[3957] born on June 22, 1985
>> Krystal Dianna Harris[3958] born on September 12, 1986

3422. CINDY RENAE HARRIS (see Descendants (183)) was born on July 9, 1976 to Jimmy Junior Harris[2240] and Audi Mae Dukes[2239].

3423. GREGORY RANDALL HUCKABAA (see Descendants (185)) was born on April 6, 1971, in Andalusia, Covington, Alabama, USA, to Randall Ike Huckabaa[2243] and Syble Diane Morgan[2244].
3424. TERESA BRADY was born on May 22, 1972, in Montgomery, Montgomery, Alabama, USA.
> Gregory Randall Huckabaa[3423], aged 18, married Teresa Brady, aged 17, on August 5, 1989 in Andalusia, Covington, Alabama, USA. They had four children:
>> Joseph Michael Huckabaa[3959] born on April 28, 1990 in Andalusia, Covington, Alabama, USA
>> Tessa Leann Huckabaa[3960] born on January 1, 1993 in Andalusia, Covington, Alabama, USA
>> Brett Allen Huckabaa[3961] born on December 29, 1995
>> Brent Randall Huckabaa[3962] born on December 29, 1995

3425. ANGELEA HUCKABAA (see Descendants (185)) was born on December 27, 1974 to Randall Ike Huckabaa[2243] and Syble Diane Morgan[2244].

3426. LESIA NICOLE HUCKABAA (see Descendants (186)) was born on October 3, 1975 to Oscar Cleveland Huckabaa[2245] and Lyndell Freeman[2246].

3427. CHRISTI LYNN HUCKABAA (see Descendants (186)) was born on December 11, 1978 to Oscar Cleveland Huckabaa[2245] and Lyndell Freeman[2246].

3428. GORDON HEATH HUCKABAA (see Descendants (187)) was born on July 3, 1975, in Andalusia, Covington, Alabama, USA, to Gordon Huckabaa[2247] and Emily Henderson[2248].

3429. HEATHER ?.

Gordon Heath Huckabaa[3428] married Heather ?. They had two children:
Shelby Huckabaa[3963]
Jamison Huckabaa[3964]

3430. BOBBY WAYNE HUCKABAA (see Descendants (187)) was born on August 15, 1987, in Andalusia, Covington, Alabama, USA, to Gordon Huckabaa[2247] and Rebecca Dean[2249].

3431. KERRY LYNN CREECH (see Descendants (188)) was born on May 17, 1975 to Ronnie Creech[2251] and Beverly Jean Huckabaa[2250].

3432. AMANDA KAY SANDERS (see Descendants (188)) was born on October 16, 1984, in Montgomery, Montgomery, Alabama, USA, to Lamar Sanders[2252] and Beverly Jean Huckabaa[2250].

3433. KAYLA ANN HUCKABAA (see Descendants (189)) was born on December 14, 1983, in Andalusia, Covington, Alabama, USA, to Rusty Lamar Huckabaa[2253] and Dorthy Ann Kendrix[2254].

3434. CHRISTOPHER ALLEN HUCKABAA (see Descendants (189)) was born on May 14, 1985, in Andalusia, Covington, Alabama, USA, to Rusty Lamar Huckabaa[2253] and Dorthy Ann Kendrix[2254].

3435. CHRISTOPHER SHANE PETTY (see Descendants (190)) was born on September 14, 1978, in Montgomery, Montgomery, Alabama, USA, to Leon Petty[2257] and Sandra Elaine Kimbril[2255].

3436. DANIEL LAMAR KIMBRIL (see Descendants (191)) was born on July 27, 1978, in Andalusia, Covington, Alabama, USA, to Timmy Lamar Kimbril[2258] and Erldean Carowell[2259].

3437. JOSEPH LOKESH KIMBRIL (see Descendants (191)) was born on February 14, 1980, in India, to Timmy Lamar Kimbril[2258] and Erldean Carowell[2259].

3438. SAMUEL LAKSHAW KIMBRIL (see Descendants (191)) was born on August 15, 1980, in India, to Timmy Lamar Kimbril[2258] and Erldean Carowell[2259].

3439. ANDREW LUCAS KIMBRIL (see Descendants (191)) was born on May 9, 1984, in India, to Timmy Lamar Kimbril[2258] and Erldean Carowell[2259].

3440. GRACE LORAINE KIMBRIL (see Descendants (191)) was born on June 11, 1987, in Hong Kong, to Timmy Lamar Kimbril[2258] and Erldean Carowell[2259].

3441. JIMMY EARL BOUTWELL (see Descendants (192)) was born on May 3, 1982, in Brewton, Escambia, Alabama, USA, to Jimmy Ray Boutwell[2265] and Teresa Jane Huckabaa[2264].

3442. GLEN DAY BIDDLE JR. (see Descendants (194)) was born on October 18, 1983, in Geneva, Geneva, Alabama, USA, to Glen Day Biddle[2269] and Redda Kay Huckabaa[2268]. Glen Day became known as "Bo".
3443. TERRI ?.
Glen Day Biddle Jr.[3442] married Terri ?.

3444. SHON LEE BIDDLE (see Descendants (194)) was born on November 20, 1985, in Pensacola, Escambia, Florida, USA, to Glen Day Biddle[2269] and Redda Kay Huckabaa[2268].
3445. BJ ?.

Direct Relations

Shon Lee Biddle[3444] married BJ ?.

3446. LORI LUCAS (see Descendants (195)) was born on February 18, 1984 to Dan Howard Lucas[2272] and Laura Lynn Huckabaa[2271].
Lori was the partner of her fourth cousin, once removed, David Brent Glidewell[2927].
David Brent Glidewell[2927] and Lori Lucas had two sons:
Jayden Glidewell[3797]
Daughton Glidewell[3798]

3447. AMANDA DAWN LUCAS (see Descendants (195)) was born on January 27, 1985 to Dan Howard Lucas[2272] and Laura Lynn Huckabaa[2271].

3448. AARON R HUCKABAA (see Descendants (196)) was born on December 25, 1990, in Andalusia, Covington, Alabama, USA, to Eddie Ray Huckabaa[2273] and Angelia Renee Ramsey[2274].

3449. CIJI HUCKABAA (see Descendants (197)) was born on September 14, 1984, in Andalusia, Covington, Alabama, USA, to Tracy Lamar Huckabaa[2275] and Kimberly Dawn Wise[2276].

3450. BRIDGET ROCHELL HUCKABAA (see Descendants (197)) was born on February 2, 1985 to Tracy Lamar Huckabaa[2275] and Sandra Fay Butts[2277]. She died on November 12, 1985, aged 0.

3451. LESLIE ANN SCHOFIELD (see Descendants (45)) was born on September 26, 1975, in Fort Walton Beach, Okaloosa, Florida, USA, to Clifford Schofield[2283] and Peggy Joyce Garrett[2282].
3452. HAYWARD CLARENCE NORRIS was born on August 29, 1970, in DeFuniak Springs, Walton, Florida, USA.
Hayward Clarence Norris, aged 19, married Leslie Ann Schofield[3451], aged 14, on March 7, 1990 in DeFuniak Springs, Walton, Florida, USA. They had one daughter:
Tiffany Ann Norris[3965] born on February 8, 1992 in Panama City, Bay, Florida, USA

3453. THOMAS JEFFERSON SCHOFIELD (see Descendants (45)) was born on January 17, 1979, in Fort Walton Beach, Okaloosa, Florida, USA, to Clifford Schofield[2283] and Peggy Joyce Garrett[2282].

3454. SHARLENE SUZETTE SMITH (see Descendants (45)) was born on February 9, 1966, in Niceville, Okaloosa, Florida, USA, to Billie Mack Smith[2284] and Shirley ?[2285].

3455. RODNEY FENTON COOK (see Descendants (45)) was born on May 11, 1965, in Niceville, Okaloosa, Florida, USA, to Fenton Broome Cook[2287] and Billie Jo Smith[2286].
3456. MS. ?.
Rodney Fenton Cook[3455] married Ms. ?. They had one son:
Christopher M. Cook[3966] born on September 17, 1990 in Eglin Air Force Base, Okaloosa, Florida, USA

3457. ARNOLD RANDALL COOK (see Descendants (45)) was born on August 7, 1969, in Fort Walton Beach, Okaloosa, Florida, USA, to Fenton Broome Cook[2287] and Billie Jo Smith[2286].

3458. NICHOLAS TYLER GILMEN (see Descendants (45)) was born on August 22, 1992, in Eglin Air Force Base, Okaloosa, Florida, USA, to Mr. ?[2289] and Barbara Payline Gilmen[2288].

3459. JASON DEREK ROWELL (see Descendants (46)) was born on November 18, 1980, in Tallahassee, Leon, Florida, USA, to Russell Edward Rowell[2298] and Kathy Renee Joyner[2299].

3460. CHRISTOPHER M. ROWELL (see Descendants (46)) was born on May 4, 1982, in Tallahassee, Leon, Florida, USA, to Russell Edward Rowell[2298] and Kathy Renee Joyner[2299].

3461. ASHLYN MORGAN CRAWFORD (see Descendants (50)) was born on December 4, 1988 to John Kenneth Crawford[2328] and Carol Yvonne Morgan[2329].

3462. APRYL MICHELLE CRAWFORD (see Descendants (50)) was born on April 26, 1990 to John Kenneth Crawford[2328] and Carol Yvonne Morgan[2329].

3463. JESSE TANNER CRAWFORD (see Descendants (50)) was born on April 17, 1992 to John Kenneth Crawford[2328] and Carol Yvonne Morgan[2329].

3464. DILLON JOHN CRAWFORD (see Descendants (50)) was born on December 15, 1993 to John Kenneth Crawford[2328] and Carol Yvonne Morgan[2329].

3465. HANK DALLAS BASS JR. (see Descendants (54)) was born on March 27, 1992 to Hank Dallas Bass Sr.[2343] and Mary Ann Behm[2344].

3466. BRITTANY LEANN VADINO.
> Hank Dallas Bass Jr.[3465], aged 27, married Brittany Leann Vadino on September 21, 2019. They had three children:
>> Leanne Avery Bass[3967] born on June 14, 2014
>> Connor Matthew Bass[3968] born on January 5, 2016
>> Payton Harper Bass[3969] born on December 20, 2019

3467. MICHAEL ANTHONY BASS (see Descendants (54)) was born on December 28, 1993 to Hank Dallas Bass Sr.[2343] and Mary Ann Behm[2344].

3468. TREASA ANN BASS (see Descendants (54)) was born on December 14, 1995 to Hank Dallas Bass Sr.[2343] and Mary Ann Behm[2344].

3469. ZACHARY DANIEL BASS (see Descendants (54)) was born on August 28, 1997 to Hank Dallas Bass Sr.[2343] and Mary Ann Behm[2344].

3470. WILLIAM ISSAC NEWMANN (see Descendants (57)) was born on October 23, 1973 to William Earl Newmann[2358] and Peggy Lee Huckabaa[2357].

3471. LORRIE LEIGH NEWMANN (see Descendants (57)) was born on June 26, 1982, in Clearwater, Pinellas, Florida, USA, to William Earl Newmann[2358] and Peggy Lee Huckabaa[2357].

3472. DAVID LEE HUCKABAA (see Descendants (57)) was born on July 12, 1984, in Georgia, USA, to Donnie Lee Huckabaa[2359] and Shiela Little[2360].

3473. BILLY J HUCKABAA (see Descendants (57)) was born on December 4, 1986, in Belgium, to Donnie Lee Huckabaa[2359] and Shiela Little[2360].

3474. DEBORAH SUE HUCKABAA (see Descendants (57)) was born on October 11, 1981, in Sarasota, Sarasota, Florida, USA, to Demas Mark Huckabaa[2362] and Deborah Ingram[2363].

3475. DEMAS JAMES HUCKABAA (see Descendants (57)) was born on September 22, 1993, in Pensacola, Escambia, Florida, USA, to Demas Mark Huckabaa[2362] and Teresa Hargabus[2364].

3476. CORA MARIE MACKO (see Descendants (57)) was born on April 4, 1990, in Ozark, Dale, Alabama, USA, to Mark Macko[2366] and Phyllis Ann Huckabaa[2365].

3477. JASON HUGH HUCKABAA (see Descendants (57)) was born on March 5, 1984, in Walton, Florida, USA, to Edgar Hugh Huckabaa[2367] and Beverly Lynn Wittmyer[2368].

3478. CRYSTAL LYNN HUCKABAA (see Descendants (57)) was born on July 8, 1988, in Walton, Florida, USA, to Edgar Hugh Huckabaa[2367] and Beverly Lynn Wittmyer[2368].

3479. ASHLI CHERE HUCKABAA (see Descendants (57)) was born on January 24, 1986, in Ozark, Dale, Alabama, USA, to James Rudolf Huckabaa[2369] and Ms. Trisha[2370].

3480. DAVID C. SNELLGROVE (see Descendants (198)) was born on October 16, 1970 to Michael C. Walters[2372] and Betty June Snellgrove[2371].

3481. MICHAEL SHANE WALTERS (see Descendants (198)) was born on July 26, 1975 to Michael C. Walters[2372] and Betty June Snellgrove[2371].

3482. TRAVIS SNELLGROVE (see Descendants (199)) was born on January 11, 1979 to Rudy Von Snellgrove[2373] and Ms. ?[2374].

3483. TRISTAN L. SNELLGROVE (see Descendants (199)) was born on September 12, 1984 to Rudy Von Snellgrove[2373] and Ms. ?[2374].

3484. AMANDA MAE SNELLGROVE (see Descendants (200)) was born on April 7, 1980 to Roger Henry Snellgrove[2375] and Rebecca Lonoel[2376].

3485. KATIE LUCRIETA SNELLGROVE (see Descendants (200)) was born on December 5, 1983 to Roger Henry Snellgrove[2375] and Rebecca Lonoel[2376].

3486. KEISHA LYNN BARNES (see Descendants (201)) was born on September 23, 1977 to John William Scott[2378] and Judy Ann Snellgrove[2377].

3487. CRYSTAL SHEREE BARNES (see Descendants (201)) was born on September 24, 1980 to John William Scott[2378] and Judy Ann Snellgrove[2377].

3488. SHARLEY JO SCOTT (see Descendants (201)) was born on December 10, 1990 to John William Scott[2378] and Judy Ann Snellgrove[2377].

3489. JOHN TIMBERLAKE SCOTT (see Descendants (201)) was born on May 16, 1994 to John William Scott[2378] and Judy Ann Snellgrove[2377].

3490. RANDY SCARBROUGH (see Descendants (202)) was born to Sherri Leigh Wilson[2384].

3491. ERIC ? (see Descendants (202)) was born to Sherri Leigh Wilson[2384].

3492. TIFFANY ? (see Descendants (202)) was born to Sherri Leigh Wilson[2384].

3493. TIMOTHY ? (see Descendants (202)) was born to Sherri Leigh Wilson[2384].

3494. DALE EDGAR ANSLEY (see Descendants (203)) was born on April 16, 1990 to Dale Edgar Ansley[2385] and Christine Alford[2386].

3495. TIFFANY LEIGHANN ANSLEY (see Descendants (203)) was born on December 12, 1990 to Dale Edgar Ansley[2385] and Christine Alford[2386].

3496. MARY ELIZABETH GUTHRIE (see Descendants (204)) was born on March 15, 1980 to Kenneth Allen Guthrie[2388] and Joanne Marie Ansley[2387].

3497. JACQUELINE MARIE GUTHRIE (see Descendants (204)) was born on October 18, 1981 to Kenneth Allen Guthrie[2388] and Joanne Marie Ansley[2387].

3498. CARRIE DENISE ANSLEY (see Descendants (205)) was born on January 6, 1983 to Lyvon Walter Ansley[2390] and Celetha Dianne Schofield[2391].

3499. SUMMER LYVON ANSLEY (see Descendants (205)) was born on June 12, 1985 to Lyvon Walter Ansley[2390] and Celetha Dianne Schofield[2391].

3500. BRITTANY NASH HUCKABA (see Descendants (207)) was born on October 26, 1988 to Mr. ?[2396] and Shonda Denise Huckaba[2394].

3501. JOEY RODRIGUES.
    Joey Rodrigues married Brittany Nash Huckaba[3500]. They had three children:
        Tenley Martin Rodrigues[3970] born on February 27, 2012
        Evelee Ember Rodrigues[3971] born on June 20, 2017
        Huxley Nash Rodrigues[3972] born on June 22, 2019

3502. ZACHARIAH TYLER PERMENTER (see Descendants (207)) was born on August 30, 1990 to Mr. ?[2397] and Shonda Denise Huckaba[2394].

3503. AMBER LYNN BIGGER (see Descendants (208)) was born on June 3, 1986 to David Bigger[2399] and Tiresa Lynn Huckaba[2398].

3504. ERIC GILLIS was born on March 26, 1985.
> Eric Gillis, aged 19, married Amber Lynn Bigger[3503], aged 18, on November 4, 2004. They had two sons:
>> Elisha Levi Gillis[3973] born on April 20, 2007
>> Ezekiel Isaiah Gillis[3974] born on August 26, 2008

3505. ANGELA TONYA BIGGER (see Descendants (208)) was born on August 3, 1986 to David Bigger[2399] and Tiresa Lynn Huckaba[2398].

3506. MR. ?.
> Mr. ? married Angela Tonya Bigger[3505]. They had two children:
>> Molly Madison Sheffield[3975] born on February 17, 2009; died on July 17, 2019
>> Mason James Patriquin[3976] born on January 31, 2015

3507. AARON ELI STOUT (see Descendants (208)) was born on January 4, 1993 to Kurt Allen Stout[2400] and Tiresa Lynn Huckaba[2398].

3508. AUSTEN JAMES HUCKABA (see Descendants (209)) was born on March 5, 1993 to Earl Flyn Huckaba II[2403] and Tanya Rae Ceynar[2404].

3509. JAYDEN EARL HUCKABA (see Descendants (209)) was born on March 3, 1994 to Earl Flyn Huckaba II[2403] and Tanya Rae Ceynar[2404].

3510. HARLEE FAY HUCKABA (see Descendants (209)) was born on October 8, 2002 to Earl Flyn Huckaba II[2403] and Amy Micha Windham[2405].

3511. SAMANTHA DIANE HUCKABA (see Descendants (209)) was born to Earl Flyn Huckaba II[2403] and Amy Micha Windham[2405].
Samantha Diane married twice. She was married to Brandon Mulkey[3512] and Ryan DeVane[3513].

3512. BRANDON MULKEY.
> Brandon Mulkey married Samantha Diane Huckaba[3511] from September 20, 2008 to 2015. They had two children:
>> Braydon Noah Mulkey[3977] born on January 8, 2010
>> Khloe Autumn Mulkey[3978] born on February 26, 2015

3513. RYAN DEVANE.
> Ryan DeVane married Samantha Diane Huckaba[3511] on February 17, 2017. They had one son:
>> Bentley Greyson Huckaba[3979] born on February 10, 2018

3514. SARAH JANE POSEY (see Descendants (58)) was born on August 22, 1985, in North Carolina, USA, to Kimmie Dallas Posey[2407] and Pamela Hicks[2408].

3515. JAMES PRESTON FRIDAY POSEY (see Descendants (58)) was born on May 20, 1987, in Raleigh, Wake, North Carolina, USA, to Kimmie Dallas Posey[2407] and Pamela Hicks[2408].

3516. MATTHEW PAUL BENOIT (see Descendants (58)) was born on July 21, 1988, in North Carolina, USA, to Bobby Benoit[2410] and Mary Katherine Posey[2409].

3517. CALEB JOSEPH BENOIT (see Descendants (58)) was born on March 11, 1992, in North Carolina, USA, to Bobby Benoit[2410] and Mary Katherine Posey[2409].

3518. JENNY NICOLE BOOKER (see Descendants (58)) was born on April 29, 1983, in Crestview, Okaloosa, Florida, USA, to Joe Booker[2412] and Diane Faye Posey[2411].

3519. AARON LEE DEATON (see Descendants (61)) was born on June 18, 1989, in Pensacola, Escambia, Florida, USA, to Christopher John Deaton[2435] and Shelia Diane Stewart[2434].

3520. CORY EUGENE DEATON (see Descendants (61)) was born on May 3, 1990, in Pensacola, Escambia, Florida, USA, to Christopher John Deaton[2435] and Shelia Diane Stewart[2434].

3521. DILLON WAYNE ADAMS (see Descendants (210)) was born on January 16, 1992 to Dusty W. Adams[2473] and Joanna Nichole Griffith[2472].

3522. LAYLA ADAMS (see Descendants (212)) was born to Devin Phillips Adams[2481] and Ms. ?[2482].

3523. NATHAN WILLIS (see Descendants (212)) was born in 2009 to Christopher Willis[2484] and Lindsey Nichole Adams[2483].

3524. CANDACE WILLIS (see Descendants (212)) was born in 2012 to Christopher Willis[2484] and Lindsey Nichole Adams[2483].

3525. HUDSON ADAMS (see Descendants (212)) was born on May 24, 2013 to Devin Randal Adams[2485] and Ashley Johnson Adams[2486].

3526. EVERETT ADAMS (see Descendants (212)) was born on March 8, 2020 to Devin Randal Adams[2485] and Ashley Johnson Adams[2486].

3527. WILLIAM COOPER BASS (see Descendants (214)) was born on May 23, 2000 to John William Bass Jr.[2490] and Kelly Pusey[2491].

3528. ALEXANDER RILEY BASS (see Descendants (214)), also recorded as Caroline Riley Bass, was born on December 5, 2003 to John William Bass Jr.[2490] and Kelly Pusey[2491].

3529. AVA CLAIRE BASS (see Descendants (214)) was born on February 14, 2006 to John William Bass Jr.[2490] and Kelly Pusey[2491].

3530. FARRAR COURTNEY BASS (see Descendants (215)) was born on September 16, 2004 to Joel Farrar Bass[2492] and Allison McCorkle[2493].

3531. DRAY ROLEN BASS (see Descendants (215)) was born on October 19, 2007 to Joel Farrar Bass[2492] and Allison McCorkle[2493].

3532. MR./MS. LEONARD (see Descendants (216)) was born to Mr. Leonard[2501] and Jennifer Michelle Monarch[2500].

3533. AMBERLY KIRA MOORE (see Descendants (217)) was born on August 4, 2002 to Mr. Moore[2510] and Alanna Nicole Bass[2509].

3534. LAKIN MOORE (see Descendants (217)) was born on December 23, 2002 to Mr. Moore[2510] and Alanna Nicole Bass[2509].

3535. EDITH MARIE GLADSON (see Descendants (219)) was born on February 3, 2016 to Nathan Michael Gladson[2515] and Stacey Elaine McVay[2514]. Edith Marie became known as "Edie".

3536. AMANDA LYNN WILLIAMSON was born on February 5, 1984 to Charles Anthony Williamson[2516] and Beverly ?[2517].

3537. AUSTIN BREWTON was born on December 13, 1991.
Austin Brewton, aged 25, married Amanda Lynn Williamson[3536], aged 33, on April 19, 2017. They had two children:

Peyton Elise McIntyre[3980] born on October 17, 2014
Carson Blake Brewton[3981] born on December 20, 2017

3538. KRISTEN MICHELLE BARNHILL was born on June 25, 1991 to Shane Barnhill[2520] and Sandra Michelle Williamson[2519].

3539. MR. ?.
Mr. ? and Kristen Michelle Barnhill[3538] had two daughters:
Cameron Michael McMillan[3982] born on September 22, 2015
Olivia Jean McMillan[3983] born on May 31, 2019
The following information is also recorded for this family:
• Unknown Relationship.

3540. TAYLOR NICOLE BARNHILL was born on December 12, 1993 to Shane Barnhill[2520] and Sandra Michelle Williamson[2519].

3541. AARON O'NEAL was born on February 8, 1993.
Aaron O'Neal, aged 21, married Taylor Nicole Barnhill[3540], aged 20, on May 31, 2014. They had three children:
Asheton Alexander O'Neal[3984] born on January 26, 2013
Aiden Blake O'Neal[3985] born on September 27, 2015
Lailynn Raine O'Neal[3986] born on May 9, 2019

3542. CHASE ALLEN BARNHILL was born on October 22, 1996 to Shane Barnhill[2520] and Sandra Michelle Williamson[2519].
Chase Allen had two partnerships. He was married to Cierra McKenzie ?[3543]. He was also the partner of Clarissa Rena Thompson[3544].

3543. CIERRA MCKENZIE ? was born on August 15, 2000.
Chase Allen Barnhill[3542], aged 25, married Cierra McKenzie ?, aged 21, on May 17, 2022. They assumed parenthood of one daughter:
Kinsley Grace Barnhill[3987] by adoption

3544. CLARISSA RENA THOMPSON.
Chase Allen Barnhill[3542] and Clarissa Rena Thompson had three children:
Brentley Allen Barnhill[3988] born on November 15, 2015
River Edward Barnhill[3989] born on January 28, 2018
Kinsley Grace Barnhill[3987] born on September 14, 2021
The following information is also recorded for this family:
• Unknown Relationship.

3545. MEAGAN MICHELLE WILLIAMSON was born on February 8, 1989 to Gordon Michael Williamson[2521] and Mary Michelle Lucas[2522].

3546. LUIS BARRAGAN was born on October 5, 1990.
Luis Barragan, aged 28, married Meagan Michelle Williamson[3545], aged 29, on December 2, 2018. They had one daughter:
Emily Kate Barragan[3990] born on August 26, 2020

3547. GARRETT MICHAEL WILLIAMSON was born on December 7, 1991 to Gordon Michael Williamson[2521] and Mary Michelle Lucas[2522].

3548. MS. ?.
Garrett Michael Williamson[3547] and Ms. ? had one son:
Easton Reese Lee Williamson[3991] born on September 22, 2017
The following information is also recorded for this family:
• Unknown Relationship.

3549. LIAM WYATT WILLIAMSON (see Descendants (220)) was born on August 27, 2008 to Shane Eric Williamson[2523] and Traci Locklar[2524].

3550. FINLEY SCOTT WILLIAMSON (see Descendants (220)) was born on January 27, 2012 to Shane Eric Williamson[2523] and Traci Locklar[2524].

3551. ETHAN MICHAEL MCVAY (see Descendants (221)) was born on July 26, 2001 to Jeffery Michael McVay[2525] and Traci Beth Thorne[2526].

Direct Relations

3552. MICAH RUNAE MCVAY (see Descendants (221)) was born on September 28, 2000 to Jeremy Wayne McVay[2527] and Chelsi Nicole Garrett[2528].
3553. NICHOLAS PRICE was born on December 8, 1998.
>Nicholas Price, aged 22, married Micah Runae McVay[3552], aged 20, on February 14, 2021. They had one son: Nicholas Layne McVay[3992]

3554. GARRETT WAYNE MCVAY (see Descendants (221)) was born on January 26, 2002 to Jeremy Wayne McVay[2527] and Chelsi Nicole Garrett[2528].
3555. MADISON CLAIR NEWELL.
>Garrett Wayne McVay[3554], aged 18, married Madison Clair Newell on November 20, 2020.

3556. ELIJAH ADAM OWENS (see Descendants (222)) was born on March 4, 2009 to Jonathan Owens[2531] and Suzanne Lea McVay[2530].

3557. JOSIAH SAMUEL OWENS (see Descendants (222)) was born on May 20, 2011 to Jonathan Owens[2531] and Suzanne Lea McVay[2530].

3558. IZABELA CLAIR OWENS (see Descendants (222)) was born on November 20, 2013 to Jonathan Owens[2531] and Suzanne Lea McVay[2530]. Izabela Clair became known as "Izzy".

3559. HAILEY JUNE MOYER (see Descendants (223)) was born on September 17, 2009 to Abraham Joshua Moyer[2533] and Julie Crystal Qualls[2532].

3560. LILY JAICYN MOYER (see Descendants (223)) was born on September 15, 2015 to Abraham Joshua Moyer[2533] and Julie Crystal Qualls[2532].

3561. CASSANDRA JAI MOYER (see Descendants (223)) was born on February 3, 2004 to Mr. ?[2534] and Julie Crystal Qualls[2532].

3562. LANDON ALLEN QUALLS (see Descendants (223)) was born on March 27, 2015 to Cody Allen Qualls[2535] and Jennifer Christine ?[2536].

3563. EVERHETT STONE QUALLS (see Descendants (223)) was born on February 13, 2019 to Cody Allen Qualls[2535] and Jennifer Christine ?[2536]. Everhett Stone became known as "Rhett".

3564. MACKENZIE GRACE MCCARVER (see Descendants (224)) was born on October 6, 2005 to Zachary Reese McCarver[2542] and Natalie Melinda McVay[2541]. Mackenzie Grace became known as "Kenzie".

3565. MACON REESE MCCARVER (see Descendants (224)) was born on July 1, 2020 to Zachary Reese McCarver[2542] and Natalie Melinda McVay[2541].

3566. NOLAN JARED MCVAY (see Descendants (224)) was born on January 28, 2009 to Nathan Jared McVay[2543] and Britney Suzanne Gregory[2544].

3567. BRAELYN SADIE MCVAY (see Descendants (224)) was born on September 6, 2012 to Nathan Jared McVay[2543] and Britney Suzanne Gregory[2544].

3568. WESTLYNN GRACE MCVAY (see Descendants (225)) was born on March 28, 2017 to Joshua Mark McVay[2546] and Taylor Nicole Jackson[2547].

3569. HANNAH MARIE MCVAY (see Descendants (225)) was born on April 22, 2009 to Joshua Mark McVay[2546] and Ms. ?[2548].

3570. BRENTON MARK LANE MCVAY (see Descendants (225)) was born on December 7, 2011 to Joshua Mark McVay[2546] and Kayla ?[2549].

3571. BAISLEY RENEE MCVAY (see Descendants (225)) was born on April 28, 2015 to Joshua Mark McVay[2546] and Kayla ?[2549].

3572. MEREDITH HOPE BASS (see Descendants (226)) was born to Marcus Stephen Bass[2553] and Melanie Hoffman[2554].

3573. MARCUS CHRISTIAN BASS (see Descendants (226)) was born to Marcus Stephen Bass[2553] and Melanie Hoffman[2554].

3574. JOHN STEPHEN BASS (see Descendants (226)) was born to Marcus Stephen Bass[2553] and Melanie Hoffman[2554].

3575. HUNTER SCOTT BASS (see Descendants (226)) was born to James Scott Bass[2555] and Elizabeth Mancuso[2556].

3576. HOLLY SUZANNE BASS (see Descendants (226)) was born to James Scott Bass[2555] and Elizabeth Mancuso[2556].

3577. EDEN KELLY SMITH (see Descendants (226)) was born to Christopher Aaron Smith[2560] and Kelly Suzanne Bass[2559].

3578. HUDSON SMITH (see Descendants (226)) was born to Christopher Aaron Smith[2560] and Kelly Suzanne Bass[2559].

3579. NICHOLAS KOZAK (see Descendants (227)) was born to Jerry Kozak[2562] and Lori Marie Stockton[2561].

3580. DYLAN KOZAK (see Descendants (227)) was born to Jerry Kozak[2562] and Lori Marie Stockton[2561].

3581. SHAWN THOMAS STOCKTON (see Descendants (227)) was born to Marshall Kevin Stockton[2563] and Suzy Fuqua[2564].

3582. LEVI STOCKTON (see Descendants (227)) was born to Marshall Kevin Stockton[2563] and Suzy Fuqua[2564].

3583. BECKHAM CEESE BASS (see Descendants (230)) was born on June 22, 2016 to Brian Royce Bass[2570] and Marlee Fuqua[2571].

3584. AUGUST BEAU BASS (see Descendants (230)) was born on December 9, 2020 to Brian Royce Bass[2570] and Marlee Fuqua[2571].

3585. ELIZA BRAY BASS (see Descendants (230)) was born to Brian Royce Bass[2570] and Marlee Fuqua[2571].

3586. RYLEE ALAINE WINGARD (see Descendants (230)) was born on August 25, 2011 to Tyler Joel Wingard[2573] and Holley Alaine Bass[2572].

3587. WYATT CARL WINGARD (see Descendants (230)) was born on March 26, 2013 to Tyler Joel Wingard[2573] and Holley Alaine Bass[2572].

3588. COY BENNETT WINGARD (see Descendants (230)) was born on April 9, 2016 to Tyler Joel Wingard[2573] and Holley Alaine Bass[2572].

3589. SADIE E BAEHR (see Descendants (232)) was born on March 9, 2006 to James Richard Baehr[2576] and Amy A Democker[2577].

3590. ANNIE O. BAEHR (see Descendants (232)) was born on April 26, 2007 to James Richard Baehr[2576] and Amy A Democker[2577].

3591. MYA M. BAEHR (see Descendants (232)) was born on August 12, 2009 to James Richard Baehr[2576] and Amy A Democker[2577].

3592. BENJAMIN R. NOLETTE (see Descendants (232)) was born on May 7, 2004 to Mr. Nolette[2580] and Susan Jean Baehr[2578].

3593. CORY JOE LETURGEY (see Descendants (233)) was born on August 10, 1994 to Joshua Alan Bass[2581] and Ondrea Leturgey[2582].

3594. SIERRA RESENDIZ.
 Cory Joe Leturgey[3593] married Sierra Resendiz. They had one daughter:
  Lilith Ella Leturgey[3993] born on October 3, 2019

3595. JAXON RILEY BASS (see Descendants (233)) was born on August 5, 2011 to Joshua Alan Bass[2581] and Nicole ?[2583].

3596. TEGAN JO VOLPE (see Descendants (234)) was born on August 30, 1999 to Joseph F. Volpe[2587] and Stacie Ann Maclam[2586].

3597. ANTHONY VOLPE (see Descendants (234)) was born on June 4, 2004 to Joseph F. Volpe[2587] and Stacie Ann Maclam[2586].

3598. MS. RHEA (see Descendants (244)) was born to John Spencer Rhea[2607] and Christy ?[2608].

3599. ABELIA JANE RHEA (see Descendants (244)) was born on January 17, 2023 to John Spencer Rhea[2607] and Christy ?[2608].
 Note: *8lb 1oz 21 inches.*
  (Birth)

3600. MR. RHEA (see Descendants (244)) was born to John Spencer Rhea[2607] and Christy ?[2608].

3601. EMBERLYNN CRYSTAL CHRZASTEK-BASS (see Descendants (1)) was born on October 20, 2022 to Joseph Blaze Chrzastek Bass[2619] and Alyssa Stark[2620].
 Note: *7pounds 3 ounces, 20 and 2/4 inches.*
  (Birth)

3602. SETH WARD (see Descendants (68)) was born on August 6, 1996 to David Carter Ward[2623] and Anita ?[2625].

3603. SYDNEY TAYLOR WARD (see Descendants (68)) was born on September 8, 2000 to David Carter Ward[2623] and Anita ?[2625].

3604. LINCOLN NATHAN MOORMAN (see Descendants (68)) was born on November 23, 2012 to Nate Moorman[2629] and Bethany Ann Stuart[2628].

3605. BENNETT OWEN MOORMAN (see Descendants (68)) was born on August 13, 2014 to Nate Moorman[2629] and Bethany Ann Stuart[2628].

3606. ELIJAH COFFMAN (see Descendants (68)) was born in 2013 to Gregory Cline Coffman[2631] and Angel ?[2632].

3607. CARTUR COFFMAN (see Descendants (68)) was born in 2017 to Gregory Cline Coffman[2631] and Angel ?[2632].

3608. MORGAN E. OLDS (see Descendants (69)) was born to Robert Olds[2642] and Linda Ann Bass[2641].

3609. ERIN LENAE BASS (see Descendants (70)) was born on May 12, 1973, in Tallahassee, Leon, Florida, USA, to Richard Edward Bass[2644] and Denese McIntire[2645].

3610. MATTHEW EVAN BASS (see Descendants (70)) was born on November 29, 1979, in Tallahassee, Leon, Florida, USA, to Richard Edward Bass[2644] and Denese McIntire[2645].

3611. MONICA ? was born on October 20, 1970.
   Matthew Evan Bass[3610], aged 37, married Monica ?, aged 46, on April 8, 2017.

3612. PATRICIA ANN BASS (see Descendants (70)) was born on April 20, 1973, in tallahassee, Leon, Florida, USA, to Charles Edward Bass[2646] and Barbara Jones[2647].
   The following information is also recorded for Patricia Ann:
      Association.
   Note: *by first Marriage.*
      (Association)

3613. RACHEL SUZANNE BASS (see Descendants (70)) was born on June 13, 1984, in Tallahassee, Leon, Florida, USA, to Charles Edward Bass[2646] and Barbara Jones[2647].

3614. BROOK RENEE LEWIS (see Descendants (70)) was born on October 22, 1982, in Tallahassee, Leon, Florida, USA, to Alvin Donnald Lewis[2649] and Linda Elizabeth Bass[2648].

3615. JOSH STRICKLAND was born to Jimmy Hamilton[2664] and Cheryl Kaye Bass[2663].

3616. NATALIE WESTERLING was born to Jimmy Hamilton[2664] and Cheryl Kaye Bass[2663].

3617. MELISSA KAY JOHNSON (see Descendants (71)) was born on June 28, 1971, in Andalusia, Covington, Alabama, USA, to Raymon Johnson[2670] and Cynthia Louise Bass[2669].
3618. THOMAS W BABBINTON.
   Thomas W Babbinton married Melissa Kay Johnson[3617], aged 21, on February 3, 1993.

3619. RAYMON BRIAN JOHNSON (see Descendants (71)) was born on May 24, 1973, in Selma, Dallas, Alabama, USA, to Raymon Johnson[2670] and Cynthia Louise Bass[2669]. Raymon Brian became known as "BJ".

3620. ANDREA NICOLE POWELL was born on June 23, 1980, in Andalusia, Covington, Alabama, USA, to Reggie Lawshe Powell[2671] and Ms. ?. Andrea Nicole was adopted by Reggie Lawshe Powell[2671] and Cynthia Louise Bass[2669].

3621. HALEY ELYSE POWELL was born on July 14, 1987, in Opp, Covington, Alabama, USA, to Reggie Lawshe Powell[2671] and Ms. ?. Haley Elyse was adopted by Reggie Lawshe Powell[2671] and Cynthia Louise Bass[2669].
3622. BRIAN CAPPS.
   Brian Capps married Haley Elyse Powell[3621], aged 19, on May 26, 2007.

3623. JOSHUA ADAM MCCURLEY (see Descendants (71)) was born on January 26, 1978, in Andalusia, Covington, Alabama, USA, to Gary Allen McCurley[2674] and Susan Dianne Bass[2673].

3624. TOWANNA JOY MCCURLEY (see Descendants (71)) was born on July 9, 1979, in Andalusia, Covington, Alabama, USA, to Gary Allen McCurley[2674] and Susan Dianne Bass[2673].

3625. BROOK ADAMS (see Descendants (85)) was born to Anthony Phillip Adams[2702] and Dianne Logan[2703].

3626. ARIC ADAMS (see Descendants (85)) was born to Anthony Phillip Adams[2702] and Dianne Logan[2703].

3627. MR. JACKSON (see Descendants (85)) was born to Louis Jackson[2707] and Ms. ?[2708].

3628. DANNY JACKSON (see Descendants (85)) was born to Louis Jackson[2707] and Ms. ?[2708].
   The following information is also recorded for Danny:
      Twin.

3629. DAVID JACKSON (see Descendants (85)) was born to Louis Jackson[2707] and Ms. ?[2708].
   The following information is also recorded for David:
      Twin.

3630. CHRISTY JACKSON (see Descendants (85)) was born to Louis Jackson[2707] and Ms. ?[2708].

3631. JAMES BRETT HARRISON (see Descendants (85)) was born on March 14, 1977, in Enterprise, Coffee, Alabama, USA, to James Marvin Harrison[2718] and Cynthia Mae Thomasson[2717].

Direct Relations

3632. CHARLES BRIAN HARRISON (see Descendants (85)) was born on August 9, 1979, in Enterprise, Coffee, Alabama, USA, to James Marvin Harrison[2718] and Cynthia Mae Thomasson[2717].

3633. BRITTNEY LAUREN HARRISON (see Descendants (85)) was born on March 6, 1986, in Dothan, Dale, Alabama, USA, to James Marvin Harrison[2718] and Cynthia Mae Thomasson[2717].

3634. CHARLES MICHAEL THOMASSON (see Descendants (85)) was born on July 25, 1984 to Charles Rocky Thomasson[2719] and Kimberly Ann Walker[2720].

3635. CASSANDRA NICOLE THOMASSON (see Descendants (85)) was born on January 8, 1990 to Charles Rocky Thomasson[2719] and Kimberly Ann Walker[2720].

3636. AMBER LYNELL TATE (see Descendants (85)) was born on February 13, 1986 to Mark Nelson Tate[2722] and Celia Lynn Thomasson[2721].

3637. ADAM NELSON TATE (see Descendants (85)) was born on April 15, 1989 to Mark Nelson Tate[2722] and Celia Lynn Thomasson[2721].

3638. ARIC CHARLES TATE (see Descendants (85)) was born on March 25, 1992 to Mark Nelson Tate[2722] and Celia Lynn Thomasson[2721].
The following information is also recorded for Aric Charles:
- Twin on March 25, 1992, as an infant.

3639. ANDREW NELSON TATE (see Descendants (85)) was born on March 25, 1992 to Mark Nelson Tate[2722] and Celia Lynn Thomasson[2721].
The following information is also recorded for Andrew Nelson:
- Twin on March 25, 1992, as an infant.

3640. JERROD RANDAL HANCOCK (see Descendants (85)) was born on February 15, 1985 to James Robert Hancock[2724] and Carol Sue Thomasson[2723].

3641. JORDAN ROBERT HANCOCK (see Descendants (85)) was born on July 25, 1987 to James Robert Hancock[2724] and Carol Sue Thomasson[2723].

3642. JAMES RYNE HANCOCK (see Descendants (85)) was born on May 1, 1990 to James Robert Hancock[2724] and Carol Sue Thomasson[2723].

3643. HAILEY HANCOCK (see Descendants (85)) was born on January 12, 1993 to James Robert Hancock[2724] and Carol Sue Thomasson[2723].

3644. LORI ROGERS (see Descendants (86)) was born on August 24, 1991 to Alvin Rodgers[2732] and Jana ?[2733].

3645. KIM HALL (see Descendants (86)) was born to Jerry Hall[2739] and Joyce Rodgers[2738].

3646. GREG HALL (see Descendants (86)) was born to Jerry Hall[2739] and Joyce Rodgers[2738].

3647. JOSEPH BYRON THOMPSON JR. (see Descendants (87)) was born on March 21, 1973, in Andalusia, Covington, Alabama, USA, to Josheph Byran Thompson[2744] and Aletha Jean Blackwell[2743].
3648. BECKY JEAN SPIVEY was born on December 23, 1971.
> Joseph Byron Thompson Jr.[3647], aged 17, married Becky Jean Spivey, aged 18, in June 1990. They had one son:
>> Joseph Byron Thompson III[3994]

3649. SONYA MICHELLE THOMPSON (see Descendants (87)) was born on September 1, 1974 to Josheph Byran Thompson[2744] and Aletha Jean Blackwell[2743].
3650. DONALD KEVIN BUTLER was born on June 20, 1976.
> Donald Kevin Butler, aged 19, married Sonya Michelle Thompson[3649], aged 21, on September 9, 1995. They had one son:
>> Kyle Butler[3995] born on September 19, 1990

3651. KIMBERLY NICOLE THOMPSON (see Descendants (87)) was born on November 14, 1979 to Josheph Byran Thompson[2744] and Aletha Jean Blackwell[2743].

3652. CHARIS WEAVER.
> Charis Weaver married Kimberly Nicole Thompson[3651]. They had two children:
>> Andrew O'Neal Weaver[3997] born on December 15, 1999
>> Kayden Weaver[3998]

3653. CAPERS THOMPSON (see Descendants (87)) was born to Josheph Byran Thompson[2744] and Aletha Jean Blackwell[2743].

3654. CHRISTOPHER ALLEN LEE SR. (see Descendants (87)) was born on February 19, 1980 to Allen Jack Lee[2746] and Demisia Blackwell[2745].
> Christopher Allen had two partnerships. He was married to Tasha Nicole Piland[3656]. He was also the partner of Kalise Erwin[3655].

3655. KALISE ERWIN.
> Christopher Allen Lee Sr.[3654] and Kalise Erwin had one daughter:
>> DeAnna Michelle Lee[3999] born on April 18, 1997
>
> The following information is also recorded for this family:
> • Unknown Relationship.

3656. TASHA NICOLE PILAND.
> Christopher Allen Lee Sr.[3654] married Tasha Nicole Piland. They had six children:
>> Kaitlin Labecca Lee[4001] born on October 30, 2000
>> Christopher Allen Lee Jr.[4004] born on September 30, 2002; died on December 18, 2016
>> Corey Dewayne Lee[4005] born on July 3, 2004
>> Shaun Even Lee[4006] born on July 3, 2004; died on July 3, 2004
>> Chrislyn Skyler Shyann Lee[4007] born on July 18, 2007
>> Tony Kyler Lee[4008] born on January 15, 2009

3657. CASEY LEE (see Descendants (87)) was born on February 6, 1990 to Allen Jack Lee[2746] and Demisia Blackwell[2745].

3658. JOSHUA GARRETT.
> Joshua Garrett married Casey Lee[3657]. They had one son:
>> Allen Garrett[4009] born about October 19, 2006

3659. MICHAEL STEVEN PEACOCK (see Descendants (87)) was born on August 11, 1974 to Steve Peacock[2747] and Demisia Blackwell[2745].

3660. MS. ?.
> Michael Steven Peacock[3659] married Ms. ?. They had two sons:
>> Cody Peacock[4010] born on July 26, 1997
>> Caleb Peacock[4011] born on December 4, 1998

3661. TONY BOYETT (see Descendants (87)) was born to Al Boyett[2749] and Cornelia Ann Blackwell[2748].

3662. MS. ?.
> Tony Boyett[3661] married Ms. ?. They had three daughters:
>> Ms. Boyett[4012]
>> Ms. Boyett[4013]
>> Ms. Boyett[4014]

3663. AL BOYETT JR. (see Descendants (87)) was born to Al Boyett[2749] and Cornelia Ann Blackwell[2748].

3664. DELORES FINDLEY (see Descendants (87)) was born to Doug Findley[2751] and Deborah Lynn Blackwell[2750].

3665. JOHNNY LAMAR DOUGLAS.
> Johnny Lamar Douglas married Delores Findley[3664]. They had two daughters:
>> Courtney Douglas[4015] born on May 19, 1994
>> Caylee Douglas[4016]

3666. GEORGE WILLIAM EVANS III (see Descendants (87)) was born to George William Evans Jr.[2752] and Deborah Lynn Blackwell[2750]. George William became known as "Billy".

3667. CARMEN ? was born in Panama.

Direct Relations

> George William Evans III[3666] married Carmen ?. They had one daughter:
>> Anna Evans[4017]

3668. **CRYSTAL GAIL EVANS** (see Descendants (87)) was born to George William Evans Jr.[2752] and Deborah Lynn Blackwell[2750].

3669. **JOHN NALLEY**.
> John Nalley married Crystal Gail Evans[3668]. They had two children:
>> Mallorie Nalley[4018]
>> Tyler Nalley[4019]

3670. **REBECCA LYNN EVANS** (see Descendants (87)) was born to George William Evans Jr.[2752] and Deborah Lynn Blackwell[2750].
> Rebecca Lynn had two partnerships. She was married to Troy Stinson[3671]. She was also the partner of Steven Cender[3672].

3671. **TROY STINSON**.
> Troy Stinson married Rebecca Lynn Evans[3670].

3672. **STEVEN CENDER**.
> Steven Cender and Rebecca Lynn Evans[3670] had one son:
>> Trenton Stone Cender[4020]
> The following information is also recorded for this family:
> • Unknown Relationship.

3673. **SUSAN MICHELLE CANNON** (see Descendants (87)) was born on May 7, 1981 to James Randall Cannon[2754] and Teresa Blackwell[2753].
> Susan Michelle married three times. She was married to Derek Adams[3674], Ronald Whitehurst[3675] and Dustin Fontenot[3676].

3674. **DEREK ADAMS**.
> Derek Adams married Susan Michelle Cannon[3673]. They had one daughter:
>> Hailey Michelle Adams[4021]

3675. **RONALD WHITEHURST**.
> Ronald Whitehurst married Susan Michelle Cannon[3673]. They had one daughter:
>> Abby Suzann Whitehurst[4022]

3676. **DUSTIN FONTENOT**.
> Dustin Fontenot married Susan Michelle Cannon[3673].

3677. **JENNIFER NICOLE CANNON** (see Descendants (87)) was born on February 10, 1984 to James Randall Cannon[2754] and Teresa Blackwell[2753].

3678. **ROBERT ERIC TRAHAN**.
> Robert Eric Trahan married Jennifer Nicole Cannon[3677], and they were divorced. They had one daughter:
>> Kyra Trahan[4023] born about 2006

3679. **STEPHANIE DYAN CANNON** (see Descendants (87)) was born on January 14, 1990 to James Randall Cannon[2754] and Teresa Blackwell[2753].

3680. **MELISSA RABON** (see Descendants (87)) was born to Ferrell Rabon[2757] and Shela Dianna Blackwell[2756].

3681. **LINDSEY EKHOMM** (see Descendants (88)) was born to Ralph Donald Ekhomm[2765] and Sharon Jean Bass[2764].

3682. **MARK EKHOMM** (see Descendants (88)) was born to Ralph Donald Ekhomm[2765] and Sharon Jean Bass[2764].

3683. **ROBERT JULIUS BASS II** (see Descendants (88)) was born to Julius Randall Bass[2766] and Shirley Ann Bennett[2767].

3684. **MEGAN CHRISTINA BASS** (see Descendants (88)) was born to Julius Randall Bass[2766] and Connie Sue West[2768].

3685. **DAVID DIXON**.
> David Dixon married Megan Christina Bass[3684] on October 19, 2019.

3686. **CHRISTOPHER RANDALL DICKHUT** was born on August 11, 1982, in Rochester, Olmstead, Minnesota, USA, to Mr. Dickhut and Connie Sue West[2768]. Christopher Randall was adopted by Julius Randall Bass[2766] and Connie Sue West[2768].

3687. PHILLIP LE BRANDON BARRY (see Descendants (88)) was born to Edward Michael Bass[2769] and Donna Denise Rushing[2770].

3688. WESLEY DARYL KING II (see Descendants (88)) was born on January 30, 1987 to Wesley Darryl King[2772] and Robin Taiwan Bass[2771].

3689. JUSTIN LEE KING (see Descendants (88)) was born on January 18, 1989 to Wesley Darryl King[2772] and Robin Taiwan Bass[2771].

3690. ZACHARY RYAN KING (see Descendants (88)) was born on June 22, 1996 to Wesley Darryl King[2772] and Robin Taiwan Bass[2771].

3691. JASON CHRISTOPHER BASS (see Descendants (88)) was born on March 13, 1985, in West Palm Beach, Florida, USA, to Richard Christopher Bass[2773] and Randi Elizabeth Robertson[2774].

3692. JOSHUA RYAN BASS (see Descendants (88)) was born on November 14, 1987, in West Palm Beach, Florida, USA, to Richard Christopher Bass[2773] and Randi Elizabeth Robertson[2774].

3693. AMANDA LYNN NIENHOUSE (see Descendants (88)) was born on September 18, 1981, in West Palm Beach, Florida, USA, to George John Nienhouse Jr.[2776] and Kimberly Ruth Bass[2775].

3694. TRAVIS GEORGE NIENHOUSE (see Descendants (88)) was born on January 27, 1985, in West Palm Beach, Florida, USA, to George John Nienhouse Jr.[2776] and Kimberly Ruth Bass[2775].

3695. MCLAIN A BACHUS (see Descendants (88)) was born on June 2, 1995, in Chattanooga, Hamilton, Tennessee, USA, to James Edward Bachus[2778] and Leigh Ann Williams[2777].

3696. MARY ALEXANDRA BACHUS (see Descendants (88)) was born on May 6, 2004, in Chattanooga, Hamilton, Tennessee, USA, to James Edward Bachus[2778] and Leigh Ann Williams[2777].

3697. ASHLEY LONG (see Descendants (89)) was born to Sydney Long[2781] and Rhonda Lynn Harrelson[2780].

3698. JENNIFER LYNN LONG (see Descendants (89)) was born on September 28, 1981 to Sydney Long[2781] and Rhonda Lynn Harrelson[2780].

3699. ERICA HARRELSON (see Descendants (89)) was born on December 12, 1990 to Robert Olen Harrelson[2784] and Laurie ?[2785].

3700. LEIGH ANN HARRELSON (see Descendants (89)) was born to Robert Olen Harrelson[2784] and Laurie ?[2785].

3701. ALLISON MCLEOD (see Descendants (89)) was born on July 1, 1989 to Mochael McLeod[2787] and Cindy Rene Harrelson[2786].

3702. EMILY BROOK MCLEOD (see Descendants (89)) was born on December 14, 1994 to Mochael McLeod[2787] and Cindy Rene Harrelson[2786].

3703. PEYTON MICHELLE HARRELSON (see Descendants (89)) was born on April 16, 1994 to Russel Allen Harrelson[2789] and Laura Jeanette Haslip[2790].

3704. CAROLINA HARRELSON (see Descendants (89)) was born to Charles Rhett Harrelson[2791] and Stephanie ?[2792].

3705. CJ HARRELSON (see Descendants (89)) was born to Charles Rhett Harrelson[2791] and Stephanie ?[2792].

3706. JEFFERY ALLEN DOUGLAS HARRELSON (see Descendants (89)) was born on September 1, 1978 to Randall Keith Harrelson[2797] and Sandra Elaine Douglas[2798].

3707. JAMES TRAVIS HARRELSON (see Descendants (89)) was born on October 28, 1983 to Randall Keith Harrelson[2797] and Sandra Elaine Douglas[2798].

3708. RANDI NICOLE HARRELSON (see Descendants (89)) was born on March 27, 1990 to Randall Keith Harrelson[2797] and Sandra Elaine Douglas[2798].

3709. HANNAH ELIZABETH HARRELSON (see Descendants (89)) was born on October 3, 1989 to James Ricky Harrelson[2801] and Mary Beth Walker[2802].

3710. JESSICA SUEANN HARRELSON (see Descendants (89)) was born on December 11, 1983, in Andalusia, Covington, Alabama, USA, to Renda Sue Harrelson[2804].

3711. STEWART BRANDON CARR. Stewart Brandon became known as "Brandon".
Stewart Brandon Carr married Jessica Sueann Harrelson[3710], aged 22, on April 8, 2006. They had two children:
Jackson Alexander Carr[4024] born on February 23, 2009 in Andalusia, Covington, Alabama, USA
Renleigh Elizabeth Carr[4025] born on July 11, 2018 in Dothan, Alabama, USA

3712. DOUGLAS MATHEW SMITH (see Descendants (90)) was born on December 6, 1995, in Andalusia, Covington, Alabama, USA, to Lloyde Mathew Smith Jr.[2808] and Stephanie Sue Powell[2809].

3713. KATELYN SUE SMITH (see Descendants (90)) was born on April 8, 1997, in Andalusia, Covington, Alabama, USA, to Lloyde Mathew Smith Jr.[2808] and Stephanie Sue Powell[2809].

3714. JONATHAN KEITH SMITH (see Descendants (90)) was born on November 16, 1993, in Dothan, Houston, Alabama, USA, to Gregory Keith Smith[2810] and Cynthia Denise Tisdale[2811].

3715. ZACHARY PAUL SMITH (see Descendants (90)) was born on November 21, 1997, in Dothan, Houston, Alabama, USA, to Gregory Keith Smith[2810] and Cynthia Denise Tisdale[2811].

3716. MEGAN REBECCA SMITH (see Descendants (90)) was born on October 5, 1999, in Dothan, Houston, Alabama, USA, to Gregory Keith Smith[2810] and Cynthia Denise Tisdale[2811].

3717. SARA GRACE SMITH (see Descendants (90)) was born on March 21, 2001, in Dothan, Houston, Alabama, USA, to Gregory Keith Smith[2810] and Cynthia Denise Tisdale[2811].

3718. TREVER KYLE WILLIAMS (see Descendants (90)) was born on December 6, 1997, in Green County, Mississippi, USA, to Jason Darren Smith[2812] and Natasha Lynn[2813].

3719. SHELBY BREANNA SMITH (see Descendants (90)) was born on April 13, 2004, in Andalusia, Covington, Alabama, USA, to Jason Darren Smith[2812] and Natasha Lynn[2813].

3720. JESSICA DAILY SMITH (see Descendants (90)) was born on May 22, 2008 to Jason Darren Smith[2812] and Natasha Lynn[2813].

3721. GARRETT LAMAR BURTON (see Descendants (90)) was born on September 21, 1998, in Montgomery, Montgomery, Alabama, USA, to Robert Lamar Burton[2817] and Melinda Gayle Barrow[2816].

3722. JOHN GRANT BURTON (see Descendants (90)) was born on October 30, 2001, in Montgomery, Montgomery, Alabama, USA, to Robert Lamar Burton[2817] and Melinda Gayle Barrow[2816].

3723. EMILY KAY WISMER (see Descendants (90)) was born on August 20, 1999, in Montgomery, Montgomery, Alabama, USA, to James William Wismer[2819] and Angela Lynn Barrow[2818].
The following information is also recorded for Emily Kay:
Twin.

3724. HANNAH ELIZABETH WISMER (see Descendants (90)) was born on August 20, 1999, in Montgomery, Montgomery, Alabama, USA, to James William Wismer[2819] and Angela Lynn Barrow[2818].
The following information is also recorded for Hannah Elizabeth:
Twin.

3725. MADALYN JEAN WISMER (see Descendants (90)) was born on May 29, 2001, in Montgomery, Montgomery, Alabama, USA, to James William Wismer[2819] and Angela Lynn Barrow[2818].

3726. AMBER NALL (see Descendants (93)) was born on November 8, 1977 to Denny Nall[2827] and Connie Wiggins[2826].
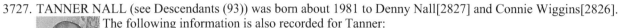
The following information is also recorded for Amber:
• Military Service.

3727. TANNER NALL (see Descendants (93)) was born about 1981 to Denny Nall[2827] and Connie Wiggins[2826].

The following information is also recorded for Tanner:
• Military Service.

3728. TANNA ?.

Tanner Nall[3727] married Tanna ?. They had two sons:
   Mr. Nall[4026]
   Mr. Nall[4027]

3729. ROBIN RENEE STACEY (see Descendants (93)) was born on August 15, 1987, in Warner Robins, Houston, Alabama, USA, to Martin Eugene Stacey[2829] and Robin Denise Henderson[2828].

3730. SETH EUGENE STACEY (see Descendants (93)) was born on May 9, 1989, in Warner Robins, Houston, Alabama, USA, to Martin Eugene Stacey[2829] and Robin Denise Henderson[2828].

3731. KATHERINE MARIE MURPHY (see Descendants (93)) was born on April 7, 1991, in Brunswick, Glenn, Georgia, USA, to Kenneth Charles Murphy[2831] and Donna Katrise Henderson[2830].

3732. AUSTIN THOMAS OTT (see Descendants (94)) was born on September 16, 1995, in Christianna, Delaware, USA, to Todd Allison Ott[2835] and Stacey Jean Blair[2836].

3733. CARLIE CIERRA OTT (see Descendants (94)) was born on February 12, 1998, in The woods, Montgomery, Texas, USA, to Todd Allison Ott[2835] and Stacey Jean Blair[2836].

3734. JUSTIN TODD SMITH (see Descendants (94)) was born on December 9, 1992, in Conroe, Montgomery, Texas, USA, to John Franklin Smith Jr.[2838] and Kam Renae Ott[2837].

3735. AARON HOPE INEZ SMITH (see Descendants (94)) was born on November 9, 1996, in Conroe, Montgomery, Texas, USA, to John Franklin Smith Jr.[2838] and Kam Renae Ott[2837].

3736. DYLAN MCKAY SMITH (see Descendants (94)) was born on March 10, 1998, in Woodlands, Montgomery, Texas, USA, to John Franklin Smith Jr.[2838] and Kam Renae Ott[2837].

3737. MADISON TAYLOR SMITH (see Descendants (94)) was born on November 6, 1999, in Conroe, Montgomery, Texas, USA, to John Franklin Smith Jr.[2838] and Kam Renae Ott[2837].

3738. HEATHER OTT (see Descendants (94)) was born to James Allen Ott Jr.[2840] and Vicky Renee Matheny[2841].

3739. MICHAEL BENNETT CREWS (see Descendants (95)) was born to Michael Allen Crews[2844] and Dana Butler[2845]. Michael Bennett became known as "Mikey".

Direct Relations

3740. MS. ?.
: Michael Bennett Crews[3739] married Ms. ?. They had one son:
  : Brayden Michael Crews[4028]

3741. SUMMER CREWS (see Descendants (95)) was born to Michael Allen Crews[2844] and Dana Butler[2845].

3742. MR./MS. BARKER (see Descendants (95)) was born to Mr. Barker[2847] and Angie Crews[2846].

3743. MR./MS. BARKER (see Descendants (95)) was born to Mr. Barker[2847] and Angie Crews[2846].

3744. MR./MS. BARKER (see Descendants (95)) was born to Mr. Barker[2847] and Angie Crews[2846].

3745. AUSTIN BASS (see Descendants (95)) was born to Shawn Bass[2848] and Ms. ?[2849].
The following information is also recorded for Austin:
- Military Service.

3746. SHELBY ?.
: Austin Bass[3745] married Shelby ?.

3747. MATHEW MANGHAM (see Descendants (96)) was born to Matthew Mangham[2851] and Marla Kim Bass[2850].

3748. MICHELLE MANGHAM (see Descendants (96)) was born to Matthew Mangham[2851] and Marla Kim Bass[2850].

3749. JESSICA ANN TYLER (see Descendants (96)) was born on March 10, 1985, in Dothan, Dale, Alabama, USA, to Michael Wayne Tyler[2853] and Barbara Ann Fairman[2854].

3750. CATHLEEN DOREN TYLER (see Descendants (96)) was born on March 5, 1987, in Dothan, Dale, Alabama, USA, to Michael Wayne Tyler[2853] and Barbara Ann Fairman[2854].

3751. RODGER CAFFEY was born on November 18, 1988, in Brewton, Escambia, Alabama, USA.
: Rodger Caffey, aged 27, married Cathleen Doren Tyler[3750], aged 29, on October 17, 2016.

3752. JUSTIN FAIRMAN TYLER (see Descendants (96)) was born on November 12, 1989 to Michael Wayne Tyler[2853] and Barbara Ann Fairman[2854]. He died on November 12, 1989, as an infant.

3753. MICHAEL FAIRMAN TYLER (see Descendants (96)) was born on May 8, 1991, in Andalusia, Covington, Alabama, USA, to Michael Wayne Tyler[2853] and Barbara Ann Fairman[2854].

3754. HANNA ELIZABETH VEASEY (see Descendants (96)) was born on October 19, 1987 to Bruce Kelley Veasey[2857] and Melissa Bates[2858].

3755. WILLIAM ALLEN BUMPERS III was born on October 10, 1985.
: Note: *Will and I both started working for the same company within six months or so of each other. So, I've gotten to know him a little and have one story that almost seems to be impossible not to include. A while after Will joined the company some of the guys here got him interested in diving. The group would go spear fishing in rivers and bays pretty regular, probably out in the gulf too. Will joined them a few times, but the last time was on a river. While he was down exploring or fishing on his turn in the rotation, some of the other guys were waiting and keeping an eye on him a little. At some point he surfaced for just a second and went right back down. Quickly the watcher decided that something was wrong and jumped into action. A few of them went down to check on him, or as it turns out retrieve him. Something had gone wrong and he'd lost air and passed out. For whatever period of time he was under water with no air. When they got him out of the water, they quickly realized he was not breathing and seemed to agree that he also had no pulse. Somehow, they were able to resuscitate him and he pretty quickly recovered. So Will is not a diver, since it killed him once.* -Nicholas Bass.

William Allen Bumpers III, aged 24, married Hanna Elizabeth Veasey[3754], aged 22, on August 28, 2010.
They had two daughters:
: Caroline Elizabeth Bumpers[4029] born on April 15, 2013
: Charlotte Clair Bumpers[4030] born on December 17, 2015

3756. ANDREW BRUCE VEASEY (see Descendants (96)) was born on November 2, 1990 to Bruce Kelley Veasey[2857] and Melissa Bates[2858].

3757. TAYLOR LYNN DONALDSON was born on February 16, 1993.
> Andrew Bruce Veasey[3756], aged 30, married Taylor Lynn Donaldson, aged 28, on April 10, 2021. They had one daughter:
>> Katherine Elizabeth Veasey[4031] born on May 2, 2022

3758. LAURA AMANDA PARRISH (see Descendants (98)) was born on April 17, 1981 to Anthony Lee Parrish[2862] and Belinda Crawford[2864].
3759. JEREMY MCDADE was born on November 25, 1974.
> Jeremy McDade married Laura Amanda Parrish[3758].

3760. CELESTE PARRISH (see Descendants (98)) was born on December 19, 1981 to Anthony Lee Parrish[2862] and Belinda Crawford[2864].
3761. ZACHARY MORANT was born on January 11, 1979.
> Zachary Morant married Celeste Parrish[3760]. They had one son:
>> Kaden Morant[4032]

3762. SHELBY ANNE PARRISH (see Descendants (98)) was born on March 29, 1999 to Anthony Lee Parrish[2862] and Belinda Crawford[2864].

3763. HOPE DANIELLE HOLLAND (see Descendants (98)) was born on March 14, 1981 to Danny Ward Holland[2866] and Rebecca Lynn Parrish[2865].

3764. HANNAH ELIZABETH HOLLAND (see Descendants (98)) was born on September 10, 1985 to Danny Ward Holland[2866] and Rebecca Lynn Parrish[2865].

3765. HEATHER LEE HOLLAND (see Descendants (98)) was born on September 10, 1985 to Danny Ward Holland[2866] and Rebecca Lynn Parrish[2865].
3766. MR. ?.
> Mr. ? married Heather Lee Holland[3765]. They had one daughter:
>> Haylee Elizabeth ?[4033] born on January 22, 2007

3767. BRETT ANDREW BASS (see Descendants (265)) was born in 1987 to Brett Zan Bass[2880] and Amy Hawks[2881].
3768. FRANCIS ?.
> Brett Andrew Bass[3767] married Francis ?. They had one son:
>> Zane Andrew Bass[4034] born in 2012

3769. CAMRIN ZAN BASS (see Descendants (265)) was born in 1993 to Brett Zan Bass[2880] and Becky Parker[2882].

3770. DYLAN WAYNE SCOTT (see Descendants (266)) was born on May 26, 1993, in Milton, Santa Rosa, Florida, USA, to Stephen Michael Scott[2884] and Brandy Lane Bass[2883].

3771. DIESEL WAYNE BASS (see Descendants (267)) was born on March 15, 2011 to Devin Lee Bass[2887] and Ms. Watson[2888].

3772. CONSTANTINOS ARGERIS (see Descendants (267)) was born on June 1, 2017 to Constantinos Argeris[2890] and Sheleiah Lynn Bass[2889].

3773. HRISTOS ARGERIS (see Descendants (267)) was born on November 12, 2019 to Constantinos Argeris[2890] and Sheleiah Lynn Bass[2889].

3774. JAMESON ? (see Descendants (268)) was born in 2010 to Mr. ?[2892] and Miranda Bass[2891].

3775. JACKSON TUTTEROW (see Descendants (272)) was born to Jeffery Scott Tutterow[2896] and Hannah LeNelle Bass[2895].

3776. CAMERON HIMES (see Descendants (272)) was born to Kevin Vance Himes[2899] and Tina Darlene Bass[2898].

3777. KENDRICK HIMES (see Descendants (272)) was born to Kevin Vance Himes[2899] and Tina Darlene Bass[2898].

3778. PATRICK O'CONNOR (see Descendants (272)) was born to Shawn Patrick O'Connor[2900] and Tina Darlene Bass[2898].

3779. LORETTA VONCILE MCVAY (see Descendants (274)) was born to William McVay[2902] and Lori Nicole Lee[2901].

3780. MS. MCVAY (see Descendants (274)) was born to William McVay[2902] and Lori Nicole Lee[2901].

3781. COURTNEY INGRAM (see Descendants (275)) was born to Tony Ingram[2906] and LaDonice Darnell Barnett[2905].

3782. JOSHUA TYLER INGRAM (see Descendants (275)) was born to Tony Ingram[2906] and LaDonice Darnell Barnett[2905].

3783. MS. ?.
> Joshua Tyler Ingram[3782] married Ms. ?. They had one son:
> Joshua Brody Ingram[4035]

3784. JOHNNY ROBERT BOLES JR. (see Descendants (276)) was born on January 6, 2005 to Johnny Robert Boles Sr.[2914] and Brandi Lee Presley[2913]. Johnny Robert became known as "JJ".

3785. BROOKLYNN LEE BOLES (see Descendants (276)) was born on November 1, 2012 to Johnny Robert Boles Sr.[2914] and Brandi Lee Presley[2913].

3786. CIERA ELIZABETH PRESLEY (see Descendants (276)) was born on April 12, 1999 to Christopher Edwin Presley[2915] and Donna Wise[2916].

3787. CHEYENNE ERIN PRESLEY (see Descendants (276)) was born on February 12, 2001 to Christopher Edwin Presley[2915] and Donna Wise[2916].

3788. BRIANNA TEGAN PRESLEY (see Descendants (276)) was born on September 4, 2008 to Christopher Edwin Presley[2915] and Dorenda Richards[2917].

3789. SYDNEY NICOLE CRAWFORD MORRIS (see Descendants (276)) was born on March 2, 2011 to Mr. Crawford[2920] and Lindsey Presley[2918].

3790. EMMALEIGH MADDISON RAY (see Descendants (277)) was born to Casey Levon Ray[2922] and Starlette Dawn Russell[2921].

3791. KIP RILEY RUSSELL (see Descendants (277)) was born to Raymond Randall Russell Jr.[2923] and Mary Ann Chance[2924].

3792. AMBER NICOLE RUSSELL (see Descendants (277)) was born to Raymond Randall Russell Jr.[2923] and Mary Ann Chance[2924].

3793. PAYTON BREANNA RUSSELL (see Descendants (277)) was born to Raymond Randall Russell Jr.[2923] and Mary Ann Chance[2924].

3794. KAYLA BROOK RUSSELL (see Descendants (277)) was born to Raymond Randall Russell Jr.[2923] and Mary Ann Chance[2924].

3795. MICHAEL TYLER GOODSON (see Descendants (277)) was born to Michael Dewayne Goodson[2926] and Sonya Leann Russell[2925].

3796. CORY RYAN GOODSON (see Descendants (277)) was born to Michael Dewayne Goodson[2926] and Sonya Leann Russell[2925].

3797. JAYDEN GLIDEWELL (see Descendants (195)) was born to David Brent Glidewell[2927] and Lori Lucas[3446].

3798. DAUGHTON GLIDEWELL (see Descendants (195)) was born to David Brent Glidewell[2927] and Lori Lucas[3446].

3799. CADEN KILPATRICK (see Descendants (278)) was born to Jerry Kilpatrick[2929] and Christy Lee Glidewell[2928].

3800. MASON ALLEN GINDLESPERGER (see Descendants (279)) was born on February 23, 2004, in Snellville, Georgia, USA, to Mitchell Allen Gindlesperger[2930] and Melissa Ann Boles[2931].

3801. MILES AVERY GINDLESPERGER (see Descendants (279)) was born on May 19, 2006, in Snellville, Georgia, USA, to Mitchell Allen Gindlesperger[2930] and Melissa Ann Boles[2931].

3802. MERRITT ANDERSON GINDLESPERGER (see Descendants (279)) was born on August 24, 2008, in Snellville, Georgia, USA, to Mitchell Allen Gindlesperger[2930] and Melissa Ann Boles[2931].

3803. DALTO MICHAEL MADDOX (see Descendants (280)) was born on October 2, 2000, in Montgomery, Montgomery, Alabama, USA, to Michael Maddox[2937] and April Ann King[2936].

3804. BRODIE JAMES MADDOX (see Descendants (280)) was born on April 24, 2004, in Montgomery, Montgomery, Alabama, USA, to Michael Maddox[2937] and April Ann King[2936].

3805. LANDON PREVITO (see Descendants (100)) was born to Trey Previto[2951] and Ms. ?[2952].

3806. JOEY PREVITO (see Descendants (100)) was born to Trey Previto[2951] and Ms. ?[2952].

3807. JULIA MELVIN (see Descendants (103)) was born to Merwyn T. Melvin I[2960] and Louise Adams[2961].
3808. TIMOTHY PELTIER.
   Timothy Peltier married Julia Melvin[3807].

3809. MERWYN T. MELVIN II (see Descendants (103)) was born to Merwyn T. Melvin I[2960] and Louise Adams[2961]. Merwyn T. became known as "Mel".
3810. MARCIE DUPUY.
   Merwyn T. Melvin II[3809] married Marcie Dupuy.

3811. VINCENT J. MELVIN (see Descendants (103)) was born to Merwyn T. Melvin I[2960] and Louise Adams[2961].
3812. DAPHNE THERIOT.
   Vincent J. Melvin[3811] married Daphne Theriot.

3813. AARON MELVIN (see Descendants (103)) was born to Merwyn T. Melvin I[2960] and Louise Adams[2961]. Aaron became known as "Bogie".

Direct Relations

3814. CHARLENE CHIASSON.
>Aaron Melvin[3813] married Charlene Chiasson.

3815. TREG SIMMONS (see Descendants (104)) was born to Roy Simmons[2963] and Ellen Francis Shaw[2962].

3816. KEVIN CORRIGAN.
>Kevin Corrigan married Treg Simmons[3815].

3817. MAJ. MR. SADLIER (see Descendants (105)) was born to Richard Sadlier[2965] and Artemis Diane Vagias[2964]. The following information is also recorded for Mr. Sadlier:
- Military Service.

Note: *U.S. Marine.*
>*(Military Service)*

3818. MR./MS. SADLIER (see Descendants (105)) was born to Richard Sadlier[2965] and Artemis Diane Vagias[2964].

3819. MR./MS. SADLIER (see Descendants (105)) was born to Richard Sadlier[2965] and Artemis Diane Vagias[2964].

3820. MR./MS. SADLIER (see Descendants (105)) was born to Richard Sadlier[2965] and Artemis Diane Vagias[2964].

3821. CAROLYN WAYMAN (see Descendants (105)) was born to Mr. Wayman[2966] and Artemis Diane Vagias[2964].

3822. ERIC BLAYLOCK.
>Eric Blaylock married Carolyn Wayman[3821]. They had two sons:
>>Mr. Blaylock[4036]
>>Mr. Blaylock[4037]

3823. KATHERINE WAYMAN (see Descendants (105)) was born to Mr. Wayman[2966] and Artemis Diane Vagias[2964].

3824. RANDY MAIN.
>Randy Main married Katherine Wayman[3823]. They had three children:
>>Mr. Main[4038]
>>Mr. Main[4039]
>>Ms. Main[4040]

3825. LOUIS VAGIAS III (see Descendants (105)) was born to Louis Vagias Jr.[2967] and Janet Casselberry[2968]. Louis became known as "Zach".

3826. MARY VALDES (see Descendants (106)) was born to Arthur Valdes[2971] and Joan Quinn[2970].

3827. MR. ?.
>Mr. ? married Mary Valdes[3826]. They had one child:
>>Mr./Ms. ?[4041]

3828. ARTHUR VALDES (see Descendants (106)) was born to Arthur Valdes[2971] and Joan Quinn[2970].

3829. ELIZABETH ?.
>Arthur Valdes[3828] married Elizabeth ?. They had three children:
>>Ms. Valdes[4042]
>>Ms. Valdes[4043]
>>Mr. Valdes[4044]

3830. JONATHAN ERIC MCLEOD (see Descendants (124)) was born to Jerry McLeod[2988] and Karen Cook[2986].

3831. BRANDON DEWAYNE ADAMS (see Descendants (124)) was born to Donald Wayne Adams[2989] and Karen Cook[2986].

3832. KENYON KOLE COOK (see Descendants (124)) was born to Keith Cook[2991] and Kathy Douglas[2992].

3833. KAYLA MICHELLE COOK (see Descendants (124)) was born to Keith Cook[2991] and Kathy Douglas[2992].

3834. KRISTOPHER LYNN COOK (see Descendants (124)) was born to Keith Cook[2991] and Kathy Douglas[2992].

3835. MELINDA RODERUS (see Descendants (124)) was born to Ernest Leroy Newton[2995] and Christine Roderus[2996].

3836. CHRISTY LYNN NEWTON (see Descendants (124)) was born to Ernest Leroy Newton[2995] and Christine Roderus[2996].

3837. JOSEPH MCCOMBS (see Descendants (290)) was born on January 31, 1977 to Lionel McCombs[2998] and Bridget Belinda Newton[2997].

3838. JESSICA MCCOMBS (see Descendants (290)) was born on June 3, 1981 to Lionel McCombs[2998] and Bridget Belinda Newton[2997].

3839. HEATHER ? (see Descendants (291)) was born to Mr. ?[3000] and Missouri Mae Newton[2999].

3840. JAY FLETCHER SPICER (see Descendants (292)) was born on November 8, 1976 to Jay Oliver Spicer[3002] and Sherry Denise Newton[3001].

3841. PHILLIP CLAYTON (see Descendants (292)) was born on February 10, 1993 to Jay Oliver Spicer[3002] and Sherry Denise Newton[3001].

3842. WAYLON GAINEY (see Descendants (293)) was born to Darrell Gainey[3006] and Barabara Sue Beck[3005].

3843. NICOLE GAINEY (see Descendants (293)) was born to Darrell Gainey[3006] and Barabara Sue Beck[3005].

3844. BRITTANY LANDINGHAM (see Descendants (294)) was born to Alan Landingham[3008] and Tamara Michelle Beck[3007].

3845. NATASHA CHESSHER (see Descendants (295)) was born to Terry Lee Chessher[3013] and Sandra Hudson[3014].

3846. CHRISTINA CHESSHER (see Descendants (295)) was born to Terry Lee Chessher[3013] and Sandra Hudson[3014].

3847. CHELSEY LEANNE CHESSHER (see Descendants (295)) was born on September 16, 1994 to Terry Lee Chessher[3013] and Ann Edge[3015].

3848. AARON JOHNSON (see Descendants (127)) was born to Dallas Johnson[3041] and Deborah Cahill[3042].

3849. HILLARY PAGE THAMES (see Descendants (128)) was born on November 26, 1992 to Christopher Thames[3047] and Karen Schofield[3048].

3850. CLAY DANIEL THAMES (see Descendants (128)) was born on September 20, 1993 to Christopher Thames[3047] and Karen Schofield[3048].

3851. DUSTIN MICHEAL THAMES (see Descendants (128)) was born on November 29, 1995 to Christopher Thames[3047] and Karen Schofield[3048].

3852. TABITHA DAWN CARNLEY (see Descendants (129)) was born on September 16, 1985 to James Micheal Carnley[3053] and Lynda Jeanne Turner[3051].

3853. JOHN RAYMOND WIGGINS.
    John Raymond Wiggins married Tabitha Dawn Carnley[3852]. They had six children:
        Kenly Madison Wiggins[4045]
        Michael Layne Grantham[4046]
        Kaden Andrew Wiggins[4047]
        Emma-Leigh Katherine Grantham[4048]
        Heidi Rae Wiggins[4049]
        Saydee Mae Wiggins[4050]

3854. TRENTON MICHAEL CARNLEY (see Descendants (129)) was born on October 2, 1989, in Enterprise, Coffee, Alabama, USA, to James Micheal Carnley[3053] and Lynda Jeanne Turner[3051].

3855. SERA PELHAM.
    Trenton Michael Carnley[3854] married Sera Pelham.

3856. MADISON JADE TURNER (see Descendants (129)) was born to Amos Dalton Turner Jr.[3054] and Brenda Gail Booker[3055].

Direct Relations

3857. STERLING JO HUGGINS.
Sterling Jo Huggins married Madison Jade Turner[3856].

3858. TAYLOR GRACE TURNER (see Descendants (129)) was born on January 19, 2000 to Amos Dalton Turner Jr.[3054] and Brenda Gail Booker[3055].

3859. TYLER JAYNES (see Descendants (129)) was born on May 15, 2000 to Mr. Jaynes[3057] and Beverly Shea Turner[3056].

3860. JOSHUA ALLEN MILLS (see Descendants (130)) was born on August 17, 1988, in Winter Haven, Polk, Florida, USA, to James Allen Mills[3058] and Jacqueline Kay Mullinnex[3060].

3861. MICHAEL ADAMS MILLS (see Descendants (130)) was born on September 7, 1991, in Canton, Stark, Ohio, USA, to James Allen Mills[3058] and Jacqueline Kay Mullinnex[3060].

3862. JOHNATHAN DAVID MILLS (see Descendants (130)) was born on January 1, 1992 to Joseph Donald Mills[3062] and Angela Rene Elliot[3063].

3863. JORDAN NONOVON MILLS (see Descendants (130)) was born on January 31, 1994 to Joseph Donald Mills[3062] and Angela Rene Elliot[3063].

3864. DEWEY WENDELL HOLMES III (see Descendants (130)) was born on December 21, 1991, in Lakeland, Polk, Florida, USA, to Dewey Wendell Holmes Jr.[3064] and Corrie L. Campbell[3065].

3865. DILLON GENE HUNT (see Descendants (130)) was born on January 10, 1990 to Wendell Gene Hunt[3067] and Melinda Dianna Holmes[3066].

3866. TRENTON WAYNE HUNT (see Descendants (130)) was born on July 20, 1991 to Wendell Gene Hunt[3067] and Melinda Dianna Holmes[3066].

3867. JENNIFER NICHOLE BLOOMFIELD (see Descendants (130)) was born on August 31, 1982, in Winter Haven, Polk, Florida, USA, to Kevin Shawn Bloomfield Sr.[3069] and Patricia Gail Holmes[3068].

3868. KEVIN SHAWN BLOOMFIELD JR. (see Descendants (130)) was born on September 2, 1983, in Lakeland, Polk, Florida, USA, to Kevin Shawn Bloomfield Sr.[3069] and Patricia Gail Holmes[3068].

3869. CRAIG ALLEN BLOOMFIELD (see Descendants (130)) was born on October 8, 1984, in Winter Haven, Polk, Florida, USA, to Kevin Shawn Bloomfield Sr.[3069] and Patricia Gail Holmes[3068].

3870. TERA LYNN WALKER (see Descendants (130)) was born on August 26, 1988, in Las Vegas, Clark, Nevada, USA, to Garry Thomas Walker[3071] and Lena Dianne Mills[3070]. She died on August 26, 1988, aged 0, in Las Vegas, Clark, Nevada, USA.

3871. BRANNON CHASE WALKER (see Descendants (130)) was born on October 25, 1990, in Las Vegas, Clark, Nevada, USA, to Garry Thomas Walker[3071] and Lena Dianne Mills[3070].

3872. TRISTA SHEALYNN WALKER (see Descendants (130)) was born on July 31, 1992, in Las Vegas, Clark, Nevada, USA, to Garry Thomas Walker[3071] and Lena Dianne Mills[3070].

3873. BROC JORDAN RATHBURN (see Descendants (130)) was born on April 10, 1991, in Denver, Colorado, USA, to Robert Kenner Rathburn[3074] and Shawnee Lynn Mills[3073].

3874. JOSHUA ALAN SILVA PATTERSON (see Descendants (296)) was born on September 27, 1984, in Boca Raton, Palm Beach, Florida, USA, to Thomas Patterson[3079] and Donna Kay Mills[3078].

3875. AMBER BROOK PATTERSON (see Descendants (296)) was born on April 20, 1986, in Boca Raton, Palm Beach, Florida, USA, to Thomas Patterson[3079] and Donna Kay Mills[3078].

3876. THOMAS CHESTER PATTERSON (see Descendants (296)) was born on April 23, 1987, in Jacksonville, Duval, Florida, USA, to Thomas Patterson[3079] and Donna Kay Mills[3078].

Wilson Bass

3877. SHANE DONOVAN PATTERSON (see Descendants (296)) was born on May 2, 1988, in Boca Raton, Palm Beach, Florida, USA, to Thomas Patterson[3079] and Donna Kay Mills[3078].

3878. TRACIE RENAE MILLS (see Descendants (130)) was born on January 11, 1994 to Donell Joseph Mills[3080] and Stephanie ?[3081].

3879. EDWARD CLIFTON JENSEN (see Descendants (297)) was born on August 2, 1986, in Sarasota, Florida, USA, to Eric Jensen[3083] and Darla Lynn Mills[3082].

3880. MATTHEW ALAN JENSEN (see Descendants (297)) was born on November 24, 1989, in Orange Park, Clay, Florida, USA, to Eric Jensen[3083] and Darla Lynn Mills[3082].

3881. PAULA MARIAN LYNN JENSEN (see Descendants (297)) was born on October 6, 1991, in Orange Park, Clay, Florida, USA, to Eric Jensen[3083] and Darla Lynn Mills[3082].

3882. KYLE KENNETH PHILLIPS (see Descendants (131)) was born on March 27, 1996 to Kenneth Paul Phillips[3085] and Sonia Darlene Homan[3086].

3883. AARON FLORENCE COBB (see Descendants (131)) was born on September 25, 1990 to James Bartlett Cobb Jr.[3087] and Jacky Mondora[3088].

3884. ANTHONY JOSEPH COBB (see Descendants (131)) was born on June 3, 1993 to James Bartlett Cobb Jr.[3087] and Jacky Mondora[3088].

3885. ZACKERY TYLER HUNT (see Descendants (131)) was born on August 18, 1993 to Gary Hunt[3090] and Martine Michelle Cobb[3089].

3886. LOGAN SWANEY EDMONDSON (see Descendants (132)) was born on May 21, 1999 to Michael Jerome Edmondson[3092] and Stephanie Lynn Swaney[3093].

3887. ZACKARY MICHAEL EDMONDSON (see Descendants (132)) was born on October 12, 2001 to Michael Jerome Edmondson[3092] and Stephanie Lynn Swaney[3093].

3888. ETHAN JACK EDMONDSON (see Descendants (132)) was born on January 4, 2004 to Michael Jerome Edmondson[3092] and Stephanie Lynn Swaney[3093].

3889. BROCK MARTIN EDMONDSON (see Descendants (132)) was born on June 10, 2005 to Michael Jerome Edmondson[3092] and Stephanie Lynn Swaney[3093].

3890. JASON WYATT EDMONDSON (see Descendants (132)) was born on February 15, 2008 to Jason Lee Edmondson[3094] and Misty Sue Abrams[3095].

3891. LAKEN GRACE EDMONDSON (see Descendants (132)) was born on November 11, 2015 to Jason Lee Edmondson[3094] and Misty Sue Abrams[3095].

3892. JOSHUA DWAYNE COLLIER (see Descendants (133)) was born on May 11, 1983 to Robert Dwayne Collier[3102] and Joanna Lee Scoffield[3103].

3893. JESSIE LEE COLLIER (see Descendants (133)) was born on October 22, 1987 to Robert Dwayne Collier[3102] and Joanna Lee Scoffield[3103].

3894. ANGELICA LYNN COLLIER (see Descendants (133)) was born on August 26, 1990 to Robert Dwayne Collier[3102] and Joanna Lee Scoffield[3103].

3895. CHRISTY ALAYNE COLLIER (see Descendants (133)) was born on February 2, 1993 to Robert Dwayne Collier[3102] and Joanna Lee Scoffield[3103].

3896. TIMOTHY IAN PORTER (see Descendants (133)) was born on March 4, 1981 to Joesph Porter[3105] and Rhonda Delaine Collier[3104].

3897. JOESPH CAMERON PORTER (see Descendants (133)) was born on September 7, 1989 to Joesph Porter[3105] and Rhonda Delaine Collier[3104].

Direct Relations

3898. SHANNON NICOLE PRATT (see Descendants (133)) was born on June 23, 1984 to Jeffery Pratt[3108] and Angie Powell[3107].

3899. JEFFERY WADE TURNER II (see Descendants (136)) was born on June 10, 1982, in Opp, Covington, Alabama, USA, to Jeffery Wade Turner[3151] and Janet Sexton[3152].

3900. LILLI ROSEANN TURNER (see Descendants (136)) was born on July 26, 1984, in Opp, Covington, Alabama, USA, to Jeffery Wade Turner[3151] and Janet Sexton[3152].

3901. JOSHUA B. HARPER (see Descendants (136)) was born on May 23, 1984, in Dothan, Houston, Alabama, USA, to Hershel E. Harper[3156] and Janet Sylvia Turner[3155].

3902. JEREMY W. HARPER (see Descendants (136)) was born on April 23, 1986, in Dothan, Houston, Alabama, USA, to Hershel E. Harper[3156] and Janet Sylvia Turner[3155].

3903. F. NICOLE HARPER (see Descendants (136)) was born on August 6, 1990, in Dothan, Houston, Alabama, USA, to Hershel E. Harper[3156] and Janet Sylvia Turner[3155].

3904. JAMES MURRAY EDWARDS (see Descendants (138)) was born to James Murriell Edwards[3172] and Phyllis Jane Parks[3173].

3905. STEVEN MURRIELL EDWARDS (see Descendants (138)) was born to Donald Eugene Edwards[3174] and Sarah Aldie Qualls[3175].

3906. MARY KATHERINE BARNES (see Descendants (298)) was born on June 17, 2003, in Homewood, Alabama, USA, to Phillip Michael Barnes[3192] and Cheryl Anne Kemp[3193].

3907. HANNAH MARIE BARNES (see Descendants (298)) was born on December 15, 2008, in Homewood, Alabama, USA, to Phillip Michael Barnes[3192] and Cheryl Anne Kemp[3193].

3908. BENSON GRAY BARNES (see Descendants (299)) was born in 2016 to Samuel Brad Barnes[3194] and Bethany Hope Bochette[3195].

3909. TROY BARNES (see Descendants (299)) was born to Samuel Brad Barnes[3194] and Bethany Hope Bochette[3195].

3910. JOEL RYAN BASS was born on December 25, 1998, in Andalusia, Covington, Alabama, USA, to Elizabeth Corinne Barringer[3197].
    • Joel Ryan was adopted by Nicholas Bruce Bass[3196] and Elizabeth Corinne Barringer[3197].

3911. WILLSON BRUCE BASS (see Descendants (300)) was born on June 8, 2006, in Opp, Alabama, USA, to Nicholas Bruce Bass[3196] and Elizabeth Corinne Barringer[3197].

3912. AUBREE CLAIRE POWELL (see Descendants (301)) was born on August 3, 2007, in Crestview, Okaloosa, Florida, USA, to Paul Edwin Powell Jr.[3199] and Ashly Rena Bass[3198].

3913. PAUL EDWIN POWELL III (see Descendants (301)) was born on October 24, 2010, in Crestview, Okaloosa, Florida, USA, to Paul Edwin Powell Jr.[3199] and Ashly Rena Bass[3198]. Paul Edwin became known as "Eddisen".

3914. RIGGS ROOSIVELT RAY (see Descendants (301)) was born on January 5, 2023, in Crestview, Okaloosa County, Florida, USA, to Barney Kieth Ray[3200] and Ashly Rena Bass[3198].
Note: *6 pounds 15 ounces.*
(Birth)

3915. BRODIE LAWSON LAMB (see Descendants (302)) was born on March 19, 2007, in Georgia, USA, to John Joe Lamb[3202] and Stacie Partain Bass[3201].

3916. HARPER KATE GORUM (see Descendants (304)) was born to Jeffrey Douglas Gorum[3206] and Kayla Kinsaul[3205].

3917. STELLA RUTH GORUM (see Descendants (304)) was born on December 17, 2016 to Jeffrey Douglas Gorum[3206] and Kayla Kinsaul[3205].

3918. CLARE ELIZABETH PATRICK (see Descendants (305)) was born to Damon Andrew Patrick[3210] and Tera Ashleigh Henderson[3209].

3919. MASON THOMAS HENDERSON (see Descendants (305)) was born on April 5, 2007 to Bret Thomas Henderson[3211] and Emily Jean Youngblood[3212].

3920. IRIS TREDWELL (see Descendants (305)) was born to Mr. Tredwell[3216] and Erin Lajune Henderson[3215].

3921. ELLE TREDWELL (see Descendants (305)) was born to Mr. Tredwell[3216] and Erin Lajune Henderson[3215].

3922. EMILY TAYLOR (see Descendants (306)) was born on July 21, 2004 to Anthony Taylor[3218] and Laura Bass[3217].

3923. JONATHAN RUSSELL CHRZASTEK was born to Whittly Vivian Russell[3219].

3924. GERRY ETHAN RUSSELL was born to Whittly Vivian Russell[3219].

3925. BLAKELEE BASS (see Descendants (307)) was born to Johnathan Blake Bass[3220] and Brittany Edwards[3221]. She died (Stillborn).

3926. EMERSON BASS (see Descendants (307)) was born to Johnathan Blake Bass[3220] and Brittany Edwards[3221].

3927. BENTLEE BASS (see Descendants (307)) was born to Johnathan Blake Bass[3220] and Brittany Edwards[3221].

3928. ANISTON BASS (see Descendants (307)) was born to Johnathan Blake Bass[3220] and Brittany Edwards[3221].

3929. LEEAM HUDSON BASS (see Descendants (307)) was born on April 24, 2017 to Johnathan Blake Bass[3220] and Brittany Edwards[3221].
Note: *8lbs 4 oz. 21 inches, at 5:08pm.*
(Birth)

3930. TREY ? (see Descendants (307)) was born to Mandie Marie Bass[3222].

3931. CHARLIE ? (see Descendants (307)) was born to Mandie Marie Bass[3222].

3932. CHESTON BASS (see Descendants (308)) was born to Zach Bass[3223] and Janet Lee Taylor[3224].

3933. EMBRIE LYNN BASS (see Descendants (308)) was born on September 20, 2016 to Zach Bass[3223] and Janet Lee Taylor[3224].

3934. LYNNLI KATE MOCK (see Descendants (308)) was born in 2018 to Cole Mock[3227] and Allison Bass[3225].

3935. DECLAN RYAN BASS (see Descendants (309)) was born on October 26, 2015 to Anthony Gabriel Bass[3229] and Whitney Greene[3230].

3936. JOSIAH SAMUEL BASS (see Descendants (309)) was born on February 23, 2014 to Nathaniel Drew Bass[3231] and Micgayle Holmes[3232].

3937. ROY TAFT JOHNSON (see Descendants (143)) was born in October 2019 to Christopher Johnson[3254] and Kathryn Wilken[3255].

8th Generation of Descendants

3938. MR. PEREZ (see Descendants (2)) was born to Mr. Perez[3270] and Jennifer Ramer[3269].

3939. HANNAH DANIELLE BURLISON (see Descendants (34)) was born to Timmy Wayne Burlison II[3298] and Holly Christina Lord[3299].

3940. ALYSA L. WINTERS (see Descendants (34)) was born on January 20, 1992 to Ryan Winters[3302] and Renee S. Cain[3301].

3941. TYLER R. WINTERS (see Descendants (34)) was born on August 4, 1994 to Ryan Winters[3302] and Renee S. Cain[3301].

3942. LOGAN TAYLOR WINTERS (see Descendants (34)) was born on September 4, 1996 to Ryan Winters[3302] and Renee S. Cain[3301].

3943. DAMION T. HENDRIX (see Descendants (34)) was born on May 31, 1996 to Kacey A. Cain[3304] and Ms. Hendrix[3305].

3944. ELIJAH HENDRIX (see Descendants (34)) was born on May 31, 1998 to Kacey A. Cain[3304] and Ms. Hendrix[3305].

3945. BLAYNE CHRISTIAN MILSTEAD (see Descendants (151)) was born on March 13, 2000 to Aubrey Gene Milstead[3310] and Heather ?[3311].

3946. BROOKE LEIGHANNE BAYLIS (see Descendants (152)) was born on May 14, 1999 to Andrew Baylis[3313] and Danita Ann Milstead[3312].

3947. KENNETH RENEE LEWIS (see Descendants (165)) was born on August 3, 1995 to Kenneth Demon Lewis[3350] and Melynda Reanee Riggins[3349].

3948. CALLI SAUTTER (see Descendants (167)) was born to Chris Sautter[3358] and Shaun Michelle Haveard[3357].

3949. JOSEPH EDWIN HAVEARD (see Descendants (167)) was born on April 13, 2000 to Chris Sautter[3358] and Shaun Michelle Haveard[3357].

3950. DUTTON LEE HUDSON (see Descendants (41)) was born on March 28, 2023 to Brett Aubrey Hudson[3403] and Kayla Lynn Inabinett[3402].

3951. DANA KERVIN (see Descendants (180)) was born on August 20, 1987, in Andalusia, Covington, Alabama, USA, to Guy Kervin[3407] and Elizabeth Ann Davidson[3406].

3952. PATRICK KERVIN (see Descendants (180)) was born on September 9, 1988, in Andalusia, Covington, Alabama, USA, to Guy Kervin[3407] and Elizabeth Ann Davidson[3406].

3953. CORBREY KERVIN (see Descendants (180)) was born on November 2, 1989, in Andalusia, Covington, Alabama, USA, to Guy Kervin[3407] and Elizabeth Ann Davidson[3406].

3954. JESSICA DANIEL FULLER (see Descendants (182)) was born on August 4, 1988, in Dothan, Houston, Alabama, USA, to Bobby Fuller[3417] and Glenda Fay Davis[3416].

3955. ANDREW SERY FULLER (see Descendants (182)) was born on April 13, 1990, in Dothan, Houston, Alabama, USA, to Bobby Fuller[3417] and Glenda Fay Davis[3416].

3956. JOHN AUBREY DAVIS (see Descendants (182)) was born on September 28, 1990 to J. W. Davis[3418] and Allie Margent Carrington[3419].

3957. JAMES BRANDON HARRIS (see Descendants (183)) was born on June 22, 1985 to James Edward Harris[3420] and Rebecca Merritte[3421].

3958. KRYSTAL DIANNA HARRIS (see Descendants (183)) was born on September 12, 1986 to James Edward Harris[3420] and Rebecca Merritte[3421].

Direct Relations

3959. JOSEPH MICHAEL HUCKABAA (see Descendants (185)) was born on April 28, 1990, in Andalusia, Covington, Alabama, USA, to Gregory Randall Huckabaa[3423] and Teresa Brady[3424].

3960. TESSA LEANN HUCKABAA (see Descendants (185)) was born on January 1, 1993, in Andalusia, Covington, Alabama, USA, to Gregory Randall Huckabaa[3423] and Teresa Brady[3424].

3961. BRETT ALLEN HUCKABAA (see Descendants (185)) was born on December 29, 1995 to Gregory Randall Huckabaa[3423] and Teresa Brady[3424].

3962. BRENT RANDALL HUCKABAA (see Descendants (185)) was born on December 29, 1995 to Gregory Randall Huckabaa[3423] and Teresa Brady[3424].

3963. SHELBY HUCKABAA (see Descendants (187)) was born to Gordon Heath Huckabaa[3428] and Heather ?[3429].

3964. JAMISON HUCKABAA (see Descendants (187)) was born to Gordon Heath Huckabaa[3428] and Heather ?[3429].

3965. TIFFANY ANN NORRIS (see Descendants (45)) was born on February 8, 1992, in Panama City, Bay, Florida, USA, to Hayward Clarence Norris[3452] and Leslie Ann Schofield[3451].

3966. CHRISTOPHER M. COOK (see Descendants (45)) was born on September 17, 1990, in Eglin Air Force Base, Okaloosa, Florida, USA, to Rodney Fenton Cook[3455] and Ms. ?[3456].

3967. LEANNE AVERY BASS (see Descendants (54)) was born on June 14, 2014 to Hank Dallas Bass Jr.[3465] and Brittany Leann Vadino[3466].

3968. CONNOR MATTHEW BASS (see Descendants (54)) was born on January 5, 2016 to Hank Dallas Bass Jr.[3465] and Brittany Leann Vadino[3466].

3969. PAYTON HARPER BASS (see Descendants (54)) was born on December 20, 2019 to Hank Dallas Bass Jr.[3465] and Brittany Leann Vadino[3466].

3970. TENLEY MARTIN RODRIGUES (see Descendants (207)) was born on February 27, 2012 to Joey Rodrigues[3501] and Brittany Nash Huckaba[3500].

3971. EVELEE EMBER RODRIGUES (see Descendants (207)) was born on June 20, 2017 to Joey Rodrigues[3501] and Brittany Nash Huckaba[3500].

3972. HUXLEY NASH RODRIGUES (see Descendants (207)) was born on June 22, 2019 to Joey Rodrigues[3501] and Brittany Nash Huckaba[3500].

3973. ELISHA LEVI GILLIS (see Descendants (208)) was born on April 20, 2007 to Eric Gillis[3504] and Amber Lynn Bigger[3503].

3974. EZEKIEL ISAIAH GILLIS (see Descendants (208)) was born on August 26, 2008 to Eric Gillis[3504] and Amber Lynn Bigger[3503].

3975. MOLLY MADISON SHEFFIELD (see Descendants (208)) was born on February 17, 2009 to Mr. ?[3506] and Angela Tonya Bigger[3505]. She died on July 17, 2019, aged 10.

3976. MASON JAMES PATRIQUIN (see Descendants (208)) was born on January 31, 2015 to Mr. ?[3506] and Angela Tonya Bigger[3505].

3977. BRAYDON NOAH MULKEY (see Descendants (209)) was born on January 8, 2010 to Brandon Mulkey[3512] and Samantha Diane Huckaba[3511].

3978. KHLOE AUTUMN MULKEY (see Descendants (209)) was born on February 26, 2015 to Brandon Mulkey[3512] and Samantha Diane Huckaba[3511].

3979. BENTLEY GREYSON HUCKABA (see Descendants (209)) was born on February 10, 2018 to Ryan DeVane[3513] and Samantha Diane Huckaba[3511].

3980. PEYTON ELISE MCLNTYRE was born on October 17, 2014 to Austin Brewton[3537] and Amanda Lynn Williamson[3536].

3981. CARSON BLAKE BREWTON was born on December 20, 2017 to Austin Brewton[3537] and Amanda Lynn Williamson[3536].

3982. CAMERON MICHAEL MCMILLAN was born on September 22, 2015 to Mr. ?[3539] and Kristen Michelle Barnhill[3538].

3983. OLIVIA JEAN MCMILLAN was born on May 31, 2019 to Mr. ?[3539] and Kristen Michelle Barnhill[3538].

3984. ASHETON ALEXANDER O'NEAL was born on January 26, 2013 to Aaron O'Neal[3541] and Taylor Nicole Barnhill[3540].

3985. AIDEN BLAKE O'NEAL was born on September 27, 2015 to Aaron O'Neal[3541] and Taylor Nicole Barnhill[3540].

3986. LAILYNN RAINE O'NEAL was born on May 9, 2019 to Aaron O'Neal[3541] and Taylor Nicole Barnhill[3540].

3987. KINSLEY GRACE BARNHILL was born on September 14, 2021 to Chase Allen Barnhill[3542] and Clarissa Rena Thompson[3544]. Kinsley Grace was adopted by Chase Allen Barnhill[3542] and Cierra McKenzie ?[3543].

3988. BRENTLEY ALLEN BARNHILL was born on November 15, 2015 to Chase Allen Barnhill[3542] and Clarissa Rena Thompson[3544].

3989. RIVER EDWARD BARNHILL was born on January 28, 2018 to Chase Allen Barnhill[3542] and Clarissa Rena Thompson[3544].

3990. EMILY KATE BARRAGAN was born on August 26, 2020 to Luis Barragan[3546] and Meagan Michelle Williamson[3545].

3991. EASTON REESE LEE WILLIAMSON was born on September 22, 2017 to Garrett Michael Williamson[3547] and Ms. ?[3548].

3992. NICHOLAS LAYNE MCVAY (see Descendants (221)) was born to Nicholas Price[3553] and Micah Runae McVay[3552].

3993. LILITH ELLA LETURGEY (see Descendants (233)) was born on October 3, 2019 to Cory Joe Leturgey[3593] and Sierra Resendiz[3594].

3994. JOSEPH BYRON THOMPSON III (see Descendants (249)) was born to Joseph Byron Thompson Jr.[3647] and Becky Jean Spivey[3648].

3995. KYLE BUTLER (see Descendants (250)) was born on September 19, 1990 to Donald Kevin Butler[3650] and Sonya Michelle Thompson[3649].
3996. JESSICA FAYE ?.
    Kyle Butler[3995] married Jessica Faye ?. They had two children:
        Mr./Ms. Butler[4051]
        Mr./Ms. Butler[4052]

3997. ANDREW O'NEAL WEAVER (see Descendants (251)) was born on December 15, 1999 to Charis Weaver[3652] and Kimberly Nicole Thompson[3651].

3998. KAYDEN WEAVER (see Descendants (251)) was born to Charis Weaver[3652] and Kimberly Nicole Thompson[3651].

3999. DEANNA MICHELLE LEE (see Descendants (252)) was born on April 18, 1997 to Christopher Allen Lee Sr.[3654] and Kalise Erwin[3655].
4000. JACOB BISHOP.
    Jacob Bishop married DeAnna Michelle Lee[3999]. They had two children:
        McKinlee Bishop[4053] born on November 22, 2015
        Mr./Ms. Bishop[4054]

4001. KAITLIN LABECCA LEE (see Descendants (252)) was born on October 30, 2000 to Christopher Allen Lee Sr.[3654] and Tasha Nicole Piland[3656].
Kaitlin Labecca had two partnerships. She was married to Evan Kade Mercer[4003]. She was also the partner of Hunter Demond Johns[4002].
4002. HUNTER DEMOND JOHNS.
    Hunter Demond Johns and Kaitlin Labecca Lee[4001] had one son:
        Sawyer Allen Johns[4055] born on June 24, 2017
    The following information is also recorded for this family:
      • Unknown Relationship.
4003. EVAN KADE MERCER.
    Evan Kade Mercer married Kaitlin Labecca Lee[4001]. They had one daughter:
        Katalena Eloise Mercer[4056] born on July 13, 2020

4004. CHRISTOPHER ALLEN LEE JR. (see Descendants (252)) was born on September 30, 2002 to Christopher Allen Lee Sr.[3654] and Tasha Nicole Piland[3656]. He died on December 18, 2016, aged 14.

4005. COREY DEWAYNE LEE (see Descendants (252)), also recorded as Johnny Sexton Jr., was born on July 3, 2004 to Christopher Allen Lee Sr.[3654] and Tasha Nicole Piland[3656].
The following information is also recorded for Corey Dewayne:
  Twin.

4006. SHAUN EVEN LEE (see Descendants (252)) was born on July 3, 2004 to Christopher Allen Lee Sr.[3654] and Tasha Nicole Piland[3656].
    • He died (At young age) on July 3, 2004, as an infant.
The following information is also recorded for Shaun Even:
  Twin.
Note: *About six hours old.*
    (Death)

4007. CHRISLYN SKYLER SHYANN LEE (see Descendants (252)) was born on July 18, 2007 to Christopher Allen Lee Sr.[3654] and Tasha Nicole Piland[3656].

4008. TONY KYLER LEE (see Descendants (252)) was born on January 15, 2009 to Christopher Allen Lee Sr.[3654] and Tasha Nicole Piland[3656].

4009. ALLEN GARRETT (see Descendants (253)) was born about October 19, 2006 to Joshua Garrett[3658] and Casey Lee[3657].

4010. CODY PEACOCK (see Descendants (254)) was born on July 26, 1997 to Michael Steven Peacock[3659] and Ms. ?[3660].

4011. CALEB PEACOCK (see Descendants (254)) was born on December 4, 1998 to Michael Steven Peacock[3659] and Ms. ?[3660].

4012. MS. BOYETT (see Descendants (255)) was born to Tony Boyett[3661] and Ms. ?[3662].

4013. MS. BOYETT (see Descendants (255)) was born to Tony Boyett[3661] and Ms. ?[3662].

4014. MS. BOYETT (see Descendants (255)) was born to Tony Boyett[3661] and Ms. ?[3662].

4015. COURTNEY DOUGLAS (see Descendants (256)) was born on May 19, 1994 to Johnny Lamar Douglas[3665] and Delores Findley[3664].

4016. CAYLEE DOUGLAS (see Descendants (256)) was born to Johnny Lamar Douglas[3665] and Delores Findley[3664].

4017. ANNA EVANS (see Descendants (257)) was born to George William Evans III[3666] and Carmen ?[3667].

4018. MALLORIE NALLEY (see Descendants (258)) was born to John Nalley[3669] and Crystal Gail Evans[3668].

4019. TYLER NALLEY (see Descendants (258)) was born to John Nalley[3669] and Crystal Gail Evans[3668].

4020. TRENTON STONE CENDER (see Descendants (259)) was born to Steven Cender[3672] and Rebecca Lynn Evans[3670].

4021. HAILEY MICHELLE ADAMS (see Descendants (260)) was born to Derek Adams[3674] and Susan Michelle Cannon[3673].

4022. ABBY SUZANN WHITEHURST (see Descendants (260)) was born to Ronald Whitehurst[3675] and Susan Michelle Cannon[3673].

4023. KYRA TRAHAN (see Descendants (261)) was born about 2006 to Robert Eric Trahan[3678] and Jennifer Nicole Cannon[3677].

4024. JACKSON ALEXANDER CARR (see Descendants (89)) was born on February 23, 2009, in Andalusia, Covington, Alabama, USA, to Stewart Brandon Carr[3711] and Jessica Sueann Harrelson[3710].

4025. RENLEIGH ELIZABETH CARR (see Descendants (89)) was born on July 11, 2018, in Dothan, Alabama, USA, to Stewart Brandon Carr[3711] and Jessica Sueann Harrelson[3710].

4026. MR. NALL (see Descendants (93)) was born to Tanner Nall[3727] and Tanna ?[3728].

4027. MR. NALL (see Descendants (93)) was born to Tanner Nall[3727] and Tanna ?[3728].

4028. BRAYDEN MICHAEL CREWS (see Descendants (262)) was born to Michael Bennett Crews[3739] and Ms. ?[3740].

4029. CAROLINE ELIZABETH BUMPERS (see Descendants (96)) was born on April 15, 2013 to William Allen Bumpers III[3755] and Hanna Elizabeth Veasey[3754].

4030. CHARLOTTE CLAIR BUMPERS (see Descendants (96)) was born on December 17, 2015 to William Allen Bumpers III[3755] and Hanna Elizabeth Veasey[3754].

4031. KATHERINE ELIZABETH VEASEY (see Descendants (96)) was born on May 2, 2022 to Andrew Bruce Veasey[3756] and Taylor Lynn Donaldson[3757].

4032. KADEN MORANT (see Descendants (98)) was born to Zachary Morant[3761] and Celeste Parrish[3760].

4033. HAYLEE ELIZABETH ? (see Descendants (264)) was born on January 22, 2007 to Mr. ?[3766] and Heather Lee Holland[3765].

4034. ZANE ANDREW BASS (see Descendants (265)) was born in 2012 to Brett Andrew Bass[3767] and Francis ?[3768].

4035. JOSHUA BRODY INGRAM (see Descendants (275)) was born to Joshua Tyler Ingram[3782] and Ms. ?[3783].

4036. MR. BLAYLOCK (see Descendants (105)) was born to Eric Blaylock[3822] and Carolyn Wayman[3821].

4037. MR. BLAYLOCK (see Descendants (105)) was born to Eric Blaylock[3822] and Carolyn Wayman[3821].

4038. MR. MAIN (see Descendants (105)) was born to Randy Main[3824] and Katherine Wayman[3823].

4039. MR. MAIN (see Descendants (105)) was born to Randy Main[3824] and Katherine Wayman[3823].

4040. MS. MAIN (see Descendants (105)) was born to Randy Main[3824] and Katherine Wayman[3823].

4041. MR./MS. ? (see Descendants (106)) was born to Mr. ?[3827] and Mary Valdes[3826].

4042. MS. VALDES (see Descendants (106)) was born to Arthur Valdes[3828] and Elizabeth ?[3829].

4043. MS. VALDES (see Descendants (106)) was born to Arthur Valdes[3828] and Elizabeth ?[3829].

4044. MR. VALDES (see Descendants (106)) was born to Arthur Valdes[3828] and Elizabeth ?[3829].

4045. KENLY MADISON WIGGINS (see Descendants (129)) was born to John Raymond Wiggins[3853] and Tabitha Dawn Carnley[3852].

4046. MICHAEL LAYNE GRANTHAM (see Descendants (129)) was born to John Raymond Wiggins[3853] and Tabitha Dawn Carnley[3852].

4047. KADEN ANDREW WIGGINS (see Descendants (129)) was born to John Raymond Wiggins[3853] and Tabitha Dawn Carnley[3852].

4048. EMMA-LEIGH KATHERINE GRANTHAM (see Descendants (129)) was born to John Raymond Wiggins[3853] and Tabitha Dawn Carnley[3852].

4049. HEIDI RAE WIGGINS (see Descendants (129)) was born to John Raymond Wiggins[3853] and Tabitha Dawn Carnley[3852].

4050. SAYDEE MAE WIGGINS (see Descendants (129)) was born to John Raymond Wiggins[3853] and Tabitha Dawn Carnley[3852].

9th Generation of Descendants

4051. MR./MS. BUTLER (see Descendants (250)) was born to Kyle Butler[3995] and Jessica Faye ?[3996].

4052. MR./MS. BUTLER (see Descendants (250)) was born to Kyle Butler[3995] and Jessica Faye ?[3996].

4053. MCKINLEE BISHOP (see Descendants (252)) was born on November 22, 2015 to Jacob Bishop[4000] and DeAnna Michelle Lee[3999].

4054. MR./MS. BISHOP (see Descendants (252)) was born to Jacob Bishop[4000] and DeAnna Michelle Lee[3999].

4055. SAWYER ALLEN JOHNS (see Descendants (252)) was born on June 24, 2017 to Hunter Demond Johns[4002] and Kaitlin Labecca Lee[4001].

4056. KATALENA ELOISE MERCER (see Descendants (252)) was born on July 13, 2020 to Evan Kade Mercer[4003] and Kaitlin Labecca Lee[4001].

Ralph Caephus Bass sitting in his tree.

4. INDEX

Ref.	Name (Relationship)
2396	?, Mr..
2181	. Ms..
2849	. Ms..
2397	. Mr..
3740	. Ms..
3827	. Mr..
1865	. Ms..
3293	. Mr..
1660	. Mr./Ms..
2059	. Ms..
1994	. Mr..
2548	. Ms..
3660	. Ms..
2033	. Ms..
2540	. Mr..
3539	. Mr..
2708	. Ms..
2534	. Mr..
3548	. Ms..
3456	. Ms..
1761	. Ms..
2138	. Mr..
3506	. Mr..
2892	. Mr..
2177	. Ms..
4041	. Mr./Ms..
2064	. Ms..
1658	. Ms..
1555	. Ms..
2062	. Ms..
2122	. Mr..
3000	. Mr..
2030	. Ms..
3662	. Ms..
1893	. Ms..
2053	. Ms..
2482	. Ms..
1945	. Ms..
2289	. Mr..
3766	. Mr..
2952	. Ms..
3783	. Ms..
2538	. Mr..
2374	. Ms..
1500	. Alice.
2633	. Amanda.
2632	. Angel.
2625	. Anita.
2042	. Barbara.
1545	. Becky.
2229	. Betty.
1387	. Betty.
3262	. Betty.
1535	. Betty J..
2517	. Beverly.
3445	. BJ.
2735	. Bonnie.
3097	. Brandy.
2191	. Carin.

Ref.	Name (Relationship)
3667	?, Carmen.
1569	. Carry Ann.
2028	. Casey.
880	. Catherine.
3931	. Charlie.
2608	. Christy.
3543	. Cierra McKenzie.
2912	. Daniel.
2431	. Denise.
1219	. Donna.
3153	. Donna L..
2731	. Dorothy.
1523	. Elaine.
3829	. Elizabeth.
3491	. Eric.
3768	. Francis.
4033	. Haylee Elizabeth.
3429	. Heather.
3311	. Heather.
3839	. Heather.
3774	. Jameson.
2733	. Jana.
2536	. Jennifer Christine.
3996	. Jessica Faye.
2219	. John Jeffery Sowell.
2052	. Joy.
2549	. Kayla.
3099	. Kenya.
2785	. Laurie.
231	. Mamie Ada.
1471	. Maxine C.
3611	. Monica.
2583	. Nicole.
1580	. Patricia.
1512	. Peggy.
2046	. Rachel.
1688	. Rita.
3275	. Rose.
1510	. Ruth.
1571	. Ruth.
1693	. Sandra J..
3746	. Shelby.
2285	. Shirley.
2792	. Stephanie.
3081	. Stephanie.
2	. Susannah.
1842	. Sylvia.
3728	. Tanna.
3443	. Terri.
3492	. Tiffany.
3493	. Timothy.
3280	. Todd.
3263	. Tommy.
3277	. Tony.
3930	. Trey.
2626	. Vicki.
3101	. Whitney.
408	AARON, William.
1572	ABNEY, Ann.

Index

Ref.	Name (Relationship)
1574	ABNEY, Glenda.
568	.... Glenn M, Jr..
1570	.... Glenn Maurice, III.
3095	ABRAMS, Misty Sue.
1434	ADAMS, Aaron Lee.
2711	.... Angela Patrice.
2704	.... Angina Valentine.
1432	.... Annette.
2702	.... Anthony Phillip.
3626	.... Aric.
2700	.... Arlis Chapman, Jr..
1428	.... Arlis Chapman, Sr..
2486	.... Ashley Johnson.
1430	.... Atris C.
1436	.... Audie Mae.
3831	.... Brandon Dewayne.
3625	.... Brook.
2709	.... Danny Lee.
3674	.... Derek.
2481	.... Devin Phillips.
2485	.... Devin Randal.
3521	.... Dillon Wayne.
2989	.... Donald Wayne.
2473	.... Dusty W..
3526	.... Everett.
4021	.... Hailey Michelle.
1213	.... Harold DeWayne.
407	.... Harold Jack.
3525	.... Hudson.
2487	.... Kayla Danielle.
1568	.... Kimi Sue.
3522	.... Layla.
2483	.... Lindsey Nichole.
2961	.... Louise.
494	.... Luie Claude.
2425	.... Melanie Jean.
2713	.... Pamela Jean.
1586	.... Sandra.
1210	.... Sharon.
2715	.... Timothy Alan.
1214	.... Walter Dean.
1217	.... William Aaron.
1332	ADKINS, Johnny McCarsey.
2621	.... Shannon Michele.
2279	ADKISON, Helen.
1121	ALEXANDER, William.
2386	ALFORD, Christine.
1039	.... Delores J.
2133	ALLEN, Teresa.
1289	ALLPORT, Ann.
2315	ALVEREZ, Harry.
476	ANDERSON, Andrew Erastus.
2506	.... Ashley Leigh.
1422	.... Elna F.
1419	.... Lucine Dalton.
1246	.... Ray Elliot.
2505	.... Sean.
1418	.... Swenson Edwin.
1420	.... William F.

Ref.	Name (Relationship)
1526	ANDREWS, Deborah.
1706	.... James Dale.
2981	.... Kelly Lynn.
1524	.... Lucia Dianne.
1522	.... Lucian Hibbard, III.
527	.... Lucian Hibbard, Jr..
1528	.... Rebecca.
3498	ANSLEY, Carrie Denise.
2385	.... Dale Edgar.
3494	.... Dale Edgar.
1110	.... James Walter.
2392	.... James William.
2387	.... Joanne Marie.
2390	.... Lyvon Walter.
3499	.... Summer Lyvon.
3495	.... Tiffany Leighann.
3772	ARGERIS, Constantinos.
2890	.... Constantinos.
3773	.... Hristos.
827	ARMSTRONG, Pete.
2016	.... Troyce.
397	ATKINS, Charlotte.
2710	BABB, Deborah.
3618	BABBINTON, Thomas W.
2778	BACHUS, James Edward.
3696	.... Mary Alexandra.
3695	.... Mclain A.
3590	BAEHR, Annie O..
2576	.... James Richard.
3591	.... Mya M..
1291	.... Richard Kenneth.
3589	.... Sadie E.
2578	.... Susan Jean.
1992	BAILEY, Mr..
2666	.... Scott.
1594	BAKER, Donald.
582	.... Mary Nell.
2105	BALIUS, John Ernest.
3318	.... Justin Eugene.
3319	.... Megan Catherine.
108	BALLARD, Jonnie Lillian.
2852	BARELARE, Mr..
3742	BARKER, Mr./Ms..
2847	.... Mr..
3743	.... Mr./Ms..
3744	.... Mr./Ms..
2453	BARKSDALE, Susan Claire.
1174	.... William J..
3908	BARNES, Benson Gray.
1899	.... Billy Gray.
622	.... Charlotte Marilla.
3487	.... Crystal Sheree.
3191	.... David Brian.
3907	.... Hannah Marie.
3486	.... Keisha Lynn.
3906	.... Mary Katherine.
3192	.... Phillip Michael.
3194	.... Samuel Brad.
3909	.... Troy.

Ref.	Name (Relationship)
2907	BARNETT, Buffie Deanna.
575	.... George R.
1587	.... Gloria Dianne.
2909	.... Gloria Lynn.
2905	.... LaDonice Darnell.
2911	.... Melissa Ann.
2908	.... Rickey Darnell, Jr..
1583	.... Rickie Donnel, Sr..
1589	.... Teresa LaGail.
1592	.... Wanda June.
848	BARNEYCASTLE, Benjamin Wilson.
2037	.... Bennie Mae.
847	.... Cynthia Lillian.
253	.... Elzie.
845	.... Ester C.
860	.... Eula.
2034	.... Hazel Marie.
854	.... Isabelle.
850	.... James William.
247	.... John Curtis.
856	.... L. C., 1st Lt.
859	.... Lula.
851	.... Martin Luther.
853	.... Nobie.
2035	.... Sue Adele.
858	.... Todd, S Sgt.
2326	BARNHILL, Angelia.
3988	.... Brentley Allen.
3542	.... Chase Allen.
2327	.... Darlene.
3987	.... Kinsley Grace.
3538	.... Kristen Michelle.
1057	.... Merlin.
2323	.... Merlin.
2324	.... Mikie.
3989	.... River Edward.
2520	.... Shane.
2325	.... Tammie.
3540	.... Taylor Nicole.
3990	BARRAGAN, Emily Kate.
3546	.... Luis.
3197	BARRINGER, Elizabeth Corinne.
1127	BARRON, Jacqueline Dianne.
2818	BARROW, Angela Lynn.
1486	.... Harold Jerome.
740	.... Julia Ann.
2820	.... Kevin Jerome.
2816	.... Melinda Gayle.
1086	.... Sharon Treasa.
3687	BARRY, Phillip Le Brandon.
889	BARTON, A. Bruce.
276	.... Alpha B..
738	.... Barbara.
892	.... Dixie.
890	.... Grant B.
891	.... Mary Etta.
2879	BASS, Mr..
1350	.... Mr..
248	.... Mr..

Ref.	Name (Relationship)
249	BASS, Mr..
872	.... Mr..
871	.... Mr..
2467	.... Adam Dean.
562	.... Addie Ruth.
2509	.... Alanna Nicole.
3528	.... Alexander Riley.
1363	.... Alice Lillian.
1393	.... Alice Marie.
1359	.... Alice Nanette.
2676	.... Alicia Marie.
1617	.... Alivia LaShelle.
265	.... Allen Milford.
3225	.... Allison.
862	.... Alvin Leon.
2471	.... Amy Elizabeth.
532	.... Andrew Bennett.
2821	.... Angela Beth.
3928	.... Aniston.
2049	.... Annette.
531	.... Annie Laura.
1918	.... Anthony Edd.
3229	.... Anthony Gabriel.
493	.... Arrie Bernice.
3198	.... Ashly Rena.
440	.... Audrey Rebecca.
3584	.... August Beau.
3745	.... Austin.
665	.... Autray Alto.
3529	.... Ava Claire.
1487	.... Barbara Eleanor.
659	.... Beatrice Izora.
1463	.... Beatrice Lucile.
3583	.... Beckham Ceese.
2336	.... Becky Rene.
885	.... Ben E.
272	.... Benjamin Edward.
257	.... Benjamin Eli.
60	.... Benjamin Wilson.
106	.... Bennett Bridges, III.
20	.... Bennett Bridges, Jr..
3	.... Bennett Bridges, Sr..
523	.... Bennett Ray.
3927	.... Bentlee.
128	.... Bertie B.
357	.... Bessie Luvine.
526	.... Bessie May.
1373	.... Betty.
438	.... Betty Irene.
1457	.... Betty Jean.
1383	.... Betty June.
1326	.... Beverly Lynn.
1063	.... Billy Ray.
3925	.... Blakelee.
1509	.... Bob.
1557	.... Bobby.
2883	.... Brandy Lane.
2043	.... Brenda.
1203	.... Brenda.

Ref.	Name (Relationship)
3767	BASS, Brett Andrew.
2880	.... Brett Zan.
2460	.... Brian.
1224	.... Brian Joseph.
2570	.... Brian Royce.
720	.... Bruce James.
402	.... Calvin Winston.
3769	.... Camrin Zan.
1531	.... Carol.
400	.... Carolyn.
3283	.... Casandra.
1368	.... Catherine Carlene.
88	.... Catherine Elizabeth.
164	.... Catherine Emma.
431	.... Cecil Edwin.
2349	.... Chad Howard.
406	.... Charity Delores.
176	.... Charles.
2646	.... Charles Edward.
1369	.... Charles Edward.
1484	.... Charlotte.
1532	.... Cheryl.
1405	.... Cheryl Dianne.
2663	.... Cheryl Kaye.
3932	.... Cheston.
329	.... Christian Ottie Lee.
1452	.... Christine.
2615	.... Christopher Troy.
818	.... Clara M.
519	.... Claude Bruce.
1892	.... Clinton Duranne.
714	.... Clinton Albert.
1723	.... Clyde Kermit, Jr..
657	.... Clyde Kermit, Sr..
1940	.... Columbus Barry.
3968	.... Connor Matthew.
735	.... Coy Bennett.
1937	.... Coy Bennett, Jr..
246	.... Cynthia Lillian.
2669	.... Cynthia Louise.
1935	.... Cynthia Michelle.
2330	.... Cynthia Renee.
269	.... Daniel Materson.
875	.... Daniel Materson, Jr..
2041	.... Daniel S.
1222	.... Danne Louise.
1562	.... Danny Kay.
1488	.... David Leon.
1083	.... Debbie Sue.
3935	.... Declan Ryan.
125	.... Dennis Bridges.
2950	.... Derrick Lamar.
2887	.... Devin Lee.
391	.... Dewey Franklin.
3771	.... Diesel Wayne.
1902	.... Don Jeffery, I.
3203	.... Don Jeffery, II.
550	.... Donald.
1556	.... Donald.

Ref.	Name (Relationship)
1390	BASS, Donald Gene.
1353	.... Donald Willis.
2759	.... Donna Carol.
2871	.... Donna Lynne.
2678	.... Donnie Lee.
1536	.... Doris Jean.
866	.... Dorothy.
883	.... Dorothy.
1187	.... Dottie Lynn.
259	.... Douglas U.
3531	.... Dray Rolen.
1189	.... Dudley Dean.
1351	.... Earnest True, Jr..
454	.... Earnest True, Sr..
727	.... Edd.
392	.... Edith Florine.
513	.... Edith Inez.
564	.... Edna Inez.
2769	.... Edward Michael.
2672	.... Edwin Durwood, Jr..
1388	.... Edwin Durwood, Sr..
112	.... Elijah L..
3585	.... Eliza Bray.
264	.... Eliza Jane.
24	.... Elizabeth.
2480	.... Elizabeth Ann.
1485	.... Elizabeth Louise.
3933	.... Embrie Lynn.
3926	.... Emerson.
1581	.... Emily Gwendolyn.
1458	.... Emmie Elvira.
1354	.... Ennis Rudolph.
2463	.... Eric Douglas.
1225	.... Eric Richard.
2468	.... Erin Leigh.
3609	.... Erin Lenae.
2886	.... Erin Lynn.
1349	.... Ernest True, Jr..
591	.... Esther Frances.
274	.... Etta Mary.
398	.... Eula Virginia.
723	.... Eunice.
496	.... Eva Allie.
281	.... Eva Elizabeth.
819	.... Eva Mae.
667	.... Fannie Esther.
3530	.... Farrar Courtney.
409	.... Farrell Dale.
179	.... Flora.
130	.... Florence.
171	.... Florence.
181	.... Florine Dorothy.
663	.... Floyd Irwin.
517	.... Frank Stewart.
737	.... Franklin Jerry.
1943	.... Franklin Scott.
3285	.... Gary.
1520	.... Gary Dean, Col..
1288	.... Gary Wayne.

Ref.	Name (Relationship)
1472	BASS, Gayle Ann.
322	.... Genola.
571	.... George Washington.
1094	.... Gerald Howard, Jr..
372	.... Gerald Howard, Sr..
868	.... Glenn Donald "Johnny".
716	.... Gordon L..
1715	.... Greer Ellen.
1511	.... Greg.
1292	.... Gregory Alan.
434	.... Grover Alcus.
262	.... Gustavus.
870	.... Gwendolyn.
3465	.... Hank Dallas, Jr..
2343	.... Hank Dallas, Sr..
2895	.... Hannah LeNelle.
1381	.... Harold Eugene.
415	.... Harvey Middleton.
1451	.... Hazel.
731	.... Hazel.
881	.... Hazel Louise.
655	.... Henry Grady.
121	.... Henry Harrelson.
466	.... Henry Obie, Captain.
552	.... Henry Walton.
733	.... Herman.
362	.... Hillary J..
712	.... Hiram J.
1891	.... Hiram, Jr..
17	.... Holland Middleton.
2572	.... Holley Alaine.
96	.... Holley Middleton.
3576	.... Holly Suzanne.
821	.... Horace Presley.
555	.... Howard Eugine.
442	.... Hubert Lee.
3575	.... Hunter Scott.
89	.... Isabell.
1248	.... Jacqueline.
3251	.... James Bennett.
174	.... James Bennett.
1913	.... James Benny.
1077	.... James Dallas.
92	.... James Dallas.
2742	.... James Dewayne.
1088	.... James Edward.
2346	.... James Edward, Jr..
1449	.... James Ervin.
1223	.... James Farris.
359	.... James Henry.
19	.... James Hilliard.
2459	.... James Holley.
1447	.... James Ivey.
2877	.... James Lynn.
429	.... James Marcus.
1179	.... James Michael.
2555	.... James Scott.
394	.... James Verlin.
40	.... James W..

Ref.	Name (Relationship)
1550	BASS, James William.
113	.... James Wilson.
498	.... Jamie Ike.
1253	.... Janet.
2470	.... Janet Kay.
2340	.... Janet Louise.
1905	.... Janet Marie.
1403	.... Janiee Marilyn.
2616	.... Jasmine Leigh.
3691	.... Jason Christopher.
1074	.... Jasper Daniel.
2339	.... Jasper Danniel, Jr..
3595	.... Jaxon Riley.
2557	.... Jeffery Philip.
1513	.... Jeffery W..
1185	.... Jeffrey Marlin.
1717	.... Jennifer Lee.
1554	.... Jerry.
530	.... Jesse Ruban.
505	.... Jessie D.
1087	.... Jimmie Ray.
1375	.... JoAnne Charlotte.
412	.... Joe Farris.
2492	.... Joel Farrar.
3910	.... Joel Ryan.
417	.... Joel Sidney.
2494	.... Joel Sidney, III.
1228	.... Joel Sidney, Jr..
41	.... John.
2045	.... John.
115	.... John Bridges.
366	.... John Clayton.
1576	.... John Dennis.
528	.... John Irvin.
267	.... John Riley.
100	.... John Riley.
3574	.... John Stephen.
425	.... John Thomas.
1250	.... John Thomas, Jr..
2490	.... John William, Jr..
1226	.... John William, Sr..
3220	.... Johnathan Blake.
1084	.... Johnny Ray.
500	.... Joseph Aaron.
98	.... Joseph Alexander.
279	.... Joseph Carson.
2984	.... Joseph Michael.
2581	.... Joshua Alan.
2345	.... Joshua Edmund.
3692	.... Joshua Ryan.
3936	.... Josiah Samuel.
865	.... Joyce Imogene.
1245	.... Judith.
2008	.... Judith Ellica.
1718	.... Judson Levon.
2983	.... Judson Levon, Jr..
2495	.... Julia Elizabeth.
501	.... Julius Clarence.
1459	.... Julius Ike.

Ref.	Name (Relationship)
2766	BASS, Julius Randall.
3252	.... Kameron Baylea.
2665	.... Karan Lainye.
1295	.... Karen Mae.
3253	.... Karson Ann.
873	.... Katherine Gladys.
1200	.... Kathy.
1290	.... Kathy Jean.
127	.... Katie.
2876	.... Katie Diane.
2559	.... Kelly Suzanne.
565	.... Kenneth Bridges.
1377	.... Kenneth Kirby.
1564	.... Kenneth Lee.
2051	.... Kenneth Riley, Jr..
878	.... Kenneth Riley, Sr..
2897	.... Kevin.
2775	.... Kimberly Ruth.
2350	.... Kyle.
3217	.... Laura.
574	.... Laura Frances.
117	.... Laura Lee.
134	.... Lawrence.
3967	.... Leanne Avery.
3929	.... Leeam Hudson.
652	.... Leilla Mae.
1321	.... Leland Samuel.
507	.... Leon Pendry.
16	.... Levina.
83	.... Levina.
1724	.... Lewis Arnold.
585	.... Lewis W.
183	.... Lillie May.
1518	.... Linda.
2641	.... Linda Ann.
1621	.... Linda C.
2648	.... Linda Elizabeth.
1407	.... Linda Kay.
2469	.... Lorin Holly.
261	.... Louis O.
363	.... Magdaline.
817	.... Maggie M.
3222	.... Mandie Marie.
3573	.... Marcus Christian.
2553	.... Marcus Stephen.
867	.... Margaret.
419	.... Margueritte Catherine.
436	.... Margueritte Elizabeth.
587	.... Marjorie.
2575	.... Mark Daron William.
1725	.... Mark Napoleon.
2850	.... Marla Kim.
396	.... Marlin Holley.
1897	.... Marlon Hugh.
1534	.... Marlon Jerome.
1720	.... Marron Grady.
283	.... Martha.
421	.... Martha Ann.
104	.... Martha Christian.

Wilson Bass

Ref.	Name (Relationship)
26	BASS, Martha Jane.
327	.... Martha Naomi.
250	.... Martin Luther.
1085	.... Marvin Dallas, Jr..
368	.... Marvin Dallas, Sr..
9	.... Mary.
209	.... Mary A..
94	.... Mary Alice.
503	.... Mary Annie.
661	.... Mary Bonnie.
589	.... Mary Elizabeth.
160	.... Mary Elizabeth.
110	.... Mary Elizabeth.
277	.... Mary Etta.
557	.... Mary Idell.
464	.... Mary Leona.
1356	.... Mary Ruth.
263	.... Mary Susannah.
1552	.... Mathew Gerald.
3610	.... Matthew Evan.
177	.... Mattie O..
1325	.... Maurice Seiwell.
427	.... Mavis Earline.
324	.... Maxie Milo.
3684	.... Megan Christina.
579	.... Melisa Juanita.
2348	.... Melissa.
3572	.... Meredith Hope.
2878	.... Michael.
3467	.... Michael Anthony.
1208	.... Michael Douglas.
2874	.... Michael Gerald.
2331	.... Michael Zoree.
1896	.... Mike.
567	.... Mildred E. Griffen.
170	.... Minnie Josephine.
2891	.... Miranda.
1357	.... Morgan Bennett.
468	.... Morgan Bennett.
583	.... Murry Cecil.
1619	.... Murry Lamar.
710	.... Myrtice.
2885	.... Nanci L..
1533	.... Nancy.
5	.... Nancy.
14	.... Nancy.
1894	.... Nancy Carolyn.
168	.... Nancy Jane.
86	.... Nancy Jane Middleton.
1911	.... Nancy Madonna.
669	.... Nannie Ruth.
3231	.... Nathaniel Drew.
1371	.... Nell.
3196	.... Nicholas Bruce.
2047	.... Nita.
1362	.... Obbie.
1367	.... Olive Marie.
495	.... Ollie Albert.
331	.... Ossie Mae.

Index

Ref.	Name (Relationship)
2872	BASS, Pamela Renea.
3612	.... Patricia Ann.
1181	.... Patricia Annelle.
1548	.... Patricia Lucille.
1082	.... Paul Howard.
2873	.... Paula Kay.
3969	.... Payton Harper.
444	.... Quinton Gene.
3613	.... Rachel Suzanne.
725	.... Ralph Caephus.
1910	.... Randall Ralph.
2893	.... Randi Lynn.
1890	.... Randy Joe.
1567	.... Randy Lynn.
877	.... Ray Leonard.
364	.... Ray-Monde.
1098	.... Rhonda.
2337	.... Rhonda Elaine.
2651	.... Rhonda Theresa.
1507	.... Richard.
2332	.... Richard Allen.
458	.... Richard Carl, Sr..
1365	.... Richard Carle, Jr..
2652	.... Richard Charles.
2773	.... Richard Christopher.
1470	.... Richard Clarence.
2644	.... Richard Edward.
2335	.... Rickey Thomas.
1900	.... Ricky Bruce.
44	.... Riley.
123	.... Riley B.
1726	.... Riley Bennett.
172	.... Riley John.
1220	.... Robert.
2650	.... Robert Carl.
2341	.... Robert Dom.
1361	.... Robert Earl.
2640	.... Robert Ernest.
1465	.... Robert Julius.
3683	.... Robert Julius, II.
1323	.... Robin Naomi.
2771	.... Robin Taiwan.
1489	.... Roger Clayton.
1218	.... Roger Dale.
2488	.... Roger Dale, Jr..
1183	.... Roger Douglas.
1530	.... Ronald.
2985	.... Ronald Joe.
576	.... Rossie Lee.
1915	.... Royce Caephus.
558	.... Ruby Lee.
2667	.... Sabin Craig.
2479	.... Sam Michael.
2574	.... Sara Suzanne.
370	.... Sarah Christian.
864	.... Sarah Francis.
166	.... Savannah.
3190	.... Serrie.
3284	.... Seth.

Ref.	Name (Relationship)
2464	BASS, Seth Jeffrey.
2054	.... Sharon.
2764	.... Sharon Jean.
2848	.... Shawn.
2677	.... Shawn Lee.
119	.... Sheila Josephine.
2889	.... Sheleiah Lynn.
1546	.... Shelia Pamelia.
1539	.... Shirley Ann.
432	.... Sibyl Louise.
509	.... Snyder Clayton.
3201	.... Stacie Partain.
102	.... Stacy Bibner.
1944	.... Stanley Brian.
404	.... Stephen Durward.
1274	.... Stephen Gene.
3282	.... Steve.
1207	.... Steve Elvin.
1559	.... Steve Walden.
1895	.... Sue Marie.
2673	.... Susan Dianne.
2338	.... Susan Elizabeth.
1279	.... Susan Lynn.
252	.... Susan Viola.
2584	.... Teri Lyn.
3286	.... Terry.
260	.... Thelma B.
1066	.... Theresa.
1068	.... Theresa Annette.
1067	.... Thomas.
1072	.... Thomas Franklin.
1221	.... Thomas Matthew.
256	.... Thomas Watson.
2056	.... Timothy.
2898	.... Tina Darlene.
2010	.... Tommy Author.
1100	.... Tonya.
3468	.... Treasa Ann.
1401	.... Trina Elaine.
650	.... Veilla Maine.
813	.... Velma.
511	.... Velma Bertha.
551	.... Virginia.
560	.... Virginia.
1909	.... Vivian Ann.
1455	.... Voncile.
1722	.... Vonda Vinor.
1096	.... Wanda.
1898	.... Wanda Arlene.
729	.... Wavie Lee.
2894	.... Waylon.
2761	.... Waymon Julius.
718	.... Wayne.
1615	.... Wendy Brynell.
1920	.... Wendy Learvene.
1329	.... Wesley Alan.
863	.... William Andrew.
815	.... William Barney.
2675	.... William Bennett.

Ref.	Name (Relationship)
84	BASS, William Bennett.
461	.... William Bennett.
553	.... William Columbus.
3527	.... William Cooper.
1080	.... William Dallas.
1385	.... William Edward.
1578	.... William Gary.
2875	.... William Henry.
162	.... William Henry.
42	.... William M..
7	.... William Riley.
64	.... William Riley.
28	.... William Riley.
211	.... William Riley.
1360	.... William Walter.
3911	.... Willson Bruce.
1	.... Wilson.
12	.... Wilson Bennett.
254	.... Wilson Lafayette.
1916	.... Winfred Lynn.
581	.... Winston Byran.
708	.... Wylene.
1205	.... Yvonne.
3223	.... Zach.
3469	.... Zachary Daniel.
4034	.... Zane Andrew.
2858	BATES, Melissa.
931	BATSON, Billie.
2081	.... David Jonathan.
2083	.... Robin Mario.
3295	.... Zackareah Jonathan.
879	BATTEN, Martha L..
561	BATZINGER, Allen.
934	BAUGHMAN, Phyllis D..
3313	BAYLIS, Andrew.
3946	.... Brooke Leighanne.
1476	BEARDEN, Betty Jean.
459	BEASLEY, Alice Lucille.
1614	.... Daniel Lewellyn.
970	.... Tammy Sue.
3004	BECK, Alan.
3005	.... Barabara Sue.
674	.... Benjamin Otis.
3010	.... Christopher Shane.
3026	.... Cindy Lynn.
1758	.... Collie.
3025	.... Deborah Elaine.
1760	.... Edward C.
672	.... Ernest Terry.
1734	.... Janice L.
3011	.... Margaret.
1756	.... Marie.
3028	.... Marilyn.
1762	.... Marylin Maxine.
1743	.... Quinton W.
1738	.... Reginald E.
3012	.... Rickey Davon.
1750	.... Ronald Eugene.
3027	.... Sandra.

Ref.	Name (Relationship)
3009	BECK, Shannon Leon.
1736	.... Shirley A.
3007	.... Tamara Michelle.
1746	.... Theron Leon.
1752	.... Vivian Diane.
1431	BECKWORTH, Jessie.
93	BEDGOOD, Amie Isabel.
2344	BEHM, Mary Ann.
1229	BEHR, Gina Joy.
2579	BEISWENGER, Mr..
195	BELL, Flossie.
1681	BENNETT, Ms..
2120	.... Christy Rene.
2767	.... Shirley Ann.
2410	BENOIT, Bobby.
3517	.... Caleb Joseph.
3516	.... Matthew Paul.
1626	BEVERLY, Ms..
1573	BEVERS, Kenneth.
3261	BICANEK, Carol Jean.
3259	.... George J., Jr..
1989	.... George J., Sr..
3260	.... Joan Diane.
2269	BIDDLE, Glen Day.
3442	.... Glen Day, Jr..
3444	.... Shon Lee.
3503	BIGGER, Amber Lynn.
3505	.... Angela Tonya.
2399	.... David.
1410	BIGGS, Beulah Mae.
1412	.... Lessie Myrl.
1409	.... Minnie Elizabeth.
470	.... William Albert.
4054	BISHOP, Mr./Ms..
1844	.... Annie Louise.
4000	.... Jacob.
4053	.... McKinlee.
216	BLACK, Eula Mae.
2743	BLACKWELL, Aletha Jean.
1456	.... Clifton Curtis.
2755	.... Clifton Joseph.
2748	.... Cornelia Ann.
2750	.... Deborah Lynn.
2745	.... Demisia.
2756	.... Shela Dianna.
2698	.... Sue.
2753	.... Teresa.
1453	.... W. Edward.
734	BLAIR, Mary Ann.
303	.... Rupert Harrelson.
2836	.... Stacey Jean.
2267	.... Tamela Renee.
1216	.... Tammy Theford.
4036	BLAYLOCK, Mr..
4037	.... Mr..
3822	.... Eric.
1751	BLOCKER, Velma.
3869	BLOOMFIELD, Craig Allen.
3867	.... Jennifer Nichole.

Ref.	Name (Relationship)
3868	BLOOMFIELD, Kevin Shawn, Jr..
3069	.... Kevin Shawn, Sr..
2040	BLUME, Donna Lee.
874	.... Kenneth Lynell.
3195	BOCHETTE, Bethany Hope.
467	BODIFORD, Ajetta.
1230	BOLDING, Margueritte Dawn.
420	.... Mark Anthony.
3785	BOLES, Brooklynn Lee.
3784	.... Johnny Robert, Jr..
2914	.... Johnny Robert, Sr..
2931	.... Melissa Ann.
1955	BOLLING, Larry.
1596	BONEY, Belinda Jo.
3055	BOOKER, Brenda Gail.
3518	.... Jenny Nicole.
2412	.... Joe.
2125	BORDERS, Cindy.
1355	BORGIOLI, Linda Barbara.
1855	BOSHELL, George.
3147	.... Gregory Alan.
2419	BOTTS, Laurin.
3441	BOUTWELL, Jimmy Earl.
2265	.... Jimmy Ray.
1805	BOWMAN, Janet.
4013	BOYETT, Ms..
4014	.... Ms..
4012	.... Ms..
2749	.... Al.
3663	.... Al, Jr..
3661	.... Tony.
834	BOZEMAN, Bennie.
1840	.... Essie Orene.
660	.... Grover.
1727	.... Margaret Ann.
796	BRADLEY, Bertha Lois.
3410	.... Crystal Darlene.
1169	.... Deborah Joann.
779	.... Delia Adeline.
923	.... Henryetta Nadine.
3409	.... Tony Wayne.
2231	.... Wayne.
457	BRADY, Ms..
3424	.... Teresa.
3537	BREWTON, Austin.
3981	.... Carson Blake.
2551	BRISOLARA, Sara.
1683	BROADWAY, Mr..
2716	BROCK, Cynthia Delores.
2084	.... Dawn Denise.
932	.... Oscar L..
822	BROOKS, Avie.
825	.... J. B..
662	.... Joe M..
2012	.... Lester.
2015	.... Sandra.
2014	.... Sherry.
2013	.... Sue.
1654	BROWN, Mr./Ms..

Ref.	Name (Relationship)
1655	BROWN, Mr./Ms..
1435	.... Betty Jean.
985	.... Bonnie.
634	.... Frank.
2987	.... George.
152	.... Laura L..
1651	BRUNSON, Jean.
626	.... Jesse E.
1416	BRYAN, Edwin.
1415	.... Judson.
1417	.... Loraine.
474	.... Newton Dudley.
1414	.... Zella.
1076	BUCKLEY, Maurine Beth.
52	BULGER, Illinoy.
1612	BULLARD, Terry.
4029	BUMPERS, Caroline Elizabeth.
4030	.... Charlotte Clair.
3755	.... William Allen, III.
1273	BURGDORF, Debbie.
1370	BURK, Mae.
3939	BURLISON, Hannah Danielle.
3300	.... Shaun Michael.
2088	.... Timmy Wayne.
3298	.... Timmy Wayne, II.
976	BURNETT, Mary Beth.
3721	BURTON, Garrett Lamar.
3722	.... John Grant.
2817	.... Robert Lamar.
3126	BUSBEE, Angie.
3124	.... Donald Eugene.
1822	.... Elton.
1829	.... Eula Vee.
1825	.... James Curtis.
3121	.... Janet.
1837	.... Jean.
1823	.... Noma.
3123	.... Peggie.
1833	.... Polly.
3135	.... Randy.
3128	.... Rickie.
3127	.... Rusty.
1827	.... Shelby Ray.
3122	.... Sue.
1820	.... Thelma Lee.
3136	.... Tonya.
1835	.... Walan.
3125	.... Wanda.
693	.... William Roy.
1831	.... Winnie Fay.
390	BUSBY, Ida May.
1553	BUSH, Mary Lou.
515	BUTKISS, Allan.
4052	BUTLER, Mr./Ms..
4051	.... Mr./Ms..
2845	.... Dana.
3650	.... Donald Kevin.
3995	.... Kyle.
869	.... Olis Geneva.

Ref.	Name (Relationship)
2277	BUTTS, Sandra Fay.
1012	BYERS, Viola.
326	BYRD, Lucile.
1232	.... Lynda Ann.
1234	.... Mychaelle Joy.
1236	.... Nancy Jane.
422	.... William Mullina.
451	CADENHEAD, Elizabeth Virginia.
3751	CAFFEY, Rodger.
3042	CAHILL, Deborah.
3304	CAIN, Kacey A..
2090	.... Kenneth A..
3306	.... Kenneth A., II.
3301	.... Renee S..
3303	.... Renee S..
1606	CALHOUN, Cindy.
63	CAMERON, E. A..
2395	CAMP, Chris.
798	CAMPBELL, Claude C..
3065	.... Corrie L..
450	.... Emma June.
799	.... Mary R.
204	.... William Nicholas.
800	.... William Nicholas, Jr..
1901	CANANT, Donna Rena.
2558	CANCILLA, Renee.
2754	CANNON, James Randall.
3677	.... Jennifer Nicole.
700	.... Pearl.
3679	.... Stephanie Dyan.
3673	.... Susan Michelle.
3622	CAPPS, Brian.
3053	CARNLEY, James Micheal.
3852	.... Tabitha Dawn.
3854	.... Trenton Michael.
1748	CAROLYN, Ms..
2259	CAROWELL, Erldean.
2233	CARPENTER, Cynthia J..
4024	CARR, Jackson Alexander.
1789	.... Martha Ray.
4025	.... Renleigh Elizabeth.
3711	.... Stewart Brandon.
3419	CARRINGTON, Allie Margent.
664	CARROLL, Avis.
1202	.... Jerry.
666	.... Joyce.
116	.... Nancy Amy.
921	CARY, Carolyn.
2080	.... Edwin Kieth.
309	.... Orlando Dudley.
922	.... Richard Derhyl.
962	CASCONE, Marie Antonette.
1247	CASEY, Rick.
280	CASH, Winnetta.
2973	CASON, Mr..
1689	.... Carolyn.
647	.... Coleman R..
1662	.... Dasy May.
643	.... Grady J..

Ref.	Name (Relationship)
1690	CASON, Grady J., Jr..
1696	.... James David.
161	.... James Hillard.
1697	.... Jimmy Ray.
645	.... John F..
1691	.... Johnny Ray.
1685	.... Kathleen.
1694	.... Leon.
1687	.... Lindsey.
637	.... Mary Florence.
1698	.... Rhett.
1692	.... Robert Gerald.
649	.... Syble G..
1695	.... Sylvia Jean.
641	.... William Charles.
639	.... Zonnie Bell.
2968	CASSELBERRY, Janet.
3393	CAUSEY, Brandon Lee.
2202	.... David Lee.
3391	.... Tawana Lynn.
3390	CAUSIE, Deborah Jane.
2195	.... Judy Ann.
981	.... Ray.
3672	CENDER, Steven.
4020	.... Trenton Stone.
1099	CEURVELS, Mr..
2353	.... Heather Lee.
2354	.... Jessica.
2404	CEYNAR, Tanya Rae.
2206	CHAMPION, Lisa Perl.
2924	CHANCE, Mary Ann.
762	CHAPPLE, James.
1981	.... James Douglas.
1980	.... Linda James.
1665	CHAVER, Mr..
2504	CHELETTE, Bronwyn Elise.
1244	.... Herman Edward, III.
3045	CHESSER, Dale.
525	.... Frances Alice Hester.
3847	CHESSHER, Chelsey Leanne.
3846	.... Christina.
1753	.... Jerry.
3017	.... Michael Anthony.
3845	.... Natasha.
3016	.... Nolan Dewrell.
3003	.... Raymond.
3013	.... Terry Lee.
3814	CHIASSON, Charlene.
831	CHILDS, Jean.
1392	CHOI, Bok Suk.
2619	CHRZASTEK BASS, Joseph Blaze.
1330	CHRZASTEK, Donna.
3923	.... Jonathan Russell.
3601	CHRZASTEK-BASS, Emberlynn Crystal.
1302	CLARK, Tamara Leigh.
2095	.... Terri S..
2445	.... Tracy.
227	.... Vera.
132	CLARY, Dennis William.

Ref.	Name (Relationship)
598	CLARY, John D.
599	.... Mary Frances.
597	.... William D.
3294	CLAUSER, Ella Alesia.
3841	CLAYTON, Phillip.
717	CLEMENTS, Joyce.
1406	CLIFTON, Lee.
233	CLOSON, H..
3883	COBB, Aaron Florence.
1802	.... Annie Pearl.
3884	.... Anthony Joseph.
687	.... Bartlett Lorenzo.
472	.... Grover Cleveland.
3087	.... James Bartlett, Jr..
1804	.... James Bartlett, Sr..
3089	.... Martine Michelle.
1473	.... Terry Lee.
3091	.... Victoria Amanda.
2242	COBURN, Mary.
1380	COCKERHAM, Beth.
3607	COFFMAN, Cartur.
3606	.... Elijah.
2631	.... Gregory Cline.
1339	.... Jeffery Lee.
1609	COLEMAN, Sandra Elaine.
3894	COLLIER, Angelica Lynn.
3895	.... Christy Alayne.
3893	.... Jessie Lee.
3892	.... Joshua Dwayne.
3104	.... Rhonda Delaine.
3102	.... Robert Dwayne.
1811	.... Robert Dwayne.
65	COLLINS, Frances Elizabeth.
354	COLLINSWORTH, Joyce.
1776	COLVIN, Dollie.
960	COOK, Alfred, Jr..
3018	.... Alician Dian.
3457	.... Arnold Randall.
1754	.... Charles.
3966	.... Christopher M..
1190	.... Donna.
2287	.... Fenton Broome.
2432	.... Jason Wayne.
2161	.... Jennifer Nell.
2986	.... Karen.
3833	.... Kayla Michelle.
2991	.... Keith.
2993	.... Kenyon.
3832	.... Kenyon Kole.
3834	.... Kristopher Lynn.
1089	.... Linda.
2158	.... Lisa Marie.
3455	.... Rodney Fenton.
1735	.... Stanley.
2433	.... Terry Lynn.
1138	.... Thurman Paul.
2160	.... Yevette Lee.
1974	COON, Diane.
212	COOPER, Augusta.

Ref.	Name (Relationship)
1508	COOPER, Milli.
2938	CORNELL, Angela Kay.
1602	.... Randel Glenn.
3816	CORRIGAN, Kevin.
2422	COTTON, Jennifer Denise.
977	.... Mary Annice.
510	COULTER, Viola Ruth.
414	COURTNEY, Betty.
702	COVINGTON, Mattilene.
2661	COX, Carel Jeanette.
2659	.... Edward Clayton.
2657	.... June Lorraine.
1376	.... Leslie Clayton.
2145	CRABILL, April Lee.
1342	CRABTREE, Jackie Elaine.
2920	CRAWFORD, Mr..
2319	.... Anita Marie.
3462	.... Apryl Michelle.
707	.... Arlene.
3461	.... Ashlyn Morgan.
2864	.... Belinda.
1056	.... Betty Jean.
2320	.... Cheryl Lynn.
2313	.... Debbie.
2321	.... Deborah Ann.
3464	.... Dillon John.
1050	.... Edna Mae.
2310	.... Eugene.
1062	.... Gerald H.
1060	.... Glinda.
1054	.... Herbert L.
2322	.... Herbert, Jr..
1052	.... James Edmund.
3463	.... Jesse Tanner.
1058	.... John Dallas.
358	.... John Henry.
2328	.... John Kenneth.
2317	.... Juanita Gale.
1048	.... Lonnie.
2309	.... Lonnie Ray, Jr..
2308	.... Nancy Lee.
2318	.... Patricia Jane.
2312	.... Sandra.
2311	.... Tina.
1670	CREECH, Mr..
1871	.... Annis.
689	.... Jewel.
3431	.... Kerry Lynn.
2251	.... Ronnie.
2846	CREWS, Angie.
4028	.... Brayden Michael.
1519	.... James Harold.
2844	.... Michael Allen.
3739	.... Michael Bennett.
3741	.... Summer.
763	CROSBY, Baby.
184	.... T. Laban.
2019	CROSS, Billy.
829	.... Cecil.

Ref.	Name (Relationship)
2018	CROSS, Donna.
2017	.... Jerry.
202	.... Laura Elizabeth.
1130	CRUMPLER, Mr..
1113	CUMMINGS, Donna Ann.
1270	CUNNINGHAM, Matthew Wayne.
2173	CUPP, Dorothy Leigh.
966	.... James Charles.
2172	.... James Landre.
2170	.... Kimberly Ann.
3373	.... Lindsey Danielle.
1079	CURBELLO, Albert.
365	.... Albert Bartley.
1078	.... Joel Maurice.
596	CURTIS, Clifford M.
593	.... James Harold.
594	.... Thelma Olline.
131	.... William Chester.
804	CUSHING, Clyde L.
715	.... Cozette.
803	.... John Jefferson.
206	.... John Jefferson.
801	.... William D "Willie".
802	.... Woodrow.
1618	DANFORD, Johnny Mack.
2949	.... Randy.
1272	DANIELS, Tammy E..
2437	DANLEY, Michelle Lane.
1143	.... Mikeal Wayne.
2438	.... Sherry Denise.
1275	DARST, Josephine Anne.
2227	DAVIDSON, Edward.
3406	.... Elizabeth Ann.
789	.... Rachel.
290	DAVIS, Athen.
1046	.... Benjamin Franklin.
1607	.... Brenda.
777	.... Charlie C.
292	.... Elma.
293	.... Ethel Louise.
1044	.... Georgiann Isabel.
3416	.... Glenda Fay.
1043	.... Hazel Alita.
3418	.... J. W..
806	.... Jack Columbus.
910	.... James C.
807	.... James Rudalph.
1859	.... Janice Frances.
3956	.... John Aubrey.
288	.... John Sumpter.
72	.... John Walter.
208	.... Joseph Josh.
1818	.... Judy Louis.
285	.... Lena Mae.
908	.... Louvenia.
909	.... Marvette Faye.
289	.... Mirtice.
808	.... Nannie Ruth.
287	.... Nora.

Ref.	Name (Relationship)
1917	DAVIS, Rhonda.
1740	.... Shelia.
547	.... Stanislaw Edward.
1047	.... Terry Allen.
356	.... Troy.
1045	.... Troy, Jr..
286	.... Willie Ophellia.
2238	.... Winfred.
3033	DAW, Jimmy.
2182	DAWSON, Duane Allen, III.
972	.... Duane Allen, Jr..
1281	DAY, Barbara Elaine.
433	.... Cecil Larry.
1284	.... Cecil Larry, II.
2569	.... Christopher Stacy.
1285	.... George Anthony.
2691	.... Shirley.
2692	.... Shirley Ann.
1287	.... Tammy Joy.
2568	.... Timothy Patrick.
2249	DEAN, Rebecca.
3519	DEATON, Aaron Lee.
1711	.... Andy.
2435	.... Christopher John.
3520	.... Cory Eugene.
2466	DEGRAAF, Amanda Michelle.
2465	.... Jason Kyle.
1188	.... Jerry.
2660	DELS, Denise.
2577	DEMOCKER, Amy A.
1739	DEMORIS, Geraldine.
619	DESTIN, Leonard, III.
142	.... Leonard, Jr..
1648	.... Linda.
617	.... Mary Ellen.
1647	.... Sylvia.
3513	DEVANE, Ryan.
3686	DICKHUT, Christopher Randall.
2426	DIEGLEMAN, Barbara Renee.
2427	.... Bonnie Marie.
2429	.... Brian Scott.
1135	.... Don P..
2428	.... Rhondel London.
1929	DILMORE, Larry.
3239	.... Nathaniel Hayes.
3240	.... Timothy.
3372	DIMARIA, Jackson Phillip.
2171	.... John Paul Victor, Jr..
3371	.... Sarah Lindsay.
2439	DISHMAN, Angela Crystal.
1146	.... Roger.
1783	DIXON, Dale.
3685	.... David.
610	DOBBS, Katie Vera.
3757	DONALDSON, Taylor Lynn.
1462	DORMAN, Donna.
1425	DORTCH, Ms..
3348	DOTSON, Amanda Lynn.
3345	.... Amber Nicole.

Ref.	Name (Relationship)
3344	DOTSON, Dixie Lee.
399	.... Glenn.
1192	.... Gloria Sue.
950	.... Jerry.
3346	.... Morgan Bailey.
3347	.... Neil.
2132	.... Ted.
2134	.... Tracy.
1623	DOUGLAS, Albert R., Jr..
588	.... Albert R., Sr..
4016	.... Caylee.
4015	.... Courtney.
1924	.... Jeanie Lorene.
1624	.... Jo Carrol.
1010	.... Johnnie Mae.
3665	.... Johnny Lamar.
2992	.... Kathy.
2798	.... Sandra Elaine.
3131	DOWNS, Alan.
1832	.... Carl.
1320	DOZIER, Austin Lamar.
2613	.... John Tyler.
2614	.... Kathryn Rebecca.
572	DRIGGERS, Lorretta Voncile.
1584	DUBOSE, Doris Ann.
1266	.... Tracie Renea.
1468	DUCKER, Peggy.
1322	DUCOTE, Cheri Lynn.
1483	DUKE, Barbara Sue.
1001	DUKES WARD, Allie Mae.
2237	DUKES, Alta.
2239	.... Audi Mae.
1003	.... Hubert.
3248	DULIN, Ike Collins, III.
3361	DUNLAP, Gabrie Coen.
2149	.... Will.
3810	DUPUY, Marcie.
775	DURDEN, Eva Irene.
3228	DYE, Devin.
3015	EDGE, Ann.
3889	EDMONDSON, Brock Martin.
3888	.... Ethan Jack.
3094	.... Jason Lee.
3890	.... Jason Wyatt.
1807	.... Jerome Aubray.
3891	.... Laken Grace.
3886	.... Logan Swaney.
3092	.... Michael Jerome.
3887	.... Zackary Michael.
1882	EDWARDS, Barbara Ann.
1868	.... Billie Wayne.
3221	.... Brittany.
704	.... Correne.
1881	.... Diane.
3174	.... Donald Eugene.
701	.... Early.
1860	.... Edna Pearl.
706	.... Ervin Hartley.
3167	.... Eugene.

Wilson Bass

Ref.	Name (Relationship)
699	EDWARDS, Harry.
1862	.... Harry, Jr..
3165	.... James.
3904	.... James Murray.
3172	.... James Murriell.
694	.... Janie.
2402	.... Jerry.
3169	.... Jerry.
692	.... Josephine E.
3177	.... Judith Ann.
3166	.... Kenneth.
1864	.... Lesley Riley, Jr..
169	.... Leslie Riley, Sr..
1880	.... Linda.
1866	.... Margarette.
1869	.... Martha Jane.
1870	.... Murray.
703	.... Murry.
3162	.... Pauline.
3160	.... Rhett.
3161	.... Rick.
696	.... Rossa.
3168	.... Roy.
3164	.... Ruby Carol.
3176	.... Sheryl Diane.
3905	.... Steven Murriell.
1477	EILAND, Christine Reba.
3681	EKHOMM, Lindsey.
3682	.... Mark.
2765	.... Ralph Donald.
1038	ELDRIDGE, Darlene.
3063	ELLIOT, Angela Rene.
2567	ELLIS, Cliff.
2155	.... Sandra Estelle.
987	ELMORE, Bobby Wayne.
2211	.... Clayborn Lee.
2210	.... John Thomas Wade.
2212	.... Robert L..
1759	.... Virginia.
2689	EPLEY, Chuck.
1199	ERMY, Anthony F..
2476	.... Daniel P..
2475	.... Michael A..
3655	ERWIN, Kalise.
146	ETHERIDGE, Lucy L.
159	.... Maggie Lou.
4017	EVANS, Anna.
3668	.... Crystal Gail.
3666	.... George William, III.
2752	.... George William, Jr..
2048	.... Jim.
3670	.... Rebecca Lynn.
3115	EVERIDGE, Chris.
1821	.... Porter.
852	FAIRCLOTHE, Prudie Lee.
2854	FAIRMAN, Barbara Ann.
3180	FARMER, Phillip.
1227	FARRAR, Celia Anne.
876	FARRIS, Dorothy Victoria.

Ref.	Name (Relationship)
3394	FERGUSON, Lena LaRae.
2203	.... Michael C..
3664	FINDLEY, Delores.
2751	.... Doug.
2956	.... Michael Rena.
1630	.... Norman Russell.
2957	.... Robby Lynn.
2955	.... Troy Lynne.
3340	FLEMING, Alex.
944	.... Eugene.
3110	.... Jeffery.
2128	.... Karen Lorine.
2126	.... Laura Lenelle.
2123	.... Phillip Eugene.
3339	.... Phillip Logan.
899	FLICKINGER, Betty Jean.
1719	FLOYD, Alice.
284	.... Bennett Abner.
69	.... James A..
3397	.... Kenneth A., III.
2208	.... Kenneth A., Jr..
3676	FONTENOT, Dustin.
59	FORMAN, Mr..
1939	FOWLER FRANTZ, Candy M..
3266	FOWLER, Mr..
2005	.... Mr..
820	.... Dallas Clinton.
3267	.... Stanley Ray.
1710	FOXWORTH, Mary Jane.
653	.... Robert Lehmon.
1709	.... Ruby Mildred.
1780	FRANKLIN, Arlee.
3044	.... Leigh Ann.
360	.... Margaret Charity.
3046	.... Tracey Lynn.
453	FREDRICK, Henry Eugene.
1346	.... Marilyn.
1348	.... Mark Forman.
1347	.... Martin Eugene.
446	.... Vivian Jo.
2246	FREEMAN, Lyndell.
3955	FULLER, Andrew Sery.
3417	.... Bobby.
3954	.... Jessica Daniel.
1426	FUQUA, Deward.
1427	.... Evelyn.
484	.... Frank A..
915	.... Jewel Gertrude.
1742	.... JoAnn.
2571	.... Marlee.
2564	.... Suzy.
749	FUTUAL, Margaret.
3006	GAINEY, Darrell.
3843	.... Nicole.
1747	.... Ola Mae.
3842	.... Waylon.
1585	GAMBELLS, Barbara.
1479	GANUS, Betty June.
2726	GARNER, Jim.

Ref.	Name (Relationship)
4009	GARRETT, Allen.
2528	.... Chelsi Nicole.
3658	.... Joshua.
2446	.... Lana Joyce Posey.
2444	.... Lynn Jesse, Jr..
1165	.... Lynn Jesse, Sr..
2280	.... Nellie June.
2282	.... Peggy Joyce.
1019	.... Thomas Jefferson.
2278	.... Thomas Jefferson, Jr..
1460	GARVIN, Carolyn.
165	.... Elzy Henderson.
1765	.... Laverne Fay.
1767	.... Lonia.
671	.... Nancy Christian.
678	.... Odessa.
677	.... Ollie.
675	.... Sherman.
1766	.... Therese.
673	.... Willier.
1763	.... Yvonne.
1310	GIANETTO, John.
1771	GIBSON, Kathryn.
3117	GILLEY, Carol.
3130	.... Deborah.
1824	.... Donnell.
3119	.... Gary.
3120	.... Gloria.
3129	.... Kathy.
3118	.... Mike.
1830	.... Roy Frank.
3116	.... Sheila.
786	GILLIS, Alton.
3973	.... Elisha Levi.
3504	.... Eric.
3974	.... Ezekiel Isaiah.
122	.... Katie Mae.
2288	GILMEN, Barbara Payline.
2291	.... Deborah Leigh.
3458	.... Nicholas Tyler.
1025	.... Russell Lee.
2290	.... Russell Lee, Jr..
1875	GILMORE, Janie.
2932	GINDLESPERGER, Andrew Grant.
1595	.... Dale Allen, Jr..
577	.... Dale Allen, Sr..
2934	.... Derek Ashley.
3800	.... Mason Allen.
3802	.... Merritt Anderson.
3801	.... Miles Avery.
2930	.... Mitchell Allen.
3535	GLADSON, Edith Marie.
2515	.... Nathan Michael.
2928	GLIDEWELL, Christy Lee.
3798	.... Daughton.
1593	.... David.
2927	.... David Brent.
3797	.... Jayden.
1091	GLOVER, Dena.

Ref.	Name (Relationship)
1793	GLOVER, Gloria Jean.
300	GODWIN, George Henry.
188	.... Lucy.
187	.... Nancy G..
488	.... Nell.
34	.... Samuel.
1744	GOLDEN, Judy.
1778	GOLSON, Faye.
2281	GOMILLION, Sherward.
2107	GOOD, Donna Lee.
198	GOODLETT, Charles Henry.
787	.... Lucille.
3796	GOODSON, Cory Ryan.
2926	.... Michael Dewayne.
3795	.... Michael Tyler.
3916	GORUM, Harper Kate.
3206	.... Jeffrey Douglas.
3917	.... Stella Ruth.
4048	GRANTHAM, Emma-Leigh Katherine.
4046	.... Michael Layne.
2617	GREENE, Mr..
3230	.... Whitney.
2758	GREER, Charles.
2544	GREGORY, Britney Suzanne.
120	.... Charles Augustus, Sr..
548	.... Corinne.
542	.... Garvin.
543	.... Henry Ervin.
545	.... Juliatte C.
544	.... Lloyd Edison.
546	.... Martha Kathleen.
2067	GRESKO, Mr..
3292	.... Chastity Deannia Inez.
2065	.... Edward Cecil.
2066	.... Etta Celia.
2060	.... Myrna E.
3291	.... Ronald Kay.
2063	.... Ronald Kay.
887	.... William.
2061	.... William Mark.
2933	GRIDER, Amanda Leigh.
411	GRIES, Carol.
569	GRIFFIN, Mr..
1095	.... Teresa.
1193	GRIFFITH, Carl Manuel.
2472	.... Joanna Nichole.
405	.... Loretta.
367	.... Louise.
401	.... Otis C.
1194	.... Roger Joseph.
1195	.... Ronald Lawrence.
2474	.... Stacie Renee.
1196	.... Stephen Dale.
1198	.... Theresa Ann.
2870	GRISSETT, Keith Lavon.
1549	.... Kenneth Lavon.
2869	.... Marquita Lynn.
2868	.... Ritchie Dean.
1798	GULETT, Brenda Kay.

Ref.	Name (Relationship)
745	GUNNER, Annie Ruth.
2006	GUNNIS, Ms..
628	GUNTER, Charles Clyde.
499	.... Cleo.
155	.... James Ottis.
629	.... Otto Lee.
3497	GUTHRIE, Jacqueline Marie.
2388	.... Kenneth Allen.
3496	.... Mary Elizabeth.
905	GUYMON, Ronald Perkins.
590	GWIN, Jerry W.
1877	HAGCE, Teresa.
997	HAIR, Sara Ann.
1366	HALE, Mary Elizabeth.
2142	.... Nancy.
3646	HALL, Greg.
2739	.... Jerry.
2737	.... Jimmy.
3645	.... Kim.
291	.... Lottie Johnson.
61	.... Matilda.
1444	.... Opal.
2664	HAMILTON, Jimmy.
736	HAMMOCK, Margaret Faye.
3643	HANCOCK, Hailey.
2724	.... James Robert.
3642	.... James Ryne.
3640	.... Jerrod Randal.
3641	.... Jordan Robert.
2159	HANKINS, Chris.
3368	.... Kaliee.
1976	HARBUCK, Allen.
756	.... Arnold.
1973	.... Frankie.
1975	.... Johnnie.
2036	HARDCASTLE, Edmond.
3274	.... Edmond, Jr..
3281	.... Greta.
3279	.... Pamela.
3276	.... Susan.
3278	.... Timothy.
462	HARE, Ora Della.
2364	HARGABUS, Teresa.
946	HARNESS, Judith.
3903	HARPER, F. Nicole.
3156	.... Hershel E..
3902	.... Jeremy W..
3901	.... Joshua B..
882	HARREL, John Henry.
220	HARRELSON, Bessie.
3704	.... Carolina.
2791	.... Charles Rhett.
2786	.... Cindy Rene.
3705	.... CJ.
3699	.... Erica.
504	.... George Rufus.
3709	.... Hannah Elizabeth.
2803	.... Jacqueline Carolyn.
2801	.... James Ricky.

Ref.	Name (Relationship)
3707	HARRELSON, James Travis.
3706	.... Jeffery Allen Douglas.
3710	.... Jessica Sueann.
3700	.... Leigh Ann.
2795	.... Michael Rex.
1475	.... Olen Rex.
3703	.... Peyton Michelle.
2800	.... Rae Suzanne.
1478	.... Ralph Marlon.
1480	.... Ramond Teuell.
2797	.... Randall Keith.
3708	.... Randi Nicole.
2783	.... Regina.
2804	.... Renda Sue.
2780	.... Rhonda Lynn.
2806	.... Rita Ann.
2784	.... Robert Olen.
1482	.... Ronnie Ray.
2789	.... Russel Allen.
901	HARRIS, Bernadette.
3422	.... Cindy Renae.
897	.... David Joseph.
1191	.... Debra.
1136	.... Donald.
2805	.... James.
3957	.... James Brandon.
3420	.... James Edward.
2068	.... Janis Mary.
2240	.... Jimmy Junior.
902	.... John Paul.
278	.... Joseph Doyle.
895	.... Joseph Riley.
3958	.... Krystal Dianna.
894	.... Leo Patrick.
900	.... Mary Etta.
896	.... Mary Patricia.
898	.... Michael James.
2069	.... Nancy Kathryn.
903	.... Robert Thomas.
1560	.... Saundra Gail.
893	.... Vincent.
1848	.... Virginia.
1107	HARRISON, Betty Jean.
3633	.... Brittney Lauren.
3632	.... Charles Brian.
2552	.... Deidre.
1813	.... Earl.
3112	.... Hank.
3631	.... James Brett.
2718	.... James Marvin.
3106	.... Michael Earl.
1358	.... Minnie M.
203	HART, Ada Alabama.
199	.... Alice Rebecca.
780	.... Allen Trammel.
776	.... Birdie H.
39	.... Columbus Daniel.
616	.... Dewey H.
805	.... Eleanor D..

Ref.	Name (Relationship)
773	HART, Ellen.
1983	.... Eugene.
138	.... George W..
609	.... Grover Cleveland.
614	.... Ina May.
613	.... Ivey W.
1985	.... James B.
778	.... James Travis.
194	.... James William.
196	.... John C.
1987	.... Julia A.
785	.... Jynelle.
772	.... Lella Mae.
782	.... Leonard V..
1984	.... Mabel Erline.
615	.... Maggie.
74	.... Margaret Josephine.
612	.... Marshall.
207	.... Mary Nora.
771	.... Maudie Aline.
205	.... Nancy Lena.
76	.... Rob.
201	.... Rubin Richard.
1986	.... Sherley L.
197	.... Virginia.
784	.... W C.
774	.... William Daniel.
1982	.... William Daniel.
1178	HARVEY, Jada.
2790	HASLIP, Laura Jeanette.
101	HASSEL, Mamie Annie.
1429	HASSELL, Annie Maude.
924	.... Carol Jean.
316	.... Frank Pete.
927	.... Jerry Donald.
926	.... Jimmie Joe.
928	.... Sharon A.
1850	HATAWAY, Dave.
1055	HATCHCOCK, Peggy.
2147	HAVEARD, Joe.
3949	.... Joseph Edwin.
3357	.... Shaun Michelle.
750	HAWKINS, Betty.
463	.... Betty Jean.
2881	HAWKS, Amy.
1391	HAYERBERG, Pamela Jane.
658	HAYES, Mamie Lelie.
1014	.... Mamie Louise.
506	HEAD, Eileen.
1243	HEAL, Paul.
369	HEATH, Kathleen L.
482	HEDGEKOFF, Kathleen.
1826	HELMS, Betty.
3226	.... Cody.
424	.... T. D..
1443	HENDERSON, Annice.
995	.... Bobby D..
3211	.... Bret Thomas.
2834	.... Chad.

Ref.	Name (Relationship)
3035	HENDERSON, Danae.
2830	.... Donna Katrise.
2248	.... Emily.
2833	.... Eric.
3215	.... Erin Lajune.
1494	.... Fredrick.
342	.... Helen.
1496	.... Judith Lynn.
3213	.... Kyle Jordan.
2222	.... Laura Rebecca.
2124	.... Linda.
418	.... Mary Elizabeth.
3919	.... Mason Thomas.
1498	.... Phillip.
1492	.... Redessa L.
2223	.... Rhonda Leigh.
2828	.... Robin Denise.
1773	.... Ronnie.
2224	.... Sonia Denise.
3209	.... Tera Ashleigh.
724	.... Thomas Harold, I.
1907	.... Thomas Harold, II.
1282	.... William Dwight.
512	.... William Turner.
3305	HENDRIX, Ms..
3943	.... Damion T..
3944	.... Elijah.
758	.... Katheryn Elizabeth.
979	HENLEY, Betty.
1335	HENRY, Brenda.
953	.... Eloise.
1505	.... Karren Regina.
936	.... Nellie.
3380	HERRIN, Mr./Ms..
3382	.... Mr./Ms..
3375	.... Mr./Ms..
3377	.... Mr./Ms..
3379	.... Mr./Ms..
3376	.... Mr./Ms..
3374	.... Mr./Ms..
2175	.... Mr..
3381	.... Mr./Ms..
2179	.... Mr..
795	HERRING, Gladys.
1491	.... Rhonda.
2078	HERRINGTON, Jimmie T.
2079	.... Joseph A.
2076	.... Larry Bradley.
912	.... Orange Arnold.
3214	HICKMAN, McLean.
2408	HICKS, Pamela.
1879	HILL, Janet Sylvia.
3776	HIMES, Cameron.
3777	.... Kendrick.
2899	.... Kevin Vance.
2554	HOFFMAN, Melanie.
1611	HOGAN, Ansel.
2946	.... Tyler Ansel.
624	HOGEBOOM, Andrew Gay.

Ref.	Name (Relationship)
4	HOGG, Mary Elizabeth.
2866	HOLLAND, Danny Ward.
1442	.... Fannie Merle.
3764	.... Hannah Elizabeth.
3765	.... Heather Lee.
3763	.... Hope Danielle.
339	HOLLOWAY, Mary L..
3864	HOLMES, Dewey Wendell, III.
3064	.... Dewey Wendell, Jr..
1791	.... Dewey Wendell, Sr..
3066	.... Melinda Dianna.
3232	.... Micgayle.
3068	.... Patricia Gail.
3086	HOMAN, Sonia Darlene.
857	HOOKS, Inez.
2477	.... Nathinal.
1204	.... Roger.
602	HOOMES, Nannie Jewl.
2590	HOOPER, Christopher Lindsay.
2589	.... William Adam.
1298	.... William F..
1117	HOPE, Brenda F..
1836	.... Rochella.
1294	HOPKINS, Kimberly Layne.
1293	.... Yvonna Christine.
1394	HORN, Gerald Van.
266	HORTON, Minnie.
50	HOWARD, Ella Melissa.
48	.... Florence Missouri.
747	.... Jeanette.
2452	.... Stefanie Marshann.
1171	.... William Jesse.
1741	HOWELL, Dorothy.
713	.... L. Ruth.
426	.... Roberta.
355	HUCKABA, Addie Irene.
3508	.... Austen James.
3979	.... Bentley Greyson.
3500	.... Brittany Nash.
2382	.... Connie Arlene.
2380	.... Craig Alan.
1111	.... Earl Flyn.
2403	.... Earl Flyn, II.
1106	.... Edward Ervin.
353	.... Eugene.
3510	.... Harlee Fay.
375	.... James Edgar.
1102	.... James Harold.
3509	.... Jayden Earl.
1114	.... Jimmy David.
1041	.... John Russell.
2381	.... Karen Elizabeth.
2383	.... Myra Lorraine.
2379	.... Randy Michael.
1042	.... Robin Rena.
3511	.... Samantha Diane.
2394	.... Shonda Denise.
2398	.... Tiresa Lynn.
1040	.... Willie Eugene.

Ref.	Name (Relationship)
3448	HUCKABAA, Aaron R.
3425	.... Angelea.
3479	.... Ashli Chere.
1008	.... Baby.
2250	.... Beverly Jean.
3473	.... Billy J.
3430	.... Bobby Wayne.
3413	.... Brenda.
3962	.... Brent Randall.
3961	.... Brett Allen.
3450	.... Bridget Rochell.
2260	.... Carolyn Dianne.
2230	.... Charlene.
3427	.... Christi Lynn.
3434	.... Christopher Allen.
3449	.... Ciji.
1104	.... Clara Mae.
3478	.... Crystal Lynn.
2235	.... Curtis.
1006	.... Daris Lee.
3472	.... David Lee.
3474	.... Deborah Sue.
3475	.... Demas James.
2362	.... Demas Mark.
3414	.... Dennis.
3415	.... Derek.
2266	.... Donald Earl.
1011	.... Donald Travis.
2359	.... Donnie Lee.
2262	.... Dorthy Jean.
1013	.... Earl C..
2273	.... Eddie Ray.
2367	.... Edgar Hugh.
2247	.... Gordon.
3428	.... Gordon Heath.
3423	.... Gregory Randall.
1009	.... Henry Clayton.
2263	.... Henry Clayton, Jr..
514	.... Homer.
2241	.... Hubet C..
2234	.... Jack Berry.
2236	.... James Larry.
2369	.... James Rudolf.
3964	.... Jamison.
3477	.... Jason Hugh.
2228	.... Jerry Wayne.
3959	.... Joseph Michael.
3433	.... Kayla Ann.
1005	.... L. B..
2271	.... Laura Lynn.
1004	.... Lener Bell.
3426	.... Lesia Nicole.
2261	.... Linda Joyce.
3411	.... Marsha.
2232	.... Martin Van Buren, Jr..
1000	.... Martin Van Buren, Sr..
2226	.... Mary Evelyn.
1109	.... Mary Opal.
2245	.... Oscar Cleveland.

Ref.	Name (Relationship)
2357	HUCKABAA, Peggy Lee.
2365	.... Phyllis Ann.
2243	.... Randall Ike.
2268	.... Redda Kay.
1017	.... Robert Thomas.
2253	.... Rusty Lamar.
3963	.... Shelby.
2264	.... Teresa Jane.
3960	.... Tessa Leann.
3408	.... Tina.
2275	.... Tracy Lamar.
3412	.... William.
91	.... William Benjamin.
346	.... William Martin.
1015	.... William Ray.
3403	HUDSON, Brett Aubrey.
3950	.... Dutton Lee.
3014	.... Sandra.
3857	HUGGINS, Sterling Jo.
3865	HUNT, Dillon Gene.
3090	.... Gary.
3866	.... Trenton Wayne.
3067	.... Wendell Gene.
3885	.... Zackery Tyler.
210	HUTCHESON, Liston Thomas.
811	HUTCHISON, Harold A.
810	.... Harris G.
812	.... Myrtle E.
809	.... William E.
586	HUTTO, Avis.
114	.... Emmie Cornelia.
3405	INABINETT, Brayden John.
3404	.... Dallas Lawson.
3402	.... Kayla Lynn.
2217	.... Michael Todd.
3781	INGRAM, Courtney.
2363	.... Deborah.
4035	.... Joshua Brody.
3782	.... Joshua Tyler.
2906	.... Tony.
1352	IRELAND, Catherine Nadine.
3627	JACKSON, Mr..
1966	.... Alex Neal.
1958	.... Carson.
3630	.... Christy.
1968	.... Dale O'Marr.
3628	.... Danny.
3629	.... David.
2705	.... Deborah.
1967	.... Debra Lynn.
2706	.... Dewayne.
584	.... Elizabeth Ann.
1969	.... Eric James.
307	.... Eula May.
753	.... Florine Jackson.
1433	.... Frank.
751	.... Haward James, MSgt.
748	.... Hillary Dalton.
1961	.... Hillary Kim.

Ref.	Name (Relationship)
1956	JACKSON, Hollis Mitchell, Jr..
744	.... Hollis Mitchell, Sr..
746	.... Horris Carson.
1016	.... Iver June.
1960	.... James Dalton.
1970	.... Kimberly K..
1957	.... Loretta.
2707	.... Louis.
1954	.... Martha Judson.
180	.... Quillie.
1963	.... Richard Tad.
1962	.... Richard Todd.
1965	.... Tammy Gayle.
2547	.... Taylor Nicole.
1959	.... Tony Ray.
1964	.... Tracy Allen.
2903	.... Willis Gene.
2729	JACOBS, Donna.
1440	.... John Mandrak.
2727	.... Ronald.
2725	.... Sherry.
2728	.... Tim.
1071	JAKUBCIN, George.
2822	JAMES, Mike.
3057	JAYNES, Mr..
3859	.... Tyler.
3879	JENSEN, Edward Clifton.
3083	.... Eric.
3880	.... Matthew Alan.
3881	.... Paula Marian Lynn.
157	JERAULD, James E, Capt..
630	.... James E, Jr..
3187	JERNIGAN, Britton.
705	.... Burris Clyde.
3189	.... Darren.
1933	.... David.
3245	.... Ethan Tyler.
1566	.... Jennifer.
3246	.... Kylee.
1876	.... Larry.
3186	.... Lindsey.
3188	.... Melissa.
3242	.... Myranda Nichole.
3244	.... Natalie Danielle.
1872	.... Phyllis.
1878	.... Roger.
1874	.... Ronnie.
352	JINKS, James T..
1215	JO, Mary.
2039	JOHNNIE, Ms..
855	.... Clarence.
4002	JOHNS, Hunter Demond.
1167	.... Jeffery Alan.
2448	.... Jeffery Alan, Jr..
2449	.... Joseph Aaron.
4055	.... Sawyer Allen.
3848	JOHNSON, Aaron.
380	.... Addie Lee.
537	.... Addie Lee Johnson.

Ref.	Name (Relationship)
305	JOHNSON, Autrey Lewis.
538	.... Bernice.
540	.... Bert Jerome.
1031	.... Billie Jean.
3032	.... Carrol.
1851	.... Charles Mitchell.
3254	.... Christopher, Dr..
1949	.... Christy.
1847	.... Cleveland.
3034	.... Crista.
3041	.... Dallas.
1843	.... Dalton Lee.
3039	.... Danny.
1948	.... Dudley Franklin.
739	.... Dudley Sadie, Dr..
3141	.... Elaine.
695	.... Fletcher.
1845	.... Frances Elaine.
1777	.... Gary Lynn.
3043	.... Gary Lynn, Jr..
534	.... Gussie Josephine.
3137	.... Hardy Lee.
1839	.... Heyward Ivin.
1852	.... Jean Ray.
1768	.... Joel.
178	.... John Henry.
1946	.... John Taft, M.D., Dr..
3256	.... Julia Adele.
741	.... Kenneth Ray, Dr..
3139	.... Lesley Mitchel.
1841	.... Lewis Edward.
3140	.... Lewis Edward, Jr..
2115	.... Lois Anette.
1775	.... Luvert.
1542	.... Marcus Gene.
541	.... Martha Lou.
430	.... Mary Louise.
223	.... Mattie Lucile.
3617	.... Melissa Kay.
743	.... Monia Ruth.
118	.... Morgan Jerome.
1952	.... Nancy Ann.
1769	.... Nick.
1795	.... Patricia Ann.
3138	.... Patrisha Ann.
3146	.... Patrisha Lee.
2082	.... Paula Jean.
2670	.... Raymon.
3619	.... Raymon Brian.
1849	.... Roseliner.
940	.... Roy H..
3937	.... Roy Taft.
1951	.... Sally.
1772	.... Sheila.
676	.... Unogar.
679	.... Walun Nick.
918	.... Wayne Carroll.
536	.... Willie Morgan.
2518	JOINER, Conny Lynn.

Ref.	Name (Relationship)
2647	JONES, Barbara.
907	.... Betty Ann.
2334	.... Connie Denise.
1448	.... Fay Agnes.
1069	.... Horace Emmete.
2696	.... James.
1745	.... Linda Lee.
2333	.... Theresa Darlyne.
3233	JORDAN, Annette Eula.
1908	.... Carol Jane.
191	.... Della.
85	.... Emily Estelle.
3029	.... Gail.
190	.... Henry.
189	.... Ida.
1922	.... Jay.
37	.... John Elbert.
193	.... Mary.
2100	.... Mary Belinda.
3031	.... Melissa Glyn.
35	.... Robert Francis.
1764	.... Roland.
3030	.... Ronald Sherman.
413	JORGENSON, Kay.
518	JOSEY, Ms..
2299	JOYNER, Kathy Renee.
1402	KAIN, Bruce R.
849	KEELS, Lola Mae.
2000	KELLEY, Mr..
1996	.... Barbara Gene.
794	.... Columbus Daniel.
791	.... Daniel.
1988	.... Eloise.
788	.... Fred Columbus.
1995	.... Fred Ronald.
1997	.... George D.
200	.... George Washington.
1999	.... James.
793	.... John.
1993	.... Joyce Marie.
1551	.... Louise.
797	.... Mildred Hazel.
1998	.... Patricia Ann.
792	.... Rubie L.
1990	.... Ruth Hazel.
790	.... William Allen.
1991	.... Wynelle D.
3193	KEMP, Cheryl Anne.
2254	KENDRIX, Dorthy Ann.
964	KENNEDY, Judy Gail.
3324	.... Kristen Nicole.
3325	.... Stephanie Michelle.
2112	.... V. W..
1404	KENNEL, Richard.
1770	KENNEY, Kathryn.
3953	KERVIN, Corbrey.
3951	.... Dana.
3407	.... Guy.
3952	.... Patrick.

Ref.	Name (Relationship)
1242	KILCREASE, Angelia Renee.
1238	.... George Stephen.
423	.... James Woodrow.
1239	.... Kathleen Ann.
2114	.... Patricia Ann.
1241	.... Phillip Wayne.
3799	KILPATRICK, Caden.
2929	.... Jerry.
1382	KILPRATRIE, Thelina Gail.
3439	KIMBRIL, Andrew Lucas.
3436	.... Daniel Lamar.
3440	.... Grace Loraine.
1007	.... Homer.
3437	.... Joseph Lokesh.
3438	.... Samuel Lakshaw.
2255	.... Sandra Elaine.
2258	.... Timmy Lamar.
2936	KING, April Ann.
1251	.... Dorothy.
1598	.... James B.
1286	.... Joyce.
3689	.... Justin Lee.
1450	.... Opal Louise.
2772	.... Wesley Darryl.
3688	.... Wesley Daryl, II.
3690	.... Zachary Ryan.
107	KINLAW, Alice.
1233	KINMAN, Gary Glenn.
2498	.... Heather Amanda.
1906	KINSAUL, Benjamin Doyle.
3207	.... Hunter Doyle.
3205	.... Kayla.
3208	.... Rollin Benjamin.
82	KIRKLIN, John.
1716	KNIPP, Bill.
2982	.... Michael Henry Knipp.
1306	KNOWLES, Jeffery Ted.
1653	KOHR, Mr./Ms..
1652	.... Patricia Tracie.
632	.... Rex Ray.
1384	KOVAL, John Joseph.
2668	.... Joseph Kenneth.
3580	KOZAK, Dylan.
2562	.... Jerry.
3579	.... Nicholas.
1799	KUCERA, Judith A..
2057	LABOVE, Juanita.
1212	LAHAMMANN, Larry.
1622	LAKOTOS, Vic.
3915	LAMB, Brodie Lawson.
3202	.... John Joe.
3008	LANDINGHAM, Alan.
3844	.... Brittany.
2101	LANDIS, Tamara Sue.
1049	LANGLEY, Genevieve.
2662	LANGSTON, Ricky Allen.
3289	LASKER, Mr./Ms..
3288	.... Mr./Ms..
884	.... Mr..

Ref.	Name (Relationship)
3290	LASKER, Mr..
2058	.... Mr..
3287	.... Mr..
1884	LASSITER, Jimmy.
1591	.... Richard Dewight.
273	LAUGHLIN, Hazel Mae.
1515	LAW, Mr./Ms..
1514	.... Mr./Ms..
1517	.... Mr./Ms..
1516	.... Mr./Ms..
522	.... Cecil Athaniel.
521	.... Sarah Clyde.
2807	LAWSON, Carl Marvin, Jr..
721	.... Catherine.
2218	.... Karen Lynn.
573	.... Mary Emma.
991	.... Marzette Alford.
2216	.... Sandra Dianne.
1172	LAZZARO, Mr..
1408	LEAK, Ronnie.
2746	LEE, Allen Jack.
1755	.... Aubrey.
3657	.... Casey.
4007	.... Chrislyn Skyler Shyann.
2815	.... Christine.
4004	.... Christopher Allen, Jr..
3654	.... Christopher Allen, Sr..
4005	.... Corey Dewayne.
3999	.... DeAnna Michelle.
3331	.... Jason.
4001	.... Kaitlin Labecca.
271	.... Katherine Gladys.
1582	.... Kenneth E.
2116	.... Leonard.
2901	.... Lori Nicole.
3332	.... Nathan.
4006	.... Shaun Even.
2904	.... Tanner.
4008	.... Tony Kyler.
1155	LEFEBVRE, Gary.
3386	LEGER, Jason Sloan.
1925	LEGG, Monette.
2939	LEHMANN, Clay.
3532	LEONARD, Mr./Ms..
2501	.... Mr..
3593	LETURGEY, Cory Joe.
3993	.... Lilith Ella.
2582	.... Ondrea.
2649	LEWIS, Alvin Donnald.
3614	.... Brook Renee.
1075	.... Judith Ann.
3350	.... Kenneth Demon.
3947	.... Kenneth Renee.
2763	.... Patricia Smith.
1497	.... Ronnie.
2832	.... Stephanie.
2447	LINAM, Joel.
2462	LINCOLN, Elizabeth Annelle.
1182	.... John Richard.

Ref.	Name (Relationship)
2461	LINCOLN, John Stephen.
56	LINDSEY, Wes.
2740	LITTLE, Mr..
1673	.... Mr..
2974	.... Chester Dale.
646	.... Flora Mavis.
1700	.... James Calvin.
2975	.... James Curtis.
2977	.... Karen Regina.
2976	.... Lanney Ray.
2360	.... Shiela.
3163	LOCKE, Floyd.
2524	LOCKLAR, Traci.
2153	LOFTUS, Anna.
2703	LOGAN, Dianne.
1027	LOMBARD, Rhonda.
3697	LONG, Ashley.
3698	.... Jennifer Lynn.
2781	.... Sydney.
2376	LONOEL, Rebecca.
3299	LORD, Holly Christina.
563	LOVELL, Ellis.
1201	LOWERY, Kenny.
2799	.... Rebecca Ann.
3447	LUCAS, Amanda Dawn.
2272	.... Dan Howard.
3446	.... Lori.
2522	.... Mary Michelle.
1129	LURTON, Walter William.
2813	LYNN, Natasha.
3476	MACKO, Cora Marie.
2366	.... Mark.
2588	MACLAM, Bethany Marie.
1296	.... David Laverne.
2586	.... Stacie Ann.
1053	MADDEN, Ola Bell.
3804	MADDOX, Brodie James.
3803	.... Dalto Michael.
2937	.... Michael.
1134	MADRON, Ronnie.
4040	MAIN, Ms..
4038	.... Mr..
4039	.... Mr..
3824	.... Randy.
1276	MALPHRUS, Susan.
2220	MANCIL, Kelley Michelle.
2221	.... Mendy Leigh.
993	.... Thomas Randall.
2556	MANCUSO, Elizabeth.
1314	MANDELVILLE, John Richard.
2603	.... Matthew Tyler.
3747	MANGHAM, Mathew.
2851	.... Matthew.
3748	.... Michelle.
2940	MANN, Ashton Nicole.
1599	.... Barbara Jane.
1601	.... Betty Jean.
2942	.... Cole Michael.
2943	.... Dakota.

Ref.	Name (Relationship)
1605	MANN, Dennis Keith.
1608	.... Michael Wayne.
578	.... Otis RC.
2944	.... Piper.
2941	.... Seth Allen Mann.
1597	.... Sue Ann.
2945	.... Taylor.
1713	MANNING, Mr..
2499	MANRY, Bo.
1521	MAPES, Dora.
2760	MARAMAN, Mr..
846	MARCONTELL, Alford L.
621	MARLER, Aquilla.
1650	.... Aquilla Jr.
1649	.... Audrey.
144	.... George Sanford.
625	.... Madeline M.
623	.... Pricilla.
1299	MARTIN, Danna Elizabeth.
1297	.... Deborah Lee.
2593	.... Elizabeth Leigh.
2594	.... Whitney Danielle.
437	.... Willard Daniel.
1301	.... Willard Daniel, Jr..
3052	.... William Todd.
2316	MASON, Barbara Payline.
1051	.... Robert.
2314	.... Shirley.
2841	MATHENY, Vicky Renee.
2167	MATHIS, Robert Lee.
556	MAUD, Annie M.
338	MAUGHON, Eula Lee.
1613	MAUND, Amelia Delaine.
580	.... Columbus Franklin.
1610	.... Linda Fay.
1304	MCALEER, James.
2148	MCAULIFFE, Kevin.
3360	.... Kristen Leigh.
1421	MCCAIN, Ms..
1781	MCCARTY, Max.
3564	MCCARVER, Mackenzie Grace.
3565	.... Macon Reese.
2542	.... Zachary Reese.
1787	MCCLINTOCK, Emma Viola.
3838	MCCOMBS, Jessica.
3837	.... Joseph.
2998	.... Lionel.
2493	MCCORKLE, Allison.
529	MCCORQUODAL, Minnie Jewel.
1604	MCCOY, Patrick.
1785	MCCURLEY, Dorothy.
2674	.... Gary Allen.
3623	.... Joshua Adam.
3624	.... Towanna Joy.
3759	MCDADE, Jeremy.
1411	MCDONALD, Charles D.
2682	.... Junior.
2680	.... Lucille.
2679	.... Robert.

Ref.	Name (Relationship)
2681	MCDONALD, Voncille.
2352	MCGILL, Aaron.
2351	.... Anthony.
1097	.... James Anthony.
2502	MCGLAMERY, Amanda Ryan.
2503	.... Mychaelle Ann.
1237	.... Sidney T..
978	MCGLAUN, Bobby.
2225	.... Carol Ann.
994	.... Doris Irene.
2193	.... Erin.
998	.... Guinda.
3388	.... Holly.
340	.... Ineta.
87	.... James Egie Nardis.
333	.... James Hollie.
984	.... James Kenneth.
3395	.... James Kenneth, III.
2205	.... James Kenny, Jr..
2204	.... James Tony.
2188	.... Joel Ray.
990	.... Joyce Marie.
3396	.... Kimberly Ann.
996	.... Lamar Ray.
2192	.... Lee.
2207	.... Lisa Rena.
986	.... Margie Ree.
3387	.... Martial.
982	.... Mary Etta.
2189	.... Mike Dewayne.
341	.... Orbey Ray.
999	.... Orion Dewayne.
343	.... Orion T.
988	.... Patricia Ann.
2190	.... Randy Lamar.
980	.... Ruby Nell.
992	.... Sheila Dianne.
2201	.... Vickey Yvone.
337	.... Virgil Lee.
335	.... Willie Oscar.
492	MCGRAW, Auburn E..
2645	MCINTIRE, Denese.
1119	MCKEE, John Richard.
2055	MCKINNEY, Thomas.
3701	MCLEOD, Allison.
3702	.... Emily Brook.
2988	.... Jerry.
3830	.... Jonathan Eric.
1268	.... Linda Gail.
2787	.... Mochael.
3980	MCLNTYRE, Peyton Elise.
3982	MCMILLAN, Cameron Michael.
3983	.... Olivia Jean.
3179	MCNEAR, Michael.
3780	MCVAY, Ms..
2545	.... Alexander Jace.
3571	.... Baisley Renee.
3567	.... Braelyn Sadie.
3570	.... Brenton Mark Lane.

Ref.	Name (Relationship)
1264	MCVAY, David Micah.
3551	.... Ethan Michael.
3554	.... Garrett Wayne.
428	.... Gaston Durell.
3569	.... Hannah Marie.
2550	.... Jacob Daniel.
2525	.... Jeffery Michael.
2527	.... Jeremy Wayne.
1258	.... Joan Marie.
1271	.... Jonathan Mark.
2546	.... Joshua Mark.
3779	.... Loretta Voncile.
1255	.... Loyce Elaine.
2539	.... Malesha Nicole.
3552	.... Micah Runae.
1260	.... Michael Ray.
1269	.... Miriam Lois.
2541	.... Natalie Melinda.
2543	.... Nathan Jared.
1267	.... Nathaniel Joel.
3992	.... Nicholas Layne.
3566	.... Nolan Jared.
1256	.... Richard Wayne.
1262	.... Samuel Paul.
2514	.... Stacey Elaine.
2529	.... Stephanie Jane.
2530	.... Suzanne Lea.
2537	.... Talitha Renea.
3568	.... Westlynn Grace.
2902	.... William.
2025	MEAD, Linda.
2011	MEDOWS, Kathy Ann.
3813	MELVIN, Aaron.
1645	.... Bennie Margaret.
1643	.... Carolyn.
1641	.... Gwen.
3807	.... Julia.
2960	.... Merwyn T., I.
3809	.... Merwyn T., II.
1639	.... Odem Thomas, Jr., Capt..
618	.... Odem Thomas, Sr., Capt..
3811	.... Vincent J..
465	MERCER, Boone.
4003	.... Evan Kade.
1399	.... James B..
4056	.... Katalena Eloise.
1397	.... Mary Margaret.
1503	MERREL, Joann.
508	MERRILL, Clipp F.
3421	MERRITTE, Rebecca.
3401	MESSICK, Amber Maria.
1249	.... Charles Manuel.
2213	.... James Edward.
989	.... Ricard Edward.
2215	.... Richard Brian.
2508	.... Roberta Ruth.
2507	.... Russell Eastman Bass.
2948	MILES, Brian.
1616	.... David.

Wilson Bass

Ref.	Name (Relationship)
2947	MILES, Mary.
654	MILLER, Edward L..
1712	.... Mary Deborah.
2143	.... Patti.
1714	.... William Michael.
1792	MILLS, Charles Earl.
685	.... Charles Oresta.
3076	.... Daniel Edward.
3082	.... Darla Lynn.
3075	.... Debbie Diane.
1797	.... Donell Franklin.
3080	.... Donell Joseph.
3078	.... Donna Kay.
1790	.... Evelyn Juanita.
1794	.... Gene Verlon.
3058	.... James Allen.
3061	.... John Douglas.
3862	.... Johnathan David.
3863	.... Jordan Nonovon.
3062	.... Joseph Donald.
3860	.... Joshua Allen.
3070	.... Lena Dianne.
3861	.... Michael Adams.
1801	.... Oresta, Jr..
3072	.... Richard Earl.
3077	.... Sean Verlon.
3073	.... Shawnee Lynn.
3878	.... Tracie Renae.
2157	.... William.
1788	.... William James.
3310	MILSTEAD, Aubrey Gene.
3945	.... Blayne Christian.
3312	.... Danita Ann.
2098	.... Frank James.
2196	MIMS, Clyde Henry, Jr..
3234	.... Eric Michael.
730	.... Leon Gade.
3237	.... Megan Hayley.
3235	.... Tony Justin.
1923	.... Tony Leon.
3236	.... William Brandon.
1324	MISSILDINE, Johnny Jason.
258	MITCHELL, Bernice.
1461	.... Fay.
2863	MIXSON, Kara.
2796	MMITH, Shirley Ann.
1125	MOBLEY, Linda.
3227	MOCK, Cole.
3934	.... Lynnli Kate.
1235	MONARCH, Gary Anthony.
2500	.... Jennifer Michelle.
2714	MONCRIEF, Donald Raymond.
3088	MONDORA, Jacky.
1034	MONEY, Eva Rosalind.
1037	.... Jimmy Ronald.
2307	.... Kelli Kaye.
2306	.... Ronald Dewayne.
351	.... Ruben A..
1032	.... Ruben Arnold, Jr..

Ref.	Name (Relationship)
2303	MONEY, Scott.
2302	.... Sherri.
2585	MONTAGUE, Benjamin Daved.
948	MOONEY, William.
2510	MOORE, Mr..
3533	.... Amberly Kira.
3534	.... Lakin.
1469	.... Sara.
3605	MOORMAN, Bennett Owen.
3604	.... Lincoln Nathan.
2629	.... Nate.
4032	MORANT, Kaden.
3761	.... Zachary.
2329	MORGAN, Carol Yvonne.
455	.... Lillian.
456	.... Ruth Valentine.
2244	.... Syble Diane.
2356	MORRELL, Brittany.
2355	.... Kaitlyn.
1101	.... Steven C..
726	MORRIS, Annie Joyce.
3038	.... Jeffery.
2301	.... Jennifer.
2919	.... John Michael.
3037	.... Michael Zoree.
1774	.... Ronnie.
3789	.... Sydney Nicole Crawford.
3158	MORROLL, Debbie.
3159	.... Rickey.
3157	.... Tim.
99	MOUNT, Carrie Lou.
2533	MOYER, Abraham Joshua.
3561	.... Cassandra Jai.
3559	.... Hailey June.
3560	.... Lily Jaicyn.
2415	MOYLAN, Brett Bernard.
1123	.... Patrick Bernard.
3512	MULKEY, Brandon.
3977	.... Braydon Noah.
3978	.... Khloe Autumn.
2788	MULLEN, Tim.
3060	MULLINNEX, Jacqueline Kay.
1153	MURDY, Jerry N..
1176	MURPHREE, Pamela Jane.
1979	MURPHY, Bobby.
760	.... Bobby Euell.
757	.... Charles Alton.
1977	.... Charles Alton, II.
1978	.... Daniel Patrick.
755	.... Dorthy E..
761	.... Edna Earl.
182	.... Everett Stanley.
1934	.... Joe.
3731	.... Katherine Marie.
2831	.... Kenneth Charles.
759	.... Lilly May.
251	.... Marvel May.
448	MURRAY, Lelia.
2070	MYERS, Kevin.

Ref.	Name (Relationship)
1163	MYSIK, Julie.
4027	NALL, Mr..
4026	.... Mr..
3726	.... Amber.
1093	.... Dennis Ray.
2827	.... Denny.
502	.... Mildred.
1090	.... Ronald Duane.
2347	.... Ronnie Duane, II.
3727	.... Tanner.
1092	.... Terry Maurice.
371	.... Victor Eugene.
1277	NALLEN, Terry Carol.
3669	NALLEY, John.
4018	.... Mallorie.
4019	.... Tyler.
861	NEEL, Walter Lee.
648	NEESE, Runell.
3022	NELSON, Brenda.
3020	.... Carlton.
3019	.... Carolyn.
3023	.... Franklin.
1757	.... Lamar.
1261	.... Nancy Runae.
3021	.... Ralph.
3024	.... Wanda.
656	NEMET, Ruth A.
3555	NEWELL, Madison Clair.
480	NEWMAN, Caudie.
1061	NEWMANN, Johnny.
3471	.... Lorrie Leigh.
2358	.... William Earl.
3470	.... William Issac.
2997	NEWTON, Bridget Belinda.
3836	.... Christy Lynn.
2995	.... Ernest Leroy.
1737	.... James.
2994	.... James Jerry.
722	.... Mildred Carlise.
2999	.... Missouri Mae.
3001	.... Sherry Denise.
611	NICHOLS, Cora Mattie.
1197	.... Pam.
3693	NIENHOUSE, Amanda Lynn.
2776	.... George John, Jr..
3694	.... Travis George.
1112	NIX, Angela Crusel.
416	NIXON, Aleatha.
2151	NOLAN, Debra Jean.
1150	NOLANA, Ms..
2580	NOLETTE, Mr..
3592	.... Benjamin R..
3452	NORRIS, Hayward Clarence.
2214	.... Sheivella Maria.
3965	.... Tiffany Ann.
1904	NORSWORTHY, Gail.
1184	NUNN, Pamela.
1558	O'BRIEN, Dianna.
559	.... O.B..

Ref.	Name (Relationship)
3778	O'CONNOR, Patrick.
2900	.... Shawn Patrick.
53	ODOM, Savannah.
969	OGLE, Roberta Marie.
1846	OGLESBY, Duval Milford.
3145	.... Milford Gene.
3143	.... Nancy Elizabeth.
3142	.... Riley Lee.
3144	.... Sharron.
620	.... Viola B.
1947	OHLMEYER, Karen.
3608	OLDS, Morgan E..
2642	.... Robert, Dr..
2861	OLIVE, Ann.
1543	.... Ann.
1544	.... Bobby.
2860	.... Chris.
549	.... Robert H, Capt..
2496	OLVANY, Dennis Michael.
1231	.... Dennis Paul.
2497	.... Matthew Stephen.
3541	O'NEAL, Aaron.
3985	.... Aiden Blake.
3984	.... Asheton Alexander.
3986	.... Lailynn Raine.
3399	O'NEIL, Hope Rena.
3400	.... Joshua Aaron.
3398	.... Ronald Joseph.
2209	.... Ronald Leon.
1395	ORBACK, John A.
1676	ORSA, Andrew.
3732	OTT, Austin Thomas.
3733	.... Carlie Cierra.
3738	.... Heather.
2840	.... James Allen, Jr..
1504	.... James Allen, Sr..
1506	.... John Byron.
2837	.... Kam Renae.
2843	.... Karren Michelle.
516	.... Millard Allison.
1501	.... Millard Allison, Jr..
2842	.... Reagan Edward.
2835	.... Todd Allison.
2839	.... William Gilbert.
2108	OTTLEY, Kelli Ann.
2007	OWENS, Ms..
3050	.... Brandy Keith.
3556	.... Elijah Adam.
3558	.... Izabela Clair.
1577	.... Janice Darlene.
2531	.... Jonathan.
3557	.... Josiah Samuel.
2958	PADGETT, Mr..
2959	.... Mr..
298	.... Annie Bell.
607	.... Claude Ray.
608	.... Clyde Dean.
1887	.... D. Jerome.
1885	.... Dorothy Jean.

Ref.	Name (Relationship)
36	PADGETT, Elizabeth H..
80	.... Ella.
1888	.... Gwendolyn J..
32	.... Henry.
1637	.... Herbert Wayne.
1634	.... Ivalou Jeanetta.
1633	.... James Clinton.
30	.... Jane.
711	.... Jean.
1638	.... Jimmy Cecil.
23	.... Josiphine.
21	.... Julia.
33	.... Levinta.
311	.... Margaret Mae.
600	.... Marvin Greely.
22	.... Mary Frances.
38	.... Nancy Ann.
605	.... Narvi Lee.
1632	.... O. B..
816	.... Ruby Lena.
1889	.... Steven Wayne.
135	.... Thomas Sonny.
606	.... Willia Daisy.
6	.... William.
1635	.... William Thomas.
1631	.... William Thomas.
601	.... Willie Thermon.
1157	PAINTER, Roger.
124	PALMER, Gussie.
383	.... Juanita.
2882	PARKER, Becky.
1972	.... Carrie Elaine.
1861	.... Edwin.
1863	.... Edwina.
1971	.... Mitchell Quillie.
754	.... William Adolphus.
3173	PARKS, Phyllis Jane.
2972	PARRISH, Mr./Ms..
1656	.... Mr..
1659	.... Mr..
1661	.... Mr..
2862	.... Anthony Lee.
627	.... Bobbie.
1547	.... Carmon Lee.
3760	.... Celeste.
145	.... Charles W..
156	.... Ella.
143	.... Emeline.
153	.... Fanny A..
631	.... Genevieve.
27	.... George Washington, Rev..
633	.... Geraldine.
158	.... James Albert, Capt..
1657	.... James Albert, III.
635	.... James Albert, Jr..
149	.... John Robert.
2867	.... Jon Kevin.
3758	.... Laura Amanda.
154	.... Leanna.

Ref.	Name (Relationship)
147	PARRISH, Martha Jane.
141	.... Mary Ellen.
524	.... Mary Rae.
2865	.... Rebecca Lynn.
3762	.... Shelby Anne.
151	.... Tolbert Tillis, Capt..
1903	PARTAIN, Treva.
1819	PATE, Andrea.
3918	PATRICK, Clare Elizabeth.
3210	.... Damon Andrew.
3976	PATRIQUIN, Mason James.
3875	PATTERSON, Amber Brook.
3874	.... Joshua Alan Silva.
2762	.... Ralph Levon, Jr..
1464	.... Ralph Levon, Sr..
833	.... Richard Junior.
3877	.... Shane Donovan.
3079	.... Thomas.
3876	.... Thomas Chester.
1728	PAUL, Hubert.
2256	PAULK, Glen.
4011	PEACOCK, Caleb.
4010	.... Cody.
3659	.... Michael Steven.
2747	.... Steve.
1386	PEARL, Margaret Louise.
1600	PELHAM, Gary Wayne.
3855	.... Sera.
3808	PELTIER, Timothy.
1921	PENG, Sheng Xiang.
533	PERDUE, Florence.
3270	PEREZ, Mr..
3938	.... Mr..
3502	PERMENTER, Zachariah Tyler.
781	PERRY, Annie P.
2129	.... Lance.
3342	.... Magnolia.
3343	.... Wyatt Chance.
2643	PETERSON, Elizabeth Sharon.
1364	.... Elwynne Phillip.
1640	PETIT, Beulah.
3435	PETTY, Christopher Shane.
2257	.... Leon.
1803	PHILLIPS, Edward Earl.
3084	.... Gregory Scott.
3085	.... Kenneth Paul.
3882	.... Kyle Kenneth.
1263	PICIRILLI, Mary June.
3258	PIERSON, Roland.
1029	.... Shelby D..
1953	.... Todd.
3257	.... Vivian.
3656	PILAND, Tasha Nicole.
140	PIPPINS, Nettie.
1265	PITTMAN, Judith Ann.
349	.... Laura.
2194	POLZIN, Mr..
3389	.... Mr./Ms..
2401	POOL, David.

Wilson Bass

Ref.	Name (Relationship)
3264	POOLE, Brenda.
2004	.... Carroll.
3265	.... Debbie.
2003	.... Eddie.
814	.... Horace E.
2001	.... Max Earl.
3105	PORTER, Joesph.
3897	.... Joesph Cameron.
3896	.... Timothy Ian.
1806	POSEY, Althea Darlene.
384	.... Bonnie Lee.
1808	.... Carolyn Dianne.
2417	.... Casey Lauren.
1168	.... Ceavie Edward, Jr..
379	.... Chester.
389	.... Cleavy Edward, Sr..
376	.... Clifton.
386	.... Cora Lee.
680	.... Cora Nolia.
1128	.... Debra K..
2411	.... Diane Faye.
1120	.... Dorothy Faye.
684	.... Gussie Lee.
381	.... Holland Middleton.
2414	.... Hope Mychelle.
1115	.... James Edward.
167	.... James Ocie.
3515	.... James Preston Friday.
2451	.... Jason Edward.
1170	.... Jennifer Kim.
1164	.... Joyce Marie.
2407	.... Kimmie Dallas.
1126	.... Larry Denton.
1122	.... Linda Louise.
374	.... Mae Belle.
1166	.... Marsha Ann.
95	.... Martin Edward.
1124	.... Martin James.
387	.... Mary Evelyn.
686	.... Mary Francis.
1118	.... Mary Jane.
2409	.... Mary Katherine.
2420	.... Nathan Edward.
682	.... Pearlie Mae.
377	.... Preston Dallas.
3514	.... Sarah Jane.
2416	.... Shanna Michelle.
2413	.... Shawn Michael.
2450	.... Stacie LeAnn.
382	.... Stacy Denton.
690	.... Vianna Catherine.
688	.... William Albert.
2418	.... William Denton.
1636	POUCHER, Mary Louise.
3620	POWELL, Andrea Nicole.
3107	.... Angie.
3912	.... Aubree Claire.
1704	.... Fredrick Harold.
3621	.... Haley Elyse.

Ref.	Name (Relationship)
1816	POWELL, Jimmy.
1389	.... Margaret Louise.
2980	.... Michelle Katherine.
3913	.... Paul Edwin, III.
3199	.... Paul Edwin, Jr..
2671	.... Reggie Lawshe.
2809	.... Stephanie Sue.
2103	PRATER, Ecki Alexander.
1108	.... Gayle.
3316	.... Isla Noel.
3317	.... Robert Calvin.
3315	.... Wade Nathan.
3108	PRATT, Jeffery.
3898	.... Shannon Nicole.
1588	PRESLEY, Arthur Lynn.
2913	.... Brandi Lee.
3788	.... Brianna Tegan.
3787	.... Cheyenne Erin.
2915	.... Christopher Edwin.
3786	.... Ciera Elizabeth.
2918	.... Lindsey.
3806	PREVITO, Joey.
2954	.... Kristina.
3805	.... Landon.
2953	.... Leah E.
1625	.... Leonard Raymond, Jr..
592	.... Leonard Raymond, Sr..
2951	.... Trey.
3553	PRICE, Nicholas.
968	PROCKTOR, Wanda.
1400	PROLIST, Margie.
2856	PRUIT, Mark Edward.
1073	PRUITT, Bobbie Ann.
163	PURVIS, Dora Alice.
2491	PUSEY, Kelly.
2535	QUALLS, Cody Allen.
3563	.... Everhett Stone.
2532	.... Julie Crystal.
3562	.... Landon Allen.
3175	.... Sarah Aldie.
2910	QUEENS, Steve.
1646	QUINN, Harry.
2969	.... Hary, Jr..
2970	.... Joan.
2757	RABON, Ferrell.
3680	.... Melissa.
1252	RABREN, Freida.
1334	RABY, Kathy.
1699	RALEY, Addie Vivian.
1708	.... Alvin Lester.
1682	.... Audry.
1678	.... Clement.
640	.... Daniel L.
1679	.... Douglas.
1707	.... Henry Edgar.
1705	.... Julia Yuvone.
1701	.... Lois Jewel.
1703	.... Mary Alice.
325	.... Mollie.

Ref.	Name (Relationship)
1680	RALEY, Muriel.
1684	.... Patricia Ann.
651	.... William Lester.
275	RALSTON, Alexander Gilbert.
886	.... Jean.
888	.... Mark.
838	RAMER, Ms..
230	.... Albert Farrell.
57	.... Alfred Calvin.
225	.... Athon, Sr..
239	.... Beulah.
839	.... Buddy.
238	.... Claude A.
842	.... Derward.
222	.... Dewey William.
841	.... Dorothy.
234	.... Homer Closon.
51	.... Jacob D.
25	.... Jake.
837	.... James.
54	.... James W.
237	.... James W.
221	.... James William.
3269	.... Jennifer.
2023	.... Jerry Edward.
232	.... Jesse C.
49	.... John.
139	.... John.
226	.... John Bennett.
11	.... John W.
3268	.... Justin.
224	.... Lena Zelma.
58	.... Mae.
245	.... Maggie Mae.
241	.... Major.
2026	.... Margaret.
242	.... Mary Dovie.
228	.... Mary E.
840	.... Mildred.
244	.... Millard.
137	.... Nancy A..
55	.... Nancy Elizabeth.
235	.... Savannah Irene.
236	.... Walter Otis.
47	.... William Albert.
229	.... William Calvin.
2024	.... Winford Eugene, Jr..
835	.... Winford Eugene, Sr..
2274	RAMSEY, Angelia Renee.
570	RANDALL, Fred.
1209	RANKIN, Suzanne.
3873	RATHBURN, Broc Jordan.
3074	.... Robert Kenner.
2935	RAW, Kelly Melissa.
3200	RAY, Barney Kieth.
2922	.... Casey Levon.
373	.... Doris.
3790	.... Emmaleigh Maddison.
1065	.... Nancy Lee Carswell.

Ref.	Name (Relationship)
3914	RAY, Riggs Roosivelt.
3359	REDDICK, Michael David.
2511	REDDISH, Kristina Lynn.
1254	.... Lynn David.
2512	.... Shane Stelmon.
1603	REED, Ronald.
334	REEDER, Anna.
766	REEVES, Johnnie.
767	.... Oscar B.
186	.... Oscar H..
765	.... Priscilla.
764	.... William.
3333	REGISTER, Alisha.
3336	.... Augusta Grace.
942	.... Billy.
3338	.... Brandie.
3335	.... Jeremiah D..
3334	.... Jessica E..
2117	.... Marcus Dean.
2121	.... Martha Grace.
2119	.... Matthew Ward.
3337	.... Mattilyn Rose.
3594	RESENDIZ, Sierra.
3600	RHEA, Mr..
3598	.... Ms..
3599	.... Abelia Jane.
2605	.... Amanda Kate.
2604	.... Jenny Lynn.
2607	.... John Spencer.
1316	.... Richard Curtis.
2606	.... Richard Zachary.
1490	RICE, Lily Esther.
2658	RICHARD, Art.
1749	RICHARDS, Brenda.
2917	.... Dorenda.
1180	RIDGE, Linda.
1575	RIEGEL, Darrell.
3352	RIGGINS, Brandon Haywood.
2139	.... Haywood.
3351	.... Kirstie Lea.
3349	.... Melynda Reanee.
1499	RILEY, Rebecca.
2305	RINE, Kristopher Lee.
1036	.... Thomas Lee.
2653	RINEHART, Donna Marie.
2654	.... Myra Nell.
1372	.... O. C..
770	ROBERTS, Marguerite E.
769	.... Mary K.
752	.... Nora Fay.
768	.... Thomas H.
192	.... Thomas Rueben.
2774	ROBERTSON, Randi Elizabeth.
1423	ROBINSON, Jane.
1495	.... Jeanette.
478	.... John W.
2996	RODERUS, Christine.
3835	.... Melinda.
2732	RODGERS, Alvin.

Ref.	Name (Relationship)
2741	RODGERS, Brenda.
1441	.... Evans.
2736	.... Jo Anne.
2734	.... John Glenn.
497	.... John Thomas Evans.
2738	.... Joyce.
1445	.... Ollie Kenneth.
2009	.... Richard Ronald, Sr..
1446	.... Ross Burton.
1439	.... Sibyl.
2730	.... Thomas.
1438	.... Thomas Lloyd, PFC.
3971	RODRIGUES, Evelee Ember.
3972	.... Huxley Nash.
3501	.... Joey.
3970	.... Tenley Martin.
1035	ROETING, James B..
2304	.... James Phillop.
3644	ROGERS, Lori.
2701	.... Mary.
2618	.... William Bryan, III.
1328	.... William Bryan, Jr..
2406	ROPER, Bobbie Fay.
604	ROSS BARLOW, Grace.
1379	ROWE, Jane.
103	ROWELL, Alline Naomi.
2292	.... April.
3460	.... Christopher M..
2296	.... Coreen.
1028	.... Ervunus.
1023	.... Eva Mae.
350	.... Eva Mae.
175	.... Flara Annie.
2293	.... Gary.
1022	.... Harold D..
1026	.... Henry Eral.
2295	.... Hope.
345	.... Ida Mae.
90	.... James Henry.
2300	.... James Randall.
3459	.... Jason Derek.
2294	.... Kimberly.
348	.... Leroy.
347	.... Lettie V..
1030	.... Ray Lee.
2298	.... Russell Edward.
2297	.... Tereasa.
1018	.... Trudy.
1020	.... Willie V..
1529	RUMBAUGH, Andy.
2770	RUSHING, Donna Denise.
435	RUSK, Dorothy June.
1938	.... Kelly Ann.
3792	RUSSELL, Amber Nicole.
1912	.... Gerry.
3924	.... Gerry Ethan.
1064	.... Joyce Merline.
3794	.... Kayla Brook.
3791	.... Kip Riley.

Ref.	Name (Relationship)
3793	RUSSELL, Payton Breanna.
1590	.... Raymond Randall.
2923	.... Raymond Randall, Jr..
2925	.... Sonya Leann.
2921	.... Starlette Dawn.
3219	.... Whittly Vivian.
1151	SABLE, Judy.
3820	SADLIER, Mr./Ms..
3819	.... Mr./Ms..
3818	.... Mr./Ms..
3817	.... Unknown, Maj..
2965	.... Richard.
698	SAHRIA, Walter.
1396	SALAIZ, Rudy.
2183	SALTER, Demetrius LaRoy.
974	.... Donnie Leroy.
1667	SANDERS, Mr..
3432	.... Amanda Kay.
2252	.... Lamar.
403	SANFORD, Marilyn.
3948	SAUTTER, Calli.
3358	.... Chris.
97	SAVAGE, Jessie.
3490	SCARBROUGH, Randy.
925	SCHMIDT, Barbara Burns.
315	.... Fredrick Harling, Lt Col.
62	SCHMITT, Frieda Kamilla.
2391	SCHOFIELD, Celetha Dianne.
336	.... Clara Mae.
2283	.... Clifford.
3048	.... Karen.
3451	.... Leslie Ann.
3453	.... Thomas Jefferson.
644	SCOFFIELD, Emmie.
3103	.... Joanna Lee.
1327	SCOTT, Anthony.
3770	.... Dylan Wayne.
3489	.... John Timberlake.
2378	.... John William.
3488	.... Sharley Jo.
2884	.... Stephen Michael.
2782	SCROGGINS, Gary.
1919	.... Sherry Lynn.
1886	SECKLER, Daniel A..
410	SEES, Barbara Kay.
443	SEIWELL, Shirley.
1312	SELF, Andrea Leedy.
3152	SEXTON, Janet.
270	SHAFER, Ione.
2127	SHAUD, David Eugene.
3341	.... Matthew Reed.
2962	SHAW, Ellen Francis.
1642	.... Theo.
268	.... Viola Mae.
3975	SHEFFIELD, Molly Madison.
2393	SHEPPRA, DE, Chandra Jean.
3392	SHERRER, Stanley Adam.
1398	SHORES, Robert.
1257	SHORT, Alice Drucilla.

Ref.	Name (Relationship)
1148	SHORT, Thomas.
109	SHULER, Rosa Lee.
2110	SICKLER, VAN, Christina.
2990	SIMMONS, Billy.
150	.... Patsy Mae.
2963	.... Roy.
742	.... Sally Marilyn.
2135	.... Tamara Lynn.
3815	.... Treg.
2361	SIMON, Susan.
1561	SIMPSON, Paula.
1732	SMITH, Mr..
1663	.... Mr..
1240	.... Mr..
3735	.... Aaron Hope Inez.
1672	.... Annice.
1378	.... Barbara Sue.
1525	.... Ben, III.
1675	.... Bessie.
2286	.... Billie Jo.
2284	.... Billie Mack.
1024	.... Bobbie Jean.
1668	.... Bonnie.
2560	.... Christopher Aaron.
1671	.... Clenna.
2092	.... Corinne Sue.
2342	.... Debbie Lynn.
3712	.... Douglas Mathew.
3736	.... Dylan McKay.
3577	.... Eden Kelly.
1677	.... Gary.
1666	.... Gladys.
2810	.... Gregory Keith.
2712	.... Harvey Valnor.
638	.... Hollie Matthew.
3578	.... Hudson.
1454	.... Jack.
2812	.... Jason Darren.
3720	.... Jessica Daily.
1527	.... Joe.
2838	.... John Franklin, Jr..
3714	.... Jonathan Keith.
3734	.... Justin Todd.
3713	.... Katelyn Sue.
1674	.... Lloyd Mathew.
2808	.... Lloyde Mathew, Jr..
1021	.... Mack.
3737	.... Madison Taylor.
173	.... Maggie.
642	.... Mary Ann.
2002	.... Mary Ann.
1796	.... Mary Ellen.
3716	.... Megan Rebecca.
361	.... Minnie Walton McKnight.
1669	.... Nellie Ruth.
1081	.... Patricia Ann.
1664	.... Rosa Bell.
3717	.... Sara Grace.
3454	.... Sharlene Suzette.

Ref.	Name (Relationship)
3719	SMITH, Shelby Breanna.
3715	.... Zachary Paul.
3484	SNELLGROVE, Amanda Mae.
2371	.... Betty June.
1105	.... Coley Joseph.
3480	.... David C..
2377	.... Judy Ann.
3485	.... Katie Lucrieta.
2375	.... Roger Henry.
2373	.... Rudy Von.
3482	.... Travis.
3483	.... Tristan L..
2814	SORRELL, Phylis.
1565	SORRELLS, Tammy C.
3036	SOUTHHARD, Darin.
3243	SOUTULLO, Sam.
3040	SPEIS, Belinda.
148	SPENCE, Bealaster S..
3308	.... Cara Leane.
2086	.... Carl Leon.
933	.... Clyde Autry.
2096	.... Clyde Autry, Jr..
2087	.... Dixie Irene.
2094	.... Floyd Colon.
323	.... Floyd S.
2093	.... James Scott.
930	.... Opal Virginia.
2089	.... Rhonda Sue.
2091	.... Robert Leon.
3307	.... Shannon Robert.
3309	.... Tabitha S..
3840	SPICER, Jay Fletcher.
3002	.... Jay Oliver.
2489	SPITHOULER, Tammy.
3648	SPIVEY, Becky Jean.
1278	.... Cathrine.
2829	STACEY, Martin Eugene.
3729	.... Robin Renee.
3730	.... Seth Eugene.
1620	STACKS, Donna Theresa.
1800	STALLARD, Peggy Jean.
2620	STARK, Alyssa.
460	STAUTIMIRE, Hadassah.
3327	STEELE, Bradley Shoven.
3323	.... David Austin.
2111	.... Donna Marie.
3329	.... Emily Ann.
3330	.... Erin Elizabeth.
3326	.... Jeremy Michael.
938	.... Joseph Shoven.
2106	.... Joseph Wayne.
3322	.... Kathryn Leanne.
3328	.... Kevin Charles.
2109	.... Larry Dale.
3321	.... Rebecca Ann.
3320	.... Stephanie Ann.
2113	.... Terry Michael.
2075	STEVENS, Mr..
2074	.... Mr..

Wilson Bass

Ref.	Name (Relationship)
2072	STEVENS, Ms..
2071	.... Mr..
2073	.... Ms..
282	.... Leonard Merrill.
904	.... Merrillyn.
906	.... William Reed.
1345	STEVERSON, Daniel Hal.
2639	.... Shelby Daniel.
1133	STEWART, Barbara Ann.
1137	.... Betty Sue.
1144	.... Bonnie Mae.
2430	.... Clifton Veal.
2441	.... Derrick.
385	.... Ernest.
1139	.... Ernest Dewayne.
1149	.... Ernest, Jr..
2443	.... LeaAnne.
1145	.... Mary Elizabeth.
1131	.... Patriciea Ernestine.
2436	.... Rachel Lee.
2434	.... Shelia Diane.
1142	.... Shirley Jane.
2442	.... Steven.
378	STILLER, Laura.
3671	STINSON, Troy.
3582	STOCKTON, Levi.
2561	.... Lori Marie.
2563	.... Marshall Kevin.
1280	.... Marshall Lee.
3581	.... Shawn Thomas.
78	STOKES, Addie Augusta.
554	.... Clara V.
1466	.... Doris Jean.
783	.... Ferol Janice.
1914	.... Marie.
1481	.... Shirley.
2389	.... Wayne.
1942	STONE, Terri.
3507	STOUT, Aaron Eli.
1161	.... Bobbie.
2400	.... Kurt Allen.
8	STRAUGHN, Mary.
317	STRAUGHTER, Hyram Hayes.
3615	STRICKLAND, Josh.
1337	STUART, Allen R..
2628	.... Bethany Ann.
2627	.... Jeffery Allen.
2630	.... Suzanne Marie.
1686	SUGGS, Mr..
3385	SUMMERLIN, Chad David.
2184	.... Charles David.
975	.... Clarence Devon.
332	.... Jesse David, Jr..
2186	.... Kathy Ann.
2187	.... Kimberly Jan.
603	.... Myrtle.
3384	.... Sarah M..
3093	SWANEY, Stephanie Lynn.
1853	SWANSON, Franklin Henry.

Ref.	Name (Relationship)
3247	SWITZER, Hannah Leigh.
1936	.... Jeffery Lee.
3250	.... Jonathan David.
3249	.... Timothy Michael.
395	TART, Jane Lee.
1541	.... Olivia.
535	.... William A..
3637	TATE, Adam Nelson.
3636	.... Amber Lynell.
3639	.... Andrew Nelson.
3638	.... Aric Charles.
2722	.... Mark Nelson.
486	TATUM, Benjamin Morris.
3218	TAYLOR, Anthony.
1159	.... Daniel Richard.
1162	.... David Allen.
3922	.... Emily.
1152	.... Evelyn Elaine.
1154	.... Gloria Jean.
1158	.... James Edward, Jr..
388	.... James Edward, Sr..
3224	.... Janet Lee.
1927	.... Jerral Lynn.
3238	.... Laura Elizabeth.
1140	.... Mary Jo.
1156	.... Sherry Diane.
1160	.... Thomas Patrick.
219	TEEL, Aaron.
830	.... Aaron, Jr..
318	.... Addie Lee.
297	.... Alex Richard.
70	.... Annie.
312	.... Atress.
66	.... Bennett B..
308	.... Bernice Cathleen.
67	.... Bruner.
301	.... Corine Virginia.
2021	.... Debra Kay.
2020	.... Dexter.
916	.... Donald.
302	.... Dora Margaret.
911	.... Dorothy Helen.
71	.... Elizabeth.
832	.... Frances Ida.
296	.... George Fred.
314	.... Gladys.
79	.... Henry Vauceous.
15	.... James.
217	.... James Bennett.
320	.... James Elijah.
920	.... James Jery Teel.
295	.... James Samuel.
319	.... James Vauciuos.
13	.... Jane.
215	.... Jesse Stallings.
313	.... Jimie L.
73	.... John.
919	.... John Everette.
2022	.... Keneth Ra.

Ref.	Name (Relationship)
826	TEEL, Marie.
304	.... Martha Lena.
824	.... Mary Ethel.
929	.... Mary Jane.
81	.... Mattie.
213	.... Mattie L.
299	.... Mayme Lee.
68	.... Melvine Lavina.
823	.... Myrtice Mae.
75	.... Nancy Viola.
214	.... Nora B.
218	.... Oliver B.
914	.... Richard Alex, Jr..
306	.... Ruben Everett.
917	.... Rufus Arnold Teel.
321	.... Sara Nancy.
828	.... Vera Merle.
10	.... William.
294	.... William Greeley.
45	.... William Henry.
913	.... William Olen.
77	.... William Riley.
310	.... Willie Samson.
1950	TEMPLE, Graham.
1782	THAMES, Billy Joe.
3047	.... Christopher.
3850	.... Clay Daniel.
3851	.... Dustin Micheal.
3849	.... Hillary Page.
681	.... John Lee.
1779	.... Ruby Nell.
3812	THERIOT, Daphne.
126	THOMAS, Lillie Lee.
2723	THOMASSON, Carol Sue.
3635	.... Cassandra Nicole.
2721	.... Celia Lynn.
3634	.... Charles Michael.
2719	.... Charles Rocky.
1437	.... Charles Wood.
2717	.... Cynthia Mae.
3653	THOMPSON, Capers.
3544	.... Clarissa Rena.
344	.... Evelyn.
3994	.... Joseph Byron, III.
3647	.... Joseph Byron, Jr..
2744	.... Josheph Byran.
3651	.... Kimberly Nicole.
3649	.... Sonya Michelle.
133	.... William.
2526	THORNE, Traci Beth.
2169	TILLEY, Lori Caprice.
490	TIMMERMAN, William Frank.
2687	TINDAL, Stan.
1467	TISDALE, Barbara Ann.
2811	.... Cynthia Denise.
2478	TOBIAS, Ashton.
1206	.... John L..
1141	TOMLINS, Patricia Elaine.
2050	TORREY, Les.

Ref.	Name (Relationship)
3059	TOUCHTON, Jody Lynn.
4023	TRAHAN, Kyra.
3678	.... Robert Eric.
1928	TRAWICK, Charlotte.
1926	.... Diane.
732	.... Eugene.
1932	.... Gena.
728	.... Learvene.
1930	.... Lisa.
3216	TREDWELL, Mr..
3921	.... Elle.
3920	.... Iris.
2370	TRISHA, Ms..
1033	TSURSKI, Hitomi.
2137	TULEY, Pamela Ann.
2140	.... Robert.
2136	.... Ronald Daune.
3113	TURBBEVILLE, Dewey Wayne, Jr..
3114	.... Hunter Wayne.
3109	.... Kim.
3111	.... Tracey.
1817	TURBEVILLE, Dewey Wayne.
691	.... Dewey, Rev..
1810	.... Doris Jene.
1815	.... Elaine.
1814	.... Jerry Lamar.
1812	.... Jimmie Nell.
3054	TURNER, Amos Dalton, Jr..
1786	.... Amos Dalton, Sr..
683	.... Amos Vincen.
3056	.... Beverly Shea.
595	.... Cary Preston.
3149	.... Dale.
3148	.... Derrel.
1784	.... Hyram Walace.
3154	.... Jack Milton.
1628	.... Jackie.
3155	.... Janet Sylvia.
1116	.... Janice.
1858	.... Jeff Wendell.
3151	.... Jeffery Wade.
3899	.... Jeffery Wade, II.
3900	.... Lilli Roseann.
3051	.... Lynda Jeanne.
697	.... M. A..
3856	.... Madison Jade.
3049	.... Pamela Nell.
1627	.... Rex.
1629	.... Ruby Jean.
1854	.... Sylvia.
3858	.... Taylor Grace.
3150	.... Tracy.
1856	.... William Amos.
3775	TUTTEROW, Jackson.
2896	.... Jeffery Scott.
1318	TWEEDY, Zelda Lynn.
1537	TYLER, Albert T.
2855	.... Anita Kaye.
3750	.... Cathleen Doren.

Ref.	Name (Relationship)
1538	TYLER, Henry Albert.
3749	.... Jessica Ann.
3752	.... Justin Fairman.
3753	.... Michael Fairman.
2853	.... Michael Wayne.
2979	UPTAGRAFT, Lisa Ann.
1702	.... Roy C..
2978	.... Stevan.
1070	URGELLES, Eurado Eurigue.
3466	VADINO, Brittany Leann.
2964	VAGIAS, Artemis Diane.
3825	.... Louis, III.
2967	.... Louis, Jr..
1644	.... Louis, Lt. Col..
4043	VALDES, Ms..
4044	.... Mr..
4042	.... Ms..
2971	.... Arthur.
3828	.... Arthur.
3826	.... Mary.
1283	VAN, Larry.
2565	.... Larry, Jr..
2566	.... Scarlet.
1502	VANDIVER, Jerrie Ellen.
3756	VEASEY, Andrew Bruce.
2859	.... Brandon Keith.
2857	.... Bruce Kelley.
1540	.... Bruce, Jr..
3754	.... Hanna Elizabeth.
4031	.... Katherine Elizabeth.
2793	VINCENT, Vicky.
3597	VOLPE, Anthony.
2587	.... Joseph F..
3596	.... Tegan Jo.
1931	WADE, Gregory Paul.
3241	.... Paul Joshua.
566	WALDEN, Nancy Ruth.
1733	WALICE, Jeff Alex.
670	.... Joseph Farrel.
3871	WALKER, Brannon Chase.
3071	.... Garry Thomas.
2720	.... Kimberly Ann.
2802	.... Mary Beth.
129	.... Obie Lucille.
3870	.... Tera Lynn.
3872	.... Trista Shealynn.
1563	.... Vicky.
954	WALKUP, Mary Sue.
2454	WALLACE, Amy Melissa.
2455	.... Andrew Middleton.
393	.... Aurthor.
2458	.... Chad Alexander.
2456	.... Charles William.
2457	.... Christopher Edward.
2085	.... Chuck.
3297	.... Kevin.
1175	.... Phillip Aurthur.
844	.... Richard.
1173	.... Sandra Ann.

Ref.	Name (Relationship)
3296	WALLACE, Steven.
1941	.... Tamera Renee.
1177	.... William Holley.
243	.... William Travis.
3365	WALTERS, Adam Alexander.
2150	.... Don Monwell.
958	.... Donnie Jay.
3363	.... Joshua.
2154	.... Kenneth Layne.
3367	.... Kenneth Layne, Jr..
2156	.... Kim Dawn.
3362	.... Lauren Ashley.
2372	.... Michael C..
3481	.... Michael Shane.
3366	.... Roderick Jay.
2152	.... Rodrick Jerome.
1828	.... Roslyn.
3364	.... Tristin.
452	WARD, Anna Faye.
1331	.... Betty Jane.
2636	.... Brooke Michelle.
1721	.... Carolyn O..
1344	.... Chris Lorraine.
18	.... Christian.
2623	.... David Carter.
2638	.... Deidre Nicole.
449	.... DeLeon Edward.
2637	.... Emily June.
105	.... Forman Edward.
1340	.... Fred Anthony.
445	.... Harvey Clinton.
1002	.... James Henry.
2634	.... Joseph Brandon.
1341	.... Joseph Dale.
2635	.... Maletha Adele.
185	.... Margaret Jane.
1336	.... Mary Ann.
29	.... Nancy Jane.
1343	.... Rose Marie.
3602	.... Seth.
1338	.... Shirley.
2118	.... Susan.
3603	.... Sydney Taylor.
2622	.... William Charles, III.
1333	.... William Charles, Jr..
447	.... William Charles, Sr., Rev..
31	.... William Forman.
1579	WATKINS, Louise.
2888	WATSON, Ms..
539	.... Morris Edwin.
2694	WATTS, Marilyn.
2966	WAYMAN, Mr..
3821	.... Carolyn.
3823	.... Katherine.
3997	WEAVER, Andrew O'Neal.
3652	.... Charis.
3998	.... Kayden.
636	WEBB, Zelma Elizabeth.
1873	WEBSTER, Carl.

Ref.	Name (Relationship)
3185	WEBSTER, Carrie.
3182	.... Denise.
3183	.... Scott.
3181	.... Stive.
3184	.... Tim.
3178	.... Tracey Rochelle.
3096	WEEMS, Charles Paul.
1809	.... Fred Charles, Jr..
3100	.... Justin Albert.
3098	.... Perry Matthew.
2044	WEIERHOLT, Ivar.
43	WELCH, Abigail.
136	.... Loula Jean.
2768	WEST, Connie Sue.
2656	WESTBURY, Donnie.
2655	.... Gary.
1374	.... Lewis.
3616	WESTERLING, Natalie.
2440	WESTERVELT, Heather Lynn.
1147	.... Kenny.
2685	WHATLEY, Gordon Lavaughn.
1413	.... Jay Theron.
2683	.... Myrtice Edna.
2684	.... Myrtle Maxine.
3271	WHITE, Mr..
2029	.... Mr..
2032	.... Mr..
3273	.... Mr..
2031	.... Mr..
3272	.... Mr..
240	.... Amos.
46	.... Ida D.
843	.... James Thomas, Sr..
2270	.... Kenneth James.
1838	.... Larry L..
520	.... Marline.
2027	.... Steve.
1211	.... Thomas.
4022	WHITEHURST, Abby Suzann.
3675	.... Ronald.
3204	WHITHEAD, Bethany.
2826	WIGGINS, Connie.
1493	.... Darrell.
4049	.... Heidi Rae.
3853	.... John Raymond.
4047	.... Kaden Andrew.
4045	.... Kenly Madison.
2823	.... Melony.
2077	.... Patricia June.
4050	.... Saydee Mae.
2825	.... Shannon.
2824	.... Sylvia.
1103	WILCOX, Cora Lee.
3255	WILKEN, Kathryn.
3383	WILKINSON, Mr./Ms..
3378	.... Mr./Ms..
3355	.... Alicia Raye.
2163	.... Brett Alan.
2174	.... Candace Delane.

Ref.	Name (Relationship)
2178	WILKINSON, Candace Delane.
963	.... Chadrick Earl.
2168	.... Christopher Del.
2097	.... Deborah Ann.
2099	.... Delmus Nathan.
2166	.... Dena Gail.
955	.... Dorothy Joan.
3369	.... Erika Jenelle.
937	.... Floyce Genelle.
330	.... Glen Curtis.
965	.... Glynda Carol.
957	.... Ina Mae.
943	.... Irma Arleen.
2104	.... Janet Lee.
3354	.... Jeremy Curtis.
3370	.... Jessie Cordel.
3314	.... Jordan Alexander.
2131	.... Joshua.
2102	.... Joy Denise.
941	.... Judith Elaine.
2165	.... Katrina Marie.
961	.... Lary Rodney.
2162	.... Lary Rodney, Jr..
947	.... Linda Aletha.
2164	.... Lisa Marie.
2513	.... Lorena.
939	.... Lorine Annette.
949	.... Marcia Glendolyn.
959	.... Mona Idez.
951	.... Neil Keith.
967	.... Norman Curtis.
2130	.... Rachel.
2141	.... Randall Glen.
973	.... Rebecca Louise.
3353	.... Rhainnon Rose.
945	.... Roland Douglas.
971	.... Selina Benita.
2180	.... Shane Curtis.
2176	.... Shane Curtis.
3356	.... Taylor.
935	.... Wade Nathan.
2144	.... Warren Craig.
952	.... Wenton Curtis.
328	.... Woodrow A..
471	WILLIAMS, Ada Ola.
2592	.... Andrew Douglas.
2699	.... Angela Maria.
485	.... Annie Ruth.
491	.... Buna Lucille.
2591	.... Danae Elizabeth.
2697	.... David Marcus.
3132	.... Dean.
3134	.... Douglas.
473	.... Francis Folsam.
709	.... Fred.
1300	.... G. Douglas.
479	.... Henry Gordon.
1834	.... James T..
2695	.... Jo Ann.

Ref.	Name (Relationship)
2690	WILLIAMS, Johnny Ray.
477	.... Laura May Williams.
2777	.... Leigh Ann.
1424	.... Lester.
489	.... Lillian Elizabeth.
1883	.... Linda.
475	.... Mattie Dora.
483	.... Naomi.
2686	.... Rebecca.
3133	.... Rita Lynn.
2693	.... Ronald Gordon.
2688	.... Susan Elizabeth.
1474	.... Thomas Eugene.
2779	.... Thomas Eugene, II.
3718	.... Trever Kyle.
469	.... Vinnie Janice.
111	.... William Henry.
481	.... William Marcus.
487	.... Wilmer Newton.
3536	WILLIAMSON, Amanda Lynn.
2516	.... Charles Anthony.
1259	.... Charles Herbert.
3991	.... Easton Reese Lee.
3550	.... Finley Scott.
3547	.... Garrett Michael.
2521	.... Gordon Michael.
3549	.... Liam Wyatt.
2624	.... Lorena.
2185	.... Mary Jo.
3545	.... Meagan Michelle.
2519	.... Sandra Michelle.
2523	.... Shane Eric.
3524	WILLIS, Candace.
2484	.... Christopher.
2038	.... Louis George, Jr..
3523	.... Nathan.
1319	WILSON, Audrey Michelle.
1308	.... Billy Shannon.
2598	.... Courtney Shanna.
441	.... John Lewis.
2597	.... Michael Shawn.
2612	.... Michael Travis.
1317	.... Michail Lewis.
2611	.... ReTessa Lyne.
1315	.... Sheila Diane.
2384	.... Sherri Leigh.
2610	.... Tiffany Nichole.
2609	.... Timothy Nicholas.
2599	.... William Daryl.
2405	WINDHAM, Amy Micha.
3588	WINGARD, Coy Bennett.
3586	.... Rylee Alaine.
2573	.... Tyler Joel.
3587	.... Wyatt Carl.
1857	WINSPUR, Patricia.
3940	WINTERS, Alysa L..
3942	.... Logan Taylor.
3302	.... Ryan.
3941	.... Tyler R..

Index

Ref.	Name (Relationship)
1729	WISE, Brenda Gail.
2916	.... Donna.
668	.... James Donald.
2276	.... Kimberly Dawn.
1730	.... Myra Lynn.
1731	.... Tracy Nanette.
3723	WISMER, Emily Kay.
3724	.... Hannah Elizabeth.
2819	.... James William.
3725	.... Madalyn Jean.
255	WITT, Nannie.
1186	WITTMAN, Susan.
2368	WITTMYER, Beverly Lynn.
2596	WOOD, Andrea Rebecka.
1305	.... Connie Gail.
2602	.... Emily Grace.
439	.... Gerald Wilson.
1303	.... JoAnn.
1313	.... Joyce Marie.
2601	.... Katherine Mary.
2600	.... Luke.
1309	.... Pamela Ellen.
1307	.... Rebecca Gaye.
1311	.... Russel Stacy.
2595	.... Samantha Gail.
956	WOODARD, Eugene Odell.
2146	.... Gail Denise.
2421	WOODFIN, Hudson, Jr..
1132	.... Hudson, Sr..
2424	.... Martin Edward.
2423	.... Robert Lee.
2199	WORLEY, Danny David.
2197	.... Gary Wayne.
983	.... Horace.
2198	.... Pamela Jun.
2200	.... Robin Don.
719	WORRELLS, Dewayne.
836	YATES, Nancy.
1059	YAWN, Faye.
1867	YORK, James.
3171	.... James, Jr..
3170	.... Lajaun.
3212	YOUNGBLOOD, Emily Jean.
2794	ZIVERINK, Barbara Ann.

Made in the USA
Monee, IL
20 May 2023

b55c528f-2a8c-4409-8642-7c2cefd016a4R02